Lecture Notes in Computer Science   11129

Commenced Publication in 1973
Founding and Former Series Editors:
Gerhard Goos, Juris Hartmanis, and Jan van Leeuwen

Editorial Board

More information about this series at http://www.springer.com/series/7412

Laura Leal-Taixé · Stefan Roth (Eds.)

Computer Vision – ECCV 2018 Workshops

Munich, Germany, September 8–14, 2018
Proceedings, Part I

 Springer

Editors
Laura Leal-Taixé
Technical University of Munich
Garching, Germany

Stefan Roth 🆔
Technische Universität Darmstadt
Darmstadt, Germany

ISSN 0302-9743   ISSN 1611-3349   (electronic)
Lecture Notes in Computer Science
ISBN 978-3-030-11008-6   ISBN 978-3-030-11009-3   (eBook)
https://doi.org/10.1007/978-3-030-11009-3

Library of Congress Control Number: 2018966826

LNCS Sublibrary: SL6 – Image Processing, Computer Vision, Pattern Recognition, and Graphics

This Springer imprint is published by the registered company Springer Nature Switzerland AG
The registered company address is: Gewerbestrasse 11, 6330 Cham, Switzerland

Foreword

It was our great pleasure to host the European Conference on Computer Vision 2018 in Munich, Germany. This constituted by far the largest ECCV event ever. With close to 2,900 registered participants and another 600 on the waiting list one month before the conference, participation more than doubled since the last ECCV in Amsterdam. We believe that this is due to a dramatic growth of the computer vision community combined with the popularity of Munich as a major European hub of culture, science, and industry. The conference took place in the heart of Munich in the concert hall Gasteig with workshops and tutorials held on the downtown campus of the Technical University of Munich.

One of the major innovations for ECCV 2018 was the free perpetual availability of all conference and workshop papers, which is often referred to as open access. We note that this is not precisely the same use of the term as in the Budapest declaration. Since 2013, CVPR and ICCV have had their papers hosted by the Computer Vision Foundation (CVF), in parallel with the IEEE Xplore version. This has proved highly beneficial to the computer vision community.

We are delighted to announce that for ECCV 2018 a very similar arrangement was put in place with the cooperation of Springer. In particular, the author's final version will be freely available in perpetuity on a CVF page, while SpringerLink will continue to host a version with further improvements, such as activating reference links and including video. We believe that this will give readers the best of both worlds; researchers who are focused on the technical content will have a freely available version in an easily accessible place, while subscribers to SpringerLink will continue to have the additional benefits that this provides. We thank Alfred Hofmann from Springer for helping to negotiate this agreement, which we expect will continue for future versions of ECCV.

September 2018

Horst Bischof
Daniel Cremers
Bernt Schiele
Ramin Zabih

Preface

It is our great pleasure to present these workshop proceedings of the 15th European Conference on Computer Vision, which was held during September 8–14, 2018, in Munich, Germany. We are delighted that the main conference of ECCV 2018 was accompanied by 43 scientific workshops. The ECCV workshop proceedings contain contributions of 36 workshops.

We received 74 workshop proposals on a broad set of topics related to computer vision. The very high quality and the large number of proposals made the selection process rather challenging. Owing to space restrictions, only 46 proposals were accepted, among which six proposals were merged into three workshops because of overlapping themes.

The final set of 43 workshops complemented the main conference program well. The workshop topics presented a good orchestration of new trends and traditional issues, built bridges into neighboring fields, as well as discussed fundamental technologies and novel applications. We would like to thank all the workshop organizers for their unreserved efforts to make the workshop sessions a great success.

September 2018   Stefan Roth
                                                                              Laura Leal-Taixé

Organization

General Chairs

Horst Bischof	Graz University of Technology, Austria
Daniel Cremers	Technical University of Munich, Germany
Bernt Schiele	Saarland University, Max Planck Institute for Informatics, Germany
Ramin Zabih	CornellNYCTech, USA

Program Chairs

Vittorio Ferrari	University of Edinburgh, UK
Martial Hebert	Carnegie Mellon University, USA
Cristian Sminchisescu	Lund University, Sweden
Yair Weiss	Hebrew University, Israel

Local Arrangement Chairs

Björn Menze	Technical University of Munich, Germany
Matthias Niessner	Technical University of Munich, Germany

Workshop Chairs

Stefan Roth	Technische Universität Darmstadt, Germany
Laura Leal-Taixé	Technical University of Munich, Germany

Tutorial Chairs

Michael Bronstein	Università della Svizzera Italiana, Switzerland
Laura Leal-Taixé	Technical University of Munich, Germany

Website Chair

Friedrich Fraundorfer	Graz University of Technology, Austria

Demo Chairs

Federico Tombari	Technical University of Munich, Germany
Joerg Stueckler	Technical University of Munich, Germany

Publicity Chair

Giovanni Maria   University of Catania, Italy
  Farinella

Industrial Liaison Chairs

Florent Perronnin   Naver Labs, France
Yunchao Gong   Snap, USA
Helmut Grabner   Logitech, Switzerland

Finance Chair

Gerard Medioni   Amazon, University of Southern California, USA

Publication Chairs

Albert Ali Salah   Boğaziçi University, Turkey
Hamdi Dibeklioğlu   Bilkent University, Turkey
Anton Milan   Amazon, Germany

Workshop Organizers

W01 – The Visual Object Tracking Challenge Workshop

Matej Kristan   University of Ljubljana, Slovenia
Aleš Leonardis   University of Birmingham, UK
Jiří Matas   Czech Technical University in Prague, Czechia
Michael Felsberg   Linköping University, Sweden
Roman Pflugfelder   Austrian Institute of Technology, Austria

W02 – 6th Workshop on Computer Vision for Road Scene Understanding and Autonomous Driving

Mathieu Salzmann   EPFL, Switzerland
José Alvarez   NVIDIA, USA
Lars Petersson   Data61 CSIRO, Australia
Fredrik Kahl   Chalmers University of Technology, Sweden
Bart Nabbe   Aurora, USA

W03 – 3D Reconstruction in the Wild

Akihiro Sugimoto   The National Institute of Informatics (NII), Japan
Tomas Pajdla   Czech Technical University in Prague, Czechia
Takeshi Masuda   The National Institute of Advanced Industrial Science
                             and Technology (AIST), Japan
Shohei Nobuhara   Kyoto University, Japan
Hiroshi Kawasaki   Kyushu University, Japan

W04 – Workshop on Visual Learning and Embodied Agents in Simulation Environments

Peter Anderson   Georgia Institute of Technology, USA
Manolis Savva   Facebook AI Research and Simon Fraser University, USA
Angel X. Chang   Eloquent Labs and Simon Fraser University, USA
Saurabh Gupta   University of California, Berkeley, USA
Amir R. Zamir   Stanford University and University of California, Berkeley,
                          USA
Stefan Lee   Georgia Institute of Technology, USA
Samyak Datta   Georgia Institute of Technology, USA
Li Yi   Stanford University, USA
Hao Su   University of California, San Diego, USA
Qixing Huang   The University of Texas at Austin, USA
Cewu Lu   Shanghai Jiao Tong University, China
Leonidas Guibas   Stanford University, USA

W05 – Bias Estimation in Face Analytics

Rama Chellappa   University of Maryland, USA
Nalini Ratha   IBM Watson Research Center, USA
Rogerio Feris   IBM Watson Research Center, USA
Michele Merler   IBM Watson Research Center, USA
Vishal Patel   Johns Hopkins University, USA

W06 – 4th International Workshop on Recovering 6D Object Pose

Tomas Hodan   Czech Technical University in Prague, Czechia
Rigas Kouskouridas   Scape Technologies, UK
Krzysztof Walas   Poznan University of Technology, Poland
Tae-Kyun Kim   Imperial College London, UK
Jiři Matas   Czech Technical University in Prague, Czechia
Carsten Rother   Heidelberg University, Germany
Frank Michel   Technical University Dresden, Germany
Vincent Lepetit   University of Bordeaux, France
Ales Leonardis   University of Birmingham, UK
Carsten Steger   Technical University of Munich, MVTec, Germany
Caner Sahin   Imperial College London, UK

W07 – Second International Workshop on Computer Vision for UAVs

Kristof Van Beeck   KU Leuven, Belgium
Tinne Tuytelaars   KU Leuven, Belgium
Davide Scaramuzza   ETH Zurich, Switzerland
Toon Goedemé   KU Leuven, Belgium

W08 – 5th Transferring and Adapting Source Knowledge in Computer Vision and Second VisDA Challenge

Tatiana Tommasi	Italian Institute of Technology, Italy
David Vázquez	Element AI, Canada
Kate Saenko	Boston University, USA
Ben Usman	Boston University, USA
Xingchao Peng	Boston University, USA
Judy Hoffman	Facebook AI Research, USA
Neela Kaushik	Boston University, USA
Antonio M. López	Universitat Autònoma de Barcelona and Computer Vision Center, Spain
Wen Li	ETH Zurich, Switzerland
Francesco Orabona	Boston University, USA

W09 – PoseTrack Challenge: Articulated People Tracking in the Wild

Mykhaylo Andriluka	Google Research, Switzerland
Umar Iqbal	University of Bonn, Germany
Anton Milan	Amazon, Germany
Leonid Pishchulin	Max Planck Institute for Informatics, Germany
Christoph Lassner	Amazon, Germany
Eldar Insafutdinov	Max Planck Institute for Informatics, Germany
Siyu Tang	Max Planck Institute for Intelligent Systems, Germany
Juergen Gall	University of Bonn, Germany
Bernt Schiele	Max Planck Institute for Informatics, Germany

W10 – Workshop on Objectionable Content and Misinformation

Cristian Canton Ferrer	Facebook, USA
Matthias Niessner	Technical University of Munich, Germany
Paul Natsev	Google, USA
Marius Vlad	Google, Switzerland

W11 – 9th International Workshop on Human Behavior Understanding

Xavier Alameda-Pineda	Inria Grenoble, France
Elisa Ricci	Fondazione Bruno Kessler and University of Trento, Italy
Albert Ali Salah	Boğaziçi University, Turkey
Nicu Sebe	University of Trento, Italy
Shuicheng Yan	National University of Singapore, Singapore

W12 – First Person in Context Workshop and Challenge

Si Liu	Beihang University, China
Jiashi Feng	National University of Singapore, Singapore
Jizhong Han	Institute of Information Engineering, China
Shuicheng Yan	National University of Singapore, Singapore
Yao Sun	Institute of Information Engineering, China

Yue Liao   Institute of Information Engineering, China
Lejian Ren   Institute of Information Engineering, China
Guanghui Ren   Institute of Information Engineering, China

W13 – 4th Workshop on Computer Vision for Art Analysis

Stuart James   Istituto Italiano di Tecnologia, Italy and University College
                       London, UK
Leonardo Impett   EPFL, Switzerland and Biblioteca Hertziana, Max Planck
                       Institute for Art History, Italy
Peter Hall   University of Bath, UK
João Paulo Costeira   Instituto Superior Tecnico, Portugal
Peter Bell   Friedrich-Alexander-University Nürnberg, Germany
Alessio Del Bue   Istituto Italiano di Tecnologia, Italy

W14 – First Workshop on Fashion, Art, and Design

Hui Wu   IBM Research AI, USA
Negar Rostamzadeh   Element AI, Canada
Leonidas Lefakis   Zalando Research, Germany
Joy Tang   Markable, USA
Rogerio Feris   IBM Research AI, USA
Tamara Berg   UNC Chapel Hill/Shopagon Inc., USA
Luba Elliott   Independent Curator/Researcher/Producer
Aaron Courville   MILA/University of Montreal, Canada
Chris Pal   MILA/PolyMTL, Canada
Sanja Fidler   University of Toronto, Canada
Xavier Snelgrove   Element AI, Canada
David Vazquez   Element AI, Canada
Julia Lasserre   Zalando Research, Germany
Thomas Boquet   Element AI, Canada
Nana Yamazaki   Zalando SE, Germany

W15 – Anticipating Human Behavior

Juergen Gall   University of Bonn, Germany
Jan van Gemert   Delft University of Technology, The Netherlands
Kris Kitani   Carnegie Mellon University, USA

W16 – Third Workshop on Geometry Meets Deep Learning

Xiaowei Zhou   Zhejiang University, China
Emanuele Rodolà   Sapienza University of Rome, Italy
Jonathan Masci   NNAISENSE, Switzerland
Kosta Derpanis   Ryerson University, Canada

W17 – First Workshop on Brain-Driven Computer Vision

Simone Palazzo	University of Catania, Italy
Isaak Kavasidis	University of Catania, Italy
Dimitris Kastaniotis	University of Patras, Greece
Stavros Dimitriadis	Cardiff University, UK

W18 – Second Workshop on 3D Reconstruction Meets Semantics

Radim Tylecek	University of Edinburgh, UK
Torsten Sattler	ETH Zurich, Switzerland
Thomas Brox	University of Freiburg, Germany
Marc Pollefeys	ETH Zurich/Microsoft, Switzerland
Robert B. Fisher	University of Edinburgh, UK
Theo Gevers	University of Amsterdam, Netherlands

W19 – Third International Workshop on Video Segmentation

Pablo Arbelaez	Universidad de los Andes, Columbia
Thomas Brox	University of Freiburg, Germany
Fabio Galasso	OSRAM GmbH, Germany
Iasonas Kokkinos	University College London, UK
Fuxin Li	Oregon State University, USA

W20 – PeopleCap 2018: Capturing and Modeling Human Bodies, Faces, and Hands

Gerard Pons-Moll	MPI for Informatics and Saarland Informatics Campus, Germany
Jonathan Taylor	Google, USA

W21 – Workshop on Shortcomings in Vision and Language

Dhruv Batra	Georgia Institute of Technology and Facebook AI Research, USA
Raffaella Bernardi	University of Trento, Italy
Raquel Fernández	University of Amsterdam, The Netherlands
Spandana Gella	University of Edinburgh, UK
Kushal Kafle	Rochester Institute of Technology, USA
Moin Nabi	SAP SE, Germany
Stefan Lee	Georgia Institute of Technology, USA

W22 – Second YouTube-8M Large-Scale Video Understanding Workshop

Apostol (Paul) Natsev	Google Research, USA
Rahul Sukthankar	Google Research, USA
Joonseok Lee	Google Research, USA
George Toderici	Google Research, USA

W23 – Second International Workshop on Compact and Efficient Feature Representation and Learning in Computer Vision

Jie Qin	ETH Zurich, Switzerland
Li Liu	National University of Defense Technology, China and University of Oulu, Finland
Li Liu	Inception Institute of Artificial Intelligence, UAE
Fan Zhu	Inception Institute of Artificial Intelligence, UAE
Matti Pietikäinen	University of Oulu, Finland
Luc Van Gool	ETH Zurich, Switzerland

W24 – 5th Women in Computer Vision Workshop

Zeynep Akata	University of Amsterdam, The Netherlands
Dena Bazazian	Computer Vision Center, Spain
Yana Hasson	Inria, France
Angjoo Kanazawa	UC Berkeley, USA
Hildegard Kuehne	University of Bonn, Germany
Gül Varol	Inria, France

W25 – Perceptual Image Restoration and Manipulation Workshop and Challenge

Yochai Blau	Technion – Israel Institute of Technology, Israel
Roey Mechrez	Technion – Israel Institute of Technology, Israel
Radu Timofte	ETH Zurich, Switzerland
Tomer Michaeli	Technion – Israel Institute of Technology, Israel
Lihi Zelnik-Manor	Technion – Israel Institute of Technology, Israel

W26 – Egocentric Perception, Interaction, and Computing

Dima Damen	University of Bristol, UK
Giuseppe Serra	University of Udine, Italy
David Crandall	Indiana University, USA
Giovanni Maria Farinella	University of Catania, Italy
Antonino Furnari	University of Catania, Italy

W27 – Vision Meets Drone: A Challenge

Pengfei Zhu	Tianjin University, China
Longyin Wen	JD Finance, USA
Xiao Bian	GE Global Research, USA
Haibin Ling	Temple University, USA

W28 – 11th Perceptual Organization in Computer Vision Workshop on Action, Perception, and Organization

Deepak Pathak	UC Berkeley, USA
Bharath Hariharan	Cornell University, USA

W29 – AutoNUE: Autonomous Navigation in Unconstrained Environments

Manmohan Chandraker	University of California San Diego, USA
C. V. Jawahar	IIIT Hyderabad, India
Anoop M. Namboodiri	IIIT Hyderabad, India
Srikumar Ramalingam	University of Utah, USA
Anbumani Subramanian	Intel, Bangalore, India

W30 – ApolloScape: Vision-Based Navigation for Autonomous Driving

Peng Wang	Baidu Research, USA
Ruigang Yang	Baidu Research, China
Andreas Geiger	ETH Zurich, Switzerland
Hongdong Li	Australian National University, Australia
Alan Yuille	The Johns Hopkins University, USA

W31 – 6th International Workshop on Assistive Computer Vision and Robotics

Giovanni Maria Farinella	University of Catania, Italy
Marco Leo	National Research Council of Italy, Italy
Gerard G. Medioni	University of Southern California, USA
Mohan Trivedi	University of California, USA

W32 – 4th International Workshop on Observing and Understanding Hands in Action

Iason Oikonomidis	Foundation for Research and Technology, Greece
Guillermo Garcia-Hernando	Imperial College London, UK
Angela Yao	National University of Singapore, Singapore
Antonis Argyros	University of Crete/Foundation for Research and Technology, Greece
Vincent Lepetit	University of Bordeaux, France
Tae-Kyun Kim	Imperial College London, UK

W33 – Bioimage Computing

Jens Rittscher	University of Oxford, UK
Anna Kreshuk	University of Heidelberg, Germany
Florian Jug	Max Planck Institute CBG, Germany

W34 – First Workshop on Interactive and Adaptive Learning in an Open World

Erik Rodner	Carl Zeiss AG, Germany
Alexander Freytag	Carl Zeiss AG, Germany
Vittorio Ferrari	Google, Switzerland/University of Edinburgh, UK
Mario Fritz	CISPA Helmholtz Center i.G., Germany
Uwe Franke	Daimler AG, Germany
Terrence Boult	University of Colorado, Colorado Springs, USA

Juergen Gall   University of Bonn, Germany
Walter Scheirer   University of Notre Dame, USA
Angela Yao   University of Bonn, Germany

W35 – First Multimodal Learning and Applications Workshop

Paolo Rota   University of Trento, Italy
Vittorio Murino   Istituto Italiano di Tecnologia, Italy
Michael Yang   University of Twente, The Netherlands
Bodo Rosenhahn   Leibniz-Universität Hannover, Germany

W36 – What Is Optical Flow for?

Fatma Güney   Oxford University, UK
Laura Sevilla-Lara   Facebook Research, USA
Deqing Sun   NVIDIA, USA
Jonas Wulff   Massachusetts Institute of Technology, USA

W37 – Vision for XR

Richard Newcombe   Facebook Reality Labs, USA
Chris Sweeney   Facebook Reality Labs, USA
Julian Straub   Facebook Reality Labs, USA
Jakob Engel   Facebook Reality Labs, USA
Michael Goesele   Technische Universität Darmstadt, Germany

W38 – Open Images Challenge Workshop

Vittorio Ferrari   Google AI, Switzerland
Alina Kuznetsova   Google AI, Switzerland
Jordi Pont-Tuset   Google AI, Switzerland
Matteo Malloci   Google AI, Switzerland
Jasper Uijlings   Google AI, Switzerland
Jake Walker   Google AI, Switzerland
Rodrigo Benenson   Google AI, Switzerland

W39 – VizWiz Grand Challenge: Answering Visual Questions from Blind People

Danna Gurari   University of Texas at Austin, USA
Kristen Grauman   University of Texas at Austin, USA
Jeffrey P. Bigham   Carnegie Mellon University, USA

W40 – 360° Perception and Interaction

Min Sun   National Tsing Hua University, Taiwan
Yu-Chuan Su   University of Texas at Austin, USA
Wei-Sheng Lai   University of California, Merced, USA
Liwei Chan   National Chiao Tung University, USA
Hou-Ning Hu   National Tsing Hua University, Taiwan
Silvio Savarese   Stanford University, USA

Kristen Grauman   University of Texas at Austin, USA
Ming-Hsuan Yang   University of California, Merced, USA

W41 – Joint COCO and Mapillary Recognition Challenge Workshop

Tsung-Yi Lin   Google Brain, USA
Genevieve Patterson   Microsoft Research, USA
Matteo R. Ronchi   Caltech, USA
Yin Cui   Cornell, USA
Piotr Dollár   Facebook AI Research, USA
Michael Maire   TTI-Chicago, USA
Serge Belongie   Cornell, USA
Lubomir Bourdev   WaveOne, Inc., USA
Ross Girshick   Facebook AI Research, USA
James Hays   Georgia Tech, USA
Pietro Perona   Caltech, USA
Deva Ramanan   CMU, USA
Larry Zitnick   Facebook AI Research, USA
Riza Alp Guler   Inria, France
Natalia Neverova   Facebook AI Research, France
Vasil Khalidov   Facebook AI Research, France
Iasonas Kokkinos   Facebook AI Research, France
Samuel Rota Bulò   Mapillary Research, Austria
Lorenzo Porzi   Mapillary Research, Austria
Peter Kontschieder   Mapillary Research, Austria
Alexander Kirillov   Heidelberg University, Germany
Holger Caesar   University of Edinburgh, UK
Jasper Uijlings   Google Research, UK
Vittorio Ferrari   University of Edinburgh and Google Research, UK

W42 – First Large-Scale Video Object Segmentation Challenge

Ning Xu   Adobe Research, USA
Linjie Yang   SNAP Research, USA
Yuchen Fan   University of Illinois at Urbana-Champaign, USA
Jianchao Yang   SNAP Research, USA
Weiyao Lin   Shanghai Jiao Tong University, China
Michael Ying Yang   University of Twente, The Netherlands
Brian Price   Adobe Research, USA
Jiebo Luo   University of Rochester, USA
Thomas Huang   University of Illinois at Urbana-Champaign, USA

W43 – WIDER Face and Pedestrian Challenge

Chen Change Loy	Nanyang Technological University, Singapore
Dahua Lin	The Chinese University of Hong Kong, SAR China
Wanli Ouyang	University of Sydney, Australia
Yuanjun Xiong	Amazon Rekognition, USA
Shuo Yang	Amazon Rekognition, USA
Qingqiu Huang	The Chinese University of Hong Kong, SAR China
Dongzhan Zhou	SenseTime, China
Wei Xia	Amazon Rekognition, USA
Quanquan Li	SenseTime, China
Ping Luo	The Chinese University of Hong Kong, SAR China
Junjie Yan	SenseTime, China

Contents – Part I

W02 – 6th Workshop on Computer Vision for Road Scene Understanding and Autonomous Driving

W03 – 3D Reconstruction in the Wild

**W04 – Workshop on Visual Learning and Embodied Agents
in Simulation Environments**

W05 – Bias Estimation in Face Analytics

W01 – The Visual Object Tracking Challenge Workshop

W01 – The Visual Object Tracking Challenge Workshop

This VOT2018 workshop is the sixth in a series of annual workshops on visual single-object tracking of a priori unknown objects. The challenges hosted by the workshops are the VOT-ST on RGB short-term tracking, the VOT-TIR on thermal and infrared tracking (since 2015), the VOT-RT on real-time tracking (since 2017), and the new VOT-LT on long-term tracking. This year, the VOT-ST and VOT-RT challenges received 56 trackers. The Technical Committee provided additional 16 trackers that define a baseline. All submissions qualified for inclusion in the results paper by outperforming the baseline. The submission of 56 trackers to VOT-ST/-RT is a notable 47% increase compared to 2017. VOT-LT received 11 submissions. All submissions qualified by reaching the baseline set by four additional trackers provided by the Technical Committee.

The first paper in the proceedings covers the results of the challenges, comprising work of 155 coauthors from 59 institutions. The paper (with results omitted) was shared with all coauthors who provided feedback and improved the quality. The VOT2018 workshop organizers received 15 regular submissions. Ten papers were reviewed in a double-blind process; each paper by two Program Committee members. Five papers were re-submissions of rejected ECCV papers, which included reviews, rebuttal reports, and information of improvements to the original work. These five papers were reviewed by the Organizing Committee. Eight papers were finally accepted. Three papers on correlation filtering show improvements in optimisation and feature pruning as well as an ensemble approach. Further three papers on Siamese networks discuss the use of memory and new context features for a better matching. In addition to these two prominent approaches, U. Kart, J-K. Kämäräinen and J. Matas show a novel framework to incorporate depth to RGB trackers. E. Burceanu and M. Leordeanu propose new ideas and constraints for parts-based representations.

We thank all Program Committee members for the effort, which is essential for maintaining the scientific quality of the effort, all the authors for their contributions, all the workshop participants for their valuable comments on future challenges during the panel discussion, and our sponsors – SICK AG and University Ljubljana, Faculty of Computer and Information Science – for their financial support. More information including past challenges is available on the VOT web page: http://www.votchallenge.net/vot2018/; 25/09/2018.

September 2018

Matej Kristan
Aleš Leonardis
Jiři Matas
Michael Felsberg
Roman Pflugfelder

The Sixth Visual Object Tracking VOT2018 Challenge Results

Matej Kristan[1]([✉]), Aleš Leonardis[2], Jiří Matas[3], Michael Felsberg[4],
Roman Pflugfelder[5,6], Luka Čehovin Zajc[1], Tomáš Vojíř[3], Goutam Bhat[4],
Alan Lukežič[1], Abdelrahman Eldesokey[4], Gustavo Fernández[5],
Álvaro García-Martín[44], Álvaro Iglesias-Arias[44], A. Aydin Alatan[28],
Abel González-García[47], Alfredo Petrosino[54], Alireza Memarmoghadam[53],
Andrea Vedaldi[55], Andrej Muhič[1], Anfeng He[27], Arnold Smeulders[48],
Asanka G. Perera[57], Bo Li[7], Boyu Chen[13], Changick Kim[24], Changsheng Xu[30],
Changzhen Xiong[9], Cheng Tian[16], Chong Luo[27], Chong Sun[13], Cong Hao[52],
Daijin Kim[34], Deepak Mishra[19], Deming Chen[52], Dong Wang[13],
Dongyoon Wee[31], Efstratios Gavves[48], Erhan Gundogdu[14],
Erik Velasco-Salido[44], Fahad Shahbaz Khan[4], Fan Yang[42], Fei Zhao[32,50],
Feng Li[16], Francesco Battistone[26], George De Ath[51],
Gorthi R. K. S. Subrahmanyam[19], Guilherme Bastos[45], Haibin Ling[42],
Hamed Kiani Galoogahi[35], Hankyeol Lee[24], Haojie Li[40], Haojie Zhao[13],
Heng Fan[42], Honggang Zhang[10], Horst Possegger[15], Houqiang Li[56],
Huchuan Lu[13], Hui Zhi[9], Huiyun Li[39], Hyemin Lee[34], Hyung Jin Chang[2],
Isabela Drummond[45], Jack Valmadre[55], Jaime Spencer Martin[58],
Javaan Chahl[57], Jin Young Choi[37], Jing Li[12], Jinqiao Wang[32,50], Jinqing Qi[13],
Jinyoung Sung[31], Joakim Johnander[4], Joao Henriques[55], Jongwon Choi[37],
Joost van de Weijer[47], Jorge Rodríguez Herranz[1,41], José M. Martínez[44],
Josef Kittler[58], Junfei Zhuang[8,10], Junyu Gao[30], Klemen Grm[1],
Lichao Zhang[47], Lijun Wang[13], Lingxiao Yang[17], Litu Rout[19], Liu Si[22],
Luca Bertinetto[55], Lutao Chu[39,50], Manqiang Che[9], Mario Edoardo Maresca[54],
Martin Danelljan[4], Ming-Hsuan Yang[49], Mohamed Abdelpakey[25],
Mohamed Shehata[25], Myunggu Kang[31], Namhoon Lee[55], Ning Wang[56],
Ondrej Miksik[55], P. Moallem[53], Pablo Vicente-Moñivar[44], Pedro Senna[46],
Peixia Li[13], Philip Torr[55], Priya Mariam Raju[19], Qian Ruihe[22],
Qiang Wang[30], Qin Zhou[38], Qing Guo[43], Rafael Martín-Nieto[44],
Rama Krishna Gorthi[19], Ran Tao[48], Richard Bowden[58], Richard Everson[51],
Runling Wang[33], Sangdoo Yun[37], Seokeon Choi[24], Sergio Vivas[44],
Shuai Bai[8,10], Shuangping Huang[40], Sihang Wu[40], Simon Hadfield[58],
Siwen Wang[13], Stuart Golodetz[55], Tang Ming[32,50], Tianyang Xu[23],
Tianzhu Zhang[30], Tobias Fischer[18], Vincenzo Santopietro[54], Vitomir Štruc[1],
Wang Wei[11], Wangmeng Zuo[16], Wei Feng[43], Wei Wu[36], Wei Zou[21],
Weiming Hu[30], Wengang Zhou[56], Wenjun Zeng[27], Xiaofan Zhang[52],
Xiaohe Wu[16], Xiao-Jun Wu[23], Xinmei Tian[56], Yan Li[9], Yan Lu[9],
Yee Wei Law[57], Yi Wu[20,29], Yiannis Demiris[18], Yicai Yang[40], Yifan Jiao[30],
Yuhong Li[10,52], Yunhua Zhang[13], Yuxuan Sun[13], Zheng Zhang[59],
Zheng Zhu[21,50], Zhen-Hua Feng[58], Zhihui Wang[13],
and Zhiqun He[8,10]

L. Leal-Taixé and S. Roth (Eds.): ECCV 2018 Workshops, LNCS 11129, pp. 3–53, 2019.
https://doi.org/10.1007/978-3-030-11009-3_1

[1] University of Ljubljana, Ljubljana, Slovenia
matej.kristan@fri.uni-lj.si
[2] University of Birmingham, Birmingham, UK
[3] Czech Technical University, Prague, Czech Republic
[4] Linköping University, Linköping, Sweden
[5] Austrian Institute of Technology, Seibersdorf, Austria
[6] TU Wien, Vienna, Austria
[7] Beihang University, Beijing, China
[8] Beijing Faceall Co., Beijing, China
[9] Beijing Key Laboratory of Urban Intelligent Control, Beijing, China
[10] Beijing University of Posts and Telecommunications, Beijing, China
[11] China Huayin Ordnance Test Center, Huayin, China
[12] Civil Aviation University of China, Tianjin, China
[13] Dalian University of Technology, Dalian, China
[14] EPFL, Lausanne, Switzerland
[15] Graz University of Technology, Graz, Austria
[16] Harbin Institute of Technology, Harbin, China
[17] Hong Kong Polytechnic University, Kowloon, Hong Kong
[18] Imperial College London, London, UK
[19] Indian Institute of Space Science and Technology, Thiruvananthapuram, India
[20] Indiana University, Bloomington, USA
[21] Institute of Automation, Chinese Academy of Sciences, Beijing, China
[22] Institute of Information Engineering, Beijing, China
[23] Jiangnan University, Wuxi, China
[24] KAIST, Daejeon, South Korea
[25] Memorial University of Newfoundland, St. John's, Canada
[26] Mer Mec S.p.A., Monopoli, Italy
[27] Microsoft Research Asia, Beijing, China
[28] Middle East Technical University, Ankara, Turkey
[29] Nanjing Audit University, Nanjing, China
[30] National Laboratory of Pattern Recognition, Beijing, China
[31] Naver Corporation, Seongnam, South Korea
[32] NLPR, Institute of Automation, Chinese Academy of Sciences, Beijing, China
[33] North China University of Technology, Beijing, China
[34] POSTECH, Pohang, South Korea
[35] Robotics Institute, Carnegie Mellon University, Pittsburgh, USA
[36] Sensetime, Beijing, China
[37] Seoul National University, Seoul, South Korea
[38] Shanghai Jiao Tong University, Shanghai, China
[39] Shenzhen Institute of Advanced Technology, Chinese Academy of Sciences,
Shenzhen, China
[40] South China University of Technology, Guangzhou, China
[41] Technical University of Madrid, Madrid, Spain
[42] Temple University, Philadelphia, USA
[43] Tianjin University, Tianjin, China
[44] Universidad Autónoma de Madrid, Madrid, Spain
[45] Universidade Federal de Itajubá, Itajubá, Brazil
[46] Universidade Federal do Mato Grosso do Sul, Campo Grande, Brazil
[47] Universitat Autónoma de Barcelona, Barcelona, Spain
[48] University of Amsterdam, Amsterdam, Netherlands

[49] University of California, Merced, USA
[50] University of Chinese Academy of Sciences, Beijing, China
[51] University of Exter, Exter, UK
[52] University of Illinois Urbana-Champaign, Urbana, USA
[53] University of Isfahan, Isfahan, Iran
[54] University of Naples Parthenope, Naples, Italy
[55] University of Oxford, Oxford, UK
[56] University of Science and Technology of China, Hefei, China
[57] University of South Australia, Adelaide, Australia
[58] University of Surrey, Guildford, UK
[59] Zhejiang University, Hangzhou, China

Abstract. The Visual Object Tracking challenge VOT2018 is the sixth
annual tracker benchmarking activity organized by the VOT initiative.
Results of over eighty trackers are presented; many are state-of-the-art
trackers published at major computer vision conferences or in journals in
the recent years. The evaluation included the standard VOT and other
popular methodologies for short-term tracking analysis and a "real-time"
experiment simulating a situation where a tracker processes images as
if provided by a continuously running sensor. A long-term tracking sub-
challenge has been introduced to the set of standard VOT sub-challenges.
The new subchallenge focuses on long-term tracking properties, namely
coping with target disappearance and reappearance. A new dataset has
been compiled and a performance evaluation methodology that focuses
on long-term tracking capabilities has been adopted. The VOT toolkit
has been updated to support both standard short-term and the new long-
term tracking subchallenges. Performance of the tested trackers typically
by far exceeds standard baselines. The source code for most of the trackers is publicly available from the VOT page. The dataset, the evaluation
kit and the results are publicly available at the challenge website (http://
votchallenge.net).

1   Introduction

Visual object tracking has consistently been a popular research area over the
last two decades. The popularity has been propelled by significant research challenges tracking offers as well as the industrial potential of tracking-based applications. Several initiatives have been established to promote tracking, such as
PETS [95], CAVIAR[1], i-LIDS[2], ETISEO[3], CDC [25], CVBASE[4], FERET [67],
LTDT[5], MOTC [44,76] and Videonet[6], and since 2013 short-term single target
visual object tracking has been receiving a strong push toward performance

---

[1] http://homepages.inf.ed.ac.uk/rbf/CAVIARDATA1.
[2] http://www.homeoffice.gov.uk/science-research/hosdb/i-lids.
[3] http://www-sop.inria.fr/orion/ETISEO.
[4] http://vision.fe.uni-lj.si/cvbase06/.
[5] http://www.micc.unifi.it/LTDT2014/.
[6] http://videonet.team.

evaluation standardisation from the VOT[7] initiative. The primary goal of VOT is establishing datasets, evaluation measures and toolkits as well as creating a platform for discussing evaluation-related issues through organization of tracking challenges. Since 2013, five challenges have taken place in conjunction with ICCV2013 (VOT2013 [41]), ECCV2014 (VOT2014 [42]), ICCV2015 (VOT2015 [40]), ECCV2016 (VOT2016 [39]) and ICCV2017 (VOT2017 [38]).

This paper presents the VOT2018 challenge, organized in conjunction with the ECCV2018 Visual Object Tracking Workshop, and the results obtained. The VOT2018 challenge addresses two classes of trackers. The first class has been considered in the past five challenges: single-camera, single-target, model-free, causal trackers, applied to short-term tracking. The *model-free* property means that the only training information provided is the bounding box in the first frame. The *short-term* tracking means that trackers are assumed not to be capable of performing successful re-detection after the target is lost and they are therefore reset after such an event. *Causality* requires that the tracker does not use any future frames, or frames prior to re-initialization, to infer the object position in the current frame. The second class of trackers is introduced this year in the *first VOT long-term sub-challenge*. This subchallenge considers single-camera, single-target, model-free long-term trackers. The *long-term* tracking means that the trackers are *required* to perform re-detection after the target has been lost and are therefore *not* reset after such an event. In the following, we overview the most closely related works and point out the contributions of VOT2018.

1.1   Related Work in Short-Term Tracking

A lot of research has been invested into benchmarking and performance evaluation in short-term visual object tracking [38–43, 47, 51, 61, 62, 75, 83, 92, 96, 101]. The currently most widely-used methodologies have been popularized by two benchmark papers: "Online Tracking Benchmark" (OTB) [92] and "Visual Object Tracking challenge" (VOT) [41]. The methodologies differ in the evaluation protocols as well as the performance measures.

The OTB-based evaluation approaches initialize the tracker in the first frame and let it runs until the end of the sequence. The benefit of this protocol is its implementation simplicity. But target predictions become irrelevant for tracking accuracy of short-term trackers after the initial failure, which introduces variance and bias in the results [43]. The VOT evaluation approach addresses this issue by resetting the tracker after each failure.

All recent performance evaluation protocols measure tracking accuracy primarily by intersection over union (IoU) between the ground truth and tracker prediction bounding boxes. A legacy center-based measure initially promoted by Babenko et al. [3] and later adopted by [90] is still often used, but is theoretically brittle and inferior to the overlap-based measure [83]. In the no-reset-based protocols the overall performance is summarized by the average IoU over the dataset (i.e., average overlap) [83, 90]. In the VOT reset-based protocols, two

---
[7] http://votchallenge.net.

measures are used to probe the performance: (i) accuracy and (ii) robustness. They measure the overlap during successful tracking periods and the number of times the tracker fails. Since 2015, the VOT primary measure is the expected average overlap (EAO) – a principled combination of accuracy and robustness. The VOT reports the so-called state-of-the-art bound (*SotA* bound) on all their annual challenges. Any tracker exceeding *SotA* bound is considered state-of-the-art by VOT standard. This bound was introduced to counter the trend of considering state-of-the-art only those trackers that rank number one on benchmarks. By *SotA* bound, the hope was to remove the need of fine-tuning to benchmarks and to incent community-wide exploration of a wider spectrum of trackers, not necessarily getting the number one rank.

Tracking speed was recognized as an important tracking factor in VOT2014 [42]. Initially the speed was measured in terms of equivalent filtering operations [42] to reduce the varying hardware influence. This measure was abandoned due to limited normalization capability and due to the fact that speed often varies a lot during tracking. Since VOT2017 [42] speed aspects are measured by a protocol that requires real-time processing of incoming frames.

Most tracking datasets [47,51,61,75,92] have partially followed the trend in computer vision of increasing the number of sequences. But quantity does not necessarily reflect diversity nor richness in attributes. Over the years, the VOT [38–43] has developed a dataset construction methodology for constructing moderately large challenging datasets from a large pool of sequences. Through annual discussions at VOT workshops, the community expressed a request for evaluating trackers on a sequestered dataset. In response, the VOT2017 challenge introduced a sequestered dataset evaluation for winner identification in the main short-term challenge. In 2015 VOT introduced a sub-challenge for evaluating short-term trackers on thermal and infra-red sequences (VOT-TIR2015) with a dataset specially designed for that purpose [21]. Recently, datasets focusing on various short-term tracking aspects have been introduced. The UAV123 [61] and [101] proposed datasets for tracking from drones. Lin et al. [94] proposed a dataset for tracking faces by mobile phones. Galoogahi et al. [22] introduced a high-frame-rate dataset to analyze trade-offs between tracker speed and robustness. Čehovin et al. [96] proposed a dataset with an active camera view control using omni directional videos. Mueller et al. [62] recently re-annotated selected sequences from Youtube bounding boxes [69] to consider tracking in the wild. Despite significant activity in dataset construction, the VOT dataset remains unique for its carefully chosen and curated sequences guaranteeing relatively unbiased assessment of performance with respect to attributes.

1.2   Related Work in Long-Term Tracking

Long-term (LT) trackers have received far less attention than short-term (ST) trackers. A major difference between ST and LT trackers is that LT trackers are required to handle situations in which the target may leave the field of view for a longer duration. This means that LT trackers have to detect target absence and re-detect the target when it reappears. Therefore a natural evaluation protocol for LT tracking is a no-reset protocol.

A typical structure of a long-term tracker is a short-term component with a relatively small search range responsible for frame-to-frame association and a detector component responsible for detecting target reappearance. In addition, an interaction mechanism between the short-term component and the detector is required that appropriately updates the visual models and switches between target tracking and detection. This structure originates from two seminal papers in long-term tracking TLD [37] and Alien [66], and has been reused in all subsequent LT trackers (e.g., [20,34,57,59,65,100]).

The set of performance measures in long-term tracking is quite diverse and has not been converging like in the short-term tracking. The early long-term tracking papers [37,66] considered measures from object detection literature since detectors play a central role in LT tracking. The primary performance measures were precision, recall and F-measure computed at 0.5 IoU (overlap) threshold. But for tracking, the overlap of 0.5 is over-restrictive as discussed in [37,43] and does not faithfully reflect the overall tracking capabilities. Furthermore, the approach requires a binary output – either target is present or absent. In general, a tracker can report the target position along with a presence certainty score which offers a more accurate analysis, but this is prevented by the binary output requirement. In addition to precision/recall measures, the authors of [37,66] proposed using average center error to analyze tracking accuracy. But center-error-based measures are even more brittle than IoU-based measures, are resolution-dependent and are computed only in frames where the target is present and the tracker reports its position. Thus most papers published in the last few years (e.g, [20,34,57]) have simply used the short-term average overlap performance measure from [61,90]. But this measure does not account for the tracker's ability to correctly report target absence and favors reporting target positions at every frame. Attempts were made to address this drawback [60,79] by specifying an overlap equal to 1 when the tracker correctly predicts the target absence, but this does not clearly separate re-detection ability from tracking accuracy. Recently, Lukežič et al. [56] have proposed *tracking* precision, *tracking* recall and *tracking* F-measure that avoid dependence on the IoU threshold and allow analyzing trackers with presence certainty outputs without assuming a predefined scale of the outputs. They have shown that their primary measure, the tracking F-measure, reduces to a standard short-term measure (average overlap) when computed in a short-term setup.

Only few datasets have been proposed in long-term tracking. The first dataset was introduced by the LTDT challenge (See footnote 5), which offered a collection of specific videos from [37,45,66,75]. These videos were chosen using the following definition of the long-term sequence: *"long-term sequence is a video that is at least 2 min long (at 25–30 fps), but ideally 10 min or longer"* (See footnote 5). Mueller et al. [61] proposed a UAV20L dataset containing twenty long sequences with many target disappearances recorded from drones. Recently, three benchmarks that propose datasets with many target disappearances have almost concurrently appeared on pre-pub [36,56,60]. The benchmark [60] primarily analyzes performance of short-term trackers on long sequences, and [36] proposes a huge dataset constructed from Youtube bounding boxes [69]. To cope with significant dataset size, [36] annotate the tracked object every few frames. The benchmark [60] does not distinguish between short-term and long-term trackers architectures but considers LT tracking as the ability to track long sequences attributing most of performance boosts to robust visual models. The benchmarks [36,56], on the other hand, point out the importance of re-detection and [56] uses this as a guideline to construct a moderately sized dataset with many long-term specific attributes. In fact, [56] argue that long-term tracking does not just refer to the sequence length, but more importantly to the sequence properties (number of target disappearances, etc.) and the type of tracking output expected. They argue that there are several levels of tracker types between pure short-term and long-term trackers and propose a new short-term/long-term tracking taxonomy covering four classes of ST/LT trackers. For these reasons, we base the VOT long-term dataset and evaluation protocols described in Sect. 3 on [56].

1.3   The VOT2018 Challenge

VOT2018 considers short-term as well as long-term trackers in separate sub-challenges. The evaluation toolkit and the datasets are provided by the VOT2018 organizers. These were released on April 26th 2018 for beta-testing. The challenge officially opened on May 5th 2018 with approximately a month available for results submission.

The authors participating in the challenge were required to integrate their tracker into the VOT2018 evaluation kit, which automatically performed a set of standardized experiments. The results were analyzed according to the VOT2018 evaluation methodology.

Participants were encouraged to submit their own new or previously published trackers as well as modified versions of third-party trackers. In the latter case, modifications had to be significant enough for acceptance. Participants were expected to submit a single set of results per tracker. Changes in the parameters did not constitute a different tracker. The tracker was required to run with fixed parameters in all experiments. The tracking method itself was allowed to internally change specific parameters, but these had to be set automatically by the tracker, e.g., from the image size and the initial size of the bounding box, and were not to be set by detecting a specific test sequence and then selecting the parameters that were hand-tuned for this sequence.

Each submission was accompanied by a short abstract describing the tracker, which was used for the short tracker descriptions in Appendix A. In addition, participants filled out a questionnaire on the VOT submission page to categorize their tracker along various design properties. Authors had to agree to help the VOT technical committee to reproduce their results in case their tracker was selected for further validation. Participants with sufficiently well-performing submissions, who contributed with the text for this paper and agreed to make their tracker code publicly available from the VOT page were offered co-authorship of this results paper.

To counter attempts of intentionally reporting large bounding boxes to avoid resets, the VOT committee analyzed the submitted tracker outputs. The committee reserved the right to disqualify the tracker should such or a similar strategy be detected.

To compete for the winner of VOT2018 challenge, learning from the tracking datasets (OTB, VOT, ALOV, NUSPRO and TempleColor) was prohibited. The use of class labels specific to VOT was not allowed (i.e., identifying a target class in each sequence and applying pre-trained class-specific trackers is not allowed). An agreement to publish the code online on VOT webpage was required. The organizers of VOT2018 were allowed to participate in the challenge, but did not compete for the winner of the VOT2018 challenge title. Further details are available from the challenge homepage[8].

Like VOT2017, the VOT2018 was running the main VOT2018 short-term sub-challenge and the VOT2018 short-term real-time sub-challenge, but did not run the short-term thermal and infrared VOT-TIR sub-challenge. As a significant novelty, the VOT2018 introduces a new VOT2018 long-term tracking challenge, adopting the methodology from [56]. The VOT2018 toolkit has been updated to allow seamless use in short-term and long-term tracking evaluation. In the following we overview the sub-challenges.

2 The VOT2018 Short-Term Challenge

The VOT2018 short-term challenge contains the main VOT2018 short-term sub-challenge and the VOT2018 realtime sub-challenge. Both sub-challenges used the same dataset, but different evaluation protocols.

The VOT2017 results have indicated that the 2017 dataset has not saturated, therefore *the dataset was used unchanged* in the VOT2018 short-term challenge. The dataset contains 60 sequences released to public (i.e., VOT2017 *public* dataset) and another 60 *sequestered* sequences (i.e., VOT2017 *sequestered* dataset). Only the former dataset was released to the public, while the latter was not disclosed and was used only to identify the winner of the main VOT2018 short-term challenge. The target in the sequences is annotated by a rotated bounding box and all sequences are per-frame annotated by the following visual attributes: (i) occlusion, (ii) illumination change, (iii) motion change, (iv) size change and (v) camera motion. Frames that did not correspond to any of the five attributes were denoted as (vi) unassigned.

2.1 Performance Measures and Evaluation Protocol

As in VOT2017 [38], three primary measures were used to analyze the short-term tracking performance: accuracy (A), robustness (R) and expected average overlap (EAO). In the following, these are briefly overviewed and we refer to [40, 43, 83] for further details.

---

[8] http://www.votchallenge.net/vot2018/participation.html.

The VOT short-term challenges apply a reset-based methodology. Whenever a tracker predicts a bounding box with zero overlap with the ground truth, a failure is detected and the tracker is re-initialized five frames after the failure. Accuracy and robustness [83] are the basic measures used to probe tracker performance in the reset-based experiments. The accuracy is the average overlap between the predicted and ground truth bounding boxes during successful tracking periods. The robustness measures how many times the tracker loses the target (fails) during tracking. The potential bias due to resets is reduced by ignoring ten frames after re-initialization in the accuracy measure (note that a tracker is reinitialized five frames after failure), which is quite a conservative margin [43]. Average accuracy and failure-rates are reported for stochastic trackers, which are run 15 times.

The third, primary measure, called the expected average overlap (EAO), is an estimator of the average overlap a tracker is expected to attain on a large collection of short-term sequences with the same visual properties as the given dataset. The measure addresses the problem of increased variance and bias of AO [92] measure due to variable sequence lengths. Please see [40] for further details on the average expected overlap measure. For reference, the toolkit also ran a no-reset experiment and the AO [92] was computed (available in the online results).

2.2   The VOT2018 Real-Time Sub-challenge

The VOT2018 real-time sub-challenge was introduced in VOT2017 [38] and is a variation of the main VOT2018 short-term sub-challenge. The main VOT2018 short-term sub-challenge does not place any constraint on the time for processing a single frame. In contrast, the VOT2018 real-time sub-challenge requires predicting bounding boxes faster or equal to the video frame-rate. The toolkit sends images to the tracker via the Trax protocol [10] at 20 fps. If the tracker does not respond in time, the last reported bounding box is assumed as the reported tracker output at the available frame (zero-order hold dynamic model).

The toolkit applies a reset-based VOT evaluation protocol by resetting the tracker whenever the tracker bounding box does not overlap with the ground truth. The VOT frame skipping is applied as well to reduce the correlation between resets.

2.3   Winner Identification Protocol

On the main VOT2018 short-term sub-challenge, the winner is identified as follows. Trackers are ranked according to the EAO measure on the public dataset. Top ten trackers are re-run by the VOT2018 committee on the sequestered dataset. The top ranked tracker on the sequestered dataset not submitted by the VOT2018 committee members is the winner of the main VOT2018 short-term challenge. The winner of the VOT2018 real-time challenge is identified as the top-ranked tracker not submitted by the VOT2018 committee members according to the EAO on the public dataset.

3   The VOT2018 Long-Term Challenge

The VOT2018 long-term challenge focuses on the long-term tracking properties. In a long-term setup, the object may leave the field of view or become fully occluded for a long period. Thus in principle, a tracker is required to report the target absence. To make the integration with the toolkit compatible with the short-term setup, we require the tracker to report the target position in each frame and provide a confidence score of target presence. The VOT2018 adapts long-term tracker definitions, dataset and the evaluation protocol from [56]. We summarize these in the following and direct the reader to the original paper for more details.

3.1   The Short-Term/Long-Term Tracking Spectrum

The following definitions from [56] are used to position the trackers on the short-term/long-term spectrum:

1. **Short-term tracker** (ST_0). The target position is reported at each frame. The tracker does not implement target re-detection and does not explicitly detect occlusion. Such trackers are likely to fail at the first occlusion as their representation is affected by any occluder.
2. **Short-term tracker with conservative updating** (ST_1). The target position is reported at each frame. Target re-detection is not implemented, but tracking robustness is increased by selectively updating the visual model depending on a tracking confidence estimation mechanism.
3. **Pseudo long-term tracker** (LT_0). The target position is not reported in frames when the target is not visible. The tracker does not implement explicit target re-detection but uses an internal mechanism to identify and report tracking failure.
4. **Re-detecting long-term tracker** (LT_1). The target position is not reported in frames when the target is not visible. The tracker detects tracking failure and implements explicit target re-detection.

3.2   The Dataset

Trackers are evaluated on the LTB35 dataset [56]. This dataset contains 35 sequences, carefully selected to obtain a dataset with long sequences containing many target disappearances. Twenty sequences were obtained from the UAVL20 [61], three from [37], six sequences were taken from Youtube and six sequences were generated from the omnidirectional view generator AMP [96] to ensure many target disappearances. Sequence resolutions range between 1280×720 and 290×217. The dataset contains 14687 frames, with 433 target disappearances. Each sequence contains on average 12 long-term target disappearances, each lasting on average 40 frames.

The targets are annotated by axis-aligned bounding boxes. Sequences are annotated by the following visual attributes: (i) Full occlusion, (ii) Out-of-view,

(iii) Partial occlusion, (iv) Camera motion, (v) Fast motion, (vi) Scale change, (vii) Aspect ratio change, (viii) Viewpoint change, (ix) Similar objects. Note this is per-sequence, not per-frame annotation and a sequence can be annotated by several attributes.

3.3 Performance Measures

We use three long-term tracking performance measures proposed in [56]: tracking precision (Pr), tracking recall (Re) and tracking F-score. These are briefly described in the following.

Let G_t be the ground truth target pose, let $A_t(\tau_\theta)$ be the pose predicted by the tracker, θ_t the prediction certainty score at time-step t, τ_θ be a classification (detection) threshold. If the target is absent, the ground truth is an empty set, i.e., $G_t = \emptyset$. Similarly, if the tracker did not predict the target or the prediction certainty score is below a classification threshold i.e., $\theta_t < \tau_\theta$, the output is $A_t(\tau_\theta) = \emptyset$. Let $\Omega(A_t(\tau_\theta), G_t)$ be the intersection over union between the tracker prediction and the ground truth and let N_g be the number of frames with $G_t \neq \emptyset$ and N_p the number of frames with existing prediction, i.e., $A_t(\tau_\theta) \neq \emptyset$.

In detection literature, the prediction matches the ground truth if the overlap $\Omega(A_t(\tau_\theta), G_t)$ exceeds a threshold τ_Ω, which makes precision and recall dependent on the minimal classification certainty as well as minimal overlap thresholds. This problem is addressed in [56] by integrating the precision and recall over all possible overlap thresholds[9]. The tracking precision and tracking recall at classification threshold τ_θ are defined as

$$Pr(\tau_\theta) = \frac{1}{N_p} \sum_{t \in \{t:A_t(\theta_t) \neq \emptyset\}} \Omega(A_t(\theta_t), G_t), \tag{1}$$

$$Re(\tau_\theta) = \frac{1}{N_g} \sum_{t \in \{t:G_t \neq \emptyset\}} \Omega(A_t(\theta_t), G_t). \tag{2}$$

Precision and accuracy are combined into a single score by computing the tracking F-measure:

$$F(\tau_\theta) = 2Pr(\tau_\theta)Re(\tau_\theta)/(Pr(\tau_\theta) + Re(\tau_\theta)). \tag{3}$$

Long-term tracking performance can thus be visualized by tracking precision, tracking accuracy and tracking F-measure plots by computing these scores for all thresholds τ_θ.

The primary long-term tracking measure [56] is F-score, defined as the highest score on the F-measure plot, i.e., taken at the tracker-specific optimal threshold. This avoids arbitrary manual-set thresholds in the primary performance measure.

---

[9] Note that this can be thought of as computing the area under the curve score [90] of a precision plot computed at certainty threshold τ_θ.

3.4   Re-detection Experiment

We also adapt an experiment from [56] designed to test the tracker's re-detection capability separately from the short-term component. This experiment generates an artificial sequence in which the target does not change appearance but only location. An initial frame of a sequence is padded with zeros to the right and down to the three times original size. This frame is repeated for the first five frames in the artificial sequence. For the remainder of the frames, the target is cropped from the initial image and placed in the bottom right corner of the frame with all other pixels set to zero.

A tracker is initialized in the first frame and the experiment measures the number of frames required to re-detect the target after position change. This experiment is re-run over artificial sequences generated from all sequences in the LTB35 dataset.

3.5   Evaluation Protocol

A tracker is evaluated on a dataset of several sequences by initializing on the first frame of a sequence and run until the end of the sequence without re-sets. The precision-recall graph from (1) is calculated on each sequence and averaged into a single plot. This guarantees that the result is not dominated by extremely long sequences. The F-measure plot is computed according to (3) from the average precision-recall plot. The maximal score on the F-measure plot (F-score) is taken as the long-term tracking primary performance measure.

3.6   Winner Identification Protocol

The winner of the VOT2018 long-term tracking challenge is identified as the top-ranked tracker not submitted by the VOT2018 committee members according to the F-score on the LTB35 dataset.

4   The VOT2018 Short-Term Challenge Results

This section summarizes the trackers submitted to the VOT short-term (VOT2018 ST) challenge, results analysis and winner identification.

4.1   Trackers Submitted

In all, 56 valid entries were submitted to the VOT2018 short-term challenge. Each submission included the binaries or source code that allowed verification of the results if required. The VOT2018 committee and associates additionally contributed 16 baseline trackers. For these, the default parameters were selected, or, when not available, were set to reasonable values. Thus in total 72 trackers were tested on the VOT2018 short-term challenge. In the following we briefly overview the entries and provide the references to original papers in the Appendix A where available.

Of all participating trackers, 51 trackers (71%) were categorized as ST_0, 18 trackers (25%) as ST_1, and three (4%) as LT_1. 76% applied discriminative and 24% applied generative models. Most trackers – 75% – used holistic model, while 25% of the participating trackers used part-based models. Most trackers applied either a locally uniform dynamic model[10] (76%), a nearly-constant-velocity (7%), or a random walk dynamic model (15%), while only a single tracker applied a higher order dynamic model (1%).

The trackers were based on various tracking principles: 4 trackers (6%) were based on CNN matching (ALAL A.2, C3DT A.72, LSART A.40, RAnet A.57), one tracker was based on recurrent neural network (ALAL A.2), 14 trackers (18%) applied Siamese networks (ALAL A.2, DensSiam A.23, DSiam A.30, LWDNTm A.41, LWDNTthi A.42, MBSiam A.48, SA_Siam_P A.59, SA_Siam_R A.60, SiamFC A.34, SiamRPN A.35, SiamVGG A.63, STST A.66, UpdateNet A.1), 3 trackers (4%) applied support vector machines (BST A.6, MEEM A.47, struck2011 A.68), 38 trackers (53%) applied discriminative correlation filters (ANT A.3, BoVW_CFT A.4, CCOT A.11, CFCF A.13, CFTR A.15, CPT A.7, CPT_fast A.8, CSRDCF A.24, CSRTPP A.25, CSTEM A.9, DCFCF A.22, DCFNet A.18, DeepCSRDCF A.17, DeepSTRCF A.20, DFPReco A.29, DLSTpp A.28, DPT A.21, DRT A.16, DSST A.26, ECO A.31, HMMTxD A.53, KCF A.38, KFebT A.37, LADCF A.39, MCCT A.50, MFT A.51, MRSNCC A.49, R_MCPF A.56, RCO A.12, RSECF A.14, SAP-KLTF A.62, SRCT A.58, SRDCF A.64, srdcf_deep A.19, srdcf_dif A.32, Staple A.67, STBACF A.65, TRACA A.69, UPDT A.71), 6 trackers (8%) applied mean shift (ASMS A.61, CPOINT A.10, HMMTxD A.53, KFebT A.37, MRSNCC A.49, SAPKLTF A.62) and 8 trackers (11%) applied optical flow (ANT A.3, CPOINT A.10, FoT A.33, Fragtrac A.55, HMMTxD A.53, LGT A.43, MRSNCC A.49, SAPKLTF A.62).

Many trackers used combinations of several features. CNN features were used in 62% of trackers – these were either trained for discrimination (32 trackers) or localization (13 trackers). Hand-crafted features were used in 44% of trackers, keypoints in 14% of trackers, color histograms in 19% and grayscale features were used in 24% of trackers.

4.2   The Main VOT2018 Short-Term Sub-challenge Results

The results are summarized in the AR-raw plots and EAO curves in Fig. 1 and the expected average overlap plots in Fig. 2. The values are also reported in Table 2. The top ten trackers according to the primary EAO measure (Fig. 2) are LADCF A.39, MFT A.51, SiamRPN A.35, UPDT A.71, RCO A.12, DRT A.16, DeepSTRCF A.20, SA_Siam_R A.60, CPT A.7 and DLSTpp A.28. All these trackers apply a discriminatively trained correlation filter on top of multidimensional features except from SiamRPN and SA_Siam_R, which apply siamese

---

[10] The target was sought in a window centered at its estimated position in the previous frame. This is the simplest dynamic model that assumes all positions within a search region contain the target have equal prior probability.

networks. Common networks used by the top ten trackers are Alexnet, Vgg and Resnet in addition to localization pre-trained networks. Many trackers combine the deep features with HOG, Colornames and a grayscale patch.

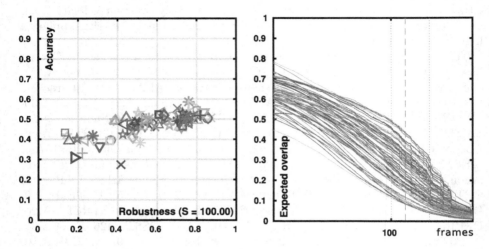

Fig. 1. The AR-raw plots generated by sequence pooling (left) and EAO curves (right). (Color figure online)

The top performer on public dataset is LADCF (A.39). This tracker trains a low-dimensional DCF by using an adaptive spatial regularizer. Adaptive spatial regularization and temporal consistency are combined into a single objective function. The tracker uses HOG, Colournames and ResNet-50 features. Data augmentation by flipping, rotating and blurring is applied to the Resnet features. The second-best ranked tracker is MFT (A.51). This tracker adopts CFWCR [31] as a baseline feature learning algorithm and applies a continuous convolution operator [15] to fuse multiresolution features. The different resolutions are trained independently for target position prediction, which, according to the authors, significantly boosts the robustness. The tracker uses ResNet-50, SE-ResNet-50, HOG and Colornames.

The top trackers in EAO are also among the most robust trackers, which means that they are able to track longer without failing. The top trackers in robustness (Fig. 1) are MFT A.51, LADCF A.39, RCO A.12, UPDT A.71, DRT A.16, LSART A.40, DeepSTRCF A.20, DLSTpp A.28, CPT A.7 and SA_Siam_R A.60. On the other hand, the top performers in accuracy are SiamRPN A.35, SA_Siam_R A.60, FSAN A.70, DLSTpp A.28, UPDT A.71, MCCT A.50, SiamVGG A.63, ALAL A.2, DeepSTRCF A.20 and SA_Siam_P A.59.

The trackers which have been considered as baselines or state-of-the-art even few years ago, i.e., MIL (A.52), IVT (A.36), Struck [28] and KCF (A.38) are positioned at the lower part of the AR-plots and at the tail of the EAO rank

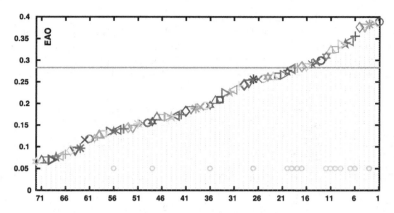

Fig. 2. Expected average overlap graph with trackers ranked from right to left. The right-most tracker is the top-performing according to the VOT2018 expected average overlap values. The dashed horizontal line denotes the average performance of ten state-of-the-art trackers published in 2017 and 2018 at major computer vision venues. These trackers are denoted by gray circle in the bottom part of the graph. (Color figure online)

list. This speaks of the significant quality of the trackers submitted to VOT2018. In fact, 19 tested trackers (26%) have been recently (2017/2018) published at computer vision conferences and journals. These trackers are indicated in Fig. 2, along with their average performance, which constitutes a very strict VOT2018 state-of-the-art bound. Approximately 26% of submitted trackers exceed this bound.

Table 1. Tracking difficulty with respect to the following visual attributes: camera motion (CM), illumination change (IC), motion change (MC), occlusion (OC) and size change (SC).

	CM	IC	MC	OC	SC
Accuracy	0.49	0.47	0.47 ③	0.40 ①	0.43 ②
Robustness	0.74	1.05 ②	0.87 ③	1.19 ①	0.61

The number of failures with respect to the visual attributes is shown in Fig. 3. The overall top performers remain at the top of per-attribute ranks as well, but none of the trackers consistently outperforms all others with respect to each attribute. According to the median robustness and accuracy over each attribute (Table 1) the most challenging attributes in terms of failures are occlusion, illumination change and motion change, followed by camera motion and scale change. Occlusion is the most challenging attribute for tracking accuracy.

The VOT-ST2018 Winner Identification. Top 10 trackers from the baseline experiment (Table 2) were selected to be re-run on the sequestered dataset.

Table 2. The table shows expected average overlap (EAO), as well as accuracy and robustness raw values (A,R) for the baseline and the realtime experiments. For the unsupervised experiment the no-reset average overlap AO [91] is used. The last column contains implementation details (first letter: (D)eterministic or (S)tohastic, second letter: tracker implemented in (M)atlab, (C)++, or (P)ython, third letter: tracker is using (G)PU or only (C)PU).

	Tracker	Baseline EAO	A	R	Realtime EAO	A	R	Unsup. AO	Impl.
1.	○ LADCF	0.389 ①	0.503	0.159 ③	0.066	0.314	1.358	0.421	D M C
2.	✕ MFT	0.385 ②	0.505	0.140 ①	0.060	0.337	1.592	0.393	D M G
3.	✳ SiamRPN	0.383 ③	0.586 ①	0.276	0.383 ①	0.586 ①	0.276 ②	0.472 ②	D P G
4.	▽ UPDT	0.378	0.536	0.184	0.068	0.334	1.363	0.454	S M C
5.	◇ RCO	0.376	0.507	0.155 ②	0.066	0.400	1.704	0.384	S M G
6.	+ DRT	0.356	0.519	0.201	0.062	0.321	1.503	0.426	D M G
7.	◁ DeepSTRCF	0.345	0.523	0.215	0.063	0.418	1.817	0.436	D M G
8.	☆ CPT	0.339	0.506	0.239	0.081	0.479	1.358	0.379	D M G
9.	▷ SA_Siam_R	0.337	0.566 ②	0.258	0.337 ②	0.566 ②	0.258 ①	0.429	D P G
10.	☐ DLSTpp	0.325	0.543	0.224	0.125	0.514	0.824	0.495 ①	S M G
11.	△ LSART	0.323	0.495	0.218	0.055	0.386	1.971	0.437	S M G
12.	✰ SRCT	0.310	0.520	0.290	0.059	0.331	1.765	0.400	D M C
13.	○ CFTR	0.300	0.505	0.258	0.062	0.319	1.601	0.375	D M G
14.	✕ CPT_fast	0.296	0.520	0.290	0.152	0.515	0.726	0.392	D M G
15.	✳ DeepCSRDCF	0.293	0.489	0.276	0.062	0.399	1.644	0.393	S M G
16.	▽ SiamVGG	0.286	0.531	0.318	0.275	0.531	0.337	0.428	D P G
17.	◇ SA_Siam_P	0.286	0.533	0.337	0.286 ③	0.533 ③	0.342	0.406	D P G
18.	+ CFCF	0.282	0.511	0.286	0.059	0.326	1.648	0.380	D M G
19.	◁ ECO	0.280	0.484	0.276	0.078	0.449	1.466	0.402	D M G
20.	☆ MCCT	0.274	0.532	0.318	0.061	0.359	1.742	0.422	D M C
21.	▷ CCOT	0.267	0.494	0.318	0.058	0.326	1.461	0.390	D M G
22.	☐ csrtpp	0.263	0.466	0.318	0.263	0.466	0.318	0.324	D C G
23.	△ LWDNTthi	0.261	0.462	0.332	0.262	0.463	0.342	0.328	D P G
24.	✰ LWDNTm	0.261	0.455	0.323	0.261	0.455	0.323	0.352	S P G
25.	○ R_MCPF	0.257	0.513	0.397	0.064	0.329	1.391	0.457	S M G
26.	✕ FSAN	0.256	0.554 ③	0.356	0.065	0.312	1.377	0.466 ③	S M G
27.	✳ CSRDCF	0.256	0.491	0.356	0.099	0.477	1.054	0.342	D C C
28.	▽ DCFCF	0.249	0.485	0.342	0.080	0.321	0.665	0.337	D M C
29.	◇ UpdateNet	0.244	0.518	0.454	0.209	0.517	0.534	0.358	D M G
30.	+ MBSiam	0.241	0.529	0.443	0.238	0.529	0.440	0.413	S P G
31.	◁ ALAL	0.232	0.533	0.475	0.067	0.404	1.667	0.405	S P G
32.	✰ CSTEM	0.226	0.467	0.412	0.239	0.472	0.379	0.316	S C C
33.	▷ BoVW_CFT	0.224	0.500	0.450	0.063	0.331	1.615	0.373	D M C
34.	☐ C3DT	0.209	0.522	0.496	0.067	0.322	1.330	0.440	D P G
35.	△ RSECF	0.206	0.470	0.501	0.074	0.414	1.569	0.319	D M G
36.	✰ DSiam	0.196	0.512	0.646	0.129	0.503	0.979	0.353	D M G
37.	○ KFebT	0.195	0.474	0.674	0.195	0.475	0.670	0.221	D C C
38.	✕ MEEM	0.192	0.463	0.534	0.072	0.407	1.592	0.328	S M C

(*continued*)

Table 2. (*continued*)

39.	* SiamFC	0.188	0.503	0.585	0.182	0.502	0.604	0.345	D M G
40.	▽ STST	0.187	0.464	0.621	0.156	0.466	0.763	0.297	S P G
41.	◇ DCFNet	0.182	0.470	0.543	0.180	0.471	0.548	0.327	D M G
42.	+ DensSiam	0.174	0.462	0.688	0.174	0.462	0.688	0.305	D P G
43.	◁ SAPKLTF	0.171	0.488	0.613	0.117	0.481	0.946	0.352	D C C
44.	☆ Staple	0.169	0.530	0.688	0.170	0.530	0.688	0.335	D M C
45.	▷ ASMS	0.169	0.494	0.623	0.167	0.492	0.632	0.337	D C C
46.	☐ ANT	0.168	0.464	0.632	0.059	0.403	1.737	0.279	D M C
47.	△ HMMTxD	0.168	0.506	0.815	0.073	0.416	1.564	0.330	D C C
48.	☆ DPT	0.158	0.486	0.721	0.126	0.483	0.899	0.315	D C C
49.	○ STBACF	0.155	0.461	0.740	0.062	0.320	0.281 ③	0.245	D M C
50.	✕ srdcf_deep	0.154	0.492	0.707	0.057	0.326	1.756	0.321	S M G
51.	* PBTS	0.152	0.381	0.664	0.102	0.411	1.100	0.265	S P C
52.	▽ DAT	0.144	0.435	0.721	0.139	0.436	0.749	0.287	D M C
53.	◇ LGT	0.144	0.409	0.742	0.059	0.349	1.714	0.225	S C C
54.	+ RAnet	0.141	0.449	0.744	0.133	0.477	0.805	0.303	S P G
55.	◁ DFPReco	0.138	0.473	0.838	0.049	0.312	0.286	0.269	D M C
56.	☆ TRACA	0.137	0.424	0.857	0.136	0.424	0.857	0.256	D M G
57.	▷ KCF	0.135	0.447	0.773	0.134	0.445	0.782	0.267	D C C
58.	☐ FoT	0.130	0.393	1.030	0.130	0.393	1.030	0.143	D C C
59.	△ srdcf_dif	0.126	0.492	0.946	0.061	0.398	1.925	0.310	D M G
60.	☆ SRDCF	0.119	0.490	0.974	0.058	0.377	1.999	0.246	S C C
61.	○ MIL	0.118	0.394	1.011	0.069	0.376	1.775	0.180	S C C
62.	✕ BST	0.116	0.272	0.881	0.053	0.271	1.620	0.149	S C C
63.	* struck2011	0.097	0.418	1.297	0.093	0.419	1.367	0.197	D C C
64.	▽ BDF	0.093	0.367	1.180	0.093	0.367	1.180	0.145	D C C
65.	◇ Matflow	0.092	0.399	1.278	0.090	0.401	1.297	0.181	S C C
66.	+ MRSNCC	0.082	0.330	1.506	0.060	0.328	2.088	0.112	S M C
67.	◁ DSST	0.079	0.395	1.452	0.077	0.396	1.480	0.172	S C C
68.	☆ IVT	0.076	0.400	1.639	0.065	0.386	1.854	0.130	S C C
69.	▷ CPOINT	0.070	0.308	1.719	0.057	0.290	1.901	0.115	S M G
70.	☐ L1APG	0.069	0.432	2.013	0.062	0.351	1.831	0.159	S M C
71.	△ FragTrack	0.068	0.390	1.868	0.068	0.316	1.480	0.180	S C C
72.	☆ Matrioska	0.065	0.414	1.939	0.000	0.000	16.740	0.004	S C C

Despite significant effort, our team was unable to re-run DRT and SA_Siam_R due to library incompatibility errors in one case and significant system modifications requirements in the other. These two trackers were thus removed from the winner identification process on the account of the code provided not being results re-production-ready. The scores of the remaining trackers are shown in Table 3. The top tracker according to the EAO is MFT A.51 and is thus the VOT2018 short-term challenge winner.

4.3   The VOT2018 Short-Term Real-Time Sub-challenge Results

The EAO scores and AR-raw plots for the real-time experiment are shown in Figs. 4 and 5. The top ten real-time trackers are SiamRPN A.35, SA_Siam_R A.60, SA_Siam_P A.59, SiamVGG A.63, CSRTPP A.25, LWD-NTm A.41, LWDNTthi A.42, CSTEM A.9, MBSiam A.48 and UpdateNet A.1. Eight of these (SiamRPN, SA_Siam_R, SA_Siam_P, SiamVGG, LWDNTm,

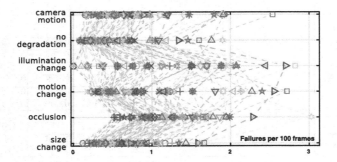

Fig. 3. Failure rate with respect to the visual attributes.

Table 3. The top eight trackers from Table 2 re-ranked on the VOT2018 sequestered dataset.

	Tracker	EAO	A	R
1.	MFT	0.2518 ①	0.5768	0.3105 ①
2.	UPDT	0.2469 ②	0.6033 ②	0.3427 ③
3.	RCO	0.2457 ③	0.5707	0.3154 ②
4.	LADCF	0.2218	0.5499	0.3746
5.	DeepSTRCF	0.2205	0.5998 ③	0.4435
6.	CPT	0.2087	0.5773	0.4238
7.	SiamRPN	0.2054	0.6277 ①	0.5175
8.	DLSTpp	0.1961	0.5833	0.4544

LWDNTthi, MBSiam, UpdateNet) are extensions of the Siamese architecture SiamFC [6]. These trackers apply pre-traind CNN features that maximize correlation localization accuracy and require a GPU. But since feature extraction as well as correlation are carried out on the GPU, they achieve significant speed in addition to extraction of highly discriminative features. The remaining two trackers (CSRTPP and CSTEM) are extensions of the CSRDCF [53] – a correlation filter with boundary constraints and segmentation for identifying reliable target pixels. These two trackers apply hand-crafted features, i.e., HOG and Colornames.

The VOT-RT2018 Winner Identification. The winning real-time tracker of the VOT2018 is the Siamese region proposal network SiamRPN [48] (A.35). The tracker is based on a Siamese subnetwork for feature extraction and a region proposal subnetwork which includes a classification branch and a regression branch. The inference is formulated as a local one-shot detection task.

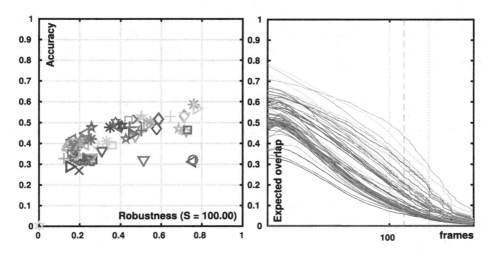

Fig. 4. The AR plot (left) and the EAO curves (right) for the VOT2017 realtime experiment. (Color figure online)

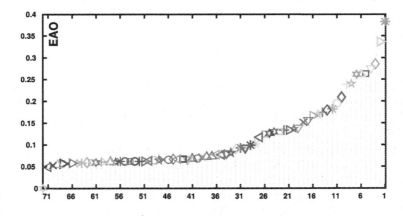

Fig. 5. The EAO plot (right) for the realtime experiment. (Color figure online)

5 The VOT2018 Long-Term Challenge Results

The VOT2018 LT challenge received 11 valid entries. The VOT2018 committee contributed additional 4 baselines, thus 15 trackers were considered in the VOT2018 LT challenge. In the following we briefly overview the entries and provide the references to original papers in the Appendix B where available.

Some of the submitted trackers were in principle ST_0 trackers. But the submission rules required exposing a target localizsation/presence certainty score which can be used by thresholding to form a target presence classifier. In this way, these trackers were elevated to LT_0 level according to the ST-LT taxonomy from Sect. 3.1. Five trackers were from the ST_0 (elevated to LT_0) class:

Table 4. List of trackers that participated in the VOT2018 long-term challenge along with their performance scores (F-score, Pr, Re), ST/LT categorization and results of the re-detection experiment in the last column with the average number of frames required for re-detection (Frames) and the percentage of sequences with successful re-detection (Success).

	Tracker	F-score	Pr	Re	ST/LT	Frames (Success)
1.	MBMD	0.610 ①	0.634 ②	0.588 ①	LT_1	1 (100%)
2.	DaSiam_LT	0.607 ②	0.627 ③	0.588 ②	LT_1	- (0%)
3.	MMLT	0.546 ③	0.574	0.521 ③	LT_1	0 (100%)
4.	LTSINT	0.536	0.566	0.510	LT_1	2 (100%)
5.	SYT	0.509	0.520	0.499	LT_1	0 (43%)
6.	PTAVplus	0.481	0.595	0.404	LT_1	0 (11%)
7.	FuCoLoT	0.480	0.539	0.432	LT_1	78 (97%)
8.	SiamVGG	0.459	0.552	0.393	$ST_0 \rightarrow LT_0$	- (0%)
9.	SLT	0.456	0.502	0.417	$ST_1 \rightarrow LT_0$	0 (100%)
10.	SiamFC	0.433	0.636 ①	0.328	$ST_0 \rightarrow LT_0$	- (0%)
11.	SiamFCDet	0.401	0.488	0.341	LT_1	0 (83%)
12.	HMMTxD	0.335	0.330	0.339	LT_1	3 (91%)
13.	SAPKLTF	0.323	0.348	0.300	LT_0	- (0%)
14.	ASMS	0.306	0.373	0.259	$ST_0 \rightarrow LT_0$	- (0%)
15.	FoT	0.119	0.298	0.074	$ST_0 \rightarrow LT_0$	0 (6%)

SiamVGG B.15, SiamFC B.5, ASMS B.11, FoT B.3 and SLT B.14. Ten trackers were from LT_1 class: DaSiam_LT B.2, MMLT B.1, PTAVplus B.10, MBMD B.8, SAPKLTF B.12, LTSINT B.7, SYT B.13, SiamFCDet B.4, FuCoLoT B.6, HMMTxD B.9.

Ten trackers applied CNN features (nine of these in Siamese architecture) and four trackers applied DCFs. Six trackers never updated *the short-term component* (DaSiam_LT, SYT, SiamFCDet, SiamVGG, SiamFC and SLT), four updated the component only when confident (MMLT, SAPKLTF, LTSINT, FuCoLoT), two applied exponential forgetting (HMMTxD, ASMS), two applied updates at fixed intervals (PTAVplus, MBMD) and one applied robust partial updates (FoT). Seven trackers never updated *the long-term component* (DaSiam_LT, MBMD, SiamFCDet, HMMTxD, SiamVGG, SiamFC, SLT), and six updated the model only when confident (MMLT, PTAVplus, SAPKLTF, LTSINT, SYT, FuCoLoT).

Results of the re-detection experiment are summarized in the last column of Table 4. MMLT, SLT, MBMD, FuCoLoT and LTSINT consistently re-detect the target while SiamFCDet succeeded in all but one sequence. Some trackers (SYT, PTAVplus) were capable of re-detection in only a few cases, which indicates a potential issue with the detector. All these eight trackers pass the re-detection test and are classified as LT_1 trackers. Trackers DaSiam_LT, SAP-KLTF, SiamVGG and SiamFC did not pass the test, which means that they do not perform image-wide re-detection, but only re-detect in a extended local region. These trackers are classified as LT_0.

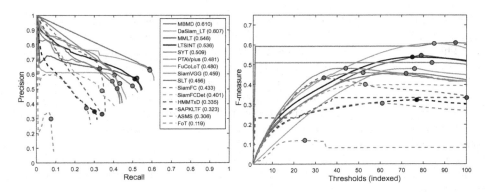

Fig. 6. Long-term tracking performance. The average tracking precision-recall curves (left), the corresponding F-score curves (right). Tracker labels are sorted according to maximum of the F-score. (Color figure online)

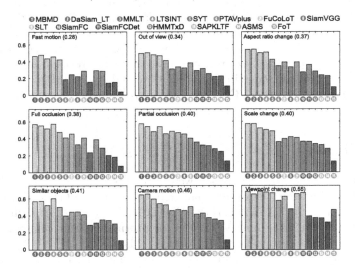

Fig. 7. Maximum F-score averaged over overlap thresholds for the visual attributes. The most challenging attributes are fast motion, out of view, aspect ratio change and full occlusion. (Color figure online)

The overall performance is summarized in Fig. 6. The highest ranked tracker is the MobileNet-based tracking by detection algorithm (MBMD), which applies a bounding box regression network and an MDNet-based verifier [64]. The bounding box regression network is trained on ILSVRC 2015 video detection dataset and ILSVRC 2014 detection dataset is used to train a regression to any object in a search region by ignoring the classification labels. The bounding box regression result is verified by MDNet [64]. If the score of regression module is below a threshold, the MDNet localizes the target by a particle filter. The MDNet is updated online, while the bounding box regression network is not updated.

The second highest ranked tracker is DaSiam_LT – an LT_1 class tracker. This tracker is an extension of a Siamese Region Proposal Network (SiamRPN) [48]. The original SiamRPN cannot recover a target after it re-appears, thus the extension implements an effective global-to-local search strategy. The search region size is gradually grown at a constant rate after target loss, akin to [55]. Distractor-aware training and inference are also added to implement a high-quality tracking reliability score.

Figure 7 shows tracking performance with respect to nine visual attributes from Sect. 3.2. The most challenging attributes are fast motion, out of view, aspect ratio change and full occlusion.

The VOT-LT2018 Winner Identification. According to the F-score, MBMD (F-score = 0,610) is slightly ahead of DaSiam_LT (F-score = 0,607). The trackers reach approximately the same tracking recall (0,588216 for MBMD vs 0,587921 for DaSiam_LT), which implies a comparable target re-detection success. But MBMD has a greater tracking precision which implies better target localization capabilities. Overall, the best tracking precision is obtained by SiamFC, while the best tracking recall is obtained by MBMD. According to the VOT winner rules, the VOT2018 long-term challenge winner is therefore MBMD B.8.

6   Conclusion

Results of the VOT2018 challenge were presented. The challenge is composed of the following three sub-challenges: the main VOT2018 short-term tracking challenge (VOT-ST2018), the VOT2018 real-time short-term tracking challenge (VOT-RT2018) and VOT2018 long-term tracking challenge (VOT-LT2018), which is a new challenge introduced this year.

The overall results of the challenges indicate that discriminative correlation filters and deep networks remain the dominant methodologies in visual object tracking. Deep features in DCFs and use of CNNs as classifiers in the trackers have been recognized as efficient tracking ingredients already in VOT2015. But their use among top performers has become wide-spread over the following years. In contrast to previous years we observe a wider use of localization-trained CNN features and CNN trackers based on Siamese architectures. Bounding box regression is being used in trackers more frequently than in previous challenges as well.

The top performer on the VOT-ST2018 *public dataset* is LADCF (A.39) – a regularized discriminative correlation filter trained on a low-dimensional projection of ResNet50, HOG and Colornames features. The top performer on the sequestered dataset and the VOT-ST2018 challenge winner is

MFT (A.51) – a continuous convolution discriminative correlation filter with per-channel independently trained localization learned features. This tracker uses ResNet-50, SE-ResNet-50, HOG and Colornames.

The top performer and the winner of the VOT-RT2018 challenge is SiamRPN (A.35) – a Siamese region proposal network. The tracker requires a GPU, but otherwise has the best tradeoff between robustness and processing speed. Note that nearly all top ten trackers on realtime challenge applied Siamese nets (two applied DCFs and run on CPU). The dominant methodology in real-time tracking therefore appears to be Siamese CNNs.

The top performer and the winner of the VOT-LT2018 challenge is MBMD (B.8) – a bounding box regression network with MDNet [64] for regression verification and localization upon target loss. This tracker is from LT_1 class, identifies a potential target loss, performs target re-detection and applies conservative updates of the visual model.

The VOT primary objective is to establish a platform for discussion of tracking performance evaluation and contributing to the tracking community with verified annotated datasets, performance measures and evaluation toolkits. The VOT2018 was a sixth effort toward this, following the very successful VOT2013, VOT2014, VOT2015, VOT2016 and VOT2017.

Acknowledgements. This work was supported in part by the following research programs and projects: Slovenian research agency research programs P2-0214, P2-0094, Slovenian research agency project J2-8175. Jiři Matas and Tomáš Vojíř were supported by the Czech Science Foundation Project GACR P103/12/G084. Michael Felsberg and Gustav Häger were supported by WASP, VR (EMC2), SSF (SymbiCloud), and SNIC. Roman Pflugfelder and Gustavo Fernández were supported by the AIT Strategic Research Programme 2017 Visual Surveillance and Insight. The challenge was sponsored by Faculty of Computer Science, University of Ljubljana, Slovenia.

A   VOT2018 Short-Term Challenge Tracker Descriptions

In this appendix we provide a short summary of all trackers that were considered in the VOT2018 short-term challenges.

A.1   Adaptive Object Update for Tracking (UpdateNet)

L. Zhang, A. Gonzalez-Garcia, J. van de Weijer, F. S. Khan
{lichao, agonzalez, joost}@cvc.uab.es, fahad.khan@liu.se
UpdateNet tracker uses an update network to update the tracked object appearance during tracking. Since the object appearance constantly changes as the video progresses, some update mechanism is necessary to maintain an accurate model of the object appearance. The traditional correlation tracker updates the object appearance by using a fixed update rule based on a single hyperparameter. This approach, however, cannot effectively adapt to the specific update requirement necessary for every particular situation. UpdateNet extends the correlation tracker of SiamFC [6] to include a network component specially

trained to update the object appearance which is an advantage with respect to the traditional fixed rule update used for tracking.

A.2   Anti-decay LSTM with Adversarial Learning Tracker (ALAL)

F. Zhao, Y. Wu, J. Wang, M. Tang
{fei.zhao, jqwang, tangm}@nlpr.ia.ac.cn, ywu.china@gmail.com

The ALAL tracker contains two CNNs: a regression CNN and a classification CNN. For each search patch, the former CNN predicts a response map which reflects the location of the target. The latter CNN distinguishes the target from the candidates. A modified LSTM which is trained by the adversarial learning is also added on the former network. The modified LSTM can extract the features of the target in long-term without the decay of the feature.

A.3   ANT (ANT)

Submitted by VOT Committee

The ANT tracker is a conceptual increment to the idea of multi-layer appearance representation that is first described in [82]. The tracker addresses the problem of self-supervised estimation of a large number of parameters by introducing controlled graduation in estimation of the free parameters. The appearance of the object is decomposed into several sub-models, each describing the target at a different level of detail. The sub models interact during target localization and, depending on the visual uncertainty, serve for cross-sub-model supervised updating. The reader is referred to [84] for details.

A.4   Bag-of-Visual-Words Based Correlation Filter Tracker (BoVW_CFT)

P. M. Raju, D. Mishra, G. R. K. S. Subrahmanyam
{priyamariyam123, vr.dkmishra}@gmail.com, rkg@iittp.ac.in

The BoVW-CFT is a classifier-based generic technique to handle tracking uncertainties in correlation filter trackers. The method is developed using ECO [15] as the base correlation tracker. The classifier operates on Bag of Visual Words (BoVW) features and SVM with training, testing and update stages. For each tracking uncertainty, two output patches are obtained, one each from the base tracker and the classifier. The final output patch is the one with highest normalized cross-correlation with the initial target patch.

A.5   Best Displacement Flow (BDF)

M. E. Maresca, A. Petrosino
mariomaresca@hotmail.it, alfredo.petrosino@uniparthenope.it

Tracker BDF is based on the idea of Flock of Trackers [86] in which a set of local tracker responses are robustly combined to track the object. The reader is referred to [58] for details.

A.6 Best Structured Tracker (BST)

F. Battistone, A. Petrosino, V. Santopietro
{francesco.battistone, alfredo.petrosino, vincenzo.santopietro}@uniparthenope.it
BST is based on the idea of Flock of Trackers [86]: a set of five local trackers tracks a little patch of the original target and then the tracker combines their information in order to estimate the resulting bounding box. Each local tracker separately analyzes the Haar features extracted from a set of samples and then classifies them using a structured Support Vector Machine as Struck [28]. Once having predicted local target candidates, an outlier detection process is computed by analyzing the displacements of local trackers. Trackers that have been labeled as outliers are reinitialized. At the end of this process, the new bounding box is calculated using the Convex Hull technique. For more detailed information, please see [5].

A.7 Channel Pruning for Visual Tracking (CPT)

M. Che, R. Wang, Y. Lu, Y. Li, H. Zhi, C. Xiong
cmq_mail@163.com, {1573112241, 1825650885}@qq.com,
liyan1994626@126.com, 1462714176@qq.com, xczkiong@163.com
In order to improve the tracking speed, the tracker CPT is proposed. The tracker introduces an effective channel pruning based VGG network to fast extract the deep convolutional features. In this way, it can obtain deeper convolutional features for better representations of various objects' variations without worrying about the speed of suppression. To further reduce the redundancy features, the Average Feature Energy Ratio is proposed to extract effective convolutional channel of the selected deep convolution layer and increase the tracking speed. The method also ameliorates the optimization process in minimizing the location error as adaptive iterative optimization strategy.

A.8 Channel Pruning for Visual Tracking (CPT_fast)

M. Che, R. Wang, Y. Lu, Y. Li, H. Zhi, C. Xiong
cmq_mail@163.com, {1573112241, 1825650885}@qq.com,
liyan1994626@126.com, 1462714176@qq.com, xczkiong@163.com
The fast CPT (called CPT_fast) method is based on CPT tracker A.7 and the DSST [12] method which is applied to estimate the tracking object's scale.

A.9 Channels-Weighted and Spatial-Related Tracker with Effective Response-Map Measurement (CSTEM)

Z. Zhang, Y. Li, J. Ren, J. Zhu
{zzheng1993, liyang89, zijinxuxu, jkzhu}@zju.edu.cn
Motivated by CSRDCF tracker [53], CSTEM has designed an effective measurement function to evaluate the quality of filter response. As a theoretical guarantee of effectiveness, CSTEM tracker scheme chooses different filter models

according to the different scenarios using the measurement function. Moreover, a sophisticated strategy is employed to detect occlusion, and then decide how to update the filter models in order to alleviate the drifting problem. In addition, CSTEM takes advantage of both log-polar approach [50] and pyramid-like method [12] to accurately estimate the scale changes of the tracking target. For the detailed information, please see [99].

A.10   Combined Point Tracker (CPOINT)

A. G. Perera, Y. W. Law, J. Chahl
asanka.perera@mymail.unisa.edu.au, {yeewei.law, javaan.chahl}@unisa.edu.au

CPOINT tracker combines 3 different trackers to predict and correct the target location and size. In the first level, four types of key-point features (SURF, BRISK, KAZE and FAST) are used to localize and scale up or down the bounding box of the target. The size and the location of the initial estimation is averaged out with another level of corner point tracker which also uses optical flow. Predictions with insufficient image details are handled by a third level histogram-based tracker.

A.11   Continuous Convolution Operator Tracker (CCOT)

Submitted by VOT Committee

C-COT learns a discriminative continuous convolution operator as its tracking model. C-COT poses the learning problem in the continuous spatial domain. This enables a natural and efficient fusion of multi-resolution feature maps, e.g. when using several convolutional layers from a pre-trained CNN. The continuous formulation also enables highly accurate localization by sub-pixel refinement. The reader is referred to [17] for details.

A.12   Continuous Convolution Operators with Resnet Features (RCO)

Z. He, S. Bai, J. Zhuang
{he010103, baishuai}@bupt.edu.cn, junfei.zhuang@faceall.cn

The RCO tracker is based on an extension of CFWCR [31]. A continuous convolution operator is used to fuse multi-resolution features synthetically, which improves the performance of correlation filter based tracker. Shallower and deeper features from convolution neural network focus on different target information. In order to improve the cooperative solving method and make full use of diverse features a multi-solution is proposed. To predict the target location RCO optimally fuses the obtained multi-solutions. RCO tracker uses CNN features extracted from Resnet50.

A.13   Convolutional Features for Correlation Filters (CFCF)

E. Gundogdu, A. Alatan
erhan.gundogdu@epfl.ch, alatan@metu.edu.tr
The tracker CFCF is based on the feature learning study in [26] and the correlation filter based tracker C-COT [17]. The proposed tracker employs a fully convolutional neural network (CNN) model trained on ILSVRC15 video dataset [71] by the learning framework introduced in [26] which is designed for correlation filter [12]. To learn features, convolutional layers of VGG-M-2048 network [11] trained on [19] are applied. An extra convolutional layer is used for fine-tuning on ILSVRC15 dataset. The first, fifth and sixth convolutional layers of the learned network, HOG [63] and Colour Names (CN) [89] are integrated to the C-COT tracker [17].

A.14   Correlation Filter with Regressive Scale Estimation (RSECF)

L. Chu, H. Li
{lt.chu, hy.li}@siat.ac.cn
RSECF addresses the problems of poor scale estimation in state of art DCF trackers by learning separate discriminative correlation filters for translation estimation and bounding box regression for scale estimation. The scale filter is learned online using the target appearance sampled at a set of different aspect ratios. Contrary to standard approaches, RSECF directly searches for continuous scale space, which can predict any scale without being limited by manually specified number of scales. RSECF generalizes the original single-channel bounding box regression to multi-channel situations, which allows for more efficient employment of multi-channel features. The correlation filter is ECOhc [15] without fDSST [16], which locates the target position.

A.15   Correlation Filter with Temporal Regression (CFTR)

L. Rout, D. Mishra, R. K. Gorthi
liturout1997@gmail.com, deepak.mishra@iist.ac.in, rkg@iittp.ac.in
CFTR tracker proposes a different approach to regress in the temporal domain based on the Tikhonov regularization. CFTR tracker applies a weighted aggregation of distinctive visual features and feature prioritization with entropy estimation in a recursive fashion. A statistics based ensembler approach is proposed for integrating the conventionally driven spatial regression results (such as from CFCF [26]), and the proposed temporal regression results to accomplish better tracking.

A.16   Correlation Tracking via Joint Discrimination and Reliability Learning (DRT)

C. Sun, Y. Zhang, Y. Sun, D. Wang, H. Lu
{waynecool, zhangyunhua, rumsyx} @mail.dlut.edu.cn,
{wdice, lhchuan} @dlut.edu.cn

DRT uses a novel CF-based optimization problem to jointly model the discrimination and reliability information. First, the tracker treats the filter as the element-wise product of a base filter and a reliability term. The base filter is aimed to learn the discrimination information between the target and backgrounds, and the reliability term encourages the final filter to focus on more reliable regions. Second, the DRT tracker introduces a local response consistency regular term to emphasize equal contributions of different regions and avoid the tracker being dominated by unreliable regions. The tracker is based on [77].

A.17   CSRDCF with the Integration of CNN Features and Handcrafted Features (DeepCSRDCF)

Z. He
he010103@bupt.edu.cn

DeepCSRDCF adopts CSRDCF tracker [53] as the baseline approach. CNN features are integrated into hand-crafted features, which boosts the performance compared to the baseline tracker CSRDCF. To avoid the model drift, an adaptive learning rate is applied.

A.18   DCFNET: Discriminant Correlation Filters Network for Visual Tracking (DCFNet)

J. Li, Q. Wang, W. Hu
jli24@outlook.com, wangqiang2015@ia.ac.cn, wmhu@nlpr.ia.ac.cn

DCFNet is a tracker with the end-to-end lightweight network architecture, which learned the convolutional features and performed the correlation tracking process simultaneously. Specifically, DCF is treated as a special correlation filter layer added in a Siamese network. The back-propagation through the network is derived by defining the network output as the probability heat-map of the object location. Since the derivation is still carried out in Fourier frequency domain, the efficiency property of DCF is preserved. For more detailed information on this tracker, please see reference [88].

A.19   Deep Enhanced Spatially Regularized Discriminative Correlation Filter (srdcf_deep)

J. Rodríguez Herranz, V. Štruc, K. Grm
j.rodriguezherranz@gmail.com, {vitomir.struc, klemen.grm} @fe.uni-lj.si

The Deep Enhanced Spatially Regularized Discriminative Correlation Filter (srdcf_deep) is based on the E-SRDCF tracker incorporating the constrained correlation filter from [13] and a motion model based on frame differences. While E-SRDCF uses only hand-crafted features (HOGs, colour names and grey-scale images), DE-SRDCF also exploits learned CNN-based features. Specifically, the CNN model used for feature extraction is an auto-encoder with a similar architecture as VGG-m [11]. The features used are taken from the first and fifth convolutional layer. More information on DE-SRDCF tracker can be found in [33].

A.20   DeepSTRCF (DeepSTRCF)

W. Zuo, F. Li, X. Wu, C. Tian, M.-H. Yang
cswmzuo@gmail.com, fengli_hit@hotmail.com, xhwu.cpsl.hit@gmail.com, tcoperator@163.com, mhyang@ucmerced.edu
DeepSTRCF implements a variant of STRCF tracker [49] with deep CNN features. STRCF addresses the computational inefficiency problem of SRDCF tracker from two aspects: (i) a temporal regularization term to remove the need of formulation on large training sets, and (ii) an ADMM algorithm to solve the STRCF model efficiently. Therefore, it can provide more robust models and much faster solutions than SRDCF thanks to the online Passive-Aggressive learning and ADMM solver, respectively.

A.21   Deformable Part Correlation Filter Tracker (DPT)

Submitted by VOT Committee
DPT is a part-based correlation filter composed of a coarse and mid-level target representations. Coarse representation is responsible for approximate target localization and uses HOG as well as colour features. The mid-level representation is a deformable parts correlation filter with fully-connected parts topology and applies a novel formulation that threats geometric and visual properties within a single convex optimization function. The mid level as well as coarse level representations are based on the kernelized correlation filter from [32]. The reader is referred to [54] for details.

A.22   Dense Contrastive Features for Correlation Filters (DCFCF)

J. Spencer Martin, R. Bowden, S. Hadfield
{jaime.spencer, r.bowden, s.hadfield}@surrey.ac.uk
Dense Contrastive Features for Correlation Filters (DCFCF) extends on previous work based on correlation filters applied to feature representations of the tracked object. A new type of dense feature descriptors is introduced which is specifically trained for the comparison of unknown objects. These generic comparison features lead to a more robust representation of a priori unknown objects, largely increasing the resolution compared to intermediate layers, whilst maintaining a reasonable dimensionality. This results in a slight increase in performance, along with a higher resistance to occlusions or missing targets.

A.23 Densely Connected Siamese Architecture for Robust Visual Tracking (DensSiam)

M. Abdelpakey, M. Shehata
{mha241, mshehata}@mun.ca

DensSiam is a new Siamese architecture for object tracking. It uses the concept of dense layers and connects each dense layer to all layers in a feed-forward fashion with a similarity-learning function. DensSiam uses non-local features to represent the appearance model in such a way that allows the deep feature map to be robust to appearance changes. DensSiam allows different feature levels (e.g. low level and high-level features) to flow through the network layers without vanishing gradients and improves the generalization capability [1].

A.24 Discriminative Correlation Filter with Channel and Spatial Reliability (CSRDCF)

Submitted by VOT Committee

The CSRDCF [53] improves discriminative correlation filter trackers by introducing two concepts: spatial reliability and channel reliability. It uses colour segmentation as spatial reliability to adjust the filter support to the part of the object suitable for tracking. The channel reliability reflects the discriminative power of each filter channel. The tracker uses HoG and colour-names features.

A.25 Discriminative Correlation Filter with Channel and Spatial Reliability - C++ (csrtpp)

Submitted by VOT Committee

The csrtpp tracker is the C++ implementation of the Discriminative Correlation Filter with Channel and Spatial Reliability (CSR-DCF) tracker A.24.

A.26 Discriminative Scale Space Tracker (DSST)

Submitted by VOT Committee

The Discriminative Scale Space Tracker (DSST) [12] extends the Minimum Output Sum of Squared Errors (MOSSE) tracker [9] with robust scale estimation. The DSST additionally learns a one-dimensional discriminative scale filter, that is used to estimate the target size. For the translation filter, the intensity features employed in the MOSSE tracker is combined with a pixel-dense representation of HOG-features.

A.27 Distractor-Aware Tracking (DAT)

H. Possegger
possegger@icg.tugraz.at

The Tracker DAT [68] is an appearance-based tracking-by-detection approach. It relies on a generative model using colour histograms to distinguish the object from its surroundings. Additionally, a distractor-aware model term suppresses visually similar (i.e. distracting) regions whenever they appear within the field-of-view, thus reducing tracker drift.

A.28   DLSTpp: Deep Location-Specific Tracking++ (DLSTpp)

L. Yang
lingxiao.yang717@gmail.com
     The DLSTpp is a tracker based on DLST tracker which decomposes the tracking problem into a localization and a classification task. The localization is achieved by ECOhc. The classification network is the same as MDNet, but their weights are fine-tuned on ImageNet VID dataset.

A.29   Dynamic Fusion of Part Regressors for Correlation Filter-Based Visual Tracking (DFPReco)

A. Memarmoghadam, P. Moallem
{a.memarmoghadam, p_moallem}@eng.ui.ac.ir
     Employing both global and local part-wise appearance models, a robust tracking algorithm based on weighted fusion of several CF-based part regressors is proposed. Importance weights are dinamically assigned to each part via solving a multi-linear ridge regression optimization problem towards achieving a more discriminative target-level confidence map. Additionally it is presented an accurate size estimation method that jointly provides object scale and aspect ratio by analyzing relative deformation cost of importance pair-wise parts. A single-patch ECO tracker [15] (but without object scale mechanism) is applied as baseline approach for each part which expeditiously makes track of target object parts.

A.30   Dynamic Siamese Network Based Tracking (DSiam)

Q. Guo, W. Feng
{tsingqguo, wfeng}@tju.edu.cn
     DSiam [27] locates an interested target by matching an online updated template with a suppressed search region. This is achieved by adding two transformations to the two branches of a pretained network that can be SiamFC, VGG19, VGG16, etc. The two transformations can be efficiently online learned in frequency domain. Instead of using the pretrained network in [27], the presented tracker uses the network introduced in [81] to extract deep features.

A.31   ECO (ECO)

Submitted by VOT Committee
     ECO addresses the problems of computational complexity and over-fitting in state of the art DCF trackers by introducing: (i) a factorized convolution operator, which drastically reduces the number of parameters in the model; (ii) a compact generative model of the training sample distribution, that significantly reduces memory and time complexity, while providing better diversity of samples; (iii) a conservative model update strategy with improved robustness and reduced complexity. The reader is referred to [15] for more details.

A.32   Enhanced Spatially Regularized Discriminative Correlation Filter (srdcf_dif)

J. Rodríguez Herranz, V. Štruc, K. Grm
j.rodriguezherranz@gmail.com, {vitomir.struc, klemen.grm}@fe.uni-lj.si

The Enhanced Spatially Regularized Discriminative Correlation Filter (srdcf_dif) is based on the constrained correlation filter formulation from [13], but incorporates an additional motion model to improve tracking performance. The motion model takes again the form of a constrained correlation filter, but is computed over frame differences instead of static frames. The standard SRDCF tracker and motion model are combined using a weighted sum over the correlation outputs. Both E-SRDCF parts exploit HOG, colour names and grey scale image features during filter construction. For more details the reader is referred to [33].

A.33   Flock of Trackers (FoT)

Submitted by VOT Committee
The Flock of Trackers (FoT) is a tracking framework where the object motion is estimated from the displacements or, more generally, transformation estimates of a number of local trackers covering the object. Each local tracker is attached to a certain area specified in the object coordinate frame. The local trackers are not robust and assume that the tracked area is visible in all images and that it undergoes a simple motion, e.g. translation. The FoT object motion estimate is robust if it is from local tracker motions by a combination which is insensitive to failures.

A.34   Fully-Convolutional Siamese Network (SiamFC)

L. Bertinetto, J. Valmadre, J. Henriques, A. Vedaldi, P. Torr
{luca.bertinetto,   joao.henriques,   andrea.vedaldi,   philip.torr}@eng.ox.ac.uk,
jack.valmadre@gmail.com

SiamFC applies a fully-convolutional deep Siamese conv-net to locate the best match for an exemplar image within a larger search image. The deep conv-net is trained offline on video detection datasets to address a general similarity learning problem.

A.35   High Performance Visual Tracking with Siamese Region Proposal Network (SiamRPN)

Q. Wang, Z. Zhu, B. Li, W. Wu, W. Hu, W. Zou
{wangqiang2015, zhuzheng2014}@ia.ac.cn, lbvictor2013@gmail.com,
wuwei@sensetime.com, wmhu@nlpr.ia.ac.cn, wei.zou@ia.ac.cn

The tracker SiamRPN consists of a Siamese sub-network for feature extraction and a region proposal sub-network including the classification branch and regression branch. In the inference phase, the proposed framework is formulated as a local one-shot detection task. The template branch of the Siamese sub-network is pre-computed while correlation layers are formulated as convolution layers to perform online tracking [48]. What is more, SiamRPN introduces an effective sampling strategy to control the imbalanced sample distribution and make the model focus on the semantic distractors [102].

A.36 Incremental Learning for Robust Visual Tracking (IVT)

Submitted by VOT Committee

The idea of the IVT tracker [70] is to incrementally learn a low-dimensional sub-space representation, adapting on-line to changes in the appearance of the target. The model update, based on incremental algorithms for principal component analysis, includes two features: a method for correctly updating the sample mean, and a forgetting factor to ensure less modelling power is expended fitting older observations.

A.37 Kalman Filter Ensemble-Based Tracker (KFebT)

P. Senna, I. Drummond, G. Bastos
pedro.senna@ufms.br, isadrummond@unifei.edu.br, sousa@unifei.edu.br

The tracker KFebT [72] fuses the result of two out-of-the box trackers, a mean-shift tracker that uses colour histogram (ASMS) [87] and a kernelized correlation filter (KCF) [32] by using a Kalman filter. Compared from last year submission, current version includes a partial feedback and an adaptive model update. Code available at https://github.com/psenna/KF-EBT.

A.38 Kernelized Correlation Filter (KCF)

Submitted by VOT Committee

This tracker is a C++ implementation of Kernelized Correlation Filter [32] operating on simple HOG features and Colour Names. The KCF tracker is equivalent to a Kernel Ridge Regression trained with thousands of sample patches around the object at different translations. It implements multi-thread multi-scale support, sub-cell peak estimation and replacing the model update by linear interpolation with a more robust update scheme. Code available at https://github.com/vojirt/kcf.

A.39 Learning Adaptive Discriminative Correlation Filter on Low-Dimensional Manifold (LADCF)

T. Xu, Z.-H. Feng, J. Kittler, X.-J. Wu
tianyang_xu@163.com, {z.feng, j.kittler}@surrey.ac.uk,
wu_xiaojun@jiangnan.edu.cn

LADCF utilises adaptive spatial regularizer to train low-dimensional discriminative correlation filters [93]. A low-dimensional discriminative manifold space is designed by exploiting temporal consistency, which realises reliable and flexible temporal information compression, alleviating filter degeneration and preserving appearance diversity. Adaptive spatial regularization and temporal consistency are combined in an objective function, which is optimised by the augmented Lagrangian method. Robustness is further considered by integrating HOG, Colour Names and ResNet-50 features. For ResNet-50 features, data augmentation [8] is adopted using flip, rotation and blur. The tracker is implemented on MatLab running on the CPU.

A.40   Learning Spatial-Aware Regressions for Visual Tracking (LSART)

C. Sun, Y. Sun, S. Wang, D. Wang, H. Lu, M.-H. Yang
{waynecool, rumsyx, wwen9502}@mail.dlut.edu.cn,
{wdice, lhchuan}@dlut.edu.cn, mhyang@ucmerced.edu

The LSART tracker exploits the complementary kernelized ridge regression (KRR) and convolution neural network (CNN) for tracking. A weighted cross-patch similarity kernel for the KRR model is defined and the spatially regularized filter kernels for the CNN model is used. While the former focuses on the holistic target, the latter focuses on the small local regions. The distance transform is exploited to pool layers for the CNN model, which determines the reliability of each output channel. Three kinds of features are used in the proposed method: Conv4-3 of VGG-16, Hog, and Colour naming. The LSART tracker is based on [78].

A.41   Lightweight Deep Neural Network for Visual Tracking (LWDNTm)

H. Zhao, D. Wang, H. Lu
zhaohj@stumail.neu.edu.cn, {wdice, lhchuan}@dlut.edu.cn

LWDNT-VGGM exploits lightweight deep networks for visual tracking. A lightweight fully convolutional network based on VGG-M-2048 is designed and trained on the ILSVRC VID dataset using mutual learning (between VGG-M and VGG-16). In online tracking, the proposed model outputs a response map regarding the target, based on which the target can be located by finding the peak of the response map. Besides, the scale estimation scheme proposed in DSST [12] is used.

A.42   Lightweight Deep Neural Network for Visual Tracking (LWDNTthi)

H. Zhao, D. Wang, H. Lu
zhaohj@stumail.neu.edu.cn, {wdice, lhchuan}@dlut.edu.cn

LWDNTthi exploits lightweight deep networks for visual tracking. To be specific, a lightweight fully convolutional network based on ThiNet is designed, and it is trained on the ILSVRC VID dataset directly. In online tracking, our model outputs a response map regarding the target, based on which the target can be located by finding the peak of the response map. The scale estimation scheme proposed in DSST [12] is also used.

A.43 Local-Global Tracking tracker (LGT)

Submitted by VOT Committee
The core element of LGT is a coupled-layer visual model that combines the target global and local appearance by interlacing two layers. By this coupled constraint paradigm between the adaptation of the global and the local layer, a more robust tracking through significant appearance changes is achieved. The reader is referred to [82] for details.

A.44 L1APG (L1APG)

Submitted by VOT Committee
L1APG [4] considers tracking as a sparse approximation problem in a particle filter framework. To find the target in a new frame, each target candidate is sparsely represented in the space spanned by target templates and trivial templates. The candidate with the smallest projection error after solving an ℓ_1 regularized least squares problem. The Bayesian state inference framework is used to propagate sample distributions over time.

A.45 Matrioska (Matrioska)

M. E. Maresca, A. Petrosino
mariomaresca@hotmail.it, alfredo.petrosino@uniparthenope.it
The Matrioska's confidence score is based on the number of keypoints found inside the object in the initialization.

A.46 Matrioska Best Displacement Flow (Matflow)

M. E. Maresca, A. Petrosino
mariomaresca@hotmail.it, alfredo.petrosino@uniparthenope.it
MatFlow enhances the performance of the first version of Matrioska [59] with response given by the short-term tracker BDF (see A.5).

A.47 MEEM (MEEM)

Submitted by VOT Committee
MEEM [97] uses an online SVM with a re-detection based on the entropy of the score function. The tracker creates an ensamble of experts by storing historical snapshots while tracking. When needed the tracker can be restored by the best of these experts, selected using an entropy minimization criterion.

A.48   MobileNet Combined with SiameseFC (MBSiam)

Y. Zhang, L. Wang, D. Wang, H. Lu
{zhangyunhua, wlj}@mail.dlut.edu.cn, {wdice, lhchuan}@dlut.edu.cn
MBSiam uses a bounding box regression network to assist SiameseFC during online tracking. SiameseFC determines the center of the target and the size of the target is further predicted by the bounding box regression network. The SiameseFC network is similar to Bertinetto's work [6] using AlexNet architecture. Bounding box regression network uses SSD-MobileNet architecture [35,52] and it aims to regress the tight bounding box of the target object in a region during tracking given the target's appearance in the first frame.

A.49   Multi Rotate and Scale Normalized Cross Correlation Tracker (MRSNCC)

A. G. Perera, Y. W. Law, J. Chahl
asanka.perera@mymail.unisa.edu.au, {yeewei.law, javaan.chahl}@unisa.edu.au
The tracker MRSNCC performs multiple stages of rotation and scaling up and down to the region of interest. The target location is localized with a normalized cross correlation filter. This tracking is combined with a corner point tracker and a histogram based tracker to handle low confident estimations.

A.50   Multi-Cue Correlation Tracker (MCCT)

N. Wang, W. Zhou, H. Li
wn6149@mail.ustc.edu.cn, {zhwg, lihq}@ustc.edu.cn
The multi-cue correlation tracker (MCCT) is based on the discriminative correlation filter framework. By combining different types of features, the proposed approach constructs multiple experts and each of them tracks the target independently. With the proposed robustness evaluation strategy, the suitable expert is selected for tracking in each frame. Furthermore, the divergence of multiple experts reveals the reliability of the current tracking, which helps updating the experts adaptively to keep them from corruption.

A.51   Multi-solution Fusion for Visual Tracking (MFT)

S. Bai, Z. He, J. Zhuang
{baishuai, he010103}@bupt.edu.cn, junfei.zhuang@faceall.cn
MFT tracker is based on correlation filtering algorithm. Firstly, different multi-resolution features with continuous convolution operator [15] are combined. Secondly, in order to improve the robustness a multi-solution using different features is trained and multi-solutions are optimally fused to predict the target location. Lastly, different combinations of Res50, SE-Res50, Hog, and CN features are applied to the different tracking situations.

A.52 Multiple Instance Learning Tracker (MIL)

Submitted by VOT Committee

MIL tracker [3] uses a tracking-by-detection approach, more specifically Multiple Instance Learning instead of traditional supervised learning methods and shows improved robustness to inaccuracies of the tracker and to incorrectly labelled training samples.

A.53 Online Adaptive Hidden Markov Model for Multi-Tracker Fusion (HMMTxD)

Submitted by VOT Committee

The HMMTxD method fuses observations from complementary out-of-the box trackers and a detector by utilizing a hidden Markov model whose latent states correspond to a binary vector expressing the failure of individual trackers. The Markov model is trained in an unsupervised way, relying on an online learned detector to provide a source of tracker-independent information for a modified Baum-Welch algorithm that updates the model w.r.t. the partially annotated data.

A.54 Part-Based Tracking by Sampling (PBTS)

George De Ath, Richard Everson
{gd295, r.m.everson} @exeter.ac.uk

PBTS [18] describes objects with a set of image patches which are represented by pairs of RGB pixel samples and counts of how many pixels in the patch are similar to them. This empirically characterises the underlying colour distribution of the patches and allows for matching using the Bhattacharyya distance. Candidate patch locations are generated by applying non-shearing affine transforms to the patches' previous locations, which are then evaluated for their match quality, and the best of these are locally optimised in a small region around each patch.

A.55 Robust Fragments Based Tracking Using the Integral Histogram - FragTrack (FT)

Submitted by VOT Committee

FragTrack represents the model of the object by multiple image fragments or patches. The patches are arbitrary and are not based on an object model. Every patch votes on the possible positions and scales of the object in the current frame, by comparing its histogram with the corresponding image patch histogram. A robust statistic is minimized in order to combine the vote maps of the multiple patches. The algorithm overcomes several difficulties which cannot be handled by traditional histogram-based algorithms like partial occlusions or pose change.

A.56   Robust Multi-task Correlation Particle Filter (R_MCPF)

J. Gao, T. Zhang, Y. Jiao, C. Xu
{gaojunyu2012, yifanjiao1227}@gmail.com, {tzzhang, csxu}@nlpr.ia.ac.cn
R_MCPF is based on the MCPF tracker [98] with a more robust fusion strategy for deep features.

A.57   ROI-Align Network (R_Anet)

S. Yun, D. Wee, M. Kang, J. Sung
{sangdoo.yun, dongyoon.wee, myunggu.kang, jinyoung.sung}@navercorp.com
This tracker is based on tracking-by-detection approach using CNNs. To make the tracker faster, a new tracking framework using RoIAlign technique is proposed.

A.58   Salient Region Weighted Correlation Filter Tracker (SRCT)

H. Lee, D. Kim
{lhmin, dkim}@postech.ac.kr
SRCT is the ensemble tracker composed of Salient Region-based Tracker [46] and ECO tracker [15]. The score map of Salient Region based Tracker is weighted to the score map of ECO tracker in spatial domain.

A.59   SA_Siam_P - An Advanced Twofold Siamese Network for Real-Time Object Tracking (SA_Siam_P)

A. He, C. Luo, X. Tian, W. Zeng
heanfeng@mail.ustc.edu.cn, {cluo, wezeng}@microsoft.com, xinmei@ustc.edu.cn
SA_Siam_P is an implementation of the SA-Siam tracker as described in [30]. Some bugs in the original implementation were fixed. In addition, for sequences where the target bounding box is not upright in the first frame, the reported tracking results are bounding boxes with the same tilt angle as the box in the first frame.

A.60   SA_Siam_R: A Twofold Siamese Network for Real-Time Object Tracking With Angle Estimation (SA_Siam_R)

A. He, C. Luo, X. Tian, W. Zeng
heanfeng@mail.ustc.edu.cn, {cluo, wezeng}@microsoft.com, xinmei@ustc.edu.cn
SA_Siam_R is a variation of the Siamese network-based tracker SA-Siam [30]. SA_Siam_R adopts three simple yet effective mechanisms, namely angle estimation, spatial mask, and template update, to achieve a better performance than SA-Siam. First, the framework includes multi-scale multi-angle candidates for search region. The scale change and the angle change of the tracked object are implicitly estimated according to the response maps. Second, spatial mask is

applied when the aspect ratio of the target is apart from 1:1 to reduce background noise. Last, moving average template update is adopted to deal with hard sequences with large target deformation. For more details, the reader is referred to [29].

A.61   Scale Adaptive Mean-Shift Tracker (ASMS)

Submitted by VOT Committee

The mean-shift tracker optimizes the Hellinger distance between template histogram and target candidate in the image. This optimization is done by a gradient descend. ASMS [87] addresses the problem of scale adaptation and presents a novel theoretically justified scale estimation mechanism which relies solely on the mean-shift procedure for the Hellinger distance. ASMS also introduces two improvements of the mean-shift tracker that make the scale estimation more robust in the presence of background clutter – a novel histogram colour weighting and a forward-backward consistency check. Code available at https://github.com/vojirt/asms.

A.62   Scale Adaptive Point-Based Kanade Lukas Tomasi Colour-Filter (SAPKLTF)

R. Martín-Nieto, Á. García-Martín, J. M. Martínez, Á. Iglesias-Arias, P. Vicente-Moñivar, S. Vivas, E. Velasco-Salido
{rafael.martinn, alvaro.garcia, josem.martinez, alvaro.iglesias, pablo.vicente, sergio.vivas, erik.velasco}@uam.es

The SAPKLTF [85] tracker is based on an extension of PKLTF tracker [24] with ASMS [87]. SAPKLTF is a single-object long-term tracker which consists of two phases: The first stage is based on the Kanade Lukas Tomasi approach (KLT) [73] choosing the object features (colour and motion coherence) to track relatively large object displacements. The second stage is based on scale adaptive mean shift gradient descent [87] to place the bounding box into the exact position of the object. The object model consists of a histogram including the quantized values of the RGB colour components and an edge binary flag.

A.63   SiamVGG (SiamVGG)

Y. Li, C. Hao, X. Zhang, H. Zhang, D. Chen
leeyh@illinois.edu, hc.onioncc@gmail.com, xiaofan3@illinois.edu,
zhhg@bupt.edu.cn, dchen@illinois.edu

SiamVGG adopts SiamFC [6] as the baseline approach. It applies a fully-convolutional Siamese network to allocate the target in the search region using a modified VGG-16 network [74] as the backbone. The network is trained offline on both ILSVRC VID dataset [71] and Youtube-BB dataset end-to-end.

A.64   Spatially Regularized Discriminative Correlation Filter Tracker (SRDCF)

Submitted by VOT Committee

Standard Discriminative Correlation Filter (DCF) based trackers such as [12,14,32] suffer from the inherent periodic assumption when using circular correlation. The Spatially Regularized DCF (SRDCF) alleviates this problem by introducing a spatial regularization function that penalizes filter coefficients residing outside the target region. This allows the size of the training and detection samples to be increased without affecting the effective filter size. By selecting the spatial regularization function to have a sparse Discrete Fourier Spectrum, the filter is efficiently optimized directly in the Fourier domain. For more details, the reader is referred to [13].

A.65   Spatio-Temporal Background-Aware Correlation Filter for Visual Tracking (STBACF)

A. Memarmoghdam, H. Kiani Galoogah
a.memarmoghadam@eng.ui.ac.ir, hamedkg@gmail.com

Recently, the discriminative BACF approach [23] efficiently tracks the target object via training a correlation filter by exploiting real negative examples densely sampled from its surrounding background. To further improve its robustness, especially against drastic changes of the object model during track, STBACF tracker simultaneously updates the filter while training by incorporating temporal regularization into the original BACF formulation. In this way, a temporally consistent filter is efficiently solved in each frame via an iterative ADMM method. Furthermore, to suppress unwanted non-object information of the target bounding box, an elliptical binary mask is applied during online training.

A.66   Spatio-Temporal Siamese Tracking (STST)

F. Zhao, Y. Wu, J. Wang, M. Tang
{fei.zhao, jqwang, tangm}@nlpr.ia.ac.cn, ywu.china@gmail.com

The tracker STST applies 3D convolutional block to extract the temporal features of the target appearing in different frames, and it uses the dense correlation layer to match the feature maps of the target patch and the search patch.

A.67   Staple: Sum of Template and Pixel-Wise LEarners (Staple)

L. Bertinetto, J. Valmadre, S. Golodetz, O. Miksik, P. Torr
{luca.bertinetto, stuart.golodetz, ondrej.miksik, philip.torr}@eng.ox.ac.uk,
jack.valmadre@gmail.com

Staple is a tracker that combines two image patch representations that are sensitive to complementary factors to learn a model online that is inherently robust to both colour changes and deformations. For more details, we refer the reader to [7].

A.68   Struck: Structured Output Tracking with Kernels (struck2011)

Submitted by VOT Committee

Struck [28] is a framework for adaptive visual object tracking based on structured output prediction. The method uses a kernelized structured output support vector machine (SVM), which is learned online to provide adaptive tracking.

A.69   TRAcker Based on Context-Aware Deep Feature Compression with Multiple Auto-Encoders (TRACA)

J. Choi, H. J. Chang, T. Fischer, S. Yun, Y. Demiris, J. Y. Choi
jwchoi.pil@gmail.com, {hj.chang, t.fischer, y.demiris}@imperial.ac.uk,
{yunsd101, jychoi}@snu.ac.kr

The proposed TRACA consists of multiple expert auto-encoders, a context-aware network, and correlation filters. The expert auto-encoders robustly compress raw deep convolutional features from VGG-Net. Each of them is trained according to a different context, and thus performs context-dependent compression. A context-aware network is proposed to select the expert auto-encoder best suited for the specific tracking target. During online tracking, only this auto-encoder is running. After initially adapting the selected expert auto-encoder for the tracking target, its compressed feature map is utilized as an input of correlation filters which tracks the target online.

A.70   Tracking by Feature Select Adversary Network (FSAN)

W. Wei, Q. Ruihe, L. Si
wang_wei.buaa@163.com, {qianruihe, liusi}@iie.ac.cn

The tracker FSAN consists of an offline trained convolutional network and a feature channels selecting adversary network. Image patches are extracted and multiple channels feature of each patch in each frame are computed. Then, the more stable discriminative feature in is selected by a channel mask generate network. The generate network can filter out the most discriminative feature channels in current frame. In the adversarial learning, the robustness of the discriminative network is increased by using examples in which the feature channels are enhanced or removed by the generate network.

A.71   Unveiling the Power of Deep Tracking (UPDT)

G. Bhat, J. Johnander, M. Danelljan, F. Khan, M. Felsberg
{goutam.bhat, joakim.johnander, martin.danelljan, fahad.khan,
michael.felsberg}@liu.se

UPDT learns independent tracking models for deep and shallow features to fully exploit their complementary properties. The deep model is trained with an emphasis on achieving higher robustness, while the shallow model is trained to achieve high accuracy. The scores of these individual models are then fused using a maximum margin based approach to get the final target prediction. For more details, the reader is referred to [8].

A.72   3D Convolutional Networks for Visual Tracking (C3DT)

H. Li, S. Wu, Y. Yang, S. Huang
haojieli_scut@foxmail.com,   eesihang@mail.scut.edu.cn,   yychzw@foxmail.com,
eehsp@scut.edu.cn
The tracker C3DT improves the existing tracker MDNet [64] by introducing spatio-temporal information using the C3D network [80]. MDNet treats the tracking as classification and regression, which utilizes the appearance feature from the current frame to determine which candidate frame is object or background, and then gets an accurate bounding box by a linear regression. This network ignores the importance of spatio-temporal information for visual tracking. To address this problem C3DT tracker adopts two-branch network to extract features. One branch is used to get features from the current frame by the VGG-S [11]; another is the C3D network, which extracts spatio-temporal information from the previous frames.

B   VOT2018 Long-Term Challenge Tracker Descriptions

In this appendix we provide a short summary of all trackers that were submitted to the long-term challenge.

B.1   A Memory Model Based on the Siamese Network for Long-term Tracking (MMLT)

H. Lee, S. Choi, C. Kim
{*hankyeol, seokeon, changick*}*@kaist.ac.kr*
MMLT consists of three parts: memory management, tracking, and re-detection. The structure of the memory model for long-term tracking, which is inspired by the well-known Atkinson-Shiffrin model [2], is divided into the short-term and long-term stores. Tracking and re-detection processes are performed based on this memory model. In the tracking step, the bounding box of the target is estimated by combining the features of the Siamese network [6] in both short-term and long-term stores. In the re-detection step, features in the long-term store are employed. A coarse-to-fine strategy is adopted that collects candidates with similar semantic meanings in the entire image and then it refines the final position based on the Siamese network.

B.2   DaSiameseRPN_long-term (DaSiam_LT)

Z. Zhu, Q. Wang, B. Li, W. Wu, Wei Zou
{*zhuzheng2014, wangqiang2015, wei.zou*}*@ia.ac.cn,*
{*libo, wuwei*}*@sensetime.com*
The tracker DaSiam_LT adopts Siamese Region Proposal Network (SiamRPN) A.35 as the baseline. It extends the SiamRPN approach by introducing a simple yet effective local-to-global search region strategy. Specifically, the

size of search region is iteratively growing with a constant step when failed tracking is indicated. The distractor-aware training and inference are added to enable high-quality detection score to indicate the quality of tracking results [102].

B.3   Flock of Trackers (FoT)

Submitted by VOT Committee
For a tracker description, the reader is referred to A.33.

B.4   Fully-Convolutional Siamese Detector (SiamFCDet)

J. Valmadre, L. Bertinetto, N. Lee, J. Henriques, A. Vedaldi, P. Torr
jack.valmadre@gmail.com, {luca.bertinetto, namhoon.lee, joao.henriques, andrea.vedaldi, philip.torr}@eng.ox.ac.uk
SiamFCDet uses SiamFC to search the entire image at multiple resolutions in each frame. There is no temporal component.

B.5   Fully-Convolutional Siamese Network (SiamFC)

J. Valmadre, L. Bertinetto, N. Lee, J. Henriques, A. Vedaldi, P. Torr
jack.valmadre@gmail.com, {luca.bertinetto, namhoon.lee, joao.henriques, andrea.vedaldi, philip.torr}@eng.ox.ac.uk
For a tracker description, the reader is referred to A.34.

B.6   Fully Correlational Long-Term Tracker (FuCoLoT)

Submitted by VOT Committee
FuCoLoT is a Fully Correlational Long-term Tracker. It exploits the novel DCF constrained filter learning method to design a detector that is able to re-detect the target in the whole image efficiently. Several correlation filters are trained on different time scales that act as the detector components. A mechanism based on the correlation response is used for tracking failure estimation.

B.7   Long-Term Siamese Instance Search Tracking (LTSINT)

R. Tao, E. Gavves, A. Smeulders
{rantao.mail, efstratios.gavves}@gmail.com, a.w.m.smeulders@uva.nl
The tracker follows the Siamese tracking framework. It has two novel components. One is a hybrid search scheme which combines local search and global search. The global search is a three-step procedure following a coarse-to-fine scheme. The tracker switches from local search to global search when the similarity score of the detected box is below a certain threshold (0.3 for this submission). The other novel component is a cautious model updating which updates the similarity function online. Model updates are permissible when the similarity score of the detected box is above a certain threshold (0.5 for this submission).

B.8   MobileNet Based Tracking by Detection Algorithm (MBMD)

Y. Zhang, L. Wang, D. Wang, J. Qi, H. Lu
{zhangyunhua, wlj}@mail.dlut.edu.cn, {wdice, jinqing, lhchuan}@dlut.edu.cn

The proposed tracker consists of a bounding box regression network and a verifier network. The regression network regresses the target object's bounding box in a search region given the target in the first frame. Its outputs are several candidate boxes and each box's reliability is evaluated by the verifier to determine the predicted target box. If the predicted scores of both networks are below the thresholds, the tracker searches the target in the whole image. The regression network uses SSD-MobileNet architecture [35,52] and its parameters are fixed during online tracking. The verifier is similar to MDNet [64] and is implemented by VGGM pretrained on ImageNet classification dataset. The last three layers' parameters of the verifier are updated online to filter the distractors for the tracker.

B.9   Online Adaptive Hidden Markov Model for Multi-Tracker Fusion (HMMTxD)

Submitted by VOT Committee
For a tracker description, the reader is referred to A.53.

B.10   Parallel Tracking and Verifying Plus (PTAVplus)

H. Fan, F. Yang, Q. Zhou, H. Ling
{hengfan, fyang, hbling}@temple.edu, zhou.qin.190@sjtu.edu.cn

PTAVplus is an improvement of PTAV [20] by combining a tracker and a strong verifier for long-term visual tracking.

B.11   Scale Adaptive Mean-Shift Tracker (ASMS)

Submitted by VOT Committee
For a tracker description, the reader is referred to A.61.

B.12   Scale Adaptive Point-Based Kanade Lukas Tomasi Colour-Filter (SAPKLTF)

R. Martín-Nieto, Á. García-Martín, J. M. Martínez, Á. Iglesias-Arias, P. Vicente-Moñivar, S. Vivas, E. Velasco-Salido
{rafael.martinn, alvaro.garcia, josem.martinez, alvaro.iglesias, pablo.vicente, sergio.vivas, erik.velasco}@uam.es

For a tracker description, the reader is referred to A.62.

B.13   Search Your Object with Siamese Network (SYT)

P. Li, Z. Wang, D. Wang, B. Chen, H. Lu
{907508458,   2805825263}@qq.com,   wdice@dlut.edu.cn,   476732833@qq.com,
lhchuan@dlut.edu.cn

In long-term tracking, few trackers can re-detect the object after tracking failures. SYT utilises the siamese network as base tracker and it introduces the Single Shot MultiBox Detector for re-detection. A verifier with the initial frame to output the tracking score is trained. When the score is larger than zero, the tracker result is utilised; otherwise, the detector to re-find the object in the whole images is used.

B.14   Siamese Long-Term Tracker (SLT)

J. Zhuang, S. Bai, Z. He
junfei.zhuang@facell.cn, {baishuai, he010103}@bupt.edu.cn

Siamese Long-term tracker (SLT) is composed of two main components. The first part is short-term tracker based on SiamFC-3s [6]. The role of this part is tracking target before it disappears from view. The second part is a detector which aims to re-detect the target when it reappears, and it is also based on Siamese network structure. For this part, a modified VGG-M model is employed to extract target features from the first frame and whole image features from other frames, then target features are compared with whole image features to locate target position in a new frame.

B.15   SiamVGG (SiamVGG)

Y. Li, C. Hao, X. Zhang, H. Zhang, D. Chen
leeyh@illinois.edu, hc.onioncc@gmail.com, xiaofan3@illinois.edu,
zhhg@bupt.edu.cn, dchen@illinois.edu

For a tracker description, the reader is referred to A.63.

References

1. Abdelpakey, M.H., Shehata, M.S., Mohamed, M.M.: Denssiam: End-to-end densely-siamese network with self-attention model for object tracking. arXiv:1809.02714, September 2018
2. Atkinson, R.C., Shiffrin, R.M.: Human memory: a proposed system and its control processes1. Psychol. Learn. Motiv. **2**, 89–195 (1968)
3. Babenko, B., Yang, M.H., Belongie, S.: Robust object tracking with online multiple instance learning. IEEE Trans. Pattern Anal. Mach. Intell. **33**(8), 1619–1632 (2011)
4. Bao, C., Wu, Y., Ling, H., Ji, H.: Real time robust L1 tracker using accelerated proximal gradient approach. In: CVPR (2012)
5. Battistone, F., Petrosino, A., Santopietro, V.: Watch out: embedded video tracking with BST for unmanned aerial vehicles. J. Sig. Process. Syst. **90**(6), 891–900 (2018). https://doi.org/10.1007/s11265-017-1279-x

6. Bertinetto, L., Valmadre, J., Henriques, J.F., Vedaldi, A., Torr, P.H.S.: Fully-convolutional siamese networks for object tracking. In: Hua, G., Jégou, H. (eds.) ECCV 2016. LNCS, vol. 9914, pp. 850–865. Springer, Cham (2016). https://doi.org/10.1007/978-3-319-48881-3_56
7. Bertinetto, L., Valmadre, J., Golodetz, S., Miksik, O., Torr, P.H.S.: Staple: complementary learners for real-time tracking. In: Proceedings of the IEEE Conference on Computer Vision and Pattern Recognition, pp. 1401–1409 (2016)
8. Bhat, G., Johnander, J., Danelljan, M., Khan, F.S., Felsberg, M.: Unveiling the power of deep tracking. In: Ferrari, V., Hebert, M., Sminchisescu, C., Weiss, Y. (eds.) ECCV 2018. LNCS, vol. 11206, pp. 493–509. Springer, Cham (2018). https://doi.org/10.1007/978-3-030-01216-8_30
9. Bolme, D.S., Beveridge, J.R., Draper, B.A., Lui, Y.M.: Visual object tracking using adaptive correlation filters. In: Proceedings of the IEEE Conference on Computer Vision and Pattern Recognition (2010)
10. Čehovin, L.: TraX: the visual tracking eXchange protocol and library. Neurocomputing 260, 5–8 (2017). https://doi.org/10.1016/j.neucom.2017.02.036
11. Chatfield, K., Simonyan, K., Vedaldi, A., Zisserman, A.: Return of the devil in the details: delving deep into convolutional nets. In: BMVC (2014)
12. Danelljan, M., Häger, G., Khan, F.S., Felsberg, M.: Accurate scale estimation for robust visual tracking. In: Proceedings of the British Machine Vision Conference BMVC (2014)
13. Danelljan, M., Häger, G., Khan, F.S., Felsberg, M.: Learning spatially regularized correlation filters for visual tracking. In: International Conference on Computer Vision (2015)
14. Danelljan, M., Khan, F.S., Felsberg, M., Van de Weijer, J.: Adaptive color attributes for real-time visual tracking. In: Computer Vision and Pattern Recognition (2014)
15. Danelljan, M., Bhat, G., Khan, F.S., Felsberg, M.: ECO: efficient convolution operators for tracking. In: CVPR (2017)
16. Danelljan, M., Häger, G., Khan, F.S., Felsberg, M.: Discriminative scale space tracking. IEEE Trans. Pattern Anal. Mach. Intell. 39, 1561–1575 (2016)
17. Danelljan, M., Robinson, A., Shahbaz Khan, F., Felsberg, M.: Beyond correlation filters: learning continuous convolution operators for visual tracking. In: Leibe, B., Matas, J., Sebe, N., Welling, M. (eds.) ECCV 2016. LNCS, vol. 9909, pp. 472–488. Springer, Cham (2016). https://doi.org/10.1007/978-3-319-46454-1_29
18. De Ath, G., Everson, R.: Part-Based Tracking by Sampling. arXiv:1805.08511, May 2018
19. Deng, J., Dong, W., Socher, R., Li, L.J., Li, K., Fei-Fei, L.: Imagenet: a large-scale hierarchical image database. In: CVPR (2009)
20. Fan, H., Ling, H.: Parallel tracking and verifying: a framework for real-time and high accuracy visual tracking. In: ICCV (2017)
21. Felsberg, M., Berg, A., Häger, G., Ahlberg, J., et al.: The thermal infrared visual object tracking VOT-TIR2015 challenge results. In: ICCV 2015 Workshop Proceedings, VOT2015 Workshop (2015)
22. Galoogahi, H.K., Fagg, A., Huang, C., Ramanan, D., Lucey, S.: Need for speed: a benchmark for higher frame rate object tracking. CoRR abs/1703.05884 (2017). http://arxiv.org/abs/1703.05884
23. Galoogahi, H.K., Fagg, A., Lucey, S.: Learning background-aware correlation filters for visual tracking. In: ICCV, pp. 1144–1152 (2017)

24. González, A., Martín-Nieto, R., Bescós, J., Martínez, J.M.: Single object long-term tracker for smart control of a PTZ camera. In: Proceedings of the International Conference on Distributed Smart Cameras, p. 39. ACM (2014)
25. Goyette, N., Jodoin, P.M., Porikli, F., Konrad, J., Ishwar, P.: Changedetection.net: a new change detection benchmark dataset. In: CVPR Workshops, pp. 1–8. IEEE (2012)
26. Gundogdu, E., Alatan, A.A.: Good features to correlate for visual tracking. IEEE Trans. Image Process. **27**(5), 2526–2540 (2018). https://doi.org/10.1109/TIP.2018.2806280
27. Guo, Q., Feng, W., Zhou, C., Huang, R., Wan, L., Wang, S.: Learning dynamic Siamese network for visual object tracking. In: ICCV (2017)
28. Hare, S., Saffari, A., Torr, P.H.S.: Struck: structured output tracking with kernels. In: Metaxas, D.N., Quan, L., Sanfeliu, A., Gool, L.J.V. (eds.) International Conference on Computer Vision, pp. 263–270. IEEE (2011)
29. He, A., Luo, C., Tian, X., Zeng, W.: Towards a better match in siamese network based visual object tracker. In: Leal-Taixé, L., Roth, S. (eds.) ECCV 2018 Workshops. LNCS, vol. 11129, pp. 132–147. Springer, Cham (2019)
30. He, A., Luo, C., Tian, X., Zeng, W.: A twofold siamese network for real-time object tracking. In: The IEEE Conference on Computer Vision and Pattern Recognition (CVPR), June 2018
31. He, Z., Fan, Y., Zhuang, J., Dong, Y., Bai, H.: Correlation filters with weighted convolution responses. In: Proceedings of the IEEE Conference on Computer Vision and Pattern Recognition, pp. 1992–2000 (2017)
32. Henriques, J., Caseiro, R., Martins, P., Batista, J.: High-speed tracking with kernelized correlation filters. PAMI **37**(3), 583–596 (2015)
33. Herranz, J.R.: Short-term single target tracking with discriminative correlation filters. Master thesis, University of Ljubljana/Technical University of Madrid (2018)
34. Hong, Z., Chen, Z., Wang, C., Mei, X., Prokhorov, D., Tao, D.: Multi-store tracker (muster): a cognitive psychology inspired approach to object tracking. In: Proceedings of the IEEE Conference on Computer Vision and Pattern Recognition, pp. 749–758 (2015)
35. Howard, A.G., et al.: Mobilenets: efficient convolutional neural networks for mobile vision applications. arXiv preprint arXiv:1704.04861 (2017)
36. Jack, V., et al.: Long-term tracking in the wild: a benchmark. arXiv:1803.09502 (2018)
37. Kalal, Z., Mikolajczyk, K., Matas, J.: Tracking-learning-detection. IEEE Trans. Pattern Anal. Mach. Intell. (TPAMI) **34**(7), 1409–1422 (2012). https://doi.org/10.1109/TPAMI.2011.239
38. Kristan, M., et al.: The visual object tracking vot2017 challenge results. In: ICCV 2017 Workshops, Workshop on Visual Object Tracking Challenge (2017)
39. Kristan, M., et al.: The visual object tracking VOT2016 challenge results. In: Hua, G., Jégou, H. (eds.) ECCV 2016. LNCS, vol. 9914, pp. 777–823. Springer, Cham (2016). https://doi.org/10.1007/978-3-319-48881-3_54
40. Kristan, M., et al.: The visual object tracking vot2015 challenge results. In: ICCV 2015 Workshops, Workshop on Visual Object Tracking Challenge (2015)
41. Kristan, M., et al.: The visual object tracking vot2013 challenge results. In: ICCV 2013 Workshops, Workshop on Visual Object Tracking Challenge, pp. 98–111 (2013)
42. Kristan, M., et al.: The visual object tracking VOT2014 challenge results. In: Agapito, L., Bronstein, M.M., Rother, C. (eds.) ECCV 2014. LNCS, vol. 8926,

pp. 191–217. Springer, Cham (2015). https://doi.org/10.1007/978-3-319-16181-5_14

43. Kristan, M., et al.: A novel performance evaluation methodology for single-target trackers. IEEE Trans. Pattern Anal. Mach. Intell. **38**(11), 2137–2155 (2016)

44. Leal-Taixé, L., Milan, A., Reid, I.D., Roth, S., Schindler, K.: Motchallenge 2015: Towards a benchmark for multi-target tracking. CoRR abs/1504.01942 (2015). http://arxiv.org/abs/1504.01942

45. Lebeda, K., Bowden, R., Matas, J.: Long-term tracking through failure cases. In: Visual Object Tracking Challenge VOT2013, in Conjunction with ICCV2013 (2013)

46. Lee, H., Kim, D.: Salient region-based online object tracking. In: 2018 IEEE Winter Conference on Applications of Computer Vision (WACV), pp. 1170–1177. IEEE (2018)

47. Li, A., Li, M., Wu, Y., Yang, M.H., Yan, S.: Nus-pro: a new visual tracking challenge. IEEE-PAMI **38**, 335–349 (2015)

48. Li, B., Yan, J., Wu, W., Zhu, Z., Hu, X.: High performance visual tracking with siamese region proposal network. In: The IEEE Conference on Computer Vision and Pattern Recognition (CVPR), June 2018

49. Li, F., Tian, C., Zuo, W., Zhang, L., Yang, M.H.: Learning spatial-temporal regularized correlation filters for visual tracking. In: CVPR (2018)

50. Li, Y., Zhu, J., Song, W., Wang, Z., Liu, H., Hoi, S.C.H.: Robust estimation of similarity transformation for visual object tracking with correlation filters (2017)

51. Liang, P., Blasch, E., Ling, H.: Encoding color information for visual tracking: algorithms and benchmark. IEEE Trans. Image Process. **24**(12), 5630–5644 (2015)

52. Liu, W., et al.: SSD: single shot multibox detector. In: Leibe, B., Matas, J., Sebe, N., Welling, M. (eds.) ECCV 2016. LNCS, vol. 9905, pp. 21–37. Springer, Cham (2016). https://doi.org/10.1007/978-3-319-46448-0_2

53. Lukežič, A., Vojíř T., Zajc, L.Č., Matas, J., Kristan, M.: Discriminative correlation filter with channel and spatial reliability. In: The IEEE Conference on Computer Vision and Pattern Recognition (CVPR), pp. 6309–6318, July 2017

54. Lukežič, A., Zajc, L.Č., Kristan, M.: Deformable parts correlation filters for robust visual tracking. IEEE Trans. Cybern. **PP**(99), 1–13 (2017)

55. Lukezic, A., Zajc, L.C., Vojír, T., Matas, J., Kristan, M.: FCLT - A fully-correlational long-term tracker. CoRR abs/1711.09594 (2017). http://arxiv.org/abs/1711.09594

56. Lukezic, A., Zajc, L.C., Vojír, T., Matas, J., Kristan, M.: Now you see me: evaluating performance in long-term visual tracking. CoRR abs/1804.07056 (2018). http://arxiv.org/abs/1804.07056

57. Ma, C., Yang, X., Zhang, C., Yang, M.H.: Long-term correlation tracking. In: CVPR (2015)

58. Maresca, M.E., Petrosino, A.: Clustering local motion estimates for robust and efficient object tracking. In: Agapito, L., Bronstein, M.M., Rother, C. (eds.) ECCV 2014. LNCS, vol. 8926, pp. 244–253. Springer, Cham (2015). https://doi.org/10.1007/978-3-319-16181-5_17

59. Maresca, M.E., Petrosino, A.: MATRIOSKA: a multi-level approach to fast tracking by learning. In: Petrosino, A. (ed.) ICIAP 2013. LNCS, vol. 8157, pp. 419–428. Springer, Heidelberg (2013). https://doi.org/10.1007/978-3-642-41184-7_43

60. Moudgil, A., Gandhi, V.: Long-term visual object tracking benchmark. arXiv preprint arXiv:1712.01358 (2017)

61. Mueller, M., Smith, N., Ghanem, B.: A benchmark and simulator for UAV tracking. In: Leibe, B., Matas, J., Sebe, N., Welling, M. (eds.) ECCV 2016. LNCS, vol. 9905, pp. 445–461. Springer, Cham (2016). https://doi.org/10.1007/978-3-319-46448-0_27

62. Müller, M., Bibi, A., Giancola, S., Al-Subaihi, S., Ghanem, B.: Trackingnet: A large-scale dataset and benchmark for object tracking in the wild. CoRR abs/1803.10794 (2018). http://arxiv.org/abs/1803.10794

63. Dalal, N., Triggs, B.: Histograms of oriented gradients for human detection. In: CVPR, vol. 1, pp. 886–893, June 2005

64. Nam, H., Han, B.: Learning multi-domain convolutional neural networks for visual tracking. In: CVPR, pp. 4293–4302 (2016)

65. Nebehay, G., Pflugfelder, R.: Clustering of Static-Adaptive correspondences for deformable object tracking. In: Computer Vision and Pattern Recognition. IEEE (2015)

66. Pernici, F., del Bimbo, A.: Object tracking by oversampling local features. IEEE Trans. Pattern Anal. Mach. Intell. **36**(12), 2538–2551 (2013). https://doi.org/10.1109/TPAMI.2013.250

67. Phillips, P.J., Moon, H., Rizvi, S.A., Rauss, P.J.: The feret evaluation methodology for face-recognition algorithms. IEEE Trans. Pattern Anal. Mach. Intell. **22**(10), 1090–1104 (2000)

68. Possegger, H., Mauthner, T., Bischof, H.: In defense of color-based model-free tracking. In: Proceedings of the IEEE Conference on Computer Vision and Pattern Recognition (2015)

69. Real, E., Shlens, J., Mazzocchi, S., Pan, X., Vanhoucke, V.: YouTube-BoundingBoxes: a large high-precision human-annotated data set for object detection in video. In: Computer Vision and Pattern Recognition, pp. 7464–7473 (2017)

70. Ross, D.A., Lim, J., Lin, R.S., Yang, M.H.: Incremental learning for robust visual tracking. Int. J. Comput. Vis. **77**(1–3), 125–141 (2008)

71. Russakovsky, O., et al.: Imagenet large scale visual recognition challenge. IJCV **115**(3), 211–252 (2015). https://doi.org/10.1007/s11263-015-0816-y

72. Senna, P., Drummond, I.N., Bastos, G.S.: Real-time ensemble-based tracker with kalman filter. In: 2017 30th SIBGRAPI Conference on Graphics, Patterns and Images (SIBGRAPI), pp. 338–344, October 2017. https://doi.org/10.1109/SIBGRAPI.2017.51

73. Shi, J., Tomasi, C.: Good features to track. In: Computer Vision and Pattern Recognition, pp. 593–600, June 1994

74. Simonyan, K., Zisserman, A.: Very deep convolutional networks for large-scale image recognition. arXiv preprint arXiv:1409.1556 (2014)

75. Smeulders, A.W.M., Chu, D.M., Cucchiara, R., Calderara, S., Dehghan, A., Shah, M.: Visual tracking: an experimental survey. TPAMI **36**, 1442–1468 (2013). https://doi.org/10.1109/TPAMI.2013.230

76. Solera, F., Calderara, S., Cucchiara, R.: Towards the evaluation of reproducible robustness in tracking-by-detection. In: Advanced Video and Signal Based Surveillance, pp. 1–6 (2015)

77. Sun, C., Wang, D., Lu, H., Yang, M.H.: Correlation tracking via joint discrimination and reliability learning. In: Proceedings of the IEEE Conference on Computer Vision and Pattern Recognition, pp. 489–497 (2018)

78. Sun, C., Wang, D., Lu, H., Yang, M.H.: Learning spatial-aware regressions for visual tracking. In: Proceedings of the IEEE Conference on Computer Vision and Pattern Recognition, pp. 8962–8970 (2018)

79. Tao, R., Gavves, E., Smeulders, A.W.M.: Tracking for half an hour. CoRR abs/1711.10217 (2017). http://arxiv.org/abs/1711.10217
80. Tran, D., Bourdev, L., Fergus, R., Torresani, L., Paluri, M.: Learning spatiotemporal features with 3D convolutional networks. In: 2015 IEEE International Conference on Computer Vision (ICCV), pp. 4489–4497, December 2015. https://doi.org/10.1109/ICCV.2015.510
81. Valmadre, J., Bertinetto, L., Henriques, J.F., Vedaldi, A., Torr, P.H.: End-to-end representation learning for correlation filter based tracking. arXiv preprint arXiv:1704.06036 (2017)
82. Čehovin, L., Kristan, M., Leonardis, A.: Robust visual tracking using an adaptive coupled-layer visual model. IEEE Trans. Pattern Anal. Mach. Intell. **35**(4), 941–953 (2013). https://doi.org/10.1109/TPAMI.2012.145
83. Čehovin, L., Leonardis, A., Kristan, M.: Visual object tracking performance measures revisited. IEEE Trans. Image Process. **25**(3), 1261–1274 (2015)
84. Čehovin, L., Leonardis, A., Kristan, M.: Robust visual tracking using template anchors. In: WACV. IEEE, March 2016
85. Velasco-Salido, E., Martínez, J.M.: Scale adaptive point-based kanade lukas tomasi colour-filter tracker. Under Review (2017)
86. Vojíř, T., Matas, J.: The enhanced flock of trackers. In: Cipolla, R., Battiato, S., Farinella, G.M. (eds.) Registration and Recognition in Images and Videos. SCI, vol. 532, pp. 113–136. Springer, Heidelberg (2014). https://doi.org/10.1007/978-3-642-44907-9_6
87. Vojíř, T., Noskova, J., Matas. J.: Robust scale-adaptive mean-shift for tracking. Pattern Recognit. Lett. **49**, 250–258 (2014)
88. Wang, Q., Gao, J., Xing, J., Zhang, M., Hu, W.: DCFNet: discriminant correlation filters network for visual tracking. arXiv preprint arXiv:1704.04057 (2017)
89. Van de Weijer, J., Schmid, C., Verbeek, J., Larlus, D.: Learning color names for real-world applications. IEEE Trans. Image Process. **18**(7), 1512–1523 (2009)
90. Wu, C., Zhu, J., Zhang, J., Chen, C., Cai, D.: A convolutional treelets binary feature approach to fast keypoint recognition. In: Fitzgibbon, A., Lazebnik, S., Perona, P., Sato, Y., Schmid, C. (eds.) ECCV 2012. LNCS, vol. 7576, pp. 368–382. Springer, Heidelberg (2012). https://doi.org/10.1007/978-3-642-33715-4_27
91. Wu, Y., Lim, J., Yang, M.H.: Online object tracking: a benchmark. In: Computer Vision and Pattern Recognition (2013)
92. Wu, Y., Lim, J., Yang, M.H.: Object tracking benchmark. PAMI **37**(9), 1834–1848 (2015)
93. Xu, T., Feng, Z.H., Wu, X.J., Kittler, J.: Learning adaptive discriminative correlation filters via temporal consistency preserving spatial feature selection for robust visual tracking. arXiv preprint arXiv:1807.11348 (2018)
94. Yiming, L., Shen, J., Pantic, M.: Mobile face tracking: a survey and benchmark. arXiv:1805.09749v1 (2018)
95. Young, D.P., Ferryman, J.M.: PETS metrics: on-line performance evaluation service. In: ICCCN 2005 Proceedings of the 14th International Conference on Computer Communications and Networks, pp. 317–324 (2005)
96. Zajc, L.Č., Lukežič, A., Leonardis, A., Kristan, M.: Beyond standard benchmarks: parameterizing performance evaluation in visual object tracking. ICCV abs/1612.00089 (2017). http://arxiv.org/abs/1612.00089
97. Zhang, J., Ma, S., Sclaroff, S.: MEEM: robust tracking via multiple experts using entropy minimization. In: Fleet, D., Pajdla, T., Schiele, B., Tuytelaars, T. (eds.) ECCV 2014. LNCS, vol. 8694, pp. 188–203. Springer, Cham (2014). https://doi.org/10.1007/978-3-319-10599-4_13

98. Zhang, T., Xu, C., Yang, M.H.: Learning multi-task correlation particle filters for visual tracking. IEEE Trans. Pattern Anal. Mach. Intell. 1–14 (2018)
99. Zhang, Z., Li, Y., Ren, J., Zhu, J.: Effective occlusion handling for fast correlation filter-based trackers (2018)
100. Zhu, G., Porikli, F., Li, H.: Tracking randomly moving objects on edge box proposals (2015)
101. Zhu, P., Wen, L., Bian, X., Haibin, L., Hu, Q.: Vision meets drones: a challenge. arXiv preprint arXiv:1804.07437 (2018)
102. Zhu, Z., Wang, Q., Li, B., Wu, W., Yan, J., Hu, W.: Distractor-aware siamese networks for visual object tracking. In: Ferrari, V., Hebert, M., Sminchisescu, C., Weiss, Y. (eds.) ECCV 2018. LNCS, vol. 11213, pp. 103–119. Springer, Cham (2018). https://doi.org/10.1007/978-3-030-01240-3_7

On the Optimization of Advanced DCF-Trackers

Joakim Johnander[1,2]($\boxtimes$), Goutam Bhat[1], Martin Danelljan[1], Fahad Shahbaz Khan[1,3], and Michael Felsberg[1]

[1] CVL, Department of Electrical Engineering, Linköping University, Linköping, Sweden
joakim.johnander@liu.se
[2] Zenuity, Gothenburg, Sweden
[3] Inception Institute of Artificial Intelligence, Abu Dhabi, UAE

Abstract. Trackers based on discriminative correlation filters (DCF) have recently seen widespread success and in this work we dive into their numerical core. DCF-based trackers interleave learning of the target detector and target state inference based on this detector. Whereas the original formulation includes a closed-form solution for the filter learning, recently introduced improvements to the framework no longer have known closed-form solutions. Instead a large-scale linear least squares problem must be solved each time the detector is updated. We analyze the procedure used to optimize the detector and let the popular scheme introduced with ECO serve as a baseline. The ECO implementation is revisited in detail and several mechanisms are provided with alternatives. With comprehensive experiments we show which configurations are superior in terms of tracking capabilities *and* optimization performance.

1 Introduction

Visual tracking is the computer vision problem of estimating a target trajectory in a video, given only its initial state. This is a challenge occurring in a wide range of vision problems seen for instance in autonomous cars, UAVs, and surveillance. For such applications, there is often a real-time constraint coupled with a desire to track objects undergoing challenging appearance changes. In recent years trackers based on Discriminative Correlation Filters (DCF) have shown promising tracking performance while often attaining good speed [16,17]. These trackers have repeatedly improved the state-of-the-art, recently due to the use of powerful features [9,20] and more sophisticated models [7,8,12,19].

The aim in DCFs is to learn a filter that, when applied to an input sample, produces a sharp and distinct peak at the target location. This is formulated as an objective over the filter coefficients. Via application of Parseval's formula, this problem is transformed into a linear least squares loss over the Fourier coefficients. In the general case, there is no solution in closed form, and the loss is minimized with an iterative solver. A standard method for such situations is the method of conjugate gradients (CG). A major advantage is that CG is able

© Springer Nature Switzerland AG 2019
L. Leal-Taixé and S. Roth (Eds.): ECCV 2018 Workshops, LNCS 11129, pp. 54–69, 2019.
https://doi.org/10.1007/978-3-030-11009-3_2

to handle the large size of the problem. Each iteration is linear in the number of parameters and it is known to converge to approximate solutions in a small number of iterations.

The effectiveness of the DCF-framework coupled with CG is well-supported empirically. In the most recent visual object tracking challenge [17], four of the top five trackers employed CG within the DCF-framework. Recent approaches investigate: more powerful features and how they can be learnt; changes to the model inference such as how scales are best handled; and additional components or alterations to the loss. In this work we instead shift our gaze toward the optimization procedure itself. The visual tracking scenario contains repeated filter optimizations of a loss that changes slowly over time, a very particular situation unlike what is usually studied in optimization literature. This leads not only to considerations regarding the objective, but also how previous optimizations are best exploited to warm-start future optimizations. As the target may undergo appearance changes, an additional concern is overfitting. A better optimization method may yield improved performance in some cases, but may lead to severe overfitting in others.

Our Contributions: In this work we present a thorough description of the implementation and optimization procedure employed in many state-of-the-art visual tracking methods. Several new variants of this method are presented, with different approaches to select the search-direction, step-length, and perform warm-starts. We present comprehensive experiments and provide an analysis of the different methods both from a tracking performance perspective, and from an optimization perspective.

2   Related Work

In visual tracking, DCF-based methods have shown promising performance across several benchmarks. In essence the DCF is a linear regressor, which is trained in a supervised fashion to predict the classification score of the target object. There are two unique characteristics of the DCF paradigm that are credited for its success and popularity. First, the DCF implicitly performs a dense sampling of training patches by modeling detection as a convolution operation. This is particularly important for tracking, where labeled training data is scarce. Secondly, the convolution operation is approximated by a circular convolution, which enables efficient training and detection to be performed in the Fourier domain and exploitation of the $\mathcal{O}(n \log n)$ FFT algorithm. Furthermore, the negative effects of the circular (i.e. periodic) assumption can be effectively mitigated using windowing [2] and spatial regularization [7].

Since the DCF loss is convex, the minimizer can be expressed in closed form as the solution of the set of linear normal equations. There are however two special cases which admit particularly simple closed form expression. These only require element-wise operations, enabling simple and efficient $\mathcal{O}(n)$ implementations. The two cases are: (1) multiple training samples with a single feature dimension [2], and (2) a single training sample with multiple feature dimensions [6]. In practice, however, it is essential to use both multiple samples and multi-dimensional features to obtain a discriminative appearance model. As no closed form solution is known for the general case, early works update the filter sequentially using simple update rules (KCF [15], ACT [10], DSST [6]). However, these update schemes rely on harsh assumptions leading to suboptimal filters with significantly reduced discriminability. Further, these methods cannot address the periodic artifacts using spatial regularization [7] or constraints [12].

Several recent works employ iterative optimization strategies in order to minimize the full DCF objective in an online manner for tracking [7,8,12]. These methods enjoy two key advantages. First, they benefit from asymptotic convergence to the optimal filter, leading to a more discriminative model. Second, alternate regularization approaches and filter constraints can be integrated, which is important for addressing the periodic artifacts. While previous optimization based approaches [7,8,12] suffered from significantly increased computational complexity, recent work [5,19] have demonstrated that state-of-the-art results can be obtained at impressive frame rates.

3   DCF-Formulation Revisited

The DCF-paradigm solves the visual tracking task by constructing a correlation or convolution filter that, when applied to an image, discriminates the target from the background. The filter is learnt in the first frame where a label of the target location is available, and is usually updated in subsequent frames treating earlier frames with corresponding predictions as training data. For the training, the formulation of a suitable loss is essential. In this section we formulate the loss employed by several state-of-the-art trackers in the filter construction [5,8, 13,14]. We proceed to discuss appropriate methods of minimizing this loss.

3.1   Formulation of the Loss

The aim is to find the filter f that is the best fit to a set of sample-label pairs $\{(x^1, y^1), (x^2, y^2), \ldots, (x^C, y^C)\}$. Each sample $x^c \in \mathbb{R}^{D \times T_1 \times T_2}$ is a multidimensional feature map, with D feature channels and spatial extent $T_1 \times T_2$. The corresponding label $y^c \in \mathbb{R}^{T_1 \times T_2}$ attains a high value at the target location and low values otherwise. This is achieved by a Gaussian function with low variance. The DCF-framework finds the filter $f \in \mathbb{R}^{D \times T_1 \times T_2}$ by minimizing the loss

$$\epsilon(f) = \sum_{c=1}^{C} \mu^c \left\| \sum_{d=1}^{D} x_d^c * f_d - y^c \right\|_2^2 + \lambda \sum_{d=1}^{D} \|f_d\|_2^2, \tag{1}$$

where each sample is weighted by μ^c. The convolution ($*$) is applied per dimension, where x_d^c and f_d denote the d'th feature channel of the sample and filter respectively. The second term of (1) regularizes the filter weights with some parameter λ. In DCFs, convolution is a key concept as it performs a dense sampling of negative training data while being efficient to calculate. The Fourier basis diagonalizes the convolution operation into multiplication, while the transform itself is quick to calculate with the Fast Fourier Transform (FFT). There is a caveat, however, in that the convolution is cyclic, introducing boundary effects which hampers performance and may allow the filter to learn the background, rather than the target appearance. Two ways have been proposed to deal with this. Galoogahi et al. propose to constrain filter coefficients far away from the center to zero [12]. They solve the constrained minimization problem with the Alternating Direction Method of Multipliers (ADMM) [3]. A disadvantage of this approach is that it requires repeated transitions between the spatial and Fourier domain, adding a substantial computational cost. An alternative proposed by Danelljan et al. [7] is to replace the filter weight regularization with a term that depends on the filter coefficients' distance to the center

$$\epsilon(f) = \sum_{c=1}^{C} \mu^c \left\| \sum_{d=1}^{D} x_d^c * f_d - y^c \right\|_2^2 + \sum_{d=1}^{D} \|w f_d\|_2^2. \tag{2}$$

The second term applies a cost $w_{i,j}$ to each filter coefficient, depending on its position. The regularization function w typically attains small values in the filter center, and increases as the position moves towards the borders. Experimental results show that the spatial regularization indeed leads to a filter that further emphasizes the target while obtaining improved tracking performance [7,19].

Previously, the samples x^c comprised handcrafted features such as Histogram of Oriented Gradients (HOG) or Color Names (CN). However, with the advent of deep learning, there emerged a desire to employ features extracted from deep convolutional neural networks (CNN). The features extracted from the deeper layers of a CNN exhibit robustness to severe appearance changes which would otherwise lead to tracking failure. They are however of low resolution, and in order to obtain accurate detections we have to rely on low level information when it is available. We would therefore like to utilize shallow features, such as HOG, CN, or features extracted from the earlier layers of a CNN. In order to combine features of different resolutions, Danelljan et al. [8] proposed to view the components of (2) as continuous functions. That is, the filter and the labels f_d, y^c are functions of two variables (t_1, t_2). The extracted feature maps x^c are interpolated to the continuous domain with some interpolation kernel b. The continuous interpretation is possible as the DCF-formulation works with a Fourier basis. A continuous function can be written as its Fourier series which may be truncated for a finite representation. The loss is transformed into the Fourier domain via Parseval's formula,

$$\epsilon(f) = \sum_{c=1}^{C} \mu^c \left\| \sum_{d=1}^{D} \mathrm{DFT}\{x_d^c\}\hat{b}\hat{f}_d - \hat{y}^c \right\|_2^2 + \sum_{d=1}^{D} \|\hat{w} * \hat{f}_d\|_2^2, \tag{3}$$

where $\hat{\cdot}$ denotes the Fourier coefficients and DFT the Discrete Fourier Transform.

3.2   DCF-Loss Vectorization

In order to solve (3) a finite representation of the included terms is required. The continuous functions are represented with infinite sequences of Fourier coefficients, which may be truncated. We use the first K coefficients from each feature channel, a total of $N^2 = (2K + 1)^2$ coefficients per channel. We note that including the same number of coefficients in each dimension is inefficient, as fewer coefficients are required with decreasing feature channel resolution. This will however not be a problem as we may constrain those coefficients to zero in the formulation and employ an optimization scheme which exploits sparsity. We will now rewrite the loss into matrix-vector-form in order to apply standard optimization techniques. The vectorized filter is rewritten as

$$\hat{\mathbf{f}} = \begin{bmatrix} \hat{\mathbf{f}}_1 \\ \hat{\mathbf{f}}_2 \\ \vdots \\ \hat{\mathbf{f}}_D \end{bmatrix} , \text{ where } \hat{\mathbf{f}}_d = \begin{bmatrix} \hat{f}_d[-K, -K] \\ \vdots \\ \hat{f}_d[-K, K] \\ \vdots \\ \hat{f}_d[K, K] \end{bmatrix} , \tag{4}$$

which is a DN^2 sized vector. The feature map components are contained in a $CN^2 \times DN^2$ sized matrix

$$A = \begin{bmatrix} A_{1,1} & A_{1,2} & \dots & A_{1,D} \\ A_{2,1} & A_{2,2} & \dots & A_{2,D} \\ \vdots & \vdots & \ddots & \vdots \\ A_{C,1} & A_{C,2} & \dots & A_{C,D} \end{bmatrix} , \tag{5}$$

where

$$A_{c,d} = \text{diag} \begin{bmatrix} \text{DFT}\{x_d^c\}[-K, -K] \cdot \hat{b}[-K, -K] \\ \vdots \\ \text{DFT}\{x_d^c\}[-K, K] \cdot \hat{b}[-K, K] \\ \vdots \\ \text{DFT}\{x_d^c\}[K, K] \cdot \hat{b}[K, K] \end{bmatrix} . \tag{6}$$

Here, diag is the transformation from a vector to a corresponding diagonal matrix. The labels are stored in a size CN^2 vector

$$\hat{\mathbf{y}} = \begin{bmatrix} \hat{\mathbf{y}}^1 \\ \hat{\mathbf{y}}^2 \\ \vdots \\ \hat{\mathbf{y}}^C \end{bmatrix} , \text{ where } \hat{\mathbf{y}}^c = \begin{bmatrix} \hat{y}^c[-K, -K] \\ \vdots \\ \hat{y}^c[-K, K] \\ \vdots \\ \hat{y}^c[K, K] \end{bmatrix} . \tag{7}$$

The sample weights are stored in the diagonal matrix

$$
\mu = \begin{bmatrix} \mu^1 I_{N^2} & & & \\ & \mu^2 I_{N^2} & & \\ & & \ddots & \\ & & & \mu^C I_{N^2} \end{bmatrix}, \tag{8}
$$

where I_{N^2} is the identity matrix of size $N^2 \times N^2$. Lastly, the spatial regularization is rewritten as

$$
\begin{bmatrix} \hat{w} * \hat{f}_1 \\ \vdots \\ \hat{w} * \hat{f}_D \end{bmatrix} = W\hat{\mathbf{f}}, \tag{9}
$$

where W is the block-diagonal matrix where each block is a convolution matrix containing the elements of $\hat{w}$. With these definitions, the objective (3) is expressed as

$$
\begin{aligned}
\epsilon(f) &= \left\| \sqrt{\Gamma} A\hat{\mathbf{f}} - \hat{\mathbf{y}} \right\|_2^2 + \|W\hat{\mathbf{f}}\|_2^2 \\
&= (A\hat{\mathbf{f}} - \hat{\mathbf{y}})^H \Gamma (A\hat{\mathbf{f}} - \hat{\mathbf{y}}) + \hat{\mathbf{f}}^H W^H W\hat{\mathbf{f}} \\
&= \hat{\mathbf{f}}^H (A^H \Gamma A + W^H W)\hat{\mathbf{f}} - 2\hat{\mathbf{y}}^H \Gamma A\hat{\mathbf{f}} + \hat{\mathbf{y}}^H \Gamma \hat{\mathbf{y}},
\end{aligned} \tag{10}
$$

where $\cdot^H$ denotes conjugate transpose. The difference between (3) and (10) is the truncation of the Fourier coefficients, and it is assumed that the difference is small. In order to minimize the loss, we note that the problem is unconstrained and convex. We can therefore set the derivative to zero and solve the arising normal equations. The derivative is found as

$$
\frac{\partial \epsilon(f)}{\partial \hat{\mathbf{f}}} = 2\hat{\mathbf{f}}^H (A^H \Gamma A + W^H W) - 2\hat{\mathbf{y}}^H \Gamma A, \tag{11}
$$

and setting the derivative to zero leads to

$$
(A^H \Gamma A + W^H W)\hat{\mathbf{f}} = A^H \Gamma \hat{\mathbf{y}}. \tag{12}
$$

It is important to note here that the left-hand side contains two terms with exploitable properties. Namely, (i) the matrix-vector product $A^H \Gamma A\hat{\mathbf{f}}$ is very sparse if it is calculated in the order $A^H(\Gamma(A\hat{\mathbf{f}}))$; and (ii) the product $W\hat{\mathbf{f}}$ corresponds to a convolution that, if the kernel is small, is efficient to calculate.

3.3   The Conjugate Gradient Method

The size of the equation system (12) depends on the number of training instances C and the feature dimensionality D. If the high-dimensional deep features are employed, D can be very large. Furthermore, C should be sufficiently large in order for the model to generalize the target appearance. The number of equations and the number of variables may each be in the order 10^5, and we would therefore like to employ a first order optimization method that can exploit sparsity. Danelljan et al. [8] proposed to employ the method of Conjugate Gradients (CG), which fulfills these priorities. It is a first order line-search method, which applies a Gram-Schmidt procedure to the steepest descent direction. This makes sure that the step directions are orthogonal with respect to a special inner product. For this method, linear convergence has been proven and typically an acceptable solution is reached in very few steps. CG furthermore does not need to store or form any additional matrices like second order methods would. We will briefly describe the method in order to later describe design choices. Details and proofs regarding the convergence of CG are available in [22].

The idea is to apply CG to the normal equations (12). To simplify notation, we apply the notation found in [21,22]. Consider a system of n equations and n variables

$$A\mathbf{x} = \mathbf{b}. \tag{13}$$

It should be noted that CG enjoys nice convergence properties if and only if the left-hand side is positive definite. This is the case for normal equations such as (12). The CG method solves the system by iteratively performing the update

$$\mathbf{x}_{k+1} = \mathbf{x}_k + \alpha_k \mathbf{p}_k, \tag{14}$$

that is, taking a step along direction $\mathbf{p}_k$ of some step-length α_k. The step directions are found as

$$\mathbf{p}_k = \mathbf{r}_k - \sum_{i<k} \frac{\mathbf{p}_i^H A \mathbf{r}_k}{\mathbf{p}_i^H A \mathbf{p}_i} \mathbf{p}_i, \tag{15}$$

where $\mathbf{p}_i$ are previous search directions, and $\mathbf{r}_k = \mathbf{b} - A\mathbf{x}_k$ is the residual in the k'th iteration. This step is the component of the negative gradient that is orthogonal to all earlier steps, with respect to the inner product $\langle \mathbf{u}, \mathbf{v} \rangle = \mathbf{u}^T A \mathbf{v}$. This is called *conjugacy* and lets CG avoid the inefficient zig-zag pattern that often emerges with steepest descent. The step lengths α_k are found as

$$\alpha_k = \frac{\mathbf{p}_k^H \mathbf{b}}{\mathbf{p}_k^H A \mathbf{p}_k}. \tag{16}$$

The step directions $\mathbf{p}$ form a basis and it is possible to show that our choice of α leads to the minimizer in n steps. The convergence is typically much faster however, and depends directly on the distribution of the eigenvalues of A. It is therefore common to apply a preconditioner M to the system of equations, which clusters the eigenvalues. In this case, we instead solve the system

$$E^{-1}A(E^{-1})^H \mathbf{x}' = E^{-1}\mathbf{b}, \tag{17}$$

where $\mathbf{x}' = E^T \mathbf{x}$ and $EE^T = M$. The solution will remain the same, but the convergence is faster if $E^{-1}A(E^{-1})^T$ has a more favorable distribution of eigenvalues than A. A common choice for the preconditioner that is efficient to calculate is the diagonal preconditioner M that keeps the diagonal elements of A, but is zero everywhere else. It is not obvious what preconditioner should be used, as a more sophisticated preconditioner may yield faster convergence but will instead be more expensive to calculate.

As storing all the search directions $\mathbf{p}_k$ would lead to quadratic memory consumption, an equivalent recursive implementation is utilized instead [22]. The step length and step direction are found as

$$\alpha_k = \frac{\mathbf{r}_k^H \mathbf{z}_k}{\mathbf{p}_k^H A \mathbf{p}_k}, \quad \mathbf{p}_k = \mathbf{z}_k + \beta_{k-1} \mathbf{p}_{k-1}, \tag{18}$$

with

$$\mathbf{r}_k = \mathbf{r}_{k-1} - \alpha_{k-1} A \mathbf{p}_{k-1}, \tag{19a}$$

$$\mathbf{z}_k = M^{-1} \mathbf{r}_k, \tag{19b}$$

$$\beta_{k-1} = \frac{\mathbf{z}_k^H \mathbf{r}_k}{\mathbf{z}_{k-1}^H \mathbf{r}_{k-1}}. \tag{19c}$$

The initial values of $\mathbf{r}$, $\mathbf{z}$, and $\mathbf{p}$ are

$$\mathbf{r}_0 = \mathbf{b} - A\mathbf{x}_0, \tag{20a}$$

$$\mathbf{z}_0 = M^{-1} \mathbf{r}_0, \tag{20b}$$

$$\mathbf{p}_0 = \mathbf{z}_0. \tag{20c}$$

Next we look at how CG is applied to the normal equations in the DCF-framework.

3.4   Applying CG to the DCF-problem

The conjugate gradient formulation is efficient as it only performs vector-vector products, except for two cases. In the updates of α in (18) and $\mathbf{r}$ in (19a), the matrix-vector products needs to be computed. As previously mentioned, the sample matrix A is sparse, and the application of W can be done via a small-kernel convolution as long as it is possible to represent the spatial regularization function w with few Fourier coefficients.

The matrix-vector product performed by the CG method when applied to the normal equations (12) is

$$\mathbf{q} = (A^H \Gamma A + W^H W)\mathbf{p}. \tag{21}$$

From (4) and (5) we obtain [8]

$$A^H \Gamma A \mathbf{p} = A^H \begin{bmatrix} \mu^1 \left(\sum_{d=1}^D A_{1,d} \mathbf{p} \right) \\ \vdots \\ \mu^C \left(\sum_{d=1}^D A_{C,d} \mathbf{p} \right) \end{bmatrix} = \begin{bmatrix} \left(\sum_{c=1}^C \bar{A}_{c,1} \mu^c \left(\sum_{d=1}^D A_{c,d} \mathbf{p} \right) \right) \\ \vdots \\ \left(\sum_{c=1}^C \bar{A}_{c,D} \mu^c \left(\sum_{d=1}^D A_{c,d} \mathbf{p} \right) \right) \end{bmatrix}. \tag{22}$$

That is, the calculation relies only on matrix-vector products with the diagonal blocks $A_{c,d}$ and is implemented as a vector-vector product. We also avoid storing the entire matrix A. For the second part of the matrix-vector product, we note that there is no need for the spatial regularization function w to contain high frequences. A smooth function is sufficient, and we therefore select a regularizer that is well represented by a few low frequency components. We then calculate

$$W^H W \hat{\mathbf{f}} = \begin{bmatrix} \hat{w} * \hat{w} * \hat{f}_1 \\ \vdots \\ \hat{w} * \hat{w} * \hat{f}_D \end{bmatrix}, \tag{23}$$

which is efficient as the filter $\hat{w}$ contains few coefficients. The conjugate transpose of the leftmost W was discarded here, as the functions w are usually symmetric and real. Hence, the conjugate gradient method can exploit the sparsity and performs only vector-vector products.

3.5   Subsequent Optimizations

In visual tracking we have a single labeled sample from which a model is learned to track an object in subsequent frames. For that case, we apply the CG-procedure and in a few iterations obtain an acceptable solution and information required for the warm-starts. In order to improve the model, samples extracted from subsequent frames and their labels are treated as additional training data. The tracker ECO for instance, updates its model every five frames. As the loss (2) does not change dramatically between subsequent optimizations, we warm-start CG. As an initial guess, the previous filter vector $\hat{\mathbf{f}}$ is used. An additional component of ECO is that the final search direction of the previous optimization is used to select the initial components. The variables $\mathbf{p}_{old}, \mathbf{z}_{old}, \mathbf{r}_{old}$ are used to modify the initialization (20) into

$$\mathbf{p}_0 = \mathbf{z}_0 + \beta_{-1} \mathbf{p}_{old}, \tag{24}$$

where the denominator of the formula for β is calculated as

$$\mathbf{z}_{k-1}^H \mathbf{r}_{k-1} = (1-\lambda)^{-\gamma} \mathbf{z}_{old}^H \mathbf{r}_{old}. \tag{25}$$

The learning rate λ is the same learning rate as that used to recursively weight samples, and γ is a hyperparameter that describes the decay of the previous search direction.

CG has remarkable convergence properties when minimizing a linear least squares loss and employing a constant preconditioner. The presented procedure introduces a somewhat different situation. It may be viewed as minimizing a loss that changes slightly over time. The preconditioners will not be constant, and the assumptions on which CG relies are violated. The literature proposes a way to deal with loss nonlinearities and non-constant preconditioners, which may be beneficial for our case. The strategy is to replace the β formula (19c), referred to as the *Fletcher-Reeves* formula, with the *Polak-Ribiere* formula

$$\beta_{k-1} = \frac{\mathbf{z}_k^H (\mathbf{r}_k - \mathbf{r}_{k-1})}{\mathbf{z}_{k-1} \mathbf{r}_{k-1}}. \tag{26}$$

As the case presented in the literature differs somewhat from the DCF-framework case, it is not obvious whichever is superior. For completeness, we also include the *gradient descent* method. This is actually easily incorporated into the CG framework by selecting $\beta_k = 0$ as $\mathbf{z}_k$ is the negative gradient of the preconditioned loss. In this case, the way α_k is selected within CG is the optimal step length along the negative gradient. A fourth alternative is to employ the *Barzilai-Borwein* method [1], which has shown favorable performance in practice. We integrate it in the CG-framework by noting that the method takes steps in the direction of the negative gradient, where the step length is based on the change of the parameters and the gradients

$$\mathbf{s}_k = \mathbf{x}_k - \mathbf{x}_{k-1}, \quad \mathbf{y}_k = \mathbf{z}_k - \mathbf{z}_{k-1}. \tag{27}$$

The step-length is selected by interleaving the updates

$$\alpha_k = \frac{\mathbf{s}_k^H \mathbf{s}_k}{\mathbf{s}_k^H \mathbf{y}_k}, \quad \alpha_k = \frac{\mathbf{s}_k^H \mathbf{y}_k}{\mathbf{y}_k^H \mathbf{y}_k}. \tag{28}$$

The motivation behind this choice is that it approximates the secant equation of the quasi-Newton methods. Next we describe our experiments, where we compare the four different updates and the impact of the conjugate direction warm-start.

4 Experiments

We analyze the optimization scheme and several of its components based on tracking performance and the behaviour of the loss. First we introduce the eight tracker configurations employed in our experiments including their respective rationale.

4.1 Optimizer Configurations

In order to minimize the loss resulting from the continuous, spatially regularized DCF-formulation, ECO relies on the conjugate gradient method with a special heuristic for warm-starting filter optimizations subsequent the initial one. We investigate the impact of this heuristic by comparing it with the two extremes: (i) warm-starting subsequent optimizations only with the previous solution and not with the previous search direction, that is, setting the forgetting rate $\gamma = \infty$; and (ii) fully keeping the initial step conjugate to the final search direction of the previous optimization, setting $\gamma = 0$. We further investigate the mechanism to ensure conjugacy: (i) Fletcher-Reeves formula; (ii) Polak-Ribiere formula;

(iii) the removal of this mechanism, equivalent to gradient descent; and (iv) the replacement of this mechanism by another way of selecting the step-length, namely the Barzilai-Borwein method. They are described in Table 1. The importance of the preconditioner is asserted via its removal. Finally, we try to hamper the baseline CG-method by always multiplying its calculated step-length with a factor 0.8. The intuition is that a lower loss not necessarily provides improved tracking capabilities, and such a heuristic could have a regularizing effect.

Table 1. The strategies to calculate α and β are shown for four configurations.

	Fletcher-Reeves	Polak-Ribiere	Gradient Descent	Barzilai-Borwein
α	Eq. (18)	Eq. (18)	Eq. (18)	Eq. (28)
β	Eq. (19c)	Eq. (26)	0	0

4.2 Evaluation Methodology

We run experiments on two tracking benchmarks. First we utilize the public VOT2018-benchmark, where performance is measured in terms of Accuracy and Robustness. Robustness measures the tracking failure rate and can be interpreted as the probability of succesful tracking for S frames, where S is a constant. Accuracy is the average overlap during successfully tracked frames. A more thorough description and analysis of the measures is given in [4]. There is typically a trade-off between accuracy and robustness, and one may be improved at cost of the other. Additionally we run experiments on a larger dataset formed by pooling the sequences of OTB-2015 [23], TempleColor [18], and NFS [11]. Overlapping sequences are removed, leaving a total of 286 sequences. Performance is measured in terms of area-under-the-curve (AUC) of the success plots.

We run each tracking algorithm at four different iteration configurations: (i) the baseline setting where the initial filter optimization runs for 150 iterations, and subsequent optimizations for 5 iterations; (ii) a fast setting where we run 90 and 3 iterations respectively; (iii) a setting with 30 initial iterations and only a single iteration in subsequent runs; (iv) and an overfitting setting with 150 iterations are used initially, and 100 iterations in subsequent runs.

The trackers are analyzed based on their performance on the two benchmarks. We would furthermore like to gain some insight on how well the different methods minimize the loss and the relationship between this and tracking performance. Therefore we run an additional experiment on the pooled dataset where the loss is considered. The value of the loss after each optimization is stored as $L_{i,j}$ where i enumerates the N sequences and j the M_i frames in sequence i. A single performance number of the loss is obtained as

$$\bar{L} = \frac{1}{N} \sum_{i=1}^{N} \frac{1}{M_i} \sum_{j=1}^{M_i} L_{i,j}. \tag{29}$$

Our initial experiments revealed that the value of the loss is heavily correlated with the tracking performance, possibly due to contamination of the training set after a tracking failure. As our intention is to study the optimization performance, we provide all trackers with the same training set: the ground truth.

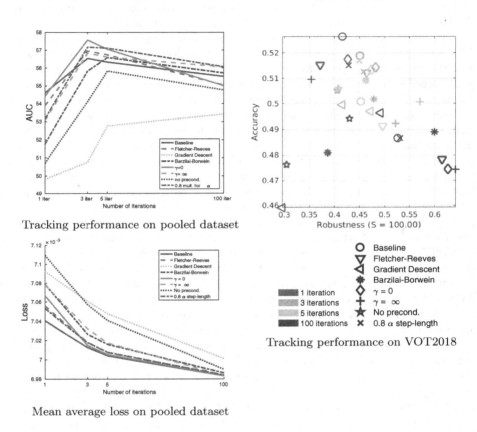

Tracking performance on pooled dataset

Mean average loss on pooled dataset

Tracking performance on VOT2018

Fig. 1. The results of the eight configurations are shown. The tracking performance (a) and the mean average loss (b) on the pooled dataset are shown as a function of the number of optimizer iterations. This dataset is the union of the OTB-2015, TempleColor, and NFS datasets. The performance on the public VOT2018 benchmark is shown in terms of accuracy and robustness (c).

4.3   Results

Figure 1a and c show the results on the VOT2018 benchmark and the pooled dataset, respectively. The average loss on the pooled dataset is shown in Fig. 1b. We first consider the effect of the conjugacy warm-start. Removing the conjugacy warm-start ($\gamma = \infty$) provides reduced performance on VOT2018 in the single iteration setting, both in terms of accuracy and robustness. For 3 or more iterations it is the most robust amongst all settings, but its accuracy is still hampered. On the pooled dataset it performs slightly better than the baseline. Instead setting the first search direction in each optimization to be fully conjugate to the previous ($\gamma = 0$), leads to slightly improved robustness in all cases compared to the baseline. The accuracy is decreased in the single iteration setting, but the gap closes for 3 iterations and the accuracy is actually improved for 5 iterations. This setting is Pareto optimal for 1, 3, and 5 iterations. On the pooled dataset, it outperforms the baseline for 3 and 5 iterations. Its average loss is very close to the baseline loss for 3, 5, and 100 iterations, whereas removing the conjugacy warm-start leads to significantly higher loss for 1, 3, and 5 iterations.

The alternative conjugacy mechanism, Fletcher-Reeves, provides inferior performance compared to the baseline for the single-iteration setting on VOT2018. However, its robustness increases with the number of iterations and surpasses the baseline for 3 iterations. On the pooled dataset, its performance is worse for 1 and 100 iterations and slightly improved for 3 and 5 iterations. The average loss is higher than that of the baseline in the 1 iteration setting, but the gap decreases with the number of iterations. Gradient descent, which lacks the conjugacy mechanism, leads to slow convergence, something reflected in the high average loss value. Performance is greatly diminished on the pooled dataset, and on VOT2018 for 1 and 3 iterations. For 5 iterations it achieves slightly improved robustness, and for 100 iterations improved accuracy at the cost of robustness.

The preconditioning is imperative in order to obtain a low loss. On the pooled dataset its removal results in lower performance for any number of iterations. On VOT2018, this leads to worse performance for 1 and 3 iterations, and improved accuracy at the cost of robustness. Hampering CG by reducing the step-lengths to 0.8α leads to reduced accuracy for 1 iteration. For 3 iterations this gap is diminished, and for 5 iterations this results in higher accuracy. For 100 iterations, they perform roughly the same. On the pooled dataset the hampering leads to reduced performance for 1 iteration, but improved performance for 3, 5, and 100 iterations. The average loss is close to that of the Fletcher-Reeves configuration.

The alternative optimization method, Barzilai-Borwein, leads to a higher loss than that of CG, close to that of removing the conjugacy warm-start from CG. On the pooled dataset, their performance is similar for 5 iterations, but Barzilao-Borwein is outperformed for 1, 3, and 100 iterations. On the VOT2018 dataset, Barzilai-Borwein leads to reduced performance compared to full conjugacy warm-start for 1, 3, and 5 iterations. For 100 iterations however, it provides significantly improved accuracy at the cost of robustness.

4.4 Analysis

The experiments suggest that the partial conjugacy warm-start heuristic in the baseline does not in general improve performance. Instead, making the initial search direction fully conjugate to the last search direction of the previous optimization improves performance for most cases, while resulting in a similar loss value. Not warm-starting the conjugacy seems to lead to slower convergence, but improved robustness if sufficiently many iterations are run. This remains a competetive alternative. The performance of the Fletcher-Reeves formula appears sensitive to the number of iterations used. Removing the conjugacy mechanism strongly deteriorates performance in most cases, as is expected. There is a surprising exception on VOT2018 for 5 iterations, where robustness slightly increased at a small cost of accuracy. Removing the preconditioner also leads to significant deterioration of performance, which is expected as normal equations have a problematic distribution of eigenvalues. The step-length multiplier did not hamper performance as much as expected, and actually improved performance for the 5-iteration case on both benchmarks. Tampering with the step-length leads to a method that does not converge to a solution. Possibly, the effect is attenuated with the repeated optimizations, and that running 5 iterations with the baseline leads to a case of overfitting that this heuristic is able to alleviate. For the case of visual tracking, conjugate gradient seems to outperform Barzilai-Borwein. It should be mentioned that the comparison is not entirely fair as the Barzilai-Borwein method has not been as thoroughly investigated as CG.

Overall, the full conjugacy warm-start ($\gamma = 0$) seems to provide a good trade-off between accuracy and robustness on VOT2018 while providing the best performance on the pooled dataset. In comparison, removing the conjugacy warm-start ($\gamma = \infty$) leads to a more robust but less accurate tracker. Both these settings outperform the baseline. The merit of the baseline is its performance from an optimization perspective, and if a very fast tracker is desired it is probably a good alternative.

The baseline attained the lowest loss for all iteration configurations. In the single-iteration setting it obtains the best performance on the pooled dataset while providing a very good trade-off between accuracy and robustness on VOT2018. For 3 iterations the Fletcher-Reeves, $\gamma = 0$, and 0.8α step-length settings provide the lowest loss values except for the baseline. These configurations obtains the top 3 best performance on the pooled dataset, and all provide a good accuracy and robustness on VOT2018. A lower loss does seem to provide increases to tracking performance in these cases, but as the number of iterations increase this ceases to be true. An explanation for this is overfitting, and as future work it may be beneficial to investigate strategies for stopping the optimization process when an acceptable solution has been obtained, instead of running the process for a fixed number of iterations.

5   Conclusion

In this paper we analyzed the optimization procedure of the popular ECO-tracker. The procedure was described in detail and several mechanisms were compared with their alternatives. Supported by experiments on the VOT2018-benchmark and a large pooled dataset, we showed the impact of the different configurations both in terms of tracking performance and in terms of optimization performance. We showed that a lower loss corresponds fairly well to improved tracking performance when the optimizers are run for a sufficiently low number of iterations. However, as the number of iterations increases, inferior optimizers may provide superior tracking performance.

Acknowledgments. This work was supported by Swedish Foundation for Strategic Research (SymbiCloud); Swedish Research Council (EMC 2, starting grant 2016-05543); CENIIT grant (18.14); Swedish National Infrastructure for Computing; and Wallenberg AI, Autonomous Systems and Software Program (WASP) funded by the Knut and Alice Wallenberg Foundation.

References

1. Barzilai, J., Borwein, J.M.: Two-point step size gradient methods. IMA J. Numer. Anal. **8**(1), 141–148 (1988)
2. Bolme, D.S., Beveridge, J.R., Draper, B.A., Lui, Y.M.: Visual object tracking using adaptive correlation filters. In: CVPR (2010)
3. Boyd, S., Parikh, N., Chu, E., Peleato, B., Eckstein, J., et al.: Distributed optimization and statistical learning via the alternating direction method of multipliers. Found. Trends® Mach. Learn. **3**(1), 1–122 (2011)
4. Cehovin, L., Kristan, M., Leonardis, A.: Is my new tracker really better than yours? In: 2014 IEEE Winter Conference on Applications of Computer Vision (WACV), pp. 540–547. IEEE (2014)
5. Danelljan, M., Bhat, G., Shahbaz Khan, F., Felsberg, M.: ECO: Efficient convolution operators for tracking. In: CVPR (2017)
6. Danelljan, M., Hager, G., Khan, F.S., Felsberg, M.: Discriminative scale space tracking. IEEE Trans. Pattern Anal. Mach. Intell. **39**, 1561–1575 (2016)
7. Danelljan, M., Häger, G., Shahbaz Khan, F., Felsberg, M.: Learning spatially regularized correlation filters for visual tracking. In: ICCV (2015)
8. Danelljan, M., Robinson, A., Shahbaz Khan, F., Felsberg, M.: Beyond correlation filters: learning continuous convolution operators for visual tracking. In: Leibe, B., Matas, J., Sebe, N., Welling, M. (eds.) ECCV 2016. LNCS, vol. 9909, pp. 472–488. Springer, Cham (2016). https://doi.org/10.1007/978-3-319-46454-1_29
9. Danelljan, M., Shahbaz Khan, F., Felsberg, M., van de Weijer, J.: Adaptive color attributes for real-time visual tracking. In: CVPR (2014)
10. Felsberg, M.: Enhanced distribution field tracking using channel representations. In: ICCV Workshop (2013)
11. Galoogahi, H.K., Fagg, A., Huang, C., Ramanan, D., Lucey, S.: Need for speed: a benchmark for higher frame rate object tracking. In: 2017 IEEE International Conference on Computer Vision (ICCV), pp. 1134–1143. IEEE (2017)
12. Galoogahi, H.K., Sim, T., Lucey, S.: Correlation filters with limited boundaries. In: CVPR (2015)
13. Gundogdu, E., Alatan, A.A.: Good features to correlate for visual tracking. IEEE Trans. Image Process. **27**(5), 2526–2540 (2018)
14. He, Z., Fan, Y., Zhuang, J., Dong, Y., Bai, H.: Correlation filters with weighted convolution responses. In: ICCV Workshops, pp. 1992–2000 (2017)
15. Henriques, J.F., Caseiro, R., Martins, P., Batista, J.: High-speed tracking with kernelized correlation filters. TPAMI **37**(3), 583–596 (2015)
16. Kristan, M., et al.: The visual object tracking VOT2016 challenge results. In: Hua, G., Jégou, H. (eds.) ECCV 2016. LNCS, vol. 9914, pp. 777–823. Springer, Cham (2016). https://doi.org/10.1007/978-3-319-48881-3_54

17. Kristan, M., et al.: The visual object tracking VOT2017 challenge results. In: ICCV Workshop (2017)
18. Liang, P., Blasch, E., Ling, H.: Encoding color information for visual tracking: algorithms and benchmark. TIP **24**(12), 5630–5644 (2015)
19. Lukezic, A., Vojír, T., Zajc, L.C., Matas, J., Kristan, M.: Discriminative correlation filter tracker with channel and spatial reliability. Int. J. Comput. Vis. **126**(7), 671–688 (2018). https://doi.org/10.1007/s11263-017-1061-3
20. Ma, C., Huang, J.B., Yang, X., Yang, M.H.: Hierarchical convolutional features for visual tracking. In: ICCV (2015)
21. Nocedal, J., Wright, S.J.: Numerical Optimization, 2nd edn. Springer, New York (2006). https://doi.org/10.1007/978-0-387-40065-5
22. Shewchuk, J.R.: An introduction to the conjugate gradient method without the agonizing pain. Technical report, Pittsburgh, PA, USA (1994)
23. Wu, Y., Lim, J., Yang, M.H.: Object tracking benchmark. TPAMI **37**(9), 1834–1848 (2015)

Channel Pruning for Visual Tracking

Manqiang Che, Runling Wang, Yan Lu, Yan Li, Hui Zhi,
and Changzhen Xiong[✉]

North China University of Technology, Beijing, China
xczkiong@163.com

Abstract. Deep convolutional feature based Correlation Filter trackers have achieved record-breaking accuracy, but the huge computational complexity limits their application. In this paper, we derive the efficient convolution operators (ECO) tracker which obtains the top rank on VOT-2016. Firstly, we introduce a channel pruned VGG16 model to fast extract most representative channels for deep features. Then an Average Feature Energy Ratio method is put forward to select advantageous convolution channels, and an adaptive iterative strategy is designed to optimize object location. Finally, extensive experimental results on four benchmarks OTB-2013, OTB-2015, VOT-2016 and VOT-2017, demonstrate that our tracker performs favorably against the state-of-the-art methods.

Keywords: Correlation filter · Deep feature · Channel pruning · Iterative optimization

1 Introduction

Visual tracking is one of the fundamental problems in computer vision. Tracking of objects or feature points plays a crucial role in real-time vision applications, such as traffic control, smart surveillance, human-computer interactions, to name a few. Even though significant progress has been made in this area, it is still a challenging problem due to fast motions, occlusions, deformations, illumination variations and etc.

Correlation Filter (CF) based trackers have attracted considerable attention due to the high computational efficiency. Feature representations such as grayscale templates [24], HOG [1] and Color Names (CN) [2] have successfully been employed in CF based trackers. Deep convolutional neural networks (CNNs) are also resorted to visual tracking for robust target representation [3,4,7]. Deep features based correlation filter can effectively increase the tracking accuracy [3,15,25], but the huge computational complexity limits their application. In order to solve this problem, Wang et al. [14] propose a real time tracker via

Electronic supplementary material The online version of this chapter (https://doi.org/10.1007/978-3-030-11009-3_3) contains supplementary material, which is available to authorized users.

© Springer Nature Switzerland AG 2019
L. Leal-Taixé and S. Roth (Eds.): ECCV 2018 Workshops, LNCS 11129, pp. 70–82, 2019.
https://doi.org/10.1007/978-3-030-11009-3_3

convolutional channel reduction. ECO tracker [6] applies a combination of the deep features along with HOG and CN features to tracking task and proposes a generative sample space model for higher precision. It also introduces a factorized convolution operator to dramatically decrease parameters and an efficient model update strategy to improve the speed. Then it obtains the highest tracking accuracy at that time, but the speed is far from real-time requirement.

We can find that deep features selected in ECO are not robust for fast motion and serious changes in appearance of objects on some videos, such as the objects in Fig. 1. And ECO tracker adopts the fixed channel number for selected convolutional layers, which is not suitable for all tested video sequences. Consequently, this paper proposes a channel pruning tracker (CPT) via channel pruned model and feature maps. Experiments on popular datasets display that our proposed CPT has better robustness (see Fig. 1 for visualized tracking results).

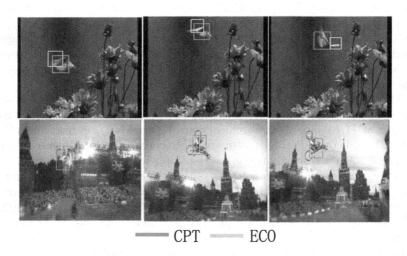

Fig. 1. Comparisons of tracking results with ECO. Example frames are from butterfly (top row) and motocross1 (bottom row) video sequences. CPT tracker with deeper features can handle such variations successfully, improving both the accuracy and robustness.

Our main contributions are four folds:

- Our work is the first attempt to apply channel pruned VGG model to visual tracking field. Thus CPT tracker can use more deep convolutional layers with rich semantic features and will not cause a decline in speed.
- An Average Feature Energy Ratio method is proposed to adaptively reduce the dimensions of convolution channels. It can effectively extract different dimensions of convolutional features for different video sequences.
- An adaptive iteration strategy is applied to adaptively terminate the optimization process of target location. It can further speed up the tracker without a precision reduction.

- We extensively validate our algorithm on four benchmarks, OTB-2013, OTB-2015, VOT-2016 and VOT-2017. Our CPT tracker performs favorably against state-of-the-art trackers.

2   Related Work

In this section, we briefly introduce trackers based on correlation filters and CNN accelerating methods related to our work.

CF based methods have shown superior performances on object tracking benchmarks [18–20, 22]. The MOSSE tracker [24] learns a minimum output sum of squared error filter for fast tracking, making researchers fully realize the advantages of correlation filters in speed. Then several extensions have been put forward to substantially promote the tracking precisions including CSK method [26] based on intensity features, KCF approach [1] with HOG descriptors and CN tracker [2] using colour attributes, showing a remarkable tracking speed. Bertinetto et al. [9] propose a tracker based on HOG and colour histograms integration for targets appearance representation. Danelljan et al. [30] introduce a spatial regularization component to penalize the filter coefficients near the boundary regions to suppress the boundary effect.

As the surge deep learning, more and more state-of-the-art visual trackers have benefited from deep CNN model owing to its powerfulness in feature extraction. Ma et al. [4, 13] extract hierarchical convolutional features from the VGG19 network [21] and combine three feature maps to correlation filter tracker. Danelljan et al. [3] learn a continuous convolution filter for tracking, with multi-scale deep features and hand-crafted features as HOG and CN, to account for appearance variations and considerably improve the tracking accuracy. In order to improve the speed of deep features based trackers, Wang et al. [14] make full use of multi-resolution deep features for precise location and remove the redundancy by reducing the channel number so as to obtain a practical speed. ECO tracker [6] introduces a factorized convolution operator to simplify the multi-channel filters of C-COT [3] and achieves a satisfactory tracking accuracy and speed. However, the fixed channel number for selected layers in ECO is not suitable for all tested video sequences.

There has been numerous work on accelerating CNNs [21] using channel pruning that removes redundant channels on feature maps. [28] regularizes networks to improve accuracy. Channel-wise SSL [28] prunes first few convolutional layers to reach high compression. Some model compression based methods [27, 29] focus on pruning the fully connected layers. [23] proposes an inference-time approach to prune redundancy inter channels. Combining with tensor factorization, it obtains 5× speed-up VGG16 model while with only 0.3% increase of error. It is worth mentioning that this work has achieved considerable results in the area of detection, but unfortunately has not been introduced into the visual tracking field. Consequently, we introduce the channel pruned VGG16 into the visual tracking field.

3   Proposed Algorithm

3.1   Channel Pruned VGG Model

Earlier convolutional layers provide more spatial information, while the latter layers encode rich semantic features [4]. The ECO tracker has achieved high tracking accuracy by fusing the shadow spatial information (Conv1) and deep semantic features (Conv5) of VGG-M. Moreover, CFWCR [11] assigns larger weight for the feature map extracted from the Conv5 layer and gains better robustness in VOT-2016. DRT [25] uses the Conv4-3 layer of VGG16 and the Conv1 layer of VGG-M to obtain higher tracking accuracy. Thus, aiming for higher precision, more deep semantic features are needed. But it will inevitably cause a decline in tracking speed. Consequently, we introduce a pruned VGG16 model obtained in [23] to fast extract more deep semantic features. With an iterative two-step algorithm (LASSO regression and Least Square Reconstruction), channels of layers from the original VGG16 network are pruned to a desired number. It dramatically decreases the feature channels and accelerates the VGG16 model by 5× speed-up in object detections [23]. For advantageous reason, we attempt to apply it to tracking field. As shown in Fig. 2, pruned channels of VGG16 network from Conv1-1 to Conv4-3 layers are marked, e.g. channels of Conv1-1 layer have pruned from 64 to 24 dimensions. Additionally, the set part of the pruned VGG16 is Conv5 layer, whose feature maps are pruned with another novel method for more effective information. Details are described in Sect. 3.2.

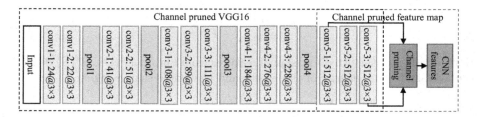

Fig. 2. Feature maps extraction framework using channel pruning.

3.2   Channel Pruned Feature Map

In our work, the Conv5-1 and Conv5-3 from channel pruned VGG16 network are selected as our tracking layers for feature extraction, which are full of semantic information to handle large appearance changes. Then an Average Feature Energy Ratio method is utilized to prune the ineffective channels as the factorized convolution operator does in ECO.

For a new frame, the correlation filter based trackers acquire the search region according to the localization of the previous frame, followed by extracting the search regions features and obtaining the response map. As shown in Fig. 3, the wanted feature map should have larger energy value of target and smaller that of other area in the search region. However, there exist large amount of features containing backgrounds information and make interferences to the tracking task. Moreover, a vast majority of features contain negligible energy. These latter two categories of features can hardly contribute to target localization, but cause a set number of calculations.

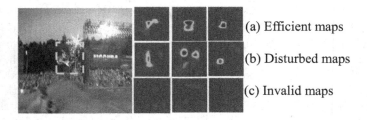

(a) Efficient maps

(b) Disturbed maps

(c) Invalid maps

Fig. 3. Feature maps in different channels. The input search region image is from the challenging motocross1 sequence. The target is in yellow dotted bounding box. (a) Efficient features for tracking task. (b) Features with noises in search region. (c) Invalid features containing negligible energy. (Color figure online)

Consequently, we explore a response map evaluation mechanism called the Average Feature Energy Ratio (AFER) method which is defined as

$$AFER_l^d = \frac{F_l^d(O)}{1 + F_l^d(S)} \tag{1}$$

Here, d indicates the dth dimension of features from l layer. $F_l^d(O)$, $F_l^d(S)$ denote the average feature energy of the object and the whole search region.

$$F_l^d(A) = \frac{\sum\limits_{i,j}^{I,J} P(i,j)}{I \bullet J} \tag{2}$$

where I and J indicate the width, height of the region A. $P(i,j)$ is the value (energy) of the location (i,j) after convolution operation. AFER indicates the validity of the response maps and the confidence level of the tracking object. The larger the AFER value is, the more effective the acquired features are, while the smaller the AFER value is, the more background interferences exist. Consequently, we adaptively select convolution channels whose AFER is greater than the given threshold for target location to prune ineffective channel. On the other hand, we put forward the channel screening approach to exclude duplicate features from different layers while at the same channel. For the reason we consider that features from the neighboring hierarchical layers while at the same channel are similar. Specifically, when there are same channels in the adjacent two-layer after feature map channel pruning, we only select the features of the lower layer and discard the features of the upper layer of this channel. Figure 4 shows channel pruned Conv5-1 feature maps from the first frame of Basketball on VOT-2016 benchmark. In this way, our tracker extracts useful information for tracking task and significantly increases the tracking speed.

Note that ours channel pruning is different from channel reliability of [8]. The latter estimates the channel reliability whose scores are used for weighting the per-channel filter responses in localization in each frame. However, our AFER is only calculated by feature energies of target and search regions in the initial frame. It focuses more on the evaluation of features by the first frame of the input video in order to prune invalid channels.

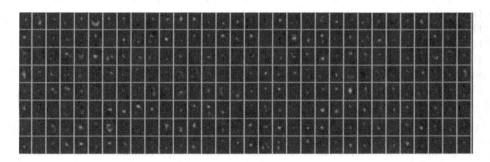

Fig. 4. Visualization of the selected features. We prune the ineffective or duplicated convolution channels, adaptively retaining the most advantageous channels for deep features.

3.3   Adaptive Iterative Optimization Strategy

The real-time performance of visual tracking mainly depends on the amount of calculations in feature extraction, filter training and position location. At the stage of the last one, C-COT and ECO tracker first perform a grid search, where the score function is evaluated at the discrete locations to obtain the initialization position p_0. Then they employ the standard Newton iteration method to predict optimal object position $p_t(x, y)$ under fixed number of iterations. In theory, the more iteration numbers, the closer solution is to the true one, the greater the amounts of calculations are. However, when iteration reaches a certain number, minimal changes to the optimization have little or no effect on the final results. At this time, the extra number of iterations will not only significantly increase the amount of calculation but also cause a waste of resources.

In order to reduce the redundancy of iterations, an adaptive Newton iterative optimization strategy is designed to adaptively terminate the iterative process. The main idea is to calculate the position difference between two consecutive iterations and find a suitable position error threshold τ. When it satisfies $sum(|p_t(x, y) - p_{t-1}(x, y)|) < \tau$, the iterative process stops, here t denotes the iteration numbers. This strategy can speed up our tracker with hardly no decline in precision.

4   Experiments

We evaluate our proposed tracking method on OTB-2013 [19], OTB-2015 [18], VOT-2016 [20] and VOT-2017 [22] benchmarks. The algorithm is implemented in Matlab R2015b, using MatConvNet toolbox, with an Intel Core i7-7800XCPU, 16 GB RAM, and a GTX1080Ti GPU card.

We select Conv5-1 and Conv5-3 layers of channel pruned VGG16 as our feature extraction layers. The AFER thresholds are 1.1 and 1.5. The position error threshold is set to $\tau = 10^{-6}$. In addition, in order to improve the performance of the filter, the bandwidth of Gaussian labeled function for training sample is set to 0.15, the learning rate is set to 0.0115, the search region is set to 3.5 times of the target size. The model updating gap is 3 frames. Other parameters are the same as ECO tracker [6]. Code is available at https://github.com/chemanqiang/CPT.

4.1   Evaluation on VOT-2016

We evaluate our tracker on VOT-2016 challenge that contains 60 annotated videos with substantial variations and measure the performance using Expected Average Overlap (EAO). Then compared the proposed tracking algorithm with four state-of-the-art methods, namely ECO [6], C-COT [3], CFWCR [11] and TCNN [10]. For clarity, we display the results in Table 1. CPT_fast algorithm here is a variation of our proposed. The difference between CPT and CPT_fast is that the latter regards the location and scale as two problems. It applies the location filter firstly to predict the targets position and then trains another 1D filter for scale estimation with the scale pyramid [17] based on the predicted position. Our CPT tracker outperforms all the trackers in VOT2016 challenge with an EAO score of 0.410, achieving a relative performance gain of 4.86% compared with CFWCR. Moreover, our CPT tracker acquires an improvement over the baseline ECO with a relative gain of 9.63% in EAO. Note that our CPT_fast tracker with an EAO of 0.394, which is also competitive among the state-of-the-art trackers in the experiment.

Table 1. Experimental results on VOT-2016. Our tracker achieves a substantial improvement over the baseline ECO method. The first and second best trackers are highlighted in red and blue, respectively.

Tracker	CPT	CPT_fast	CFWCR	ECO	C-COT	TCNN
EAO	0.41	0.394	0.391	0.374	0.331	0.327
Acc. Raw	0.56	0.55	0.58	0.55	0.54	0.53
Fail. Raw	0.68	0.77	0.81	0.87	0.89	0.90

4.2   Evaluation on VOT-2017

The VOT-2017 benchmark obtained 10 pairs of new sequences not present in other benchmarks and replaced 10 least challenging sequences in VOT-2016. Figure 5 illustrates the excellent performance of CPT tracker with four top ranked trackers including ECO [6], LSART [15], CFWCR [11] and CFCF [16]. In addition, we evaluate the compared trackers in terms of EAO, Accuracy Ranks (Ar) and Robustness Ranks (Rr). The detailed results are in Table 2. There is a large gap between other algorithms and ours, which illustrates our CPT tracker performs best against the evaluated trackers. Specially, the CPT and CPT_fast improve the ECO tracker by 24.2% and 6.05% in the metric of EAO, respectively.

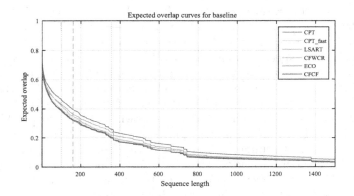

Fig. 5. Expected Overlap curves on VOT-2017 for baseline. When there are challenges of camera motion, occlusion, size change and etc., our CPT tracker has much better performance than the compared trackers.

Table 2. Experimental performances on VOT-2017. The first and second best trackers are highlighted in red and blue, respectively.

Tracker	CPT	CPT_fast	LSART	CFWCR	CFCF	ECO
EAO	0.349	0.298	0.323	0.303	0.286	0.281
Acc. Raw	0.50	0.52	0.49	0.48	0.50	0.48
Fail. Raw	1.04	1.20	0.94	1.21	1.17	1.12

Moreover, to better demonstrate the superiority of our tracker, we show the compared EAO ranking plot and accuracy-robustness results in Fig. 6. Note that, the better trackers are located at the upper-right corner according to the protocol. Clearly, the proposed tracker obtains the rightmost position in the plot. Overall, our CPT achieves the appealing performance results both in accuracy and robustness on VOT-2017 dataset.

4.3   Evaluation on OTB

For completeness, we also display the evaluation results on OTB-2013 and its extensive dataset OTB-2015, which contain 11 various challenging factors such as deformation, occlusion, scale variation and etc. We employ the one-pass evaluation (OPE) with precision and success plots metrics. The precision metric measures the frame locations rate within a certain threshold distance from ground truth locations while the success plot metric measures the overlap rate between the predicted bounding boxes and the ground truth. Then compare our algorithm with another seven state-of-the-art trackers including ECO [6], VITAL [12], HCFTS [13], C-COT [3], LMCF [5], CSR-DCF [8] and Staple [9]. Figure 7 illustrates the precision and success plots based on center location error and bounding box overlap ratio, respectively. It clearly demonstrates that our CPT and CPT_fast gain the first and second top in precision on OTB-2013 and OTB-2015, outperforming the state-of-the-art trackers significantly.

We evaluate the speed and effectiveness for channel pruned model, channel pruned feature map component of our approach on OTB-2015 benchmark. The notation CPT_VGG16 donates the method using the original VGG16 model. Another strategy is the same as earlier introduced CPT_fast tracker using channel pruned VGG16 model. The results are shown in Fig. 8. From this figure, the CPT_fast tracker wins the highest precision and fastest speed, showing the advantages of channel pruning and accurate scale estimation using hand-craft features. CPT_VGG16 runs slower than CPT_fast, which illustrates the channel pruned VGG16 model effectively improves the computational speed. We also investigate our visual tracking version without adaptive iterative optimization strategy (CPT_fast_noAI) based on CPT_fast. Consequently, we can conclude that the process of adaptive iteration improves the running speed effectively

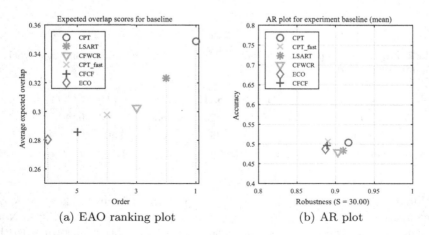

(a) EAO ranking plot   (b) AR plot

Fig. 6. A comparison for accuracy-robustness results on VOT2017 dataset. (a) The plot of EAO ranking for experiment baseline. (b) The plot of accuracy and robustness scores (AR). Apparently, our CPT gains a superior result.

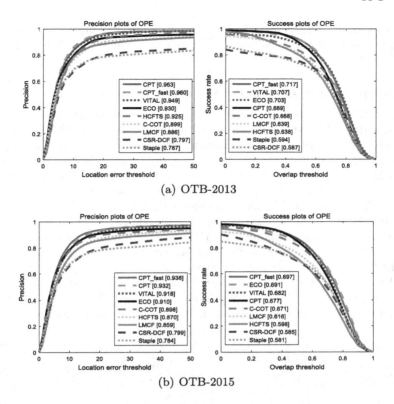

(a) OTB-2013

(b) OTB-2015

Fig. 7. Precision and success plots on OTB-2013 and OTB-2015. The numbers in the legend indicate the representative precisions at 20 pixels for precision plot and the area-under-curve scores for success plot. The proposed CPT and CPT_fast gain satisfactory results.

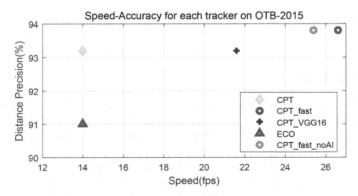

Fig. 8. Comparision on speed and accuracy of our three trackers and ECO. All our three trackers outperform the ECO tracker in speed and accuracy. Our CPT_fast tracker is the best.

with hardly no change of precision. All our four trackers outperform the ECO tracker. Our trackers gain the best results and show the favorable performances in precision and real-time application.

4.4   Comparison of CPT and CPT_fast

CPT tracker only predict 7 different scales for fast scale variations by CNN features, while CPT_fast has 33 predicted scales calculated by HOG. Therefore, when locating the target center is accurate to some extent, CPT_fast tracker can predict more accurate and faster than CPT, especially in complex scenes with multi-scale deformations. We show several different cases between CPT and CPT_fast in Fig. 9. When subject to dramatic scale variations, CPT_fast tracker with more predicted scales can quickly find the appropriate scale to mark object in a larger scale range. Besides, violent non-rigid deformation leads to serious changes in target's appearance. However, CPT_fast constantly learns new features and loses more original features, which can make CPT_fast fail easily. CPT tracker does not have notable scale-predicted interference so that it can track object more robust. As a result, CPT has better stability than CPT_fast, while CPT_fast has better scale adaptability than CPT. That is also the reason why the OTB and VOT datasets exhibit different tracking performances.

CPT   **CPT_fast**

Fig. 9. Differences of CPT and CPT_fast (zebrafish1 and human4)

5   Conclusions

We present a novel and robust channel pruning tracker (CPT) in this paper. Firstly, channel pruned VGG model is applied to fast extract deeper convolutional features with rich semantic information. Then we utilize the Average Feature Energy Ratio to further prune the redundant convolution channels, which are from the feature extraction layers and adaptive iterative strategy to optimize target location. Finally, we evaluate our CPT method on the OTB-2013, OTB-2015, VOT-2016 and VOT-2017 datasets. Extensive experiments demonstrate that the proposed CPT tracker outperforms the state-of-the-art trackers over all four benchmarks. The tracking of speed of CPT_fast tracker achieves 26 fps on OTB-2015. Our trackers gain the best results and show the favorable performances in precision and real-time application.

References

1. Henriques, J.F., Caseiro, R., Martins, P., Batista, J.: High-speed tracking with kernelized correlation filters. IEEE Trans. Pattern Anal. Mach. Intell. **37**(3), 583–596 (2015)
2. Danelljan, M., Shahbaz Khan, F., Felsberg, M., Weijer, J.: Adaptive color attributes for real-time visual tracking. In: Proceedings of the IEEE Conference on Computer Vision and Pattern Recognition, pp. 1090–1097 (2014)
3. Danelljan, M., Robinson, A., Shahbaz Khan, F., Felsberg, M.: Beyond correlation filters: learning continuous convolution operators for visual tracking. In: Leibe, B., Matas, J., Sebe, N., Welling, M. (eds.) ECCV 2016. LNCS, vol. 9909, pp. 472–488. Springer, Cham (2016). https://doi.org/10.1007/978-3-319-46454-1_29
4. Ma, C., Huang, J.B., Yang, X., Yang, M.H.: Hierarchical convolutional features for visual tracking. In: Proceedings of the 2015 IEEE International Conference on Computer Vision, pp. 3074–3082 (2015)
5. Wang, M., Liu, Y., Huang, Z.: Large margin object tracking with circulant feature maps. In: Proceedings of the IEEE Conference on Computer Vision and Pattern Recognition, pp. 4800–4808 (2017)
6. Danelljan, M., Bhat, G., Shahbaz Khan, F., Felsberg, M.: ECO: efficient convolution operators for tracking. In: Proceedings of the IEEE Conference on Computer Vision and Pattern Recognition, pp. 6931–6939 (2017)
7. Wang, L., Ouyang, W., Wang, X., Lu, H.: Visual tracking with fully convolutional networks. In: Proceedings of the IEEE International Conference on Computer Vision, pp. 3119–3127 (2015)
8. Lukezic, A., Vojr, T., Cehovin Zajc, L., Matas, J., Kristan, M.: Discriminative correlation filter with channel and spatial reliability. In: Proceedings of the IEEE Conference on Computer Vision and Pattern Recognition, pp. 4847–4856 (2017)
9. Bertinetto, L., Valmadre, J., Golodetz, S., Miksik, O., Torr, P.H.S.: Staple: complementary learners for real-time tracking. In: Proceedings of IEEE Conference on Computer Vision and Pattern Recognition, pp. 1401–1409 (2016)
10. Kang, K., et al.: T-CNN: tubelets with convolutional neural networks for object detection from videos. IEEE Trans. Circuits Syst. Video Technol., 1 (2017)
11. He, Z., Fan, Y., Zhuang, J., Dong, Y., Bai, H.: Correlation filters with weighted convolution responses. In: Proceedings of the IEEE International Conference on Computer Vision Workshops, pp. 1992–2000 (2017)
12. Song, Y., et al.: VITAL: VIsual Tracking via Adversarial Learning. In: Computer Vision and Pattern Recognition (2018 Spotlight)
13. Ma, C., Huang, J.B., Yang, X., Yang, M.H.: Robust visual tracking via hierarchical convolutional features. arXiv preprint (2017)
14. Wang, X., Li, H., Li, Y., Shen, F., Porikli, F.: Robust and real-time deep tracking via multi-scale domain adaptation. In: International Conference on Multimedia and Expo, pp. 1338–1343 (2017)
15. Sun, C., Wang, D., Lu, H., Yang, M.H.: Learning spatial-aware regressions for visual tracking. In: Computer Vision and Pattern Recognition (2018 Spotlight)
16. Gundogdu, E., Alatan, A.A.: Learning attentions: good features to correlate for visual tracking. arXiv preprint (2017)
17. Danelljan, M., Hager, G., Shahbaz Khan, F., Felsberg, M.: Accurate scale estimation for robust visual tracking. In: British Machine Vision Conference (BMVC), pp. 1–11. British Machine Vision Association, Durham (2014)

18. Wu, Y., Lim, J., Yang, M.: Object tracking benchmark. TPAMI **37**(9), 1834–1848 (2015)
19. Wu, Y., Lim, J., Yang, M.: Online object tracking: a benchmark. In: Computer Vision and Pattern Recognition (2013)
20. Kristan, M., et al.: The visual object tracking VOT2016 challenge results. In: Hua, G., Jégou, H. (eds.) ECCV 2016. LNCS, vol. 9914, pp. 777–823. Springer, Cham (2016). https://doi.org/10.1007/978-3-319-48881-3_54
21. Simonyan, K., Zisserman, A.: Very deep convolutional networks for large-scale image recognition. Comput. Sci. **1**(2), 3 (2014)
22. Kristan, M., Leonardis, A., Matas, J., et al.: The visual object tracking VOT2017 challenge results. In: ICCV Workshops (2017)
23. He, Y., Zhang, X., Sun, J.: Channel pruning for accelerating very deep neural networks. In: International Conference on Computer Vision (ICCV), pp. 1398–1406 (2017)
24. Bolme, D.S., Beveridge, J.R., Draper, B.A., et al.: Visual object tracking using adaptive correlation filters. In: Proceedings of European Conference on Computer Vision, pp. 2544–2550 (2010)
25. Sun, C., Wang, D., Lu, H., Yang, M.: Correlation tracking via joint discrimination and reliability learning. In: Proceedings of European Conference on Computer Vision (2018)
26. Henriques, J.F., Caseiro, R., Martins, P., Batista, J.: Exploiting the circulant structure of tracking-by-detection with kernels. In: Fitzgibbon, A., Lazebnik, S., Perona, P., Sato, Y., Schmid, C. (eds.) ECCV 2012. LNCS, vol. 7575, pp. 702–715. Springer, Heidelberg (2012). https://doi.org/10.1007/978-3-642-33765-9_50
27. Hu, H., Peng, R., Tai, Y.W., et al.: Network trimming: a data-driven neuron pruning approach towards efficient deep architectures. arXiv preprint arXiv:1607.03250 (2016)
28. Wen, W., Wu, C., Wang, Y., et al.: Learning structured sparsity in deep neural networks. In: Proceedings of Advances in Neural Information Processing Systems, pp. 2074–2082 (2016)
29. Zhou, H., Alvarez, J.M., Porikli, F.: Less is more: towards compact CNNs. In: Leibe, B., Matas, J., Sebe, N., Welling, M. (eds.) ECCV 2016. LNCS, vol. 9908, pp. 662–677. Springer, Cham (2016). https://doi.org/10.1007/978-3-319-46493-0_40
30. Danelljan, M., Häger, G., Khan, F.S., Felsberg, M.: Learning spatially regularized correlation filters for visual tracking. In: Proceedings of International Conference on Computer Vision, pp. 4310–4318 (2015)

WAEF: Weighted Aggregation with Enhancement Filter for Visual Object Tracking

Litu Rout[1], Deepak Mishra[1],
and Rama Krishna Sai Subrahmanyam Gorthi[2(✉)]

[1] Department of Avionics, Indian Institute of Space Science and Technology,
Thiruvananthapuram 695 547, Kerala, India
`liturout1997@gmail.com, deepak.mishra@iist.ac.in`
[2] Department of Electrical Engineering, Indian Institute of Technology Tirupati,
Tirupati 517 506, Andhra Pradesh, India
`rkg@iittp.ac.in`

Abstract. In the recent years, convolutional neural networks (CNN) have been extensively employed in various complex computer vision tasks including visual object tracking. In this paper, we study the efficacy of temporal regression with Tikhonov regularization in generic object tracking. Among other major aspects, we propose a different approach to regress in the temporal domain, based on weighted aggregation of distinctive visual features and feature prioritization with entropy estimation in a recursive fashion. We provide a statistics based ensembler approach for integrating the conventionally driven spatial regression results (such as from ECO), and the proposed temporal regression results to accomplish better tracking. Further, we exploit the obligatory dependency of deep architectures on provided visual information, and present an image enhancement filter that helps to boost the performance on popular benchmarks. Our extensive experimentation shows that the proposed weighted aggregation with enhancement filter (WAEF) tracker outperforms the baseline (ECO) in almost all the challenging categories on OTB50 dataset with a cumulative gain of 14.8%. As per the VOT2016 evaluation, the proposed framework offers substantial improvement of 19.04% in occlusion, 27.66% in illumination change, 33.33% in empty, 10% in size change, and 5.28% in average expected overlap.

Keywords: Enhancement filter · Temporal regression ·
Weighted aggregation · Feature prioritization ·
Tikhonov regularization · Ensembler

Electronic supplementary material The online version of this chapter (https://doi.org/10.1007/978-3-030-11009-3_4) contains supplementary material, which is available to authorized users.

L. Leal-Taixé and S. Roth (Eds.): ECCV 2018 Workshops, LNCS 11129, pp. 83–99, 2019.
https://doi.org/10.1007/978-3-030-11009-3_4

1   Introduction

Visual object tracking is one of the widely investigated problems by the computer vision community. The goal of this task is to estimate various attributes of an object with the sole supervision of a bounding box given in the first frame of a sequence. A possible approach to address this issue is to learn unique representation of the target object and employ discriminative power of deep similarity networks [28], or correlation filters [5,14] for efficient estimation of target attributes, often include target position and size. Though the tracking community has achieved significant progress in the recent years, especially after the widespread success of deep CNN in various vision challenges, the complexity of the problem still persists. The difficulty in tracking generic objects in an unconstrained environment still remains at a high level due to several rationale such as occlusion, deformation etc. Getting better at resolving these issues usually has a very good impact on various cross platforms that involves video surveillance, traffic monitoring, human computer interaction etc.

Despite the effort devoted by a large part of the community, there are still several challenges yet to be conquered. To overcome such challenges, most of the previously proposed trackers focus on some of the key components in tracking, including robust feature extraction for learning better representation [1,20,25,34], accurate scale estimation [5], rotation adaptiveness [17,27], motion models [16] etc. There are several other state-of-the-art trackers such as SRDCF [7], and CCOT [8] that implement additional constraint on the residual sum of errors to enforce higher degree of smoothness on the physical movement of the object. In the pursuit of accurate tracking, some of the proposed frameworks [9,34] are predominantly attributed by sophisticated features and complex models. Further, the emergence of deep CNN has replaced the low-level hand-crafted features which are not robust enough to discriminate significant appearance changes. The success of deep learning based trackers such as MDNet [23] and TCNN [22] on popular tracking benchmarks such as OTB [33] and VOT [15] is a clear indication of the distinctive feature extraction ability of deep CNN. In spite of the popularity, these feature extractors still lack high quality visual inputs that can further boost the performance. Therefore, one of the major aspects of this paper is to study the effect of enhancing visual inputs prior to feature extraction. In some sequences like Matrix (ref. Fig. 1), the hand-crafted and CNN features, as used in ECO, also fail to track the target, whereas image enhancement leads to sophisticated feature extraction that helps in tracking under such conditions.

Though deep learning based models have gained a lot of attention on account of their accuracy and robustness, the inherent scarcity of data, and required time for training these networks online, leave such models a step behind the correlation filter (CF) trackers. For this reason, a proper synthesis of CNN as feature extractor, and CF as detector has been doing exceedingly well in most of the challenging sequences. However, most of these fusion based trackers [4,8], being supervised regressors, learns to maximize the spatial correlation between target and candidate image patches. Due to spatial regularization, as in SRDCF [7],

Fig. 1. The groundtruth of Matrix sequence of VOT2016 is shown in blue. The ECO (green) tracker fails to track the object because of drastic appearance changes. However, our ECO_EF (red) can handle the abrupt transition in appearance, mainly due to enhanced visual information provided before feature extraction, and tracks successfully. (Color figure online)

such trackers are capable of searching in a large spatial region that produces a significant gain in performance. But, these classifiers give minimal consideration to regress in temporal domain. Therefore, we exploit the temporal regression (TR) ability of a simple, yet effective model considering weighted aggregation of preceding features. The proposed technical and theoretical contributions can be summarized as following:

- A simple and effective enhancement filter (EF) (Sect. 3.2) is proposed to alleviate the adverse conditions in visual inputs prior to feature extraction. By this approach, the proposed tracker is able to perform against the state-of-the-art on VOT2016 dataset with an improvement of 5.2% in Average Expected Overlap (AEO) over the baseline approach.
- Although a lot of methods have been developed based on spatial regression, TR still remains a relatively less explored method in tracking. Therefore, in this paper, a detailed analysis on impacts of employing TR in single object tracking is undertaken.
- For efficient learning of TR parameters, a weighted aggregation (Sect. 3.3) based approach is proposed to suppress the dominance of un-correlated frames while regressing in temporal domain. Also, the training features are further organised based on average information content (Sect. 3.3). To our knowledge, this is in contrast to the conventional linear regressions in which equal [14], or more preference [30] is given to the historic frames. In order to generalize better, and control over-fitting in temporal domain, we have embedded the whole TR framework in Tikhonov regularization (Sect. 3.3).

Though we have demonstrated the importance of contributions through integrating with ECO, the proposed framework is generic, and can be integrated with other trackers to tackle some of the aforementioned tracking challenges with certain improvement in accuracy. This paper is structured as following. At first we discuss the previous methods which intend to address similar issues as ours (Sect. 2), followed by the proposed methodology (Sect. 3). After describing fundamental concepts of the proposed contributions, we detail our experiments and draw essential inferences (Sect. 4) to assess the overall performance.

2   Related Works

Correlation Filter (CF) based trackers have gained a lot of attention due to their low computational cost, high accuracy, and robustness. The regression of circularly shifted input features with a Gaussian kernel makes it plausible for implementation in Fourier domain, which in fact is the predominant cause of low computational cost. The object representation models, as adapted by many such trackers, have emerged gradually with colour attributes [25], HOG [3], SIFT [34], sparse based [20], CNN [6], and hierarchical CNN [18]. These methods have assisted in diminishing the adverse effects of ill-posed visual inputs. In this paper, our proposed enhancement filter, in a loose sense, contributes towards alleviating this issue further by pre-processing the inputs prior to feature extraction.

Among spatio-temporal models, the Spatio-Temporal context model based Tracker (STT) [32] proposes a temporal appearance model that captures historical appearances to prevent the tracker from drifting into the background. Also, STT proposes a spatial appearance model that creates a supporting field which gives much more information than the appearance of the target, and thus, ensures robust tracking. The Recurrently Target-attending Tracker (RTT) [2] exploits the essential components of the target in the long-range contextual cues with the help of a Recurrent Neural Network (RNN). The close form solution used in RTT is computationally less intensive, and more importantly, it helps in mitigating occlusion cases upto a great extent. The deep architecture proposed in [29] consists of three networks: a Feature Net, a Temporal Net, and a Spatial Net which assist in learning better representation model, establishing temporal correspondence, and refining the tracking state, respectively. The Context Tracker [10] explores the context on-the-fly by a sequential randomized forest, an online template based appearance model, and local features. The distracters and supporters, as proposed in Context Tracker, are very much useful in verifying genuine targets in case of resumption. The TRIC-track [31] algorithm uses incrementally learned cascaded regression to directly predict the displacement between local image patches and part locations. The Local Evidence Aggregation [19], as per the discussion in TRIC-track, determines the confidence level which is used to update the model. The Recurrent YOLO (ROLO) [24] tracker studies the regression ability of RNN in temporal domain.

In a nutshell, most of the trackers try to incorporate temporal information either by enforcing filters of previous frames to be somehow similar or by combining the model through a convex combination, which often leads to low performance and high time complexity. In other words, the model possess dual responsibility of detecting the object and maintaining temporal correspondence. However, the proposed method suggests that regularization over the augmented version of two complementary spaces, one encompassing temporal feature space and another enforcing the spatial smoothness through temporal regression over the position variations, can lead to substantial gain in various challenging categories including illumination variation, size change and occlusion. In such case, one model is specifically trained to smoothly localize the object in spatial domain and the other model, to maintain the temporal correspondence in feature space.

Thereafter, the mean ensemble of these two models leverage the spatio-temporal information to localize the target object. Though the idea of temporal regularization has been used before in correlation filters, relatively less attention has been paid in decomposing the model so as to enforce higher degree of smoothness on the motion model. Therefore, we propose to reduce the under performance of correlation filter trackers by decomposing the model into two separate models. The detailed description is given in the following Sect. 3.

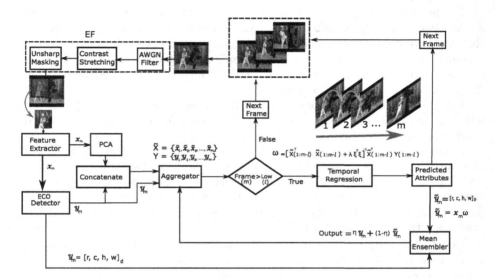

Fig. 2. Temporal regression with weighted aggregation and enhancement filter as proposed in this paper (Sect. 3). Each frame is passed through enhancement filter (EF) before feature extraction. The detector (ECO) uses the extracted features and predicts the target attributes based on spatial correlation. The extracted features are projected into a low dimensional space where these are concatenated with target attributes. The concatenated features are then aggregated based on temporal correspondence and used in learning the parameters (ω) of temporal regression. The TR model predicts the target attributes based on temporal information. Finally, the location of the target object is determined based on weighted mean ensemble of spatial and temporal predictions.

3   Proposed Methodology

The overall architecture of our method is shown in Fig. 2. As discussed in the contributions and the preceding sections we enhance the visual inputs before feature extraction through an EF (Sect. 3.2), and thereafter, the essential processing required for TR (Sect. 3.3) is depicted. For the sake of experimentation, we integrate the proposed methodology in ECO tracker, and showcase the efficacy by comparing with various state-of-the-art trackers on various benchmarks.

We specifically provide a systematic approach based on well known regularization framework for incorporating temporal information in DCF trackers. The framework provides a proportionate weight-age across the previous frames based on their similarity with current frame and also considers feature prioritization based on the average information content in temporal domain.

At the beginning, we apply EF to each frame. After enhancement of visual information, the search region from each frame is fed to the feature extractor. The search region is decided based on the previous position and scale as implemented in [4]. The high dimensional CNN features, as extracted in [4], are projected onto a low dimensional space, aiming at reduction of time complexity. To achieve this, we have applied principal component analysis (PCA) with 90% captured variance. The compressed features are then concatenated with ECO detector outputs, and thereafter, these concatenated features with weighted aggregation (Sect. 3.3) are accumulated in the aggregator.

Let X be a collection of feature vectors in m frames $\{x_1, x_2, \ldots, x_m\} \in \mathbb{R}^{1 \times n}$, where n represents the number of features extracted from the highly correlated patch in each frame. Let Y be a collection of regression targets of the corresponding m frames $\{y_1, y_2, \ldots, y_m\} \in \mathbb{R}^{1 \times p}$, where p represents the dimension of attributes in the order of target centroid $(row, column)$ and size $(height, width)$, i.e., (r, c, h, w). The matrix Y contains the output y_m of the detector and X contains the corresponding input features to the detector. For robust prediction of $\widetilde{y}_m = x_m \omega$, we learn the regressor parameters $\omega \in \mathbb{R}^{n \times p}$ by accumulating the previous estimates of target attributes $Y(1 : m - 1)$, and the associated features with controlled suppression of uncorrelated frames $\widetilde{X}(1 : m-1)$. Then we propose to augment the spatial ECO detector output y_m, with temporal regression output $\widetilde{y}_m$, by considering weighted mean ensemble $(\eta y_m + (1 - \eta)\widetilde{y}_m)$ consistently. The ensemble attributes are then fed back to the aggregator, which are used to update the accumulated attributes in Y and X. The main reason for including target attributes as input features is to enhance the degree of smoothness on the trajectory of the target object. However, updating target attributes in both Y and X may unfairly emphasize falsely tracked targets due to marginal inclusion of detector outputs. Therefore, we either update the concatenated detector outputs in X by $x_m(end - p - 1 : end) \leftarrow (\eta y_m + (1 - \eta)\widetilde{y}_m)$ or regression targets in Y by $y_m \leftarrow (\eta y_m + (1 - \eta)\widetilde{y}_m)$. This is indeed the case as our experiments show that updating X turns out to be more effective than the other counter parts. First, we discuss briefly the fundamental working principles of ECO (Sect. 3.1), and thereafter, the detailed contributions as shown in Fig. 2.

3.1   Baseline Approach: ECO

The ECO [4] tracker, which we have adopted as our baseline, has performed well on various benchmarks [15, 21, 33]. The introduction of factorized convolution operators in ECO, has reduced the parameters in the DCF model drastically. Apart from efficient convolution operators, the ECO tracker proposes a method for feasible memory consumption by reducing the number of training samples, while maintaining diversity. Moreover, the efficient model update strategy, as proposed in ECO, reduces the unfavourable sudden appearance changes as a result of illumination variation, out-of-view, and deformation. As per the comprehensive experimentation, the ECO tracker with deep features outperforms all the previous trackers that rely on DCF formulation. Motivated by these findings, we have integrated the proposed framework into baseline ECO with deep settings in light of further improvement, and demonstrated that the newly developed approach offers significant gain in numerous challenging sequences.

3.2   Enhancement Filter (EF)

In real world scenarios, it is intractable to obtain high quality visual information due to stochastic nature of the environment. To combat several random fluctuations, while preserving the fine/sharp details of the information content in images, we employ edge adaptive Gaussian smoothing. The AWGN Filter block in Fig. 2 represents edge preserved Gaussian smoothing of additive white Gaussian noise (AWGN) with three channel or 3D multi variate Gaussian kernel of standard deviation close to 0 each (here, 0.1), in order not to smooth the edges. A detailed description on AWGN filters can be found in [26]. To span the whole intensity from 0 to 255, while rectifying the contrast imbalance in each channel, we have employed linear contrast stretching after AWGN removal.

Low frequency interference arises when the visual information is gathered under variable illumination. This holds in almost all indoor scenes because of the inverse square law of light propagation. Arguably, the outdoor scenes do not suffer from this effect, because the sun is so far away, that all the tiny regions in an image appear to be at equal distance from it. However, other illuminating sources may produce low frequency interference in an unconstrained environment. Also, we may sometimes be interested in minute details of a scene, or scenes that manifest in high frequencies such as object boundaries. Therefore, it is often desirable to suppress the unwanted low frequencies to leverage high variations in a scene. While this issue has been studied extensively in image processing tasks [26], even in state-of-the-art trackers, as per our knowledge, the necessary attention for the same is not paid explicitly. So we intend to introduce the popular algorithm, local unsharp masking on visual object tracking paradigm, which is shown in Eq. (1). A detail description of these methods along with essential comparisons can be found in [26].

$$g(x, y) = A[f(x, y) - m(x, y)] + m(x, y) \qquad (1)$$

where $A = \frac{kM}{\sigma(x,y)}$, k is a scalar, M is the average intensity of the whole image, $\sigma(x, y)$ represents variance of the window. $g(x, y)$, $f(x, y)$, and $m(x, y)$ represent resulting image, input image, and low pass version of $f(x, y)$, respectively.

3.3   Temporal Regression by Tikhonov Regularization in Tracking

Here, we elaborate our Temporal Regression (TR) framework with detailed analysis of each key components such as Weighted Aggregation, Feature Prioritization, Tikhonov Regularization, and Mean Ensembler.

Weighted Aggregation (WA) in Temporal Regression: Here, we illustrate the weighted aggregation strategy, which brings substantial gain on a diverse set of tough sequences. Let $\alpha \in \mathbb{R}^{m \times 1}$ represent the coefficients for modulating the m frames in temporal domain. The elements of α are computed based on the projection of x_m onto X which consists of m vectors in $\mathbb{R}^{1 \times n}$. An important point to remember here is, even if m frames are modulated based on this correlation metric, the frame x_m remains unaltered due to maximal correlation, and also, it is excluded from training set. The underlying hypothesis is to learn from the weighted aggregation of preceding features based on similarity measure with the test frame x_m, and predict the current attributes $\widetilde{y_m}$. Thereby, we inhibit the dominance of dissimilar frames in voting for target attributes in the current frame. In other words, features from only those frames are amplified which have a contextual correspondence with the test frame in the temporal domain. We squash the elements of α using sigmoid activation in order to map the correlation values to a fixed smooth range between 0 and 1 for all frames, reason for which is understandable. Thus, the coefficients α can be computed using Eq. (2).

$$\alpha = sigmoid(\frac{X x_m^T}{n}),\tag{2}$$

where $X \in \mathbb{R}^{m \times n}$, $x_m \in \mathbb{R}^{1 \times n}$, and $\alpha \in \mathbb{R}^{m \times 1}$.

The features from preceding m frames are modulated by α to enhance the contribution of highly correlated frames, while suppressing the contribution of uncorrelated ones. Thereby, efficient aggregation of past information is utilized in learning the parameters of regressor, which leads to robust prediction of target attributes in the subsequent frames. The modulated training samples are computed by Eq. (3).

$$\widetilde{X} = X. * \alpha \tag{3}$$

where .$*$ represents row wise multiplication with corresponding scalar value of α, i.e., $\widetilde{X}(i, :) = X(i, :) * \alpha(i), i = 1, 2, \ldots, m$ and $*$ represents element wise multiplication.

In a nutshell, the temporal regression model uses the information over several frames to determine which frames it should pay more, or less attention to. The proposed modulating factor determines the attention values while learning the representation. Thus, the WA block enforces selective learning of representation based on temporal correspondence. Figure 3 shows the aggregation coefficients of Ironman sequence from OTB50. After obtaining $\widetilde{X} = \{\widetilde{x_1}, \widetilde{x_2}, \ldots, \widetilde{x_m}\}$, the training features are further regulated based on entropy of the associated random variables (Sect. 3.3).

Feature Prioritization Through Entropy Estimation (FPEE): In this section, we briefly discuss an efficient feature engineering approach as part of WA, taking into account the uncertainty preserved in each feature in the temporal domain. The hypothesis is to estimate the entropy of each feature in $\widetilde{X}$ across all m frames, and use this information content to enhance the contribution of

Fig. 3. Coefficients of aggregation α, which are used to modulate the preceding features of the corresponding frames based on similarity rational. Here, x_{36} has been projected onto $X(1:35)$, where $n = 3140, m = 36$, i.e., $x_i \in \mathbb{R}^{1 \times 3140}, i = 1, 2, \ldots, m$, $X \in \mathbb{R}^{36 \times 3140}$, $Y \in \mathbb{R}^{36 \times 4}$, and $\omega \in \mathbb{R}^{3140 \times 4}$. Note that the current frame has higher correlation with the distant frames than the immediate previous ones.

that particular set of features towards estimation of target attributes. This can be achieved by modulating each column of $\widetilde{X}$, which is in contrast to row wise modulation, as done by α. Let $f_i \in \mathbb{R}^{1 \times m}, i = 1, 2, \ldots, n$ represent a random variable with observations drawn from the ith feature of all m frames. For the ease of experimentation, the observations of these random variables are used to estimate the distribution based on normalized histogram counts. For better understanding, we have visualized the histogram of two random variables, f_1 and f_{104} in Fig. 4.

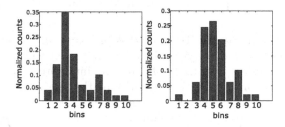

Fig. 4. The histogram of features are computed with fixed number of bins (here, 10). The normalized count is used as probability density $\mathbb{P}_{f_i}$. The distributions of f_1 (left) and f_{104} (right) are used to quantify the average information content.

The basic intuition is, learning that an unlikely event has occurred is more informative than a likely event has occurred. Therefore, we define self-information of event $f = \mathrm{f}$ by $I(\mathrm{f}) = -\log \mathbb{P}_f(\mathrm{f})$, with base e, as characterized in information theory. The self-information deals with a single outcome which leads to several drawbacks, such as an event with unity density has zero self-information, despite it is not guaranteed to occur. Therefore, we have opted Shannon entropy,

$$H(f) = \mathbb{E}_{f \sim \mathbb{P}_f} \left[I(\mathrm{f}) \right] = -\mathbb{E}_{f \sim \mathbb{P}_f} \left[\log \mathbb{P}_f(\mathrm{f}) \right],$$

which is used to deal with such issues [12], to quantify the amount of uncertainty conserved in the entire distribution. We use this uncertainty measure to enhance, or suppress the training features in $\widetilde{X} = f_1, f_2, \ldots, f_n$ by Eq. (4).

$$\widetilde{f}_i = f_i * H(f_i), i = 1, 2, \ldots, n \tag{4}$$

Consequently, the parameters (ω) of temporal regression are computed with the updated training features $\widetilde{X} = \left\{ \widetilde{f_1}, \widetilde{f_2}, \ldots, \widetilde{f_n} \right\}$.

Tikhonov Regularization in Temporal Regression: Here, we describe the context in which we employ standard Tikhonov regularization. To ensure smooth variation of temporal weights (ω), we have penalized the coefficients with larger norms. In our formulation, $\lambda\xi$ represents the standard Tikhonov operator. For equal preference, we have set ξ to be an identity matrix $I \in \mathbb{R}^{m \times n}$, and λ to be 1000. Thus, after incorporating temporal correspondence by WA and FPEE, the standard ridge regression has been updated to Eq. (5).

$$J = \left\| \widetilde{X}\omega - Y \right\|_2^2 + \lambda \left\| \xi\omega \right\|_2^2 \tag{5}$$

The closed-form solution of J can be obtained as following.

$$\nabla_\omega \left\{ \left\| \widetilde{X}\omega - Y \right\|_2^2 + \lambda \left\| \xi\omega \right\|_2^2 \right\} = 0 \implies \omega = \left[\widetilde{X}^T\widetilde{X} + \lambda\xi^T\xi \right]^{-1} \widetilde{X}^TY,$$

where $\omega \in \mathbb{R}^{n \times p}$, and the predicted attributes are computed by $\widetilde{y_m} = x_m\omega$.

Mean Ensembler for Spatio-Temporal Aggregation: This section depicts the theoretical background on the efficacy of mean ensemble. The proposed dynamic model comprises two models having minimal interdependence in their way of implementation. The detector works in the spatial domain with efficient training and robust model update strategy. On the contrary, the regression model operates in the temporal domain maximizing the correspondence with visual features from the current frame, and capturing the physically meaningful movement variables, such as position and angular displacement. Hence, the composition of these two models with bootstrap aggregation would be beneficial in lessening the overall error [12]. Assume there are k models with error $\delta_i \sim \mathcal{N}(\mu = 0, \sigma^2 = v)$, $i = 1, 2, \ldots, k$. Let the covariance $\mathbb{E}[\delta_i\delta_j] = c$. The error made by the mean ensembler output would be $\frac{1}{k}\sum_{i=1}^{k}\delta_i$. The expected squared error predicted by the ensembler would be

$$\mathbb{E}\left[\left(\frac{1}{k}\sum_{i=1}^{k}\delta_i \right)^2 \right] = \mathbb{E}\left[\frac{1}{k^2}\sum_{i=1}^{k}\left(\delta_i^2 + \sum_{j=1, j\neq i}^{k}\delta_i\delta_j \right) \right] = \frac{v}{k} + \frac{k-1}{k}c.$$

If the models are perfectly correlated, i.e., $\mathbb{E}[\delta_i\delta_j] = c = v$, then there will not be any improvement in expected squared error v. However, the uncorrelated models, i.e., $\mathbb{E}[\delta_i \delta_j] = 0$ would shrink the expected squared error by k times. Thus, the proposed dynamic model would perform significantly better than the individual models due to ensemble of two partially uncorrelated models. In addition, the speed will not degrade much due to closed-form solution of the temporal weights.

4   Experiments

Here, we detail our experiments and draw essential inferences to validate our methodology. In all our experiments, we use VOT toolkit and OTB toolkit for evaluation on VOT2016 and OTB50 benchmark, respectively. We develop our algorithm by progressively integrating the contributions into baseline. We demonstrate the impact of individual components by performing ablation studies on OTB50. We compare our top-performing trackers with state-of-the-art trackers and show compelling results in all the challenging categories of OTB50. Figure 5 shows the qualitative analysis of the proposed framework.[1]

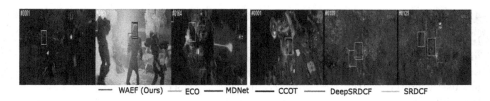

Fig. 5. Comparison on two of the toughest sequences from OTB50 dataset: Ironman (left) and Soccer (right). The WAEF tracker localizes the target under severe deformation, occlusion and illumination variations, unlike the compared trackers.

4.1   Implementation Details

To avoid the ambiguity caused by numerical computation of different machines, we evaluate both the baseline and our proposed trackers on the same machine with exactly same experimental setup. We use the exact parameter settings of ECO [4], including feature extraction, factorized convolution and optimization, for generating detector output. All the experiments are conducted on a single machine: Intel(R) Xeon(R) CPU E3-1225 v2 @ 3.20 GHz, 4 Core(s), 4 Logical Processor(s), 44 GB RAM and NVIDIA GPU (GeForce GTX 1080 Ti). The proposed tracker has been implemented on MATLAB with Matconvnet. We observed that elimination of immediate past frame $((m-1)^{th})$ during training of the TR model provides improvement over inclusion of that particular frame. One possible hypothesis is that the output of the tracker may sometimes lead to false positive bounding box which will incrementally allow it to drift away

---

[1] For more results on OTB and VOT, please refer to supplementary material.

from the actual target. In other words, the trajectory of an object, moving in a straight line, may become curved during regression due to the outlier in $(m-1)^{th}$ frame. To avoid this, one can eliminate few past frames from TR, but this would restrain the learning of recent appearance changes. Therefore, we propose to remove only the last frame from training TR model, which would capture the actual straight line trajectory, and thus, will assist in few scenarios where drastic change is a major concern. We have eliminated the experiments with removal of more immediate frames based on qualitative analysis, and showcase the efficacy of removing immediate past frame on whole OTB50 dataset. However, this approach may become troublesome when the actual trajectory has abrupt deviation from previous estimates. So, the weighted mean ensemble of spatial detector, which is mostly right (more weightage, $\eta = 0.7$), and TR would be useful to tackle this issue. The weights have been determined by employing a grid search from 0 to 1 with step size 0.1. The TR model requires a minimum of $\text{Low}(l) = 2$ frames for a meaningful regression. We consider only past 50 frames for training TR model to meet the computational requirement.

4.2 Ablation Studies

In Table 1, we analyse the performance of ablative trackers on OTB50 benchmark. TR1 and TR2 denote the temporal regression with training features from $\max(m-50, 1)$ to $m-1$ and $m-2$, respectively. Note that the TR1 and TR2 do not use weighted aggregation while computing ω. It is evident that TR2 is better than TR1 both in accuracy and robustness, which validates our hypothesis of excluding immediate previous frame from training TR model in order to supress the adverse effect of outliers up to some extent. Despite the weak performance of TR, the composition tracker TREF outperforms the baseline in Success rate and Precision. Further, the WA and TREF consolidate into Weighted Aggregation with Enhancement Filter (WAEF) which again achieves substantial gain over baseline. In WAEF1, WAEF2 and WAEF, we update x_m & y_m, y_m, and x_m, respectively. It is evident that WAEF performs better than its counterparts, which validates our claim of updating x_m alone in order to enforce smooth transition from previous frame. We report that the WAEF tracker exceeds the baseline with a gain of 1.24% in success rate, and 0.69% in precision.

Table 1. The success and precision area under the curve (AUC) of the individual components of our proposed framework on OTB50.

Tracker	WAEF	TREF	ECO	TR2	TR1	WAEF1	WAEF2
Success rate	0.651	0.648	0.643	0.627	0.619	0.615	0.610
Precision	0.880	0.877	0.874	0.849	0.839	0.825	0.814

4.3 Comparison with the State of the Arts

Evaluation on OTB50: In Fig. 6, we compare our top-performing trackers with the state-of-the-art trackers. Among the compared trackers, our WAEF tracker does exceedingly well, outperforming the winner on OTB50. We observe that the proposed framework is robust enough to tackle the typical challenging issues in object tracking. In Table 2, we show the categorical comparison of area under the curve (AUC) and success rate, which are the standard metrics on benchmark results. The WAEF tracker provides substantial cumulative gain of 14.8% over all the crucial categories on OTB50. Moreover, the proposed architecture does not deteriorate the baseline performance in either of the aforementioned categories.

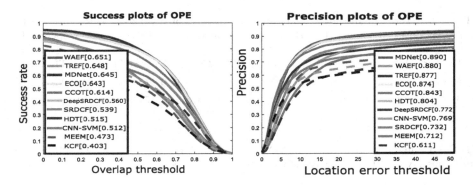

Fig. 6. The success and precision plots of our proposed WAEF, TREF, and several state-of-the-art trackers on OTB50 dataset.

Table 2. The success and precision plots in various category of our proposed WAEF, TREF, and several state-of-the-art trackers on OTB50 dataset.

Tracker	**WAEF**	**TREF**	MDNet	ECO	CCOT	DeepSRDCF	SRDCF	HDT	KCF
Out of view	0.657	0.654	0.617	0.644	0.636	0.551	0.512	0.479	0.368
Occlusion	0.654	0.652	0.631	0.643	0.632	0.555	0.532	0.504	0.405
Illumination variation	0.632	0.628	0.625	0.623	0.594	0.530	0.509	0.488	0.386
Low resolution	0.626	0.623	0.608	0.617	0.613	0.511	0.486	0.471	0.334
Background clutter	0.638	0.636	0.625	0.629	0.588	0.535	0.517	0.494	0.388
Deformation	0.634	0.634	0.627	0.621	0.602	0.532	0.520	0.488	0.399
Out-of-plane rotation	0.646	0.642	0.627	0.636	0.605	0.549	0.516	0.503	0.399
FastMotion	0.645	0.643	0.620	0.637	0.625	0.554	0.523	0.499	0.365

Evaluation on VOT2016: We also evaluate the WAEF tracker on VOT2016 dataset, and compare the results in Table 3. The WAEF tracker offers remarkable achievement, improving 5.28% AEO, 6.31% accuracy rank, and 7.75% robustness rank relative to baseline. In particular, the WAEF tracker provides substantial

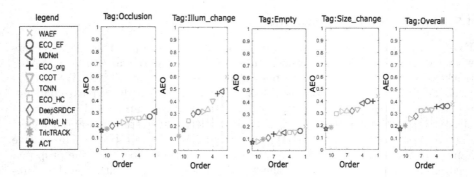

Fig. 7. Average Expected Overlap (AEO) analysis of our WAEF tracker and several other state-of-the-art trackers in various challenging categories of VOT2016.

Table 3. Overall quantitative analysis of few trackers on VOT2016. AEO, Ar, and Rr represents average expected overlap, accuracy rank, and robustness rank, respectively.

Tracker	**WAEF**	**ECO_EF**	MDNet	ECO	CCOT	DeepSRDCF	TricTRACK
AEO	0.3750	0.3616	0.3584	0.3563	0.3310	0.2763	0.1995
Ar	1.78	2.13	1.40	1.90	2.13	2.47	5.90
Rr	2.38	2.38	2.70	2.58	2.77	4.00	6.92

Table 4. Quantitative analysis on VOT2018 benchmark. The proposed CFTR tracker performs favourably against the state-of-the-art trackers.

Trackers	LSART	CFWCR	**CFTR**	CFCF	ECO	GNET	CCOT	CRT
AEO	0.323	0.303	0.301	0.286	0.280	0.274	0.267	0.244
Accuracy	0.50	0.49	0.51	0.51	0.48	0.50	0.49	0.46
Robustness	46.53	57.00	55.00	59.00	59.00	59.00	68.0	71.93
Raw FPS	1.72	1.80	0.62	0.32	3.71	1.29	0.15	3.24

improvement of 19.04% in occlusion, 27.66% in illumination change, 33.33% in empty, and 10% in size change category of VOT2016, as can be inferred from Fig. 7. Also, to validate the usefulness of EF, we have experimented ECO with EF alone. We observe that the enhancement filter assists in shaping the visual information which eventually leads to a notable gain of 1.48% in AEO. This implicates that the robust feature extractors still lack high quality visual inputs that may boost the overall performance.

Evaluation on VOT2018: Here, we build the proposed TR around a different framework CFCF [13], namely Correlation Filter with Temporal Regression (CFTR) and show that the performance consistently improves irrespective of the framework. The CFTR tracker achieves 3.44% and 7.27% gain in AEO and

Robustness relative to baseline CFCF, respectively. The decomposed network runs almost double the speed of baseline without degrading the overall performance (Table 4).

5 Concluding Remarks

In this study, we demonstrated that enhancing the visual information prior to feature extraction, as proposed in this paper, can yield significant gain in performance. We analysed the impact of ridge regression with Tikhonov regularization in temporal domain, and showed promising results on popular benchmarks. Further, we introduced an approach to regress in the temporal domain based on weighted aggregation and entropy estimation, which provided drastic improvement in various challenging categories of popular benchmarks. Moreover, the proposed framework is generic, and can accommodate other detectors with simultaneously leveraging the spatial and temporal correspondence while localizing the target object. Our future scope will include robust feature selection based on sophisticated density estimation. Also, we will assimilate the performance of the proposed contributions on other publicly available datasets [11,21].

References

1. Bengio, Y., Courville, A., Vincent, P.: Representation learning: a review and new perspectives. IEEE Trans. Pattern Anal. Mach. Intell. **35**(8), 1798–1828 (2013)
2. Cui, Z., Xiao, S., Feng, J., Yan, S.: Recurrently target-attending tracking. In: Proceedings of the IEEE Conference on Computer Vision and Pattern Recognition, pp. 1449–1458 (2016)
3. Dalal, N., Triggs, B.: Histograms of oriented gradients for human detection. In: 2005 IEEE Computer Society Conference on Computer Vision and Pattern Recognition, CVPR 2005, vol. 1, pp. 886–893. IEEE (2005)
4. Danelljan, M., Bhat, G., Khan, F.S., Felsberg, M.: ECO: efficient convolution operators for tracking. In: Proceedings of the 2017 IEEE Conference on Computer Vision and Pattern Recognition (CVPR), Honolulu, HI, USA, pp. 21–26 (2017)
5. Danelljan, M., Häger, G., Khan, F., Felsberg, M.: Accurate scale estimation for robust visual tracking. In: British Machine Vision Conference, Nottingham, 1–5 September 2014. BMVA Press (2014)
6. Danelljan, M., Hager, G., Shahbaz Khan, F., Felsberg, M.: Convolutional features for correlation filter based visual tracking. In: Proceedings of the IEEE International Conference on Computer Vision Workshops, pp. 58–66 (2015)
7. Danelljan, M., Hager, G., Shahbaz Khan, F., Felsberg, M.: Learning spatially regularized correlation filters for visual tracking. In: Proceedings of the IEEE International Conference on Computer Vision, pp. 4310–4318 (2015)
8. Danelljan, M., Robinson, A., Shahbaz Khan, F., Felsberg, M.: Beyond correlation filters: learning continuous convolution operators for visual tracking. In: Leibe, B., Matas, J., Sebe, N., Welling, M. (eds.) ECCV 2016. LNCS, vol. 9909, pp. 472–488. Springer, Cham (2016). https://doi.org/10.1007/978-3-319-46454-1_29
9. Danelljan, M., Shahbaz Khan, F., Felsberg, M., Van de Weijer, J.: Adaptive color attributes for real-time visual tracking. In: Proceedings of the IEEE Conference on Computer Vision and Pattern Recognition, pp. 1090–1097 (2014)

10. Dinh, T.B., Vo, N., Medioni, G.: Context tracker: exploring supporters and distracters in unconstrained environments. In: 2011 IEEE Conference on Computer Vision and Pattern Recognition (CVPR), pp. 1177–1184. IEEE (2011)
11. Galoogahi, H.K., Fagg, A., Huang, C., Ramanan, D., Lucey, S.: Need for speed: a benchmark for higher frame rate object tracking. arXiv preprint arXiv:1703.05884 (2017)
12. Goodfellow, I., Bengio, Y., Courville, A.: Deep Learning, vol. 1. MIT Press, Cambridge (2016)
13. Gundogdu, E., Alatan, A.A.: Good features to correlate for visual tracking. IEEE Trans. Image Process. 27(5), 2526–2540 (2018)
14. Henriques, J.F., Caseiro, R., Martins, P., Batista, J.: High-speed tracking with kernelized correlation filters. IEEE Trans. Pattern Anal. Mach. Intell. 37(3), 583–596 (2015)
15. Kristan, M., et al.: A novel performance evaluation methodology for single-target trackers. IEEE Trans. Pattern Anal. Mach. Intell. 38(11), 2137–2155 (2016). https://doi.org/10.1109/TPAMI.2016.2516982
16. Kwon, J., Lee, K.M.: Tracking by sampling trackers. In: 2011 IEEE International Conference on Computer Vision (ICCV), pp. 1195–1202. IEEE (2011)
17. Liu, T., Wang, G., Yang, Q.: Real-time part-based visual tracking via adaptive correlation filters. In: Proceedings of the IEEE Conference on Computer Vision and Pattern Recognition, pp. 4902–4912 (2015)
18. Ma, C., Huang, J.B., Yang, X., Yang, M.H.: Hierarchical convolutional features for visual tracking. In: Proceedings of the IEEE International Conference on Computer Vision, pp. 3074–3082 (2015)
19. Martinez, B., Valstar, M.F., Binefa, X., Pantic, M.: Local evidence aggregation for regression-based facial point detection. IEEE Trans. Pattern Anal. Mach. Intell. 35(5), 1149–1163 (2013)
20. Mei, X., Ling, H.: Robust visual tracking and vehicle classification via sparse representation. IEEE Trans. Pattern Anal. Mach. Intell. 33(11), 2259–2272 (2011)
21. Mueller, M., Smith, N., Ghanem, B.: A benchmark and simulator for UAV tracking. In: Leibe, B., Matas, J., Sebe, N., Welling, M. (eds.) ECCV 2016. LNCS, vol. 9905, pp. 445–461. Springer, Cham (2016). https://doi.org/10.1007/978-3-319-46448-0_27
22. Nam, H., Baek, M., Han, B.: Modeling and propagating CNNs in a tree structure for visual tracking. arXiv preprint arXiv:1608.07242 (2016)
23. Nam, H., Han, B.: Learning multi-domain convolutional neural networks for visual tracking. In: Proceedings of the IEEE Conference on Computer Vision and Pattern Recognition, pp. 4293–4302 (2016)
24. Ning, G., et al.: Spatially supervised recurrent convolutional neural networks for visual object tracking. In: 2017 IEEE International Symposium on Circuits and Systems (ISCAS), pp. 1–4. IEEE (2017)
25. Pérez, P., Hue, C., Vermaak, J., Gangnet, M.: Color-based probabilistic tracking. In: Heyden, A., Sparr, G., Nielsen, M., Johansen, P. (eds.) ECCV 2002. LNCS, vol. 2350, pp. 661–675. Springer, Heidelberg (2002). https://doi.org/10.1007/3-540-47969-4_44
26. Petrou, M., Petrou, C.: Image Enhancement, Chap. 4. Wiley, New York (2010)
27. Rout, L., Manyam, G.R., Mishra, D., et al.: Rotation adaptive visual object tracking with motion consistency. In: 2018 IEEE Winter Conference on Applications of Computer Vision (WACV), pp. 1047–1055, March 2018. https://doi.org/10.1109/WACV.2018.00120

28. Tao, R., Gavves, E., Smeulders, A.W.: Siamese instance search for tracking. In: Proceedings of the IEEE Conference on Computer Vision and Pattern Recognition, pp. 1420–1429 (2016)
29. Teng, Z., Xing, J., Wang, Q., Lang, C., Feng, S., Jin, Y.: Robust object tracking based on temporal and spatial deep networks. In: Proceedings of the IEEE Conference on Computer Vision and Pattern Recognition, pp. 1144–1153 (2017)
30. Valmadre, J., Bertinetto, L., Henriques, J., Vedaldi, A., Torr, P.H.S.: End-to-end representation learning for correlation filter based tracking. In: The IEEE Conference on Computer Vision and Pattern Recognition (CVPR), July 2017
31. Wang, X., Valstar, M., Martinez, B., Haris Khan, M., Pridmore, T.: TRIC-track: tracking by regression with incrementally learned cascades. In: Proceedings of the IEEE International Conference on Computer Vision, pp. 4337–4345 (2015)
32. Wen, L., Cai, Z., Lei, Z., Yi, D., Li, S.Z.: Robust online learned spatio-temporal context model for visual tracking. IEEE Trans. Image Process. **23**(2), 785–796 (2014)
33. Wu, Y., Lim, J., Yang, M.H.: Online object tracking: a benchmark. In: IEEE Conference on Computer Vision and Pattern Recognition (CVPR) (2013)
34. Zhou, H., Yuan, Y., Shi, C.: Object tracking using sift features and mean shift. Comput. Vis. Image Underst. **113**(3), 345–352 (2009)

A Memory Model Based on the Siamese Network for Long-Term Tracking

Hankyeol Lee⬥, Seokeon Choi⬥, and Changick Kim$^{(\boxtimes)}$⬥

School of Electrical Engineering, KAIST, Daejeon, Republic of Korea
{hankyeol,seokeon,changick}@kaist.ac.kr

Abstract. We propose a novel memory model using deep convolutional features for long-term tracking to handle the challenging issues, including visual deformation or target disappearance. Our memory model is separated into short- and long-term stores inspired by Atkinson-Shiffrin Memory Model (ASMM). In the tracking step, the bounding box of the target is estimated by the Siamese features obtained from both memory stores to accommodate changes in the visual appearance of the target. In the re-detection step, we take features only in the long-term store to alleviate the drift problem. At this time, we adopt a coarse-to-fine strategy to detect the target in the entire image without the dependency of the previous position. In the end, we employ Regional Maximum Activation of Convolutions (R-MAC) as key criteria. Our tracker achieves an F-score of 0.52 on the LTB35 dataset, which is 0.04 higher than the performance of the state-of-the-art algorithm.

Keywords: Long-term tracking · Atkinson-Shiffrin Memory Model · Siamese network · Regional Maximum Activation of Convolutions

1 Introduction

Visual object tracking is one of the most popular tasks in computer vision with many applications such as surveillance, traffic control, and autonomous driving. Given a target with a bounding box in the first frame, the goal of visual tracking is to estimate the bounding boxes of the target in the remaining frames of a video sequence. In particular, short-term object tracking, which assumes that the target is always located in the image, has greatly advanced with various tracking benchmarks [20,29,33] and visual object tracking challenges [9,18] over the last decade.

Meanwhile, long-term tracking has also received increasing attention with the introduction of a new benchmark [24]. Unlike in short-term tracking, the target could disappear over time in long-term tracking due to full occlusion or out-of-view. The long-term tracking task also involves a variety of challenging

---

H. Lee and S. Choi—Authors contributed equally.

© Springer Nature Switzerland AG 2019
L. Leal-Taixé and S. Roth (Eds.): ECCV 2018 Workshops, LNCS 11129, pp. 100–115, 2019.
https://doi.org/10.1007/978-3-030-11009-3_5

problems (e.g., viewpoint change, object deformation, and fast motion), because it deals with a relatively long sequence. Therefore, additional procedures are required to achieve robust performance in long-term tracking.

Convolutional Neural Networks (CNNs) have recently demonstrated remarkable performance in many computer vision tasks [12,15,34] and many CNN-based short-term trackers have been proposed [2,3,26,30]. SiamFC [2], one of the successful CNN-based trackers, has especially achieved high performance in real-time on the short-term tracking benchmarks by using a fully-convolutional Siamese network. However, although SiamFC could exploit the expressive power of deep convolutional networks, it is difficult to handle the challenging issues in long-term tracking without additional procedures.

The reason why SiamFC is not suitable for long-term tracking is as follows. Firstly, SiamFC easily fails to track the target if the target appearance changes significantly since tracking works with only the target appearance given in the first frame without an online learning process. Secondly, the target re-detection process is not implemented explicitly, so the re-entered target must be detected in the same way as tracking. However, the tracking process in SiamFC not only exploits the prior knowledge about the target position, but also covers a region of interest which is the neighbor region of the target position estimated in the previous frame. Eventually, this manner causes a strong dependency on the previous position, which may lead to re-detection failure when the target re-enters far from its previous position.

In this paper, we propose a Memory Model via the Siamese network for Long-term Tracking (MMLT) to address the problem for target appearance variation and the dependency on the previous position. Our long-term tracker is a novel approach that applies deep features extracted from the Siamese and VGG networks to Atkinson-Shiffrin Memory Model (ASMM) [1], unlike MUSTer [14] based on the traditional descriptors such as HOG [10] and SIFT [21]. MMLT consists of three parts: tracking, re-detection, and memory management. The structure of the memory for long-term tracking is divided into short- and long-term stores depending on period and manner in which the memory is stored. Tracking and re-detection processes are performed based on this memory model.

In the tracking process, the position of the target is estimated based on the response map of the Siamese network. At this time, we take a weighted sum of the features in both short- and long-term stores to effectively capture appearance variations. In contrast, we employ features only in the long-term store to constrain the drift problem in the re-detection process. Furthermore, we adopt a coarse-to-fine strategy to detect the target in the entire image without the dependency of the previous position. Firstly, we collect several candidates that retain similar semantic meanings with the target to pick out coarse positions in the entire image. Next, we select the final candidate and refine the target position by applying the Siamese network in the long-term store to each candidate. Regional Maximum Activation of Convolutions (R-MAC) [31], which has been proposed for image retrieval, is applied to determine whether the re-detected object is the target or not. We demonstrate that our tracker achieves the state-of-the-art performance on the long-term tracking benchmark [24].

2   Related Works

Long-term tracking is characterized by the disappearance of the target object, so re-detection is required as a key process. In addition, since the length of long-term tracking sequence is considerably longer than that of the short-term, the updating scheme capable of accommodating changes in the visual appearance of the target greatly affects performance. Therefore, we briefly introduce how recent long-term trackers [14,17,23] are used to overcome the critical issues of long-term tracking.

Kalal *et al.* [17] proposed a new tracking framework, TLD, that decomposes long-term tracking into tracking (T), learning (L), and detection (D). First, the tracker estimates the position of the moving object based on the median-flow tracker [16]. Next, the detector determines the presence of the target in a cascade manner over the entire area of the image and modifies the tracker if necessary. At this time, three processes are performed for detection: patch variance, ensemble classifier, and NN-classifier. Assuming that the tracker and detector may fail, the learning process estimates errors based on P-N learning and learns the tracker and detector more robustly.

Hong *et al.* [14] firstly adopted Atkinson-Shiffrin Memory Model (ASMM) [1], also known as the multi-store model, for long term tracking to cope with appearance changes of the object. The MUlti-Store Tracker (MUSTer) consists of short- and long-term memory stores. An Integrated Correlation Filter (ICF), which is based on Kernelized Correlation Filter (KCF) [13] and Discriminative Scale Space Correlation Filter (DSSCF) [4], is used for short-term tracking. Furthermore, they add a complementary element based on keypoint matching-tracking [27] and MLESAC estimation [32] as a long-term component. In the end, they design a forgetting curve to model remembering-forgetting [7].

Lukežič *et al.* [23] suggested a Fully-Correlated Long-term Tracker (FCLT) that applies discriminative correlation filters to long-term tracking. This is decomposed into the short-term tracker and detector. These two components are modeled by learning DCFs at different time scales. Especially, the problem that the correlation filter could not be applied to detection is solved efficiently.

3   Memory Model for Long-Term Tracking (MMLT)

According to Atkinson-Shiffrin Memory Model (ASMM) [1], human memory is divided into three separate components: a sensory register, a short-term store, and a long-term store. The sensory register acts as a buffer for passing information to the short-term store. The short-term store retains the information for a short time, and repeated memories in the short-term store are transferred to the long-term store with semantic information. These memories can be recalled by the retrieval process as needed.

Inspired by this memory model, we propose a memory model for long-term tracking, which is divided into short- and long-term stores. It is not the first time that this multi-store model has been used for long-term tracking. The MUlti-Store Tracker (MUSTer) [14] is a representative long-term tracker based on ASMM, which is described in detail in the previous section. They employ the traditional descriptors (e.g., HOG [10], color attributes [6], and SIFT [21]) as sensory information, whereas we incorporate rich features extracted from deep neural networks into the memory model to accommodate large changes in the visual appearance of the target.

In this paper, we introduce a novel Memory Model based on the Siamese network for Long-term Tracking (MMLT) to effectively deal with the problems for visual deformation and target disappearance. The short-term store $\mathcal{S}$ retains the Siamese features of the target, and the long-term store $\mathcal{L}$ holds both the Siamese features and semantic features as follows:

$$\mathcal{S} = \{f(z_{S_i})\}_{i=1}^{N_S}, \quad \mathcal{L} = \{f(z_{L_i}), g(z_{L_i})\}_{i=1}^{N_L}, \tag{1}$$

where $f(\cdot)$ and $g(\cdot)$ denote the Siamese feature and the semantic feature extracted from deep neural networks. z is an exemplar image that covers a larger region than the estimated bounding box, which is discussed in SiamFC [2]. We note that the exemplar image z and the estimated target region $\hat{z}$ (e.g., bounding box) are different. S_i and L_i indicate the frame index of the stored features, and i indicates the order entered in each memory store. The memory capacities of the short- and long-term stores are $N_S(=60)$ and $N_L(=40)$, respectively.

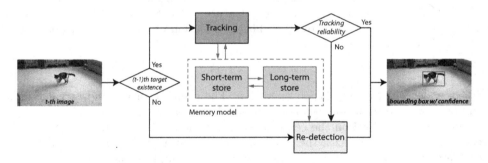

Fig. 1. The overall flowchart of our tracker. The black arrows represent how the tracking and re-detection procedures work depending on two main conditions, and the red arrows indicate how memory is stored and delivered. (Color figure online)

The entire tracking process including re-detection is executed based on this memory model, which is depicted in Fig. 1. The proposed long-term tracker comprises three parts: tracking, re-detection, and memory management. If the target position in the previous frame is successfully estimated, the tracking process is performed with the Siamese features in the short- and long-term stores (Sect. 3.1). On the contrary, if this estimation fails in the previous frame or if

Algorithm 1. Tracking

1: **Input**: Searching region x, short-term store $\mathcal{S}$, long-term store $\mathcal{L}$, P-Net f
2: **Output**: Estimated target $\hat{z}$, *tracking reliability flag*
3: Compute the response using Eq. (3)
4: **if** (Satisfy Eq. (6)) **then**
5:     *Tracking reliability flag* $\leftarrow 1$
6:     Estimated target $\leftarrow \hat{z}$
7:     $N_T \leftarrow N_T + 1$
8: **else**
9:     *Tracking reliability flag* $\leftarrow 0$
10:    Estimated target $\leftarrow \emptyset$
11:    $N_T \leftarrow 0$
12: **end if**

---

the current tracking result is unreliable, the re-detection process is operated based on the features in the long-term store (Sect. 3.2). In the end, Sect. 3.3 gives details on how memory is stored in the short-term store, how short-term memory is transferred to long-term memory, and memory limits for the short- and long-term stores.

3.1 Tracking

Our network for tracking is the same as SiamFC [2]. Thus, we briefly review the process of SiamFC. They denote an exemplar image given in the first frame and a searching region as z and x, which have a dimension of $127 \times 127 \times 3$ and $255 \times 255 \times 3$, respectively. The output feature of the Siamese network, which we call it P-Net, is denoted by $f(\cdot)$. The formulation of the SiamFC to obtain response map can be written as:

$$y = f(z) * f(x), \tag{2}$$

where $*$ denotes the correlation operation. The center position and target size can be estimated from this response map. And, the searching region x of the next frame is formed based on the center position of the estimated target. However, since SiamFC only utilizes the exemplar image given in the first frame, it is difficult to capture target appearance variations during the tracking.

To address this problem, $f(z)$ in Eq. (2) is replaced by combining the output features of P-Net in the short- and long-term stores. Thus, the response map can be calculated by the following equation,

$$y = f_M(\mathcal{S}, \mathcal{L}) * f(x), \tag{3}$$

where $f_M(\mathcal{S}, \mathcal{L})$ denotes the combined features of the short- and long-term stores. $f_M(\mathcal{S}, \mathcal{L})$ is obtained as a weighted sum of short-term features $f_S(\mathcal{S})$ and long-term features $f_L(\mathcal{L})$:

$$f_M(\mathcal{S}, \mathcal{L}) = \lambda \exp(-\frac{N_T}{h_M}) f_S(\mathcal{S}) + (1 - \lambda \exp(-\frac{N_T}{h_M})) f_L(\mathcal{L}), \tag{4}$$

where λ denotes a weight parameter to control the relative importance between short-term memory and long-term memory, h_M is a constant to control the strength of the time, and N_T is the number of successive frames with reliable tracking results. According to this equation, as the number of consecutive frames with reliable tracking results increases, the weight of $f_S(\mathcal{S})$ decreases and that of $f_L(\mathcal{L})$ increases. It means that the tracker initially focuses on short-term memory to accommodate changes in the visual appearance of the target, but switch focus to long-term memory since reliable information is transferred to the long-term store over time. Each feature is calculated as a combination of exemplar images extracted from selected frames as follows:

$$f_S(\mathcal{S}) = \frac{\sum_{i=1}^{N_S} \exp(-\frac{i}{h_S}) f(z_{S_i})}{\sum_{i=1}^{N_S} \exp(-\frac{i}{h_S})}, \quad f_L(\mathcal{L}) = \alpha_L f(z_{L_1}) + (1 - \alpha_L) \frac{\sum_{i=2}^{N_L} f(z_{L_i})}{N_L - 1},$$
(5)

where h_S is a constant to control the impact of the short-term store length. $f_S(\mathcal{S})$ is computed by assigning a higher weight to the features according to the order entered early in the short-term store to alleviate the drift problem. On the other hand, we give only the first frame a high weight α_L since the first stored long-term memory ($L_1 = 1$) is always ground truth. We note that the first stored short-term memory might not be ground truth since short-term memory is often reset, which is discussed in the next section.

We need to decide whether or not the re-detection process should be applied, so we set a criterion to decide if the tracking result is reliable. To determine whether the tracking result is reliable, we use the maximum value of the response map $y^* = \max(f_M(\mathcal{S}, \mathcal{L}) * f(x))$. Let $\bar{y}$ be the average maximum value of the response maps calculated by the recent 40 reliable frames. We assume that the tracking result is reliable if the ratio between y^* and $\bar{y}$ is higher than a predefined threshold τ_1 (=0.6) for comparison of the Siamese features, i.e.,

$$y^*/\bar{y} > \tau_1.$$
(6)

If this criterion is satisfied, then the center position and target size are estimated from the response map in the same manner as in SiamFC (e.g., upsampling for accurate localization and searching over five scales). Thus, we can get the target region $\hat{z}$ from the above information. However, target estimation is postponed to the re-detection step if it fails to satisfy the criterion, which is introduced in the next section. The overall process of tracking is summarized in Algorithm 1.

3.2   Re-detection

If the criterion of Eq. (6) is not satisfied, the tracking result is considered unreliable and eventually the re-detection step proceeds. We adopt a coarse-to-fine strategy to detect the target in the entire image without the dependency of the position estimated in the previous frame. Only the information in the long-term store is employed to re-detect the target, and the short-term store is reset to handle the drift problem.

Algorithm 2. Re-detection

1: **Input**: Image I, long-term store $\mathcal{L}$, P-Net f, S-Net g
2: **Output**: Estimated target $\hat{z}$, *target existence flag*
3: Short-term store $\mathcal{S}$ is reset
4: Get candidates using Eq. (7)
5: Select the one candidate using Eq. (8)
6: Estimated target $\leftarrow \hat{z}$
7: **if** (Satisfy Eq. (9) and Eq. (10) and Eq. (11)) **then**
8:      *Target existence flag* $\leftarrow 1$
9: **else**
10:      *Target existence flag* $\leftarrow 0$
11: **end if**

Firstly, we use the last layer ($conv5$) of the pre-trained VGGNet to collect the coarse positions of the candidates which have similar semantic meanings with the target in the entire image. This is denoted by $g(\cdot)$, and we call it S-Net. Let I denote the entire image, which has a size of $W \times H \times 3$. The spatial size of the output features $g(I)$ is reduced to the size of $\frac{W}{16} \times \frac{H}{16} \times 512$ due to the existence of pooling layers. Then, the semantic response maps are calculated as follows:

$$y_i^s = g(z_{L_i}) * g(I), \quad i = 1, \ldots, N_L. \tag{7}$$

Since the spatial size of the features is smaller than that of the entire image, we could not estimate the exact position from the semantic response map y_i^s. So, we only obtain the coarse searching regions x_k of N_D (=3) candidates with high response values. After that, the best candidate is selected by P-Net as follows:

$$x = \underset{x_k}{\operatorname{argmax}} \left(\max(f_L(\mathcal{L}) * f(x_k)) \right), \quad k = 1, \ldots, N_D, \tag{8}$$

where x_k is the searching region of each candidate. Unlike searching for the target over five scales, we change it to fifteen scales to effectively deal with scale variations in the re-detection process. Eventually, the searching region x of the best candidate is selected by Eq. (8), and then the target region $\hat{z}$ of this candidate is estimated from the maximum value of $f_L(\mathcal{L}) * f(x)$.

To determine whether the final candidate is the target, three criteria are defined. The first is how the Siamese feature of the final candidate and that of exemplar images in the long-term store are similar, which is expressed as follows:

$$\frac{\max(f_L(\mathcal{L}) * f(x))}{\sum_{i=1}^{N_L} f(z_{L_i}) * f(z_{L_i})/N_L} > \tau_2, \tag{9}$$

where τ_2 (=0.35) is a certain threshold for comparison of the Siamese features. Short-term memory is not considered because it has been reset.

The second is related to the retrieval process occurring in ASMM [1]. We use the Regional Maximum Activation of Convolutions (R-MAC) vector [31], which has been proposed for image retrieval. The R-MAC feature vector $\mathbf{h}(\cdot)$ is a compact representation of the CNN response map $g(\cdot)$ with semantic meaning. It is robust to scale and translation due to sampling the response map at multiple scales and aggregating the regional vectors. The second criterion based on the semantic meaning regardless of position and size is described as follows:

$$\frac{1}{N_L}\sum_{i=1}^{N_L}\langle \mathbf{h}(g(z_{L_i})), \mathbf{h}(g(z))\rangle > \tau_h, \tag{10}$$

where $\langle \cdot, \cdot \rangle$ denotes the cosine similarity between two vectors. τ_h ($=0.6$) is a threshold for comparison of the R-MAC vectors, and we call it the R-MAC threshold.

The third is designed to prevent the tracker from being confused by background objects with similar appearance. We extract the exemplar images $\{z_j^n\}_{j=1}^{N_n}$ of $N_n(=16)$ negative samples in the first frame, which are target-like distractors chosen based on P-Net and S-Net. To prevent the target from accidentally being classified as a negative sample, the negative samples are extracted only in the first frame. The third criterion is computed as follows:

$$\max(f_L(\mathcal{L}) * f(x)) > \max(f(z_j^n) * f(x)), \quad j = 1, \dots, N_n. \tag{11}$$

According to the equation, the final candidate must be more similar to the positive samples in the long-term store than all the negative samples.

If the final candidate satisfies these three criteria, we determine the candidate as the target and proceed with the tracking process from the next frame. The overall of the re-detection process is summarized in Algorithm 2.

3.3 Memory Management

According to the memory management in ASMM [1], only a limited amount of the information can be held in the short-term store. Repeated memories among them are moved to the long-term store, and they are reset in the short-term store over time. Unlike the short-term store, memories in the long-term store are maintained for a long time. In particular, the frequently used memory lasts long, but the memory that is not used often is forgotten.

In this section, we model how memory information moves and disappears from memory stores based on the above memory model. The memory management step proceeds only when the tracking result of the current frame is reliable. Firstly, acceptable information from the sensory register is transferred to the short-term store as Siamese features via the following criterion as follows:

$$\frac{\max(f_M(\mathcal{S}, \mathcal{L}) * f(x))}{\sum_{i=1}^{N_L} f(z_{L_i}) * f(z_{L_i})/N_L} > \tau_3, \tag{12}$$

where τ_3 ($=0.5$) is a certain threshold. If the short-term store is full, the short-term store is managed in the first in/first out manner during tracking since the short-term store has a limited capacity of $N_S(=60)$. However, if the tracking result is unreliable, all short-term memories disappear entirely.

Algorithm 3. Memory management
1: **Input**: Estimated target $\hat{z}$, short-term store $\mathcal{S}$, long-term store $\mathcal{L}$
2: **Output**: Short-term store $\mathcal{S}$, long-term store $\mathcal{L}$
3: **if** (Satisfy Eq. (12)) **then**
4:    z is transferred to the short-term store $\mathcal{S}$
5:    **if** (Satisfy Eq. (10) and Eq. (11)) **then**
6:        z is transferred to the long-term store $\mathcal{L}$
7:    **end if**
8: **end if**

On the other hand, moving the short-term information to the long-term store need to be treated more carefully. Therefore, the information is transferred only when the criterion for Eq. (11) succeeds after Eq. (10) is satisfied consecutively during 10 frames. At this time, both the Siamese and semantic features are transferred to the long-term store. This is summarized in Algorithm 3.

In the end, we set the forgetting curve [7] for each long-term memory. If additional memory is entered after long-term memory capacity is full, the memory with the smallest forgetting curve value disappears. However, we always keep the first memory in the long-term store since it is the ground truth given in the first frame. This forgetting curve is modeled as follows:

$$c_i = \begin{cases} \min(1, k_c c_i), & \text{if } \langle \mathbf{h}(g(z_{L_i})), \mathbf{h}(g(z)) \rangle > \tau_h, \\ p_i \exp(-a_i/h_c), & \text{otherwise,} \end{cases} \quad i = 2, \dots, N_L, \quad (13)$$

where c_i denotes the forgetting curve of the i-th long-term memory, k_c (>1) represents the reinforcement parameter, and h_c indicates the memory strength parameter. a_i is the age value that is initialized to 0 ($a_i = 0$) if the above condition is satisfied, otherwise it is increased by 1 ($a_i = a_i + 1$). p_i is the baseline of the forgetting curve, which has a value of 1 ($p_i = 1$) when memory is initially stored, but it is re-initialized to a reinforced value $p_i = \min(1, k_c c_i)$ if the above condition is satisfied. In summary, when the newly entered memory is similar to the existing stored memory, it means that the forgetting curve value c_i corresponding to the existing memory is strengthened by k times and the age value a_i is initialized. Otherwise, the age value a_i is increased by 1, and the forgetting curve value c_i of that memory decreases depending on the age.

3.4   Tracking with MMLT

Our three main parts introduced in the previous sections are now integrated as a long-term tracker, which is summarized in Algorithm 4. For the interaction of these three parts, we designate two flags called *tracking reliability* and *target existence flag*. Our tracker is initialized by transferring the ground truth information given in the first frame to the short- and long-term stores. Unlike short-term tracking, which only predicts the bounding box of the target, long-term tracking requires not only the bounding box prediction but also the confidence score

---

Algorithm 4. MMLT

1: **Input:** Images I, target in the first frame $\hat{z}_1$
2: **Output:** Estimated target $\hat{z}$, confidence score v
3: Initialization
4: *Target existence flag* & *Tracking reliability flag* $\leftarrow 1$
5: **for** $t = 2, 3, \ldots, N$ **do**
6:     **if** (*Target existence flag* $= 1$) **then**
7:         Forgetting curve c_i management using Eq. (13)
8:         Tracking (Algorithm 1)
9:         **if** (*Tracking reliability flag* $= 1$) **then**
10:            Memory management (Algorithm 3)
11:         **end if**
12:     **end if**
13:     **if** (*Target existence flag* $= 0$) or (*Tracking reliability flag* $= 0$) **then**
14:         Re-detection (Algorithm 2)
15:     **end if**
16:     Compute the confidence score on the estimated target using Eq. (14)
17: **end for**

---

assignment to the estimated bounding box. The confidence score should be high if the target is present and vice versa. Thus, we assign the confidence score differently depending on whether the target exists or not as follows:

$$v = \begin{cases} \frac{1}{N_L} \sum_{i=1}^{N_L} \langle \mathbf{h}(g(z_{L_i})), \mathbf{h}(g(z)) \rangle, & \text{if } target\ existence\ flag = 1, \\ \frac{\alpha_v}{N_L} \sum_{i=1}^{N_L} \langle \mathbf{h}(g(z_{L_i})), \mathbf{h}(g(z)) \rangle, & \text{otherwise.} \end{cases} \quad (14)$$

Since $\alpha_v = \frac{\max(f_L(\mathcal{L}) * f(x))}{\sum_{i=1}^{N_L} f(z_{L_i}) * f(z_{L_i})/N_L}$ is always smaller than 1, the confidence score is assigned a small value when the target does not exist.

4 Experimental Results

4.1 Dataset

We experimented with a long-term tracking dataset, called LTB35 [24], to compare the proposed MMLT to other trackers. The LTB35 dataset is officially used in the VOT2018 long-term challenge [19] and has the following characteristics: It contains a total of 146,847 frames with more than 1,000 frames for each sequence of 35 categories. Two sequences (*following* and *liverRun*) are even more than 10,000 frames. The number of frames in each sequence is much longer than the previous short-term datasets [20, 29, 33], which makes the task challenging. In addition, since the target disappears for an average of about 12.4 times, a re-detection process is considered to be particularly important. The resolution of the sequences is between 1280×720 and 290×217, and the size of the target is different for each image and continuously changes over time. The target of each sequence is annotated with an axis-aligned bounding-box, and various objects are categorized such as persons, animals, and vehicles.

Table 1. The maximum F-score for each tracker.

Method	Type	Maximum F-score
MMLT	LT_1	0.52
FCLT [23]	LT_1	0.48
SiamFC [2]	ST_1	0.40
ECO [3]	ST_1	0.35
ECOhc [3]	ST_1	0.33
CSRDCF [22]	ST_0	0.33
CREST [30]	ST_0	0.33
PTAV [8]	LT_0	0.31
BACF [11]	ST_0	0.31
MUSTER [14]	LT_1	0.29
KCF [13]	ST_0	0.27
TLD [17]	LT_1	0.27
SRDCF [5]	ST_0	0.26
LCT [25]	LT_0	0.25
CMT [28]	LT_1	0.22

4.2   Evaluation Protocol

The proposed MMLT was evaluated by the evaluation protocol of the VOT2018 long-term challenge [19], which tracks a target from the first frame to the end of the sequence without re-sets. This evaluation protocol was automatically performed by the VOT toolkit [19], which automatically computed the highest F-score for each sequence based on a detection-like precision-recall plot by using confidence scores assigned to bounding boxes of the target. The experiments were performed using MATLAB R2017a on a system with Intel(R) core(TM) i7-4770 3.40 GHz processor and a single NVIDIA GTX 1080 Ti with 11 GB RAM.

4.3   The VOT-LT2018 Benchmark

We compared the tracking performance of our MMLT to that of various trackers based on the maximum F-score. Table 1 shows the maximum F-scores of the state-of-the-art trackers which have been reported in the LTB35 dataset paper [24]. Evaluated trackers are separated into four categories as follows: short-term tracker (ST_0), short-term tracker with conservative updating (ST_1), pseudo long-term tracker (LT_0), and re-detecting long-term tracker (LT_1). The following taxonomy has been introduced explicitly in [24].

The proposed MMLT algorithm can be classified as the re-detecting long-term tracker (LT_1) since our tracker judges tracking failure and performs target re-detection. FCLT [23], which is also the re-detecting long-term tracker (LT_1), achieved the highest performance among the existing methods. However, we achieved an F-score of 0.52 on the LTB35 dataset, which is 0.04 higher than the performance of the state-of-the-art algorithm. Other long-term trackers, however, produced lower performance than existing short-term trackers. This indicates how important and careful the process of re-detection or updating the visual model should be.

We have selected several trackers to analyze the qualitative results with our tracker, which are visualized in Fig. 2. The tracking results for a total of seven sequences are arranged in descending order for the number of target disappearances. The best performer among short-term trackers, ECO [3], tracked the target well even though the viewpoint and scale changed significantly in the *Car* sequence. The correlation filter-based trackers like ECO present a strong advantage in the sequences where the target object does not disappear from the image. On the other hand, SiamFC [2], one of the famous CNN-based short-term trackers, did not adapt as well as ECO to visual appearance variation because an online updating module was not implemented.

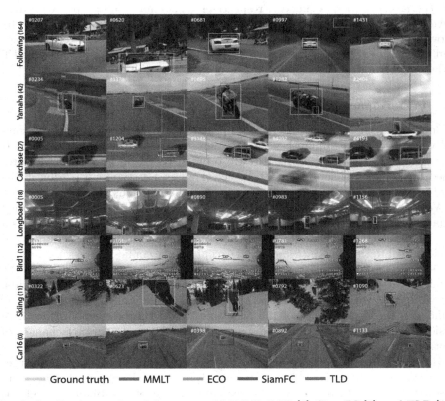

Fig. 2. Qualitative results of the proposed MMLT, ECO [3], SiamFC [2], and TLD [17] in representative frames of challenging seven sequences. Sequences are sorted based on the number of target disappearances, which are indicated by the number in parentheses.

In the remaining six sequences in Fig. 2, ECO has easily drifted to other objects or background because it did not deal with the process of overcoming the disappearance of the target. SiamFC often detected objects in the *Yamaha* sequence where the background clutter was relatively small and the target was noticeable compared to the background. TLD has often succeeded in detecting the target in the *Carchase* sequence where the target often disappears but performance was not as good. In short, all of the existing trackers solved the problem only in some attributes and their performance degraded significantly in challenging problems involving complex attributes.

On the other hand, the proposed MMLT achieved robust tracking performance even in challenging sequences where the target frequently disappears and the visual appearance of the object changes significantly. In particular, in the *Bird* sequence, all previous algorithms completely failed to detect and track the target, whereas the proposed MMLT method obtained better performance by the reliable re-detection procedure and online updating manner based on ASMM. We also achieved F-scores of 0.50, 0.44, 0.40, and 0.51 for *Following*, *Yamaha*, *Longboard*, and *Skiing* sequences, respectively. Therefore, the proposed MMLT proved to be a robust long-term tracker compared to the existing methods. The following results demonstrated that MMLT is a more robust long-term tracker than conventional methods. In the end, the average execution speed of MMLT in the long-term experiment provided by the VOT toolkit [19] achieved 6.15 fps.

4.4   Performance Analysis of Detailed Algorithms

To analyze the sub-algorithms of the proposed MMLT in detail, we created several versions. The maximum F-score for each sequence was calculated, which is summarized in Fig. 3. All sequences are ordered based on how much the proposed final version is superior to the other versions, i.e., the final version in the *Car16* sequence was the most superior to the other versions.

Various versions are distinguished based on whether to perform the online updating and re-detection processes. The leftmost version of each sequence is a version that does not perform both the re-detection and update procedures, and it is identical to the existing SiamFC [2] except for the confidence scoring method and specific parameters. We set this version as a baseline and transformed the update process into three ways as follows: always update with the same weights, always update with an exponential forgetting scheme, and update only when confident. The performance of the last version was the best among the three versions, which was notable in the sequences with large appearance changes of the target such as *Nissan*, *Car1*, and *Cat2*.

However, the four versions described above were difficult to detect the target if the tracking object disappeared frequently or for a long period. The main reason for the problem is that the searching range of the Siamese model is limited. Therefore, we applied only the re-detection procedure without updating to verify the performance of re-detection. The performance has greatly improved by the ability to re-detect the target even if the tracker misses the target due to full occlusion and camera motion changes. In the end, the final version further improved performance by adding an online update process and the results were remarkable in *Car16, Group2, LiverRun, Longboard, Carchase, Person14*, and *skiing* sequences.

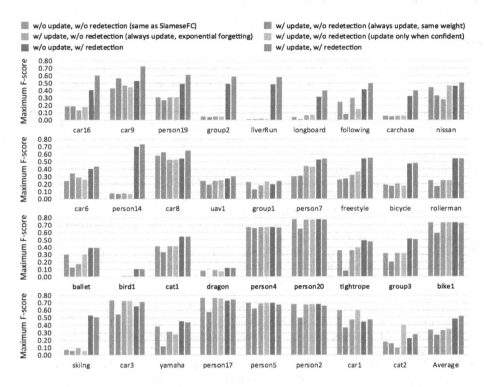

Fig. 3. The maximum F-score for various versions of the proposed MMLT. All sequences are listed based on the order in which the performance of the proposed final version is superior to that of the other versions.

5 Conclusion

In this paper, we have proposed a memory model based on the Siamese network for long-term tracking (MMLT). Memory stores in MMLT are divided into short- and long-term stores depending on each characteristic. The tracking process is operated by taking a weighted sum of the features in both the short- and long-term stores. On the other hand, in the re-detection, only the information in the long-term store is utilized, and the target is detected in the entire image by adopting a coarse-to-fine strategy. As such, memory stores play a crucial role in the tracking and re-detection parts, and the short- and long-term stores are managed differently. The short-term memory is managed in the first in/first out manner, and the forgetting curve is employed for managing the long-term memory. Regional Maximum Activations of Convolutions (R-MAC) is applied to determine the existence of the target and to compute the confidence score. The experimental results on the long-term tracking benchmark show that MMLT achieves state-of-the-art performance.

References

1. Atkinson, R.C., Shiffrin, R.M.: Human memory: a proposed system and its control processes1. In: Psychology of Learning and Motivation, vol. 2, pp. 89–195. Elsevier (1968)
2. Bertinetto, L., Valmadre, J., Henriques, J.F., Vedaldi, A., Torr, P.H.S.: Fully-convolutional siamese networks for object tracking. In: Hua, G., Jégou, H. (eds.) ECCV 2016. LNCS, vol. 9914, pp. 850–865. Springer, Cham (2016). https://doi.org/10.1007/978-3-319-48881-3_56
3. Danelljan, M., Bhat, G., Khan, F.S., Felsberg, M.: ECO: efficient convolution operators for tracking. In: Proceedings of the 2017 IEEE Conference on Computer Vision and Pattern Recognition (CVPR), Honolulu, HI, USA, pp. 21–26 (2017)
4. Danelljan, M., Häger, G., Khan, F., Felsberg, M.: Accurate scale estimation for robust visual tracking. In: British Machine Vision Conference, Nottingham, 1–5 September 2014. BMVA Press (2014)
5. Danelljan, M., Hager, G., Shahbaz Khan, F., Felsberg, M.: Learning spatially regularized correlation filters for visual tracking. In: Proceedings of the IEEE International Conference on Computer Vision, pp. 4310–4318 (2015)
6. Danelljan, M., Shahbaz Khan, F., Felsberg, M., Van de Weijer, J.: Adaptive color attributes for real-time visual tracking. In: Proceedings of the IEEE Conference on Computer Vision and Pattern Recognition, pp. 1090–1097 (2014)
7. Ebbinghaus, H.: Memory: a contribution to experimental psychology. Ann. Neurosci. **20**(4), 155 (2013)
8. Fan, H., Ling, H.: Parallel tracking and verifying: a framework for real-time and high accuracy visual tracking. arXiv preprint arXiv:1708.00153 (2017)
9. Felsberg, M., et al.: The thermal infrared visual object tracking VOT-TIR2016 challenge results. In: Hua, G., Jégou, H. (eds.) ECCV 2016. LNCS, vol. 9914, pp. 824–849. Springer, Cham (2016). https://doi.org/10.1007/978-3-319-48881-3_55
10. Felzenszwalb, P.F., Girshick, R.B., McAllester, D., Ramanan, D.: Object detection with discriminatively trained part-based models. IEEE Trans. Pattern Anal. Mach. Intell. **32**(9), 1627–1645 (2010)
11. Galoogahi, H.K., Fagg, A., Lucey, S.: Learning background-aware correlation filters for visual tracking. In: Proceedings of the 2017 IEEE Conference on Computer Vision and Pattern Recognition (CVPR), Honolulu, HI, USA, pp. 21–26 (2017)
12. He, K., Gkioxari, G., Dollár, P., Girshick, R.: Mask R-CNN. In: 2017 IEEE International Conference on Computer Vision (ICCV), pp. 2980–2988. IEEE (2017)
13. Henriques, J.F., Caseiro, R., Martins, P., Batista, J.: High-speed tracking with kernelized correlation filters. IEEE Trans. Pattern Anal. Mach. Intell. **37**(3), 583–596 (2015)
14. Hong, Z., Chen, Z., Wang, C., Mei, X., Prokhorov, D., Tao, D.: MUlti-Store Tracker (MUSTer): a cognitive psychology inspired approach to object tracking. In: Proceedings of the IEEE Conference on Computer Vision and Pattern Recognition, pp. 749–758 (2015)
15. Hu, J., Shen, L., Sun, G.: Squeeze-and-excitation networks. arXiv preprint arXiv:1709.01507 (2017)

16. Kalal, Z., Mikolajczyk, K., Matas, J.: Forward-backward error: automatic detection of tracking failures. In: 2010 20th International Conference on Pattern Recognition (ICPR), pp. 2756–2759. IEEE (2010)
17. Kalal, Z., Mikolajczyk, K., Matas, J.: Tracking-learning-detection. IEEE Trans. Pattern Anal. Mach. Intell. **34**(7), 1409–1422 (2012)
18. Kristan, M., et al.: The visual object tracking VOT2017 challenge results. In: 2017 IEEE International Conference on Computer Vision Workshops (ICCVW), pp. 1949–1972, October 2017. https://doi.org/10.1109/ICCVW.2017.230
19. Kristan, M., et al.: A novel performance evaluation methodology for single-target trackers. IEEE Trans. Pattern Anal. Mach. Intell. **38**(11), 2137–2155 (2016). https://doi.org/10.1109/TPAMI.2016.2516982
20. Liang, P., Blasch, E., Ling, H.: Encoding color information for visual tracking: algorithms and benchmark. IEEE Trans. Image Process. **24**(12), 5630–5644 (2015)
21. Lowe, D.G.: Distinctive image features from scale-invariant keypoints. Int. J. Comput. Vis. **60**(2), 91–110 (2004)
22. Lukezic, A., Vojir, T., Zajc, L.C., Matas, J., Kristan, M.: Discriminative correlation filter with channel and spatial reliability. In: Proceedings of the IEEE Conference on Computer Vision and Pattern Recognition, vol. 2 (2017)
23. Lukežič, A., Zajc, L.Č., Vojíř, T., Matas, J., Kristan, M.: FCLT-a fully-correlational long-term tracker. arXiv preprint arXiv:1711.09594 (2017)
24. Lukežič, A., Zajc, L.Č., Vojíř, T., Matas, J., Kristan, M.: Now you see me: evaluating performance in long-term visual tracking. arXiv preprint arXiv:1804.07056 (2018)
25. Ma, C., Yang, X., Zhang, C., Yang, M.H.: Long-term correlation tracking. In: 2015 IEEE Conference on Computer Vision and Pattern Recognition (CVPR), pp. 5388–5396. IEEE (2015)
26. Nam, H., Han, B.: Learning multi-domain convolutional neural networks for visual tracking. In: 2016 IEEE Conference on Computer Vision and Pattern Recognition (CVPR), pp. 4293–4302. IEEE (2016)
27. Nebehay, G., Pflugfelder, R.: Consensus-based matching and tracking of keypoints for object tracking. In: 2014 IEEE Winter Conference on Applications of Computer Vision (WACV), pp. 862–869. IEEE (2014)
28. Nebehay, G., Pflugfelder, R.: Clustering of static-adaptive correspondences for deformable object tracking. In: Proceedings of the IEEE Conference on Computer Vision and Pattern Recognition, pp. 2784–2791 (2015)
29. Smeulders, A.W., Chu, D.M., Cucchiara, R., Calderara, S., Dehghan, A., Shah, M.: Visual tracking: an experimental survey. IEEE Trans. Pattern Anal. Mach. Intell. **36**(7), 1442–1468 (2014)
30. Song, Y., Ma, C., Gong, L., Zhang, J., Lau, R.W., Yang, M.H.: CREST: convolutional residual learning for visual tracking. In: 2017 IEEE International Conference on Computer Vision (ICCV), pp. 2574–2583. IEEE (2017)
31. Tolias, G., Sicre, R., Jégou, H.: Particular object retrieval with integral max-pooling of CNN activations. arXiv preprint arXiv:1511.05879 (2015)
32. Torr, P.H., Zisserman, A.: MLESAC: a new robust estimator with application to estimating image geometry. Comput. Vis. Image Underst. **78**(1), 138–156 (2000)
33. Wu, Y., Lim, J., Yang, M.H.: Object tracking benchmark. IEEE Trans. Pattern Anal. Mach. Intell. **37**(9), 1834–1848 (2015)
34. Zhao, H., Shi, J., Qi, X., Wang, X., Jia, J.: Pyramid scene parsing network. In: IEEE Conference on Computer Vision and Pattern Recognition (CVPR), pp. 2881–2890 (2017)

Multiple Context Features in Siamese Networks for Visual Object Tracking

Henrique Morimitsu$^{(\boxtimes)}$ (iD)

Univ. Grenoble Alpes, Inria, CNRS, Grenoble INP, LJK, 38000 Grenoble, France
hmorimitsu@outlook.com

Abstract. Siamese networks have been successfully utilized to learn a robust matching function between pairs of images. Visual object tracking methods based on siamese networks have been gaining popularity recently due to their robustness and speed. However, existing siamese approaches are still unable to perform on par with the most accurate trackers. In this paper, we propose to extend the SiamFC tracker [1] to extract features at multiple context and semantic levels from very deep networks. We show that our approach effectively extracts complementary features for siamese matching from different layers, which provides a significant performance boost when fused. Experimental results on VOT and OTB datasets show that our multi-context tracker is comparable to the most accurate methods, while still being faster than most of them. In particular, we outperform several other state-of-the-art siamese methods.

Keywords: Object tracking · Siamese network · ResNet

1 Introduction

Visual object tracking consists of estimating the trajectory of an object along a continuous video sequence. Usually, only the first frame is annotated with a bounding box, which provides very limited information about the object to be tracked. In real situations, the target often undergoes complex transformations which cause its appearance to significantly change over time. Until recently, the majority of trackers tackled this challenge by constantly updating a classifier throughout the video [7,9,13]. In fact, when combined with deep network models, this strategy still produces the most accurate results on standard benchmarks [4,23,26]. However, updating the classifier online presents challenges of its own. Firstly, constantly updating a large model causes a significant drop in speed. Secondly, as the update depends on previous predictions, the classifier is prone to drift and contamination [6,19,31].

Lately, however, siamese networks have shown that compelling results can be achieved without updating the model [1,10,12]. Siamese trackers are trained on a large set of image pairs to learn a robust matching function that is able to re-identify the object even when its appearance changes significantly. Nonetheless,

L. Leal-Taixé and S. Roth (Eds.): ECCV 2018 Workshops, LNCS 11129, pp. 116–131, 2019.
https://doi.org/10.1007/978-3-030-11009-3_6

although they are usually fast, there is still a gap in accuracy when compared to the top-performing trackers.

In this paper, we show that this gap can be significantly decreased by collecting features containing different context and semantic levels from a deep network. Unlike traditional multi-layer tracking approaches which only exploit the different semantic levels [24, 28, 30], we extract features with multiple context levels by applying a crop on the feature maps, which we refer to as *multi-context features*. In the scope of this work, *context* refers to the amount of background that is included with the object. Figure 1b shows an example of an object with different context levels. Since the receptive field is different at each layer, cropping the maps allows each feature to collect information from different context sizes. We hypothesize, and show through experiments, that multi-context features are particularly suitable for siamese networks.

In the siamese formulation proposed in SiamFC [1], two images, an exemplar z and an instance x, are forwarded through two identical networks with shared weights, yielding features $\varphi(z)$ and $\varphi(x)$ respectively. When matching the features, $\varphi(z)$ can be interpreted as a filter to be applied over $\varphi(x)$ to produce a prediction. If we use multi-layer features, it is possible to obtain multiple filters $\varphi_l(z)$ and $\varphi_l(x)$. However, standard multi-layer features can only provide different global representations for the same image. On the other hand, as explained in Sect. 3.2, by considering *multi-context features*, filters from different layers can be more diverse, focusing on different regions of the image. As discussed in previous works [1, 10, 29], the amount of context can play a significant role in the tracking performance. And our proposed tracker, SiamMCF, allows to leverage it at multiple levels in a single pass.

The contributions of this paper are two-fold: (i) a novel extension to the siamese formulation which leverages multiple context and semantic levels in a single forward pass, and (ii) we demonstrate that the multi-context features provide a significant increase in performance when compared to standard multi-layer ones.

2 Related Work

2.1 Siamese Tracking

SINT [27] is one of the earliest siamese trackers that presented some really compelling results. It consists of a siamese network trained for matching patches of images. For the tracking stage, a patch of the first frame is matched to patches collected around the previous position. Although its results are still among the best siamese trackers, it is much slower than other approaches. GOTURN [12], on the other hand, is able to track at 100 fps. It works by extracting deep features from two crops: one from the object and another from the area centered on the previous position. These features are concatenated and used to solve a regression problem to estimate the relative motion of the target relative to the previous frame. The high speed does compromise the performance, as its results are not as accurate as other siamese approaches.

SiamFC [1] is one of the most balanced options, as it presents one of the best compromises between accuracy and speed. The SiamFC tracker employs a pair of AlexNets [18] with shared weights. A smaller exemplar image and a larger instance are forwarded to generate high-level features. By correlating the exemplar feature over every instance position, a spatial prediction map is obtained.

Several improvements [8,10,14,29] were proposed over the initial SiamFC tracker. CFNet [29] proposes to include a trainable correlation filter layer on top of the siamese network. By introducing a differentiable solution to the deep correlation filter in the Fourier domain, the tracker can be efficiently trained end-to-end with gradient descent. DSiam [8] tackles the model updating problem in siamese networks. Two transformation terms are independently applied to both branches before the matching. The first term updates the model by encouraging it to be similar to the previous observation. The second one is used to suppress background activations in the current frame. EAST [14] proposes to speed-up SiamFC by trying to avoid forwarding the images until the last layer. For this, reinforcement learning is applied to train a classifier that decides at which layer forwarding can be stopped while still retaining a discriminative representation for the given image. SA-Siam [10] leverages appearance and semantic features for tracking. This is done by using two networks, a SiamFC and an AlexNet trained for classification. The authors show that the features obtained from each net are complementary and better results are obtained by combining their predictions.

2.2   Tracking with Multi-layer Representations

Multi-layer features have been applied to object tracking in different ways. Wang et al. [30] showed that different layers effectively produce complementary features for tracking. By leveraging information collected from different layers, tracking results were improved. Chi et al. [3] also exploited this property to obtain predictions from multiple layers. Some other methods [22,28] have used deeper layers to first roughly estimate the target position and then project it to shallower layers. The rationale is that early layers provide less coarse features which can improve the detection accuracy. HDT [24] applies an adaptive hedge method to assign different confidence levels to each layer based on its previous results. C-COT [7] employs an implicit interpolation model to cast the feature maps into the continuous space. In this way, features from different layers with different sizes can be merged to train a correlation filter.

All of the previous approaches still use the whole feature maps for the predictions. Therefore, complementarity between layers is somewhat restricted, as all layers are global representations of the image and do not fully exploit information related to more localized patches. Some recent works [5,21] have demonstrated that, by suppressing or masking the features maps, more robust representations can be obtained. In this work, we propose to combine multi-layer features with spatially constrained maps to obtain multi-context features. SA-Siam [10] has exploited this property to some extent by concatenating features from two layers and then cropping. However, that was applied to consecutive layers of an AlexNet [18], which are not very deep and too close to each other. SINT [27] adopts a strategy to extract multi-layer features which is similar to ours. However, there are some important differences to be pointed out. Firstly, we apply cropping on the exemplar branch, in which the object is known, whereas SINT uses ROI pooling on the instance branch, in which the real object position is uncertain. Secondly, ROI pooling in SINT performs a rescaling (into a 7×7 region) with a max-pooling directly in the lower-resolution feature space, while we rescale the input image before forwarding and always crop a region of the same size, which is less prone to suffer from the negative effects of discretization. We show through experiments that our approach obtains significantly better results than other previous siamese approaches, including SINT and SiamFC-R [15], which also uses a very deep network as a backbone.

3   Our Approach

3.1   Siamese Tracker

In the standard SiamFC [1] formulation, two images are provided as inputs: the exemplar from the first frame z and the current tracking frame, the instance x. Let the prime symbol represent a crop operation over an image. The siamese network receives the cropped regions z' and x' which are then forwarded to produce the features $\varphi(z')$ and $\varphi(x')$ respectively. The feature $\varphi(z')$ is then used as a correlation filter over $\varphi(x')$, thus yielding a prediction map

$$g(x', z') = \varphi(x') \star \varphi(z'). \tag{1}$$

3.2   Siamese Tracker with Multi-context Features

For our SiamMCF tracker, we adapt the prediction map function to work at different layers and extract features with different contexts from each layer. Figure 1 illustrates our proposed approach. The context amount is controlled by cropping the feature map. Since the receptive field at each layer is different, as long as the crop sizes in different layers are not proportional to the receptive field changes, we are able to extract features that consider different areas of the input image. In particular, we can extract features with different contexts by cropping regions of the same size from all the layers. Figure 1b shows the effective region corresponding to crops at different layers.

Given a set of selected layers $L = \{l\}$, prediction maps are estimated as

$$g_l(x', z') = \mathbb{1}\gamma_l \odot (\varphi_l(x') \star \varphi_l'(z')) + \mathbb{1}\beta_l, \tag{2}$$

where $\varphi_l(\cdot)$ represents the feature obtained by forwarding until layer l, and $\odot$ indicates element-wise multiplication. We also learn normalization parameters γ_l and β_l to stabilize the magnitude of the predictions. Notice that we use the cropped filter $\varphi_l'(z')$ to collect exemplars with different context sizes.

Since the backbone network in SiamFC is based on AlexNet [18], which is relatively shallow, extracting multi-level features does not provide very different

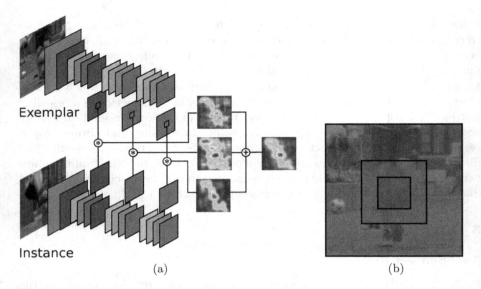

Exemplar

Instance

(a)   (b)

Fig. 1. Illustration of our tracking framework. (a) Proposed network with multi-context features. (b) Receptive fields of different layers superposed over the image. Deeper layers encode larger contexts. Best viewed in colors.

representations. Therefore, we replace the backbone with a deeper network. In particular, we conduct experiments with a ResNet-50 [11]. The original ResNet, however, has a large output stride of 32, which is not ideal for the siamese formulation as both images are largely reduced. Therefore, we reduce the output stride to 8 by setting the convolution stride to 1 in blocks 2 and 3 of the ResNet, and by applying dilated convolutions [2].

It is important to mention that the original SiamFC is based on the fully-convolutional formulation [1]. This formulation ensures that the output features generated by the network commute with translation. Therefore, if the exemplar image is a crop of a region of the instance, then the exemplar output features will also correspond to a region of instance features. In other words, the exemplar image can be found in the instance simply by looking for the region with the maximum similarity. One important caveat is that this formulation can only hold as long as the employed network does not use padding operations, which severely restricts the choice of available architectures.

A ResNet, however, is very deep and requires padding. In fact, the receptive field in the last layer is usually larger than the input image, thus generating an asymmetry when processing images of different sizes (e.g. 127 and 255 for the exemplar and instance branches) which, in turn, break the fully-convolutional formulation. We hypothesize, and show by experiments, that the use of multi-context features alleviates this issue, by using images of the same size, and by extracting cropped intermediate features which: (i) are comparable due to same size inputs, and (ii) also include features whose receptive field are smaller than the input (earlier layers).

We further modify the network by adding residual adaptation modules on top of each of the $|L|$ base layers from the backbone network. A residual adaptation module consists of an additional bottleneck residual unit [11] followed by a convolution. The residual unit has the same properties (number of channels, dilation rate, etc.) as the base ResNet layer it is connected to. The role of this module is to provide more capacity for the extracted features to adapt to the siamese matching at each layer and also to decrease the dimensionality for faster cross-correlation. We show experimentally that the addition of residual units for adaptation positively affects the results.

Final predictions are obtained by computing the average map:

$$g(x', z') = \frac{1}{|L|} \sum_{l \in L} g_l(x', z').$$ (3)

3.3   Training

We compute an individual loss to each layer prediction $g_l(x', z')$. Let i indicate the index of the element (pixel) in a map. Then the loss of each prediction is the average of the logistic losses ℓ_l:

$$\mathcal{L}_l = \sum_i w(y_i)\ell_l(g_l(x_i', z_i'; \theta), y_i),$$ (4)

where $w(y_i)$ is a weighting function applied on the labels y_i that leverages the imbalance between positive and negative samples. This weighting function is defined as:

$$w(y_i) = \frac{0.5y_i}{n_{\text{pos}}} + \frac{0.5(1 - y_i)}{n_{\text{neg}}},$$ (5)

where n_{pos} and n_{neg} are the number of positive and negative samples respectively.

The network is then trained with gradient descent to find the set of parameters θ that minimizes the global loss:

$$\theta^* = \arg\min_{\theta} \sum_{l \in L} \mathcal{L}_l(g_l(x_i', z_i'; \theta), y_i) + \lambda\|\theta\|_2^2.$$ (6)

4   Experimental Results

4.1   Datasets and Evaluation Protocols

We evaluate our tracker on two widely-adopted public datasets: the visual object tracking (VOT) and the online tracking benchmark (OTB).

VOT. Both VOT16 and VOT17 [15–17] are composed of 60 sequences annotated with rotated bounding boxes. The standard evaluation criterion is focused on short-term tracking, where trackers are reinitialized whenever their IoU is zero.

Trackers are ranked mainly according to three measures: Expected Average Overlap, Accuracy and Robustness. It also provides a normalized speed value (EFO) which can be used to compare tracker speeds disregarding the influence of the hardware, to some extent. (we refer to [16] for more details about the metrics).

OTB. We use two versions of the OTB dataset: OTB13 [32] and OTB15 [33]. The former contains 51 objects to be tracked, while the latter is a superset of OTB13 with 100 objects. The trackers are evaluated by two measures: precision and success. Precision estimates the average distance between the center of the predicted bounding box and the groundtruth. Success is used for obtaining the average Intersection-over-Union (IoU) of the predicted boxes. We use OTB13 for our ablation experiments, while OTB15 is kept for comparing with state-of-the-art trackers.

4.2   Implementation Details

Network. Our backbone network is a ResNet [11] with 50 layers. We initialize its weights from a model trained on ImageNet [25] classification. As mentioned before, we decrease the network output stride from 32 to 8. In order to keep the input size compatible with the stride, we resize the input images to 248×248 pixels. In our formulation, both the exemplar and the instance images are of the same size and they include a large context, which is obtained by cropping an area 16 times larger than the object. The output features generated by the network have dimensions $31 \times 31 \times 64$. For the multi-context features, we crop the central 7×7 region from each of the feature maps $\varphi_l(z')$. Our set of chosen layers L is composed of the outputs of each of the 4 residual blocks of the ResNet.

Training. During training, the weights from the ResNet are frozen, and only the residual adaptation modules are trained. We briefly experimented with training ResNet layers as well, but we did not observe any noticeable improvement. The training follows the same protocol as in the SiamFC [1], by learning to match pairs of images collected from the ImageNet VID challenge. This dataset contains around 4000 sequences divided into 30 categories, which accounts for more than one million frames. One important point to notice is that, since ResNets use padded convolutions, the training targets must not always be centered, as it is done in SiamFC. Otherwise, the network will learn a positional bias. Therefore, we augment the training set with random cropping, as well as color distortion, horizontal flipping, and small resizing perturbations. The weights are optimized using gradient descent with a momentum term of 0.9. The learning rate is continually decayed exponentially from 10^{-3} to 10^{-6}. The network is trained during 50000 iterations with a mini-batch size of 8 pairs of images.

Testing. Tracking is conducted in the same manner as in the SiamFC [1]. Therefore, the matching is conducted independently at each frame and spatial consistency between frames is enforced by applying a Hann window over the prediction map. In order to obtain more precise predictions, we upsample the correlation output by a factor of 8 using bicubic interpolation. We handle scale changes by forwarding three images at different scales. For a fair comparison, all hyperparameters are kept the same as in SiamFC.

We implement our tracker using Python and Tensorflow 1.4. The experiments were conducted on a machine with an Intel Xeon E5 CPU and a GeForce GTX 1080Ti GPU. The average tracking speed during the experiments is around 20 frames per second. The code will be made available on http://github.com/hmorimitsu/siam-mcf.

4.3   Ablation Study

We verify the contribution of each of our design choices by evaluating the results of different configurations on the OTB13 dataset. Our main interests were to verify the impacts of (i) replacing the AlexNet in SiamFC by a ResNet, (ii) using different layers from the ResNet for the matching, (iii) using large context inputs with late feature cropping, and (iv) including residual adaptation modules. For the third test, when large-context and cropping are not used, we input an exemplar image whose size is 120×120 pixels. This image also contains a reduced context size, corresponding to an area four times larger than the object, which is the same setting used in SiamFC. For the fourth test, if residual adaptation is not used, we add and train only a single convolutional layer on top of the ResNet outputs. Table 1 summarizes our results.

Table 1. Ablation results on OTB13 dataset. L1–L4 indicates that features from those levels are being used for matching.

ResNet	L1	L2	L3	L4	Feat. crop	Res adapt.	IoU	Prec.
✓	✓					✓	0.517	0.671
✓		✓				✓	0.549	0.704
✓			✓			✓	0.584	0.782
✓				✓		✓	0.506	0.718
✓	✓	✓	✓	✓		✓	0.612	0.801
✓	✓	✓	✓	✓			0.577	0.748
✓	✓				✓	✓	0.592	0.775
✓		✓			✓	✓	0.654	0.846
✓			✓		✓	✓	0.654	0.871
✓				✓	✓	✓	0.535	0.740
✓	✓	✓	✓		✓	✓	0.676	0.876
✓	✓	✓	✓	✓	✓	✓	**0.692**	**0.894**
✓	✓	✓	✓	✓	✓		0.688	0.879
Baseline SiamFC							0.606	0.807

The last row corresponds to the result obtained by the baseline SiamFC. The results show that simply replacing the backbone with a ResNet actually generates worse results. This can be explained by the violation of the fully-convolutional formulation discussed in Sect. 3.2. Even by considering multi-layer features, the performance is only on par with the baseline. However, as illustrated by the results in the bottom part of the table, multi-context features obtained with feature cropping from multiple layers produce noticeably better results. In fact, even when applied to some layers individually, the results are already better than the baseline. However, we see that by combining it with multiple layers we have significantly better performance. It is interesting to remark that, although using L4 by itself usually leads to worse results, removing it from the multi-features set actually generates slightly worse results. One reason is that, in sequences such as Ironman, MotorRolling, and Skating1, L4 is actually better than other layers. We observe a similar behavior when comparing L123 with L1234, thus showing that L4 predictions are beneficial to the model. Lastly, we observe that dropping the residual adaptation does decrease the results, thus demonstrating its contribution.

We select the model with multi-context features and residual adaptation module, which generated the best results, as our SiamMCF to perform the experiments against the state-of-the-art methods.

4.4 Comparison with the Start-of-the-Art

We validate the performance of our tracker by comparing its results with some state-of-the-art trackers. We selected some of the currently best performing trackers in general, as well as other recent siamese proposals. We evaluate our results on three datasets: VOT16, VOT17, and OTB15.

VOT16. We compare our results using SiamMCF on VOT 2016 with the best contenders in the competition (C-COT, TCNN, SSAT, MLDF). We also include the results of other trackers, including SA-Siam [10] and SiamRPN [20], two recent siamese trackers, and SiamFC-R [15], a SiamFC modified to use ResNet as a backbone. The results are summarized in Table 2.

Table 2. Results on the VOT16 dataset. The arrows indicate whether higher or lower values are better.

Tracker		SiamMCF	SiamRPN	C-COT	TCNN	SSAT	SA-Siam	SiamFC-R	SiamFC-A
EAO	↑	**0.361**	0.344	0.331	0.325	0.321	0.291	0.277	0.235
Acc.	↑	**0.58**	0.56	0.54	0.55	0.58	0.54	0.55	0.53
Rob.	↓	1.05	1.08	0.89	**0.83**	1.05	1.08	1.36	1.91
EFO	↑	5.5	**23.3**	0.5	1.0	0.5	<9	5.4	9.2

We can see that SiamMCF outperforms all compared trackers, including the best tracker in the competition, C-COT, and recent siamese methods SiamRPN and SA-Siam. On the other hand, we still cannot obtain better robustness than the methods using online updating, although we outperform all siamese entries. By analyzing the ranking results in Fig. 2, we see that occlusion is the main reason for the drop in performance. This result is understandable, as in such situation, the tracker tends to present higher activations in the surrounding area than in the occluded region, thus causing drifting. It is important to notice that the contributions of SiamMCF are orthogonal to siamese updating strategies, for example, as proposed by DSiam [8]. Therefore, it is possible that even better performance could be obtained by applying those updating strategies to our tracker.

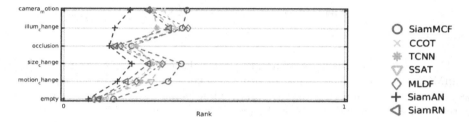

Fig. 2. EAO ranking on VOT16 according to sequence attributes. Each row corresponds to an attribute. The horizontal axis shows the EAO according to the corresponding attribute. Our SiamMCF obtain the best results most of the time.

We also compare our tracker on the unsupervised setting of the VOT benchmark. Different from the standard settings, the trackers are not reinitialized after they drift away from the target. This evaluation focuses on longer-term tracking, as it penalizes more heavily trackers which are unable to recover from a temporary target loss. Figure 3 shows the precision and success plots of the One-Pass Evaluation (OPE) on the VOT16 dataset. We can see that SiamMCF also achieves state-of-the-art results on this test, being very close to the best method SSAT.

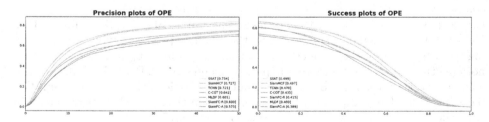

Fig. 3. OPE results on the VOT16 dataset.

VOT17. As in the previous benchmark, we also select the top trackers from the competition (LSART, CFWCR, CFCF, ECO) and siamese trackers (SiamDCF,

SA-Siam, SiamFC). From the results in Table 3 we see that our tracker also performs very favorably on VOT17 as well, being seconded only by LSART, while retaining the highest accuracy. Once again we outperform all other siamese trackers.

Table 3. Results on the VOT17 dataset. The arrows indicate whether higher or lower values are better.

Tracker		SiamMCF	LSART	CFWCR	CFCF	ECO	SiamDCF	SA-Siam	SiamFC
EAO	↑	0.304	**0.323**	0.303	0.286	0.280	0.249	0.236	0.183
Acc.	↑	**0.53**	0.49	0.48	0.51	0.48	0.50	0.50	0.50
Rob.	↓	1.31	**0.94**	1.21	1.17	1.12	1.87	-	2.05

The unsupervised results shown in Fig. 4 are also encouraging. In this dataset, SiamMCF actually outperforms all other trackers when considering the Intersection over Union metric (success plots), while being close to the best method in terms of the center distance of the predictions (precision plots).

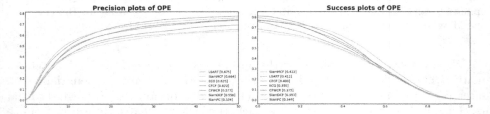

Fig. 4. OPE results on the VOT17 dataset.

OTB15. We further verify the results of SiamMCF on OTB15 (Fig. 5). We show comparative results against state-of-the-art trackers that use multi-layer features (ECO [4], C-COT [7], HDT [24]) and siamese networks (SINT+ [27], SiamFC [1], CFNet [29]). Once again we outperform other siamese proposals while approaching the other state-of-the-art methods, which rely on online updating. It is worth noticing that ECO adopts different hyperparameters for OTB and VOT datasets, whereas we keep them fixed for all evaluations. Particularly, we kept SiamFC parameters for fair comparison, thus it is possible that a further improvement could be obtained with a careful hyperparameter search.

We also show the results on some more specific attributes in Fig. 6. Similarly to what was observed on VOT, videos containing occluded or out-of-view objects are responsible for the largest differences in performance. On the other hand,

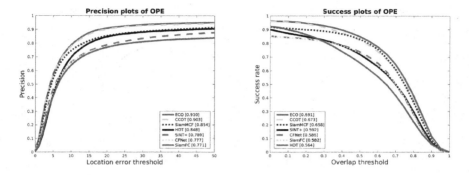

Fig. 5. Results on the OTB15 dataset.

our tracker performs remarkably well on low-resolution videos. This seems to be a feature of trackers based on SiamFC, as both SiamFC itself and CFNet also perform relatively better in this type of sequence. Some qualitative results are displayed in Fig. 7.

We can see that SiamMCF is quite robust to diverse challenging situations, including change of lighting, rotation and scale changes. From the results of the fourth sequence, we see that the use of deeper networks provide additional robustness to rotation, as both our method and HDT show good results. Nonetheless, we observe that our proposal is still overall more robust than HDT, correctly tracking the target in sequences 2 and 3. The qualitative results also confirm that our approach is more robust than the SiamFC baseline, as it works correctly in many sequences where SiamFC loses the target. We also verify that we are able to better handle some sequences where the top performer ECO has difficulties.

The last two sequences present some failure cases for our tracker. We can see that sometimes when the target appearance changes significantly, or if fast motion and blur happen, we are still unable to keep tracking the target. Occlusion also presents difficulties, which may cause the tracker to drift away from the target.

5   Summary

This paper proposed to extend SiamFC to exploit multi-context features in visual object tracking, which is obtained by applying cropping on features maps of different layers. In this way, each layer contributes not only with different semantic levels, but also focus on regions of different sizes of the input image. We showed that by incorporating these features into a deep siamese network tracker we are able to obtain outstanding results in short-term tracking, by outperforming almost all other methods on the newest VOT benchmarks. We are also able to

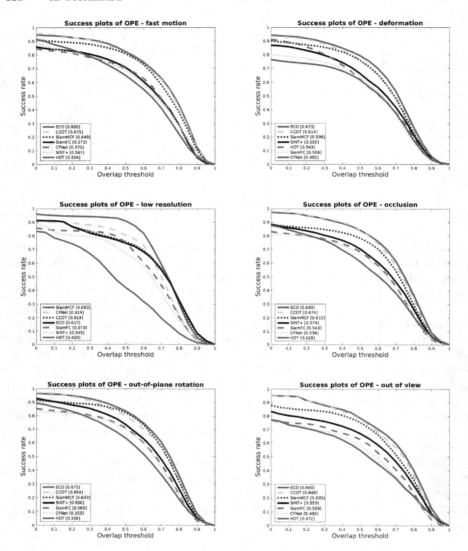

Fig. 6. OTB15 success plots for different attributes.

outperform the state-of-the-art siamese trackers on OTB while getting close to the most accurate methods. Even with the use of multi-context features and deep networks, our tracker remains faster than many of the top-performing methods, running at almost real-time speeds.

SiamMCF   ECO   CCOT   HDT   SiamFC   SINT+   CFNet

Fig. 7. Qualitative results on sequences from OTB15 using the selected trackers.

Acknowledgements. This work was supported in part by Indo-French project EVEREST (no. 5302-1) funded by CEFIPRA. I offer my most sincere regards to Dr. Karteek Alahari and Dr. Cordelia Schmid for providing invaluable insights and support for concluding this project. I also thank Rafael Eller Cruz for providing comments to improve this manuscript.

References

1. Bertinetto, L., Valmadre, J., Henriques, J.F., Vedaldi, A., Torr, P.H.S : Fully-convolutional siamese networks for object tracking. In: Hua, G., Jégou, H. (eds.) ECCV 2016. LNCS, vol. 9914, pp. 850–865. Springer, Cham (2016). https://doi.org/10.1007/978-3-319-48881-3_56
2. Chen, L.C., Papandreou, G., Kokkinos, I., Murphy, K., Yuille, A.L.: DeepLab: semantic image segmentation with deep convolutional nets, atrous convolution, and fully connected CRFs. IEEE TPAMI **40**(4), 834–848 (2018)
3. Chi, Z., Li, H., Lu, H., Yang, M.H.: Dual deep network for visual tracking. IEEE TIP **26**(4), 2005–2015 (2017)
4. Danelljan, M., Bhat, G., Khan, F.S., Felsberg, M.: ECO: efficient convolution operators for tracking. In: CVPR, pp. 6638–6646 (2017)
5. Danelljan, M., Hager, G., Shahbaz Khan, F., Felsberg, M.: Learning spatially regularized correlation filters for visual tracking. In: ICCV, pp. 4310–4318 (2015)
6. Danelljan, M., Hager, G., Shahbaz Khan, F., Felsberg, M.: Adaptive decontamination of the training set: a unified formulation for discriminative visual tracking. In: CVPR, pp. 1430–1438 (2016)
7. Danelljan, M., Robinson, A., Shahbaz Khan, F., Felsberg, M.: Beyond correlation filters: learning continuous convolution operators for visual tracking. In: Leibe, B., Matas, J., Sebe, N., Welling, M. (eds.) ECCV 2016. LNCS, vol. 9909, pp. 472–488. Springer, Cham (2016). https://doi.org/10.1007/978-3-319-46454-1_29
8. Guo, Q., Feng, W., Zhou, C., Huang, R., Wan, L., Wang, S.: Learning dynamic siamese network for visual object tracking. In: ICCV, pp. 1763–1771 (2017)
9. Hare, S., et al.: Struck: structured output tracking with kernels. IEEE TPAMI **38**(10), 2096–2109 (2016)
10. He, A., Luo, C., Tian, X., Zeng, W.: A twofold siamese network for real-time object tracking. In: CVPR, pp. 4834–4843 (2018)
11. He, K., Zhang, X., Ren, S., Sun, J.: Deep residual learning for image recognition. In: CVPR, pp. 770–778 (2016)
12. Held, D., Thrun, S., Savarese, S.: Learning to track at 100 FPS with deep regression networks. In: Leibe, B., Matas, J., Sebe, N., Welling, M. (eds.) ECCV 2016. LNCS, vol. 9905, pp. 749–765. Springer, Cham (2016). https://doi.org/10.1007/978-3-319-46448-0_45
13. Henriques, J.F., Caseiro, R., Martins, P., Batista, J.: High-speed tracking with kernelized correlation filters. IEEE TPAMI **37**(3), 583–596 (2015)
14. Huang, C., Lucey, S., Ramanan, D.: Learning policies for adaptive tracking with deep feature cascades. In: ICCV, pp. 105–114 (2017)
15. Kristan, M., et al.: The visual object tracking VOT2016 challenge results. In: Hua, G., Jégou, H. (eds.) ECCV 2016. LNCS, vol. 9914, pp. 777–823. Springer, Cham (2016). https://doi.org/10.1007/978-3-319-48881-3_54
16. Kristan, M., et al.: The visual object tracking VOT2017 challenge results. In: Visual Object Tracking Workshop (2017)

17. Kristan, M., et al.: A novel performance evaluation methodology for single-target trackers. IEEE TPAMI **38**(11), 2137–2155 (2016)
18. Krizhevsky, A., Sutskever, I., Hinton, G.E.: ImageNet classification with deep convolutional neural networks. In: NIPS, pp. 1097–1105 (2012)
19. Kwon, J., Timofte, R., Van Gool, L.: Leveraging observation uncertainty for robust visual tracking. Comput. Vis. Image Underst. **158**, 62–71 (2017)
20. Li, B., Yan, J., Wu, W., Zhu, Z., Hu, X.: High performance visual tracking with siamese region proposal network. In: CVPR, pp. 8971–8980 (2018)
21. Lukezic, A., Vojír, T., Zajc, L.C., Matas, J., Kristan, M.: Discriminative correlation filter with channel and spatial reliability. In: CVPR, vol. 8, pp. 6309–6318 (2017)
22. Ma, C., Huang, J.B., Yang, X., Yang, M.H.: Hierarchical convolutional features for visual tracking. In: ICCV, pp. 3074–3082 (2015)
23. Nam, H., Han, B.: Learning multi-domain convolutional neural networks for visual tracking. In: CVPR, pp. 4293–4302 (2016)
24. Qi, Y., Zhang, S., Qin, L., Yao, H., Huang, Q., Lim, J., Yang, M.H.: Hedged deep tracking. In: CVPR, pp. 4303–4311 (2016)
25. Russakovsky, O., et al.: Imagenet large scale visual recognition challenge. IJCV **115**(3), 211–252 (2015)
26. Sun, C., Wang, D., Lu, H., Yang, M.H.: Learning spatial-aware regressions for visual tracking. In: CVPR, pp. 8962–8970 (2018)
27. Tao, R., Gavves, E., Smeulders, A.W.M.: Siamese instance search for tracking. In: CVPR, pp. 1420–1429 (2016)
28. Teng, Z., Xing, J., Wang, Q., Lang, C., Feng, S., Jin, Y.: Robust object tracking based on temporal and spatial deep networks. In: CVPR, pp. 1144–1153 (2017)
29. Valmadre, J., Bertinetto, L., Henriques, J.F., Vedaldi, A., Torr, P.H.S.: End-to-end representation learning for correlation filter based tracking. In: CVPR, pp. 5000–5008 (2017)
30. Wang, L., Ouyang, W., Wang, X., Lu, H.: Visual tracking with fully convolutional networks. In: ICCV, pp. 3119–3127 (2015)
31. Wang, N., Shi, J., Yeung, D.Y., Jia, J.: Understanding and diagnosing visual tracking systems. In: ICCV, pp. 3101–3109 (2015)
32. Wu, Y., Lim, J., Yang, M.H.: Online object tracking: a benchmark. In: CVPR, pp. 2411–2418 (2013)
33. Wu, Y., Lim, J., Yang, M.H.: Object tracking benchmark. IEEE TPAMI **37**(9), 1834–1848 (2015)

Towards a Better Match in Siamese Network Based Visual Object Tracker

Anfeng He[1], Chong Luo[2(✉)], Xinmei Tian[1], and Wenjun Zeng[2]

[1] CAS Key Laboratory of Technology in Geo-Spatial Information Processing and Application System, University of Science and Technology of China, Hefei, Anhui, China
heanfeng@mail.ustc.edu.cn, xinmei@ustc.edu.cn
[2] Microsoft Research, Beijing, China
{cluo,wezeng}@microsoft.com

Abstract. Recently, Siamese network based trackers have received tremendous interest for their fast tracking speed and high performance. Despite the great success, this tracking framework still suffers from several limitations. First, it cannot properly handle large object rotation. Second, tracking gets easily distracted when the background contains salient objects. In this paper, we propose two simple yet effective mechanisms, namely angle estimation and spatial masking, to address these issues. The objective is to extract more representative features so that a better match can be obtained between the same object from different frames. The resulting tracker, named Siam-BM, not only significantly improves the tracking performance, but more importantly maintains the realtime capability. Evaluations on the VOT2017 dataset show that Siam-BM achieves an EAO of 0.335, which makes it the best-performing realtime tracker to date.

Keywords: Realtime tracking · Siamese network ·
Deep convolutional neural networks

1 Introduction

Generic visual object tracking is a challenging and fundamental task in the area of computer vision and artificial intelligence. A tracker is initialized with only the bounding box of an unknown target in the first frame. The task of the tracker is to predict the bounding boxes of the target in the following frames. There are numerous applications of object tracking, such as augmented reality, surveillance and autonomous systems. However, robust and precise tracking is still an open problem.

A. He—This work is carried out while Anfeng He is an intern in MSRA.

Electronic supplementary material The online version of this chapter (https://doi.org/10.1007/978-3-030-11009-3_7) contains supplementary material, which is available to authorized users.

© Springer Nature Switzerland AG 2019
L. Leal-Taixé and S. Roth (Eds.): ECCV 2018 Workshops, LNCS 11129, pp. 132–147, 2019.
https://doi.org/10.1007/978-3-030-11009-3_7

- In the past a few years, with the penetration of deep convolutional neural networks (DCNN) in various vision problems, there emerge a large number of DCNN-based trackers [2,3,5,7,11–13,20–22,24,25], among which the siamese network based trackers have received great attention. The pioneering work in this category is the SiamFC tracker [2]. The basic idea is to use the same DCNN to extract features from the target image patch and the search region, and to generate a response map by correlating the two feature maps. The position with the highest response indicates the position of the target object in the search region. The DCNN is pre-trained and remains unchanged during testing time. This allows SiamFC to achieve high tracking performance in realtime. Follow-up work of SiamFC includes SA-Siam, SiamRPN, RASNet, EAST, DSiam, CFNET and SiamDCF [10,12,14,18,25,26,29] (Fig. 1).

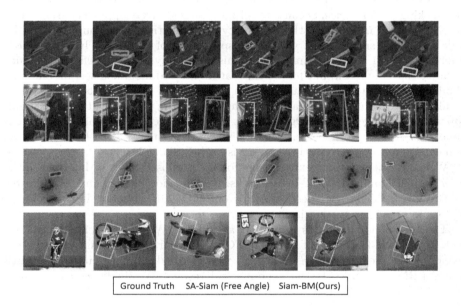

Fig. 1. Comparison with our tracker and baseline tracker. Best view in color.

Despite the great success of siamese network-based trackers, there are still some limitations in this framework. First, as previous research [15,23,32] pointed out, the CNN features are not invariant to large image transformations such as scaling and rotation. Therefore, SiamFC does not perform well when the object has large scale change or in-plane rotation. This problem is exaggerated when the tracked object is non-square, because there is no mechanism in the SiamFC framework that can adjust the orientation or the aspect ratio of the tracked object bounding box. Second, it is hard to determine the spatial region from which DNN features should be extracted to represent the target object. Generally speaking, including a certain range of the surrounding context is helpful to tracking, but too many of them could be unprofitable especially when the background contains distracting objects. Recently, Wang et al. [26] also observed this problem and they propose to train a feature mask to highlight the features of the target object.

In this paper, we revisit the SiamFC tracking framework and propose two simple yet effective mechanisms to address the above two issues. The computational overhead of these two mechanisms is kept low, such that the resulting tracker, named Siam-BM, can still run in real-time on GPU.

First, our tracker not only predicts the location and the scale of the target object, but also predicts the angle of the target object. This is simply achieved by enumerating several angle options and computing DCNN features for each option. However, in order to maintain the high speed of the tracker, it is necessary to trim the explosive number of (scale, angle) combinations without tampering the tracking performance. Second, we propose to selectively apply a spatial mask to CNN feature maps when the possibility of distracting background objects is high. We apply such a mask when the aspect ratio of the target bounding box is far apart from 1:1. This simple mechanism not only saves the efforts to train an object-specific mask, but allows the feature map to include a certain amount of information of the background, which is in general helpful to tracking. Last, we also adopt a simple template updating mechanism to cope with the gradual appearance change of the target object. All these mechanisms are toward the same goal to achieve a better match between the same object from different frames. Therefore, the resulting tracker is named Siam-BM.

We carry out extensive experiments for the proposed Siam-BM tracker, over both the OTB and the VOT benchmarks. Results show that Siam-BM achieves an EAO of 0.335 at the speed of 32 fps on VOT-2017 dataset. It is the best-performing realtime tracker in literature.

The rest of the paper is organized as follows. We review related work in Sect. 2. In Sect. 3, we revisit the SiamFC tracking framework and explain the proposed two mechanisms in details. Section 4 provides implementation details of Siam-BM and presents the experimental results. We finally conclude with some discussions in Sect. 5.

2   Related Work

Visual object tracking is an important computer vision problem. It can be modeled as a similarity matching problem. In recent years, with the widespread use of deep neural networks, there emerge a bunch of Siamese network based trackers, which performs similarity matching based on extracted DCNN features. The pioneering work in this category is the fully convolutional Siamese network (SiamFC) [2]. SiamFC extract DCNN features from the target patch and the search region using AlexNet. Then, a response map is generated by correlating the two feature maps. The object is tracked to the location where the highest response is obtained. A notable advantage of this method is that it needs no or little online training. Thus, real-time tracking can be easily achieved.

There are a large number of follow-up work [8,10,12,14,18,24–26,29,30] of SiamFC. EAST [14] attempts to speed up the tracker by early stopping the feature extractor if low-level features are sufficient to track the target. CFNet [29] introduces correlation filters for low level CNNs features to speed up tracking without accuracy drop. SINT [24] incorporates the optical flow information and achieves better performance. However, since computing optical flow is computationally expensive, SINT only operates at 4 frames per second (fps). DSiam [10] attempts to online update the embeddings of tracked target. Significantly better performance is achieved without much speed drop. HP [8] tries to tune hyperparameters for each sequence in SiamFC [2] by optimizing it with continuous Q-Learning. RASNet [26] introduces three kinds of attention mechanisms for SiamFC [2] tracker. The authors share the same vision with us to look for more precise feature representation for the tracked object. SiamRPN [18] includes a region proposal subnetwork to estimate the aspect ratio of the target object. This network will generate a more compact bounding box when the target shape changes. SA-Siam [12] utilizes complementary appearance and semantic features to represent the tracked object. A channel-wise attention mechanism is used for semantic feature selection. SA-Siam achieves a large performance gain at a small computational overhead.

Apparently we are not the first who concerns transformation estimation in visual object tracking. In correlation filter based trackers, DSST [4] and SAMF [19] are early work that estimates the scale change of the tracked object. DSST [4] does so by learning separate discriminative correlation filters for translation and scale estimation. SAMF [19] uses a scale pyramid to search corresponding target scale. Recently, RAJSSC [31] proposes to perform both scale and angle estimation in a unified correlation tracking framework by using the Log-Polar transformation. In SiamFC-based trackers, while the scale estimation has been considered in the original SiamFC tracker, angle estimation has not been considered before.

There are also a couple of previous research efforts to suppress the background noise. SRDCF [6] and DeepSRDCF [5] reduce background noise by introducing the spatial regularization term in loss function during the online training of correlation filters. RASNet [26] and SA-Siam [12] are two SiamFC-based trackers. They adopt spatial attention or channel-wise attention in the feature extraction network. They both need careful training of the attention blocks.

3   Siam-BM Tracker

Our tracker Siam-BM is built upon the recent SA-Siam tracker [12], which is in turn built upon the SiamFC tracker [2]. The main difference between SA-Siam and SiamFC trackers is that the former extracts semantic features in addition to appearance features for similarity matching. In this section, we will first revisit the SiamFC tracking framework and then present the two proposed mechanisms in Siam-BM towards a better matching of object features.

3.1   An Overview of the SiamFC Tracking Framework

Figure 2 shows the basic operations in the SiamFC tracking framework. The input of the tracker is the target object bounding box B_0 in the first frame F_1. A bounding box can be described by a four-tuple (x, y, w, h), where (x, y) is the center coordinates and w, h are the width and the height, respectively. SiamFC crops the target patch T from the first frame, which is a square region covering B_0 and a certain amount of surrounding context. When the tracker comes to the ith frame, several candidate patches $\{C_1, C_2, ...C_M\}$ are drawn, all of which are centered at the tracked location of the previous frame, but differ in scales. In the original SiamFC [2] work, M is set to 3 or 5 to deal with 3 or 5 different scales.

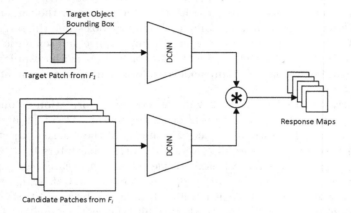

Fig. 2. The SiamFC tracking framework

Both the target patch and the candidate patches go through the same DCNN network, which is fixed during testing time. The process of extracting DCNN features can be described by a function $\phi(\cdot)$. Then, $\phi(T)$ is correlated with $\phi(C_1)$ through $\phi(C_M)$ and M response maps $\{R_1, R_2, ...R_M\}$ are computed. The position with the highest value in the response maps is determined by:

$$(x_i, y_i, m_i) = \arg\max_{x,y,m} R_m, \quad (m = 1...M), \tag{1}$$

where x_i, y_i are the coordinates of the highest-value position and m is the index of the response map from which the highest value is found. Then, the tracking result is given by $B_i = (x_i, y_i, s_{m_i} \cdot w, s_{m_i} \cdot h)$, where s_{m_i} is the scale factor of the m_i^{th} candidate patch.

In this process, SiamFC tracker only determines the center position and the scale of the target object, but keeps the orientation and aspect ratio unchanged. This becomes a severe limitation of SiamFC tracker.

3.2   Angle Estimation

As previous research [15,23,32] has pointed out, DCNN features are not invariant to large image transformations, such as scaling and rotation. While scaling has been handled in the original SiamFC tracker, the rotation of the target object is not considered. Ideally, the change of object angle, or object rotation, can be similarly addressed as object scaling. Specifically, one could enumerate several possible angle changes and increase the number of candidate patches for similarity matching. However, with M scale choices and N angle choices, the number of candidate patches becomes $M \times N$. It is quite clear that the tracker speed is inversely proportional to the number of candidate patches. Using contemporary GPU hardware, a SiamFC tracker becomes non-realtime even when $M = N = 3$.

Knowing the importance of realtime tracking, we intend to find a mechanism to reduce the number of candidate patches without tampering the performance of the tracker. The solution turns out to be a simple one: the proposed Siam-BM tracker adjusts the properties (scale or angle) of the tracked object only one at a time. In other words, Siam-BM can adjust both scale and angle in two frames, if necessary. As such, the number of candidate patches is reduced from $M \times N$ to $M + N - 1$. In our implementation, $M = N = 3$, so only 5 candidate patches are involved in each tracking process.

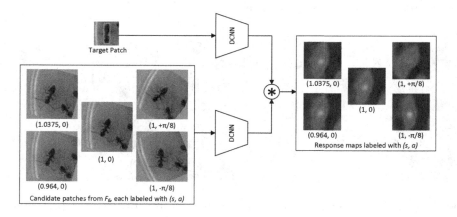

Fig. 3. Illustrating the scale and angle estimation in Siam-BM.

Mathematically, each candidate patch is associated with an (s, a) pair, where s is the scaling factor and a is the rotation angle. It is forced that $s = 1$ (no scale change) when $a \neq 0$ (angle change), and $a = 0$ when $s \neq 1$. Similarly, the tracked object is determined by:

$$(x_i, y_i, k_i) = \underset{x,y,k}{\arg\max} \, R_k, \quad (k = 1, 2, ..., K), \tag{2}$$

where $K = M + N - 1$ is the number of candidate patches. (x_i, y_i) gives the center location of the tracked object and k_i is associated with an (s, a) pair, giving an estimation of the scale and angle changes. Both types of changes are accumulated during the tracking process.

Figure 3 illustrates the scale and angle estimation in the proposed Siam-BM tracker. In the figure, each candidate patch and each response map are labeled with the corresponding (s, a) pair. We can find that, when the target object has the same orientation in the target patch as in the candidate patch, the response is dramatically increased. In this example, the highest response in the map with $(1, -\pi/8)$ is significantly higher than the top values in other maps.

3.3   Spatial Mask

Context information is helpful during tracking. However, including too much context information could be distracting when the background has salient objects or prominent features. In the SiamFC framework, the target patch is always a square whose size is determined only by the area of the target object. Figure 4 shows some examples of target patches containing objects with different aspect ratios. It can be observed that, when the target object is a square, the background is made up of narrow stripes surrounding the target object, so the chance of having an integral salient object in it is small. But when the aspect ratio of the target object is far apart from 1 (vertical or horizontal), it is more likely to have salient objects in the background area.

Fig. 4. Some examples of target patches containing objects with different aspect ratios. Target patches tend to include salient background objects when the object aspect ratio is far apart from 1:1.

We propose to selectively apply spatial mask to the target feature map. In particular, when the aspect ratio of the target object exceeds a predefined threshold th_r, a corresponding mask is applied. We have mentioned that the proposed Siam-BM tracker is built upon a recent tracker named SA-Siam [12]. In SA-Siam, there is an attention module which serves a similar purpose. However, we find that the spatial mask performs better and is more stable than the channel-wise attention scheme. Therefore, we replace the channel attention model in SA-Siam with spatial masking in Siam-BM.

3.4 The Siam-BM Tracker

Siam-BM is built upon SA-Siam [12], which contains a semantic branch and an appearance branch for feature extraction. The target patch has a size of 127×127 as in SiamFC, and the candidate patches have a size of 255×255. We set $M = N = 3$, so that there are 5 candidate patches and their corresponding scale and angle settings are $(s, a) = (1.0375, 0), (0.964, 0), (1, 0), (1, \pi/8), (1, -\pi/8)$. Correspondingly, five response maps are generated after combining semantic and appearance branches. Similar to SiamFC and SA-Siam, normalization and cosine window are applied to each of the five response maps. An angle penalty of 0.975 is applied when $a \neq 0$ and a scale penalty of 0.973 is applied when $s \neq 1$.

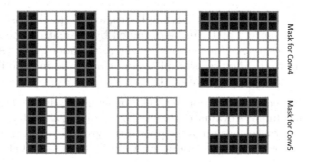

Fig. 5. Spatial feature mask when the aspect ratio of target object exceeds a predefined threshold. Left two masks: $h/w > th_r$; right two masks: $w/h > th_r$; middle two masks: $\max\{w/h, h/w\} < th_r$.

Following SA-Siam, both conv4 and conv5 features are used, and the spatial resolutions are 8×8 and 6×6, respectively. Spatial mask is applied when the aspect ratio is greater than $th_r = 1.5$. Figure 5 shows the fixed design of spatial masks when $\max\{\frac{w}{h}, \frac{h}{w}\} > th_r$. The white grids indicate a coefficient of 1 and the black grids indicate a coefficient of 0.

In addition, we perform template updating in Siam-BM. The template for frame t, denoted by $\phi(T_t)$ is defined as followings:

$$\phi(T_t) = \lambda_S \times \phi(T_1) + (1 - \lambda_S) \times \phi(T_t^u), \tag{3}$$

$$\phi(T_t^u) = (1 - \lambda_U) \times \phi(T_{t-1}^u) + \lambda_U \times \hat{\phi}(T_{t-1}). \tag{4}$$

where $\hat{\phi}(T_{t-1})$ is the feature of the tracked object in frame $t - 1$. It can be cropped from the feature map of candidate regions of frame $t - 1$. $\phi(T_t^u)$ is the moving average of feature maps with updating rate λ_U. λ_S is the weight of the first frame. In our implementation, we set $\lambda_S = 0.5$, $\lambda_U = 0.006$.

Note that the spatial mask is only applied to the semantic branch. This is because semantic responses are more sparse and centered than appearance responses, and it is less likely to exclude important semantic responses with spatial masks. The attention module in SA-Siam is removed.

4   Experiments

In this section, we evaluate the performance of Siam-BM tracker against state-of-the-art realtime trackers and carry out ablation studies to validate the contribution of angle estimation and spatial masking.

4.1   Datasets and Evaluation Metrics

OTB: The object tracking benchmarks (OTB) [27,28] consist of two major datasets, namely OTB-2013 and OTB-100, which contain 51 and 100 sequences respectively. The two standard evaluation metrics on OTB are success rate and precision. For each frame, we compute the IoU (intersection over union) between the tracked and the groundtruth bounding boxes, as well as the distance of their center locations. A success plot can be obtained by evaluating the success rate at different IoU thresholds. Conventionally, the area-under-curve (AUC) of the success plot is reported. The precision plot can be acquired in a similar way, but usually the representative precision at the threshold of 20 pixels is reported.

VOT: We use the recent version of the VOT benchmark, denoted by VOT2017 [17]. The VOT benchmarks evaluate a tracker by applying a reset-based methodology. Whenever a tracker has no overlap with the ground truth, the tracker will be re-initialized after five frames. Major evaluation metrics of VOT benchmarks are accuracy (A), robustness (R) and expected average overlap (EAO). A good tracker has high A and EAO scores but low R scores.

In addition to the evaluation metrics, VOT differs from OTB in groundtruth labeling. In VOT, the groundtruth bounding boxes are not always upright. Therefore, we only evaluate the full version of Siam-BM on VOT. OTB is used to validate the effectiveness of spatial mask.

4.2   Training Siam-BM

Similar to SA-Siam, the appearance network and the fuse module in semantic branch are trained using the ILSVRC-2015 video dataset (only color images are used). The semantic network uses the pretrained model for image classification on ILSVRC. Among a total of more than 4,000 sequences, there are around 1.3 million frames and about 2 million tracked objects with groundtruth bounding boxes. We strictly follow the separate training strategy in SA-Siam and the two branches are not combined until testing time.

We implement our model in TensorFlow [1] 1.7.0 framework in Python 3.5.2 environment. Our experiments are performed on a PC with a Xeon E5-2690 2.60 GHz CPU and a Tesla P100 GPU.

4.3   Ablation Analysis

Angle Estimation: We first evaluate whether angle estimation improves the performance on the VOT benchmark. Spatial masking is not added, so our method is denoted by Siam-BM (w/o mask). There are two baseline methods. In addition to vanilla SA-Siam, we implement a variation of SA-Siam, denoted by SA-Siam (free angle). Specifically, when the bounding box of the tracked object is not upright in the first frame, the reported tracking results are tilted by the same angle in all the subsequent frames. Table 1 shows the EAO as well as accuracy and robustness of the three comparing schemes. Note that the performance of SA-Siam is slightly better than that reported in their original paper, which might due to some implementation differences. We can find that angle estimation significantly improves the tracker performance even when it is compared with the free angle version of SA-Siam.

Table 1. Comparison between Siam-BM (w/o mask) and two baseline trackers shows the effectiveness of angle estimation.

Trackers	EAO	Accuracy	Robustness
SA-Siam (vanilla)	0.261	0.505	1.276
SA-Siam (free angle)	0.287	0.529	1.234
Siam-BM (w/o mask)	0.301	0.544	1.305

Spatial Mask: We use the OTB benchmark for this ablation study. Angle estimation is not added to the trackers evaluated in this part, therefore our method is denoted by Siam-BM (mask only). For all the 100 sequences in OTB benchmark, we compute the aspect ratio of the target object using $r = \max(\frac{h}{w}, \frac{w}{h})$, where w and h are the width and height of the groundtruth bounding box in the first frame. We set a threshold th_r, and if $r > th_r$, the object is called an *elongated object*. Otherwise, we call the object a *mediocre object*. At the testing stage, Siam-BM (mask only) applies spatial mask to elongated objects. At the training stage, we could either use the full feature map or the masked feature map for elongated objects. For mediocre objects, mask is not applied in training or testing. The comparison between different training and testing choices are included in Table 2. Comparing (3)(4) with (5)(6) in the Table, we can conclude that applying spatial mask significantly improves the tracking performance for elongated objects. Comparison between (3) and (4) shows that training with spatial mask will further improve the performance for elongated objects, which agrees with the common practice to keep the consistency of training and testing. An interesting finding is obtained when we comparing (1) with (2). If we apply spatial mask to elongated objects during training, the Siamese network seems to be trained in a better shape and the tracking performance for mediocre objects is also improved even though no spatial mask is applied during testing time.

We then compare the performance of Siam-BM (mask only) with the state-of-the-art realtime trackers on OTB-2013 and OTB-100, and the results are shown in Table 3 and Fig. 6. The improvement of Siam-BM (mask only) with respect to SA-Siam demonstrates that the simple spatial masking mechanism is indeed effective.

Table 2. Comparison between training and testing choices with or without spatial mask.

Training	Testing		
	Mediocre object	Elongated object	
	No mask	w/mask	w/o mask
w/mask	0.681 (1)	0.654 (3)	0.581 (5)
w/o mask	0.665 (2)	0.644 (4)	0.609 (6)

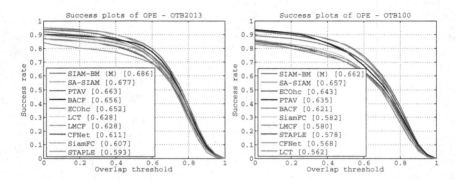

Fig. 6. Comparing SiamBM (Mask only) with other high performance and real-time trackers

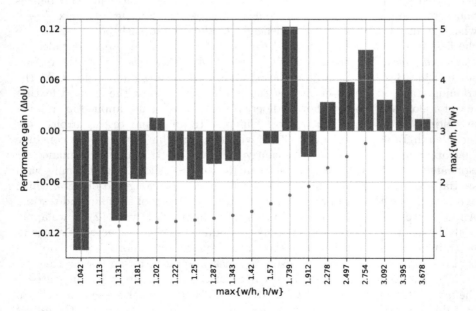

Fig. 7. Performance gain of feature masking is positively correlated with the deviation of aspect ratio from 1.

Figure 7 shows the relationship between the object aspect ratio and the performance gain of spatial masking. Consistent with our observation, when the aspect ratio is far apart from 1, doing spatial masking is helpful. However, when the object is a mediocre one, masking the features is harmful. In general, the performance gain of feature masking is positively correlated with the deviation of aspect ratio from 1.

Table 3. Comparing SiamBM (mask only) with other high performance and real-time trackers

Trackers	OTB2013		OTB100		FPS
	AUC	Prec.	AUC	Prec.	
ECOhc [3]	0.652	0.874	0.643	0.856	60
BACF [16]	0.656	0.859	0.621	0.822	35
PTAV [9]	0.663	0.895	0.635	0.849	25
SA-Siam [12] (baseline)	0.677	0.896	0.657	0.865	50
Siam-BM (mask only)	**0.686**	**0.898**	**0.662**	**0.864**	48

Siam-BM: Finally, we show in Table 4 how the performance of Siam-BM is gradually improved with our proposed mechanisms. The EAO of the full-fledged Siam-BM reaches 0.335 on VOT2017, which is a huge improvement from 0.287 achieved by SA-Siam. Of course, as we add more mechanisms in Siam-BM, the tracking speed also drops, but the full-fledged Siam-BM still runs in realtime.

Table 4. Analysis of our tracker Siam-BM on the VOT2017. The impact of progressively integrating one contribution at a time is depicted.

	Baseline SA-Siam $\Longrightarrow$	Angle Estimation $\Longrightarrow$	Spatial Mask $\Longrightarrow$	Template Updating
EAO	0.287	0.301	0.322	**0.335**
Accuracy	0.529	0.544	0.551	**0.563**
Robustness	1.234	1.305	1.07	**0.977**
FPS	50	35	34	32

4.4   Comparison with the State-of-the-Art Trackers

We evaluate our tracker in VOT2017 main challenge and realtime subchallenge. The final model in this paper combines all components mentioned in previous section. We do not evaluate the final model in OTB because the groundtruth labeling in OTB is always upright bounding boxes and applying rotation does not produce a higher IoU even when the tracked bounding box is more precise and tight.

As shown in Fig. 8, our Siam-BM tracker is among the best trackers even when non-realtime trackers are considered. From Fig. 9, we can see that Siam-BM outperforms all realtime trackers in VOT2017 challenge by a large margin. The Accuracy-Robustness plot in Fig. 10 also shows the superiority of our tracker.

We also compare the EAO value of our tracker with some of the latest trackers. RASNet [26] achieves an EAO number of 0.281 in the main challenge and 0.223 in the realtime subchallenge. SiamRPN [18] achieves an EAO number of 0.243 in the realtime subchallenge. The EAO number achieved by Siam-BM is much higher.

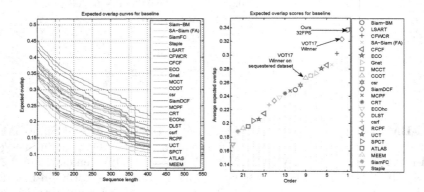

Fig. 8. EAO curves and rank in VOT17 main challenge. FA represents Free Angle here.

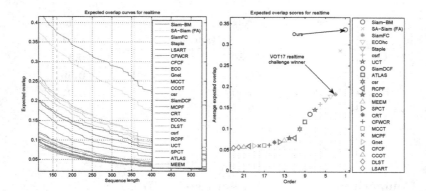

Fig. 9. EAO curves and rank in VOT17 realtime challenge. FA represents Free Angle here.

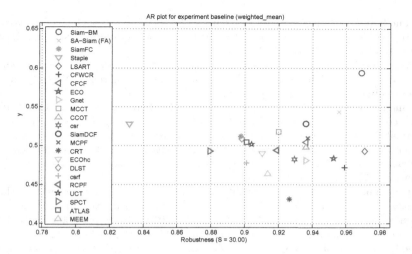

Fig. 10. Accuracy and robustness plots in VOT17 main challenge. Best trackers are closer to the topright corner. FA represents Free Angle here.

5 Conclusion

In this paper, we have designed a SiamFC-based visual object tracker named Siam-BM. The design goal is to achieve a better match between feature maps of the same object from different frames. In order to keep the realtime capability of the tracker, we propose to use low-overhead mechanisms, including parallel scale and angle estimation, fixed spatial mask and moving average template updating. The proposed Siam-BM tracker outperforms state-of-the-art realtime trackers by a large margin on the VOT2017 benchmark. It is even comparable to the best non-realtime trackers. In the future, we will investigate the adaptation of object aspect ratio during tracking.

Acknowledgement. This work was supported in part by National Key Research and Development Program of China 2017YFB1002203, NSFC No. 61572451, No. 61390514, and No. 61632019, Youth Innovation Promotion Association CAS CX2100060016, and Fok Ying Tung Education Foundation WF2100060004.

References

1. Abadi, M., et al.: Tensorflow: large-scale machine learning on heterogeneous distributed systems. arXiv preprint arXiv:1603.04467 (2016)
2. Bertinetto, L., Valmadre, J., Henriques, J.F., Vedaldi, A., Torr, P.H.S.: Fully-convolutional siamese networks for object tracking. In: Hua, G., Jégou, H. (eds.) ECCV 2016. LNCS, vol. 9914, pp. 850–865. Springer, Cham (2016). https://doi.org/10.1007/978-3-319-48881-3_56

3. Danelljan, M., Bhat, G., Shahbaz Khan, F., Felsberg, M.: Eco: efficient convolution operators for tracking. In: The IEEE Conference on Computer Vision and Pattern Recognition (CVPR), July 2017

4. Danelljan, M., Häger, G., Khan, F., Felsberg, M.: Accurate scale estimation for robust visual tracking. In: British Machine Vision Conference, Nottingham, 1–5 September 2014. BMVA Press (2014)

5. Danelljan, M., Hager, G., Shahbaz Khan, F., Felsberg, M.: Convolutional features for correlation filter based visual tracking. In: Proceedings of the IEEE International Conference on Computer Vision Workshops, pp. 58–66 (2015)

6. Danelljan, M., Hager, G., Shahbaz Khan, F., Felsberg, M.: Learning spatially regularized correlation filters for visual tracking. In: Proceedings of the IEEE International Conference on Computer Vision, pp. 4310–4318 (2015)

7. Danelljan, M., Robinson, A., Shahbaz Khan, F., Felsberg, M.: Beyond correlation filters: learning continuous convolution operators for visual tracking. In: Leibe, B., Matas, J., Sebe, N., Welling, M. (eds.) ECCV 2016. LNCS, vol. 9909, pp. 472–488. Springer, Cham (2016). https://doi.org/10.1007/978-3-319-46454-1_29

8. Dong, X., Shen, J., Wang, W., Liu, Y., Shao, L., Porikli, F.: Hyperparameter optimization for tracking with continuous deep q-learning. In: The IEEE Conference on Computer Vision and Pattern Recognition (CVPR), June 2018

9. Fan, H., Ling, H.: Parallel tracking and verifying: a framework for real-time and high accuracy visual tracking. In: The IEEE International Conference on Computer Vision (ICCV), October 2017

10. Guo, Q., Feng, W., Zhou, C., Huang, R., Wan, L., Wang, S.: Learning dynamic siamese network for visual object tracking. In: The IEEE International Conference on Computer Vision (ICCV), October 2017

11. Han, B., Sim, J., Adam, H.: Branchout: regularization for online ensemble tracking with convolutional neural networks. In: The IEEE Conference on Computer Vision and Pattern Recognition (CVPR), July 2017

12. He, A., Luo, C., Tian, X., Zeng, W.: A twofold siamese network for real-time object tracking. In: The IEEE Conference on Computer Vision and Pattern Recognition (CVPR), June 2018

13. Held, D., Thrun, S., Savarese, S.: Learning to track at 100 FPS with deep regression networks. In: Leibe, B., Matas, J., Sebe, N., Welling, M. (eds.) ECCV 2016. LNCS, vol. 9905, pp. 749–765. Springer, Cham (2016). https://doi.org/10.1007/978-3-319-46448-0_45

14. Huang, C., Lucey, S., Ramanan, D.: Learning policies for adaptive tracking with deep feature cascades. In: The IEEE International Conference on Computer Vision (ICCV), October 2017

15. Jaderberg, M., Simonyan, K., Zisserman, A., et al.: Spatial transformer networks. In: Advances in Neural Information Processing Systems, pp. 2017–2025 (2015)

16. Kiani Galoogahi, H., Fagg, A., Lucey, S.: Learning background-aware correlation filters for visual tracking. In: The IEEE International Conference on Computer Vision (ICCV), October 2017

17. Kristan, M., et al.: The visual object tracking vot2015 challenge results. In: Proceedings of the IEEE International Conference on Computer Vision Workshops (2017)

18. Li, B., Yan, J., Wu, W., Zhu, Z., Hu, X.: High performance visual tracking with siamese region proposal network. In: The IEEE Conference on Computer Vision and Pattern Recognition (CVPR), June 2018

19. Li, Y., Zhu, J.: A scale adaptive kernel correlation filter tracker with feature integration. In: Agapito, L., Bronstein, M.M., Rother, C. (eds.) ECCV 2014. LNCS, vol. 8926, pp. 254–265. Springer, Cham (2015). https://doi.org/10.1007/978-3-319-16181-5_18
20. Lukezic, A., Vojir, T., Cehovin Zajc, L., Matas, J., Kristan, M.: Discriminative correlation filter with channel and spatial reliability. In: The IEEE Conference on Computer Vision and Pattern Recognition (CVPR), July 2017
21. Ma, C., Huang, J.B., Yang, X., Yang, M.H.: Hierarchical convolutional features for visual tracking. In: Proceedings of the IEEE International Conference on Computer Vision, pp. 3074–3082 (2015)
22. Nam, H., Han, B.: Learning multi-domain convolutional neural networks for visual tracking. In: Proceedings of the IEEE Conference on Computer Vision and Pattern Recognition, pp. 4293–4302 (2016)
23. Shen, X., Tian, X., He, A., Sun, S., Tao, D.: Transform-invariant convolutional neural networks for image classification and search. In: Proceedings of the 2016 ACM on Multimedia Conference, pp. 1345–1354. ACM (2016)
24. Tao, R., Gavves, E., Smeulders, A.W.: Siamese instance search for tracking. In: Proceedings of the IEEE Conference on Computer Vision and Pattern Recognition, pp. 1420–1429 (2016)
25. Wang, Q., Gao, J., Xing, J., Zhang, M., Hu, W.: DCFNet: discriminant correlation filters network for visual tracking. arXiv preprint arXiv:1704.04057 (2017)
26. Wang, Q., Teng, Z., Xing, J., Gao, J., Hu, W., Maybank, S.: Learning attentions: residual attentional siamese network for high performance online visual tracking. In: The IEEE Conference on Computer Vision and Pattern Recognition (CVPR), June 2018
27. Wu, Y., Lim, J., Yang, M.H.: Online object tracking: a benchmark. In: Proceedings of the IEEE Conference on Computer Vision and Pattern Recognition, pp. 2411–2418 (2013)
28. Wu, Y., Lim, J., Yang, M.H.: Object tracking benchmark. IEEE Trans. Pattern Anal. Mach. Intell. 37(9), 1834–1848 (2015)
29. Xu, H., Gao, Y., Yu, F., Darrell, T.: End-to-end learning of driving models from large-scale video datasets. In: The IEEE Conference on Computer Vision and Pattern Recognition (CVPR), July 2017
30. Yang, T., Chan, A.B.: Recurrent filter learning for visual tracking. In: The IEEE International Conference on Computer Vision (ICCV), October 2017
31. Zhang, M., Xing, J., Gao, J., Shi, X., Wang, Q., Hu, W.: Joint scale-spatial correlation tracking with adaptive rotation estimation. In: Proceedings of the IEEE International Conference on Computer Vision Workshops, pp. 32–40 (2015)
32. Zhou, Y., Ye, Q., Qiu, Q., Jiao, J.: Oriented response networks. In: 2017 IEEE Conference on Computer Vision and Pattern Recognition (CVPR), pp. 4961–4970. IEEE (2017)

How to Make an RGBD Tracker?

Uğur Kart[1]([✉])[iD], Joni-Kristian Kämäräinen[1][iD], and Jiří Matas[2][iD]

[1] Laboratory of Signal Processing, Tampere University of Technology,
Tampere, Finland
{ugur.kart,joni.kamarainen}@tut.fi
[2] The Center for Machine Perception, Czech Technical University,
Prague, Czech Republic
matas@cmp.felk.cvut.cz

Abstract. We propose a generic framework for converting an arbitrary short-term RGB tracker into an RGBD tracker. The proposed framework has two mild requirements − the short-term tracker provides a bounding box and its object model update can be stopped and resumed. The core of the framework is a depth augmented foreground segmentation which is formulated as an energy minimization problem solved by graph cuts. The proposed framework offers two levels of integration. The first requires that the RGB tracker can be stopped and resumed according to the decision on target visibility. The level-two integration requires that the tracker accept an external mask (foreground region) in the target update. We integrate in the proposed framework the Discriminative Correlation Filter (DCF), and three state-of-the-art trackers − Efficient Convolution Operators for Tracking (ECOhc, ECOgpu) and Discriminative Correlation Filter with Channel and Spatial Reliability (CSR-DCF). Comprehensive experiments on Princeton Tracking Benchmark (PTB) show that level-one integration provides significant improvements for all trackers: DCF average rank improves from 18th to 17th, ECOgpu from 16th to 10th, ECOhc from 15th to 5th and CSR-DCF from 19th to 14th. CSR-DCF with level-two integration achieves the top rank by a clear margin on PTB. Our framework is particularly powerful in occlusion scenarios where it provides 13.5% average improvement and 26% for the best tracker (CSR-DCF).

Keywords: Visual object tracking · RGBD tracking

1 Introduction

Short-term visual object tracking has been an active research topic in computer vision due to its widespread application areas. In recent years, the community has witnessed rapid development and seen many successful trackers emerging thanks to standardized evaluation protocols and publicly available benchmarks and competitions [1–6]. In order to adapt to target appearance changes, short-term trackers update their tracking models over time. However, that makes them

© Springer Nature Switzerland AG 2019
L. Leal-Taixé and S. Roth (Eds.): ECCV 2018 Workshops, LNCS 11129, pp. 148–161, 2019.
https://doi.org/10.1007/978-3-030-11009-3_8

prone to model corruption and drifting in case of persistent occlusions when the tracker adapts to the occluding object and starts to track it.

To avoid corruption, a tracker should be able to discriminate between the target object and the rest of the scene so that it can stop model updating if the target is occluded. However, this is a challenging task in the RGB space if there are occluders with similar visual appearance. To alleviate this issue, adding the depth cue to short-term trackers is intuitive; even if a tracked object is occluded by another object with similar appearance, the difference in their depth levels will be distinctive and will help to detect the occlusion. The availability of affordable depth sensors makes adoption of the depth cue even more attractive.

Since the depth channel lacks texture, depth itself may not provide useful information for visual tracking. On the other hand, RGB trackers perform competitively as long as no occlusions occur (see Table 1). Therefore, our work aims at benefiting from the huge amount of effort that has been put on generic short-term RGB trackers and adopts depth as means for occlusion detection. As a novel solution, we propose a generic framework that can be used with any VOT compliant [6] short-term tracker to convert it into an RGBD tracker with depth-augmented occlusion detection. By applying the proposed framework through a clear interface and not changing the internal structure of a short-term tracker, a fast integration is ensured and the framework will benefit from ever improving short-term tracker performance in the future.

The proposed framework contains two main components: *short-term failure detection* and *recovery from occlusion*. Short-term failure detector continuously evaluates the target region to decide whether to allow the short-term tracker to update its model or switch to the recovery from occlusion mode. The framework also contains an optional, powerful third component which can be used with RGB trackers that accepts *foreground masks* that explicitly indicate occluded regions that do not belong to the target(*e.g.* CSR-DCF [7]).

The main contributions of this paper are:

- A generic framework to convert an arbitrary RGB short-term tracker into an RGBD tracker.
- Formulation of the framework's core component - *non-occluded foreground segmentation* - as an energy function of three terms, depth, color and spatial prior, which is optimized using graph cuts.
- RGBD versions of one baseline and three state-of-the-art short-term RGB trackers: DCF [8], ECO (ECOhc and ECOgpu variants) [9] and CSR-DCF [7]

The rest of the paper is organized as follows; Sect. 2 summarizes existing literature on generic, short-term tracking and RGBD trackers, Sect. 3 explains the proposed framework in detail, Sect. 4 provides the experiments and finally Sect. 5 concludes the paper.

2   Related Work

The aim of the provided generic framework is to convert any existing short-term RGB tracker into an RGBD tracker. We are motivated by the facts that the field

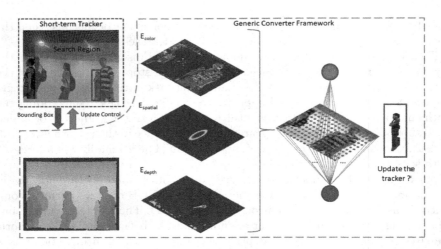

Fig. 1. Overview of the proposed framework. The short-term RGB tracker provides bounding box coordinates to the framework to be used for segmenting the visible target region with the help of depth. Using the ratio of the visible region to the bounding box, occlusions are detected hence, short-term tracker update is stopped and recovery mode is started. If the object is re-detected during recovery, the RGB tracker is resumed.

of short-term RGB tracking progresses on a steady basis and RGB provides a strong cue for tracking. On the other hand, we also believe that depth can be used as a complementary cue to instruct when a short-term tracker should be stopped and switched to recovery mode. In this sense, the proposed framework benefits from state-of-the-art short-term trackers which are briefly surveyed in addition to the recent RGBD trackers (Fig. 1).

RGB Trackers – generic, short-term visual object tracking on RGB videos is a well-established research topic in computer vision and the main approaches can be grouped under two main categories. In *Generative Trackers*, a target model is stored and the goal is to find the best matching region in the next frame. A few descriptive examples for this category are Incremental Visual Tracking (IVT) [10], Structural Sparse Tracking (SST) [11] and kernel-based object tracking [12]. On the other hand, *Discriminative Trackers* continuously train a classifier using positive and negative samples that are acquired during the tracking process. Prominent examples of this category are Tracking-Learning-Detection (TLD) [13], Continuous Convolutional Operators Tracking (CCOT) [14], Multi-Domain Convolutional Neural Networks (MDNet) [15], Efficient Convolution Operators for Trackers (ECO) [9], and Discriminative Correlation Filter with Channel and Spatial Reliability (CSR-DCF) [7]. Due to their success in the last few years, discriminative trackers have been widely adopted in the recent works. For example, in the VOT 2017 challenge, 67% of the submissions were from this category [6]. However, training a classifier can be computationally expensive which has prompted the adoption of simple yet powerful methods for the training stage. Starting with the seminal work of Bolme *et al.* [16], Discriminative Correlation Filter (DCF) based trackers have gained momentum due to their performance, fast model update (training) and mathematical elegance. Henriques *et al.* [17] proposed a method for efficient training of multiple samples that improves performance while providing very high FPS. To suppress the border artefacts resulting from circular correlation, Galoogahi *et al.* [8] posed the DCF learning as a more complex optimization problem which can still be efficiently solved with the help of the Augmented Lagrangian Method (ALM). Lukezic *et al.* [7] further improved their idea by introducing spatial reliability maps to extract unpolluted foreground masks. In VOT 2017, DCF based algorithms constitute almost 50% of the submitted trackers [6] with ECO [9] and CSR-DCF [7] being among the top performers while CSR-DCF C++ implementation won the best real-time tracker award.

RGBD Trackers – as compared to generic, short-term tracking on RGB, RGBD tracking is a relatively unexplored area. This can be partly attributed to the lack of datasets with groundtruths until recently. Song *et al.* [18] captured and annotated a dataset consisting of 100 videos with an online evaluation system and their benchmark is still the largest available. They also provided multiple baseline algorithms under two main categories; *depth as an additional cue* and *point cloud tracking.* Depth as an additional cue trackers treat depth as an extra channel to HOG features [19] whereas point cloud tracking methods use 3D point clouds for generating 3D bounding boxes. Among the ten proposed variations the one with RGBD HOG features and boosted by optical flow and occlusion detector achieved the best performance.

The seminal work of Song *et al.* inspired many followups. Meshgi *et al.* [20] proposed an occlusion-aware particle filter based tracker that can handle persistent occlusions in a probabilistic manner. Bibi *et al.* [21] also used a particle filter framework with sparse parts for appearance modeling. In their model, each particle is a sparse, linear combination of 3D cuboids which stays fixed during the tracking. Without occlusion, they first make a coarse estimation of the target location using 2D optical flow and then sample particles over the rotation R and translation T spaces. Occlusion is detected by counting the number of points in the 3D cuboid representation. Success of the DCF approach naturally caught the attention in the RGBD community as well. To the best of our knowledge, the first DCF based RGBD tracker was proposed by Camplani *et al.* [22]. They first cluster the depth histogram and then apply a single Gaussian distribution to model the tracked object in the depth space. To extract the foreground object, they assume that the cluster with the smallest mean is the object. The second method using DCF was proposed by An *et al.* [23] where Kernelized Correlation Filters (KCF) are used in conjunction with depth based segmentation for target localization. Heuristic approaches were adopted for detecting whether an object is in the occlusion state or not.

Recently, Kart *et al.* [24] proposed an algorithm for using the depth as a means to generate masks for DCF updates. Although this work is in a similar spirit, our method differs from theirs in multiple, fundamental aspects; first of all, the authors incorporate neither color nor spatial cues for the mask creation. This results with the loss of very vital information sources. Especially in sequences where the target object and the occluding object have similar depth levels, it is very likely that the algorithm will not be able to discriminate in between even if they have different colors. Secondly, their foreground segmentation consists of a simple thresholding of depth probabilities which is an ad-hoc approach that requires careful fine tuning. Finally, the authors propose a brute force, full-frame grid search for recovering from the occlusion state whereas we propose to use the motion history of the target object to adaptively generate significantly smaller search areas to avoid redundant computational complexity.

3   RGBD Converter Framework

The proposed framework offers two levels of integration with the level-two being optional for trackers that can use a foreground mask in their model update. In the *level-one integration*, the framework continuously calculates the visibility state of a target object by casting the visibility problem as a pixel-wise foreground-background segmentation from multiple information sources: color, spatial proximity and depth. The segmentation result is the *foreground mask*. Without interfering with the internal structure of an RGB tracker, the framework uses the tracker output and bounding box to obtain a region of interest (ROI) for the segmentation step. If the ratio between the visible and occluded pixels is below a threshold, model updating of the RGB tracker is stopped and the framework goes into occlusion recovery mode. In the occlusion recovery mode, model update is stopped and the search region is continuously expanded around the last known location of the target. The search is performed by running the RGB tracker in a coarse-to-fine manner to find its maximum response r in the search region. The score is compared to the mean of last N valid responses (Sect. 3.4, Algorithm 1). Once the target is detected, RGB tracker updating resumes. The *level-two integration* is available for trackers that use foreground masks in their model update.

For foreground segmentation, we adopt the energy minimization formulation in [25]:

$$E(f) = E_{smooth}(f) + E_{data}(f) \tag{1}$$

The goal is to find a pixel-wise labeling f (foreground/background) that minimizes the energy. E_{smooth} represents smoothness prior that penalizes neighboring pixels being labeled differently and E_{data} represents the observed data based energy. For E_{smooth}, we adopt the efficient computation of smoothed priors in [26] and E_{data} we formulate as

$$E_{data}(f) = E_{color}(f) + E_{spatial}(f) + E_{depth}(f) \tag{2}$$

where E_{color} measures the likelihood of observed pixel color given the target color model, E_{depth} models target region's depth and finally $E_{spatial}$ the spatial prior which is driven by the tracker location in the current frame. At the core

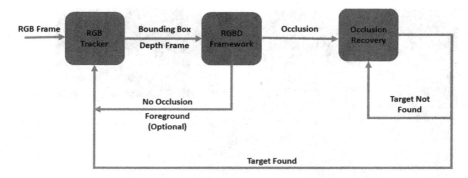

Fig. 2. The workflow diagram of the proposed framework. The framework uses bounding box coming from the RGB tracker and the depth frame to make a decision whether the target object is visible or not. In case it is visible, it allows the RGB tracker to update its model and continue tracking. If the target disappears, the framework runs the occlusion recovery module where the target object is searched using the last valid target model of the RGB tracker.

of our approach are proper formulations of E_{color} (Sect. 3.1), E_{depth} (Sect. 3.2) and $E_{spatial}$ (Sect. 3.3) so that the global optimum can be computed efficiently using the graph cuts algorithms [25, 27] (Fig. 2).

An example of the segmentation process is given in Fig. 3. As it can be seen, color based segmentation assigns both the target and the occluding object high confidence. However, the depth component is able to discriminate between the two while spatial component ensures high probability for the pixels that are close to the center of the tracking window.

3.1   Color-Based Target-Background Model E_{color}

In our formulation, E_{color} represents conditional dependencies between random variables (pixel fg/bg labels) for which we adopt a conditional random field formulation. The formulation uses the foreground/background probabilities as

$$E_{color} = \sum_{i \in \mathcal{V}} \psi_i(x_i) \tag{3}$$

where i is a graph vertex index (pixel) and x_i its corresponding label. ψ_i is encoded as a probability term

$$\begin{aligned}
\psi_i(x_i = 0) &= -\log\left(p(x_i \notin fg)\right) \\
\psi_i(x_i = 1) &= -\log\left(p(x_i \in fg)\right)
\end{aligned} \tag{4}$$

Since tracking is a temporal process, we need to add the frame number indicator to our notation $x_i \Rightarrow x_i^{(t)}$ where (t) is the current and $(t-1)$ the previous frame.

The probabilities $p(\cdot)$ can be efficiently computed using the color histograms of the foreground and background, h_f and h_b, respectively. It should be noted

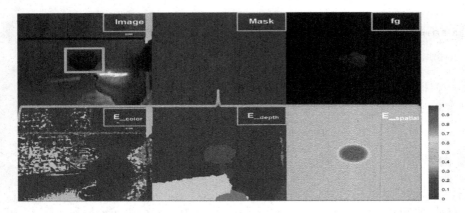

Fig. 3. Energy components in (2) and the segmentation output. The depth provides a strong cue even if the tracked and the occluding object have a very similar appearance.

that these histograms are updated after processing every frame for adapting to appearance changes. Therefore during processing frame t, the most recent color histograms are represented as h_f^{t-1} and h_b^{t-1}. Now, the color probability term is

$$p\left(x_i^t \in fg\right) = p\left(x_i^t = 1 \mid \mathrm{hsv}(x_i^t), h_f^{(t-1)}, h_b^{(t-1)}\right). \tag{5}$$

where the $hsv(\cdot)$ function returns the HSV color space value of the pixel corresponding the label x_i in the current frame. The histograms are computed in 3D using $8 \times 8 \times 8 = 512$ uniformly distributed bins.

3.2   Depth-Based Target-Background Model E_{depth}

We model the depth induced energy E_{depth} similar to color using depth histograms $\hat{h}_f$ and $\hat{h}_b$

$$p\left(x_i^t \in fg\right) = p\left(x_i^t = 1 \mid \mathrm{depth}(x_i^t), \hat{h}_f^{(t-1)}, \hat{h}_b^{(t-1)}\right) \tag{6}$$

where the depth probability is defined via the Bayesian rule (we use d to denote $\mathrm{depth}(x_i^{(t)})$ for more compact representation)

$$p\left(x_i^{(t)} = 1 \mid d, \hat{h}_f^{(t-1)}, \hat{h}_b^{(t-1)}\right) = \frac{p\left(x_i^{(t)} = 1 \mid d, \hat{h}_f^{(t-1)}\right)}{p\left(x_i^{(t)} = 1 \mid d, \hat{h}_f^{(t-1)}\right) + p\left(x_i^{(t)} = 0 \mid d, \hat{h}_b^{(t-1)}\right)} \tag{7}$$

The above depth histograms are computationally efficient, but strongly biased against unseen depth levels. To be more precise, since probabilities for previously seen depth levels are high, the current frame (t) pixels with the same depth levels are more likely to be assigned to the foreground and the model easily fails to introduce new depth levels. For tackling this problem, we add foreground and background distribution priors in the spirit of Bayesian estimation theory. For the foreground histogram estimation prior, we adopt the triangle function which has a maximum at the foreground depth mode (d denotes depth(x_i) for more compact notation and $|| \cdot ||$ is the length of the histogram)

$$\Psi_f(d) = tri(d) = \left(1 - \frac{|d - \text{mode}(\hat{h}_f^{(t-1)})|}{||\hat{h}_f^{(t-1)}||}\right) * \gamma \tag{8}$$

and for the background histogram estimation, we adopt the uniform distribution as a non-informative prior

$$\Psi_b(d) = \text{unif}(x_i) = \frac{1}{||\hat{h}_b^{(t-1)}||} * \theta \tag{9}$$

γ and θ are constants that control the prior gains. The choice of using a triangle distribution for foreground and uniform distribution for background stems from the following; in case of the foreground depth levels, it is expected that the newly seen depth levels will be similar to the current depth (e.g. a rotating object) and depth values in general are concentrated around the mode/mean. However, we cannot make any assumptions about the background and therefore we adopt the non-informative prior in (9).

To ensure continuous depth levels while not compromising from quick updates, we propose to apply a smoothening filter $g^t(d)$ to the observed histogram in the updating stage where $g^t(d)$ is a single Gaussian function centered at the histogram mode. By suppressing depth values that are highly unlikely to belong to the current observation, it provides a safety mechanism against wrong detections and drifting. Thus, the depth histogram updating process takes the following online update form:

$$\begin{aligned} \hat{h}_f^{(t)} &= \alpha \hat{h}_f^{(t-1)} + \left((1-\alpha)\hat{h}_f^{(t)}\right) \odot g^t(d) \\ \hat{h}_b^{(t)} &= \alpha \hat{h}_b^{(t-1)} + \left((1-\alpha)\hat{h}_b^{(t)}\right) \end{aligned} \tag{10}$$

3.3 Spatial Prior $E_{spatial}$

The third energy term in our model is a spatial prior that gives preference to foreground labels near the object center suggested by the short-term tracker;

$$p\left(x_i^t \in fg\right) = p\left(x_i^t = 1 \mid \boldsymbol{x}(x_i^t)\right) = k\left(\boldsymbol{x}(x_i^t); \sigma\right) \tag{11}$$

where $\boldsymbol{x}(\cdot)$ provides the spatial location (x,y) of the label x_i and $k(x;\sigma)$ is a clipped Epanechnikov kernel commonly used in kernel density estimation.

3.4   Occlusion Recovery

Given the energy terms E_{color}, E_{depth} and $E_{spatial}$, graph cut [25] provides labeling of each pixel in the tracker window by minimizing the energy. If the number of foreground pixels falls below a threshold τ, the tracker is stopped and recovery process started. To this end, we propose to use the trained RGB model M^t as an object detector since the depth information is no longer reliable, especially when the occlusion is persistent.

The proposed recovery strategy is based on three principles: (i) target object will be found again near the spatial location where it was previously seen, (ii) tracker response of a recovered object must be similar (proportional by Ω) to the previous tracked frames ($N = 30$ in our experiments), and (iii) each region must be expanded with a speed proportional to the object's average speed before the object was lost. By expanding the search region adaptively, computational redundancy of processing irrelevant spatial regions is avoided. Algorithm 1 summarizes the occlusion recovery process.

Algorithm 1. Occlusion Recovery

Require: Current frame I^t, response threshold constant Ω and target information
  before occlusion: $\{x_i, bb_i, r_i\}_{i=t-1,...,t-10}$ (centroid, bounding box and response)
  Initialization: $n = 0$ {# of frames in recovery mode}
  Compute target speed $S = \max\left(5, \sum_{i=t-10}^{t-1} ||x_i - x_{i-1}||\right)$
  while max response $r^n < \Omega * \text{mean}(r_i)$ **do**
    Expand $W^n = n * S + 2 * bb(1)$
    Expand $H^n = n * S + 2 * bb(2)$
    Extract patch $I^{W^n \times H^n} \subset I^t$ centered at x_{t-1}
    $n = n + 1$
    Find the tracker maximum response r^n in $I^{W^n \times H^n}$
    Move to the next frame $t + 1$
  end while
  Reset depth histograms: $\hat{h}_f^{(t)}$ and $\hat{h}_b^{(t)}$
  Resume tracking with the short-term RGB tracker

3.5   Target-Background Mask Extension for CSR-DCF

This section is related to the *level-two integration* explained in the beginning of Sect. 3 and as the example case we use the CSR-DCF tracker in [7]. Since the original idea of Discriminative Correlation Filter (DCF) for tracking [16,28], many improvements have been proposed. An efficient solution in the Fourier domain was proposed by Henriques *et al.* [29] and their work was followed by an important extension by Galoogahi *et al.* [8] who relaxed the assumption of circular symmetrical filters. These extensions were adopted in CSR-DCF [7] which constructs a reliability mask that is used to mask out background regions during tracker updates. Intuitively, the CSR mask can be replaced with the proposed foreground mask which is the output of graph cuts optimization (see Fig. 3 for an example mask). In our experiments, it turns out that this significantly improves the performance of CSR-DCF since the proposed depth-based mask avoids model pollution more effectively. The level-two integration of our framework to CSR-DCF is simple: CSR mask is replaced with the mask produced by minimizing (1).

4 Experiments

In this section, we present the results for various trackers augmented with the proposed framework. Four generic, short-term trackers due to their proven success and efficiency are chosen; DCF [8], ECO [9] and CSR-DCF [7]. Since ECO has two variants, we applied the proposed framework to both ECO-gpu (deep features) and ECO-hc (hand crafted features).

4.1 Experimental Setup

Implementation Details – All experiments were run on a single laptop using a non-optimized Matlab code with Intel Core i7 3.6 GHz and Ubuntu 16.04 OS. The parameters for the proposed algorithm were empirically set and kept constant during the experiments. Tracking parameters were as in the original works with the exception of DCF and CSR-DCF filter learning update rates were set to 0.03 and the number of bins for color histograms to 512. The rest of the parameters can be found in the publicly available code of our framework [32].

Dataset – For validating the proposed framework we conducted experiments on the Princeton Tracking Benchmark (PTB) [18]. The dataset consists of 95 evaluation sequences and 5 validation sequences from 11 tracking categories, namely *human, animal, rigid, large, small, slow, fast, occlusion, no occlusion, passive motion* and *active motion*. The videos have been recorded with a standard Kinect 1.0 device and all frames annotated manually.

Evaluation Metrics – We use the metrics as they are provided by PTB [18].
However, the evaluation sequences do not contain publicly available ground truths except for the initial frame. To facilitate a fair comparison, Song *et al.* [18] also provide an online system where the resulting coordinates are uploaded for obtaining the final scores and ranking. The results of other methods in our paper were taken from the online system's website with the exception of DLST [23] who have not registered their methods. DLST scores were obtained from its paper. Bibi *et al.* [21] depth images are adopted in the experiments.

4.2 Comparison to State-of-the-Art

The results of the converted short-term trackers and the other top performing trackers on the PTB dataset are given in Table 1. Since the evaluation server did not allow multiple simultaneous submissions, we submitted each method separately and generated the leaderboard using the official protocol; methods were first ranked in each category and then the average rank was calculated.

Table 1. Comparison of short-term RGB and RGBD tracking methods on the Princeton Tracking Benchmark (PTB) [18]. DCF [8] and three state-of-the-art trackers were used within the framework – ECOgpu [9], ECOhc [9] and CSR-DCF [7]; their level-one RGBD extensions are denoted DCF-rgbd, ECO-rgbd and CSR-DCF-rgbd, the level-two CSR-DCF integration where the original RGB-based mask is replaced by the proposed foreground mask (Sect. 3.5) is denoted CSR-DCF-rgbd++. (The table shows results for the Princeton Benchmark as of June 15, 2018)

Method	Avg Rank	Human	Animal	Rigid	Large	Small	Slow	Fast	Occ.	No-Occ.	Passive	Active
⋆CSR-DCF-rgbd++	**3.64**	0.77(2)	0.65(5)	0.76(6)	0.75(4)	**0.73(1)**	0.80(3)	0.72(3)	0.70(3)	0.79(5)	0.79(5)	0.72(3)
OAPF [20]	5.27	0.64(14)	**0.85(1)**	0.77(4)	0.73(6)	0.73(2)	**0.85(1)**	0.68(8)	0.64(8)	**0.85(1)**	0.78(9)	0.71(4)
3D-T [21]	5.36	**0.81(1)**	0.64(7)	0.73(15)	**0.80(1)**	0.71(6)	0.75(8)	**0.75(1)**	**0.73(1)**	0.78(11)	0.79(6)	0.73(2)
RGBDOcc+OF [18]	5.55	0.74(5)	0.63(9)	0.78(2)	0.78(3)	0.70(7)	0.76(5)	0.72(4)	0.72(2)	0.75(17)	0.82(2)	0.70(5)
∘ECOhc-rgbd	6.18	0.70(7)	0.55(15)	**0.81(1)**	0.69(9)	0.72(4)	0.78(4)	0.68(7)	0.65(6)	0.79(6)	**0.83(1)**	0.66(8)
DSKCF-Shape [30]	6.64	0.71(6)	0.71(3)	0.74(11)	0.74(5)	0.70(8)	0.76(6)	0.70(6)	0.65(7)	0.81(4)	0.77(11)	0.70(6)
DLST [23]	6.73	0.77(3)	0.69(4)	0.73(16)	0.80(2)	0.70(9)	0.73(14)	0.74(2)	0.66(5)	0.85(2)	0.72(16)	**0.75(1)**
DM-DCF [24]	6.73	0.76(4)	0.58(12)	0.77(5)	0.72(8)	0.73(3)	0.75(10)	0.72(5)	0.69(4)	0.78(13)	0.82(3)	0.69(7)
DSKCF [22]	9.36	0.67(10)	0.61(10)	0.76(8)	0.69(10)	0.70(10)	0.75(9)	0.67(9)	0.63(9)	0.78(12)	0.79(7)	0.66(9)
∘ECOgpu-rgbd	9.82	0.66(11)	0.58(11)	0.76(7)	0.65(14)	0.71(5)	0.81(2)	0.64(14)	0.62(10)	0.77(14)	0.78(8)	0.65(12)
DSKCF-CPP [22]	10.36	0.65(12)	0.64(8)	0.74(12)	0.66(13)	0.69(12)	0.76(7)	0.65(13)	0.60(12)	0.79(7)	0.80(4)	0.64(14)
RGBD+OF [18]	11.36	0.64(15)	0.65(6)	0.75(9)	0.72(7)	0.65(17)	0.73(15)	0.66(10)	0.60(13)	0.79(8)	0.74(15)	0.66(10)
hiob [31]	11.64	0.53(19)	0.72(2)	0.78(3)	0.61(16)	0.70(11)	0.72(16)	0.64(15)	0.53(16)	0.85(3)	0.77(12)	0.62(15)
⋆CSR-DCF-rgbd	11.91	0.68(9)	0.57(13)	0.74(10)	0.68(11)	0.68(14)	0.74(12)	0.65(12)	0.62(11)	0.75(16)	0.77(10)	0.64(13)
∘ECOhc [9]	12.18	0.69(8)	0.56(14)	0.72(17)	0.67(12)	0.68(13)	0.74(11)	0.65(11)	0.59(14)	0.78(9)	0.74(14)	0.65(11)
∘ECOgpu [9]	15.36	0.58(16)	0.54(16)	0.73(13)	0.59(18)	0.65(15)	0.73(13)	0.58(17)	0.51(17)	0.78(10)	0.69(17)	0.60(17)
•DCF-rgbd	15.45	0.64(13)	0.54(17)	0.73(14)	0.65(15)	0.65(16)	0.71(17)	0.63(16)	0.59(15)	0.74(18)	0.76(13)	0.61(16)
•DCF [8]	18.09	0.56(17)	0.52(19)	0.66(18)	0.60(17)	0.59(19)	0.65(18)	0.57(18)	0.48(18)	0.74(19)	0.68(18)	0.56(18)
⋆CSR-DCF [7]	18.36	0.54(18)	0.53(18)	0.64(19)	0.56(19)	0.59(18)	0.61(19)	0.56(19)	0.44(19)	0.76(15)	0.64(19)	0.55(19)

The symbols •, ⋆, ⋄, and ∘ in Table 1 mark the trackers that our framework applied to. As it can be observed, the proposed method clearly has a big impact on overall rankings for all three trackers. Especially in sequences with occlusions, this impact becomes more visible. CSR-DCF improves 8 ranks, ECOgpu ranking sees 7 ranks improvement and ECOhc rank improves by 8. In terms of accuracy, the improvement is as strong as in rankings. When the proposed framework (without foreground masked updates) is applied to CSR-DCF, its performance in occlusion sequences increases 18% while ECOhc grows by 6% and ECOgpu 11%. The level-two integration further boosts occlusion sequences accuracy for CSR-DCF to a total of 26%.

Unlike other top performing methods, CSR-DCF-rgbd++ also maintains a well-balanced performance over all the categories by staying among the top in every one. This suggests that it does not overfit to specific categories but it provides similar performance for different scenarios which makes it a very suitable candidate for real-life applications.

Figure 4 shows that the proposed framework adds to tracker's occlusion resilience to both short-term and long-term occlusions. For example, ECOhc-rgbd was able to detect the occlusion and it also re-detected the target object

Fig. 4. Short-term and long-term occlusion examples comparing the original methods (red) and their RGBD versions (green). Top row – DCF, second row – ECOgpu, third row – ECOhc, bottom row – CSR-DCF. (Color figure online)

when it reappeared in the scene instead of drifting due to model pollution. As a good example of long-term recovery example, CSR-DCF-rgbd++ was able to recover even after 35 frames of occlusion state since it avoided model corruption and expanded the search region gradually.

The reason why CSR-DCF-rgbd++ performs better than the other RGBD methods can be possibly explained by its masked DCF update mechanism which uses the foreground provided by the framework. In the discriminative tracking paradigm, the tracker's target model is updated over the time for coping with the visual changes. However, when a rectangular bounding box is used for this purpose, it is likely to include background and occluding object's pixels as well. This results with learning of irrelevant information that may cause drifting. Whereas in the masked update approach, the updates are done only using the pixels that are confidently belong to the target object. Thus, the target model stays uncorrupted which results with better performance.

5   Conclusions

A generic framework was proposed for converting existing short-term RGB trackers into RGBD trackers. The framework is easy to adopt as it only requires control of model updating (stop/resume) and a tracking bounding box which are both provided in any tracker that is VOT compliant [6]. At the core of the framework is a foreground model which uses depth, color and spatial cues to efficiently detect occluded regions which are utilized at two-levels: occlusion detection and optionally, masked tracker updates. In all experiments, existing RGB trackers improved their ranks in the publicly available Princeton tracking benchmark [18]. CSR-DCF tracker which allows level-two integration of the proposed foreground model achieved state-of-the-art accuracy and was ranked the best on the day of submission. The full source code of the framework is publicly available [32].

Acknowledgements. Uğur Kart was supported by two projects: Business Finland Project "360 Video Intelligence - For Research Benefit" with Nokia, Lynx, JJ-Net, BigHill, Leonidas and Business Finland - FiDiPro Project "Pocket - Sized Big Visual Data". Jiří Matas was supported by the OP VVV MEYS project CZ.02.1.01/0.0/0.0/16_019/ 0000765 "Research Center for Informatics".

References

1. Wu, Y., Lim, J., Yang, M.H.: Online object tracking: a benchmark. In: CVPR (2013)
2. Kristan, M., Pflugfelder, R., Leonardis, A., Matas, J., Porikli, F., et al.: The visual object tracking VOT2013 challenge results. In: CVPR Workshops (2013)
3. Kristan, M., et al.: The visual object tracking VOT2014 challenge results. In: Agapito, L., Bronstein, M.M., Rother, C. (eds.) ECCV 2014. LNCS, vol. 8926, pp. 191–217. Springer, Cham (2015). https://doi.org/10.1007/978-3-319-16181-5_14
4. Kristan, M., Matas, J., Leonardis, A., Felsberg, M., Cehovin, L., et al.: The visual object tracking VOT2015 challenge results. In: ICCV Workshops (2015)
5. Kristan, M., et al.: The visual object tracking VOT2016 challenge results. In: Hua, G., Jégou, H. (eds.) ECCV 2016. LNCS, vol. 9914, pp. 777–823. Springer, Cham (2016). https://doi.org/10.1007/978-3-319-48881-3_54
6. Kristan, M., Leonardis, A., Matas, J., Felsberg, M., Pflugfelder, R., et al.: The visual object tracking VOT2017 challenge results. In: ICCV Workshops (2017)
7. Lukezic, A., Vojir, T., Cehovin, L., Matas, J., Kristan, M.: Discriminative correlation filter with channel and spatial reliability. In: CVPR (2017)
8. Galoogahi, H., Sim, T., Lucey, S.: Correlation filters with limited boundaries. In: CVPR (2015)
9. Danelljan, M., Bhat, G., Shahbaz Khan, F., Felsberg, M.: ECO: efficient convolution operators for tracking. In: CVPR (2017)
10. Ross, D.A., Lim, J., Lin, R.S., Yang, M.H.: Incremental visual tracking. Int. J. Comput. Vis. (IJCV) **77**, 125–141 (2008)
11. Zhang, T., et al.: Structural sparse tracking. In: CVPR (2015)
12. Comaniciu, D., Ramesh, V., Meer, P.: Kernel-based object tracking. IEEE PAMI **25**, 564–567 (2003)
13. Kalal, Z., Mikolajczyk, K., Matas, J.: Tracking-learning-detection. IEEE PAMI **34**, 1409–1422 (2011)

14. Danelljan, M., Robinson, A., Shahbaz Khan, F., Felsberg, M.: Beyond correlation filters: learning continuous convolution operators for visual tracking. In: Leibe, B., Matas, J., Sebe, N., Welling, M. (eds.) ECCV 2016. LNCS, vol. 9909, pp. 472–488. Springer, Cham (2016). https://doi.org/10.1007/978-3-319-46454-1_29
15. Nam, H., Han, B.: Learning multi-domain convolutional neural networks for visual tracking. In: CVPR (2016)
16. Bolme, D.S., Beveridge, J., Draper, B.A., Lui, Y.M.: Visual object tracking using adaptive correlation filters. In: CVPR (2010)
17. Henriques, J., Caseiro, R., Martins, P., Batista, J.: High-speed tracking with kernelized correlation filters. IEEE PAMI **37**, 1–14 (2014)
18. Song, S., Xiao, J.: Tracking revisited using RGBD camera: unified benchmark and baselines. In: ICCV (2013)
19. Dalal, N., Triggs, B.: Histograms of oriented gradients for human detection. In: CVPR (2005)
20. Meshgi, K., Maeda, S.I., Oba, S., Skibbe, H., Li, Y.Z., Ishii, S.: An occlusion-aware particle filter tracker to handle complex and persistent occlusions. CVIU **150**, 81–94 (2016)
21. Bibi, A., Zhang, T., Ghanem, B.: 3D part-based sparse tracker with automatic synchronization and registration. In: CVPR (2016)
22. Camplani, M., et al.: Real-time RGB-D tracking with depth scaling kernelised correlation filters and occlusion handling. In: BMVC (2015)
23. An, N., Zhao, X.G., Hou, Z.G.: Online RGB-D tracking via detection-learning-segmentation. In: ICPR (2016)
24. Kart, U., Kämäräinen, J.K., Matas, J., Fan, L., Cricri, F.: Depth masked discriminative correlation filter. In: ICPR (2018)
25. Boykov, Y., Veksler, O., Zabih, R.: Fast approximate energy minimization via graph cuts. IEEE PAMI **23**(11), 1222–1239 (2001)
26. Diplaros, A., Vlassis, N., Gevers, T.: A spatially constrained generative model and an EM algorithm for image segmentation. IEEE Trans. Neural Netw. **18**(3), 798–808 (2007)
27. Rother, C., Kolmogorov, V., Blake, A.: GrabCut interactive foreground extraction using iterated graph cuts. In: SIGGRAPH (2004)
28. Hester, C., Casasent, D.: Multivariant technique for multiclass pattern recognition. Appl. Optics **19**, 1758–1761 (1980)
29. Henriques, J.F., Caseiro, R., Martins, P., Batista, J.: Exploiting the circulant structure of tracking-by-detection with kernels. In: Fitzgibbon, A., Lazebnik, S., Perona, P., Sato, Y., Schmid, C. (eds.) ECCV 2012. LNCS, vol. 7575, pp. 702–715. Springer, Heidelberg (2012). https://doi.org/10.1007/978-3-642-33765-9_50
30. Hannuna, S., et al.: DS-KCF: a real-time tracker for RGB-D data. J. Real-Time Image Process. 1–20 (2016). https://link.springer.com/article/10.1007/s11554-016-0654-3
31. Springstübe, P., Heinrich, S., Wermter, S.: Continuous convolutional object tracking. In: ESANN (2018)
32. https://github.com/ugurkart/rgbdconverter

Learning a Robust Society of Tracking Parts Using Co-occurrence Constraints

Elena Burceanu[1,2,3(✉)] and Marius Leordeanu[1,2,4]

[1] Bitdefender, Bucharest, Romania
eburceanu@bitdefender.com
[2] Institute of Mathematics of the Romanian Academy, Bucharest, Romania
[3] Mathematics and Computer Science, University of Bucharest, Bucharest, Romania
[4] Automatic Control and Computer Science, University Politehnica of Bucharest, Bucharest, Romania
marius.leordeanu@cs.pub.ro

Abstract. Object tracking is an essential problem in computer vision that has been researched for several decades. One of the main challenges in tracking is to adapt to object appearance changes over time and avoiding drifting to background clutter. We address this challenge by proposing a deep neural network composed of different parts, which functions as a society of tracking parts. They work in conjunction according to a certain policy and learn from each other in a robust manner, using co-occurrence constraints that ensure robust inference and learning. From a structural point of view, our network is composed of two main pathways. One pathway is more conservative. It carefully monitors a large set of simple tracker parts learned as linear filters over deep feature activation maps. It assigns the parts different roles. It promotes the reliable ones and removes the inconsistent ones. We learn these filters simultaneously in an efficient way, with a single closed-form formulation, for which we propose novel theoretical properties. The second pathway is more progressive. It is learned completely online and thus it is able to better model object appearance changes. In order to adapt in a robust manner, it is learned only on highly confident frames, which are decided using co-occurrences with the first pathway. Thus, our system has the full benefit of two main approaches in tracking. The larger set of simpler filter parts offers robustness, while the full deep network learned online provides adaptability to change. As shown in the experimental section, our approach achieves state of the art performance on the challenging VOT17 benchmark, outperforming the published methods both on the general EAO metric and in the number of fails, by a significant margin.

Keywords: Unsupervised tracking · Co-occurrences · Part-based tracker

Electronic supplementary material The online version of this chapter (https://doi.org/10.1007/978-3-030-11009-3_9) contains supplementary material, which is available to authorized users.

L. Leal-Taixé and S. Roth (Eds.): ECCV 2018 Workshops, LNCS 11129, pp. 162–178, 2019.
https://doi.org/10.1007/978-3-030-11009-3_9

1   Introduction

Object tracking is one of the first and most fundamental problems that has been addressed in computer vision. While it has attracted the interest of many researchers over several decades of computer vision, it is far from being solved [17,18,23,32,36]. The task is hard for many reasons. Difficulties could come from severe changes in object appearance, presence of background clutter and occlusions that might take place in the video. The only ground-truth knowledge given to the tracker is the bounding box of the object in the first frame. Thus, without knowing in advance the properties of the object being tracked, the tracking algorithm must learn them on the fly. It must adapt correctly and make sure it does not jump toward other objects in the background. That is why the possibility of drifting to the background poses on of the main challenges in tracking.

Our proposed model, at the conceptual level, is composed of a large group of different tracking parts, functioning like a society, each with different roles and powers over the final decisions. They learn from each other using certain co-occurrence rules and are monitored according to their reliability. The way they function together gives them robustness. From a structural point of view, they are all classifiers within a large deep neural network structure, composed of two pathways, namely the FilterParts and the ConvNetPart pathways (see Fig. 2). While the first insures robustness through the co-occurrence of a large number of smaller tracker parts, the second pathway insures the ability to adapt to subtle object changes. The ConvNetPart is fully trained online, end-to-end, and uses as ground-truth high confidence tracker responses that are decided together with the whole society of parts. We will refer to the frames of high confident tracker responses as Highly Confident Frames (HCFs). We provide more details in Sect. 3.2. Using as ground-truth only a small set of high precision points is also related to the recent work on unsupervised object discovery in video [14].

Our approach is based on two key insights. One is the organization of the whole tracker into a large group of different types of classifiers, simpler and more complex, at multiple scales and with different levels of depth, as part of a larger neural network structure, that make decisions together based on mutual agreements. The second idea is the usage of co-occurrence constraints as basis for ensuring robustness, both for online training of the overall tracker, as well as for frame by frame inference.

Relation to Prior Work: Existing trackers in the literature differ in terms of type of target region, appearance model, mathematical formulation and optimization. Objects can be represented by boxes, ellipses [19], superpixels [35] or blobs [13]. The appearance model can be described as one feature set over the region or as an array of features, one for each part of the target [12,20,30].

In recent years, trackers based on discriminative correlation filters (DCF), such as MOSSE [1] and KCF [16], achieved the best results on public benchmarks. Newer models like Staple [4], CCOT [9] and ECO [7] provide consistent improvements by adding to the DCF model different components, such as multi-channel feature maps and robust scale estimation [8,33]. CCOT, for instance, proposes to learn continuous convolution parameters by optimizing a function that results from transforming the original feature space into a continuous one and applying onto it the continuous convolutions. While learning the parameters continuously, provides adaptability to the tracker, overfitting to noise and drifting could pose a threat. To reduce overfitting, ECO comes with a generative model over training samples. Nevertheless, most recent tracking approaches still suffer from overfitting to background noise, which causes tracker failure.

A common approach for top trackers in the recent literature is to model object features with deep convolutional networks (CNNs). To address the issue of robustness against background noise in the case of online training of CNNs, the TCNN [26] algorithm, for example, maintains stability of appearance through a tree structure of CNNs. MLDF [17] uses discriminative multi-level deep features between foreground and background together with a Scale Prediction Network. Another approach, MDNET [27] is used as starting point for many CNN trackers. For instance, SSAT [17] uses segmentation to properly fit the bounding box and builds a separate model to detect whether the target in the frame is occluded or not. It uses this to consider frames for training the shape segmentation model.

Other line of object tracking research is the development of part-based models, which are more resistant to appearance changes and occlusions. Their multipart nature gives them robustness against noisy appearance changes in the video. In recent benchmarks however, they did not obtain the top results. For instance, in VOT16 [17] challenge, while the number of part-based trackers, such as DPCF [3], CMT [28], DPT [21], BDF [2], was relatively high (25%), the best one of the group, SHCT [11], is on the 14th place overall. SHCT [11] is a complex system using a graph structure of the object that models higher order dependencies between object parts, over time. As it is the case with deep networks, we believe complex systems are prone to overfitting to background noise without a high precision way of selecting their unsupervised online training frames.

Our proposed model combines the best of two worlds. On one hand it uses a powerful deep convolutional network trained on high confidence frames, in order to learn features that better capture and adapt to object appearance changes. On the other hand, it uses the power of a large group of simpler classifiers that are learned, monitored, added and replaced based on co-occurrence constraints. Our approach is validated by the very low failure rate of our tracker, relative to the competition on the VOT2017 and VOT16 benchmarks.

Our Main Contributions: (1) Our first contribution is the design of a tracker as a dual-pathway network, with FilterParts and ConvNetPart pathways working in complementary ways within a robust society of tracking parts. FilterParts is more robust to background noise and uses many different and relatively simple trackers learned on top of deep feature activation maps. ConvNetPart is better capable to learn object appearance and adapt to its changes. It employs a deep convolutional network that is learned end to end during tracking using unsupervised high confidence frames for ground-truth. (2) Our second contribution is that every decision made for learning and inference of the tracker is based on robust co-occurrence constraints. Through co-occurrences over time we learn which FilterParts classifiers are reliable or not. Thus we can change their roles and add new ones. Also, through co-occurrences between the vote maps of the two pathways, we decide which frames to choose for training the ConvNetPart path along the way. Last but not least, through co-occurrences we decide the next object center by creating a combined vote map from all reliable parts.

(3) Our third contribution addresses a theoretical point, in Sect. 3.1. We show that the efficient closed-form formulation for learning object parts simultaneously in a one sample vs. all fashion is equivalent to the more traditional, but less efficient, balanced one vs. all formulation.

2   Intuition and Motivation

A tracking model composed of many parts, with different degrees of complexity, could use the co-occurrences of their responses in order to monitor over time, which parts are reliable and which are not. This would provide **stability**. They could also be used to train the more complex ConvNetPart pathway only on high-confidence frames on which the two pathway responses strongly co-occur in the same region. Thus, they could provide **robust adaptability**. Last but not least, by taking in consideration only where sufficient parts votes co-occur for the object center, we could also achieve **robust frame to frame performance**. We discuss each aspect in turn, next:

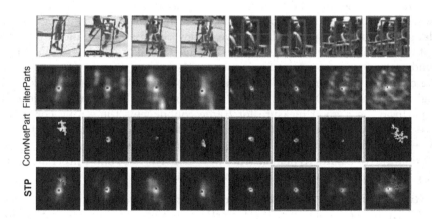

Fig. 1. Qualitative comparisons between FilterParts, ConvNetPart and the final (STP) voting maps. Often, in complicated scenarios, the ConvNetPart vote could be of better quality. There are also relatively simple cases where the ConvNetPart activation map look bad, and we need the stability of the FilterParts. The final vote map (STP), provides a more robust maximum. The blue point represent the center of the final vote. (Color figure online)

(1) Stability Through Steadiness: A part classifier is a discriminative patch detector (detailed in Sect. 3.1). We consider a part to be reliable if it has showed independently and frequently enough agreement in voting with the majority of the other parts - a statistically robust measure. A certain part is at the beginning monitored as a **candidate part**, and not used for deciding the next tracker move. It is only after a candidate part's vote for the object center co-occurred frequently enough at the same location with the majority vote, we promote the candidate to become a **reliable part**. From then on its vote will participate in the final vote map. Tracking parts that display consistent reliable behaviour over relatively long periods of time are promoted to the status of **gold members** - they will permanently have the right to vote, they cannot be downgraded and will not be monitored. In similar fashion, for the ConvNetPart, we always keep the tracker output from the first frames (=20) in video during the learning updates of the convolutional net. We further ensure robustness by favoring current tracker prediction to be close to the previous one. We use a tracker location uncertainty mask, centered around the previous center location.

(2) Robust Adaptation: the tracker is able to continuously adapt by adding candidate parts and removing unreliable ones. It also adapts by learning the ConvNetPart on high confidence frames accumulated over time. For object parts along the FilterParts pathway, gaining reliability, loosing it or becoming a gold member, can happen only over time. It is the temporal buffer, when tracking parts are monitored, which ensures both stability and the capacity to adapt to new conditions in a robust way. In time, the second pathway has access to a larger and larger set of reliable HCFs that are monitored through co-occurrences between the voted tracker centers of the two pathways. By training the net on larger sets of high quality frames we achieve both stability and capacity to adapt to true object appearance changes. As mentioned previously, HCFs used as ground-truth comes from past frames where the center given by the FilterParts alone co-occurred at the same location (within a very small distance) with the one given by the ConvNetPart. In Fig. 3 we show why the distance between the two pathways is a good measure for frame confidence - the strong correlation between the distance between the tracker and the ground-truth and the distance between the centers voted along the two pathways is evident. In Fig. 1 we also show qualitative results to demonstrate how ConvNetPart and FilterParts could better work together in conjunction, than separately.

(3) Robust Frame to Frame Tracking: Each part produces a prediction map for the object center. For the FilterParts pathway, an average vote map is obtained from all reliable parts. That map is then added to the ConvNetPart final vote map, with a strong weight given to the FilterParts pathway. This is the final object center map in which the peak is chosen as the next tracker location. It is thus only through the same strong **co-occurrences** of votes at a single location that we robustly estimate the next move.

3   The Tracker Structure, Function and Learning

Tracker Structure: At the structural level, the Society of Tracking Parts (STP) has two pathways: FilterParts and ConvNetPart (Fig. 2). The first pathway is formed of smaller object parts that are linear classifiers over activation maps, from a pre-learned convolutional net. The ConvNetPart pathway is a deep convolutional net, with the same structure as the first pathway up to a given depth. Now we present the actual CNNs structures of the two pathways:

The ConvNetPart is a fully convolutional network, where the first part (common as architecture with FilterParts features extractor) has 7 convolutional layers, with 3×3 filters (each followed by ReLU) and 2 maxpooling layers (2×2). It is inspired from the VGG architecture [31]. The second part, is composed of 4 convolutional layers with 3×3 filters, having the role to gradually reduce the number of channels and computing the segmentation mask for object center prediction. We could have tested with different, more recent architectures, but in our experiments this architecture was strong enough.

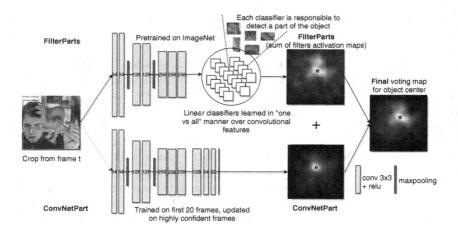

Fig. 2. STP overview: The tracker functions as a society of parts. It combines the vote for center maps from all parts over two main pathways, FilterParts and ConvNetPart. The two pathways are learned differently. The FilterParts classifiers once learned are fixed individually but adapt as a group. The ConvNetPart is trained end-to-end with back-propagation over unsupervised tracker outputs from previous highly confident frames (HCFs).

Tracking by Co-occurrences of Part Votes: The tracker always chooses as its next move at time t, the place (the center of the bounding box) l_{t+1} where there is the largest accumulation of votes in P_t, its final object center prediction map. For each filter part i, along the FilterParts pathway, there is an activation map F_{ti}, computed as the response of the classifier c_i corresponding to that part over the search region. The activation maps of filter parts are each shifted with the part displacement from object center and added together to form the overall F_t. When all filter parts are in strong agreement, all votes from F_t focus around a point. For the second pathway, the object center prediction map C_t is the output of the ConvNetPart network, given the same image crop input as to FilterParts. After smoothing F_t with a small Gaussian filter, it is added to C_t. The final prediction map P_t is then obtained by multiplying pixelwise the linear combination of C_t and F_t, with a center uncertainty mask M_c, around the center in the previous frame. M_c is a circular soft mask, with exponential decay in weights, as the distance from the previous center prediction increases. Thus, $P_t = (\alpha F_t + (1 - \alpha)C_t) \cdot M_c$, where $\cdot$ denotes pixelwise multiplication. M_c encourages small center movements at the expense of large, sharp, abrupt ones. The maximum in P_t is chosen as the next center location l_{t+1}.

3.1   Learning Along the FilterParts Pathway

STP chooses in the FilterParts update phase new parts to add as candidates. They are classifiers, of different sizes and locations, represented as linear filters over activation maps of deep features. To each part it corresponds a patch, within the tracker's main bounding box. Only patch classifiers that are highly discriminative from the rest are selected. One is considered discriminative if the ratio between the response on its own corresponding patch (the positive patch) and the maximum response over negatives is larger than a threshold t_d. Positive patches are selected from the inside of the bounding box, while (hard) negatives are selected as patches from outside regions with high density of edges. We sample patches from a dense grid (2 pixels stride) of 3 sizes. The small ones will see local appearance and the larger ones will contain some context. A point in grid is covered only by one selected discriminative patch, at one size. The smaller ones have priority and we search the next size for the patch centered in the grid point only if the smaller patch is not discriminative enough. The object box is completely covered when each pixel is covered by any given patch. A simple budgeting mechanism is added, in order to limit the speed impact. When too many parts of a certain patch size become reliable $> N_{max}$, we remove the new reliable ones which are most similar to older parts, based on simple dot product similarity for the corresponding classifiers.

Mathematical Formulation for Filter Parts Classifiers: We introduce the mathematical formulation for learning the part classifiers in FilterParts. For a given feature type let $\mathbf{d}_i \in \mathbb{R}^{1 \times k}$ be the i-th descriptor, with k real elements, corresponding to an patch window at a certain scale and location relative to the object bounding box. In our case, the descriptor $\mathbf{d}_i$ is a vector version of the specific patch concatenated over all activation map channels over the considered layers of depth in the FilterParts pathway. Our formulation is general and does not depend on a specific level of depth - features could as well be simple pixel values of any image channel. Let then $\mathbf{D}$ be the data matrix, formed by putting all descriptors in the image one row below the other.

We learn the optimal linear classifier $\mathbf{c}_i$ that separates $\mathbf{d}_i$ from the rest of the patches, according to a regularized linear least squares cost, which is both fast and accurate. Classifier $\mathbf{c}_i$ minimizes the following cost ([25] Chap. 7.5):

$$\min \frac{1}{n}\|\mathbf{D}\mathbf{c}_i - \mathbf{y}_i\|^2 + \lambda\mathbf{c}_i^\top\mathbf{c}_i. \tag{1}$$

In classification tasks the number of positives and negatives should be balanced, according to their prior distributions and the specific classifier used. Different proportions usually lead to different classifiers. In linear least squares formulations weighting differently the data samples could balance learning.

Learning with One Sample Versus All: The idea of training one classifier for a single positively labeled data sample has been successfully used before, for example, in the context of SVMs [24]. When using very few positive samples for training a ridge regression classifier, weighting is applied to balance the data. Here we show that it is possible, when a single positive sample is used, to obtain the same result with a single positive sample without weighting, as if balancing was applied. We show a novel result, that while the magnitude of the corresponding classifier vector is different for the single positive data sample case, its direction remains unchanged w.r.t. the balanced case.

Theorem 1. *For any positive weight w_i given to the positive i-th sample, when the negative labels considered are 0 and the positive label is 1 and all negatives have the same weight 1, the solution vector to the weighted least squares version of Eq. 1 will have the same direction and it might differ only in magnitude. In other words, it is invariant under L2 normalization.*

Proof. Let $\mathbf{c}_i$ be the solution to Eq. 1. At the optimum the gradient vanishes, thus the solution respects the following equality $(\mathbf{D}^\top\mathbf{D} + \lambda\mathbf{I}_k)\mathbf{c}_i = \mathbf{D}^\top\mathbf{y}_i$. Since $y_i(i) = 1$ and $y_i(j) = 0$ for $j \neq i$, it follows that $(\mathbf{D}^\top\mathbf{D} + \lambda\mathbf{I}_k)\mathbf{c}_i = \mathbf{d}_i$. Since the problem is convex, with a unique optimum, a point that obeys such an equality must be the solution. In the weighted case, a diagonal weight $n \times n$ matrix $\mathbf{W}$ is defined, with different weights on the diagonal $w_j = \mathbf{W}(j, j)$, one for each data sample. In that case, the objective cost optimization in Eq. 1 becomes:

$$\min \frac{1}{n}\|\mathbf{W}^{\frac{1}{2}}(\mathbf{D}\mathbf{c}_i - \mathbf{y}_i)\|^2 + \lambda\mathbf{c}_i^\top\mathbf{c}_i. \tag{2}$$

We consider when all negative samples have weight 1 and the positive one is given w_i. Now we show that for any w_i, if $\mathbf{c}_i$ is an optimum of Eq. 1 then there is a real number q such that $q\mathbf{c}_i$ is the solution of the weighted case. The scalar q exists if it satisfies $(\mathbf{D}^\top\mathbf{D} + \mathbf{d}_i\mathbf{d}_i^\top(w_i-1) + \lambda\mathbf{I}_k)q\mathbf{c}_i = w_i\mathbf{d}_i$. And, indeed, it can be verified that $q = \frac{w_i}{1+(w_i-1)(\mathbf{d}_i^\top\mathbf{c}_i)}$ satisfies the required equality. In the **supplementary material** we have provided a detailed proof.

Efficient Multi-class Filter Learning: The fact that the classifier vector direction is invariant under different weighting of the positive sample suggests that training with a single positive sample will provide a robust and stable separator. The classifier can be re-scaled to obtain values close to 1 for the positive samples. Theorem 1 also indicates that we could reliably compute filter classifiers for all positive patches in the bounding box at once, by using a single data matrix $\mathbf{D}$. We form the target output matrix $\mathbf{Y}$, with one target labels column $\mathbf{y}_i$ for each corresponding sample $\mathbf{d}_i$. Note that $\mathbf{Y}$ is, in fact, the $\mathbf{I}_n$ identity matrix. We now write the multi-class case of the ridge regression model and finally obtain the matrix of one versus all classifiers, with one column classifier for each tracking part: $\mathbf{C} = (D^\top D + \lambda \mathbf{I}_k)^{-1} \mathbf{D}^\top$. Note that $\mathbf{C}$ is a regularized pseudo-inverse of $\mathbf{D}$. $\mathbf{D}$ contains one patch descriptor per line. In our case, the descriptor length is larger than the number of positive and negative samples, so we use the Matrix Inversion Lemma [25](Chap. 14.4.3.2) and compute $\mathbf{C}$ in an equivalent form:

$$\mathbf{C} = \mathbf{D}^\top (\mathbf{D}\mathbf{D}^\top + \lambda \mathbf{I}_n)^{-1}. \tag{3}$$

Now the matrix to be inverted is significantly smaller ($n \times n$ instead of $k \times k$).

Reliability States: The reliability of a filter part i is estimated as the frequency f_i at which the maximum activation of a given part is in the neighborhood of the maximum in the final activation P_t where the next tracker center l_{t+1} is chosen. If a part is selected for the first time, it is considered a candidate part. Every U frames, the tracker measures the reliability of a given part, and promotes parts with a reliability larger than a threshold $f_i > p_+$, from candidate state (C) to reliable state (R) and from reliable (R) to gold (G). Parts that do not pass the test $f_i \leq p_-$ are removed, except for gold ones which are permanent.

3.2   Learning Along the ConvNetPart Pathway

The end output of the ConvNetPart pathway is an object center prediction map, of the same size as the one produced along the FilterParts pathway. Different from FilterParts, the second pathway has a deeper architecture and a stronger representation power, being trained end-to-end with back-propagation along the video sequence. First, we train this net for the first 20 frames, using as ground-truth the FilterParts center prediction (expected to be highly accurate). Afterwards, the ConvNetPart is considered to be reliable part and it will contribute, through its center prediction, to the final tracker prediction.

From then on, the ConvNetPart will be fine-tuned using as ground-truth the final tracker predictions on highly confident frames (HCFs). This will ensure that we keep the object appearance up to date, and we won't drift in cases of local occlusion or distractors. Results from Table 4 supports our decision.

Selecting Training Samples from Highly Confident Frames: We call HCF (Highly Confident Frame) a frame on which the distance between FilterParts and ConvNetPart votes for object center prediction is very small. When the two pathways vote almost on the same center location, we have high confidence that the vote is correct. In order to balance efficiently the number of updates with keeping track of object appearance changes, we do the following. First, we accumulate frames of high confidence and second, at regular intervals, we fine tune the network using the accumulated frames. The assumption we made is that on HCFs, our tracker is closer to ground-truth than in the other frames. This is confirmed in Fig. 3. 11% of all frames are HCFs. More extensive tests for validating HCF usefulness are described in Sect. 4.

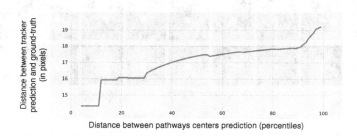

Fig. 3. The plot shows the expected distance to ground-truth for a given distance between the centers predicted by the two pathways. As seen, the correlation is strong and is therefore used for selecting in an unsupervised way high confidence frames. We choose HCFs from the first 11% percentile. (Color figure online)

Technical Details for Training the ConvNetPart: For each training frame, we use as input an image crop around the object (Fig. 4). The ground-truth is given as a segmentation map of the same size, with a circle stamp in the center. We increase robustness and generalization by randomly shifting the image along with its ground-truth - thus we also augment the data by providing two such randomly shifted pairs, per frame. We use the Adam optimizer (Pytorch [29]), with learning rate lr, at first for k epochs on the first $N(=20)$ frames, then on k epochs on each update, after each U frames. In the update step, we always use as samples the last N HCFs and the first N frames - thus we combine the new changes with the initial appearance. The training loss was $MSE = \frac{\sum(x_i - y_i)^2}{n}$. Note that we did not experiment with many architectures or loss functions, which might have further improve performance.

Parameters: we use the following parameters values in all our experiments from Sect. 4: $\alpha = 0.6$, $U = 10$ frames, $t_d = 1.4$, $p_+ = 0.2$, $p_- = 0.1$, $k = 10$ epochs, $N = 20$ frames, $lr = 1e - 5$ and $N_{max} = 200$ parts for each scale size.

4   Experimental Analysis

Results on VOT17 and VOT16 Benchmarks: We tested our tracker on the top visual object tracking benchmarks, VOT17 [18] and VOT16 [17]. VOT16 contains 60 video sequences, containing many difficult cases of occlusion, illumination change, motion change, size change and camera motion. The VOT17 dataset replaces sequences from VOT16 that were solved by most trackers with

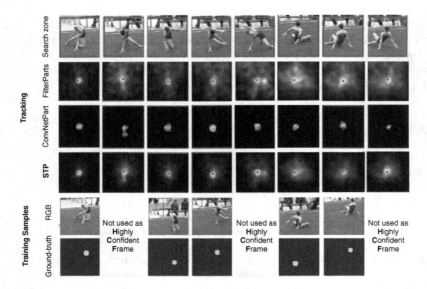

Fig. 4. The voting maps for FilterParts, ConvNetPart and the final (STP), respectively. We also show the qualitative view of training samples selection for ConvNetPart. Frame is not Highly Confident if pathways votes centers are distanced. Best seen in colors.

new and more difficult ones. For computing the final EAO evaluation score, VOT setup is re-initializing the tracker when it completely misses the target.

In Table 1 we present the results after running our tracker through the VOT toolkit. We compared our method against top published tracking methods: ECO [7], CCOT [9], CFWCR [15], Staple [4], ASMS [34], EBT [38], CCCT [6], CSRDCF [22], MCPF [37], ANT [5], some with reported results on both benchmarks. Our STP outperforms the current state of the art methods on VOT17, and is in the top three on VOT16. Note that we used the exact same set of parameters on all videos from both VOT17 and VOT16. What distinguishes our tracker the most from the rest is the much lower failure rate (R is 0.76 vs. second best 1.13, on VOT17). We think this is due to the robustness gained by the use of co-occurrence constraints in all aspects of learning and inference, and the dual-pathway structure, with each pathway having complementary advantages. In the **supplementary material** we present visual results of our tracker on VOT17 and comparisons on different challenging cases, as tagged by VOT evaluation. We are in top first or second on 4 out of 5 special cases, while being the first overall as shown in the Table 1. VOT16 [17] and VOT17 [18] identify occlusion as the most difficult case, on which we strongly outperform the others. Next we show how each design choice influenced the strong performance of our tracker.

Combining the FilterParts and ConvNetPart Pathways: In Table 2 we test the effect of combining the two pathways on the overall tracker. Each path-

Table 1. Top published trackers in terms of Expected Average Overlap (EAO), Robustness and Accuracy (R, R^* and A). We computed R in two ways: (1) R as initially computed by VOT and also reported by our main competitors, ECO [7] and CFWCR [15]; and (2) R^*, a more complex robustness metric, as currently computed in the VOT benchmark. Note that our tracker outperforms the published methods in terms of both robustness measures R, R^* on both VOT17 and VOT16 by a significant margin. We obtain the state of the art final EAO metric on VOT17 and the 3rd EAO score on VOT16. Our overlap score (A) is slightly lower as we did not explicitly learn object shape or mask. Note that we obtained these results with the exact same tracker and parameters for both VOT17 and VOT16. We will make our code available.

Tracker	Dataset							
	VOT17 [18]				VOT16 [17]			
	EAO	$R\downarrow$	$A\uparrow$	$R^*\downarrow$	EAO	$R\downarrow$	$A\uparrow$	$R^*\downarrow$
STP (ours)	0.309	0.76	0.44	0.206	0.361	0.47	0.48	0.140
CFWCR [15]	0.303	1.2	0.48	0.267	0.39	0.81	0.58	-
ECO [7]	0.28	1.13	0.48	0.276	0.374	0.72	0.54	0.200
CCOT [9]	0.267	1.31	0.49	0.318	0.331	0.85	0.52	0.238
Staple [4]	0.169	2.5	0.53	0.688	0.295	1.35	0.54	0.378
ASMS [34]	0.169	2.23	0.49	0.623	0.212	1.925	0.5	0.522
CCCT [6]	–	–	–	–	0.223	1.83	0.442	0.461
EBT [38]	–	–	–	–	0.291	0.9	0.44	0.252
CSRDCF [22]	0.256	1.368	0.491	0.356	–	–	–	–
MCPF [37]	0.248	1.548	0.510	0.427	–	–	–	–
ANT [5]	0.168	2.16	0.464	0.632	–	–	–	–

way is let by itself to guide the tracker. In the "FilterParts only" line, we have results where the first pathway becomes the tracker, with no influence from ConvNetPart ($\alpha = 1$). On the second we show the opposite case, when the tracker is influenced only by ConvNetPart ($\alpha = 0$). In that case the ConvNetPart is trained on the first 20 frames, then continuously updated on its own output, with no influence from the FilterParts pathway.

In general, the FilterParts pathway is more robust and resistant to drifting because it incorporates new information slower, after validating the candidates in time. It is also based on stronger pre-trained features on ImageNet [10]. It is more stable (lower failure rate) but less capable of learning about object appearance (lower accuracy, as IOU w.r.t ground-truth). The ConvNetPart pathway is deeper and more powerful, but as it is continuously trained on its own tracker output it is prone to overfitting to background noise, resulting in many failures.

When using both components, the two pathways work in conjunction and learn from each other using their outputs' co-occurrence constraints. The deeper pathway (ConvNetPart) is learning from the less flexible but more robust pathway (FilterParts). The numbers confirm our intuition and show that the two paths work in complementary, each bringing important value to the final tracker. The boost in performance after combining them is truly significant.

Table 2. In "FilterParts only" experiment, the second pathway is not used at all. In "ConvNetPart only" experiment, we use the FilterParts pathway only for the first 20 frames, to initialize the network, and not use it afterwards. In the absence of high confidence frames selection, the ConvNetPart is trained on each frame, using its own predictions as ground-truth.

Version	Dataset					
	VOT17			VOT16		
	EAO	$R \downarrow$	$A \uparrow$	EAO	$R \downarrow$	$A \uparrow$
FilterParts only	0.25	0.99	0.42	0.306	0.80	0.44
ConvNetPart only	0.205	2.09	0.43	0.265	1.53	0.46
Combined	**0.309**	**0.765**	**0.44**	**0.361**	**0.47**	**0.48**

Using Different Part Roles in FilterParts Pathway: In this case all filters have one single role. Instead of considering candidates, reliable and gold parts, which ensure stability over time, now all parts added over the sequence have the right to vote at any time. In Table 3 we see that the impact of multiple roles for filter parts, depending on their validation in time is high, bringing a 5% increase in terms of EAO, comparing to the basic one role for all version.

Table 3. Impact of different part roles used in FilterParts pathway. Considering roles based on parts credibility over time (candidate, reliable, gold), which is measured using spatial and temporal co-occurrences, is of great benefit to the tracker. It brings an advantage of 5% in EAO over the vanilla, "one role for all" case.

Version	Dataset					
	VOT17			VOT16		
	EAO	$R \downarrow$	$A \uparrow$	EAO	$R \downarrow$	$A \uparrow$
One role	0.262	0.99	0.44	0.31	0.715	0.47
All roles	**0.309**	**0.765**	**0.44**	**0.361**	**0.47**	**0.48**

Learning with Highly Confident Frames on ConvNetPart Pathway: In order to better appreciate the value of HCFs in training the ConvNetPart, we have tested it against the cases of training on all frames (all frames are good for training) and that of training only on the first 20 frames (no frame is good, except for the first 20 when the ConvNetPart is initialized). As we can see in Table 4, the "Full continuous update" regime on all frames is worst or at most similar in performance with "No update" at all. This shows that the model can overfit very quickly, immediately resulting in drifting (high failure rate). The idea to learn only from Highly Confident Frames is of solid value, bringing a 2% improvement in the final metric EAO, and a large cut off in failure rate. Even when we randomly select frames to be HCFs, of the same number as in the case of the true HCF measure, we again obtained the same drop of 2% in performance. These results, along with the statistical correlation between HCF and the ground-truth presented previously in Fig. 3 validate experimentally the value of considering only a smaller set of high precision frames for training, even when that set might be just a small portion of all high quality frames.

Speed: The "No update" version runs in realtime, at 30 fps on GTX TITAN X, for 600 filter parts. The performance of the "No update" compared to our best version, the "HCFs update", is only 2% lower, in terms of EAO, on both benchmarks, as presented in Table 4.

Table 4. Comparison in performance on VOT17 and VOT16, between updating the ConvNetPart only on Highly Confident Frames (HCF update), not updating it at all (No update), or updating it on every frame (Full update). We mention that in all our experiments we used the top 11% past frames, in confidence score, to perform training at a given time.

Version	Dataset					
	VOT17			VOT16		
	EAO	$R\downarrow$	$A\uparrow$	EAO	$R\downarrow$	$A\uparrow$
No update	0.28	0.95	0.43	0.34	0.7	**0.48**
Full update	0.284	0.92	**0.44**	0.327	0.66	0.46
HCFs update	**0.309**	**0.765**	**0.44**	**0.361**	**0.47**	**0.48**

Our top version, the "HCFs update", runs at 4 fps due to the updates of the ConvNetPart, which happen in 5% of the frames. The computational time needed by these updates depend on the GPU technology we use and is expected to drop in the near future as GPUs are getting faster. The top "HCFs update" can run at 30 fps if the updates and the tracking are done in parallel, such that when the ConvNetPart update is performed the "No update" version continues tracking. The performance of the parallel version drops by about 1%, situated between the top sequential "HCFs update" and the "No update" versions.

5   Conclusions

We proposed a deep neural network system for object tracking that functions as a society of tracking parts. Our tracker has two main deep pathways, one that is less flexible but more robust, and another that is less robust but more capable of adapting to complex changes in object appearance. Each part uses co-occurrences constraints in order to keep its robustness high over time, while allowing some degree of adaptability. The two pathways are also combined in a robust manner, by joining their vote maps and picking the locations where their votes co-occurred the most. From a technical point of view, the novelty aspects of our system include: **(1)** the way the classifiers in the FilterParts pathway are learned and ascribed different roles, depending on their degree of reliability. These roles relate to the idea of a society, where some parts are candidates that are being monitored, others are reliable voters, while those who proved their reliability long enough become gold members; **(2)** another novelty aspect represents the way we train the ConvNetPart on high confidence frames only, by selecting for training only those frames where the two different and complementary pathways agree; and **(3)** we provide a novel theoretical result, which proves that the efficient one sample vs. all strategy employed for learning in the FilterParts path, is stable - it basically gives the same classifier as in the balanced case. In experiments we provide solid validation of our design choices and show state of the art performance on VOT17 and top three on VOT16, while staying on top on both in terms of robustness (R and R^*, which measure the failure rate), by a significant margin.

Acknowledgements. This work was supported in part by UEFISCDI, under projects PN-III-P4-ID-ERC-2016-0007 and PN-III-P1-1.2-PCCDI-2017-0734.

References

1. Visual object tracking using adaptive correlation filters (2010). https://doi.org/10.1109/CVPR.2010.5539960
2. Agapito, L., Bronstein, M.M., Rother, C. (eds.): Computer Vision - ECCV 2014 Workshops - Zurich, Switzerland, September 6–7 and 12, 2014, Proceedings, Part II. LNCS, vol. 8926. Springer, Cham (2015). https://doi.org/10.1007/978-3-319-16181-5
3. Akin, O., Erdem, E., Erdem, A., Mikolajczyk, K.: Deformable part-based tracking by coupled global and local correlation filters. J. Vis. Commun. Image Represent. **38**, 763–774 (2016). https://doi.org/10.1016/j.jvcir.2016.04.018
4. Bertinetto, L., Valmadre, J., Golodetz, S., Miksik, O., Torr, P.H.S.: Staple: complementary learners for real-time tracking. In: 2016 IEEE Conference on Computer Vision and Pattern Recognition, CVPR 2016, Las Vegas, NV, USA, 27–30 June 2016 (2016). https://doi.org/10.1109/CVPR.2016.156
5. Cehovin, L., Leonardis, A., Kristan, M.: Robust visual tracking using template anchors. In: 2016 IEEE Winter Conference on Applications of Computer Vision, WACV 2016, Lake Placid, NY, USA, 7–10 March 2016 (2016). https://doi.org/10.1109/WACV.2016.7477570
6. Chen, D., Yuan, Z., Wu, Y., Zhang, G., Zheng, N.: Constructing adaptive complex cells for robust visual tracking. In: IEEE International Conference on Computer Vision, ICCV 2013, Sydney, Australia, 1–8 December 2013 (2013). https://doi.org/10.1109/ICCV.2013.142
7. Danelljan, M., Bhat, G., Khan, F.S., Felsberg, M.: ECO: efficient convolution operators for tracking. In: 2017 IEEE Conference on Computer Vision and Pattern Recognition, CVPR 2017, Honolulu, HI, USA, 21–26 July 2017 (2017). https://doi.org/10.1109/CVPR.2017.733

8. Danelljan, M., Häger, G., Khan, F.S., Felsberg, M.: Discriminative scale space tracking. IEEE Trans. Pattern Anal. Mach. Intell. **39**(8), 1561–1575 (2017). https://doi.org/10.1109/TPAMI.2016.2609928

9. Danelljan, M., Robinson, A., Shahbaz Khan, F., Felsberg, M.: Beyond correlation filters: learning continuous convolution operators for visual tracking. In: Leibe, B., Matas, J., Sebe, N., Welling, M. (eds.) ECCV 2016. LNCS, vol. 9909, pp. 472–488. Springer, Cham (2016). https://doi.org/10.1007/978-3-319-46454-1_29

10. Deng, J., Dong, W., Socher, R., Li, L.J., Li, K., Fei-Fei, L.: ImageNet: a large-scale hierarchical image database. In: CVPR (2009)

11. Du, D., Qi, H., Li, W., Wen, L., Huang, Q., Lyu, S.: Online deformable object tracking based on structure-aware hyper-graph. IEEE Trans. Image Process. **25**(8), 3572–3584 (2016). https://doi.org/10.1109/TIP.2016.2570556

12. Forsyth, D.A.: Object detection with discriminatively trained part-based models. IEEE Comput. **47**, 1–7 (2010)

13. Godec, M., Roth, P.M., Bischof, H.: Hough-based tracking of non-rigid objects. Comput. Vis. Image Underst. **117**, 1245–1256 (2011)

14. Haller, E., Leordeanu, M.: Unsupervised object segmentation in video by efficient selection of highly probable positive features. In: IEEE International Conference on Computer Vision, ICCV 2017, Venice, Italy, 22–29 October 2017 (2017). https://doi.org/10.1109/ICCV.2017.544

15. He, Z., Fan, Y., Zhuang, J., Dong, Y., Bai, H.: Correlation filters with weighted convolution responses. In: The IEEE International Conference on Computer Vision (ICCV) Workshops, October 2017

16. Henriques, J.F., Caseiro, R., Martins, P., Batista, J.: High-speed tracking with kernelized correlation filters. CoRR abs/1404.7584 (2014). http://arxiv.org/abs/1404.7584

17. Kristan, M., et al.: The visual object tracking VOT2016 challenge results. In: Hua, G., Jégou, H. (eds.) ECCV 2016. LNCS, vol. 9914, pp. 777–823. Springer, Cham (2016). https://doi.org/10.1007/978-3-319-48881-3_54

18. Kristan, M., et al.: The visual object tracking vot2017 challenge results. In: The IEEE International Conference on Computer Vision (ICCV) Workshops, October 2017

19. Kuo, C.H., Nevatia, R.: How does person identity recognition help multi-person tracking? In: CVPR (2011)

20. Kwon, J., Lee, K.M.: Tracking of a non-rigid object via patch-based dynamic appearance modeling and adaptive basin hopping Monte Carlo sampling. In: 2009 IEEE Computer Society Conference on Computer Vision and Pattern Recognition (CVPR 2009), 20–25 June 2009, Miami, Florida, USA (2009). https://doi.org/10.1109/CVPRW.2009.5206502

21. Lukezic, A., Cehovin, L., Kristan, M.: Deformable parts correlation filters for robust visual tracking. CoRR abs/1605.03720 (2016). http://arxiv.org/abs/1605.03720

22. Lukezic, A., Vojir, T., Zajc, L.C., Matas, J., Kristan, M.: Discriminative correlation filter with channel and spatial reliability. In: 2017 IEEE Conference on Computer Vision and Pattern Recognition, CVPR 2017, Honolulu, HI, USA, 21–26 July 2017 (2017). https://doi.org/10.1109/CVPR.2017.515

23. Luo, W., Zhao, X., Kim, T.: Multiple object tracking: a review. CoRR abs/1409.7618 (2014). http://arxiv.org/abs/1409.7618

24. Malisiewicz, T., Gupta, A., Efros, A.A.: Ensemble of exemplar-SVMs for object detection and beyond. In: 2011 IEEE International Conference on Computer Vision (ICCV). IEEE (2011)

25. Murphy, K.P.: Machine Learning - A Probabilistic Perspective. Adaptive Computation and Machine Learning Series. MIT Press (2012)

26. Nam, H., Baek, M., Han, B.: Modeling and propagating CNNs in a tree structure for visual tracking. CoRR abs/1608.07242 (2016). http://arxiv.org/abs/1608.07242

27. Nam, H., Han, B.: Learning multi-domain convolutional neural networks for visual tracking. In: 2016 IEEE Conference on Computer Vision and Pattern Recognition, CVPR 2016, Las Vegas, NV, USA, 27–30 June 2016 (2016). https://doi.org/10.1109/CVPR.2016.465

28. Nebehay, G., Pflugfelder, R.P.: Clustering of static-adaptive correspondences for deformable object tracking. In: IEEE Conference on Computer Vision and Pattern Recognition, CVPR 2015, Boston, MA, USA, 7–12 June 2015 (2015). https://doi.org/10.1109/CVPR.2015.7298895

29. Paszke, A., Gross, S., Chintala, S., Chanan, G.: Pytorch (2017)

30. Shu, G., Dehghan, A., Oreifej, O., Hand, E., Shah, M.: Part-based multiple-person tracking with partial occlusion handling. In: CVPR (2012)

31. Simonyan, K., Zisserman, A.: Very deep convolutional networks for large-scale image recognition. CoRR abs/1409.1556 (2014). http://arxiv.org/abs/1409.1556

32. Smeulders, A.W.M., Chu, D.M., Cucchiara, R., Calderara, S., Dehghan, A., Shah, M.: Visual tracking: an experimental survey. IEEE Trans. Pattern Anal. Mach. Intell. 36, 1442–1468 (2014)

33. Valstar, M.F., French, A.P., Pridmore, T.P. (eds.): British Machine Vision Conference, BMVC 2014, Nottingham, UK, 1–5 September 2014. BMVA Press (2014)

34. Vojir, T., Noskova, J., Matas, J.: Robust scale-adaptive mean-shift for tracking. Pattern Recognit. Lett. 49, 250–258 (2014). https://doi.org/10.1016/j.patrec.2014.03.025

35. Wang, S., Lu, H., Yang, F., Yang, M.H.: Superpixel tracking. In: ICCV (2011)

36. Wu, Y., Lim, J., Yang, M.H.: Object tracking benchmark. IEEE Trans. Pattern Anal. Mach. Intell. 37, 1834–1848 (2015)

37. Zhang, T., Xu, C., Yang, M.: Multi-task correlation particle filter for robust object tracking. In: 2017 IEEE Conference on Computer Vision and Pattern Recognition, CVPR 2017, Honolulu, HI, USA, 21–26 July 2017 (2017). https://doi.org/10.1109/CVPR.2017.512

38. Zhu, G., Porikli, F., Li, H.: Beyond local search: tracking objects everywhere with instance-specific proposals. In: 2016 IEEE Conference on Computer Vision and Pattern Recognition, CVPR 2016, Las Vegas, NV, USA, 27–30 June 2016 (2016). https://doi.org/10.1109/CVPR.2016.108

W02 – 6th Workshop on Computer Vision for Road Scene Understanding and Autonomous Driving

W02 – 6th Workshop on Computer Vision for Road Scene Understanding and Autonomous Driving

The goal of the workshop on Computer Vision for Road Scene Understanding and Autonomous Driving (CVRSUAD) is to allow researchers in these fields to present their progress and discuss novel ideas that will shape the future of this area. In particular, we aim for this workshop to bridge the gap between the community that develops novel theoretical approaches for road scene understanding and the community that builds working real-life systems performing in real-world conditions. To this end, we regularly invite speakers covering different continents and coming from both academia and industry. This series of workshops started in 2013 in conjunction with ICCV, with the initial name Workshop on Computer Vision for Autonomous Driving. Since then, the workshop has been organized every year, in conjunction with ECCV and ICCV alternatively.

For this 6th edition of CVRSUAD, on September 14, 2018, we had 5 great invited speakers: Prof. Mohan Trivedi from UCSD, USA, Dr. Henning Hammer from Continental, Germany, Prof. Dariu Gavrila from TU Delft, The Netherlands, Prof. Arnaud de La Fortelle from Mines ParisTech, France, and Dr. Oscar Beijbom from nuTonomy, USA. With their diverse backgrounds and affiliations, they covered a wide range of themes within the general topic of the workshop. Nevertheless, the development of new datasets emerged as a recurring theme, common to both academia and industry.

When it comes to paper contributions, we initially received 15 submissions by July 9, 2018. Each submission was reviewed by three independent referees, drawn from a pool of 46 program committee members and assigned to the papers by the workshop organizers. The reviews were then moderated by the workshop organizers, and we ended up with 8 accepted papers. These papers were presented during a 2 hour poster session at the workshop, the goal of favoring posters over oral presentations being to facilitate discussions. We believe that this was a success, observing constant discussions between the authors and the audience around the posters during the entire session.

Altogether, we believe that this edition of CVRSUAD was a success, with high-quality talks and contributed papers and a good audience, reaching more than 100 people simultaneously in the room despite the workshop being held after the main conference. We are glad to see that this topic still attracts much interest in the community and hope that this trend will continue in the future.

September 2018

Mathieu Salzmann
José Alvarez
Lars Petersson
Fredrik Kahl
Bart Nabbe

Semantic Segmentation of Fisheye Images

Gregor Blott[1,2(✉)] [iD], Masato Takami[1], and Christian Heipke[2] [iD]

[1] Computer Vision Research Lab, Robert Bosch GmbH, Hildesheim, Germany
{gregor.blott,masato.takami}@de.bosch.com
[2] Institute of Photogrammetry and GeoInformation, Leibniz Universität Hannover,
Hannover, Germany
{blott,heipke}@ipi.uni-hannover.de

Abstract. Semantic segmentation of fisheye images (e.g., from action-cameras or smartphones) requires different training approaches and data than those of rectilinear images obtained using central projection. The shape of objects is distorted depending on the distance between the principal point and the object position in the image. Therefore, classical semantic segmentation approaches fall short in terms of performance compared to rectilinear data. A potential solution to this problem is the recording and annotation of a new dataset, however this is expensive and tedious. In this study, an alternative approach that modifies the augmentation stage of deep learning training to re-use rectilinear training data is presented. In this way we obtain a considerably higher semantic segmentation performance on the fisheye images: +18.3% intersection over union (IoU) for action-camera test images, +8.3% IoU for artificially generated fisheye data, and +18.0% IoU for challenging security scenes acquired in bird's eye view.

Keywords: Semantic segmentation · Fisheye images · Deep learning

1 Introduction

Semantic segmentation (SemSeg) of images is a research topic of increasing interest. Several tasks, e.g. in the automotive domain [3], in action localization [13], person re-identification [19], background modeling [16], and remote sensing [18] address SemSeg in a pre-processing step before the actual domain-specific work is conducted. Various SemSeg approaches incl. those from the knowledge-based domain, graphical models, and machine learning have been published in recent years, see the survey [17]. A large and representative amount of training data is required before such approaches can be successfully applied to unseen data. Obtaining this required level of training data is expensive and tedious, since all images have to be annotated before conducting supervised learning.

We address a SemSeg procedure for ultra-wide-angle view images with fisheye (FE) effects. FE lenses are used in the automotive, robotic, consumer, and security domains to obtain a larger field of view with a single camera. Examples of corresponding sensors are action-cameras, recently published smartphones, and

L. Leal-Taixé and S. Roth (Eds.): ECCV 2018 Workshops, LNCS 11129, pp. 181–196, 2019.
https://doi.org/10.1007/978-3-030-11009-3_10

security-cameras. As a drawback of using such lenses, rectilinearity in images is not maintained and the projection depends heavily on the lens design. In particular, the ratio of pixels per degree for equidistant fisheye projection is constant, whereas the ratio for central projection depends on the angle between the optical axis and the ray of the observed image point in space. Therefore, object shape in images obtained using FE lenses depends on the distance to the principal point and the position in the image. Consequently, training material, e.g., from an object located next to the principal point in image space will look different than the same object located next to the image border. It is thus not recommended for FE training to use rectilinear data since the model can then never learn the FE peculiarities, especially those towards the image border.

Our approach for FE SemSeg (cf. Fig. 1) exploits the projection model underlying FE images and a publicly available dataset containing central projection images and annotations (MS COCO [10]) and transforms those images and annotations into FE geometry before training. Thus, the focus of our study is on obtaining rectilinear dataset performance for FE images without ever having seen an image actually captured in FE geometry during training and validation.

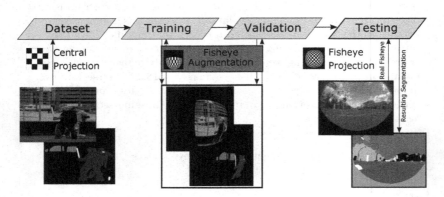

Fig. 1. Our approach for FE SemSeg. Images and annotations using central projection are augmented into FE images for training and validation with six degree of freedom. Real FE images are used only for testing. Credit central projection images [10].

The rest of the paper is structured as follows: work related to this study and the state of-the-art are discussed further in this section. The methods we developed are described in Sect. 2, and the results of the experiments are reported and discussed in Sect. 3. Finally, conclusions are provided in Sect. 4.

1.1 State-of-the-Art and Related Work

Three approaches can be designed for FE SemSeg. These are: (1) separate recording, annotation (labeling), and training with a FE dataset using well-known SemSeg approaches. However, this task is expensive and tedious, and is therefore not addressed in this paper. (2) Pre-training of a classifier (typically a deep learning architecture would be employed today) on rectilinear data and re-training of the last layers on a diverse amount of FE images and annotations. In this approach, the effort related to generating data and creating annotations is much lower but it is still tangible for the purpose of this study. (3) Although generic in nature, a FE image can be re-projected (de-warped) into a rectilinear view, resulting in an equivalent to an image taken by a virtual camera with central projection (cf. Fig. 2). Here, a trade-off has to be found between image quality, field of view, and de-warping artifacts. The outer FE image areas are frequently suppressed, since squeezed FE regions cannot be de-warped with sufficient quality into a rectilinear image. A SemSeg model pre-trained on rectilinear data can subsequently be run on the generated rectilinear data as long as de-warping artifacts are acceptable.

Fig. 2. De-warping of a FE image: Left to right: original FE image and rectilinear de-warped images with decreasing focal length of the virtual camera. By increasing the focal length of the virtual camera, the field of view decreases and information content from the FE image is lost.

To the best of our knowledge there exists only one reference dealing directly with FE SemSeg. This approach, which is related to the goal of our work is published in [5]. In this work, the authors focus on finding a specialized architecture for handling FE images. Due to a lack of FE images with provided SemSeg annotations, images from *Cityscapes* dataset [3] are transformed into images taken using a virtual FE camera exploiting a theoretical FE approximation. The resulting FE images are classified pixel wise via a Convolutional Neural Network (CNN) approach. Additionally *Zoom Augmentation* (one degree of freedom), by varying the focal length of the virtual FE camera, is employed. Validation of real FE data is not performed.

Our work differs fundamentally from the above described approach, since we want to train a network, which achieves superior performance on FE images, without the need of creating an expensive training dataset of annotated FE images. Furthermore, we want to avoid de-warping and enable segmentation also in the outer FE image area where de-warping cannot be performed. In contrast to [5], we use six degrees of freedom (DoF) for augmentation, focus on obtaining rectilinear SemSeg performance on FE images and our FE model is adapted for real manufactured camera lenses.

2   Methods

Our approach is based on the fact that a rectilinear image taken under central projection and its corresponding annotation can be de-warped (transformed) to a FE image by exploiting a commonly used projection model. Additionally, by varying the exterior camera orientation (pose), various artificial (augmented) FE images can be created which will look like a real camera image. After a transformation into FE geometry, vignetting effects resulting in black areas, which are typical for FE images, occur towards the corners and borders and also for non-illuminated pixels caused by the augmentation. These pixels are masked out (we call them "ignore pixels"), which means, that they will not be used for parameter optimization in training and neither be evaluated in validation nor in testing. Our augmentation contains six DoF (cf. Fig. 3 (c)-(h)); the resulting non-illuminated pixel coordinates can be pre-computed for every augmented image. In theory, we can extend our DoF using additional parameters describing the interior camera orientation. However, in this paper, we use six parameters and train exactly for the camera model that we will use for evaluation later (Note that our FE augmentation differs from central projection augmentation (e.g. scaling or shifting) since object shape is distorted differently with increasing distance to the principal point. Using central projection, the shape itself is consistent and, typically, only similarity transformation, flipping, and cropping are used for augmentation [6]).

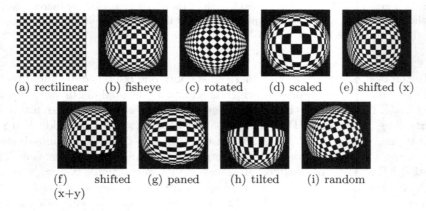

(a) rectilinear   (b) fisheye   (c) rotated   (d) scaled   (e) shifted (x)

(f)   shifted   (g) paned   (h) tilted   (i) random
(x+y)

Fig. 3. DoF effects of augmentation. (a) Original rectilinear input image, (b): augmented and centered FE image, (c): (b)+ rotated by 45°, (d): (b)+ scaled, (e): (b)+ horizontally shifted, (f): (b)+ horizontally and vertically shifted, (g): (b)+ paned, (h): (b)+ tilted, (i) 6 degrees of freedom randomly applied.

For the augmentation, we use the projection model introduced by Mei [11] including his notation, which is an extension of [1,7]. As described in the following equations, up to a certain scale, points in 3D space can be transformed into a FE image and vice versa. We use this model to enable indirect coordinate mapping of the rectilinear image and the related annotation via a look-up-table (LUT). Bilinear interpolation for the image and nearest neighbor interpolation for the annotation are used to keep values consistent. For every tuple consisting of an image and its corresponding annotation, 25 randomly chosen augmentations are created. Coordinates from a source image (rectilinear image) are mapped to the destination image (FE) by applying the following transformation (cf. Fig. 4), [11][1]:

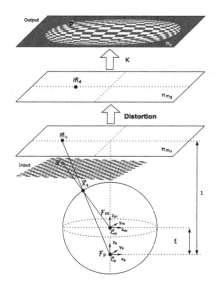

Fig. 4. Projection model from [11] (see footnote 1) adapted for this study

1. An image plane (rectilinear image) is located in the coordinate system (C_m), whereby the exact position of the plane is varied due to the augmentation. The plane is randomly rotated (three DoF) and shifted (three DoF) with respect to the coordinate system origin and axes. This allows to move the rectilinear image content to different locations in the FE image, depending on the randomly chosen plane position and orientation.
2. Points from the image plane are projected onto a unit sphere,

$$(\vec{X})_{\mathcal{F}_m} \rightarrow (\vec{X_S})_{\mathcal{F}_m} = \frac{\vec{X}}{||\vec{X}||} = (X_S, Y_S, Z_S). \tag{1}$$

3. The points are then changed to a new reference frame centered at $\vec{C}_p = (0, 0, \xi)$, where ξ is a lens depending parameter (cf. [11]),

$$(\vec{X_S})_{\mathcal{F}_m} \rightarrow (\vec{X_S})_{\mathcal{F}_p} = (X_S, Y_S, Z_S + \xi). \tag{2}$$

---

[1] http://www.robots.ox.ac.uk/~cmei/articles/projection_model.pdf.

4. The points are then projected onto the normalized image plane (π_{m_u}). The coordinates on the normalized image plane are given by:

$$\vec{m}_u = (\frac{X_S}{Z_S + \xi}, \frac{Y_S}{Z_S + \xi}, 1). \tag{3}$$

5. Radial and tangential distortions are added with the distortion model introduced by Brown [2] with three radial and two tangential coefficients. The coordinates on the distortion affected image plane (π_{m_d}) are then:

$$\vec{m}_d = \vec{m}_u + D(\vec{m}_u, \mathbf{V}), \tag{4}$$

where D describes the coordinate depending distortion with the distortion coefficients $\mathbf{V}$.

6. The final projection involves a generalized camera projection matrix $\mathbf{K}$ (with the generalized focal length f, (u_0, v_0) as the principal point, s as the skew, and r as the aspect ratio). The coordinates on the fisheye image plane (π_p) are finally:

$$\vec{p} = \mathbf{K} \cdot \vec{m}_d. \tag{5}$$

In our study, we used the interior calibration parameters (ξ, u_0, v_0, f, s, r, $\mathbf{V}$) obtained from the target FE camera based on [15].

For the actual augmentation, the inverse transformation is implemented to enable indirect mapping (see above).

3   Experimental Evaluation

In this section, the results of experiments to investigate the described method are reported. The goals of the experiments can be divided into three parts and are summarized in Table 1:

Table 1. Structure of this section

Section	Goal
3.1	**Training and validation**
	- Baseline: Training on public MSCOCO dataset separately with (w/A) and without (wo/A) rectilinear augmentation
	- Training on the same dataset with FE augmentation (w/FEA)
3.2	**Testing on FE images (consumer-camera images)**
	- Testing the models trained in Sect. 3.1 on real and artificially generated FE images
3.3	**Re-training and testing on FE images (security-camera images)**
	- Re-training and testing the models trained in Sect. 3.1 with 400 security-camera images using central projection to obtain domain adaptation
	(the public dataset does not contain a security-camera pose)

Semantic Segmentation Methodology: We choose the commonly used architecture from the Visual Geometry Group, *VGG16* [14], to create baseline results against which we evaluate our experiments. The feature extractor is initialized with weights, which we obtain by pre-training on the ImageNet Dataset [4]. To output a semantic segmentation the last two fully connected layers are converted into fully convolutional layers and skip layers are introduced up to FCN8s as described in [12]. We freeze the weights from all layers prior to the originally fully connected layers and therefore only re-train the last layers of the network. Training is run with a batch size of five samples, using the adaptive optimizer ADAM [9].

While there are several other approaches, which potentially deliver better results on SemSeg, the scope of this work is to introduce and evaluate a method for improving SemSeg on FE images compared to a SemSeg output from a network, which is solely trained on rectilinear images. For this purpose the absolute accuracy and thus the choice of deep learning network architecture is seen as less important.

Key Performance Indicator: We optimize our network with the cross entropy loss and evaluate the resulting SemSeg image with the intersection over union (IoU) as used in many SemSeg benchmarks, e.g. the Cityscapes Dataset [3]. Furthermore, we report the average IoU, which is the average IoU over all class IoUs and the F1-score, followed by the true positive and true negative rates.

Test Images: Since training and testing material is limited in the FE domain, especially in the SemSeg domain, we create and annotate three datasets for our study. MSCOCO-FE (Sect. 3.2) constitutes 37,504 images and annotations from the original MSCOCO [10] dataset, which we transform to 937,600 artificially generated FE images with pre-defined interior orientation parameters. GoPro-FE (Sect. 3.2) constitutes 50 real images taken using a *GoPro Hero 4* full frame, ultra-wide-angle view FE camera (4000 × 3000 pixels resolution, down-sampled to 640 × 480 pixels). The dataset consists of persons, animals, cars, bicycles, and furniture. The interior orientation of this camera is used for MSCOCO-FE; a bundle adjustment based on [15] is used to determine these parameters. However, since the GoPro camera does not have a fixed focal length, we use the averaged camera parameters for our projection model and do not consider variations. Security-Dome (Sect. 3.3) constitutes 12 challenging real FE images (640 × 640 pixels) taken using a circular FE security-camera in bird's eye view pose. While being a dataset with only a small number of images, each image comprises a lot of information with 25–55 persons being present per image.

Augmentation: Performances between networks where augmentation was used during training can not be fairly compared to networks trained without augmentation. By using augmentation during training, a bigger variability is introduced to the training data and if correctly used, it will be beneficial for the network. Therefore, we not only implemented a FE augmented training as used in Sect. 3.1, but also an augmentation for the rectilinear images. By applying this to our baseline experiment trained on rectilinear images without augmentations (wo/A), we get a model trained on rectilinear images with augmentations (w/A), which can be better compared to our FE augmented model (w/FEA). This augmentation on the baseline experiment are arbitrary combinations of similarity transformations like translation (2D) or flipping. For both augmentation approaches (baseline and FE), the angle of rotation (see Fig. 3(c)) is limited to $-20° < \alpha < +20°$, because the shape of objects in the test set is expected to be in this range.

3.1   Training and Validation

Training Data: Microsoft COCO (MSCOCO) [10], is a diverse dataset containing consumer-camera images collected from the Flickr website. The dataset provides 80 object classes and one background class for instance-based SemSeg. The official test set of the dataset is not published and evaluation is only possible by submitting to the evaluation servers. Due to our final goal of training networks specialized for FE images such an evaluation is not of interest. Instead, we reduce the class set to the classes, which are relevant for the FE test dataset and subdivide the validation set of the publicly available dataset including annotations into a customized validation and test set. We remap the 80 to 16 coarser classes[2] for non-instance-based SemSeg. Training is performed based on 82,783 images, 3,000 images for validation, and 37,504 images for testing (the original MSCOCO validation image size minus our used validation images). As we do not carry out instance-based SemSeg, we do not apply the official evaluation metric, which is the average precision and average recall on instance-based segmentation, but use the IoU evaluation following the Cityscapes [3] evaluation protocol instead, because we are primarily interested in the impact of our method on FE images. Furthermore, all images are normalized by subtraction of the mean and division by the standard deviation.

Validation Procedure: The standard procedure is to only apply augmentations during training and to leave the validation images untouched to measure the improvements in every subsequent epoch. For rectilinear augmentations this is reasonable, because the validation set consists of real images. However, in our case, we are not searching for the best performance on real images. Instead, we want to validate the performance on virtual FE images, where all transformations from rectilinear images represent a 'real' FE image on its own. Therefore, we perform random FE transformations also on the validation images. Due to reasons of comparability we do the same for the experiment using rectilinear augmentations.

Validation Results: In Fig. 5 the average IoU as a function of the training epochs on the validation data for the different training strategies is shown, where

---

[2] Background, person, bicycle, car, motorcycle, airplane, bus, train, truck, boat, traffic light, furniture, animal, bagpack, handbag, and suitcase.

we choose an epoch size of 8000 images. Because of the reduction to 16 classes, we have to deal with an over-representation of the background class in the MSCOCO dataset, which is why training tends to get stuck in a local minimum resulting in background as the only output. To overcome this issue, we carry out training and validation for the first 100 epochs using the original training and validation images (without augmentation) and subsequently use the resulting weights to initialize the networks of the augmentation based experiments. Another option would have been to introduce class weights.

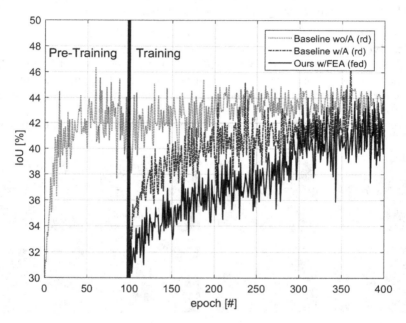

Fig. 5. Average IoU as function of training epoch. Training is performed on rectilinear data (rd) and artificially (augmented) generated FE data (fed). (Color figure online)

The red curve in Fig. 5 shows the IoU for the rectilinear training without augmentation (wo/A), the blue curve shows the IoU for rectilinear augmentation (w/A). The drop in IoU percentage (red vs. blue curve) results in the difference between training and validation images caused by the augmentation introduced after 100 epochs. On average, both models obtain around 42% IoU during the last epochs on the respective validation data. While the baseline model without augmentation converges after approximately 70 epochs, the training incorporating augmentation needs considerably longer to converge. This is not surprising if taking into account that here, in contrast to the standard procedure, the validation images are also augmented. The black curve shows the IoU of the approach presented in this work, using augmented FE images. After around 300 epochs, no significant improvement is noted for both augmentation-based models. In our experiment the FE augmented model and the rectilinear augmented model eventually end up at roughly the same performance. This shows that regardless of the different augmentations, the model performances does not seem to differ as long as the same type of transformations are used in training and validation.

3.2   Testing on FE Images

In this section, we evaluate our SemSeg performance on real fisheye images for models trained with rectilinear images against models trained with our augmented FE images and present qualitative and quantitative results.

Qualitative Evaluation: Figure 6 shows examples for the two models (w/A and w/FEA) trained on MSCOCO deployed on our new dataset (GoPro-FE). The images obtained using the baseline approach suffer from mis-classifications in the outer image area. Since this model is not trained on FE images, the number of incorrectly segmented pixels rises with increasing distance to the principal point due to stronger FE effects. Images segmented from the model trained with

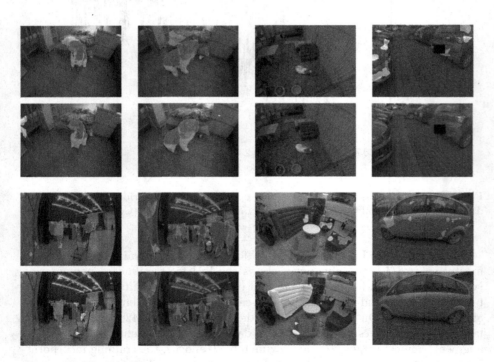

Fig. 6. Qualitative results on images randomly picked from our dataset. Odd line numbers show the result with the best rectilinear model; even line numbers correspond to the results for the model trained with our FE model and augmentation. Class visualization: person - red, animal - orange, car - blue, furniture - white. (Color figure online)

our approach show improved results in particular in the outer image areas (1st and 2nd line, 1st image from the right). In the image showing the furniture (3rd and 4th line, 2nd image from the right) the result of explicitly learned FE effects can be observed for the curved couch and the zebra image in the back.

Quantitative Evaluation: Table 2 shows the quantitative results for our 50 real FE test images (GoPro-FE). Our model considerably outperforms the two baseline models ($+18.3\%\ \overline{IoU}$) while using the same raw training material as the baseline with augmentation. All classes are better classified by our approach, evidenced by an F1-score of $+18.8\%$, a true positive rate of $+27.8\%$, and a true negative rate of $+7.7\%$. The large margin compared to the baseline is not surprising since the baseline model is not trained for FE data. Notably, we observe that we can use rectilinear images plus augmentation to obtain much higher IoU on FE images.

Table 2. Quantitative evaluation on our own FE dataset. $\star$ indicates not countable.

	# instances	Baseline wo/A	Baseline w/A	Ours w/FEA
IoU (average)	175	33.9	37.3	**55.6**
Background	$\star$	90.5	90.3	**94.7**
Person	49	51.0	59.8	**75.5**
Bicycle	28	12.1	13.9	**27.6**
Car	75	30.0	29.8	**45.4**
Sitting furniture	6	0.0	4.9	**39.1**
Animal	17	19.9	25.1	**51.1**
F1	175	42.8	50.0	**68.8**
True positive rate	175	31.4	34.2	**62.0**
True negative rate	175	89.0	87.9	**95.6**

Evaluation on Artificial FE Images: In this section, we report the performance for the FE SemSeg obtained for images that are from the same domain than the ones used during training (MSCOCO-FE), but not used for training and validation. We use artificially generated images since the test material is limited. To do so we also transform the MSCOCO test dataset, which is split (original validation dataset minus the 3,000 images that we only use for our validation), into FE geometry. We transform all of the 37,504 images and the label images each to 25 randomly generated FE image versions using the projection model introduced in Sect. 2, resulting in 937,600 test images.

Figure 7 shows four example images from MSCOCO augmented to FE images, whereas Table 3 lists the SemSeg results. The results show that our augmentation is very powerful. We obtain $+8.3\%$ more IoU than the other two tested approaches on the same test images with our augmentation. Using the

(a) Original#1   (b) Original#2   (c) Original#3   (d) Original#4

(e) Augmented#1 (f) Augmented#2 (g) Augmented#3 (h) Augmented#4

Fig. 7. Four randomly picked original images from the MSCOCO dataset and corresponding fisheye images.

Table 3. Quantitative evaluation on an artificially generated **FE** test set. The used augmented test dataset constitutes 937,600 images.

	Baseline wo/A (↑)	Baseline w/A(↑)	Ours w/FEA (↑)
IoU (average)	34.0	34.7	**43.0**
Background	90.1	89.9	**92.9**
Person	65.1	58.9	**73.1**
Bicycle	23.5	24.7	**30.2**
Car	24.4	30.5	**35.2**
Motorcycle	36.8	48.1	**48.9**
Airplane	33.3	34.8	**43.5**
Bus	48.5	48.4	**66.4**
Train	46.8	44.4	**63.1**
Truck	28.0	26.3	**41.1**
Boat	15.3	18.2	**22.8**
Traffic light	22.5	25.4	**31.2**
Furniture	24.6	19.7	**26.4**
Animal	64.9	57.8	**75.3**
Bagpack	0.0	6.6	**16.0**
Handbag	**4.1**	1.9	0.0
Suitcase	16.2	19.6	**23.2**
F1-score	46.5	48.0	**56.1**
True positive rate	42.2	42.9	**52.1**
True negative rate	97.8	97.5	**98.5**

proposed method, all classes, except the handbag class, are considerably better classified in comparison to using the baseline approaches. The class handbag is the class with the lowest number of pixels, and therefore an adequate training of this class is challenging. Moreover, our true positive rate is +9.2% and F1-score +8.1% higher than those obtained for the other two approaches. It is also noticeable, that the two baseline models show almost identical performance. This indicates, that it is not sufficient to add variability by any arbitrary augmentation. To gain performance on the target images, it is crucial to choose augmentations which suit the camera model. We will underline this further in Sect. 3.3.

3.3   Testing on FE Images in the Security-Camera Domain

In this Section, we show that it is crucial to choose the correct underlying camera model when applying our FE augmentation method. Therefore, we evaluate our approach on our Security-Dome test dataset, which consists of challenging real dome security-camera images. Compared to the GoPro-FE dataset, the FE effect is much stronger and we are dealing with a bird's eye view. First, to create our baseline experiment, we evaluate the baseline model (w/A) and the model trained with FE-augmentations (w/FEA) on the Security-Dome dataset. As expected, the w/FEA model achieved higher performance, but especially facing some issues towards the borders of the image. Since not having many persons captured from the bird's eye view in the MSCOCO dataset, we decided to use an already annotated dataset Security-Recti which consists of 400 rectilinear images also from the security domain. To evaluate the importance of correct augmentation, we now re-train our w/FEA model for 100 epochs with the same FE-augmentation as used for the GoPro and a FE-augmentation, which uses the transformation parameters from the dome security-camera. For completion, we also re-trained the w/A-model with the Security-Recti images. In Table 4, the high impact of the augmentations can be observed. With the baseline approach for rectilinear images an IoU of 17.4% is achieved, while the use of our

Table 4. Measures for class person in the challenging Security-Dome dataset.

Class person	w/A	w/A +re-train	w/FEA (GoPro)	w/FEA +re-train (GoPro)	w/FEA +re-train (Sec.-Cam.)
		Baseline	Baseline	(Wrong cam.)	(Wrong cam.)	(Correct cam.)
IoU	15.1	17.4	20.4	27.1	**35.4**
F1-score	26.2	29.7	35.2	42.6	**52.3**
True positive rate	16.4	19.5	22.3	29.0	**38.2**
True negative rate	99.0	98.7	99.1	99.2	**99.2**

FE-augmentation method is already giving a 10% gain even with the parameters for the GoPro-camera. Now applying the correct augmentation, the performance reaches 35.4% IoU. This is quite impressive on the Security-Dome with its very strong distortions and extreme viewpoint considering that not a single image from this domain was was recorded and annotated. Qualitative results can be seen in Fig. 8.

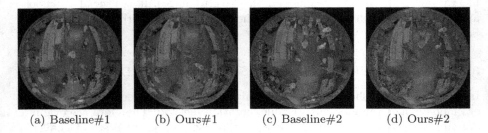

(a) Baseline#1   (b) Ours#1   (c) Baseline#2   (d) Ours#2

Fig. 8. SemSeg for FE images. Two input images are segmented with w/A (Baseline) and with w/FEA (Ours) both re-trained on Security-Recti.

4   Conclusion

Training data for fisheye (FE) semantic segmentation is limited and recording and annotation for supervised learning is expensive and tedious. Additionally, much more training data is required than for rectilinear data, since, depending on the employed lens, the shape of objects varies with the position of the object in the image. We presented an approach to re-use rectilinear training material to enable semantic segmentation on FE images obtained from action cameras, smartphones or security cameras. In particular, we introduce rectlinear-to-FE transformations to the augmentation stage in training. Additional annotations or specially tailored deep learning architectures are not necessary. On average our approach is +18.3% IoU (trained on MSCOCO) better on real full-frame fisheye images (n = 50 images) and +8.3% IoU better on artificially generated FE images (n = 937,600 images) when using the same raw training material as the baseline with rectilinear augmentations. Furthermore, we obtained +18.0% *IoU* on a new, very challenging dome security-camera dataset (circular FE) where the camera is mounted in bird's eye view.

One further effect, which we realized was that in our experiment the FE augmented model and the rectilinear augmented model eventually end up roughly at the same performance on the respective dataset. This shows that regardless of the different augmentations, the model performance does not seem to differ as long as the same type of transformation is used in training and validation.

In the future, we will increase the DoF for augmentation and investigate, how the deep learning model architecture can be tailored for further improvements on FE SemSeg. Another direction, we want to explore is the use of Generative

Adversarial Networks (GANs) [8] to do semantic segmentation on FE images: instead of employing an explicit sensor model (see Eqs. (1) to (5)) we want to train a GAN with the aim to transform arbitrary FE images to rectilinear images and the segmentation back to the FE image. The segmentation network is then only trained with the original training set of rectilinear images. We will compare obtained segmentation performance with our FE augmented model.

References

1. Barreto, J.P., Araujo, H.: Issues on the geometry of central catadioptric image formation. In: CVPR, pp. 422–427. IEEE (2001)
2. Brown, D.C.: Decentering distortion of lenses. Photogram. Eng. **130**, 444–462 (1966). http://www.close-range.com/docs/Decentering_Distortion_of_Lenses_Brown_1966_may_444-462.pdf
3. Cordts, M., et al.: The cityscapes dataset for semantic urban scene understanding. In: CVPR, pp. 3213–3223. IEEE (2016)
4. Deng, J., Dong, W., Socher, R., Li, L.J., Li, K., Fei-Fei, L.: ImageNet: a large-scale hierarchical image database. In: CVPR, pp. 248–255. IEEE (2009)
5. Deng, L., Yang, M., Qian, Y., Wang, C., Wang, B.: CNN based semantic segmentation for urban traffic scenes using fisheye camera. In: Intelligent Vehicles Symposium (IV), pp. 231–236. IEEE (2017)
6. Garcia-Garcia, A., Orts-Escolano, S., Oprea, S., Villena-Martinez, V., Rodríguez, J.G.: A review on deep learning techniques applied to semantic segmentation. CoRR abs/1704.06857 (2017)
7. Geyer, C., Daniilidis, K.: A unifying theory for central panoramic systems and practical implications. In: Vernon, D. (ed.) ECCV 2000. LNCS, vol. 1843, pp. 445–461. Springer, Heidelberg (2000). https://doi.org/10.1007/3-540-45053-X_29
8. Goodfellow, I.J., et al.: Generative adversarial networks. CoRR abs/1406.2661 (2014)
9. Kingma, D.P., Ba, J.: Adam: a method for stochastic optimization. CoRR abs/1412.6980 (2014)
10. Lin, T.-Y., et al.: Microsoft COCO: common objects in context. In: Fleet, D., Pajdla, T., Schiele, B., Tuytelaars, T. (eds.) ECCV 2014. LNCS, vol. 8693, pp. 740–755. Springer, Cham (2014). https://doi.org/10.1007/978-3-319-10602-1_48
11. Mei, C.: Couplage vision omnidirectionnelle et télémétrie laser pour la navigation en robotique/laser-augmented omnidirectional vision for 3D localisation and mapping. Ph.D. thesis, INRIA Sophia Antipolis, Project-team ARobAS (2007)
12. Shelhamer, E., Long, J., Darrell, T.: Fully convolutional networks for semantic segmentation. CoRR abs/1605.06211 (2016)
13. Shou, Z., Chan, J., Zareian, A., Miyazawa, K., Chang, S.: CDC: convolutional-de-convolutional networks for precise temporal action localization in untrimmed videos. CoRR abs/1703.01515 (2017)
14. Simonyan, K., Zisserman, A.: Very deep convolutional networks for large-scale image recognition. CoRR abs/1409.1556 (2014)
15. Strauß, T., Ziegler, J., Beck, J.: Calibrating multiple cameras with non-overlapping views using coded checkerboard targets. In: ITSC, pp. 2623–2628. IEEE (2014)

16. Su, T.-F., Chen, Y.-L., Lai, S.-H.: Over-segmentation based background modeling and foreground detection with shadow removal by using hierarchical MRFs. In: Kimmel, R., Klette, R., Sugimoto, A. (eds.) ACCV 2010. LNCS, vol. 6494, pp. 535–546. Springer, Heidelberg (2011). https://doi.org/10.1007/978-3-642-19318-7_42
17. Thoma, M.: A survey of semantic segmentation. CoRR abs/1602.06541 (2016)
18. Wei, X., Guo, Y., Gao, X., Yan, M., Sun, X.: A new semantic segmentation model for remote sensing images. In: IEEE International Geoscience and Remote Sensing Symposium (IGARSS), pp. 1776–1779. IEEE (2017)
19. Yang, Y., Yang, J., Yan, J., Liao, S., Yi, D., Li, S.Z.: Salient color names for person re-identification. In: Fleet, D., Pajdla, T., Schiele, B., Tuytelaars, T. (eds.) ECCV 2014. LNCS, vol. 8689, pp. 536–551. Springer, Cham (2014). https://doi.org/10.1007/978-3-319-10590-1_35

Complex-YOLO:
An Euler-Region-Proposal for Real-Time
3D Object Detection on Point Clouds

Martin Simon[1,2]([✉]), Stefan Milz[1], Karl Amende[1,2], and Horst-Michael Gross[2]

[1] Valeo Schalter und Sensoren GmbH, Bietigheim-Bissingen, Germany
{martin.simon,stefan.milz,karl.amende}@valeo.com
[2] Ilmenau University of Technology, Ilmenau, Germany
horst-michael.gross@tu-ilmenau.de

Abstract. Lidar based 3D object detection is inevitable for autonomous driving, because it directly links to environmental understanding and therefore builds the base for prediction and motion planning. The capacity of inferencing highly sparse 3D data in real-time is an ill-posed problem for lots of other application areas besides automated vehicles, e.g. augmented reality, personal robotics or industrial automation. We introduce Complex-YOLO, a state of the art real-time 3D object detection network on point clouds only. In this work, we describe a network that expands YOLOv2, a fast 2D standard object detector for RGB images, by a specific complex regression strategy to estimate multi-class 3D boxes in Cartesian space. Thus, we propose a specific Euler-Region-Proposal Network (E-RPN) to estimate the pose of the object by adding an imaginary and a real fraction to the regression network. This ends up in a closed complex space and avoids singularities, which occur by single angle estimations. The E-RPN supports to generalize well during training. Our experiments on the KITTI benchmark suite show that we outperform current leading methods for 3D object detection specifically in terms of efficiency. We achieve state of the art results for cars, pedestrians and cyclists by being more than five times faster than the fastest competitor. Further, our model is capable of estimating all eight KITTI-classes, including Vans, Trucks or sitting pedestrians simultaneously with high accuracy.

Keywords: 3D object detection · Point cloud processing · Lidar · Autonomous driving

1 Introduction

Point cloud processing is becoming more and more important for autonomous driving due to the strong improvement of automotive Lidar sensors in the recent years. The sensors of suppliers are capable to deliver 3D points of the surrounding environment in real-time. The advantage is a direct measurement of the

© Springer Nature Switzerland AG 2019
L. Leal-Taixé and S. Roth (Eds.): ECCV 2018 Workshops, LNCS 11129, pp. 197–209, 2019.
https://doi.org/10.1007/978-3-030-11009-3_11

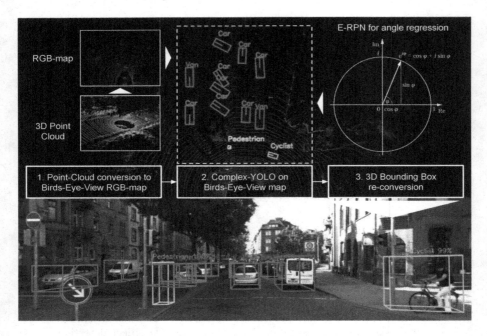

Fig. 1. Complex-YOLO is a very efficient model that directly operates on Lidar only based birds-eye-view RGB-maps to estimate and localize accurate 3D multiclass bounding boxes. The upper part of the figure shows a bird view based on a Velodyne HDL64 point cloud (Geiger et al. [1]) such as the predicted objects. The lower one outlines the re-projection of the 3D boxes into image space. Note: Complex-YOLO needs no camera image as input, it is Lidar based only.

distance of encompassing objects [1]. This allows us to develop object detection algorithms for autonomous driving that estimate the position and the heading of different objects accurately in 3D [2–9]. Compared to images, Lidar point clouds are sparse with a varying density distributed all over the measurement area. Those points are unordered, they interact locally and could mainly be not analyzed isolated. Point cloud processing should always be invariant to basic transformations [10,11].

In general, object detection and classification based on deep learning is a well known task and widely established for 2D bounding box regression on images [12–21]. Research focus was mainly a trade-off between accuracy and efficiency. In regard to automated driving, efficiency is much more important. Therefore, the best object detectors are using region proposal networks (RPN) [3,15,22] or a similar grid based RPN-approach [13]. Those networks are extremely efficient, accurate and even capable of running on a dedicated hardware or embedded devices. Object detections on point clouds are still rarely, but more and more important. Those applications need to be capable of predicting 3D bounding boxes. Currently, there exist mainly three different approaches using deep learning [3]:

1. Direct point cloud processing using Multi-Layer-Perceptrons [5,10,11,23,24]
2. Translation of Point-Clouds into voxels or image stacks by using Convolutional Neural Networks (CNN) [2–4,6,8,9,25,26]
3. Combined fusion approaches [2,7]

1.1 Related Work

Recently, Frustum-based Networks [5] have shown high performance on the KITTI Benchmark suite. The model is ranked[1] on the second place either for 3D object detections, as for birds-eye-view detection based on cars, pedestrians and cyclists. This is the only approach, which directly deals with the point cloud using Point-Net [10] without using CNNs on Lidar data and voxel creation. However, it needs a pre-processing and therefore it has to use the camera sensor as well. Based on another CNN dealing with the calibrated camera image, it uses those detections to minimize the global point cloud to frustum-based reduced point cloud. This approach has two drawbacks: (i). The models accuracy strongly depends on the camera image and its associated CNN. Hence, it is not possible to apply the approach to Lidar data only; (ii). The overall pipeline has to run two deep learning approaches consecutive, which ends up in higher inference time with lower efficiency. The referenced model runs with a too low frame-rate at approximately 7 fps on a NVIDIA GTX 1080i GPU [1].

In contrast, Zhou et al. [3] proposed a model that operates only on Lidar data. In regard to that, it is the best ranked model on KITTI for 3D and birds-eye-view detections using Lidar data only. The basic idea is an end-to-end learning that operates on grid cells without using hand crafted features. Grid cell inside features are learned during training using a Pointnet approach [10]. On top builds up a CNN that predicts the 3D bounding boxes. Despite the high accuracy, the model ends up in a low inference time of 4 fps on a TitanX GPU [3].

Another highly ranked approach is reported by Chen et al. [5]. The basic idea is the projection of Lidar point clouds into voxel based RGB-maps using handcrafted features, like points density, maximum height and a representative point intensity [9]. To achieve highly accurate results, they use a multi-view approach based on a Lidar birds-eye-view map, a Lidar based front-view map and a camera based front-view image. This fusion ends up in a high processing time resulting in only 4 fps on a NVIDIA GTX 1080i GPU. Another drawback is the need of the secondary sensor input (camera).

1.2 Contribution

To our surprise, no one is achieving real-time efficiency in terms of autonomous driving so far. Hence, we introduce the first slim and accurate model that is capable of running faster than 50 fps on a NVIDIA TitanX GPU. We use the multi-view idea (MV3D) [5] for point cloud pre-processing and feature extraction. However, we neglect the multi-view fusion and generate one single birds-eye-view RGB-map (see Fig. 1) that is based on Lidar only, to ensure efficiency.

---

[1] The ranking refers to the time of submission: 14th of march in 2018.

On top, we present Complex-YOLO, a 3D version of YOLOv2, which is one of the fastest state-of-the-art image object detectors [13]. Complex-YOLO is supported by our specific E-RPN that estimates the orientation of objects coded by an imaginary and real part for each box. The idea is to have a closed mathematical space without singularities for accurate angle generalization. Our model is capable to predict exact 3D boxes with localization and an exact heading of the objects in real-time, even if the object is based on a few points (e.g. pedestrians). Therefore, we designed special anchor-boxes. Further, it is capable to predict all eight KITTI classes by using only Lidar input data. We evaluated our model on the KITTI benchmark suite. In terms of accuracy, we achieved on par results for cars, pedestrians and cyclists, in terms of efficiency we outperform current leaders by minimum factor of 5. The main contributions of this paper are:

1. This work introduces Complex-YOLO by using a new E-RPN for reliable angle regression for 3D box estimation.
2. We present real-time performance with high accuracy evaluated on the KITTI benchmark suite by being more than five times faster than the current leading models.
3. We estimate an exact heading of each 3D box supported by the E-RPN that enables the prediction of the trajectory of surrounding objects.
4. Compared to other Lidar based methods (e.g. [3]) our model efficiently estimates all classes simultaneously in one forward path.

2   Complex-YOLO

This section describes the grid based pre-processing of the point clouds, the specific network architecture, the derived loss function for training and our efficiency design to ensure real-time performance.

2.1   Point Cloud Preprocessing

The 3D point cloud of a single frame, acquired by Velodyne HDL64 laser scanner [1], is converted into a single birds-eye-view RGB-map, covering an area of 80 m × 40 m (see Fig. 4) directly in front of the origin of the sensor. Inspired by Chen et al. (MV3D) [5], the RGB-map is encoded by height, intensity and density. The size of the grid map is defined with $n = 1024$ and $m = 512$. Therefore, we projected and discretized the 3D point clouds into a 2D grid with resolution of about $g = 8$ cm. Compared to MV3D, we slightly decreased the cell size to achieve less quantization errors, accompanied with higher input resolution. Due to efficiency and performance reasons, we are using only one instead of multiple height maps. Consequently, all three feature channels (z_r, z_g, z_b with $z_{r,g,b} \in \mathbb{R}^{m \times n}$) are calculated for the whole point cloud $\mathcal{P} \in \mathbb{R}^3$ inside the covering area Ω. We consider the Velodyne within the origin of $\mathcal{P}_\Omega$ and define:

$$\mathcal{P}_\Omega = \{\mathcal{P} = [x, y, z]^T | x \in [0, 40m], y \in [-40m, 40m], z \in [-2m, 1.25m]\} \quad (1)$$

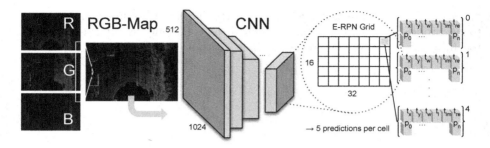

Fig. 2. Complex-YOLO Pipeline. We present a slim pipeline for fast and accurate 3D box estimations on point clouds. The RGB-map is fed into the CNN (see Table 1). The E-RPN grid runs simultaneously on the last feature map and predicts five boxes per grid cell. Each box prediction is composed by the regression parameters t (see Fig. 3) and object scores p with a general probability p_0 and n class scores $p_1...p_n$.

We choose $z \in [-2m, 1.25m]$, considering the Lidar z position of 1.73m [1], to cover an area above the ground to about 3 m height, expecting trucks as highest objects. With the aid of the calibration [1], we define a mapping function $\mathcal{S}_j = f_{\mathcal{PS}}(\mathcal{P}_{\Omega i}, g)$ with $\mathcal{S} \in \mathbb{R}^{m \times n}$ mapping each point with index i into a specific grid cell $\mathcal{S}_j$ of our RGB-map. A set describes all points mapped into a specific grid cell:

$$\mathcal{P}_{\Omega i \to j} = \{\mathcal{P}_{\Omega i} = [x, y, z]^T | \mathcal{S}_j = f_{\mathcal{PS}}(\mathcal{P}_{\Omega i}, g)\} \qquad (2)$$

Hence, we can calculate the channel of each pixel, considering the Velodyne intensity as $I(\mathcal{P}_\Omega)$:

$$\begin{aligned} z_g(\mathcal{S}_j) &= \max(\mathcal{P}_{\Omega i \to j} \cdot [0, 0, 1]^T) \\ z_b(\mathcal{S}_j) &= \max(I(\mathcal{P}_{\Omega i \to j})) \\ z_r(\mathcal{S}_j) &= \min(1.0, \log(N+1)/64) \quad N = |\mathcal{P}_{\Omega i \to j}| \end{aligned} \qquad (3)$$

Here, N describes the number of points mapped from $\mathcal{P}_{\Omega i}$ to $\mathcal{S}_j$, and g is the parameter for the grid cell size. Hence, z_g encodes the maximum height, z_b the maximum intensity and z_r the normalized density of all points mapped into $\mathcal{S}_j$ (see Fig. 2).

2.2 Architecture

The Complex-YOLO network takes a birds-eye-view RGB-map (see Sect. 2.1) as input. It uses a simplified YOLOv2 [13] CNN architecture (see Table 1), extended by a complex angle regression and E-RPN, to detect accurate multi-class oriented 3D objects while still operating in real-time.

Euler-Region-Proposal. Our E-RPN parses the 3D position $b_{x,y}$, object dimensions (width b_w and length b_l) as well as a probability p_0, class scores

$p_1...p_n$ and finally its orientation b_ϕ from the incoming feature map. In order to get proper orientation, we have modified the commonly used Grid-RPN approach, by adding a complex angle $arg(|z|e^{ib_\phi})$ to it:

$$b_x = \sigma(t_x) + c_x$$
$$b_y = \sigma(t_y) + c_y$$
$$b_w = p_w e^{t_w} \tag{4}$$
$$b_l = p_l e^{t_l}$$
$$b_\phi = arg(|z|e^{ib_\phi}) = \arctan_2(t_{Im}, t_{Re})$$

With the help of this extension the E-RPN estimates accurate object orientations based on an imaginary and real fraction directly embedded into the network. For each grid cell (32×16 see Table 1) we predict five objects including a probability score and class scores resulting in 75 features each, visualized in Fig. 2.

Anchor Box Design. The YOLOv2 object detector [13] predicts five boxes per grid cell. All were initialized with beneficial priors, i.e. anchor boxes, for better convergence during training. Due to the angle regression, the degrees of freedom, i.e. the number of possible priors increased, but we did not enlarge the number of predictions for efficiency reasons. Hence, we defined only three different sizes and two angle directions as priors, based on the distribution of boxes within the KITTI dataset: (i) vehicle size (heading up); (ii) vehicle size (heading down); (iii) cyclist size (heading up); (iv) cyclist size (heading down); (v) pedestrian size (heading left).

Complex Angle Regression. The orientation angle for each object b_ϕ can be computed from the responsible regression parameters t_{im} and t_{re}, which correspond to the phase

Table 1. Complex-YOLO design. Our nal model has 18 convolutional and 5 maxpool layers, as well as 3 intermediate layers for feature reorganization respectively.

Layer	Filters	Size	Input	Output
conv	24	$3 \times 3/1$	$1024 \times 512 \times 3$	$1024 \times 512 \times 24$
max		$2 \times 2/2$	$1024 \times 512 \times 24$	$512 \times 256 \times 24$
conv	48	$3 \times 3/1$	$512 \times 256 \times 24$	$512 \times 256 \times 48$
max		$2 \times 2/2$	$512 \times 256 \times 48$	$256 \times 128 \times 48$
conv	64	$3 \times 3/1$	$256 \times 128 \times 48$	$256 \times 128 \times 64$
conv	32	$1 \times 1/1$	$256 \times 128 \times 64$	$256 \times 128 \times 32$
conv	64	$3 \times 3/1$	$256 \times 128 \times 32$	$256 \times 128 \times 64$
max		$2 \times 2/2$	$256 \times 128 \times 64$	$128 \times 64 \times 64$
conv	128	$3 \times 3/1$	$128 \times 64 \times 64$	$128 \times 64 \times 128$
conv	64	$3 \times 3/1$	$128 \times 64 \times 128$	$128 \times 64 \times 64$
conv	128	$3 \times 3/1$	$128 \times 64 \times 64$	$128 \times 64 \times 128$
max		$2 \times 2/2$	$128 \times 64 \times 128$	$64 \times 32 \times 128$
conv	256	$3 \times 3/1$	$64 \times 32 \times 128$	$64 \times 32 \times 256$
conv	256	$1 \times 1/1$	$64 \times 32 \times 256$	$64 \times 32 \times 256$
conv	512	$3 \times 3/1$	$64 \times 32 \times 256$	$64 \times 32 \times 512$
max		$2 \times 2/2$	$64 \times 32 \times 512$	$32 \times 16 \times 512$
conv	512	$3 \times 3/1$	$32 \times 16 \times 512$	$32 \times 16 \times 512$
conv	512	$1 \times 1/1$	$32 \times 16 \times 512$	$32 \times 16 \times 512$
conv	1024	$3 \times 3/1$	$32 \times 16 \times 512$	$32 \times 16 \times 1024$
conv	1024	$3 \times 3/1$	$32 \times 16 \times 1024$	$32 \times 16 \times 1024$
conv	1024	$3 \times 3/1$	$32 \times 16 \times 1024$	$32 \times 16 \times 1024$
route	12			
reorg		/2	$64 \times 32 \times 256$	$32 \times 16 \times 1024$
route	22 20			
conv	1024	$3 \times 3/1$	$32 \times 16 \times 2048$	$32 \times 16 \times 1024$
conv	75	$1 \times 1/1$	$32 \times 16 \times 1024$	$32 \times 16 \times 75$
E-RPN			$32 \times 16 \times \mathbf{75}$	

of a complex number, similar to [27]. The angle is given simply by using $\arctan_2(t_{im}, t_{re})$. On one hand, this avoids singularities, on the other hand this results in a closed mathematical space, which consequently has an advantageous impact on generalization of the model. We can link our regression parameters directly into the loss function (7).

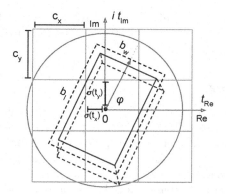

Fig. 3. 3D bounding box regression. We predict oriented 3D bounding boxes based on the regression parameters shown in YOLOv2 [13], as well as a complex angle for box orientation. The transition from 2D to 3D is done by a predefined height based on each class.

2.3 Loss Function

Our network optimization loss function $\mathcal{L}$ is based on the the concepts from YOLO [12] and YOLOv2 [13], who defined $\mathcal{L}_{\text{Yolo}}$ as the sum of squared errors using the introduced multi-part loss. We extend this approach by an Euler regression part $\mathcal{L}_{\text{Euler}}$ to get use of the complex numbers, which have a closed mathematical space for angle comparisons. This neglect singularities, which are common for single angle estimations:

$$\mathcal{L} = \mathcal{L}_{\text{Yolo}} + \mathcal{L}_{\text{Euler}} \tag{5}$$

The Euler regression part of the loss function is defined with the aid of the Euler-Region-Proposal (see Fig. 3). Assuming that the difference between the complex numbers of prediction and ground truth, i.e. $|z|e^{ib_\phi}$ and $|\hat{z}|e^{i\hat{b}_\phi}$ is always located on the unit circle with $|z| = 1$ and $|\hat{z}| = 1$, we minimize the absolute value of the squared error to get a real loss:

$$\mathcal{L}_{\text{Euler}} = \lambda_{coord} \sum_{i=0}^{S^2} \sum_{j=0}^{B} \mathbb{1}_{ij}^{obj} \left| (e^{ib_\phi} - e^{i\hat{b}_\phi})^2 \right| \tag{6}$$

$$= \lambda_{coord} \sum_{i=0}^{S^2} \sum_{j=0}^{B} \mathbb{1}_{ij}^{obj} \left[(t_{im} - \hat{t}_{im})^2 + (t_{re} - \hat{t}_{re})^2 \right] \tag{7}$$

where λ_{coord} is a scaling factor to ensure stable convergence in early phases and $\mathbb{1}_{ij}^{obj}$ denotes that the jth bounding box predictor in cell i has highest intersection over union (IoU) compared to ground truth for that prediction. Furthermore the comparison between the predicted box P_j and ground truth G with IoU $\frac{P_j \cap G}{P_j \cup G}$, where $P_j \cap G = \{x : x \in P_j \wedge x \in G\}$, $P_j \cup G\{x : x \in P_j \vee x \in G\}$ is adjusted to handle rotated boxes as well. This is realized by the theory of intersection of two 2D polygon geometries and union respectively, generated from the corresponding box parameters b_x, b_y, b_w, b_l and b_ϕ.

2.4   Efficiency Design

The main advantage of the used network design is the prediction of all bounding boxes in one inference pass. The E-RPN is part of the network and uses the output of the last convolutional layer to predict all bounding boxes. Hence, we only have one network, which can be trained in an end-to-end manner without specific training approaches. Due to this, our model has a lower runtime than other models that generate region proposals in a sliding window manner [22] with prediction of offsets and the class for every proposal (e.g. Faster R-CNN [15]). In Fig. 5 we compare our architecture with some of the leading models on the KITTI benchmark. Our approach achieves a way higher frame rate while still keeping a comparable mAP (mean Average Precision). The frame rates were directly taken from the respective papers and all were tested on a Titan X or Titan Xp. We tested our model on a Titan X and an NVIDIA TX2 board to emphasize the real-time capability (see Fig. 5).

3   Training and Experiments

We evaluated Complex-YOLO on the challenging KITTI object detection benchmark [1], which is divided into three subcategories 2D, 3D and birds-eye-view object detection for *Cars*, *Pedestrians* and *Cyclists*. Each class is evaluated based on three difficulty levels *easy*, *moderate* and *hard* considering the object size, distance, occlusion and truncation. This public dataset provides 7,481 samples for training including annotated ground truth and 7,518 test samples with point clouds taken from a Velodyne laser scanner, where annotation data is private. Note that we focused on birds-eye-view and do not ran the 2D object detection benchmark, since our input is Lidar based only.

3.1   Training Details

We trained our model from scratch via stochastic gradient descent with a weight decay of 0.0005 and momentum 0.9. Our implementation is based on modified version of the Darknet neural network framework [28]. First, we applied our preprocessing (see Sect. 2.1) to generate the birds-eye-view RGB-maps from Velodyne samples. Following the principles from [2,3,29], we subdivided the training set with public available ground truth, but used ratios of 85% for training and 15% for validation, because we trained from scratch and aimed for a model that is capable of multi-class predictions. In contrast, e.g. VoxelNet [3] modified and optimized the model for different classes. We suffered from the available ground truth data, because it was intended for camera detections first. The class distribution with more than 75% *Car*, less than 4% *Cyclist* and less than 15%

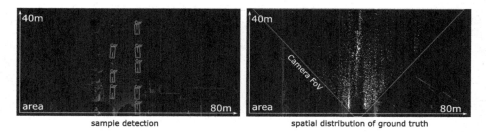

sample detection   spatial distribution of ground truth

Fig. 4. Spatial ground truth distribution. The figure outlines the size of the birds-eye-view area with a sample detection on the left. The right shows a 2D spatial histogram of annotated boxes in [1]. The distribution outlines the horizontal field of view of the camera used for annotation and the inherited blind spots in our map.

Pedestrian is disadvantageous. Also, more than 90% of all the annotated objects are facing the car direction, facing towards the recording car or having similar orientations. On top, Fig. 4 shows a 2D histogram for spatial object locations from birds-eye-view perspective, where dense points indicate more objects at exactly this position. This inherits two blind spot for birds-eye-view map. Nevertheless we saw surprising good results for the validation set and other recorded unlabeled KITTI sequences covering several use case scenarios, like urban, highway or inner city.

For the first epochs, we started with a small learning rate to ensure convergence. After some epochs, we scaled the learning rate up and continued to gradually decrease it for up to 1,000 epochs. Due to the fine grained requirements, when using a birds-eye-view approach, slight changes in predicted features will have a strong impact on resulting box predictions. We used batch normalization for regularization and a linear activation $f(x) = x$ for the last layer of our CNN, apart from that the leaky rectified linear activation:

$$f(x) = \begin{cases} x, & x > 0 \\ 0.1x, & \text{otherwise} \end{cases} \tag{8}$$

3.2 Evaluation on KITTI

We have adapted our experimental setup and follow the official KITTI evaluation protocol, where the IoU thresholds are 0.7 for class *Car* and 0.5 for class *Pedestrian* and *Cyclist*. Detections that are not visible on the image plane are filtered, because the ground truth is only available for objects that also appear on the image plane of the camera recording [1] (see Fig. 4). We used the average precision (AP) metric to compare the results. Note, that we ignore a small number of objects that are outside our birds-eye-view map boundaries with more than 40 m to the front, to keep the input dimensions as small as possible for efficiency reasons.

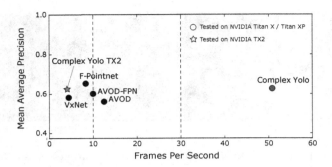

Fig. 5. Performance comparison. This plot shows the mAP in relation to the run-time (fps). All models were tested on a Nvidia Titan X or Titan Xp. Complex-Yolo achieves accurate results by being five times faster than the most effective competitor on the KITTI benchmark [1]. We compared to the five leading models and measured our network on a dedicated embedded platform (TX2) with reasonable efficiency (4 fps) as well. Complex-Yolo is the first model for real-time 3D object detection.

Birds-Eye-View. Our evaluation results for the birds-eye-view detection are presented in Table 2. This benchmark uses bounding box overlap for comparison. For a better overview and to rank the results, similar current leading methods

Table 2. Performance comparison for birds-eye-view detection. APs (in %) for our experimental setup compared to current leading methods. Note that our method is validated on our splitted validation dataset, whereas all others are validated on the official KITTI test set.

Method	Modality	FPS	Car			Pedestrian			Cyclist		
			Easy	Mod.	Hard	Easy	Mod.	Hard	Easy	Mod.	Hard
MV3D [2]	Lidar+Mono	2.8	86.02	76.90	68.49	-	-	-	-	-	-
F-PointNet [5]	Lidar+Mono	5.9	88.70	84.00	75.33	**58.09**	**50.22**	**47.20**	**75.38**	61.96	54.68
AVOD [7]	Lidar+Mono	12.5	86.80	**85.44**	77.73	42.51	35.24	33.97	63.66	47.74	46.55
AVOD-FPN [7]	Lidar+Mono	10.0	88.53	83.79	**77.90**	50.66	44.75	40.83	62.39	52.02	47.87
VoxelNet [3]	Lidar	4.3	**89.35**	79.26	77.39	46.13	40.74	38.11	66.70	54.76	50.55
Complex-YOLO	Lidar	**50.4**	85.89	77.40	77.33	46.08	45.90	44.20	72.37	**63.36**	**60.27**

Table 3. Performance comparison for 3D object detection. APs (in %) for our experimental setup compared to current leading methods. Note that our method is validated on our splitted validation dataset, whereas all others are validated on the official KITTI test set.

Method	Modality	FPS	Car			Pedestrian			Cyclist		
			Easy	Mod.	Hard	Easy	Mod.	Hard	Easy	Mod.	Hard
MV3D [2]	Lidar+Mono	2.8	71.09	62.35	55.12	-	-	-	-	-	-
F-PointNet [5]	Lidar+Mono	5.9	81.20	70.39	62.19	**51.21**	**44.89**	**40.23**	**71.96**	56.77	50.39
AVOD [7]	Lidar+Mono	12.5	73.59	65.78	58.38	38.28	31.51	26.98	60.11	44.90	38.80
AVOD-FPN [7]	Lidar+Mono	10.0	**81.94**	**71.88**	**66.38**	46.35	39.00	36.58	59.97	46.12	42.36
VoxelNet [3]	Lidar	4.3	77.47	65.11	57.73	39.48	33.69	31.51	61.22	48.36	44.37
Complex-YOLO	Lidar	**50.4**	67.72	64.00	63.01	41.79	39.70	35.92	68.17	**58.32**	**54.30**

are listed as well, but performing on the official KITTI test set. Complex-YOLO consistently outperforms all competitors in terms of runtime and efficiency, while still manages to achieve comparable accuracy. With about 0.02 s runtime on a Titan X GPU, we are 5 times faster than AVOD [7], considering their usage of a more powerful GPU (Titan Xp). Compared to VoxelNet [3], which is also Lidar based only, we are more than 10 times faster and MV3D [2], the slowest competitor, takes 18 times as long (Fig. 6).

Fig. 6. Visualization of complex-YOLO results. Note that predictions are exclusively based on birds-eye-view images generated from point clouds. The re-projection into camera space is for illustrative purposes only.

3D Object Detection. Table 3 shows our achieved results for the 3D bounding box overlap. Since we do not estimate the height information directly with regression, we ran this benchmark with a fixed spatial height location extracted from ground truth similar to MV3D [2]. Additionally as mentioned, we simply injected a predefined height for every object based on its class, calculated from the mean over all ground truth objects per class. This reduces the precision for all classes, but it confirms the good results measured on the birds-eye-view benchmark.

4   Conclusion

In this paper we present the first real-time efficient deep learning model for 3D object detection on Lidar based point clouds. We highlight our state of the art results in terms of accuracy (see Fig. 5) on the KITTI benchmark suite with an outstanding efficiency of more than 50 fps (NVIDIA Titan X). We do not need additional sensors, e.g. camera, like most of the leading approaches. This breakthrough is achieved by the introduction of the new E-RPN, an Euler regression approach for estimating orientations with the aid of the complex numbers. The closed mathematical space without singularities allows robust angle prediction.

Our approach is able to detect objects of multiple classes (e.g. cars, vans, pedestrians, cyclists, trucks, tram, sitting pedestrians, misc) simultaneously in one forward path. This novelty enables deployment for real usage in self driving cars and clearly differentiates to other models. We show the real-time capability even on dedicated embedded platform NVIDIA TX2 (4 fps). In future work, it is planned to add height information to the regression, enabling a real independent 3D object detection in space, and to use tempo-spatial dependencies within point cloud pre-processing for a better class distinction and improved accuracy.

Acknowledgement. First, we would like to thank our main employer Valeo, especially Jörg Schrepfer and Johannes Petzold, for giving us the possibility to do fundamental research. Additionally, we would like to thank our colleague Maximillian Jaritz for his important contribution on voxel generation. Last but not least, we would like to thank our academic partner the TU-Ilmenau for having a fruitful partnership.

References

1. Geiger, A.: Are we ready for autonomous driving? the KITTI vision benchmark suite. In: Proceedings of the 2012 IEEE Conference on Computer Vision and Pattern Recognition (CVPR) CVPR 2012, pp. 3354–3361. IEEE Computer Society, Washington (2012)
2. Chen, X., Ma, H., Wan, J., Li, B., Xia, T.: Multi-view 3D object detection network for autonomous driving. CoRR abs/1611.07759 (2016)
3. Zhou, Y., Tuzel, O.: VoxelNet: end-to-end learning for point cloud based 3D object detection. CoRR abs/1711.06396 (2017)
4. Engelcke, M., Rao, D., Wang, D.Z., Tong, C.H., Posner, I.: Vote3Deep: fast object detection in 3D point clouds using efficient convolutional neural networks. CoRR abs/1609.06666 (2016)

5. Qi, C.R., Liu, W., Wu, C., Su, H., Guibas, L.J.: Frustum PointNets for 3D object detection from RGB-D data. CoRR abs/1711.08488 (2017)
6. Wang, D.Z., Posner, I.: Voting for voting in online point cloud object detection. In: Proceedings of Robotics: Science and Systems, Rome July 2015
7. Ku, J., Mozifian, M., Lee, J., Harakeh, A., Waslander, S.: Joint 3D proposal generation and object detection from view aggregation. arXiv preprint arXiv:1712.02294 (2017)
8. Li, B., Zhang, T., Xia, T.: Vehicle detection from 3D lidar using fully convolutional network. CoRR abs/1608.07916 (2016)
9. Li, B.: 3D fully convolutional network for vehicle detection in point cloud. CoRR abs/1611.08069 (2016)
10. Qi, C.R., Su, H., Mo, K., Guibas, L.J.: PointNet: deep learning on point sets for 3D classification and segmentation. CoRR abs/1612.00593 (2016)
11. Qi, C.R., Yi, L., Su, H., Guibas, L.J.: PointNet++: beep hierarchical feature learning on point sets in a metric space. CoRR abs/1706.02413 (2017)
12. Redmon, J., Divvala, S.K., Girshick, R.B., Farhadi, A.: You only look once: unified, real-time object detection. CoRR abs/1506.02640 (2015)
13. Redmon, J., Farhadi, A.: YOLO9000: better, faster, stronger. CoRR abs/1612.08242 (2016)
14. Liu, W., et al.: SSD: single shot multibox detector. CoRR abs/1512.02325 (2015)
15. Ren, S., He, K., Girshick, R.B., Sun, J.: Faster R-CNN: towards real-time object detection with region proposal networks. CoRR abs/1506.01497 (2015)
16. Cai, Z., Fan, Q., Feris, R.S., Vasconcelos, N.: A unified multi-scale deep convolutional neural network for fast object detection. CoRR abs/1607.07155 (2016)
17. Ren, J.S.J., et al.: Accurate single stage detector using recurrent rolling convolution. CoRR abs/1704.05776 (2017)
18. Chen, X., Kundu, K., Zhang, Z., Ma, H., Fidler, S., Urtasun, R.: Monocular 3D object detection for autonomous driving. In: IEEE CVPR (2016)
19. Girshick, R.B., Donahue, J., Darrell, T., Malik, J.: Rich feature hierarchies for accurate object detection and semantic segmentation. CoRR abs/1311.2524 (2013)
20. He, K., Zhang, X., Ren, S., Sun, J.: Deep residual learning for image recognition. CoRR abs/1512.03385 (2015)
21. Chen, X., Kundu, K., Zhu, Y., Ma, H., Fidler, S., Urtasun, R.: 3D object proposals using stereo imagery for accurate object class detection. CoRR abs/1608.07711 (2016)
22. Girshick, R.B.: Fast R-CNN. CoRR abs/1504.08083 (2015)
23. Li, Y., Bu, R., Sun, M., Chen, B.: PointCNN (2018)
24. Wang, Y., Sun, Y., Liu, Z., Sarma, S.E., Bronstein, M.M., Solomon, J.M.: Dynamic graph CNN for learning on point clouds (2018)
25. Xiang, Y., Choi, W., Lin, Y., Savarese, S.: Data-driven 3D voxel patterns for object category recognition. In: Proceedings of the IEEE International Conference on Computer Vision and Pattern Recognition (2015)
26. Wu, Z., Song, S., Khosla, A., Tang, X., Xiao, J.: 3D shapenets for 2.5D object recognition and next-best-view prediction. CoRR abs/1406.5670 (2014)
27. Beyer, L., Hermans, A., Leibe, B.: Biternion nets: continuous head pose regression from discrete training labels. In: Gall, J., Gehler, P., Leibe, B. (eds.) GCPR 2015. LNCS, vol. 9358, pp. 157–168. Springer, Cham (2015). https://doi.org/10.1007/978-3-319-24947-6_13
28. Redmon, J.: DarkNet: open source neural networks in c. http://pjreddie.com/darknet/ (2013–2016)
29. Chen, X., et al.: 3D object proposals for accurate object class detection. In: NIPS (2015)

It's Not All About Size: On the Role of Data Properties in Pedestrian Detection

Amir Rasouli$^{(\boxtimes)}$ ⓘ, Iuliia Kotseruba ⓘ, and John K. Tsotsos ⓘ

Department of Electrical Engineering and Computer Science and Center for Vision Research, York University, Toronto, ON M3J 1P3, Canada
{aras,yulia_k,tsotsos}@eecs.yorku.ca

Abstract. Pedestrian detection is central in applications such as autonomous driving. The performance of algorithms tailored to solve this problem has been extensively evaluated on benchmark datasets, such as Caltech, which do not adequately represent the diversity of traffic scenes. Consequently, the true performance of algorithms and their limitations in practice remain understudied.

To this end, we conduct an empirical study using 7 classical and state-of-the-art algorithms on the recently proposed JAAD dataset augmented with 16 additional labels for pedestrian attributes. Using this data we show that the relative performance of the algorithms varies depending on the properties of the training data.

We analyze the contribution of weather conditions and pedestrian attributes to performance changes and examine the major sources of detection errors. Finally, we show that the diversity of the training data leads to better generalizability of the algorithms across different datasets even with a smaller number of samples.

Keywords: Pedestrian detection · Data properties · Pedestrian attributes · Benchmark dataset · Evaluation framework · Autonomous driving

1 Introduction

1.1 Pedestrian Detection

With the rise of autonomous driving systems, visual perception algorithms are facing a new dilemma, that is the ability to detect and recognize objects in highly varying scenes. Among typical objects present in traffic scenes, pedestrians are particularly challenging for identification because they assume different poses, have high variability of appearance and can be easily confused with other objects with similar properties [25].

In the past decades numerous pedestrian detection algorithms [1,7,8,25,31] have been proposed, the majority of which have been tested on the publicly available datasets such as Caltech [5] and KITTI [11]. Although these datasets contain

L. Leal-Taixé and S. Roth (Eds.): ECCV 2018 Workshops, LNCS 11129, pp. 210–225, 2019.
https://doi.org/10.1007/978-3-030-11009-3_12

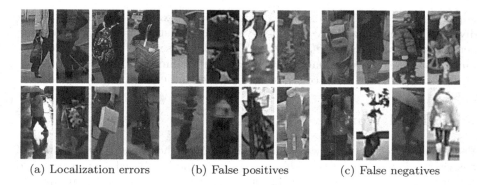

(a) Localization errors   (b) False positives   (c) False negatives

Fig. 1. Different sources of detection errors due to the variability in the appearance of the pedestrians and scenes: (a) shows localization errors due to the presence of bags, backpack and umbrellas which are commonly associated with pedestrians observed in the scenes; (b) false positives caused by various environmental factors such as reflections on wet surfaces, over-exposure as well as the presence of objects resembling pedestrians; and (c) false negatives due to variation in shape, e.g. children who have different aspect ratio compared to adults, and appearance, e.g. pedestrians wearing hooded jackets, holding umbrellas or carrying bulky backpacks.

an adequately large amount of data for evaluating the performance of pedestrian detection algorithms, they lack sufficient variability in scene properties such as different lighting conditions and pedestrians' appearance corresponding to different weather conditions.

Given the dynamic nature of driving and the fact that autonomous vehicles should be able to handle a wide range of conditions robustly (see examples in Fig. 1), there is a need to examine the performance of pedestrian detection algorithms and measure their limitations under various visual conditions.

A number of past studies have investigated the role of data properties, such as deformation and occlusion [17], ground truth annotation [23,30], and scale [18] in pedestrian detection algorithms. What is missing, however, is determining the effects of visual appearances due to pedestrian attributes and environmental conditions.

The newly proposed detection datasets collected under various conditions, such as CityPersons [32] and JAAD [20], provide the opportunity to further investigate the role of data properties in the performance of pedestrian detection algorithms. To this end, we analyze the performance of state-of-the-art pedestrian detection algorithms using the publicly available JAAD dataset for which we annotated all pedestrian samples with information regarding their appearance, such as clothing, accessories, objects being carried and pose.

Using the newly annotated dataset together with available properties of JAAD, we show performance variation in detection algorithms as a result of the changes in train/test data. In particular, we investigate the influence of weather conditions under which the data is collected and attributes that impact appearance and visibility of pedestrians. We also examine the effect of data diversity on generalizability by cross-evaluating the state-of-the-art pedestrian detection algorithms on the JAAD and Caltech datasets. As part of our contribution, we release an evaluation framework for training and testing pedestrian detection algorithms using common benchmarks and evaluation metrics.

2   Related Works

Pedestrian detection is a well-studied field. Over the years, a wide range of algorithms have been developed, ranging from models based on hand-crafted features [7,14,31] to modern convolutional neural networks [1,8,29], and hybrid algorithms benefitting from a combination of both of these techniques [15,28].

The modern pedestrian detection algorithms use various techniques to overcome the challenges of identifying pedestrians in the wild. For example, Tian et al. [24] propose a part-based detection algorithm to deal with occlusion. The model consists of a number of part detectors, combinations of which determine the existence of a pedestrian in a given location. In [25], the authors use semantic information of the scene in the form of pedestrian attributes, e.g. carrying a backpack, and scene attributes such as trees or vehicles to distinguish the pedestrians from the background.

In [29] the authors use bootstrapping techniques to mine hard negative samples to minimize confusions caused by background while detecting pedestrians. The proposed algorithm uses features learned by a region proposal network (RPN) to train a cascaded boosted forest for the final hard negative mining and classification. In a more recent approach, Brazil et al. [1] show that jointly training a Faster R-CNN network and semantic segmentation network on pedestrian bounding boxes can improve the overall detection results.

As the performance of state-of-the-art pedestrian detection algorithms on benchmark datasets began to saturate (e.g. 7–9% miss rate reported on Caltech [5]), attention has shifted towards the effects of data properties on detection performance. A recent study on generic object recognition tasks shows that order of magnitude increase in the size of training samples can enhance performance even in the presence of up to 20% error in ground truth annotation [22].

As for pedestrian detection algorithms, the effect of occlusion and sample size [17], the balance between negative and positive samples [12], and the cleanness of ground truth annotations [23] have been investigated. Zhang et al. [30], for example, demonstrate that the percentage of miss-classification and localization error varies significantly depending on the algorithm. Through experimental evaluations, the authors show that simply by improving the quality of ground truth annotations, localization errors can be significantly reduced resulting in the overall performance boost of more than 7% miss rate in state-of-the-art pedestrian detection algorithms.

2.1   Datasets

There are a number of publicly available pedestrian detection datasets among which some, namely the Caltech [5] and KITTI [11] datasets, are widely used for evaluating the performance of pedestrian detection algorithms. These datasets, although large in scale, lack the diversity in data properties such as weather conditions, geographical locations, pedestrian attributes, etc. For example, Caltech contains 10 h of driving footage collected under sunny and clear weather conditions in streets of Los Angles. Likewise, KITTI is collected under similar weather conditions in streets of Karlsruhe in Germany.

Recently, we have witnessed the emergence of more diverse pedestrian detection datasets. For instance, CityPersons [32] is a pedestrian detection dataset comprised of data collected in various cities across Germany, in different seasons and under different weather conditions. Another pedestrian detection dataset, JAAD [20] is a set of high resolution image sequences collected in different countries and contains video footage recorded under clear and extreme weather conditions such as heavy rain.

The recently proposed datasets provide a variety of scenery and pedestrian samples suitable for studying the limitations of pedestrian detection algorithms under different conditions. Examples of errors caused by the changes data properties are illustrated in Fig. 1.

Despite the introduction of diverse pedestrian detection datasets, there are very few attempts on quantifying the effect of data properties on pedestrian detection algorithms. To this end, in this paper we analyze the effect of data properties in two ways: their impact on the performance of state-of-the-art, and generalizability of the algorithms across different datasets. More specifically, the contributions of this paper are as follows:

1. We introduce a large dataset of pedestrian attributes by annotating the pedestrian samples from the JAAD dataset [20] to study the effect of pedestrian appearance changes on detection algorithms.
2. We examine the performance of state-of-the-art pedestrian detection algorithms with respect to dataset properties and highlight changes in their behavior with respect to different training and testing samples.
3. We perform a cross-evaluation of the state-of-the-art algorithms on the JAAD and Caltech datasets to measure the generalizability of algorithms and datasets based on different properties of the data.
4. We propose a software framework for experimentation and benchmarking classical and state-of-the-art pedestrian detection algorithms using publicly available pedestrian datasets.

3   The Attribute Dataset

There are a number of existing pedestrian attribute datasets that provide fine-grained attributes (e.g. RAP [13], PETA [4]). These datasets primarily cater to applications such as surveillance and identification tasks, and, as a result,

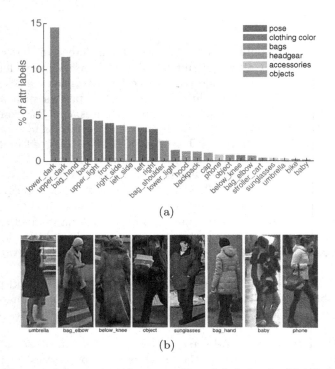

Fig. 2. (a) Types and frequency of new attribute labels in the JAAD dataset color-coded based on the attribute type (e.g. pose, clothing color, accessories); (b) Samples of pedestrians with select attribute labels shown. (Color figure online)

often contain indoor scenes or are recorded using on-site security cameras. Such characteristics make these datasets unsuitable for analyzing pedestrian detection algorithms for applications such as autonomous driving.

Tian *et al.* [25] introduced pedestrian attribute information for the Caltech dataset. The authors augmented the dataset with 9 attributes on 2.7K pedestrian samples. As was mentioned earlier, the Caltech dataset has insufficient variability of weather and scenery properties, hence the attributes lack diversity as well.

To investigate the effect of pedestrian attributes and data properties on detection algorithms, we utilized the publicly available JAAD dataset. The JAAD dataset is a naturalistic driving dataset which comprises videos gathered under different weather and road conditions and contains annotations for video properties, as well as some characteristics of pedestrians (e.g. their age and gender).

We further extended these annotations by adding 16 attributes for each of the 392K pedestrian samples, a total of 900K new attribute labels, summarized in Fig. 2(a)[1]. There are attributes for coarse pose (*left*, *right*, *back*, *front*), clothing

---

[1] The JAAD attributes are available at https://github.com/ykotseruba/JAAD_pedestrian.

color (*upper_dark* and *lower_dark*) and length (*below_knee* for long coats and skirts).

There are also several attributes for the presence and location of bags and their type: whether they are worn on the *left_side* or *right_side* relative to pedestrian's body and carried on the shoulder (*bag_shoulder*), elbow (*bag_elbow*), back (*backpack*) or held in the hand (*bag_hand*). In addition, we add labels for hooded clothing (*hood*) and caps (*cap*), accessories (e.g. *phone*, *sunglasses*) and various objects that pedestrians can hold in their hands (e.g. *object*, *baby*).

The attributes were selected based on their appropriateness for the driving tasks. For instance, pose of the pedestrian and color of their clothing affect visibility; long clothing obscures the shape and movement of the human body; caps, hoods, and sunglasses occlude pedestrian's face and may limit their view of the traffic scene as well; carrying large bags, backpacks or other objects may not only change appearance and shape of the pedestrian but limit their mobility; holding a phone does not change the pose significantly, but can be used to determine pedestrian's distraction [19], etc.

Clothing color and pose are the only attributes provided for all bounding boxes in the JAAD dataset and form the minimum attribute set. As can be seen from the bar plot in Fig. 2(a), most pedestrians in the dataset are wearing dark clothes, for instance, nearly 70% of pedestrians have both *upper_dark* and *lower_dark* attributes present.

Pose attributes, *left*, *right*, *back*, and *front*, are nearly equally distributed. Aside from clothing color and pose, the *bags* category is the most represented. In fact, nearly 50% of all pedestrians carry a bag or a backpack. In the following sections, we will consider the effect of the diversity and uneven distribution of attributes in the training data on detection.

4   Experimental Setup

4.1   Evaluation Framework

Our framework provides a unified API[2] for experimentation with 10 classical and state-of-the-art pedestrian detection algorithms including SPP+ [16], ACF+ [7], Faster-RCNN [21], CCF [28], Checkerboards [31], DeepPed [26], RPN+BF [29], LDCF+ [14], MS-CNN [2], and SDS-RCNN [1]. All algorithms in the API have training and testing code except SPP+ and DeepPed which only have test code as no official training code has been released by the authors.

The proposed framework is compatible with major publicly available pedestrian detection datasets including INRIA [3], ETH [10], TUD-Brussels [27], Daimler [9], Caltech [5], KITTI [11], CityPersons [32], and JAAD [20]. It allows the manipulation of these datasets in terms of scale, balancing training and testing samples, selection of ground truth, etc. The results can be evaluated using common metrics for pedestrian detection.

---

[2] The API is available at https://github.com/aras62/PBF.

The software is implemented in Matlab and is based on the code published by the authors of the corresponding algorithms. The training and testing functions are modified for the ease of use from a single API. Our framework uses the original and modified versions of the Piotr toolbox [6] and follows the Caltech benchmark standards [5].

4.2 Algorithms

For the experimental evaluations in this paper we chose three classical algorithms as baselines including ACF+ and its variation LDCF+ [7], and LDCF++ [14], and four state-of-the-art algorithms including RPN+BF [29], MS-CNN [2], SDS-RPN and SDS-RCNN [1] (the top performing algorithm as of ICCV 2017). From RPN+BF algorithm, we only report the results of its RPN component to highlight how the weak segmentation approach proposed in SDS-RPN would behave under different conditions.

The algorithms were trained on the subsets of the JAAD dataset using the default parameters proposed by the authors for the Caltech dataset. The only exception is that we modified the width of training and testing images to maintain the aspect ratio of the images in JAAD. For cross-evaluation with the Caltech dataset, we used the pre-trained models published by the authors of corresponding algorithms.

4.3 Data

The JAAD dataset contains HD quality images with dimensions of 1080×1920 pixels. To maximize the performance of the detection algorithms using default parameters tuned on Caltech, we resized all images to half-scale of 540×960. For evaluation and training, we selected samples with reasonable scale (bounding box height of 50 pixels or more) with partial occlusion (visibility of 75% or more).

For experimental evaluations, we divided JAAD into four different train/test subsets according to the property of the data in terms of weather conditions including *clear*, *cloudy*, *cloudy+clear* (*c+c*) and *mix*. As the names imply, *clear* and *cloudy* subsets only include training images collected under clear and cloudy skies with no rain/snow, and *mix* contains all weather conditions including clear and cloudy, and more extreme weather conditions such as rain/snow. It should be noted that we excluded the videos from the JAAD dataset that were collected under very poor visibility conditions such as nighttime and heavy rain.

The training images for each subset are generated by uniformly sampling 50% of the videos that are recorded under the given condition. Each training subset contains approximately 6.5K pedestrian samples. The remainder of the videos (which may include all weather conditions) are also uniformly sampled and divided into validation and test set.

4.4 Metrics

To report the performance of the algorithms, we use log-average miss rate over the precision range of $[10^{-2}, 10^0]$ (MR_2) and $[10^{-4}, 10^0]$ (MR_4) false positives

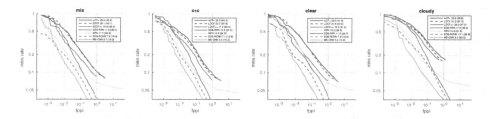

Fig. 3. ROC curves for all algorithms trained and tested on *mix*, *clear*, *cloudy* and *c+c* (clear and cloudy) datasets with detection threshold set to 0.5 IoU. Legends for each plot show the names of algorithms together with $MR_2(MR_4)$ measures. In each plot legend the algorithms are sorted by MR_2 in a descending order.

per image (FPPI) as in [29,30]. We also follow [30] and apply two oracle test cases to measure the contributions of background and localization errors. The localization oracle excludes all false positives that overlap with ground truth from evaluation thus reflecting the contribution of background error. The background oracle does not count false positives that do not overlap with ground truth hence showing the amount of localization error. All of our results are presented using the matching criterion of intersection over union (IoU) ≥ 0.5, unless otherwise stated.

5   Data Properties and Detection Accuracy

5.1   Weather

Weather conditions have multiple effects on the visibility of the pedestrians (e.g. due to rain) and their appearance (e.g. presence of sunglasses or umbrellas). In addition, the appearance of the scene itself may be altered by different lighting conditions, precipitation, reflections, sharp shadows, etc., leading to detection errors as illustrated in Fig. 1. In order to quantify these effects, we trained and tested all pedestrian detection algorithms on different subsets of JAAD dataset split by weather conditions as explained in Sect. 4.

We begin by reporting the ROC curves along with MR_2 and MR_4 metrics. As can be seen in Fig. 3, despite the changes in the overall performance of the algorithms, the rankings are the same across different subsets. The only exception is in the *clear* case where SDS-RPN outperforms RPN.

The main difference between SDS-RPN and regular RPN is that the former adds a weak segmentation component utilizing binary masks from bounding box annotations. It is apparent that using this technique is only effective under clear weather conditions which correspond to the properties of the Caltech dataset that this algorithm was originally tested on (see Table 2). Under different weather conditions, however, the weak segmentation results in a poorer performance compared to the regular RPN.

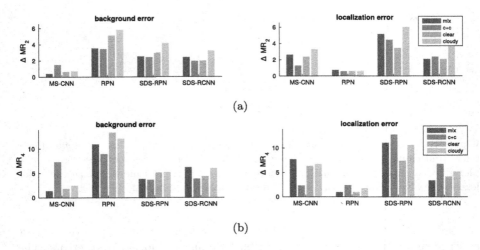

(a)

(b)

Fig. 4. The relative contribution of background and localization errors to the performance of the pedestrian detection algorithms. The errors are calculated as changes in (a) MR_2 and (b) MR_4 measures for algorithms trained and tested on different subsets of JAAD.

Another observation is that the MS-CNN algorithm (which according to [1] is not among top five performing algorithms on Caltech) achieves the best performance by a large margin (up to 2% on *mix, clear* and *c+c* subsets and more than 5% on *cloudy*) compared to state-of-the-art SDS-RCNN.

To further understand the underlying factors impacting the performance of each algorithm, we report background and localization errors under different weather conditions. As depicted in Fig. 4, testing and training on the subsets of JAAD with different properties reveal inconsistencies in the performance of each detection algorithm as well as their relative performance compared to other algorithms. For example, in the case of *c+c*, MS-CNN reaches its highest background error while at the same time it achieves the lowest localization error compared to others.

For RPN-based models the same trend does not hold as they all perform poorly in terms of localization error, when trained and tested on *c+c*. Comparatively, MS-CNN has the lowest background error on the *mix, clear* and *cloudy* subsets and the second worst on *c+c*.

Likewise, on average, RPN performs best in terms of localization error, however, it is the worst in terms of background error. One interesting observation is the added benefit of the weak segmentation component to RPN (in SDS-RPN) which helps improve the background error but at the price of reducing its localization accuracy.

Table 1. The performance of pedestrian detection algorithms in the presence of individual attributes. The results are reported as MR_4 metric. The top performing algorithms for each attribute are highlighted in bold.

Algorithms	Attributes										
	female	male	pose_back	pose_front	pose_left	pose_right	child	backpack	bag	cap_hood	umbrella
ACF+	38.96	34.66	39.71	38.28	34.70	33.91	60.92	38.88	36.00	40.21	69.18
LDCF+	37.02	33.84	35.27	37.24	32.90	30.94	55.02	33.50	33.94	38.27	68.16
LDCF++	30.09	28.30	34.41	31.79	26.44	26.71	55.16	32.76	26.69	33.29	56.64
MS-CNN	**13.49**	**14.03**	17.77	**14.00**	15.20	**11.19**	45.37	16.01	**10.77**	**14.08**	31.06
RPN	21.99	25.79	28.03	26.82	22.72	21.34	53.59	24.59	19.48	28.97	37.35
SDS-RPN	24.31	22.57	26.58	23.67	21.51	22.74	52.54	19.50	20.12	24.61	31.68
SDS-RCNN	14.30	15.77	**17.72**	15.29	**14.46**	13.60	**43.14**	**15.85**	12.25	15.68	**25.57**

5.2   Pedestrian Attributes

In this section, we evaluate the contribution of select attributes (shown in Table 1) on the performance of detection algorithms trained and tested on the *mix* dataset.

Due to the fact that many attributes often appear together in various combinations, it is very hard to disentangle the effect of the individual attributes on the overall detection accuracy of each algorithm. However, major differences can be observed in the relative performances of the algorithms in the presence of certain attributes in the scene.

As one would expect, the performance of classical models is inferior compared to CNN-based algorithms, particularly with respect to some of the rarely occurring attributes such as *child* and *umbrella*. The performance of the state-of-the-art also varies on different attributes. For example, MS-CNN, which shows the highest results on the *mix* subset of JAAD, underperforms compared to SDS-RCNN on select attributes such as *umbrella, backpack, child, pose-back*.

To investigate the common causes of error for MS-CNN and SDS-RCNN we group false positive (FP) and false negative (FN) detections at 0.1 FPPI by the object present in the bounding box as shown in Fig. 5.

With respect to FP, SDS-RCNN and MS-CNN differ greatly not only in the relative contributions of background and localization errors but also in terms of the objects they commonly confuse with pedestrians. Aside from annotation errors, MS-CNN is much more distracted by elongated objects often found in the street scenes, such as tree trunks, hydrants and parking meters.

Many of the localization errors for both MS-CNN and SDS-RCNN are caused by not being able to distinguish pedestrians in groups of 2 or more, particularly when children are also present (attribute *group child* in Fig. 5b). SDS-RCNN also has a higher tendency to place bounding boxes on body parts of the pedestrians or objects they carry (e.g. bags) than MS-CNN. Finally, for both MS-CNN and SDS-RCNN, partially occluded pedestrians, groups of pedestrians and children stand out as main sources of false negative detections.

Note that despite individual sensitivities to certain attributes, both MS-CNN and SDS-RCNN have trouble detecting children and pedestrians with infrequently occurring attributes such as backpacks, umbrellas, hooded clothing, etc.

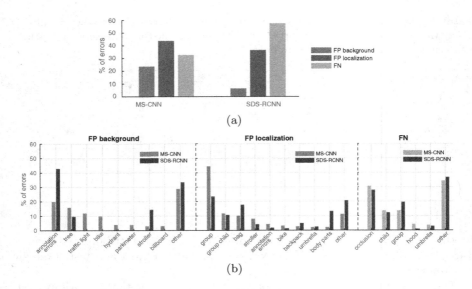

(a)

(b)

Fig. 5. Error analysis for MS-CNN and SDS-RCNN trained and tested on the *mix* reasonable subset of JAAD. Plot (a) shows the relative percentages of false positives (FP) and false negatives (FN) for each algorithm at 0.1 FPPI. FP is further split into localization and background errors depending on whether the detected bounding box overlaps with the ground truth or not. Plot (b) shows a detailed breakdown of false positive and false negative errors grouped by the corresponding attributes.

There is also evidence that algorithms may learn the appearance of common attributes such as bags instead of the pedestrian itself leading to poor localization.

The former issue may be addressed by increasing the variability of the training data either by explicitly ensuring the presence of certain hard attributes or implicitly, by gathering data under different weather conditions, which in turn affect the appearance of the pedestrians. On the other hand, explicitly learning the attributes may also help, as demonstrated by [25].

5.3   Generalizability Across Different Datasets

Here, our goal is to identify the link between the generalizability of the dataset and its properties, i.e. we want to measure whether using training data from a diverse dataset can improve the performance of detection algorithms on other datasets with more uniform properties.

For this purpose, we employed the widely used Caltech dataset [5] and JAAD. We evaluated the algorithms trained on Caltech using the test data from the *mix* subset of JAAD, and also the models trained on different subsets of JAAD using Caltech test set. All the tests are done on a reasonable set of pedestrians with the height of 50 pixels and above. The minimum allowable visibility is set to 75% on the Caltech test set to match the partial occlusion of the JAAD dataset.

Table 2. The performance of state-of-the-art pedestrian detection algorithms on the Caltech and JAAD *mix* datasets. The table shows the results for algorithms trained and tested on the same dataset. The performances on the Caltech test set are reported on both old (MR^O) and new (MR^N) annotations. The best results are highlighted with blue color.

	$C \rightarrow C$ $MR_2^N (MR_2^O)$	$mix \rightarrow mix$ MR_2
ACF+	26.27 (30.55)	23.36
LDCF+	23.07 (25.79)	23.07
LDCF++	13.66 (16.10)	16.90
RPN	11.71 (14.33)	11.71
MS-CNN	9.47 (11.21)	5.70
SDS-RPN	8.15 (9.27)	11.89
SDS-RCNN	6.58 (7.59)	7.78

Table 3. The performance of state-of-the-art pedestrian detection algorithms on the Caltech and different subsets of the JAAD dataset. The results show the performance of the algorithms trained on Caltech and tested on JAAD $(C \rightarrow mix)$ and trained on different subsets of JAAD and tested on Caltech $(J \rightarrow C)$. The performances on the Caltech test set are reported on both old (MR^O) and new (MR^N) annotations. The best and second best results are highlighted with blue and green color respectively.

	$C \rightarrow mix$ MR_2	$J \rightarrow C$ $MR_2^N (MR_2^O)$			
		mix	c+c	cloudy	clear
ACF+	77.94	46.97 (53.63)	49.52 (55.06)	70.79 (74.06)	49.99 (55.23)
LDCF+	54.82	43.61 (49.93)	44.89 (50.85)	59.18 (64.11)	47.29 (52.54)
LDCF++	47.94	37.66 (46.04)	40.41 (48.54)	54.86 (60.72)	44.77 (51.93)
RPN	40.15	27.80 (41.19)	25.74 (38.18)	34.67 (47.34)	28.75 (40.05)
MS-CNN	35.09	22.87 (34.83)	26.30 (38.11)	31.55 (46.35)	29.49 (41.64)
SDS-RPN	43.40	24.24 (30.84)	26.64 (33.61)	35.62 (42.90)	30.85 (38.52)
SDS-RCNN	25.45	21.47 (27.73)	25.29 (32.69)	35.20 (42.35)	23.81 (31.75)

Given that a large portion of the original bounding box annotations in the Caltech dataset are poorly localized, following the advice of [30], we report the results on both the original and newly clean Caltech test set. We denote the miss rate results as MR^O and MR^N for old and new annotations respectively. All detections are calculated on $IoU \geq 0.5$. The results of the evaluations of the algorithms trained and tested on the same dataset are summarized in Table 2 and the results of cross-evaluation between algorithms trained and tested on Caltech and subsets of JAAD are shown in Table 3.

The first observation is that the performance of algorithms on a uniform dataset compared to a diverse one varies significantly. SDS-RCNN algorithm that achieves state-of-the-art performance on Caltech is the second best in JAAD and its counterpart, SDS-RPN, which has the second-best performance on Caltech, performs worse compared to the regular RPN algorithm. MS-CNN, on the other hand, performs best on the *mix* subset, even though on Caltech it is the third best in our evaluation and not even in top five in the latest benchmarks [1].

As was mentioned earlier, the Caltech dataset contains images collected during daylight under the clear sky. Surprisingly, we observe that the *clear* subset of JAAD that has similar properties does not generalize best to Caltech. Besides having the second-best performance on SDS-RCNN models, it ranks third in other cases. In fact, we can see that diversifying the data by training on $c+c$ and further adding extreme weather conditions such as rainy and snowy samples achieves the best results on the Caltech dataset.

Partly, such performance improvement is owing to better localization. For instance, MS-CNN and SDS-RCNN on average have IoUs of 0.73 and 0.75 respectively when trained on JAAD *clear* and 0.74 and 0.76 when trained on JAAD *mix*. The same models trained on Caltech, however, have an average IoU of 0.73.

It should be noted that the CNN-based models in the table are trained on Caltech10x [31] which contains over 45K images with more than 16K training samples. The diverse *mix* dataset contains less than 7K samples, yet generalizes better on Caltech than vice versa.

6   Discussion

In this paper, we conducted a series of experiments to investigate the effect of dataset diversity on the performance of pedestrian detection algorithms (see some qualitative examples in Fig. 6). Using the newly proposed JAAD dataset, we showed that the performance measures reported on the classical benchmark

| GT | Clear | Cloudy | C + C | Mix |

Fig. 6. Examples of the performance of state-of-the-art pedestrian detection algorithms on samples with different weather conditions and pedestrian attributes. From left to right, the ground truth (GT) and the results of algorithms trained on different subsets of the JAAD dataset are shown. Colors green, red and blue correspond to the ground truth, MS-CNN and SDS-RCNN respectively. The results show that the behaviors of both detection algorithms are affected based on the changes in the training data, but in different and somewhat unpredictable ways. For instance, in the example in the second row, SDS-RCNN performs better when trained on the *mix* subset whereas MS-CNN does so when trained on the *clear* subset. (Color figure online)

datasets, such as Caltech, do not necessarily reflect the true potential of detection algorithms in dealing with a wider range of environmental conditions. For instance, MS-CNN which does not even rank top five in the recent state-of-the-art benchmarks, outperforms the current top ranking algorithm, SDS-RCNN, by a significant margin on all subsets of the JAAD dataset.

We showed that the changes in relative performance can be attributed to different properties of the datasets, e.g. depending on what types of weather conditions are represented in the training data. For example, SDS-RPN outperforms the classical RPN on the Caltech dataset owing to the use of a weak segmentation technique, however, it shows inferior results on the JAAD dataset under all weather conditions except clear (which is the most similar to Caltech).

Similar fluctuations in the performance of detection algorithms can be seen with respect to pedestrian attributes. Particularly, rarely occurring attributes such as *child, backpack* and *umbrella* are associated with the highest miss rate for all algorithms. On the other hand, some of the most frequently occurring attributes such as hand bags are shown to be frequently localized instead of the pedestrians.

The diversity of training data also leads to the better generalization of pedestrian detection algorithms across different datasets. Our empirical results suggest that mixing samples with different properties can improve the performance of algorithms even on a more uniform dataset. For example, the MS-CNN algorithm trained on the *mix* subset of JAAD had 7% and 3% lower miss rates on Caltech compared to the models trained on the *clear* and *c+c* subsets respectively.

A carefully selected dataset can also reduce the need for a large volume of training data. For example, the models trained on the *mix* subset of JAAD using only 7K training samples performed better on the Caltech dataset compared to models that were trained on more than 16K training samples from Caltech and tested on the JAAD *mix*.

In conclusion, our study shows that the selection of benchmark datasets for the evaluation of pedestrian detection algorithms for practical applications such as autonomous driving should be revisited to properly assess their performance and limitations under different conditions, and to better reflect the nature of generalizability that is desired.

Using larger datasets certainly benefits the training of the algorithms as does balancing the data with respect to underrepresented weather conditions and pedestrian categories. On the other hand, overrepresented attributes in the data can cause detection errors which should be taken into account when designing pedestrian detection algorithms.

Acknowledgement. This research was supported by several sources, via grants to the senior author, for which the authors are grateful: Air Force Office of Scientific Research USA (FA9550-18-1-0054), the Canada Research Chairs Program (950-231659), and the Natural Sciences and Engineering Research Council of Canada (RGPIN-2016-05352), and the NSERC Canadian Field Robotics Network (NETGP-417354-11).

References

1. Brazil, G., Yin, X., Liu, X.: Illuminating pedestrians via simultaneous detection & segmentation. In: ICCV, pp. 4950–4959 (2017)
2. Cai, Z., Fan, Q., Feris, R.S., Vasconcelos, N.: A unified multi-scale deep convolutional neural network for fast object detection. In: Leibe, B., Matas, J., Sebe, N., Welling, M. (eds.) ECCV 2016. LNCS, vol. 9908, pp. 354–370. Springer, Cham (2016). https://doi.org/10.1007/978-3-319-46493-0_22
3. Dalal, N., Triggs, B.: Histograms of oriented gradients for human detection. In: CVPR, vol. 1, pp. 886–893 (2005)
4. Deng, Y., Luo, P., Loy, C.C., Tang, X.: Pedestrian attribute recognition at far distance. In: The ACM International Conference on Multimedia, pp. 789–792 (2014)
5. Dollár, P., Wojek, C., Schiele, B., Perona, P.: Pedestrian detection: a benchmark. In: CVPR, pp. 304–311 (2009)
6. Dollár, P.: Piotr's Computer Vision Matlab Toolbox (PMT). https://github.com/pdollar/toolbox
7. Dollár, P., Appel, R., Belongie, S., Perona, P.: Fast feature pyramids for object detection. PAMI **36**(8), 1532–1545 (2014)
8. Du, X., El-Khamy, M., Lee, J., Davis, L.: Fused DNN: a deep neural network fusion approach to fast and robust pedestrian detection. In: Winter Conference on Applications of Computer Vision (WACV), pp. 953–961 (2017)
9. Enzweiler, M., Gavrila, D.M.: Monocular pedestrian detection: survey and experiments. PAMI **31**(12), 2179–2195 (2009)
10. Ess, A., Leibe, B., Schindler, K., van Gool, L.: A mobile vision system for robust multi-person tracking. In: CVPR, pp. 1–8 (2008)
11. Geiger, A., Lenz, P., Stiller, C., Urtasun, R.: Vision meets robotics: the KITTI dataset. Int. J. Robot. Res. (IJRR) **32**(11), 1231–1237 (2013)
12. Jung, S.I., Hong, K.S.: Deep network aided by guiding network for pedestrian detection. Pattern Recognit. Lett. **90**, 43–49 (2017)
13. Li, D., Zhang, Z., Chen, X., Ling, H., Huang, K.: A richly annotated dataset for pedestrian attribute recognition. arXiv:1603.07054 (2016)
14. Ohn-Bar, E., Trivedi, M.M.: To boost or not to boost? on the limits of boosted trees for object detection. In: ICPR, pp. 3350–3355 (2016)
15. Ouyang, W., Wang, X.: Joint deep learning for pedestrian detection. In: ICCV, pp. 2056–2063 (2013)
16. Paisitkriangkrai, S., Shen, C., van den Hengel, A.: Strengthening the effectiveness of pedestrian detection with spatially pooled features. In: Fleet, D., Pajdla, T., Schiele, B., Tuytelaars, T. (eds.) ECCV 2014. LNCS, vol. 8692, pp. 546–561. Springer, Cham (2014). https://doi.org/10.1007/978-3-319-10593-2_36
17. Rajaram, R.N., Ohn-Bar, E., Trivedi, M.M.: An exploration of why and when pedestrian detection fails. In: International Conference on Intelligent Transportation Systems (ITSC), pp. 2335–2340 (2015)
18. Rajaram, R.N., Ohn-Bar, E., Trivedi, M.M.: Looking at pedestrians at different scales: a multiresolution approach and evaluations. IEEE Trans. Intell. Transp. Syst. **17**(12), 3565–3576 (2016)
19. Rangesh, A., Ohn-Bar, E., Yuen, K., Trivedi, M.M.: Pedestrians and their phones-Detecting phone-based activities of pedestrians for autonomous vehicles. In: International Conference on Intelligent Transportation Systems (ITSC), pp. 1882–1887 (2016)

20. Rasouli, A., Kotseruba, I., Tsotsos, J.K.: Are they going to cross? a benchmark dataset and baseline for pedestrian crosswalk behavior. In: ICCV, pp. 206–213 (2017)
21. Ren, S., He, K., Girshick, R., Sun, J.: Faster R-CNN: towards real-time object detection with region proposal networks. In: Advances in Neural Information Processing Systems (NIPS), pp. 91–99 (2015)
22. Sun, C., Shrivastava, A., Singh, S., Gupta, A.: Revisiting unreasonable effectiveness of data in deep learning era. In: ICCV, pp. 843–852 (2017)
23. Taiana, M., Nascimento, J., Bernardino, A.: On the purity of training and testing data for learning: the case of pedestrian detection. Neurocomputing **150**, 214–226 (2015)
24. Tian, Y., Luo, P., Wang, X., Tang, X.: Deep learning strong parts for pedestrian detection. In: ICCV, pp. 1904–1912 (2015)
25. Tian, Y., Luo, P., Wang, X., Tang, X.: Pedestrian detection aided by deep learning semantic tasks. In: CVPR, pp. 5079–5087 (2015)
26. Tomè, D., Monti, F., Baroffio, L., Bondi, L., Tagliasacchi, M., Tubaro, S.: Deep convolutional neural networks for pedestrian detection. Signal Process.: Image Commun. **47**, 482–489 (2016)
27. Wojek, C., Walk, S., Schiele, B.: Multi-cue onboard pedestrian detection. In: 2009 IEEE Conference on Computer Vision and Pattern Recognition, pp. 794–801 (2009)
28. Yang, B., Yan, J., Lei, Z., Li, S.Z.: Convolutional channel features. In: ICCV, pp. 82–90 (2015)
29. Zhang, L., Lin, L., Liang, X., He, K.: Is faster R-CNN doing well for pedestrian detection? In: ECCV, pp. 443–457 (2016)
30. Zhang, S., Benenson, R., Omran, M., Hosang, J., Schiele, B.: How far are we from solving pedestrian detection? In: CVPR, pp. 1259–1267 (2016)
31. Zhang, S., Benenson, R., Schiele, B.: Filtered channel features for pedestrian detection. In: CVPR, pp. 1751–1760 (2015)
32. Zhang, S., Benenson, R., Schiele, B.: CityPersons: a diverse dataset for pedestrian detection. In: CVPR, pp. 3213–3221 (2017)

Real-Time Point Cloud Alignment for Vehicle Localization in a High Resolution 3D Map

Balázs Nagy[1,2(✉)] and Csaba Benedek[1,2]

[1] Machine Perception Research Laboratory,
Institute for Computer Science and Control, Kende u. 13-17, Budapest 1111, Hungary
{balazs.nagy,csaba.benedek}@sztaki.mta.hu
[2] Faculty of Information Technology and Bionics,
Pázmány Péter Catholic University, Práter utca 50/A, Budapest 1083, Hungary

Abstract. In this paper we introduce a Lidar based real time and accurate self localization approach for self driving vehicles (SDV) in high resolution 3D point cloud maps of the environment obtained through Mobile Laser Scanning (MLS). Our solution is able to robustly register the sparse point clouds of the SDVs to the dense MLS point cloud data, starting from a GPS based initial position estimation of the vehicle. The main steps of the method are robust object extraction and transformation estimation based on multiple keypoints extracted from the objects, and additional semantic information derived from the MLS based map. We tested our approach on roads with heavy traffic in the downtown of a large city with large GPS positioning errors, and showed that the proposed method enhances the matching accuracy with an order of magnitude. Comparative tests are provided with various keypoint selection strategies, and against a state-of-the-art technique.

Keywords: Lidar · Point cloud · Registration · Scene understanding

1 Introduction

Self driving vehicles (SDV) offer several benefits for the society ensuring for example a decreased number of road accidents, and more effective traffic distribution on heavy roads. Since these vehicles are equipped with various sensors, apart from their original transportation functionality, they can also contribute to solving environment monitoring, mapping, surveillance, and change detection tasks [1,7]. Taking the advantage of these massive, moving sensor parks on the roads, algorithms can forecast traffic jams, and they can automatically notify the community about particular or unusual events such as accidents, or police actions.

Accurate and robust localization and environment mapping are key challenges in autonomous driving. Although the GPS-based position information is

L. Leal-Taixé and S. Roth (Eds.): ECCV 2018 Workshops, LNCS 11129, pp. 226–239, 2019.
https://doi.org/10.1007/978-3-030-11009-3_13

usually suitable for helping human drivers, its accuracy is not sufficient for navigating a self driving vehicle. Instead, the accurate position and orientation of the SDV should be calculated by registering the measurements of its onboard visual or range sensors to available 3D high definition (HD) city maps [9,17].

Rotating Multi-beam (RMB) Lidar laser scanners [2,3] mounted on vehicle tops are efficient candidates to ensure robust positioning of SDVs. RMB Lidars measure directly the range information, and as active light based sensors, they efficiently perform under different illumination and weather conditions, offering accurate point cloud data with a large field of view in real-time. Although RMB Lidars provide strong geometric features about the environment, the captured point cloud data is quite sparse and inhomogeneous. In addition due to nature of the scanning process, objects are effected by occlusions and motion artifacts, thus robust object detection and classification on such measurements are not straightforward [2]. The point clouds of RMB Lidars are originally obtained in the sensor's local coordinate system, which can be shifted with the actually measured GPS position of the SDV. However in urban environments, due to lack of accurate navigation signals the error of GPS-based position estimation may be often around 2–10 m.

We can also witness a quick improvement of up to date HD map generation technologies. Mobile Laser Scanning (MLS) can rapidly provide very dense and detailed 3D maps of the cities, however economic (*offline*) filtering and semantic labeling, and *real time* exploitation of the raw MLS data are currently a highly challenging problems [18].

(a) RMB Lidar scan   (b) MLS point cloud   (c) Segmented MLS cloud

Fig. 1. Point cloud scenes captured at a downtown area using a Velodyne HDL64E Rotating Multi-Beam (RMB) Lidar sensor and a Riegl VMX450 Mobile Laser Scanning (MLS) system. Class color codes in the segmented cloud; black: *facade*, dark gray: *ground*, mid gray: *tall column*, bright gray: *street furniture*, green: *tree crowns* (Color figure online)

In this paper, we utilize the measurements of the Velodyne HDL64E RMB Lidar sensor and the Riegl VMX450 MLS system. The Velodyne sensor was originally designed to help real time perception of autonomous vehicles or robots. It provides a stream of relatively sparse ($60 - 100 \times 10^3$ points/frame) point clouds with a temporal frequency of 10–15 fps. The spatial accuracy is around 1–2 cm in the sensor's own coordinate system, but the point density quickly decreases as a function of the distance from the sensor. As a result of the rotating multi-beam scanning approach, the point clouds show typical ring patterns (Fig. 1(a)).

The Riegl VMX450 MLS system is highly appropriate for city mapping, urban planning and road survaillance applications. It integrates two Riegl laser scanners, a well designed calibrated camera platform, and a high performance Global Navigation Satellite System (GNSS). It provides extremely dense, accurate (up to global accuracy of a few centimetres) and feature rich data with relatively uniform point distribution as shown in Fig. 1(b).

For self localization of the SDV, we have to register the sparse Velodyne data with GPS based coarse initial position estimation to the dense and accurate MLS point cloud, used as HD map. While point cloud registration is a deeply explored topic, matching 3D measurements with such different point density and characteristics is a highly challenging task. In our approach, we propose an accurate and fast object based alignment algorithm between the RMB Lidar point clouds and the MLS HD map.

2   Previous Work on Point Cloud Registration

Normal Distribution Transform (NDT) [8] and Iterative Closest Point (ICP) [19] algorithms are among the most cited methods in the field of point cloud registration. ICP has several different versions with various improvements: [6] extend the ICP with geometric constraints derived from local point neighborhoods, [10] use color information and [5] make improvements via tracking. However all of these methods are quite sensitive to the different density characteristics of the point clouds, particularly the typical ring pattern of the Velodyne sensor may mislead the registration process. Moreover all of the mentioned methods have a critical precondition: ICP based methods locally minimize the error, so they need a sufficiently accurate pre-alignment between the point clouds. In practice, the GPS based initial alignment with an error of several metres does not prove sufficiently good enough for this purpose. Other techniques focus on applications with larger displacement between between the point clouds: [15] and [11] extract local feature descriptors to find global correspondences, which approach can also be used to find an initial pre-alignment before the ICP process. However, as bottleneck, these algorithms have large computational cost even working with smaller point cloud parts, thus in real-time mapping, SLAM and localization applications they are not efficient. A technique has been introduced for scan alignment based on ICP [3], which solves data mapping at the object level by explicitly matching segments across scans rather than using standard point-to-point type of search. This method proved to be efficient for matching Velodyne frames, however the computational time remained 3–15 s per scan pair. Registering point clouds with different modalities and density characteristics has a limited bibliography. A sequential technique for cross modal point cloud alignment has be proposed in [4], which extracts first abstract object patches in both point clouds, then it calculates a coarse alignment between the frames purely based on the estimated object centers, finally an NDT based point level refinement process is applied. As drawbacks, the object level matching may fail in case of several diverse object types, and the additional NDT steps induces significant computational overload.

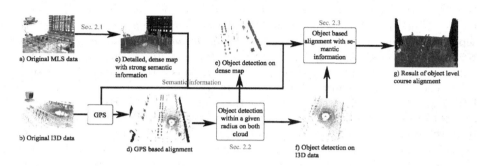

Fig. 2. The workflow of the proposed algorithm.

3   Proposed Approach

We propose a real-time, robust object based alignment technique between sparse RMB Lidar measurements and dense MLS point clouds. The workflow of the new approach is shown in Fig. 2. As a preliminary step, we perform a semantic segmentation of the MLS data, and jointly exploit the raw point cloud and the extracted labels as a High Definition map, to support the registration process. For estimating the optimal scan matching transform, we adopt the fingerprint minutia matching algorithm [4, 14], which is able to find a robust transformation between two point sets even if the size of the point sets are different. However, as a novel contribution, instead of considering the object centers only which only enable coarse frame matching [4], we recommend a new key point selection technique that yields an accurate alignment without the computationally expensive point-level refinement step, and also provides more stable results in scenes with several - often only partially extracted - objects. In addition, we also apply semantic constraints for matching the object candidates obtained by a quick segmentation and patch analysis of the actual RMB Lidar frame, and the preliminary extracted segmentation labels of the HD map.

3.1   Creating the Reference High Definition Map

The Riegl VMX450 system rapidly provides detailed and very dense MLS point cloud data from large-scale outdoor environments. The captured data is geo-referenced, therefore following semantic segmentation it can be directly used as a 3D High Definition (HD) map. Although manual labeling of billions of points is a highly resource intensive task, deep learning based point cloud classification approaches such as the PointNet++ [13] offer promising way to automate the process. However, dealing with urban MLS data a number of particular challenges appear - such as the phantom effect caused independent object motions [12] - , which are not handled by general point clouds segmentation algorithms. For this reason, we extended here a 3D convolutional neural network based technique [12] developed particularly for MLS data filtering, by accommodating it to separate various urban classes such as *ground, facade, phantom, vehicle, pedestrian, vegetation* (bushes and tree crowns), *tall column* (including traffic sign holders and tree trunks) and *street furniture* (various further street objects such as benches, dustbins, short columns). Figure 1(c) demonstrates the result of the labeling process. Object separation in the segmented MLS HD map is quite straightforward: object samples, such as a particular traffic sign, are obtained from the corresponding segmented class regions by Euclidean clustering [16] in an offline way. For the subsequent scene registration process, we will use the objects of the MLS based map as landmarks in background model, therefore will ignore all dynamic (*phantom, vehicle, pedestrian*) or time-varying objects (*vegetation*), as well as classes of large regions (i.e. *ground* and *facade*). As a consequence, for scene matching we will rely on the extracted object samples of the *tall column*, and *street furniture* classes, which all have a static appearance, compact shape thus can be used as landmarks.

(a) Landmark objects of the HD map   (b) Detected objects in RMB Lidar frame

Fig. 3. Extracted objects used for the alignment calculation. Color codes are the following (a) different landmark objects of the HD map are displayed with different color (b) red: ground/road, other colors: different detected objects in the RMB Lidar frame (Color figure online)

3.2   Real Time Object Detection in the RMB Lidar Point Clouds

Since we are dealing with object based point cloud alignment, accurate and robust object detection is also essential in the RMB Lidar frames. On the other hand, the task is highly challenging here, due to the low and inhomogeneous point density, several partially scanned object shapes, occlusions and the real time requirement of the process. First, we only keep the points within a $r = 30\,m$ radius region around the sensor's rotation axis (parameter r was optimized for Velodyne HDL64), as the distant regions are too sparse for reliable scene analysis.

The next step is ground removal. On one hand, the typical ring patterns of RMB Lidars particularly affect the ground regions, which phenomena can mislead the registration process. Furthermore, separation of field objects is facilitated by eliminating the ground which connects the object candidates in the raw frames. Planar ground models are often used in the literature based on robust plane estimation methods such as RANSAC, however, they are less efficient in cases of significant elevation differences within the observed terrain parts (e.g. uphill and downhill roads). Instead, we apply a cell based locally adaptive terrain modeling approach based on [2]. First, we fit a regular 2-D grid with 0.2 m rectangle width (i.e. grid distance) - optimized to urban environment according to [2] - onto the P_z horizontal plane of the RMB Lidar point cloud's local Euclidean coordinate system. We assign each point to the corresponding cell, which contains its projection to P_z. We mark the cells as ground (road) candidate cells where the differences of the observed maximal and minimal point elevation values are lower than 10 cm, which condition admits up to 26° ground slope within a cell. Next, for obtaining a local elevation map, we calculate for the previously marked ground candidate cells the average of the included point elevation coordinates. To eliminate outlier values in the elevation map, resulted by e.g. flat car roofs, we apply a median filter considering neighboring ground cells. For the remaining non-ground cells - which presumptively contain the field objects - the local ground elevation value z_0 is interpolated using the neighboring ground cells, and all included points with elevation z_p are denoted as non-ground points, where $z_p - z_0 > \tau$ (used $\tau = 10\,cm$).

After ground removal, we cluster corresponding *non-ground* points to separate individual object candidates. This process is implemented in the 2D cell map with a region growing algorithm, where empty cells act as stopping criterion. Although in this way, some adjacent objects may be merged together due to the limited resolution of the grid, this 2D object detection approach proved to be faster with two orders of magnitude than traditional kd-tree based 3D Euclidean clustering algorithms. Let us note again, that unlike by offline HD map generation, here the processing speed should fulfill the real time requirements.

Figure 3(b) allows us a qualitative analysis of the object detection step. Field object such as vehicles, columns or tree samples usually appear as separated blobs, while large facade regions are separated into smaller wall segments. Nevertheless, considering the above detailed limitations of the RMB Lidar point clouds, we do not perform a strict classification of the extracted object blobs, and will use all of them in the subsequent scene matching process.

3.3   Object Based Alignment

In this section, we aim to estimate the optimal geometric transform for registering the sparse *observation frame* recorded by the RMB Lidar to the MLS based HD map data. First, we use the GPS-based coarse position estimation of the vehicle (p_0) for an initial positioning of the *observation frame*'s center in the HD map's global coordinate system. To make the bounding area of the two adjustable point clouds equal, we also cut a 30m radius region from the MLS cloud around the current p_0 position.

Exploiting that the Lidar sensors provide direct measurements in the 3D Euclidean space up to cm accuracy, the estimated spatial transform between the two frames can be represented as a rigid similarity transform with a translation and a rotation component. On one hand, we search for a 3D translation vector (dx, dy and dz), which is equal to the originally unknown position error of the GPS sensor. On the other hand, we have experienced that assuming a locally planar road segment within the search region, the road's local normal vector can be fairly estimated in an analytical way from the MLS point cloud, thus only the rotation component α around the vehicle's up vector should be estimated via the registration step. In summary, we model the optimal transform between the two frames by the following homogeneous matrix:

$$
T_{dx,dy,dz,\alpha} \begin{pmatrix} x \\ y \\ z \\ 1 \end{pmatrix} = \begin{bmatrix} \cos\alpha & \sin\alpha & 0 & dx \\ -\sin\alpha & \cos\alpha & 0 & dy \\ 0 & 0 & 1 & dz \\ 0 & 0 & 0 & 1 \end{bmatrix} \begin{bmatrix} x \\ y \\ z \\ 1 \end{bmatrix}
$$

For limiting the parameter space, we allow a maximum 45° degree rotation (α) in both directions, since from the GPS data, we already know an approximate driving direction. For parameters dx and dy we allow ±12 m offsets, while for the vertical translation ±2 m.

We continue with the description of the transformation estimation algorithm. Instead of aligning the raw point clouds, our proposed registration technique matches various keypoints extracted from the *landmark objects* of the HD map (Sect. 3.1), and the *observed object candidates* in the RMB Lidar frame (Sect. 3.2). In addition, exploiting the semantic information stored in the HD, we only attempt to match keypoints which correspond to *compatible* objects. Therefore the remaining part of the algorithm consists of three steps, presented in the following subsections: (i) *keypoint selection*, (ii) defining *compatibility constrains between observed and landmark objects*, (iii) *optimal transform estimation* based on compatible pairs of keypoints.

Keypoint Selection: A critical step of the proposed approach is keypoint extraction from the observed and landmark objects. A straightforward choice [4] is extracting a single keypoint from each object, taken as the center of mass of the object's blob (see Fig. 4(a) and (b)). However, as discussed earlier, the observed RMB Lidar point clouds contain several partially scanned objects, thus the shape

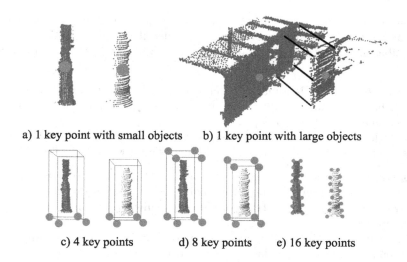

Fig. 4. Choosing key points for registration.

of their point cloud blobs may be significantly different from the more complete MLS point cloud segments of the same object, yielding that the extracted center points are often very different.

For the above reasons, we have implemented various multiple keypoint selection strategies. Beyond the single keypoint based registration approach, we tested the algorithm's performance using 4, 8 and 16 keypoints, whose alignment is demonstrated in Fig. 4(c),(d) and (e). As shown there, using the 4- and 8-keypoint strategies, the feature points are derived as corner points of the 3D bounding boxes of the *observed* and *landmark* objects. For the 16-keypoint case, we divide the 3D bounding box of the object into $2 \times 2 \times 4$ equal cuboid regions, and in each region we select the mass center of the object boundary points as keypoint.

Our expectation is here, that using several keypoints we can obtain correct matches even from partially extracted objects, if certain corners of the (incomplete) bounding box are appropriately detected. On the other hand using a larger number of keypoints induces some computational overload, while due to the increased number of possible point-to-point matching options, it may also cause a false optimum of the estimated transform.

Compatibility Constrains Between Observed and Landmark Objects:
As discussed earlier, we estimate the optimal transform between two frames via sets of keypoints. Since we implement an object based alignment process, our approach allows us to filter out several false keypoint matches based on object level knowledge. More specifically, we will only match point pairs extracted from *compatible* objects of the scene. According to the HD map generation process (Sect. 3.1), we can distinguish *tall column* and *street furniture* samples among

the landmark objects, thus all landmark keypoints are derived from samples of the above two object types. Although such detailed object classification was not feasible in the RMB Lidar frame, we prescribe the following compatibility constraints:

- A *tall column* MLS landmark object is compatible with RMB Lidar blobs, which have a column shaped bounding box, i.e. its height is at least twice longer than its width and depth.
- The ratio of the bounding volumes of compatible RMB Lidar objects and *street furniture* MLS landmark objects must be between 0.75 and 1.25.

Applying the above pre-defined constraint we increase of the evidence of a given transformation only if the objects pairs show similar structures, moreover in this way by skipping many transformation calculations we increase the speed of the algorithm.

Note that the RMB Lidar point clouds may contain various dynamic objects such as pedestrians and vehicles, which fulfill the above matching criteria with certain landmark objects of the MLS based map. These objects will generate outlier matches during the transformation estimation step, thus their effect should be eliminated at higher level.

Optimal Transform Estimation: Let us denote the sets of all *observed* and *landmark* objects by $\mathcal{O}_o$ and $\mathcal{O}_l$ respectively.

Using the 3D extension of the Hough transform based schema [14], we search for the best transformation between the two object keypoint sets by a voting process (Fig. 5). We discretize the transformation space between the minimal and maximal allowed values of each parameter, using 0.2 m disrectization steps for the translation components and 0.25° steps for rotation.

Next we allocate a four dimensional array to summarize the votes for each possible (dx, dy, dz, α) discrete quadruple, describing a given transformation. We set zero initial values of all elements of this array.

During the voting process, we visit all the possible O_o, O_l pairs of *compatible* objects from $\mathcal{O}_o \times \mathcal{O}_l$. Then, we attempt to match each keypoint of O_o to the corresponding keypoint in O_l, so that for such a keypoint pair o_o, o_l, we add a vote for every possible $T_{dx,dy,dz,\alpha}$ transform, which maps o_o to o_l. Here we iterate over all the discrete $\alpha^* \in [-45°, +45°]$ values one by one, and for each α^* we rotate o_o with the actual α^*, and calculate a corresponding translation vector $[dx^*, dy^*, dz^*]^T$ as follows:

$$
\begin{bmatrix} dx^* \\ dy^* \\ dz^* \end{bmatrix} = o_l - \begin{bmatrix} \cos\alpha^* & \sin\alpha^* & 0 \\ -\sin\alpha^* & \cos\alpha^* & 0 \\ 0 & 0 & 1 \end{bmatrix} o_o
$$

Thereafter we increase the number of votes given for the $T_{dx^*,dy^*,dz^*,\alpha^*}$ transform candidate. Finally at the end of the iterative voting process, we find the maximum value of the 4-D vote array, whose $(\alpha, dx, dy$ and $dz)$ parameters represent the optimal transform between the two object sets.

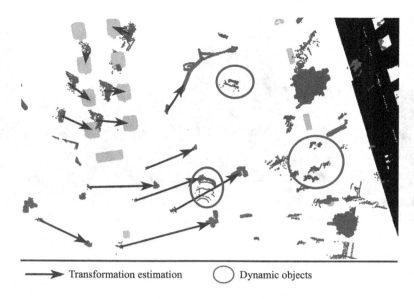

⟶ Transformation estimation   ◯ Dynamic objects

Fig. 5. Illustration of the output of the proposed object matching algorithm based on the *fingerprint minutiae* approach [14]. Red points mark the objects observed in the RMB Lidar frame. (Color figure online)

4 Evaluation

We evaluated the proposed method on different scenarios from dense city areas, some qualitative results are shown in Fig. 6. During quantitative evaluation we compared the different keypoint selection strategies using our proposed model, and also compared our approach to the state-of-the-art technique [4]. As evaluation metrics we used the average distance of the keypoints after the optimal point cloud alignment, since following our subjective visual verification this metrics proved to be relevant for numerical comparison of different matches.

Figure 7 demonstrates the result of the method comparison in 25 different RMB Lidar frames, where we displayed the calculated transformation scores in a logarithmic scale. Regarding the keypoint selection, Fig. 7 shows that the optimal strategy proved to be the 8-keypoint approach (shown in Fig. 4(d)), with an average error between 0.15 and 0.5 m for the different frames. We can observe that using 1 or 4 keypoints, the resulting error is slightly higher than with applying the 8-point version. On the other hand, 16 keypoint selection suffers from ovefitting problems, since it yields large errors in some of the frames.

By comparing the proposed method to [4], we can experience the clear superiority of our new technique with any keypoint selection variants. On one hand, the reference technique [4] only used the 2D object centers from a top-view projection to find the optimal transform, which solution was only appropriate to find a coarse matching between the two point cloud frames. On the other hand, [4] did not use any object specific knowledge from the HD map, that highly con-

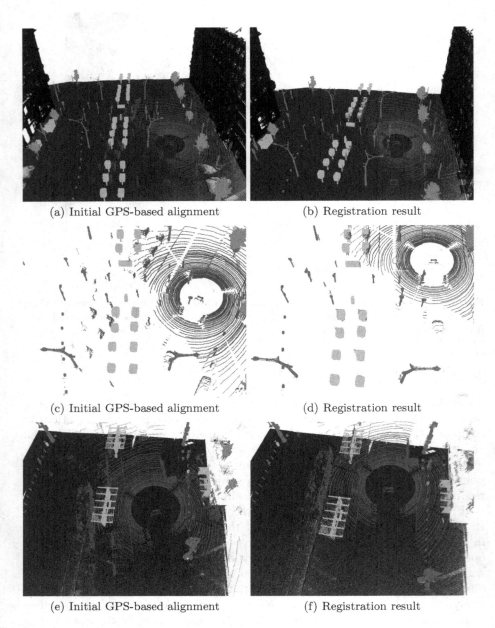

(a) Initial GPS-based alignment

(b) Registration result

(c) Initial GPS-based alignment

(d) Registration result

(e) Initial GPS-based alignment

(f) Registration result

Fig. 6. Results of the proposed registration approach with 8 keypoint selection strategy. RMB Lidar point clouds are displayed with red, while the MLS data is shown with multiple colors depending on the segmentation class. First two rows correspond to the same scene, just ground and facades are not displayed in the 2nd row for better visualization of the object based alignment (Color figure online)

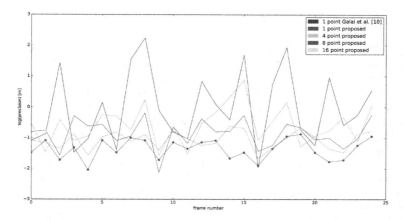

Fig. 7. Evaluation of the proposed approach with various keypoint selection strategies and comparison to [4]

tributed to eliminate false matches in our present model. In addition, since our method does not use the computationally expensive point level NDT refinement step, it is able to run with 10 frame/seconds (fps) on a desktop computer, in contrast to the 0.5 fps speed of [4].

5   Conclusions

We have proposed an object based algorithm for accurate localization of self driving vehicles (SDV) equipped with a RMB Lidar sensor. Assuming that a High Definition (HD) point cloud map is available from the environment obtained by Mobile Laser Scanning technology, the problem is to solve the registration of point clouds with significantly different density characteristics. Apart from exploiting semantic information from the HD map, various keypoint selection strategies have been proposed and compared. We have experienced that the 8-keypoint approach yields a highly efficient solution for the problem, which is superior over other keypoint selection strategies and also over a state-of-the-art method.

Acknowledgment. This work was supported by the National Research, Development and Innovation Fund (grants NKFIA K-120233 and KH-125681), and by the Széchenyi 2020 Program (grants EFOP-3.6.2-16-2017-00013 and 3.6.3-VEKOP-16- 2017-00002). Cs. Benedek also acknowledges the support of the Janos Bolyai Research Scholarship of the Hungarian Academy of Sciences.

References

1. Bayat, B., Crasta, N., Crespi, A., Pascoal, A.M., Ijspeert, A.: Environmental monitoring using autonomous vehicles: a survey of recent searching techniques. Curr. Opin. Biotechnol. **45**, 76–84 (2017). https://doi.org/10.1016/j.copbio.2017.01.009. http://www.sciencedirect.com/science/article/pii/S0958166916302312
2. Börcs, A., Nagy, B., Benedek, C.: Fast 3-D urban object detection on streaming point clouds. In: Agapito, L., Bronstein, M.M., Rother, C. (eds.) ECCV 2014. LNCS, vol. 8926, pp. 628–639. Springer, Cham (2015). https://doi.org/10.1007/978-3-319-16181-5_48
3. Douillard, B., et al.: Scan segments matching for pairwise 3D alignment. In: IEEE International Conference on Robotics and Automation (ICRA), pp. 3033–3040. St. Paul, May 2012. https://doi.org/10.1109/ICRA.2012.6224788
4. Gálai, B., Nagy, B., Benedek, C.: Crossmodal point cloud registration in the Hough space for mobile laser scanning data. In: International Conference on Pattern Recognition (ICPR), pp. 3374–3379. IEEE, Cancun (2016)
5. Gressin, A., Cannelle, B., Mallet, C., Papelard, J.P.: Trajectory-based registration of 3D LIDAR point clouds acquired with a mobile mapping system. In: ISPRS Annals of Photogrammetry Remote Sensing and Spatial Information Sciences, pp. 117–122, July 2012. https://doi.org/10.5194/isprsannals-I-3-117-2012
6. Gressin, A., Mallet, C., David, N.: Improving 3D LIDAR point cloud registration using optimal neighborhood knowledge. In: ISPRS Annals of Photogrammetry, Remote Sensing and Spatial Information Sciences, pp. 111–116, July 2012. https://doi.org/10.5194/isprsannals-I-3-111-2012
7. Kang, M., Hur, S., Jeong, W., Park, Y.: Map building based on sensor fusion for autonomous vehicle. In: International Conference on Information Technology: New Generations, pp. 490–495. Las Vegas, April 2014. https://doi.org/10.1109/ITNG.2014.30
8. Magnusson, M.: The Three-Dimensional Normal-Distributions Transform - an Efficient Representation for Registration, Surface Analysis, and Loop Detection. Ph.D. thesis, Örebro University (December 2009)
9. Matthaei, R., Bagschik, G., Maurer, M.: Map-relative localization in lane-level maps for ADAS and autonomous driving. In: IEEE Intelligent Vehicles Symposium Proceedings, pp. 49–55, Dearborn, June 2014. https://doi.org/10.1109/IVS.2014.6856428
10. Men, H., Gebre, B., Pochiraju, K.: Color point cloud registration with 4D ICP algorithm. In: IEEE International Conference on Robotics and Automation (ICRA), pp. 1511–1516, Shanghai, May 2011. https://doi.org/10.1109/ICRA.2011.5980407
11. Mian, A., Bennamoun, M., Owens, R.: On the repeatability and quality of keypoints for local feature-based 3D object retrieval from cluttered scenes. Int. J. Comput. Vis. **89**(2), 348–361 (2010). https://doi.org/10.1007/s11263-009-0296-z
12. Nagy, B., Benedek, C.: 3D CNN based phantom object removing from mobile laser scanning data. In: International Joint Conference on Neural Networks (IJCNN), pp. 4429–4435, Anchorage, May 2017
13. Qi, C., Yi, L., Su, H., Guibas, L.: PointNet++: deep hierarchical feature learning on point sets in a metric space. In: Conference on Neural Information Processing Systems (NIPS), pp. 5105–5114. Long Beach (2017)
14. Ratha, N.K., Karu, K., Chen, S., Jain, A.K.: A real-time matching system for large fingerprint databases. IEEE Trans. Pattern Anal. Mach. Intell. **18**(8), 799–813 (1996). https://doi.org/10.1109/34.531800

15. Rusu, R.B., Blodow, N., Beetz, M.: Fast point feature histograms (FPFH) for 3D registration. In: IEEE International Conference on Robotics and Automation (ICRA), pp. 3212–3217, Kobe, May 2009. https://doi.org/10.1109/ROBOT.2009. 5152473

16. Rusu, R.B., Cousins, S.: 3D is here: point cloud library (PCL). In: IEEE International Conference on Robotics and Automation (ICRA), pp. 1–4, Shanghai, May 2011. https://doi.org/10.1109/ICRA.2011.5980567

17. Seif, H.G., Hu, X.: Autonomous driving in the iCity—HD maps as a key challenge of the automotive industry. Engineering **2**(2), 159–162 (2016). https://doi. org/10.1016/J.ENG.2016.02.010, http://www.sciencedirect.com/science/article/ pii/S2095809916309432

18. Yu, Y., Li, J., Guan, H., Wang, C.: Automated detection of three-dimensional cars in mobile laser scanning point clouds using DBM-hough-forests. IEEE Trans. Geosci. Rem. Sens. **54**(7), 4130–4142 (2016). https://doi.org/10.1109/TGRS.2016. 2537830

19. Zhang, Z.: Iterative point matching for registration of free-form curves and surfaces. Int. J. Comput. Vis. **13**(2), 119–152 (1994)

Exploiting Single Image Depth Prediction
for Mono-stixel Estimation

Fabian Brickwedde[1,2]($\boxtimes$) (iD), Steffen Abraham[1] (iD), and Rudolf Mester[2] (iD)

[1] Robert Bosch GmbH, Hildesheim, Germany
{Fabian.Brickwedde,Steffen.Abraham}@de.bosch.com
[2] VSI Laboratory, Goethe University, Frankfurt, Germany
mester@vsi.cs.uni-frankfurt.de

Abstract. The stixel-world is a compact and detailed environment representation specially designed for street scenes and automotive vision applications. A recent work proposes a monocamera based stixel estimation method based on the structure from motion principle and scene model to predict the depth and translational motion of the static and dynamic parts of the scene. In this paper, we propose to exploit the recent advantages in deep learning based single image depth prediction for mono-stixel estimation. In our approach, the mono-stixels are estimated based on the single image depth predictions, a dense optical flow field and semantic segmentation supported by the prior knowledge about the characteristic of typical street scenes. To provide a meaningful estimation, it is crucial to model the statistical distribution of all measurements, which is especially challenging for the single image depth predictions. Therefore, we present a semantic class dependent measurement model of the single image depth prediction derived from the empirical error distribution on the Kitti dataset.

Our experiments on the Kitti-Stereo'2015 dataset show that we can significantly improve the quality of mono-stixel estimation by exploiting the single image depth prediction. Furthermore, our proposed approach is able to handle partly occluded moving objects as well as scenarios without translational motion of the camera.

Keywords: Mono-stixel · Single image depth prediction ·
Scene reconstruction · Scene flow · Monocamera · Automotive

1 Introduction

Autonomous vehicles and driver assistance systems need to understand their environment including a geometric representation of the distances and motions as well as a semantic representation of the classification of each object. Additionally, to reduce the computational effort for higher-level vision applications, this representation should be compact.

Therefore, the stixel-world was introduced by Badino et al. [1] and extended to a multi-layer stixel-world by Pfeiffer et al. [21]. The stixel-world represents

© Springer Nature Switzerland AG 2019
L. Leal-Taixé and S. Roth (Eds.): ECCV 2018 Workshops, LNCS 11129, pp. 240–255, 2019.
https://doi.org/10.1007/978-3-030-11009-3_14

the scene as a composition of thin stick like elements, the stixels. Each stixel corresponds to a vertical rectangle in the image and stores the distance to the camera assuming an upright orientation of object stixel and lying orientation of ground stixel. Additionally to the type, segmentation and distance each stixel segment can consist of a label for the semantic class [23] and the motion of each stixel can be estimated using a Kalman-filter based tracking approach [20]. The mentioned works use stereo depth measurements to estimate the stixel-world. A recent work by Brickwedde et al. [2] presents the mono-stixel approach, a monocamera based stixel-model and estimation method. The mono-stixel model directly estimates the 2D-translational motion of each stixel as part of the segmentation problem and introduces a further mono-stixel type by distinguishing static and potentially moving object stixel. The mono-stixels are estimated based on a dense optical flow field and semantic segmentation leveraging the structure from motion principle for the static environment and the scene model assumption that moving objects stand on the ground plane. However, there are two limitations of the mono-stixel estimation approach in [2]. First, a translational motion of the camera is required. Second, the projection of a potentially moving object stixel on the ground plane only works as long as this part of the object really stands on the ground, the ground contact point is not occluded and the surface of the ground plane is estimated with high quality.

To overcome these limitations and improve the quality, we propose to exploit a deep learning based single image depth prediction for mono-stixel estimation as a further information. Thereby, the mono-stixel estimation serves as a fusion of an optical flow field, single image depth prediction and semantic segmentation supported by scene model assumptions. By exploiting the single image depth prediction the approach is able to handle partly occluded objects and a translational motion of the camera is not required anymore as shown in Fig. 1.

Fig. 1. Example depth prediction of our mono-stixel estimation. Top to bottom: image, ground truth depth, and our mono-stixel depth estimation. The color encodes the inverse depth from close (red) to far (dark blue). The ego vehicle is standing in the images of the third and fourth column. By exploiting the single image depth prediction our mono-stixel estimation approach provides reliable depth estimates even for partly occluded vehicles and scenarios without translational motion of the camera. (Color figure online)

2   Related Work

Traditionally stixel estimation methods use stereo depth measurements like [1,21]. Levi et al. [15] and Garnett et al. [9] propose a convolutional neural network, called the Stixel-Net for a monocamera based stixel estimation method. The convolutional neural network predicts the segment and depth of the closest stixel in each column, but does not provide a depth representation of the whole image and is more related to a freespace segmentation method. As discussed in the introduction, the mono-stixel approach by Brickwedde et al. [2] is highly related to our approach as a multi-layer mono-stixel estimation based on the structure from motion or multi-view geometry principle [12]. The 3D-position of static points in the scene can be reconstructed based on the image correspondences and the camera motion by triangulation. For example, SLAM methods like [18] and [5] jointly estimate the camera motion and image correspondences including their 3D-position in the scene. In general, this reconstruction is only known up to an unknown scale of the scene and camera motion in a monocamera setup. However, in autonomous applications the unknown scale can be estimated based on the known camera height above the ground [6,19] or derived from an inertial measurement unit. But, there are still limitations of the structure from motion principle for moving objects or scenarios without translational motion of the camera. By exploiting the epipolar geometry or scene constraints some independent moving objects (IMO) are detectable based on the optical flow and camera motion [14,22]. But some IMOs like oncoming vehicle are still not detectable. Therefore, the mono-stixel estimation approach in [2] proposes to distinguish static and potentially moving objects like vehicles based on a semantic segmentation. To reconstruct these objects some methods [2,22] exploit the scene model assumption that these objects are connected with the surrounding static environment, for example, that a vehicle stands on the ground plane.

In the recent years, deep learning methods show impressive results for predicting the depth of the scene for a single image. Thus, these methods exploit totally different information than the multi-view approaches. These methods potentially learn the typical shape and size of objects and structures as well as the contextual information. One of the pioneering work is presented by Eigen et al. [4]. They propose a supervised learning approach for single image depth prediction, but it can also be trained in an unsupervised or self-supervised manner [8,11,30]. Providing additionally the statistical distribution of the predicted depth is still challenging. Kendall and Gal [13] distinguish two types of uncertainties: the aleatoric uncertainty, that refers to sensor noise and can not be reduced even with more training data and the epistemic or model uncertainty that could be explained away given enough training data. They propose to learn to predict the aleatoric uncertainty as part of a supervised learning approach and use Monte Carlo dropout to derive the epistemic uncertainty.

Single-view and multi-view depth predictions exploit totally different information with different benefits and drawbacks. This makes it powerful to fuse both depth prediction approaches [7,25]. Alternatively, the methods [27,28] propose to learn the multi-view and structure from motion principle directly. Thereby, the convolutional network can additionally exploit the single-view depth cues and seen as a fusion as well.

The contributions of our work are as follows: We present a mono-stixel estimation that fuses single image depth predictions with a dense optical flow field and semantic segmentation. Thereby, we significantly outperform previous mono-stixel estimation methods and overcome two main limitations. Our mono-stixel estimation method is able to provide reliable depth estimates even for scenarios without translational motion of the camera and is able to reconstruct moving objects even if the ground contact point is occluded. Furthermore, our approach can be seen as a fusion scheme that is supported by a semantic segmentation and scene model assumptions. For a statistical meaningful fusion, it is crucial to know the error distribution, which is especially challenging for the single image depth predictions. Therefore, we present a semantic class dependent measurement model for the single image depth prediction derived from the empirical error distribution on the Kitti dataset [17]. This analysis additionally gives some insights which parts of the scene are challenging for single image depth prediction.

3   Method

In this chapter, we present our mono-stixel estimation method. We mainly follow the mono-stixel model and segmentation algorithm proposed by Brickwedde et al. [2]. In the first section, we give a brief overview of that method and present how to adapt it to exploit the single image depth prediction for mono-stixel estimation. Thereby, our mono-stixel approach uses a pixel-wise semantic segmentation, dense optical flow field, and single image depth prediction as inputs. Furthermore, the camera motion is assumed to be known. In the second chapter, we derive a measurement model of the single image depth prediction based on the error statistic on the Kitti-Stereo'15 dataset [17]. Finally, the last chapter presents how to solve the mono-stixel segmentation problem.

3.1   Mono-stixel Segmentation as Energy Minimization Problem

We follow the mono-stixel model proposed in [2] that defines a mono-stixel as a thin stick-like planar and rigid moving element in the scene. To represent the whole scene the image of width w and height h is divided into columns of a fixed width w_s and each column k is segmented into N_k mono-stixels separately:

$$\mathbf{s}_k = \{s_i \mid 1 \leq i \leq N_k \leq h\}$$
$$\text{with } s_i = (v_i^b, v_i^t, c_i, p_i, \mathbf{t}_i, m_i) \tag{1}$$

Each mono-stixel s_i consists of labels for the segmentation, represented by the bottom v_i^b and top v_i^t point in that column, a label for the semantic class c_i, labels to encode the inverse depth p_i and 2D-translational motion over the ground $\mathbf{t}_i$ and is of a given mono-stixel type m_i. The four mono-stixel types m_i are ground, static object, dynamic object, and sky stixel as defined in [2]. Each semantic class

c_i is directly associated with one mono-stixel type m_i. Thus, a ground stixel could be of the semantic class road, sidewalk or terrain, a static object stixel could be of the semantic class building, pole or vegetation, a dynamic object stixel could be of the type vehicle, two-wheeler or person and the sky stixels are of the semantic class sky. Furthermore, assumptions of the geometry and motion are defined for each stixel type. A ground stixel has a lying orientation, an object stixel has an upright orientation facing the camera center and a sky stixel is at infinite distance $p_i = 0$. The dynamic object stixel is the only type with independent motion, the other stixel types are assumed to be static $t_i = 0$.

The mono-stixel segmentation is defined as a 1D-energy minimization problem [2] for each column k:

$$\hat{\mathbf{s}} = \arg\min_{\mathbf{s}} E(\mathbf{s}, \mathbf{f}, \mathbf{l})$$
$$= \arg\min_{\mathbf{s}} \left(\Psi(\mathbf{s}) + \Phi(\mathbf{s}, \mathbf{f}, \mathbf{l}, \mathbf{d}) \right), \tag{2}$$

where $\Psi(\mathbf{s})$ represents the prior knowledge of the typical structure of street scenes. It consists of a gravity prior to encode that most of the objects typically stand on the ground plane, an ordering constraint to regard that one object might occlude another one and a flat ground plane prior which prefers small discontinuities of the height in the ground plane. Additionally, a constant value is added for each new stixel to prevent over-segmentation and regulates the model complexity. To model the scene prior we follow exactly the same equations as defined in [2] and refer the interested reader to that paper.

The data likelihood $\Phi(\mathbf{s}, \mathbf{f}, \mathbf{l}, \mathbf{d})$ rates the consistency of the stixel hypothesis based on the semantic segmentation $\mathbf{l}$, the optical flow $\mathbf{f}$ and single image depth prediction $\mathbf{d}$:

$$\Phi(\mathbf{s}, \mathbf{f}, \mathbf{l}, \mathbf{d}) = \sum_{i=1}^{N_k} \sum_{v=v_i^b}^{v_i^t} \left(\lambda_L \Phi_L(s_i, \mathbf{l}_v) + \lambda_F \Phi_F(s_i, \mathbf{f}_v, v) + \lambda_{SI} \Phi_{SI}(s_i, d_v) \right) \tag{3}$$

The probability is assumed to be independent across the rows v in that column and each data likelihood term is weighted by λ. The data likelihood terms $\Phi_L(s_i, \mathbf{l}_v)$ and $\Phi_F(s_i, \mathbf{f}_v, v)$ are defined as in [2]: $\Phi_L(s_i, \mathbf{l}_v)$ prefers stixels having a semantic class c_i with high class scores $\mathbf{l}_v(c_i)$ in the semantic segmentation and $\Phi_F(s_i, \mathbf{f}_v, v)$ rates the consistency of the stixel based on the optical flow $\mathbf{f}_v$. Therefore, the expected optical flow $\mathbf{f}_{exp,v}(s_i)$ at row v given a stixel hypothesis s_i is computed based on its inverse depth, relative motion to the camera and orientation defined by its mono-stixel type. This computation can be expressed by a stixel-homography [2]. The data likelihood $\Phi_F(s_i, \mathbf{f}_v, v)$ rates the difference between the expected $\mathbf{f}_{exp,v}(s_i)$ and measured optical flow $\mathbf{f}_v$ as the negative logarithm of the measurement model which is defined as a mixture model consisting of a normal distribution for inliers and a uniform distribution for outliers.

We propose to extend the data likelihood for the input of the single image depth prediction by $\Phi_{SI}(s_i, d_v)$. The output of our single image depth prediction is defined as a dense disparity map with $d_v = \frac{1}{Z_v}$, where Z_v is the z-coordinate of the 3D-position in camera coordinates. The data likelihood rates the difference between expected disparity $d_{exp,v}(s_i)$ of the corresponding stixel hypothesis s_i and the disparity measurement d_v of single image depth prediction for the pixel at row v. The expected disparity $d_{exp,v}(s_i)$ of the stixel hypothesis s_i is defined by the inverse depth p_i and stixel type m_i as:

$$d_{exp,v}(s_i) = \begin{cases} \frac{p_i(\mathbf{x}\cdot\mathbf{n}_i)}{\mathbf{x}_z}, & \text{if } m_i \in \{\text{static object, dynamic object, ground}\} \\ 0, & \text{if } m_i = \text{sky} \end{cases} \quad (4)$$

where $\mathbf{x}$ is the ray of the pixel corresponding to row v and $\mathbf{n}_i$ is the normal vector defined by the orientation of the mono-stixel type m_i.

The measurement model of the single image depth prediction derived in the next section defines the statistical distribution of a disparity error dependent on the semantic class $p(d_{error}|c)$. Switching to the log-domain $\Phi_{SI}(s_i, d_v)$ is defined as the negative logarithm of this probability:

$$\Phi_{SI}(s_i, d_v) = -\log\left(p(d_v' - d_{exp,v}(s_i)|c_i)\right)$$
$$= -\log\left(p(d_{error,v}|c_i)\right) \quad (5)$$

3.2 Measurement Model of Single Image Depth Prediction

To achieve a high performance of the mono-stixel estimation and meaningful fusion with the optical flow, it is crucial to model the statistical distribution of the disparity error of the single image depth prediction. Supervised learning methods are limited to the ground truth provided by the sensor which is typically limited by a certain range and view. For example, the Velodyne sensor in the Kitti dataset [17] only provides ground truth up to around 80 m and only for the lower part of the image. Consequently, we propose to use a self-supervised learning method and follow the approach of Godard et al. [11]. However, this method does not provide uncertainties of the predicted depth and the aleatoric uncertainty estimation presented by Kendall and Gal [13] is not applicable for a self-supervised learning approach.

Therefore, to derive a measurement model we analyzed the empirical error distribution of the single image depth prediction approach by [11] on the Kitti dataset [17]. The error distribution shown in Fig. 2 mainly consists of two parts. First, a part with slowly decreasing tails that mainly models the distribution of large errors and has a triangular shape on a logarithmic scale. Second, one part that corresponds to a peak and high probabilities for small errors. To approximate this characteristic of the empirical density function we propose a mixture model that consists of a Laplacian distribution that mainly models the probability of large errors and a Gaussian distribution mainly for the low errors:

$$p(d_{error}) = \frac{1-\lambda}{\sqrt{2\pi}\sigma}e^{-\frac{d_{error}^2}{2\sigma^2}} + \frac{\lambda}{2b}e^{-\frac{|d_{error}|}{b}} \quad (6)$$

Fig. 2 shows the approximated density function as an orange line for $\sigma = 0.0042$, $b = 0.02$ and $\lambda = 0.2$.

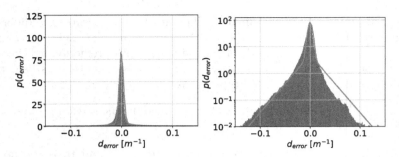

Fig. 2. Statistical distribution of the disparity error of the single image depth prediction [11]. The blue histograms show the empirical distribution of the error on Kitti-Stereo'15 [17] and the orange curve the approximated measurement model. The distribution is shown with a logarithmic scale of the frequency in the right diagram. (Color figure online)

Furthermore, we identified that the error distribution highly depends on the semantic class as shown in Fig. 3. Especially roads, sidewalks, and vehicles work quite well. These classes follow strict model assumptions regarding surface, shape or size and are frequently represented in the training dataset. This observation motivates to model a class dependent measurement model. Therefore, we estimate the parameters σ_{c_i}, b_{c_i} and λ_{c_i} separately for each class as shown in Table 1, which correspond to the density functions in Fig. 3 colored in orange.

Table 1. Class-dependent measurement model of single image depth prediction

Class c_i	Road	Sidewalk	Terrain	Building	Pole	Vegetation	Vehicle
σ_{c_i}	0.0032	0.006	0.007	0.0075	0.008	0.008	0.005
b_{c_i}	0.01	0.02	0.02	0.025	0.03	0.03	0.015
λ_{c_i}	0.15	0.1	0.1	0.2	0.3	0.3	0.2

For the semantic classes two-wheeler, person and sky there is not enough data for a reliable analysis of the statistical distribution. Therefore, we use the overall distribution in Fig. 2 for these classes. Based on the derived class dependent measurement model the term $\Phi_{SI}(s_i, d_v)$ in Eq. 5 is defined as:

$$\Phi_{SI}(s_i, d_v) = -\log\left(p(d_{error}|c_i)\right)$$
$$\approx min\left(-\log\left(\frac{1-\lambda_{c_i}}{\sqrt{2\pi}\sigma_{c_i}}\right) + \frac{d_{error}^2}{2\sigma_{c_i}^2}, \ -\log\left(\frac{\lambda_{c_i}}{2b_{c_i}}\right) + \frac{|d_{error}|}{b_{c_i}}\right) \qquad (7)$$

3.3 Solving the Mono-stixel Segmentation Problem

The mono-stixel segmentation problem is defined as the energy minimization problem in Eq. 2. To solve this segmentation problem we follow the proposed

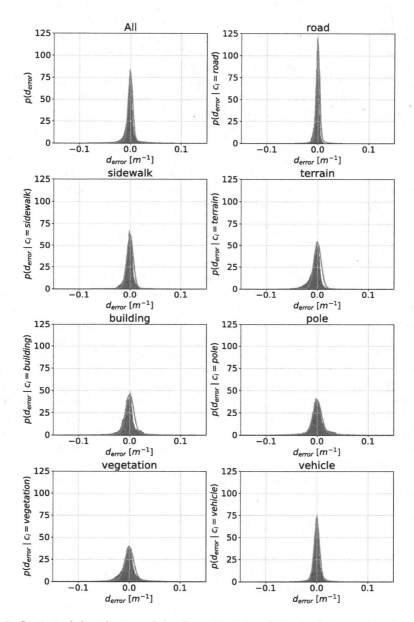

Fig. 3. Statistical distribution of the disparity error of the single image depth prediction [11] dependent on the semantic class. The blue histograms show the empirical distribution of the error on Kitti-Stereo'15 [17] and the orange curve the approximated measurement model. (Color figure online)

method in [2]. The optimization of the stixel types m_i and segmentation labels v_i^b, v_i^t is formulated as a minimum path problem solved via dynamic programming. Each edge in the minimum path problem corresponds to a mono-stixel hypothesis of a given segmentation v_i^b, v_i^t and type m_i. To reduce the computational effort the semantic class c_i, inverse depth p_i and translational motion $\mathbf{t}_i$ are locally optimized for the corresponding image segment. We take that semantic class c_i that minimized $\Phi_L(s_i, \mathbf{l}_v)$ considering the association between semantic classes and the mono-stixel type m_i. Thereby, the semantic segmentation supports the segmentation as well as the distinction of the different mono-stixel types.

To estimate the inverse depth p_i and translational motion $\mathbf{t}_i$ we use a MLESAC-based approach [26] which, in contrast to the approach in [2], minimizes the optical flow as well as the single image depth prediction based data likelihood and serves as a statistical fusion:

$$\hat{p}_i, \hat{\mathbf{t}}_i = \arg\min_{p_i, \mathbf{t}_i} \sum_{v=v_i^b}^{v_i^t} \left(\lambda_F \Phi_F(s_i, \mathbf{f}_v, v) + \lambda_{SI} \Phi_{SI}(s_i, d_v) \right) \qquad (8)$$

For static objects and ground stixels both data likelihood terms depend solely on the inverse depth p_i as the translational motion $\mathbf{t}_i$ is zero by definition. Therefore, the MLESAC-based estimation serves as a fusion and takes that inverse depth defined by one optical flow vector or one single image depth estimate in the corresponding image segment v_i^b, v_i^t that minimizes the cost term defined in Eq. 8. For dynamic object stixel the optical flow related-data likelihood term depends on two degrees of freedom, namely the linear combination of inverse depth and relative 2D-translation of that stixel to the camera $\tilde{\mathbf{t}}_i = p_i \mathbf{t}_{i,cam}$ as shown in [2]. But one degree of freedom, for example, the inverse depth p_i can be chosen freely. In contrast to that, the data likelihood term of the single image depth prediction only depends on the inverse depth p_i of the stixel, but is independent of the translational motion. Consequently, we separate the estimation in two parts. First, we take that inverse depth p_i defined by one single image depth estimate in the corresponding image segment v_i^b, v_i^t, that minimizes the following cost term:

$$\hat{p}_i = \arg\min_{p_i} \sum_{v=v_i^b}^{v_i^t} \left(\lambda_{SI} \Phi_{SI}(s_i, d_v) \right) \qquad (9)$$

Second, we take that labels for the translational motion $\mathbf{t}_i$ defined by one optical flow vector in the corresponding image segment v_i^b, v_i^t that minimizes the optical flow based data likelihood for the given depth $\hat{p}_i$:

$$\hat{\mathbf{t}}_i = \arg\min_{\mathbf{t}_i} \sum_{v=v_i^b}^{v_i^t} \left(\lambda_F \Phi_F(s_i, \mathbf{f}_v, v) \right) \qquad (10)$$

A hypothesis of the 2D-translational motion or inverse depth based on one optical flow vector can be estimated using the direct linear transform of the stixel-homography as explained in [2]. For each single image depth estimate, we can derive a hypothesis of the inverse depth of a stixel given its type by the inversion of Eq. 4. The scene model additionally rates the consistency of the estimated depth during optimization as a minimum path problem and prefers a mono-stixel segmentation consistent to the defined scene model.

4   Experiments

In this chapter, the performance of our proposed mono-stixel estimation method is analyzed. First, we describe our experimental setup including the used metric. Second, we present the experimental results of our performance evaluation as well as some example results.

4.1   Setup and Metric

The inputs of our method, the dense optical flow field, camera motion estimation, pixel-wise semantic labeling, and single image depth prediction are implemented as follows: For the dense optical flow we use the public available DeepFlow [29], the camera motion is provided by the method described in [10] and for the single image depth prediction we use the method proposed by Godard et al. [11] as discussed in Sect. 3.2. For the semantic segmentation, we train our own fully convolutional network [16] based on the VGG-architecture [24]. We pretrain the network on the cityscape dataset [3] and fine-tune it on 470 annotated images of the Kitti dataset [17] as proposed in [2,23].

Our experiments are performed on the Kitti-Stereo'15 dataset [17]. The dataset consist of 200 short sequences in street scenes with ground truth depth maps provided by a Velodyne laser scanner and 3D-CAD models for moving vehicles. In the first setup the optical flow and camera motion is computed on keyframes with a minimum driven distance of 0.5 m. These keyframes exist for 171 sequences. In the second setup, the optical flow and camera motion is computed on two consecutive images for all 200 sequences. This means that in the second setup also scenarios without or with a quite small translational motion of the camera are included in the dataset.

As a first baseline, we use the mono-stixel estimation approach described in [2] with the same optical flow and camera motion estimation as inputs. Comparing to that baseline shows if we can improve the performance of mono-stixel estimation by exploiting the single image depth predictions. The implemented baseline is exactly the approach described in [2]. However, due to some parameter tuning, we were able to achieve slightly better results than stated in the original paper. The baseline approach and our approach both use a stixel width of $w_s = 5$ and exactly the same parameters, for example, to define the scene model. Furthermore, we present the performance of both inputs to analyze if our approach serves as a suitable fusion of both information. Therefore, we implement a traditional structure from motion (SFM) approach [12] by triangulating each optical flow vector based on the camera motion. Again, the same optical flow and camera motion are used as for our approach. Additionally, the quality of the single image depth prediction in [11] is shown.

Moreover, we perform the experiments for three different measurement models for the single image depth prediction. First, our semantic class dependent mixture model proposed in Sect. 3.2 (ours-SemMixture). Second, the same mixture model but independent of the semantic class (ours-Mixture). Third, a measurement model assuming a normal distribution of the inverse depth error (ours-Normal). The variance of the normal distribution is determined by the mean squared error of the inverse depth.

The results are compared using the depth metric by [4]. The metric measures the root mean squared error (RMSE) of the depth prediction, the mean absolute relative error (Rel. Error) and percentage of depths that fulfill some threshold δ. Note, that the metric is computed in the depth space and not in the inverse depth or disparity space.

4.2 Results

Figure 4 shows some example outputs of our proposed method. The segmentation of each mono-stixel is visualized by a white boundary and the color represents the semantic class or depth of that pixel encoded by the mono-stixel.

Image	Mono-Stixel - Semantics	Mono-Stixel - Depth

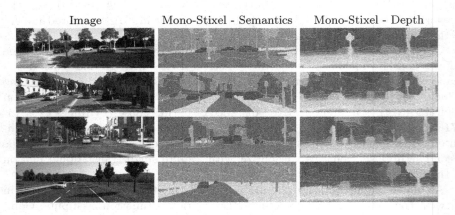

Fig. 4. Example depth and semantic scene representation of our proposed mono-stixel estimation method. The stixel color encodes the semantic class following [3] or the inverse depth from close (red) to far (dark blue), respectively. (Color figure online)

In Fig. 5 the performance of the depth representation is compared to the mentioned baselines. The first image shows that our approach is able to predict reliable depth estimates even for vehicles partly occluded by the image boundary or other objects. This is not the case for the mono-stixel approach in [2] that needs to observe the ground contact point of the mono-stixel for a reasonable depth estimate. The images in the second and third column show that the fusion

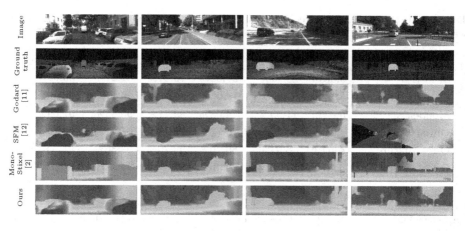

Fig. 5. Example performance of the depth reconstruction of our proposed mono-stixel estimation method compared to the mono-stixel estimation method of Brickwedde et al. [2], structure from motion (SFM) [12] and single image depth prediction by Godard et al. [11]. The color encodes the inverse depth from close (red) to far (dark blue). Invalid negative depth values are colored black. The ego vehicle is standing in the scenario of the last column. (Color figure online)

supported by the scene model is able to correct errors of one of the inputs in many cases. For example, in the second column of Fig. 5 the depth of the bushes and building in the right part of the image mainly follows the depth defined by the optical flow. But, our approach is also able to correct errors in the optical flow as shown in the third column behind the vehicle or for the guideline on the right side, even though these are parts of the scene with high parallax. The last column additionally shows a scenario with standing ego vehicle. The structure from motion baseline completely fails in that situation, the mono-stixel approach in [2] reconstructs a flat ground plane, projects the dynamic objects on that plane, but fails for the static objects, whereas our approach provides a reasonable depth reconstruction of the whole scene.

Including the single image depth prediction does not have a significant effect on the number of mono-stixels and thus the compactness of the representation. The mean number of mono-stixels per image of the approach in [2] is 1853 which corresponds to 7.4 mono-stixels per column. Compared to that our approach gives out 1944 mono-stixels per image or 7.8 mono-stixels per column in average. Note, that the parametrization is more focused on quality than on compactness. By changing the parameter the number of mono-stixel could be reduced significantly but at the expense of the quality due to higher discretization effects.

Table 2 shows the performance of our method compared to the mentioned baselines for the keyframe-based subset evaluated for all parts of the scene. The results show that our proposed semantic class dependent measurement model outperforms the class independent counterpart and especially the measurement model assuming a normal distribution. Furthermore, our approach significantly

Table 2. Results on Kitti-Stereo'15 for the 171 keyframes evaluated on all parts of the scene

Method	RMSE	Rel. error	$\delta < 1.1$	$\delta < 1.25$	$\delta < 1.25^2$	$\delta < 1.25^3$
SFM [12]	9.36 m	29.11%	67.02%	76.81%	82.21%	86.02%
Godard [11]	5.14 m	9.84%	71.00%	87.52%	96.17%	98.56%
Mono-stixel [2]	6.05 m	11.99%	74.08%	89.71%	95.85%	97.64%
Ours-Normal	4.71 m	8.37%	79.73%	92.58%	97.31%	98.76%
Ours-Mixture	**4.57 m**	8.01%	80.76%	92.70%	97.36%	**98.79%**
Ours-SemMixture	**4.57 m**	**7.97%**	**81.36%**	**93.04%**	**97.45%**	**98.79%**

improves the quality of the mono-stixel estimation by exploiting the single image depth prediction and serves as a suitable fusion, which is shown by the fact, that the performance is better than each input solely. In Tables 3 and 4 the same experiment is evaluated for the static and moving parts of the scene separately. For moving objects the structure from motion baseline fails completely and therefore our depth estimation mainly follows the single image depth prediction. Due to the discretization effect and errors in the semantic segmentation, our performance is slightly lower than the single image depth prediction for moving objects. However, for the whole scene, our approach is significantly better as shown in Table 2, the representation is more compact and the translational motion of the moving object stixels is additionally provided. Furthermore, compared to the mono-stixel estimation approach in [2], we show that our approach significantly outperforms the scene model-based reconstruction of moving objects.

Table 3. Results on Kitti-Stereo'15 for the 171 keyframes evaluated on static parts of the scene

Method	RMSE	Rel. error	$\delta < 1.1$	$\delta < 1.25$	$\delta < 1.25^2$	$\delta < 1.25^3$
SFM [12]	7.02 m	16.11%	76.67%	87.49%	92.77%	94.98%
Godard [11]	5.38 m	10.26%	69.32%	86.23%	95.78%	98.43%
Mono-stixel [2]	6.01 m	11.20%	77.54%	90.81%	96.03%	97.71%
Ours-SemMixture	**4.51 m**	**7.79%**	**81.29%**	**92.63%**	**97.37%**	**98.81%**

In Table 5 the same experiment is shown, but with the optical flow and camera motion computed on consecutive frames. Thus, there are still many scenarios with a moving camera, but also some cases without any or a quite small translational motion. Consequently, the performance of the SFM and mono-stixel [2] baselines drop significantly. For example by around 7% and 5% for the accuracy threshold of $\delta < 1.1$. Our approach is still able to handle situations without translational motion and thereby the quality only decreases slightly by around 1% for the same accuracy threshold. The small deterioration is explainable by

Table 4. Results on Kitti-Stereo'15 for the 171 keyframes evaluated on moving objects

Method	RMSE	Rel. error	$\delta < 1.1$	$\delta < 1.25$	$\delta < 1.25^2$	$\delta < 1.25^3$
SFM [12]	18.51 m	115.17%	3.12%	6.15%	12.36%	26.71%
Godard [11]	**3.2 m**	**7.1%**	**82.18%**	**96.07%**	**98.81%**	**99.48%**
Mono-stixel [2]	6.32 m	17.21%	51.14%	82.43%	94.65%	97.21%
Ours-SemMixture	4.98 m	9.17%	81.83%	95.73%	97.98%	98.68%

the fact, that there are lower parallax configurations for the consecutive frames. However, the optical flow is still useful even in standstill situations to support the distinction between static and moving objects and to estimate the translational motion of the moving objects.

Table 5. Results on Kitti-Stereo'15 for the 200 consecutive frames evaluated on all parts of the scene

Method	RMSE	Rel. error	$\delta < 1.1$	$\delta < 1.25$	$\delta < 1.25^2$	$\delta < 1.25^3$
SFM [12]	16.06 m	59.20%	59.55%	69.71%	76.27%	81.31%
Godard [11]	5.20 m	9.68%	71.63%	87.91%	96.25%	98.58%
Mono-stixel [2]	7.26 m	13.90%	69.68%	87.09%	94.53%	96.80%
Ours-SemMixture	**4.88 m**	**8.24%**	**80.27%**	**92.60%**	**97.28%**	**98.73%**

5   Conclusions

We have presented an extension of the mono-stixel estimation by exploiting the recent advantages in single image depth prediction. The mono-stixel estimation serves as a statistical fusion of the single image depth prediction and optical flow supported by scene model assumptions and semantic segmentation. For a statistically reasonable fusion, we tackle the challenging problem of providing a statistical error distribution for deep learning based single image depth estimates in a self-supervised learning approach and proposed a semantic class dependent measurement model derived by the empirical error distribution.

Our approach is able to significantly improve the quality of mono-stixel estimation and handle partly occluded moving objects as well as scenarios without translational motion of the camera. Both cases might be highly relevant for a driver assistance system or autonomous vehicles.

References

1. Badino, H., Franke, U., Pfeiffer, D.: The stixel world - a compact medium level representation of the 3D-world. In: Denzler, J., Notni, G., Süße, H. (eds.) DAGM 2009. LNCS, vol. 5748, pp. 51–60. Springer, Heidelberg (2009). https://doi.org/10.1007/978-3-642-03798-6_6
2. Brickwedde, F., Abraham, S., Mester, R.: Mono-Stixels: monocular depth reconstruction of dynamic street scenes. In: 2018 IEEE International Conference on Robotics and Automation (ICRA), pp. 1–7. IEEE (2018)
3. Cordts, M., et al.: The cityscapes dataset for semantic urban scene understanding. In: Proceedings of the IEEE Conference on Computer Vision and Pattern Recognition, pp. 3213–3223 (2016)
4. Eigen, D., Puhrsch, C., Fergus, R.: Depth map prediction from a single image using a multi-scale deep network. In: Advances in Neural Information Processing Systems, pp. 2366–2374 (2014)
5. Engel, J., Schöps, T., Cremers, D.: LSD-SLAM: large-scale direct monocular SLAM. In: Fleet, D., Pajdla, T., Schiele, B., Tuytelaars, T. (eds.) ECCV 2014. LNCS, vol. 8690, pp. 834–849. Springer, Cham (2014). https://doi.org/10.1007/978-3-319-10605-2_54
6. Fanani, N., Stürck, A., Ochs, M., Bradler, H., Mester, R.: Predictive monocular odometry (PMO): What is possible without RANSAC and multiframe bundle adjustment? Image Vis. Comput. **68**, 3–13 (2017)
7. Fcil, J.M., Concha, A., Montesano, L., Civera, J.: Single-view and multi-view depth fusion. IEEE Robot. Autom. Lett. **2**(4), 1994–2001 (2017). https://doi.org/10.1109/LRA.2017.2715400
8. Carneiro, G., Reid, I., Garg, R.B.G.V.K., et al.: Unsupervised CNN for single view depth estimation: geometry to the rescue. In: Leibe, B., Matas, J., Sebe, N., Welling, M. (eds.) ECCV 2016. LNCS, vol. 9912, pp. 740–756. Springer, Cham (2016). https://doi.org/10.1007/978-3-319-46484-8_45
9. Garnett, N., et al.: Real-time category-based and general obstacle detection for autonomous driving. In: The IEEE International Conference on Computer Vision (ICCV), October 2017
10. Geiger, A., Ziegler, J., Stiller, C.: Stereoscan: dense 3D reconstruction in real-time. In: 2011 IEEE Intelligent Vehicles Symposium (IV), pp. 963–968. IEEE (2011)
11. Godard, C., Mac Aodha, O., Brostow, G.J.: Unsupervised monocular depth estimation with left-right consistency. In: The IEEE Conference on Computer Vision and Pattern Recognition (CVPR), July 2017
12. Hartley, R., Zisserman, A.: Multiple View Geometry in Computer Vision. Cambridge University Press, Cambridge (2003)
13. Kendall, A., Gal, Y.: What uncertainties do we need in Bayesian deep learning for computer vision? In: Advances in Neural Information Processing Systems, pp. 5574–5584 (2017)
14. Klappstein, J.: Optical-flow based detection of moving objects in traffic scenes. Ph.D. thesis (2008)
15. Levi, D., Garnett, N., Fetaya, E., Herzlyia, I.: StixelNet: a deep convolutional network for obstacle detection and road segmentation. In: BMVC, pp. 109:1 (2015)
16. Long, J., Shelhamer, E., Darrell, T.: Fully convolutional networks for semantic segmentation. In: Proceedings of the IEEE Conference on Computer Vision and Pattern Recognition, pp. 3431–3440 (2015)

17. Menze, M., Geiger, A.: Object scene flow for autonomous vehicles. In: Conference on Computer Vision and Pattern Recognition (CVPR) (2015)
18. Mur-Artal, R., Montiel, J.M.M., Tardos, J.D.: ORB-SLAM: a versatile and accurate monocular SLAM system. IEEE Trans. Robot. **31**(5), 1147–1163 (2015)
19. Pereira, F.I., Ilha, G., Luft, J., Negreiros, M., Susin, A.: Monocular visual odometry with cyclic estimation. In: 2017 30th SIBGRAPI Conference on Graphics, Patterns and Images (SIBGRAPI), pp. 1–6. IEEE (2017)
20. Pfeiffer, D., Franke, U.: Modeling dynamic 3D environments by means of the Stixel World. IEEE Intell. Transp. Syst. Mag. **3**(3), 24–36 (2011)
21. Pfeiffer, D., Franke, U.: Towards a global optimal multi-layer stixel representation of dense 3D data. In: BMVC, vol. 11, pp. 51–1 (2011)
22. Ranftl, R., Vineet, V., Chen, Q., Koltun, V.: Dense monocular depth estimation in complex dynamic scenes. In: Proceedings of the IEEE Conference on Computer Vision and Pattern Recognition, pp. 4058–4066 (2016)
23. Schneider, L., et al.: Semantic stixels: depth is not enough. In: 2016 IEEE Intelligent Vehicles Symposium (IV), pp. 110–117. IEEE (2016)
24. Simonyan, K., Zisserman, A.: Very deep convolutional networks for large-scale image recognition. arXiv preprint arXiv:1409.1556 (2014)
25. Tateno, K., Tombari, F., Laina, I., Navab, N.: CNN-SLAM: real-time dense monocular SLAM with learned depth prediction. In: Proceedings of the IEEE Conference on Computer Vision and Pattern Recognition (CVPR), vol. 2 (2017)
26. Torr, P.H., Zisserman, A.: MLESAC: a new robust estimator with application to estimating image geometry. Comput. Vis. Image Underst. **78**(1), 138–156 (2000)
27. Ummenhofer, B., et al.: DeMoN: depth and motion network for learning monocular stereo. In: The IEEE Conference on Computer Vision and Pattern Recognition (CVPR), July 2017
28. Vijayanarasimhan, S., Ricco, S., Schmid, C., Sukthankar, R., Fragkiadaki, K.: SfM-Net: learning of structure and motion from video. arXiv preprint arXiv:1704.07804 (2017)
29. Weinzaepfel, P., Revaud, J., Harchaoui, Z., Schmid, C.: DeepFlow: large displacement optical flow with deep matching. In: Proceedings of the IEEE International Conference on Computer Vision, pp. 1385–1392 (2013)
30. Zhou, T., Brown, M., Snavely, N., Lowe, D.G.: Unsupervised learning of depth and ego-motion from video. In: CVPR (2017)

EL-GAN: Embedding Loss Driven Generative Adversarial Networks for Lane Detection

Mohsen Ghafoorian$^{(\boxtimes)}$, Cedric Nugteren, Nóra Baka, Olaf Booij,
and Michael Hofmann

TomTom, Amsterdam, The Netherlands
{mohsen.ghafoorian,cedric.nugteren,nora.baka,
olaf.booij,michael.hofmann}@tomtom.com

Abstract. Convolutional neural networks have been successfully applied to semantic segmentation problems. However, there are many problems that are inherently not pixel-wise classification problems but are nevertheless frequently formulated as semantic segmentation. This ill-posed formulation consequently necessitates hand-crafted scenario-specific and computationally expensive post-processing methods to convert the per pixel probability maps to final desired outputs. Generative adversarial networks (GANs) can be used to make the semantic segmentation network output to be more *realistic* or better *structure-preserving*, decreasing the dependency on potentially complex post-processing.

In this work, we propose EL-GAN: a GAN framework to mitigate the discussed problem using an *embedding loss*. With EL-GAN, we discriminate based on learned embeddings of both the labels and the prediction at the same time. This results in much more stable training due to having better discriminative information, benefiting from seeing both 'fake' and 'real' predictions at the same time. This substantially stabilizes the adversarial training process. We use the TuSimple lane marking challenge to demonstrate that with our proposed framework it is viable to overcome the inherent anomalies of posing it as a semantic segmentation problem. Not only is the output considerably more similar to the labels when compared to conventional methods, the subsequent post-processing is also simpler and crosses the competitive 96% accuracy threshold.

1 Introduction

Convolutional neural networks (CNNs) have been successfully applied to various computer vision problems by posing them as an image segmentation problem. Examples include road scene understanding for autonomous driving [18,20,23] and medical imaging [2,3,8,13,19,22]. The output of such a network is an image-sized map, representing per-pixel class probabilities. However, in many cases the

Electronic supplementary material The online version of this chapter (https://doi.org/10.1007/978-3-030-11009-3_15) contains supplementary material, which is available to authorized users.

L. Leal-Taixé and S. Roth (Eds.): ECCV 2018 Workshops, LNCS 11129, pp. 256–272, 2019.
https://doi.org/10.1007/978-3-030-11009-3_15

problem itself is not directly a pixel-classification task, and/or the predictions need to preserve certain qualities/structures that are not enforced with the high degrees of freedom of a per-pixel classification scheme. For instance, if the task at hand is to detect a single straight line in an image, a pixel-level loss cannot easily enforce high-level qualities such as thinness, straightness or the uniqueness of the detected line. The fundamental reason behind this is the way the training loss is formulated (e.g. per-pixel cross entropy), such that each output pixel in the segmentation map is evaluated independently of all others, i.e. no explicit inter-pixel consistency is enforced. Enforcing these qualities often necessitates additional post-processing steps. Examples of post-processing steps include applying a conditional random field (CRF) [14], additional separately trained networks [20], or non-learned problem-specific algorithms [1]. Drawbacks of such approaches are that they require effort to construct, can have many hyper-parameters, are problem specific, and might still not capture the final objective. For example, CRFs need to be trained separately and either only capture local consistencies or are computationally expensive at inference time with long-range dependencies.

A potential solution for the lack of structure enforcement in semantic segmentation problems is to use generative adversarial networks (GANs) [5] to 'learn' an extra loss function that aims to model the desired properties. GANs work by training two networks in an alternating fashion in a minimax game: a *generator* is trained to produce results, while a *discriminator* is trained to distinguish produced data ('fake') from ground truth labels ('real'). GANs have also been applied to semantic segmentation problems to try to address the aforementioned issues with the per-pixel loss [18]. In such a case, the generator would produce the semantic segmentation map, while the discriminator alternately observes ground truth labels and predicted segmentation maps. There are issues with this approach, as also observed by [28]: the single binary prediction of the discriminator does not provide stable and sufficient gradient feedback to properly train the networks.

In prior work, the discriminator in a GAN observes either 'real' or 'fake' data in an alternating fashion (e.g. [18]), due to its inherently unsupervised nature. However, in the case of a semantic segmentation problem, we do have access to the ground truth data corresponding to a prediction. The intuition behind our work is that by feeding both the predictions and the labels at the same time, it is possible for a discriminator to obtain much more useful feedback to steer the training of the segmentation network in the direction of more realistic labels. In other words, the discriminator can be taught to learn a supervised loss function.

In this work, we propose such an architecture for enforcing structure in semantic segmentation output. In particular, we propose EL-GAN ('Embedding loss GAN'), in which the discriminator takes as input the source data, a prediction map and a ground truth label, and is trained to minimize the difference between embeddings of the predictions and labels. The more useful gradient feedback and increased training stability in EL-GAN enables us to successfully train semantic segmentation networks using a GAN architecture. As a result, our segmentation predictions are structurally much more similar to the training

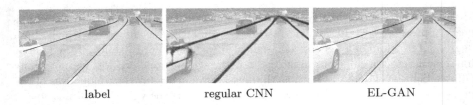

label   regular CNN   EL-GAN

Fig. 1. Illustration of using EL-GAN for lane marking segmentation: an example ground truth label (left), its corresponding raw prediction by a conventional segmentation network based on [11] (middle), and a prediction by EL-GAN (right). Note how EL-GAN matches the thin-line style of the labels in terms of certainty and connectivity (Color figure online)

labels without requiring additional problem-specific loss terms or post-processing steps. The benefits of our approach are illustrated in Fig. 1, in which we show an example training label and compare it to predictions of a regular segmentation network and our EL-GAN framework. Our contributions are:

- We propose a novel method to impose structure on problems that are badly posed as semantic segmentation, by using a generative adversarial network architecture with a discriminator that is trained on both predictions and labels at the same time. We introduce EL-GAN, an instance of the above, which uses an L_2 loss on embeddings of the segmentation network predictions and the ground truth labels.
- We show that the embedding loss substantially stabilizes training and leads to more useful gradient feedback compared to a normal adversarial loss formulation. Compared to conventional segmentation networks, this requires no extra engineered loss terms or complex post-processing, leading to better label-like prediction qualities.
- We demonstrate the usefulness of EL-GAN for autonomous driving applications, although the method is generic and can be applied to other segmentation problems as well. We test on the TuSimple lane marking detection dataset and show competitive accuracy scores, but also show that EL-GAN visually produces results more similar to the ground truth labels.

2 Related Work

Quality Preserving Semantic Segmentation. Several methods have proposed to add property-targeted loss terms [2,22] or to use pair-wise or higher-order term CRFs [14,27,31], to enforce neural networks to preserve certain qualities such as smoothness, topology and neighborhood consistency. In contrast to our work, such approaches are mostly only capable of preserving lower-level consistencies and also impose additional costs at inference time. Hand-engineering extra loss terms that target enforcing certain qualities is often challenging as identifying the target qualities in the first place and then coming up with efficient differentiable loss terms is often not straight-forward.

Adversarial Training for Semantic Segmentation. The principal underlying idea of GANs [5] is to enable a neural network to learn a target distribution for generating samples by training it in a minimax game with a competing discriminator network. Luc et al. [18] employed adversarial training for segmentation to ensure higher-level semantic consistencies. Their work involves using a discriminator that provides feedback to the segmentation network (generator) based on differences between distributions of labels and predictions. This differs from aforementioned works in the sense that the additional loss term is being learned by the discriminator rather than having fixed hand-crafted loss terms. The same mechanism was later applied to image-to-image translation [10], medical image analysis [3,8,13,17,19,24,28,29] and other segmentation tasks [21]. In contrast to our work, this formulation of adversarial training does not use the pairing information of images and labels. Based on this, some works [7,30] suggest using a GAN in a semi-supervised fashion, with the additional assumption that the unlabeled data is coming from the same distribution as the labeled ones. Our work also stems from the same intuition that this formulation does not leverage the pairing information; we instead change the method such that the pairing information is exploited. Another related work is [28], which proposes an L_1 loss term for GAN-based medical image segmentation, but interpretations and extensive ablation studies are not provided. Our method differs in the input the discriminator receives, as well as the loss term that is used to train it. In concurrent work, Hwang et al. [9] uses adversarial training for structural matching between the ground-truth and the predicted image. In contrast to our work, [9] does not condition the discriminator on the input image, nor uses a pixel-level loss to steer the training of the segmenter network. As a consequence, the discriminator representations need to be kept low-level to ensure a segmenter that attends to low-level details. Furthermore, we provide extensive ablation studies in order to better understand, discuss and interpret the characteristics and benefits of the method.

Feature matching, as proposed in [26], also learns features to maximize the difference between the real and fake distributions. However, a difference is that Salimans et al. are matching fake/real distribution features statistics (e.g. mean) rather than matching the embeddings directly, which is not possible in unsupervised image generation.

Perceptual Loss. Several recent works [4,12,25], in particular targeting image super-resolution, are based on the idea that pixel-level objective losses are often not sufficient to ensure high-level semantics of a generated image. Therefore, they suggest to capture higher-level representations of images from the representations of a separate network at a given layer. In image super-resolution, the corresponding ground truth label for a given low-resolution image is often available. Therefore, a difference measure (e.g. L_2) between the high-level representations of the reconstructed and ground truth images is considered as an extra loss term. Our work is inspired by this idea: similarly, we propose to use the difference between the labels and predictions in a high-level embedding space.

Lane Marking Detection. Since the evaluation of our work focuses on lane marking detection, we also discuss other related approaches for this problem, while we refer the reader to a recent survey for a broader overview [1]. An example of a successful lane marking detection approach is by Pan et al. [23]. In their work, they train a problem-specific spatial CNN and add hand-crafted post-processing. Lee et al. [15] use extra vanishing-point labels to guide the network toward a more structurally consistent lane marking detection. Another recent example is the work by Neven et al. [20], in which a regular segmentation network is used to obtain lane marking prediction maps. They then train a second network to perform a constrained perspective transformation, after which curve fitting is used to obtain the final results. We compare our work in more detail to the studies above [20, 23] that are similarly conducted on the Tusimple challenge, in Sect. 6.1.

3 Method

In this section we introduce EL-GAN: adversarial training with embedding loss for semantic segmentation. This method is generic and can be applied to various segmentation problems. The detailed network architecture and training set-up is discussed in Sect. 4.

3.1 Baseline: Adversarial Training for Semantic Segmentation

Adversarial training can be used to ensure a higher level of label resembling qualities such as smoothness, preserving neighborhood consistencies, and so on. This is done by using a discriminator network that learns a loss function for these desirable properties over time rather than formulating these properties explicitly. A typical approach for benefiting from adversarial training for semantic segmentation [10, 18] involves formulating a loss function for the segmentation network (generator) that consists of two terms: one term concerning low-level pixel-wise prediction/label fitness ($\mathcal{L}_{\text{fit}}$) and another (adversarial) loss term for preserving higher-level consistency qualities ($\mathcal{L}_{\text{adv}}$), conditioned on the input image:

$$\mathcal{L}_{\text{gen}}(x, y; \theta_{\text{gen}}, \theta_{\text{disc}}) = \mathcal{L}_{\text{fit}}(G(x; \theta_{\text{gen}}), y) + \lambda \mathcal{L}_{\text{adv}}(G(x; \theta_{\text{gen}}); x, \theta_{\text{disc}}), \quad (1)$$

where x and y are the input image and the corresponding label map respectively, θ_{gen} and θ_{disc} are the set of parameters for the generator and discriminator networks, $G(x; \theta)$ represents a transformation on input image x, imposed by the generator network parameterized by θ, and λ indicates the relative importance of the adversarial loss term. The loss term $\mathcal{L}_{\text{fit}}$ is often formulated with a pixel-wise categorical cross entropy loss, $\mathcal{L}_{\text{cce}}(G(x; \theta_{\text{gen}}), y)$, where $\mathcal{L}_{\text{cce}}(\hat{y}, y) = \frac{1}{wh} \sum_i^{wh} \sum_j^c y_{i,j} \ln(\hat{y}_{i,j})$ with c representing the number of target classes and w and h being the width and height of the image.

The adversarial loss term, $\mathcal{L}_{\mathrm{adv}}$ indicates how successful the discriminator is in rejecting the (fake) dense prediction maps produced by the generator and is often formulated with a binary cross entropy loss between zero and the binary prediction of the discriminator for a generated prediction map: $\mathcal{L}_{\mathrm{bce}}(D(G(x; \theta_{\mathrm{gen}}); \theta_{\mathrm{disc}}), 0)$, where $\mathcal{L}_{\mathrm{bce}}(\hat{z}, z) = -z \ln(\hat{z}) - (1 - z) \ln(1 - \hat{z})$ and D is the transformation imposed by the discriminator network.

While the generator is trained to minimize its adversarial loss term, the discriminator tries to maximize it, by minimizing its loss defined as:

$$\mathcal{L}_{\mathrm{disc}}(x, y; \theta_{\mathrm{gen}}, \theta_{\mathrm{disc}}) = \mathcal{L}_{\mathrm{bce}}(D(G(x; \theta_{\mathrm{gen}}); \theta_{\mathrm{disc}}), 0) + \mathcal{L}_{\mathrm{bce}}(D(y; \theta_{\mathrm{disc}}), 1). \quad (2)$$

By alternating between the training of the two networks, the discriminator learns the differences between the label and prediction distributions, while the generator tries to change the qualities of its predictions, similar to that of the labels, such that the two distributions are not distinguishable. In practice, it is often observed that the training of the adversarial networks tends to be more tricky and unstable compared to training normal networks. This can be attributed to the mutual training of the two networks involved in a minimax game where the training dynamics of each affect the training of the other. The discriminator gives feedback to the generator based on how plausible the generator images are. There are two important issues with the frequently used adversarial training framework for semantic segmentation:

1. The notion of plausibility and fake-ness of these prediction maps comes from the discriminator's representation of these concepts and how its weights encode these qualities; This encoding is likely to be far from perfect, resulting in gradients in directions that are likely not improving the generator.
2. The conventional adversarial loss term does not exploit the valuable piece of information on image/label pairing that is often available for many of the supervised semantic segmentation tasks.

3.2   Adversarial Training with Embedding Loss

Given the two issues above, one can leverage the image/label pairing to base the plausibility/fake-ness not only on the discriminator's understanding of these notions but also on a true plausible label map. One way to utilize this idea is to use the discriminator to take the prediction/label maps into a higher-level description and define the adversarial loss as their difference in embedding space:

$$\mathcal{L}_{\mathrm{gen}}(x, y; \theta_{\mathrm{gen}}, \theta_{\mathrm{disc}}) = \mathcal{L}_{\mathrm{fit}}(G(x; \theta_{\mathrm{gen}}), y) + \lambda \mathcal{L}_{\mathrm{adv}}(G(x; \theta_{\mathrm{gen}}), y; x, \theta_{\mathrm{disc}}), \quad (3)$$

where we suggest to formulate $\mathcal{L}_{\mathrm{adv}}(G(x; \theta_{\mathrm{gen}}), y; x, \theta_{\mathrm{disc}})$ with embedding loss $\mathcal{L}_{\mathrm{emb}}(G(x; \theta_{\mathrm{gen}}), y; x, \theta_{\mathrm{disc}})$ defined as a distance over embeddings (e.g. L_2):

$$\mathcal{L}_{\mathrm{emb}}(\hat{y}, y; x, \theta_{\mathrm{disc}}) = \|D_e(y; x, \theta_{\mathrm{disc}}) - D_e(\hat{y}; x, \theta_{\mathrm{disc}})\|_2, \quad (4)$$

where $D_e(\hat{y}; x, \theta)$ represents the embeddings extracted from a given layer in the network D parameterized with θ, given the prediction $\hat{y}$ and x as its inputs.

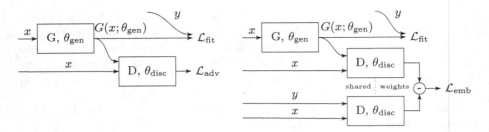

Fig. 2. Illustration of the novel training set-up for the generator loss: left for a conventional GAN (Eq. 1), right when using the embedding loss (Eqs. 3 and 4)

We name this the EL-GAN architecture, in which the adversarial loss and the corresponding gradients are computed based on a difference in high-level descriptions (embeddings) of labels and predictions. While the discriminator learns to minimize its loss on the discrimination between real and fake distributions, and likely learns a set of discriminative embeddings, the generator tries to minimize this embedding difference. This formulation of generator training is illustrated in Fig. 2 on the right-hand side, in which we also show the regular generator training set-up on the left-hand side for comparison.

Apart from the mentioned change in computing the adversarial loss for the generator updates, Eq. 2 for discriminator updates can optionally be rewritten with a similar idea as:

$$\mathcal{L}_{\text{disc}}(x, y; \theta_{\text{gen}}, \theta_{\text{disc}}) = -\mathcal{L}_{\text{emb}}(G(x, \theta_{\text{gen}}), y; x, \theta_{\text{disc}}). \qquad (5)$$

However, in our empirical studies we have found that using the cross entropy loss for updating the discriminator parameters gives better results.

4   Experimental Setup

In this section we elaborate on the datasets and metrics used for evaluating our method, followed by details of the network architectures and training methods.

4.1   Evaluation Datasets and Metrics

We focus our evaluation on the application domain of autonomous driving, but stress that our method is generic and can be applied to other semantic segmentation problems as well. One of the motivations of this work is to be able to produce predictions resembling the ground truth labels as much as possible. This is in particular useful for the TuSimple lane marking detection data set with thin structures, reducing the need for complicated post-processing.

The TuSimple lane marking detection dataset[1] consists of 3626 annotated 1280×720 front-facing road images images on US highways in the San Diego

---

[1] TuSimple dataset details: http://benchmark.tusimple.ai/#/t/1.

area divided over four sequences, and a similar set of 2782 test images. The annotations are given in the form of polylines of lane markings: those of the ego-lane and the lanes to the left and right of the car. The polylines are given at fixed height-intervals every 20 pixels. To generate labels for semantic segmentation, we convert these to segmentation maps by discretizing the lines using smooth interpolation with a Gaussian with a sigma of 1 pixel wide. An example of such a label is shown in red in the left of Fig. 1.

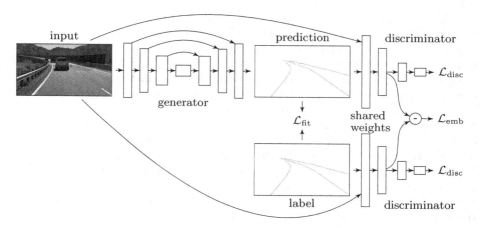

Fig. 3. Overview of the EL-GAN architecture, illustrating both the training of the generator and discriminator with examples from the TuSimple lane marking challenge

The dataset is evaluated on results in the same format as the labels, namely multiple polylines. For our evaluation we use the official metrics as defined in the challenge (See footnote 1), namely accuracy, false positive rate, and false negative rate. We report results on the official test set as well as on a validation set which is one of the labeled sequences with 409 images ('0601'). We note that performance on this validation set is perhaps not fully representative, because of its small size. A different validation sequence also has its drawbacks, since the other three are much larger and will considerably reduce the size of the already small data set.

Since our network still outputs segmentation maps rather than the required polylines, we do apply post-processing, but keep it as simple as possible: after binarizing, we transform each connected component into a separate polyline by taking the mean x-index of a sequence of non-zero values at each y-index. We refer to this method as 'basic'. We also evaluate a 'basic++' version which also splits connected components in case it detects that multiple sequences of non-zero values occur at one sampling location.

4.2 Network Architectures and Training

In this section we discuss the network and training set-up used for our experiments. A sketch of the high-level network architecture with example data is shown in Fig. 3, which shows the different loss terms used for either the generator or discriminator training, or both.

For the generator we use a fully-convolutional U-Net style network with a downwards and an upwards path and skip connections. In particular, we use the Tiramisu DenseNet architecture [11] for lane marking detection, configured with 7 up/down levels for a total of 64 3 × 3 convolution layers.

For the discriminator we use a DenseNet architecture [6] with 7 blocks and a total of 32 3 × 3 convolution layers, followed by a fully-convolutional *patch-GAN* classifier [16]. We use a two-headed network for the first 2 dense blocks to separately process the input image from the labels or predictions, after which we concatenate the feature maps. We take the embeddings after the final convolution layer, but explore other options in Sect. 5.2.

We first pre-train the generator models until convergence, which we also use as our baseline non-GAN model for Sect. 5. Using a batch size of 8, we then pre-train the discriminator for 10k iterations, after which alternate between 300 and 200 iterations of generator and discriminator training, respectively. The generator is trained with the Adam optimizer, while the discriminator training was observed to be more stable using SGD. We train the discriminator using the regular cross entropy loss (Eq. 2), while we train the generator with the adversarial embedding loss with $\lambda = 1$ (Eqs. 3 and 4). We did not do any data augmentation nor pre-train the model on other data.

5 Results

In this section we report the results on the TuSimple datasets using the experimental set-up as discussed in Sect. 4. Additionally, we perform three ablation studies: evaluating the training stability, exploring the options for the training losses, and varying the choice for embedding loss layer.

5.1 TuSimple Lane Marking Challenge

In this section we report the results of the TuSimple lane marking detection challenge and compare them with our baseline and the state-of-the-art.

We first evaluated EL-GAN and our baseline on the validation set using both post-processing methods. The results in Table 1 show that the basic post-processing method is not suitable for the baseline model, while the improved basic++ method performs a lot better. Still, EL-GAN outperforms the baseline, in particular with the most basic post-processing method.

Some results on the validation set are shown in Fig. 4, which compares the two methods in terms of raw prediction maps and post-processed results using the basic++ method. Clearly, EL-GAN produces considerably thinner and more label-like output with less noise, making post-processing easier in general.

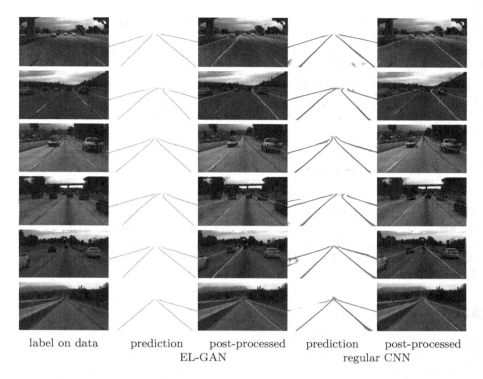

label on data	prediction	post-processed	prediction	post-processed
	EL-GAN		regular CNN	

Fig. 4. Example results for lane marking segmentation: the labels on top of the data (left column), the prediction and final results of EL-GAN (next two columns), and results of the regular CNN baseline [11] using the same post-processing (right two columns). The colors of the lines have no meaning other than to distinguish them from each other. Details are best viewed on a computer screen when zoomed in (Color figure online)

Furthermore, we train EL-GAN and the baseline on the entire labeled dataset, and evaluate using the basic++ post-processing on the official test set of the TuSimple challenge. Table 2 shows the results, which includes all methods in the top 6 (only two of which are published, to the best of our knowledge) and their rank on the leaderboard as of March 14, 2018. We rank 4th based

Table 1. Results on TuSimple lane marking validation set

Method	Post-processing	Accuracy (%)	FP	FN
Baseline (no GAN)	basic	86.2	0.089	0.213
Baseline (no GAN)	basic++	94.3	0.084	0.070
EL-GAN	basic	93.3	0.061	0.104
EL-GAN	basic++	**94.9**	**0.059**	**0.067**

Table 2. TuSimple lane marking challenge leaderboard (test set) as of March 14, 2018

Rank	Method	Name on board	Extra data	Accuracy (%)	FP	FN
#1	Unpublished	leonardoli	?	**96.87**	0.0442	0.0197
#2	Pan et al. [23]	XingangPan	Yes	96.53	0.0617	**0.0180**
#3	Unpublished	aslarry	?	96.50	0.0851	0.0269
#5	Neven et al. [20]	DavyNeven	No	96.38	0.0780	0.0244
#6	Unpublished	li	?	96.15	0.1888	0.0365
#14	Baseline (no GAN)	N/A	No	94.54	0.0733	0.0476
#4	EL-GAN	TomTom EL-GAN	No	96.39	**0.0412**	0.0336

on accuracy with a difference less than half a percent to the best, and obtain the lowest false positive rate. Compared to the baseline, our adversarial training algorithm improves ~2% on the accuracy (decrease of error by 38%), decreases the FPs by more than 55% and FNs by 30% on the private challenge test set. These improvements take the baseline from 14th rank to 4th.

5.2 Ablation Studies

Table 3 compares the use of embedding/cross entropy as different choices for adversarial loss term for training of the generator and the discriminator networks. To compare the stability of the training, statistics over validation accuracies are reported. Figure 5 furthermore illustrates the validation set F-score mean, and standard deviation over 5 training runs. These results show that using the embedding loss for the generator makes GAN training stable. We observed similar behavior when training with other hyper-parameters.

Table 3. TuSimple validation set accuracy statistics over different training iterations (every 10K), comparing the stability of different choices for adversarial losses

Loss		Accuracy statistics			Equations
Generator	Discriminator	Mean	Var	Max	
Cross entropy	Cross entropy	33.84	511.71	58.11	1 and 2
Cross entropy	Embedding	0.00	**0.00**	0.02	1 and 5
Embedding	Cross entropy	93.97	0.459	94.65	3, 4 and 2
Embedding	Embedding	**94.17**	0.429	**94.98**	3, 4 and 5

The features used for the embedding loss can be taken at different locations in the discriminator. In this section we explore three options: taking the features either after the 3rd, 5th, or 7th dense block. We note that the 3rd block contains the first shared convolution layers with both the image input and the predictions or labels, and that the 7th block contains the final set of convolutions before

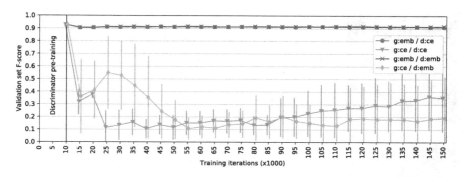

Fig. 5. A comparison of training stability for using different adversarial loss terms (embedding/cross entropy) on the validation f-score. For each method the central point represents the mean f-score and the bars on each side illustrate the standard deviation. It should be noted that in the *g:emb/d:ce* and *g:emb/d:emb* cases the std bars are not visible due to tiny variations among different runs.

the classifier of the network. Results for the TuSimple lane marking detection validation set are given in Table 4 and in Fig. 6. From the results, we conclude that the later we take the embeddings, the better the score and the more similar the predictions are to the labels.

Table 4. Ablation study on embedding extraction layer

Embedding loss after block #	Accuracy (%)	FP	FN
Dense block 3 (first block after joining)	93.91	0.1013	0.1060
Dense block 5	94.01	0.0733	0.0878
Dense block 7 (before classifier)	**94.94**	**0.0592**	**0.0673**

6 Discussion

6.1 Comparison with Other Lane Marking Detection Methods

In Table 2 we showed the results on the TuSimple lane marking data set with EL-GAN ranking 4th on the leaderboard. In this section, we compare our method in more detail to the other two published methods: Pan et al. [23] (ranking 2nd) and Neven et al. [20] (ranking 5th).

Neven et al. [20] argue in their work that post-processing techniques such as curve fitting are preferably not done on the output of the network, but rather in a birds-eye perspective. To this extent they train a separate network to learn a homography to find a perspective transform for which curve fitting is easier. In our work we show that it is possible to achieve comparable accuracy results without having to perform curve fitting at all, thus omitting the requirement for training and evaluating a separate network for this purpose.

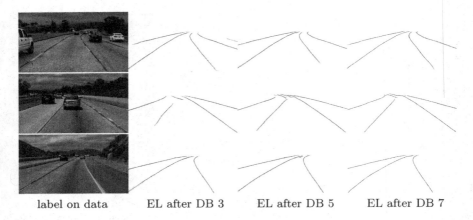

label on data   EL after DB 3   EL after DB 5   EL after DB 7

Fig. 6. Comparison of taking the embedding loss (EL) after a particular dense block (DB): the data and the label (left) and the prediction results of the different settings (right three images). Details are best viewed on a computer screen when zoomed in

Pan et al. [23] use a multi-class approach to lane marking detection, in which each lane marking is a separate class. Although this eases post-processing, it requires more complexity in label creation and makes the task more difficult for the network: it should now also learn which lane is which, requiring a larger field of view and yielding ambiguities at lane changes. In contrast, with our GAN approach, we can learn a simpler single-class problem without requiring complex post-processing to separate individual markings. Pan et al. [23] also argue that problems such as lane marking detection can benefit from spatial consistency and message passing before the final predictions are made. For this reason they propose to feed the output of a regular segmentation network into a problem specific 'spatial CNN' with message passing convolutions in different directions. This does indeed result in a better accuracy on the TuSimple data set compared to EL-GAN, however, it is unclear how much is attributed to their spatial CNN and how much to the fact that they train on a non-public data set which is 20 times larger than the regular TuSimple data set.

6.2   Analysis of the Ablation Study

As we observed in the comparison of the different adversarial loss terms as presented in Table 3 and Fig. 5, using the embedding loss for the generator makes the training more stable and prevents collapses. The embedding loss, in contrast to the usual formulation with the cross entropy loss, provides stronger signals as it leverages the existing ground-truth rather than basing it only on the discriminator's internal representations of fake-ness and plausibility.

Therefore, using a normal cross entropy loss can result in collapses, in which the generator starts to explore samples in the feature space where the discriminator's fake/real comprehension is not well formed. In contrast, using the embed-

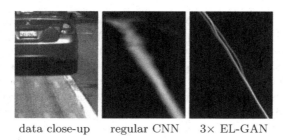

data close-up   regular CNN   3× EL-GAN

Fig. 7. Example detail of input data (left), a regular semantic segmentation output (center), and three different EL-GAN models trained with the same settings shown as red, green, and blue channels (right) (Color figure online)

ding loss, such noise productions result in high differences in the embedding space and is strictly penalized by the embedding loss. Furthermore, having an overwhelming discriminator that can perfectly distinguish the fake and real distributions results in training collapses and instability. Hence, using an embedding loss with better gradients that flow back to the generator likely results in a more competent generator. Similarly, it is no surprise that using an embedding loss for the discriminator and not for the generator results in a badly diverging behavior due to a much more dominating discriminator and a generator that is not penalized much for producing noise.

In the second ablation study, as presented in Table 4 and Fig. 6, we observed that using deeper representations for extracting the embeddings results in better performance. This is perhaps due to a larger receptive field of the embeddings that better enables the generator to improve on the higher-level qualities and consistencies.

6.3 GANs for Semantic Segmentation

Looking more closely at the comparison between a regular CNN and EL-GAN (Fig. 4), we see a distinct difference in the nature of their output. The non-GAN network produces a probabilistic output with a probability per class per pixel, while EL-GAN's output is similar to a possible label, without expressing any uncertainty. One might argue that the lack of being able to express uncertainty hinders further post-processing. However, the first step of commonly applied post-processing schemes is removing the probabilities by thresholding or applying argmax (e.g. [20,23]). In addition, the independent per-pixel probabilistic output of the regular CNN might hide inter-pixel correlation necessary for correct post-processing. The cross entropy loss pushes the network to output a segmentation distribution that does not lie on the manifold of possible labels.

In EL-GAN and other GANs for semantic segmentation, networks are trained to output a sample of the distribution of possible labels conditioned on the input image. An example is shown in Fig. 7, from which we clearly see the selection of a sample once the lane marking is occluded and the network becomes more uncertain. Although this sacrifices the possibility to express uncertainty, we argue that the fact that it lies on, or close to, the manifold of possible labels, it can make post-processing easier and more accurate. For the task of lane marking detection we indeed have shown that the semantic segmentation does not need to output probabilities. However, for other applications this might not be the case. A straightforward approach to re-introduce expressing uncertainty by a GAN, would be to simply run it multiple times conditioned on extra random input or use an ensemble of EL-GANs. The resulting samples which model the probability on the manifold of possible labels would then be the input to post-processing.

7   Conclusions

In this paper, we proposed, studied and compared EL-GAN as a method to preserve label-resembling qualities in the predictions of the network. We showed that using EL-GAN results in a more stable adversarial training process. Furthermore, we achieved state-of-the-art results on the TuSimple challenge, without using any extra data or complicated hand-engineered post-processing pipelines, as opposed to the other competitive methods.

Acknowledgments. The authors would like to thank Nicolau Leal Werneck, Stefano Secondo, Jihong Ju, Yu Wang, Sindi Shkodrani and Bram Beernink for their contributions and valuable feedback.

References

1. Bar Hillel, A., Lerner, R., Levi, D., Raz, G.: Recent progress in road and lane detection: a survey. Mach. Vis. Appl. **25**(3), 727–745 (2014). https://doi.org/10.1007/s00138-011-0404-2
2. BenTaieb, A., Hamarneh, G.: Topology aware fully convolutional networks for histology gland segmentation. In: Ourselin, S., Joskowicz, L., Sabuncu, M.R., Unal, G., Wells, W. (eds.) MICCAI 2016. LNCS, vol. 9901, pp. 460–468. Springer, Cham (2016). https://doi.org/10.1007/978-3-319-46723-8_53
3. Dai, W., et al.: Scan: structure correcting adversarial network for chest x-rays organ segmentation. arXiv preprint arXiv:1703.08770 (2017)
4. Dosovitskiy, A., Brox, T.: Generating images with perceptual similarity metrics based on deep networks. In: NIPS: Advances in Neural Information Processing Systems, pp. 658–666 (2016)
5. Goodfellow, I., et al.: Generative adversarial nets. In: Ghahramani, Z., Welling, M., Cortes, C., Lawrence, N.D., Weinberger, K.Q. (eds.) Advances in Neural Information Processing Systems 27, pp. 2672–2680. Curran Associates, Inc. (2014). http://papers.nips.cc/paper/5423-generative-adversarial-nets.pdf
6. Huang, G., Liu, Z., Weinberger, K.Q.: Densely connected convolutional networks. In: CVPR: Computer Vision and Pattern Recognition (2017)
7. Hung, W.C., Tsai, Y.H., Liou, Y.T., Lin, Y.Y., Yang, M.H.: Adversarial learning for semi-supervised semantic segmentation. arXiv e-prints, February 2018

8. Huo, Y., et al.: Splenomegaly segmentation using global convolutional kernels and conditional generative adversarial networks. In: Proceedings of SPIE, vol. 10574, pp. 10574–10574-7 (2018). https://doi.org/10.1117/12.2293406

9. Hwang, J.J., Ke, T.W., Shi, J., Yu, S.X.: Adversarial structure matching loss for image segmentation. arXiv preprint arXiv:1805.07457 (2018)

10. Isola, P., Zhu, J.Y., Zhou, T., Efros, A.A.: Image-to-image translation with conditional adversarial networks. In: CVPR: Computer Vision and Pattern Recognition (2017)

11. Jegou, S., Drozdzal, M., Vazquez, D., Romero, A., Bengio, Y.: The one hundred layers tiramisu: fully convolutional DenseNets for semantic segmentation. In: CVPRW: IEEE Conference on Computer Vision and Pattern Recognition Workshops, pp. 1175–1183, July 2017. https://doi.org/10.1109/CVPRW.2017.156

12. Johnson, J., Alahi, A., Fei-Fei, L.: Perceptual losses for real-time style transfer and super-resolution. In: Leibe, B., Matas, J., Sebe, N., Welling, M. (eds.) ECCV 2016. LNCS, vol. 9906, pp. 694–711. Springer, Cham (2016). https://doi.org/10.1007/978-3-319-46475-6_43

13. Kohl, S., et al.: Adversarial networks for the detection of aggressive prostate cancer. arXiv preprint arXiv:1702.08014 (2017)

14. Krähenbühl, P., Koltun, V.: Efficient inference in fully connected CRFs with Gaussian edge potentials. In: Advances in Neural Information Processing Systems, pp. 109–117 (2011)

15. Lee, S., et al.: VPGNet: vanishing point guided network for lane and road marking detection and recognition. In: 2017 IEEE International Conference on Computer Vision (ICCV), pp. 1965–1973. IEEE (2017)

16. Li, C., Wand, M.: Precomputed real-time texture synthesis with markovian generative adversarial networks. In: Leibe, B., Matas, J., Sebe, N., Welling, M. (eds.) ECCV 2016. LNCS, vol. 9907, pp. 702–716. Springer, Cham (2016). https://doi.org/10.1007/978-3-319-46487-9_43

17. Li, Z., Wang, Y., Yu, J.: Brain tumor segmentation using an adversarial network. In: Crimi, A., Bakas, S., Kuijf, H., Menze, B., Reyes, M. (eds.) BrainLes 2017. LNCS, vol. 10670, pp. 123–132. Springer, Cham (2018). https://doi.org/10.1007/978-3-319-75238-9_11

18. Luc, P., Couprie, C., Chintala, S., Verbeek, J.: Semantic segmentation using adversarial networks. In: NIPS Workshop on Adversarial Training, Barcelona, Spain, December 2016. https://hal.inria.fr/hal-01398049

19. Moeskops, P., Veta, M., Lafarge, M.W., Eppenhof, K.A.J., Pluim, J.P.W.: Adversarial training and dilated convolutions for brain MRI segmentation. In: Cardoso, M.J., et al. (eds.) DLMIA/ML-CDS -2017. LNCS, vol. 10553, pp. 56–64. Springer, Cham (2017). https://doi.org/10.1007/978-3-319-67558-9_7

20. Neven, D., De Brabandere, B., Georgoulis, S., Proesmans, M., Van Gool, L.: Towards end-to-end lane detection: an instance segmentation approach. arXiv e-prints, February 2018

21. Nguyen, V., Vicente, T.F.Y., Zhao, M., Hoai, M., Samaras, D.: Shadow detection with conditional generative adversarial networks. In: ICCV: IEEE International Conference on Computer Vision, pp. 4520–4528. IEEE (2017)

22. Oktay, O., et al.: Anatomically constrained neural networks (ACNN): application to cardiac image enhancement and segmentation. IEEE Trans. Med. Imaging 37(2), 384–395 (2017)

23. Pan, X., Shi, J., Luo, P., Wang, X., Tang, X.: Spatial as deep: spatial CNN for traffic scene understanding. In: AAAI Conference on Artificial Intelligence, February 2018

24. Sadanandan, S.K., Karlsson, J., Whlby, C.: Spheroid segmentation using multi-scale deep adversarial networks. In: ICCVW: IEEE International Conference on Computer Vision Workshops, pp. 36–41, October 2017. https://doi.org/10.1109/ICCVW.2017.11

25. Sajjadi, M.S., Scholkopf, B., Hirsch, M.: EnhanceNet: single image super-resolution through automated texture synthesis. In: CVPR: IEEE Conference on Computer Vision and Pattern Recognition, pp. 4491–4500 (2017)

26. Salimans, T., Goodfellow, I., Zaremba, W., Cheung, V., Radford, A., Chen, X.: Improved techniques for training GANs. In: Advances in Neural Information Processing Systems, pp. 2234–2242 (2016)

27. Schwing, A.G., Urtasun, R.: Fully connected deep structured networks. arXiv e-prints, March 2015

28. Xue, Y., Xu, T., Zhang, H., Long, R., Huang, X.: SegAN: adversarial network with multi-scale L_1 loss for medical image segmentation. arXiv e-prints, June 2017

29. Yang, D., et al.: Automatic liver segmentation using an adversarial image-to-image network. In: Descoteaux, M., Maier-Hein, L., Franz, A., Jannin, P., Collins, D.L., Duchesne, S. (eds.) MICCAI 2017. LNCS, vol. 10435, pp. 507–515. Springer, Cham (2017). https://doi.org/10.1007/978-3-319-66179-7_58

30. Zhang, Y., Yang, L., Chen, J., Fredericksen, M., Hughes, D.P., Chen, D.Z.: Deep adversarial networks for biomedical image segmentation utilizing unannotated images. In: Descoteaux, M., Maier-Hein, L., Franz, A., Jannin, P., Collins, D.L., Duchesne, S. (eds.) MICCAI 2017. LNCS, vol. 10435, pp. 408–416. Springer, Cham (2017). https://doi.org/10.1007/978-3-319-66179-7_47

31. Zheng, S., et al.: Conditional random fields as recurrent neural networks. In: ICCV: International Conference on Computer Vision, pp. 1529–1537 (2015)

Scale Drift Correction of Camera Geo-Localization Using Geo-Tagged Images

Kazuya Iwami[1]([⊠])(iD), Satoshi Ikehata[2](iD), and Kiyoharu Aizawa[1](iD)

[1] The University of Tokyo, Tokyo, Japan
{iwami,aizawa}@hal.t.u-tokyo.ac.jp
[2] National Institute of Informatics, Tokyo, Japan
sikehata@nii.ac.jp

Abstract. Camera geo-localization from a monocular video is a fundamental task for video analysis and autonomous navigation. Although 3D reconstruction is a key technique to obtain camera poses, monocular 3D reconstruction in a large environment tends to result in the accumulation of errors in rotation, translation, and especially in scale: a problem known as scale drift. To overcome these errors, we propose a novel framework that integrates incremental structure from motion (SfM) and a scale drift correction method utilizing geo-tagged images, such as those provided by Google Street View. Our correction method begins by obtaining sparse 6-DoF correspondences between the reconstructed 3D map coordinate system and the world coordinate system, by using geo-tagged images. Then, it corrects scale drift by applying pose graph optimization over Sim(3) constraints and bundle adjustment. Experimental evaluations on large-scale datasets show that the proposed framework not only sufficiently corrects scale drift, but also achieves accurate geo-localization in a kilometer-scale environment.

Keywords: 3D reconstruction · Localization · Street View

1 Introduction

Camera geo-localization from a monocular video in a kilometer-scale environment is a essential technology for AR, video analysis, and autonomous navigation. To achieve accurate geo-localization, 3D reconstruction from a video is a key technique. Incremental structure from motion (SfM) and visual simultaneous localization and mapping (visual SLAM) achieve large-scale 3D reconstructions by simultaneously localizing camera poses with six degrees-of-freedom (6-DoF) and reconstructing a 3D environment map [7,19].

Unlike for a stereo camera, an absolute scale of the real world cannot be derived using a single observation from a monocular camera. Although it is possible to estimate an environment's relative scale from a series of monocular

© Springer Nature Switzerland AG 2019
L. Leal-Taixé and S. Roth (Eds.): ECCV 2018 Workshops, LNCS 11129, pp. 273–288, 2019.
https://doi.org/10.1007/978-3-030-11009-3_16

observations, errors in the relative scale estimation accumulate over time, and this is referred to as scale drift [6,22].

For an accurate geo-localization not affected by scale drift, prior information in a geographic information system (GIS) has been utilized in previous studies. For example, point clouds, 3D models, building footprints, and road maps have been proven to be efficient for correcting reconstructed 3D maps [4,5,18,23,24]. However, these priors are only available in limited situations, e.g., in an area that is observed in advance, or in an environment consisting of simply-shaped buildings. Therefore, there is a good chance that other GIS information can help to extend the area in which a 3D map can be corrected.

Hence, in this paper, motivated by the recent availability of massive public repositories of geo-tagged images taken all over the world, we propose a novel framework for correcting the scale drift of monocular 3D reconstruction by utilizing geo-tagged images, such as those in Google Street View [1], and achieve accurate camera geo-localization. Owing to the high coverage of Google Street View, our proposal is more scalable than those in previous studies.

The proposed framework integrates incremental SfM and a scale drift correction method utilizing geo-tagged images. Our correction method begins by computing 6-DoF correspondences between the reconstructed 3D map coordinate system and the world coordinate system, by using geo-tagged images. Owing to significant differences in illumination, viewpoint, and the environment resulting from differences in time, it tends to be difficult to acquire correspondences between video frames and geo-tagged images (Fig. 2). Therefore, a new correction method that can deal with the large scale drift of a 3D map using a limited number of correspondences is required. Bundle adjustment with constraints of global position information, which represents one of the most important correction methods, cannot be applied directly. This is because bundle adjustment tends to get stuck in a local minimum when starting from a 3D map including large errors [22]. Hence, the proposed correction method consists of two coarse-to-fine steps: pose graph optimization over Sim(3) constraints, and bundle adjustment. In these steps, our key idea is to extend the pose graph optimization method proposed for the loop closure technique of monocular SLAM [22], such that it incorporates the correspondences between the 3D map coordinate system and the world coordinate system. This step corrects the large errors, and enables bundle adjustment to obtain precise results. After implementing this framework, we conducted experiments to evaluate the proposal.

The contributions of this work are as follows. First, we propose a novel framework for camera geo-localization that can correct scale drift by utilizing geo-tagged images. Second, we extend the pose graph optimization approach to dealing with scale drift using a limited number of correspondences to geotags. Finally, we validate the effectiveness of the proposal through experimental evaluations on kilometer-scale datasets.

2 Related Work

2.1 Monocular 3D Reconstruction

Incremental SfM and visual SLAM are important approaches to reconstructing 3D maps from monocular videos. Klein *et al.* proposed PTAM for small AR workspaces [11]. Mur-Artal *et al.* developed ORB-SLAM, which can reconstruct large-scale outdoor environments [19]. For accurate 3D reconstruction, the loop closure technique has commonly been employed in recent SLAM approaches [19,22]. Loop closure deals with errors that accumulate between two camera poses that occur at the same location, i.e., when the camera trajectory forms a loop. Lu and Milios [16] formulated this technique as a pose graph optimization problem, and Strasdat *et al.* [22] extended pose graph optimization to deal with scale drift for monocular visual SLAM. It is certain that loop closure can significantly improve 3D maps, but this is only effective if a loop exists in the video.

2.2 Geo-Registration of Reconstructions

Correcting reconstructed 3D maps by using geo-referenced information has been regarded as a geo-registration problem. Kaminsky *et al.* proposed a method that aligns 3D reconstructions to 2D aerial images [10]. Wendel *et al.* used an overhead digital surface model (DSM) for the geo-registration of 3D maps [26]. Similar to our work, Wang *et al.* used Google Street View geo-tagged images and a Google Earth 3D model for the geo-registration of reconstructed 3D maps [25]. However, because all these methods focus on estimating a best-fitting similarity transformation to geo-referenced information, they only correct the global scale in terms of 3D map correction.

Methods for geo-registration using non-linear transformations have also been proposed. To integrate GPS information, Lhuillier *et al.* proposed incremental SfM using bundle adjustment with constraints from GPS [14], and Rehder *et al.* formulated a global pose estimation problem using stereo visual odometry, inertial measurements, and infrequent GPS information as a 6-DoF pose graph optimization problem [20]. In terms of correcting camera poses using sparse global information, Rehder's method is similar to our pose graph optimization approach. However, our 7-DoF pose graph optimization differs in focusing on scale drift resulting from monocular 3D reconstruction, and in utilizing geo-tagged images. In addition to GPS information, various kinds of reference data have been used for the non-linear geo-registration or geo-localization of a video, such as point clouds [5,18], 3D models [23], building footprints [24], and road maps [4]. In this paper, we address a method that introduces geo-tagged images to the non-linear geo-registration of 3D maps.

3 Proposed Method

Figure 1 provides a flowchart of the proposed framework, which is roughly divided into three parts. The first part is incremental SfM, and is described

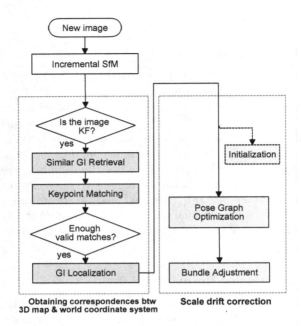

Fig. 1. A flowchart of our proposal. KF and GI denote a keyframe and geo-tagged image, respectively. Initialization is performed only once in a whole reconstruction.

in Sect. 3.2. The second part computes 6-DoF correspondences between the 3D map coordinate system and the world coordinate system (as defined below), by making use of geo-tagged images (Sect. 3.3). The third part then uses the correspondences to correct the scale drift of the 3D map, by applying pose graph optimization over Sim(3) constraints (Sect. 3.5) and bundle adjustment (Sec. 3.6) incrementally. The initialization of the scale drift correction method is described in Sect. 3.4.

3.1   World Coordinate System

In this paper, the world coordinates are represented by 3D coordinates (x, y, z), where the xz-plane corresponds to the Universal Transverse Mercator (UTM) coordinate system, which is an orthogonal coordinate system using meters, and y corresponds to the height from the ground in meters. The UTM coordinates can be converted into latitude and longitude if necessary.

3.2   Incremental SfM

As large-scale incremental SfM, we use ORB-SLAM [19] (with no real-time constraints). This is one of the best-performing monocular SLAM systems. Frames

Fig. 2. Examples of keypoint matches between keyframes (without blue squares) and geo-tagged images of Google Street View (with blue squares) after kVLD validation. Top: pairs of images where valid matches are found. Yellow lines denote kVLD graph structures, which are composed of inliers. Bottom: rejected pairs of images where a sufficient number of matches is not found because of differences in illumination, viewpoint, and environment, despite being taken in almost the same location. (Color figure online)

that are important for 3D reconstruction are selected as keyframes by ORB-SLAM. Every time a new keyframe is selected, our correction method is performed, and the 3D map reconstructed up to that point is corrected. In the 3D reconstruction, we identify 3D map points and their corresponding 2D keypoints in the keyframes (collectively denoted by $C_{\text{map-kf}}$).

Our proposed framework does not depend on a certain 3D reconstruction method, and can be applied to the other monocular 3D reconstruction methods, such as incremental SfM and feature-based visual SLAM.

3.3 Obtaining Correspondences Between 3D Map and World Coordinates

Here, we describe the second part of the proposed method, which uses geo-tagged images to compute a 6-DoF correspondence, $C_{\text{map-world}}$, between the 3D map and world coordinate system. For this purpose, we modify Agarwal's method [2] to integrate it into ORB-SLAM. This part consists of the following four steps: geo-tagged image collection, similar geo-tagged image retrieval, keypoint matching, and geo-tagged image localization.

Geo-Tagged Image Collection. Google Street View [1] is a browsable street-level GIS, which is one of the largest repositories of global geo-tagged images (i.e., images and their associated geo-tags). All images are high-resolution RGB panorama images, containing highly accurate world positions [12]. We make use of this data by converting each panorama image into eight rectilinear images with the same field-of-view as our input video, with eight horizontal directions. Note that because each geo-tag has a position and rotation in the world coordinates,

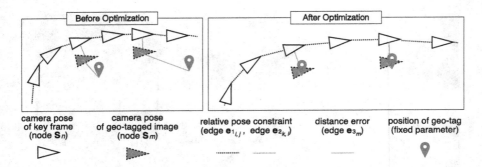

Fig. 3. An example of the proposed pose graph optimization. This optimization maintains overall relative poses, except for gradual scale changes, and keeps camera poses of geo-tagged images close to the positions of the corresponding geo-tags.

we can obtain the 6-DoF correspondences between the 3D map coordinate system and world coordinate system if geo-tagged images are localized in the 3D map coordinate system.

Similar Geo-Tagged Image Retrieval. When a new keyframe is selected, we retrieve the top-k similar geo-tagged images. The retrieval system employs a bag-of-words approach based on SIFT descriptors [2].

Keypoint Matching. Given the pairs of keyframes and retrieved geo-tagged images, we detect ORB keypoints [21] from the pairs and perform keypoint matching. Because the matching between video frames and Google Street View images tends to include many outliers [17], we use a virtual line descriptor (kVLD) [15], which can reject outliers by using a graph matching method even when inlier rate is around 10.

Geo-Tagged Image Localization. To compute $C_{\text{map-world}}$, we first compute 3D-to-2D correspondences $C_{\text{map-geo}}$ between 3D map points and their corresponding 2D keypoints in geo-tagged images. In particular, we obtain $C_{\text{map-geo}}$ by combining the 2D keypoint matches (computed in the previous step) with the correspondences $C_{\text{map-kf}}$ between 3D map points and their corresponding 2D keypoints in keyframes (computed in 3D reconstruction). Then, we obtain the 6-DoF camera poses of geo-tagged images in the 3D map coordinate system by minimizing the re-projection errors of $C_{\text{map-geo}}$, using the LM algorithm. Finally, we obtain $C_{\text{map-world}}$ by combining the camera poses of geo-tagged images and 6-DoF camera poses of the associated geo-tags.

3.4   Initialization (INIT)

As the initialization, two kinds of linear transformations are performed on the 3D map, because the positions and scales of the 3D map coordinates and world coordinates are significantly different. Initialization is applied once, when the i-th geo-tagged image is localized. We set $i = 4$.

Given the first to i-th $C_{\text{map-world}}$, the first transformation assumes that all camera poses are approximately located in one plane, and rotates the 3D map to align that plane to the world xz-plane. The best-fitting plane can be estimated by a principal component analysis.

Next, we estimate the best-fitting transformation matrix given by Eq. 1, which transforms a point in the 3D map coordinate system $\mathbf{p}_{\text{SLAM},k}$ to be closer to a corresponding point in the world coordinate system $\mathbf{p}_{world,k}$ ($\mathbf{p}_{\text{SLAM},k}$ and $\mathbf{p}_{world,k}$ are denoted using a homogeneous representation):

$$\mathbf{A} = \begin{bmatrix} s*\cos(\theta) & 0 & -s*\sin(\theta) & a \\ 0 & s & 0 & 1 \\ s*\sin(\theta) & 0 & s*\cos(\theta) & b \\ 0 & 0 & 0 & 1 \end{bmatrix} \tag{1}$$

Using the first to i-th $C_{\text{map-world}}$, we estimate the four matrix parameters $[a, b, s, \theta]$ by minimizing the following cost using RANSAC [8] and the Levenberg-Marquart (LM) algorithm:

$$E = \sum_{k \in 1,2\ldots i} \|\mathbf{p}_{world,k} - \mathbf{A}\mathbf{p}_{\text{SLAM},k}\|^2 \tag{2}$$

The camera poses of the geo-tagged images in $C_{\text{map-world}}$, keyframes, and 3D map point can then be transformed using the resulting matrix.

3.5 Pose Graph Optimization over Sim(3) Constraints (PGO)

We correct the 3D map focusing on scale drift by using the newest three of $C_{\text{map-world}}$. This correction is performed every time a new $C_{\text{map-world}}$ is found after initialization. Then, we propose a graph-based non-linear optimization method (pose graph optimization) on Lie manifolds, which simultaneously corrects the scale drift and aligns the 3D map with the world coordinates.

Notation. A 3D rigid body transformation $\mathbf{G} \in \text{SE}(3)$ and a 3D similarity transformation $\mathbf{S} \in \text{Sim}(3)$ are defined by Eq. 3, where $\mathbf{R} \in \text{SO}(3)$, $\mathbf{t} \in \mathbb{R}^3$, and $s \in \mathbb{R}^+$. Here, SO(3), SE(3), and Sim(3) are Lie groups, and $\mathfrak{so}(3)$, $\mathfrak{se}(3)$, and $\mathfrak{sim}(3)$ are their corresponding Lie algebras. A Lie group can be transformed into a Lie algebra using its exponential map, and the inverse transformation is defined by the inverse logarithm map. Each Lie algebra is represented by a vector of its coefficients. For example, $\mathfrak{sim}(3)$ is represented as the seven-vector $\boldsymbol{\xi} = (\omega_1, \omega_2, \omega_3, \sigma, \nu_1, \nu_2, \nu_3)^{\text{T}} = (\boldsymbol{\omega}, \sigma, \boldsymbol{\nu})^{\text{T}}$, and the exponential map $\exp_{\text{Sim}(3)}$ and logarithm map $\log_{\text{Sim}(3)}$ are defined as in Eqs. 4 and 5, respectively, where $\mathbf{W}$ is a term similar to Rodriguez's formula. Further details of Sim(3) are given in [22].

$$\mathbf{G} = \begin{bmatrix} \mathbf{R} & \mathbf{t} \\ \mathbf{0} & 1 \end{bmatrix} \qquad \mathbf{S} = \begin{bmatrix} s\mathbf{R} & \mathbf{t} \\ \mathbf{0} & 1 \end{bmatrix} \tag{3}$$

$$\exp_{\text{Sim}(3)}(\boldsymbol{\xi}) = \begin{bmatrix} e^{\sigma} \exp_{\text{SO}(3)}(\boldsymbol{\omega}) & \mathbf{W}\boldsymbol{\nu} \\ \mathbf{0} & 1 \end{bmatrix} = \mathbf{S} \tag{4}$$

$$\log_{\text{Sim}(3)}(\mathbf{S}) = \exp_{\text{Sim}(3)}^{-1}(\mathbf{S}) = \boldsymbol{\xi} \tag{5}$$

Proposed Pose Graph Optimization. In a general pose graph optimization approach [16,20], camera poses and relative transformations between two camera poses are represented as elements of SE(3). However, in our approach, 6-DoF camera poses and relative transformations are converted into 7-DoF camera poses, represented by elements of Sim(3). This is achieved by leaving the rotation R and translation $\mathbf{t}$ of a camera pose unchanged, and setting the scale s to 1. The idea that camera poses and relative pose constraints can be handled in Sim(3) was proposed by Strasdat et al. [22], for dealing with the scale drift problem in monocular SLAM. In this paper, we introduce 7-DoF pose graph optimization, which has previously only been used in the context of loop closure, to correct 3D reconstruction by utilizing sparse correspondences between two coordinate systems. Our pose graph contains two kinds of nodes and three kinds of edges, as follows (see Fig. 3):

- Node $\mathbf{S}_n \in \text{Sim}(3)$, where $n \in C_1$: the camera pose of the nth keyframe.
- Node $\mathbf{S}_m \in \text{Sim}(3)$, where $m \in C_2$: the camera pose of the mth geo-tagged image.
- Edge $\mathbf{e}_{1_{i,j}}$, where $(i,j) \in C_3$: the relative pose constraint between the ith and j^{th} keyframes (Eq. 6).
- Edge $\mathbf{e}_{2_{k,l}}$, where $(k,l) \in C_4$: the relative pose constraint between the kth keyframe and the lth geo-tagged image (Eq. 7).
- Edge $\mathbf{e}_{3_m}$, where $m \in C_2$: the distance error between the position of the mth geo-tagged image and the world position $\mathbf{y}_m$ of the corresponding geo-tag (Eq. 8).

$$\mathbf{e}_{1_{i,j}} = \log_{\text{Sim}(3)}(\Delta \mathbf{S}_{i,j} \cdot \mathbf{S}_i \cdot \mathbf{S}_j^{-1}) \in \mathbb{R}^7 \tag{6}$$

$$\mathbf{e}_{2_{k,l}} = \log_{\text{Sim}(3)}(\Delta \mathbf{S}_{k,l} \cdot \mathbf{S}_k \cdot \mathbf{S}_l^{-1}) \in \mathbb{R}^7 \tag{7}$$

$$\mathbf{e}_{3_m} = \text{trans}(\mathbf{S}_m) - \mathbf{y}_m \in \mathbb{R}^3 \tag{8}$$

where $\text{trans}(\mathbf{S}) \equiv (\mathbf{S}_{1,4}, \mathbf{S}_{2,4}, \mathbf{S}_{3,4})^{\text{T}}$. Here, N is the total number of keyframes, and M is the total number of geo-tagged images that have correspondences to keyframes. The set C_1 contains all the keyframes positioned between the two that have the newest and the third newest $C_{\text{map-world}}$. The set C_2 contains the newest three of $C_{\text{map-world}}$. The set C_3 contains the pairs of keyframes that observe the same 3D map point in 3D reconstruction, and C_4 contains pairs of keyframes and their corresponding geo-tagged images. Finally, $\Delta \mathbf{S}_{i,j}$ is the converted Sim(3) relative transformation between $\mathbf{S}_i$ and $\mathbf{S}_j$, which is calculated before the optimization and remains fixed during the optimization.

Note that we newly introduced the nodes $\mathbf{S}_m$, edges $\mathbf{e}_{2_{k,l}}$, and edges $\mathbf{e}_{3_m}$ to Strasdat's pose graph optimization. Minimizing $\mathbf{e}_{1_{i,j}}$ and $\mathbf{e}_{2_{k,l}}$ suppresses changes in the relative transformations between camera poses, with the exception of gradual scale changes. Minimizing $\mathbf{e}_{3_m}$ keeps the positions of the geo-tagged images close to the positions obtained from the associated geo-tags. Our overall cost function E_{PGO} is defined as follows:

$$E_{PGO}\left(\left\{\mathbf{S}_i\right\}_{i \in C_1 \cup C_2}\right) = \lambda_1 \sum_{(i,j) \in C_3} \mathbf{e}_{1_{i,j}}^{\mathrm{T}} \mathbf{e}_{1_{i,j}}$$
$$+ \lambda_2 \sum_{(k,l) \in C_4} \mathbf{e}_{2_{k,l}}^{\mathrm{T}} \mathbf{e}_{2_{k,l}} + \lambda_3 \sum_{m \in C_2} \mathbf{e}_{3_m}^{\mathrm{T}} \mathbf{e}_{3_m} \tag{9}$$

The corrected camera poses of keyframes $\mathbf{S}_n$ and geo-tagged images $\mathbf{S}_m$ are obtained by minimizing the cost function E_{PGO} on Lie manifolds using the LM algorithm. Following this optimization, we also reflect this correction in the 3D map points, as in [22].

3.6 Bundle Adjustment (BA)

Following the pose graph optimization, we refine the 3D reconstruction by applying bundle adjustment with the constraints of the geo-tagged images. Bundle adjustment is a classic method that jointly refines the 3D structure and camera poses (and camera intrinsic parameters) by minimizing the total re-projection errors. Each re-projection error $\mathbf{r}_{i,j}$ between the ith 3D point and j^{th} camera is defined as:

$$\mathbf{r}_{i,j} = \mathbf{x_i} - \pi(\mathbf{R}_j \mathbf{X}_i + \mathbf{t}_j) \tag{10}$$

$$\pi(\mathbf{p}) = [f_x \frac{\mathbf{P}_x}{\mathbf{P}_z} + c_x, \ f_y \frac{\mathbf{P}_y}{\mathbf{P}_z} + c_y]^{\mathrm{T}} \tag{11}$$

where $\mathbf{X}_i$ is a 3D point and $\mathbf{x}_i$ is the 2D observation of that 3D point; $\mathbf{R}_j$ and $\mathbf{t}_j$ are the rotation and translation of the jth camera pose, respectively; $\mathbf{p} = [\mathbf{p}_x, \mathbf{p}_y, \mathbf{p}_z]^{\mathrm{T}}$ is a 3D point; $\pi(\cdot) : \mathbb{R}^3 \mapsto \mathbb{R}^2$ is the projection function; (f_x, f_y) is the focal length; and (c_x, c_y) is the center of projection.

To incorporate global position information of geo-tagged images with bundle adjustment, we add a penalty term corresponding to the constraint for a geo-tagged image [14]. The total cost function with this constraint is given by:

$$E_{BA}\left(\left\{\mathbf{X}_i\right\}_{i \in C_5}, \left\{\mathbf{T}_j\right\}_{j \in C_1}\right) = \sum_{(i,j) \in C_{\text{map-kf}}} \rho(\mathbf{r}_{i,j}^{\mathrm{T}} \mathbf{r}_{i,j}) + \lambda \sum_{m \in C_3} \|\mathbf{t}_m - \mathbf{y}_m\|^2 \tag{12}$$

where $\mathbf{T}$ is a camera pose of a keyframe represented as an element of SE(3), ρ is the Huber robust cost function, C_5 consists of map points observed by keyframes in C_1, and C_1 and C_3 are defined in Sect. 3.5. Both the positions of 3D points and the camera poses of keyframes are optimized by minimizing the cost function on Lie manifolds using the LM algorithm. This step can potentially correct the 3D map more precisely when it starts from a reasonably good 3D map.

4   Experiments

In this section, we evaluate the proposed method on the Málaga dataset [3], using geo-tagged images obtained from Google Street View. We also investigate the performance of pose graph optimization and bundle adjustment using the KITTI Dataset [9].

4.1   Implementation

We obtained geo-tagged images from Google Street View at intervals of 5 m within the area where the video was captured. We set the cost function weights to $\lambda_1 = \lambda_2 = 1.0 \times 10^5$ and $\lambda_3 = 1.0$, and we employed the g2o library [13] for the implementation of the pose graph optimization and bundle adjustment.

4.2   Performance of the Proposed Method

To verify the practical effectiveness of the proposed method, we evaluate it on the Málaga dataset using geo-tagged images obtained from Google Street View.

The Málaga Stereo and Laser Urban Data Set (the Málaga dataset) [3]—a large-scale video dataset that captures Street-View-usable areas—is employed in this experiment. The Málaga dataset contains a driving video captured at a resolution of 1024×768 at 20 fps in a Spanish urban area. We extracted two video clips (video 1 and video 2) from the video, and used these for the evaluation. The two video clips contain no loops, and their trajectories are over 1 km long. All frames in the videos contain inaccurate GPS positions, which are sometimes confirmed to contain errors of more than 10 m. Because of the inaccuracies, we manually assigned the ground truth positions to some selected keyframes by referring to the videos, inaccurate GPS positions, and Google Street View 3D Map. Figure 4 presents an example of inaccurate GPS data and our assigned ground truth. Because the ground truth positions are assigned by taking into account the lane from which the video was taken, the errors in the ground truth are considered to be within 2 m, and these errors are sufficiently small for this experiment.

We evaluated the proposed method on the two videos by comparing the proposal and a baseline method that uses a similarity transformation (like a part of [25]). For the baseline method, we apply the initialization (INIT: described in Sect. 3.4) without applying pose graph optimization and bundle adjustment. We did not employ a global similarity transformation as a baseline because it cannot be applied until the end of the whole 3D reconstruction.

To evaluate the proposed method quantitatively, we considered the average (Ave) and standard deviation (SD) of 2D distances between the ground truth positions and corresponding keyframe positions in the UTM coordinate system (in meters).

Table 1 presents the quantitative results, and Fig. 5 visualizes the results on Google Maps. As is clearly shown in these results, the baseline results accumulate scale errors, resulting in large errors of over 50 m. This is because the trajectories

Fig. 4. The left figure shows an example of inaccurate GPS data (brown dots) and manually assigned ground truth positions (back crosses) on Google Maps. Although we use Google Maps to visualize the results clearly, the shapes of roads are not sufficiently accurate. Our ground truth positions are always assigned in the appropriate lane of the road, as seen in the satellite image (white crosses in the center figure). The right figure shows an example of a video frame captured at the left of the two ground truth positions in the left figure. (Color figure online)

Table 1. Results of our proposed method on the Málaga dataset using Google Street View.

	Video 1		Video 2	
	Ave [m]	SD	Ave [m]	SD
Baseline (INIT)	54.8	141.3	142.5	249.8
Ours	6.7	5.6	6.0	3.0

of these videos are long (greater than 1 km) and contain no loops. The proposed method sufficiently corrects scale drift, and significantly improves the 3D map by using geo-tagged images. In (b) and (e) of the visualized results, the 3D map points corrected using the proposed method are projected onto Google Maps, and it is shown that the 3D map points are correctly aligned to the map. To visualize all the correspondences between the 3D map coordinate system and the world coordinate system used in the proposal, we present the correspondences between the positions of geo-tagged images transformed by initialization and the positions of the corresponding geo-tags. These correspondences are employed incrementally for the correction.

4.3 Performance of PGO and BA

To investigate the performance of the pose graph optimization and the bundle adjustment in our proposed method, we evaluated the performance using different combinations of these when varying the interval of $C_{\text{map-world}}$.

Through the previous experiment, we found that the geo-tag location information of Google Street View and the manually assigned ground truths of the Málaga dataset occasionally had errors of several meters. In this experiment, we control the interval of $C_{\text{map-world}}$, and use high-accuracy ground truths and geo-tags by using the KITTI dataset. The odometry benchmark of KITTI dataset [9]

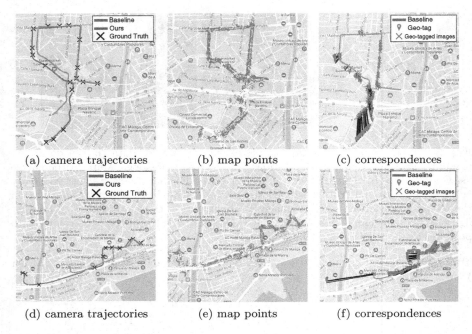

(a) camera trajectories   (b) map points   (c) correspondences

(d) camera trajectories   (e) map points   (f) correspondences

Fig. 5. Results of our proposed method visualized on Google Maps. Top: results on video 1. Bottom: results on video 2. In (a) and (d), red and blue dots—which appear like lines—indicate the positions of keyframes corrected using a global similarity transformation (INIT) and our proposed method (Ours), respectively. In (b) and (e), 3D map points corrected by our method are depicted by green dots. (c) and (f) show all of the employed correspondences between the positions of geo-tagged images transformed using a global similarity transformation (green crosses) and the positions of the corresponding geo-tags (red pin icons). The correspondences are applied incrementally for scale drift correction in our proposed method. (Color figure online)

contains 11 sequences of stereo videos and precise location information obtained from RTK-GPS/IMU, and unfortunately Google Street View is not available in Germany where this dataset was captured. The experiment was conducted on two sequences, which include the largest and second-largest errors when applying ORB-SLAM: sequences 02 and 08 (containing 4660 and 4047 frames, respectively). The left images of the stereo videos are used as input, and pairs of a right image and location information are identified as geo-tagged images. All the location information associated with keyframes is used as the ground truth. In this experiment with KITTI dataset, we can compare the performances of correction methods accurately for the following reasons: geo-tag information and ground truths are sufficiently precise (open sky localization errors of RTK-GPS/IMU < 5 cm); and errors in geo-tagged image localization are sufficiently small, because keypoint matching between corresponding left and right images performs very well.

Table 2. Results of the experiments on the KITTI dataset: sequences 02 and 08. Values denote average 2D errors between ground truth positions and the corresponding keyframe positions [m]. Ours consists of INIT, PGO, and BA.

	Geotag interval (#02)					Geotag interval (#08)				
	100	200	300	400	500	100	200	300	400	500
INIT + BA	1.15	2.22	65.86	164.17	96.66	0.45	1.24	18.43	148.17	52.40
INIT + PGO	4.57	4.26	7.54	10.89	11.96	0.93	2.83	4.64	5.44	9.11
Ours	2.27	2.51	4.87	6.89	12.35	0.50	2.06	2.84	4.19	6.38

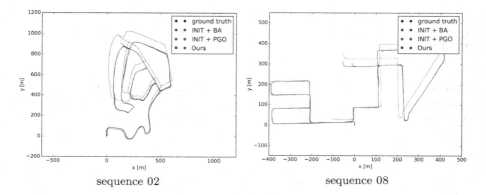

sequence 02   sequence 08

Fig. 6. Results of the experiment on the KITTI dataset when the interval of geo-tagged images is 300 frames. Keyframe trajectories estimated by INIT+BA, INIT+PGO, and Ours are visualized.

For the comparison, we present the results of the methods employing the initialization + the pose graph optimization (INIT+PGO), and initialization + the bundle adjustment (INIT+BA). The correction method of INIT + BA is the same as [14], which is often used with a GPS location information. Ours includes the initialization, the pose graph optimization and the bundle adjustment. We changed the interval of geo-tagged images from 100 frames to 500 frames. For an equal initialization, we set geo-tagged images in the interval of 50 frames from the first to the 200th frame.

Figure 6 visualizes the ground truth and keyframe trajectories estimated by INIT+BA, INIT+PGO, and Ours when the interval of geo-tagged images is 300 frames. Table 2 presents the quantitative results of the experiment, where the values represent the average 2D errors between ground truth positions and the corresponding keyframe positions in the UTM coordinate system (in meters). Moreover, we report the errors of the global linear transformation on the sequence 02 and 08 by aligning the keyframe trajectory obtained by ORB-SLAM with ground truths through a similarity transformation: 20.15 and 25.12, respectively. The results show that bundle adjustment with geo-tag constraints, which is typically employed in the fusion of 3D reconstruction and GPS information [14], is not

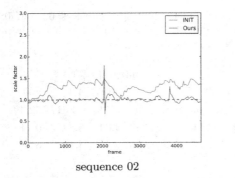 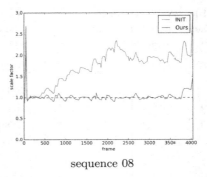

sequence 02   sequence 08

Fig. 7. Change in scale factor of the proposed method on the KITTI dataset sequences 02 and 08.

suitable when the interval of $C_{\text{map-world}}$ is large. It can also be seen that Ours (the combination of initialization, pose graph optimization, and bundle adjustment) often estimates the keyframe positions more accurately than any other method.

4.4 Scale Drift Correction

To confirm that scale drift is corrected incrementally, we visualize the change in scale factor of the proposed method on the KITTI dataset sequences 02 and 08. Figure 7 shows that ORB-SLAM with the initialization accumulates scale errors, and our method can keep the scale factor around 1.

5 Conclusion

In this paper, we propose a novel framework for camera geo-localization that can correct scale drift by utilizing massive public repositories of geo-tagged images, such as those provided by Google Street View. By virtue of the expansion of such repositories, this framework can be applied in many countries around the world, without requiring the user to observe an environment. The framework integrates incremental SfM and a scale drift correction method utilizing geo-tagged images. In the correction method, we first acquire sparse 6-DoF correspondences between the 3D map coordinate system and the world coordinate system by using geo-tagged images. Then, we apply pose graph optimization over Sim(3) constraints and bundle adjustment. Our experiments on large-scale datasets show that the proposed framework sufficiently improves the 3D map by using geo-tagged images.

Note that our framework not only corrects the scale drift of 3D reconstruction, but also accurately geo-localizes a video. Our results are no less accurate than those of mobile devices (between 5 and 8.5 m) that use a cellular network and low-cost GPS [27], and those using monocular video and road network maps [4] (8.1 m in the KITTI sequence 02 and 45 m in sequence 08). This implies that geo-localization using geo-tagged images is sufficiently useful compared with methods using other GIS information.

Acknowledgement. This work was partially supported by VTEC laboratories Inc.

References

1. Google street view. https://www.google.com/streetview/
2. Agarwal, P., Burgard, W., Spinello, L.: Metric localization using Google street view. In: 2015 IEEE/RSJ International Conference on Intelligent Robots and Systems (IROS), pp. 3111–3118. IEEE (2015)
3. Blanco-Claraco, J.L., Moreno-Dueñas, F.Á., González-Jiménez, J.: The málaga urban dataset: high-rate stereo and LiDAR in a realistic urban scenario. Int. J. Robot. Res. **33**(2), 207–214 (2014)
4. Brubaker, M.A., Geiger, A., Urtasun, R.: Map-based probabilistic visual self-localization. IEEE Trans. Pattern Anal. Mach. Intell. **38**(4), 652–665 (2016)
5. Caselitz, T., Steder, B., Ruhnke, M., Burgard, W.: Monocular camera localization in 3D LiDAR maps. In: 2016 IEEE/RSJ International Conference on Intelligent Robots and Systems (IROS), pp. 1926–1931. IEEE (2016)
6. Clemente, L.A., Davison, A.J., Reid, I.D., Neira, J., Tardós, J.D.: Mapping large loops with a single hand-held camera. In: Robotics: Science and Systems, vol. 2 (2007)
7. Engel, J., Schöps, T., Cremers, D.: LSD-SLAM: large-scale direct monocular SLAM. In: Fleet, D., Pajdla, T., Schiele, B., Tuytelaars, T. (eds.) ECCV 2014. LNCS, vol. 8690, pp. 834–849. Springer, Cham (2014). https://doi.org/10.1007/978-3-319-10605-2_54
8. Fischler, M.A., Bolles, R.C.: Random sample consensus: a paradigm for model fitting with applications to image analysis and automated cartography. Commun. ACM **24**(6), 381–395 (1981)
9. Geiger, A., Lenz, P., Urtasun, R.: Are we ready for autonomous driving? The KITTI vision benchmark suite. In: 2012 IEEE Conference on Computer Vision and Pattern Recognition (CVPR), pp. 3354–3361 (2012)
10. Kaminsky, R.S., Snavely, N., Seitz, S.M., Szeliski, R.: Alignment of 3D point clouds to overhead images. In: CVPR Workshops 2009 IEEE Computer Society Conference on Computer Vision and Pattern Recognition Workshops, pp. 63–70 (2009)
11. Klein, G., Murray, D.: Parallel tracking and mapping for small AR workspaces. In: 6th IEEE and ACM International Symposium on Mixed and Augmented Reality, ISMAR 2007, pp. 225–234. IEEE (2007)
12. Klingner, B., Martin, D., Roseborough, J.: Street view motion-from-structure-from-motion. In: Proceedings of the IEEE International Conference on Computer Vision, pp. 953–960 (2013)
13. Kümmerle, R., Grisetti, G., Strasdat, H., Konolige, K., Burgard, W.: g2o: a general framework for graph optimization. In: 2011 IEEE International Conference on Robotics and Automation (ICRA), pp. 3607–3613. IEEE (2011)
14. Lhuillier, M.: Incremental fusion of structure-from-motion and GPS using constrained bundle adjustments. IEEE Trans. Pattern Anal. Mach. Intell. **34**(12), 2489–2495 (2012)
15. Liu, Z., Marlet, R.: Virtual line descriptor and semi-local matching method for reliable feature correspondence. In: British Machine Vision Conference 2012, p. 16-1 (2012)

16. Lu, F., Milios, E.: Globally consistent range scan alignment for environment mapping. Auton. Robots 4(4), 333–349 (1997)

17. Majdik, A.L., Albers-Schoenberg, Y., Scaramuzza, D.: MAV urban localization from Google street view data. In: 2013 IEEE/RSJ International Conference on Intelligent Robots and Systems (IROS), pp. 3979–3986. IEEE (2013)

18. Middelberg, S., Sattler, T., Untzelmann, O., Kobbelt, L.: Scalable 6-DOF localization on mobile devices. In: Fleet, D., Pajdla, T., Schiele, B., Tuytelaars, T. (eds.) ECCV 2014. LNCS, vol. 8690, pp. 268–283. Springer, Cham (2014). https://doi.org/10.1007/978-3-319-10605-2_18

19. Mur-Artal, R., Montiel, J.M.M., Tardos, J.D.: ORB-SLAM: a versatile and accurate monocular SLAM system. IEEE Trans. Robot. 31(5), 1147–1163 (2015)

20. Rehder, J., Gupta, K., Nuske, S., Singh, S.: Global pose estimation with limited GPS and long range visual odometry. In: 2012 IEEE International Conference on Robotics and Automation (ICRA), pp. 627–633 (2012)

21. Rublee, E., Rabaud, V., Konolige, K., Bradski, G.: ORB: an efficient alternative to SIFT or SURF. In: 2011 IEEE International Conference on Computer Vision (ICCV), pp. 2564–2571. IEEE (2011)

22. Strasdat, H., Montiel, J., Davison, A.J.: Scale drift-aware large scale monocular SLAM. In: Robotics: Science and Systems VI (2010)

23. Tamaazousti, M., Gay-Bellile, V., Collette, S.N., Bourgeois, S., Dhome, M.: Nonlinear refinement of structure from motion reconstruction by taking advantage of a partial knowledge of the environment. In: 2011 IEEE Conference on Computer Vision and Pattern Recognition (CVPR), pp. 3073–3080. IEEE (2011)

24. Untzelmann, O., Sattler, T., Middelberg, S., Kobbelt, L.: A scalable collaborative online system for city reconstruction. In: Proceedings of the IEEE International Conference on Computer Vision Workshops, pp. 644–651 (2013)

25. Wang, C.P., Wilson, K., Snavely, N.: Accurate georegistration of point clouds using geographic data. In: 2013 International Conference on 3DTV-Conference, pp. 33–40 (2013)

26. Wendel, A., Irschara, A., Bischof, H.: Automatic alignment of 3D reconstructions using a digital surface model. In: 2011 IEEE Computer Society Conference on Computer Vision and Pattern Recognition Workshops (CVPRW), pp. 29–36. IEEE (2011)

27. Zandbergen, P.A., Barbeau, S.J.: Positional accuracy of assisted GPS data from high-sensitivity GPS-enabled mobile phones. J. Navig. 64(3), 381–399 (2011)

Distant Vehicle Detection: How Well Can Region Proposal Networks Cope with Tiny Objects at Low Resolution?

Ann-Katrin Fattal[1,2(✉)], Michelle Karg[3], Christian Scharfenberger[3], and Jürgen Adamy[1]

[1] Institute for Control Methods and Robotics, Technische Universität Darmstadt, Darmstadt, Germany
[2] Systems and Technology for Chassis and Safety, Continental AG, Frankfurt, Germany
ann-katrin.fattal@continental-corporation.com
[3] BU Advanced Driver Assistance Systems, Continental AG, Lindau, Germany

Abstract. High-performance faster R-CNN has been applied to many detection tasks. Detecting tiny objects at very low resolution remains a challenge, however, and a few studies addressed explicitly the detection of such objects yet. Focusing on distant object detection at very low resolution images for driver assistance systems, we introduce post-trained net surgery to (1) analyze the network activation patterns, (2) study the potential of prior information to improve localization and binary classification performance, and (3) to support the development of priors for improving the network performance.

We use post-trained net surgery to analyze the feature maps used for bounding box regression and classification for RPNs in detail, and to discuss the complexity of the network activation patterns. Using these findings, we show that incorporating prior maps into the network architecture improves the performance of bounding box regression and binary classification for small object detection in low resolution images.

Keywords: Saliency maps · Region proposal network · Low resolution · Object detection

1 Introduction

Deep learning-based detection approaches combine three stages in one architecture for high efficiency: (1) feature extraction, (2) region proposals/localization and (3) object classification. The objective of feature extraction is to learn a meaningful set of features representing target objects. Region proposal methods use the features to identify potential object regions and to reduce the number of regions fed into an expensive classification stage. Approaches to proposing regions are of great importance due to the need of detecting regions containing distant objects very quickly for the purpose of robust object detection for

© Springer Nature Switzerland AG 2019
L. Leal-Taixé and S. Roth (Eds.): ECCV 2018 Workshops, LNCS 11129, pp. 289–304, 2019.
https://doi.org/10.1007/978-3-030-11009-3_17

Fig. 1. The feature quality depends highly on the image resolution (from left to right: 443×421 px, 222×211 px, 111×106 px, 55×53 px, 28×27 px, 14×14 px). For this reason, detection of low resolution objects is a challenging task.

autonomous driving. Hardware and cost constraints on the sensor set-up impose the need for an inexpensive yet still accurate algorithm. Classical approaches such as [1–3] make use of hand-crafted models to identify object regions. Recent work on neural networks with trained features for object detection showed better results in localization and classification, where trained filters in layers decompose input information and produce feature maps for each layer.

The Fast R-CNN [4] combines localization and classification in one architecture and shows good results on a variety of data sets for object detection. In [5], a first concept for bounding box regression using features solely from the CNN was proposed. Other architectures such as Faster R-CNN [6], YOLO [7], Overfeat [8] and SSD [9] combine trained feature extraction and region proposals in neural network architectures (RPN). The detection of small objects in low-resolution images, however, remains a challenge for all approaches presented. Li *et al.* [10] use feature maps from different layers of the convolutional feature extractor for bounding box regression to consider more low-level features. The performance of this approach depends strongly on the feature maps chosen, and is hardly feasible for detecting small objects in low resolution images. Brazil *et al.* [11] apply a ground-truth mask on the feature maps inside an RPN during training to help the network focus on relevant object regions, resulting in less cluttered feature maps. However, a dedicated segmentation branch is needed for this approach. Huang *et al.* [12] evaluate different CNN architectures and show the excellent accuracy of Faster R-CNN [6] over a variety of convolutional object localizers. Faster R-CNN [6] makes use of feature maps from a convolutional feature extractor which may base on any fully convolutional network architecture such as ZF-Net or VGG16. The RPN uses an extra layer to extract objectiveness-specific features feeding two consecutive branches for bounding box regression and binary object classification (BCN). A set of base anchors, fitted to the data sets properties, are set on each location of the last feature map inside the RPN. The bounding box regression learns the deviation to the base anchors pre-defining position, width, and height. Finally, the binary classification branch derives a score for objectiveness, i.e., how likely an object is present in each base anchor.

The analysis of convolutional object detection performed by Huang *et al.* [12] showed that the detection of small objects with dimensions smaller than 20 pixels is three times worse than the detection of medium-sized objects. Zhang *et al.* [13] emphasized that small objects are the most common source of false negatives. This has a high relevance to distant vehicle detection for assisted/autonomous driving, and implies a low miss rate for distant objects that can only be achieved when the Recall of the region proposal network is high. The Hypernet [14] and the Feature Pyramid Network [15] use feature maps at higher resolution with more low level features to detect small objects. However, in the case of a low resolution images, using different feature maps is difficult as object regions provide weak local features.

In this work, we wish to make explicit use of incorporating prior information into a Faster R-CNN [6] to improve the overall network performance with focus on very small objects in low-resolution for driver assistance systems. As shown in Fig. 1, vehicles in 130 m distance to the camera may occupy only 8×8 pixels on the camera image. In particular, we introduce *post-trained net surgery* to (1) cluster network activation patterns, (2) to study the potential of prior information to improve localization and classification performance, and (3) to support the development of priors for improving an overall network performance of RPNs. We further study the impact of the feature maps and priors on bounding box regression and binary object classification for very small objects. First, we evaluate the importance of the feature maps by clustering them based on their correlation to the task specific ground truth data. The clustered feature maps show that very few maps cover the most features of the small objects and contribute the most to the overall localization and classification performance of an RPN. Second, we incorporate different external priors into the RPN chain before bounding box regression and binary classification and study their contributions to the overall performance of the RPN.

This analysis allows for several important conclusions: Post trained net surgery, with selecting the most important cluster of feature maps, helps identify the important feature maps for bounding box regression and binary classification, and understand the contribution of features to obtain decent feature maps. This allows to adapt priors or external data to the most prominent features to increase the Recall for the task of improving distant, and hence object detection in low-resolution images. Finally, evaluations demonstrate the need for incorporating priors into the network architecture to increase the Recall for small object detection significantly.

2 Network Architecture

We wish to choose a network architecture for evaluation purposes that is designed and optimized for the detection of small objects such as distant vehicles for assisted and autonomous driving. Given the limited computational resources on embedded systems for driver assistance systems, small and inexpensive neural networks are preferred over larger and more complex architectures.

Faster-RCNN with ZF Net. We chose the Faster R-CNN [6] as it combines a region proposal network (RPN) and a binary classification network (BCN) in one architecture and achieves higher detection accuracies than single-shot architectures like Yolo or SSD [12].

Faster R-CNN uses a common feature representation for both the RPN and BCN, is learned in an end-to-end fashion and shares convolutional layers between the RPN and BCN to compute locally restricted feature maps for feature extraction [16]. Different core network architectures can be used for feature extraction. Here, we choose as a small network architecture the ZF-Net to meet the limited computational resources for running CNNs on embedded devices for automotive applications. The ZF-Net consists of five convolutional layers, with two pooling and two fully connected layers. The stride of the network is 16 px, however the input image is upscaled by a factor of 2.4 as suggested by Fan *et al.* [17] to improve the performance. This still allows learning of important features due to the down-sampling layers as well to use pre-trained networks of the shelf.

Region Proposal Network (RPN). An RPN proposes bounding boxes for the subsequent binary classification network (BCN). The RPN aims to decrease the false negative detection rate, resulting in a high Recall, and the BCN reduces the false positive detection rate, resulting in a high Precision [11]. Since a high Recall is prerequisite for detecting small and distant objects, we focus on improving the performance of the RPN in this work.

The RPN consists of the three main stages: (1) a set of convolutional layers for feature extraction, (2) binary classification to compute a score indicating the object probability in each anchor, and (3) bounding box regression for the center coordinates (x, y), width and height of each anchor. Overall, refining the bounding boxes using regression improves the overall classification results.

A set of N anchors predefines aspect ratio and scale and is fitted to the application. Binary classification and bounding box regression are computed for each anchor at each position in the final feature map of the RPN, including two scores for the presence of objects and four values for the bounding box. Given the fix locations of anchor areas, the deviation to the object region center in x and y direction and the deviation of the bounding boxes in height and width are considered in the network.

For the special use case of small object detection at low resolution, the anchor sizes and scales are fitted to the data set. Furthermore, the input image size is upscaled. As the number of positions with sufficiently overlapping anchors is smaller for small objects, the batch size during training is reduced drastically to obtain a better balanced RPN training set. The minimal allowed scaled bounding boxes are chosen to be larger than the stride of the feature map within the RPN because the stride defines the smallest possible detected object. Table 1 summarizes the adapted parameters for small object detection.

The output size of the 1×1 convolutional layer is $2 \times N$ for the classification, and $4 \times N$ for bounding box regression. The input size is the number of feature maps of the last convolutional layer of the RPN. To investigate the capacity of this 1×1 convolutional layer for binary classification and bounding box regression, we alter the input of the last convolutional layer in the RPN by both removing feature maps using net surgery and by providing prior information.

Table 1. Weights: pretrained RPN weights, anch.-o.: original anchors, anch.-a.: adjusted anchors, 2.4x: upscaling by factor 2.4x, batchs.256: batchsize of 256 within the RPN, batchs.20: adjusted batchsize of 20 within the RPN.

Parameters						Mean recall in % for object sizes			
Weights	anch.-o	anch.-a	2.4x	batchs.256	batchs.20	8–20 px	20–30 px	30–60 px	60–100 px
-	✓	-	-	✓	-	16.89	70.32	87.95	87.88
✓	✓	-	-	✓	-	18.84	74.24	87.23	85.61
✓	-	✓	-	✓	-	29.03	71.24	82.31	90.91
✓	-	✓	-	-	✓	32.93	75.00	86.23	93.18
✓	-	✓	✓	✓	-	56.74	83.39	94.71	95.13
✓	-	✓	✓	-	✓	**68.54**	**90.93**	**96.51**	**99.57**

3   Net Surgery

To analyze the feature representation prior to binary classification and bounding box regression in detail, we propose two extensions to net surgery. The first extension addresses the clustering of feature maps of similar relevance and the second extension addresses the search for the optimal representation of prior information.

3.1   Relevance-Based Clustering of Feature Maps

Understanding the underlying functionality of CNNs has attracted the interest of the research community. This interest is driven by the fact that neural network architectures are generally understood as black-box technologies. Understanding of this functionality is especially relevant for safety-critical applications such as autonomous driving. Zeiler *et al.* [18] introduced the use of back-propagation to generate the optimal input image for a convolutional network given the desired output. Using this method, it is possible to understand which kernel filters are responding maximal for different object classes. We are interested in how many feature maps include class-relevant information, in the redundancy of the class-relevant information, and whether or not the information content is depended on object attributes such as size. For this reason, we introduce post-trained, relevance-based clustering of feature maps, where only a subset of feature maps is used during inference.

Clustering of RPN Feature Maps. Given that several feature maps evolve similar features [18], we wish to make use of clustering to merge feature maps with similar content. Clustering can be based on several characteristics such as homogeneity or correlation to external data. In this work, we chose correlation to ground truth as our cluster criterion, such as shown in Fig. 2.

Clustering is conducted for each trained model using the data of the test set. For each test-image$_i$, the absolute correlation is calculated for each feature

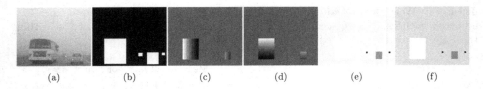

| (a) | (b) | (c) | (d) | (e) | (f) |

Fig. 2. Visualization of the ground truths for the RPN: (a) original image, (b) ground truth for the classification and pre-processed ground truth for the bounding box regression: (c, d) deviation to the center in x and y direction, (e, f) deviation of width and height

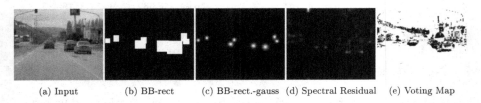

(a) Input   (b) BB-rect   (c) BB-rect.-gauss (d) Spectral Residual   (e) Voting Map

Fig. 3. (a) Shows the original image, (b) the ground truth in BB-rect, (c) ground truth BB-rect smoothed by Gaussians, (d) spectral residual saliency map [19] and (e) the voting map [3].

map $\text{fm}_{i,j}$ and ground truth BB-rect_i as shown in Fig. 3b. The feature maps are then sub-divided into Q equally large groups q where the feature maps with the highest correlation score is assigned to the group with the highest z_Q with $z_q \in [1, \cdots, q, \cdots, Q]$. This is done for all images in the test set. The final cluster is then computed by finding the highest occurrence of z_q for each fm_j.

Cluster-Based Inference. With the different feature map clusters, it is now possible to determine the influence of each cluster to the performance of the RPN to find the most important features. With net surgery, only feature maps in cluster q are contributing to following layers inside the network. A filter kernel in a convolutional neural network is described by its size K, with its depth the number of input data channels (here feature maps). X kernel use then all feature maps fm_m of layer output m, and after a convolution it produces X new feature maps fm_{m+1}. During net surgery, the input data of the kernel is modified so that only feature maps within certain clusters are processed. To perform net surgery with cluster q, the weights inside the kernel are set to zero except for weights that correspond to all feature maps fm_j with $\text{cl}_j == z_q$. Hence, only feature maps fm_m within cluster q transport information to fm_{m+1}. Then, it is possible to evaluate the performance of the network based on different feature clusters. In this work, net surgery is performed on the bounding box regression kernel and/or binary classification kernel. Figure 4 visualizes the net surgery.

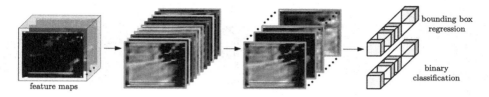

Fig. 4. The feature maps of the last layer of the RPN are clustered using the similarity between the feature map activation and ground truth as cluster criterion. We analyzed the features maps within each cluster regarding: their contribution to the bounding box regression and binary classification.

3.2 Incorporation of Prior Information

Using the idea of net surgery we wish to study the positive impact of external data on the performance of an RPN. Figure 5 shows three different ways of incorporating of prior information during feed-forward and training phase into the last layer of the region proposal network.

Motivated by improving the performance of the RPN by incorporating prior feature maps, as in [20], we study the potential performance gain that can be obtained when incorporating perfect feature maps. To estimate such an upper bound, prior information is computed based on ground truth data. The effect of feature representation is studied for the 1×1 convolutions for binary classification and bounding box regression. Hence, the optimal feature maps are incorporated using net surgery prior to bounding box regression (Fig. 5a), pior to classification (Fig. 5b), and prior to both classification and bounding box regression (Fig. 5c). In doing so, we analyze how efficient the information from additional feature maps can be learned by the 1×1 convolutions for binary classification and bounding box regression using stochastic gradient descent. Furthermore, this approach enables studying the optimal representation for prior information. In the following, a set of different representations for priors are summarized, both for theoretically studying the optimal performance gain using the ground truth as prior and for application-relevant priors, such as saliency maps.

Adapted Ground Truth Data. The ground truth data for binary classification and bounding box regression are different due to the different nature of the underlying task. The ground truth for only binary classification architectures as shown in Fig. 5b are created by setting all pixel values inside an object region to one and zero otherwise (see Fig. 3b). This form of ground truth is called *BB-rectangular*. The BB-rectangular data is designed in the same way as the label data for the binary classification branch during the training phase of the RPN. The ground truth data for the bounding box regression branch as shown in architectures of Fig. 5a follows another pattern which is based on the underlying anchor size. It contains the deviation of the anchor center (x_a, y_a) to the object center (x, y), and the deviation of the anchor size (h_a, w_a) in height and width to fit the objects size (h, w) as shown in Fig. 2(c)–(f) [21]. The ground truth data $t_{x,y,w,h}$ for the regression is then given as following

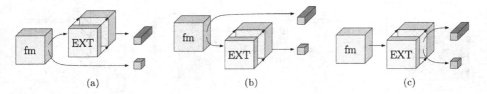

Fig. 5. Prior information is added as external data (EXT) to the output of the last convolutional layer (fm) of the RPN for either (a) bounding box regression, (b) binary classification, or (c) both bounding box regression and binary classification. The blue boxes represent data from the feature map, the yellow boxes external data and green and pink boxes the 1×1 kernels for regression (green) or classification (pink). (Color figure online)

$$t_x = (x - x_a)/w_a \qquad t_w = log(w/w_a)$$
$$t_y = (y - y_a)/h_a \qquad t_h = log(h/h_a)$$

"BB-rectangular" refers to the ground truth suitable for classification, "GT-adjusted" refers to the transformed ground truth for bounding box regression.

Gauss-Degradation to Blobs. To examine the influence of degradation of the quality on the ground truth data as external priors, the ground truth bounding boxes are transformed to Gaussian blobs which follow the elongation of the object based on ground truth labels. The center of each object obtains the highest overall pixel value within the data map, and all remaining data is reduced following the multivariate normal distribution:

$$y = \frac{1}{\sqrt{|\Sigma|(2\pi)^d}} \cdot exp\left(-0.5(x - \mu)\Sigma^{-1}(x - \mu)'\right)$$

where y is the pixel value on the data map, and Σ a $d \times d$ symmetric positive definite matrix.

For each object region at an object center position $d = 2$, $\mu = 0$ and Σ

$$\Sigma = \begin{bmatrix} w & 0 \\ 0 & h \end{bmatrix}$$

For all external data, that is degraded by such distribution the flag "-gauss" is added.

Saliency-Inspired Maps. All previous presented external data is based on the knowledge of the ground truth and can therefore only be used hypothetically for analysis. Saliency-inspired maps can be calculated without any ground truth knowledge as the fundamental idea of saliency maps is to focus on the essential information within an image. Hence, saliency maps can be computed directly on the image and can be considered as external data. Potential priors that can

Table 2. Details of the used data set. The table illustrates the number of images used for training, test and validation, and the distribution of object sizes.

Data set	Train	Val	Test	Object width (px)	8–20	20–30	30–60	60–100	>100
# Samples	826	104	104	# Samples	2792	2770	1767	631	332

be computed in real-time are Spectral Residual [19] and a Voting Scheme [3]. The Spectral Residual map analyses anomalies in the frequency spectrum of an image. Since regions containing small objects exhibit high spatial frequencies when compared to background, this map is suitable for detecting small objects. The Voting Map is adaptively modeling the background within an image with few homogeneous areas to distinguish between background and possible foreground. This approach is tailored to the task of guiding detection towards small object regions in motorway scenarios. Both the Spectral Residual and Voting maps are chosen as saliency-inspired external data in this study.

4 Experiments

The proposed approach is evaluated on a motorway and highway traffic data set that includes many distant cars and trucks. The evaluation includes the results for the model without any external data or net surgery as well as different architectures including net surgery or external data.

4.1 Data Set and Data Augmentation

A data set for distant vehicle detection has been recorded and includes 1034 different motor- and highway scenes. The data set contains over 5.000 distant cars and trucks with object sizes smaller than a width of 30 px, and is subdivided into training, validation and test set as illustrated in Table 2. Objects that are occluded by less than 50% are included in the data set. The image size is 1024 × 640 px. Table 2 shows the occurrence of object widths within the data set. In addition, data set augmentation is used for both training and testing to avoid over-fitting during training. Therefore, 10 crops of size 300 × 250 px are taken from each image using a random jittering inside the image, ensuring that each crop includes at least one object and no objects are truncated. Additionally each image/crop is flipped vertically.

4.2 Network Architecture and Training Details

A ZF-net architecture with weights pre-trained on the ImageNet and Kitti data set is used as the core network for the Faster R-CNN. The input size of the Faster R-CNN using the ZF-net is 600 × 720 px. The image crops are upscaled by a factor of 2.4 as suggested by Fan et al. [17] to improve the performance especially for the task of small object detection. For our data set the best ratios

Table 3. Details of the training parameters to train the RPN and classification head of the faster RCNN for a data set with small objects

Parameter	Value
Iterations within the RPN	9.000
Upscaling factor	2.4
Max value of external data	10
RPN batchsize	20
Anchor sizes	10, 20, 40 px
Anchor ratios	[0.5, 1, 2]
Minimum bounding box	8 px

are [0.5, 1, 2] as it contains trucks as well as cars from the side. The anchor sizes are set to [10, 20, 40] px to suit especially small object regions, and to fit to the object occurrence. Forward feed allowed 8 px wide boxes. For the following experiments the faster RCNN was trained as proposed in [6] with original parameter set-up. The trained weights of this base model are then frozen except for the binary classification and bounding box regression branch in the RPN. During all following experiments only the RPN is refined in one stage. To fit to the data set with many small objects, the batch size for the RPN is reduced drastically to 20 to generate a balanced foreground/background set of possible anchors during training (Table 3).

4.3 Evaluation Metrics

The performance is evaluated using the Recall metric based on the Intersection over Unit (IoU $= 0.5$). The Recall measures how many of the relevant objects are successfully detected:

$$\text{Recall} = \frac{TP}{TP + FN}$$

TP is the number of relevant matches retrieved, and FN the number of relevant matches missed. As the RPN is the localizer of the Faster R-CNN, the Recall representing the number of object regions detected initially is of interest only. We compute the Recall for each object size over the number of selected bounding boxes, for an IoU equal to 0.5 and 600 proposed bounding boxes.

4.4 Results of the Net Surgery

To understand the diversity and spread of information of the RPN within the feature maps, the absolute correlation of the feature maps and ground truth as BB-rect data (see Fig. 3b) is used. The clustering uses the absolute correlation values, and 3, 5 and 10 clusters are formed. In Fig. 6, the Recall of the different active feature map clusters for 5 clusters is shown. The Recall is decreased in all object size classes for just some of the clusters activated.

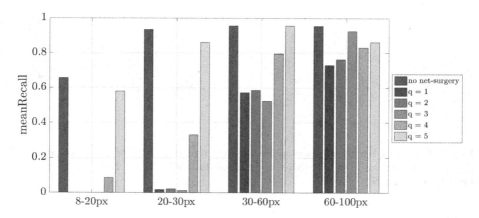

Fig. 6. The Recall for cluster-based net surgery for 600 boxes and 5 different clusters is shown. For each cluster q, the feature maps with highest range of absolute correlation to BB-rectangular are activated. The red bar corresponds to an architecture without net-surgery, while each bar to the left represents a different activated cluster with increasing correlation. We can see that different features impact the performance for detecting differently sized objects. (Color figure online)

Table 4. The table shows the potential of branch size reduction Δbranch-size and reduction of recall Δq_{max} for the different object sizes and different number of clusters Q. The baseline is the model without any net surgery.

Q	Δq_{max}[tiny, small, medium, large objects]	Δbranch-size
3	$-7.2\%, -5\%, -5.1\%, -3.6\%$	-66%
5	$-12.8\%, -13.5\%, -6\%, -2.7\%$	-80%
10	$-36\%, -31\%, -19\%, -13.8\%$	-90%

It can be seen that the feature map cluster with highest absolute correlation value (yellow bars) contains the most valuable features for the RPN among the object sizes 8–60 px. For larger object sizes the feature maps with the 40–60% highest absolute correlation value shows the highest Recall among the model which were modified by net surgery. Here, it is shown that different feature maps evolve object size specific feature. Hence, the relevance of a feature map cluster depends on the size of the object detected, where feature maps including fine-grained information support the detection of small objects, and feature maps omitting detailed information the detection of larger objects. For small objects a high similarity to the BB-rectangular data is most favorable. This can be used when e.g. a large network is trained on several object classes/sizes but only certain sizes/classes are of interest. Then all feature maps not useful for the interesting object-size/class can be removed or added as needed.

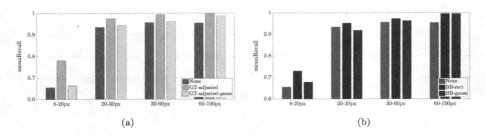

Fig. 7. (a) Mean Recall with ground truth external data only for the bounding box regression branch and (b) with BB-rect external data only for the binary classification branch of the RPN.

Execution Time. Using cluster-based network surgery it is possible to reduce the size of the network architecture while only loosing comparable low Recall. This reduces the computational cost or execution time of the branches. In Table 4 it is shown that the branch size can be reduced by e.g. 66% during net surgery with 3 clusters while the Recall decreases only in average 5.2%. Hence, the execution time/computational cost can be decreased also by 66%. Especially in the automotive environment the reduction of network size due to limited computational power while keeping the performance high is desired [22].

4.5   Influence of External Data on the Recall

In two experiments the bounding box regression or binary classification branch uses ground truth external data as additional information to understand the capability of each branch and to determine a upper bound of performance. In the last experiment both RPN branches were trained and executed using several different external data maps. In Fig. 5 the different architectures are shown.

Comparison of Only Regression or Classification Branch. Figure 7a shows the Recall for different external data composed with ground truth knowledge in the regression branch only (architecture as in Fig. 5a). It can be seen that especially for small objects with 8–20 px width the external data increases the overall Recall by more than 10%. For objects larger than 20 px, the increase is 5% in Recall. For Gaussian degraded ground truth the performance degrades and shows that Gaussian blobs are less suitable features for the regression branch.

When only the binary classification branch is trained with external ground truth data, Fig. 7b, performance only increases for the BB-rectangle format of the ground truth. This shows that the binary classification branch can only transform external data with a high similarity to the BB-rectangle format and even gauss-degraded ground truth data is not improving recall values.

Comparing both architectures with each corresponding ground truth respectively, it shows that the ground truth adjusted for the regression branch improves

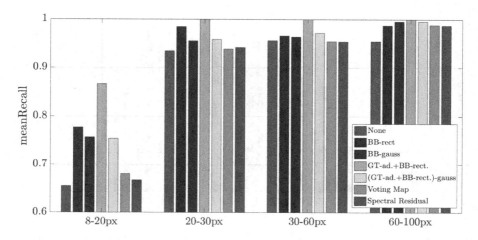

Fig. 8. The Recall for low resolution objects is significantly lower than for objects with a minimum size of 20 px. Adding prior maps as input to bounding box regression and binary classification improves the recall and the localization of low resolution objects dramatically, where ground truth prior maps estimate upper bounds.

the overall recall more, than the ground truth BB-rectangular for the binary classification. This finding shows that the features for the regression seems to be less evolved inside the feature maps of the region proposal network than the features for binary classification. This applies especially for objects smaller than 20 px but is also present for larger objects. Neither of the branches exhibits a recall of 100% which showed as well, that the improvement of only one branch is not sufficient to reach high Recall values.

Bounding Box Regression and Classification Branch. In Fig. 8 the Recall of the RPN is shown where both branches of the RPN use external data during training and testing. It shows that the RPN has in general less Recall when the objects get smaller. For object sizes larger than 20 px in width the average Recall is more than 93% without any external data, while it is only 65.5% for objects smaller than 20 px in width. Here it shows that the adjusted ground truth (GT & BB-rect) optimal for both branches reaches in all objects sizes best results as expected. However, even for objects smaller than 20 px only 86.6% of Recall is reached and is an indicator, that small objects are even with best possible data difficult to detect for the RPN. To understand the gap of performance even with best possible data it is important to discuss the evaluation metric. E.g. a bounding box proposal of correct object size with a 3 px displaced center has an IoU of 0.65 for an object of size 20 px, while the IoU is only 0.45 for an object of 8 px size. Hence, any dislocation or error in box size to the object is more severe for small objects than for larger ones. The external saliency-like maps increase the Recall for small objects down to 8 px by 2.6%, while it only slightly increase the Recall for larger objects up to 30 px. Figure 9 visualizes the

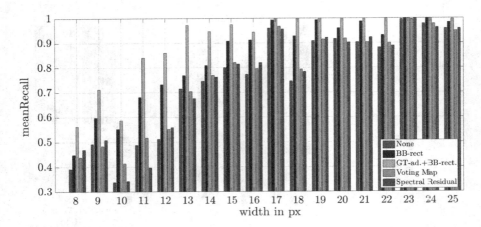

Fig. 9. Detailed visualization of the mean Recall for small objects of sizes 8–25 px width.

Recall in detail for objects of a width between 8–25 px. Performance of the region proposal network decreases substantially for objects smaller than 13 px showing a technical boundary for the detection of small objects.

Especially in this challenging region, saliency maps as external data improve the Recall. The reasons is that both saliency-like maps are well suited for small object detection. In addition, the maps require few computations during testing time and are, hence, suitable for real-time applications.

5   Conclusions

This work studies the final feature maps of an RPN before bounding box regression and binary classification is applied to improve the overall detection performance, with the following key findings:

(1) Feature map clustering and net surgery exhibit key feature maps that contribute individually to different object sizes.
(2) Post-trained net surgery is used to cluster maps with similar activation patterns. For the task of detecting single objects, the information from a larger group of final feature maps is relevant. This group often includes redundant information and allows to reduce the network size by considering the key feature maps only.
(3) Additional feature maps/priors improve the detection performance for very small objects. We studied a variety of prior maps to gain further understanding on how to efficiently incorporate additional prior information into the RPN. It is shown that the incorporation of additional prior information resulted in a higher performance gain for smaller than larger objects.

Finally, bounding box regression and binary classification require a different feature representation strategy, whose more detailed elaboration will be part of future work.

References

1. Alexe, B., Deselaers, T., Ferrari, V.: Measuring the objectness of image windows. IEEE Trans. Pattern Anal. Mach. Intell. **34**(11), 2189–2202 (2012)
2. Uijlings, J.R., Van De Sande, K.E., Gevers, T., Smeulders, A.W.: Selective search for object recognition. Int. J. Comput. Vis. **104**(2), 154–171 (2013)
3. Batzer, A.K., Scharfenberger, C., Karg, M., Lueke, S., Adamy, J.: Generic hypothesis generation for small and distant objects. In: 2016 IEEE 19th International Conference on Intelligent Transportation Systems (ITSC), pp. 2171–2178. IEEE (2016)
4. Girshick, R.: Fast R-CNN. In: Proceedings of the IEEE International Conference on Computer Vision, pp. 1440–1448 (2015)
5. Lenc, K., Vedaldi, A.: R-CNN minus R. BMVC (2015)
6. Ren, S., He, K., Girshick, R., Sun, J.: Faster R-CNN: towards real-time object detection with region proposal networks. In: Advances in Neural Information Processing Systems, pp. 91–99 (2015)
7. Redmon, J., Divvala, S., Girshick, R., Farhadi, A.: You only look once: unified, real-time object detection. In: Proceedings of the IEEE Conference on Computer Vision and Pattern Recognition, pp. 779–788 (2016)
8. Sermanet, P., Eigen, D., Zhang, X., Mathieu, M., Fergus, R., LeCun, Y.: OverFeat: integrated recognition, localization and detection using convolutional networks. arXiv preprint arXiv:1312.6229 (2013)
9. Liu, W., et al.: SSD: single shot MultiBox detector. In: Leibe, B., Matas, J., Sebe, N., Welling, M. (eds.) ECCV 2016. LNCS, vol. 9905, pp. 21–37. Springer, Cham (2016). https://doi.org/10.1007/978-3-319-46448-0_2
10. Li, W., Breier, M., Merhof, D.: Recycle deep features for better object detection. arXiv preprint arXiv:1607.05066 (2016)
11. Brazil, G., Yin, X., Liu, X.: Illuminating pedestrians via simultaneous detection & segmentation. In: Proceedings of the IEEE Conference on Computer Vision and Pattern Recognition, pp. 4950–4959 (2017)
12. Huang, J., et al.: Speed/accuracy trade-offs for modern convolutional object detectors. In: IEEE CVPR (2017)
13. Zhang, S., Benenson, R., Omran, M., Hosang, J., Schiele, B.: How far are we from solving pedestrian detection? In: Proceedings of the IEEE Conference on Computer Vision and Pattern Recognition, pp. 1259–1267 (2016)
14. Kong, T., Yao, A., Chen, Y., Sun, F.: Hypernet: towards accurate region proposal generation and joint object detection. In: Proceedings of the IEEE Conference on Computer Vision and Pattern Recognition, pp. 845–853 (2016)
15. Lin, T.Y., Dollar, P., Girshick, R., He, K., Hariharan, B., Belongie, S.: Feature pyramid networks for object detection. In: CVPR, vol. 1, p. 4 (2017)
16. Luo, W., Li, Y., Urtasun, R., Zemel, R.: Understanding the effective receptive field in deep convolutional neural networks. In: Advances in Neural Information Processing Systems, pp. 4898–4906 (2016)
17. Fan, Q., Brown, L., Smith, J.: A closer look at faster R-CNN for vehicle detection. In: 2016 IEEE Intelligent Vehicles Symposium (IV), pp. 124–129. IEEE (2016)

18. Zeiler, M.D., Fergus, R.: Visualizing and understanding convolutional networks. In: Fleet, D., Pajdla, T., Schiele, B., Tuytelaars, T. (eds.) ECCV 2014. LNCS, vol. 8689, pp. 818–833. Springer, Cham (2014). https://doi.org/10.1007/978-3-319-10590-1_53
19. Hou, X., Zhang, L.: Saliency detection: a spectral residual approach. In: IEEE Conference on Computer Vision and Pattern Recognition, CVPR 2007, pp. 1–8. IEEE (2007)
20. Fattal, A.K., Karg, M., Scharfenberger, C., Adamy, J.: Saliency-guided region proposal network for CNN based object detection. In: 2017 IEEE 20th International Conference on Intelligent Transportation Systems (ITSC), pp. 1–8. IEEE (2017)
21. Girshick, R., Donahue, J., Darrell, T., Malik, J.: Rich feature hierarchies for accurate object detection and semantic segmentation. In: Proceedings of the IEEE Conference on Computer Vision and Pattern Recognition, pp. 580–587 (2014)
22. Molchanov, P., Tyree, S., Karras, T., Aila, T., Kautz, J.: Pruning convolutional neural networks for resource efficient transfer learning. In: ICLR 2016 (2016)

W03 – 3D Reconstruction in the Wild

W03 – 3D Reconstruction in the Wild

Research on 3D reconstruction has long focused on recovering 3D information from multi-view images captured in ideal conditions. However, the assumption of ideal acquisition conditions severely limits the deployment possibilities for reconstruction systems, as typically several external factors need to be controlled, intrusive capturing devices have to be used or complex hardware setups need to be operated to acquire image data suitable for 3D reconstruction. In contrast, 3D reconstruction in unconstrained settings (referred to as 3D reconstruction in the wild) usually imposes only little restrictions on the data acquisition procedure and/or on data capturing environments, but, therefore, represents a far more challenging task.

The goal of this workshop was to foster the development of 3D reconstruction techniques that are robust and real-time, and consequently perform well on a variety of environments with different characteristics. To this end, we organized this workshop with interests in all parts of 3D reconstruction techniques ranging from multi-camera calibration, feature extraction, matching, data fusion, depth learning, and meshing techniques to 3D modeling approaches capable of operating on image data captured in the wild.

At the workshop, we invited five distinguished researchers working on 3D reconstruction. Long Quan (Hong Kong University of Science and Technology) presented "Computer Vision, Visual Learning, and 3D Reconstruction," Andrea Fusiello (Università di Udine) presented "The Long March of 3D Reconstruction: from Tabletop to Outer Space", Yaser Sheikh (Oculus Research and Carnegie Mellon University) talked about "Social Perception with Machine Vision", Michael Zollhöfer (Stanford University) presented "Born in the Wild: Self-supervised 3D Face Model Learning". The talk by Jan-Michael Frahm (University of North Carolina at Chapel Hill) was titled "Towards Bringing 3D World Models to Life Leveraging Crowd Sourced Data", and Srikumar Ramalingam (University of Utah) gave a talk on "Depth, Semantics, and Localization for Autonomous Driving Applications". Besides the invited talks, 13 contributed papers were presented as posters and intensively discussed. The workshop was attended by almost 100 participants. We would like to thank all the people involved in the workshop preparation, as well as speakers, authors, reviewers, and participants for their contributions to the success of the workshop.

September 2018

Akihiro Sugimoto
Tomas Pajdla
Shohei Nobuhara
Hiroshi Kawasaki
Takeshi Masuda

Deep Depth from Defocus: How Can Defocus Blur Improve 3D Estimation Using Dense Neural Networks?

Marcela Carvalho[1]([✉]), Bertrand Le Saux[1], Pauline Trouvé-Peloux[1],
Andrés Almansa[2], and Frédéric Champagnat[2]

[1] DTIS, ONERA, Université Paris-Saclay, 91123 Palaiseau, France
{marcela.carvalho,bertrand.saux,pauline.trouve}@onera.fr
[2] Université Paris Descartes, 75006 Paris, France
{andres.almansa,frederic.champagnat}@parisdescartes.fr

Abstract. Depth estimation is critical interest for scene understanding and accurate 3D reconstruction. Most recent approaches with deep learning exploit geometrical structures of standard sharp images to predict depth maps. However, cameras can also produce images with defocus blur depending on the depth of the objects and camera settings. Hence, these features may represent an important hint for learning to predict depth. In this paper, we propose a full system for single-image depth prediction in the wild using depth-from-defocus and neural networks. We carry out thorough experiments real and simulated defocused images using a realistic model of blur variation with respect to depth. We also investigate the influence of blur on depth prediction observing model uncertainty with a Bayesian neural network approach. From these studies, we show that out-of-focus blur greatly improves the depth-prediction network performances. Furthermore, we transfer the ability learned on a synthetic, indoor dataset to real, indoor and outdoor images. For this purpose, we present a new dataset with real all-focus and defocused images from a DSLR camera, paired with ground truth depth maps obtained with an active 3D sensor for indoor scenes. The proposed approach is successfully validated on both this new dataset and standard ones as NYUv2 or Depth-in-the-Wild. Code and new datasets are available at https://github.com/marcelampc/d3net_depth_estimation.

Keywords: Depth from defocus · Domain adaptation · Depth estimation · Single-image depth prediction

1 Introduction

3D reconstruction has a large field of applications such as in human computer interaction, augmented reality and robotics, which have driven research on the topic. This reconstruction usually relies on accurate depth estimates to process the 3D shape of an object or a scene. Traditional depth estimation approaches

© Springer Nature Switzerland AG 2019
L. Leal-Taixé and S. Roth (Eds.): ECCV 2018 Workshops, LNCS 11129, pp. 307–323, 2019.
https://doi.org/10.1007/978-3-030-11009-3_18

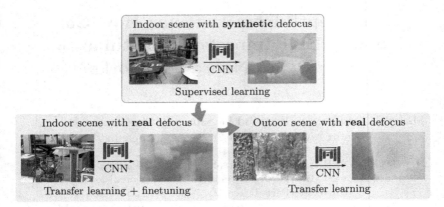

Fig. 1. Depth estimation with synthetic and real defocused data on indoor and outdoor challenging scenes. These results show the flexibility to new datasets of a model trained with a synthetically defocused indoor dataset, finetuned on a real DSLR indoor set and finally tested in outdoor scenes without further training.

exploit different physical aspects to extract 3D information from perception, such as stereoscopic vision, structure from motion, structured light and other depth cues in 2D images [1,2]. However, some of these techniques depend on the environment (*e.g.* sun, texture) or even require several devices (*e.g.* camera, projector), leading to cumbersome systems. Many efforts have been made to make them compact: *e.g.* the light-field cameras which use a microlens array in front of the sensor, from which a depth map can be extracted [3] (Fig. 1).

In recent years, several approaches for depth estimation based on deep learning (deep depth estimation), have been proposed [4]. These methods use a single image and thus lead to compact, standard systems. Most of them exploit depth cues in the image based on geometrical aspects of the scene to estimate the 3D structure with the use of convolutional neural networks (CNNs) [5–8]. A few ones can also make use of additional depth cues such as stereo information to train the network [9] and improve predictions.

Another important cue for depth estimation is defocus blur. Indeed, Depth from Defocus (DFD) has been widely investigated [10–15]. It led to various analytical methods and corresponding optical systems for depth prediction. However, conventional DFD suffers from ambiguity in depth estimation with respect to the focal plane and dead zone, due to the camera depth of field where no blur can be measured. Moreover, DFD requires a scene model and an explicit calibration between blur level and depth value to estimate 3D information. Thus, it is tempting to integrate defocus blur with the power of neural networks, which leads to the question: does defocus blur improve deep depth estimation performances?

In this paper, we use a dense neural network, D3-Net [16], in order to study the influence of defocus blur on depth estimation. First it is tested on a synthetically defocused dataset created from NYUv2 with optically realistic blur variation, which allows to compare several optical settings. We further examine the uncertainty of the CNN predictions with and without blur. We then explore real defocused data with a new dataset which comprises indoor all-in-focus and defocused images, and corresponding depth maps. Finally, we verify how the deep model behaves when confronted to challenging images in the wild with the Depth-in-the-Wild [17] dataset and further outdoor images.

These experiments show that defocused information is exploited by neural networks and is indeed an important hint to improve deep depth estimation. Moreover, the joint use of structural and blur information proposed in this paper overcomes current limitations of single-image DFD. Finally, we show that these findings can be used in a dedicated device with real defocus blur to actually predict depth indoors and outdoors with good generalization.

2 Related Work

Deep Monocular Depth Estimation. Several works have been developed to perform monocular depth estimation based on techniques of machine learning. One of the first solutions was presented by Saxena *et al.* [18], which formulate the depth estimation for the Make3D dataset as a Markov Random Field (MRF) problem with horizontally aligned images using a multi-scale architecture. More recent solutions are based on CNNs to exploit spatial correlation by enforcing a local connectivity. Eigen *et al.* [4,5] proposed a multi-scale architecture capable of extracting global and local information from the scene. In [19], Cao *et al.* used a Conditional Random Field (CRF) to post-process the output of a deep residual network (ResNet) [20] in order to improve the reliability of the predictions. Xu *et al.* [21] adopted a deeply supervised approach connecting intermediate outputs of a ResNet to a continuous CRF fusion module to combine depth prediction at different scales achieving higher performance. Also adopting residual connections, Laina *et al.* [22] proposed an encoder-decoder architecture with fast up-projection blocks. More recently, Jung *et al.* [23] introduced generative adversarial networks [24] (GANs) adapting an adversarial loss to refine the depth map predictions. With a different strategy, [9,25,26] propose to investigate the epipolar geometry using CNNs. DeMoN [9] jointly estimates a depth map and camera motion given a sequential pair of images with optical flow. [25,26] use unsupervised learning to reconstruct stereo information and predict depth. More recently, Kendall and Gal [27] and Carvalho *et al.* [16] explore the reuse of feature maps, building upon an encoder decoder with dense and skip connections [28]. While [27] propose a regression function that captures the uncertainty of the data, [16] uses an adversarial loss.

The aforementioned techniques for monocular depth estimation with neural networks base their learning capabilities on structured information (*e.g.*, textures, linear perspective, statistics of objects and their positions). However, depth perception can use another well-know cue: defocus blur. We present in the following section state-of-the-art approaches from this domain.

Depth Estimation Using DFD. In computational photography, several works investigated the use of defocus blur to infer depth [10]. Indeed, the amount of defocus blur of an object can be related to its depth using geometrical optics $\epsilon = Ds \cdot \left| \frac{1}{f} - \frac{1}{d_{out}} - \frac{1}{s} \right|$, where f stands for the focal length, d_{out} the distance of the object with respect to the lens, s the distance between the sensor and the lens and D the lens diameter. $D = f/N$, where N is the f-number (Fig. 2).

Recent works usually use DFD with a single image (SIDFD). Although the acquisition is simple, it leads to more complex processing as both the scene and the blur are unknown. State of the art approaches use analytical models for the scene such as sharp edges models [15] or statistical scene Gaussian priors [12,29]. Coded apertures have also been proposed to improve depth estimation accuracy [11, 14,30,31].

Nevertheless, SIDFD suffers from two main limitations: first, there is an *ambiguity* related to the object's position in front or behind the in-focus plane; second, blur variation cannot be measured in the camera depth of field, leading to a *dead zone*.

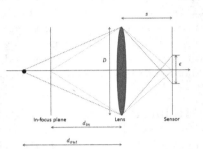

Fig. 2. Illustration of the DFD principle. Rays originating from the out of focus point (black dot) converge before the sensor and spread over a disc of diameter ϵ.

Ambiguity can be solved using asymmetrical coded aperture [14], or even by setting the focus at infinity. Second, dead zones can be overcome using several images with various in-focus planes. In a single snapshot context, this can be obtained with unconventional optics such as a plenoptic camera [32] or a lens with chromatic aberration [12,33], but both at the cost of image quality (low resolution or chromatic aberration).

Indeed, inferring depth from the amount of defocus blur with model-based techniques requires a tedious explicit calibration step, usually conducted using point sources or a known high frequency pattern [11,34] at each potential depth. These constraints lead us to investigate data-based methods using deep learning techniques to explore structured information together with blur cues.

Learning Depth from Defocus Blur. The existence of common datasets for depth estimation [1,32,35], containing pairs of RGB images and corresponding depth maps, facilitates the creation of synthetic defocused images using real camera parameters. Hence, a deep learning approach can be used. To the best of our knowledge, only a few papers in the literature use defocus blur as a cue in learning depth from a single image. Srinivasan *et al.* [36] uses defocus blur to train a network dedicated to monocular depth estimation: the model measures the consistency of simulated defocused images, generated from the estimated depth map and all-in-focus image, with true defocused images. However, the final network is used to conduct depth estimation from all-in-focus images. Hazirbas *et al.* [32] propose to use a focal stack, which is more related to depth from focus approaches than DFD. Finally, [37] presents a network for depth estimation and deblurring using a single defocused image. This work shows that networks can integrate blur interpretation. However, [37] creates a synthetically defocused dataset from real NYUv2 images without a realistic blur variation with respect to the depth, nor sensor settings (*e.g.*, camera aperture, focal distance). However, there has not been much investigation about how defocus blur influence on depth estimation, nor how can these experiments improve depth prediction in the wild.

In contrast to previous works, to the best of our knowledge, we present the first system for deep depth from defocus (Deep-DFD): *i.e.* single-image depth prediction in the wild using deep learning and depth-from-defocus. In Sect. 3, we study the influence of defocus blur on deep depth estimation performances. (i) We run tests on a synthetically defocused dataset generated from a set of true depth maps and all-in-focus images. The amount of defocus blur with respect to depth varies according to a physical optical model to relate to realistic examples. (ii) We also compare performances of deep depth estimation with several optical settings: we compare all-in-focus images with defocused images of three different focus settings. (iii) We analyse the influence of defocus blur on neural networks using uncertainty maps and diagrams of errors per depth. In Sect. 4, (iv) we carry out validation and analysis on a new dataset created with a Digital Single Lens Reflex (DSLR) camera and a calibrated RGB-D sensor. At last, in Sect. 5, (v) we show the network is able to generalize to images in the wild.

3 Learning DFD to Improve Depth Estimation

In this section, we perform a series of experiments with synthetic and real defocused data exploring the power of deep learning to depth prediction. As we are interested in using blur as a cue, we do not apply any image processing for data augmentation capable of modifying out-of-focus information. Hence, for all experiments, we extract random crops of 224 × 224 from the original images and apply horizontal flip with a probability of 50%. Tests are realized using the full-resolution image.

3.1 D3-Net Architecture

To perform such tests, we adopt the D3-Net architecture from [16], illustrated in Fig. 3. We use the PyTorch framework on a NVIDIA TITAN X GPU with 12 GB of memory. We initialize the D3-Net encoder, corresponding to DenseNet-121, with pretrained weights on Imagenet dataset and D3-Net decoder with random weights from a normal distribution with zero-mean and 0.2 variance. We add dropout [39] regularization with a probability of 0.5 to the first four convolutional layers of the decoder as we noticed it improves generalization. We also adopt dropout layers to posteriorly study model's uncertainty.

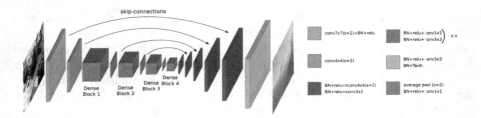

Fig. 3. D3-Net architecture from [16]. The encoder part corresponds to a DenseNet-121 [28], with $n = 6, 12, 24, 16$, respectively for indicated Dense Blocks. The encoder-decoder structure is based on U-Net [38] to explore the reuse of feature maps.

3.2   Synthetic NYUv2 with Defocus Blur

The NYU-Depth V2 (NYUv2) dataset [35] has approximately 230k pairs of images from 249 scenes for training and 215 scenes for testing. In [16], D3-Net reaches its best performances when trained with the complete dataset. However, NYUv2 also contains a smaller split with 1449 pairs of aligned RGB and depth images, of which 795 pairs are used for training and 654 pairs for testing. Therefore, experiments in this section were performed using this smaller dataset to fasten experiments. Original frames from Microsoft Kinect output have the resolution of 640 × 480. Pairs of images from the RGB and Depth sensors are posteriorly aligned, cropped and processed to fill-in invalid depth values. Final resolution is 561 × 427.

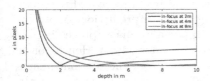

Fig. 4. Blur diameter variation vs depth for the in-focus settings: 2 m, 4 m and 8 m tests on the NYUv2.

To generate physically realistic out-of-focus images, we choose the parameters corresponding to a synthetic camera with a focal length of 15 mm, f-number 2.8 and pixel size of 5.6 µm. Three settings of in-focus plane are tested, respectively at 2 m, 4 m and 8 m from the camera. Figure 4 shows the variation of the blur diameter ϵ with respect to depth, for both settings and Fig. 5 shows examples of synthetic defocused images. As illustrated in Fig. 4, setting the in-focus plane at 2 m corresponds to a camera with small depth of field. The objects in the depth range from 1 to 10 m will present small defocus blur amounts, apart from the objects in the camera depth of field, which remain sharp. Note that this configuration suffers from depth ambiguity caused by the blur estimation. Setting the in-focus plane at a larger depth, here 4 m or 8 m, corresponds to a camera with larger depth of field. Only the closest objects will show defocus blur, with a comparatively larger blur ammount between 0–3 m than previous setting. This can be observed in the extracted details in Fig. 5.

To create the out-of-focus dataset, we adopt the layered approach of [40] where each defocused image $\widehat{L}$ is the sum of K blurred images multiplied by masks, A_k, related to local object depth, k, and occlusion of foreground objects:

$$\widehat{L} = \sum_k \left[(A_k L + A_k^* L_k^*) * h(k)\right] M_k, \tag{1}$$

where $h(k)$ is the defocus blur at distance k, L is the all-in-focus image and $A_k^* L_k^*$, the layer extension behind occluders, obtained by inpainting. Finally M_k models the cumulative occlusions defined as:

$$M_k = \prod_{k'=k+1}^{K} (1 - A_{k'} * h(k')). \tag{2}$$

Following [36], we chose to model the blur as a disk function which the diameter varies with the depth.

As will be discussed later, the proposed approach can be disputable as the true depth map is used to generate the out-of focus image. However, this strategy allows us easily perform various experiments to analyze the influence of blur corresponding to different in-focus settings in the image.

Fig. 5. Examples of synthetic defocused images generated from an image of the NYUv2 database for two camera in-focus plane settings: 2 and 8 m.

3.3   Performance Results

Table 1 shows performance of D3-Net first using all-in-focus and then defocused images with proposed settings. As illustrated in Fig. 4, when the in-focus plane is at 8 m, there is no observable ambiguity. Hence performance comparison with SIDFD methods can then be made. So, we include the performances of two methods from the SIDFD literature [15,41] which estimate the amount of local blur using either sharp edge model or gaussian prior on the scene gradients.

Several conclusions can be drawn from Table 1. First, as already stated by Anwar *et al.*, there is a significant improvement on depth estimation when using out-of-focus images instead of all-in-focus images. Second, D3-Net outperforms the standard model-based SIDFD methods, which can also be observed in Fig. 8, without requiring an analytical scene model nor explicit blur calibration. Furthermore, there is also a sensitivity of the depth estimation performance with respect to the position of the in-focus plane. The best setting for these tests is

Table 1. Performance comparison of D3-Net using all-in-focus and defocused images with different settings, and two SIDFD approaches [15,41] for the 8 m focus setting.

Methods	Error↓				Accuracy↑		
	rel	log10	rms	rmslog	$\delta < 1.25$	$\delta < 1.25^2$	$\delta < 1.25^3$
Original RGB images							
D3-Net All-in-focus	0.226	-	0.706	-	65.8%	89.2%	96.7%
RGB images with additional blur							
D3-Net 2 m focus	0.068	0.028	0.274	0.110	96.1%	99.0%	99.6%
D3-Net 4 m focus	0.085	0.036	0.398	0.125	92.5%	99.0%	99.8%
D3-Net 8 m focus	0.060	-	0.324	-	95.2%	99.1%	99.9%
Zhuo et al. [15] 8 m focus	0.273	-	0.981	-	51.7%	83.1%	95.1%
Trouvé et al. [41] 8 m focus	0.429	0.289	1.743	0.956	39.2%	52.7%	61.5%
RGB images with additional blur proposed by [37]							
Anwar et al. [37]	0.094	0.039	0.347	-	-	-	-
D3-Net	0.036	0.016	0.144	0.054	99.3%	100.0%	100.0%

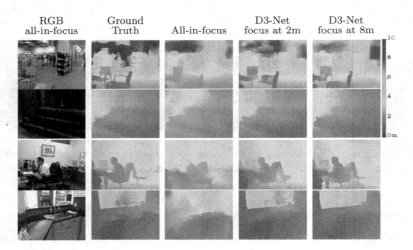

Fig. 6. Qualitative comparison for different predictions with the proposed defocus blur configurations.

with the in-focus plane at 2 m. This corresponds to a significant amount of blur for most of the objects but near the focal plane. And shows that the network actually uses blur cues and is able to overcome depth ambiguity using geometrical structural information. Figure 8 also illustrates this conclusion: the scene has mainly three depth levels with a foreground, a background, and an intermediate level around 2 m. The corresponding out-of-focus image is generated using an in-focus plane at 2 m. Using [15], the background and the foreground are at the same depth, while D3-Net shows no such error in the depth map.

Finally, we also trained and tested D3-Net with the dataset proposed in [37]. However, differently from the method explored in our paper, the out-of-focus images were generate without any regard to camera settings. The last two lines from Table 1 shows that D3-Net also outperforms the network in [37].

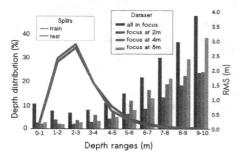

Fig. 7. Distribution of pixels on different depth ranges and RMS performance of D3-Net trained with and without defocus blur.

Also, Fig. 6 and columns 3 and 6 from Fig. 9 show that estimations from out-of-focus images are sharper than from all-in-focus images. Indeed, defocus blur provides extra local information to the network leading to a better depth segmentation.

Per Depth Error Analysis. There is an intrinsic relation between the number of examples a network can learn from and its performance when tested on similar samples. Here, we compare the prediction error per depth range between all-in-focus and defocused images. We observe the relation to depth data distribution. Figure 7 shows in the same plot repartition the RMS per depth in meters and the depth distribution for testing and training images with NYUv2.

For all-in-focus images, the errors seem to be highly correlated to the number of examples in the dataset. Indeed, a minimum error is obtained for 2 m, corresponding to the depth with the highest number of examples. On the other hand, using defocus blur, errors repartition is more similar to a quadratic increase of error with depth, which is the usual error repartition of passive depth estimation.

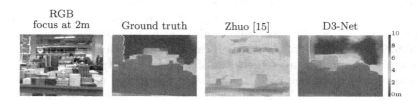

Fig. 8. Comparison between D3-Net estimation and Zhuo [15] for images with the focus plane at 2 m.

Furthermore, the 2 m focus setting does not show an error increase at its focal plane position, though it corresponds to the dead zone of SIDFD. This surprising result shows that the proposed approach overcomes this issue probably because the neural network also relies on context and geometric features. In general, 2 m, 4 m and 8 m focus have similar performance for depth range between 0 to 3 m. After this depth, the 2 m focus presents the lowest errors. When focus is at 4 m,

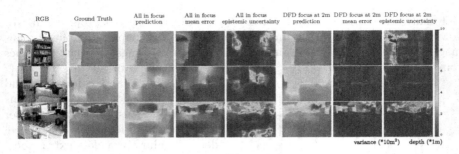

Fig. 9. Qualitative comparison of all focus and DFD with 2 m focus prediction, mean error and epistemic uncertainty with NYUv2 dataset. Lower values of depth and uncertainties are represented by warmer colors. (Color figure online)

we observe a drop in all metrics performances compared to 2 m and 8 m. The reason can be observed when comparing both Figs. 4 and 7. This configuration presents worst RMS performances between 3 and 7 m, when blur information is too small to be used by the network and there is not enough data to overcome the missing cue, but enough to worsen results. The same happens to the model at 8 m, where results are more prone to errors after approximately 7 m.

3.4   Uncertainties on the Depth Estimation Model

To go further in the analysis of understanding the influence of blur in depth prediction, we present a study on model uncertainties following [27, 42, 43]. More precisely, we evaluate the epistemic uncertainty of the deep network model, or how ignorant is the model with respect to the dataset probabilistic distribution.

To perform this experiment, we place a prior distribution over the network weights to replace the deterministic weight parameters at test time [27]. We adopt the Monte Carlo dropout method [43] to measure variational inference placing dropout layers during train and also during test phases. Following [42], we produce 50 samples for each image, calculate the mean prediction and the variance of these predictions to generate the model uncertainty.

Figure 9 presents examples of the network prediction, mean error and epistemic uncertainty for the NYUv2 dataset with sharp images and with focus at 2 m. Mean error is produced using the ground truth image, while the variance only depends on the model's prior distribution. For both configurations, highest variances are observed in non-textured areas and edges, as predictable. However, the model with blur has less diffuse uncertainty: it is concentrated on the object edges, and these objects are better segmented. In the second row of the figure, we observe that the all-in-focus model has difficulties to find an object near the window, while this is overcome with blur cues present on the defocused model. In the first row, we observe high levels of uncertainty at the zones near the bookcase, defocused model reduce some of this variance with defocus information. Finally, the last row presents a hard example where both models have high prediction variances mainly in the top middle part, where there is a hole. However the all-in-focus model also presents high mean error and variance in the bottom zone unlike the model with blur.

4   Experiments on a Real Defocused Dataset

In Sect. 3, several experiments were performed using a synthetic version of NYUv2. However, when adopting convolutional neural networks, it can be a little tricky to use the desired output (depth) to create blur information on the input of the network. So, in this section, we propose to validate our method on real defocused data from a DSLR camera paired with the respective depth map from a calibrated RGB-D sensor.

Dataset Creation. To create a DFD dataset, we paired a DSLR Nikon D200 with an Asus Xtion sensor to produce out-of-focus data and corresponding depth maps, respectively. Our platform can be observed in Fig. 10. We carefully calibrate the depth sensor to the DSLR coordinates to produce RGB images alligned with the corresponding depth map. The proposed dataset contains 110 images from indoor scenes, with 81 images for training and 29 images for testing. Each scene is acquired with two camera apertures: $N = 2.8$ and $N = 8$, providing respectively out-of-focus and all-in-focus images.

Fig. 10. Experimental platform with Xtion PRO sensor coupled to a DSLR Nikon camera.

As the DFD dataset contains a small amount of images, we pretrain the network using simulated images from NYUv2 dataset and then conduct a finetuning of the network using the real dataset. The DSLR camera originally captures images of high resolution 3872×2592; but to reduce the calculation burden, we downsample them to 645×432. In order to simulate defocused images from NYUv2 as similar as possible to DSLR's, the images from the Kinect are upsampled and cropped to have the same resolution and the same field of view as the downsampled DSLR images. Then defocus blur is applied to the images using the same method as in Sect. 3 but with a blur variation with that fits the real blur variation of the DSLR, obtained experimentally.

Performance Results. Using the new dataset, we perform three experiments: first we train D3-Net with the in-focus and defocused dataset respectively, using same patch approach from last experiments. We also test D3-Net with the in-focus dataset using an strategy that explores the global information of the scene and a series of preprocessing methods: we resize input images to 320×256 and performance data augmentation suggested in [4] to improve generalization.

In Table 2, the performances from the proposed models can be compared. The results show that defocus blur does improve the network performance increasing 10 to 20 percentual points in accuracy and also gives qualitative results with better segmentation as illustrated in Fig. 11.

The network is capable to find a relation between depth and defocus blur and predict better results, even thought the it may miss from global information

RGB   Ground   DSLR   DSLR   DSLR
all-in-focus Truth   DFD N=2.8   N=8   N=8 (resize)

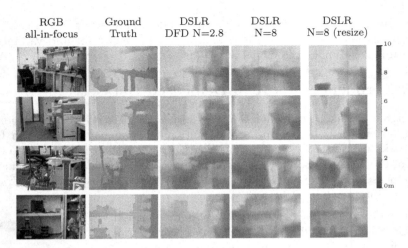

Fig. 11. Qualitative comparison of D3-Net trained on defocused and all-focused images from a DSLR camera.

Table 2. Performance comparison of D3-Net using all-in-focus and defocused images on a real DSLR dataset.

Methods	Error↓				Accuracy↑		
	rel	log10	rms	rmslog	$\delta < 1.25$	$\delta < 1.25^2$	$\delta < 1.25^3$
$N = 2.8$	0.157	0.065	0.546	0.234	80.9%	94.4%	97.6%
$N = 8$	0.225	0.095	0.730	0.285	60.2%	87.7%	98.0%
$N = 8$ (resize)	0.199	0.084	0.654	0.259	69.6%	91.6%	97.4%

when being trained with small patches. When feeding the network with resized images, filters from the last layers of the encoder, as from the first layers of the decoder, can understand the global information as they are fed with feature maps from the entire scene in a low resolution. However, this relation is not enough to give better predictions. As we can observe in the first examples of the third row in Fig. 11, the DFD D3-Net used defocus to find the contours of the object, meanwhile the standard D3-Net wrongly predicts the form of a chair, as it is an object constantly present in front of a desk. Our experiments show that the Deep-DFD model is more robust to generalization and less prone to overfitting than traditional methods trained and finetuned on all-in-focus images.

5   Depth "in the Wild"

In the era of autonomous driving vehicles (on land, on water, or in the air), there has been an increasing demand of less intrusive, more robust sensors and processing techniques to embed in systems able to evolve in the wild. Previously, we validated our approach with several experiments on indoor scenes and we proved that blur can be learned by a neural network to improve prediction and also to improve the model's confidence to its estimations. In this section, we now propose to tackle the general case of uncontrolled scenes. We first assess the ability of the standard D3-Net, trained without defocus blur, to generalize to "in-the-wild" images using the Depth-in-the-Wild dataset [17] (DiW). Second, we use the whole system, D3-Net trained on indoor defocused images and the DSLR camera described from Sect. 4, in uncontrolled, outdoor environments.

Depth-in-the-Wild Dataset (DiW). The ground truth of the DiW dataset is not dense; indeed, only two points of each RGB image are relatively annotated as being closer or farther from the camera, or at the same distance. To adapt the network, we replace the objective function of D3-Net by the one proposed by the authors of the dataset [17]. Then, for training, we take the weights of D3-Net trained on all-in-focus NYUv2 [16], and finetune the model on DiW using the modified network. We show the results of this model on the test set of DiW in Fig. 12. The predicted depths present sharp edges for people and objects and give plausible estimates of the 3D structure of the given scenes. However, as the network was mostly trained on indoor scenes, it cannot give accurate depth predictions on sky regions. This shows that the a neural network has inherent capacity to predict depth in the wild. We will now see that we can improve this capacity by integrating physical cues of the sensor.

RGB   Prediction

Fig. 12. Examples of depth prediction using DIW dataset with D3-Net trained on NYUv2.

Deep-DFD in the Wild. We now observe how deep models trained with blurred indoor images behave when confronted to challenging outdoor scenes. These experiments explore the model's capability to adapt predictions to new scenarios, never seen during training. To perform our tests, we first acquire new data using the DSLR camera with defocus optics (from Sect. 4) and keeping the same camera settings. As the depth sensor from the proposed platform works poorly outdoor, this new set of images does not contain respective depth ground truth. Thus, the model is neither trained on the new data, nor finetuned. Indeed, we use directly the models finetuned on indoor data with defocus blur (Sect. 4).

Results from the CNN models and from Zhuo's [15] analytical method are shown in Fig. 13. With D3-Net trained on all-in-focus images, the model constantly fails to extract information from new objects, as can be observed in the images with the road and also with the tree trunk. As expected, this model tries to base prediction on objects similar to what those seen during training or during finetuning, which are mostly non-existent in these new scenes. On the contrary, though the model trained with defocus blur information has equally never seen these new scenarios, the predictions give results relatively close to the expected depth maps. Indeed, the Deep-DFD model notably extracts and uses blur information to help prediction, as geometric features are unknown for the trained network. Finally, Zhuo's method also gives encouraging results, but constantly fails duo to defocus blur ambiguity to the focal plane (as on the handrail on the top left example of Fig. 13). As can be deduced from our experiments, the combined use of geometric, statistical and defocus blur is a promising method to generalize learning capabilities.

RGB   D3-Net   D3-Net N=8 (resize)   Zhuo [15] N=2.8
        N=2.8

Fig. 13. Depth estimation methods: from left to right, D3-Net trained on defocused images, all-in-focus images and a classical Depth from Defocus approach by [15].

6   Conclusion

In this paper, we have studied the influence of defocus blur as a cue in a monocular depth estimation using a deep learning approach. We have shown that the use of blurred images outperforms the use of all-in-focus images, without requiring any scene model nor blur calibration. Besides, the combined use of defocus blur and geometrical structure information on the image, brought by the use of a deep network, avoids the classical limitations of DFD with a conventional camera (*e.g.*, depth ambiguity, dead zones). We have proposed different tools to visualize the benefit of defocus blur on the network performance, such as per depth error statistics and uncertainty maps. These tools have shown that depth estimation with defocus blur is most significantly improved at short depths, resulting in better depth map segmentations. We have also compared performance of Deep-DFD with several optical settings to better understand the influence of the camera parameters to deep depth prediction. In our tests, the best performances were obtained for a close in-focus plane, which leads to really small camera depths of field and thus defocus blur on most of the objects in the dataset.

Besides synthetic data, this paper also provides excellent results on both indoor and outdoor real defocused images from a new set of DSLR images. These experiments on real defocused data proved that defocus blur combined to neural networks are more robust to training data and domain generalization, reducing possible constraints of actual acquisition models with active sensors and stereo systems. Notably, results on the challenging domain of outdoor scenes without further calibration, or finetuning prove that this new system can be used in the wild to combine physical information (defocus blur) and geometry and perspective cues already used by standard neural networks. These observations open the way to further studies on the optimization of the camera parameters and acquisition modalities for 3D estimation using defocus blur and deep learning.

References

1. Saxena, A., Sun, M., Ng, A.Y.: Make3D: learning 3D scene structure from a single still image. IEEE Trans. Pattern Anal. Mach. Intell. **31**(5), 824–840 (2009)
2. Calderero, F., Caselles, V.: Recovering relative depth from low-level features without explicit T-junction detection and interpretation. Int. J. Comput. Vis. **104**(1), 38–68 (2013)
3. Ng, R., Levoy, M., Brédif, M., Duval, G., Horowitz, M., Hanrahan, P.: Light field photography with a hand-held plenoptic camera. Computer Science Technical report (2005)
4. Eigen, D., Puhrsch, C., Fergus, R.: Depth map prediction from a single image using a multi-scale deep network. In: NIPS (2014)
5. Eigen, D., Fergus, R.: Predicting depth, surface normals and semantic labels with a common multi-scale convolutional architecture. In: ICCV (2015)
6. Li, B., Shen, C., Dai, Y., Van Den Hengel, A., He, M.: Depth and surface normal estimation from monocular images using regression on deep features and hierarchical CRFs (2015)
7. Wang, P., Shen, X., Lin, Z., Cohen, S., Price, B., Yuille, A.L.: Towards unified depth and semantic prediction from a single image. In: CVPR (2015)
8. Chakrabarti, A., Shao, J., Shakhnarovich, G.: Depth from a single image by harmonizing overcomplete local network predictions. In: NIPS (2016)
9. Ummenhofer, B., et al.: DeMoN: depth and motion network for learning monocular stereo. arXiv preprint arXiv:1612.02401 (2016)
10. Pentland, A.P.: A new sense for depth of field. IEEE Trans. PAMI **9**(4), 523–531 (1987)
11. Levin, A., Fergus, R., Durand, F., Freeman, W.T.: Image and depth from a conventional camera with a coded aperture. ACM Trans. Graph. **26**, 70 (2007)
12. Trouvé, P., Champagnat, F., Le Besnerais, G., Sabater, J., Avignon, T., Idier, J.: Passive depth estimation using chromatic aberration and a depth from defocus approach. Appl. Opt. **52**(29), 7152–7164 (2013)
13. Martinello, M., Favaro, P.: Single image blind deconvolution with higher-order texture statistics. In: Cremers, D., Magnor, M., Oswald, M.R., Zelnik-Manor, L. (eds.) Video Processing and Computational Video. LNCS, vol. 7082, pp. 124–151. Springer, Heidelberg (2011). https://doi.org/10.1007/978-3-642-24870-2_6
14. Sellent, A., Favaro, P.: Which side of the focal plane are you on? In: ICCP (2014)

15. Zhuo, S., Sim, T.: Defocus map estimation from a single image. Pattern Recognit. **44**, 1852–1858 (2011)
16. Carvalho, M., Saux, B.L., Trouvé-Peloux, P., Almansa, A., Champagnat, F.: On regression losses for deep depth estimation. In: ICIP (2018, to appear)
17. Chen, W., Fu, Z., Yang, D., Deng, J.: Single-image depth perception in the wild. In: NIPS, pp. 730–738 (2016)
18. Saxena, A., Chung, S.H., Ng, A.Y.: Learning depth from single monocular images. In: NIPS (2006)
19. Cao, Y., Wu, Z., Shen, C.: Estimating depth from monocular images as classification using deep fully convolutional residual networks. IEEE Trans. Circuits Syst. Video Technol. **28**(11), 3174–3182 (2017)
20. He, K., Zhang, X., Ren, S., Sun, J.: Deep residual learning for image recognition. In: CVPR, pp. 770–778 (2016)
21. Xu, D., Ricci, E., Ouyang, W., Wang, X., Sebe, N.: Multi-scale continuous CRFs as sequential deep networks for monocular depth estimation. arXiv preprint arXiv:1704.02157 (2017)
22. Laina, I., Rupprecht, C., Belagiannis, V., Tombari, F., Navab, N.: Deeper depth prediction with fully convolutional residual networks. In: 2016 Fourth International Conference on 3D Vision (3DV), pp. 239–248. IEEE (2016)
23. Jung, H., Kim, Y., Min, D., Oh, C., Sohn, K.: Depth prediction from a single image with conditional adversarial networks. In: ICIP (2017)
24. Goodfellow, I., et al.: Generative adversarial nets. In: NIPS (2014)
25. Godard, C., Mac Aodha, O., Brostow, G.J.: Unsupervised monocular depth estimation with left-right consistency. arXiv preprint arXiv:1609.03677 (2016)
26. Garg, R., B.G., V.K., Carneiro, G., Reid, I.: Unsupervised CNN for single view depth estimation: geometry to the rescue. In: Leibe, B., Matas, J., Sebe, N., Welling, M. (eds.) ECCV 2016. LNCS, vol. 9912, pp. 740–756. Springer, Cham (2016). https://doi.org/10.1007/978-3-319-46484-8_45
27. Kendall, A., Gal, Y.: What uncertainties do we need in Bayesian deep learning for computer vision? arXiv preprint arXiv:1703.04977 (2017)
28. Huang, G., Liu, Z., van der Maaten, L., Weinberger, K.Q.: Densely connected convolutional networks. In: CVPR (2017)
29. Levin, A., Weiss, Y., Durand, F., Freeman, W.: Understanding and evaluating blind deconvolution algorithms. In: CVPR, pp. 1–8 (2009)
30. Veeraraghavan, A., Raskar, R., Agrawal, A., Mohan, A., Tumblin, J.: Dappled photography: mask enhanced cameras for heterodyned light fields and coded aperture refocusing. ACM Trans. Graph. **26**, 69 (2007)
31. Chakrabarti, A., Zickler, T.: Depth and deblurring from a spectrally-varying depth-of-field. In: Fitzgibbon, A., Lazebnik, S., Perona, P., Sato, Y., Schmid, C. (eds.) ECCV 2012. LNCS, vol. 7576, pp. 648–661. Springer, Heidelberg (2012). https://doi.org/10.1007/978-3-642-33715-4_47
32. Hazirbas, C., Leal-Taixé, L., Cremers, D.: Deep depth from focus. arxiv preprint arXiv:1704.01085, April 2017
33. Guichard, F., Nguyen, H.P., Tessières, R., Pyanet, M., Tarchouna, I., Cao, F.: Extended depth-of-field using sharpness transport across color channels. In: Rodricks, B.G., Süsstrunk, S.E. (eds.) IS&T/SPIE Electronic Imaging, International Society for Optics and Photonics, pp. 72500N–72500N-12, January 2009
34. Delbracio, M., Musé, P., Almansa, A., Morel, J.: The non-parametric sub-pixel local point spread function estimation is a well posed problem. Int. J. Comput. Vis. **96**, 175–194 (2012)

35. Silberman, N., Hoiem, D., Kohli, P., Fergus, R.: Indoor segmentation and support inference from RGBD images. In: Fitzgibbon, A., Lazebnik, S., Perona, P., Sato, Y., Schmid, C. (eds.) ECCV 2012. LNCS, vol. 7576, pp. 746–760. Springer, Heidelberg (2012). https://doi.org/10.1007/978-3-642-33715-4_54
36. Srinivasan, P.P., Garg, R., Wadhwa, N., Ng, R., Barron, J.T.: Aperture supervision for monocular depth estimation. arXiv preprint arXiv:1711.07933 (2016)
37. Anwar, S., Hayder, Z., Porikli, F.: Depth estimation and blur removal from a single out-of-focus image. In: BMVC (2017)
38. Ronneberger, O., Fischer, P., Brox, T.: U-net: convolutional networks for biomedical image segmentation. In: Navab, N., Hornegger, J., Wells, W.M., Frangi, A.F. (eds.) MICCAI 2015. LNCS, vol. 9351, pp. 234–241. Springer, Cham (2015). https://doi.org/10.1007/978-3-319-24574-4_28
39. Srivastava, N., Hinton, G.E., Krizhevsky, A., Sutskever, I., Salakhutdinov, R.: Dropout: a simple way to prevent neural networks from overfitting. J. Mach. Learn. Res. 15(1), 1929–1958 (2014)
40. Hasinoff, S.W., Kutulakos, K.N.: A layer-based restoration framework for variable-aperture photography. In: 2007 IEEE 11th International Conference on Computer Vision, pp. 1–8, October 2007
41. Trouvé, P., Champagnat, F., Le Besnerais, G., Idier, J.: Single image local blur identification. In: IEEE ICIP (2011)
42. Kendall, A., Badrinarayanan, V., Cipolla, R.: Bayesian SegNet: model uncertainty in deep convolutional encoder-decoder architectures for scene understanding. arXiv preprint arXiv:1511.02680 (2015)
43. Gal, Y., Ghahramani, Z.: Dropout as a Bayesian approximation: representing model uncertainty in deep learning. In: ICML, pp. 1050–1059 (2016)

Deep Modular Network Architecture for Depth Estimation from Single Indoor Images

Seiya Ito, Naoshi Kaneko[✉], Yuma Shinohara, and Kazuhiko Sumi

Aoyama Gakuin University, Kanagawa, Japan
{ito.seiya,shinohara.yuma}@vss.it.aoyama.ac.jp,
{kaneko,sumi}@it.aoyama.ac.jp

Abstract. We propose a novel deep modular network architecture for indoor scene depth estimation from single RGB images. The proposed architecture consists of a main depth estimation network and two auxiliary semantic segmentation networks. Our insight is that semantic and geometrical structures in a scene are strongly correlated, thus we utilize global (i.e. room layout) and mid-level (i.e. objects in a room) semantic structures to enhance depth estimation. The first auxiliary network, or *layout network*, is responsible for room layout estimation to infer the positions of walls, floor, and ceiling of a room. The second auxiliary network, or *object network*, estimates per-pixel class labels of the objects in a scene, such as furniture, to give mid-level semantic cues. Estimated semantic structures are effectively fed into the depth estimation network using newly proposed *discriminator networks*, which discern the reliability of the estimated structures. The evaluation result shows that our architecture achieves significant performance improvements over previous approaches on the standard NYU Depth v2 indoor scene dataset.

Keywords: Depth estimation · Convolutional Neural Network

1 Introduction

Depth estimation is one of the fundamental problems of 3D scene structure analysis in computer vision. Traditional approaches including structured lights [27], time-of-flight [8], multi-view stereo [28], and structure from motion [3] have been extensively studied for decades. Most of these approaches are built upon stereo geometry and rely on reliable correspondences between multiple observations.

In contrast, depth estimation from a single RGB image is a relatively new task and has been actively studied for the last decade. Without prior knowledge or geometrical assumption, the problem is known as ill-posed, since numerous real-world spaces may produce the same image measurement. Early studies tackled this problem using Markov Random Fields (MRF) to infer the depth values of

---

S. Ito and N. Kaneko—The authors assert equal contribution and joint first authorship.

© Springer Nature Switzerland AG 2019
L. Leal-Taixé and S. Roth (Eds.): ECCV 2018 Workshops, LNCS 11129, pp. 324–336, 2019.
https://doi.org/10.1007/978-3-030-11009-3_19

image patches [25] or the planar parameters of superpixels [26]. Later, approaches based on Conditional Random Fields (CRF) emerged [22,36]. More recently, the task has enjoyed rapid progress [1,4,5,13,20,21,23,33,37] thanks to the recent advances of deep architectures [16,31] and large-scale datasets [9,24,30]. Without a doubt, the deep architectures, especially Convolutional Neural Networks (CNN), greatly contribute to the performance boost.

In this paper, we propose a novel deep modular network architecture for monocular depth estimation of indoor scenes. Our insight is that semantic and geometrical structures in a scene are strongly correlated, therefore, we use the semantic structures to enhance depth prediction. Interestingly, while the insight itself is not new [12], there are relatively few works [13,33] that use both deep architectures and semantic structure analysis. We will show that the proposed architecture, which effectively merges the semantic structure into the depth prediction, clearly outperforms previous approaches on the standard NYU Depth v2 benchmark dataset.

The proposed architecture is composed of a main depth estimation network and two auxiliary semantic segmentation networks. The first auxiliary network, or *layout network*, gives us the global (i.e. room layout) semantic structure of a scene by inferring the positions of walls, floor, and ceiling. The second auxiliary network, or *object network*, provides the mid-level (i.e. objects in a room) cues by estimating per-pixel class labels of the objects. To effectively merge the estimated structures into the depth estimation, we also introduce *discriminator networks*, which discern the reliability of the estimated structures. Each semantic structure is weighted by the respective reliability score and this process reduces the adverse effect on the depth estimation when the estimation quality of semantic segmentation is insufficient.

To summarize, we present:

- A novel deep modular network architecture which considers global and mid-level semantic structures.
- Discriminator networks to effectively merge the semantic structures into the depth prediction.
- Significant performance improvements over previous methods on the standard indoor depth estimation benchmark dataset.

2 Related Work

One of the first studies of single image depth estimation was done by Saxena et al. [25]. This method used hand-crafted convolutional filters to extract a set of texture features from an input image and solved the depth estimation problem using Markov Random Fields (MRF). The authors later proposed Make3D [26] to estimate 3D scene structure from a single image by inferring a set of planar parameters for superpixels using MRF. This approach depends on the horizontal consistency of the image and suffers from lack of versatility.

Instead of directly estimating depth, Hoiem et al. [12] assembled a simple 3D model of a scene by classifying the regions in an image as a geometrical structure such as sky or ground, and indirectly estimating the depths of the image. Liu et al. [19] used predicted semantic labels of a scene to guide depth estimation and solved a simpler problem with MRF. Ladicky et al. [18] proposed a pixel-wise classification model to jointly estimate the semantic labels and the depth of a scene, and showed that semantic classification and depth estimation can benefit each other.

Liu et al. [22] proposed a discrete-continuous Conditional Random Fields (CRF) model to consider relationships between neighbouring superpixels. Zhuo et al. [36] extended the CRF model to a hierarchical representation to model local depth jointly with mid-level and global scene structures. These methods lack generality in that they rely on nearest neighbour initialization from a training set. Besides, all of the above techniques used hand-crafted features.

In recent years, methods based on deep neural networks have become successful. Eigen et al. [5] proposed a robust depth estimation method using multi-scale Convolutional Neural Networks (CNN), and later extended it to a network structure that can also estimate the semantic labels and the surface orientation of a scene [4]. Thanks to the learning capability of multi-scale CNN and the availability of large-scale datasets, their latter work showed prominent performance. There are several works that combine CNN with CRF based regularization [20,21,33]. Liu et al. [20,21] tackled the problem with Deep Convolutional Neural Fields which jointly learn CNN and continuous CRF. Wang et al. [33] used two separate CNN to obtain regional and global potentials of a scene and fed them into hierarchical CRF to jointly estimate the depth and the semantic labels. Roy and Todorovic [23] showed that random forests can also be used as a regularizer. While the majority of existing approaches trained the estimator with supervised learning using metric depth, there are some works that used relative depth [1,37] or semi/unsupervised learning [10,17].

In the literature, the method closest to our approach was proposed by Jafari et al. [13]. They first performed depth prediction and semantic segmentation using existing methods [4,29] and then merged them through a Joint Refinement Network (JRN). Compared to [13], our architecture differs in two aspects. First, in addition to the mid-level object semantics, we consider the room layout of a scene as a global semantic structure for more consistent depth estimation. Second, we propose simple yet effective discriminator networks, which discern the reliability of the estimated structures, to further improve the performance.

3   Modular Network Architecture

This section presents the details of the proposed indoor scene depth estimation architecture. Figure 1 shows an overview of the proposed method. Taking a single RGB image as an input, we first estimate the global (i.e. room layout) and the mid-level (i.e. objects in a room) semantic structures of a scene using two separate semantic segmentation networks. The layout labels are estimated by the layout network N_L, and the object labels are estimated by the object network N_O. To treat the different number of classes in the same domain, we convert

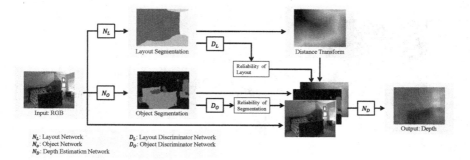

Fig. 1. Proposed depth estimation architecture. First, an input RGB image is fed into two separate semantic segmentation networks N_L and N_O to estimate room layout and object class labels, respectively. Then, discriminator networks D_L and D_O discern the reliability of the estimated layout and object labels. Lastly, the depth estimation network N_D take the input image, two label images, and two reliability scores as inputs to infer the final depth values.

the estimated labels to 3-channel label images using a predefined colour palette. Then, the layout label image and the object label image are respectively fed into the discriminator networks D_O and D_L which estimate the reliability scores of these images; i.e. how *real* the estimated label images are. Before feeding the layout label image into the depth estimation network, we apply edge extraction and distance transform [7] to it. Lastly, the depth estimation network N_D takes the input image, two label images, and two reliability scores as inputs to infer the final depth values. Each label image does not directly flow into N_D, but is weighted by the respective reliability score. This weighting process reduces the adverse effect on the depth estimation when the estimation quality of semantic segmentation is insufficient.

3.1 Semantic Segmentation

In the proposed method, two types of semantic segmentation are performed: (1) room layout segmentation to estimate the positions of walls, floor, and ceiling of a room and (2) object segmentation to recognize the items in a room such as furniture (hereinafter referred to as layout estimation and object recognition, respectively). We utilize Pyramid Scene Parsing Network (PSPNet) [35] for both segmentations.

In the layout estimation, we train the layout network N_L with five room layout classes: Ceiling, Floor, Right Wall, Left Wall, and Front Wall. The trained network infers dense labelling of the layout classes as depicted in Fig. 1.

Object recognition gives us a more detailed, mid-level semantic structure of a scene. 11 object classes including Bed, Chair, Table, etc., are used to train the object network N_O. The estimated mid-level cues support the depth estimation network to make object depths consistent. Figure 1 shows the estimated object labels.

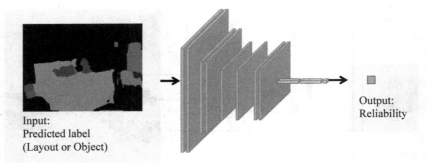

Fig. 2. Structure of the discriminator network. It takes the estimated label image and provides the reliability of the estimation in the interval $[0, 1]$.

To treat different numbers of classes in the same domain, we convert the estimated labels to 3-channel label images using a predefined colour palette.

3.2 Reliability Estimation

Since most CNN architectures assume that all of the input information is equally reliable, the input signals are not weighted. Rather, their reliability, or the amount of influence, is *implicitly* learned in the network. However, in the proposed modular architecture, where the layout estimation and the object recognition results are received as inputs, their quality may affect the final depth estimation result. Therefore, instead of implicit learning, we perform *explicit* weighting to reduce the influence of erroneous results.

We propose a reliability estimation network, which takes the estimated label image and provides the reliability of the estimation. The proposed reliability estimation network is inspired by the discriminator of Generative Adversarial Networks (GAN) [11] which discerns a given instance as being fake or real. Thus, we refer to this network as *discriminator network*. Figure 2 shows the network structure. We built it upon the AlexNet [16] with some modifications. We reduce the dimensions of the first two fully connected layers to 2,048 and set the output dimension to 1. The output reliability is activated by a sigmoid function.

The discriminator network is trained to output a value 1 for the ground truth label image and 0 for the estimated label image. We denote a training example as $\{l, \hat{l}\}$, where l denotes the estimated label image and $\hat{l}$ denotes the corresponding ground truth label image. We define the loss function L_{dis} for the discriminator network as follows:

$$L_{dis} = -\frac{1}{m} \sum_{i=1}^{m} \left\{ \log(D(l_i)) + \log(1 - D(\hat{l}_i)) \right\} \tag{1}$$

where m is the mini-batch size, i is the index of each label image in the mini-batch, and $D(\cdot)$ is the reliability in the interval $[0, 1]$ estimated by the discriminator network. Note that the two discriminator networks D_L and D_O in the

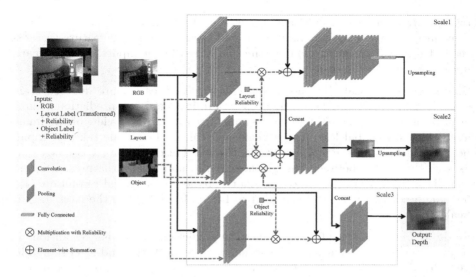

Fig. 3. Structure of the depth estimation network. Each scale takes different semantic information as the inputs. The layout label image is fed into Scale 1 and 2, and the object recognition label image is given to Scale 2 and 3. The layout label image produces the global semantic structure of a scene, while the object recognition label image gives the mid-level semantic structure.

proposed architecture are individually trained with the results of the layout estimation and the object recognition, respectively.

3.3 Extension of Depth Estimation Network

Taking the original image, two label images, and their reliabilities as inputs, our depth estimation network N_D infers the detailed depth of a cluttered indoor scene. Figure 3 shows a conceptual diagram of the network structure. Our network is based on the multi-scale CNN [4] and is extended to consider semantic structures. Through preliminary experiments, we found that preprocessing the layout estimation label image before feeding it to the depth network yields better performance. Specifically, we apply edge extraction and distance transform [7] to the label image. For ease of notation, we refer to the transformed layout estimation label image and the object recognition label image as global semantics and mid-level semantics, respectively.

Scale 1. The first scale provides a coarse global set of features over the entire image region by processing low-level image features with convolutional layers followed by two fully connected layers which introduce global relations. To enhance the global consistency of the depth prediction, we feed both the global semantics and the RGB image to this scale. The two input signals are separately mapped to feature spaces by the dedicated input convolutional layers. Then, the global semantics is weighted by multiplication with the estimated reliability score. The two feature maps are fused by element-wise summation and are processed by 11 convolutional layers and two fully connected layers. The output feature vector of the last layer is reshaped to 1/16 of the spatial size of the inputs, then bilinearly upsampled to 1/4 the scale.

Scale 2. As the scale increases, the network captures a more detailed scene structure. In the second scale, the network produces a depth prediction at mid-level resolution by combining feature maps from a narrower view of the image along with the global features provided by Scale 1. This scale takes as inputs both the global and the mid-level semantics in addition to the RGB image, and acts as the bridge between the global and the mid-level structures. The last convolutional layer outputs a coarse depth prediction of spatial resolution 74 × 55. The predicted depth is upsampled to 148 × 110 and fed to the later stage of Scale 3.

Scale 3. The third scale further refines the prediction to a higher resolution. To recover the detailed structure of a scene, we feed both the mid-level semantics and the RGB image to this final scale. After merging the two input signals, we concatenate the output from Scale 2 with the feature maps to incorporate multi-scale information. The final output is a depth prediction of size 148 × 110.

We train the network using the loss function motivated by [4]. We denote training examples as $\{Y, \hat{Y}\}$, where Y denotes the predicted depth map and $\hat{Y}$ denotes the ground truth depth map. Putting $d = Y - \hat{Y}$ to be their difference, the loss function L_{depth} is defined as:

$$L_{depth}(\hat{D}, D^*) = \frac{1}{n} \sum_i d_i^2 - \frac{1}{2n^2} \left(\sum_i d_i \right)^2$$
$$+ \frac{1}{n} \sum_i \left[(\nabla_x d_i)^2 + (\nabla_y d_i)^2 \right] \tag{2}$$

where n represents the total number of valid pixels in the image (we mask out the pixels where the ground truth is missing), i represents the pixel index, and $\nabla_x d_i$ and $\nabla_y d_i$ are the image gradients of the difference in the horizontal and vertical directions. We convolve a simple 1×3 filter to calculate $\nabla_x d_i$ and use its transposed version to calculate $\nabla_y d_i$.

4   Experiments

We evaluate our depth estimation architecture on the standard NYU Depth v2 indoor scene depth estimation dataset [30] which contains 654 test images. We compare our architecture with the published results of recent methods [4,5,13, 20,23,33]. For quantitative evaluation, we report the following commonly used metrics:

- Absolute relative difference (abs rel): $\frac{1}{n} \sum_i \frac{|y_i - \hat{y}_i|}{y_i}$
- Squared relative difference (sqr rel): $\frac{1}{n} \sum_i \frac{\|y_i - \hat{y}_i\|^2}{y_i}$

- RMSE (rms(linear)): $\sqrt{\frac{1}{n}\sum_i \|y_i - \hat{y}_i\|^2}$
- RMSE in log space (rms(log)): $\sqrt{\frac{1}{n}\sum_i \|\log(y_i) - \log(\hat{y}_i)\|^2}$
- Average $\log_{10}$ error (log10): $\frac{1}{n}\sum_i |\log_{10}(y_i) - \log_{10}(\hat{y}_i)|$
- Threshold: % of y_i s.t. $\max\left(\frac{y_i}{\hat{y}_i}, \frac{\hat{y}_i}{y_i}\right) = \delta < thr$, where $thr \in \{1.25, 1.25^2, 1.25^3\}$

where y_i is the predicted depth value of a pixel i, $\hat{y}_i$ is the ground truth depth, and n is the total number of pixels. The next subsection describes training procedures and datasets used to train the network modules.

4.1 Implementation Details

Layout Estimation. We train the layout estimation network N_L with the LSUN layout estimation dataset [34], which contains 4,000 indoor images. Following the procedure of [2], we assign dense semantic layout labels to the images and train the network as a standard semantic segmentation task. Since the dataset contains images of various sizes, we apply bicubic interpolation to resize the images to 321×321 pixels. We utilize the PSPNet model [35] and initialize its parameters using pre-trained weights (trained with the Pascal VOC2012 [6]) which is publicly available[1]. We set the base learning rate for the SGD solver to 0.0001 and apply polynomial decay of power 0.9 to this rate at each iteration during the whole training. Momentum and weight decay rate are set to 0.9 and 0.0001, respectively. Due to physical memory limitations on our graphics card, we set the mini-batch size to 2.

Object Recognition. We use almost the same set-up as for the layout estimation, except for training dataset. We train the object recognition network N_O with 5,285 training images from SUN RGB-D semantic segmentation dataset [32]. We apply no resizing to this dataset and feed the original 640×480 images to the network. We modify the standard 37 object categories by mapping to 13 categories [4] and removing duplicated layout classes (i.e. Wall, Floor, Ceiling). In addition, we add a 'background' class and assign the above removed categories to this class. This results in 11 classes. To improve the segmentation quality, we use a fully-connected CRF [15] for post-processing.

Reliability Estimation. We train two discriminator networks D_L and D_O using the LSUN dataset [34] and the SUN RGB-D dataset [32], respectively. We use the same training procedure for D_L and D_O. For ease of notation, we omit the subscripts in the following explanation. First, we acquire estimation results from a training set of the dataset using the trained semantic segmentation network N. The estimated labels and the corresponding ground truth labels are colourised using a predefined colour palette. Then, we assign a label 0 for the estimated label image and 1 for the ground truth label image. Finally, we train the discriminator

---

[1] https://github.com/hszhao/PSPNet.

Table 1. Quantitative comparison against previous approaches on the NYU Depth v2 dataset.

Method	Error (lower is better)					Accuracy (higher is better)		
	abs rel	sqr rel	rms(linear)	rms(log)	log10	$\delta < 1.25$	$\delta < 1.25^2$	$\delta < 1.25^3$
Eigen et al. [5]	0.215	0.212	0.907	0.285	-	0.611	0.887	0.971
Joint HCRF [33]	0.220	0.210	0.745	0.262	0.094	0.605	0.890	0.970
Liu et al. [20]	0.230	-	0.824	-	0.095	0.614	0.883	0.971
Eigen and Fergus [4]	0.158	0.121	0.641	0.214	-	0.769	0.950	0.988
Roy and Todorovic [23]	0.187	-	0.744	-	0.078	-	-	-
Jafari et al. [13]	0.157	0.123	0.673	0.216	0.068	0.762	0.948	0.988
Ours	**0.151**	**0.107**	**0.601**	0.203	**0.061**	**0.801**	**0.969**	**0.992**
Ours w/o Disc.	0.163	0.127	0.631	0.207	0.064	0.794	0.963	0.991
Objects + Disc.	0.155	0.119	0.619	**0.202**	0.065	0.780	0.961	**0.992**
Layout + Disc.	**0.151**	0.112	0.643	**0.202**	0.071	0.778	0.959	**0.992**
Distance trans. + Disc.	0.161	0.121	0.626	0.206	0.063	0.774	0.959	0.991

D using the loss function defined in Eq. 1. We use Adam optimizer [14] and set the learning rate to 10^{-10}.

Depth Estimation. Following [4,5], we train our depth estimation network N_D using the raw distribution of the NYU Depth v2 dataset [30] which contains many additional images. We extract 16K synchronized RGB-depth image pairs using the toolbox provided by the authors[2]. We downsample the RGB images from 640×480 to 320×240 pixels. The ground truth depth maps are converted into log space and resized to the network output size 148×110. We train the network using the SGD solver with mini-batches of size 8. Learning rate and Momentum are set to 10^{-6} and 0.9, respectively. Note that, our training is done by end-to-end learning instead of the incremental learning in [4].

4.2   Results on the NYU Depth v2

Table 1 shows the quantitative comparison of the proposed architecture against previous approaches on the NYU Depth v2 dataset [30]. The proposed architecture shows the best performance in most metrics. Comparing to the baseline [4], which our architecture is built upon, we achieve consistent improvements in all metrics. To evaluate the proposed architecture in detail, we conduct experiments with several settings. As shown in Table 1, using the object recognition (Objects + Disc.) has positive impacts on all metrics. Interestingly, in the individual case, using the layout estimation without distance transform (Layout + Disc.) performs better than the distance transformed layout (Distance trans. + Disc.). However, we found that the distance transformed layout provides better results when it is integrated into the whole architecture. More importantly, one can see the discriminator networks play an important role in our architecture (Ours w/o Disc.). These results validate the effectiveness of our modular architecture.

---

[2] https://cs.nyu.edu/~silberman/datasets/nyu_depth_v2.html.

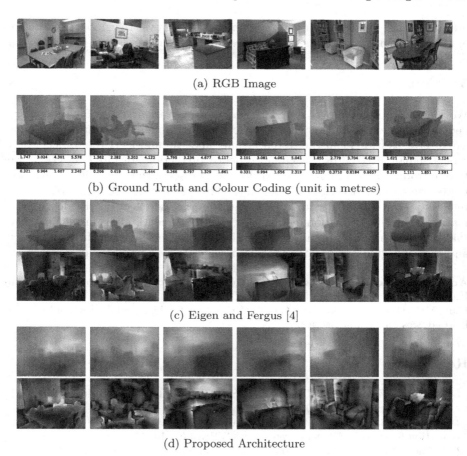

(a) RGB Image

(b) Ground Truth and Colour Coding (unit in metres)

(c) Eigen and Fergus [4]

(d) Proposed Architecture

Fig. 4. Depth estimation results for the NYU Depth v2 dataset. We show the depth maps in upper rows and the corresponding error maps in lower rows.

Figure 4 presents the qualitative comparison between the proposed architecture and the prediction of [4]. For detailed comparison, we also visualize the errors in the depth maps. In addition to the quantitative performance improvements, we found that the proposed architecture is more robust to the appearance changes inside objects. In the second scene from the left, the sticky notes pasted on a computer change its appearance and [4] produces large estimation error. In contrast, our architecture consistently estimates the depth inside the object. A similar effect appears in the centre of the fourth scene from the left, where a shadow changes the appearance of a wall.

One drawback of our architecture is "blur effect" in object boundaries. The visualized results show that feeding the object recognition label image into the depth estimation contributes to the accuracy improvement. Nevertheless, the object boundaries become unclear due to imperfect segmentation results. The layout estimation has similar effects. Although it improves the global consistency of the prediction, it smooths out the local object boundaries.

5   Conclusions

We have proposed a novel deep modular network architecture for monocular depth estimation of indoor scenes. Two auxiliary semantic segmentation networks give us the global (i.e. room layout) and the mid-level (i.e. objects in a room) semantic structure to enhance depth prediction. Inspired by GAN, we have introduced discriminator networks, which discern the reliability of the estimated semantic structures. Each semantic structure is weighted by the respective reliability score, and this process reduces the adverse effect on the depth estimation when the estimation quality of semantic segmentation is insufficient. We evaluated the proposed architecture on the NYUD Depth v2 benchmark dataset and showed significant performance improvements over previous approaches.

Acknowledgments. This work was partially supported by Aoyama Gakuin University-Supported Program "Early Eagle Program". The authors are grateful to Prof. M.J. Dürst from Aoyama Gakuin University for his careful proofreading and kind advices on the manuscript.

References

1. Chen, W., Fu, Z., Yang, D., Deng, J.: Single-image depth perception in the wild. In: NIPS, pp. 730–738 (2016)
2. Dasgupta, S., Fang, K., Chen, K., Savarese, S.: Delay: robust spatial layout estimation for cluttered indoor scenes. In: CVPR, pp. 616–624 (2016)
3. Dellaert, F., Seitz, S.M., Thorpe, C.E., Thrun, S.: Structure from motion without correspondence. In: CVPR, pp. 557–564 (2000)
4. Eigen, D., Fergus, R.: Predicting depth, surface normals and semantic labels with a common multi-scale convolutional architecture. In: ICCV, pp. 2650–2658 (2015)
5. Eigen, D., Puhrsch, C., Fergus, R.: Depth map prediction from a single image using a multi-scale deep network. In: NIPS, pp. 2366–2374 (2014)
6. Everingham, M., Van Gool, L., Williams, C.K.I., Winn, J., Zisserman, A.: The PASCAL Visual Object Classes Challenge 2012 (VOC2012) Results. http://www.pascal-network.org/challenges/VOC/voc2012/workshop/index.html
7. Felzenszwalb, P., Huttenlocher, D.: Distance transforms of sampled functions. Technical report, Cornell University (2004)
8. Foix, S., Alenya, G., Torras, C.: Lock-in time-of-flight (ToF) cameras: a survey. IEEE Sens. J. **11**(9), 1917–1926 (2011)
9. Geiger, A., Lenz, P., Stiller, C., Urtasun, R.: Vision meets robotics: the KITTI dataset. Int. J. Robot. Res. **32**(11), 1231–1237 (2013)
10. Godard, C., Mac Aodha, O., Brostow, G.J.: Unsupervised monocular depth estimation with left-right consistency. In: CVPR, pp. 270–279 (2017)
11. Goodfellow, I., et al.: Generative adversarial nets. In: NIPS, pp. 2672–2680 (2014)
12. Hoiem, D., Efros, A.A., Hebert, M.: Automatic photo pop-up. ACM Trans. Graph. **24**(3), 577–584 (2005)

13. Jafari, O.H., Groth, O., Kirillov, A., Yang, M.Y., Rother, C.: Analyzing modular CNN architectures for joint depth prediction and semantic segmentation. In: ICRA, pp. 4620–4627 (2017)
14. Kingma, D., Ba, J.: Adam: a method for stochastic optimization. In: ICLR (2015)
15. Krähenbühl, P., Koltun, V.: Efficient inference in fully connected CRFs with Gaussian edge potentials. In: NIPS, pp. 109–117 (2011)
16. Krizhevsky, A., Sutskever, I., Hinton, G.E.: Imagenet classification with deep convolutional neural networks. In: NIPS, pp. 1097–1105 (2012)
17. Kuznietsov, Y., Stückler, J., Leibe, B.: Semi-supervised deep learning for monocular depth map prediction. In: CVPR, pp. 6647–6655 (2017)
18. Ladicky, L., Shi, J., Pollefeys, M.: Pulling things out of perspective. In: CVPR, pp. 89–96 (2014)
19. Liu, B., Gould, S., Koller, D.: Single image depth estimation from predicted semantic labels. In: CVPR, pp. 1253–1260 (2010)
20. Liu, F., Shen, C., Lin, G.: Deep convolutional neural fields for depth estimation from a single image. In: CVPR, pp. 5162–5170 (2015)
21. Liu, F., Shen, C., Lin, G., Reid, I.: Learning depth from single monocular images using deep convolutional neural fields. IEEE Trans. Pattern Anal. Mach. Intell. **38**(10), 2024–2039 (2016)
22. Liu, M., Salzmann, M., He, X.: Discrete-continuous depth estimation from a single image. In: CVPR, pp. 716–723 (2014)
23. Roy, A., Todorovic, S.: Monocular depth estimation using neural regression forest. In: CVPR, pp. 5506–5514 (2016)
24. Russakovsky, O., et al.: Imagenet large scale visual recognition challenge. Int. J. Comput. Vis. **115**(3), 211–252 (2015)
25. Saxena, A., Chung, S.H., Ng, A.Y.: Learning depth from single monocular images. In: NIPS, pp. 1161–1168 (2005)
26. Saxena, A., Sun, M., Ng, A.Y.: Make3D: learning 3D scene structure from a single still image. IEEE Trans. Pattern Anal. Mach. Intell. **31**(5), 824–840 (2009)
27. Scharstein, D., Szeliski, R.: High-accuracy stereo depth maps using structured light. In: CVPR, pp. 195–202 (2003)
28. Seitz, S.M., Curless, B., Diebel, J., Scharstein, D., Szeliski, R.: A comparison and evaluation of multi-view stereo reconstruction algorithms. In: CVPR, pp. 519–528 (2006)
29. Shelhamer, E., Long, J., Darrell, T.: Fully convolutional networks for semantic segmentation. IEEE Trans. Pattern Anal. Mach. Intell. **39**(4), 640–651 (2017)
30. Silberman, N., Hoiem, D., Kohli, P., Fergus, R.: Indoor segmentation and support inference from RGBD images. In: Fitzgibbon, A., Lazebnik, S., Perona, P., Sato, Y., Schmid, C. (eds.) ECCV 2012. LNCS, vol. 7576, pp. 746–760. Springer, Heidelberg (2012). https://doi.org/10.1007/978-3-642-33715-4_54
31. Simonyan, K., Zisserman, A.: Very deep convolutional networks for large-scale image recognition. In: ICLR (2015)
32. Song, S., Lichtenberg, S.P., Xiao, J.: SUN RGB-D: a RGB-D scene understanding benchmark suite. In: CVPR (2015)
33. Wang, P., Shen, X., Lin, Z., Cohen, S., Price, B., Yuille, A.L.: Towards unified depth and semantic prediction from a single image. In: CVPR, pp. 2800–2809 (2015)
34. Yu, F., Zhang, Y., Song, S., Seff, A., Xiao, J.: LSUN: construction of a large-scale image dataset using deep learning with humans in the loop. arXiv preprint arXiv:1506.03365 (2015)

35. Zhao, H., Shi, J., Qi, X., Wang, X., Jia, J.: Pyramid scene parsing network. In: CVPR, pp. 2881–2890 (2017)
36. Zhuo, W., Salzmann, M., He, X., Liu, M.: Indoor scene structure analysis for single image depth estimation. In: CVPR, pp. 614–622 (2015)
37. Zoran, D., Isola, P., Krishnan, D., Freeman, W.T.: Learning ordinal relationships for mid-level vision. In: ICCV, pp. 388–396 (2015)

Generative Adversarial Networks for Unsupervised Monocular Depth Prediction

Filippo Aleotti, Fabio Tosi, Matteo Poggi$^{(\boxtimes)}$, and Stefano Mattoccia

University of Bologna, Viale del Risorgimento 2, Bologna, Italy
{filippo.aleotti2,fabio.tosi5,m.poggi,stefano.mattoccia}@unibo.it

Abstract. Estimating depth from a single image is a very challenging and exciting topic in computer vision with implications in several application domains. Recently proposed deep learning approaches achieve outstanding results by tackling it as an image reconstruction task and exploiting geometry constraints (e.g., epipolar geometry) to obtain supervisory signals for training. Inspired by these works and compelling results achieved by Generative Adversarial Network (GAN) on image reconstruction and generation tasks, in this paper we propose to cast unsupervised monocular depth estimation within a GAN paradigm. The generator network learns to infer depth from the reference image to generate a warped target image. At training time, the discriminator network learns to distinguish between fake images generated by the generator and target frames acquired with a stereo rig. To the best of our knowledge, our proposal is the first successful attempt to tackle monocular depth estimation with a GAN paradigm and the extensive evaluation on CityScapes and KITTI datasets confirm that it enables to improve traditional approaches. Additionally, we highlight a major issue with data deployed by a standard evaluation protocol widely used in this field and fix this problem using a more reliable dataset recently made available by the KITTI evaluation benchmark.

1 Introduction

Accurate depth estimation is of paramount importance for many computer vision tasks and for this purpose active sensors, such as LIDARs or Time of Flight sensors, are being extensively deployed in most practical applications. Nonetheless, passive depth sensors based on conventional cameras have notable advantages compared to active sensors. Thus, a significant amount of literature aims at tackling depth estimation with standard imaging sensors. Most approaches reply on multiple images acquired from different viewpoints to infer depth through binocular stereo, multi-view stereo, structure from motion and so on. Despite their

Electronic supplementary material The online version of this chapter (https://doi.org/10.1007/978-3-030-11009-3_20) contains supplementary material, which is available to authorized users.

L. Leal-Taixé and S. Roth (Eds.): ECCV 2018 Workshops, LNCS 11129, pp. 337–354, 2019.
https://doi.org/10.1007/978-3-030-11009-3_20

effectiveness, all of them rely on the availability of multiple acquisitions of the sensed environment (e.g., binocular stereo requires two synchronized images) (Fig. 1).

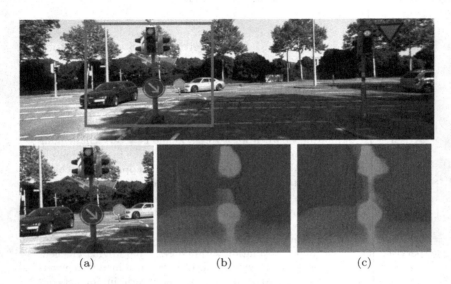

(a)   (b)   (c)

Fig. 1. Estimated depth maps from single image. On top, frame from KITTI 2015 dataset, on bottom (a) detail from reference image (red rectangle), (b) depth predicted by Godard et al. [13] and (c) by our GAN architecture. (Color figure online)

Monocular depth estimation represents an appealing alternative to overcome such constraint and recent works in this field achieved excellent results leveraging machine learning [6,13,21,24]. Early works tackled this problem in a supervised manner [6,21,24] by training on a large amount of images with pixel-level depth labels. However, is well known that gathering labeled data is not trivial and particularly expensive when dealing with depth measurements [11,12,30,38]. More recent methods [13,54] aim to overcome this issue casting monocular depth estimation as an image reconstruction problem. In [54] inferring camera ego-motion in image sequences and in [13] leveraging a stereo setup. In both cases, difficult to source labeled depth data are not required at all for training. The second method yields much better results outperforming even supervised methods [6,21,24] by a large margin.

Recently, Generative Adversarial Networks (GANs) [14] proved to be very effective when dealing with high-level tasks such as image synthesis, style transfer and more. In this framework, two architectures are trained to solve competitive tasks. The first one, referred to as *generator*, produces a new image from a given input (e.g., a synthetic frame from noise, an image with a transferred style, etc.) while the second one called *discriminator* is trained to distinguish between real images and those generated by the first network. The two models play a *min-max* game, with the generator trained to produce outputs good enough to fool the discriminator and this latter network trained to not being fooled by the generator.

Considering the methodology adopted by state-of-the-art methods for unsupervised monocular depth estimation and the intrinsic ability of GANs to detect inconsistencies in images, in this paper we propose to infer depth from monocular images by means of a GAN architecture. Given a stereo pair, at training time, our generator learns to produce meaningful depth representations, with respect to left and right image, by exploiting the epipolar constraint to align the two images. The warped images and the real ones are then forwarded to the discriminator, trained to distinguish between the two cases. The rationale behind our idea is that a generator producing accurate depth maps will also lead to better reconstructed images, harder to be distinguished from original unwarped inputs. At the same time, for the discriminator will be harder to be fooled, pushing the generator to build more realistic warped images and thus more accurate depth predictions.

In this paper, we report extensive experimental results on the KITTI 2015 dataset, which provides a large amount of unlabeled stereo images and thus it is ideal for unsupervised training. Moreover, we highlight and fix inconsistencies in the commonly adapted split of Eigen [6], replacing Velodyne measurements with more accurate labels recently made available on KITTI [40]. Therefore, our contribution is threefold:

- Our framework represents, to the best of our knowledge, the first method to tackle monocular depth estimation within a GAN paradigm
- It outperforms traditional methods
- We propose a more reliable evaluation protocol for the split of Eigen et al. [6].

2   Related Work

Depth estimation from images has a long history in computer vision. Most popular techniques rely on synchronized image pairs [39], multiple acquisitions from different viewpoints [9], at different time frames [35] or in presence of illumination changes [45]. Although certainly relevant to our work, these methods are not able to infer depth from a single image while recent methods casting depth prediction as a learning task and applications of GANs to other fields are strictly related to our proposal.

Learning-Based Stereo. Traditional binocular stereo algorithms perform a subset of steps as defined in [39]. The matching cost computation phase is common to all approaches, encoding an initial similarity score between pixels on reference image, typically the left, and matching candidates on the target. The seminal work by Zbontar and LeCun [50,51] computes matching costs using a CNN trained on image patches and deploys such strategy inside a well-established stereo pipeline [15] achieving outstanding results. In a follow-up work, Luo et al.

[25] obtained more accurate matching representation casting the correspondence search as a multi-class classification problem. A significant departure from this strategy is represented by DispNet [29], a deep architecture aimed at regressing per-pixel disparity assignments after an end-to-end training. These latter methods require a large amount of labeled images (i.e., stereo pairs with ground-truth disparity) for training [29]. Other works proposed novel CNN-based architectures inspired by traditional stereo pipeline as GC-Net [18] and CLR [31].

Supervised Monocular Depth Estimation. Single image depth estimation is an ill-posed problem due to the lack of geometric constraints and thus it represents a much more challenging task compared to depth from stereo. Saxena et al. [37] proposed Make3D, a patch-based model estimating 3D location and orientation of local planes by means of a MRF framework. This technique suffers in presence of thin structures and lack of global context information often useful to obtain consistent depth estimations. Liu et al. [24] trained a CNN to tackle monocular depth estimation, while Ladicky et al. [21] exploited semantic information to obtain more accurate depth predictions. In [17] Karsch et al. achieved more consistent predictions at testing time by copying entire depth images from a training set. Eigen et al. [6] proposed a multi-scale CNN trained in supervised manner to infer depth from a single image. Differently from [24], whose network was trained to compute more robust data terms and pairwise terms, this approach directly infers the final depth map from the input image. Following [6] other works enabled more accurate estimations by means of CRF regularization [23], casting the problem as a classification task [2], designing more robust loss functions [22] or using scene priors for plane normals estimation [43]. Luo et al. [26] formulated monocular depth estimation as a stereo matching problem in which the right view is generated by a view-synthesis network based on Deep 3D [46]. Fu et al. [8] proposed a very effective depth discretization strategy and a novel ordinal regression loss achieving state-of-the-art results on different challenging benchmarks. Kumar et al. [4] demonstrated that recurrent neural networks (RNNs) can learn spatio-temporally accurate monocular depth prediction from video sequences. Atapour et al. [1] take advantage of style transfer and adversarial training on synthetic data to predict depth maps from real-world color images. Lastly, Ummenhofer et al. [41] proposed DeMoN, a deep model to infer both depth and ego-motion from a pair of subsequent frames acquired by a single camera. As for deep stereo models all these techniques require a large amount of labeled data at training time to learn meaningful depth representation from a single image.

Unsupervised Monocular Depth Estimation. Pertinent to our proposal are some recent works concerned with view synthesis. Flynn et al. [7] proposed DeepStereo, a deep architecture trained on images acquired by multiple cameras in unsupervised manner to generate novel view points. Deep3D by Xie et al. [46] generates corresponding target view from an input reference image in the context of binocular stereo, by learning a distribution over all possible disparities for each pixel on the source frame and training their model with a reconstruction loss. Similarly, Garg et al. [10] trained a network for monocular depth

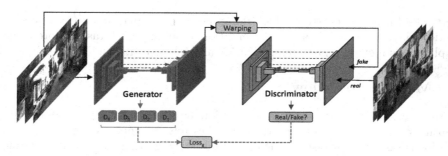

Fig. 2. Proposed adversarial model. Given a single input frame, depth maps are produced by a Generator (blue) and used to warp images. Discriminator (gray) process both raw and warped images, trying to classify the former as real and the latter as fake. The generator is pushed to improve depth prediction to provide a more realistic warping to fool the discriminator. At the same time the discriminator learns to improve its ability to perform this task. (Color figure online)

estimation using a reconstruction loss over a stereo pair. To make their model fully differentiable they used Taylor approximation to make their loss linear, resulting in a more challenging objective to optimize. Godard et al. [13] overcome this problem by using a bilinear sampling [16] to generate images from depth prediction. At training time, this model learns to predict depth for both images in a stereo pair thus enabling to enforce a left-right consistency constraint as supervisory signal. A simple post-processing step allows to refine depth prediction. This approach was extended by including additional temporal information [52] and by training with semi-supervised data [20,48]. While previous method requires rectified stereo pairs for training, Zhou et al. [54] proposed to train a model to infer depth from unconstrained video sequences by computing a reconstruction loss between subsequent frames and predicting, at the same time, the relative pose between them. This strategy removes the requirement of stereo pairs for training but produces a less accurate depth estimation. Wang et al. [42] proposed a simple normalization strategy that circumvent problems in the scale sensitivity of the depth regularization terms employed during training and empirically demonstrated that the incorporation of a differentiable implementation of Direct Visual Odometry (DVO) improves previous monocular depth performance [54]. Mahjourian et al. [27] used a novel approximate ICP based loss to jointly learn depth and camera motion for rigid scenes, while Yin et al. [47] proposed a learning framework for jointly training monocular depth, optical flow and camera motion from video. [52]. Concurrently with our work, Poggi et al. [32] deployed a thin model for depth estimation on CPU and proposed a trinocular paradigm [33] to improve unsupervised approaches based on stereo supervision, while Ramirez et al. [49] proposed a semi-superised framework for joint depth and semantic estimation.

Generative Adversarial Networks. GANs [14] recently gained popularity by enabling to cast computer vision problems as a competitive task between two

networks. Such methodology achieved impressive performance for image generalization [5,34], editing [55] and representation learning [28,34] tasks. More recent
applications include text-to-image [36,53] and image-to-image [56] translations.

3   Method Overview

In this section we describe our adversarial framework for unsupervised monocular
depth estimation. State-of-the-art approaches rely on single network to accomplish this task. In contrast, at the core of our strategy there is a novel loss function based on a two players min-max game between two adversarial networks,
as shown in Fig. 2. This is done by using both a generative and a discriminative
model competing on two different tasks, each one aimed at prevailing the other.
This section discusses the geometry of the problem and how it is used to take
advantages of 2D photometric constraints with a generative adversarial approach
in a totally unsupervised manner. We refer to our framework as *MonoGAN*.

3.1   Generator Model for Monocular Depth Estimation

The main goal of our framework is to estimate an accurate depth map from a single image without relying on hard to find ground-truth depth labels for training.
For this purpose, we can model this problem as a domain transfer task: given an
input image x, we want to obtain a new representation $y = G(x)$ in the depth
domain. In other contexts, GAN models have been successfully deployed for
image-to-image translation [56]. For our purpose a generator network, depicted
in blue in Fig. 2, is trained to learn a transfer function $G : \mathcal{I} \rightarrow \mathcal{D}$ mapping
an input image from $\mathcal{I}$ to $\mathcal{D}$, respectively, the RGB and the depth domain. To
do so, it is common practice to train the generator with loss signals enforcing
structure consistency across the two domains to preserve object shapes, spatial
consistency, etc. Similarly, this can be done for our specific goal by exploiting
view synthesis. That is, projecting RGB images into 3D domain according to
estimated depth and then back-projecting to new synthesized view for which
we need a real image to compare with. To make it possible, for each training
sample at least two images from different points of view are required to enable
the image reconstruction process described so far. In literature, this strategy is
used by other unsupervised techniques for monocular depth estimation, exploiting both unconstrained sequences [54] or stereo imagery [13]. In this latter case,
given two images i^l and i^r acquired by a stereo setup, the generator estimates
inverse depth (i.e., disparity) d^l used to obtain a synthesized image $\tilde{i}^l$ by warping i^r with bilinear sampler function [16] being it fully differentiable and thus
enabling end-to-end training. If d^l is accurate, shapes and structures are preserved after warping, while an inaccurate estimation would lead to distortion
artifacts as shown on the right of Fig. 3. This process is totally unsupervised
with respect to the $\mathcal{D}$ domain and thus it does not require at all ground-truth
labels at training time. Moreover, by estimating a second output d^r, representing
the inverse mapping from i^l to i^r, allows to use additional supervisory signals by
enforcing consistency in the $\mathcal{D}$ domain (i.e., Left-Right consistency constraint).

3.2 Discriminator Model

To successfully accomplish domain transfer, GANs rely on a second network trained to distinguish images produced by the generator from those belonging to the target domain, respectively *fake* and *real* samples. We follow the same principle using the gray model in Fig. 2, but acting differently from other approaches. In particular, to discriminate synthesized images from real ones we need a large amount of samples in the target domain. While for traditional domain transfer applications this does not represent an issue (requiring images without annotation), this becomes a limitation when depth is the target domain being ground-truth label difficult to source in this circumstance. To overcome this limitation, we train a discriminator to work on the RGB domain to tell original input images from synthesized ones. Indeed, if estimated disparity by the generator is not accurate, the warping process would reproduce distortion artifacts easily detectable by the discriminator. On the other hand, an accurate depth prediction would lead to a reprojected image harder to be recognized from a real one. Figure 3 shows, on the left, an example of real image and, on the right, a warped one synthesized according to an inaccurate depth estimation. For instance, by looking at the tree, we can easily tell the real image from the warped one. By training the discriminator on this task, the generator is constantly forced to produce more accurate depth maps thus leading to a more realistic reconstructed image in order to fool it. At the same time the discriminator is constantly pushed to improve its ability to tell real images from synthesized ones. Our proposal aims at such *virtuous behavior* by properly modeling the adversarial contribution of the two networks as described in detail in the next section.

4 Adversarial Formulation

To train the framework outlined so far in end-to-end manner we define an objective function $\mathcal{L}(G, D)$ sum of two terms, a $\mathcal{L}_{GAN}$ expressing the min-max game between generator G and discriminator D:

$$\mathcal{L}_{GAN} = \min_G \max_D V(G, D) = \mathbb{E}_{i_0 \sim \mathcal{I}}[\log(D(i_0))]$$
$$+ \mathbb{E}_{i_1 \sim \tilde{\mathcal{I}}}[\log(1 - D(i_1))] \tag{1}$$

with i_0 and i_1 belonging, respectively, to real images $\mathcal{I}$ and fake images $\tilde{\mathcal{I}}$ domains being the latter obtained by bilinear warping according to depth estimated by G and a data term $\mathcal{L}_{data}$ resulting in:

$$\mathcal{L}(G, D) = \mathcal{L}_{GAN} + \mathcal{L}_{data} \tag{2}$$

According to this formulation, generator G and discriminator D are trained to minimize loss functions $\mathcal{L}_G$ and $\mathcal{L}_D$:

$$\mathcal{L}_G = \mathcal{L}_{data} + \alpha_{adv}\mathbb{E}_{i_0,i_1 \sim \tilde{\mathcal{I}}}[\log(D(i_1))] \tag{3}$$

Fig. 3. Example of real (top) and warped (bottom) image according to an estimated depth. We can clearly notice how inaccurate predictions lead to warping artifacts on the reprojected frame (e.g., distorted trees) not perceivable elsewhere.

$$\mathcal{L}_D = -\frac{1}{2}\mathbb{E}_{i_0 \sim \mathcal{I}} \log(D(i_0)) - \frac{1}{2}\mathbb{E}_{i_1 \sim \tilde{\mathcal{I}}} \log(1 - D(i_1)) \tag{4}$$

To give an intuition, G is trained to minimize the loss from data term and the probability that D will classify a warped image $i_1 \sim \tilde{\mathcal{I}}$ as fake. This second contribution is weighted according to α_{adv} factor, hyper-parameter of our framework. Consistently, D is trained to classify a raw image $i_0 \sim \mathcal{I}$ as real and a warped one as fake. Despite our framework processes a transfer from $\mathcal{I}$ to depth domain $\mathcal{D}$, we highlight how in the proposed adversarial formulation the discriminator does not process any sample from domain $\mathcal{D}$, neither fake nor real. Thus it does not require any ground-truth depth map and perfectly fits with an unsupervised monocular depth estimation paradigm.

4.1   Data Term Loss

We define the data term $\mathcal{L}_{data}$ part of the generator loss function $\mathcal{L}_G$ as follows:

$$\mathcal{L}_{data} = \beta_{ap}(\mathcal{L}_{ap}) + \beta_{ds}(\mathcal{L}_{ds}) + \beta_{lr}(\mathcal{L}_{lr}) \tag{5}$$

where the loss consists in the weighted sum of three terms. The first one, namely *appearence* term, measures the reconstruction error between warped image $\tilde{I}$ and real one I by means of SSIM [44] and L1 difference of the two

$$\mathcal{L}_{ap} = \frac{1}{N}\sum_{i,j} \gamma \frac{1 - SSIM(I_{i,j}, \tilde{I}_{i,j})}{2} + (1 - \gamma)\|I_{i,j} - \tilde{I}_{i,j}\|_1 \tag{6}$$

The second term is a *smoothness* constraint that penalizes large disparity differences between neighboring pixels along the x and y directions unless a strong intensity gradients in the reference image I occurs

$$\mathcal{L}_{ds} = \frac{1}{N} \sum_{i,j} |\delta_x d_{i,j}| e^{-||\delta_x I_{i,j}||} + |\delta_y d_{i,j}| e^{-||\delta_y I_{ij}||} \tag{7}$$

Finally, by building the generator to output a second disparity map d^r, we can add the term proposed in [13] as third supervision signal, enforcing left-right consistency between the predicted disparity maps, d^l and d^r, for left and right images:

$$\mathcal{L}_{lr}^l = \frac{1}{N} \sum_{i,j} |d_{i,j}^l - d_{i,j+d_{i,j}^l}^r| \tag{8}$$

Moreover, estimating d^r also enables to compute the three terms for both images in a training stereo pair.

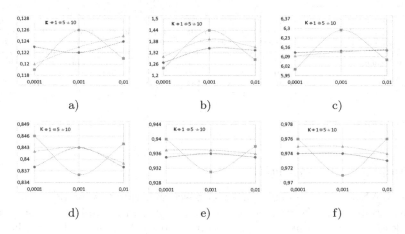

Fig. 4. Analysis of hyper-parameters α_{adv} and k of our GAN model, on x axis α_{adv}, on y axis an evaluation metric. (a) Abs Rel, (b) Sq Rel and (c) RMSE metrics (lower is better). (d) $\delta < 1.25$, (e) $\delta < 1.25^2$, (f) $\delta < 1.25^3$ metrics (higher is better). Interpolation is used for visualization purpose only. We can notice how our proposal using a weight α_{adv} of 0.0001 and a step k of 5 achieves the best performance with all metrics.

5   Experimental Results

In this section we assess the performance of our proposal with respect to literature. Firstly, we describe implementation details of our model outlining the architecture of generator and discriminator networks. Then, we describe the training protocols followed during our experiments reporting an exhaustive comparison on KITTI 2015 stereo dataset [30] with state-of-the-art method [13]. This evaluation clearly highlights how the adversarial formulation proposed is beneficial when tackling this unsupervised monocular depth estimation. Moreover, we compare our proposal with other frameworks known in literature, both supervised and unsupervised, on the split of data used by Eigen et al. [6]. In this latter case we provide experimental results on the standard Eigen split as well as on a similar one made of more reliable data. This evaluation highlights once again the effectiveness of our proposal.

Table 1. Results on KITTI stereo 2015 [30]. We compare MonoGAN with [13] using different training schedules, respectively only KITTI sequences (K), only CityScapes (CS) and both sequentially (CS + K). Adversarial contribution always improves the results. We indicate with pp results obtained after applying the final post-processing step proposed in [13].

Exp.	Method	Dataset	Abs Rel	Sq Rel	RMSE	RMSE log	D1-all	$\delta < 1.25$	$\delta < 1.25^2$	$\delta < 1.25^3$
			Proposed method			Lower is better		Higher is better		
i)	Godard et al. [13]	K	0.124	1.388	6.125	0.217	30.272	0.841	0.936	0.975
	MonoGAN	K	**0.119**	**1.239**	**5.998**	**0.212**	**29.864**	**0.846**	**0.940**	**0.976**
ii)	Godard et al. [13]	CS	0.699	10.060	14.445	0.542	94.757	0.053	0.326	0.862
	MonoGAN	CS	**0.668**	**9.488**	**14.051**	**0.526**	**94.092**	**0.063**	**0.394**	**0.876**
iii)	Godard et al. [13]	CS+K	0.104	1.070	5.417	0.188	25.523	0.875	0.956	0.983
	MonoGAN	CS+K	**0.102**	**1.023**	**5.390**	**0.185**	**25.081**	**0.878**	**0.958**	**0.984**
iv)	Godard et al. [13] + pp	CS+K	0.100	0.934	**5.141**	0.178	25.077	0.878	0.961	0.986
	MonoGAN + pp	CS+K	**0.098**	**0.908**	5.164	**0.177**	**23.999**	**0.879**	0.961	0.986

5.1   Implementation Details

For our GAN model, we deploy a VGG-based generator as in [13] counting 31 million parameters. We designed the discriminator in a similar way but, since the task of the discriminator is easier compared to the one tackled by the generator, we reduced the amount of feature maps extracted by each layer by a factor of two to obtain a less complex architecture. In fact, it counts about 8 million parameters, bringing the total number of variables of the overall framework to 39 million at training time. At test time, the discriminator is no longer required, restoring the same network configuration of [13] and thus the same computational efficiency.

For a fair comparison, we tune hyper-parameters such as learning rate or weights applied to loss terms to match those in [13], trained with a multi-scale data term while the adversarial contribution is computed at full resolution only. Being the task of D easier compared to depth estimation performed by G, we interleave the updates applied to the two. To this aim we introduce a further hyper-parameter k as the ratio between the number of training iterations performed on G and those on D, in addition to α_{adv}. In other words, discriminator weights are updated only every k updates of the generator. We will report

Table 2. Results for unsupervised techniques on the original Eigen et al. [6] split based on raw Velodyne data.

Method	cap	Dataset	Proposed method Abs Rel	Lower is better Sq Rel	RMSE	RMSE log	Higher is better $\delta < 1.25$	$\delta < 1.25^2$	$\delta < 1.25^3$
Zhou et al. [54]	80 m	CS+K	0.198	1.836	6.565	0.275	0.718	0.901	0.960
Mahjourian et al. [27]	80 m	CS+K	0.159	1.231	5.912	0.243	0.784	0.923	0.970
Yin et al. [47]	80 m	CS+K	0.153	1.328	5.737	0.232	0.802	0.934	0.972
Wang et al. [42]	80 m	CS+K	0.148	1.187	5.496	0.226	0.812	0.938	0.975
Poggi et al. [32] (200)	80 m	CS+K	0.146	1.291	5.907	0.245	0.801	0.926	0.967
Godard et al. [13]	80 m	CS+K	0.124	1.076	5.311	0.219	0.847	0.942	0.973
MonoGAN	80 m	CS+K	0.124	1.055	5.289	0.220	0.847	0.942	0.973
Godard et al. [13] + pp	80 m	CS+K	**0.118**	0.923	5.015	**0.210**	0.854	0.947	**0.976**
MonoGAN + pp	80 m	CS+K	**0.118**	**0.908**	**4.978**	**0.210**	**0.855**	**0.948**	**0.976**
Garg et al. [10]	50 m	K	0.169	1.080	5.104	0.273	0.740	0.904	0.962
Zhou et al. [54]	50 m	CS+K	0.190	1.436	4.975	0.258	0.735	0.915	0.968
Mahjourian et al. [27]	50 m	CS+K	0.151	0.949	4.383	0.227	0.802	0.935	0.974
Poggi et al. [32] (200)	50 m	CS+K	0.138	0.937	4.488	0.230	0.815	0.934	0.972
Godard et al. [13]	50 m	CS+K	0.117	0.762	3.972	0.206	0.860	0.948	0.976
MonoGAN	50 m	CS+K	0.118	0.761	3.995	0.208	0.860	0.949	0.976
Godard et al. [13] + pp	50 m	CS+K	**0.112**	0.680	3.810	**0.198**	0.866	**0.953**	**0.979**
MonoGAN + pp	50 m	CS+K	**0.112**	**0.673**	**3.804**	**0.198**	**0.868**	**0.953**	**0.979**

evaluations for different values of parameter k. To jointly train both generator and discriminator we use two instances of Adam optimizer [19], with $\beta_1 = 0.9$, $\beta_2 = 0.99$ and $\epsilon = 10^{-8}$. The learning rate is the same for both instances: it is set at $\lambda = 10^{-4}$ for the first 30 epochs and then halved each 10 epochs. Number of epochs is set to 50 as for [13]. Training data are extracted from both KITTI raw sequences [30] and CityScapes dataset [3] providing respectively about 29000 and 23000 stereo pairs, these latter samples are cropped to remove lower part of the image frames (depicting a portion of the car used for acquisition) as in [13]. Moreover, as in [13] we perform data augmentation by randomly flipping input images horizontally and applying the following transformations: random gamma correction in [0.8, 1.2], additive brightness in [0.5, 2.0], and color shifts in [0.8, 1.2] for each channel separately. The same procedure is applied before forwarding images to both generator and discriminator.

5.2 Hyper-parameters Analysis

As mentioned before, our GAN model introduces two additional hyper-parameters: the weight α_{adv} applied to the adversarial loss acting on the generator and the iteration interval k between subsequent updating applied to the discriminator. Figure 4 reports an analysis aimed at finding the best configuration (α_{adv}, k). On each plot, we report an evaluation metric used to measure accuracy in the field of monocular depth estimation (e.g., in [13]) as a function of both α_{adv} and k. Respectively, on top we report from left to right Abs Rel, Sq Rel and RMSE (lower scores are better), on bottom $\delta < 125$, $\delta < 125^2$ and $\delta < 125^3$ (higher scores are better). These results were obtained training MonoGAN on the 29000 KITTI stereo images [30], with α_{adv} set to 0.01, 0.001 and 0.0001 and k to 1, 5 and 10, for a total of 9 models trained and evaluated in Fig. 4. We can notice how the configuration $\alpha_{adv} = 0.0001$ and $k = 5$ achieves the best performance with all evaluated metrics. According to this analysis we use these hyper-parameters in the next experiments, unless otherwise stated. It is worth to note that despite the much smaller magnitude of α_{adv} compared to weights α_{ap}, α_{ds} and α_{lr} in data term (5), its contribution will affect significantly depth estimation accuracy as reported in the remainder.

(a)   (b)

Fig. 5. Qualitative comparison between (a) reprojected raw Velodyne points as done in the original Eigen split for results reported in Table 2 and (b) reprojected ground-truth labels filtered according to [40], available on the KITTI website, deployed for our additional experiments reported in Table 3. Warmer colors encode closer points.

5.3   Evaluation on KITTI Dataset

Table 1 reports experimental results on the KITTI 2015 stereo dataset. For this evaluation, 200 images with provided ground-truth disparity from KITTI 2015 stereo dataset are used for validation, as proposed in [13]. We report results for different training schedules: running 50 epochs on data from KITTI only (K), from CityScapes only (CS) and 50 epochs on CityScapes followed by 50 on KITTI (CS + K). We compare our proposal to state-of-the-art method for unsupervised monocular depth estimation proposed by Godard et al. [13] reporting for this method the outcome of the evaluation available in the original paper. Table 1 is divided into four main sections, representing four different experiments. In particular, (i) compares MonoGAN with [13] when both trained on K. We can observe how our framework significantly outperforms the competitor on all metrics. Experiment (ii) concerns the two models trained on CityScapes data [3] and evaluated on KITTI stereo images, thus measuring the generalization capability across different environments. In particular, CityScapes and KITTI images differ

Table 3. Results for MonoGAN and Godard et al. [13] on 93.5% of Eigen et al. [6] split using accurate ground-truth labels [40] recently made available by KITTI evaluation benchmark.

Method	cap	Dataset	Proposed method	Lower is better			Higher is better		
			Abs Rel	Sq Rel	RMSE	RMSE log	$\delta <1.25$	$\delta < 1.25^2$	$\delta < 1.25^3$
Godard et al. [13]	80 m	CS+K	0.097	0.728	4.279	0.151	0.898	0.973	0.991
MonoGAN	80 m	CS+K	**0.096**	**0.699**	**4.236**	**0.150**	**0.899**	**0.974**	**0.992**
Godard et al. [13] + pp	80 m	CS+K	0.092	0.596	3.977	0.145	0.902	0.975	0.992
MonoGAN + pp	80 m	CS+K	**0.090**	**0.566**	**3.911**	**0.143**	**0.906**	**0.977**	**0.993**
Godard et al. [13]	50 m	CS+K	0.095	0.607	**4.100**	0.149	0.896	0.975	0.992
MonoGAN	50 m	CS+K	**0.094**	**0.600**	4.110	**0.148**	**0.897**	**0.976**	**0.993**
Godard et al. [13] + pp	50 m	CS+K	0.091	0.544	3.996	0.145	0.899	0.976	0.993
MonoGAN + pp	50 m	CS+K	**0.089**	**0.522**	**3.958**	**0.143**	**0.902**	**0.978**	**0.994**

not only in terms of scene contents but also for the camera setup. We can notice that MonoGAN better generalizes when dealing with different data. In (iii), we train both models on CityScapes first and then on KITTI, showing that Mono-GAN better benefits from using different datasets at training time compared to [13] thus confirming the positive trend outlined in the previous experiments. Finally, in (iv) we test the network trained in (iii) refining the results with the same post-processing step described in [13]. It consists in predicting depth for both original and horizontally flipped input image, then taking 5% right-most pixels from the first and 5% left-most from the second, while averaging the two predictions for remaining pixels. With such post-processing, excluding one case out of 6 (i.e., with the RMSE metric) MonoGAN has better or equivalent performance compared to [13]. Overall, the evaluation on KITTI 2015 dataset highlights the effectiveness of the proposed GAN paradigm. In experiments (iii) and (iv), we exploited adversarial loss only during the second part of the training (i.e., on K) thus starting from the same model of [13] trained as in experiment (ii), with the aim to assess how the discriminator improves the performance of a pre-trained model. Moreover, when fine-tuning we find beneficial to change the α_{adv} weight, similarly to traditional learning rate decimation techniques. In particular, we increased the adversarial weight α_{adv} from 0.0001 to 0.001 after 150k iterations (out of 181k total).

5.4   Evaluation on Eigen Split

We report additional experiments conducted on the split of data proposed by Eigen et al. in [6]. This validation set is made of 697 depth maps obtained by projecting 3D points inferred by a Velodyne laser into the left image of the acquired stereo pairs in 29 out of 61 scenes. The remaining 32 scenes are used to extract 22600 training samples. We compare to other monocular depth estimation framework following the same protocol proposed in [13] using the same crop dimensions and parameters.

Table 2 reports a detailed comparison of unsupervised methods. On top, we evaluated depth maps up to a maximum distance of 80 m. We can observe how MonoGAN performs on par or better than Godard et al. [13] outperforming it in terms of Sq Rel and RMSE errors and $\delta < 1.25$, $\delta < 1.25^2$ metrics. On the bottom of the table, we evaluate up to 50 m maximum distance to compare with Garg et al. [10]. This evaluation substantially confirms the previous trend. As for experiments on KITTI 2015 stereo dataset, we find out that increasing by a factor 10 the adversarial weight α_{adv} from 0.0001 to 0.001 after 150k iterations out of 181k total increases the accuracy of MonoGAN. Apparently, the margin between MonoGAN and [13] is much lower on this evaluation data. However, as already pointed out in [13] and [40], depth data obtained through Velodyne projection are affected by errors introduced by the rotation of the sensor, the motion of the vehicle and surrounding objects and also incorrect depth readings due to occlusion at object boundaries. Therefore, to better assess the performance of our proposal with respect to state-of-the-art we also considered the same split of images with more accurate ground-truth labels made available by Uhrig et al. [40] and now officially distributed as depth ground-truth maps by KITTI benchmark. These maps are obtained by filtering Velodyne data with disparity obtained by the Semi Global Matching algorithm [15] so as to remove outliers from the original measurements. Figure 5 shows a qualitative comparison between depth labels from raw Velodyne data reprojected into the left image, deployed in the original Eigen split, and labels provided by [40], deployed for our additional evaluation. Comparing (a) and (b) to the reference image at the top we can easily notice in (a) several outliers close to the tree trunk border not detectable in (b). Unfortunately, accurate ground-truth maps provided by [40] are not available for 45 images of the original Eigen split. Therefore, the number of testing images is reduced from 697 to 652. However, at the expense of a very small reduction of validation samples (i.e., 6.5%) we get much more reliable ground-truth data according to [40]. With such accurate data, Table 3 reports a comparison between [13] and MonoGAN with and without post-processing, thresholding at 80 and 50 m as for previous experiment on standard Eigen split. From Table 3 we can notice how with all metrics, excluding one case, MonoGAN on this more reliable dataset outperforms [13] confirming the trend already reported in Table 1 on the accurate KITTI 2015 benchmark.

6   Conclusions

In this paper, we proposed to tackle monocular depth estimation as an image generation task by means of a Generative Adversarial Networks paradigm. Exploiting at training time stereo images, the generator learns to infer depth from the reference image and from this data to generate a warped target image. The discriminator is trained to distinguish between real images and fake ones generated by the generator. Extensive experimental results confirm that our proposal outperforms known techniques for unsupervised monocular depth estimation.

Acknowledgement. We gratefully acknowledge the support of NVIDIA Corporation with the donation of the Titan X Pascal GPU used for this research.

References

1. Atapour-Abarghouei, A., Breckon, T.P.: Real-time monocular depth estimation using synthetic data with domain adaptation via image style transfer. In: The IEEE Conference on Computer Vision and Pattern Recognition (CVPR) (2018)
2. Cao, Y., Wu, Z., Shen, C.: Estimating depth from monocular images as classification using deep fully convolutional residual networks. IEEE Trans. Circuits Syst. Video Technol. (2017)
3. Cordts, M., et al.: The cityscapes dataset for semantic urban scene understanding. In: Proceedings of the IEEE Conference on Computer Vision and Pattern Recognition, pp. 3213–3223 (2016)
4. Kumar, A.C.S., Bhandarkar, S.M., Mukta, P.: DepthNet: a recurrent neural network architecture for monocular depth prediction. In: 1st International Workshop on Deep Learning for Visual SLAM (CVPR) (2018)
5. Denton, E.L., Chintala, S., Fergus, R., et al.: Deep generative image models using a Laplacian pyramid of adversarial networks. In: Advances in Neural Information Processing Systems, pp. 1486–1494 (2015)
6. Eigen, D., Puhrsch, C., Fergus, R.: Depth map prediction from a single image using a multi-scale deep network. In: Advances in Neural Information Processing Systems, pp. 2366–2374 (2014)
7. Flynn, J., Neulander, I., Philbin, J., Snavely, N.: DeepStereo: learning to predict new views from the world's imagery. In: Proceedings of the IEEE Conference on Computer Vision and Pattern Recognition, pp. 5515–5524 (2016)
8. Fu, H., Gong, M., Wang, C., Batmanghelich, K., Tao, D.: Deep ordinal regression network for monocular depth estimation. In: The IEEE Conference on Computer Vision and Pattern Recognition (CVPR) (2018)
9. Furukawa, Y., Hernández, C., et al.: Multi-view stereo: a tutorial. Found. Trends® Comput. Graph. Vis. 9(1–2), 1–148 (2015)
10. Garg, R., Carneiro, G., Reid, I., Vijay Kumar, B.G., et al.: Unsupervised CNN for Single View Depth Estimation: Geometry to the Rescue. In: Leibe, B., Matas, J., Sebe, N., Welling, M. (eds.) ECCV 2016. LNCS, vol. 9912, pp. 740–756. Springer, Cham (2016). https://doi.org/10.1007/978-3-319-46484-8_45
11. Geiger, A., Lenz, P., Stiller, C., Urtasun, R.: Vision meets robotics: the KITTI dataset. Int. J. Robot. Res. (IJRR) 32, 1231–1237 (2013)
12. Geiger, A., Lenz, P., Urtasun, R.: Are we ready for autonomous driving? The KITTI vision benchmark suite. In: 2012 IEEE Conference on Computer Vision and Pattern Recognition (CVPR), pp. 3354–3361. IEEE (2012)
13. Godard, C., Mac Aodha, O., Brostow, G.J.: Unsupervised monocular depth estimation with left-right consistency. In: CVPR, vol. 2, p. 7 (2017)
14. Goodfellow, I., et al.: Generative adversarial nets. In: Advances in Neural Information Processing Systems, pp. 2672–2680 (2014)
15. Hirschmuller, H.: Accurate and efficient stereo processing by semi-global matching and mutual information. In: 2005 IEEE Computer Society Conference on Computer Vision and Pattern Recognition. CVPR 2005, vol. 2, pp. 807–814. IEEE (2005)
16. Jaderberg, M., Simonyan, K., Zisserman, A., et al.: Spatial transformer networks. In: Advances in Neural Information Processing Systems, pp. 2017–2025 (2015)
17. Karsch, K., Liu, C., Kang, S.: Depth transfer: depth extraction from video using non-parametric sampling. IEEE Trans. Pattern Anal. Mach. Intell. 36(11), 2144–2158 (2014)

18. Kendall, A., et al.: End-to-end learning of geometry and context for deep stereo regression. In: The IEEE International Conference on Computer Vision (ICCV), October 2017
19. Kingma, D., Ba, J.: Adam: a method for stochastic optimization. arXiv preprint arXiv:1412.6980 (2014)
20. Kuznietsov, Y., Stuckler, J., Leibe, B.: Semi-supervised deep learning for monocular depth map prediction. In: The IEEE Conference on Computer Vision and Pattern Recognition (CVPR), July 2017
21. Ladicky, L., Shi, J., Pollefeys, M.: Pulling things out of perspective. In: Proceedings of the IEEE Conference on Computer Vision and Pattern Recognition, pp. 89–96 (2014)
22. Laina, I., Rupprecht, C., Belagiannis, V., Tombari, F., Navab, N.: Deeper depth prediction with fully convolutional residual networks. In: 2016 Fourth International Conference on 3D Vision (3DV), pp. 239–248. IEEE (2016)
23. Li, B., Shen, C., Dai, Y., van den Hengel, A., He, M.: Depth and surface normal estimation from monocular images using regression on deep features and hierarchical CRFs. In: Proceedings of the IEEE Conference on Computer Vision and Pattern Recognition, pp. 1119–1127 (2015)
24. Liu, F., Shen, C., Lin, G., Reid, I.: Learning depth from single monocular images using deep convolutional neural fields. IEEE Trans. Pattern Anal. Mach. Intell. **38**(10), 2024–2039 (2016)
25. Luo, W., Schwing, A.G., Urtasun, R.: Efficient deep learning for stereo matching. In: Proceedings of the IEEE Conference on Computer Vision and Pattern Recognition, pp. 5695–5703 (2016)
26. Luo, Y., et al.: Single view stereo matching. In: The IEEE Conference on Computer Vision and Pattern Recognition (CVPR) (2018)
27. Mahjourian, R., Wicke, M., Angelova, A.: Unsupervised learning of depth and ego-motion from monocular video using 3D geometric constraints. In: The IEEE Conference on Computer Vision and Pattern Recognition (CVPR) (2018)
28. Mathieu, M.F., Zhao, J.J., Zhao, J., Ramesh, A., Sprechmann, P., LeCun, Y.: Disentangling factors of variation in deep representation using adversarial training. In: Advances in Neural Information Processing Systems, pp. 5040–5048 (2016)
29. Mayer, N., et al.: A large dataset to train convolutional networks for disparity, optical flow, and scene flow estimation. In: Proceedings of the IEEE Conference on Computer Vision and Pattern Recognition, pp. 4040–4048 (2016)
30. Menze, M., Geiger, A.: Object scene flow for autonomous vehicles. In: Conference on Computer Vision and Pattern Recognition (CVPR) (2015)
31. Pang, J., Sun, W., Ren, J.S., Yang, C., Yan, Q.: Cascade residual learning: a two-stage convolutional neural network for stereo matching. In: The IEEE International Conference on Computer Vision (ICCV), October 2017
32. Poggi, M., Aleotti, F., Tosi, F., Mattoccia, S.: Towards real-time unsupervised monocular depth estimation on CPU. In: IEEE/JRS Conference on Intelligent Robots and Systems (IROS) (2018)
33. Poggi, M., Tosi, F., Mattoccia, S.: Learning monocular depth estimation with unsupervised trinocular assumptions. In: 6th International Conference on 3D Vision (3DV) (2018)
34. Radford, A., Metz, L., Chintala, S.: Unsupervised representation learning with deep convolutional generative adversarial networks. arXiv preprint arXiv:1511.06434 (2015)

35. Ranftl, R., Vineet, V., Chen, Q., Koltun, V.: Dense monocular depth estimation in complex dynamic scenes. In: Proceedings of the IEEE Conference on Computer Vision and Pattern Recognition, pp. 4058–4066 (2016)
36. Reed, S., Akata, Z., Yan, X., Logeswaran, L., Schiele, B., Lee, H.: Generative adversarial text to image synthesis. arXiv preprint arXiv:1605.05396 (2016)
37. Saxena, A., Sun, M., Ng, A.Y.: Make3d: learning 3d scene structure from a single still image. IEEE Trans. Pattern Anal. Mach. Intell. **31**(5), 824–840 (2009)
38. Scharstein, D., et al.: High-resolution stereo datasets with subpixel-accurate ground truth. In: Jiang, X., Hornegger, J., Koch, R. (eds.) GCPR 2014. LNCS, vol. 8753, pp. 31–42. Springer, Cham (2014). https://doi.org/10.1007/978-3-319-11752-2_3
39. Scharstein, D., Szeliski, R.: A taxonomy and evaluation of dense two-frame stereo correspondence algorithms. Int. J. Comput. Vision **47**(1–3), 7–42 (2002)
40. Uhrig, J., Schneider, N., Schneider, L., Franke, U., Brox, T., Geiger, A.: Sparsity invariant CNNs. In: International Conference on 3D Vision (3DV) (2017)
41. Ummenhofer, B., et al.: Demon: depth and motion network for learning monocular stereo. In: IEEE Conference on Computer Vision and Pattern Recognition (CVPR), vol. 5 (2017)
42. Wang, C., Buenaposada, J.M., Zhu, R., Lucey, S.: Learning depth from monocular videos using direct methods. In: The IEEE Conference on Computer Vision and Pattern Recognition (CVPR) (2018)
43. Wang, X., Fouhey, D., Gupta, A.: Designing deep networks for surface normal estimation. In: Proceedings of the IEEE Conference on Computer Vision and Pattern Recognition, pp. 539–547 (2015)
44. Wang, Z., Bovik, A.C., Sheikh, H.R., Simoncelli, E.P.: Image quality assessment: from error visibility to structural similarity. IEEE Trans. Image Process. **13**(4), 600–612 (2004)
45. Woodham, R.J.: Photometric method for determining surface orientation from multiple images. Opt. Eng. **19**(1), 191139 (1980)
46. Xie, J., Girshick, R., Farhadi, A.: Deep3D: fully automatic 2D-to-3D video conversion with deep convolutional neural networks. In: Leibe, B., Matas, J., Sebe, N., Welling, M. (eds.) ECCV 2016. LNCS, vol. 9908, pp. 842–857. Springer, Cham (2016). https://doi.org/10.1007/978-3-319-46493-0_51
47. Yin, Z., Shi, J.: GeoNet: unsupervised learning of dense depth, optical flow and camera pose. In: The IEEE Conference on Computer Vision and Pattern Recognition (CVPR) (2018)
48. Yang, N., Wang, R., Stückler, J., Cremers, D.: Deep virtual stereo odometry: leveraging deep depth prediction for monocular direct sparse odometry. In: Ferrari, V., Hebert, M., Sminchisescu, C., Weiss, Y. (eds.) ECCV 2018. LNCS, vol. 11212, pp. 835–852. Springer, Cham (2018). https://doi.org/10.1007/978-3-030-01237-3_50
49. Ramirez, P.Z., Poggi, M., Tosi, F., Mattoccia, S., Stefano, L.D.: Geometry meets semantic for semi-supervised monocular depth estimation. In: 14th Asian Conference on Computer Vision (ACCV) (2018)
50. Zbontar, J., LeCun, Y.: Computing the stereo matching cost with a convolutional neural network. In: Proceedings of the IEEE Conference on Computer Vision and Pattern Recognition, pp. 1592–1599 (2015)
51. Zbontar, J., LeCun, Y.: Stereo matching by training a convolutional neural network to compare image patches. J. Mach. Learn. Res. **17**(1–32), 2 (2016)
52. Zhan, H., Garg, R., Weerasekera, C.S., Li, K., Agarwal, H., Reid, I.: Unsupervised learning of monocular depth estimation and visual odometry with deep feature reconstruction. In: The IEEE Conference on Computer Vision and Pattern Recognition (CVPR) (2018)

53. Zhang, H., et al.: StackGAN: text to photo-realistic image synthesis with stacked generative adversarial networks. In: IEEE International Conference Computer Vision (ICCV), pp. 5907–5915 (2017)
54. Zhou, T., Brown, M., Snavely, N., Lowe, D.G.: Unsupervised learning of depth and ego-motion from video. In: CVPR, vol. 2, p. 7 (2017)
55. Zhu, J.-Y., Krähenbühl, P., Shechtman, E., Efros, A.A.: Generative visual manipulation on the natural image manifold. In: Leibe, B., Matas, J., Sebe, N., Welling, M. (eds.) ECCV 2016. LNCS, vol. 9909, pp. 597–613. Springer, Cham (2016). https://doi.org/10.1007/978-3-319-46454-1_36
56. Zhu, J.-Y., Park, T., Isola, P., Efros, A.A.:. Unpaired image-to-image translation using cycle-consistent adversarial networks. arXiv preprint arXiv:1703.10593 (2017)

Combination of Spatially-Modulated ToF and Structured Light for MPI-Free Depth Estimation

Gianluca Agresti[(✉)] and Pietro Zanuttigh

Department of Information Engineering, University of Padova, Padova, Italy
{gianluca.agresti,zanuttigh}@dei.unipd.it

Abstract. Multi-path Interference (MPI) is one of the major sources of error in Time-of-Flight (ToF) camera depth measurements. A possible solution for its removal is based on the separation of direct and global light through the projection of multiple sinusoidal patterns. In this work we extend this approach by applying a Structured Light (SL) technique on the same projected patterns. This allows to compute two depth maps with a single ToF acquisition, one with the Time-of-Flight principle and the other with the Structured Light principle. The two depth fields are finally combined using a Maximum-Likelihood approach in order to obtain an accurate depth estimation free from MPI error artifacts. Experimental results demonstrate that the proposed method has very good MPI correction properties with state-of-the-art performances.

Keywords: ToF sensors · Multi-path · Structured Light · Depth acquisition · Data fusion

1 Introduction

Continuous-wave Time-of-Flight (ToF) cameras attracted a large attention both from the research community and for commercial applications due to their ability to robustly measure the scene depth in real-time. They have been employed for many computer vision applications including human body tracking, 3D scene reconstruction, robotics, object detection and hand gesture recognition [1–4]. The success of this kind of systems is given by their benefits, e.g., the simplicity of processing operations for the estimation of the depth maps, the absence of moving components, the possibility to generate a dense depth map, the absence of artifacts due to occlusions and scene texture. Other depth estimation systems as Structured Light (SL) and stereo vision systems have weaknesses due to these aspects and so it is preferable to use ToF cameras in many situations [5].

Beside these good aspects, ToF cameras have also some limitations for which they need to be further analyzed and improved. Some of these limitations are

Electronic supplementary material The online version of this chapter (https://doi.org/10.1007/978-3-030-11009-3_21) contains supplementary material, which is available to authorized users.

© Springer Nature Switzerland AG 2019
L. Leal-Taixé and S. Roth (Eds.): ECCV 2018 Workshops, LNCS 11129, pp. 355–371, 2019.
https://doi.org/10.1007/978-3-030-11009-3_21

a low spatial resolution due to the complexity of pixel hardware required for the depth estimation, the presence of a maximum measurable distance, estimation artifacts on the edges and corners and the wrong depth estimation due to the Multi-Path Interference (MPI) phenomenon. The latter corresponds to the fact that ToF cameras work under the hypothesis that each pixel of the sensor observes a single optical ray emitted by the ToF projector and reflected only once in the scene [6], the so called direct component of the light. This hypothesis is often violated and since a part of the emitted light (called the global component of the light) could experience multiple reflections inside the scene, the rays related to different paths are received by a pixel leading to wrong estimation of the corresponding depth [5,7,8]. MPI is one of the major sources of error in ToF camera depth measurements. Many works in the literature (see Sect. 2) deal with this problem, but the removal of MPI error remains a challenging issue. A possible approach for this problem is based on the separation of the direct and global component of the light through the projection of multiple sinusoidal patterns as proposed by Whyte et al. [8]. This allows to correct a wide range of MPI phenomena as inter-reflection, surface scattering and lens flare but the obtained depth estimations are noisier if compared with standard ToF system. This work starts from this rationale but goes further by combining a ToF system based on this idea with a SL depth estimation approach. The presented technique gives the possibility to compute two depth maps, one with the ToF approach and the other with the SL approach, using a single acquisition. Then a statistical fusion between the two depth maps is described. In order to evaluate the performance of the proposed method we tested it on a synthetic dataset. Similarly to [9], we rendered different 3D synthetic scenes using *Blender* [10] and ToF data have been extracted from these using the *ToF Explorer* simulator realized by Sony EuTEC starting from the work of Meister et al. [11], able to reproduce various ToF acquisition issues including global illumination. Experimental results show very good MPI correction properties and the higher accuracy of the depth estimation compared with Whyte method [8] and with standard ToF cameras.

After presenting the main methods for MPI correction proposed in the literature in Sect. 2, we analyze the ToF depth acquisition process and the MPI removal by illuminating the scene with time varying high spatial frequency patterns in Sect. 3. The same patterns can be exploited for the computation of a second depth map with a SL approach as it will be described in Sect. 4. This depth map will prove to be less noisy than the Whyte method (STM-ToF) in the near range. Finally, the STM-ToF and SL depths will be fused together using a statistical approach exploiting the estimated noise statistics (Sect. 5). The experimental results in Sect. 6 show how the proposed method is able to reduce the MPI effect and outperform state-of-the-art methods.

2   Related Works

Many methods have been proposed in order to try to estimate the direct component of the light and thus remove the MPI error but this task in Continuous-Wave

ToF systems is particularly complex. This is due to various reasons: first of all, when a light with sinusoidal intensity modulation hits a scene element its modulation frequency is not modified and only the amplitude and the phase of the modulation wave are affected [7]. A consequence is that all the interfering light rays have the same modulation frequency and when some of them are summed together (direct light summed to the global light) the resulting waveform is another sinusoid with the same frequency of the projected modulated light but different phase and amplitude. Thus MPI effects can not be detected only by looking at the received waveform. Moreover MPI effects are related to the scene geometry and materials. From this rationale it follows that MPI correction is a ill-posed problem in standard ToF systems without hardware modifications or not using multiple modulation frequencies. Since MPI is one of the major sources of errors in ToF cameras [7, 12–14] and its effects can dramatically corrupt the depth estimation, different algorithms and hardware modifications have been proposed: an exhaustive review of the methods can be found in [15].

A first family of methods tries to model the light as the summation of a finite number of interfering rays. A possible solution is to use multiple modulation frequencies and exploit the frequency diversity of MPI to estimate the depth related to the direct component of the light as shown by Freedman et al. in [14] and by Bhandari et al. in [12]. In [14] an iterative method for the correction of MPI on commercial ToF systems is proposed based on the idea of using $m = 3$ modulation frequencies and exploiting the fact that the effects of MPI are frequency dependent. Bhandari et al. presented in [12] a closed form solution for MPI correction and a theoretically lower bound for the number of modulation frequencies required to solve the interference of a fixed number of rays. This method is effective against specular reflections but it requires a pre-defined maximum number of interfering rays as initial hypothesis. Differently, the method proposed by Kadambi et al. [13] computes a time profile of the incoming light for each pixel to correct MPI. The method requires to modulate the single frequency ToF waveforms with random on-off codes but the ToF acquisitions last about 4 s. O'Toole et al. [16] proposed a ToF system for global light transport estimation with a modified projector that emits a spatio-temporal signal.

Another approach to correct MPI is to use single frequency ToF data and to exploit a reflection model in order to estimate the geometry of the scene and correct MPI. Fuchs et al. presented in [17] a method where a 2 bounces scenario is considered. In [18], this method is improved by taking in account materials with multiple albedo and reflections. Jimenez et al. [19] proposed a method based on a similar idea implemented as a non-linear optimization.

Some recent methods use data driven approaches based on machine learning for MPI removal on single frequency ToF acquisitions [20, 21]. In [20], the target was to solve MPI in small scenes acquired from a robotic arm. In [21], a CNN with an auto-encoder structure is trained in 2 phases, first using real world depth data without ground truth, then keeping fixed the encoder part and re-training the decoder with a synthetic dataset whose true depth is known in order to learn how to correct MPI. In [22–24], CNNs are trained on synthetic datasets with the task of estimating a refined depth map from multi-frequency ToF data and in [22] a quantitative analysis on real ToF data is carried out.

Other approaches are based on the main assumption that the light is described as the summation of only two sinusoidal waves, one related to the direct component while the other groups together all the sinusoidal waves related to global light. In [7] the analysis is focused on the relationships between the global light component and the modulation frequency of the ToF systems. The authors discussed that the global response of the scenes is temporally smooth and it can be assumed band-limited in case of diffuse reflections. By consequence, if the employed modulation frequency is higher than a certain threshold that is scene-depend, the global sinusoidal term is going to vanish. This observation is used to theoretically model a MPI correction method, however this method requires very high modulation frequencies (~1 GHz) not possible with nowadays ToF cameras. The method that we are going to present in this paper, as also the ones of Naik et al. [25] and of Whyte et al. [8] (from which we started for the ToF estimation part of Sect. 3), uses a modified ToF projector able to emit a spatial high frequency pattern in order to separate the global and direct component of the light and so correct MPI. These methods rely on the studies of Nayar et al. [26] and allow to correct MPI in case of diffuse reflections.

3   Time-of-Flight Depth Acquisition with Direct and Global Light Separation

3.1   Basic Principles of ToF Acquisition

Continuous-Wave ToF cameras use an infra-red projector to illuminate the scene with a periodic amplitude modulated light signal, e.g., a sinusoidal wave, and evaluate the depth from the phase displacement between the transmitted and received signal. The projected light signal can be represented as

$$s_t(t) = \frac{1}{2}a_t\big(1 + \sin(\omega_r t)\big) \qquad (1)$$

where t is the time, ω_r is the signal angular frequency equal to $\omega_r = 2\pi f_{mod}$ and a_t is the maximum power emitted by the projector. The temporal modulation frequency f_{mod} is in nowadays sensors in the range [10 MHz; 100 MHz]. The received light signal can be modeled as:

$$s_r(t) = b_r + \frac{1}{2}a_r\big(1 + \sin(\omega_r t - \phi)\big) \qquad (2)$$

where b_r is the light offset due to the ambient light, $a_r = \alpha a_t$ with α equal to the channel attenuation and ϕ is the phase displacement between the transmitted and received signal. The scene depth d can be computed from ϕ through the well known relation $d = \frac{\phi c_l}{2\omega_r}$ where c_l is the speed of light. The ToF pixels are able to compute the correlation function between the received signal and a reference one, e.g., a rectangular wave at the same modulation frequency

$rect_{\omega_r}(t) = H\big(\sin(\omega_r t)\big)$, where $H(\cdot)$ represents the Heaviside function. The correlation function sampled in $\omega_r \tau_i \in [0; 2\pi)$ can be modelled as

$$c(\omega_r \tau_i) = \int_0^{\frac{1}{f_{mod}}} s_r(t) rect_{\omega_r}(t + \tau_i) dt = \frac{1}{f_{mod}} \left[\frac{b_r}{2} + \frac{a_r}{4} + \frac{a_r}{2\pi} \cos(\omega_r \tau_i + \phi) \right]. \quad (3)$$

$c(\omega_r \tau_i)$ represents a measure of the number of photons accumulated during the integration time. By sampling the correlation function in different points (nowadays ToF cameras usually acquire 4 samples at $\omega_r \tau_i \in \{0; \frac{\pi}{2}; \pi; \frac{3\pi}{2}\}$), we have:

$$\phi = atan2\left(c(\frac{3\pi}{2}) - c(\frac{\pi}{2}), \; c(0) - c(\pi) \right). \quad (4)$$

The ToF depth estimation is correct if the light received by the sensor is reflected only once inside the scene (direct component of the light), but in real scenarios a part of the light emitted and received by the ToF system can also experience multiple reflections (global component of the light). Each of these reflections carries a sinusoidal signal with a different phase offset proportional to the length of the path followed by the light ray. In this scenario the correlation function can be modelled as

$$c(\omega_r \tau_i) = \frac{1}{f_{mod}} \left[\frac{b_r}{2} + \frac{a_r}{4} + \frac{a_r}{2\pi} \cos(\omega_r \tau_i + \phi_d) + \frac{b_{r,g}}{2} + \frac{a_{r,g}}{\pi} \cos(\omega_r \tau_i + \phi_g) \right] \quad (5)$$

where the first sinusoidal term is related to the direct component of the light and the second to the global one, $a_{r,g}$ and $b_{r,g}$ are respectively proportional to the amplitude and intensity of the global light waveform due to MPI. The superimposition of the direct and global components is the so called MPI phenomenon and corrupts the ToF depth generally causing a depth overestimation.

3.2   Direct and Global Light Separation

The key issue in order to obtain a correct depth estimation is to separate the direct component of the light from the global one. The approach we exploited is inspired by the method described by Whyte and Dorrington in [8, 27], but extends it taking into account the fact that most real world ToF cameras work with square wave modulations. The system presented in [8, 27] is composed by a standard ToF sensor and a modified ToF projector that emits a periodic light signal (Fig. 1): the standard temporally modulated ToF signal of (1) is also spatially modulated by a predefined intensity pattern. The projector and the camera are assumed to have parallel image planes. In the developed method we are going to consider the sinusoidal intensity pattern

$$L_{x,y}(\omega_r \tau_i) = \frac{1}{2}\left(1 + \cos\left(l\omega_r \tau_i - \theta_{x,y} \right) \right) \quad (6)$$

where (x, y) denote a pixel position on the projected image, $\theta_{x,y} = \frac{2\pi x}{p} + \sin\left(\frac{2\pi y}{q}\right)$ is the pattern phase offset at the projector pixel (x, y), p and q are respectively

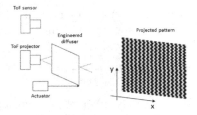

Fig. 1. ToF acquisition system for direct and global light separation.

	$i = 0$	$i = 1$	$i = 2$	$i = 3$	$i = 4$	$i = 5$	$i = 6$	$i = 7$	$i = 8$
Sampling point of the ToF correlation function $\omega_r \tau_i$	0	$\dfrac{2\pi}{9}$	$\dfrac{4\pi}{9}$	$\dfrac{6\pi}{9}$	$\dfrac{8\pi}{9}$	$\dfrac{10\pi}{9}$	$\dfrac{12\pi}{9}$	$\dfrac{14\pi}{9}$	$\dfrac{16\pi}{9}$
Phase shift of the projected pattern $l\omega_r \tau_i, \; l=3$	0	$\dfrac{2\pi}{3}$	$\dfrac{4\pi}{3}$	0	$\dfrac{2\pi}{3}$	$\dfrac{4\pi}{3}$	0	$\dfrac{2\pi}{3}$	$\dfrac{4\pi}{3}$
Employed pattern									

Fig. 2. Synchronization between phase shift of the projected pattern and phase sample of the ToF correlation function.

the periodicity of the pattern in the horizontal and in the vertical direction, l is a positive integer number and $\omega_r \tau_i \in [0; 2\pi)$ is a sampling point of the ToF correlation function as defined in (3). Notice that for each computed sample of the ToF correlation function a specific pattern is used to modulate the standard ToF signal of Eq. (1). Denoting the angular modulation frequency of the ToF camera as $\omega_r = 2\pi f_{mod}$, the projected pattern $L(\omega_r \tau_i)$ is phase shifted with angular frequency $l\omega_r$. Figure 2 shows the pattern projection sequence for the case in which $l = 3$ and the ToF camera evaluates 9 samples of the correlation function. When the ToF signal is modulated by the phase shifted patterns depicted in Fig. 2 considering the proposed synchronization between the pattern phase offsets and the ToF correlation sampling points, and by assuming that the spatial frequency of the projected patterns is high enough to separate the direct and global component of the light [26] (this holds in case of absence of specular reflections), it results that only the direct component of the light is modulated by the patterns. In this case the ToF correlation function (5) computed by the ToF camera on a generic pixel can be modelled as:

$$c(\omega_r \tau_i) = B + A\cos(\omega_r \tau_i + \phi_d) + A_g \cos(\omega_r \tau_i + \phi_g) + \frac{\pi A}{2} \cos(l\omega_r \tau_i - \theta)$$
$$+ \frac{A}{2}\Big[\cos\big((l-1)\omega_r \tau_i - \phi_d - \theta\big) + \cos\big((l+1)\omega_r \tau_i + \phi_d - \theta_{x,y}\big)\Big] \quad (7)$$

where $B = \frac{1}{f_{mod}}\left(\frac{b_r}{2} + \frac{a_r}{8} + \frac{b_{r,g}}{2}\right)$ is an additive constant that represents the received light offset, $A = \frac{a_r}{4\pi f_{mod}}$ is proportional to the power of the direct component of the received light, $A_g = \frac{a_{r,g}}{\pi f_{mod}}$ is proportional to the power of the global component of the received light, ϕ_d is the phase offset related to the direct component of the light (not affected by MPI), ϕ_g is the phase offset related to the MPI phenomenon and $\theta_{x,y}$ is the phase offset of the projected pattern on the specific scene point observed by the considered ToF pixel. Notice that both ϕ_d (through the ToF model of Sect. 3.1) and $\theta_{x,y}$ (through the SL approach of Sect. 4) can be used to estimate the depth at the considered location. In the following of this paper we are going to consider $l = 3$ since it avoids aliasing with 9 samples of the correlation function and no other value of l brings to a smaller number of acquired samples. By using these setting and opportunely arranging the acquisition process, the projector has to update the emitted sinusoidal patterns at 30 fps in order to produce depth images at 10 fps.

A first difference with the analysis carried out in [8,27] is that in these works the reference signal used for correlation by the ToF camera is a sine wave without offset, instead in our model we use a rectangular wave since this is the waveform used by most real world ToF sensors. This choice in the model brings to an harmonic at frequency $l = 3$ that was not considered in [8,27], and this harmonic is informative about the pattern phase offset θ. In the next section and more in detail in the *additional material* we will show that by estimating θ from this harmonic allows a more accurate estimation than computing it from the $(l-1) - th$ and $(l+1) - th$ harmonics. In order to estimate a depth map of the scene free from MPI we are going to apply Fourier analysis on the retrieved ToF correlation signal of (7) as also suggested in [8,27]. By labelling with φ_k the phase of the $k - th$ harmonic retrieved from the Fourier analysis we have that:

$$\phi_d = (\varphi_4 - \varphi_2)/2, \quad \theta = -\varphi_3 \tag{8}$$

By estimating ϕ_d as mentioned above we can retrieve a depth map of the scene that is not affected by MPI but the result appears to be noisier than standard ToF acquisitions as discussed in the next subsection. We are going to name the approach for MPI correction described in this section as *Spatially Temporally Modulated* ToF (STM-ToF). In Sect. 4, θ will be used for SL depth estimation.

3.3   Error Propagation Analysis

In order to evaluate the level of noise of the depth estimation with STM-ToF acquisition, we used an error propagation analysis to predict the effects of the noise acting on ToF correlation samples on the phase estimation. In particular, we consider the effects of the *photon shot* noise. The noise variance in standard ToF depth acquisitions can be computed with the classical model of [28–30]:

$$\sigma^2_{d_{std}} = \left(\frac{c}{4\pi f_{mod}}\right)^2 \frac{B_{std}}{2A^2_{std}}. \tag{9}$$

In a similar way we can estimate the level of noise in the proposed system.

If we assume to use 9 ToF correlation samples $c(\omega_r \tau_i)$ with $\omega_r \tau_i = \frac{2\pi}{9}i$ for $i = 0, ..., 8$ affected by photon shot noise it is possible to demonstrate (the complete derivation of the model through error propagation is in the *additional material*) that the mean value of the noise variance in the proposed approach is

$$\bar{\sigma}^2_{d_{noMPI}} = \left(\frac{c}{4\pi f_{mod}}\right)^2 \frac{4B}{9A^2}. \tag{10}$$

Here we are considering only the mean value of the noise variance for the estimated depth map, since the complete formulation contains also sinusoidal terms which depend on the scene depth and the pattern phase offset.

By comparing Eqs. (9) and (10) and opportunely considering the scaling effects due to the modulating projected pattern, if $b_r >> a_r$ (usually the case) we have that $\bar{\sigma}^2_{d_{noMPI}}/\sigma^2_{d_{std}} = 3.56$, i.e., the noise variance obtained by using the approach in [8] is around 4 times nosier if compared with a standard ToF camera that uses the same peak illumination power.

4   Applying Structured Light to ToF Sensors

In this section, we propose to use the pattern phase offset θ observed by the whole ToF sensor in order to estimate a second depth map of the scene with a Structured Light (SL) approach. The phase image θ can be estimated with the approach of Sect. 3.2, i.e., from Eq. (8). Notice that our model considers a rectangular wave as reference signal (that is typically the case in commercial ToF cameras) and we could exploit the harmonic at frequency $l = 3$ of Eq. (7), allowing to obtain a higher accuracy than using the second and the fourth harmonics as in [8]. More in detail, if we compare the level of noise in estimating θ from the second and fourth harmonics (i.e., as done in [8]) with the noise in the estimation from the third harmonic (as we propose), we have that:

$$\bar{\sigma}^2_{\varphi_2,\varphi_4} = \frac{4B}{9A^2}, \quad \bar{\sigma}^2_{\varphi_3} = \frac{8B}{9\pi^2 A^2}. \tag{11}$$

Thus θ estimated from the third harmonic has a noise variance about 4 times smaller if compared with the estimation from the second and fourth harmonics.

The estimated pattern phase offset can be used to compute the second depth map of the scene with the SL approach. If the pattern phase image θ_{ref} is captured on a reference scene for which the distance d_{ref} from the camera is known, e.g., a straight wall orthogonal to the optical axis of the camera, then it is possible to estimate the depth of any target scene by comparing pixel by pixel the estimated phase image θ_{target} with the reference one (see Fig. 3).

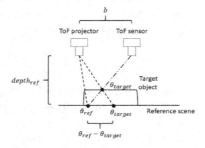

Fig. 3. Geometry of the SL acquisition on target and reference scenes.

A similar approach has been exploited by Xu et al. in [31] for standard color cameras. In that case a phase unwrapping of the phase images has to be applied before being able to estimate the depth. This can be obtained by projecting multiple lower frequency patterns on the scene. Assuming that θ_{ref} and θ_{target} have been phase unwrapped in θ_{ref}^{PU} and θ_{target}^{PU}, the depth of the target scene can be estimated as:

$$d_{SL} = d_{ref}\left(1 + \frac{Q}{b}\left(\theta_{ref}^{PU} - \theta_{target}^{PU}\right)\right)^{-1} \tag{12}$$

where d_{ref} is the distance between the reference scene and the ToF camera, Q is a parameter related to the acquisition system setup that can be estimated by calibration and b is the baseline between the camera and the projector, 3 cm in the proposed setup. In standard SL systems a bigger baseline (e.g., 10 cm) is required to reliably estimate depth in the far range, here we can afford a smaller one since we have also ToF data (more reliable in the far range) in the fusion process described in Sect. 5. Moreover, a smaller baseline reduces the problem of occlusions of standard SL estimation. Here we avoid the use of additional patterns for phase unwrapping by employing the ToF depth map computed with the method of Sect. 3. The idea is to use for implicit phase unwrapping the phase image θ_{ToF} that would have produced the ToF depth map in case of a SL acquisition. We can compute the depth with the SL approach assisted by the ToF estimation as:

$$d_{SL} = d_{ref}\left(1 + \frac{d_{ref} - d_{ToF}}{d_{ToF}} + \frac{Q}{b}\left(\theta_{ToF} - \theta_{target}\right)_{[-\pi;\pi]}\right)^{-1} \tag{13}$$

where:

$$\theta_{ToF} = \theta_{ref} - \frac{b}{Q} \cdot \frac{d_{ref} - d_{ToF}}{d_{ToF}} \tag{14}$$

In this approach we are using θ_{ToF} as a new reference phase offset to be used to estimate the SL depth map related to θ_{target}. We report the complete derivation of the SL implicit phase unwrapping in the *additional material*.

In this case the variance of the noise corrupting d_{SL} can be computed from error propagation analysis (see the *additional material* for more details):

$$\sigma_{d_{SL}}^2 = \left(Q\frac{d_{target}^2}{d_{ref}b}\right)^2 \sigma_\theta^2. \tag{15}$$

From Eq. (15) it is possible to notice that the depth estimation accuracy improves if we increase the baseline between the sensor and the projector and it degrades with the increase of the depth that we are going to estimate. This is a common behavior for SL systems. The reference scene distance d_{ref} has no effect in the accuracy since Q is directly proportional to d_{ref}.

5   Fusion of ToF and SL Depth Maps

The approaches of Sects. 3 and 4 allow to compute two different depth maps, one based on the Time-of-Flight estimation with MPI correction (the STM-ToF acquisition) and one based on a SL approach. In the final step the two depth maps must be fused into a single accurate depth image of the scene. The exploited fusion algorithm is based on the Maximum Likelihood (ML) principle [32]. The idea is to compute two functions representing the likelihoods of the possible depth values given the data computed by the two approaches and then look for the depth value Z that maximizes at each location the joint likelihood that is assumed to be composed by the independent contributions of the 2 depth sources [33,34]:

$$d_{fus}(i,j) = argmax_Z P\big(I_{ToF}(i,j)|Z\big) P\big(I_{SL}(i,j)|Z\big) \tag{16}$$

where $P\big(I_{ToF}(i,j)|Z\big)$ and $P\big(I_{SL}(i,j)|Z\big)$ are respectively the likelihoods for the STM-ToF and SL acquisitions for the pixel (i,j) while $I_{ToF}(i,j)$ and $I_{SL}(i,j)$ are the computed data (in our case the depth maps and their error variance maps). The variance maps are computed using the error propagation analysis made in Sects. 3.3 and 4 starting from the data extracted from the Fourier analysis of the ToF correlation function. They allow to estimate the depth reliability in the two computed depth maps and are fundamental in order to guide the depth fusion method towards obtaining an accurate depth estimation. Different likelihood structures can be used, in this work we used a *Mixture of Gaussians* model. For each pixel and for each estimated depth map (from SL or STM-ToF approach), the likelihood is computed as a weighted sum of Gaussian distributions estimated on a patch of size $(2w_h + 1) \times (2w_h + 1)$ centred on the considered sample. For each pixel of the patch we model the acquisition as a Gaussian random variable centred at the estimated depth value with variance equal to the estimated error variance. The likelihood is given by a weighted sum of the Gaussian distributions of the samples in the patch with weights depending on the Euclidean distance from the central pixel. The employed model in the case of the ToF measure is given by the following equation:

$$P(I_{ToF}(i,j)|Z(i,j)) \propto \sum_{o,u=-w_h}^{w_h} \frac{e^{-\frac{||(o,u)||_2}{2\sigma_s^2}}}{\sigma_{ToF}(i+o,j+u)} e^{-\frac{\big(d_{ToF}(i+o,j+u)-Z(i,j)\big)^2}{2\sigma_{ToF}^2(i+o,j+u)}} \tag{17}$$

where $\sigma_{ToF}(i,j)$ is the standard deviation of the depth estimation noise for pixel (i,j) as computed in Sect. 3.3, σ_s manages the decay of the distribution weights with the spatial distance in the considered neighbourhood of (i,j). In our experiments we fixed $\sigma_s = 1.167$ and $w_h = 3$, i.e., we considered data in a 7×7 neighbourhood of each pixel. The likelihood $P(I_{SL}(i,j)|Z(i,j))$ for the SL depth is evaluated in the same way just by replacing ToF data with SL data.

In order to speed up the fusion of the 2 depth maps, we restricted the candidates for $d_{fus}(i,j)$ in a range of 3 times the standard deviation from the computed depth values for both the ToF and SL estimations.

6   Experimental Results

In this section we are going to the discuss the performance of the proposed method in comparison with standard ToF acquisitions, with the spatio-temporal modulation implemented on the ToF system (STM-ToF) introduced in [8] and described in Sect. 3.2 and finally with the multi-frequency method of Freedman et al. (SRA) [14]. For the comparison with [14] we performed the experiments using 3 modulation frequencies, i.e., 4.4, 13.3 and 20 MHz in order to have the maximum frequency equal to the one we used for a fair comparison and the others selected with scaling factors similar to those used in [14]. We have used a synthetic dataset for which the ground truth geometry of the scenes can be accurately extracted to test the different approaches. In this way a reference depth ground truth for the ToF acquisitions is available and can be used for the numerical evaluation. The synthetic dataset has been generated with Blender [10] while the ToF acquisitions are faithfully reproduced with the *Sony ToF Explorer* simulator that models the various ToF error sources, including the *read-out noise*, the effects of the *photon shot-noise*, the *pixel cross-talk*, and in particular the effects of the multiple reflections of the light inside the scenes (MPI). The camera parameters used in the simulations are taken from a commercial ToF camera. We simulated 21 ToF acquisitions (some examples are shown in Fig. 4) on scenes with complex textures and objects with different shape and size, in order to test the methods on various illumination and MPI conditions. Each scene has a maximum depth smaller or equal to 4 m.

Fig. 4. Samples of the synthetic test scene used for evaluating the proposed approach. The figure shows a color view of some selected scenes from the dataset. (Color figure online)

We are going to discuss the performance of the proposed method first from a qualitative and then from a quantitative point of view. Figure 5 shows the depth maps and the corresponding error maps for the different components of our approach on 4 synthetic scenes. In particular, the first and the second columns show respectively the depth maps and the error maps (equal to the acquired depth minus the true depth) for a standard ToF camera using 4 samples of the correlation function. The third and the fourth columns show the results for the STM-ToF approach based on [8] and implemented as discussed in Sect. 3.2. In the fifth and sixth columns instead we collected the depth and the error maps obtained with the SL approach on ToF acquisitions as described in Sect. 4. The output of the proposed fusion approach given by the combination of the MPI correction method based on [8] with the SL depth maps by exploiting the statistical distribution of the error is represented in the seventh and eighth column of Fig. 5. Notice that the two depth fields going to be fused are captured together with a single ToF acquisition as described in Sect. 3.2. The last column contains the ground truth values.

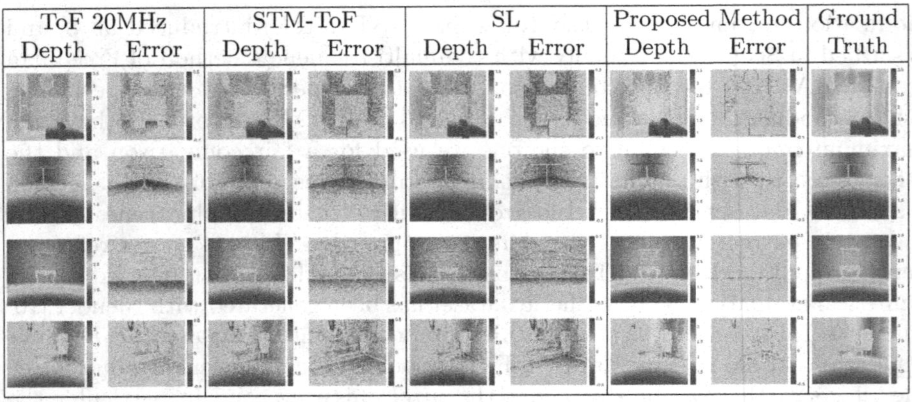

ToF 20MHz		STM-ToF		SL		Proposed Method		Ground
Depth	Error	Depth	Error	Depth	Error	Depth	Error	Truth

Fig. 5. Qualitative comparison for STM-ToF, SL and their fusion on some sample scenes. All the values are measured in meters. In the error maps, dark red is equivalent to 0.5 cm, dark blue to −0.5 cm and green to no error. (Color figure online)

As it is possible to observe from Fig. 5, the standard ToF acquisitions are characterized by a dramatic overestimation of the depth near to the corners caused by the MPI phenomenon. Differently, by using the STM-ToF approach the depth overestimation due to MPI is reduced (no more uniform red regions in the error maps) as it can be seen in rows 2 and 3 from the corners composed by the floor and walls. On the other side, the data appears to be much more noisy, in particular in regions where only a small amount of light is reflected back (e.g., distant corners and the borders of the tiles on the floor in row 2). This problem of the STM-ToF approach was already pointed out in Sect. 3.3, indeed the depth generated with this approach has an error variance that is about 4 times higher than a standard ToF acquisition with the same settings. Concerning the depth maps estimated with the *SL* approach, also in this case the overestimation due to MPI is absent, but there are artifacts not present in standard ToF acquisitions. The overestimation close to corners is almost completely removed and the amount of noise on flat surfaces is less than in the ToF approach. On the other side there are artifacts in heavily textured regions (e.g., on the back in row 1) and sometimes the color patterns can propagate to the depth estimation (we will discuss this issue in the following of this section). By observing the depth and error maps obtained with the proposed fusion approach, it is possible to see that both the MPI corruption and the *zero-mean* error have been reduced obtaining a much higher level of precision and accuracy when compared with the other approaches. In particular, notice how there is much less zero-mean noise, the MPI corruption is limited to the points extremely close to the corners and artifacts of both methods like the ones on the border of the tiles have been removed, without losing the small details in the scenes.

Table 1. Mean Absolute Error (MAE) for the compared approaches on the synthetic dataset averaged on the 21 scenes (measured in millimeters).

	MAE (*all*)	MAE (*valid**)
ToF 20 MHz	73.9	56.8
STM-ToF [8]	93.4	65.2
SL	80.8	49.7
SRA [14]	-	50.8
Proposed	**21.8**	**14.2**

*The minimization used by SRA does not give an outcome for all points, for a fair comparison we also show the results on the subset computed by SRA.

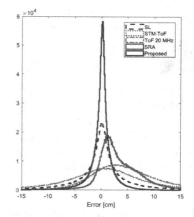

Fig. 6. Histogram of the error distribution for the considered methods.

The qualitative discussion is confirmed by the quantitative comparison. We used the *Mean Absolute Error* (MAE) as metric for the comparison. Table 1 collects the results averaged on the 21 scenes that compose the dataset while Fig. 6 contains a pictorial representation of the error histogram.

The MAE values and the histogram show that standard ToF acquisition has a bias due to the overestimation caused by MPI. This bias is much reduced by the STM-ToF, SL, SRA and proposed methods. The STM-ToF [8] strongly reduces MPI but have an high MAE due to the increased noise level. Concerning SRA, it reduces the positive bias in the error due to MPI but not so effectively as the proposed method. The main reasons for this not optimal behavior of SRA are that it is susceptible to noise and that the sparseness assumption for the global component is not completely fulfilled in a diffuse reflection scenario. Finally, it is possible to notice that the proposed method outperforms all the other approaches achieving a lower MAE and removing MPI. Furthermore, the histogram in Fig. 6 shows that the initial biased error of the standard ToF estimation is moved close to 0 by the proposed method and that the overall variance is much smaller for our approach compared to all the others.

In Fig. 7 instead we depicted a couple of critical cases in which the proposed method able to reduce the overall level of error, but adds some small undesired distortions. In the first case (row 1), the SL estimation is corrupted in the regions that present a strong local variation of the color (see the vertical stripe in the *color view*), a well-known problem of *Structured Light* systems. In the fusion process the effect of this issue are reduced but not completely removed. The second line of Fig. 7 shows that the SL estimation adds a distortion near to the center of the corner due to the refection of the patterns. This is a second well-known issue related to the systems which employ SL approach [35]. This could

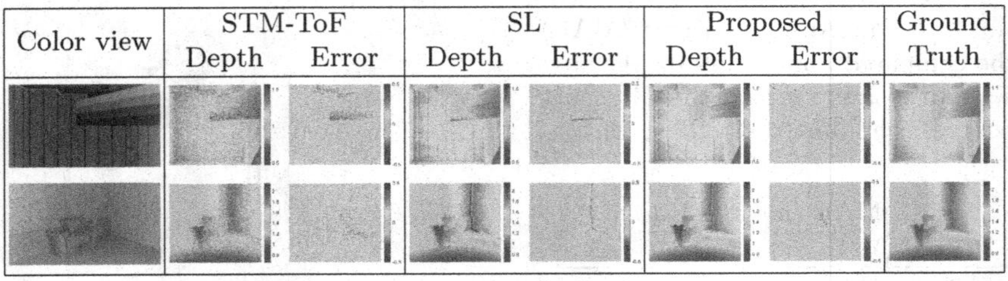

| Color view | STM-ToF | | SL | | Proposed | | Ground |
	Depth	Error	Depth	Error	Depth	Error	Truth

Fig. 7. Critical cases in which the method reduces the overall level of error but adds small distortions. All the values are measured in meters. In the error map dark red is equivalent to 0.5 cm, dark blue to −0.5 cm and green to no error. (Color figure online)

be solved by increasing the spatial frequency of the projected patterns but the small resolution of current ToF camera makes this solution challenging to apply. The aforementioned distortions are reduced but not completely corrected by the proposed fusion approach.

7   Conclusions

In this paper we presented a method for MPI correction and noise reduction for ToF sensors. The method starts from the idea of separating the direct and global component of the light by projecting high frequency sinusoidal patterns instead of a uniform light as in standard ToF sensors. We applied an error analysis on this approach showing the critical increase of zero-mean error if compared with standard ToF acquisitions, and we propose to exploit the projected patterns to estimate a second depth map of the scene with the structured light principle by using the data acquired with the same ToF acquisition. Finally we proposed a maximum likelihood fusion framework to estimate a refined depth map of the scene from the 2 aforementioned depth estimates and the related error variances that we estimated through error propagation analysis. We tested the presented method on a synthetic dataset for which the true depth is known and we have shown that it is able to remove MPI corruption and reduce the overall level of noise if compared with standard ToF acquisitions, with SRA [14] and with the STM-ToF approach [8].

Future work will be devoted to the development of a more refined fusion framework that models more accurately the issues related to the ToF and SL acquisitions. Furthermore, we will consider to test the method on real world data building a prototype camera using a modified ToF device in combination with a DMD projector as also done by O'Toole et al. in [16].

Acknowledgment. We would like to thank the Computational Imaging Group at the Sony European Technology Center (EuTEC) for allowing us to use their *ToF Explorer* simulator and Muhammad Atif, Oliver Erdler, Markus Kamm and Henrik Schaefer for their precious comments and insights.

References

1. Schwarz, L.A., Mkhitaryan, A., Mateus, D., Navab, N.: Human skeleton tracking from depth data using geodesic distances and optical flow. Image Vis. Comput. **30**(3), 217–226 (2012)
2. Van den Bergh, M., Van Gool, L.: Combining RGB and ToF cameras for real-time 3D hand gesture interaction. In: 2011 IEEE Workshop on Applications of Computer Vision (WACV), pp. 66–72. IEEE (2011)
3. Memo, A., Zanuttigh, P.: Head-mounted gesture controlled interface for human-computer interaction. Multimedia Tools Appl. **77**(1), 27–53 (2018)
4. Hussmann, S., Liepert, T.: Robot vision system based on a 3D-ToF camera. In: 2007 IEEE Instrumentation and Measurement Technology Conference Proceedings, IMTC 2007, pp. 1–5. IEEE (2007)
5. Schmidt, M.: Analysis, modeling and dynamic optimization of 3D time-of-flight imaging systems. Ph.D. thesis (2011)
6. Zanuttigh, P., Marin, G., Dal Mutto, C., Dominio, F., Minto, L., Cortelazzo, G.M.: Time-of-Flight and Structured Light Depth Cameras. Springer, Cham (2016). https://doi.org/10.1007/978-3-319-30973-6
7. Gupta, M., Nayar, S.K., Hullin, M.B., Martin, J.: Phasor imaging: a generalization of correlation-based time-of-flight imaging. ACM Trans. Graph. (TOG) **34**(5), 156 (2015)
8. Whyte, R., Streeter, L., Cree, M.J., Dorrington, A.A.: Resolving multiple propagation paths in time of flight range cameras using direct and global separation methods. Opt. Eng. **54**(11), 113109 (2015)
9. Agresti, G., Minto, L., Marin, G., Zanuttigh, P.: Deep learning for confidence information in stereo and ToF data fusion. In: Geometry Meets Deep Learning ICCV Workshop, pp. 697–705 (2017)
10. The Blender Foundation: Blender website. https://www.blender.org/. Accessed 7 July 2018
11. Meister, S., Nair, R., Kondermann, D.: Simulation of time-of-flight sensors using global illumination. In: Bronstein, M., Favre, J., Hormann, K. (eds.) Vision, Modeling and Visualization. The Eurographics Association (2013)
12. Bhandari, A., et al.: Resolving multipath interference in time-of-flight imaging via modulation frequency diversity and sparse regularization. Opt. Lett. **39**(6), 1705–1708 (2014)
13. Kadambi, A., et al.: Coded time of flight cameras: sparse deconvolution to address multipath interference and recover time profiles. ACM Trans. Graph. (TOG) **32**(6), 167 (2013)
14. Freedman, D., Smolin, Y., Krupka, E., Leichter, I., Schmidt, M.: SRA: fast removal of general multipath for ToF sensors. In: Fleet, D., Pajdla, T., Schiele, B., Tuytelaars, T. (eds.) ECCV 2014. LNCS, vol. 8689, pp. 234–249. Springer, Cham (2014). https://doi.org/10.1007/978-3-319-10590-1_16
15. Whyte, R., Streeter, L., Cree, M.J., Dorrington, A.A.: Review of methods for resolving multi-path interference in time-of-flight range cameras. In: IEEE Sensors, pp. 629–632. IEEE (2014)

16. O'Toole, M., Heide, F., Xiao, L., Hullin, M.B., Heidrich, W., Kutulakos, K.N.: Temporal frequency probing for 5D transient analysis of global light transport. ACM Trans. Graph. (TOG) **33**(4), 87 (2014)

17. Fuchs, S.: Multipath interference compensation in time-of-flight camera images. In: Proceedings of IEEE International Conference on Pattern Recognition (ICPR), pp. 3583–3586. IEEE (2010)

18. Fuchs, S., Suppa, M., Hellwich, O.: Compensation for multipath in ToF camera measurements supported by photometric calibration and environment integration. In: Chen, M., Leibe, B., Neumann, B. (eds.) ICVS 2013. LNCS, vol. 7963, pp. 31–41. Springer, Heidelberg (2013). https://doi.org/10.1007/978-3-642-39402-7_4

19. Jiménez, D., Pizarro, D., Mazo, M., Palazuelos, S.: Modeling and correction of multipath interference in time of flight cameras. Image Vis. Comput. **32**(1), 1–13 (2014)

20. Son, K., Liu, M.Y., Taguchi, Y.: Learning to remove multipath distortions in time-of-flight range images for a robotic arm setup. In: Proceedings of IEEE International Conference on Robotics and Automation (ICRA), pp. 3390–3397 (2016)

21. Marco, J., et al.: DeepToF: off-the-shelf real-time correction of multipath interference in time-of-flight imaging. ACM Trans. Graph. (TOG) **36**(6), 219 (2017)

22. Agresti, G., Zanuttigh, P.: Deep learning for multi-path error removal in ToF sensors. In: Geometry Meets Deep Learning ECCV Workshop (2018)

23. Su, S., Heide, F., Wetzstein, G., Heidrich, W.: Deep end-to-end time-of-flight imaging. In: Proceedings of the IEEE Conference on Computer Vision and Pattern Recognition, pp. 6383–6392 (2018)

24. Guo, Q., Frosio, I., Gallo, O., Zickler, T., Kautz, J.: Tackling 3D ToF artifacts through learning and the FLAT dataset. In: Ferrari, V., Hebert, M., Sminchisescu, C., Weiss, Y. (eds.) ECCV 2018. LNCS, vol. 11205, pp. 381–396. Springer, Cham (2018). https://doi.org/10.1007/978-3-030-01246-5_23

25. Naik, N., Kadambi, A., Rhemann, C., Izadi, S., Raskar, R., Bing Kang, S.: A light transport model for mitigating multipath interference in time-of-flight sensors. In: Proceedings of IEEE Conference on Computer Vision and Pattern Recognition (CVPR), pp. 73–81 (2015)

26. Nayar, S.K., Krishnan, G., Grossberg, M.D., Raskar, R.: Fast separation of direct and global components of a scene using high frequency illumination. ACM Trans. Graph. (TOG) **25**(3), 935–944 (2006)

27. Dorrington, A.A., Whyte, R.Z.: Time of flight camera system which resolves direct and multi-path radiation components. US Patent 9,874,638, 23 January 2018

28. Lange, R., Seitz, P., Biber, A., Lauxtermann, S.C.: Demodulation pixels in CCD and CMOS technologies for time-of-flight ranging. In: Sensors and Camera Systems for Scientific, Industrial, and Digital Photography Applications, vol. 3965. International Society for Optics and Photonics, pp. 177–189 (2000)

29. Mufti, F., Mahony, R.: Statistical analysis of measurement processes for time-of-flight cameras. In: Videometrics, Range Imaging, and Applications X, vol. 7447, p. 74470I. International Society for Optics and Photonics (2009)

30. Spirig, T., Seitz, P., Vietze, O., Heitger, F.: The lock-in CCD-two-dimensional synchronous detection of light. IEEE J. Quantum Electron. **31**(9), 1705–1708 (1995)

31. Xu, Y., Ekstrand, L., Dai, J., Zhang, S.: Phase error compensation for three-dimensional shape measurement with projector defocusing. Appl. Opt. **50**(17), 2572–2581 (2011)

32. Dal Mutto, C., Zanuttigh, P., Cortelazzo, G.: A probabilistic approach to ToF and stereo data fusion. In: 3DPVT, Paris, France, May 2010

33. Mutto, C.D., Zanuttigh, P., Cortelazzo, G.M.: Probabilistic ToF and stereo data fusion based on mixed pixels measurement models. IEEE Trans. Pattern Anal. Mach. Intell. **37**(11), 2260–2272 (2015)
34. Zhu, J., Wang, L., Gao, J., Yang, R.: Spatial-temporal fusion for high accuracy depth maps using dynamic MRFs. IEEE Trans. Pattern Anal. Mach. Intell. **32**(5), 899–909 (2010)
35. Gupta, M., Nayar, S.K.: Micro phase shifting. In: Proceedings of IEEE Conference on Computer Vision and Pattern Recognition (CVPR), pp. 813–820. IEEE (2012)

Robust Structured Light System Against Subsurface Scattering Effects Achieved by CNN-Based Pattern Detection and Decoding Algorithm

Ryo Furukawa[1(✉)], Daisuke Miyazaki[1], Masashi Baba[1], Shinsaku Hiura[1], and Hiroshi Kawasaki[2]

[1] Hiroshima City University, Hiroshima, Japan
`ryo-f@hiroshima-cu.ac.jp`
[2] Kyushu University, Fukuoka, Japan

Abstract. To reconstruct 3D shapes of real objects, a structured-light technique has been commonly used especially for practical purposes, such as inspection, industrial modeling, medical diagnosis, etc., because of simplicity, stability and high precision. Among them, oneshot scanning technique, which requires only single image for reconstruction, becomes important for the purpose of capturing moving objects. One open problem of oneshot scanning technique is its instability, when captured pattern is degraded by some reasons, such as strong specularity, subsurface scattering, inter-reflection and so on. One of important targets for oneshot scan is live animal, which includes human body or tissue of organ, and has subsurface scattering. In this paper, we propose a learning-based approach to solve pattern degradation caused by subsurface scattering for oneshot scan. Since patterns are significantly blurred by subsurface scattering, robust decoding technique is required, which is effectively achieved by separating the decoding process into two parts, such as pattern detection and ID recognition in our technique; both parts are implemented by CNN. To efficiently achieve robust pattern detection, we convert a line detection into segmentation problem. For robust ID recognition, we segment all the region into each ID using U-Net. In the experiments, it is shown that our technique is robust against strong subsurface scattering compared to state of the art technique.

1 Introduction

In order to reconstruct 3D shapes of real objects, mainly two approaches exist, one is camera only algorithm and the other is camera and active-lighting based algorithm. Although there are several important advantages on camera only algorithm, *i.e.*, systems can be compact and low energy consumption, critical limitations exists, such as textureless objects cannot be recovered. Because of the limitation, it is difficult to apply the camera only algorithm to practical purposes, such as inspection, industrial modeling or medical diagnosis. To the

L. Leal-Taixé and S. Roth (Eds.): ECCV 2018 Workshops, LNCS 11129, pp. 372–386, 2019.
https://doi.org/10.1007/978-3-030-11009-3_22

contrary, camera and active-lighting algorithm do not have such limitation and wide varieties of products have been developed. Among them, structured-light technique is most popular because of its simplicity, stability and high precision. Along a long history of structured light, problems on scanning static objects with smooth and Lambertian surfaces have been mostly solved. One important remaining problem is a reconstruction of moving objects and it has been intensively researched recently. Most popular solution is based on static pattern projection with single image capture, which is called oneshot scan [12,16].

Generally, to retrieve correspondences between the captured image and the original illuminated patterns of a projector for oneshot scan systems, features and codes are extracted from the captured image. For this purpose, common feature detection methods such as edge/corner detection are the first choice. Since projected patterns for recent oneshot scan techniques usually consist of simple structures, such as grids or dots [12,16,26], using the prior knowledge of such structure is used to improve the detection accuracy. After feature extraction, unique correspondences between the projected pattern and the captured image are retrieved by using spatial distribution of those features. To achieve efficient and stable matching between the patterns and the captured images, many existing oneshot methods embed a distinctive "codes" into local area of pattern. These codes are detected from the captured image (*i.e.*, decoding) and used for matching. If these codes are detected with smaller error rate than the assumption of the matching algorithm, the matching process succeeds. One practical issue of oneshot scan is that since the codes are embedded as spatial pattern distribution, reconstruction accuracy is severely affected by degradation of the captured pattern; note that such degradation is frequently caused by common physical phenomena, such as specularity, strong subsurface scattering or inter-reflection.

In this paper, we propose a learning-based approach to solve subsurface scattering effect, which is typical on live animals including human body and tissue or organ. Since patterns are significantly blurred out by subsurface scattering effects, robust decoding technique is required, which is efficiently achieved by separating the decoding process into two parts, such as pattern detection and ID recognition part. Both parts are implemented by CNN to avoid analyzing complicated phenomena of subsurface scattering and related effects. In the paper, we further propose a robust line detection algorithm by converting the problem into a segmentation problem, where lines are detected as a boundary of two segments; note that CNN works surprisingly well on segmentation and our technique can take full advantage of it. We also propose a robust ID recognition technique which is achieved by segmenting all the region into each ID using U-Net.

In the experiments, it is shown that our technique is robust to strong subsurface scattering effects compared to state of the art technique. The advantages of our approach are as follows: (1) Novel CNN-based technique for detecting and decoding projected patterns, where grid-structures of patterns are detected by two line-detection CNNs, and ID recognition CNN, is proposed. (2) Line detection problem is solved by segmentation algorithm. (3) The CNNs are trained by examples with strong subsurface scattering properties and the stability of the method against blurring of the projected patterns are confirmed.

2   Related Work

There are two major shape recovery techniques using active light, such as photometric stereo and structured light. Photometric stereo recovers the surface normal of each pixel using multiple images captured by a camera while changing the light source direction [9,10]. Although photometric stereo can recover surface normals, they need usually more than 40 images for stable reconstruction and cannot be used for oneshot scan [11,27]. The structured-light technique has been used for practical applications [17,22,27]. There are two primary approaches to encode positional information into patterns, such as temporal and spatial encoding. Because temporal encoding requires multiple images, it is not suitable for capturing moving objects [23,25]. Spatial encoding requires only a single image and is possible to capture fast-moving objects [12,15,16,20,26] and recently draw a wide attention. One severe problem for spatial encoding method is that they encode positional information into small regions, patterns tend to be complicated and easily degraded by environmental conditions, such as noise, specularity, blur, etc. To avoid such limitations, some techniques are based on geometric constraints rather than decoding [13,14,18,21,26], but not considered for strong degradation like subsurface scattering. There are several techniques for compensation of such degradation [5–7], however, they assume capturing multiple images with projecting multiple patterns, thus cannot be applied to oneshot scan. Recently, solution for subsurface scattering objects is proposed [4], but it requires a specifically designed pattern and more general technique for wide variations of patterns is strongly demanded.

Recently, CNNs have become common tools for vision applications. Image segmentation is one of the most successful examples of such applications [3,8]. U-Net [19] is an architecture of FCNN (Fully convolutional neural network), which can receive an image and produces a pixel-wise labeled image. It has contracting paths (signal flow where image resolution becomes coarse) to capture large-scale context information and symmetric expanding path (signal flow where low-resolution features are merged into high-resolution features) to realize precise localization. It is known to outperform previous FCNN architectures such as sliding window convolutional networks [2] in segmentation tasks of medical images. Song *et al.* proposed to detect code information of structured light using a CNN [24]. We not only use CNNs for classifying codes of the structured light, but also use them for detecting structures of the pattern such as lines that form grid-like structures.

3   Overview

3.1   System Configuration

The proposed 3D measurement system consists of a camera and a projector as shown in Fig. 1(a). The camera and the projector are assumed to be calibrated

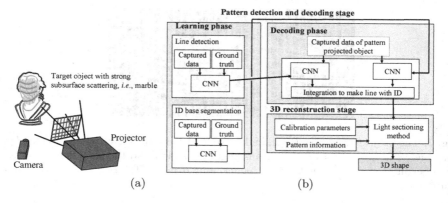

Fig. 1. Projector-camera scanning system and algorithm overview: (a) Scanning system: patterns are projected onto the objects including strong subsurface scattering. Geometric features of patterns, such as lines or intersections, are detected and used for reconstruction. (b) Algorithm overview of CNN-based decoding and 3D reconstruction for oneshot scan. Note that we have two CNNs for vertical and horizontal line detections, and another CNN for decoding IDs of grid points.

(*i.e.*, the intrinsic parameters of the devices and their relative positions and orientations are known). The projector pattern is fixed and does not change, so no synchronization is required. Some geometric patterns are projected from the projector and captured by the camera. In the work of spatial encoding method, the projected pattern is extracted from the captured image and the accuracy of such pattern detection is the key for accuracy and stability of 3D reconstruction. In the method, pixel-wise pattern information is efficiently decoded by CNN-based technique.

3.2   Algorithm

Our method consists of two stages: pattern decoding stage and 3D reconstruction stage as shown in Fig. 1(b).

The pattern decoding stage can also be divided into two phases, such as a learning phase and a decoding phase. In the pattern learning phase, first, actual patterns are projected onto the strong subsurface scattering objects and captured by a camera. Then, correct lines and code IDs are manually given as for the ground truth. It is a tough task even for humans, thus, learning data augmentations such as image translations or rotations are used to decrease the burden. Then, parameters and kernels of U-net [19] are estimated for lines and IDs independently using deep learning framework so that cost functions are minimized. The cost function is basically a difference between an output of U-net and the ground truth.

In the decoding phase, the captured image is first applied to CNNs for vertical and horizontal line detections. At the same time, the image is also applied

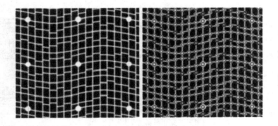

Fig. 2. The projected pattern (top), and embedded codewords of S colored in red, L in blue, and R in green (bottom). S means edges of the left and the right sides have the same height, L means the left side is higher, and R means the right is higher. (Color figure online)

to CNN for region-wise classification of local feature codes embedded into the pattern. Then, both results are combined to produce final output, *i.e.*, detected lines with estimated local codes in the pattern.

Finally, by using the image with detected lines with pattern ID as the input, 3D shapes are recovered in the 3D reconstruction stage. Since a single local code is not sufficient for unique decision of correspondences, information of connectivity and the epipolar constraints are used with a voting scheme to increase robustness, similarly as [4]. Once correspondences are retrieved, 3D shapes are reconstructed by light sectioning method.

4   CNN-Based Feature Detection and Decode for Active Stereo

In this paper, we use "grid pattern with gapped codes" described in [4], which is claimed to be robust to defocus on projection. The pattern is shown in Fig. 2. A major feature of this pattern is a grid-like structure and discrete codes given to each grid point. The grid-like structure is composed of vertical and horizontal line segments. In the pattern, a discrete feature (gap code) is attached to each of the grid point represented by the level gap between the left and right edges of the grid point. The classes of the code are either of S/L/R as shown in different color in Fig. 2 (right).

We believe such a grid-like structure is suited for CNN-based detection framework. Because pattern structures are repetitive, common features of different points can be easily extracted. Moreover, the grid-structure itself can be a large help for detecting local features such as lines, even in disturbances such as noise or blurring.

4.1   Detection of Grid Structure

In this paper, we propose to extract grid-structure and gap-code information using U-Nets [19], which is a kind of FCNN (fully convolutional neural network). The structure of the U-Net is shown in Fig. 3. The numbers in the figure

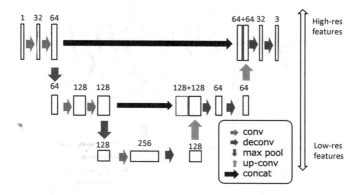

Fig. 3. Structure of U-Nets.

represents dimensions of the feature maps. For example, the 1-D image (intensity image) of the input is converted to a 64-D feature map by applying 2-steps of convolutions. Then, the spatial size of the feature map is sub-sampled to become a lower resolution (1/2 for both x and y-axis) feature map by max pooling. This coarse resolution feature map is later up-sampled by up-convolution and concatenated with the high-resolution feature maps. The information flow in the feature map looks as if "U" character in Fig. 3, thus, it is called "U-Net". Because of this network structure, both fine and coarse resolution features are accounted for in the outputs of U-Nets.

U-Nets are originally used for pixel-wise labeling or segmentation of images. Applying a U-Net to an image, it finally produces a feature map of the same size. In the resulting N-dimensional feature maps, each pixel is an N-D vector. By taking the index of the maximum element for each N-D vector, image of N-labels is obtained.

The training process of a U-Net for detecting vertical lines is as follows. First, image samples of the pattern-illuminated scene is collected. Then, the vertical line locations for the image samples are designated manually as curves of 1-dot widths. The 1-dot width curves are too sparse and narrow to be directly used as regions of teacher data. Thus, regions with 5-dot width of left and right side of the thin curves are extracted, and labeled as 1 and 2, respectively, as shown in Fig. 4. The rest of the pixels are labeled as 0. These 3 labeled images are used as teacher data. Then, a U-Net is trained to produce such labeled regions using the loss function of the softmax entropy between the 3-labeled teacher data and the 3-D feature map produced by the trained U-Net.

By applying the trained U-Net to the image, we can get the 3-labeled image, where left and right side of the vertical curves are labeled as 1 and 2, respectively. Thus, by extracting the 2 horizontally-adjacent pixels where the left is 1 and the right is 2, and connecting those pixels vertically, vertical curve detection is achieved.

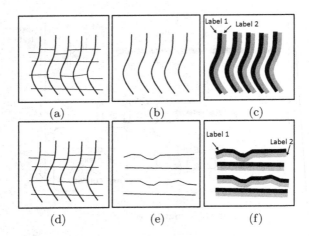

Fig. 4. Teacher data for vertical line detection (a–c), and horizontal line detection (d–f). (a), (d): Sample image of the projected pattern. (b), (e) Vertical lines that are manually annotated. (c), (f) Labeled regions used as training data. For horizontal line detection, discontinuities at the grid points are intentionally connected in the teacher data.

The horizontal curve detection is achieved similarly. However, the horizontal edges may be disconnected due to the gaps at the grid points. Even in those cases, teacher data is provided as continuous curves that go through the center point of the gaps as shown in Fig. 4(e). By training a U-Net using such teacher data, we can expect results where horizontal curves are detected as continuous at grid points, even if they are actually disconnected by gap codes.

An advantage of using U-Net for line detection of the grid structure is stability to disturbances such as blur, noise, or specularity. Figure 5 show an example to show the stability of the line detection ability using a surface of a squid. In the examples, strong noise is added to the image, however, the line-detection result does not degrade significantly. We think that the stability comes from that the CNN uses features extracted by image convolution, which is known to be stable to small noises. In addition, we think that the U-Net uses global information such as grid-like structures for detecting local features of line, because the lines that are almost completely wiped out by the noise and saturation are also detected.

On the contrary, we have found that the line detection of U-Net can be disturbed by scale changes that are not trained. In Fig. 6, we used U-Net that are trained for patterns with about 20×20 (pixel) grid size, and we can see that the result of U-Net was disturbed by scale changes (40×40 grid size) of input image for this example. This problem can be solved by adding training data with proper sizes, for example, if the grid sizes of the input images may be as large as 40×40, then training data with this size should be included. This can be achieved by data augmentation.

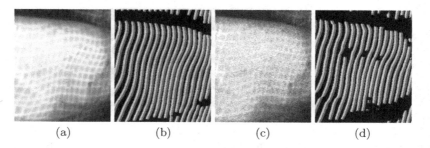

(a)   (b)   (c)   (d)

Fig. 5. Stability to noised image. (a) Sample image (squid surface). (b) CNN (vertical line detection) result of (a). (c) Noised image of (a). (d) CNN (vertical line detection) result of (c).

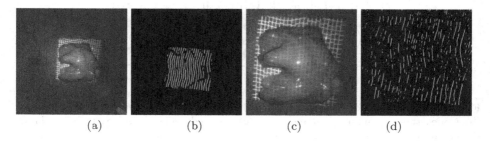

(a)   (b)   (c)   (d)

Fig. 6. Scale mismatch of the input image. (a) Input image with matched scale (about 20×20 grid size). (b) CNN (vertical line detection) result of (a). (c) Input image with mismatched scale (about 40×40 grid size). (d) CNN (vertical line detection) result of (c).

Another advantage of using U-Net for grid detection is that the horizontal edges that are actually disconnected by the gaps are intentionally detected as continuous curves by providing such training data (Fig. 7). Such a task is not easy for conventional line detection algorithms. Thanks to the continuously-detected horizontal curves, analysis of grid-structure becomes much simpler than the previous work [4].

The max pooling and up convolution of the U-Net provide feature maps for different resolutions. For line detection process, we use 4 different resolutions. In the coarsest resolutions, the size of a "pixel" feature map is 8×8 pixels of the original image. Thus, the convolution in this resolution uses information of about 24×24 pixel patches, which is larger than typical grid size that is about 20×20 of the original image. Thus, the U-Net is considered to use information of the grid structures for local line detections.

4.2 Detection of Pattern Codes

In the proposed method, identification of gap codes is processed by directly applying U-Net to the image signal, not from the line detection results. Thus,

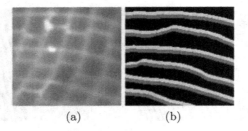

(a)   (b)

Fig. 7. Detection of discontinuous lines with gaps as continuous lines. (a) Input image (squid surface). (b) CNN (horizontal line detection) result of (a).

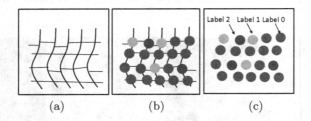

(a)   (b)   (c)

Fig. 8. Teacher data for code detection. (a): Sample image of the projected pattern. (b) Codes that are manually annotated. (c) Labeled regions used as training data. Background pixels are treated as "don't care" data for the loss function.

the gap code estimation does not depend on line segment detection, which is advantageous for stable detection of gap codes. Note that such a direct method is not easy to implement by conventional image processing.

The training data generation is shown in Fig. 8. In the training process, the white background pixels of Fig. 8(c) are treated as "don't care" regions.

The advantage of directly detecting the pattern code is that the stability of the code detection. Since, in the previous work [4], identification of gap codes have been achieved by using results of line detection, failure of line detection or failure of grid-structure analysis consequently leads to code-detection failures. The proposed method is free from such problems of sequential processing.

5   Experiment

5.1   Evaluation Using Subsurface Scattering Objects

To examine the ability of our technique, we actually scan multiple objects, which also exhibit subsurface scattering effects, by using the system as shown in Fig. 9. The 3D points on the projected lines are calculated by triangulation. Since the lines are sparse points, we filled space between the lines using interpolation based on RBFs (radial-basis functions) [1].

For the training of U-Nets, we have captured images of several materials with subsurface scattering (*e.g.*, bio-tissues , squids, or candles) while projecting the

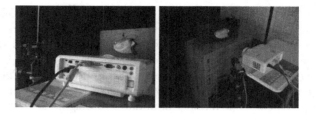

Fig. 9. Actual objects capturing setup. A camera and a projector are precisely calibrated in advance.

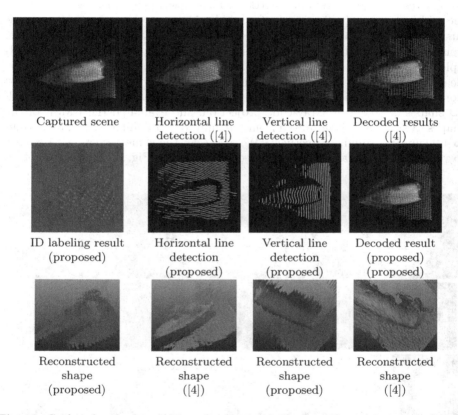

| Captured scene | Horizontal line detection ([4]) | Vertical line detection ([4]) | Decoded results ([4]) |

| ID labeling result (proposed) | Horizontal line detection (proposed) | Vertical line detection (proposed) | Decoded result (proposed) |

| Reconstructed shape (proposed) | Reconstructed shape ([4]) | Reconstructed shape (proposed) | Reconstructed shape ([4]) |

Fig. 10. Grid and code detection results for squid: Top row: Source images and line detection and decoding results of [4]. Middle row: ID segmentation, line detection and decoding results of our method. Bottom row: Shape reconstructed results. Since encoding pattern is as same as Fig. 13(f), it is confirmed that our decoding result is more correct than [4]. Further, from 3D reconstruction results, it is confirmed that our method achieves dense and smooth reconstruction without any smoothing algorithm, whereas previous method [4] creates many holes and bumps.

grid pattern of Fig. 2. Then the vertical and horizontal lines are annotated by human hands, and teacher data samples shown in Fig. 4 are generated from the data. Teacher data of code detection (Fig. 8) are also generated from human annotation. The numbers of the annotated images were 42, 40, and 42, respectively for the vertical lines, horizontal lines, and codes detection. The U-Nets are trained with image patches with size of 80 extracted from the training data set, and with batch size of 50. The number of updates of weights of U-Nets were 2000 for each of the three nets. In this training process, we augment the training data by adding noise and scaling the intensity, since the intensity of the illuminated patterns may change significantly.

The tested objects are squid, bottled milk and wax materials. Figure 10 shows the grid and code detection results for squid using our technique as well as previous technique [4]. The code error were improved 15% by applying our technique from [4]. Figure 11 shows all the reconstruction results, where objects are multiple times scanned in order to increase their density. From the results, it is clearly shown that reconstruction quality and density are significantly improved from previous technique [4]. We have compared the results with ground truth 3D shapes obtained by Gray-code projection, and evaluated the RMSE of the shapes. RMSE value is improved from 1.70 mm to 1.27 mm for milk and 1.78 mm to 1.44 mm for squid, respectively. We also scan the same objects with Kinect to verify the subsurface scattering effect. As shown in Fig. 12, shapes cannot be

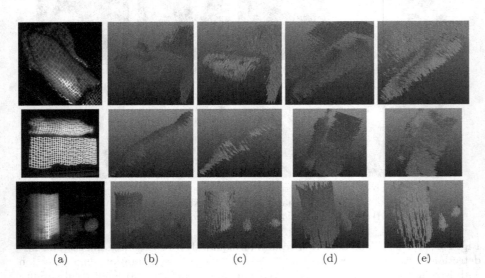

  (a)   (b)   (c)   (d)   (e)

Fig. 11. Reconstruction results compared to previous technique [4]. Top row: squid, middle row: bottled milk, and bottom row: waxed objects. Left to right: (a) scanning scene, (b) and (d) shape reconstructed by our method, and (c) and (e) shape reconstructed by [4]. It is confirmed that our method achieves dense and smooth reconstruction, whereas previous method [4] creates many holes and bumps.

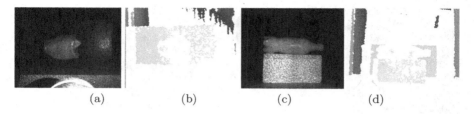

(a)   (b)   (c)   (d)

Fig. 12. Objects with strong subsurface scattering effects scanned by Kinect. (a): Infrared image of squid. (b) Depth image of scene (a), where it is shown that the depth of the squid cannot be retrieved. (c): Infra-red image of bottled milk. (d) Depth image of scene (c), where it is shown that the depth of the bottled milk cannot be retrieved.

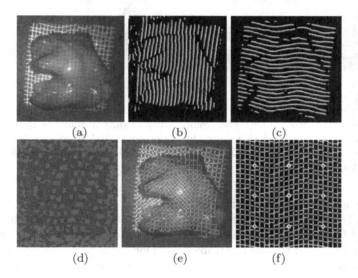

(a)   (b)   (c)

(d)   (e)   (f)

Fig. 13. Grid and code detection results for measuring a piece of organ tissue: (a): Source image. (b) Output label image for vertical line detection. (c) Output label image for horizontal line detection. (d) Output label image for code detection (Note that, since the background regions are trained as "Don't care", the background pixels are labeled arbitrary). (e) Extracted grid-structures and codes for grid points from (b), (c) and (d). (f) Original gap codes with same coloring with (e). To evaluate correctness of (e), compare the color arrangements of (e) with (f). (Color figure online)

recovered because of strong subsurface scattering effect, such effect are clearly shown in infra-red images (it increases speckle noise to intervene correct decoding process).

5.2   Bio-Tissue Scanning

Next, to demonstrate practicability of the proposed method, we measured an actual organ tissue using endoscopic camera system. Bio-tissues such as organ

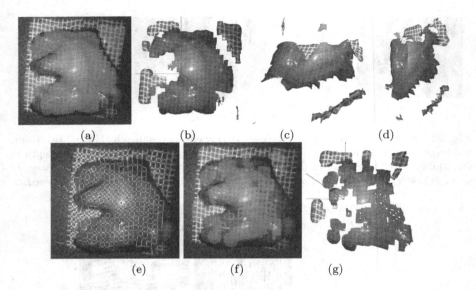

(a)   (b)   (c)   (d)

(e)   (f)   (g)

Fig. 14. 3D reconstruction of Fig. 13. (a–d) The results using the proposed grid and code detection algorithm. (e–g) The results using a conventional line detection algorithms of [4]. (a) Reconstructed regions. (b–d) Reconstructed 3D shapes. (e) Extracted grid-structures and codes for grid points based with a conventional method [4]. (f) Reconstructed regions with [4]. (g) Reconstructed shape with [4].

tissues are generally problematic material, because they have strong subsurface scattering, but important for medical diagnosis and have strong demand.

Figure 13 shows the results of grid detection and code detection. Note that, since the background regions are trained as "Don't care", the background pixels are labeled arbitrarily in (d). Also, to qualitatively evaluate correctness of (e), compare the color arrangements of (e) with (f).

For quantitative evaluation of the accuracy of the code detection, we manually counted the number of erroneous code detection in Fig. 13(e), and the error rate was 1.6%. It is shown that, despite the effects of subsurface scattering, which causes strong blurring on the projected lines or bright regions between the lines, the grid structures and the codes in the projected pattern are stably detected.

Figure 14 (a–d) shows the results of the proposed algorithm. For comparison, Fig. 13 (e–g) shows grid and code detection results and the 3D reconstruction result with line detection algorithm of [4]. The reconstructed area of the proposed method is far wider than the result of of [4].

6   Conclusion

This paper proposed a CNN-based grid pattern detection algorithm for active stereo to solve pattern degradation problem caused by subsurface scattering. Two independent networks are constructed and trained for both line detection and code based segmentation purposes, respectively. They are integrated to retrieve robust and accurate line detection results with pattern IDs. With our experiments using several target objects with strong subsurface scattering and specular effects, the proposed method shows stable detection of the grid structure and codes that are embedded into the grid points. In addition, 3D shapes of strong subsurface scattering objects are successfully reconstructed, which is only scarcely reconstructed even with the previous technique which is designed to robust to blurring effects. In the future, scale dependencies would be addressed by analyzing the training data sets.

Acknowledgment. This work was supported by JSPS/KAKENHI 16H02849, 16KK0151, 18H04119, 18K19824, and MSRA CORE14.

References

1. Carr, J.C., et al.: Reconstruction and representation of 3D objects with radial basis functions. In: Proceedings of the 28th Annual Conference on Computer Graphics and Interactive Techniques, SIGGRAPH 2001, pp. 67–76. ACM, New York (2001)
2. Ciresan, D., Giusti, A., Gambardella, L.M., Schmidhuber, J.: Deep neural networks segment neuronal membranes in electron microscopy images. In: Advances in Neural Information Processing Systems, pp. 2843–2851 (2012)
3. Dai, J., He, K., Sun, J.: Convolutional feature masking for joint object and stuff segmentation. In: Proceedings of the IEEE Conference on Computer Vision and Pattern Recognition, pp. 3992–4000 (2015)
4. Furukawa, R., Morinaga, H., Sanomura, Y., Tanaka, S., Yoshida, S., Kawasaki, H.: Shape acquisition and registration for 3D endoscope based on grid pattern projection. In: Leibe, B., Matas, J., Sebe, N., Welling, M. (eds.) ECCV 2016. LNCS, vol. 9910, pp. 399–415. Springer, Cham (2016). https://doi.org/10.1007/978-3-319-46466-4_24
5. Gupta, M., Agrawal, A., Veeraraghavan, A., Narasimhan, S.G.: A practical approach to 3D scanning in the presence of interreflections, subsurface scattering and defocus. Int. J. Comput. Vision **102**, 33–55 (2013)
6. Gupta, M., Nayar, S.K.: Micro phase shifting. In: IEEE Conference on Computer Vision and Pattern Recognition (CVPR), pp. 1–8, June 2012
7. Gupta, M., Yin, Q., Nayar, S.K.: Structured light in sunlight. In: The IEEE International Conference on Computer Vision (ICCV), December 2013
8. Hariharan, B., Arbeláez, P., Girshick, R., Malik, J.: Simultaneous detection and segmentation. In: Fleet, D., Pajdla, T., Schiele, B., Tuytelaars, T. (eds.) ECCV 2014. LNCS, vol. 8695, pp. 297–312. Springer, Cham (2014). https://doi.org/10.1007/978-3-319-10584-0_20
9. Horn, B.K.P.: Obtaining shape from shading information. In: Shape From Shading, pp. 123–171. MIT Press, Cambridge (1989)
10. Ikeuchi, K.: Determining surface orientations of specular surfaces by using the photometric stereo method. IEEE Trans. Pattern Anal. Mach. Intell. **6**, 661–669 (1981)
11. Inoshita, C., Mukaigawa, Y., Matsushita, Y., Yagi, Y.: Shape from single scattering for translucent objects. In: Fitzgibbon, A., Lazebnik, S., Perona, P., Sato, Y., Schmid, C. (eds.) ECCV 2012. LNCS, vol. 7573, pp. 371–384. Springer, Heidelberg (2012). https://doi.org/10.1007/978-3-642-33709-3_27

12. Kawasaki, H., Furukawa, R., Sagawa, R., Yagi, Y.: Dynamic scene shape reconstruction using a single structured light pattern. In: CVPR, pp. 1–8, 23–28 June 2008
13. Kawasaki, H., Ono, S., Horita, Y., Shiba, Y., Furukawa, R., Hiura, S.: Active one-shot scan for wide depth range using a light field projector based on coded aperture. In: Proceedings of the IEEE International Conference on Computer Vision, pp. 3568–3576 (2015)
14. Koninckx, T.P., Van Gool, L.: Real-time range acquisition by adaptive structured light. IEEE Trans. Pattern Anal. Mach. Intell. **28**(3), 432–445 (2006)
15. Mesa Imaging AG. SwissRanger SR-4000 (2011). http://www.swissranger.ch/index.php
16. Microsoft. Xbox 360 Kinect (2010). http://www.xbox.com/en-US/kinect
17. O'Toole, M., Achar, S., Narasimhan, S.G., Kutulakos, K.N.: Homogeneous codes for energy-efficient illumination and imaging. ACM Trans. Graph. **34**(4), 35:1–35:13 (2015)
18. Proesmans, M., Van Gool, L.: One-shot 3D-shape and texture acquisition of facial data. In: Bigün, J., Chollet, G., Borgefors, G. (eds.) AVBPA 1997. LNCS, vol. 1206, pp. 411–418. Springer, Heidelberg (1997). https://doi.org/10.1007/BFb0016022
19. Ronneberger, O., Fischer, P., Brox, T.: U-Net: convolutional networks for biomedical image segmentation. In: Navab, N., Hornegger, J., Wells, W.M., Frangi, A.F. (eds.) MICCAI 2015. LNCS, vol. 9351, pp. 234–241. Springer, Cham (2015). https://doi.org/10.1007/978-3-319-24574-4_28
20. Ryan Fanello, S., et al.: HyperDepth: learning depth from structured light without matching. In: CVPR, June 2016
21. Sagawa, R., Ota, Y., Yagi, Y., Furukawa, R., Asada, N., Kawasaki, H.: Dense 3D reconstruction method using a single pattern for fast moving object. In: ICCV, pp. 1779–1786 (2009)
22. Salvi, J., Pages, J., Batlle, J.: Pattern codification strategies in structured light systems. Pattern Recognit. **37**(4), 827–849 (2004)
23. Sato, K., Inokuchi, S.: Three-dimensional surface measurement by space encoding range imaging. J. Rob. Syst. **2**, 27–39 (1985)
24. Song, L., Tang, S., Song, Z.: A robust structured light pattern decoding method for single-shot 3D reconstruction. In: 2017 IEEE International Conference on Real-time Computing and Robotics (RCAR), pp. 668–672, July 2017
25. Taguchi, Y., Agrawal, A., Tuzel, O.: Motion-aware structured light using spatio-temporal decodable patterns. In: Fitzgibbon, A., Lazebnik, S., Perona, P., Sato, Y., Schmid, C. (eds.) ECCV 2012. LNCS, vol. 7576, pp. 832–845. Springer, Heidelberg (2012). https://doi.org/10.1007/978-3-642-33715-4_60
26. Ulusoy, A., Calakli, F., Taubin, G.: One-shot scanning using de bruijn spaced grids. In: Proceedings of the 2009 IEEE International Workshop on 3-D Digital Imaging and Modeling (2009)
27. Wang, J., Sankaranarayanan, A.C., Gupta, M., Narasimhan, S.G.: Dual structured light 3D using a 1D sensor. In: Leibe, B., Matas, J., Sebe, N., Welling, M. (eds.) ECCV 2016. LNCS, vol. 9910, pp. 383–398. Springer, Cham (2016). https://doi.org/10.1007/978-3-319-46466-4_23

Robust 3D Pig Measurement in Pig Farm

Kumiko Yoshida[1] and Kikuhito Kawasue[2]([✉])

[1] KOYO Plant Services Co., Ltd., Nobeoka, Japan
[2] University of Miyazaki, 1-1 Gakuen Kibanadai-nishi, Miyazaki 889-2192, Japan
kawasue@cc.miyazaki-u.ac.jp

Abstract. On a pig farm, the shipment of pigs of proper weight is very important for increasing profit. However, in order to reduce labor costs, many farmers ship pigs without weighing them. Therefore, an automatic sorting system that selects pigs that have reached the proper weight by measuring the weight of each pig has been developed. In the present paper, a weight estimation system using a camera for pig sorting is introduced. Three-dimensional visual information on a pig captured in a single image is used to estimate its weight. The proposed method is robust and practical for the measurement of a moving animal in a poor environment of pig farms.

Keywords: Pig measurement · Computer vision ·
Three dimensional · Weight estimation · Multiple slits laser ·
Random dots

1 Introduction

As the weight of a pig at shipment is an indicator of price, it is very important to ship pigs of proper weight. For economic reasons, the best weight for shipping pigs is approximately 115 kg. However, in order to reduce labor costs, many farmers ship pigs without measuring their weight. Therefore, the price of pigs has decreased, which is a significant management problem.

In order to deal with this problem, automatic sorting systems for selecting pigs of appropriate weight have been developed, primarily in Europe and United States [1,2]. Although load cells are generally used as weight sensors, pigs must remain still during measurement in order to avoid errors. This increases the measurement time. Sawdust is often used as a matting material in pig houses. Although sawdust is comfortable for the pigs, it often gets under the load-cell baseboard, which causes mechanical errors.

In order to cope with these issues, the development of a weight measurement method using a camera is required. Some systems have been developed to measure some parts on a pig body using camera to estimate the pig weight from 2D information. Kashiha et al. [3] estimated the pig weight by measuring the top view body area and Schofield et al. [4] identified differences in the measured area to weight relationships for the three strains. Wang et al. [5] developed walk-through weighing system of pigs using computer vision. Traditionally, the weight

© Springer Nature Switzerland AG 2019
L. Leal-Taixé and S. Roth (Eds.): ECCV 2018 Workshops, LNCS 11129, pp. 387–400, 2019.
https://doi.org/10.1007/978-3-030-11009-3_23

of a pig can be accurately estimated by manually measuring specific parts, such as body length and chest circumference [6,7]. The purpose of the present study is to measure these parts on a pig body using a camera, and thereby estimate the weight of the pig. In order to simulate manual measurement on a computer, extraction of these parts in three dimensions is needed. Moreover, since it is difficult to keep a pig still during measurement, instantaneous measurement is required.

Although color-coded structured light projection methods [8–11] have been introduced to perform instantaneous measurement, under practical conditions, these methods are easily influenced by ambient light. Recently, RGB-D cameras such as KINECT or Xtion sensors have been used in a number of applications to obtain instantaneous three-dimensional (3D) data for motion capture [12–15]. KINECT has been applied to cattle measurement and satisfactory results have been obtained [16,17]. The Xtion sensor has also been used for pig measurement [18]. Although using RGB-D cameras to obtain instantaneous 3D shape information has been proposed, there is a limit to the maximum length of the USB cable. A USB3 cable should be less than 5 m in length. As such, the computer used to control the KINECT sensor must be nearby. In general, the environment of a pig house is not good for computers. Temperature, humidity and dust cause computer trouble in a couple of days. Over 1 mm dust is accumulated in a day. Therefore, the use of RGB-D cameras in pig house is not practical.

In the proposed method, Gig-Ethernet camera and multiple slits laser with random dots are used to obtain instantaneous shape data. Using this camera and laser system, remote control is possible, and instantaneous 3D shape data can be acquired without the need to sweep the laser. Many cross sections on multiple slits of the laser can be captured simultaneously. In order to convert the cross-sectional shape into global coordinates, the direction of each slit should be recognized. In this method, the pattern of random dots around each slit is used to identify the slit. The use of random dots is also adequate to extract the pig body robustly from background as it shows the big difference between the images with a pig and without a pig under the nature light condition. This method is appropriate for use in a pig sorting system because it enables robust measurement under the poor environmental conditions in a pig house. In the present paper, a method for extracting a pig body shape from a captured image and reconstructing the 3D surface to estimate the weight of the pig is introduced.

2   Pig Sorting System

2.1   Sorting Process

Figure 1 shows a schematic illustration of the pig sorting system. A pig passes through (a) the entrance and enters (b) the camera and sorting area, which is located in the center of the figure. The camera system estimates the weight of the pig. If the pig has not reached the proper weight (around 115 kg), then the pig is guided to (c) the food zone on the left-hand side of the figure. In the food zone, there is (d) a one-way path to (e) the relaxation zone. The pig moves from the food zone to the relaxation zone after eating food. When the pig becomes hungry, it reenters (a) the camera and sorting area. The pigs repeat these actions (from (a) to (e)), and when the pig has reached the proper weight for shipment, the pig is guided to (f) a shipping zone located on the right-hand side of the figure. Figure 2 shows a photograph of the developed sorting system. In this system, a rotary mechanism is used to separate pigs. This is an effective way of avoiding multiple pigs becoming jammed at the exit.

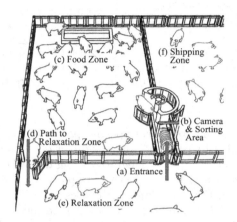

Fig. 1. Pig sorting system. Pigs repeatedly move from (a) to (e), and when a pig has reached the proper weight for shipment, the pig is automatically guided to (f) the shipping zone.

2.2   Camera Settings for Weight Estimation

Generally, the weight of an animal is measured by a load cell. However, load cells are not appropriate for automatic animal measurement because pigs do not remain still during measurement. Sawdust is often used for matting in pig houses. However, sawdust can get under the load-cell baseboard, causing mechanical errors. Therefore, a computer vision system is more appropriate for use in pig weight measurement. Upon implementing the system, quick measurement is also required. The proposed system uses a computer and laser projectors to project a pattern of multiple slits and random dots in the same area. In a practical situation, the use of a laser projector with a specific wavelength is recommended for robustness. The random dot projector is effective for distinguishing laser lights from ambient light because it forms distinguishable structured light over the entire surface of a pig. Figure 3 shows an image of the measurement area. Multiple slits with random dots (wavelength: 660 nm) are projected from the top of the system. A Gig-Ethernet camera with a bandpass filter is also placed at the top of the system. A magnified image captured by the camera is shown

Fig. 2. Photograph of the pig sorting system (2018). A computer is placed outside of the pig room, and the system is controlled by a LAN connection. A Gig-Ethernet camera system is placed at the top of the system and observes the movement of the pigs.

in the figure. The random dots form specific patterns along each slit. These patterns are used to identify each slit, and the direction of each slit is estimated. Both the slits and random dots are generated using diffractive optical elements placed at the laser projector. The projectors are placed vertically on the holder. The separation between the two projectors causes a slight displacement on the surface of the target, as shown in Fig. 4. However, identification of the slits is not influenced by this shift, because the displacement is along the laser slit direction.

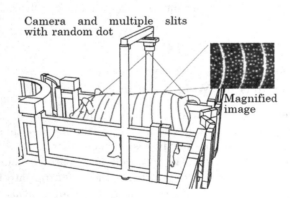

Fig. 3. Multiple slits with random dots are projected onto the surface of the pig from the top of the sorting system. The random dots are used to identify the direction and number of slits.

2.3   Identification of Slit

The direction of each slit from the projector has to be identified to estimate the global data for a triangulation. Reference image that include multiple slits

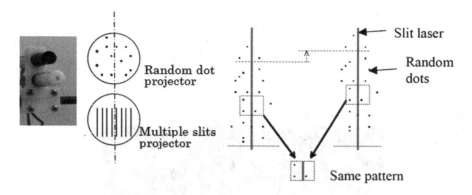

Fig. 4. Shift of the random dot pattern along the slit direction.

with slit number and random dots pattern is recorded first as initial setting. The example of the reference image is shown in Fig. 5. This reference image is set on the computer memory and is used to allocate the slit address number on the measurement process.

Initially, Epipolar equation [19, 20] is determined between measurement image and reference image. The relation between measurement image $m(u',v')$ and reference image $r(u,v)$ is shown as Eq. (1).

$$[u'\ v'\ 1] \begin{bmatrix} m_{11} & m_{12} & m_{13} \\ m_{21} & m_{22} & m_{23} \\ m_{31} & m_{32} & m_{33} \end{bmatrix} \begin{bmatrix} u \\ v \\ 1 \end{bmatrix} = 0 \tag{1}$$

where m_{11}–m_{33} is a rotational and translational matrix, these parameter can be determined by setting over 8 corresponding pairs of points between measurement image and reference image. By setting the point (u',v') in the measurement image, the Epipolar line in the reference image is determined. as following,

$$(u'm_{11} + v'm_{21} + m_{31})u + (u'm_{12} + v'm_{22} + m_{32})v + u'm_{13} + v'm_{23} + 1 = 0 \tag{2}$$

After obtaining the measurement image, small size of template such as Fig. 3 is selected and the same arrangement of the random dots are searched in the reference image. Therefore, the slit address number in measurement image is determined by finding the slit address with the same random pattern on the reference image. Once the slit address number is determined the global coordinate can be calculated by the triangulation as the ordinary slit ray projection method. Equation (3) is a relation ship between measurement image (u,v) and global coordinates (x,y,z) . $(c_{11}$–$c_{33})$ are camera parameters that include rotational and translational matrix and ρ is a scale factor between images [21].

$$\rho \begin{bmatrix} u \\ v \\ 1 \end{bmatrix} = \begin{bmatrix} c_{11} & c_{12} & c_{13} & c_{14} \\ c_{21} & c_{22} & c_{23} & c_{24} \\ c_{31} & c_{32} & c_{33} & 1 \end{bmatrix} \begin{bmatrix} x \\ y \\ z \\ 1 \end{bmatrix} \tag{3}$$

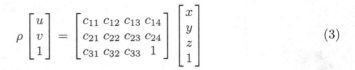

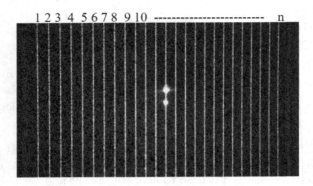

Fig. 5. Example of reference image that has include the slit numbers and random dot pattern. The slit number is allocated in the measurement image by finding the same random dot pattern in this image.

Figure 6 shows the example of the slit segment. Some points are randomly selected on each slit segment and the small template are defined that has a selected point as center. Epipolar equation is used for quick processing. Figure 7 shows the image of Epipolar line calculated for the selected point. Computer calculate the cross points between the Epipolar line and slit line on the reference image. The candidates of matching points are limited in these cross points. The same arrangement of the random dots with the template are searched in the reference image and the evaluation value for the matching is recorded. Finally, the slit address number is allocated by this process on selecting the address number with the maximum evaluation value of matching. This process enables us a quick processing.

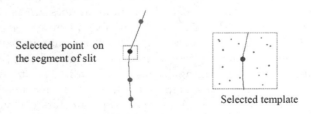

Selected point on the segment of slit

Selected template

Fig. 6. Template setting. Dot pattern around segment is used for identification of each slit

The relation between global coordinates and slit with address number n is as following [21].

$$
\alpha \begin{bmatrix} n \\ 1 \end{bmatrix} = \begin{bmatrix} p_{11} & p_{12} & p_{13} & p_{14} \\ p_{21} & p_{22} & p_{23} & 1 \end{bmatrix} \begin{bmatrix} x \\ y \\ z \\ 1 \end{bmatrix}
\tag{4}
$$

where $(p_{11}\text{--}p_{23})$ are projector parameters that include rotational and translational matrix and α is a scale factor between global coordinates and reference number. Finally, the global coordinates can be calculated by Eq. (5) using Eqs. (3) and (4).

$$
\begin{bmatrix} x \\ y \\ z \end{bmatrix} = \begin{bmatrix} c_{11} - c_{31}u & c_{12} - c_{32}u & c_{13} - c_{33}u \\ c_{21} - c_{31}v & c_{22} - c_{32}v & c_{23} - c_{33}v \\ p_{11} - p_{21}n & p_{12} - p_{22}n & p_{13} - p_{23}n \end{bmatrix}^{-1} \begin{bmatrix} u - c_{14} \\ v - c_{24} \\ n - p_{14} \end{bmatrix}
\tag{5}
$$

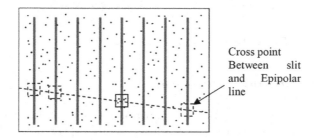

Cross point
Between   slit
and   Epipolar
line

Fig. 7. Cross points between slits and Epipolar line are extracted and template matching processing is executed among them

2.4 Extraction of Pig Images

For practical use, robust extraction of the target from a captured image is required. Image subtraction is a basic approach to extraction. The use of a specific laser wavelength and a bandpass filter on the camera is effective at preventing interference due to ambient light. In the present system, random dots (wavelength: 660 nm) are the main light source for the camera. The use of random dots is effective to extract the pig body robustly from background as it shows the big difference between the images with a pig and without a pig under the nature light condition. The random dots are dispersed in the measurement area and they are displaced depend on the depth. The displacements are used to extract the pig body from the image without being affected by the nature light. In order to reduce the noises, a median filter is used to construct the filled area of the pig image.

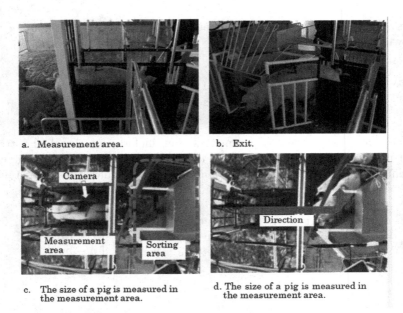

a. Measurement area.   b. Exit.

c. The size of a pig is measured in   d. The size of a pig is measured in
    the measurement area.   the measurement area.

Fig. 8. Experimental setup in the pig house.

3   Experiment and Discussion

Figure 8 is an experimental system in the pig house. When a pig enter the measurement area, the image of the pig is automatically captured and the image is sent to a computer. The sorting direction of the pig is determined by the result of a weight estimation processing.

Figure 9 is the example of extraction result of a pig from captured image. As the random dots are displaced according to the depth, the pig body is easy to be extracted from a back ground image using subtracting procedure. This extracted single image is used for 3D processing.

The specific points to be measured on the body of a pig are shown in Fig. 10. The body length from ears to tail and the girth are highly correlated with the weight of the pig [6,7]. The proposed measurement system has been developed to measure the body length and girth automatically.

The laser has a wavelength of 660 nm, and the bandpass filter of the camera is centered on this wavelength of 660 nm. A multiple-laser projector and a random dot projector are arranged vertically on one side of the rod, and the camera (Basler acA1300 60 fps) is placed at the other side of the rod. When the entire body of the pig is captured in the camera image, and computer starts processing. The software was developed using Visual Studio 2015 and Open CV 3.1.0.

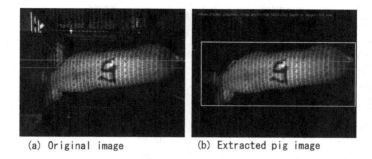

| (a) Original image | (b) Extracted pig image |

Fig. 9. Extraction process of a pig in the system (a) Original Image (b) Extracted pig image using the proposed subtraction method.

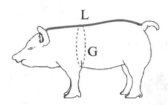

Fig. 10. Specific points to be measured. These points have a high correlation with the weight of the pig.

3.1 Conversion of Slit Images to Three Dimensional Data

In order to obtain the three dimensional information from the image, the address have to be allocated to each slit for the triangulations. For slit line address allocation, points on each slit in the measurement image are randomly selected and the template around the point is selected. Figure 11 shows an image of the candidate points corresponding to the selected point from among the intersection points between the Epipolar line and the slits in the reference image. Pattern matching is performed among these intersection points. In order to assure the allocation, 10 dots were selected from one segment in order to perform pattern matching, and the highest degree of matching was allocated for the selected segment from among the 10 randomly selected points. Table 1 shows the allocation result of the image. There are 25 segments in the measurement image to be allocated the slit address. On the allocation process, evaluation values on template matching used for the reallocation. The slit address with highest evaluation value is selected for the final address of the segment. The processing time to allocate line numbers to these 25 segments took 1.5 s. Points on the slit segment with global coordinates are calculated by Eq. (5) after the slit number is allocated. These data with global coordinate are used to extract the specific parameters for estimating the pig weight.

Table 1. Allocation result of slit address

Randomly selected point	Preallocated address number	Correlation value	Final allocation
A_0	2	0.529	2
A_1	10	0.201	
A_2	2	0.539*	
A_3	2	0.526	
A_4	2	0.249	
A_5	2	0.347	
A_6	2	0.411	
A_7	2	0.511	
A_8	2	0.487	
A_9	18	0.221	

*highest correlation value

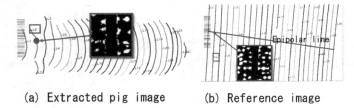

(a) Extracted pig image   (b) Reference image

Fig. 11. Pig image extracted from the measured and reference images. The selected point generates the epipolar line in the reference image, and the corresponding point is selected from the candidates at the intersection points between the epipolar line and the slit lines. In this image, colors indicate corresponding slit numbers between images. (Color figure online)

3.2   Estimation of Body Length

Length of the pig body is calculated after the global coordinates on the slit are obtained. Figure 12 shows the procedure of the length estimation. The point with the highest point in each segment is selected and curved line along these selected points is generated by connecting these selected points. The length of the body is calculated using this curved line.

3.3   Estimation of Pig Girths

Girth as well as a body length is an important parameter to estimate the weight of the pig. The image captured from upper side of a pig is used in our system since the back shape of a pig reflects the carcass shape. Figure 13 shows the estimation procedure of girths. As the cross sections of the pig is close to circle, each segment on the body is estimated by circle. These estimated circles are

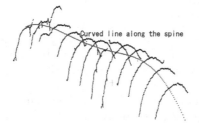

Fig. 12. Estimation of body length. The point with maximum z value is selected from each segment of slit and the curved line along the spine is generated by connecting these selected points. Length of the body is calculated using this curved line.

arranged along the pig body and the pig body is reconstructed as (c) in Fig. 13. Around ear of pig, approximation is missed by the image noises, but the data can be smoothed by taking the average of these circles. The reconstructed of the pig body has similar shape with the carcass data as (d). As the final price of a pig is determined by the weight of the carcass, this similarity shows the extra feature of our proposed method. Though more data and more discussions from the view point of an animal science are needed to establish our assumption, it has a possibility that the price of the pig can be estimated before shipping.

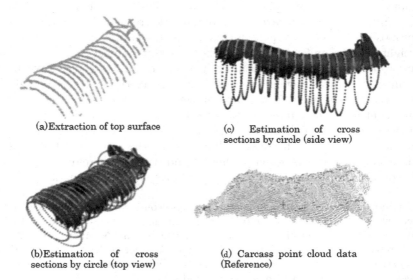

(a)Extraction of top surface

(c) Estimation of cross sections by circle (side view)

(b)Estimation of cross sections by circle (top view)

(d) Carcass point cloud data (Reference)

Fig. 13. Estimation of girths from the upper side image. Girths are estimated by circle approximation using the arc that captured. The reconstruction of the pig body has similar shape with the carcass data (d).

3.4   Accuracy Evaluation

To estimate the accuracy of the proposed system, the depth measurement accuracy was checked first using a plain board. A plain board was placed at a distance of 1 m in front of the measurement system and the deviation was checked. The average deviation was 0.7 mm.

The accuracy of weight estimation was conducted using real pigs. The number of pig was five and they were randomly passed the measurement area. 60 pig images were used by comparing the ground truth weights that were measured by the load cell. The range of the weight was from 95.0 kg to 124.5 kg. The weight was estimated by the measured body length and girth. The equation developed to estimate the weight was as follows.

$$W = 0.103 * L + 0.122 * G - 101.4 \tag{6}$$

where L [mm] is the length , G [mm] the girth width of the pig and the W [kg] is the estimated weight of the pig. The correlation coefficient between the estimated weight and the ground truth weight was 0.92.

4   Conclusion

A 3D measurement method for a pig sorting system that uses a single image to estimate the weight of a pig was introduced. The projection of multiple slits enables the simultaneous measurement of multiple cross sections of the pig body. The proposed method is adequate for extracting the parameters used to estimate the weight of a pig, and subtraction of the background image using random dots enables robust practical measurement in a pig farm. Since pigs take various pose during the measurement, the measurement method that is not affected by the posture is needed. The image processing method to realize the stable measurement for various posture was introduced.

In this paper, the performance of the proposed method was shown from the engineering view point. The relationship between the result and the measured data may be changed depend on pig houses and strains. Therefore, it have to be discussed also from the animal science view point on the next step.

Acknowledgement. All animal experiments were conducted in compliance with the protocol which was reviewed by the Institutional Animal Care and Use Committee and approved by the President of University of Miyazaki (Permit Number: 2017-021).

This research was supported by grants from the Project of the NARO Bio-oriented Technology Research Advancement Institution (the special scheme project on vitalizing management entities of agriculture, forestry and fisheries).

References

1. Lee, S.Y., Song, C.H., Choe, Y.C.: The convergence of ICT and automatic sorting system: a quantitative performance analysis. Adv. Sci. Technol. Lett. **49**(1), 229–235 (2014)
2. Salak-Johnson, J.L.: Impact of auto-sort systems on pig welfare, vol. 31, no. 2, pp. 1–17. North Carolina Swine Extension (2008)
3. Kashiha, M., Bahr, C., Ott, S., Moons, C.P., Niewold, T.A.: Automatic weight estimation of individual pigs using image analysis. Comput. Electron. Agric. **107**, 38–44 (2014)
4. Schofield, C., Marchant, J., White, R., Brandl, N., Wilson, M.: Monitoring pig growth using a prototype imaging system. J. Agric. Eng. Res. **72**(3), 205–210 (1999)
5. Wang, Y., Yang, W., Winter, P., Walkder, L.: Walk-through weighing of pigs using machine vision and an artificial neural network. Biosyst. Eng. **100**(1), 117–125 (2008)
6. Asai, T., Ueyama, K., Yamanae, T., Maruyama, M., Segaki, H.: A simpler estimating method of the body weight for growing finishing swine of large type breed (in Japanese). Jpn. Pork J. **6**(1), 1–5 (1969)
7. Nadiope, G., Stock, J., Stalder, K.J., Pezo, D.: Prediction of live body weight using various body measurements in Ugandan village pigs. Livest. Res. Rural. Dev. **26**(5), 1–7 (2014)
8. Geng, Z.J.: Rainbow three dimensional camera: new concept of high speed three dimensional vision systems. Opt. Eng. **35**(2), 376–383 (1996)
9. Boyer, K.L., Kak, A.C.: Color-encoded structured light for rapid active ranging. IEEE Trans. Pattern Anal. Mach. Intell. **9**(1), 14–28 (1987)
10. Durdle, N.G., Thayyoor, J., Raso, V.J.: An improved structured light technique for surface reconstruction of the human trunk. In: IEEE Canadian Conference on Electrical and Computer Engineering, vol. 2, pp. 874–877 (1998)
11. Petriu, E.M., Sakr, Z., Spoelder, H.J.W., Moica, A.: Object recognition using pseudo-random color encoded structured light. In: Conference Record - IEEE Instrumentation and Measurement Technology Conference, vol. 3, pp. 1237–1241 (2000)
12. Dal Mutto, C., Zanuttigh, P., Cortelazzo, G.M.: Time-of-Flight Cameras and Microsoft Kinect^{TM}, 1st edn. Springer, Heidelberg (2012). https://doi.org/10.1007/978-1-4614-3807-6
13. Webster, D., Celik, O.: Experimental evaluation of Microsoft Kinect's accuracy and capture rate for stroke re-habilitation applications. In: Proceedings of Haptics Symposium, no. 1, pp. 455–460. IEEE (2014)
14. Nagayama, R., Kazuma, T., Endo, T., He, A.: A basic study of human face direction estimation using depth sensor. In: Proceedings of International Joint Conference on Awareness Science and Technology and Ubi-Media Computing, pp. 644–648 (2013)
15. Zhang, Z.: Microsoft kinect sensor and its effect. IEEE Multimedia **19**, 4–10 (2012)
16. Kawasue, K., Ikeda, T., Tokunaga, T., Harada, H.: Three-dimensional shape measurement system for black cattle using kinect sensor. Int. J. Circuit Signal Process. **7**(4), 220–230 (2013)
17. Kawasue, K., Win, K.D., Yoshida, K., Tokunaga, T.: Black cattle body shape and temprature measurement using themography and kinect sensor. Artif. Life Robot. **22**(4), 464–470 (2017)

18. Guo, H., et al.: 3D scanning of live pigs system and its application in body measurements. Proc. Int. Arch. Photogramm. Remote. Sens. Spat. Inf. Sci. **42**, 211–217 (2017)
19. Zhang, Z.: Determining the epipolar geometry and its uncertainty. IJCV **27**(2), 161–198 (1998)
20. Chai, J., Ma, S.: Robust epipolar geometry estimation using genetic algorithm. PRL **19**(9), 829–838 (1998)
21. Torras, C.: Computer Vision: Theory and Industrial Applications. Springer, Heidelberg (1992). https://doi.org/10.1007/978-3-642-48675-3

SConE: Siamese Constellation Embedding Descriptor for Image Matching

Tomasz Trzcinski[1,2], Jacek Komorowski[1(✉)], Lukasz Dabala[1],
Konrad Czarnota[1], Grzegorz Kurzejamski[1], and Simon Lynen[3]

[1] Warsaw University of Technology, Warsaw, Poland
jacek.komorowski@pw.edu.pl
[2] Tooploox, Wrocław, Poland
[3] Google, Mountain View, USA

Abstract. Numerous computer vision applications rely on local feature descriptors, such as SIFT, SURF or FREAK, for image matching. Although their local character makes image matching processes more robust to occlusions, it often leads to geometrically inconsistent keypoint matches that need to be filtered out, e.g. using RANSAC. In this paper we propose a novel, more discriminative, descriptor that includes not only local feature representation, but also information about the geometric layout of neighbouring keypoints. To that end, we use a Siamese architecture that learns a low-dimensional feature embedding of keypoint constellation by maximizing the distances between non-corresponding pairs of matched image patches, while minimizing it for correct matches. The 48-dimensional floating point descriptor that we train is built on top of the state-of-the-art FREAK descriptor achieves significant performance improvement over the competitors on a challenging TUM dataset.

Keywords: Feature descriptor · Image matching · Siamese networks

1 Introduction

Matching images with local feature descriptors is a fundamental part of many computer vision applications, including 3D reconstruction [1], panorama stitching [2] and monocular Simultaneous Localization and Mapping [3]. This topic has therefore gained significant attention from the research community [4–7]. While traditional approaches rely on hand-crafted features [4–7], more recent descriptors use machine learning techniques such as boosting [8] or deep learning [9,10] to train discriminative transformation-invariant representations. Although using local feature descriptors proposed in the literature increases robustness of image matching methods to partial occlusions, it often leads to incorrect descriptor matches, as presented in the upper right part of Fig. 1. In this paper, we propose a more discriminative feature descriptor by encoding information about constellation of keypoints, as shown in Fig. 1. To that end, we use a Siamese neural network that learns low-dimensional feature embeddings by minimizing distance

© Springer Nature Switzerland AG 2019
L. Leal-Taixé and S. Roth (Eds.): ECCV 2018 Workshops, LNCS 11129, pp. 401–413, 2019.
https://doi.org/10.1007/978-3-030-11009-3_24

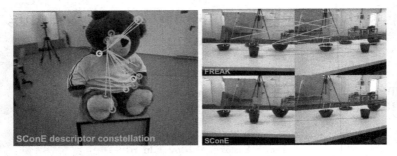

Fig. 1. Our proposed SConE descriptor uses information about neighbouring keypoints (left figure) to construct a discriminative low-dimensional embedding of a keypoint constellation. This way matching images with SConE reduces the number of incorrect matches found with respect to those found using a standard feature descriptor FREAK (coloured red in the top right figure) and increases the quality of resulting matches (bottom right figure). (Color figure online)

between similar keypoint constellations, while maximizing it for non-matching pairs. Instead of relying on a local intensity patch around the detected keypoint, we construct our embedding by feeding into the neural network information on a central keypoint and its nearest neighbourhood keypoints on the image. The resulting 48-dimensional Siamese Constellation Embedding descriptor, dubbed SConE for simplicity, is built using FREAK [5] as a base descriptor, however our framework is agnostic to descriptor types and can be generalized to other descriptors. Evaluation of our descriptor on the challenging TUM dataset [11] shows that despite its compact nature, SConE outperforms its competitors, while decreasing the computational cost of matching by eliminating the need for a geometrical verification step.

In the remainder of this paper, we first discuss related work in Sect. 2. We then describe the details of our method in Sect. 3. Finally, in Sect. 4 we show that our descriptor is able to outperform the state-of-the-art descriptors on a real-life dataset and we conclude the paper in Sect. 5.

2   Related Work

Due to the role of local features descriptors in many computer vision tasks, significant amount of work has been focused on building those representations effectively and efficiently [4–6,8,9]. Floating-point descriptors, such as SIFT [4] or SURF [6], typically offer better performance at a higher computational cost. Their binary competitors, such as FREAK [5] or ORB [7] approximate many operations and simplify the resulting representation to a binary output. Our proposed method is built on top of the binary FREAK descriptor, which offers an efficient yet powerful alternative to floating-point competitors. Nevertheless, the framework proposed in this paper is general enough to be applicable also to other descriptors.

Recently, due to their success in other domains, deep neural networks have also been used to train feature descriptors [9,10]. For instance, LIFT [10] uses a neural network architecture to handle full pipeline of feature extraction and computation. Another method called MatchNet uses Siamese neural network to jointly learn feature representation and matching procedure [12]. In [13], they use a triplet loss function coupled with convolutional neural network that aims at training context-augmented descriptors based on FREAK. In our work, we use a Siamese architecture to learn low-dimensional feature embeddings based on FREAK descriptors. But instead of using an image patch around detected keypoints, we incorporate data on the neighbourhood keypoints.

[14,15] apply convolutional neural networks to graph data to learn useful features. However our input data does not have a graph structure defined by an adjacency matrix. Spatial positions of neighbourhood keypoints and its attributes (binary descriptor, position and orientation) are important, not the structural relationships between keypoints.

Once keypoint descriptors are extracted, they are typically matched with each other to find correspondences between image regions. Depending on the final application, the matching can be done using brute-force or approximate nearest neighbour (ANN) search methods [16,17]. Heuristic techniques (e.g. two nearest neighbour ratio test [4]) are used to filter out outliers. In the final stage, putative matches are typically subject to geometric validation using epipolar constraint with a robust parameter estimation method, such as RANSAC [18] or its extension USAC [19]. A recently proposed approach called GMS (Grid-based Motion Statistics) [20] also aims at filtering out geometrically incorrect matches using a simple heuristic based on the number of matches in the keypoint neighbourhood. Although often effective, above methods require additional computational cost. In our method we propose to embed the geometrical information useful for filtering the matches within the descriptor itself. This way we can avoid the unnecessary post-processing step and increase the efficiency of the image matching pipeline.

3 Method

Our method aims at improving precision of the descriptor matching step. Instead of matching raw descriptors (e.g. 512-bit FREAK descriptors), we compare more discriminative representations of keypoint constellations. We define a *constellation* as a set of nearby keypoints in an image. It consists of a *central keypoint* and its k nearest, in Euclidean distance sense, keypoints detected on the same image. An exemplary constellation is visualized on Fig. 1. The following information is taken into account when constructing a *constellation*: binary descriptor, scale and orientation of a central keypoint; and binary descriptors, relative position (with respect to the central keypoint), scale and orientation of each of its k nearest neighbours. In this work, based on an initial experiments, we set $k = 20$.

Dimensionality of the data constituting a constellation is rather high. We find low dimensional constellation embeddings by training the Siamese neural network [21]. This produces low dimensional, real valued, embeddings that can be efficiently stored and processed. High-level architecture of our Siamese neural network is depicted on Fig. 2. The network consists of two identical Siamese modules (same network architecture with shared weights) that compute low dimensional constellation embeddings. Representations computed by Siamese modules can be matched using standard Euclidean distance between them.

The network is trained by presenting mini-batches consisting of pairs of similar and dissimilar constellations. We consider two constellations similar if their central keypoint is a projection of the same 3D scene point (landmark). Otherwise constellations are dissimilar. We use a contrastive loss function, as formulated in [22]. Let X_1, X_2 be a pair of constellations in the training set and Y a binary label assigned to this pair. $Y = 0$ if constellations X_1 and X_2 are similar, and $Y = 1$ if they are dissimilar. D_W is a parametrized distance function between constellations X_1 and X_2, defined as an Euclidean distance between learned constellation embeddings G_W.

$$D_W (X_1, X_2) = ||G_W (X_1) - G_W (X_2)||_2 \qquad (1)$$

The loss $\mathcal{L}$ function minimized during the training is defined as:

$$\mathcal{L} = \sum_{i=1}^{P} L\left(W, (Y, X_1, X_2)^i\right), \qquad (2)$$

with

$$L\left(W, (Y, X_1, X_2)^i\right) = (1 - Y) L_S\left(D_W^i\right) + Y L_D\left(D_W^i\right) \qquad (3)$$

where $(Y, X_1, X_2)^i$ is the i-th sample composed of a pair of constellations X_1, X_2 and a binary label. $L_s = \frac{1}{2}(D_W)^2$ is a partial loss function for a pair of similar constellations and $L_D = \frac{1}{2}(\max\{0, margin - D_W\})^2$ is a partial loss function for a pair of dissimilar constellations.

As shown in Fig. 2, a constellation is fed to the *constellation embedding module* as a high dimensional vector. We process binary descriptor (512 dimensions for FREAK), scale and orientation (2 dimensions) of the central descriptor. For each neighbourhood keypoint, we use its binary feature descriptor (512 dimensions) and relative position, scale and orientation (4 dimensions). For a constellation consisting of the central descriptor and its 20 nearest neighbours, this gives $514 + 20 \times 516 = 10834$ dimensions. We designed the *constellation embedding module* (see bottom of Fig. 2) in a modular fashion. The design was based on an extensive series of experiments to help us identify the best architecture of each component. The best performing architecture is described below. The twin *constellation embedding module* first computes k 32-dimensional embeddings of k neighbour binary descriptors. The resulting embeddings are concatenated with k neighbours relative position, relative orientation and relative scale with respect to the central keypoint. This gives a sequence of k 36-dimensional vectors which are further processed by RNN (recurrent neural network) module producing 32-dimensional neighbourhood representation. Then neighbourhood representation

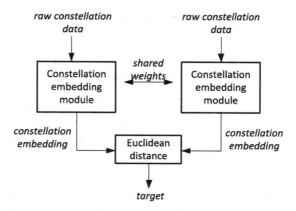

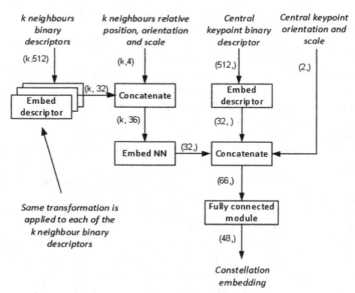

Fig. 2. (Top) High level architecture of the Siamese neural network computing constellation embeddings. (Bottom) Architecture of a constellation embedding module of a Siamese neural network. We feed into the network information on central keypoint and its nearest, in Euclidean distance sense, neighbourhood keypoints on the image. Central keypoint FREAK descriptor, orientation and scale are used along with nearest neighbours, in Euclidean distance sense, informations. That include FREAK descriptors, their relative positions, orientations and scales with respect to the central keypoint. Hence, our resulting SConE descriptor of the central keypoint offers better performance of descriptor matching at a lower computational cost than competing descriptors.

is concatenated with the central keypoint binary descriptor, orientation and scale resulting in 66-dimensional vector. This is processed by a final fully connected module resulting in the 48-dimensional constellation embedding called SConE

Table 1. Components of a twin constellation embedding module from Fig. 2. Scaled Exponential Liner Unit (SELU) [23] activation is used after each fully-connected layer.

Component name	Details
Embed descriptor	3 fully-connected layers with 512/256/32 units
Embed NN	2 layer bidirectional LSTM [24] with 32/32 units followed by 3 fully-connected layers with 64/64/32 units
Fully-connected module	3 fully-connected layers with 64/64/48 units

for Siamese Constellation Embedding descriptor. Details of each component are given in Table 1. The size of the final embedding (48 real values) was chosen as a compromise between the descriptor discriminative power and the storage requirements.

Siamese neural network training is conducted using data acquired with structure-from-motion solution embedded in a Google Tango tablet. The device produces datasets containing keypoints and feature descriptors detected on the recorded video sequences. Camera poses and scene structure, in the form of sparse 3D point sets, are reconstructed using reliable structure-from-motion techniques. The training set was constructed by concatenating samples from multiple video sequences. It consists of almost 10 thousand keyframes with over 4 million FREAK descriptors linked with 259 thousand landmarks. The validation sequence, used to measure the performance of the trained networks, contains almost 5 thousand keyframes with over 2 million feature descriptors linked with 120 thousand landmarks. In both sequences, almost half of the feature descriptors are linked with reconstructed 3D scene points (landmarks) whereas the rest of them is not linked with any landmark.

We experimentally choose the number of neighbours used to form the constellation, that produces the most discriminative SConE descriptor. This is done by training the Siamese network multiple times using constellations of various size and evaluating the performance of the trained network. We use nearest neighbour search precision on the embeddings of the validation set as the performance measure. The precision is calculated as follows. First, embeddings of validation set elements are calculated using the constellation embedding module of the trained Siamese network. Then 10 thousand embeddings is randomly chosen from the validation set. For each sampled embedding, its nearest neighbour in embedding space (that is in Euclidean space, as embeddings are real-valued vectors) is found. If the nearest neighbour is linked with the same 3D scene point (landmark) as the sampled element we declare a match. *Precision* is calculated as the percentage of correct matches. The results are depicted on Fig. 3. As the number of neighbours increases the precision grows, to reach a maximum for 20 neighbours. Compared to using raw FREAK descriptors we get increase of nearest neighbour search precision from 0.807 to 0.851 on our validation set.

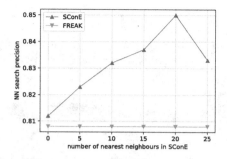

Fig. 3. The influence of k nearest neighbours on the nearest neighbour search precision in the validation set. The best results are achieved when 20 neighbourhood keypoints are used to form a constellation.

4   Evaluation

This section describes evaluation procedure and its results. The evaluation dataset is described in Sect. 4.1. In Sect. 4.2 we present our evaluation protocol. Finally, in Sect. 4.3 we show the results of our evaluations.

4.1   Dataset

For the evaluation procedure, we use a challenging TUM dataset [11], often used in other works to compare descriptors' performance [20]. TUM is a large dataset with sequences recorded using Microsoft Kinect sensor and we choose seven of them for evaluation: `fr1/plant`, `fr2/dishes`, `fr2/metallic_sphere2`, `ft3/cabinet`, `fr3/large_cabinet`, `fr2/flowerbouquet` and `fr3/teddy`. Sample sequences can be seen in top of Fig. 4. In addition to images, sensor ground-truth trajectory and depth-maps are provided. We divide each sequence into 100 long subsequences. First frame is treated as a reference and 99 others are used for matching. Bottom of Fig. 4 presents four different frames from a sequence. They differ significantly, the last one being rotated almost 360°. It makes it hard for matchers to find any correct matches between first and last frame in such scenario.

Due to a lot of blurred images and changes in lighting, the TUM dataset is considered to be rather challenging. Additional difficulty comes from the fact that color images, depth maps and camera positions are not perfectly consistent. They were collected in different moments of time, so timestamps cannot be perfectly aligned and to address this problem we approximate them to minimize the time gaps between frames. Furthermore, due to the limitation of the capturing device, a large portion of depth maps does not provide correct depth values, especially on the edges of objects where a large portion of keypoints is detected. Hence we use an epipolar geometry condition and ground truth camera poses to verify correctness of a match.

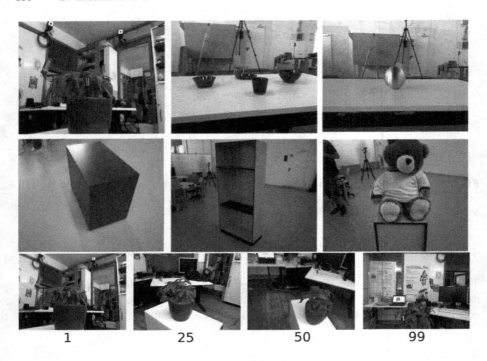

Fig. 4. (Top) Exemplary images from TUM [11] video sequences used in evaluation of our method. (Bottom) 1st, 25th, 50th and 99th keyframes from one test sequence (`fr1/plant`). There's a large viewpoint variation in frames forming one sequence.

4.2 Evaluation Procedure

We test our descriptor in a demanding scenario of a real application, strictly connected with SLAM and Structure from Motion pipelines. We use TUM's ground truth presented as a trajectory and calibration data for each camera in the set. The TUM dataset is specifically designed to evaluate Structure from Motion algorithms and therefore its frame resolution is low and graphical content is often lacking the details necessary to track dense feature sets. Nevertheless, such characteristics create a demanding benchmark for camera pose estimation and we therefore use it in our evaluation.

We compare our method to the state-of-the-art methods for image matching: FREAK [5], SURF [6], SIFT [4], ORB [7] (implementations comes from OpenCV [25] package), GMS [20] and embeddings calculated by our custom artificial neural network (SConE). For SConE, we first use FAST [26] key point detection algorithm. Then we compute FREAK feature descriptors at detected keypoints. SConE descriptors are calculated using the constellation embedding module of the trained Siamese network. The network training is performed as described in Sect. 3. For each 100 frame subsequence from the evaluated TUM sequence, we compute matches between the first frame and all others, resulting in 99 image

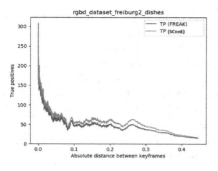
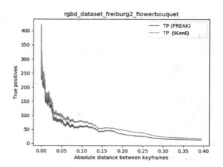

Fig. 5. Number of true positives in matching feature descriptors between a pair of images as a function of an angular distance between keyframes. Results on `fr2/dishes` (left) `fr2/flowerbouquet` (right) sequences from TUM [11] dataset are presented. SConE consistently yields better results than FREAK descriptor due to encoding additional information about the neighbourhood keypoints.

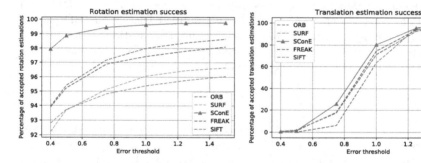

Fig. 6. Pose estimation errors on TUM [11] dataset for SConE and competing descriptors. SConE outperforms the state-of-the-art descriptors, including SIFT and SURF, across all error thresholds.

pair matches. For each image pair we find pairs of corresponding features with a brute-force approach. Matches are then filtered using standard ratio-test.

We compute essential matrix from the key point correspondences for each image pair. From them we estimate relative camera pose for each pair of images in form of a rotation matrix and translation vector. We use the OpenCV [25] implementation with RANSAC for this purpose.

RANSAC is needed in the process because of two reasons. The first is its ability to filter out matches considered good given a 3D model, but giving perturbations in affine transformation estimation. This situation happens when the scene contains moving or deforming objects. The second factor is connected with a level of locality in SConE. SConE makes use of constellation, incorporating structural data of a bigger area than the base descriptor itself, but still is considered as a local descriptor. If duplicate elements of the scene appear, SConE is prone to generate bad matches. Feature duplicates can be seen in various real case scenarios where textures contain patterns or multiple features of the same appearance, for instance in windows or buildings' facades.

We compare the relative pose recovered using abovementioned procedure against ground truth and calculate qualitative metric for each image pair. The metric is presented as an error in translation and rotation estimation, calculated according to the procedure described in the Odometry Development Kit from KITTI benchmark [27]. KITTI benchmark defines a method of error calculation for 3D tracks with six degrees of freedom with asynchronous sampling. In our case the data is synchronized, so the formulas are straightforward. Error in translation is calculated as a translation vector difference in 3D. Error for rotation is calculated from relative 3×3 rotation matrix dR according to the formula:

$$d = \frac{tr\,(dR) - 1.0}{2} \tag{4}$$

$$R_{err} = acos\,(\max\,(\min\,(d, 1.0)\,, -1.0)) \tag{5}$$

In addition to GMS and basic matchers, we use DeepMatching (DM [28]), Bilateral Functions Matching (BM [29]) and Bounded Distortion (BD [30]) as state-of-the-art image matchers. We use original implementations of its authors, so its computational efficiency may be considered as far from optimal. Where possible, we use only one computing thread for better comparison.

4.3   Results

We analyse our results using pose estimation errors obtained for various descriptors. Figure 6 shows the results of this experiment. SConE outperforms all basic features with ratio tests. The performance gap is substantial, and shows gain over basic FREAK descriptor. SConE uses FREAK keypoints as a base descriptor for learning, thus it has the same keypoints pool before filtering stage. This characteristic lets us build simple comparison based solely on true positives after ratio test. Figure 5 shows number of true positives on FREAK keypoint locations, using both FREAK descriptors and SConE embeddings. The X-axis contains absolute distance between frames calculated as the difference between quaternion rotations for each camera position.

SConE gives very good results in comparison with advanced matching methods, as shown in Fig. 7. All of the descriptors give very similar results in translation estimation. Rotation estimation is much more prone to keypoint localization perturbations, thus shows more variance between methods. Our approach outperforms GMS with its default keypoints pool (10 000 ORB keypoints).

Furthermore, we evaluate the computational complexity of our proposed SConE descriptor-based matching and compare it with the competing methods. We measure both descriptor extraction and matching times. For raw descriptors we use brute force matcher. Figure 8 shows the results of this comparison. SConE adds very little overhead to FREAK computation, which is used as base. It's much faster then GMS, while obtaining better results.

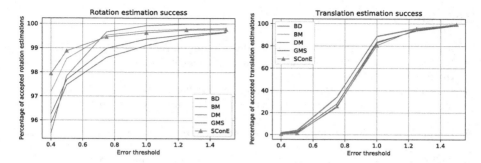

Fig. 7. Pose estimation errors on TUM dataset for SConE and significantly more complex matching procedures. Performance of SConE is au pair with much more advanced keypoint matching procedures.

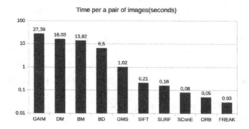

Fig. 8. Descriptor extraction and matching time for matching descriptors between a pair of images. SConE offers very competitive performance compared to more sophisticated matching methods.

5 Conclusions

In this paper, we propose a novel low-dimensional feature descriptor that incorporates geometrical information about the layout of neighbouring keypoints. This way we are able to reduce the importance of additional post-processing step that typically aims at filtering out incorrect matches. To train our descriptor we use Siamese neural network architecture and feed it with central keypoint descriptor, as well as neighbouring keypoints and their descriptors, relative position, orientation and scale. Although our framework is agnostic to descriptor type, we use as our base descriptor FREAK and show that the SConE descriptor generated by our neural network outperforms competitors on a challenging TUM dataset.

Acknowledgement. This research was supported by Google Sponsor Research Agreement under the project "Efficient visual localization on mobile devices".

The Titan X Pascal used for this research was donated by the NVIDIA Corporation.

References

1. Agarwal, S., et al.: Building Rome in a day. Commun. ACM **54**(10), 105–112 (2011)
2. Brown, M., Lowe, D.G.: Automatic panoramic image stitching using invariant features. IJCV **74**(1), 59–73 (2007)
3. Lynen, S., Sattler, T., Bosse, M., Hesch, J.A., Pollefeys, M., Siegwart, R.: Get out of my lab: large-scale, real-time visual-inertial localization. In: Robotics: Science and Systems (2015)
4. Lowe, D.G.: Distinctive image features from scale-invariant keypoints. IJCV **60**(2), 91–110 (2004)
5. Alahi, A., Ortiz, R., Vandergheynst, P.: FREAK: fast retina keypoint. In: CVPR (2012)
6. Bay, H., Tuytelaars, T., Van Gool, L.: SURF: speeded up robust features. In: Leonardis, A., Bischof, H., Pinz, A. (eds.) ECCV 2006. LNCS, vol. 3951, pp. 404–417. Springer, Heidelberg (2006). https://doi.org/10.1007/11744023_32
7. Rublee, E., Rabaud, V., Konolige, K., Bradski, G.: ORB: an efficient alternative to sift or surf. In: ICCV (2011)
8. Trzcinski, T., Christoudias, M., Lepetit, V., Fua, P.: Boosting binary keypoint descriptors. In: CVPR (2013)
9. Simo-Serra, E., Trulls, E., Ferraz, L., Kokkinos, I., Fua, P., Moreno-Noguer, F.: Discriminative learning of deep convolutional feature point descriptors. In: ICCV (2015)
10. Yi, K.M., Trulls, E., Lepetit, V., Fua, P.: LIFT: learned invariant feature transform. In: Leibe, B., Matas, J., Sebe, N., Welling, M. (eds.) ECCV 2016. LNCS, vol. 9910, pp. 467–483. Springer, Cham (2016). https://doi.org/10.1007/978-3-319-46466-4_28
11. Sturm, J., Engelhard, N., Endres, F., Burgard, W., Cremers, D.: A benchmark for the evaluation of RGB-D SLAM systems. In: IROS (2012)
12. Han, X., Leung, T., Jia, Y., Sukthankar, R., Berg, A.C.: MatchNet: unifying feature and metric learning for patch-based matching. In: CVPR (2015)
13. Loquercio, A., Dymczyk, M., Zeisl, B., Lynen, S., Gilitschenski, I., Siegwart, R.: Efficient descriptor learning for large scale localization. In: ICRA (2017)
14. Niepert, M., Ahmed, M., Kutzkov, K.: Learning convolutional neural networks for graphs. In: Proceedings of the 33rd International Conference on International Conference on Machine Learning, ICML 2016, vol. 48, pp. 2014–2023. JMLR.org (2016)
15. Defferrard, M., Bresson, X., Vandergheynst, P.: Convolutional neural networks on graphs with fast localized spectral filtering. In: Proceedings of the 30th International Conference on Neural Information Processing Systems, NIPS 2016, USA, pp. 3844–3852. Curran Associates, Inc. (2016)
16. Muja, M., Lowe, D.G.: Fast matching of binary features. In: Computer and Robot Vision (CRV) (2012)
17. Muja, M., Lowe, D.G.: Scalable nearest neighbor algorithms for high dimensional data. TPAMI **36**(11), 2227–2240 (2014)
18. Fischler, M.A., Bolles, R.C.: Random sample consensus: a paradigm for model fitting with applications to image analysis and automated cartography. Commun. ACM **24**(6), 381–395 (1981)
19. Raguram, R., Chum, O., Pollefeys, M., Matas, J., Frahm, J.M.: USAC: a universal framework for random sample consensus. TPAMI **35**(8), 2022–2038 (2013)

20. Bian, J., Lin, W.Y., Matsushita, Y., Yeung, S.K., Nguyen, T.D., Cheng, M.M.: GMS: grid-based motion statistics for fast, ultra-robust feature correspondence. In: CVPR (2017)
21. Bromley, J., Guyon, I., LeCun, Y., Säckinger, E., Shah, R.: Signature verification using a "siamese" time delay neural network. In: NIPS (1993)
22. Hadsell, R., Chopra, S., LeCun, Y.: Dimensionality reduction by learning an invariant mapping. In: CVPR (2006)
23. Klambauer, G., Unterthiner, T., Mayr, A., Hochreiter, S.: Self-normalizing neural networks. In: Guyon, I., et al. (eds.) Advances in Neural Information Processing Systems 30, pp. 971–980. Curran Associates, Inc. (2017)
24. Hochreiter, S., Schmidhuber, J.: Long short-term memory. Neural Comput. 9(8), 1735–1780 (1997)
25. https://opencv.org/
26. Rosten, E., Drummond, T.: Machine learning for high-speed corner detection. In: Leonardis, A., Bischof, H., Pinz, A. (eds.) ECCV 2006. LNCS, vol. 3951, pp. 430–443. Springer, Heidelberg (2006). https://doi.org/10.1007/11744023_34
27. Geiger, A., Lenz, P., Urtasun, R.: Are we ready for autonomous driving? The KITTI vision benchmark suite. In: CVPR (2012)
28. Weinzaepfel, P., Revaud, J., Harchaoui, Z., Schmid, C.: DeepFlow: large displacement optical flow with deep matching. In: ICCV (2013)
29. Lin, W.-Y.D., Cheng, M.-M., Lu, J., Yang, H., Do, M.N., Torr, P.: Bilateral functions for global motion modeling. In: Fleet, D., Pajdla, T., Schiele, B., Tuytelaars, T. (eds.) ECCV 2014. LNCS, vol. 8692, pp. 341–356. Springer, Cham (2014). https://doi.org/10.1007/978-3-319-10593-2_23
30. Lipman, Y., Yagev, S., Poranne, R., Jacobs, D.W., Basri, R.: Feature matching with bounded distortion. ACM Trans. Graph. 33(3), 26:1–26:14 (2014)

RGB-D SLAM Based Incremental Cuboid Modeling

Masashi Mishima[1]($\boxtimes$), Hideaki Uchiyama[1], Diego Thomas[1],
Rin-ichiro Taniguchi[1], Rafael Roberto[2], João Paulo Lima[2,3],
and Veronica Teichrieb[2]

[1] Kyushu University, Fukuoka, Japan
{mishima,uchiyama,thomas}@limu.ait.kyushu-u.ac.jp
rin@kyudai.jp
[2] Universidade Federal de Pernambuco, Recife, Brazil
{rar3,jpsml,vt}@cin.ufpe.br
[3] Universidade Federal Rural de Pernambuco, Recife, Brazil
http://limu.ait.kyushu-u.ac.jp/

Abstract. This paper present a framework for incremental 3D cuboid modeling combined with RGB-D SLAM. While performing RGB-D SLAM, planes are incrementally reconstructed from point clouds. Then, cuboids are detected in the planes by analyzing the positional relationships between the planes; orthogonality, convexity, and proximity. Finally, the position, pose and size of a cuboid are determined by computing the intersection of three perpendicular planes. In addition, the cuboid shapes are incrementally updated to suppress false detections with sequential measurements. As an application of our framework, an augmented reality based interactive cuboid modeling system is introduced. In the evaluation at a cluttered environment, the precision and recall of the cuboid detection are improved with our framework owing to stable plane detection, compared with a batch based method.

Keywords: Geometric shape · Cuboid ·
Incrementally structural modeling · Point cloud

1 Introduction

Owing to the advance of visual odometry and simultaneous localization and mapping (SLAM), the automated control of cars, drones and robots has been achieved by generating a point cloud based map. Although the localization can be performed by using the map, the map does not represent semantics in the environment. For 3D scene understanding, it is important to convert a point cloud into an object-level representation. Planes, cylinders and spheres are examples

Electronic supplementary material The online version of this chapter (https://doi.org/10.1007/978-3-030-11009-3_25) contains supplementary material, which is available to authorized users.

L. Leal-Taixé and S. Roth (Eds.): ECCV 2018 Workshops, LNCS 11129, pp. 414–429, 2019.
https://doi.org/10.1007/978-3-030-11009-3_25

of a parametric object representation. The recognition of such primitive shapes is an important process for obstacle avoidance and object grasping [21].

A cuboid is also considered as an informative shape representation because there exist many cuboids in our environment. For instance, delivery boxes used in logistics and product packages in markets can be represented by cuboids. To achieve automated robot manipulation in such environments, the techniques to recognize cuboid objects are often required. In the literature, the cuboid detection has been performed by using an RGB image [1,6–8,26] or a point cloud generated with an RGB-D image or LIDAR [5,9,10,13,16,18–20]. Generally, these methods are based on an off-line batch processing such that the recognition is performed only with a single observation. Because of noisy observations, they often suffer from both false positives and false negatives. To suppress the false detections, an on-line sequential approach is investigated in our framework because it can incorporate multiple observations with temporal filtering.

In this paper, we propose a framework for incremental cuboid modeling combined with RGB-D SLAM. At every frame, planes are incrementally reconstructed from points clouds acquired from an RGB-D SLAM based approach [17], and used as input to our framework. Then, the planes are clustered to compose a cuboid by analyzing three plane positional relationships; orthogonality, convexity, and proximity. To accurately reconstruct a cuboid, a cluster of three perpendicular planes is first selected, and their intersection is computed [4]. By determining three perpendicular cuboid edges from both the intersection and the normal vectors of each face, the width, height and depth are finally computed. Since the plane parameters are incrementally updated [17], the positional relationships are analyzed in every frame not only for newly-detected planes but also for previously-detected cuboids. False detections can be suppressed with this sequential processing such that a falsely-detected cuboid face can be replaced with a correct one. Also, a new cuboid face can be assigned to a previously-detected cuboid as a forth one. As another advantage of our incremental approach, we introduce an interactive cuboid modeling system to assist users to reconstruct cuboids with augmented reality (AR) based affordance. In the evaluation, the accuracy of our framework was quantitatively evaluated by using some boxes with their ground truth sizes. Also, the comparison between a batch based method and our incremental one was investigated to show the effectiveness of our incremental approach at a cluttered environment. Finally, the computational cost was investigated to show that our framework can run in real time at a room-scale environment. The contributions of our paper are summarized as follows.

- A cuboid reconstruction is performed by searching three perpendicular planes and computing the intersection of the planes.
- A framework for incremental cuboid modeling based on cuboid detection and mapping is proposed.
- An application for AR based interactive cuboid modeling is presented.

2 Related Work

The cuboid detection has been investigated in semantic 3D scene understanding. In this section, we review the literature from the aspects of devices used for the detection.

Recognizing cuboids from a single RGB image has been proposed [1,3,6–8,26]. Hedau *et al.* reconstructed a cuboid based room layout by using vanishing points [6,7]. First, wall, ceiling and furniture contours were extracted from an input image, and then vanishing points were estimated from orthogonal three straight lines. Finally, a bounding box was aligned to a rectangular area to recognize a cuboid object. Del *et al.* proposed to use the Manhattan world property such that many surfaces in a room were parallel to three principle ones [1]. This assumption is valid only when cuboids are placed on a floor and parallel to walls. Xiao *et al.* proposed to first detect vertices on a cuboid based on histograms of oriented gradients, and then detect a cuboid by finding connected edges [26]. Hejrati and Ramanan investigated the performance of several feature representations for categorizing cuboid objects [8]. Dwibedi *et al.* proposed a deep learning based region proposal method for the cuboid detection [3]. Basically, the cuboid detection using a RGB image is an ill-posed problem, and the accuracy is largely degraded under occlusions.

A point cloud acquired from RGB-D images or LIDAR has also been used for the cuboid detection [5,9,10,13,15,16,18–20]. Shape descriptors for arbitrary 3D objects were proposed for object classification including cuboids [18–20]. For indoor environments, the prior knowledge of a room layout was incorporated to globally optimize the object arrangement including cuboids in the room [13,19]. To detect buildings as cuboids, a closed polyhedral model is searched from planes detected in a point cloud [15]. An optimization based approach was proposed by designing a cost function with surfaces, volumes and their layout to detect cuboids in an RGB-D image [5,9,10]. Compared with the approach using a RGB image, the one using a point cloud can provide the size and pose of a cuboid in a scene. However, it still suffers from the false detections in the presence of sensor noises and registration error. To improve the stability and accuracy of the cuboid detection, we propose an incremental approach by fusing multiple measurements captured from different viewpoints without using any constraint on the object arrangement.

3 Overview

We start by explaining the main steps of our algorithm. First, a plane map, which is composed of oriented planes, is incrementally generated from point clouds, and used as input to our framework. This reconstruction process is based on an existing method [17] that applies a shape detection method [22] to incoming point clouds acquired from RGB-D SLAM [12]. This method can incrementally reconstruct accurate parametric shapes including planes, and largely contribute to our stable cuboid modeling.

From the plane map, a cuboid map, which is composed of cuboids with positions, poses, and sizes, is generated. As described in Sect. 4, cuboid faces are detected among a group of planes by cuboid check based on analyzing plane positional relationships. A cuboid is a convex polyhedron comprising six quadrilateral faces. Also, the adjacent faces of a cuboid are perpendicularly connected. By analyzing these relationships, cuboids can be detected. The procedure of the cuboid detection is illustrated in Fig. 1. First, the orthogonality of all the pairs of two planes in the plane map is investigated by brute force searching. Next, a pair of two perpendicular planes is selected to search their third plane by using the cross product of the two plane normals. Finally, the proximity between the planes is checked. When a set of these three planes passes the cuboid check, the planes are classified as composing a cuboid. By computing the intersection of the planes, the position, pose, and size of a cuboid are determined.

To generate an accurate cuboid map, an incremental reconstruction process is proposed, as described in Sect. 5. At every frame, the status of the planes in the plane map is classified into planes assigned to cuboids and unassigned ones, as illustrated in Fig. 2. The cuboid check is performed for the cuboids in the cuboid map to check the positional relationships of the cuboid faces in every frame because their parameters are incrementally updated [17], This process is specifically referred to as cuboid update. For the unassigned planes, the cuboid check with the cuboid faces in the cuboid map is first performed so that the faces in the cuboid map can be replaced with new planes or an undetected cuboid face such as a fourth plane can be assigned to a cuboid in the cuboid map. Then, the cuboid detection is performed for the remaining unassigned planes. This incremental process allows users to make modeling succeed with AR based affordance.

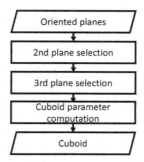

Fig. 1. Cuboid detection. From oriented planes, two planes are first selected as a plane pair by checking their positional relationships. Then, the third plane perpendicular to the pair is searched by using the cross product of the two plane normals. Finally, the cuboid shape parameters are computed from these three planes.

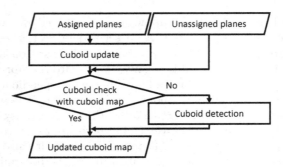

Fig. 2. Cuboid mapping. The status of the planes in the plane map is classified into planes assigned to cuboids or not. For the assigned planes, the cuboid check is performed for the cuboids in the map in every frame, as cuboid update. For the unassigned planes, the cuboid check with the cuboids in the map is first performed, and then the cuboid detection is performed if necessary.

4   Cuboid Detection

Next, we explain the detail of detecting a cuboid from planes. The first process is to select two perpendicular planes by analyzing the positional relationships. The second process is to search the third plane by using the cross product of the two plane normals. After three perpendicular faces are determined, cuboid shape parameters are also determined by computing the intersection of the three planes.

4.1   Second Plane Selection

In this process, sets of two planes composing a cuboid are searched in a brute force manner. An i-th plane in the plane map is parameterized with the center of mass p_i and the normal vector n_i [17]. First, the inner products between a target plane and all of the other planes are computed, as orthogonality check. A plane is selected if the angle computed from the inner product is perpendicular with an error tolerance (e.g. 5°). However, the orthogonality is not sufficient for the cuboid detection because there are two possibilities of the positional relationship between two planes; concave and convex. Also, a plane can be selected even if it is far from the target plane and does not compose a cuboid in the environment. Therefore, in the latter processes, these criteria are considered to select an appropriate plane.

For the plane selected by the orthogonality check, the convexity with the target plane is analyzed by using [25], as convexity check. If the relationship between two planes is concave, they do not compose a cuboid because we assume that only outer cuboid faces are captured. Since each plane has the center of mass and the normal vector, the convexity can be computed from them. In Fig. 3, n_1 and n_2 are the normal vectors, and p_1 and p_2 are the centers, and α_1 and α_2 are the angles between a vector $p_1 - p_2$ and each normal vector n_1 and n_2, respectively. When α_1 is smaller than α_2, the relationship between two planes is convex. Otherwise, the relationship is concave. Therefore, a plane is selected when it satisfies this convex condition: $\alpha_1 < \alpha_2$.

After performing both orthogonality and convexity checks, there may be multiple candidates for the second plane of a cuboid. In this case, the plane closest to the target plane is finally selected. The distance between each candidate and the target plane is computed by using the center of mass, as proximity check. All of these checks between two planes are referred to as cuboid check.

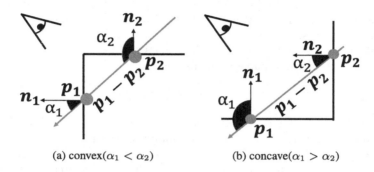

(a) convex($\alpha_1 < \alpha_2$)   (b) concave($\alpha_1 > \alpha_2$)

Fig. 3. Convexity check. The convexity is analyzed by using the centers of mass and the normal vectors [25].

4.2   Third Plane Selection

From the two perpendicular planes, it is possible to infer a cuboid by using the bounding box for both planes. However, the inference may be incorrect because 3D edge regions of a cuboid cannot normally be degraded in depth images. To accurately reconstruct a cuboid, three perpendicular planes are used to determine cuboid shape parameters.

First, the normalized normal vectors for all of the planes in the plane map are indexed by using a kd-tree, as a plane normal space for fast approximated nearest neighbor searching. Then, the cross product of the two perpendicular planes is computed, and is used as a query to the kd-tree to search the third plane of a cuboid. In other words, planes orthogonal to both of the two planes are searched in the space. By using the radius search in the kd-tree with a threshold (e.g. 0.1 for L2 norm between two vectors), the candidates for the third plane are retrieved. Then, the convexity with each of the two planes is checked for each candidate. Finally, the third plane is selected from the candidates according to the proximity check.

4.3   Cuboid Parameter Estimation

To reconstruct an accurate cuboid shape, the shape parameters are computed from the three perpendicular planes. In our framework, the parameters are the origin vertex position, three edge directions from the origin, and their lengths. In Fig. 4, π_i is an ith plane, n_i is the normal vector of π_i, and p_i is the center of mass, and p_o is the intersection of the three perpendicular planes. First, p_o is computed by using [4] as follows.

$$p_o = \frac{(p_1 \cdot n_1)(n_2 \times n_3)}{(n_1 \times n_2) \cdot n_3} + \frac{(p_2 \cdot n_2)(n_3 \times n_1)}{(n_1 \times n_2) \cdot n_3} + \frac{(p_3 \cdot n_3)(n_1 \times n_2)}{(n_1 \times n_2) \cdot n_3} \quad (1)$$

The intersection can be used as the origin of a cuboid to describe the shape parameters. After determining the intersection, the edge directions from the intersection can automatically be determined because they correspond to the plane normal vectors.

To determine the size of a cuboid, the length of each edge is computed by projecting the points on a plane onto the edge as

$$length = \max_i \{(x_i - p_o) \cdot n\} \quad (2)$$

where n is the normalized edge direction vector, and x_i is an ith point in the plane. This equation represents that the points on the plane sharing the edge are projected onto the edge, and the furthest point from the intersection on the edge is selected to compute the length. Since each edge is shared by two planes, the average of two lengths is used as a final result. It should be noted that the plane numbers i can be arbitrary determined for the three perpendicular planes.

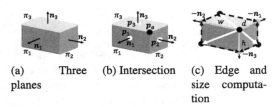

(a)   Three planes   (b) Intersection   (c) Edge and size computation

Fig. 4. Cuboid parameter estimation. The intersection of three perpendicular planes is first computed by using the centers of mass and the plane normal vectors. Edges of a cuboid are then determined by using the plane normal vectors. The width, height and depth are finally computed from the point projection from a plane to an edge.

5   Cuboid Mapping

In the plane map, the status of planes can be divided into two categories; planes assigned to one of the cuboids in the cuboid map, and the rest. The first category is referred to as assigned planes, and the other is unassigned planes. When a new plane appears in the plane map, it is first considered as an unassigned plane. As illustrated in Fig. 2, the process for each plane is different according to the status. In this section, we explain the detail of the cuboid mapping.

5.1 Cuboid Update

To reduce the false detections, the cuboid check is performed for the cuboid faces in the cuboid map. While capturing only a part of a plane, a cuboid may be wrongly detected as a false positive or a false negative at a time due to the incomplete measurement. Therefore, in every frame, the cuboid check is applied to the cuboids in the map, and cuboid shapes are updated such that some cuboids disappear or others are refined.

This cuboid update is useful for the visual feedback to users. Normally, users do not understand the best way to capture a scene and when to finish capturing it. By using an incremental approach, false positives and false negatives are visualized in an on-line manner. This helps users to complete the modeling because they can understand the progress.

As an alternative approach, it is possible to apply a batch based method to a point cloud in every frame. However, the computational cost at a frame increases according to the size of the point cloud. Also, it is redundant to search cuboids in the map in every frame because the detection result at a frame can be useful at the next frame. In terms of the computational efficiency, the incremental approach is appropriate for on-line systems.

5.2 Cuboid Check with Cuboid Map

The unassigned planes in the plain map contain both newly-detected planes and previously-detected planes that are not assigned to the cuboids. For those planes, the cuboid check with respect to all the cuboids in the map is first performed. A cuboid face in the map can be replaced with an unassigned plane when an unassigned plane passes the cuboid check, its normal vector is the same as the cuboid face one, and it is more proximate than the cuboid face. Also, the plane is assigned to the cuboid if it passes the cuboid check, and it corresponds to a missing face in the cuboid. After this process, the cuboid shape parameters are updated.

For the remaining unassigned planes, the cuboid detection is performed, as described in Sect. 4. After a set of three perpendicular planes is detected, a new cuboid is generated and inserted into the cuboid map.

6 Interactive Cuboid Modeling

Since 3D modeling using a camera is not an easy task for non-experts, interactive techniques have been proposed [24]. For instance, the result of the 3D modeling can be easily modified on user interfaces [23,27]. Also, the incompleteness of the modeling is visualized by showing a 2D slide of a point cloud for modeling a room [2] or showing an example for modeling an object [11]. Here, we introduce a simple but effective affordance for modeling a cuboid.

As illustrated in Fig. 5, the points on planes are overlaid with some colors. Blue regions and yellow ones represent detected cuboids as completed ones and two perpendicular planes as incomplete ones, respectively. In other words, the color represents the modeling progress. To model a cuboid, the user's task is to find yellow regions and then capture the remaining plane where colored points are not overlaid, as illustrated in Fig. 5a. This corresponds to the instruction for the users. Since the users are induced to capture the remaining plane from the visualization, this interaction can be regarded as AR based affordance. After the user successfully captures the cuboid, the color of the cuboid becomes blue, as illustrated in Fig. 5b. Owing to the incremental approach, it is possible to develop this type of interactive modeling systems.

(a) Incomplete (Top is missing)   (b) Completed (Top is captured)

Fig. 5. Interactive cuboid modeling. Yellow regions and blue ones represent incomplete and completed, respectively. A box is represented by yellow in (a), and the color becomes blue in (b) after the user completely captures it. (Color figure online)

7   Evaluation

To evaluate the performance of our proposed framework, we first prepared RGB-D image sequences capturing multiple boxes as our dataset because only a dataset for single views was developed in the literature [26] and there is no dataset with RGB-D sequences containing cuboid ground truth annotations. For the camera, a Kinect V1 sensor was used, and therefore the boxes were set up in the indoor environments. The size of each box was measured by a ruler as a ground truth.

For the evaluation criterion, the accuracy of each estimated cuboid shape was investigated by comparing the result with its ground truth. To investigate the effectiveness of our proposed method, a batch based cuboid detection in a point cloud was implemented as a benchmarking method, and its result was compared with our result. Finally, the computational cost of each process was measured.

7.1   Cuboid Shape Estimation

As illustrated in Fig. 6, three scenes were designed such that four cuboids with different sizes were arranged on a table and also other objects were placed as obstacles. In the Scene 1, the cuboids were rotated to face to the same direction. In the Scene 2, the cuboids were rotated not to face to the same direction except for the top face. In the Scene 3, two cuboids were inclined onto a cuboid. In all the scene, one cuboid was placed far from the table. In Fig. 6, the first column represents an example image of each scene, the second one does the shape map [17] drawn with different colors per cuboid, and the third one does our cuboid map. At each scene, an RGB-D image sequence was freely captured from one side of the table by moving around the table.

In this experiment, all of the cuboids were successfully detected regardless of the cuboid arrangements with some occlusions, and their shape parameters were also computed. The estimated size of each cuboid at each scene was described in Table 1. The error of cuboid 2 was larger than others because this cuboid was located at the furthest position from the table. This results from the accuracy degradation of depth images. Also, the shape of cuboid 2 was not completely measured because an obstacle hid the cuboid 2. In this case, the accuracy was largely decreased. For other cuboids, the error variance was relatively small.

Table 1. Estimated cuboid lengths (cm)

Cuboid 1	Depth	Width	Height	Cuboid 2	Depth	Width	Height
Ground truth	16.0	22.5	10.5	*Ground truth*	46.6	49.8	41.0
Scene1	16.8	23.5	9.8	*Scene1*	46.9	50.3	34.1
Scene2	16.8	23.1	9.6	*Scene2*	40.9	50.7	36.5
Scene3	16.3	24.6	9.8	*Scene3*	39.8	47.1	31.2
Cuboid 3	Depth	Width	Height	Cuboid 4	Depth	Width	Height
Ground truth	9.8	9.8	19.7	*Ground truth*	7.9	16.0	21.8
Scene1	10.3	10.7	19.2	*Scene1*	7.0	17.2	21.3
Scene2	10.7	11.4	19.4	*Scene2*	7.4	19.4	21.9
Scene3	9.9	10.5	19.3	*Scene3*	7.2	16.7	21.2

7.2 Cuboid Detection at a Cluttered Environment

To show the effectiveness of our incremental approach, a batch based approach was implemented as follow. A RGB-D SLAM system [12] was applied to an RGB-D image sequence to generate a full point cloud in a scene. Next, a shape detection method [22] was applied to the point cloud to detect planes in the scene. Since each plane normal vector cannot be uniquely determined, two planes having opposite normal vectors were generated from one plane. Then, the cuboid detection in Sect. 4 was applied to all the oriented planes to detect cuboids.

For this experiment, a challenging scene was designed, as illustrated in Fig. 7. In this scene, 19 cuboids were randomly arranged, and many other objects were

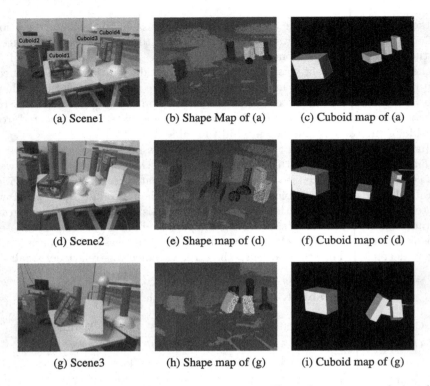

(a) Scene1	(b) Shape Map of (a)	(c) Cuboid map of (a)
(d) Scene2	(e) Shape map of (d)	(f) Cuboid map of (d)
(g) Scene3	(h) Shape map of (g)	(i) Cuboid map of (g)

Fig. 6. Cuboid shape estimation at various scenes. Three datasets were designed to investigate the accuracy of estimated cuboid shapes according to the arrangement. The first, the second, and their columns represent a scene, its shape map [17], and its cuboid map, respectively. The size of each cuboid was measured by a ruler as ground truth. (Color figure online)

also placed as a cluttered environment. The scene was captured by freely moving around the scene. It should be noted that our visual guidance system was not used to capture the dataset.

The performance of the method was evaluated in terms of precision and recall based on false positives, false negatives and true positives, as described in Table 2. Also, the results of cuboid maps were illustrated in Fig. 7. In the batch based approach, there were more false positives and false negatives, compared with our approach. Since the point cloud from RGB-D SLAM was noisy due to registration error, several false positive and false negative planes were detected. Also, the ambiguity of plane normals caused the wrong clustering of three perpendicular planes. In our approach, cuboids were correctly detected because most of the planes were accurately modeled by avoiding the influence of error accumulation in ICP based D-SLAM [17]. However, the false negatives still occurred in our approach due to the incomplete measurement of the cuboids. Therefore, our AR based guidance system is helpful to complete the modeling.

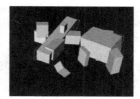

(a) A cluttered environ-   (b) A batch based ap-   (c) Our incremental ap-
ment   proach   proach

Fig. 7. Comparison between a batch based approach with our incremental one. For (a) a scene reconstructed by [12], we applied a batch based cuboid detection to the scene, and had (b) the result. Compared to (c) our result, there were many false positives and false negatives because of noisy point cloud reconstruction. The detail of the accuracy is presented in Table 2.

Table 2. Performance of cuboid detection

	Batch	Ours
Precision	0.64	0.92
Recall	0.37	0.63
Batch	*Positive*	*Negative*
True	7	-
False	4	12
Ours	*Positive*	*Negative*
True	12	-
False	1	7

7.3 Computational Cost

The computational cost was measured at the Scene 1 in Fig. 6a with 3.70 GHz of Intel (R) Xeon (R) CPU E 5-1620 v2, as illustrated in Fig. 8. In [17], the computational cost required for RGB-D SLAM and plane reconstruction was within 100-ms on average. Compared to [17], we focused on measuring the cost for the 3D cuboid modeling. In the cuboid detection, the costs of detecting three planes and computing shape parameters were separately measured. In the figure, the orange dots represent the time when a new cuboid is detected.

The shape parameter estimation needed most computational cost, especially in the process of the point projection to a line to compute edge lengths. The cost of detecting three planes gradually increased according to the number of planes in the map because planes can be detected from not only cuboids but also non-cuboids such as walls. In this case, the cuboid check was applied to the planes from non-cuboids in every frame. Therefore, this process affected the increase of the cost. Overall, the cost of our framework at a room-scale environment was sufficient for running with RGB-D SLAM.

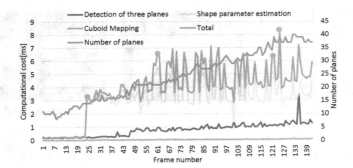

Fig. 8. Computational cost. The orange dots represent the time when a new cuboid is detected. The cost of shape parameter estimation is larger than others. The detection of three planes represents the sum of both 2nd and 3rd plane detections in Sect. 4. This cost increased as time passes because the number of unassigned planes increased. (Color figure online)

7.4   Limitation

As illustrated in Fig. 9, the cuboid detection using three perpendicular planes sometimes failed when boxes were stacked. Basically, the detection accuracy depends on the quality of the plane map. For instance, two stacked boxes can be detected as one cuboid when they are aligned. Since the faces of the two

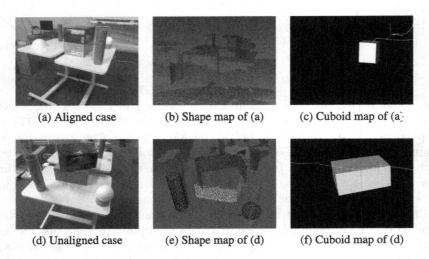

Fig. 9. Limitation. At the first row, two stacked boxes are detected as one cuboid when they are aligned. At the second row, even when two stacked boxes are not aligned, the lower box is not detected because the top face of the lower box is not sufficiently captured as a plane. The accuracy of the cuboid detection can be degraded when boxes are stacked according to the arrangement.

boxes compose a plane, they are detected as one plane. By using an image based segmentation, two boxes can be separately detected. In another case, the lower box cannot be detected even when two stacked boxes are not aligned because the top face of the lower box is still hidden by the upper box. Since three perpendicular planes are required to detect a cuboid in our framework, the detection fails.

8 Conclusions

We presented a framework for generating a cuboid map in an incremental manner. In this approach, a cuboid is first detected by analyzing the positional relationship between oriented planes. Then, it is incrementally updated to suppress false detections. An interactive cuboid modeling system was designed to assist the users to reconstruct cuboids.

The evaluation demonstrated that the cuboid modeling with our approach was more accurate than a batch-based method. Also, our method successfully detected the cuboids regardless of their arrangements. However, three perpendicular planes are required to be captured to compute the cuboid shape parameters, as our limitation.

In the future work, the performance of our framework with additional various scenes is investigated. Also, image features from RGB images will be integrated into our framework to increase the accuracy and robustness of the cuboid detection. Since the point cloud is obtained by RTAB-MAP [12] which is relatively inaccurate in terms of reconstruction quality compared with a TSDF based fusion method such as KinectFusion [14]. Our system should be combined with technique to improve the accuracy for primitive shape reconstruction quality. Additionally, the comparison of the state of the art will be done for display the advantage of our proposed method.

Acknowledgment. This work is supported by JSPS KAKENHI Grant Number JP17H01768.

References

1. Del Pero, L., Guan, J., Brau, E., Schlecht, J., Barnard, K.: Sampling bedrooms. In: 2011 IEEE Conference on Computer Vision and Pattern Recognition (CVPR), pp. 2009–2016. IEEE (2011)
2. Du, H., et al.: Interactive 3D modeling of indoor environments with a consumer depth camera. In: Proceedings of the 13th International Conference on Ubiquitous Computing, pp. 75–84. ACM (2011)
3. Dwibedi, D., Malisiewicz, T., Badrinarayanan, V., Rabinovich, A.: Deep cuboid detection: beyond 2D bounding boxes. arXiv preprint arXiv:1611.10010 (2016)
4. Goldman, R.: Intersection of three planes. In: Graphics Gems, p. 305. Academic Press Professional, Inc. (1990)
5. Hashemifar, Z.S., Lee, K.W., Napp, N., Dantu, K.: Consistent cuboid detection for semantic mapping. In: 2017 IEEE 11th International Conference on Semantic Computing (ICSC), pp. 526–531. IEEE (2017)

6. Hedau, V., Hoiem, D., Forsyth, D.: Recovering the spatial layout of cluttered rooms. In: 2009 IEEE 12th International Conference on Computer Vision, pp. 1849–1856. IEEE (2009)
7. Hedau, V., Hoiem, D., Forsyth, D.: Thinking inside the box: using appearance models and context based on room geometry. In: Daniilidis, K., Maragos, P., Paragios, N. (eds.) ECCV 2010. LNCS, vol. 6316, pp. 224–237. Springer, Heidelberg (2010). https://doi.org/10.1007/978-3-642-15567-3_17
8. Hejrati, M., Ramanan, D.: Categorizing cubes: revisiting pose normalization. In: 2016 IEEE Winter Conference on Applications of Computer Vision (WACV), pp. 1–9. IEEE (2016)
9. Jiang, H., Xiao, J.: A linear approach to matching cuboids in RGBD images. In: 2013 IEEE Conference on Computer Vision and Pattern Recognition (CVPR), pp. 2171–2178. IEEE (2013)
10. Khan, S.H., He, X., Bannamoun, M., Sohel, F., Togneri, R.: Separating objects and clutter in indoor scenes. In: 2015 IEEE Conference on Computer Vision and Pattern Recognition (CVPR), pp. 4603–4611 (2015)
11. Kim, Y.M., Mitra, N.J., Huang, Q., Guibas, L.: Guided real-time scanning of indoor objects. In: Computer Graphics Forum, vol. 32, pp. 177–186. Wiley Online Library (2013)
12. Labbé, M., Michaud, F.: Online global loop closure detection for large-scale multi-session graph-based SLAM. In: 2014 IEEE/RSJ International Conference on Intelligent Robots and Systems (IROS 2014), pp. 2661–2666. IEEE (2014)
13. Lin, D., Fidler, S., Urtasun, R.: Holistic scene understanding for 3D object detection with RGBD cameras. In: 2013 IEEE International Conference on Computer Vision (ICCV), pp. 1417–1424. IEEE (2013)
14. Newcombe, R.A., et al.: KinectFusion: real-time dense surface mapping and tracking. In: 2011 10th IEEE International Symposium on Mixed and Augmented Reality (ISMAR), pp. 127–136. IEEE (2011)
15. Nguatem, W., Drauschke, M., Mayer, H.: Finding cuboid-based building models in point clouds. ISPRS-Int. Arch. Photogramm. Remote Sens. Spat. Inf. Sci. **XXXIX-B**, 149–154 (2012). https://doi.org/10.5194/isprsarchives-XXXIX-B3-149-2012
16. Nguyen, T., Reitmayr, G., Schmalstieg, D.: Structural modeling from depth images. IEEE Trans. Vis. Comput. Graph. **21**(11), 1230–1240 (2015)
17. Olivier, N., et al.: Live structural modeling using RGB-D SLAM. In: ICRA, pp. 6352–6358 (2018)
18. Osada, R., Funkhouser, T., Chazelle, B., Dobkin, D.: Shape distributions. ACM Trans. Graph. (TOG) **21**(4), 807–832 (2002)
19. Ren, Z., Sudderth, E.B.: Three-dimensional object detection and layout prediction using clouds of oriented gradients. In: Proceedings of the IEEE Conference on Computer Vision and Pattern Recognition, pp. 1525–1533 (2016)
20. Rusu, R.B., Marton, Z.C., Blodow, N., Dolha, M., Beetz, M.: Towards 3D point cloud based object maps for household environments. Robot. Auton. Syst. **56**(11), 927–941 (2008)
21. Saxena, A., Driemeyer, J., Ng, A.Y.: Robotic grasping of novel objects using vision. Int. J. Robot. Res. **27**(2), 157–173 (2008)
22. Schnabel, R., Wahl, R., Klein, R.: Efficient RANSAC for point-cloud shape detection. In: Computer Graphics Forum, vol. 26, pp. 214–226. Wiley Online Library (2007)

23. Shao, T., Xu, W., Zhou, K., Wang, J., Li, D., Guo, B.: An interactive approach to semantic modeling of indoor scenes with an RGBD camera. ACM Trans. Graph. (TOG) **31**(6), 136 (2012)
24. Sinha, S.N., Steedly, D., Szeliski, R., Agrawala, M., Pollefeys, M.: Interactive 3D architectural modeling from unordered photo collections. In: ACM Transactions on Graphics (TOG), vol. 27, p. 159. ACM (2008)
25. Stein, S.C., Wörgötter, F., Schoeler, M., Papon, J., Kulvicius, T.: Convexity based object partitioning for robot applications. In: 2014 IEEE International Conference on Robotics and Automation (ICRA), pp. 3213–3220. IEEE (2014)
26. Xiao, J., Russell, B., Torralba, A.: Localizing 3D cuboids in single-view images. In: Advances in Neural Information Processing Systems, pp. 746–754 (2012)
27. Zhang, Y., Luo, C., Liu, J.: Walk&sketch: create floor plans with an RGB-D camera. In: Proceedings of the 2012 ACM Conference on Ubiquitous Computing, pp. 461–470. ACM (2012)

Semi-independent Stereo Visual Odometry for Different Field of View Cameras

Trong Phuc Truong[1(✉)], Vincent Nozick[1,2(✉)], and Hideo Saito[1(✉)]

[1] Graduate School of Science and Technology, Keio University, Tokyo, Japan
{ttphuc,saito}@hvrl.ics.keio.ac.jp
[2] Japanese French Laboratory for Informatics, CNRS, UMI 3527, Tokyo, Japan
vincent.nozick@u-pem.fr

Abstract. This paper presents a pipeline for stereo visual odometry using cameras with different fields of view. It gives a proof of concept about how a constraint on the respective field of view of each camera can lead to both an accurate 3D reconstruction and a robust pose estimation. Indeed, when considering a fixed resolution, a narrow field of view has a higher angular resolution and can preserve image texture details. On the other hand, a wide field of view allows to track features over longer periods since the overlap between two successive frames is more substantial. We propose a semi-independent stereo system where each camera performs individually temporal multi-view optimization but their initial parameters are still jointly optimized in an iterative framework. Furthermore, the concept of lead and follow camera is introduced to adaptively propagate information between the cameras. We evaluate the method qualitatively on two indoor datasets, and quantitatively on a synthetic dataset to allow the comparison across different fields of view.

Keywords: Stereo visual odometry · Field of view · 3D reconstruction

1 Introduction

Visual odometry (VO) and simultaneous localization and mapping (SLAM) have been popular research topics in the past decades, and have recently become a prominent part in many emerging technologies such as self-driving car, drone delivery, virtual and augmented reality. Monocular cameras are widely used for these challenging tasks due to their low hardware cost and relatively small size. However, the absolute scale is not observable by using monocular camera approaches without introducing priors, and thus leading to scale drift [4,9]. Stereo camera configurations allow to resolve this scale ambiguity by computing the depth from a known fixed-baseline [12]. In many stereo VO and SLAM using cameras with overlapping fields of view, two identical cameras are often considered to estimate more efficiently correspondences. The second camera is only used to perform static depth estimation [10,13] and/or to add a static constraint

© Springer Nature Switzerland AG 2019
L. Leal-Taixé and S. Roth (Eds.): ECCV 2018 Workshops, LNCS 11129, pp. 430–442, 2019.
https://doi.org/10.1007/978-3-030-11009-3_26

term in the optimization [3,14,17]. Temporal multi-view stereo is thus neglected for the latter since the gain of information would not be worth the computation cost.

This paper presents a proof of concept on how a strong constraint on the focal length difference between the two cameras can result in both a higher reconstruction robustness and accuracy. Indeed, when using cameras with different fields of view, performing temporal multi-view stereo for both cameras can become meaningful as the stereo system will be able to exploit more independent source of data when compared to the case of an identical pair of cameras. In theory, a wider field of view allows to avoid occlusion and it is more likely that the visible part of the scene contains well-suited information for visual methods. Visual odometry and SLAM using large field of view fish-eye cameras [2,15] demonstrate more robust pose estimation, notably during rapid motion, as there is more overlap between subsequent images such that landmarks can be tracked over longer periods. However, the angular resolution of the image decreases as the FOV increases for a fixed image resolution. In [18], Zhang et al. study the impact of the field of view for visual odometry, and show that large field of view camera should be used in confined environment since features are more evenly distributed which stabilizes the pose estimation and can be tracked for a longer time. On the other hand, due to the loss of angular resolution of higher FOV, the triangulation error is amplified with the depth range especially for large scale outdoor environment such that small FOV cameras should be preferred. In this paper, we propose a semi-independent for stereo visual odometry using cameras with different fields of view so that it can take advantage of both the large and small fields of view properties by performing temporal multi-view stereo for both of them.

1.1 Related Work

Using a stereo camera configuration, the scale becomes directly observable given the fixed-baseline, but the implied triangulation can only be estimated for correspondences from both images. As a result, a lot of stereo systems consider a configuration where the common field of view area is maximized.

An early seminal work using a stereo camera setup was proposed by Nister et al. [12], where static triangulation and sequential frame-to-frame matching for sparse features were used to estimate the motion with the correct scale of the stereo rig. In [13], Paz et al. present an approach based on extended Kalman filter that considers information from both close and far features. The former provides scale information through the stereo baseline and the latter are represented with an inverse depth parametrization that is useful to obtain angular information. More recently, Mur-Artal et al. present ORB-SLAM2 [10], an extension of their monocular SLAM framework based on ORB features [9]. The system can work with different configurations such as stereo cameras. It includes loop closing, relocalization, map reuse and follows a similar strategy to [13] by treating differently close and far points.

While these methods are solely based on sparse interest points, recently proposed semi-direct and direct methods have gained popularity due to their ability to circumvent this limitation by exploiting information from all intensity gradients in the image [4,6,11]. Forster et al. present SVO [7], a semi-direct visual odometry, that exploits both photometric error to estimate the initial motion, and geometric error to jointly optimize the camera poses as well as sparse landmarks positions over a window of frames. This method can be easily extended to multiple cameras as the motion estimation and bundle adjustment can be generalized to include measurements from other cameras given their relative pose. On the other hand, full direct methods that only optimize the photometric error also demonstrate state-of-the art results. Based on the work of Engel et al. LSD-SLAM [4], and DSO [3], extension to stereo camera systems have been presented in [5], and [17], in which the authors couple temporal stereo and static stereo in their optimization problem.

1.2 Motivation and Contribution

In this work, we propose a framework for stereo visual odometry using cameras with different yet overlapping fields of view. In particular, we consider the combination of a wide-angle ($\sim$80°) and a medium telephoto lens pinhole camera ($\sim$30°). With this stereo configuration, our system is able to recover the scale by estimating the depth using static stereo matching from the common FOV as illustrated in Fig. 1.

While our method is based on DSO [3], we extend it to work with a stereo configuration such that information between the two different FOV cameras can be shared. Furthermore, it differs from the stereo implementation presented in [17] as we do not directly introduce any constraint from static stereo in the windowed bundle adjustment pipeline. Instead, the back-end optimization is performed individually for each camera as if it were two independent monocular systems to avoid instability that could arise from photometric error depending on the difference of FOV between the cameras. In other words, the temporal multiple-view optimization is performed by both cameras allowing to take advantage of their respective properties; e.g., angular resolution and robust tracking. Furthermore, we introduce an iterative optimization pipeline such that the least reliable camera is initialized in a way that it is more likely to lie in the basin of attraction of the cost function. The front-end part is also modified to initialize the depth variance of each keyframe with static stereo matching and share the depth map used for tracking such that scale drift can be reduced.

Therefore, the proposed method is designated as semi-independent since the two cameras independently execute monocular VO but their initial parameters are jointly optimized. Our main contributions include:

- A stereo visual odometry using different fields of view that can fully exploit, on the one hand, the precision and robustness of the pose of the large FOV camera, and on the other hand, the angular resolution of the small FOV camera, while recovering the reconstruction scale from the known baseline.

(a) (b) (c) (d)

Fig. 1. Example of stereo image input with different fields of view: (a) 32° and (b) 77°. (c)–(d) Their respective color-coded depth map generated from static stereo matching. (Color figure online)

- An iterative optimization procedure with efficient front-end frame and point management to avoid the joint optimization of two dissimilar cameras.
- Quantitative evaluations on a synthetic dataset with a comparison with DSO and ORB-SLAM2.

2 Stereo Matching

Estimating the depth using images from different physical cameras but taken at the same time (i.e. static stereo) is an important part of stereo VO since it gives information about the scale as the relative position between both cameras is known. Many stereo systems such as [10,14,17] use rectified images as input so that the correspondences search can be performed efficiently along horizontal epipolar lines. However, when considering cameras with notably different focal lengths, there is a loss of the FOV for the wide-lens camera due to distortion or cropping depending on the rectification method used. As a result, rectified images cannot be directly input to our system, but they are still used during static stereo matching for computation time. It can be noted that the 3D point computed from the disparity given rectified images needs to be transformed into the original camera frame since unrectified images are fed as input for the VO pipeline.

Since commonly used matching cost functions were not robust to the difference of resolution between the two rectified images, we define an empirical cost function combining NCC with BRIEF binary descriptor [1]. It allows to avoid local maxima for the NCC by taking into account a sparse but bigger region using BRIEF descriptors. Furthermore, since rectification practically removes any rotation and scale variance, BRIEF provides a good performance under image blur for a low computation time [8]. By defining B_n as the min-max normalized L1 distance between the pixel point p_1 in image I_1 and p_2 in image I_2, and similarly NCC_n as the min-max normalized NCC for the same points, the final cost function C is defined as follows

$$C(p_1, p_2, I_1, I_2) = 1 - B_n(p_1, p_2, I_1, I_2) + \lambda NCC_n(p_1, p_2, I_1, I_2), \quad (1)$$

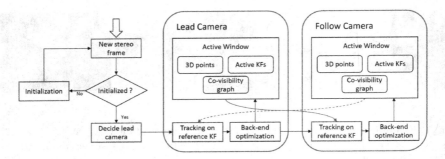

Fig. 2. Overview of our system, blue parts represent our contributions. After initialization, a lead camera is decided and is firstly optimized with the monocular visual odometry pipeline. Given additional information from the active window of the lead camera, the second camera runs, in turn, the monocular pipeline. (Color figure online)

where λ is a weighting factor to balance the influence between NCC and BRIEF. In our experiment, we use NCC with a 5×7 neighborhood, BRIEF with 256 location pairs, and $\lambda = 1$.

3   Stereo VO with Wide and Narrow FOV Cameras

We present a stereo visual odometry method using a wide-angle and a narrow-angle lens camera that combines multi-view stereo from both cameras and static stereo matching from the overlapping FOV. DSO [3] is used as the backbone visual odometry framework since it can benefit from its direct and sparse aspects. In fact, direct method can use every points with high gradient as features so that we can achieve higher resolution point cloud by exploiting the narrow-angle lens camera. Moreover, the sparse nature of DSO allows to save stereo computation time as correspondences are required for a smaller amount of points than dense methods. An overview of our system is presented in Fig. 2, where the blue parts represent our contributions.

3.1   Direct Sparse Odometry Back-End

We adopt the DSO framework as the core visual odometry in our system. DSO proposes a direct probabilistic model with joint optimization of all model parameters including camera poses, camera intrinsic and geometric parameters represented by inverse depths. It is a sparse method that does not incorporate geometric prior so that the Hessian matrix can be solved efficiently using the Schur complement. In [3], the photometric error for a point p in the reference frame I_i, observed in a target frame is defined as the weighted SSD over a 8-point neighborhood $\mathcal{N}_p$ and is formulated as

$$E_{pj} = \sum_{p \in \mathcal{N}_p} w_p \left\| (I_j[p'] - b_j) - \frac{t_j e^{a_j}}{t_i e^{a_i}} (I_i[p] - b_i) \right\|_\gamma , \qquad (2)$$

where p' is the warped point of p in I_j; t_i, t_j are the exposure times of the images I_i, I_j; a_i, a_j, b_i, b_j are brightness affine transfer function parameters; $\|.\|_\gamma$ is the Huber norm and w_p is a gradient-dependent weighting defined as

$$w_p = \frac{c^2}{c^2 + \|\nabla I_i(p)\|_2^2}. \qquad (3)$$

Each time a new keyframe is created, it is added to the active window which results in an additional energy factor for every points that can be observed by another keyframe in the window as defined (2). The full energy is optimized using Gauss-Newton method, and in order to keep the sliding window of bounded size, marginalization is employed to remove the old keyframes.

3.2   Semi-independent Stereo VO

Iterative Pipeline. Given a stereo configuration with different fields of view, we propose an iterative approach to avoid the uncertainty coming from the difference of resolution during the photometric error optimization. In fact, when comparing the pixel intensity in a reference frame and the one in a target frame from a camera with a different focal length, the impact of noisy pose or depth estimations can result in the non-convergence of the highly complex optimization. The complexity is even more accentuated as we want to perform temporal multi-view stereo for both cameras.

For these reasons, we decouple the problem by performing iteratively two monocular visual odometry pipelines with independent windowed optimizations as illustrated in Fig. 2. At each incoming frame, the most reliable camera (lead camera) is first optimized such that its refined parameters can be thereafter shared with the visual odometry front-end of the other camera (follow camera). As a result, the follow camera, that is considered less reliable, is more likely to converge during its back-end optimization process.

Visual Odometry Front-End. The front-end part of the system handles how frames and points are managed. In particular, it decides which frames and points are added and removed from the windowed optimization. Similarly to DSO, new keyframes are required when the current image becomes too distinctive compared to the last keyframe. It is based on three criteria: when the field of view is significantly different, when the translation part of the motion is high, and when the camera exposure time considerably changes. Each time a keyframe is created, well distributed candidate points with sufficient gradient are selected and their inverse depth variance is directly initialized using static stereo. The front-end also provides initializations for new parameters (camera pose, affine transform parameters, and inverse depth of candidate points) required to optimize the highly non-convex optimization in the windowed optimization.

It differs from stereo DSO [17] by taking advantage of having two semi-independent systems running iteratively. When a new keyframe is created, all active points from both windowed optimizations are projected into the latter and then dilated to create a semi-dense depth map used for tracking the pose of new frames. Since feature points are selected to be well distributed, they can be substantially different for the same area of the two cameras due to the difference of FOV, and thus resulting in denser depth map. This depth map is used to track the camera pose of new frames fed into to the system by minimizing the photometric error using direct image alignment. During this optimization, the inverse depth values are fixed and the two-frame direct image alignment is performed on an image pyramid in a coarse-to-fine order.

Moreover, instead of assuming a constant motion model for the follow system, it is directly initialized using the optimized pose of the lead camera given their constant relative pose. This process is particularly important for the narrow FOV camera as it can easily lose its tracking with respect to the last keyframe during fast motion.

Lead and Follow Camera Selection. The selection of the lead camera is critical as an incorrect pose initialization for the follow camera can result in a divergence from the optimal solution. We propose a straightforward metric to select the lead camera by comparing the latest RMSE results from the windowed optimization. Since the narrow-angle lens camera is more likely to converge to local minimum due to its limited FOV, the latter can become the lead only if the following condition

$$RMSE_{narrow} < f_c RMSE_{wide} \tag{4}$$

is respected 3 keyframes in a row to avoid local minima and maxima results from the optimization. In (4), f_c is a factor to decide which camera should be more trusted. We set $f_c = 0.8$ in our experiment to let the small FOV camera leads the large FOV only when the result of the back-end optimization is 20% lower than the one from the other camera.

3.3 Asynchronous Initialization

Bootstrapping methods for stereo setup based on an initial depth map from static stereo matching as employed in [10,17] will not work efficiently for the wide-angle lens camera. In fact, the estimated depth from static stereo is only limited to the FOV of the narrow-angle lens camera, i.e. the common FOV between the two cameras. We propose an asynchronous method to initialize both cameras in the same coordinate system considering a small overlapping FOV.

Similarly to [17], a semi-dense depth map for the first frame of the small FOV camera can be estimated from static stereo matching to initialize the system.

Once the small FOV system has created N_i keyframes, the corresponding poses for the large FOV system are computed using the relative pose. Then, the point candidates of its first frame can be tracked and their depth values are refined in the subsequent $N_i - 1$ frames by minimizing the photometric error. Moreover, to constraint this discrete search along the epipolar line, all the active points from the small FOV system are projected to the first image plane of the large FOV camera to initialize the associated variance of the candidate points. Finally, the large FOV camera is initialized using the computed depth map and the poses inferred from its counterpart so that both cameras are in the same coordinate system.

4   Evaluation

For the evaluation of our method, we first demonstrate the ability to reconstruct higher resolution point clouds with two indoor datasets, then we evaluate the odometry on a synthetic dataset to be able to compare its accuracy with ORB-SLAM2 and DSO. Since the aim of this paper is to give a proof of concept about stereo systems with different focal lengths, a runtime analysis will not be detailed. However, with an unoptimized implementation, it runs about twice as slow as DSO considering it has to compute a second time the back-end optimization and estimate stereo matches each time a keyframe is generated.

4.1   Point Cloud Reconstruction

The stereo configuration used to evaluate the point cloud accuracy is a 77° and 32° FOV camera with a ~20 cm baseline. The two datasets contain 800 frames representing around 15 s of video of an indoor environment. Some examples of input images are illustrated in Fig. 3. It also shows the estimated trajectory of the camera pair as well as the point cloud generated using our semi-independent visual odometry method. The accuracy of the registration of both system can be observed by comparing the 3D points from the large and small FOV camera represented in red and green respectively. The color mapping of the trajectory shows that for these two datasets, the camera lead was the narrow-angle lens one. It can be explained by the fact that the motion was relatively slow. However, for both datasets, the lead switches to the big FOV because of the sudden change of direction. The last row illustrates the difference of density between the 3D reconstruction of each camera. In particular, it shows that using a medium telephoto camera, the point selection of DSO can focus more on specific details of the scene. The point cloud is thus more detailed even if the camera pair is at a reasonable distance from the scene.

4.2   Odometry Accuracy

We evaluate our method on the Urban Canyon model [18], where photorealistic synthetic images were generated for a stereo pinhole camera setup with different

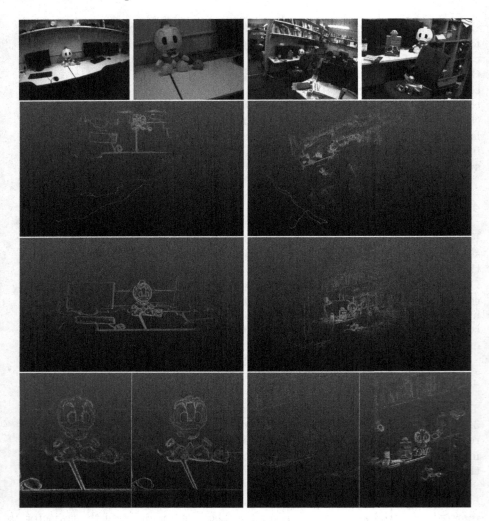

Fig. 3. Qualitative examples on two indoor datasets. (*First row*) Example of input images. (*Second and third row*) 3D reconstruction of the large and small FOV camera are shown in *red* and *green* respectively. The camera trajectory is also represented on the *top row*, and the same color mapping represents which camera was the lead. (*Last row*) A zoomed view of the 3D reconstruction of the large FOV camera displayed on the *left* and the small one on the *right* (Color figure online)

FOV (40°, 60°, and 80°) by using cycle raytracing engine implemented in Blender (Fig. 4). This way, many stereo configurations for the same trajectory can be proposed to study the impact of the field of view. We compare the accuracy of the visual odometry with ORB-SLAM2 and monocular DSO (since the stereo version is not available publicly). The trajectories are aligned to the ground truth using a rigid-body transform (6DoF) for the stereo methods and a similarity transform (7DoF) for DSO. It can be noted that to allow a fair comparison between all methods, loop closure and relocalization were disabled for ORB-SLAM2, we also disable real-time forcing and we use the default parameters for DSO and ORB-SLAM2. We use three different metrics proposed in [16] for our evaluation: the absolute translation RMSE t_{abs}, the relative translation RMSE t_{rel}, and the average relative rotation error r_{rel}.

In the remaining part of this paper, we denote the different results as follows:

- *Ours40*: our semi-independent stereo VO using 40°-80° FOV stereo camera
- *Ours60*: our semi-independent stereo VO using 60°-80° FOV stereo camera
- *DSO60*: DSO using 60° monocular camera
- *DSO80*: DSO using 80° monocular camera
- *ORB40*: ORB-SLAM2 using 40° stereo camera
- *ORB80*: ORB-SLAM2 using 80° stereo camera

Table 1 summarizes the visual odometry results for the different evaluated configurations. Their trajectory can be observed on Fig. 5. While it does not prove the versatility of our method, *Ours40* and *Ours60* have the best results for the absolute trajectory error and relative rotation error. The reason is that it is able to exploit the wide FOV camera and it slightly outperforms *DSO80* for the absolute trajectory error since information from the narrow FOV is also exploited. While ORB-SLAM2 manages to estimate correctly the relative rotation, the translational error is higher than the two other methods. A reason could be that ORB features are not suitable for this synthetic data since increasing the number of feature points resulted in higher errors in our experiment.

Table 1. Comparison of accuracy in the Urban Canyon dataset. t_{abs} absolute translation RMSE (m), t_{rel} relative translation RMSE (%), r_{rel} average relative rotation error (deg/10 m). Best results are shown as bold numbers

	t_{abs}	t_{rel}	r_{rel}
Ours40	**0.275**	1.236	0.896
Ours60	0.428	3.918	**0.486**
DSO60	0.906	1.352	0.612
DSO80	0.292	**0.439**	0.622
ORB40	1.599	2.120	0.533
ORB80	0.929	1.856	0.543

5   Discussion and Conclusion

In most of stereo VO and SLAM methods, homogeneous camera are considered to take advantage of their overlapping fields of view and the ability to efficiently

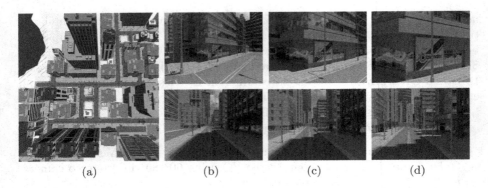

(a)   (b)   (c)   (d)

Fig. 4. (a) Top view of the Urban Canyon 3D model. Examples of synthetic images with different fields of view: (b) 80° (c) 60° (d) 40°, each row corresponds to the same camera position.

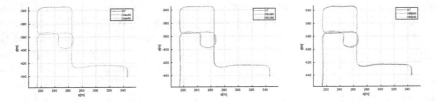

Fig. 5. Qualitative results on the Urban Canyon dataset. (*From left to right*) Trajectory of our semi-independent method, monocular DSO, and stereo ORB-SLAM2

estimate matches. As a result, temporal information from the second camera is often omitted since it does not provide additional meaningful data to the stereo system when compared to the first camera. In this paper, we suggest that, by using heterogeneous stereo camera with different focal lengths, performing temporal multi-view stereo optimization for both cameras can lead to better 3D reconstruction while having a robust pose estimation. This proof of concept is illustrated by our semi-independent stereo visual odometry for large FOV and small FOV cameras. Some preliminary results show the ability to reconstruct high detailed 3D point clouds while standing at a reasonable distance and to estimate with accuracy the camera pose when compared to DSO and ORB-SLAM2 for the proposed synthetic dataset.

While it does not prove that our method is constantly better, it exposes the ability to choose different focal lengths for a multiple cameras setup. For example, this stereo configuration is already present in many smartphones to allow depth of field rendering. Nevertheless, because of the limited range of the static stereo depth estimation due to the small baseline and the difference of FOV, most of common stereo VO and SLAM methods are not suitable. In this case, employing a semi-independent approach could result in a better performance.

References

1. Calonder, M., Lepetit, V., Strecha, C., Fua, P.: BRIEF: binary robust independent elementary features. In: Daniilidis, K., Maragos, P., Paragios, N. (eds.) ECCV 2010. LNCS, vol. 6314, pp. 778–792. Springer, Heidelberg (2010). https://doi.org/10.1007/978-3-642-15561-1_56
2. Caruso, D., Engel, J., Cremers, D.: Large-scale direct SLAM for omnidirectional cameras. In: IROS, vol. 1, p. 2 (2015)
3. Engel, J., Koltun, V., Cremers, D.: Direct sparse odometry. IEEE Trans. Pattern Anal. Mach. Intell. **4** (2017)
4. Engel, J., Schöps, T., Cremers, D.: LSD-SLAM: large-scale direct monocular SLAM. In: Fleet, D., Pajdla, T., Schiele, B., Tuytelaars, T. (eds.) ECCV 2014. LNCS, vol. 8690, pp. 834–849. Springer, Cham (2014). https://doi.org/10.1007/978-3-319-10605-2_54
5. Engel, J., Stückler, J., Cremers, D.: Large-scale direct slam with stereo cameras. In: 2015 IEEE/RSJ International Conference on Intelligent Robots and Systems (IROS), pp. 1935–1942. IEEE (2015)
6. Forster, C., Pizzoli, M., Scaramuzza, D.: SVO: fast semi-direct monocular visual odometry. In: 2014 IEEE International Conference on Robotics and Automation (ICRA), pp. 15–22. IEEE (2014)
7. Forster, C., Zhang, Z., Gassner, M., Werlberger, M., Scaramuzza, D.: SVO: semidirect visual odometry for monocular and multicamera systems. IEEE Trans. Rob. **33**(2), 249–265 (2017)
8. Heinly, J., Dunn, E., Frahm, J.-M.: Comparative evaluation of binary features. In: Fitzgibbon, A., Lazebnik, S., Perona, P., Sato, Y., Schmid, C. (eds.) ECCV 2012. LNCS, pp. 759–773. Springer, Heidelberg (2012). https://doi.org/10.1007/978-3-642-33709-3_54
9. Mur-Artal, R., Montiel, J.M.M., Tardos, J.D.: ORB-SLAM: a versatile and accurate monocular SLAM system. IEEE Trans. Rob. **31**(5), 1147–1163 (2015)
10. Mur-Artal, R., Tardós, J.D.: ORB-SLAM2: an open-source slam system for monocular, stereo, and RGB-D cameras. IEEE Trans. Rob. **33**(5), 1255–1262 (2017)
11. Newcombe, R.A., Lovegrove, S.J., Davison, A.J.: DTAM: dense tracking and mapping in real-time. In: 2011 IEEE International Conference on Computer Vision (ICCV), pp. 2320–2327. IEEE (2011)
12. Nistér, D., Naroditsky, O., Bergen, J.: Visual odometry. In: Proceedings of the 2004 IEEE Computer Society Conference on Computer Vision and Pattern Recognition, CVPR 2004, vol. 1, p. I. IEEE (2004)
13. Paz, L.M., Piniés, P., Tardós, J.D., Neira, J.: Large-scale 6-DOF SLAM with stereo-in-hand. IEEE Trans. Rob. **24**(5), 946–957 (2008)
14. Pire, T., Fischer, T., Civera, J., De Cristóforis, P., Berlles, J.J.: Stereo parallel tracking and mapping for robot localization. In: 2015 IEEE/RSJ International Conference on Intelligent Robots and Systems (IROS), pp. 1373–1378. IEEE (2015)
15. Rituerto, A., Puig, L., Guerrero, J.: Comparison of omnidirectional and conventional monocular systems for visual SLAM. In: 10th OMNIVIS with RSS (2010)
16. Sturm, J., Engelhard, N., Endres, F., Burgard, W., Cremers, D.: A benchmark for the evaluation of RGB-D SLAM systems. In: 2012 IEEE/RSJ International Conference on Intelligent Robots and Systems (IROS), pp. 573–580. IEEE (2012)

17. Wang, R., Schwörer, M., Cremers, D.: Stereo DSO: large-scale direct sparse visual odometry with stereo cameras. In: International Conference on Computer Vision (ICCV), vol. 42 (2017)
18. Zhang, Z., Rebecq, H., Forster, C., Scaramuzza, D.: Benefit of large field-of-view cameras for visual odometry. In: 2016 IEEE International Conference on Robotics and Automation (ICRA), pp. 801–808. IEEE (2016)

Improving Thin Structures in Surface Reconstruction from Sparse Point Cloud

Maxime Lhuillier[(✉)]

Université Clermont Auvergne, CNRS, SIGMA Clermont, Institut Pascal,
63000 Clermont-Ferrand, France
maxime.lhuillier@free.fr
http://maxime.lhuillier.free.fr

Abstract. Methods were proposed to estimate a surface from a sparse cloud of points reconstructed from images. These methods are interesting in several contexts including large scale scenes, limited computational resources and initialization of dense stereo. However they are deficient in presence of thin structures such as posts, which are often present in both urban and natural scenes: these scene components can be partly or even completely removed. Here we reduce this problem by introducing a pre-processing, assuming that (1) some of the points form polygonal chains approximating curves and occluding contours of the scene and (2) the direction of the thin structures is roughly known (e.g. vertical). In the experiments, our pre-processing improves the results of two different surface reconstruction methods applied on videos taken by helmet-held 360 cameras.

Keywords: Thin structures · Sparse features ·
3D Delaunay triangulation · Visibility · Environment modeling

1 Introduction

The automatic surface reconstruction from images is still an active research topic. One of the difficulties is caused by thin structures: they are partly or even completely removed by the methods that do not include specific processing. There are two kinds of thin structures: planar ones like road signs and rectilinear ones like posts. This paper only focuses on the rectilinear case, which is frequent in both urban and natural scenes. It also focuses on an input point cloud reconstructed from sparse features in images. This is useful not only for applications that do not need the high level of details of computationally expensive dense stereo, but also to initialize dense stereo in other cases. Since we have two difficulties (thin structures and sparse input) and would like a tractable problem, our method uses further information available in the images: we reconstruct curves

Electronic supplementary material The online version of this chapter (https://doi.org/10.1007/978-3-030-11009-3_27) contains supplementary material, which is available to authorized users.

L. Leal-Taixé and S. Roth (Eds.): ECCV 2018 Workshops, LNCS 11129, pp. 443–458, 2019.
https://doi.org/10.1007/978-3-030-11009-3_27

as polygonal chains in 3D from image gradient. We also assume that the thin structures have a known direction with large tolerance. The paper restricts to the vertical direction which is the dominant direction of the reconstructed curves in our terrestrial image sequences (this is partly due to the aperture problem), but it is obvious to consider several directions by alternating.

2   Previous Surface Reconstruction Methods

We summarize methods that use constraints similar to ours, whether they deal with thin structures or not, without or with a sparse point cloud.

2.1   Using Lines or Curves or Image Gradient

Methods use lines or curves and organize them as graphs, which are used as scaffolds for surface reconstruction. In [22], curves are reconstructed from image gradient and the surface is obtained by curve interpolation (lofting) and occlusion reasoning. In [24], an initial surface mesh is regularized by back-projecting linear structures that are semi-automatically selected from the images. Other methods estimate dense depth maps including pixels at occluding contours, then merge them in a voxel grid. In [18], quasi-dense depth maps of internet images are densified by encouraging depth discontinuities at image contours. In [27], the depths of video sequences are first computed in high-gradient regions including silhouettes, then they are propagated to low-gradient regions. Using a point cloud reconstructed from images of a scene with planar structures, [5] segments into inside and outside a tetrahedralization of the points by using graph-cut and two regularizations: horizontal slicing and a smoothness term based on image lines.

A very recent work [10] deals with thin rectilinear structures. First it reconstructs curves from image gradient, then integrates both dense scattered points and curve vertices in a 3D Delaunay triangulation, last segments into inside and outside by using graph-cut.

2.2   Reconstructing Trees and Roots

Methods estimate thin structures like trees [12,20] and plant roots [28]. In [12], several trees are automatically reconstructed from laser scan data assuming that the major branch structures are sampled. First every tree is modeled by a minimal spanning tree whose root is on high point density of the ground plane, vertices are input points and edge weights are Euclidean distances. Then the spanning trees are globally optimized using constraints on length, thickness and smoothness derived from biological properties. A previous method [20] reconstructs realistic-looking trees from pre-segmented images into branches/leaves/background and a more difficult point cloud estimated by quasi-dense structure-from-motion. The computation of minimum spanning trees is done for subsets of branches using weights combining two distances

(3D Euclidean and image gradient-based). Little user interaction is needed to select branch subsets and to connect subsets. The method in [28] is shortly summarized in two steps: first robustly estimate a visual hull of the plant roots (They are mostly black with white background thanks to a transparent gel container.) in a voxel grid, then repair the connectivity of the inside voxels by computing a minimal spanning tree. In these methods and [10], the connectedness constraint is essential to recover missing parts of the thin structures.

2.3   Other Surface Reconstruction Methods

Other methods are not in the classifications above. In [1], the input point cloud is first approximated by planar segments, then these segments are prolonged and assembled into a well-behaved surface using visibility constraints. The prolongations are done using prior on urban scenes including the prevalence of the vertical structures. In [6], a graph-cut method segments a tetrahedralization of the input points into inside and outside by using visibility information. Compared to [23], it favors the inside where the visibility gradient is high and improves the thin structure reconstructions, but it ignores image gradient and tends to produce more surfaces that do not correspond to real surfaces. In [16], thin structures such as stick and rope are reconstructed in a voxel grid by enforcing the inside connectedness. First an approximate visual hull including the final surface is estimated, then a voxel labeling is computed by convex optimization subject to linear constraints on the labeling derivatives such that the inside and the visual hull have similar topology. Thin planar structures [21] are not the paper topic.

2.4   Our Contribution

There are several differences between our method and the previous ones that reconstruct thin (rectilinear) structures. First we reconstruct 3D curves from image gradient (including those that approximate occluding contours) and use them to detect the thin vertical structures. Their points also complete the sparse input point cloud reconstructed by structure-from-motion (SfM). Second we partition the space by using a 3D Delaunay triangulation T of the input points with tetrahedra labeled freespace or matter. Voxel grid is used in most previous works for thin structures but is inadequate for both large scale scenes and sparse input point cloud. Third we detect the thin structures in T as vertices of vertical curves that have small matter neighborhoods in the horizontal directions. These vertices are regrouped in large enough sets to avoid false positive detections. There is only one thin structure per set. Fourth we use the connectedness constraint to complete the thin structures in the vertical direction: force to matter vertical series of tetrahedra connecting vertices of a same set. Last we adapt two previous surface reconstruction methods such that their regularizations do not cancel our matter completion.

Now we detail differences with the closest and recent work [10]. It adds to T a lot of Steiner vertices near 3D curves, which are not in the original input and do not have visibility information (i.e. rays). This is not adequate for incremental surface reconstruction methods like [11,17] and is not obvious to adapt to non-graph-cut methods. Our thin structure processing does not use such points and does not have these drawbacks. The price to pay is (1) an approximate knowledge of the direction of thin structures and (2) involved detection-completion steps of the matter tetrahedra of the thin structures. Furthermore we start with terrestrial video sequences with sparse point clouds. We believe that this experimental context is more challenging (or "wild") than that of [10], which starts from denser point clouds and still images whose view-points are selected by UAV.

3   Overview

The three first steps in Sects. 3.1, 3.2 and 3.3 estimate the curves, the vertical direction and initialize the 3D Delaunay triangulation from the output of a sparse SfM. The two next steps in Sects. 3.4 and 3.5 are the main contributions: they detect the thin vertical structures and improve their matter labeling. Last Sects. 3.6 and 3.7 explain how to update two surface reconstruction methods to take into account our matter improvement: a graph-cut method in [23] and a manifold method in [9].

3.1   Step 1: Estimate Points and Polygonal Chains

We use standard methods: detect both Harris points and Canny curves, match them in consecutive images of the sequence using correlation and the epipolar constraint [8]. A curve is approximated by a polygonal chain of points in an image such that the distance between two consecutive points is roughly constant (4 pixels in our implementation). These points are matched with points of Canny curves in other images. Then the chain points are reconstructed independently and we obtain a polygonal chain in 3D. Last all 3D points are filtered by thresholding on angles formed by their rays. (Reject a point if its angles are smaller than $10°$.) Better methods exist to reconstruct lines and curves [2,4,7,13], but this is not the paper focus. The resulting polygonal chains approximate curves in 3D and have both redundancy and inaccuracy for several reasons: failures of detection and matching, matching of 2D points that do not correspond to a single 3D point due to occluding contours, inaccurate camera calibration.

3.2   Step 2: Estimate the Vertical Direction

In the terrestrial imaging context, we observe that the main direction of the edges of the polygonal chains is vertical. (There are also a lot of horizontal curves in usual scenes, but most of them cannot be reconstructed due to the aperture problem.) Thus we compute the density of the edge directions in a histogram and assume that the direction with the largest density is vertical.

3.3   Step 3: Initialize the 3D Delaunay Triangulation

Step 3 is a by-product of the surface reconstruction methods based on 3D Delaunay triangulation and visibility constraints. First a 3D Delaunay triangulation T is build from the points generated in Sect. 3.1. Then its tetrahedra are labeled freespace or matter. In more details, each Delaunay vertex **a** has several rays and a ray is a line segment **ac** between **a** and a viewpoint **c** whose image includes a detection of **a**. The matter M is the set of tetrahedra that are not intersected by ray(s) and $T \setminus M$ is the freespace. Note that we not only have isolated points but also edges of polygonal chains. Following [3,19], a tetrahedron is freespace if it is intersected by a stereo triangle **abc** where **ab** is such an edge and **c** is a common viewpoint of **a** and **b** (more details in the supplementary material).

3.4   Step 4: Detect Vertices of the Thin Structures

For each thin structure, we would like to find (as large as possible) sets of vertices of T that are in the structure. Such a set is computed as a connected component of a graph G with vertex set V and edge set E. Since structure is vertical, all edges in E are almost vertical. The set E not only includes edges of the polygonal chains but also edges of the Delaunay triangulation. (A same structure can have many polygonal chains.) Since structure is matter, every vertex in V is in at least one matter tetrahedron in M. Since structure is thin along the vertical direction, such a vertex has a small connected component of matter tetrahedra in a horizontal neighborhood (in a slice between two horizontal planes). Section 4.2 details the definition of G.

Evidence of thin structure increases with connected component size. Thus we reject the smallest connected components of G to avoid false positive detections of thin structures. (If they have less than 6 vertices in our implementation.)

3.5   Step 5: Improve the Matter of the Thin Structures

Thin vertical structure should be approximated in T by connected set of matter tetrahedra with large size in the vertical direction and small size in the horizontal directions. However, this connectedness does not hold in practice due to several reasons: noise, lack of points and bad points that generate false positive freespace tetrahedra. We would like to improve this connectedness by using the selected connected components of G (Sect. 3.4).

Since all vertices of a connected component C of G are in a same structure, we force to matter (i.e. add to M) series of tetrahedra in T connecting vertices of C. Since structure is vertical, the forced tetrahedra cover line segments that are almost vertical. Since structure is thin, we only force to matter tetrahedra with small size in the horizontal directions. Thus there are two steps: first estimate the width (measuring the size in the horizontal directions) of the structure including C, then complete M by considering tetrahedra between pairs of vertices in C if the width of these tetrahedra are not too large compared to that of the structure. This process is detailed in Sect. 4.3.

Last we set a Boolean b_Δ for every tetrahedron Δ: b_Δ is true if and only if Δ is forced to matter by Step 5. (Whether we have $\Delta \in M$ or $\Delta \notin M$ in Step 3.)

3.6   Step 6a: Graph-Cut Surface Reconstruction

The graph-cut method [23] labels the tetrahedra of T with inside or outside. (The surface is the triangle set between outside and inside tetrahedra.) However, it removes thin structures by labeling outside several tetrahedra that are in M. There are two reasons: it has a regularization and it ignores our matter improvement. Thus we modify it such that the set of the inside tetrahedra includes the set of the tetrahedra with true Boolean b_Δ (Sect. 3.5).

We remind that it computes a minimum $s - t$ cut of a graph. This graph is the adjacency graph of T augmented by two vertices $\{s, t\}$ and edges $\{vs, vt\}$ for every vertex v of the adjacency graph. Cut is partition of the vertex set in two subsets: a subset including s and a subset including t. The details on the definition of the augmented graph and its edge weights are in [23]. We only need to know that if vt has a large weight, v and t are in the same subset, which implies that the tetrahedron associated to v is labeled inside.

Thus we modify the augmented graph (before computing the minimum cut) by adding a large value to every edge vt such that the tetrahedron Δ associated to v has a true Boolean b_Δ.

3.7   Step 6b: Manifold Surface Reconstruction

The manifold method [9] also labels the tetrahedra of T with inside or outside. It uses our matter improvement (i.e. the set M computed in Sect. 3.5), but it removes thin structures due to a regularization, which labels outside several tetrahedra that are in M.

We summarize it to correct the regularization. Let O be the set of outside tetrahedra and ∂O be its boundary, i.e. the set of triangles between outside and inside tetrahedra. First O grows in $T \setminus M$ to meet visibility constraints, then O evolves in T by the regularization. Both steps maintain the manifoldness of ∂O. The regularization removes peaks, i.e. rings of triangles in ∂O around a vertex **a** which form small solid angles. This is done in two cases: remove from O all tetrahedra including **a**, or add to O all tetrahedra including **a**. However parts of thin vertical structure can be removed in the second case: some of their matter tetrahedra can become outside the surface.

We solve this problem as follows: the regularization is prohibited in the second case if at least one of the tetrahedra added to O has a true Boolean b_Δ.

4   Detection and Improvement of the Structures

Here we detail the contributions of the paper summarized in Sects. 3.4 and 3.5.

4.1   Definitions

We remind that M is the set of the matter tetrahedra in T, which should include the thin vertical structures. Let $\mathbf{v} \in \mathbb{R}^3$ be the *vertical direction*. (We have $||\mathbf{v}|| = 1$.)

The *small matter slice* $M(\Delta_0)$ started from a tetrahedron $\Delta_0 \in M$ is computed as follows. Let P_1 and P_2 be the two horizontal planes that enclose Δ_0. (The vertex of Δ_0 with the highest or lowest altitude is in P_1 or P_2, both altitude and horizontal directions are defined using $\mathbf{v}$.) We initialize $M(\Delta_0) = \{\Delta_0\}$ and complete it by a graph traversal of the adjacency graph of M by only considering tetrahedra that intersect the area between P_1 and P_2. In more details, the following process is repeated: take a tetrahedron $\Delta \in M(\Delta_0)$ and add to $M(\Delta_0)$ every neighbor tetrahedron of Δ in M (Δ has no more than four neighbors) that intersects the area between P_1 and P_2. We only need matter slices whose number of tetrahedra is less than a small threshold M_{max}, i.e. which can be included in a thin vertical structure. (We use $M_{max} = 20$.) Thus we stop the graph traversal if $M(\Delta_0)$ becomes larger than M_{max}, then we reset $M(\Delta_0) = \emptyset$ (no slice found).

Let $\mathbf{a}$ and $\mathbf{b}$ be in $\mathbb{R}^3$. The horizontal distance $w(\mathbf{a}, \mathbf{b})$ is

$$w(\mathbf{a}, \mathbf{b}) = \sqrt{||\mathbf{a} - \mathbf{b}||^2 - (\mathbf{v}^\top(\mathbf{a} - \mathbf{b}))^2}. \tag{1}$$

Let $v(A)$ be the vertex set of a tetrahedron set $A \subseteq T$. The *maximum width* of A is measured from a base point $\mathbf{b} \in \mathbb{R}^3$:

$$w(A, \mathbf{b}) = \max\{w(\mathbf{a}, \mathbf{b}), \mathbf{a} \in v(A)\}. \tag{2}$$

We also define the *path* $p(\Delta, \mathbf{a})$ between a tetrahedron $\Delta \in T$ and a vertex $\mathbf{a} \in v(T)$: this is the set of tetrahedra in T whose interiors are intersected by the line segment joining $\mathbf{a}$ and the barycenter of Δ.

4.2   Vertex Detection

We only need to detail the definition of the graph $G = (V, E)$ introduced in Sect. 3.4. Let α be an angle threshold. Let E' be the set of the edges $\mathbf{ab}$ in the polygonal chains that are almost vertical, i.e. if

$$|\mathbf{v}^\top \frac{\mathbf{b} - \mathbf{a}}{||\mathbf{b} - \mathbf{a}||}| > \cos\alpha. \tag{3}$$

We use a large tolerance $\alpha = 20°$ is our implementation. Let V' be the vertex set of E'. We have $\mathbf{a} \in V$ if and only if $\mathbf{a} \in V'$ and there is a tetrahedron $\Delta_0 \in M$ including $\mathbf{a}$ such that $M(\Delta_0) \neq \emptyset$. We have $\mathbf{ab} \in E$ if and only if $\mathbf{a} \in V$ and $\mathbf{b} \in V$ and Eq. 3 is meet and the following condition is meet: $\mathbf{ab} \in E'$ or $\mathbf{ab}$ is an edge of the Delaunay triangulation or there is $\mathbf{c} \in V'$ such that $\mathbf{ac} \in E'$ and $\mathbf{cb} \in E'$. The last condition using $\mathbf{c} \in V'$ is useful to connect two parts of a thin structure separated by a vertex that is not in a matter tetrahedron.

4.3   Matter Improvement

First we estimate a *median width* w_C for every connected component C of G by using the horizontal distance between a vertex $\mathbf{b} \in C$ and other vertices of the small matter slices $M(\Delta_0)$ such that $\mathbf{b} \in \Delta_0$. We collect the small matter slices attached to $\mathbf{b} \in C$ in

$$M_{\mathbf{b}} = \cup_{\mathbf{b} \in \Delta_0 \in M} M(\Delta_0) \tag{4}$$

and compute

$$w_C = \mathrm{median}\{w(\mathbf{a}, \mathbf{b}), \mathbf{b} \in C, \mathbf{a} \in v(M_{\mathbf{b}}), \mathbf{a} \neq \mathbf{b}\}. \tag{5}$$

Second the vertices $\mathbf{a}_i \in C$ are ordered along the vertical direction $\mathbf{v}$: they meet $\mathbf{v}^{\top}\mathbf{a}_i \leq \mathbf{v}^{\top}\mathbf{a}_{i+1}$ for all i. We obtain one composite polygonal chain $\mathbf{a}_1\mathbf{a}_2$, $\mathbf{a}_2\mathbf{a}_3$, $\cdots$ for C, which should be included in matter tetrahedra of the thin structure (it is not expected to be exactly on the surface of the thin structure).

Third we collect in a list L for several pairs (i, j) a path between $\mathbf{a}_i$ and $\mathbf{a}_j$ that will be forced to matter. Let $\mathbf{b} = (\mathbf{a}_i + \mathbf{a}_j)/2$. We consider several paths between $\mathbf{a}_i$ and $\mathbf{a}_j$ and take one that minimizes the maximum width with respect to $\mathbf{b}$. These paths are $p(\Delta, \mathbf{a}_j)$ where $\mathbf{a}_i \in \Delta \in M$ and $p(\Delta, \mathbf{a}_i)$ where $\mathbf{a}_j \in \Delta \in M$. For example, $p(\Delta, \mathbf{a}_j)$ minimizes the maximum width for a given (i, j). If $w(p(\Delta, \mathbf{a}_j), \mathbf{b}) < cw_C$ where c is a threshold, we decide that $p(\Delta, \mathbf{a}_j)$ is thin enough to be forced to matter and we add $(\Delta, \mathbf{a}_j)$ to the list L. This is done for all C. In the experiments, we use $c = 2$ and only take $j \in \{i+1, i+2\}$.

Last the matter is improved: we add $p(\Delta, \mathbf{a}_j)$ to M for every $(\Delta, \mathbf{a}_j) \in L$. Figure 1 summarizes the construction and the use of a composite polygonal chain.

Fig. 1. Construction and use of a composite polygonal chain in a simplified case: in 2D using $j = i + 1$ without the width test. (The vertical direction is horizontal in this figure.) First there are three reconstructed polygonal chains (bold edges) in the Delaunay triangulation. The gray triangles are matter and the remainder is freespace. Second the vertices of these chains form a connected component of G and we draw the resulting composite polygonal chain (eight bold edges). Third we draw all line segments linking the barycenter of matter triangles and vertices such that $j = i + 1$. Fourth all triangles intersected by these segments are forced to matter.

5   Experiment

Steps 1–5 (our pre-processing) are described in Sect. 5.1. Sections 5.2 and 5.3 focus on step 6a (graph-cut methods) and step 6b (manifold methods), respectively. Last Sect. 5.4 shows a lot of results for all surface reconstructions methods. For fair comparisons, the experimented methods start from the same 3D

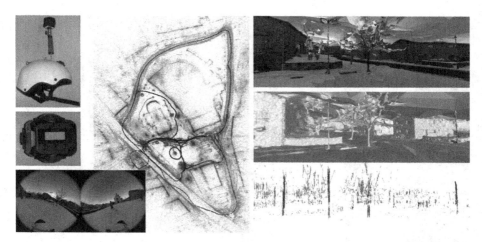

Fig. 2. Left: the helmet-held Garmin Virb 360 camera and one keyframe. Middle: a top view of the SfM point cloud and the camera trajectory. Right: a view of the final surface reconstructed by step 6b and the vertical edges (the set E') that we use.

Delaunay tetrahedralization T and end by the same Laplacian smoothing of the surface.

First we take two 2496×2496 videos at 30 Hz by walking during 473 s in a town using a helmet-held 360 camera (Garmin Virb 360). Then we apply generic SfM [14] followed by detection and closure of loops inspired by [25,26]. Last we experiment on the 1334 keyframes selected by SfM. Figure 2 shows our setup, a keyframe, a top view of the SfM result, a view of the 3D model by one of our method, and the set of vertical edges that we use.

5.1   Our Pre-processing

Step 1 generates 106k polygonal chains having 249k vertices. Step 3 builds the 3D Delaunay triangulation T. It has 1.2M vertices reconstructed from image features and 7.4M tetrahedra, 3.1M of them are matter. Step 4 is the detection step of thin structures. It only retains 25k edges of the polygonal chains that are almost vertical (the set E'). Then it finds 13k vertices in the vertex set of E' that have a small matter slice in their neighborhood (the set V). Using edges in both Delaunay triangulation and E', the graph G has 7k connected components. Last Step 4 only retains 230 of them by ignoring the smallest ones (very end of Sect. 3.4). Step 5 is the matter improvement step. It forces 10k tetrahedra to be matter. (6.5k of them were in $T \setminus M$ before.) Figure 3 shows our pre-processing: it has a noticeable improvement on a low-textured thin structure with missing matter tetrahedra and a negligible effect on a well-textured thick structure with a lot of matter tetrahedra. These results are those expected.

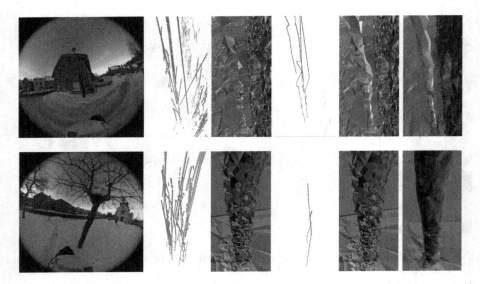

Fig. 3. Our pre-processing for a post (top) and a trunk (bottom). From left to right: one input image, reconstructed vertical edges (using $\alpha = 20°$), matter tetrahedra before our pre-processing, composite polygonal chains, matter tetrahedra after our pre-processing, final surface.

The detection and improvement steps take less than 0.6 s on a standard laptop. The feature reconstruction (both Canny and Harris points) is the most time consuming step: 40 min.

5.2 Graph-Cut Surface Reconstruction Methods

Here we compare methods "base graph-cut" and "our graph-cut". The former is in [23] and the latter is an update of the former (Sect. 3.6) preceded by our pre-processing (Sect. 3). We remind that base graph-cut estimates a surface minimizing an energy $E_{vis} + \lambda_{qual} E_{qual}$ with a visibility term E_{vis} (using $\alpha_{vis} = 1$) and a quality term E_{qual}. The greater the value of λ_{qual}, the better the surface quality in a regularization sense. Figure 4 shows a light post reconstructed by our graph-cut using $\lambda_{qual} = 2$ and base graph-cut using $\lambda_{qual} = 0.5$ and $\lambda_{qual} = 2$. The surface of the complete scene has 1.888M, 2.183M and 1.885M triangles, respectively. First we see that choosing a small λ_{qual} is a first solution to improve the post. However this solution is not satisfactory for two reasons: the post is incomplete (about 30% is lacking) and the noise increases in the background house. See the gray level variations in the left part. The smaller the value of λ_{qual}, the greater the number of surface vertices. (They include inaccurate points.) Second, we see that our graph cut provides the most complete post at the price of very small increases of triangle number and computation time. In the next experiments using base or our graph-cut, $\lambda_{qual} = 2$.

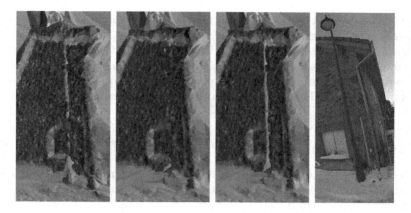

Fig. 4. Comparing three graph-cut methods. From left to right: base graph-cut using $\lambda_{qual} = 0.5$, base graph-cut using $\lambda_{qual} = 2$, our graph-cut using $\lambda_{qual} = 2$, a local view of an input image.

5.3 Manifold Surface Reconstruction Methods

Now we compare methods "base manifold" and "our manifold". The former is in [9] and the latter is an update of the former (Sect. 3.7) preceded by our preprocessing (Sect. 3). Figure 5 shows the same light post as Fig. 4 reconstructed by base manifold and our manifold. The surface of the complete scene has 1.734M and 1.739M triangles, respectively. Almost all parts of the post are removed by base manifold. In contrast to this, the post is almost complete by our manifold (at the price of very small increases of triangle number and computation time). There are two spurious handles that connect the post and the house. Thanks to other examples, we observe that the probability of such an artifact increases

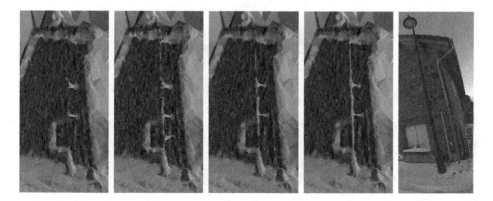

Fig. 5. Comparing four manifold methods. From left to right: base manifold, base manifold with updated regularization, our manifold with naive regularization, our manifold, a local view of an input image.

when the distance between a post and another scene component (house or wall or another post) decreases.

Figure 5 also shows base manifold with the regularization update in Sect. 3.7, and our manifold without the regularization update (i.e. base manifold with our pre-processing). In both cases, the post reconstruction is less complete than that of our manifold. This shows that both our pre-processing and regularization update are useful.

5.4   Other Experiments

In other examples we compare base graph-cut and our graph-cut, base manifold and our manifold. Figure 6 shows results for electric posts similar to that in the experiments above with different backgrounds. Our methods provide the most complete post reconstructions. Examining the background house in the top of the figure and assuming its planarity, we compare noises: the graph-cut noise is greater than the manifold noise although the total numbers of surface triangles

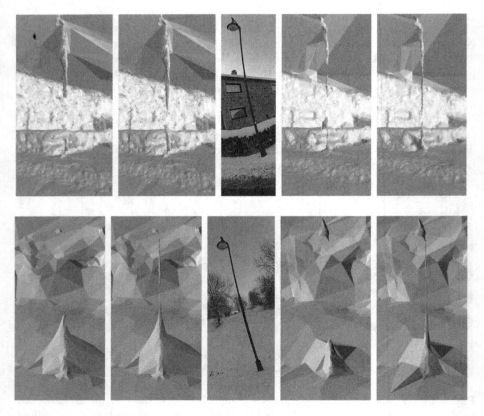

Fig. 6. Comparisons between several methods. From left to right: base graph-cut, our graph-cut, local view of input image, base manifold, our manifold.

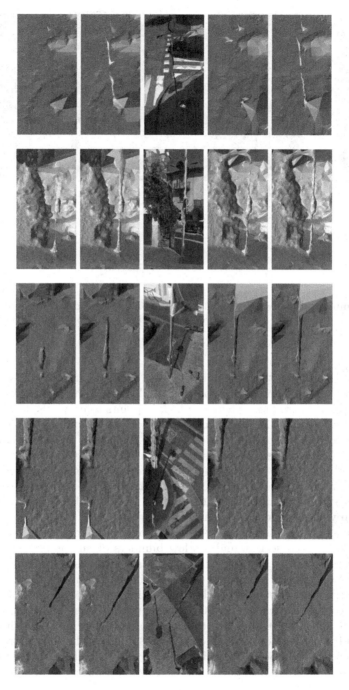

Fig. 7. Comparisons between several methods. From left to right: base graph-cut, our graph-cut, our manifold (textured), base manifold, our manifold.

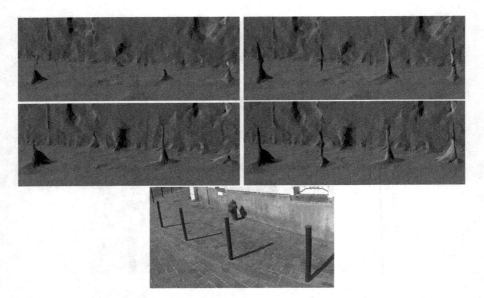

Fig. 8. Comparisons between several methods. Top: base graph-cut (left) and our graph-cut (right). Middle: base manifold (left) and our manifold (right). Bottom: local view of an input image.

are similar. Examining the post in the bottom of the figure, we note a shrinking artifact due to the Laplacian smoothing and a fattening artifact due to low texture in the background. (There is a lack of points to carve the freespace near the post bottom, thus the foreground post and background are not separated.) This holds for all methods. Figures 7 and 8 show thin structures in another dataset: a 2.5 km long sequence using four helmet-held Gopro cameras biking in a city [15]. Although our results on thin structures are not perfect, they are clearly better than those of the two base methods which omit important parts. Furthermore we remind that they are obtained in a difficult context: sparse point clouds from videos sequences taken in the wild.

We also examine the differences between base methods and our methods in overall reconstructed scenes, and see few blunders of our preprocessing due to excesses of the matter completion. There are several reasons. A first one is the conservative selection of vertices in Sect. 3.4: the small connected components of G are discarded for robustness (for both detection and w_C computation). Second our matter completion forces only 10k tetrahedra to matter. This number is small compared to the 3.1M tetrahedra that are matter by default, i.e. that are not intersected by rays or stereo triangles in Sect. 3.3. Third the tetrahedra forced to matter are selected in Sect. 4.3 such that they have smallest widths as possible in the horizontal directions. This limits the size of a potential blunder.

6   Conclusion

This paper presents a new pre-processing to improve the thin rectilinear structures in a surface reconstructed from an image sequence using a sparse cloud of features and their visibility. Starting from the traditional 3D Delaunay triangulation, we first detect vertical series of vertices in a same thin structure by reconstructing curves. Then we complete the matter label in tetrahedra between such vertices by using the connectedness constraint. Last we easily adapt two previous surface reconstruction methods such that their regularizations do not remove the thin structures that we detect and complete.

Our method has limitations and can be improved by several ways. The thin structures cannot be detected if they don't have gradient edges in the images. Since the detection step relies on polygonal chains approximating curves and occluding contours in the scene, this step can be improved thanks to previous work on curve reconstruction from images. Furthermore, the completion step should not only enforce connectedness but also geometric regularity like constant or smooth width along the thin structures. Our contributions can be applied to the incremental surface reconstruction and several directions of thin structures (although we only experiment batch surface reconstruction methods with the vertical direction). Last our pre-processing should also be generalized to other thin structures such as road signs, which are not rectilinear but planar.

References

1. Chauve, A., Labatut, P., Pons, J.: Robust piecewise-planar 3D reconstruction and completion from large-scale unstructured point data. In: CVPR 2010. IEEE (2010)
2. Fabbri, R., Kimia, B.: 3D curve sketch: flexible curve-based stereo reconstruction and calibration. In: CVPR 2010. IEEE (2010)
3. Faugeras, O., Bras-Mehlman, E.L., Boissonnat, J.: Representing stereo data with the Delaunay triangulation. Artif. Intell. **44**(1–2), 41–87 (1990)
4. Hofer, M., Wendel, A., Bischof, H.: Line-based 3D reconstruction of wiry objects. In: Computer Vision Winter Workshop (2013)
5. Holzmann, T., Fraundorfer, F., Bischof, H.: Regularized 3D modeling from noisy building reconstructions. In: 3DV 2016. IEEE (2016)
6. Jancosek, M., Pajdla, T.: Multi-view reconstruction preserving weakly-supported surfaces. In: CVPR 2011. IEEE (2011)
7. Kahl, F., August, J.: Multiview reconstruction of space curves. In: ICCV 2003. IEEE (2003)
8. Lhuillier, M., Quan, L.: Match propagation for image-based modeling and rendering. TPAMI **24**(8), 1140–1146 (2002)
9. Lhuillier, M., Yu, S.: Manifold surface reconstruction of an environment from sparse structure-from-motion data. CVIU **117**(11), 1628–1644 (2013)
10. Li, S., Yao, Y., Fang, T., Quan, L.: Reconstructing thin structures of manifold surfaces by integrating spatial curves. In: CVPR 2018. IEEE (2018)
11. Litvinov, V., Lhuillier, M.: Incremental solid modeling from sparse structure-from-motion data with improved visual artifact removal. In: ICPR 2014. IAPR (2014)

12. Livny, Y., Yan, F., Olson, M., Chen, B., Zhang, H., El-Sana, J.: Automatic reconstruction of tree skeletal structures from point clouds. In: SIGGRAPH Asia. ACM (2010)

13. Mai, F., Hung, Y.: 3D curves reconstruction from multiple images. In: International Conference on Digital Image Computing: Techniques and Applications (2010)

14. Mouragnon, E., Lhuillier, M., Dhome, M., Dekeyser, F., Sayd, P.: Generic and real-time structure from motion. In: BMVC 2007. BMVA (2007)

15. Nguyen, T., Lhuillier, M.: Self-calibration of omnidirectional multi-camera including synchronization and rolling shutter. CVIU **162**, 166–184 (2017)

16. Oswald, M.R., Stühmer, J., Cremers, D.: Generalized connectivity constraints for spatio-temporal 3D reconstruction. In: Fleet, D., Pajdla, T., Schiele, B., Tuytelaars, T. (eds.) ECCV 2014. LNCS, vol. 8692, pp. 32–46. Springer, Cham (2014). https://doi.org/10.1007/978-3-319-10593-2_3

17. Piazza, E., Romanoni, A., Matteucci, M.: Real-time CPU-based large-scale three-dimensional mesh reconstruction. Robot. Autom. Lett. **3**(3), 1584–1591 (2018)

18. Shan, Q., Curless, B., Furukawa, Y., Hernandez, C., Seitz, S.: Occluding contours for multi-view stereo. In: CVPR 2014. IEEE (2014)

19. Sugiura, T., Torii, A., Okutomi, M.: 3D surface reconstruction from point-and-line cloud. In: 3DV 2015. IEEE (2015)

20. Tan, P., Zeng, G., Wang, J., Kang, S., Quan, L.: Image-based tree modeling. Trans. Graph. **26**(3), 87 (2007)

21. Ummenhofer, B., Brox, T.: Point-based 3D reconstruction of thin object. In: ICCV 2013. IEEE (2013)

22. Usumezbas, A., Fabbri, R., Kimia, B.: The surfacing of multiview 3D drawings via lofting and occlusion reasoning. In: CVPR 2017. IEEE (2017)

23. Vu, H., Labatut, P., Pons, J., Keriven, R.: High accuracy and visibility-consistent dense multi-view stereo. TPAMI **34**(5), 889–901 (2012)

24. Wang, J., et al.: Image-based building regularization using structural linear features. IEEE Trans. Visual. Comput. Graphics **22**(6), 1 (2016)

25. Younes, G., Asmar, D., Shammas, E., Zelek, J.: Keyframe-based monocular slam: design, survey, and future directions. Robot. Auton. Syst. **98**, 67–88 (2017)

26. Yousif, K., Bab-Hadiashar, A., Hoseinnezhad, R.: An overview to visual odometry and visual slam: application to mobile robotics. Intell. Ind. Syst. **1**, 289–311 (2015)

27. Yucer, K., Kim, C., Sorkine-Hornung, A., Sorkine-Hornung, O.: Depth from gradients in dense light fields for object reconstruction. In: 3DV 2016. IEEE (2016)

28. Zheng, Y., Gu, S., Edelsbrunner, H., Tomasi, C., Benfey, P.: Detailed reconstruction of 3D plant root shape. In: ICCV 2011. IEEE (2011)

Polygonal Reconstruction of Building Interiors from Cluttered Pointclouds

Inge Coudron[✉], Steven Puttemans[✉], and Toon Goedemé[✉]

EAVISE Research Group, KU Leuven,
Jan Pieter De Nayerlaan 5, Sint-Katelijne-Waver, Belgium
{inge.coudron,steven.puttemans,toon.goedeme}@kuleuven.be

Abstract. In this paper, we propose a framework for reconstructing a compact geometric model from point clouds of building interiors. Geometric reconstruction of indoor scenes is especially challenging due to clutter in the scene, such as furniture and cabinets. The clutter may (partially) hide the structural components of the interior. The proposed framework is able to cope with this clutter by using a hypothesizing and selection strategy, in which candidate faces are firstly generated by intersecting the extracted planar primitives. Secondly, an optimal subset of candidate faces is selected by optimizing a binary labeling problem. We formulate the selection problem as a continuous quadratic optimization problem, allowing us to incorporate a cost function specifically for indoor scenes. The obtained polygonal surface is not only 2-manifold but also oriented, meaning that the surface normals of each polygon are consistently oriented towards the interior. All adjacent and coplanar faces that were selected, are merged into a single face in order to obtain a final geometric model that is as compact as possible. This compact model of the room uses less memory and allows for faster processing when used in virtual reality applications. The method of Nan et al. was used as a starting point for our proposed framework. Finally, as opposed to other state-of-the-art interior modeling approaches, the only input that is required, is the point cloud itself. We do not rely on viewpoint information, nor do we assume constrained input environments with a 2.5D or, more restrictively, a Manhattan-world structure. To demonstrate the practical applicability of our proposed method, we performed various experiments on actual scan data of building interiors.

1 Introduction

As we live in a 3D world, performing most of our activities in indoor environments, indoor scenes are familiar and essential in everyone's life. In the virtual world, 3D models of indoor scenes are used everywhere from 3D games to interior design. With the fast development of various augmented and virtual applications, the demand for realistic 3D indoor models is growing rapidly. However, obtaining such 3D models is quite difficult and challenging as opposed to outdoor scene modeling. The amount of clutter in outdoor scenes hiding the geometry of a

© Springer Nature Switzerland AG 2019
L. Leal-Taixé and S. Roth (Eds.): ECCV 2018 Workshops, LNCS 11129, pp. 459–472, 2019.
https://doi.org/10.1007/978-3-030-11009-3_28

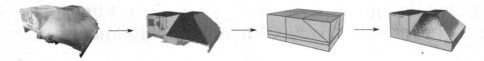

Fig. 1. Overview of the proposed pipeline. First the planar primitives are extracted from the pointcloud (Subsect. 3.1). Then candidate faces are generated (Subsect. 3.2). Finally an optimal subset of candidate faces is selected (Subsect. 3.3).

Fig. 2. Example of clutter inside a room.

building is rather low compared to indoor scenes. In indoor scenes, the clutter ranges from planar surfaces such as closets and furniture to highly irregular objects such as plants. Therefore, it is often not relevant to apply outdoor reconstruction algorithms to indoor scenes [2]. Nonetheless, we were able to adapt an outdoor reconstruction algorithm for the robust geometric modelling of indoor scenes (Fig. 2).

In this work, we focus on the reconstruction of a single room. We assume each room has been scanned separately. Therefore, when processing a complete building, each room will be processed sequentially. Hence, the problem of room segmentation is not considered here. Our goal is to reconstruct the basic geometry of the room from a point cloud obtained from a 3D consumer camera. The fact that we work with consumer cameras imposes a few extra challenges. First of all, the quality of the point clouds obtained with these scanners is often rather noisy. Secondly, the use of these consumer cameras may result in pose estimation errors during tracking which produce ghost-like double walls. Hence, the reconstruction algorithm must be robust enough to be able to cope with these imperfections. Furthermore, the scans contain a lot of clutter such as tables, doors etc. These surfaces should be ignored as well, as we are only interested in the outer geometry of the room as if it was an empty room. To obtain a compact geometric model, we approximate the room by as few piecewise planar surfaces as possible. A more compact model of the room uses less memory and allows for faster processing when used in virtual reality applications.

Our pipeline considers as input a 3D point cloud from a single room and produces as output a lightweight watertight 2-manifold oriented mesh. It requires no further information such as viewpoints. An overview of the proposed pipeline is shown in Fig. 1. Firstly, candidate faces are generated by intersecting the extracted planar primitives. Secondly, an optimal subset of candidate faces is selected. The selection of the optimal subset of candidate faces is in fact a binary labeling problem, but we cast it as a continuous quadratic programming problem in order to be able to incorporate an indoor specific cost function. The result is a 2-manifold and oriented mesh that can compactly describe the outline of a cluttered indoor scene even with slanted walls or sloped ceilings.

The remainder of this paper is organized as follows. In Sect. 2 we give an overview of the current state-of-the-art in 3D interior reconstruction and geometric modeling from point clouds. Next, in Sect. 3 we explain our proposed pipeline. The results are discussed in Sect. 4. Finally, a conclusion and future work is given in Sect. 5.

2   Related Work

Most of the research done on reconstructing building interiors from point clouds follows a 2D approach. They either assume simple vertical walls [3, 4, 6] or, even more stringent, a Manhattan world [5, 7–9]. In either case, the final model is produced by extruding a 2D floorplan with respect to the ceiling height. Some of these methods are restricted to piecewise linear floorplans [5], while others are able to capture rounded walls as well [7]. These assumptions limit the number of real-world architectures that can be reconstructed significantly. Therefore, more and more research is being done on interior reconstruction in 3D instead of 2D. One of the most promising techniques, is the work of [2]. They first determine whether the detected planar patches belong to permanent components (e.g. walls, ceiling or floor) by reasoning on a graph-based scene representation. Then the permanent components are used to build a 3D linear cell complex that is partitioned into separate rooms through a multi-label energy minimization formulation. However, this requires the prior knowledge of the scanning device poses, which is not always available. Therefore, in our approach we do not want to rely on this kind of prior knowledge.

In this paper, we want to create a geometric model of a scanned room. The model must be simple while being powerful enough to explain the scanned point cloud data. As interior rooms are mostly planar, we choose to fit a piecewise planar model to the room. In literature, reconstructing piecewise planar models from building exteriors is a well-studied problem [1, 10, 11]. However, methods such as [11] do not result in a watertight mesh, which is in fact necessary for correct shadow mapping in virtual reality. Furthermore, many of these methods ignore the problem of occlusions and missing regions due to clutter and are therefore not suited for indoor scenes. However, classifying planar patches as either clutter or structural components and simply removing them is not an option. Sometimes the structural components are completely occluded by clutter, so removing these planar patches would result in missing planes making it impossible to reconstruct a closed surface. Therefore we choose not to remove the clutter and adapt the algorithm from [1] to better handle the clutter. The main reason why this algorithm is not directly suited for indoor scenes, is that it assumes that all points belong to a piecewise planar object. However, the indoor scenes also contain clutter, which should be ignored as much as possible. Furthermore, their hypothesis generator was not robust enough for indoor scenes. In the next section we will explain how we adapted this algorithm.

3   Proposed Method

Our proposed method takes as input a point cloud of an entire room, including furniture and other objects and outputs a piecewise planar model of the room. As shown in Fig. 1, first the planar primitives are extracted from the pointcloud. Then, candidate faces are generated. Finally, an optimal subset of candidate faces is selected.

3.1   Plane Extraction

To detect planar primitives in the 3D point cloud, we use the standard RANSAC based shape detection from [12]. As the computational cost of the algorithm is relatively high for large point clouds, we first downsample the input cloud using a voxelgrid filter at a resolution of 5 cm. The result from this RANSAC based shape detection is a set of planar patches $P = \{p_i\}$. Each patch p_i consists of a set of points which lie within a distance ϵ from the best fit plane through these points.

One of the most common problems in indoor scene reconstruction from planar patches is that some of the boundary walls are undetected due the presence of clutter, door openings etc. Part of this problem can be alleviated by adding the planes from the bounding box around the point cloud to the set of planar patches. The bounding box planes are defined as the front, back, top, bottom left and right side of the bounding box. If we cannot find a plane that is close to the bounding box plane, the latter is added to the set of detected planes. By adding these planes to the set, we can ensure that it is always possible to at least generate a watertight mesh.

To check if a plane is close to a bounding box plane, we use the algorithm proposed in [10]. First we compute the angles between the detected planes and the bounding box planes. Then, starting from the plane with the smallest angle, we test if two conditions are met. On the one hand, the angle between the planes must be lower than some threshold θ_t. On the other hand, more than a specified number of points n_t must lie on the bounding box plane. If these two conditions are met we identify the detected plane as the corresponding bounding box plane. If not, we add the bounding box plane to the set. In our experiments we chose $\theta_t = 10°$ and $n_t = 20\%|p_i|$ where $|p_i|$ denotes the number of inliers of the planar patch p_i.

3.2   Candidate Face Generation

As explained by Nan et al., the hypothesis generator of [1] might introduce degenerate faces due to the limit of floating point precision. A face is called degenerate when one or more of its edges is no longer connected to an adjacent face. This degeneracy usually makes the manifold and watertight constraints impossible to be satisfied. When applying their hypothesis generator on our indoor scenes it became apparent that this is indeed a problem. Therefore, we implemented a new hypothesis generator that is able to cope with the limitations of floating point precision and does not suffer from these degeneracies.

From the previous step, we were able to identify each of our bounding box planes. These planes are used to build an initial polyhedron. As this polyhedron is always convex, the subsequent slicing of the polyhedron with the detected planes will again result in convex polyhedrons. To dynamically slice a convex polyhedron, we make use of the Sutherland-Hodgman clipping routine [13]. This routine is quite simple and very efficient. Furthermore, it can be extended to account for numerical robustness (see Fig. 3).

The two adjustments that are required to make the algorithm numerically robust are the following. First of all, the intersection point calculated from point A to point B will be slightly different than the calculation from point B to point A due to the limited precision of floating points. In order to avoid numerical issues because of this, we have to compute the intersection in a consistent manner. This is achieved by ordering the two points lexicographically: first x-coordinates are compared, if they are equal, y-coordinates are compared. Secondly, another source of numerical issues arises when checking if a point lies in front or behind the plane. Therefore we slice the plane with so-called thick planes. When a vertex of the polygon lies within a certain distance of the plane, it is as if the plane cut the polygon at this vertex.

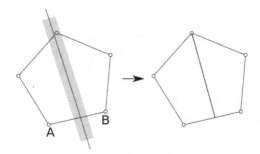

Fig. 3. Clipping a convex polygon by a plane.

To construct all candidate faces, we slice the polyhedron subsequently with each of the detected planes. Each face of the polyhedron is cut by the plane using the previously mentioned clipping routine. The result is a collection of faces belonging to the polyhedron on the positive side of the cutting plane and a set of faces belonging to the negative side. The cross section from this cut is added to both the front and back polyhedron. Each of the polyhedrons that is constructed as a result of this cut, will be subsequently cut by the next detected plane. In the end, we obtain a collection of polyhedrons that represent the candidate faces.

As opposed to the hypothesis generator from [1], we also do no longer have the problem of generating long and very thin candidate faces. By changing the distance to determine if a vertex is on the plane, we can control how long the smallest edge will minimally be. Furthermore, Finally, we do not create any degenerate faces. A face is degenerate when it contains an edge that is not connected to any other face. Selecting such a face can never lead to a manifold mesh and is therefore considered redundant. Adding these faces to the optimization problem, makes the problem size unnecessary larger.

A comparison between a set of candidate faces generated by the method in [1] and ours is shown in Fig. 4. From left to right right this image shows the input cloud, the candidate faces generated by [1], the reconstructed model from their hypothesis, the candidate faces generated by our algorithm and the reconstructed model from our hypothesis. As we can see in the first row of this figure, the top and front plane were not detected by the RANSAC approach as the number of inliers was too low. With our hypothesizing strategy we were able to cope with these missing planes. As apposed to [1] we do not only rely on the planes detected by RANSAC, but we start from a bounding volume which we subsequently slice with the detected planes. Therefore an approximation of these missing planes is added automatically to the candidate set. In Fig. 4(b) a circle is drawn around a face that was incorrectly cut, resulting in a reconstructed model that is not able to capture the actual geometry of the room.

3.3   Optimal Face Selection

Energy Terms. Each face f_i is described by two variables x_i and x_{ir}. The subscript r stands for reverse, meaning that we either select the face in its counter clockwise orientation (i.e. $x_i = 1$) or its clockwise or reversed orientation (i.e. $x_{ir} = 1$). If the face is not selected, both variables must be zero. Our objective function consists of three energy terms: data selection, model complexity and interior coverage.

First of all the data selection term evaluates how many of the points, that belong to the planar patches, are selected:

$$E_d = -\frac{1}{|P|} \sum_{i=1}^{N} (x_i + x_{ir}) \cdot inliers(f_i), \tag{1}$$

where P is the total number of inliers from the detected planar patches and $inliers(f_i)$ is the number of inliers in face f_i and N is the total number of faces that was generated. This term favourizes selecting as many faces where we found planar patches as possible. However, these planar patches also contain clutter such as closets, tables, doors etc. The data fitting term will try to select the

Input pointcloud (per plane color)	Candidate faces by L. Nan et al.	Selected faces by L. Nan et al.	Candidate faces by ours	Selected faces by ours

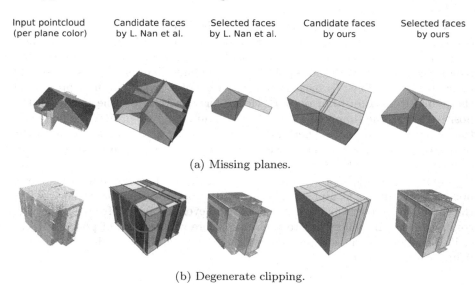

(a) Missing planes.

(b) Degenerate clipping.

Fig. 4. A comparison between the candidate face generated by [1] and our hypothesis generator. From left to right right: the input cloud, the candidate faces generated by [1], the reconstructed model from their hypothesis, the candidate faces generated by our algorithm and the reconstructed model from our hypothesis.

faces containing these objects as well. Therefore, we need to define some other energy terms to counterbalance this effect.

The second energy term we define, is a measure for the complexity of the resulting model. Selecting faces corresponding to clutter often results in gaps or protrusions. Therefore, we define the complexity of the model as the number of boundary edges that were selected. An edge is a boundary edge if the two faces adjacent to this edge do not lie on the same plane. The less boundary edges are selected, the simpler the model will be. Hence, this term discourages selecting the faces corresponding to clutter as that introduces more boundary edges. The complexity term can be written as follows:

$$E_c = \frac{1}{|E|} \sum_{i=1}^{N} \sum_{j=1, i \neq j}^{N} (x_i + x_{ir})(x_j + x_{jr}) \cdot corner(f_i, f_j), \qquad (2)$$

where E is the total number of edges and $corner(f_i, f_j)$ indicates whether the edge formed by the faces f_i and f_j is a boundary edge (i.e. $corner(f_i, f_j) = 1$) or not. However, in indoor scenes this is not sufficient because the clutter often occludes the actual room structure. As a result, the faces corresponding to the underlying structure do not contain any inliers while the clutter does. And so the first energy term will still dominate.

We define a third energy term, namely the interior coverage, that tries to compensate for the fact that the clutter results in missing data. In indoor scenes, we want as many points on the inside of the obtained model. So the uncovered regions (i.e. regions with more points on the outside than on the inside) should be as low as possible. To measure the coverage of a face f_i we first project all the points that lie in front onto f_i. Hence for x_i we project the points on the positive side of the supporting plane onto f_i and for x_{ir} we project the points on the negative side onto f_i. Then, we calculate the 2D alpha shape [14] from the projected points. The alpha shape creates a bounding area that envelops the set of projected 2D points. By changing the alpha parameter, you can manipulate the alpha shape object to tighten or loosen the fit around the points to create a non convex region. The alpha shape provides a good measure for the coverage of the candidate face by the projected points. So even if a face f_i from a structural component has no inliers due to occlusion, there will be a lot of points in front of it. Therefore, it can still provide a high coverage and gets a higher chance at being selected as well.

$$E_i = -\frac{1}{|area(M)|} \sum_{i=1}^{N} x_i \cdot (area(f_i) - area_P(f_i))$$

$$+ x_{ir} \cdot (area(f_i) - area_N(f_i)), \quad (3)$$

where $area(M)$, $area(f_i)$, $area_P(f_i)$ and $area_N(f_i)$ denote the surface areas of the bounding box, a candidate face f_i, and the area of the alphashape mesh constructed from the points on the positive or negative side of f_i respectively.

Optimization. By minimizing a weighted sum of the above mentioned energy terms, we can find the optimal subset of candidate faces. Remember that for the selection of each face f_i we defined two variables x_i and x_{ir}. They indicate in which orientation the face is selected. As we can select only one orientation, these variables are mutually exclusive. The mutual exclusion can be enforced by adding an extra term to the objective function, namely $x_i x_{ir}$. This term drives the solution towards either one or both variables of being zero. The objective function is thereby formulated as follows:

$$E = \lambda_d \cdot E_d + \lambda_c \cdot E_c + \lambda_i \cdot E_i + \sum_{i=1}^{N} x_i x_{ir}$$

$$with \quad 0 \leqslant x_i, x_{ir} \leqslant 1 \quad (4)$$

By defining two variables per face, we can ensure that the reconstructed model will have a consistent orientation. The orientation of two adjacent faces is consistent if the two vertices of the common edge are in the opposite direction (see Fig. 5). Note that the vertices of each edge are lexicographically ordered. So for each face f_i, adjacent to an edge e_j, we can determine its direction with respect to this edge. For this, we define a function $sign(x_i, e_j)$ and $sign(x_{ir}, e_j)$ as follows:

$$sign(x_i, e_j) = \begin{cases} 1 & \text{if } e_j \text{ and corresponding edge in } x_j \\ & \text{have the same direction} \\ -1 & \text{if } e_j \text{ and corresponding edge in } x_j \\ & \text{have opposite directions} \end{cases} \tag{5}$$

$$sign(x_{ir}, e_j) = -sign(x_i, e_j) \tag{6}$$

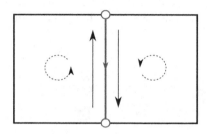

Fig. 5. Consistent ordering of the faces among an edge.

To ensure each edge will have consistently oriented faces, we define the following constraint:

$$\forall e_j : \sum_{f_i \in \mathcal{N}(e_j)} sign(x_i, ej) \cdot x_i + sign(x_{ir}, ej) \cdot x_{ir} = 0, \tag{7}$$

This constraint implies that when a face is selected with the edge in one direction, another face should be selected with the edge in the opposite direction.

To guarantee that the reconstructed model is 2-manifold either two or no faces must be selected. Therefore we define an additional constraint for each edge:

$$\forall e_j : \sum_{f_i \in \mathcal{N}(e_j)} x_i + x_{ir} \leqslant 2 \tag{8}$$

Thus the final optimization problem for selecting the best subset of candidate faces can be formulated as follows:

$$\min_{x_i, x_{ir}} \lambda_d \cdot E_d + \lambda_c \cdot E_c + \lambda_i \cdot E_i + \sum_{i=1}^{N} x_i x_{ir} \tag{9}$$

$$\text{s.t.} \begin{cases} \sum_{f_i \in \mathcal{N}(e_j)} sign(x_i, ej) \cdot x_i + \\ \qquad sign(x_{ir}, ej) \cdot x_{ir} = 0 \\ \sum_{f_i \in \mathcal{N}(e_j)} x_i + x_{ir} \leqslant 2 \\ 0 \leqslant x_i, x_{ir} \leqslant 1 \end{cases} \tag{10}$$

To obtain the final selection of candidate faces, we round the variables x_i and x_{ir} to the nearest integer. This is necessary because we are solving a continuous relaxation of the binary labeling problem. Therefore, the outcome will be close to

0 or 1 but not exactly. Each face for which either x_i and x_{ir} is 1 will be selected. The union of the selected faces comprises the final polygonal reconstruction.

Our method distinguishes from [1] in two aspects. Firstly, we implemented a hypothesis generator that is more robust for indoor scenes as explained the previous subsection. Secondly, our energy terms are able to better handle the missing or erroneous data as a result of occlusions and clutter in indoor scenes. A comparison between a reconstructed model obtained using the optimization problem of [1] and ours is shown in Fig. 6. As we can see despite the heavy clutter, our method is still able to detect the outer geometry of the room.

Fig. 6. Comparison between the optimization problem as defined in [1] and ours. From left to right: the cluttered indoor scene, the extracted planar primitives, the model reconstructed by [1], the model reconstructed by our method

4   Results

Our algorithm is implemented in C++ using the free Edition of the ALGLIB library for solving the quadratic optimization problem. To detect the planar primitives and construct the alpha shape meshes, we used the CGAL library [14]. We tested our pipeline on a set of 4 different real-world datasets from building interiors. All test were performed on a DELL XPS with an Intel Core i7 (1.8 GHz), 8 GB DDR3 RAM. Processing times for all models are given in Table 1 and vary from about 30 s to about 5 min for the complete pipeline. Note that our algorithm uses the free edition of ALGLIB and therefore runs on a single core. The planar primitive extraction is obtained using the RANSAC implementation in CGAL. For this we used the default parameter settings. The energy minimization depends on the weights λ_d, λ_c and λ_i that we fixed to 0.2, 0.3 and 0.3 respectively, which was determined empirically.

Table 1. Information on the environment (no. rooms) and overall processing time.

Dataset	#rooms	Processing time
House1	15	27 s
House2	17	313 s
Appartment1	12	38 s
House3	12	186 s

In Fig. 9 we show the output of our algorithm on 3 different datasets. The experiments show the advantages of our method. We were able to reconstruct the outer geometry of the rooms despite the clutter and missing or erroneous data. For example, if we take a closer look at the dining room from Appartment1 (see Fig. 7), we can see that the point cloud suffers from an extreme case of what we call a ghost-like double wall. Despite the erroneous data our method is able to correctly estimate the actual geometry of the room.

Fig. 7. A closeup from the dining room of Appartment1. The reconstructed model is shown in green. Despite the erroneous data the method is able to correctly estimate the geometry of the room. (Color figure online)

Fig. 8. A closeup from the bedroom on the second floor of House1. Due to a planar patch that was not detected, our method fails to reconstruct the correct geometry.

However, our method also has its limitations. We rely on the detection of planar patches from the structural components of the room to reconstruct its outer geometry. As we cannot guarantee that all planar surfaces are correctly extracted, our method will fail to correctly reconstruct the geometry in such cases as can be seen in Fig. 8. In this point cloud, the points that were not assigned to any planar patch are marked yellow. As we can see, there was no planar patch detected near the door of the bedroom. Therefore, our method was not able to correctly reconstruct the outer geometry of the room.

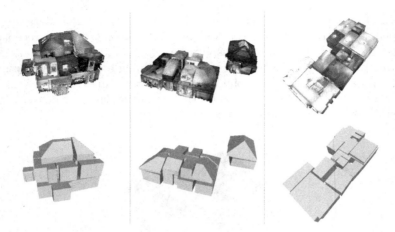

Fig. 9. Our method applied on different real life datasets: House1, House2 and Appartment1 respectively. From top to bottom: the cluttered indoor scenes, the model reconstructed by our method

In Fig. 10 we show a direct comparison between our method and the method from [1]. While their method is able to reconstruct most of the rooms, our method better describes the actual outer geometry. For example, in the close up from the living room, we can see that the method from Nan et al. Tries to overfit the clutter. The same problem was seen in the kitchen. Furthermore, some of the rooms were only constructed partially or not at all as a result of their non-robust hypothesis generator.

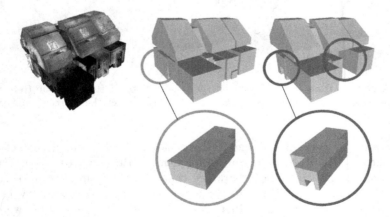

Fig. 10. Comparison between the results produced by our method and [1] on House4. From left to right: the cluttered indoor scenes, the model reconstructed by our method, the model reconstructed by [1]

5   Conclusion and Future Work

In this paper, we proposed a framework for reconstructing a lightweight polygonal surface of building interiors from cluttered point clouds. The method uses a hypothesis and selection strategy, in which candidate faces are firstly generated by intersecting the extracted planar primitives. Secondly, an optimal subset of candidate faces is selected by optimizing a binary linear programming problem. In this paper, we adapted the pipeline from [1] to make it more suitable for indoor scenes. As a first step, we implemented a hypothesis generator that is more numerically robust. Secondly, we reformulated the selection problem as a continuous quadratic optimization problem. The reformulation allowed us to incorporate a different cost function relevant for indoor scenes. Furthermore, the obtained polygonal surface is not only 2-manifold but also oriented, meaning that the surface normal of each polygon is consistently oriented towards the interior. This is especially interesting for rendering, where the shading depends on the correct orientation of the normals. Finally, as opposed to other state-of-the-art interior modeling approaches, the only input that is required, is the point cloud itself. We do not rely on viewpoint information, nor do we assume constrained input environments with a 2.5D or, more restrictively, a Manhattan-world structure.

The main limitation of our approach is that some planar surfaces that define the outer geometry of the room might still be undetected. In future work, we would like to explore the possibility to make the detection of planar surfaces more robust. Since the scenes were captured using an RGBD sensor, we can use the RGB images to detect lines as well. Next we can apply a RANSAC based method to detect planar surfaces from these line segments. The is especially suited for the missing planes due to windows or door openings which result in missing data in the depth images. To be able to better compare the results of the different reconstructions quantitavely, we will define a new metric based on the Intersection over Union. For the groundtruth mesh as well as the reconstructed mesh, we can create an occupancy grid in which each voxel is 1 if it is inside the mesh or 0 when it is on the outside. The Intersection over Union of both occupancy grids provides a good measure of the similarity of the reconstruction. If the reconstructed mesh is the same as the groundtruth mesh, the IoU will be 1.

References

1. Nan, L., Wonka, P.: PolyFit: polygonal surface reconstruction from point clouds. In: 2017 IEEE International Conference on Computer Vision (ICCV), pp. 2372–2380, October 2017
2. Mura, C., Mattausch, O., Pajarola, R.: Piecewise-planar reconstruction of multiroom interiors with arbitrary wall arrangements. In: Computer Graphics Forum (2016)

3. Turner, E., Zakhor, A.: Floor plan generation and room labeling of indoor environments from laser range data. In: Proceedings of the 9th International Conference on Computer Graphics Theory and Applications: GRAPP, VISIGRAPP 2014, INSTICC, vol. 1, pp. 22–33. SciTePress (2014)
4. Oesau, S., Lafarge, F., Alliez, P.: Indoor scene reconstruction using feature sensitive primitive extraction and graph-cut. ISPRS J. Photogramm. Remote Sens. **90**, 68–82 (2014)
5. Mura, C., Mattausch, O., Villanueva, A.J., Gobbetti, E., Pajarola, R.: Automatic room detection and reconstruction in cluttered indoor environments with complex room layouts. Comput. Graph. **44**(C), 20–32 (2014)
6. Ochmann, S., Vock, R., Wessel, R., Klein, R.: Automatic reconstruction of parametric building models from indoor point clouds. Comput. Graph. **54**(C), 94–103 (2016)
7. Turner, E., Zakhor, A.: Watertight as-built architectural floor plans generated from laser range data. In: 2012 Second International Conference on 3D Imaging, Modeling, Processing, Visualization & Transmission (3DIMPVT), pp. 316–323, October 2012
8. Ikehata, S., Yang, H., Furukawa, Y.: Structured indoor modeling. In: 2015 IEEE International Conference on Computer Vision (ICCV), pp. 1323–1331, December 2015
9. Murali, S., Speciale, P., Oswald, M.R., Pollefeys, M.: Indoor Scan2BIM: building information models of house interiors. In: 2017 IEEE/RSJ International Conference on Intelligent Robots and Systems (IROS), pp. 6126–6133, September 2017
10. Li, M., Wonka, P., Nan, L.: Manhattan-world urban reconstruction from point clouds. In: Leibe, B., Matas, J., Sebe, N., Welling, M. (eds.) ECCV 2016. LNCS, vol. 9908, pp. 54–69. Springer, Cham (2016). https://doi.org/10.1007/978-3-319-46493-0_4
11. Monszpart, A., Mellado, N., Brostow, G.J., Mitra, N.J.: RAPter: rebuilding manmade scenes with regular arrangements of planes. ACM Trans. Graph. **34**(4), 103:1–103:12 (2015)
12. Fischler, M.A., Bolles, R.C.: Random sample consensus: a paradigm for model fitting with applications to image analysis and automated cartography. Commun. ACM **24**(6), 381–395 (1981)
13. Sutherland, I.E., Hodgman, G.W.: Reentrant polygon clipping. Commun. ACM **17**(1), 32–42 (1974)
14. Da, T.K.F.: 2D alpha shapes. In: CGAL User and Reference Manual, 4.12 edn. CGAL Editorial Board (2018)

Paired 3D Model Generation with Conditional Generative Adversarial Networks

Cihan Öngün[✉] and Alptekin Temizel

Graduate School of Informatics, Middle East Technical University, Ankara, Turkey
{congun,atemizel}@metu.edu.tr

Abstract. Generative Adversarial Networks (GANs) are shown to be successful at generating new and realistic samples including 3D object models. Conditional GAN, a variant of GANs, allows generating samples in given conditions. However, objects generated for each condition are different and it does not allow generation of the same object in different conditions. In this paper, we first adapt conditional GAN, which is originally designed for 2D image generation, to the problem of generating 3D models in different rotations. We then propose a new approach to guide the network to generate the same 3D sample in different and controllable rotation angles (sample pairs). Unlike previous studies, the proposed method does not require modification of the standard conditional GAN architecture and it can be integrated into the training step of any conditional GAN. Experimental results and visual comparison of 3D models show that the proposed method is successful at generating model pairs in different conditions.

Keywords: Conditional Generative Adversarial Network (CGAN) ·
Pair generation · Joint learning · 3D voxel model

1 Introduction

While 3D technology mostly focuses on providing better tools for humans to scan, create, modify and visualize 3D data, recently there has been an interest in automated generation of new 3D object models. Scanning a real object is the most convenient way to generate digital 3D object models, however, this requires availability of real-life objects and each of these objects needs to be scanned individually. More crucially, it does not allow creating a novel object model. Creating a novel object model is a time consuming task requiring human imagination, effort and specialist skills. So it is desirable to have an automated system facilitating streamlined generation of 3D object content.

Generative models have recently become mainstream with their applications in various domains. Generative Adversarial Networks (GANs) [7] have been a recent breakthrough in the field of generative models. GANs provide a generic

L. Leal-Taixé and S. Roth (Eds.): ECCV 2018 Workshops, LNCS 11129, pp. 473–487, 2019.
https://doi.org/10.1007/978-3-030-11009-3_29

solution for various types of data leveraging the power of artificial neural networks, particularly Convolutional Neural Networks (CNN). On the other hand, use of GANs brings out several challenges. While stability is the most fundamental problem in GAN architecture, there are also domain specific challenges.

Standard GAN model generates novel samples from an input distribution. However, the generated samples are random and there is no control over them as the input noise and the desired features are entangled. While some solutions attack the entanglement problem [6], some propose new types of GANs for specific purposes. Conditional GAN [15] allows controlling the characteristics of the generated samples using a condition. While these conditions could be specified, the generated samples are random and it fails to generate pair samples in different conditions [12,14]. Keeping the input value the same while changing the condition value does not generate the same output in different conditions because of the entanglement problem. The representation between input and output sample is entangled in such a way that changing condition value changes the output completely. There are many studies for learning joint distributions to generate novel pair samples. Most of them uses modified GAN architectures, complex models or paired training data as described in the Related Works section.

In this study, we propose a new approach to generate paired 3D models with Conditional GANs. Our method is integrated as an additional training step to Conditional GAN without changing the original architecture. This generic solution provides flexibility such that it is applicable to any conditional GAN architecture as long as there is a metric to measure the similarity of samples in different conditions. Also the system can be trained with paired samples, unpaired samples and without any tuples of corresponding samples in different domains.

In Sect. 2, we describe the GAN architecture and the related work. The proposed method is given in Sect. 3 and experimental evaluation and results are provided in Sect. 4. Conclusions and future work are given in Sect. 5.

2 Related Work

GAN architecture (Fig. 1(a)) consists of a generator model G and a discriminator model D [7]. Generator model takes an input code and generates new samples. Discriminator model takes real and generated samples and tries to distinguish real ones from generated ones. Generator and discriminator are trained simultaneously so that while generator learns to generate better samples, discriminator becomes better at distinguishing samples resulting in an improved sample generation performance at the end of the training.

If GAN is trained with training data $\mathbf{x}$ for discriminator D and sampled noise z for generator G, D is used to maximize the correctly labeled real samples as real $\log(D(x))$ and generated samples as fake $\log(1 - D(G(z)))$. On the other hand, generator G tries to fool the discriminator to label the generated data as real so G is used for minimizing $\log(1 - D(G(z)))$. These two models duel each other in a min-max game with the value function $V(D, G)$. The objective of the whole system can be formulated as:

$$min_G max_D V(D, G) = E_{x \sim p_{data}(x)}[log\ D(x)]$$
$$+ E_{z \sim p_z(z)}[log\ (1 - D(G(z)))]. \tag{1}$$

Use of CNN based GANs [16] is popular in 2-D image domain with various applications. Pix2pix [8] is a general-purpose GAN based solution to image-to-image translation problems and it has been shown to be effective at problems such as synthesizing photos from label maps, reconstructing objects from edge maps, and colorizing images. It uses GANs in conditional settings for image-to-image translation tasks, where a condition is given on an input image to generate a corresponding output image. Another application of GAN is style transfer [13]. For an input image, the system can transfer the style of the reference image including time of the day, weather, season and artistic edit to the target. Perceptual Adversarial Network (PAN) [18] provides a generic framework for image-to-image transformation tasks such as removing rain streaks from an image (image de-raining), mapping object edges to the corresponding image, mapping semantic labels to a scene image and image inpainting.

The fundamental principle of GANs, i.e. using two different models trained together, causes stability problems. These two models must be in equilibrium to work together in harmony. Since the architecture is based on dueling networks, during the training phase, one of the model could overpower the other, causing a stability problem. Wasserstein GAN [3] proposes a new distance metric to calculate the discriminator loss where Wasserstein distance (Earth-Mover distance) is used to improve the stability of learning and provide useful learning curves. In [4] several approaches are introduced for regularizing the system to stabilize the training of GAN models.

Generating 3D models with GANs is a relatively new area with a limited number of studies. The first and the most popular study uses an all-convolutional neural network to generate 3D objects [19]. In this work, the discriminator mostly mirrors the generator and $64 \times 64 \times 64$ voxels are used to represent 3D models. Wasserstein distance [17] is employed by normalizing with gradient penalization as a training objective to improve multiclass 3D generation. In another study an autoencoder network is used to generate 3D representations in latent space [2]. GAN model generates new samples in this latent space and these samples are decoded using the same autoencoder network to obtain 3D point cloud samples. 3D meshes can also be used to train a GAN [9] to produce mesh-based 3D output. To overcome the difficulty of working with mesh data, input data is converted to signed distance field, then processed with two GAN architectures: low-frequency and high-frequency generator. After generating high and low-frequency samples, outputs are combined to generate a 3D mesh object.

Generator model of GAN uses a simple input noise vector $\mathbf{z}$ and it is possible that the noise will be used by the generator in a highly entangled way, causing the input vector $\mathbf{z}$ not correspond to semantic features of the output data. InfoGAN [6] is a method proposed to solve entanglement problem. To make a semantic connection between input noise vector and output data, a simple modification is presented to the generative adversarial network objective that encourages it to learn interpretable and meaningful representations. Generator network is provided with both the incompressible noise **z** and the latent code **c**, so the form of input data becomes (z, c). After necessary optimizations for combining these values, expected outputs can be generated with given parameters.

Conditional GAN (Fig. 1(b)) is an extended version of GAN [15] conditioning both generator and discriminator on some extra information. While standard GAN models generate samples from random classes, CGANs can generate samples with a predetermined class for any input distribution such as generating specific digits by using class labels as condition in MNIST dataset.

Input noise **z** and condition value **y** are concatenated to use as input to the generator G. Training data **x** and condition value **y** are concatenated to use as input to the discriminator D. With this modification, the objective function of conditional GAN can be formulated as follows:

$$
\begin{aligned}
min_G max_D V(D, G) = {} & E_{x \sim p_{data}(x)}[log \ D(x|y)] \\
& + E_{z \sim p_z(z)}[log \ (1 - D(G(z|y)))].
\end{aligned}
\tag{2}
$$

Conditional GANs can generate samples in given conditions, however they are not able to generate pairs for the same input and different condition values. Coupled GAN (CoGAN) [12] is a new network model for learning a joint distribution of multi-domain images. CoGAN consists of a pair of GANs, each having a generative and a discriminator model for generating samples in one domain. By sharing of weights, the system generates pairs of images sharing the same high-level abstraction while having different low-level realizations. DiscoGAN [10] aims to discover cross-domain relations with GANs. A similar approach is used in CycleGAN [21] where an image is used as input instead of a noise vector and it generates a new image by translating it from one domain to another. SyncGAN [5] employs an additional synchronizer model for multi-modal generation like sound-image pairs. AlignGAN [14] adopts a 2-step training algorithm to learn the domain-specific semantics and shared label semantics via alternating optimization.

3   Proposed Method

While the standard GAN model can generate realistic samples, it basically generates random samples in given input distribution and does not provide any control over these generated samples. For example, when a chair dataset is used to train the network, it generates chairs without any control over its characteristics such as its rotation. Conditional GANs provide control over the generated samples by training the system with given input conditions. For example, if rotation is used as a condition value for chair dataset, system can generate samples with a given rotation.

For both standard GAN and conditional GAN, the representation between the input and the output is highly entangled such that changing a value in the input vector changes the output in an unpredictable way. For example, for chair

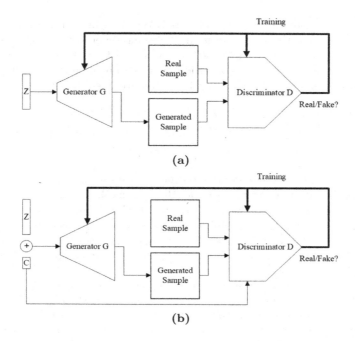

Fig. 1. (a) Standard GAN and (b) conditional GAN architectures.

dataset, each chair generated by standard GAN would be random and it would be created in an unknown orientation. Conditional GAN allows specification of a condition Input vector **z** and condition value **y** are concatenated and given together as input to the system so input becomes $(z|y)$. As the condition value **y** is also an input value, changing the condition also changes the output. Even if the input vector **z** is kept the same, the model generates different independent samples in given conditions and does not allow generating the same sample in different conditions [12, 14]. For example, for chair dataset, if the condition is rotation, system generates a chair in first rotation and a different chair in different rotation. As these objects are different, they cannot be merged at a later processing stage to create a new sample with less artifacts.

To overcome this problem, we propose incorporating an additional step in training to guide the system to generate the same sample in different conditions. The pseudo code of the method is provided in Algorithm 1 and Fig. 2 illustrates the proposed method for the 2-condition case. We use standard conditional GAN model and training procedure to generate samples by keeping the input vector **z** the same and changing the condition value. Generator function is defined as $G(z|y)$ for input vector **z** and condition value **y**. We can define the function for same input vector and n different conditions as $G(z|y_n)$ and the domain specific merging operator as $M(G(z|y_n))$. We feed the merged result to discriminator to determine if it is realistic so the output of discriminator is $D(M(G(z|y_n)))$.

Since the proposed method is an additional step to standard conditional GAN, it is a new term for the min-max game between generator and discriminator. The formulation of proposed method can be added to standard formulation to define the system as a whole. The objective function of conditional GAN with proposed additional training step can be formulated as follows:

$$
\begin{aligned}
min_G max_D V(D,G) = {} & E_{x \sim p_{data}(x)}[log\ D(x|y)] \\
& + E_{z \sim p_z(z)}[log\ (1 - D(G(z|y)))] \\
& + E_{z \sim p_z(z)}[log\ (1 - D(M(G(z|y_n))))].
\end{aligned}
\tag{3}
$$

As expected the system generates n different samples at n different rotations even though the input vector is the same. However as their rotations are specified by the condition, they are known. We then merge these samples to create a single object by first aligning these samples and then taking the average of the values for each voxel, similar to taking the intersection of 3D models. The merged model is then fed into the discriminator to evaluate whether it is realistic or not:

- If generated objects are different (as expected at the beginning), the merged model will be empty or meaningless. The discriminator will label the merged result as fake and the generator will get a negative feedback.
- If generated objects are realistic and similar, the merged model will also be very similar to them and to a realistic chair model. The discriminator is likely to label the merged object as real and the generator gets a positive feedback.

By this additional training step, even if the generated samples are realistic, system gets negative feedback unless the samples are similar. We enforce the system to generate similar and realistic samples in different conditions for the same input vector.

Note that the merge operation is domain specific and could be selected according to the target domain.

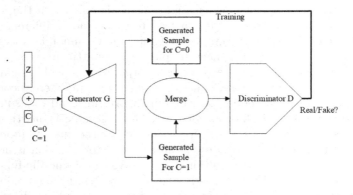

Fig. 2. Proposed method illustrated for 2-condition case.

Algorithm 1. Conditional GAN training with proposed method for n-conditions

Input: Real samples in n conditions: $X_0, X_1, \cdots, X_n$ input vector: Z, condition values: $C_0, C_1, \cdots, C_n$

Initialize network parameters for discriminator D, Generator G and merge operation M

for number of training steps **do**

// Standard conditional GAN

- Update the discriminator using $X_0, X_1, \cdots, X_n$ with $C_0, C_1, \cdots, C_n$ respectively
- Generate samples $S_0, S_1, \cdots, S_n$ using vector Z with $C_0, C_1, \cdots, C_n$ respectively
- Update the discriminator using $S_0, S_1, \cdots, S_n$ with $C_0, C_1, \cdots, C_n$ respectively
- Update the generator using $S_0, S_1, \cdots, S_n$ with $C_0, C_1, \cdots, C_n$ respectively

// Proposed method

- Align $S_1, \cdots, S_n$ with S_0
- Merge $S_0, S_1, \cdots, S_n : M(S_0, S_1, \cdots, S_n)$
- Feed merged sample to the discriminator with condition C_0
- Update the generator using the discriminator output

end for

---

4   Experiments

To test the system we used ModelNet [20] dataset to generate 3D models for different object classes (e.g. chair, bed, sofa). We adapted the conditional GAN for the problem of generation of 3D objects. We then evaluated the proposed method for 2-conditional and 4-conditional cases. Visual results as well as objective comparisons are provided at the end of this section.

ModelNet Dataset: This dataset contains a noise-free collection of 3D CAD models for objects. There are 2 manually aligned subsets with 10 and 40 classes of objects for deep networks. While the original models are in CAD format, there is also voxelized version [20]. Voxels are basically binary 3D matrices, each matrix element determines the existence of unit cube in the respective location. Voxelized models have $30 \times 30 \times 30$ resolution. The resolution is set to $32 \times 32 \times 32$ by simply zero padding one unit on each side. For the experiments 3 object classes are used: chair, bed and sofa having 989, 615 and 780 samples respectively. Each sample has 12 orientations $O_1, O_2, \cdots, O_{12}$ with 30 degrees of rotation between them. In the experiments with 2 orientations we use O_1, and O_7 which represent the object in opposite directions ($0°$ and $180°$). Experiments with 4 orientations use O_1, O_4, O_7 and O_{10} ($0°$, $90°$, $180°$ and $270°$).

While there are more object classes in the dataset, either they do not have sufficient number of training samples for the system to converge (less than 500) or objects are highly symmetric such that different orientations come out as same models (round or rectangle objects). For different rotations, the system has been tested with paired input samples, unpaired (shuffled) samples or removing any correspondence between samples in different conditions by using one half of the dataset for one condition and the other half for other condition. The tests with different variants of input dataset show no significant change on the output.

Network Structure: We designed our architecture building on a GAN architecture for 3D object generation [17]. In this architecture, the generator network uses 4 3D transposed deconvolutional layers and a sigmoid layer at the end. Layers use ReLU activation functions and the generator takes a 200 dimensional vector as input. Output of the generator network is a $32 \times 32 \times 32$ resolution 3D matrix. Discriminator network mostly mirrors the generator with 4 3D convolutional layers with leaky ReLU activation functions and a sigmoid layer at the end. It takes a $32 \times 32 \times 32$ voxel grid as input and generates a single value between 0 and 1 as output, representing the probability of a sample being real. Both networks use batch normalization between all layers. Kernel size of convolutional filters is 4 and stride is 2.

Adapting Conditional GAN for Generation of 3D Models: To generate 3D models on different rotations, we modified the aforementioned GAN architecture and converted it into a conditional GAN. Conditional value $\mathbf{y}$ is concatenated into $\mathbf{z}$ for generator input. For discriminator input, $\mathbf{y}$ is concatenated into real and generated samples as an additional channel. To train the discriminator, we feed objects on different rotations with corresponding condition values. To generate pairs, we change only the $\mathbf{y}$ and keep the $\mathbf{z}$ the same.

Training: Since generating 3D models is a more difficult task than differentiating between real and generated ones, discriminator learns faster than generator and it overpowers the generator. If the learning pace is different between generator and discriminator, it causes instability in the network and it fails to generate realistic results [7]. To keep the training in pace, we used a threshold for discriminator training. Discriminator is updated only if the accuracy is less than 95% in the previous batch. The learning rates are 0.0025 for generator and 0.00005 for discriminator. ADAM [11] is used for optimization with $\beta = 0.5$. System is trained using a batch size of 128. For 2 orientations, condition 0 and 1 are used for $0°$ and $180°$ respectively. For 4 orientations, condition 0, 1, 2 and 3 are used for $0°$, $90°$, $180°$, $270°$ respectively.

Visual results prove that, standard conditional GAN fails to generate 3D models with the same attributes in different rotations. In 2-conditional case, it generates a chair with $0°$ orientation, and a completely different chair with $180°$ orientation for the same input value. On the other hand, the proposed system can generate 3D models of the same object category with same attributes with $0°$ and $180°$ orientations. Also the result of merge operation is given to show the intersection of models. Since intersection of noise is mostly empty, merged model is also mostly noise-free. For these 3 classes, system is proven to generate pair models on different rotations.

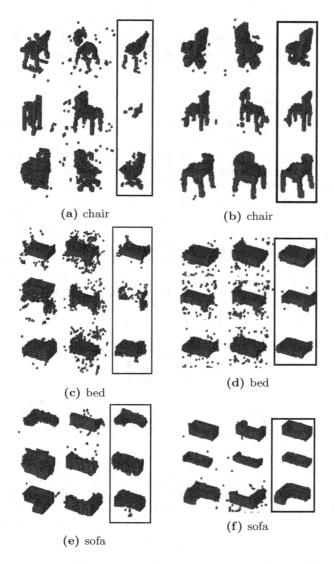

(a) chair

(b) chair

(c) bed

(d) bed

(e) sofa

(f) sofa

Fig. 3. Results with 3 classes (chair, bed and sofa) using 2-conditions (rotations). The first two samples are the generated pairs, merged results are shown in boxes. (a), (c) and (e) show the pairs generated with standard conditional GAN. It is clearly visible that the samples belong to different objects. Standard conditional GAN fails to generate the same object in different conditions (rotations) as expected and the merged results are noisy. (b), (d) and (f) show the pairs generated with the proposed method. The samples are very similar and the merged results (intersection of samples) support this observation. Merged results are also mostly noise-free and have more detail compared to standard conditional GAN.

For additional training of the proposed method, samples are generated by keeping the input vector the same and setting the condition value differently. Then the outputs are merged and fed into the discriminator. Only the generator is updated in this step. Experiments show that, also updating the discriminator in this step causes overtraining and makes the system unstable. Since this step is for enforcing the generator to generate the same sample in different conditions, training of the discriminator is not necessary.

Merge Method: Merging the generated samples is domain specific. For our case, generated samples are 3D voxelized models with values between 0 and 1 representing the probability of the existence of the unit cube on that location. First aligning the samples generated with different orientations and then simply averaging their 3D matrices, we get the merged result. In Fig. 4, we illustrate the merging procedure with a 2-conditional case with chair dataset. Generator will output two chairs with 0° and 180° rotations respectively. We can simply rotate the second model 180° to align both samples. Then, we average these 3D matrices. By averaging we get the probability of the existence of unit cubes in each location taking both outputs into account. If chairs are similar, the intersection of them will also be a similar chair (Fig. 4(a)) and if the chairs are not similar, their intersection will be meaningless (Fig. 4(b)). By feeding these merged results into the discriminator, we make the network evaluate the intersection model and train the generator using this information.

(a)   (b)

Fig. 4. Examples of merging operation. After generating pairs, one of the pairs is aligned with the other. Second sample is rotated to align with the first one in these examples. Then aligned samples are merged to form a new one. Simple averaging is applied to aligned pairs to get the intersection. (a) The result of the merging operation will be similar to the generated samples if the samples are similar, (b) the result will be meaningless if the samples are different.

Results: The proposed framework has been implemented using Tensorflow [1] version 1.4 and tested with 3 classes: chair, bed and sofa. The results are observed after training the model for 1500 epochs with the whole dataset. Dataset is divided into batches of 128 samples. For comparison, we used the conditional GAN that we adapted for 3D model generation as the baseline method. Both systems have been trained with the same parameters and same data. Results are generated with the same input and different condition values. To visualize the results, binary voxelization is used with a threshold of 0.5. Figure 3 shows the visual results. Note that the presented results are visualizations of raw output without any post processing or noise reduction.

As there is no established metric for the evaluation of generated samples, we introduce 2 different evaluation metrics: Average Absolute Difference (AAD) and Average Voxel Agreement Ratio (AVAR).

Raw outputs are 3D matrices for each generated model and each element of these matrices is a probability value between 0 and 1. For the calculation of AAD with n-conditions, first, the generated models $S_1, \ldots, S_n$ aligned with S_0 to get $S_1^R, \ldots, S_n^R$ then AAD can be formulated as follows:

$$AAD = \frac{\sum_{i=0}^{n-1} \frac{\sum_{\forall x,y,z} |S_i^R(x,y,z) - M(x,y,z)|}{total \ \# \ of \ matrix \ elements}}{n} \tag{4}$$

As a result of AAD a single difference metric is obtained for that object. A lower AAD value indicates agreement of the generated models with the merged model and it is desired to have an AAD value closer to 0.

For the calculation of Average Voxel Agreement Ratio (AVAR), first the aligned 3D matrices are binarized with a threshold of 0.5 to form voxelized S_i^{RB} M^B and then Average Voxel Agreement Ratio (AVAR) can be formulated as:

$$AVAR = \frac{\sum_{i=0}^{n-1} \frac{\sum_{\forall x,y,z} S_i^{RB}(x,y,z) \wedge M^B(x,y,z)}{\sum_{\forall x,y,z} S_i^{RB}(x,y,z)}}{n} \tag{5}$$

where $\wedge$ is the binary logical AND operator. AVAR value of 0 indicates disagreement while a value of 1 indicates agreement of the models with the merged model and it is desired to have an AVAR value closer to 1.

Table 1. Comparison of the proposed method with baseline using different object classes for 2-conditions and a batch (128) of pairs. AAD: Average Absolute Difference between generated matrices, AVAR: Average Voxel Agreement Ratio.

	Chair		Bed		Sofa	
	AAD	AVAR	AAD	AVAR	AAD	AVAR
Baseline	0.027	0.32	0.029	0.69	0.018	0.74
Proposed	0.009	0.79	0.012	0.89	0.004	0.95

Table 2. Comparison of the proposed method with baseline using different object classes for 4-conditions. The same metrics are used as in the 2-condition case.

	Chair		Bed		Sofa	
	AAD	AVAR	AAD	AVAR	AAD	AVAR
Baseline	0.034	0.36	0.043	0.65	0.034	0.62
Proposed	0.024	0.61	0.021	0.82	0.013	0.90

Results for 2-conditions and a batch of 128 pairs are given in Table 1. AAD and AVAR results are calculated separately for each pair in the batch and then averaged to get a single result for the batch. The results show that the proposed

(a) chair   (b) chair

(c) bed   (d) bed

(e) sofa   (f) sofa

Fig. 5. Visual results with 4 conditions. The first four samples are the generated objects, merged results are shown in boxes. (a), (c) and (e) show the objects and the merged result obtained with standard conditional GAN. (b), (d) and (f) show the objects and the merged result obtained with the proposed method The samples are very similar and the merged results (intersection of samples) support this claim. Merged results are also mostly noise-free and have more detail compared to standard conditional GAN.

method reduces the average difference significantly; 3, 2.4 and 4.5 times for chair, bed and sofa respectively. Here the results are highly dependent to object class. Different beds and sofas are naturally more similar than different chairs. While different bed shapes are mostly same except headboards, chairs can be very different considering stools, seats etc. Also we can see it in the results, the proposed method improved the similarity of generated chair pairs from 0.32 to 0.79. While the generated chair pairs are very different with the baseline method, the proposed method generated very similar pairs. For bed and sofa the baseline similarities are 0.69 and 0.74, relatively more similar as expected. The proposed method improved the results to 0.89 and 0.95 for bed and sofa respectively by converging to the same model.

The proposed system has also been tested with 4-conditions. For 4 orientations, condition 0, 1, 2 and 3 are used for $0°$, $90°$, $180°$ and $270°$ respectively. Also for merging operation, all generated samples are aligned with the first sample with $0°$ rotation. For that purpose 2nd, 3rd and 4th samples are rotated by $270°$, $180°$ and $90°$ respectively. After aligning all 4 samples, they are merged into a single model by averaging.

Figure 5 shows the visual results for 4-conditional case with the same experimental setup. Experimental results in terms of the same metrics are presented in Table 2. Standard conditional GAN generates 4 different chairs on 4 rotations. On the other hand the proposed method enforces the network to generate the same chair on 4 different rotations. Since the problem is more complex for 4 rotations, individual generated samples are noisier and have lower resolution. The improvement rates compared to the baseline are relatively lower than 2-condition case because of the increased complexity of the problem. To account for the increasing complexity of the model with higher number of conditions, more training data and/or higher number of epochs need to be used. While generating better samples with more training may seem crucial, it doesn't change the behavior of the networks. Conditional GAN keeps generating different samples and proposed model generates paired samples with each training iteration.

5   Conclusions and Future Work

In this paper, we presented a new approach to generate paired 3D models with conditional GAN. First, we adapted the conditional GAN to generate 3D models on different rotations. Then, we integrated an additional training step to solve problem of generation of pair samples, which is a shortcoming of standard conditional GAN. The proposed method is generic and it can be integrated into any conditional GAN. The results show the potential of the proposed method for the popular problem of joint distribution learning in GANs.

We demonstrated that proposed method works successfully for 3D voxel models on 2 and 4 orientations. Visual results and the objective evaluation metrics confirm the success of the proposed method. The difference between generated models are reduced significantly in terms of the average difference. The merged samples create noise-free high-resolution instances of the objects. This approach can also be used for generating better samples compared to traditional GAN for a particular object class.

The extension of the method to work with higher number of conditions is trivial. However, as the training of the system takes a long time, we leave the experiments with higher number of conditions and classes as a future work. The proposed solution is generic and could be applied to other types of data. As a next step, we are aiming to test the method on generation of 2D images to investigate the validity of the method for different data types.

References

1. Abadi, M., et al.: TensorFlow: large-scale machine learning on heterogeneous systems (2015). https://www.tensorflow.org/
2. Achlioptas, P., Diamanti, O., Mitliagkas, I., Guibas, L.: Representation learning and adversarial generation of 3D point clouds. arXiv preprint arXiv:1707.02392 (2017)
3. Arjovsky, M., Chintala, S., Bottou, L.: Wasserstein GAN. arXiv preprint arXiv:1701.07875 (2017)
4. Che, T., Li, Y., Jacob, A.P., Bengio, Y., Li, W.: Mode regularized generative adversarial networks. arXiv preprint arXiv:1612.02136 (2016)
5. Chen, W.C., Chen, C.W., Hu, M.C.: SyncGAN: synchronize the latent space of cross-modal generative adversarial networks. arXiv preprint arXiv:1804.00410 (2018)
6. Chen, X., Duan, Y., Houthooft, R., Schulman, J., Sutskever, I., Abbeel, P.: Info-GAN: interpretable representation learning by information maximizing generative adversarial nets. In: Advances in Neural Information Processing Systems, pp. 2172–2180 (2016)
7. Goodfellow, I., et al.: Generative adversarial nets. In: Advances in Neural Information Processing Systems, pp. 2672–2680 (2014)
8. Isola, P., Zhu, J.Y., Zhou, T., Efros, A.A.: Image-to-image translation with conditional adversarial networks. arXiv preprint arXiv:1611.07004 (2017)
9. Jiang, C., Marcus, P., et al.: Hierarchical detail enhancing mesh-based shape generation with 3D generative adversarial network. arXiv preprint arXiv:1709.07581 (2017)
10. Kim, T., Cha, M., Kim, H., Lee, J.K., Kim, J.: Learning to discover cross-domain relations with generative adversarial networks. arXiv preprint arXiv:1703.05192 (2017)
11. Kingma, D.P., Ba, J.L.: Adam: a method for stochastic optimization. In: Proceedings of the 3rd International Conference on Learning Representations (ICLR) (2015)
12. Liu, M.Y., Tuzel, O.: Coupled generative adversarial networks. In: Advances in Neural Information Processing Systems, pp. 469–477 (2016)
13. Luan, F., Paris, S., Shechtman, E., Bala, K.: Deep photo style transfer. CoRR abs/1703.07511 2 (2017)
14. Mao, X., Li, Q., Xie, H.: AlignGAN: learning to align cross-domain images with conditional generative adversarial networks. arXiv preprint arXiv:1707.01400 (2017)
15. Mirza, M., Osindero, S.: Conditional generative adversarial nets. arXiv preprint arXiv:1411.1784 (2014)

16. Radford, A., Metz, L., Chintala, S.: Unsupervised representation learning with deep convolutional generative adversarial networks. arXiv preprint arXiv:1511.06434 (2015)
17. Smith, E., Meger, D.: Improved adversarial systems for 3D object generation and reconstruction. arXiv preprint arXiv:1707.09557 (2017)
18. Wang, C., Xu, C., Wang, C., Tao, D.: Perceptual adversarial networks for image-to-image transformation. IEEE Trans. Image Process. **27**(8), 4066–4079 (2018)
19. Wu, J., Zhang, C., Xue, T., Freeman, B., Tenenbaum, J.: Learning a probabilistic latent space of object shapes via 3D generative-adversarial modeling. In: Advances in Neural Information Processing Systems, pp. 82–90 (2016)
20. Wu, Z., et al.: 3D ShapeNets: a deep representation for volumetric shapes. In: Proceedings of the IEEE Conference on Computer Vision and Pattern Recognition, pp. 1912–1920 (2015)
21. Zhu, J.Y., Park, T., Isola, P., Efros, A.A.: Unpaired image-to-image translation using cycle-consistent adversarial networks. arXiv preprint arXiv:1703.10593 (2017)

Predicting Muscle Activity and Joint Angle from Skin Shape

Ryusuke Sagawa[✉], Ko Ayusawa, Yusuke Yoshiyasu, and Akihiko Murai

National Institute of Advanced Industrial Science and Technology,
Tsukuba Central 1, 1-1-1 Umezono, Tsukuba, Ibaraki 305-8560, Japan
{ryusuke.sagawa,k.ayusawa,yusuke-yoshiyasu,a.murai}@aist.go.jp

Abstract. Muscle of human body can be a clue to recognize the behavior and intention of a person. If the muscle activity is measured only by visual observation, it is useful to estimate the state of the muscle. In this paper, a method of predicting muscle activity and joint angle of human body from skin shape is proposed. Since the muscle activity and the joint angle affect the skin shape, the both factors should be considered simultaneously. The proposed method is a learning-based approach that uses the data set of the skin shape, the muscle activity and the joint angle. It trains a linear regressor for predicting muscle activity and joint angle from skin shape. The deformation of skin shape is calculated as the feature in the active regions, which are extracted from the training data and limits the regions of the skin shape that contribute to the prediction. We acquired a lower limb with simple motion to consider the small number of factors in this paper. In the experiment, the muscle activity and joint angle are predicted even in the case that the both factors change simultaneously. The skin regions that contributes to prediction are given as the result of learning, and the distribution is reasonable from the viewpoint of biomechanics.

Keywords: Skin shape · Muscle activity · Joint angle

1 Introduction

Non-contact visual measurement using cameras can obtain various information by using the techniques of computer vision. The geometrical information, for example, shape and motion, has been one of the major topics. Shape and motion give useful information, but they are however often not sufficient to understand the real world. For example, for human-robot interaction, knowing a person's muscle activity is useful for robot's cooperative motion with the person. Motion planning of picking objects by a robot also would be easier if its physical properties such as weight and compliance are known in advance.

Electronic supplementary material The online version of this chapter (https://doi.org/10.1007/978-3-030-11009-3_30) contains supplementary material, which is available to authorized users.

© Springer Nature Switzerland AG 2019
L. Leal-Taixé and S. Roth (Eds.): ECCV 2018 Workshops, LNCS 11129, pp. 488–502, 2019.
https://doi.org/10.1007/978-3-030-11009-3_30

The physical information, such as muscle activity and weight, requires installation of additional sensors, for example force sensors, outside the vision system, while shape and motion are the information that can be directly obtained by using input images and camera parameters. Since the additional sensors are not always available especially in uncontrolled environments, it is beneficial if the physical information can be obtained by non-contact visual measurement, which is easier to apply to various situations compared to other systems that require contact with target objects.

In this paper, we focused on observing the muscle activity as one of the physical information. If the muscle activity is measured only by visual observation, it is useful to estimate the force generated by the muscle, and can be a clue to recognize the behavior and intention of the person. Since humans can estimate physical quantities only from visual clues, this approach is similar to the inference process of human.

Several visual features can be considered as the clues to estimate the muscle activity of a person such as the body pose, the articulated motion, and the muscle bulging. We measure the skin shape to observe the muscle bulging since it is expected to directly indicate the muscle activity, while the estimation from pose and motion needs the contact information with the environment.

The skin shape is not only affected by the muscle activity but also by the angle of the joint to which the muscle is attached. Even if a muscle is not activated, the length of the muscle changes according to the joint angle because the end point the muscle moves with the bone. Therefore, it is necessary to consider both the muscle activity and the joint angle. The question we tackle in this paper is if it is possible to predict muscle activity and joint angle from skin shape.

The proposed method is a learning-based approach. At the prediction step, the muscle activity and the joint angle is estimated only from the skin shape captured by non-contact sensor. At the training step, the data set of skin shape, muscle activity and joint angle is obtained, and their relationship is learned. The skin shape is captured by using a range sensor (a.k.a. depth sensor). The muscle activity is measured by electromyograph (EMG) sensors, which are attached to the skin above the target muscles, and record the electrical activity produced by muscles. The joint angle is measured by motion capture (mocap) system. Although the joint angle can be measured by a vision system without attaching markers on the human body, we used a mocap system for the accuracy at the training step.

The contribution of this paper is summarized as follows.

- It is demonstrated that visual measurement of skin shape can be used to estimate muscle activity and joint angle by a learning-based approach.
- Skin regions that corresponds to the muscles can be detectable as active regions from the training data set.
- It is succeeded to predict muscle activity, joint angle from skin shapes by linear regression of the skin deformation in the active region.

2 Related Work

The recent techniques of human motion analysis enables the estimation of the internal joint torque or muscle tension [1,2]. The joint trajectories can be computed, for example, by using the optical motion capture system which measures the trajectories from the markers attached on a human subject [3]. The joint torques are obtained from the inverse dynamics computation of an articulated body system, which is almost the same formula as mechanical system [4]. It usually requires the inertial properties of a human subject, which are estimated from literature data or identified [5]. The joint torques accentuated by muscles is extracted by subtracting the external joint torques driven by contact forces. Though the contact forces are measurable by utilizing some force sensors or force plates, the multi-contact situation makes it difficult to measure them individually; the mathematical optimization is often formulated to estimate them [2]. Each muscle tension can be estimated from the actuated joint torque with mathematical optimization techniques [2,6], or be obtained from the combination of a physiological muscle model [7,8] and EMG sensors. The mathematical optimization evaluates several physical and physiological terms in order to obtain one unique solution; however, the accurate estimation requires many reliable evaluation terms. Though EMG sensors measure individual muscle activation, they actually cannot be attached on all the muscles. The method using both mathematical optimization and EMG sensors is also investigated [9].

The articulated motion of human body can be estimated from 2D images without markers. The detection of 2D joint positions can be done using convolutional neural networks (ConvNets). Toshev et al. [10] first proposed a method based on ConvNets for detecting human pose i.e., 2D key points representing joint locations from a single image. Li et al. [11] used ConvNets to directly regress 3D human joints with an image. There are two main reasons for the improvements on accuracy of 3D human pose detection. In biomechanics and robotics, inverse kinematics has been well-studied and used to generate human pose from mocap by controlling joint angles. Previous approaches [12,13] estimated 3D human pose from 2D key points by combining a statistical model and constraints such as joint limit [14], segment length [12] and symmetry. Some methods perform regression of joint angles or axis angles [15,16] to estimate angular skeletal pose using ConvNets but the high nonlinearity prevents us from accurate prediction of joint locations. In this paper, it is assumed that the skeletal pose is given by mocap or these methods, and we used a mocap system for accuracy in the experiments.

Skin deformation according to body pose is important factor to generate a realistic model of human body in computer graphics. The methods of modeling muscles is classified to three approaches: geometrically-based, physically-based, and data-driven approaches [17]. The muscle deformation is model from the range data obtained by a depth camera in [18]. The skin deformation is learned with respect to the pose and acceleration of body parts by kernel regression in [19]. Various parts of body are modeled for graphics by simulating muscle and skin such as face [20], hand [21], lung [22] and upper body [23]. The relationship between skin shape and muscle force is learned in [24] to predict the force from skin shape while the skeletal pose is assumed to be fixed.

Skin deformation is based on nonrigid surface registration techniques, which are classified into three categories in terms of regularization that they use: smoothness regularization, isometric regularization and conformal regularization. Early approaches [25–28] are based on smoothness regularization. These techniques are very flexible to deform a template shape largely, but they are poor at preserving template details and mesh structures. Second, the isometric (as-rigid-as possible) regularization can preserve original template details and are commonly used in automatic registration techniques [29–31]. The drawback of these methods are that they are incapable of handling models with different sizes or those which undergo large local stretching. Third, the techniques based on conformal (as-similar-as possible) regularization [32–34] are proposed to achieve both flexibility in changing shapes and preservation of mesh structure. They are based on angle-preserving deformation.

3   Proposed Method

We consider the lower limb in this paper to simplify the situation, since some of the muscles are affected by various factors of multiple joints and muscles around them if they are attached to the joints of large degree of freedom like shoulder joints. The muscles of lower limb is related to the ankle joint and the movement can be controlled as the 1D motion, flexion/extension of the ankle. The motion of the ankle mainly depends on three muscles, Gastrocnemius, Soleus, Tibialis anterior muscles. Therefore, we analyze the relationship of the activity of the first two of these muscles, the ankle joint and the skin shape of lower-limb in this paper.

3.1   Data Acquisition

First, we describe how to acquire the data set to observe lower limb. Figure 1 shows the setup of the experiment. The skin shape of the lower limb of a subject is observed by using three range sensors placed around the subject. The range sensors are based on a projector-camera system [35] and capture the shape of the visible part from the sensor at 100FPS. The whole shape of the lower limb is captured by using three range sensors with a technique of reducing the crosstalk of multiple projected patterns [36]. The shape of the lower limb is reconstructed by merging range scans by Poisson reconstruction [37]. Figure 2 shows the examples of the skin shapes. The activity of muscles are low at Pose 1. The subject is standing on the toe at Pose 2, and the bulging of Gastrocnemius and Soleus muscles can be observed. The shape of EMGs on the skin is removed from the range scans and the skin shape is interpolated during merging them.

The joint angle of the ankle is measured by a mocap system. The markers are attached on the knee, ankle and toe, and the angle of the ankle joint is calculated

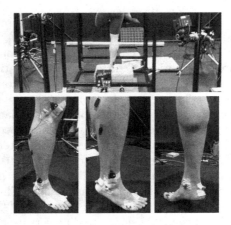

Fig. 1. The setup of the experiment: the skin shape of the lower limb of a subject is observed by using three range sensors placed around the subject. The joint angle of the ankle is measured by a mocap system. The muscle activities of lower limb are measured by EMG sensors placed on the skin above the muscles.

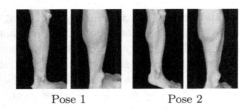

Pose 1   Pose 2

Fig. 2. Two examples of skin shapes: the activity of muscles are low at Pose 1. The subject is standing on the toe at Pose 2, and the bulging of Gastrocnemius muscle can be observed.

by solving inverse kinematics. We used the mocap system since it gives accurate and stable results, and estimating the angle without markers is one of our future work.

The muscle activities of lower limb are calculated from the data measured by EMG sensors placed on the skin above the muscles. Two EMG sensors are used simultaneously, and they are placed on Gastrocnemius and Soleus muscles. Figure 3 shows an example of the muscle activity and the ankle angle according to the motion of the lower limb. The muscle activity is defined as the integrated EMG signal normalized by the signal of the maximal voluntary contraction (MVC) [38]. If it is close to zero, the muscle is relaxed.

3.2   Calculating Deformation of Skin Shapes

The muscle activity affects the skin shape by the deformation of muscle shape under the skin. Since the skin shapes are acquired by the range scanners frame-

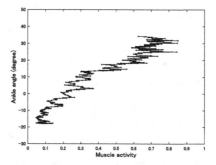

Fig. 3. The trajectory of muscle activity and ankle angle is shown for an example of the motion. The muscle activity is calculated from the data measured by a EMG sensor.

by-frame, the deformation of skin shape is needed to be calculated by finding the correspondence between the shapes. In this paper, we use a template shape to compare with each range scan. It is constructed from the one of the relaxed pose with low muscle activity.

In this paper, we used the as-conformal-as possible approach [34] to deform a template model. This method constrains the transformations of the model as similarity transformations (scale + rotation) locally as much as possible, which allows us to fit the model to the target geometry in a flexible way while preserving the mesh structure with less distortions. The cost function is defined as follows.

$$E(X) = w_{\text{ASAP}} E_{\text{ASAP}} + w_{\text{Closest}} E_{\text{Closest}}$$
$$+ w_{\text{Marker}} E_{\text{Marker}}, \tag{1}$$

where E_{ASAP} constrains deformation as similar as possible, and E_{Closest} penalizes distances between the closest points of template and target surface. E_{Marker} is the positional constraint of deformation by using mocap markers to avoid the shift during deformable registration. Four marker landmarks at the inner/outer knee and ankle are used. The energy is minimized using the alternating optimization technique where the first step optimizes the vertex positions with fixed transformations and the second step optimizes affine transformations with fixed vertex positions.

3.3 Detecting Active Regions Corresponding to Muscles

The skin actively deforms according to the motion is limited to the small number of the regions in the whole skin. The proposed method detects the regions of the skin which are deformed largely according to muscle contractions in order to use them for predicting muscle activities and joint angles.

First, the part of the lower limb is extracted from the template model that is deformed to each range scan. The deformed templates are then aligned to the original template shape by rigid transformation so as to minimize the deformation vectors. It is necessary to reduce the error of the skeletal pose estimated by the mocap system.

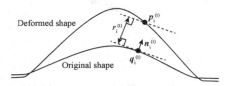

Fig. 4. The displacement caused by deformation for each vertex is calculated based on the normal vector at the vertex.

Second, the displacement caused by deformation $r_i^{(t)}$ of vertex i at sample t is calculated as follows.

$$r_i^{(t)} = n_i^{(t)} \cdot (p_i^{(t)} - q_i^{(t)}), \tag{2}$$

where $p_i^{(t)}$ and $q_i^{(t)}$ are the vertex positions of the deformed and original model, respectively. $n_i^{(t)}$ is the normal vector at the vertex $q_i^{(t)}$ as shown in Fig. 4.

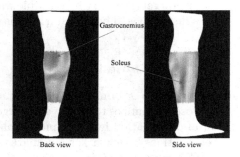

Fig. 5. The variance of the displacement for all vertices is calculated by using the training data set. The red parts indicate that the variance is large, and the regions of Gastrocnemius and Soleus muscles can be recognized from the variance. (Color figure online)

Since the active regions are assumed to deform largely according to the muscle activity and the joint angle. If the shape is captured for various poses and state of muscles, the variance of the displacement is expected to be large. Figure 5 shows the variance of the displacement calculated for all vertices by using the training data set. The red part indicates that the variance is large, and the regions of Gastrocnemius and Soleus muscles can be recognized from the variance.

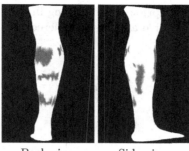

Back view   Side view

Fig. 6. The red regions are regarded as active by choosing the vertices of top 25% variance. The number of vertices are reduced to 25% of the original template by decimating the model. (Color figure online)

The top 25% vertices are chosen as the active regions that are used for prediction. Figure 6 shows the regions chosen as active. The number of vertices are reduced to 25% of the original template by decimating the model to lower the degree of freedom in this paper. For predicting the activity of Gastrocnemius and Soleus muscles, the regions around the calf are used based on the knowledge of biomechanics, while the all regions are used for predicting the ankle angle. The set of active vertices are defined as V_{act} for predicting the muscle activities and V_{ang} for predicting the ankle angle, respectively.

3.4 Predicting Muscle Activity and Joint Angle from Skin Shape

To learn the relationship between skin shape and muscle activity, a muscle model is assumed. Each muscle force along the fiber direction is often modeled as the sum of an active and passive part as shown in Hill-type models [7,8]. The passive part depends on only the elastic property of each muscle, whereas the active one is generated by the muscle activity. The active component can be represented by the products of the activity level, the length depending function, the velocity dependent function, and the constant value related to the maximum muscle contraction [39,40]. In this paper, let us assume the quasi-static muscle contraction and the linear elastic isotropic property for muscle. In the assumption, the local displacement as well as the active stress can be considered to be linear with respect to the muscle activity level. When also assuming the small change of the relative angle between the normal direction on each skin surface and the fiber direction in the nearest muscle, the displacement of each skin vertex is approximated to be linear to the corresponding muscle activity level.

Based on the above assumption, the following linear model between the skin shape, muscle activity and ankle angle is considered.

$$
\boldsymbol{y} = \boldsymbol{X}\boldsymbol{\omega}, \qquad
\boldsymbol{y} = \begin{bmatrix} \vdots \\ y^{(t)} \\ y^{(t+1)} \\ \vdots \end{bmatrix} \qquad
\boldsymbol{\omega} = \begin{bmatrix} \vdots \\ \omega_{V(i)} \\ \omega_{V(i+1)} \\ \vdots \end{bmatrix}
\tag{3}
$$

$$
\boldsymbol{X} = \begin{bmatrix} \ddots & \vdots & \vdots & \\ \cdots & r^{(t)}_{V(i)} & r^{(t)}_{V(i+1)} & \cdots \\ \cdots & r^{(t+1)}_{V(i)} & r^{(t+1)}_{V(i+1)} & \cdots \\ & \vdots & \vdots & \ddots \end{bmatrix}
$$

$y^{(t)}$ is t-th sample of the one of two muscle activities and the angle of the ankle joint, which are measured by the EMG sensors and the mocap system. $\omega_{V(i)}$ is the weight of i-th vertex in the active region $V(i)$ to be estimated from the training data set. $V(i)$ is V_{act} for predicting the muscle activities and V_{ang} for predicting the ankle angle, respectively. $r^{(t)}_{V(i)}$ is the displacement calculated for each vertex of the t-th sample. The weight vector $\boldsymbol{\omega}$ is estimated by the least square solution for three targets, two muscle activities and the ankle angle. In the step of prediction, the displacement is given by calculating deformation and the muscle activities and the ankle angle are estimated by using the weight vector.

4 Experiments

As the training data set, we acquire 8K samples of skin shape, muscles activity and joint angle. The angle of the ankle changes from 20° of dorsiflexion to 40° of plantar flexion during the acquisition. Figure 8 shows the distribution of the muscle activity and the ankle angle is used for training parameters. The muscle activity is captured so that it is distributed two-dimensionally over the value range of both the muscle activity and the ankle angle.

The decimated template consists of 3.7K vertices while the original template shape have 15K vertices. The active regions used for prediction consist of 138 and 176 vertices for estimating the muscle activities and the ankle angle, respectively.

As the validation data, we use a sequence that the subject stands up on the toe by moving the ankle from 20° of dorsiflexion to 40° of plantar flexion slowly in five seconds. Figure 7 shows the captured shape and the skeleton reconstructed from the predicted angles of the ankle joint. The red part of the shapes is used for predicting the muscle activities and the ankle angle. Although the shape of the foot and ankle is not included for prediction, the proposed method calculates the angles. The distribution of the muscle activity and the ankle angle is shown in Fig. 3.

The predicted results of two muscle activities and the ankle angle are shown in Figs. 9, 10 and 11. The red lines are the results measured by EMG sensors

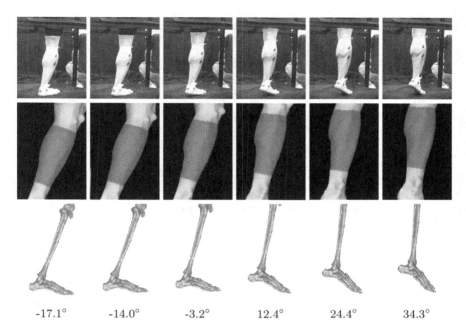

-17.1°   -14.0°   -3.2°   12.4°   24.4°   34.3°

Fig. 7. In the sequence for validation, the subject stands up on the toe by moving the ankle from 20° of dorsiflexion to 40° of plantar flexion slowly in five seconds. The middle row is the captured shape, and the bottom row is the skeleton reconstructed from the predicted angles of the ankle joint. The red part of the shape is used for predicting the muscle activities and the ankle angle. (Color figure online)

and the mocap system. The blue lines are the predicted results. 500 samples are captured in five seconds, and the average errors are 9.0% and 6.7% of the MVCs for the activities of Gastrocnemius and Soleus muscles, and 1.8° for the ankle angle, respectively.

The weight vector ω indicates how much the vertices that affect the prediction of the muscle activities and the ankle angle. Figure 12 shows the magnitude of the weight for each vertex. The red regions have large weights. With regard to Gastrocnemius muscle, the large weights exist around the upper parts of the calf where the bulges of Gastrocnemius muscle is visible on the skin. The weight for Soleus muscle is similar to that for Gastrocnemius muscle since they are both related to the motion of lowering the toe. But, there is large weight of Soleus muscle at the side of the lower limb, where the Soleus muscle is visible on the skin. The weight for predicting the ankle angle have large values on both the front and back sides of the lower limb. It indicates that it is important to observe the whole lower limb to predict the ankle angle, and is reasonable because the ankle angle is affected by the muscles on both sides, mainly by Gastrocnemius, Soleus and Tibialis anterior muscles.

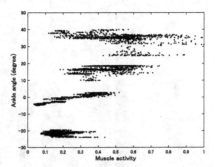

Fig. 8. The distribution of the muscle activity of Gastrocnemius muscle and the ankle angle is used for training parameters.

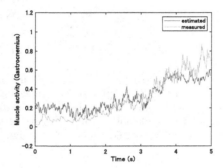

Fig. 9. The prediction result of the activity of Gastrocnemius muscle. (Color figure online)

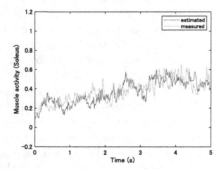

Fig. 10. The prediction result of the activity of Soleus muscle. (Color figure online)

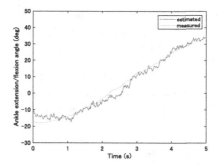

Fig. 11. The prediction result of the joint angle of the ankle. (Color figure online)

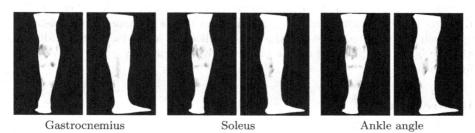

Gastrocnemius   Soleus   Ankle angle

Fig. 12. The red regions indicates that the vertex have large weights for prediction. As to Gastrocnemius muscle, the large weights exist around the upper parts of the calf where the bulges of Gastrocnemius muscle is visible on the skin. The weight for Soleus muscle is similar to that for Gastrocnemius muscle, but there is large weight at the side of the lower limb, where the Soleus muscle is visible on the skin. The weight for predicting the ankle angle have large values on both the front and back sides of the lower limb. (Color figure online)

The Gastrocnemius and Soleus muscles cooperate with respect to the ankle joints, and it is difficult to discriminate them by inverse kinematics, inverse dynamics, or mathematical optimization. Since the proposed method observes the deformation of individual muscle, the activity of the cooperative muscles can be uniquely estimated. It is one of the contributions that is meaningful from the viewpoint of the biomechanics.

5   Conclusion

In this paper, we have proposed a method of predicting muscle activity and joint angle of human body from skin shape. The both factors are needed to be considered simultaneously since the muscle activity and the joint angle affect the skin shape. The proposed method is a learning-based approach that uses the data set of the skin shape, the muscle activity and the joint angle, and trains a linear regressor for predicting muscle activity and joint angle from skin shape.

The active regions corresponding to the muscles are extracted from the training data, and the weight parameters for prediction is learned for the active regions. In this paper, we chose a simple situation of a lower limb that the ankle moves one dimensionally to lower the toe. The muscle activity and joint angle are successfully predicted even in the case that the both factors change simultaneously. The learned weights are reasonable from the viewpoint of biomechanics, and it indicates that the skin shapes gives useful information to infer the state of muscle and joint.

The approach in this paper requires the training data set to learn the regressor. Since it is costly to obtain the data for many subjects, the next step is to study a scalable approach that can predict the state of muscle and joint for many people even if they are not included in the training data set. One of the promising approaches is the prediction based on a biomechanical model by estimating the muscle structure for each individuals from the skin shape. A model-based approach are expected to reduce the cost of collecting individual data. Additionally, we plan to apply the proposed method to different part of the body in the future work.

References

1. Delp, S., Loan, J.: A computational framework for simulating and analyzing human and animal movement. IEEE Comput. Sci. Eng. **2**(5), 46–55 (2000)
2. Nakamura, Y., Yamane, K., Fujita, Y., Suzuki, I.: Somatosensory computation for man-machine interface from motion-capture data and musculoskeletal human model. IEEE Trans. Robot. **21**(1), 58–66 (2005)
3. Luh, J., Walker, M., Paul, R.: On-line computational scheme for mechanical manipulators. ASME J. Dyn. Syst. Meas. Contr. **102**(2), 69–76 (1980)
4. Gamage, S., Lasenby, J.: New least squares solutions for estimating the average centre of rotation and the axis of rotation. J. Biomech. **35**(1), 87–93 (2002)
5. Venture, G., Ayusawa, K., Nakamura, Y.: Optimal estimation of human body segments dynamics using realtime visual feedback. In: Proceedings of the IEEE/International Conference on Intelligent Robot System, pp. 1627–1632 (2009)
6. Rasmussen, J., Damsgaard, M., Voigt, M.: Muscle recruitment by the min/max criterion - a comparative numerical study. J. Biomech. **34**(3), 409–415 (2001)
7. Hill, A.: The heat of shortening and the dynamic constants of muscle. Proc. R. Soc. Lond. **126**, 136–195 (1938)
8. Stroeve, S.: Impedance characteristics of a neuro-musculoskeletal model of the human arm I: posture control. J. Biol. Cybern. **81**, 475–494 (1999)
9. Yamane, K., Fujita, Y., Nakamura, Y.: Estimation of physically and physiologically valid somatosensory information. In: Proceedings of the IEEE International Conference on Robotics and Automation, pp. 2624–2630 (2005)
10. Toshev, A., Szegedy, C.: DeepPose: human pose estimation via deep neural networks. In: Proceedings of the IEEE Conference on Computer Vision and Pattern Recognition, pp. 1653–1660 (2014)
11. Li, S., Chan, A.B.: 3D human pose estimation from monocular images with deep convolutional neural network. In: Cremers, D., Reid, I., Saito, H., Yang, M.-H. (eds.) ACCV 2014. LNCS, vol. 9004, pp. 332–347. Springer, Cham (2015). https://doi.org/10.1007/978-3-319-16808-1_23

12. Ramakrishna, V., Kanade, T., Sheikh, Y.: Reconstructing 3D human pose from 2D image landmarks. In: Fitzgibbon, A., Lazebnik, S., Perona, P., Sato, Y., Schmid, C. (eds.) ECCV 2012. LNCS, vol. 7575, pp. 573–586. Springer, Heidelberg (2012). https://doi.org/10.1007/978-3-642-33765-9_41
13. Bogo, F., Kanazawa, A., Lassner, C., Gehler, P., Romero, J., Black, M.J.: Keep it SMPL: automatic estimation of 3D human pose and shape from a single image. In: Leibe, B., Matas, J., Sebe, N., Welling, M. (eds.) ECCV 2016. LNCS, vol. 9909, pp. 561–578. Springer, Cham (2016). https://doi.org/10.1007/978-3-319-46454-1_34
14. Akhter, I., Black, M.J.: Pose-conditioned joint angle limits for 3D human pose reconstruction. In: Proceedings of the IEEE Conference on Computer Vision and Pattern Recognition, pp. 1446–1455 (2015)
15. Zhou, X., Sun, X., Zhang, W., Liang, S., Wei, Y.: Deep kinematic pose regression. In: Hua, G., Jégou, H. (eds.) ECCV 2016. LNCS, vol. 9915, pp. 186–201. Springer, Cham (2016). https://doi.org/10.1007/978-3-319-49409-8_17
16. Kanazawa, A., Black, M.J., Jacobs, D.W., Malik, J.: End-to-end recovery of human shape and pose. In: Computer Vision and Pattern Recognition (CVPR) (2018)
17. Lee, D., Glueck, M., Khan, A., Fiume, E., Jackson, K.: Modeling and simulation of skeletal muscle for computer graphics: a survey. Found. Trends Comput. Graph. Vis. 7(4), 229–276 (2012)
18. Robertini, N., Neumann, T., Varanasi, K., Theobalt, C.: Capture of arm-muscle deformations using a depth-camera. In: Proceedings of European Conference on Visual Media Production (CVMP), vol. 10 (2013)
19. Park, S., Hodgins, J.: Data-driven modeling of skin and muscle deformation. In: ACM TOG (2008)
20. Lewis, J., Anjyo, K., Rhee, T., Zhang, M., Pighin, F., Deng, Z.: Practice and theory of blendshape facial models. In: Proceedings of Eurographics 2014 - State the Art Reports (2014)
21. Sueda, S., Pai, D.K.: Dynamic simulation of the hand. In: Balasubramanian, R., Santos, V.J. (eds.) The Human Hand as an Inspiration for Robot Hand Development. STAR, vol. 95, pp. 267–288. Springer, Cham (2014). https://doi.org/10.1007/978-3-319-03017-3_13
22. Tsoli, A., Mahmood, N., Black, M.: Breathing life into shape: capturing, modeling and animating 3D human breathing. ACM Trans. Graph. 33(4), 52 (2014)
23. Lee, S.H., Sifakis, E., Terzopoulos, D.: Comprehensive biomechanical modeling and simulation of the upper body. ACM Trans. Graph. 28(4), 99 (2009)
24. Sagawa, R., Yoshiyasu, Y., Alspach, A., Ayusawa, K., Yamane, K., Hilton, A.: Analyzing muscle activity and force with skin shape captured by non-contact visual sensor. In: Bräunl, T., McCane, B., Rivera, M., Yu, X. (eds.) PSIVT 2015. LNCS, vol. 9431, pp. 488–501. Springer, Cham (2016). https://doi.org/10.1007/978-3-319-29451-3_39
25. Weise, T., Li, H., Van Gool, L., Pauly, M.: Face/off: live facial puppetry. In: Proceedings of the 2009 ACM SIGGRAPH/Eurographics Symposium on Computer Animation, pp. 7–16 (2009)
26. Yeh, I.C., Lin, C.H., Sorkine, O., Lee, T.Y.: Template-based 3D model fitting using dual-domain relaxation. IEEE Trans. Visual. Comput. Graph. 17(8), 1178–1190 (2010)
27. Allen, B., Curless, B., Popović, Z.: The space of human body shapes: reconstruction and parameterization from range scans. ACM Trans. Graph. 22(3), 587–594 (2003)
28. Amberg, B., Romdhani, S., Vetter, T.: Optimal step nonrigid ICP algorithms for surface registration. In: CVPR (2007)

29. Li, H., Sumner, R.W., Pauly, M.: Global correspondence optimization for non-rigid registration of depth scans. In: Proceedings of the Symposium on Geometry Processing, pp. 1421–1430 (2008)
30. Huang, Q.X., Adams, B., Wicke, M., Guibas, L.J.: Non-rigid registration under isometric deformations. In: Proceedings of the Symposium on Geometry Processing, pp. 1449–1457 (2008)
31. Tevs, A., Bokeloh, M., Wand, M., Schilling, A., Seidel, H.P.: Isometric registration of ambiguous and partial data. In: CVPR, pp. 1185–1192 (2009)
32. Liao, M., Zhang, Q., Wang, H., Yang, R., Gong, M.: Modeling deformable objects from a single depth camera. In: ICCV, pp. 167–174 (2009)
33. Papazov, C., Burschka, D.: Deformable 3D shape registration based on local similarity transforms. Comput. Graph. Forum 30, 1493–1502 (2011)
34. Yoshiyasu, Y., Ma, W.C., Yoshida, E., Kanehiro, F.: As-conformal-as-possible surface registration. Comput. Graph. Forum 33(5), 257–267 (2014)
35. Sagawa, R., Sakashita, K., Kasuya, N., Kawasaki, H., Furukawa, R., Yagi, Y.: Grid-based active stereo with single-colored wave pattern for dense one-shot 3D scan. In: 3DIMPVT, pp. 363–370 (2012)
36. Sagawa, R., Satoh, Y.: Illuminant-camera communication to observe moving objects under strong external light by spread spectrum modulation. In: Proceedings of CVPR (2017)
37. Kazhdan, M., Bolitho, M., Hoppe, H.: Poisson surface reconstruction. In: Proceedings of the Fourth Eurographics Symposium on Geometry Processing. SGP 2006, pp. 61–70 (2006)
38. Merletti, R.: Standards for reporting EMG data. J. Electromyogr. Kinesiol. 9(1), III–IV (1999)
39. Stroeve, S.: Impedance characteristic of a neuromusculoskeletal model of the human arm I. Posture control. Biol. Cybern. 81(5), 475–494 (1999)
40. Johansson, T., Meier, P., Blickhan, R.: A finite-element model for mechanical analysis of skeletal muscles. J. Theor. Biol. 206(1), 131–149 (2000)

W04 – Workshop on Visual Learning and Embodied Agents in Simulation Environments

W04 – Workshop on Visual Learning and Embodied Agents in Simulation Environments

Simulation environments are having a profound impact on computer vision and artificial intelligence (AI) research. Synthetic environments can be used to generate unlimited cheap, labeled data for training data-hungry visual learning algorithms for perception tasks such as 3D pose estimation, object detection and recognition, semantic segmentation, 3D reconstruction, intuitive physics modeling and text localization. In addition, visually-realistic simulation environments designed for embodied agents have reignited interest in high-level AI tasks such as visual navigation, natural language instruction following and embodied question answering. This workshop brought together researchers from computer vision, machine learning, NLP and robotics and examined the challenges and opportunities in this rapidly developing area - using simulation environments to develop intelligent embodied agents and other vision-based systems.

The workshop included two tracks, the visual learning track and the embodied agents track. All submissions to the visual learning track were handled electronically via the workshop CMT website. The reviewing process was double-blind. Each submission was reviewed by three reviewers for originality, significance, clarity, soundness, relevance and technical contents. There were in total 6 submissions received and 4 papers accepted. Among the 4 accepted papers, two would opt out the workshop post-proceedings as indicated by the authors. Submissions to the embodied agents track were reviewed in a single-blind manner. All the submissions were reviewed by at least two reviewers. There were in total 12 submissions received and all 12 papers were accepted. All the accepted papers from the embodied agent track chose to opt out the workshop post-proceedings.

We would like to express our gratitude to all the invited speakers, who had shared their inspiring thoughts with our audiences during the workshop. We would also like to thank all our colleagues for submitting their great work to the workshop.

September 2018

Li Yi
Hao Su
Qixing Huang
Cewu Lu
Leonidas J. Guibas
Peter Anderson
Manolis Savva
Angel X. Chang
Saurabh Gupta
Amir R. Zamir
Stefan Lee
Samyak Datta

Modeling Camera Effects to Improve Visual Learning from Synthetic Data

Alexandra Carlson[✉], Katherine A. Skinner, Ram Vasudevan,
and Matthew Johnson-Roberson

University of Michigan, Ann Arbor, USA
askc@umich.edu

Abstract. Recent work has focused on generating synthetic imagery to increase the size and variability of training data for learning visual tasks in urban scenes. This includes increasing the occurrence of occlusions or varying environmental and weather effects. However, few have addressed modeling variation in the sensor domain. Sensor effects can degrade real images, limiting generalizability of network performance on visual tasks trained on synthetic data and tested in real environments. This paper proposes an efficient, automatic, physically-based augmentation pipeline to vary sensor effects – chromatic aberration, blur, exposure, noise, and color temperature – for synthetic imagery. In particular, this paper illustrates that augmenting synthetic training datasets with the proposed pipeline reduces the domain gap between synthetic and real domains for the task of object detection in urban driving scenes.

Keywords: Deep learning · Image augmentation · Object detection

1 Introduction

Deep learning has enabled impressive performance increases across a range of computer vision tasks. However, this performance improvement is largely dependent upon the size and variation of labeled training datasets that are available for a chosen task. For some tasks, benchmark datasets contain millions of hand-labeled images for the supervised training of deep neural networks (DNNs) [1,2]. Ideally, we could compile a large, comprehensive training set that is representative of all domains and is labelled for all visual tasks. However, it is expensive and time-consuming to both collect and label large amounts of training data, especially for more complex tasks like detection or pixelwise segmentation [40]. Furthermore, it is practically impossible to gather a single real dataset that captures all of the variability that exists in the real world.

Two promising methods have been proposed to overcome the limitations of real data collection: graphics rendering engines and image augmentation

---

A. Carlson and K. A. Skinner—Authors contributed equally to this work.

© Springer Nature Switzerland AG 2019
L. Leal-Taixé and S. Roth (Eds.): ECCV 2018 Workshops, LNCS 11129, pp. 505–520, 2019.
https://doi.org/10.1007/978-3-030-11009-3_31

Fig. 1. Examples of object detection tested on KITTI for baseline unaugmented data (left) and for our proposed method (right). Blue boxes show correct detections; red boxes show detections missed by the baseline method but detected by our proposed approach for sensor-based image augmentation. (Color figure online)

pipelines. These approaches enable increased variability of scene features across an image set without requiring any additional manual data annotation. Recent work in rendering datasets has shown success in training DNNs with large amounts of highly photorealistc, synthetic data and testing on real data [17], [?]. Pixel-wise labels for synthetic images can be generated automatically by rendering engines, greatly reducing the cost and effort it takes to create ground truth for different tasks. Recent work on image augmentation has focused on modeling environmental effects such as scene lighting, time of day, scene background, weather, and occlusions in training images as a way to increase the representation of these visual factors in training sets, thereby increasing robustness to these cases during test time [5,6]. Another proposed augmentation approach is to increase the occurrence of objects of interest (such as cars or pedestrians) in images in order to provide more training examples of those objects in different scenes and spatial configurations [4,7].

However, even with varying spatial geometry and environmental factors in an image scene, there remain challenges to achieving robustness of task performance when transferring trained networks between synthetic and real image domains. To further understand the gaps between synthetic and real datasets, it is worthwhile to consider the failure modes of DNNs in visual learning tasks. One factor that has been shown to contribute to degradation of performance and cross-dataset generalization for various benchmark datasets is sensor bias [8–11]. The interaction between the camera model and lighting in the environment can greatly influence the pixel-level artifacts, distortions, and dynamic range induced in each image [12–14]. Sensor effects, such as blur and overexposure, have been shown to decrease performance of object detection networks in urban driving scenes [15]. Examples of failure modes caused by over exposure, manifesting as missed detections, are shown in Fig. 1. However, there still is an absence in the literature examining how to improve failure modes due to sensor effects for learned visual tasks in the wild.

In this work, we propose a novel framework for augmenting synthetic data with realistic sensor effects – effectively randomizing the sensor domain for synthetic images. Our augmentation pipeline is based on sensor effects that occur in image formation and processing that can lead to loss of information and produce failure modes in learning frameworks – chromatic aberration, blur, exposure, noise and color cast. We show that our proposed method improves performance for object detection in urban driving scenes when trained on synthetic data and tested on real data, an example of which is shown in Fig. 1. Our results demonstrate that sensor effects present in real images are important to consider for bridging the domain gap between real and simulated environments.

This paper is organized as follows: Sect. 2 presents related background work; Sect. 3 details the proposed image augmentation pipeline; Sect. 4 describes experiments and discusses results of these experiments and Sect. 5 concludes the paper. Code for this paper can be found at https://github.com/alexacarlson/SensorEffectAugmentation.

2   Related Work

Domain Randomization with Synthetic Data: Rendering and gaming engines have been used to synthesize large, labelled datasets that contain a wide variety of environmental factors that could not be feasibly captured during real data collection [3,16]. Such factors include time of day, weather, and community architecture. Improvements to rendering engines have focused on matching the photorealism of the generated data to real images, which comes at a huge computational cost. Recent work on domain randomization seeks to bridge the reality gap by generating synthetic data with sufficient random variation over scene factors and rendering parameters such that the real data falls into this range of variation, even if rendered data does not appear photorealistic. Tobin et al. [27] focus on the task of object localization trained with synthetic data. They perform domain randomization over textures, occlusion levels, scene lighting, camera field of view, and uniform noise within the rendering engine, but their experiments are limited to highly simplistic toy scenes. Building on [27], Tremblay et al. [?] generate a synthetic dataset via domain randomization for object detection of real urban driving scenes. They randomize camera viewpoint, light source, object properties, and introduce flying distractors. Our work focuses on image augmentation outside of the rendering pipeline and could be applied in addition to domain randomization in the renderer.

Augmentation with Synthetic Data: Shrivastava et al. recently developed SimGAN, a generative adversarial network (GAN) to augment synthetic data to appear more realistic. They evaluated their method on the tasks of gaze estimation and hand pose estimation [19]. Similarly, Sixt et al. proposed RenderGAN, a generative network that uses structured augmentation functions to augment synthetic images of markers attached to honeybees [20]. The augmented images are used to train a detection network to track the honeybees. Both of these approaches focus on image sets that are homogeneously structured and low resolution. We instead focus on the application of autonomous driving, which features highly varied, complex scenes and environmental conditions.

Traditional Augmentation Techniques: Standard geometric augmentations, such as rotation, translation, and mirroring, have become commonplace in deep learning for achieving invariance to spatial factors that are not relevant to the given task [24]. Photometric augmentations aim to increase robustness to differing illumination color and intensity in a scene. These augmentations induce small changes in pixel intensities that do not produce loss of information in the image. A well known example is the PCA-based color shift introduced by Krizhevsky et al. [1] to perform more realistic RGB color jittering. In contrast, our augmentations are modeled directly from real sensor effects and can induce large changes in the input data that mimics the loss of information that occurs in real data.

Sensor Effects in Learning: More generally, recent work has demonstrated that elements of the image formation and processing pipeline can have a large impact upon learned representation [10,28,29]. Andreopoulos and Tsotsos demonstrate the sensitivities of popular vision algorithms under variable illumination, shutter speed, and gain [8]. Doersch et al. show there is dataset bias introduced by chromatic aberration in visual context prediction and object recognition tasks [11]. They correct for chromatic aberration to eliminate this bias. Diamond et al. demonstrate that blur and noise degrade neural network performance on classification tasks [29]. They propose an end-to-end denoising and deblurring neural network framework that operates directly on raw image data. Rather than correcting for the effects of the camera during image formation of real images, we propose to augment synthetic images to simulate these effects. As many of these effects can lead to loss of information, correcting for them is non-trivial and may result in the hallucination of visual information in the restored image.

3   Sensor-Based Image Augmentation

Figure 2 shows a side-by-side comparison of two real benchmark vehicle datasets, KITTI [38,39] and Cityscapes [40], and two synthetic datasets, Virtual KITTI [16] and Grand Theft Auto [17,41]. Both of the real datasets share many spatial and environmental visual features: both are captured during similar times of day, in similar weather conditions, and in cities regionally close together, with the camera located on a car pointing at the road. In spite of these similarities, images from these datasets are visibly different. This suggests that these two real datasets differ in their global pixel statistics. Qualitatively, KITTI images feature more pronounced effects due to blur and over-exposure. Cityscapes has a distinct color cast compared to KITTI. Synthetic datasets such as Virtual KITTI and GTA have many spatial similarities with real benchmark datasets, but are still visually distinct from real data. Our work aims to close the gap between real and synthetic data by modelling these sensor effects that

Fig. 2. A comparison of images from the KITTI Benchmark dataset (upper left), Cityscapes dataset (upper right), Virtual KITTI (lower left) and Grand Theft Auto (lower right). Note that each dataset has differing color cast, brightness, and detail.

can cause distinct visual differences between real world datasets. Figure 3 shows the architecture of the proposed sensor-based image augmentation pipeline. We consider a general camera framework, which transforms radiant light captured from the environment into an image [30]. There are several stages that comprise the process of image formation and post-processing steps, as shown in the first row of Fig. 3. The incoming light is first focused by the camera lens to be incident upon the camera sensor. Then the camera sensor transforms the incident light into RGB pixel intensity. On-board camera software manipulates the image (e.g., color space conversion and dynamic range compression) to produce the final output image. At each stage of the image formation pipeline, loss of information can occur to degrade the image. Lens effects can introduce visual distortions in an image, such as chromatic aberration and blur. Sensor effects can introduce over- or under-saturation depending on exposure, and high frequency pixel artifacts, based on characteristic sensor noise. Lastly, post-processing effects are implemented to shift the color cast to create a desirable output. Our image augmentation pipeline focuses on five total sensor effects augmentations to model loss of information that can occur at each stage during image formation and post-processing: chromatic aberration, blur, exposure, noise, and color shift. To model how these effects manifest in images in a camera, we implement the image processing pipeline as a composition of physically-based augmentation functions across these five effects, where lens effects are applied first, then sensor effects, and finally post-processing effects:

$$I_{aug.} = \phi_{color}(\phi_{noise}(\phi_{exposure}(\phi_{blur}(\phi_{chrom.ab.}(I))))) \qquad (1)$$

Note that these chosen augmentation functions are not exhaustive, and are meant to approximate the camera image formation pipeline. Each augmentation function is described in detail in the following subsections.

3.1 Chromatic Aberration

Chromatic aberration is a lens effect that causes color distortions, or fringes, along edges that separate dark and light regions within an image. There are

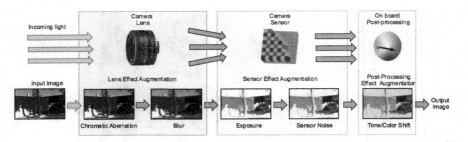

Fig. 3. A schematic of the image formation and processing pipeline used in this work. A given image undergoes augmentations that approximate the same pixel-level effects that a camera would cause in an image.

two types of chromatic aberration, longitudinal and lateral, both of which can be modeled by geometrically warping the color channels with respect to one another [31]. Longitudinal chromatic aberration occurs when different wavelengths of light converge on different points along the optical axis, effectively magnifying the RGB channels relative to one another. We model this aberration type by scaling the green color channel of an image by a value S. Lateral chromatic aberration occurs when different wavelengths of light converge to the different points within the image plane. We model this by applying translations (t_x, t_y) to each of the color channels of an image. We combine these two effects into the following affine transformation, which is applied to each (x, y) pixel location in a given color channel C of the image:

$$\begin{bmatrix} x_C^{chrom.ab.} \\ y_C^{chrom.ab.} \\ 1 \end{bmatrix} = \begin{bmatrix} S & 0 & t_x \\ 0 & S & t_y \\ 0 & 0 & 1 \end{bmatrix} \begin{bmatrix} x_C \\ y_C \\ 1 \end{bmatrix} \tag{2}$$

3.2   Blur

While there are several types of blur that occur in image-based datasets, we focus on out-of-focus blur, which can be modeled using a Gaussian filter [33]:

$$G = \frac{1}{2\pi\sigma^2} e^{-\frac{x^2+y^2}{2\sigma^2}} \tag{3}$$

where x and y are spatial coordinates of the filter and σ is the standard deviation. The output image is given by:

$$I_{blur} = I * G \tag{4}$$

3.3   Exposure

To model exposure, we use the exposure density function developed in [34, 35]:

$$I = f(S) = \frac{255}{1 + e^{-A \times S}} \qquad (5)$$

where I is image intensity, S indicates incoming light intensity, or exposure, and A is a constant value for contrast. We use this model to re-expose an image as follows:

$$S' = f^{-1}(I) + \Delta S \qquad (6)$$

$$I_{exp} = f(S') \qquad (7)$$

We vary ΔS to model changing exposure, where a positive ΔS relates to increasing the exposure, which can lead to over-saturation, and a negative value indicates decreasing exposure.

3.4   Noise

The sources of image noise caused by elements of the sensor array can be modeled as either signal-dependent or signal-independent noise. Therefore, we use the Poisson-Gaussian noise model proposed in [14]:

$$I_{noise}(x, y) = I(x, y) + \eta_{poiss}(I(x, y)) + \eta_{gauss} \qquad (8)$$

where $I(x, y)$ is the ground truth image at pixel location (x, y), η_{poiss} is the signal-dependent Poisson noise, and η_{gauss} is the signal-independent Gaussian noise. We sample the noise for each pixel based upon its location in a *GBRG* Bayer grid array assuming bilinear interpolation as the demosaicing function.

3.5   Post-processing

In standard camera pipelines, post-processing techniques, such as white balancing or gamma transformation, are nonlinear color corrections performed on the image to compensate for the presence of different environmental illuminants. These post-processing methods are generally proprietary and cannot be easily characterized [12]. We model these effects by performing translations in the CIELAB color space, also known as L*a*b* space, to remap the image tonality to a different range [36, 37]. Given that our chosen datasets are all taken outdoors during the day, we assume a D65 illuminant in our L*a*b* color space conversion.

Fig. 4. Example augmentations of GTA (left column) and VKITTI (right column) using the proposed sensor effect augmentation pipeline. Each image has a randomly sampled level of blur, chromatic aberration, exposure, sensor noise, and color temperature shift applied to it in an effort to model the visual structure/information loss caused by cameras when capturing real images.

3.6   Generating Augmented Training Data

The bounds on the sensor effect parameter regimes were chosen experimentally. The parameter selection process is discussed in more detail in Sect. 4. To augment an image, we first randomly sample from these visually realistic parameter ranges. Both the chosen parameters and the unaugmented image are then input to the augmentation pipeline, which outputs the image augmented with the camera effects determined by the chosen parameters. We augmented each image multiple times with different sets of randomly sampled parameters. Note that this augmentation method serves as a pre-processing step. Figure 4 shows sample images augmented with individual sensor effects as well as our full proposed sensor-based image augmentation pipeline. We use the original image labels as the labels for the augmented data. Pixel artifacts from cameras, like chromatic aberration and blur, make the object boundaries noisy. Thus, the original target labels are used to ensure that the network makes robust and accurate predictions in the presence of camera effects.

4   Experiments

We evaluate the proposed sensor-based image augmentation pipeline on the task of object detection on benchmark vehicle datasets to assess its effectiveness at bridging the synthetic to real domain gap. We apply our image augmentation pipeline to two benchmark synthetic vehicle datasets, each of which was rendered with different levels of photorealism. The first, Virtual KITTI (VKITTI) [16], features over 21000 images and is designed to models the spatial layout of KITTI with varying environmental factors such as weather and time of day. The second is Grand Theft Auto (GTA) [17,41], which features 21000 images and is noted for its high quality and increased photorealism compared to VKITTI. To evaluate the proposed augmentation method for 2D object detection, we used Faster R-CNN as our base network [42]. Faster R-CNN achieves relatively high performance on the KITTI benchmark test dataset, and many state-of-the-art object detection networks that improve upon these results use Faster R-CNN as their base architecture. For all experiments, we apply sensor effect augmentation pipeline to all images in the given dataset, then train an object detection network on the combination of original unaugmented data and sensor effect augmented data. We ran experiments to determine the number of sensor effect augmentations per image, and determined that optimal performance was achieved by augmenting each image in each dataset one time. To determine the bounds of the sensor effect parameter ranges from which to sample, we augmented small datasets of 2975 images by randomly sampling from increasingly larger parameter bounds and chose the ranges for each sensor effect that yielded the highest performance as well as visually realistic images. We found that the same parameter regime yielded optimal performance for both synthetic datasets. All of the trained networks are tested on a held out validation set of 1480 images from the KITTI training data and we report the Pascal VOC $AP50_{bbox}$ value for the car class. We also report the gain in $AP50_{bbox}$, which is the difference in performance relative to the baseline (unaugmented) dataset. We compare the performance of object detection networks trained on sensor-effect augmented data to object detection networks trained on unaugmented data as our baseline. For each dataset, we trained each Faster R-CNN network for 10 epochs using four Titan X Pascal GPUs in order to control for potential confounds between performance and training time.

4.1   Performance on Baseline Object Detection Benchmarks

Table 1 shows results for FasterRCNN networks trained on unaugmented synthetic data and sensor-effect augmented data for both VKITTI and GTA. Note that we provide experiments trained on the full training datasets, as well as experiments trained on subsets of 2975 images to allow comparison of performance across differently sized datasets. Synthetic data augmented with the proposed method yields significant performance gains over the baseline (unaugmented) synthetic datasets. This is expected as, in general, rendering engines do not realistically model sensor effects such as noise, blur, and chromatic aberration as accurately as our proposed approach. Another important result for the synthetic datasets (both VKITTI and GTA), is that, by leveraging our approach, we are able to outperform the networks trained on over 20000 unaugmented images with a tiny subset of 2975 images augmented with using our approach. This means that not only can networks be trained faster but also when training with synthetic data, varying camera effects can outweigh the value of simply generating more data with varied spatial features. The VKITTI baseline dataset tested on KITTI performs relatively well compared to GTA, even though GTA is a more photorealistic dataset. This can most likely be attributed to the similarity in spatial layout and image features between VKITTI and KITTI. With our proposed approach, VKITTI gives comparable performance to the network trained on the Cityscapes baseline, showing that synthetic data augmented with our proposed sensor-based image pipeline can perform comparably to real data for cross-dataset generalization.

Table 1. Object detection trained on synthetic data, tested on KITTI

Training Set	AP_{car}	Gain
Virtual KITTI		
2975 Baseline	54.60	—
2975 Prop. Method	61.88	↑ 7.28
Full Baseline (21K)	58.25	—
Full Prop. Method	62.52	↑ 4.27
GTA		
2975 Baseline	46.83	—
2975 Prop. Method	51.24	↑ 4.41
Full Baseline (21K)	49.80	—
Full Baseline (50K)	53.26	—
Full Prop. Method	55.85	↑ 6.05

4.2   Comparison to Other Augmentation Techniques

We ran experiments to compare our proposed method to photometric augmentation, specifically PCA-based color shift [1], complex spatial/geometric augmentations, specifically elastic deformation [47], standard additive gaussian noise augmentation, and a suite of standard spatial augmentations, specifically random rotations, scaling, translations, and cropping. We provide the results of training Faster-RCNN networks on the full VKITTI and GTA datasets augmented with the above methods in Table 2. All networks were tested on the same held-out set of KITTI images as used in the previous object detection experiments. Our results show that our proposed method drastically outperforms the other standard augmentation techniques, and that for certain synthetic data, spatial augmentations actually decrease performance on real data. This suggests that the proposed sensor effect augmentations capture more salient visual structure than traditional, non-photorealistic augmentation methods. We hypothesize this is because the physically-based sensor augmentations better model the information loss and the resulting global pixel-statistics that occur in real images. For example, our proposed method uses LAB space color transformation to alter the color cast of an image, where as traditional approaches use RGB space. LAB space is device independent, so it results in a more accurate, physically-based augmentation than [1].

Table 2. We provide the results of training Faster-RCNN networks on GTA and Virtual KITTI augmented with various augmentation methods. All networks were tested on KITTI.

Augmentation Method	AP_{Car}	Gain
Virtual KITTI		
Baseline	58.25	—
Prop. Method	**62.52**	↑ **4.27**
Krishevsky et al. [1]	59.09	↑ 0.84
Ronneberger et al. [47]	56.56	↓ 1.69
Additive Gaussian Noise	56.98	↓ 1.27
Random Rotation, Scale, Transl., Crop	55.11	↓ 3.14
GTA		
Baseline (21k)	49.80	—
Prop. Method (21k)	**55.85**	↑ **6.05**
Krishevsky et al. [1]	51.62	↑ 1.88
Ronneberger et al. [47]	48.94	↑ 0.14
Additive Gaussian Noise	52.01	↑ 2.21
Random Rotation, Scale, Transl., Crop	50.11	↑ 0.31

4.3   Ablation Study

To evaluate the contribution of each sensor effect augmentation on performance, we used the proposed pipeline to generate datasets with only one type of sensor effect augmentation. We trained Faster-RCNN on each of these datasets augmented with single augmentation functions, the results of which are given in Table 3. Performance increases across all ablation experiments for training on synthetic data. This further validates our hypothesis that each of the sensor effects are important for closing the gap between synthetic and real data.

4.4   Failure Mode Analysis

Figure 5 shows the qualitative results of failure modes of FasterRCNN trained on each synthetic training dataset and tested on KITTI, where the blue bounding box indicates correct detections and the red bounding box indicate a missed detection for the baseline that was correctly detected by our proposed method. Qualitatively, it appears that our method more reliably detects instances of cars that are small in the image, in particular in the far background, at a scale in which the pixel statistics of the image are more pronounced. Note that our method also improves performance on car detections for cases where the image is over-saturated due to increased exposure, which we are directly modeling through our proposed augmentation pipeline. Additionally, our method produces improved detections for other effects that obscure the presence of a car, such as

Table 3. Ablation study for object detection trained on synthetic data, tested on KITTI

Training Set	Augmentation Type	AP_{car}	Gain
Virtual KITTI			
2975 Baseline	*None*	54.60	—
2975 Prop. Method	Chrom. Ab.	61.08	↑ 6.48
2975 Prop. Method	Blur	59.72	↑ 5.12
2975 Prop. Method	Exposure	57.37	↑ 2.77
2975 Prop. Method	Sensor Noise	58.60	↑ 4.00
2975 Prop. Method	Color Shift	58.59	↑ 3.99
GTA			
2975 Baseline	*None*	46.83	—
2975 Prop. Method	Chrom. Ab.	48.92	↑ 2.09
2975 Prop. Method	Blur	49.17	↑ 2.34
2975 Prop. Method	Exposure	47.95	↑ 1.12
2975 Prop. Method	Sensor Noise	48.09	↑ 1.26
2975 Prop. Method	Color Shift	48.61	↑ 1.78

Fig. 5. Virtual KITTI examples are in the left column, GTA examples are in the right column. Blue boxes show correct detections; red boxes show detections missed by the FasterRCNN network trained on baseline, unaugmented image datasets but detected by FasterRCNNs trained on data augmented using our proposed approach for sensor-based image augmentation. (Color figure online)

occlusion and shadows, even though we do not directly model these effects. This may be attributed to increased robustness to effects that lead to loss of visual information about an object in general.

5   Conclusions

We have proposed a novel sensor-based image augmentation pipeline for augmenting synthetic training data input to DNNs for the task of object detection in real urban driving scenes. Our augmentation pipeline models a range of physically-realistic sensor effects that occur throughout the image formation and post-processing pipeline. These effects were chosen as they lead to loss of information or distortion of a scene, which degrades network performance on learned visual tasks. By training on our augmented datasets, we can effectively increase dataset size and variation in the sensor domain, without the need for further labeling, in order to improve robustness and generalizability of resulting object detection networks. We achieve significantly improved performance across a range of benchmark synthetic vehicle datasets, independent of the level of photorealism. Overall, our results reveal insight into the importance of modeling sensor effects for the specific problem of training on synthetic data and testing on real data.

Acknowledgements. This work was supported by a grant from Ford Motor Company via the Ford-UM Alliance under award N022884, and by the National Science Foundation under Grant No. 1452793.

References

1. Krizhevsky, A., Sutskever, I., Hinton, G.E.: ImageNet classification with deep convolutional neural networks. In: Advances in Neural Information Processing Systems, pp. 1097–1105 (2012)
2. Zhou, B., Lapedriza, A., Khosla, A., Oliva, A., Torralba, A.: Places: a 10 million image database for scene recognition. IEEE Trans. Pattern Anal. Mach. Intell. (2017)
3. Ros, G., Sellart, L., Materzynska, J., Vazquez, D., Lopez, A.M.: The SYNTHIA dataset: a large collection of synthetic images for semantic segmentation of urban scenes. In: Proceedings of the IEEE Conference on Computer Vision and Pattern Recognition, pp. 3234–3243 (2016)
4. Alhaija, H.A., Mustikovela, S.K., Mescheder, L., Geiger, A., Rother, C.: Augmented reality meets deep learning for car instance segmentation in urban scenes. In: Proceedings of the British Machine Vision Conference, vol. 3 (2017)
5. Zhang, H., Sindagi, V., Patel, V.M.: Image de-raining using a conditional generative adversarial network. arXiv preprint arXiv:1701.05957 (2017)
6. Veeravasarapu, V., Rothkopf, C., Visvanathan, R.: Adversarially tuned scene generation. arXiv preprint arXiv:1701.00405 (2017)
7. Huang, S., Ramanan, D.: Undefined, undefined, undefined, undefined: expecting the unexpected: training detectors for unusual pedestrians with adversarial imposters. In: 2017 IEEE Conference on Computer Vision and Pattern Recognition (CVPR), pp. 4664–4673 (2017)

8. Andreopoulos, A., Tsotsos, J.K.: On sensor bias in experimental methods for comparing interest-point, saliency, and recognition algorithms. IEEE Trans. Pattern Anal. Mach. Intell. **34**, 110–126 (2012)

9. Song, S., Lichtenberg, S.P., Xiao, J.: SUN RGB-D: a RGB-D scene understanding benchmark suite. In: Proceedings of the IEEE Conference on Computer Vision and Pattern Recognition, pp. 567–576 (2015)

10. Dodge, S., Karam, L.: Understanding how image quality affects deep neural networks. In: 2016 Eighth International Conference on Quality of Multimedia Experience (QoMEX), pp. 1–6. IEEE (2016)

11. Doersch, C., Gupta, A., Efros, A.A.: Unsupervised visual representation learning by context prediction. In: Proceedings of the IEEE International Conference on Computer Vision, pp. 1422–1430 (2015)

12. Grossberg, M.D., Nayar, S.K.: Modeling the space of camera response functions. IEEE Trans. Pattern Anal. Mach. Intell. **26**, 1272–1282 (2004)

13. Couzinie-Devy, F., Sun, J., Alahari, K., Ponce, J.: Learning to estimate and remove non-uniform image blur. In: Proceedings of the IEEE Conference on Computer Vision and Pattern Recognition, pp. 1075–1082 (2013)

14. Foi, A., Trimeche, M., Katkovnik, V., Egiazarian, K.: Practical Poissonian-Gaussian noise modeling and fitting for single-image raw-data. IEEE Trans. Image Process. **17**, 1737–1754 (2008)

15. Ramanagopal, M.S., Anderson, C., Vasudevan, R., Johnson-Roberson, M.: Failing to learn: autonomously identifying perception failures for self-driving cars. CoRR abs/1707.00051 (2017)

16. Gaidon, A., Wang, Q., Cabon, Y., Vig, E.: Virtual worlds as proxy for multi-object tracking analysis. In: Proceedings of the IEEE Conference on Computer Vision and Pattern Recognition, pp. 4340–4349 (2016)

17. Johnson-Roberson, M., Barto, C., Mehta, R., Sridhar, S.N., Rosaen, K., Vasudevan, R.: Driving in the matrix: can virtual worlds replace human-generated annotations for real world tasks? In: 2017 IEEE International Conference on Robotics and Automation (ICRA), pp. 746–753. IEEE (2017)

18. Sankaranarayanan, S., Balaji, Y., Jain, A., Lim, S., Chellappa, R.: Unsupervised domain adaptation for semantic segmentation with GANs. CoRR abs/1711.06969 (2017)

19. Shrivastava, A., Pfister, T., Tuzel, O., Susskind, J., Wang, W., Webb, R.: Learning from simulated and unsupervised images through adversarial training. arXiv preprint arXiv:1612.07828 (2016)

20. Sixt, L., Wild, B., Landgraf, T.: RenderGAN: generating realistic labeled data. arXiv preprint arXiv:1611.01331 (2016)

21. Zhu, J.Y., Park, T., Isola, P., Efros, A.A.: Unpaired image-to-image translation using cycle-consistent adversarial networks. arXiv preprint arXiv:1703.10593 (2017)

22. Eitel, A., Springenberg, J.T., Spinello, L., Riedmiller, M., Burgard, W.: Multimodal deep learning for robust RGB-D object recognition. In: 2015 IEEE/RSJ International Conference on Intelligent Robots and Systems (IROS), pp. 681–687. IEEE (2015)

23. Wu, R., Yan, S., Shan, Y., Dang, Q., Sun, G.: Deep image: scaling up image recognition. arXiv preprint arXiv:1501.02876, vol. 7, no. 8 (2015)

24. Hauberg, S., Freifeld, O., Larsen, A.B.L., Fisher, J., Hansen, L.: Dreaming more data: class-dependent distributions over diffeomorphisms for learned data augmentation. In: Artificial Intelligence and Statistics, pp. 342–350 (2016)

25. Paulin, M., Revaud, J., Harchaoui, Z., Perronnin, F., Schmid, C.: Transformation pursuit for image classification. In: 2014 IEEE Conference on Computer Vision and Pattern Recognition (CVPR), pp. 3646–3653. IEEE (2014)
26. Kim, H.E., Lee, Y., Kim, H., Cui, X.: Domain-specific data augmentation for on-road object detection based on a deep neural network. In: 2017 IEEE Intelligent Vehicles Symposium (IV), pp. 103–108. IEEE (2017)
27. Tobin, J., Fong, R., Ray, A., Schneider, J., Zaremba, W., Abbeel, P.: Domain randomization for transferring deep neural networks from simulation to the real world. In: 2017 IEEE/RSJ International Conference on Intelligent Robots and Systems (IROS), pp. 23–30. IEEE (2017)
28. Kanan, C., Cottrell, G.W.: Color-to-grayscale: does the method matter in image recognition? PloS One 7(1), e29740 (2012)
29. Diamond, S., Sitzmann, V., Boyd, S., Wetzstein, G., Heide, F.: Dirty pixels: optimizing image classification architectures for raw sensor data (2017)
30. Karaimer, H.C., Brown, M.S.: A software platform for manipulating the camera imaging pipeline. In: Leibe, B., Matas, J., Sebe, N., Welling, M. (eds.) ECCV 2016. LNCS, vol. 9905, pp. 429–444. Springer, Cham (2016). https://doi.org/10.1007/978-3-319-46448-0_26
31. Kang, S.B.: Automatic removal of chromatic aberration from a single image. In: 2007 IEEE Conference on Computer Vision and Pattern Recognition, CVPR 2007, pp. 1–8. IEEE (2007)
32. Jaderberg, M., Simonyan, K., Zisserman, A., et al.: Spatial transformer networks. In: Advances in Neural Information Processing Systems, pp. 2017–2025 (2015)
33. Cheong, H., Chae, E., Lee, E., Jo, G., Paik, J.: Fast image restoration for spatially varying defocus blur of imaging sensor. Sensors 15(1), 880–898 (2015)
34. Bhukhanwala, S.A., Ramabadran, T.V.: Automated global enhancement of digitized photographs. IEEE Trans. Consum. Electron. 40(1), 1–10 (1994)
35. Messina, G., Castorina, A., Battiato, S., Bosco, A.: Image quality improvement by adaptive exposure correction techniques. In: Proceedings of the 2003 International Conference on Multimedia and Expo, ICME 2003, vol. 1, I-549–I-552, July 2003
36. Hunter, R.S.: Accuracy, precision, and stability of new photoelectric color-difference meter. J. Opt. Soc. Am. 38, 1094 (1948)
37. Annadurai, S.: Fundamentals of Digital Image Processing. Pearson Education India, Delhi (2007)
38. Geiger, A., Lenz, P., Urtasun, R.: Are we ready for autonomous driving? The KITTI vision benchmark suite. In: 2012 IEEE Conference on Computer Vision and Pattern Recognition (CVPR), pp. 3354–3361. IEEE (2012)
39. Fritsch, J., Kuehnl, T., Geiger, A.: A new performance measure and evaluation benchmark for road detection algorithms. In: International Conference on Intelligent Transportation Systems (ITSC) (2013)
40. Cordts, M., et al.: The cityscapes dataset for semantic urban scene understanding. In: Proceedings of the IEEE Conference on Computer Vision and Pattern Recognition, pp. 3213–3223 (2016)
41. Richter, S.R., Vineet, V., Roth, S., Koltun, V.: Playing for data: ground truth from computer games. In: Leibe, B., Matas, J., Sebe, N., Welling, M. (eds.) ECCV 2016. LNCS, vol. 9906, pp. 102–118. Springer, Cham (2016). https://doi.org/10.1007/978-3-319-46475-6_7
42. Ren, S., He, K., Girshick, R., Sun, J.: Faster R-CNN: towards real-time object detection with region proposal networks. In: Advances in Neural Information Processing Systems, pp. 91–99 (2015)

43. Long, J., Shelhamer, E., Darrell, T.: Fully convolutional networks for semantic segmentation. In: The IEEE Conference on Computer Vision and Pattern Recognition (CVPR), June 2015
44. Simonyan, K., Zisserman, A.: Very deep convolutional networks for large-scale image recognition. CoRR abs/1409.1556 (2014)
45. Zhang, Y., David, P., Gong, B.: Curriculum domain adaptation for semantic segmentation of urban scenes. In: The IEEE International Conference on Computer Vision (ICCV), vol. 2, p. 6 (2017)
46. Hoffman, J., Wang, D., Yu, F., Darrell, T.: FCNs in the wild: pixel-level adversarial and constraint-based adaptation. CoRR abs/1612.02649 (2016)
47. Ronneberger, O., Fischer, P., Brox, T.: U-Net: convolutional networks for biomedical image segmentation. In: Navab, N., Hornegger, J., Wells, W.M., Frangi, A.F. (eds.) MICCAI 2015. LNCS, vol. 9351, pp. 234–241. Springer, Cham (2015). https://doi.org/10.1007/978-3-319-24574-4_28

Answering Visual *What-If* Questions: From Actions to Predicted Scene Descriptions

Misha Wagner[1], Hector Basevi[1(✉)], Rakshith Shetty[2], Wenbin Li[2],
Mateusz Malinowski[2], Mario Fritz[3], and Aleš Leonardis[1]

[1] University of Birmingham, Birmingham, UK
mishajw@gmail.com, H.R.A.Basevi@cs.bham.ac.uk
[2] Max Planck Institute for Informatics,
Saarland Informatics Campus, Saarbrücken, Germany
[3] CISPA Helmholtz Center i.G.,
Saarland Informatics Campus, Saarbrücken, Germany

Abstract. In-depth scene descriptions and question answering tasks
have greatly increased the scope of today's definition of scene understanding. While such tasks are in principle open ended, current formulations primarily focus on describing only the current state of the scenes
under consideration. In contrast, in this paper, we focus on the future
states of the scenes which are also conditioned on actions. We posit this
as a question answering task, where an answer has to be given about a
future scene state, given observations of the current scene, and a question that includes a hypothetical action. Our solution is a hybrid model
which integrates a physics engine into a question answering architecture
in order to anticipate future scene states resulting from object-object
interactions caused by an action. We demonstrate first results on this
challenging new problem and compare to baselines, where we outperform fully data-driven end-to-end learning approaches.

Keywords: Scene understanding · Visual turing test ·
Visual question answering · Intuitive physics

1 Introduction

While traditional scene understanding involves deriving bottom-up scene representations such as object bounding boxes and segmentation, in recent years
alternative approaches such as *scene captioning* and *question answering* have

---

M. Wagner and H. Basevi—Contributed equally to this work.

Electronic supplementary material The online version of this chapter (https://
doi.org/10.1007/978-3-030-11009-3_32) contains supplementary material, which is
available to authorized users.

L. Leal-Taixé and S. Roth (Eds.): ECCV 2018 Workshops, LNCS 11129, pp. 521–537, 2019.
https://doi.org/10.1007/978-3-030-11009-3_32

become increasingly popular. These do not strive for a particular type of representation of the input scene, but rather formulate an alternative task that requires a more holistic scene understanding. Such approaches have been very successful and have shown great advances in extracting the semantic scene content by deriving captions and answers about diverse scene elements.

Beyond the estimation of the "status quo" of a visual scene, recent deep learning approaches have shown improved capabilities of forecasting scenes into the future. This is particularly useful for autonomous agents (e.g., robots or driving assistants) that have to plan ahead and act safely in dynamically changing environments. Recent approaches show extrapolation of complete videos [1], edge information [2] or object trajectories [3,4]. However, with increasing time horizons and complexity of the scenes, such quantitative predictions become increasingly difficult. In addition, extrapolation of complete image data might be wasteful and overly difficult to achieve.

Furthermore, current work on anticipation and forecasting is typically not interactive, meaning that the agent is acting purely as a passive observer. However, in many real-world applications, an agent is faced with the task of evaluating multiple different potential actions that will cause diverse outcomes. The future is therefore often conditioned on the actions of the agent which is not handled by the state-of-the-art methods.

Therefore, we argue for a qualitative prediction of the future conditioned on an action. We phrase this as the *Answering Visual What-If Questions* task, where the answer is conditioned on an observation and question including a hypothetical action. This formulation allows us to evaluate a model's forecasting abilities conditioned on a hypothetical action, and at the same time allows for sparse representation of the future where not all details of the scene or object interactions have to be fully modeled.

We provide the first investigation of this challenging problem in a table top scenario where a set of objects is placed in a challenging configuration and different actions can be taken. Dependent on the action, the objects will interact according to the physics of the scene and will cause a certain outcome in terms of object trajectories. The task is to describe the outcome with respect to the action. In order to address this problem we couple the question answering approach with a physics engine – resulting in a hybrid model. While several parts of the method, such as inferring the action from the question and predicting the answer, are data-driven, the core aspect of our model that predicts future outcomes is model-based (using a physics engine).

The contributions of this paper are as follows:

- We define a new challenge called Visual *What-If* Question answering (WIQ) that brings together question answering with anticipation.
- We propose the first dataset for the WIQ task based on table-top interactions between multiple objects called TIWIQ.
- We propose the first hybrid model that uses a physics engine together with a question answering architecture.

2   Related Work

Learning Physics and Future Predictions: Coping with the physical world by predicting how objects interact with each other using rules of physics is among the pillars of human intelligence. This type of intuitive understanding of physics, often referred to as "intuitive physics" [5], is also becoming of interest to machine learning researchers. The "NeuroAnimator" is among the first learning-based architectures trained to simulate physical dynamics based on observations of physics-based models [6]. Although the "NeuroAnimator" is mainly motivated by efficiency, others have realized that learning-based architectures may be key components to learn the whole spectrum of physical reasoning that humans possess. For instance, [7] argues that a cognitive mechanism responsible for physical reasoning may resemble an engine that simulates complex interactions between different physical objects, and can be implemented by "graph neural networks" [8,9] or by an engineered physics engine [10]. In this work, our hybrid model also uses a physics engine, but unlike [10] we are less interested in inferring latent physics properties of two objects from videos, but rather in a forward model of physics for the purpose of answering questions. A complementary line of research has shown that convolutional neural networks (CNN) are capable to some extent of physical reasoning such as stability prediction [3,11,12], or future frame synthesis from RGB-D input [1,2,13] or even static images [4,14]. These approaches to physical intelligence focus on testing this understanding either by trying to extrapolate sensory data into the future (predicting video frames) or by inferring individual properties (predicting stability or physics properties). In contrast, we propose to achieve qualitative physical understanding, where we want the model to have general understanding of physical processes but not necessarily the ability to make precise prediction.

Visual Question Answering (Visual QA): This is a recently introduced research area [15,16] that attempts to build and understand if machines can learn to explain the surrounding environment only based on questions and answers. Since then, the community has seen a proliferation of various datasets [17–23], including the most popular VQA [24], as well as numerous methods [15,18,25–29]. Although most of the questions involve static scenes, and are either related to objects, attributes, or activities, there are some that require understanding of physics at the "intuitive level". Consider even such seemingly simple question as "What is on the table?". To interpret this question, understanding of "on" is needed, and this involves physical forces such as gravity. In spite of the existence of such questions in the aforementioned datasets, due to lack of interactions, it is hardly possible the learnt models can really understand them, and likely they only rely on visual correlations. In our work, through the interactions, and exploitation of physics, we can train architectures that, we hypothesize, can model physical interactions between objects.

Simulations and Machine Learning: Since it is difficult to generate realistic data that includes complex physical interactions, most approaches either rely on short videos with limited exposition to physics [1,2,13] or on synthetically generated data [8,9,12,30]. This problem of lacking good realistic environments with rich physical interactions also governs the research on reinforcement learning [31], where the community often relies on game-like environments [32–35]. Since there is no publicly available realistic environment that has rich enough physical interactions that we are interested in, we build a dataset consisting of 3D scenes, with physical interactions, and with realistically textured objects.

3   Visual *What-If* Questions (WIQ) Task

While Visual QA evaluates the scene understanding of a passive agent, this is not sufficient for an active agent that needs to anticipate the consequences of its actions and communicate about them. To study this aspect of scene understanding, we propose the task of answering "what-if" questions pertaining to a visual scene. The agent is shown an input scene with multiple objects and is given a hypothetical action description. It then has to describe what happens to different objects in the scene, given that it performs the specified action. This amounts to answering questions of the form "If I perform action A, what happens to object X?". To answer such questions the agent has to parse the natural language description of the action to infer the action type and target object on which the action is applied, along with the corresponding parameters such as the initial force. Then the agent needs to anticipate the consequences of this action on different objects in the scene, and finally verbalize its predictions. This combines the challenges involved in the standard VQA task [24] with intuitive physics [8] and the future state anticipation tasks [36].

3.1   Table-Top Interaction Visual *What-If* Questions (TIWIQ) Dataset

Existing Visual QA datasets [15,18,24] focus on static scenes, whereas datasets commonly used in future prediction tasks such as CityScapes [37] involve a passive observer (future states are not conditioned on the agent's action). Since we are interested in the question answering task involving "physical intelligence", we collect a new table-top interaction visual *what-if* questions (TIWIQ) dataset. This dataset has synthetic table-top scenes, with pairs of action descriptions and ground-truth descriptions of the outcomes of the specified action. We stick to synthetic scenes and a physics simulation engine to build this dataset as it provides physics, and enables controlled experimentation.

Scenes: To obtain the TIWIQ dataset we instantiate random table-top scenes in a physics engine, simulate actions on these scenes and collect human annotations describing the actions and the consequences. Each training sample in the TIWIQ dataset contains a table-top scene with five objects, each randomly placed upon the table. The five objects are chosen from eight items from the YCB Object Dataset [38]: a foam brick, a cheez-it box, a chocolate pudding box, a mustard bottle, a banana, a softball, a ground coffee can, and a screwdriver.

Actions: A random action is chosen to be performed on a single random object, simulated using the Bullet 3 [39] physics engine. The resulting trajectories are rendered into a video of the interactions. The actions can be one of four: 1. Push an object in a specific direction. 2. Rotate an object clockwise or anti-clockwise. 3. Remove an object from the scene. 4. Drop an object on another object.

Annotation: The objects shown in rendered videos have colored outlines, and when questions are posed to annotators, objects are referred to by their outline color rather than their name. This avoids the questions biasing the annotator's vocabulary with regard to object names.

Human Baseline: We have also collected a human performance benchmark on the visual what-if question answering task on the TIWIQ dataset. To obtain the human performance baseline, the annotators were shown a static image of the scene and a description of the action to be performed and were asked to describe what happens to different objects in the scene. We compare the performance of the model proposed in Sect. 4 to this human performance benchmark.

Dataset Statistics: We have generated and annotated 15 batches of data. Each batch has 17 examples of each action, totaling 68 examples per batch. In total, we have 1020 annotated examples. Three batches, totaling 204 examples and 20% of the dataset, are dedicated to testing. For each scene, there are four generated descriptions (one for each object that is not being acted on), therefore there are 4080 (1020 * 4) annotated descriptions. However, descriptions relate to movement or interactions between objects only around 25% of the time. This is due to the random placement of objects sometimes resulting in scenes with spatially separated objects, and therefore some actions having no impact on most objects in a scene. This results in approximately 1000 movement and interaction descriptions across the dataset. Only these annotations are used to train the description generation model.

Vocabulary Statistics: The vocabulary of the dataset is explored by counting the number of unique words used across the dataset (1-gram), as well as the number of unique n-grams for values 2 to 5 (2, 3, 4, 5-grams). This is shown in Table 1. These statistics are reported for the action description annotations, the action effect annotations, and the two together. It is worth noting that the vocabulary of the action description dataset is significantly smaller than the vocabulary of the effect description dataset. This is due to the range of actions being specified by the design of the scenario, while the range of effects has no such constraints.

4   Our Model

Recent advances in Deep Learning architectures have dominated Visual QA and image captioning tasks. The dominant approach is to use end-to-end trainable neural networks which take the inputs, e.g. image and question, and predict the answer. The whole model is learned purely from the data. Driven by sizable datasets, they have outperformed previous purely model-based approaches

Table 1. The size of the vocabulary for the action and effect descriptions and the whole TIWIQ dataset, including the average sentence length and the number of unique n-grams in each subset of the dataset.

Descriptions	Length	1-gram	2-grams	3-grams	4-grams	5-grams
Action	9.63	107	323	565	757	867
Effect	7.663	110	403	724	981	1,075
All	8.582	152	619	1,171	1,653	1,895

e.g. relying on semantic parsing or rule-based systems [15, 25]. Although latest work has also shown early success at applying this end-to-end machine learning paradigm to predicting future states of a scene, the time horizon remains limited to a few frames and rich object interactions are typically not considered, or the scenes are greatly simplified [2, 9, 11]. Therefore, we argue for a hybrid model. We use a physics engine as a backbone in order to simulate outcomes of hypothetical actions, but we embed the simulation into learning-based components that drive the simulation as well as interpret its outcome in terms of a natural language output.

4.1   Model Overview

The proposed hybrid question answering model consists of three distinct components as shown in Fig. 1. There are two inputs to the whole model. The first is a list of object types and their initial pose (position in 3-dimensional space, and a 3×3 rotation matrix) in the scene. We always assume the same table position for every case. The second input is the action description. This was provided by human annotators, and describes some action performed on one of the objects in the scene, for example "The robot pushes the mustard container to the left".

Both inputs are used by a "parser" (we use a neural network as the parser) to extract parameters of the action to be performed. This includes parsing the action type, object to be acted upon and parameters of the action. This extracted information serves as an input to a physics engine, which then simulates the parsed actions on the input scene to produce trajectories for each object in the scene. While these trajectories encode everything that happened in the simulation, they are not human readable. The description model takes these trajectories as input and produces a natural language summary of the state of each object under the influence of this action. The action parser model and description models are comprised of neural networks and their parameters are learned from the data. The physics engine is model driven and has no trainable parameters. In the following subsections we discuss each of these components and how they interact in more details.

As well as being described in this document, all models are illustrated accurately in the corresponding figures. Each component in the illustrations describes a single layer, whether it is an RNN or a fully connected layer. All details of the layers are given in the supplementary material. This includes layer sizes, dropout, and activation functions.

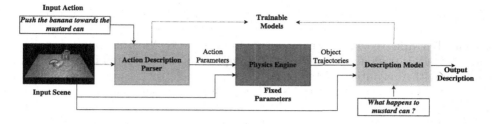

Fig. 1. Overall architecture of the proposed hybrid QA model.

4.2 Action Description Parser

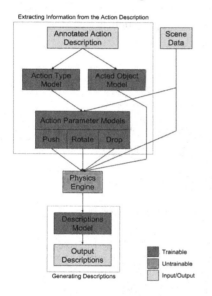

Fig. 2. Illustration of the interaction of subcomponents of the action description parser when inferring parameters of the action to be performed from input sentence.

The first step in the pipeline is parsing the exact nature of the action to be performed from the input sentence description. This model forms part of Fig. 2. It consists of three components with a total of five neural networks, shown in Fig. 3. First component is the *Action Type Model* which infers the type of the action described in the input (push, rotate, drop or remove). This is a recurrent neural network (RNN) that embeds the tokenized action description, iterates over it using a long short-term memory (LSTM) model, and puts the final output of the LSTM through a fully connected layer with softmax activation. These outputs are treated as the probability that each action type was described in the action description.

The second component is the *Acted Object Model*, which predicts the object in the input scene on which the described action is to be performed. The structure is identical to the Action Type Model, with the exception that it outputs probabilities of each class being the object to act upon.

Finally, the third component is a set of *Action Parameter Models*, which infer the exact parameters of the action depending on the action type. Depending on the inferred action type, one of four things happens. If the action type is a push, rotate, or drop action, then the corresponding parameter model is called with the action description and the input scene. If it is a remove action, no parameters need to be inferred as the object is simply removed from the scene.

There are parameter models for three of the four actions: push, rotate, and drop. Each of these models use recurrent networks for embedding the action description specific to the action type.

The *Push Parameter Model* infers the direction of the push by outputting a (x, y) push direction vector in its final layer. The activation for this layer is sigmoid in order to cap both components from -1 to 1. When the physics engine simulates this push direction, the (x, y) components are converted into an angle, removing the magnitude of the push.

The *Rotate Parameter Model* is a binary classifier which predicts whether the rotation is clockwise or anti-clockwise, using softmax activation for classification.

The *Drop Parameter Model* outputs a classification of which other object the acted object is dropped on. This also has a softmax activation for the classification, running over all possible objects.

Each component model that has text as input requires the text to be embedded. When it provided an improvement in performance, GloVe pre-trained word embeddings [40] were used. Details on which layers used pre-trained embeddings, including the size of the embeddings, is given in the supplementary material.

4.3   Physics Simulation

The Acted Object Model extracts the action type, the object of interest, and the parameters of the action. We use Bullet 3 [39] as a physics engine, with object representations from the YCB Object Dataset [38]. We use object convex decompositions for collision detection which are calculated using VHACD, an algorithm included in the Bullet 3 source code. Pushes and rotations are implemented via impulses.

The physics engine is initialized with initial object poses. The engine is run for one second of simulation time in order for objects to settle in.

The inferred action is then performed on the inferred object, and the simulation is run for a total of five seconds at a sampling rate of 300 Hz. Trajectories for each object are extracted from the simulation as a list of translation and rotation pairs, where the translation is a point in 3-dimensional space and the rotation is represented by a 3×3 rotation matrix.

We then run a simple algorithm to check if an object was affected by the action. To

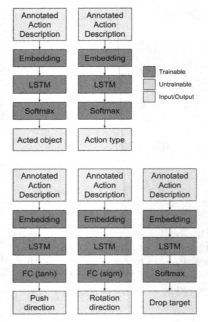

Fig. 3. Illustrations of the action parsing models. Between them, only the final fully connected (FC) layers differ.

do this, we look at the trajectory for a single object, normalize the pose using a standard deviation and mean estimated from the entire training data set, and then calculate the standard deviation of both the translation and rotation, resulting in two floating point values. We say that an object was affected by the action if either of these values exceed a certain threshold. These thresholds were calculated by running a grid search over possible threshold values for either value, and picking the pair that resulted in the best classification accuracy on the training set.

4.4   Generating Descriptions

The *Description Model* shown in Fig. 4 uses the trajectories from the physics simulation to produce a one sentence summary of the effect of the action on each object in the scene. This model is run independently for each generated description with the following inputs: 1. The action description. 2. The object class to describe. 3. The trajectory of the object to describe. 4. A list of other object classes in the scene. 5. A list of other object trajectories in the scene.

The object classes are encoded as a one-hot vector, and the trajectories are encoded as a list of points in 3-dimensional space.

At training time, ground truth trajectories are used, but when the complete hybrid model is being evaluated, predicted trajectories are generated via physics simulation.

The description model works in two stages. First the input trajectories of the target object (whose state is being described) and other objects in the scene are compared and trajectory embeddings are obtained. Then these trajectory embeddings and action description embeddings are input to a decoder LSTM language model, which generates the final description.

To obtain the trajectory embeddings we iterate over each of the other objects in the scene—that is, the ones that are not currently being described. For each object, we compute the difference between its trajectory and the trajectory of the object to be described, at each time step. These difference vectors are then embedded and iterated over using an LSTM. The initial state of this LSTM is provided by embedding both of the object classes and putting them through a fully connected layer. The final hidden state of this LSTM should encode the interactions between the two objects. This output trajectory embedding is concatenated with the object encodings of the two relevant objects. We find that including these embeddings after as well as before the trajectory encoding LSTM improves the overall model's performance.

The input action description is encoded using an LSTM (as in earlier models, such as the action description model). A fully connected layer is used to transform the concatenated trajectory embedding vector and the encoded input instruction into the right dimensions and is used to initialize the hidden state of the decoder LSTM. The input for the decoder LSTM at time t_0 is the *start of sentence* token, and the input at time t_i is the output from t_{i-1}. At each step the decoder LSTM outputs the next word and this repeats until the *end of sentence* token is predicted. This process is carried out to generate a description for each object in the scene.

4.5   Implementation Details

We have implemented the hybrid model
and all components in Python using the
Keras [41] library with the TensorFlow [42]
backend. For the description model, custom
layers were introduced into Keras using TensorFlow. Overall runtime of the system is
1.76 s, where prediction time of the Action
Description Parser and Description Generation is negligible. Almost all time is spent in
the simulation part. For reproducibility and
to stimulate more work on this challenge, we
will release code, models and setup.

5   Results

We evaluate our overall hybrid approach
as well as the individual components on
the proposed dataset as well as compare to
an end-to-end learning and human baseline.
We provide example results and analyses
that highlight the benefits of our approach.

5.1   Performance of Hybrid Model Components

We separately evaluate the performance of
the six components of the hybrid model,
using ground truth annotations at these
intermediate stages. First, we show the per-

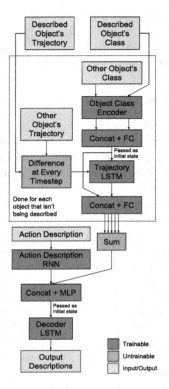

Fig. 4. An illustration of the description model. The section outlined in a
gray square is run for every object
that isn't the object that is currently
being described.

formance of the action description information extraction models (action type
model, acted object model, push/rotate/drop parameter model) in Table 2. We
created simple support vector machine (SVM) baselines in order to benchmark
the more powerful neural models. The input to these SVMs is a vector of word
counts for every word in the data vocabulary. We find that in all cases bar
one, the neural models significantly outperform SVMs, as shown in Table 2. The
exception is the rotation parameter model, which is outperformed by 5.8%. The
performance for the rotation parameter model is particularly poor due to noisy
annotations in the cases of rotation actions. Through looking at a small subset
of the rotation action annotations, we have found that 30–40% of the annotations are mislabeled in some way—either giving the wrong rotational direction,
or annotated as a push action.

To compare the push parameter model with a classification network, we discretize the angle inferred by the neural model into eight directions (e.g. left,
top-left, up). The SVM also classifies to one of those eight directions, allowing
us to compare the performance of these two models.

5.2   Quantifying the Hybrid Model Performance

We will now quantify the performance of the proposed hybrid model and baselines on the test set.

Metrics: To measure the description performance we use the standard metrics used in evaluating image captioning models such as BLEU, CIDEr, ROUGE and a custom metric COM ("Correct Objects Mentioned") that we designed for this specific problem. This metric searches the descriptions for different object names, creating a list of objects mentioned in the text. This is done for both the prediction and the ground truth. The COM metric is computed as the intersection over union of these two sets. The upper-bound for COM is 1, and occurs when all correct objects are mentioned in all predictions for a scene. Image captioning metrics such as BLEU focus on overall n-gram matching of the generated description with the ground truth, regardless of the importance of each word, whereas COM directly measures how well models identify the acting objects in a scene.

Table 2. Comparing classification accuracy of neural network based and SVM based models on different tasks.

Task	NN	SVM
Action type	**97.5%**	97%
Acted object	**94%**	90%
Push parameters	**90%**	44%
Rotation parameters	68%	**72%**
Drop parameters	**90%**	36%

Hybrid Model Compared to Baselines: We compare the performance of the hybrid model against three other baselines on the test set. The first is a pure data-driven model, an end-to-end trainable neural network illustrated in Fig. 5. The inputs to this network are the input action description, the initial scene, and the object to describe. The action description is embedded and then run through an LSTM and the final output of this LSTM is taken. Each class and pose in the initial scene is flattened into a vector, and each of these is put through a fully connected layer and summed together. The object to describe is encoded as a one-hot vector and passed through a fully connected layer. Each of these encodings are concatenated together and treated as input for the decoder LSTM, which generates a description for the specified object class.

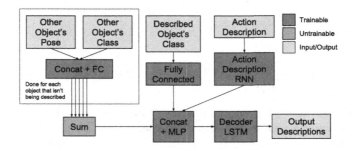

Fig. 5. Illustration of the data-driven model.

Human Baseline and "Upper Bound": The second set of descriptions is from a human baseline, mentioned in Sect. 3.1. Human annotators were shown the input scene and action description, but not the video of the action taking place. They were asked to describe what happens to each object. This simulates the same task tackled by the hybrid, and pure data-driven models. Finally, the third baseline is obtained by feeding the ground-truth trajectories to the description model. This represents an upper-bound on the hybrid model performance.

Discussion: We find that the hybrid model outperforms the data-driven model in all metrics, with an increase of 15.4% in the BLEU metric, and an increase of 20.5% in the COM metric, as illustrated in Table 3. This provides evidence for incorporating a physics engine for solving physics based anticipation problems over a pure data-driven approach. The performance of the hybrid model is close to its upper-bound description model and this gap comes from the cases where the action parsing model failed. However, there is still a gap in performance in terms of the COM metric between the proposed hybrid model and the human benchmark, indicating the scope for future improvements.

Human Baseline Discussion: Under most metrics, the hybrid model outperforms the human baseline. However, this is misleading: the human baseline contains high-quality annotations, and under domain-specific metrics such as COM, is evaluated with a near-perfect score (0.953). Its large error in BLUE, CIDEr, and ROUGE results from the differing vocabularies between the human baseline and the ground truth. For this reason, comparison between the hybrid model and the human baseline is difficult to achieve using these metrics; a similar problem is common in the image captioning domain.

Table 3. Comparison of description generating models. Best values between the hybrid model and data-driven model are highlighted. This shows that the hybrid model exceeds the data-driven model and even the human baseline in some metrics.

Model	BLEU	BLEU-1	BLEU-2	BLEU-3	BLEU-4	CIDEr	ROUGE	COM
Description model	0.280	0.439	0.345	0.203	0.133	1.118	0.421	0.671
Human baseline	0.191	0.207	0.192	0.186	0.181	1.849	0.209	0.953
Hybrid model	**0.262**	**0.407**	**0.322**	**0.184**	**0.134**	1.118	**0.396**	**0.640**
Data-driven model	0.227	0.375	0.282	0.154	0.099	0.896	0.376	0.531

5.3   Qualitative Analysis

We provide qualitative examples and analysis in Table 5. In these examples, the hybrid model can be seen generating more specific and accurate descriptions of the results of actions compared to the data-driven model. There are three main failure cases of the data-driven model.

The first of these is shown in row 1 of Table 5. In this example, the hybrid model correctly predicts the object which hits the foam (in this case the screwdriver) while the data-driven approach predicts that a different object in the scene will hit the foam. Accuracy is lost here due to the data-driven model not being able to reliably infer the object that interacted with the subject object. Our hybrid model performs better in this case, presumably because it was able to use the trajectories from the physics engine to infer the correct object.

The second main failure case is shown in row 2. Both models are correct but the hybrid model gives a more precise description, stating correctly which object hit the mustard container. The data-driven model gives a more vague description by not stating the acting object and just describing the movement.

The third failure case is shown in row 3. Often, the data-driven model produces a description where both the object being acted on and the object affecting it are the same. This could be due to the data-driven model making the best guess it can—if it knows that the class "screw driver" appears in the text but does not know what the other object could be, and it knows that the sentence should reference two objects, then it may choose to mention "screw driver" twice in the sentence. This failure case, although more prevalent in the data-driven model, shows up in the hybrid model too as seen in row 4 of Table 5.

There is a failure case unique to the hybrid model. The data-driven model was trained only on cases where the action did have an effect on the object. However, the hybrid model has to infer whether there was an effect. This results in some cases where the hybrid model misclassifies the object as "not moving" and generates the "nothing" description. An example of this case is shown in row 5 of Table 5.

5.4   Ablation Analysis

We also analyze the error introduced by the different components within the hybrid model. We do this by introducing, one-by-one, the ground truth values for a particular component instead of the predicted values. The results of this are shown in Table 4. We can see that introducing the ground-truth for whether an object moved provides the biggest increase in performance, implying that the

Table 4. Comparison of how the performance of the hybrid model improves when cumulatively adding truth values for each of the components.

Model	BLEU	CIDEr	ROUGE	COM
All Predictions:	0.262	1.118	0.396	0.640
With True Action Type:	0.264	1.126	0.398	0.644
...and True Acted Object:	0.265	1.129	0.400	0.646
...and True Action Parameters:	0.272	1.153	0.406	0.662
...and True Trajectories:	0.268	1.086	0.401	0.645
...and True Object Acted On:	0.283	1.133	0.424	0.673

Table 5. Examples of different scenes in the data set with annotations from ground truth, human baseline, the predictions from the hybrid model, and predictions from the baseline data-driven model. The hybrid can be seen giving more precise descriptions than the data-driven model.

Input Scene And Action	Output Description
 1) "the robot drops the screw driver on the foam" — what happens to the foam?	**Ground Truth** "the foam is pushed a little by the screw driver" **Human Baseline** "the foam is pushed because the screw driver drops on it" **Hybrid Model Prediction** "the foam is pushed by the screw driver" **Data-Driven Model Prediction** "the foam is pushed by the mustard container"
 2) "the robot spins the screw driver in anti-clowise direction" — what happens to the mustard container?	**Ground Truth** "the screw driver pushes the mustard container" **Human Baseline** "the mustard conatainer moves a little due to the impact of spinning screw driver" **Hybrid Model Prediction** "the screw driver pushes the mustard container" **Data-Driven Prediction** "the mustard container shakes a little from the impact"
 3) "the robot drops the cheese box on the foam" — what happens to the screw driver?	**Ground Truth** "the screw driver is pushed by the cheese box" **Human Baseline** "the screw driver is pushed by the cheese box" **Hybrid Model Prediction** "the screw driver is pushed by the cheese box" **Data-Driven Prediction** "the screw driver is pushed by the screw driver"
 4) "the robot spins the screw driver in anti-clockwise direction" — what happens to the chocolate box?	**Ground Truth** "the chocolate box is pushed by the screw driver" **Human Baseline** "the chocolate box is pushed a slightly by the screw driver" **Hybrid Model Prediction** "the chocolate box pushes the chocolate box" **Data-Driven Prediction** "the chocolate box is pushed by the screw driver"
 5) "the robot pushes the baseball to the middle of the table" — what happens to the chocolate box?	**Ground Truth** "the chocolate box is pushed by the baseball" **Human Baseline** "the chocolate box is pushed by the baseball" **Hybrid Model Prediction** "nothing" **Data-Driven Prediction** "the chocolate box is pushed by the chocolate box"
 6) "the robot rolls the baseball to the north-west side of the table and it drops off" — what happens to the banana?	**Ground Truth** "nothing" **Human Baseline** "nothing" **Hybrid Model Prediction** "nothing" **Data-Driven Prediction** N/A

hybrid model loses a lot of accuracy when predicting whether an object moved. Conversely, we can also see that the Action Type and Acted Object models introduce relatively small amounts of error, suggesting they correctly model the ground truth.

6 Conclusion

We have proposed a new task that combines scene understanding with anticipation of future scene states. We argue that this type of "physical intelligence" is a key competence of an agent that is interacting with an environment and tries to evaluate different alternatives. In contrast to prior work on quantitative predictions of future states, here, we focus on a qualitative prediction that describes the outcome for a certain object with a natural language utterance. Owing to such a formulation, we can train and evaluate our agent on long-term future anticipation, where the model can easily ignore irrelevant details of the scene or the interactions. This contrasts with future frame synthesis where all the details have to be correctly modeled.

Due to the lack of suitable datasets, we introduced the first dataset and an evaluation protocol for this challenging task. Our proposed model is the first that combines a question answering architecture with a physics engine and verbalizes different outcomes dependent on the visual and language input. In particular, our hybrid model outperforms a purely data-driven Deep Learning baseline. We believe that such hybrid models that combine a complex simulation engine with data-driven components represent an exciting avenue for further research as they allow for generalization, scalability and improved performance in challenging scenarios with a high combinatorial complexity.

Acknowledgements. We acknowledge MoD/Dstl and EPSRC for providing the grant to support the UK academics involvement in a Department of Defense funded MURI project through EPSRC grant EP/N019415/1.

References

1. Mathieu, M., Couprie, C., LeCun, Y.: Deep multi-scale video prediction beyond mean square error. In: International Conference on Learning Representations (2016)
2. Bhattacharyya, A., Malinowski, M., Schiele, B., Fritz, M.: Long-term image boundary extrapolation. In: Association for the Advancement of Artificial Intelligence (2018)
3. Lerer, A., Gross, S., Fergus, R.: Learning physical intuition of block towers by example. In: International Conference on Machine Learning (2016)
4. Mottaghi, R., Rastegari, M., Gupta, A., Farhadi, A.: "What happens if..." learning to predict the effect of forces in images. In: Leibe, B., Matas, J., Sebe, N., Welling, M. (eds.) ECCV 2016. LNCS, vol. 9908, pp. 269–285. Springer, Cham (2016). https://doi.org/10.1007/978-3-319-46493-0_17
5. McCloskey, M.: Intuitive physics. Sci. Am. **248**(4), 122–131 (1983)

6. Grzeszczuk, R., Terzopoulos, D., Hinton, G.: Neuroanimator: fast neural network emulation and control of physics-based models. In: Proceedings of the 25th Annual Conference on Computer Graphics and Interactive Techniques, pp. 9–20. ACM (1998)
7. Battaglia, P.W., Hamrick, J.B., Tenenbaum, J.B.: Simulation as an engine of physical scene understanding. Proc. Natl. Acad. Sci. **110**(45), 18327–18332 (2013)
8. Battaglia, P., Pascanu, R., Lai, M., Rezende, D.J., et al.: Interaction networks for learning about objects, relations and physics. In: Advances in Neural Information Processing Systems, pp. 4502–4510 (2016)
9. Watters, N., Tacchetti, A., Weber, T., Pascanu, R., Battaglia, P., Zoran, D.: Visual interaction networks. In: Advances in Neural Information Processing Systems (2017)
10. Wu, J., Yildirim, I., Lim, J.J., Freeman, B., Tenenbaum, J.: Galileo: perceiving physical object properties by integrating a physics engine with deep learning. In: Advances in Neural Information Processing Systems, pp. 127–135 (2015)
11. Li, W., Leonardis, A., Fritz, M.: Visual stability prediction for robotic manipulation. In: Proceedings of the IEEE International Conference on Robotics and Automation (2017)
12. Li, W., Azimi, S., Leonardis, A., Fritz, M.: To fall or not to fall: a visual approach to physical stability prediction. CoRR abs/1604.00066 (2016)
13. Ranzato, M., Szlam, A., Bruna, J., Mathieu, M., Collobert, R., Chopra, S.: Video (language) modeling: a baseline for generative models of natural videos. CoRR abs/1412.6604 (2014)
14. Mottaghi, R., Bagherinezhad, H., Rastegari, M., Farhadi, A.: Newtonian scene understanding: unfolding the dynamics of objects in static images. In: Proceedings of the IEEE Conference on Computer Vision and Pattern Recognition, pp. 3521–3529 (2016)
15. Malinowski, M., Fritz, M.: A multi-world approach to question answering about real-world scenes based on uncertain input. In: Advances in Neural Information Processing Systems, pp. 1682–1690 (2014)
16. Malinowski, M., Fritz, M.: Towards a visual turing challenge. CoRR abs/1410.8027 (2014)
17. Geman, D., Geman, S., Hallonquist, N., Younes, L.: Visual Turing test for computer vision systems. Proc. Natl. Acad. Sci. **112**(12), 3618–3623 (2015)
18. Ren, M., Kiros, R., Zemel, R.: Exploring models and data for image question answering. In: Advances in Neural Information Processing Systems (2015)
19. Yu, L., Park, E., Berg, A.C., Berg, T.L.: Visual madlibs: fill in the blank description generation and question answering. In: Proceedings of the IEEE International Conference on Computer Vision, pp. 2461–2469. IEEE (2015)
20. Zhu, Y., Groth, O., Bernstein, M., Fei-Fei, L.: Visual7W: grounded question answering in images. In: Proceedings of the IEEE Conference on Computer Vision and Pattern Recognition, pp. 4995–5004 (2016)
21. Tapaswi, M., Zhu, Y., Stiefelhagen, R., Torralba, A., Urtasun, R., Fidler, S.: MovieQA: understanding stories in movies through question-answering. In: Proceedings of the IEEE Conference on Computer Vision and Pattern Recognition, pp. 4631–4640 (2016)
22. Agrawal, A., Batra, D., Parikh, D., Kembhavi, A.: Don't just assume; look and answer: overcoming priors for visual question answering. In: Proceedings of the IEEE Conference on Computer Vision and Pattern Recognition (2018)

23. Kafle, K., Cohen, S., Price, B., Kanan, C.: DVQA: understanding data visualizations via question answering. In: Proceedings of the IEEE Conference on Computer Vision and Pattern Recognition (2018)
24. Antol, S., et al.: VQA: visual question answering. In: Proceedings of the IEEE International Conference on Computer Vision, pp. 2425–2433 (2015)
25. Malinowski, M., Rohrbach, M., Fritz, M.: Ask your neurons: a deep learning approach to visual question answering. Int. J. Comput. Vis. **125**(1–3), 110–135 (2017)
26. Yang, Z., He, X., Gao, J., Deng, L., Smola, A.: Stacked attention networks for image question answering. In: Proceedings of the IEEE Conference on Computer Vision and Pattern Recognition, pp. 21–29 (2016)
27. Fukui, A., Park, D.H., Yang, D., Rohrbach, A., Darrell, T., Rohrbach, M.: Multimodal compact bilinear pooling for visual question answering and visual grounding. CoRR abs/1606.01847 (2016)
28. Hu, R., Andreas, J., Rohrbach, M., Darrell, T., Saenko, K.: Learning to reason: end-to-end module networks for visual question answering. In: Proceedings of the IEEE International Conference on Computer Vision (2017)
29. Santoro, A., et al.: A simple neural network module for relational reasoning. In: Advances in Neural Information Processing Systems, pp. 4974–4983 (2017)
30. Ehrhardt, S., Monszpart, A., Mitra, N.J., Vedaldi, A.: Taking visual motion prediction to new heightfields. CoRR abs/1712.09448 (2017)
31. Sutton, R.S., Barto, A.G.: Reinforcement Learning: An Introduction, vol. 1. MIT Press, Cambridge (1998)
32. Beattie, C., et al.: DeepMind Lab. CoRR abs/1612.03801 (2016)
33. Kempka, M., Wydmuch, M., Runc, G., Toczek, J., Jaśkowski, W.: ViZDoom: a doom-based AI research platform for visual reinforcement learning. In: IEEE Conference on Computational Intelligence and Games, pp. 1–8. IEEE (2016)
34. Shah, S., Dey, D., Lovett, C., Kapoor, A.: AirSim: high-fidelity visual and physical simulation for autonomous vehicles. In: Hutter, M., Siegwart, R. (eds.) Field and Service Robotics. SPAR, vol. 5, pp. 621–635. Springer, Cham (2018). https://doi.org/10.1007/978-3-319-67361-5_40
35. Wu, Y., Wu, Y., Gkioxari, G., Tian, Y.: Building generalizable agents with a realistic and rich 3D environment. CoRR abs/1801.02209 (2018)
36. Finn, C., Goodfellow, I., Levine, S.: Unsupervised learning for physical interaction through video prediction. In: Advances in Neural Information Processing Systems, pp. 64–72 (2016)
37. Cordts, M., et al.: The cityscapes dataset for semantic urban scene understanding. In: Proceedings of the IEEE Conference on Computer Vision and Pattern Recognition (2016)
38. Çalli, B., Walsman, A., Singh, A., Srinivasa, S., Abbeel, P., Dollar, A.M.: Benchmarking in manipulation research: the YCB object and model set and benchmarking protocols. CoRR abs/1502.03143 (2015)
39. Coumans, E.: Bullet 3 (2018). https://github.com/bulletphysics/bullet3
40. Pennington, J., Socher, R., Manning, C.D.: GloVe: global vectors for word representation. In: Empirical Methods in Natural Language Processing (EMNLP), pp. 1532–1543 (2014)
41. Chollet, F., et al.: Keras (2015). https://github.com/keras-team/keras
42. Abadi, M., et al.: TensorFlow: large-scale machine learning on heterogeneous systems (2015). Software available from tensorflow.org

W05 – Bias Estimation in Face Analytics

W05 – Bias Estimation in Face Analytics

Welcome to the first Workshop on Bias Estimation in Face Analytics (BEFA'18), held in conjunction with ECCV in Munich, Germany. As AI technology, and Computer Vision in particular, makes advances into daily lives of people, it is being assessed for its performance not only in terms of quality and speed but also in terms of its social acceptance such as bias in its decision making favoring any particular group or subgroup. In a recently published study for example it has been shown that the gender estimation from face images is biased against dark skin females over white skin males. The core goal of the workshop has been to understand the limitations of current face analytics systems. In order to facilitate the understanding of the state of the art, we released a test dataset as a competition. Data was provided to interested research groups, without ground truth information. The dataset is borrowed from a publicly available one, from which images were selected by design in order to ensure a uniform distribution of examples across multiple attributes of facial analytics, namely age, ethnicity and gender. Out of 15 requesters, three requesters submitted their prediction results. Based on the attributes prediction accuracy across all the categories (age, gender and ethnicity), as well as their intersection, we were able to announce a winner.

We also extended the invitation to works related to the general topic of the workshop, even if not directly pertaining the competition. We received an interesting submission on bias in handling primate faces detection using current state of the art technology. In addition to the competition and paper presentation, we also had three distinguished invited talks. The first talk by Prof. Kate Saenko of Boston University entitled "Women also snowboard: Diagnosing and correcting bias in captioning models" touched upon gender bias in caption generation from images. The second talk by Prof. Dimitri Metaxas from Rutgers University focused on bias mitigation during the learning process. The final talk by Prof. Walter Scheirer from the University of Notre Dame addressed a mechanism to incorporate learning from human vision system into AI systems to lower bias.

We take this opportunity to thank all the competition participants, attendees, speakers, sponsors and ECCV. We look forward to extending this workshop at other avenues to address the public perception as well as technical challenges to address bias in face analytics systems.

September 2018

Rama Chellappa
Nalini Ratha
Rogerio Feris
Michele Merler
Vishal Patel

Exploring Bias in Primate Face Detection and Recognition

Sanchit Sinha, Mohit Agarwal, Mayank Vatsa, Richa Singh[(✉)],
and Saket Anand

IIIT-Delhi, New Delhi, India
{sanchit15083,mohit15060,mayank,rsingh,anands}@iiitd.ac.in

Abstract. Deforestation and loss of habitat have resulted in rapid decline of certain species of primates in forests. On the other hand, uncontrolled growth of a few species of primates in urban areas has led to safety issues and nuisance for the local residents. Hence, identifying individual primates has become the need of the hour - not only for conservation and effective mitigation in the wild but also in zoological parks and wildlife sanctuaries. Primates and human faces share a lot of common features like position and shape of eyes, nose and mouth. It is worth exploring whether the knowledge of human faces and recent methods learned from human face detection and recognition can be extended to primate faces. However, similar challenges relating to bias in human faces will also occur in primates. The quality and orientation of primate images along with different species of primates - ranging from monkeys to gorillas and chimpanzees will contribute to bias in effective detection and recognition. Experimental results on a primate dataset of over 80 identities show the effect of bias in this research problem.

Keywords: Animal biometrics · Deep learning · Biometrics · Bias ·
Face detection · Face recognition

1 Introduction

The population of many species of primates is fast reducing due to loss of habitat caused by deforestation. Many species of chimpanzees and gorillas have recently been added to the list of endangered and critically endangered animals in the International Union for Conservation of Nature (IUCN) Red List [1]. As deforestation sees no reduction in near future, there is an enormous risk of more primate species being added to the list or inevitable extinction of its current members. To counter these catastrophic consequences, conservation of primates is the need of the hour.

Contrarily, there are several areas of the world where current population of primates have become a nuisance to urban dwellers. The ease of getting food and

S. Sinha and M. Agarwal—Equal contribution by student authors.

© Springer Nature Switzerland AG 2019
L. Leal-Taixé and S. Roth (Eds.): ECCV 2018 Workshops, LNCS 11129, pp. 541–555, 2019.
https://doi.org/10.1007/978-3-030-11009-3_33

relatively less competition in the cities has resulted in a population explosion of such species (monkeys in particular). The growing population of monkeys is a health, safety and sanitation hazard for local population. Monkeys are known to be aggressive in nature if a human unknowingly invades their territory and mostly respond by scratching/biting them. As monkeys are known carriers of the lethal rabies disease causing virus, it is essential to minimize such incidents. Monkeys are also known to cause vandalism and have been reportedly seen vandalizing important electric/telephone connections as well as causing hazard to human lives. Hence, in this scenario, it is important to control their population.

The above two scenarios require maintaining effective track of individual primates and identify the primates which require extra care or need to be controlled using effective mitigation techniques. Hence, it is important to construct a system which can accurately identify any primate in the wild. The current systems of animal tracking are mostly invasive in nature. For example researchers have used GPS collars [3], which have to be strapped around the neck of animals and can be monitored from a remote location. Another approach of tracking is proposed by Kim et al. [13] which employs both RFID and GPS tags embedded in the body of animals to detect if they have escaped their cages in a zoo. This kind of arrangements are costly, unreliable and require a significant human intervention into the lifestyles of wild animals. In these approaches, animals have to be first drugged to put any kind of device on their bodies. Sometimes these collars/tags cause pain to the animals and hinder in their daily activities. A few more docile methods such as using a Wireless Sensor Network (WSN) to detect movements/activities of turtles in Wildlife Institute of India (WII) [12] are also employed. As investment required in an invasive technique is too high - along with problems the animals have to face, shifting to non-obtrusive and non-invasive methods for recognition is a requirement.

A step in this direction has been taken by Mason et al. [18]. They use stripe patterns of a tiger as a biometric modality to identify tigers. A similar approach has been applied to zebras in recognizing them from their patterns [14]. In the process, several new biometric modalities specific to a particular type of animal have been discovered and implemented, for example recognizing cattle from their nose-print [2]. The non-obtrusive methods are relatively cheap to set up, they only involve automatic camera traps to trigger photographs. Humans are also required to go into dangerous environments less frequently - saving time, resources and money. However, building such a system poses a different set of challenges. For instance, face recognition of tigers or monkeys may not have prior literature or database as the starting point. A very major challenge in face detection is the high amount of background clutter in the image (due to heavy cover of trees, shrubs, mud), which interferes with the detection methods. The primates are not a very docile family of mammals, most images contain a side-profile or partially-occluded faces. Hence, capturing images in a controlled environment is not feasible and images in the wild have to be considered. Another major challenge is the fact that the structure of eyes and nose of a primate are considerably different than that from a human; hence, traditional eye and nose detection methods do not work very well on them. As recognizing primates using their faces is a relatively newly pursued field, most of the research dealing with this problem have either manually cropped faces for recognition step [4] or have used traditional face detection algorithms inspired from the ones developed by Viola-Jones [23]. Few research papers have used proprietary software [5] built on the same concept as existing face detectors. Furthermore, only a handful of them have considered the problem of straightening or normalization of faces after detection [24]. However, none of the research till now has tried adapting deep learning techniques for detection. Along with the challenge of detection, to the best of our knowledge, no work has tried to find various kinds of bias affecting primate detection in the wild.

In automated face recognition, both deep learning and non-deep learning based approaches have been tried. Researchers have used a variety of techniques to extract features from the detected faces. For example, PCA [16], Fisherfaces [16], LBP features [4], and SURF [15] are utilized. Another recent research has used deep learning methods to recognize primates [9]. Similarly, the performance of recognition has not been well studied to understand the various biases.

Human face detection and recognition problem suffers from various kinds of biases arising from race [20], age [26], ethnicity [22] etc. of the subjects or the physical properties like quality [17] or orientation [25]. We conjecture that detection and recognition of primate faces also suffers from various kinds of biases arising from both intrinsic and extrinsic properties. It is worth exploring both intrinsic bias like the species of the primate to be detected or extrinsic biases like the quality of the image, orientation of the primate and amount of noise in the image. Since this domain of primate faces is relatively new and not well studied, we plan to investigate this domain further. In this paper, we present a dataset of primates, a deep learning based pipeline and experimental results that help us better understand the various biases found in primate face detection and recognition.

2   Dataset

The experiments are performed on two databases: one was provided by the Wildlife Institute of India (WII), Dehradun, India. It contained manually clicked candid images of a group of Rhesus Macaque (*Macaca mulatta*). The images are high resolution shots (3648×2736) taken by a DSLR camera. The images are an ensemble of front and side profile images with a few back profile images as well. A few images contained more than one subject especially mothers and their new born babies. The images were accompanied with manual ground truth labellings around the subject's face in an XML format. However, the number of images corresponding to a single identity were non-uniform - ranging from minimum 4 to maximum 50 images. All images are manually inspected and the ones with total occlusion were removed. Everything included, the cleaned dataset contained a total of 56 identities.

The second dataset is acquired from the Leipzig Zoo [9] and contained images of resident common chimpanzees (*Pan troglodytes*) and western gorillas (*Gorilla*

Fig. 1. Sample images of the primates in the dataset.

gorilla). Again, the images are high resolution candid shots (1936 × 1296). Once again the images are a mix of front and side profiles with a few photos containing groups of chimps and gorillas. However, there are no manual ground truth facial markings as in the previous collection. The number of images per identity are a little more uniform ranging between 10–20. There are a total of 18 identities of chimpanzees and 6 identities of gorillas.

Both the above collections (WII Database and Leipzig Zoo Database) are combined to form a unified dataset with total of 927 images spread over 80 identities. This dataset is used further in the experiments. Some example of images in the dataset are shown in Fig. 1.

3   Primate Face Detection and Recognition Framework

The method to analyze various biases in detection and recognition of primates consists of two modules: detection-normalization and recognition. The details of both the components are summarized in Fig. 2 and explained in the following two subsections.

3.1   Detection and Normalization

Currently available face detectors are primarily trained for human face detection and they are able to detect all kinds of faces including animals, sketches, and cartoons. However, in this research, we are only interested in detecting animal faces

Fig. 2. The composite pipeline used for detection, normalization and recognition.

and all other faces are considered as false positives. *Tiny Faces* [10] is a state-of-the-art face detector, which utilizes image resolution, spatial context and object scale information to detect faces. Using these novel descriptors, it fine-tunes pre-trained ImageNet models on existing deep learning architectures and achieves best results using the ResNet101 architecture. The pre-trained Tiny Faces model was used on the primates dataset. To analyze the biases due to extrinsic properties on primate detection, all images in the dataset were classified based on two properties - quality of the image and orientation of the subject primate in the image. Images with blurring, occlusion, camera shake, etc. were adjudged as bad quality images and all others with good face clarity were adjudged as good quality images. Similarly, images in which both the eyes of the subject primate were clearly visible were adjudged as good orientation images and all the others where one or both eyes are not visible due to overexposure, side profile or growth of fur were adjudged as bad orientation images. Out of the total 927 images, 77 images were found to be of bad quality and 210 images were found to have bad orientation. Similarly, the images in the dataset were segregated into the different species- monkeys, gorillas and chimpanzees. Figure 3 demonstrates sample output of the algorithm, and two sets of challenges that are observed in the results.

- Occurrence of false positives - Small patches of grass, leaves, and primate skin were mostly detected as faces. This is because Tiny Faces particularly focuses on finding smaller faces and in that process ends up detecting more false positives.
- No distinction between human and primate faces - This is due to the fact that tiny faces is primarily fine-tuned for human faces. Although the datasets considered in this research consist of all primate images only and no humans among them, this property is undesired as one would not want a human face to be detected as primate. These can be seen in Fig. 3.

Due to the above two factors, the performance of the primate face detector is lacking. Therefore, we propose to further process the outputs of Tiny Faces by following a two step approach:

1. Training an eye detector and using it on positive and negative output images to filter out the false positives. The dataset for this is prepared by manually extracting the regions containing the eyes from the detected primate faces. Along with this, negatives for the eye detector are taken as manually cropped

Fig. 3. Few examples of false positives produced by Tiny Faces detector. It can be seen that clutter in the background causes false positives. Detector can also not differentiate between human and primate faces. It is to be noted that the top two images are for illustration purposes only and they are not part of the dataset.

primate noses (to distinguish between eyes and nose) and random patches from detected face excluding eyes.

2. A CNN architecture comprising of three convolutional layers, each having 16 filters with ReLU activation function is constructed for the task of binary classification between eye and non-eye regions. The collection of about 700 cropped eye images and 1500 negatives is split randomly into train and test set (70%–30%). The train set is used to train the CNN and the accuracy of classification is computed on the test set. Finally, all the train images are combined together to retrain the CNN. A sliding window of (60 × 60) pixels is run on the output of Tiny Faces, resized to (300 × 300) pixels with the hyper-parameter of window step size set to 16 pixels both vertically and horizontally. The trained CNN model is run on this window to filter out the false positives. Only one window with the highest score is chosen among the overlapping windows detected as eyes. And finally total two such windows with highest scores are chosen for each image and identified as eyes. A few samples of the training images can be seen in Fig. 4.

3. Once the eyes are detected, the distance between the mid points of the eyes is calculated. The nose point (or the pivot point) is computed using heuristics −0.7 times the distance between eyes in this case. The position of the nose point is measured from the mid point of the line segment joining mid points of eyes. Subsequently, the rotation angle is determined as the angle formed by the line joining the nose point and mid point with the normal. The results of normalization can be seen in Fig. 6.

4. The model constructed may still not be able to distinguish between human and primate faces. Hence, a model is trained using Histogram of Oriented

Fig. 4. Samples of the eyes and negative patches (including noses) used for training the CNN. The top five images are those of eyes and the bottom five of negatives (first 3 are noses).

Gradients as features and AdaBoost as the classifier. The training data included about 350 primate images (obtained from the training dataset) and about 400 images of human faces (randomly chosen from the Labelled Faces in the Wild-LFW dataset) [11]. The model is cross-validated over 5 folds and then used on the images obtained from above (CNN).

3.2   Recognition

To study the bias in recognition experiment, we used the following existing face recognition matching algorithms and independently tested them on different training and test sets.

- Principal Component Analysis (PCA) [21] - PCA is applied on the training database to compute the eigen vectors. 115 principal components pertaining to 95% eigen-energy conservation are utilized. For testing, gallery and probe images are transformed to the trained vector space and Euclidean distance is computed from the nearest match among the gallery for each probe image.
- Linear Discriminant Analysis (LDA) [7] - 28 components are extracted pertaining to 95% eigen-energy conservation. Again, for testing, gallery and probe images are transformed to the trained vector space and Euclidean distance is used to compute the nearest match among the gallery for each probe image.
- VGG-Face [19] - It is an adapted VGG-16 architecture for recognition task trained on 2622 human identities and is one of the best models for human facial recognition. For testing, pre-trained weights of the VGG-face model are used and two different sets of features are extracted for the gallery and probe images of the test set.
  1. Last Fully Connected Layer (fc8)
  2. Second Last Fully Connected Layer (fc7) along with last MaxPool layer (pool5).
  Here cosine distance between gallery and probe feature is used to compute the nearest match.
- VGG-Face with Finetuning - All the fully-connected layers of VGG-Face model are finetuned using the training data. For testing, these finetuned weights of the model are used. Two different sets of features are extracted and cosine distance is used to compute the nearest match similar to VGG-Face.

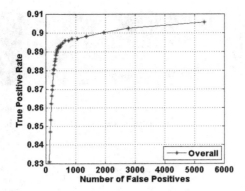

Fig. 5. ROC curve for primate face detection using Tiny Faces face detector.

4   Experiment Protocol and Results

The dataset contains 927 primate images spread over 80 identities. The experiments are performed with four times random cross-validation, with 50–50% train-test partitioning. The train and test partitions in each fold have no overlap in terms of the identities.

4.1   Detection and Normalization

For the first experiment, Tiny Faces Detector is run over all the images in the dataset with a confidence threshold of 0.5. Out of the total 927 images, the detector returned 920 true positive results. However, the total number of false positives returned were 352. The results of different biases are depicted as ROC curves in Figs. 11 and 12. Any positives less than (10×10) pixels is discarded, assuming reasonable size of faces. Once the faces are correctly detected, the true positives and the false positives are cropped out. Figure 5 shows the overall detection ROC curve. Now these identities are split into folds, similar to the one described before.

All cropped true positives are collected together and a CNN (as described in Sect. 3.1) is trained with a 70–30 split. The negatives are populated by random patches and cropped nose images (Fig. 4). The accuracy obtained on the test set is **85.58%**. Once the trained model is applied on the test set, the images classified as primates are kept and the rest are discarded.

The true positive images are again split into 70–30 splits and an AdaBoost classifier [8] using HOG features [6] is trained. As mentioned in Sect. 3.1, the classifier is trained with the 70% fold as positives and random images from LFW dataset as negatives. The classification accuracy on the 30% fold was found to be **99.08%**. The images in the test set are filtered twice, once by the CNN model and then with the AdaBoost classifier. It can be safely concluded that the images in the test set only contain primate faces. A few examples of normalized images are shown in Fig. 6.

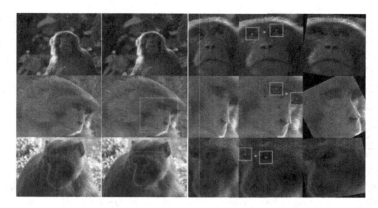

Fig. 6. Primate face detection and normalization pipeline: original image, face detection, cropped faces, eye detection, and normalization using samples from the dataset

Fig. 7. Top 5 matches for a few sample probe images.

4.2 Recognition

The recognition experiments are performed with two different gallery sizes: 2 and 5. The recognition performance is computed for ranks ranging from 1 to gallery size. Better rate on lower gallery size would mean that the trained model can learn the features well of new identities using fewer images. On the other hand, a better rate for the higher gallery size would mean that given sufficient number of images, the trained model can learn the features well for new identities. The results for recognition baselines can be seen in Figs. 8 and 9. The various results obtained on different train and test sets are shown in Table 1.

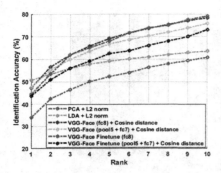 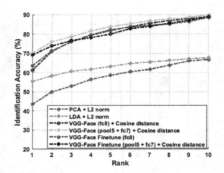

Fig. 8. CMC curve for recognition using different methods when gallery size is fixed at maximum 2 images from each identity.

Fig. 9. CMC curve for recognition using different methods when gallery size is fixed at maximum 5 images from each identity.

4.3   Bias Analysis

Detection: The results of the extrinsic bias - quality can be seen in Fig. 11 and those of orientation can be seen in Fig. 12. As can be seen, the performance of the face detector is better on good quality images than on bad quality images, as expected. Similarly, detection results on good orientation images are better than those on bad orientation. Hence, we can conclude that images which have poor quality such as have blur, pixelation, camera-shake, overexposure, occlusion, etc. are prone to detection errors such as partial or wrong detection. The results of intrinsic bias - species can be seen in Fig. 10. As, TinyFaces is predominantly trained on human faces, the species with the closest resemblance to human face-like features are the better detected.

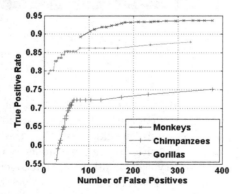

Fig. 10. ROC curve for detection across various species in the dataset - Monkeys, Chimpanzees and Gorillas.

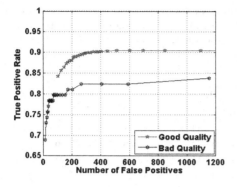
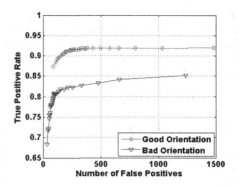

Fig. 11. ROC curve for good and bad quality images using TinyFaces face detector.

Fig. 12. ROC curve for good and bad orientation images using Tiny-Faces face detector.

Recognition: The values for the Rank 1, 3 and 5 accuracies are summarized in Table 1 for different training sets. It can be seen that the predominant species in the training set is better recognized than the less dominant ones.

- When training set consists of a single species, the test results of that species on its own test set are usually the highest among all.
- When the training set consists of multiple species, the test results on the test sets of species present in the training set are greater than the others. However, between the training species, the test results are better on the species with a larger training set.
- It must be noted that the number of images in the Gorilla set is much lower when compared to monkeys and chimpanzees. Consequently, for higher rank cases, we see that the accuracy for Gorilla faces is abnormally high, even reaching 100% at Rank-5.
- The high variability in the performance of VGG-Face model is explained due to very limited training data used for fine-tuning, which never exceeds around 350.

4.4 Scope for Improvement

Although the detection pipeline achieves good results, the presence of biases (intrinsic and extrinsic) as discussed leads to improper detection of faces. The detection does not work well if these biases of quality, occlusion, orientation, species difference etc. exist in the training images. Similarly, the recognition performance is highly sensitive to illumination and face profile as can be seen in

Table 1. Rank 1, 3 and 5 accuracy percentage values using techniques - (a) PCA, (b) LDA, (c) VGG-Face Fine-Tuned, (VF-FT) for different training and test sets - (a) M-Monkey (b) C-Chimpanzee (c) G-Gorilla. The training set includes half of the randomly chosen identities of monkeys, gorillas and chimpanzees and their unique combinations - tested over 2 folds

Train set	Technique	Rank 1			Rank 3			Rank 5		
		M	C	G	M	C	G	M	C	G
M	PCA + L2 Norm	39.62	20.10	20.22	54.94	37.50	45.21	62.09	56.52	65.42
	LDA + L2 Norm	23.04	12.50	16.49	35.30	36.95	40.96	42.73	53.26	59.04
	VF-FT (fc8)	49.03	25.00	55.32	61.11	50.00	79.79	66.77	63.04	90.43
C	PCA + L2 Norm	32.95	29.53	22.34	44.34	56.09	45.21	51.04	75.52	68.61
	LDA + L2 Norm	24.00	23.53	14.89	37.04	49.83	43.08	43.47	66.01	66.49
	VF-FT (fc8)	42.43	36.48	55.32	54.96	63.72	79.79	59.83	73.83	90.43
G	PCA + L2 Norm	31.82	15.76	35.71	44.52	35.32	87.68	51.65	49.45	100
	LDA + L2 Norm	8.35	9.78	29.82	17.74	28.80	72.13	26.43	40.76	100
	VF-FT (fc8)	42.43	25.00	61.12	54.95	50.00	92.23	59.82	63.04	100
M + C	PCA + L2 Norm	39.98	29.20	19.15	55.29	55.76	45.21	62.10	76.12	66.49
	LDA + L2 Norm	22.53	27.16	17.02	34.65	54.06	40.42	40.85	74.77	59.57
	VF-FT (fc8)	49.03	36.47	55.32	61.10	63.71	79.79	66.77	73.83	90.42
M + G	PCA + L2 Norm	40.15	20.65	38.83	55.82	37.5	83.40	62.27	57.06	100
	LDA + L2 Norm	21.65	16.85	28.36	32.51	36.95	74.72	37.66	51.08	100
	VF-FT (fc8)	49.03	25.00	61.13	61.11	50.00	92.22	66.77	63.04	100
C + G	PCA + L2 Norm	33.56	30.47	39.01	44.34	57.03	86.52	51.91	76.46	100
	LDA + L2 Norm	22.87	26.97	24.98	35.39	50.43	68.83	37.66	51.08	100
	VF-FT (fc8)	42.43	36.47	61.12	54.95	63.71	92.22	59.82	73.82	100
M + C + G	PCA + L2 Norm	39.80	29.19	41.15	55.65	56.70	84.56	62.27	75.18	100
	LDA + L2 Norm	20.96	31.27	23.89	31.86	58.24	66.75	38.31	73.22	100
	VF-FT (fc8)	48.13	32.97	64.80	61.78	63.04	93.39	67.59	74.16	100

Fig. 7 if not handled properly beforehand. Additionally, the recognition performance is significantly affected due to imbalance of training data from different species. Devising strategies for overcoming these challenges can lead to substantial increase in the recognition performance (Fig. 13).

Fig. 13. Examples of bias in primate images from the dataset. Row 1 consists of images which are bad in quality, row 2 contains images where orientation of primates is not good, denoting extrinsic biases. Row 3 contains example images of different species in the dataset, which if not balanced may lead to an intrinsic bias.

5   Conclusion and Future Work

The paper presents a method to analyze biases in primate face detection and recognition. Experimental results on a primate dataset show that a deep learning based face detector trained for humans yields satisfying outputs on primates also. However, both intrinsic as well as extrinsic biases that may exist in human face detection or recognition models, also get extended to primate faces. We observe that the face detection problems can be handled reasonably well by employing simple techniques, e.g., shallow CNN based eye detectors paired with spatial constraints, and the use of ensemble learning techniques. However, the algorithm is still not fully immune to biases that exist in primate face datasets, and requires better understanding of the work.

Further, a deep learning based architecture, VGG-face, significantly outperforms other methods given a sufficiently large gallery size. However, an ideal recognition system should perform equally well on a smaller gallery size, as well as handle different intrinsic and extrinsic biases that may exist. Our future work would comprise of coming up with such a system which is robust to the different types of biases and also where recognition rates for both higher and lower gallery sizes are comparable.

Acknowledgement. Vatsa, Singh, and Anand are partially supported through Infosys Center for AI at IIIT-Delhi. The authors acknowledge Wildlife Institute of India for sharing the database.

References

1. The IUCN red list of threatened species. version 2017–3. http://www.iucnredlist. org. Accessed 02 Jan 2018
2. Awad, A.I.: From classical methods to animal biometrics: a review on cattle identification and tracking. Comput. Electron. Agric. **123**, 423–435 (2016)
3. Clark, P.E., et al.: An advanced, low-cost, GPS-based animal tracking system. Rangel. Ecol. Manag. **59**(3), 334–340 (2006)
4. Crouse, D., et al.: Lemurfaceid: a face recognition system to facilitate individual identification of lemurs. BMC Zool. **2**(1), 2 (2017)
5. Crunchant, A.S., et al.: Automated face detection for occurrence and occupancy estimation in chimpanzees. Am. J. Primatol. **79**(3), e22627 (2017)
6. Dalal, N., Triggs, B.: Histograms of oriented gradients for human detection. In: IEEE Computer Society Conference on Computer Vision and Pattern Recognition. vol. 1, pp. 886–893 (2005)
7. Etemad, K., Chellappa, R.: Discriminant analysis for recognition of human face images. J. Opt. Soc. Am. A **14**(8), 1724–1733 (1997)
8. Freund, Y., Schapire, R.E.: A decision-theoretic generalization of on-line learning and an application to boosting. J. Comput. Syst. Sci. **55**(1), 119–139 (1997)
9. Freytag, A., Rodner, E., Simon, M., Loos, A., Kühl, H.S., Denzler, J.: Chimpanzee faces in the wild: log-euclidean CNNs for predicting identities and attributes of primates. In: Rosenhahn, B., Andres, B. (eds.) GCPR 2016. LNCS, vol. 9796, pp. 51–63. Springer, Cham (2016). https://doi.org/10.1007/978-3-319-45886-1_5
10. Hu, P., Ramanan, D.: Finding tiny faces. In: IEEE Conference on Computer Vision and Pattern Recognition, pp. 1522–1530 (2017)
11. Huang, G.B., Ramesh, M., Berg, T., Learned-Miller, E.: Labeled faces in the wild: A database for studying face recognition in unconstrained environments. Technical report 07–49, University of Massachusetts, Amherst, October 2007
12. Joshi, A., VishnuKanth, I.N., Samdaria, N., Bagla, S., Ranjan, P.: GPS-less animal tracking system. In: Fourth IEEE Conference on Wireless Communication and Sensor Networks, pp. 120–125 (2008)
13. Kim, S.H., Kim, D.H., Park, H.D.: Animal situation tracking service using RFID, GPS, and sensors. In: Second International Conference on Computer and Network Technology, pp. 153–156. IEEE (2010)
14. Lahiri, M., Tantipathananandh, C., Warungu, R., Rubenstein, D.I., Berger-Wolf, T.Y.: Biometric animal databases from field photographs: identification of individual zebra in the wild. In: Proceedings of the 1st ACM International Conference on Multimedia Retrieval, p. 6 (2011)
15. Loos, A., Ernst, A.: An automated chimpanzee identification system using face detection and recognition. EURASIP J. Image Video Process. (1), 49 (2013)
16. Loos, A., Pfitzer, M., Aporius, L.: Identification of great apes using face recognition. In: 19th European Signal Processing Conference, pp. 922–926. IEEE (2011)
17. Marciniak, T., Chmielewska, A., Weychan, R., Parzych, M., Dabrowski, A.: Influence of low resolution of images on reliability of face detection and recognition. Multimedia Tools Appl. **74**(12), 4329–4349 (2015)
18. Mason, A.D., Michalakidis, G., Krause, P.J.: Tiger nation: empowering citizen scientists. In: 6th IEEE International Conference on Digital Ecosystems Technologies, pp. 1–5 (2012)
19. Parkhi, O.M., Vedaldi, A., Zisserman, A., et al.: Deep face recognition. In: British Machine Vision Conference, vol. 1, p. 6 (2015)

20. Phillips, P.J., Jiang, F., Narvekar, A., Ayyad, J., O'Toole, A.J.: An other-race effect for face recognition algorithms. ACM Trans. Appl. Percept. **8**(2), 14 (2011)
21. Shlens, J.: A tutorial on principal component analysis. Computer Research Repository (2014). http://arxiv.org/abs/1404.1100
22. Sinha, P., Balas, B., Ostrovsky, Y., Russell, R.: Face recognition by humans: nineteen results all computer vision researchers should know about. Proc. IEEE **94**(11), 1948–1962 (2006)
23. Viola, P., Jones, M.: Rapid object detection using a boosted cascade of simple features. In: IEEE Computer Society Conference Computer Vision and Pattern Recognition, vol. 1 (2001)
24. Witham, C.L.: Automated face recognition of rhesus macaques. J. Neurosci. Methods **300**, 157–165 (2018)
25. Xiao, R., Li, M.J., Zhang, H.J.: Robust multipose face detection in images. IEEE Trans. Circuits Syst. Video Technol. **14**(1), 31–41 (2004)
26. Yadav, D., Singh, R., Vatsa, M., Noore, A.: Recognizing age-separated face images: humans and machines. Public Libr. Sci. One **9**(12), e112234 (2014)

Turning a Blind Eye: Explicit Removal of Biases and Variation from Deep Neural Network Embeddings

Mohsan Alvi[1]([✉]), Andrew Zisserman[1], and Christoffer Nellåker[2,3]

[1] Visual Geometry Group, Department of Engineering Science, University of Oxford, Oxford, UK
mohsalvi@robots.ox.ac.uk
[2] Nuffield Department of Obstetrics and Gynaecology, University of Oxford, Oxford, UK
[3] Big Data Institute, University of Oxford, Oxford, UK

Abstract. Neural networks achieve the state-of-the-art in image classification tasks. However, they can encode spurious variations or biases that may be present in the training data. For example, training an age predictor on a dataset that is not balanced for gender can lead to gender biased predicitons (e.g. wrongly predicting that males are older if only elderly males are in the training set). We present two distinct contributions:

(1) An algorithm that can remove multiple sources of variation from the feature representation of a network. We demonstrate that this algorithm can be used to remove biases from the feature representation, and thereby improve classification accuracies, when training networks on extremely biased datasets.

(2) An ancestral origin database of 14,000 images of individuals from East Asia, the Indian subcontinent, sub-Saharan Africa, and Western Europe. We demonstrate on this dataset, for a number of facial attribute classification tasks, that we are able to remove racial biases from the network feature representation.

Keywords: Dataset bias · Face attribute classification · Ancestral origin dataset

1 Introduction

The current state-of-the-art image recognition algorithms are based on convolutional neural networks [1–3]. These networks rely on large datasets of labeled images, to simultaneously generate a feature representation and a decision framework. This approach removes the need to handcraft features for any given problem but also gives rise to the question as to what feature representation the network has actually learned.

© Springer Nature Switzerland AG 2019
L. Leal-Taixé and S. Roth (Eds.): ECCV 2018 Workshops, LNCS 11129, pp. 556–572, 2019.
https://doi.org/10.1007/978-3-030-11009-3_34

These models are trained on large datasets that contain a number of biases [4,5] or spurious variations, that are irrelevant, or even problematic, for a given task (e.g. discriminating by gender or ancestral origin). One such example is face recognition. Large publicly available face datasets are often composed of celebrities, such as [6–11]. These can contain age, gender, and ancestral origin biases: for example, female celebrities tend to be younger than their male counterparts. This bias does not represent the real world outside of the movie business, reducing the usefulness of models trained on these datasets. Furthermore, in cases where large datasets are not available, training algorithms are initialized from networks that have been trained on similar tasks, for which more data is available [12–14]. This method, called fine-tuning, carries two potential issues: (1) spurious variations are learned from the small dataset, and (2) inheriting biases present in the large dataset.

The use of big data to train AI-models has, to name a few, been adopted by government agencies, institutions of law, human resources, and medical decision systems. A number of such models have been shown to make decisions based on the gender or ancestral origin of an individual, leading to concerns about their "fairness" [15–17]. With the recent enforcement of the General Data Protection Regulation laws[1], individuals have the right to know the rationale behind an automated decision concerning them. To continue the adoption of deep learning, more needs to be done to make neural networks more transparent. One way to approach this issue is to prevent models from making decisions for the wrong reasons.

To be sure that decisions are not being made due to biases, we must look beyond using accuracy as our only performance metric. An experiment by Zhao et al. [18] showed that neural networks learn and amplify biases in the training data. Women were more often depicted in kitchens than men, so the network learned that being in the kitchen was a key feature for the identification of women. Though this may have been true for the dataset the classifier was trained on, in general, this is not a reliable indicator of the presence of a woman.

In this paper, we introduce an algorithm, inspired by a domain and task adaptation approach [19], that can be used to (1) to ensure that a network is blind to a known bias in the dataset, (2) improve the classification performance when faced with an extreme bias, and (3) remove multiple spurious variations from the feature representation of a primary classification task. We use age, gender, ancestral origin, and pose information for facial images to demonstrate our framework.

As discrimination by ancestral origin is a type of spurious variation in many tasks, we have created a new labeled ancestral origin dataset, "Labeled Ancestral Origin Faces in the Wild (LAOFIW)", from publicly available images. This dataset contains 14,000 images of individuals whose ancestral origin is sub-Saharan Africa, Indian Subcontinent, Europe, and East Asia, with a variety of poses, illumination, facial expressions.

---

[1] https://www.eugdpr.org.

The rest of this paper is organized as follows. Section 3 introduces our LAOFIW dataset and other datasets we used for our experiments. Section 4 discusses the methods to remove spurious variations from the feature representation of a network. In Sect. 5.1, we present an experiment to remove a bias from the feature representation network. In Sect. 5.2, we investigate how removing an extreme bias can improve classification performance, and in Sect. 5.3, we investigate removing multiple spurious variations from a network. The results are detailed in Sect. 6. Finally, Sect. 7 summarises our findings.

2   Related Work

Image datasets are known to contain biases that cause models to generalize poorly to new, unseen data [4,5]. This has been addressed by domain adaptation that aims to minimize the difference between the source and target domains [20]. Domain adaptation has been shown to improve the generalisability of classifiers for the same task across different domains [19,21]. We draw inspiration from domain adaptation methods to make the network agnostic to spurious variations.

Learning feature representations that are invariant to certain spurious variations has been tackled in a number of ways. [22] take a multi-task learning approach to pose-invariant face recognition. They propose a novel approach to automatically weight each of the spurious variations during training. Another approach is to adjust the training data distribution at training time, to avoid learning biases [18]. This method relies on having labels for each of the spurious variations for each training instance. This is not feasible for most existing datasets, as they tend to be labeled with a single task in mind, where information about spurious variations is not available. Our method can make use of separate datasets, each labeled for distinct tasks, to remove multiple spurious variations simultaneously.

Jia et al. [23] and Raff et al. [24] draw inspiration from [25] to remove a source of variation with the use of a gradient reversal layer to update the network in opposition of a task. Instead of applying gradient reversal on the output of the softmax layer, which penalizes correct classifications, we compute the cross-entropy of the output classifier and a uniform distribution, as in [19,21]. This ensures an equally uninformative classifier across all tasks.

3   Datasets

3.1   Labeled Ancestral Origin Faces in the Wild

A new ancestral origin database was created as part of this work called "Labeled Ancestral Origin Faces in the Wild (LAOFIW)". The aim of this dataset was to (1) create a dataset for experimentation, and (2) be used as a spurious variation dataset for applications where training a network to be agnostic to ancestral origin is important. The database was assembled using the Bing Image Search API. Search terms based upon origin, e.g. "German, English, Polish, etc.", were

Fig. 1. Example images from the LAOFIW dataset for each of the four classes. In rows top to bottom: Sub-Saharan Africa, Europe, East Asia, Indian Subcontinent. The images are highly varied in age, gender, pose, lighting and expression.

submitted in conjunction with the words "man, woman; boy, girl". Additionally, results were filtered to return photographic images of faces. In total, 43 origin search terms were queried returning 20,000 images. Duplicates were removed by comparing their Histogram of Oriented Gradients [26] encoded using a Gaussian mixture model for each image. The remaining 14,000 images, were manually divided into four broad ancestral origins: sub-Saharan Africa, Indian Subcontinent, Europe, and East Asia. These classes were selected on the basis of being visually distinct from each other.

The database contains roughly the same number of male and female individuals. It also contains images with varied poses: more than a third of the images are non-frontal. Sample images are shown in Fig. 1.

3.2 Age and Gender Dataset

The IMDB dataset is a large publicly available dataset of the images contained in the profiles of the 100,000 most popular actors on the IMDb website[2] with gender and date of birth labels provided for each instance [27]. We used this dataset to investigate the effects of age and gender bias in celebrity datasets.

The labels in the IMDB dataset are noisy, with a number of individuals having both incorrect age and gender labels. This is due to the nature of how the data was collected: The authors assumed that images from an actor's profile that contained a single face would show the actor in question. As stated by the authors, however, these images often contain other actors, who co-starred in their movies [27]. As gender and date of birth are taken from the profile of the actor, this causes erroneous labels for images that show co-stars. The age of an

---

[2] https://www.imdb.com/.

individual was calculated as the difference between the timestamp of the photo and the date of birth of the subject. In some cases, the time stamps of photos predate an actor's date of birth or are otherwise unreliable.

To mitigate this problem, we used the Microsoft Azure Face API[3] to extract gender and age estimates for an identity-balanced subset of 150,000 images. We rejected all images in which the predicted gender from Azure and the IMDB gender label disagreed. We then ran the analysis for age and removed images in which the Azure age prediction differed by more than 10 years from the IMDB labels. The resulting, cleaned dataset contained 60,000 images.

In order to quantify the effectiveness of this data cleansing procedure, we trained a gender classification VGG-M network [3] on both the original 150,000 images and the cleaned 60,000 images, withholding 20% of the images for testing. The gender classification accuracies on the test images improved from 75%, before cleaning, to 99% after cleaning.

The distribution of ages for each gender in the cleaned IMDB dataset is shown in Fig. 2. We can observe a bias towards younger women and older men in the data.

A subset of the cleaned data was used to create an unbiased test dataset, which contains equal numbers of men and women for each age category. This unbiased test dataset was used to evaluate network bias and was not used during training.

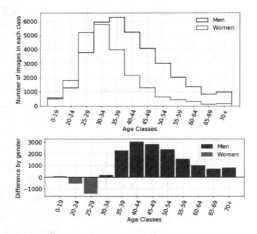

Fig. 2. Age distributions and differences for women (red) and men (blue) in the IMDB dataset. The dataset bias towards younger women and older men is visible. (Color figure online)

---

[3] https://azure.microsoft.com/en-gb/services/cognitive-services/face/.

3.3   Pose Dataset

We used the AFLW dataset [10] categorized by yaw, to train the pose classifier mentioned in Sect. 3.1. The poses were binned into five categories, "profile left, near-frontal left, frontal, near-frontal right, profile right". The non-frontal images were duplicated and flipped to augment the dataset. A class-balanced subset of 24,000 images was selected for training, and a class-balanced set of 6,000 images was reserved for testing.

4   Methods

We introduce a supervised-learning algorithm that aims to learn a single feature representation θ_{repr}, that is informative for a primary classification task, whilst simultaneously being uninformative for a number of spurious variations, that represent undesirable sources of variation. For example, we may wish to create an age classifier, that does not base its decisions on any pose, ancestral origin, or gender information.

We assume access to a primary dataset $\mathcal{D}_p = \{x_i, y_i\}_{i=1}^{n_p}$, containing n_p images, x_i, with labels $y_i \in \{1, \ldots, K\}$. And similarly, we assume access to M secondary datasets, $\mathcal{D}_s = \{\mathcal{D}_m\}_{m=1}^{M}$, each describing a single spurious variation.

4.1   Joint Learning and Unlearning

We introduce a joint learning and unlearning (JLU) algorithm to learn a primary classification task, whilst simultaneously unlearning multiple spurious variations.

Our convolutional network (CNN) architecture is depicted in Fig. 3. The primary branch has a single classification loss, the primary classification loss, which assesses the ability of the network to accurately distinguish between classes of the primary task. Each secondary branch has two losses: a classification loss and a confusion loss. These losses are used to, in turn, assess the amount of spurious variation information left in the feature representation θ_{repr} and then remove it.

Let the classification objective for a generic task with K classes and a corresponding classifier θ_c, given a feature representation θ_{repr}, be defined as the standard softmax loss:

$$L_{\mathrm{softmax}}(x, y; \theta_{\mathrm{repr}}, \theta_C) = -\sum_{k=1}^{K} \mathbb{1}[y = k] \log p_k, \tag{1}$$

where p_k is the softmax of the classifier's output assigning the input x to class k. We will refer to this loss evaluated on the primary task as $L_P(x_p, y_p; \theta_{\mathrm{repr}}, \theta_P)$ and on the m-th spurious variation as $L_m(x_m, y_m, \theta_{\mathrm{repr}}; \theta_m)$.

Inspired by [19], we introduce a confusion loss for the m-th spurious variation, $L_{\mathrm{conf}}(x_m, y_m, \theta_m; \theta_{\mathrm{repr}})$, in (2). Minimizing the confusion loss seeks to change

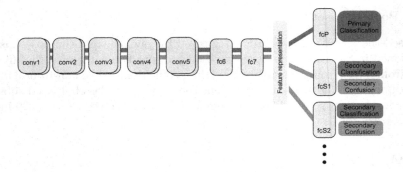

Fig. 3. Overview of CNN Architecture: We use a joint loss over primary and secondary data to learn a feature representation that simultaneously learns to classify the primary task but becomes invariant to secondary tasks, the spurious variations. The spurious variation classification loss and confusion loss act in opposition to learn the classifier on the feature embedding and change the feature embedding to confuse the classifier, respectively. The base architecture is a VGG-M network [3].

the feature representation θ_{repr}, such that it becomes invariant to the spurious variations.

$$L_{\text{conf,m}}(x_m, y_m, \theta_m; \theta_{\text{repr}}) = -\sum_{n_m} \frac{1}{n_m} \log p_{n_m}. \tag{2}$$

We compute the best classifier for each spurious variation, θ_m, and then compute the entropy between the output predicted from each of these classifiers and a uniform distribution. The complete method minimizes the joint loss function:

$$L(x_p, y_p, x_s, y_s, \theta_p, \theta_s, \theta_{\text{repr}}) = L_p(x_p, y_p; \theta_{\text{repr}}, \theta_p)$$
$$+ L_s + \alpha L_{\text{conf}}, \tag{3}$$

where α determines how strongly the confusion loss affects the overall loss, $\theta_s = \{\theta_1, ..., \theta_M\}$, and

$$L_{\text{conf}} = \frac{1}{M} \sum_{m=1}^{M} L_{\text{conf},m}(x_m, y_m, \theta_m; \theta_{\text{repr}}) \tag{4}$$

$$L_s = \sum_{m=1}^{M} \beta_m L_m(x_m, y_m, \theta_{\text{repr}}; \theta_m), \tag{5}$$

where β_m is a weight assigned to the $m-$th spurious variation. As mentioned in [19], the confusion loss (4) and the spurious variation classification loss (5) stand in opposition to one another, so they cannot be optimized in the same step. Therefore, we switch between training the spurious variation classification loss, L_s, and then the joint primary and confusion loss, $L_p(x_p, y_p; \theta_{\text{repr}}, \theta_p) + \alpha L_{conf}$. At each iteration, we find the best spurious variation classifier for the feature representation. The training procedure is shown in Algorithm 1. We used the

VGG-M architecture [28], which consists of five convolutional layers (conv 1-5) and three fully connected layers (fc6-8). The feature representation parameters θ_{repr} represents layers conv1-fc7.

Algorithm 1. Joint Learning and Unlearning

1: **procedure** min $\mathrm{L}(x_p, y_p, x_s, y_s, \theta_p, \theta_s, \theta_{\text{repr}})$
2:     **for** epochs **do**
3:         **while** $\frac{dL_s}{d\theta_s} \neq 0$ **do**
4:             min L_s
5:         **end while**
6:         min $L_p + \alpha L_{\text{conf}}$
7:     **end for**
8: **end procedure**

---

5   Experiments

In this section, we present experiments to demonstrate possible applications of our methodology and the datasets we tested them on.

Removal of a bias from a network—We train a gender-agnostic age classifier using the IMDB dataset, which contains a gender bias: female celebrities tend to be younger than their male counterparts in this dataset.

Removal of an extreme bias from a network—We train an age-agnostic gender classifier on subsets of the IMDB dataset that contain only young women and only old men, and vice versa.

Simultaneous removal of multiple spurious variations—We demonstrate our JLU algorithm's ability to simultaneously remove multiple spurious variations from the feature representation of a network trained for a primary classification task.

5.1   Removal of a Bias from a Network

We investigated the task of creating an age classifier using the cleaned IMDB dataset described in Sect. 3.2. We hypothesize that the gender bias in the distribution, where men are generally older than their female counterparts in this dataset, will be learned by the network.

We trained two networks to perform this task: (1) baseline—trained solely on age data, (2) blind—trained on age data, whilst removing gender-specific information from the network.

We evaluated both networks on the unbiased test dataset detailed in Sect. 3.2. We compared accuracies for age classification and prediction distributions for both genders.

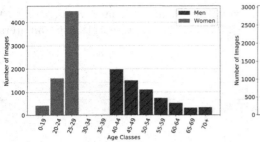
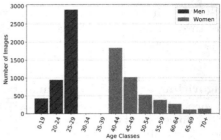

(a) EB1: women aged 0-30, men aged 40+   (b) EB2: women aged 40+, men aged 0-30

Fig. 4. Histograms showing the ages of women (red) and men (blue) in the artificially biased datasets. In both cases, individuals aged under 35 were selected for the young, and individuals aged above 45 were selected for the old set. (Color figure online)

5.2   Removal of an Extreme Bias from a Network

We train gender classifiers using the following artificially biased subsets of the cleaned IMDB data from Sect. 3.2:

1. Extreme bias 1 (EB1): women aged 0–30, men aged 40+
2. Extreme bias 1 (EB2): women aged 40+, men aged 0–30

We placed a buffer of 10 years without any individuals between the two sets to exaggerate the age difference between the genders. We hypothesize that the age bias in the distribution will be learned by the network, for example, if trained on EB1, it should falsely learn to predict that young men are in fact women. Histograms of these datasets are given in Fig. 4.

We trained a baseline network on gender only, and a blind network using our JLU algorithm to unlearn age. The trained classifiers were evaluated on the unbiased test dataset detailed in Sect. 3.2.

5.3   Simultaneous Removal of Multiple Spurious Variations

We demonstrate our algorithm's ability to remove multiple spurious variations from the feature representation of a network. The primary task and spurious variations are selected from age, gender, ancestral origin and pose. In each case, one task is selected as the primary task, and the others make up the spurious variations that we wish to remove. A baseline network was trained for each primary task without using our JLU algorithm.

We used the cleaned IMDB dataset described in Sect. 3.2 for age and gender labels. We used our LAOFIW dataset, described in Sect. 3.1 to classify ancestral origin. Finally, we used the adapted AFLW dataset (Sect. 3.3) to classify pose.

5.4   Age Classification

Since our dataset is relatively small for a deep learning task, we do not approach age estimation as a regression task. We conduct age classification by creating age bins of 5 years, or more years at either end of the distribution. The categories are shown in Fig. 2. We define predictions within one class from the true age class as a positive classification to account for errors caused by edge cases in different bins.

5.5   Implementation Details

Our base network is an adapted VGG-M network [3], pre-trained on the VGG-Face dataset [11]. In our experiments, we saw no significant improvement in updating the weights in the convolutional layers, therefore, the weights in layers conv1-conv5 were frozen for all experiments. This significantly increased the speed of the training algorithm.

The confusion loss was approximated using the Kullback-Leibler divergence between the softmax output of a classifier and a uniform distribution. The network is trained using stochastic gradient descent (SGD) with a learning rate of 1×10^{-4}. Learning rates of classification layers for each task were boosted by a factor of 10. The hyperparameter in Eq. 3 is set to a value of $\alpha = 0.1$. The spurious variation classifier hyperparameters were all set to $\beta_m = 1$. To address the imbalance in the class distributions of the training data, losses were weighted by the inverse of the relative frequency of that class. We conduct our experiments using the MatConvNet framework [29].

6   Results

6.1   Removal of a Bias from a Dataset

We computed feature representations for the class-balanced test dataset from Sect. 3.2 for both baseline and blind networks. T-SNE visualizations of these feature embeddings are shown in Fig. 5. The feature representation of the baseline network that was trained to classify age is clearly separable by gender, demonstrating that the bias in the training data was learned. After unlearning gender, the feature representation is no longer separable by gender, demonstrating that this bias has been removed.

The distributions of the age predictions and ground truth on the gender-balanced test set are shown in Fig. 6. The red and blue lines show the predicted ages for women and men, respectively. The black dashed line shows the ground truth for both genders. The distributions of predicted ages for females and males are different for the baseline network (Fig. 6a): women's ages tend to be underestimated, whereas men's ages are generally overestimated. This behaviour mimics the bias within the training data, which confirms that the classification model is making age predictions that are, to a degree, dependent on gender.

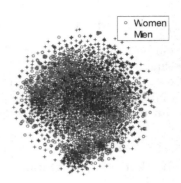

(a) Feature representation of baseline network

(b) Feature representation of blind network

Fig. 5. T-SNE visualizations of 4096-dimensional feature representation of the class-balanced test dataset for age classification networks trained on gender-biased data. (a) Baseline network without unlearning gender, (b) Blind network with gender unlearning. The feature representation is clearly separable by gender for the baseline network, showing that the network has learned the gender bias in the dataset. After unlearning, this bias is no longer pronounced.

In order for us to be sure that the network is not using gender information to predict age, both female and male prediction distributions should be similar. Figure 6b shows the distributions for the network that has been trained to no longer be able to differentiate between genders. The KL-divergence between age prediction distributions for men and women of the biased and unbiased networks are 0.049 and 0.027, respectively. The reduction in KL-divergence shows that the network has successfully unlearned gender, as the predicted age distributions for both genders are similar. Note, that we are not necessarily trying to perfectly predict the ground truth, but be confident that we are not treating men and women differently.

The average prediction accuracy for age classification on the gender-balanced test dataset for the baseline network was 78.9% (78.4% for females and 79.4% for males) and for the unbiased network was 78.1% (77.4% for females and 78.9% for males). This corresponds to a reduction in accuracy of 0.8% (1.2% for females and 0.5% for males).

6.2   Removal of an Extreme Bias from a Network

The baseline gender classification accuracy on the gender-balanced test data was 70% for a network trained on the EB1 dataset. This was improved by 16% to 86% for the blind network, where we simultaneously unlearned age information. The accuracies for networks trained on the EB2 dataset were 62% for the baseline and 82% for the blind network. This amounts to a 20% increase in classification accuracy.

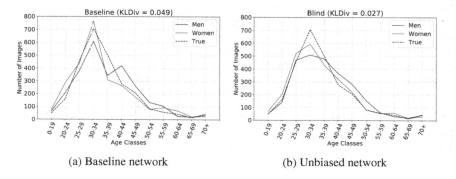

(a) Baseline network   (b) Unbiased network

Fig. 6. Prediction distributions of age for each gender compared to the ground truth (black) for men (blue) and women (red). The evaluation dataset was gender-balanced so that each class has an equal number of women and men. (a) Baseline network without unlearning gender, (b) unbiased network with gender unlearning. The red line shows the age predictions for women and the blue line shows them for men. The prediction distributions for women and men align after unlearning gender. The KL-divergence score between the prediction distributions of men and women are given for each case. The KL-Divergence score reduces, as two distributions become more similar. (Color figure online)

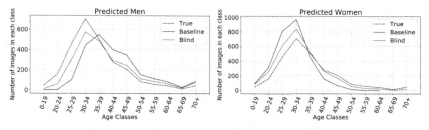

(a) Male and female predictions by age by network trained on EB1 dataset

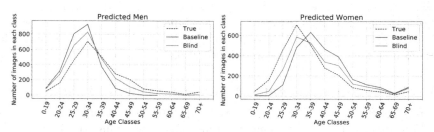

(b) Male and female predictions by age by network trained on EB2 dataset

Fig. 7. Age distributions of male and female predictions from networks trained on the biased (a) EB1 and (b) EB2 datasets, evaluated on the gender-balanced test data. The baseline network often wrongly predicts older individuals to be male and younger individuals to be female. Using the JLU algorithm reduces this bias and shifts the prediction distributions closer to the true distribution.

Table 1. Classification accuracies for each spurious variation for a baseline network and a "blind network". The baseline accuracies show the best classifiers that can be learned on the feature representation of the primary task without the JLU algorithm. The "Blind" column shows the classification accuracies after JLU. The random chance column states the target accuracy for a spurious variation classifier after JLU, corresponding to an uninformative classifier's accuracy. The % unlearned column shows the relative difference of baseline and blind accuracies to random chance.

Primary	Spurious	Baseline	Blind	% Unlearned	Random Chance
Age		0.79	0.74		
	Ancestral Origin	0.83	0.25	100%	0.25
	Gender	0.99	0.56	88%	0.50
	Pose	0.66	0.24	91%	0.20
Ancestral Origin		0.94	0.95		
	Age	0.58	0.12	92%	0.08
	Gender	0.99	0.51	98%	0.50
	Pose	0.56	0.25	86%	0.20
Gender		0.99	0.99		
	Age	0.70	0.12	94%	0.08
	Ancestral Origin	0.85	0.26	98%	0.25
	Pose	0.62	0.22	95%	0.20
Pose		0.84	0.84		
	Age	0.68	0.12	93%	0.08
	Ancestral Origin	0.88	0.39	78%	0.25
	Gender	0.99	0.57	86%	0.50

The age distributions of individuals that were predicted to be either male or female, trained on the EB1 dataset, are shown in Fig. 7. The baseline network often wrongly predicts older individuals to be male, and younger individuals to be female, in line with the training data. The age distribution of gender predictions from the JLU network, however, is closer to the true distribution. We observed similar results for the baseline network trained on the EB2 dataset, where younger individuals were more often predicted to be male, and older individuals were more often predicted to be female. The JLU network prediction distributions were closer to the true distributions.

6.3   Simultaneous Removal of Multiple Spurious Variations

Figure 8 shows how the accuracies on the test data for each attribute vary over the JLU training procedure when simultaneoulsy unlearning multiple spurious variations. For clarity, in the figure, spurious variation classification accuracies were rescaled using the equation below:

$$a = 1 - \frac{e}{e_{max}}, \tag{6}$$

where e is the mean-class error of the classifier and e_{max} corresponds to the error-rate of a classifier that draws at random. A perfect classifier corresponds

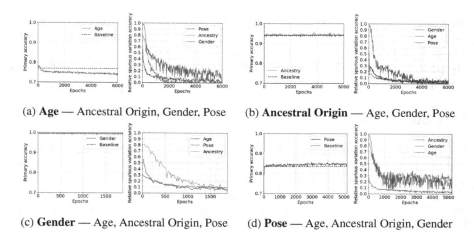

(a) **Age** — Ancestral Origin, Gender, Pose   (b) **Ancestral Origin** — Age, Gender, Pose

(c) **Gender** — Age, Ancestral Origin, Pose   (d) **Pose** — Age, Ancestral Origin, Gender

Fig. 8. Classification accuracies on test data for the primary task and spurious variations during the training procedure of the JLU algorithm. The primary classification
accuracy is compared to the baseline network accuracy (dotted). The spurious variation accuracies have been re-scaled using Eq. 6 so that zero accuracy corresponds to
the accuracy of a random chance classifier.

to a score of $a = 1$ and a random classifier corresponds to a score of $a = 0$. The
primary classification accuracy was not rescaled.

These results are summarised in Table 1 for networks trained with and without JLU. The baseline column corresponds to the accuracy of the best classifier on a feature embedding trained without JLU. The "blind" column shows
the same accuracies when using the JLU algorithm. When the classifier cannot recover meaningful information from the feature embedding the accuracy is
equivalent to random chance.

Age—The primary classification accuracy of the blind network is 5% less
than the baseline network. Information about ancestral origin was removed from
the network completely. Gender and pose information were removed by 88% and
91%, respectively.

Ancestral Origin—The primary classification accuracy of the blind network
improved by 1% compared to the baseline network. The proportions of age,
gender, and pose information that were unlearned were 92%, 98%, and 86%,
respectively.

Gender—The primary classification accuracy of the blind network is the
same as the baseline network. Age, ancestral origin, and pose information were
removed by 94%, 98% and 95%, respectively.

Pose—The primary classification accuracy of the blind network is the same
as the baseline network. Information about age, ancestral origin, and gender
were removed from the network by 93%, 78% and 86%, respectively.

Apart from the network that was trained on the primary task of age classification on data that contained a strong gender bias, all blind networks have

the same or better primary classification accuracy compared to their baseline counterparts. Spurious variations were successfully removed in most cases, with classification accuracies reducing to within 5% of random chance in 9/12 cases. The pose experiment proved the least effective, with ancestral origin information proving most difficult to remove.

7   Conclusion

The paper proposes an approach for removing multiple known dataset biases or spurious variations from a deep neural network. Similar to previous work in the field, the algorithm is inspired by domain adaptation work. Drawing inspiration from [19], we compare the cross-entropy between the output distribution of classifiers that are trained to predict spurious variations and a uniform distribution. The resulting feature representation is informative for the primary task but blind to one or more spurious variations.

We demonstrated our algorithm's efficacy on face classification tasks of age, ancestral origin, pose and gender. The resulting feature representations remained informative for one task, whilst simultaneously being uninformative for the others. When training a gender classification network on extremely age-biased data, our algorithm significantly improves (by up to 20%) classification accuracies on an unbiased test dataset. This demonstrates that our algorithm allows networks trained on biased data to generalize better to unbiased settings, by removing each known bias from the feature representation of the network.

This is a significant step towards trusting that a network definitely isn't basing its decisions on the wrong reasons. With increasing use of neural networks in government, law, and employment to make life-changing decisions, it is of great importance, that undesirable social biases are not encoded in the decision algorithm. We also created a dataset to detect ancestral origin from faces, which can be used to remove racial biases from the feature representation of a network. We will make this dataset available to the public.

Some spurious variations are easier to remove than others—applying different weights to each spurious variation classifier could account for these differences. A dynamic-weighting scheme, as in [22], to automatically weight these different tasks at different time-points during training may improve convergence.

Acknowledgments. This research was financially supported by the EPSRC programme grant Seebibyte EP/M013774/1, the EPSRC EP/G036861/1, and the MRC Grant MR/M014568/1.

References

1. He, K., Zhang, X., Ren, S., Sun, J.: Deep Residual Learning for Image Recognition, ArXiv e-prints, December 2015
2. Krizhevsky, A., Sutskever, I., Hinton, G.E.: Imagenet classification with deep convolutional neural networks. In: Advances in Neural Information Processing Systems, pp. 1097–1105 (2012)

3. Simonyan, K., Zisserman, A.: Very Deep Convolutional Networks for Large-Scale Image Recognition. ArXiv e-prints, September 2014
4. Tommasi, T., Patricia, N., Caputo, B., Tuytelaars, T.: A Deeper Look at Dataset Bias. ArXiv e-prints, May 2015
5. Torralba, A., Efros, A.A.: Unbiased look at dataset bias. In: CVPR (2011)
6. Cao, Q., Shen, L., Xie, W., Parkhi, O.M., Zisserman, A.: VGGFace2: A dataset for recognising faces across pose and age, p. 8
7. Guo, Y., Zhang, L., Hu, Y., He, X., Gao, J.: Ms-celeb-1m: Challenge of recognizing one million celebrities in the real world, February 2016
8. Huang, G.B., Ramesh, M., Berg, T., Learned-Miller, E.: Labeled faces in the wild: a database for studying face recognition in unconstrained environments. Technical report 07–49, University of Massachusetts, Amherst, October 2007
9. Kemelmacher, I., Seitz, S., Miller, D., Brossard, E.: The megaface benchmark: 1 million faces for recognition at scale, December 2015
10. Kostinger, M., Wohlhart, P., Roth, P.M., Bischof, H.: Annotated facial landmarks in the wild: a large-scale, real-world database for facial landmark localization, pp. 2144–2151. IEEE, November 2011
11. Parkhi, O., Vedaldi, A., Zisserman, A.: Deep face recognition. In: BMVC, vol. 1, no. 3, p. 6, September 2015
12. Girshick, R., Donahue, J., Darrell, T., Malik, J.: Rich feature hierarchies for accurate object detection and semantic segmentation. ArXiv e-prints, November 2013
13. Long, M., Cao, Y., Wang, J., Jordan, M.I.: Learning Transferable Features with Deep Adaptation Networks. ArXiv e-prints, February 2015
14. Oquab, M., Bottou, L., Laptev, I., Sivic, J.: Learning and transferring mid-level image representations using convolutional neural networks, pp. 1717–1724. IEEE, June 2014
15. Buolamwini, J., Gebru, T.: Gender shades: intersectional accuracy disparities in commercial gender classification. In: Friedler, S.A., Wilson, C. (eds.) Proceedings of the 1st Conference on Fairness, Accountability and Transparency. Proceedings of Machine Learning Research, PMLR, New York, NY, USA, 23–24 Feb 2018, vol. 81, pp. 77–91 (2018)
16. Ras, G., van Gerven, M., Haselager, P.: Explanation Methods in Deep Learning: Users, Values. Concerns and Challenges, ArXiv e-prints, March 2018
17. Sweeney, L.: Discrimination in Online Ad Delivery. ArXiv e-prints, January 2013
18. Zhao, J., Wang, T., Yatskar, M., Ordonez, V., Chang, K.W.: Men also like shopping: reducing gender bias amplification using corpus-level constraints. In: Proceedings of the 2017 Conference on Empirical Methods in Natural Language Processing, Copenhagen, Denmark, pp. 2979–2989. Association for Computational Linguistics, September 2017
19. Tzeng, E., Hoffman, J., Darrell, T., Saenko, K.: Simultaneous deep transfer across domains and tasks. In: 2015 IEEE International Conference on Computer Vision (ICCV), pp. 4068–4076. IEEE (2015)
20. Gretton, A., Smola, A., Huang, J., Schmittfull, M., Borgwardt, K., Schlkopf, B.: Covariate shift and local learning by distribution matching. In: Dataset Shift in Machine Learning. Biologische Kybernetik, Cambridge, MA, USA, pp. 131–160 (2009)
21. Tzeng, E., Hoffman, J., Saenko, K., Darrell, T.: Adversarial Discriminative Domain Adaptation. ArXiv e-prints, February 2017
22. Yin, X., Liu, X.: Multi-task convolutional neural network for pose-invariant face recognition. IEEE Trans. Image Process. **27**(2), 964–975 (2018)

23. Jia, S., Lansdall-Welfare, T., Cristianini, N.: Right for the Right Reason: Training Agnostic Networks. ArXiv e-prints, June 2018
24. Raff, E., Sylvester, J.: Gradient Reversal Against Discrimination. ArXiv e-prints, July 2018
25. Ganin, Y., et al.: Domain-adversarial training of neural networks. In: Csurka, G. (ed.) Domain Adaptation in Computer Vision Applications. ACVPR, pp. 189–209. Springer, Cham (2017). https://doi.org/10.1007/978-3-319-58347-1_10
26. Dalal, N., Triggs, B.: Histograms of oriented gradients for human detection. In: Proceedings of the 2005 IEEE Computer Society Conference on Computer Vision and Pattern Recognition (CVPR 2005), Washington, DC, USA, vol. 1, pp. 886–893. IEEE Computer Society (2005)
27. Rothe, R., Timofte, R., Gool, L.V.: DEX: Deep EXpectation of apparent age from a single image, pp. 252–257. IEEE, December 2015
28. Chatfield, K., Simonyan, K., Vedaldi, A., Zisserman, A.: Return of the devil in the details: delving deep into convolutional nets. In: British Machine Vision Association, pp. 6:1–6:12 (2014)
29. Vedaldi, A., Lenc, K.: Matconvnet - convolutional neural networks for matlab. In: Proceedings of the ACM International Conference on Multimedia (2015)

Mitigating Bias in Gender, Age and Ethnicity Classification: A Multi-task Convolution Neural Network Approach

Abhijit Das$^{(\boxtimes)}$, Antitza Dantcheva, and Francois Bremond

Inria, Sophia Antipolis, France
{abhijit.das,antitza.dantcheva,francois.bremond}@inria.fr

Abstract. This work explores joint classification of gender, age and race. Specifically, we here propose a Multi-Task Convolution Neural Network (MTCNN) employing joint dynamic loss weight adjustment towards classification of named soft biometrics, as well as towards mitigation of soft biometrics related bias. The proposed algorithm achieves promising results on the UTKFace and the Bias Estimation in Face Analytics (BEFA) datasets and was ranked first in the BEFA Challenge of the European Conference of Computer Vision (ECCV) 2018.

Keywords: Bias · Facial analysis · Age · Gender and race ·
Soft biometrics · Facial attributes

1 Introduction

The prevalent commercial deployment of automated face analysis systems (i.e., face recognition as a robust authentication method) has fueled increasingly the scientific attention. Current machine learning algorithms allow for a relative reliably detection, recognition, as well as categorization of face images w.r.t. age, race and gender. We note though, that training and evaluation data for such algorithms is often biased concerning factors such as age, gender, ethnicity, pose and resolution. Very recently Buolamwini and Gebru [1] reported that algorithms trained with such biased data are inherently bound to produce skewed results. This leads to a significant drop in performance of state of the art models, when applied to images of particular gender and/or ethnicity groups.

Motivated by the above, we here propose a Multi-Task Convolution Neural Network (MTCNN) employing joint dynamic loss weight adjustment targeted to jointly classify gender, age and race, as well as to minimize identified soft biometrics related bias.

The rest of the paper is organized as following: Sect. 2 reviews related work, Sect. 3 describes proposed methodology, in Sect. 4 the experimental results are presented and discussed. Finally Sect. 5 concludes the work.

© Springer Nature Switzerland AG 2019
L. Leal-Taixé and S. Roth (Eds.): ECCV 2018 Workshops, LNCS 11129, pp. 573–585, 2019.
https://doi.org/10.1007/978-3-030-11009-3_35

2   Related Work

2.1   Face Analysis

Automated FA is instrumental in a wide range of applications including face detection [2], soft biometrics/face attribute classification [3] and face recognition [4]. Prominently, such applications have been integrated into the current generation of smartphones. Simultaneously, companies such as Google, IBM, Microsoft and Face++ have released commercial software on automated FA. Moreover nowadays, FA is not restricted to face recognition, but has transgressed onto emotion analysis [5], gender classification [6], as well as other facial characteristics [7–9].

Despite of the prevalence of face analysis, accuracies of face recognition systems are lower for particular subcategories of population, such as "female, black". Particularly individuals between the age of 18 and 30 years exhibit low accuracy for face recognition systems used in US-based law enforcement, as reported by Klare et al. [10]. With regards to gender, age and race classification, it is worth mentioning that these algorithms are biased as well, depending on related attribute-subcategories. The latest report on gender classification released by National Institute for Standards and Technology (NIST) reflects on the fact that algorithms performed worse for females than males [11].

Farinella and Dugelay [12] alleged that ethnicity has no effect on gender classification, adopting a binary ethnic categorization scheme for the experimentation: Caucasian and non-Caucasian. Dwork et al. [13] demonstrated the importance of understanding sensitive characteristics such as gender and race, in order to build demographically inclusive models. Proposals for fairness have included parity, such as demographic parity, and equality measures, which require equal false negative rates and false positive rates across subgroups. In a very recent work Buolamwini and Gebru [1] investigated gender and skin type bias in two facial analysis benchmarks, IJB-A and Adience, evaluating three commercial gender classification systems and concluded that darker-skinned females are the most misclassified group. They further recommended that such substantial disparities in the accuracy of classification of gender classification systems require urgent attention, in order to ensure that *FA-systems* are built genuinely *fair, transparent and accountable*. In addition, Garvie et al. [14] observed that African-Americans were more likely to be terminated by law enforcement and subjected to have a biased face recognition searches than individuals of other ethnicity. Therefore, monitoring phenotypic and demographic accuracy of these systems is necessitated.

One further biasing factor concerning gender classification constitutes age. Cheng et al. [15] performed an initial investigation, suggesting that the discriminable features for gender classification for children and adults were significantly different. This was affirmed by Dantcheva et al. [16] and Bilinski et al. [17].

Towards eliminating bias Ranjan and Chellappa [18], as well as Ryu et al. [19] proposed the use of multi-task learning (MTL) networks, and fine-tuned a model trained for face recognition. In another work decoupled classifiers were proposed to handle bias [20], where the learning of sensitive attributes can be separated from a downstream task in order to maximize both, fairness and accuracy. In particular they employed transfer learning to tackle bias of sub-type based domain adaptation.

2.2 Available Datasets

In the context of bias estimation in FA, we note that generally publicly available datasets contain a significant demographic bias. For instance, Labeled Faces in the Wild (LFW), used widely as a benchmark, contains 77.5% male and 83.5% Caucasians [21]. While many works have reported high performance on LFW, the fine grained analysis of the performance considering race, age and gender sub-group has rarely been considered.

To mitigate these limitations, Intelligence Advanced Research Projects Activity (IARPA) introduced an initiative to release the IJB-A dataset as the most diverse set [22]. Further the Adience gender and age classification benchmark was released by Levi and Hassner [23]. As of 2017, NIST started a challenge to spur improvement in face gender classification by expanding on the former 2014–2015 study. Further, to increase the exposure of race diversity Escalera et al. [24] collected the Faces of the World (FotW) dataset, with the aim to achieve a uniform distribution across two genders and four ethnic groups.

While aforementioned datasets include annotation with gender as well as different skin color subgroups, the datasets lack the annotation for age. Consequently these datasets cannot be employed to study factors such as age, gender and race that can bias FA systems. Therefore, the UTKFace dataset was developed recently by Zhang et al. [25], consisting of all required labeling.

3   Proposed Approach

3.1   Proposed MTCNN

We propose to use MTCNN with joint dynamic weight loss to classify gender, age and race and further mitigate related bias. The proposed method utilizes disjoint features of the fully connected layers of a Deep CNN using a separated fully connected layers for fulfilling multi-task learning that operates to aim better face attribute analysis. It exploits the synergy and the disjoint features among the tasks, boosting up performances. We exploit the fact that information contained in CNN features is hierarchically distributed throughout the network. Lower layers consist of feature such as edges and corners, and therefore contain better localization features. Hence they are more suitable for learning localization and pose estimation tasks. Whereas, on the other hand, deeper layers, e.g., higher top layers are class-specific and suitable for learning complex tasks such as face recognition and the fully connected layers involve for the classification task i.e., where the end to end system can learn and attempt to discriminate the salient features for different inherent tasks in a MTCNN scenario. Given the aforementioned MTCNN-characteristic, as well as the aim of the work to enhance face attribute analysis, we propose to customize Facenet [26] for face recognition with ResNet V1 inception (as it is one of the prominent face architectures). A block diagram of the proposed MTCNN is illustrated in Fig. 1.

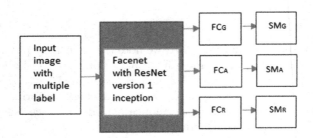

Fig. 1. Block diagram of proposed MTCNN for face attribute analysis (FC_R = fully connected layer of race classification task, FC_A = fully connected layer of age classification task, FC_G = fully connected layer of gender classification task, SM_R = Softmax layer of race classification task, SM_G = Softmax layer of gender classification task and SM_A = Softmax layer of age classification task).

The Facenet network consists of a batch of input layer and a Deep CNN architecture (ResNet V1 in our scenario) followed by L2 normalization, which results in face embedding. This is followed by the triplet loss during training. The architecture consists of a stream of convolution layers, normalization layer and pooling layers followed by 3 inception blocks and their reduction. The latter followed by dropout and a fully connected layer. At this point, we split the network into three separate branches corresponding to the different classification tasks (i.e., gender, race and age). We add three fully connected layers, one for race classification, second for gender classification and third for age classification. Finally, a Softmax layer is added to each of the branches to predict the individual task labels feature with L2 normalization and respective dropout layer. After each convolution a Rectified Linear Unit (ReLU) is deployed as activation function. The Facenet model turns an image of a face into a vector of 128 floating point numbers. These 128 embedding can be used as features for classification. While using Facenet we fine-tuned the fully connected layer.

In the MTCNN the network is split at the fully connected layer followed by individual Softmax layer of each task. Therefore an input layer tuple of the MTCNN, for a given training set T with N images contains T = Ii, Yi, where i = 1:N, where Ii is the image and Yi is a vector consisting of the labels. In MTCNNs it is challenging to define the loss weight for each task. In previous works, this was dealt either by treating all tasks equally Dong et al. [27], dynamic MTCNN Fang et al., [28], obtaining weights via brute-force search [28] or by dynamically assigning disjoint weights for the side task [29]. However neither of this strategies work in our setting. Unlike pose and illumination, gender, race and age classification are closely related facial features. Moreover, they possess varying degrees of relevance for both intra-class and inter-class variation. Such relevance depends on their intensity exhibited per samples. Hence, we seek to optimize the effect of multi-task facial attribute classification (i.e., gender, age and race) by learning them jointly and dynamically, depending on the degree of relevance of the feature present for each classification task. Specifically, the MTCNN should directly learn classification task relations from data instead of subjective task grouping. Thereby deciding weight of the task sharing. Hence, we propose a joint dynamic weighting scheme to automatically assign the loss weights for the each task during training.

First, we find the summed weight for the each classification task by brute-force search on the validation set. Further by adding a fully connected layer and a Softmax layer to each task the model gets proficient to shared features from the last common layer, which is aimed at learning the dynamic weights for each iteration depending degree of relevance of the task. Therefore we obtain the dynamic weight percentages for each task from the fully connected layer. Further, the function of the soft-max layer converts the dynamic weights to positive values that sum to 1. Consequently, the most relevant task is to contribute predominantly to the final loss and the additional task is to contribute to the relevant task, in order to reduce the loss of the most relevant task. Thereby, the MTCNN should assign a higher weight for a non-relevant task with a lower loss, in order to reduce the overall loss. A mini-batch Stochastic Gradient Descent (SGD) was employed to solve the above optimization problem of loss weight. Further, the weights were averaged for each batch.

3.2 Implementation Details

The Python library of Facenet[1] is used to calculate facial embedding of face images and developing the proposed MTCNN. The Facenet library was implemented in TensorFlow. It includes pre-trained Facenet models for face recognition. The models have been validated on the LFW database [30] and were trained on a subset of the MSCeleb-1M database [31]. The models architecture follows the Inception-ResNet-v1 network [32].

The Facenet library includes an implementation of detection, alignment and landmark estimation, as proposed by Zhang et al. [33] which we use for preprocessing for our images. The output of our proposed MTCNN is a 128 dimension floating point embedding, similar to Facenet. The Scikit-learns SVM version with RBF kernel is used with Tensorflow for classification of this embedding for face recognition. As the pre-trained model was trained on a much larger face dataset but with less similarity in respect to face attributes, we employ transfer learning. Specifically we freeze the initial layers of the pre-trained model and train the last top layers. Therefore, the top layers (which are known to contain the face attribute information) are customized to our setting of interest. During transfer learning we ensure that the final layers are not restored from the pre-trained model and we also to ensure that gradients are gated for all other parameters during training. While fine tuning the weight decay is set to 0.0005.

---

[1] https://github.com/davidsa-ndberg/facenet.

All models are trained for 10 epochs with a batch size of 20. The learning rate starts at 0.001 and reduces at 5th, 7th, and 9th epochs with a factor of 0.1.

4   Experiment Results and Discussions

We proceed to present employed datasets, experimental protocol, implementation details, obtained results obtained, as well as to discuss these. The results achieved in the ECCV 2018 BEFA challenge employing the proposed MTCNN are also explained at the end of this section.

4.1   Datasets

We report experimental results on two datasets: UTKFace and BEFA challenge dataset, which we proceed to describe.

1. **UTKFace** dataset is a large-scale face dataset (over 20,000 face images) with a population coverage of long age span ranged from 0 to 116 years. Specifically, annotation for age includes following classes: baby: 0–3 years, child: 4–12 years, teenagers: 13–19 years, young: 20–30 years, adult: 31–45 years, middle aged: 46–60 years and senior: 61 and above years. The dataset additionally contains the labeling for gender (male and female), as well as five races (White, Black, Asian, Indian and other race). UTKFace includes large variations of pose, facial expression, illumination, occlusion, and resolution.
2. **BEFA** challenge dataset[2] is the official dataset of the related challenge. It contains 13431 test images. It has been annotated for age (baby, child, teenagers, young, adults, middle age and senior), gender (male and female), and ethnicity (white, black, Asian and Indian). As per challenge goals, these soft biometric traits and trait instances are represented in a balanced manner.

4.2   Experimental Protocol

We classify gender, age and race, respectively, analyzing the trait instances of the remaining facial attributes. For instance for age classification we report the age true classification rates for males, females, as well as for each category separately.

1. **UTKFace:** The dataset consists of three parts. Part I, II and III consist of 10437, 10719 and 3252 images, respectively. We use part I for training (three forth for fine tuning and rest for training the classifier), part II for testing and part III for validation.
2. **BEFA:** The BEFA dataset was used only for testing. Training and fine tuning were performed as above. As per the challenge protocol, we classify the soft biometric traits, analyzing all possible categories. Hence all 56 are considered (i.e., one possible category being "male, young, Indian").

---

[2] https://sites.google.com/site/eccvbefa2018/.

4.3   Results and Analysis

1. **UTKFace:** The overall mean classification accuracy for race, gender and age classification is summarized in Table 1. We observe that the proposed approach significantly improves accuracies achieved by Facenet and its fine-tuned model, consistently for all attributes.

Table 1. Mean classification accuracy of the race, gender and age classification [%].

	Race	Gender	Age
Facenet	85.1	91.2	56.9
Finetuned Facanet (FFNet)	86.1	96.1	64
Proposed MTCNN	90.1	98.23	70.1

Table 2. The classification accuracy of the **race classification** considering gender and age instances [%].

	FFNet	Proposed MTCNN
Male	87	90.9
Female	84.3	89.1
Baby	100	100
Child	84.3	88.8
Teenager	85.8	89.1
Young	84.9	88.9
Adult	88.1	91.5
Middle	87.7	90.7
Senior	81.9	87.7

The results in Table 2 suggest the presence of a bias in **race classification** w.r.t. gender and age for the FFNet approach. While babies are categorized to 100% ethnically, the accuracy decreases down to 81.9% for seniors. Less profound, but similarly while females are categorized to 84.3% ethnically, males reach 87% true classification accuracy. We note, that such bias has been mitigated to a large extent by the proposed MTCNN. The remaining low level of bias still persists among the senior age category, possibly due to lower race exhibits in older subjects.

Table 3 summarizes the accuracies of **age classification**. Again, FFNet's performance indicates for a significant bias, with classification rates ranging from 61.5% for males to 78.7% for Asians. We note a classification accuracy higher for females than for males. Such bias in gender estimation has been

Table 3. The classification accuracy of the **age classification** considering race and gender instances [%].

	FFNet	Proposed MTCNN
Male	61.5	69.1
Female	66.8	70.9
White	61.8	69.6
Black	59.2	68.9
Asian	78.7	80.1
Indian	63.6	69.5
Others	64.5	66.7

nearly mitigated by the proposed MTCNN. A certain low level of bias can be still found among race instances.

The accuracies in Table 4 indicate that for gender classification, bias w.r.t. race and age can be mainly observed for the instances baby, child and teenagers employing FFNet. Again, this bias has been nearly mitigated by the proposed MTCNN. Remaining bias is accredited to low sexual dimorphism in babies.

Table 4. The classification accuracy of the **gender classification** considering gender and race instances [%].

	FFNet	Proposed MTCNN
Baby	70	80.5
Child	79.6	96.7
Teenager	92	95
Young	96.8	97
Adult	97.7	98.3
Middle	96.6	97.7
Senior	95.1	96.5
White	97	98.7
Black	95	98.6
Asian	97.5	99.3
Indian	97.8	99.1
Others	97.5	99

2. **BEFA:** The overall mean classification accuracies of the BEFA challenge dataset employing the proposed MTCNN are summarized in Table 5.

Table 5. The overall mean classification accuracy of race, gender, age and overall attribute classification on BEFA challenge dataset [%].

	All attributes	Race	Gender	Age
MTCNN	56.37	84.29	93.72	71.83

The related confusion matrices of gender, age, race classification and attribute classification considering age, gender and race along intersection for all the attributes are illustrated in Figs. 2, 3, 4 and 5. It can be concluded that age, gender and race classification performance achieved by the proposed MTCNN on the BEFA dataset is rather encouraging, whilst there are some remaining scenarios with low performance. For instance, it can be observed from Fig. 2 that the performance of gender classification was low among the baby subgroup, moreover it was worst for female babies with Asian race. In terms of age classification, we observe from Fig. 3 that the classification performance was low for the adults for most instances of race and gender, specifically with lowest accuracies for black females. Further from Fig. 4, we see that for race classification the performance is lowest for Asian and Indian seniors. While considering all attributes together (age, race and gender), the performance dropped, with lowest accuracies for teenagers and adult black females.

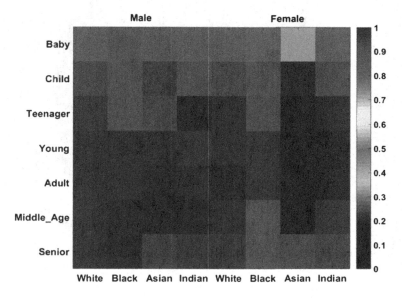

Fig. 2. Confusion matrix of gender classification along intersections of all attributes.

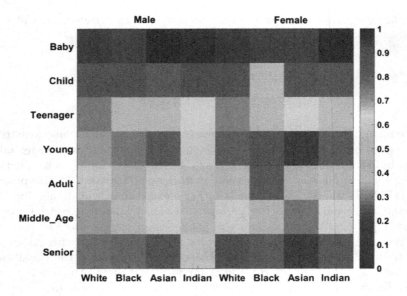

Fig. 3. Confusion matrix of age classification along intersections of all attributes.

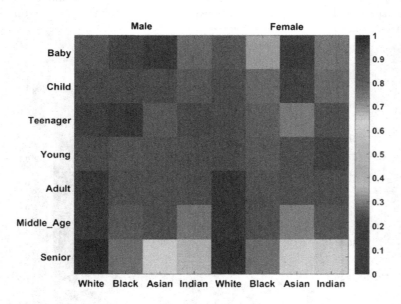

Fig. 4. Confusion matrix of race classification along intersections of all attributes.

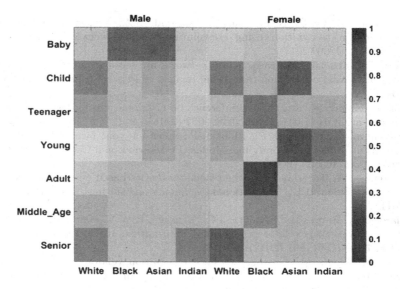

Fig. 5. Confusion matrix of attributes classification considering all attributes together (gender, age and race) along intersections of all attributes.

5   Conclusions

In this paper, we presented an approach for gender, age and race classification targeted to minimize inter-class bias. The proposed multi-task CNN approach utilized joint dynamic loss, providing promising results on the UTKFace and the Bias Estimation in Face Analytics (BEFA) challenge datasets. The proposed algorithm was ranked first in the related BEFA-challenge of the European Conference on Computer Vision (ECCV) 2018. In future work, we intend to extend the current study onto other facial attributes. In addition, we intend to explore the approach presented in this work in the context of mitigating biases in face recognition.

References

1. Buolamwini, J., Gebru, T.: Gender shades: intersectional accuracy disparities in commercial gender classification. In: Conference on Fairness, Accountability and Transparency, pp. 77–91 (2018)
2. Zafeiriou, S., Zhang, C., Zhang, Z.: A survey on face detection in the wild: past, present and future. Comput. Vis. Image Underst. **138**, 1–24 (2015)
3. Dantcheva, A., Elia, P., Ross, A.: What else does your biometric data reveal? A survey on soft biometrics. IEEE Trans. Inf. Forensics Secur. **11**, 1–26 (2015)
4. Ranjan, R., Sankaranarayanan, S., Castillo, C.D., Chellappa, R.: An all-in-one convolutional neural network for face analysis. In: 2017 12th IEEE International Conference on Automatic Face & Gesture Recognition (FG 2017), pp. 17–24. IEEE (2017)

5. Dehghan, A., Ortiz, E.G., Shu, G., Masood, S.Z.: Dager: deep age, gender and emotion recognition using convolutional neural network. arXiv preprint arXiv:1702.04280 (2017)
6. Wang, Y., Kosinski, M.: Deep neural networks are more accurate than humans at detecting sexual orientation from facial images. J. Pers. Soc. Psychol. 114(2), 246 (2018)
7. Wu, X., Zhang, X.: Automated inference on criminality using face images. arXiv preprint arXiv:1611.04135, pp. 4038–4052 (2016)
8. Dantcheva, A., Bremond, F., Bilinski, P.: Show me your face and I will tell you your height, weight and body mass index. In: International Conference on Pattern Recognition (ICPR) (2018)
9. Dantcheva, A., Dugelay, J.: Female facial aesthetics based on soft biometrics and photo-quality. In: IEEE International Conference on Multimedia and Expo (ICME) (2011)
10. Klare, B.F., Burge, M.J., Klontz, J.C., Bruegge, R.W.V., Jain, A.K.: Face recognition performance: role of demographic information. IEEE Trans. Inf. Forensics Secur. 7(6), 1789–1801 (2012)
11. Ngan, M., Ngan, M., Grother, P.: Face recognition vendor test (FRVT) performance of automated gender classification algorithms. US Department of Commerce, National Institute of Standards and Technology (2015)
12. Farinella, G., Dugelay, J.L.: Demographic classification: do gender and ethnicity affect each other? In: 2012 International Conference on Informatics, Electronics & Vision (ICIEV), pp. 383–390. IEEE (2012)
13. Dwork, C., Hardt, M., Pitassi, T., Reingold, O., Zemel, R.: Fairness through awareness. In: Proceedings of the 3rd Innovations in Theoretical Computer Science Conference, pp. 214–226. ACM (2012)
14. Clare Garvie, A.B., Frankle, J.: The perpetual line-up: unregulated police face recognition in America (2016)
15. Cheng, Y.D., O'Toole, A.J., Abdi, H.: Classifying adults' and children's faces by sex: computational investigations of subcategorical feature encoding. Cogn. Sci. 25(5), 819–838 (2001)
16. Dantcheva, A., Bremond, F.: Gender estimation based on smile-dynamics. IEEE Trans. Inf. Forensics Secur. 12(3), 719–729 (2017)
17. Bilinski, P., Dantcheva, A., Brémond, F.: Can a smile reveal your gender? In: 2016 International Conference of the Biometrics Special Interest Group (BIOSIG), pp. 1–6. IEEE (2016)
18. Ranjan, R., Castillo, C.D., Chellappa, R.: L2-constrained softmax loss for discriminative face verification. arXiv preprint arXiv:1703.09507 (2017)
19. Ryu, H.J., Adam, H., Mitchell, M.: InclusiveFaceNet: improving face attribute detection with race and gender diversity. In: Workshop on Fairness, Accountability, and Transparency in Machine Learning (FAT/ML) (2018)
20. Dwork, C., Immorlica, N., Kalai, A.T., Leiserson, M.D.: Decoupled classifiers for group-fair and efficient machine learning. In: Conference on Fairness, Accountability and Transparency, pp. 119–133 (2018)
21. Han, H., Jain, A.K.: Age, gender and race estimation from unconstrained face images. Department of Computer Science and Engineering, Michigan State University, East Lansing, MI, USA, MSU Technical report (MSU-CSE-14-5) (2014)
22. Klare, B.F., et al.: Pushing the frontiers of unconstrained face detection and recognition: Iarpa Janus benchmark a. In: Proceedings of the IEEE Conference on Computer Vision and Pattern Recognition, pp. 1931–1939 (2015)

23. Levi, G., Hassner, T.: Age and gender classification using convolutional neural networks. In: Proceedings of the IEEE Conference on Computer Vision and Pattern Recognition Workshops, pp. 34–42 (2015)
24. Escalera, S., et al.: Chalearn looking at people and faces of the world: face analysis workshop and challenge 2016. In: Proceedings of the IEEE Conference on Computer Vision and Pattern Recognition Workshops, pp. 1–8 (2016)
25. Zhang, Z., Song, Y., Qi, H.: Age progression/regression by conditional adversarial autoencoder. In: IEEE Conference on Computer Vision and Pattern Recognition (CVPR). IEEE (2017)
26. Schroff, F., Kalenichenko, D., Philbin, J.: FaceNet: a unified embedding for face recognition and clustering. In: Proceedings of the IEEE Conference on Computer Vision and Pattern Recognition, pp. 815–823 (2015)
27. Yi, D., Lei, Z., Liao, S., Li, S.Z.: Learning face representation from scratch. arXiv preprint arXiv:1411.7923 (2014)
28. Fang, Y., Ma, Z., Zhang, Z., Zhang, X.Y., Bai, X.: Dynamic multi-task learning with convolutional neural network
29. Yin, X., Liu, X.: Multi-task convolutional neural network for pose-invariant face recognition. IEEE Trans. Image Process. **27**, 964–975 (2017)
30. Huang, G.B., Mattar, M., Berg, T., Learned-Miller, E.: Labeled faces in the wild: a database for studying face recognition in unconstrained environments. In: Workshop on Faces in 'Real-Life' Images: Detection, Alignment, and Recognition (2008)
31. Guo, Y., Zhang, L., Hu, Y., He, X., Gao, J.: MS-Celeb-1M: a dataset and benchmark for large-scale face recognition. In: Leibe, B., Matas, J., Sebe, N., Welling, M. (eds.) ECCV 2016. LNCS, vol. 9907, pp. 87–102. Springer, Cham (2016). https://doi.org/10.1007/978-3-319-46487-9_6
32. Szegedy, C., Ioffe, S., Vanhoucke, V., Alemi, A.A.: Inception-v4, inception-resnet and the impact of residual connections on learning (2017)
33. Zhang, K., Zhang, Z., Li, Z., Qiao, Y.: Joint face detection and alignment using multitask cascaded convolutional networks. IEEE Signal Process. Lett. **23**(10), 1499–1503 (2016)

W06 – 4th International Workshop on Recovering 6D Object Pose

W06 – 4th International Workshop on Recovering 6D Object Pose

The 4th International Workshop on Recovering 6D Object Pose (R6D) was held in conjunction with ECCV 2018 in Munich. The workshop featured four invited talks, oral and poster presentations of accepted workshop papers, and an introduction of the BOP benchmark for 6D object pose estimation. The workshop was attended by 100+ people working on relevant topics in both academia and industry who shared up-to-date advances and discussed open problems. For more details about the workshop, please see the following summary paper. Note that this paper was not peer-reviewed.

Papers submitted to the workshop were peer-reviewed, each by 2–3 reviewers. The program committee accepted 10 out of 13 submitted papers. The winners of the best paper award are Vladimir Knyaz, Vladimir V. Kniaz, and Fabio Remondino with their work titled *Image-to-Voxel Model Translation with Conditional Adversarial Networks*.

We would like to express our gratitude to authors of the submitted papers for moving the field forward, to the reviewers for their rigorous and swift work, and to the invited speakers for their high-quality talks.

September 2018

Tomáš Hodaň
Rigas Kouskouridas
Tae-Kyun Kim
Krzysztof Walas
Jiří Matas
Carsten Rother
Frank Michel
Vincent Lepetit
Aleš Leonardis
Carsten Steger
Caner Sahin

A Summary of the 4th International Workshop on Recovering 6D Object Pose

Tomáš Hodaň[1]([✉]), Rigas Kouskouridas[2], Tae-Kyun Kim[3], Federico Tombari[4], Kostas Bekris[5], Bertram Drost[6], Thibault Groueix[7], Krzysztof Walas[8], Vincent Lepetit[9], Ales Leonardis[10], Carsten Steger[6], Frank Michel[11], Caner Sahin[3], Carsten Rother[12], and Jiří Matas[1]

[1] CTU in Prague, Prague, Czech Republic
hodantom@cmp.felk.cvut.cz
[2] Scape Technologies, London, England
[3] Imperial College London, London, England
[4] TU Munich, Munich, Germany
[5] Rutgers University, New Brunswick, USA
[6] MVTec, Munich, Germany
[7] Ecole Nationale des Ponts et Chaussées, Marne-la-Vallée, France
[8] Poznan University of Technology, Poznań, Poland
[9] University of Bordeaux, Bordeaux, France
[10] University of Birmingham, Birmingham, UK
[11] TU Dresden, Dresden, Germany
[12] Heidelberg University, Heidelberg, Germany

Abstract. This document summarizes the 4th International Workshop on Recovering 6D Object Pose which was organized in conjunction with ECCV 2018 in Munich. The workshop featured four invited talks, oral and poster presentations of accepted workshop papers, and an introduction of the BOP benchmark for 6D object pose estimation. The workshop was attended by 100+ people working on relevant topics in both academia and industry who shared up-to-date advances and discussed open problems.

1 Introduction

An accurate, fast and robust estimation of 6D object pose is of great importance to many application fields such as robotic manipulation, augmented reality, scene interpretation, and autonomous driving. In robotics, for example, the 6D object pose facilitates spatial reasoning and allows an end-effector to act upon the object. In an augmented reality scenario, object pose can be used to enhance one's perception of reality by augmenting objects with extra information such as hints for assembly.

The introduction of consumer and industrial grade RGB-D sensors have allowed for substantial improvement in 6D object pose estimation as these sensors concurrently capture both the appearance and geometry of the scene. However, there still remain challenges to be addressed, including robustness against

© Springer Nature Switzerland AG 2019
L. Leal-Taixé and S. Roth (Eds.): ECCV 2018 Workshops, LNCS 11129, pp. 589–600, 2019.
https://doi.org/10.1007/978-3-030-11009-3_36

occlusion and clutter, scalability to multiple objects, and fast and reliable object modelling, including capturing of reflectance properties. Extending contemporary methods to work reliably and with sufficient execution speed in an industrial setting is still an open problem. Many recent methods focus on specific rigid objects, but pose estimation of deformable or articulated objects and of object categories is also an important research direction.

Fig. 1. Estimation of 6D pose, i.e. 3D translation and 3D rotation, of a specific rigid object. This task is considered in the BOP benchmark [25].

The field of 6D object pose estimation has gained more attention last years. A big achievement for the field is the best paper award of ECCV 2018 given to Martin Sundermeyer, Zoltan Marton, Maximilian Durner, Manuel Brucker, and Rudolph Triebel for their work titled *Implicit 3D Orientation Learning for 6D Object Detection from RGB Images.*

The 4th edition of the International Workshop on Recovering 6D Object Pose [4][1] was organized in conjunction with ECCV 2018 and was attended by 100+ people from both academia and industry who shared up-to-date advances and discussed open problems. Four invited speakers talked about their current work (Sect. 2), the BOP benchmark for 6D object pose estimation was introduced (Sect. 3), and the accepted workshop papers were presented.

The workshop covered the following topics: (a) 6D object pose estimation (a.k.a. 3D object detection) and tracking, (b) 3D object modeling and reconstruction, (c) surface representation and registration, (d) robustness to occlusion and background clutter, (e) multiple object instance detection, (f) pose estimation of non-rigid objects and object categories, (g) robotic grasping and grasp affordances, and (h) object manipulation and interaction.

Many methods for 6D pose estimation of specific rigid objects (Fig. 1) have been published recently, but were usually compared with only a few competitors on a small subset of datasets. It had been therefore unclear which methods perform well and in which scenarios. To capture the *status quo* of the field, we organized the SIXD Challenge [5] at the 3rd workshop edition held at ICCV 2017 [3]. The results submitted to the challenge were published in the BOP benchmark paper [25] and presented at the 4th workshop edition.

Papers submitted to the workshop were peer-reviewed. Out of 13 submissions, the program committee accepted 10 papers which were introduced at the

---

[1] The previous editions were held at ICCV 2015 [1], ECCV 2016 [2], and ICCV 2017 [3].

workshop through oral and poster presentations. The best paper award was given to *Image-to-Voxel Model Translation with Conditional Adversarial Networks* by Vladimir Knyaz, Vladimir V. Kniaz, and Fabio Remondino.

2   Invited Talks

The invited talks were given by Federico Tombari from Technical University of Munich, Kostas Bekris from Rutgers University, Bertram Drost from MVTec, and Thibault Groueix from Ecole Nationale des Ponts et Chaussées. The talks are summarized below and the slides are available on the workshop website [4].

2.1   From 3D Descriptors to Monocular 6D Pose: What Have We Learned? – *Federico Tombari*

While 6D rigid pose estimation has been an important research task for more than twenty years, recently the design of new algorithms is more and more focused on overcoming the limitations provided by real world applications, so to bridge the gap between lab research and products. This translates to the necessity to move on from the simplified scenario of estimating the pose of a single object on a clutter-less planar surface, towards scenarios with high clutter and occlusion [42]. At the same time, algorithms need to process input data at a very high frame rate, so to reduce the latency of the output and avoid lagging, provide accurate pose estimation (e.g. to reduce jitter during tracking) and cope with resource-limited hardware architectures such as mobile phones or embedded computers. This is particularly motivated by applications that already have a strong market interest such as augmented reality, personal/industrial robotics and autonomous driving. A disruptive technology that strongly influenced the field of 6D rigid pose estimation in the past 5 years is deep learning. Hence, the talk presented an overview of the current trends and results regarding the use of deep learning for this task, in view of overcoming the aforementioned limitations. In particular, it highlighted two main research directions where deep learning has been leveraged to improve the state of the art: (i) the definition of 3D descriptors for 3D data; (ii) 6D object pose estimation from RGB (or monocular) data.

As for the first aspect, we briefly went over the development of 3D descriptors for unorganized 3D representations, starting from the handcrafted ones [41,46] until the more recent "learned" ones. An important aspect regarding the influence of deep learning on this field is that certain 3D representations such as point clouds and 3D meshes, frequently utilized for 6D rigid pose estimation tasks, are not well suited to convolutions due to their intrinsic unorganized nature. Hence, an important step in the direction of learning 3D features was the introduction of methods such as PointNet [35] and [50], that, conversely to approaches such as 3D Match [52] and [29], can directly operate on point clouds or meshes without the need to either voxelize or histogram the data. The recent global and fully-convolutional architecture for point cloud processing and scene understanding proposed in [40] was also introduced.

As for the second research direction, the intuition of estimating the 6D pose of an object based on monocular information relies on the fact that humans can often have a rough idea of the pose of the objects in the surrounding 3D space simply from monocular cues, provided that they are familiar with the shape of the objects. Several works have recently explored this direction, which were briefly introduced and compared in terms of characteristics. One distinctive trait that differentiates such approaches is the type of output that the network is trained to infer: from the 8 corners of the projected bounding box [36,45] to the regression of the 6D pose [15,49] or the classification of the viewpoint and in-plane rotations [27]. The method in [30] was also introduced, that proposes to learn the 6D pose refinement from pairs of RGB patches using a CNN. Finally, the extension of monocular 6D pose estimation to the autonomous driving domain was also discussed, by referencing recent directions such as [12,13].

In conclusion, deep learning appears as a powerful tool for 6D rigid pose estimation, although seems still strongly limited by open issues such as generalizability, learning of geometric invariance and computational efficiency (especially in a field where most applications need to deal with resource-limited hardware). Monocular pose estimation can be promisingly carried out via deep learning, although not yet as accurately as with a depth sensor, as also showcased by a qualitative comparison on a real sequence between the two tracking approaches in [30] (monocular) and [42] (RGB-D). Finally, deploying monocular 6D pose estimation jointly with monocular semantic SLAM such as CNN-SLAM [43], which also leverages deep learning to obtain dense semantic reconstruction, appears as an interesting direction to explore towards full (i.e. semantic + geometry) scene understanding from monocular data.

2.2   Towards Robust 6D Pose Estimation: Physics-Based Reasoning and Data Efficiency − *Kostas Bekris*

Towards the objective of robust 6 DoF pose estimation at an accuracy and speed level that allows robots to manipulate objects in their surroundings, this talk focused on warehouses tasks, such as picking from bins, packing and sorting. Warehouses can be seen as a stepping stone between the success story of robotics in manufacturing and the vision of deploying robots in everyday human environments. Warehouses involve a large variety of objects, which can appear in general, unpredictable configurations, as well as cluttered scenes and tight spaces, such as shelving units, which limit the observability of on-board sensors and introduce occlusions. They allow, however, access to known object models, which frequently correspond to standard geometric shapes, due to packaging.

In these setups, it is critical for a robot to both utilize physics-based reasoning to achieve 3D scene-level understanding as well as minimize the dependence of solutions to excessive human labeling, which negatively impacts scalability. With these priorities in mind, the talk highlighted a pipeline for robust 6D pose estimation, which includes the following four steps: (1) semantic object segmentation given physically realistic synthetic data, (2) pose hypothesis generation through robust point registration, (3) pose improvement via consideration of physical constraints at the scene level, and (4) lifelong self-learning through active physical interaction with objects.

Recently, deep learning methods, such as those employing Convolutional Neural Networks (CNN's), have become popular for object detection [37,38] and pose estimation [27,48], outperforming alternatives in most benchmarks. These results are typically obtained by training CNN's using datasets with a large number of labeled images. Such datasets, however, need to be collected in a way that captures the intricacies of the environment the robot is deployed in, such as lighting conditions, occlusion and clutter. This motivates the development of synthetic dataset that can capture the known parameters of the environment and generate data accordingly, while avoid overfitting to the unknown parameters.

The first component of the proposed pipeline is to use a physics engine in the synthetic dataset generation pipeline [33]. The physics engine defines environmental constraints on object placement, which naturally capture in the training set, the distribution of object poses that can realistically appear during testing. Furthermore, a physics engine is a convenient tool to parameterize the unknown scene features, such as illumination. A randomization over such parameters is very effective in avoiding overfitting to synthetic textures of objects.

Given semantic object segmentation, the problem of estimating the 6D object poses involves geometric reasoning regarding the position and orientation of the detected objects. Solutions that became popular in the context of the Amazon Picking Challenge (APC) [14], use a Convolutional Neural Network (CNN) for object segmentation [21,51] followed by a 3D model alignment step using point cloud registration techniques [6,31]. The quality of the pose estimate, however, can still suffer due to over-reliance on the learned models.

The second insight of the talk is that CNN output can be seen as a probability for an object to be visible at each pixel. These segmentation probabilities can then be used during the registration process to achieve robust and fast pose estimation. This requires sampling a base of points on a point cloud segment, such that all points on the base belong to the target object with high probability. The resulting approach, denoted as "Stochastic Congruent Sets" (StoCS) [32], builds a probabilistic graphical model given the obtained soft segmentation and information from the pre-processed geometric object models. The pre-processing corresponds to building a global model descriptor that expresses oriented point pair features [18]. This geometric modeling, not only biases the base samples to lie within the object bound, but is also used to constrain the search for finding the congruent sets, which provides a substantial computational benefit.

The third key observation of the talk is to treat individual-object predictions with some level of uncertainty and perform a global, scene-level optimization process that takes object interactions into account [34]. This information arises from physical properties, such as respecting gravity and friction as well as the requirement that objects do not penetrate one another. In particular, a Monte Carlo Tree Search (MCTS) process utilizes local detections to achieve scene-level optimization. It generates multiple candidate poses per object and then searches over the cartesian product of these individual object pose candidates to find the optimal scene hypothesis. The scene is evaluated according to a score defined in terms of similarity of the rendered hypothesized scenes against input data. The search performs constrained local optimization via physics correction and ICP [6]. Through this physical reasoning, the resulting pose estimates for the objects are of improved accuracy and by default consistent.

Once the system has access to an object detector and a pose estimation process, it can already be deployed for the desired task. Nevertheless, as the system performs its task, it also gets access to data in the operation domain, which it did not have access to during training. This data could be very useful in further improving the performance of the system but they are not labelled.

The fourth aspect of the talk is a solution for automatically labeling real images acquired from multiple viewpoints using a robotic manipulator [33]. A robotic manipulator autonomously collects multi-view images of real scenes and labels them automatically using the object detector trained with the above physics-based simulation tool. The key insight is the fact that the robot can often find a good viewing angle that allows the detector to accurately label the object and estimate its pose. The object's predicted pose is then used to label images of the same scene taken from more difficult and occluded views. The transformations between different views are known because they are obtained by moving the robotic manipulator. Overall, the data can be added to the existing synthetic dataset to re-train the model for better performance as part of a lifelong, self-learning procedure.

2.3   Detecting Geometric Primitives in 3D Data – *Bertram Drost*

Even though methods based on (deep) learning lead to major advances in many areas of computer vision over the last years, the top-performing methods for 6D object detection are still hand-crafted, classic methods. This is evident from the recent results on the BOP benchmark (Sect. 3).

Methods that currently perform best on BOP are based on a voting scheme that can be interpreted as a meet-in-the-middle between RANSAC and a generalized Hough transform. The base method [18] uses a local parametrization for the object pose, where an oriented scene point (reference point) is fixed and assumed to be on the target object. The remaining local parameters are then the point on the model surface that corresponds to the reference point and the rotation around the normal vector, which combined represent three degrees of freedom. The optimal local parameters are recovered using a voting scheme. For this, the reference point is paired with neighboring scene points, and similar point pairs on the model are searched using an efficient hashing scheme. Each such match then casts a vote. While the base method shows good results for 3D shapes with a distintive geometry, it has weaknesses for shapes that are symmetric of strongly self-similar. This is mostly because point pairs on such shapes are no longer very discriminative. The voting thus finds all symmetric poses simultaneously, which is both slower and less robust.

The talk presented a way of adapting the base method for geometric primitive shapes - spheres, planes, cylinders, and to some extend cones. First, the local parameter space was reduced by removing duplicate entries due to symmetries. For example, since a sphere is identical no matter the corresponding point on its surface or the rotation around the normal, the local parameter space becomes zero-dimensional, i.e. a single counter. Additionally, the local parameters can be extended by shape parameters such as the radius of a sphere or cylinder, or the opening angle of a cone. Second, instead of using a hashing scheme for matching point pairs between scene and model, an explicit point pair matching can be used thanks to the explicit nature of the geometric primitives. Those changes make the method both faster and more robust for such geometric primitives, while also allowing the recovery of shape parameters.

2.4   Parameteric Estimation of 3D Surfaces and Correspondences – *Thibault Groueix*

Pose of a rigid object has 6 degrees of freedom and is well defined. A broader class of objects are non-rigid shapes such as articulated robots or humans. Articulated robots have an additional degree of freedom for each joint. Those additional intrinsic parameters also have to be estimated. In this case, it is easy to manually design a parametrization with N degrees of freedom, where each parameter naturally encodes the angle of a joint. Humans are much harder to parameterize and doing it manually is hard. We propose to learn the parameterization [19].

To that end, we want to map each shape S of category C, represented as a point cloud, to a parameter space. A relevant prior on deformable shapes is the ability to find a neutral template, already encoding lots of general information on humans. To learn a parameterization, we use autoencoder neural networks. The encoder is a PointNet [35] and the decoder is a Shape Deformation Network [19] that deforms the template by iteratively transforming each point on the template to a point in 3D. Given correspondence annotation between a training example and the template, the L2 distance between the generated and the input point clouds is penalized. Annotation of correspondences is expensive and can be avoided through an unsupervised reconstruction loss, the chamfer distance, and a proper regularization. The parameterization is a mapping from the parameter space to the point cloud space, and is given by the learned decoder.

At test time, the parameters associated with this parametrization can be estimated using the encoder. We propose to use this estimate as an initialization for a local exploration of the parameter space through gradient descent. The learned parametrization is evaluated on the task of 3D correspondences on the FAUST dataset [7] and achieves state-of-the-art-results. It also displays strong robustness to holes and noise in the data.

The method is not limited to humans, but applies to any category of shape for which a template can be found. For broader category without natural templates such as chairs, or general furniture, the template can be replaced by a set a square patches [20]. The assumption is that any object can be reconstruct through the deformation of a set of patches. The proposed parametrization, Atlasnet, is learned on Shapenet and applied for the task of Single View Reconstruction, leading to state-of-the-art results. This confirms that learning a parametrization can be the key to extending 6D pose estimation beyond rigid objects.

3   BOP: Benchmark for 6D Object Pose Estimation

The BOP benchmark considers the task of 6D pose estimation of a rigid object from a single RGB-D input image, when the training data consists of a texture-mapped 3D object model or images of the object in known 6D poses. The benchmark comprises of: (i) eight datasets [8,16,22,23,39,44] in a unified format that cover different practical scenarios, including two new datasets focusing on varying lighting conditions, (ii) an evaluation methodology with a pose-error function that deals with pose ambiguities, (iii) an evaluation of 15 diverse recent methods that captures the state of the art, and (iv) an online evaluation system at bop.felk.cvut.cz that is open for continuous submission of new results.

The evaluation shows that methods based on point-pair features [18,47], introduced in 2010, currently perform best. They outperform template matching methods [26], learning-based methods [8,9,28,44] and methods based on 3D local features [10,11]. Occlusion is a big challenge for current methods, as shown by scores dropping swiftly already at low levels of occlusion. As another important future research directions, our analysis identified robustness against object symmetries and similarities, varying lighting conditions, and noisy depth images.

3.1   Future Plans

Various possible extensions of the BOP benchmark regarding datasets, problem statement and evaluation metrics were discussed at the workshop and are summarized in the following paragraphs.

The benchmark was started with the simple task of 6D localization of a single instance of a single object. This task allowed to evaluate most of the recent methods out of the box and is a common denominator of the other 6D localization variants – a single instance of multiple objects, multiple instances of a single object, and multiple instances of multiple objects. The plan is to move step by step and add the more complicated variants to the online evaluation system in the near future, as well as the 6D detection task, where no prior information about the object presence is provided [24]. Note that while it is easy to extend the evaluation to other tasks, it is non-trivial to extend the methods.

The plan is also to keep adding new datasets, e.g. [17], and for every new dataset to reserve a set of test images for which the ground-truth annotation will be private. The datasets that are currently included in BOP are fully public.

Another topic of discussion were the pose-error functions. In the BOP benchmark, 6D pose estimates are evaluated using the Visible Surface Discrepancy (VSD) which measures misalignment of the visible part of the object surface. One limitation of the current version of VSD is that it does not consider color. The same holds for the other pose-error functions commonly used in the literature [24]. While the alignment of color texture is less relevant for a number of robotic applications, it may be important for augmented-reality applications. The plan is to fix this limitation in a new version of VSD with an extended pixel-wise test checking not only the distance of the object surface but also its color. We are open to other feedback and discussion about the evaluation methodology.

4 Conclusions

This document summarized the 4th International Workshop on Recovering 6D Object Pose which was organized at ECCV 2018 and featured four invited talks, oral and poster presentations of accepted workshop papers, and an introduction of the BOP benchmark for 6D object pose estimation.

An accurate, fast and robust method for 6D object pose estimation is still in need, as is evident from the current scores on the BOP benchmark [25]. We would like to encourage authors of relevant methods to keep submitting results to the online evaluation system at bop.felk.cvut.cz. We will present snapshots of the leaderboards at the next workshop editions, which are planned for the upcoming major conferences.

References

1. 1st International Workshop on Recovering 6D Object Pose, ICCV 2015, Santiago. https://labicvl.github.io/3DPose-2015.html
2. 2nd International Workshop on Recovering 6D Object Pose, ECCV 2016, Amsterdam. https://labicvl.github.io/R6D
3. 3rd International Workshop on Recovering 6D Object Pose, ICCV 2017, Venice. http://cmp.felk.cvut.cz/sixd/workshop_2017/
4. 4th International Workshop on Recovering 6D Object Pose, ECCV 2018, Munich. http://cmp.felk.cvut.cz/sixd/workshop_2018/
5. SIXD challenge (2017). http://cmp.felk.cvut.cz/sixd/challenge_2017/
6. Besl, P.J., McKay, N.D.: Method for registration of 3D shapes. In: International Society for Optics and Photonics (1992)
7. Bogo, F., Romero, J., Loper, M., Black, M.J.: FAUST: dataset and evaluation for 3D mesh registration. In: CVPR (2014)
8. Brachmann, E., Krull, A., Michel, F., Gumhold, S., Shotton, J., Rother, C.: Learning 6D object pose estimation using 3D object coordinates. In: Fleet, D., Pajdla, T., Schiele, B., Tuytelaars, T. (eds.) ECCV 2014. LNCS, vol. 8690, pp. 536–551. Springer, Cham (2014). https://doi.org/10.1007/978-3-319-10605-2_35
9. Brachmann, E., Michel, F., Krull, A., Yang, M.Y., Gumhold, S., Rother, C.: Uncertainty-driven 6D pose estimation of objects and scenes from a single RGB image. In: CVPR (2016)
10. Buch, A.G., Petersen, H.G., Krüger, N.: Local shape feature fusion for improved matching, pose estimation and 3D object recognition. SpringerPlus **5**, 297 (2016)
11. Buch, A.G., Kiforenko, L., Kraft, D.: Rotational subgroup voting and pose clustering for robust 3D object recognition. In: ICCV (2017)
12. Chen, X., Kundu, K., Zhang, Z., Ma, H., Fidler, S., Urtasun, R.: Monocular 3D object detection for autonomous driving. In: CVPR (2016)

13. Chen, X., et al.: 3D object proposals for accurate object class detection. In: Advances in Neural Information Processing Systems. pp. 424–432 (2015)
14. Correll, N., et al.: Analysis and observations from the first Amazon picking challenge. IEEE Trans. Autom. Sci. Eng. (T-ASE) **15**, 172–188 (2016)
15. Do, T.T., Cai, M., Pham, T., Reid, I.: Deep-6Dpose: recovering 6D object pose from a single RGB image. arXiv preprint arXiv:1802.10367 (2018)
16. Doumanoglou, A., Kouskouridas, R., Malassiotis, S., Kim, T.K.: Recovering 6D object pose and predicting next-best-view in the crowd. In: CVPR (2016)
17. Drost, B., Ulrich, M., Bergmann, P., Härtinger, P., Steger, C.: Introducing MVTec ITODD - a dataset for 3D object recognition in industry. In: CVPR (2017)
18. Drost, B., Ulrich, M., Navab, N., Ilic, S.: Model globally, match locally: efficient and robust 3D object recognition. In: CVPR (2010)
19. Groueix, T., Fisher, M., Kim, V.G., Russell, B.C., Aubry, M.: 3D-CODED: 3D correspondences by deep deformation. In: Ferrari, V., Hebert, M., Sminchisescu, C., Weiss, Y. (eds.) ECCV 2018. LNCS, vol. 11206, pp. 235–251. Springer, Cham (2018). https://doi.org/10.1007/978-3-030-01216-8_15
20. Groueix, T., Fisher, M., Kim, V.G., Russell, B.C., Aubry, M.: AtlasNet: a Papier-Mache approach to learning 3D surface generation. arXiv preprint arXiv:1802.05384 (2018)
21. Hernandez, C., et al.: Team Delft's robot winner of the Amazon picking challenge 2016. In: Behnke, S., Sheh, R., Sarıel, S., Lee, D.D. (eds.) RoboCup 2016. LNCS (LNAI), vol. 9776, pp. 613–624. Springer, Cham (2017). https://doi.org/10.1007/978-3-319-68792-6_51
22. Hinterstoisser, S., et al.: Model based training, detection and pose estimation of texture-less 3D objects in heavily cluttered scenes. In: Lee, K.M., Matsushita, Y., Rehg, J.M., Hu, Z. (eds.) ACCV 2012. LNCS, vol. 7724, pp. 548–562. Springer, Heidelberg (2013). https://doi.org/10.1007/978-3-642-37331-2_42
23. Hodaň, T., Haluza, P., Obdržálek, Š., Matas, J., Lourakis, M., Zabulis, X.: T-LESS: an RGB-D dataset for 6D pose estimation of texture-less objects. In: WACV (2017)
24. Hodaň, T., Matas, J., Obdržálek, Š.: On evaluation of 6D object pose estimation. In: Hua, G., Jégou, H. (eds.) ECCV 2016. LNCS, vol. 9915, pp. 606–619. Springer, Cham (2016). https://doi.org/10.1007/978-3-319-49409-8_52
25. Hodaň, T., et al.: BOP: benchmark for 6D object pose estimation. In: Ferrari, V., Hebert, M., Sminchisescu, C., Weiss, Y. (eds.) ECCV 2018. LNCS, vol. 11214, pp. 19–35. Springer, Cham (2018). https://doi.org/10.1007/978-3-030-01249-6_2
26. Hodaň, T., Zabulis, X., Lourakis, M., Obdržálek, Š., Matas, J.: Detection and fine 3D pose estimation of texture-less objects in RGB-D images. In: IROS (2015)
27. Kehl, W., Manhardt, F., Tombari, F., Ilic, S., Navab, N.: SSD-6D: making RGB-based 3D detection and 6D pose estimation great again. In: ICCV (2017)
28. Kehl, W., Milletari, F., Tombari, F., Ilic, S., Navab, N.: Deep learning of local RGB-D patches for 3D object detection and 6D pose estimation. In: Leibe, B., Matas, J., Sebe, N., Welling, M. (eds.) ECCV 2016. LNCS, vol. 9907, pp. 205–220. Springer, Cham (2016). https://doi.org/10.1007/978-3-319-46487-9_13
29. Khoury, M., Zhou, Q.Y., Koltun, V.: Learning compact geometric features. In: ICCV (2017)
30. Manhardt, F., Kehl, W., Navab, N., Tombari, F.: Deep model-based 6D pose refinement in RGB. In: Ferrari, V., Hebert, M., Sminchisescu, C., Weiss, Y. (eds.) Computer Vision – ECCV 2018. LNCS, vol. 11218, pp. 833–849. Springer, Cham (2018). https://doi.org/10.1007/978-3-030-01264-9_49

31. Mellado, N., Aiger, D., Mitra, N.J.: Super4PCS fast global pointcloud registration via smart indexing. In: Computer Graphics Forum, vol. 33, pp. 205–215. Wiley Online Library (2014)
32. Mitash, C., Boularias, A., Bekris, K.E.: Robust 6D object pose estimation with stochastic congruent sets. In: British Machine Vision Conference (BMVC) (2018)
33. Mitash, C., Bekris, K.E., Boularias, A.: A self-supervised learning system for object detection using physics simulation and multi-view pose estimation. In: 2017 IEEE/RSJ International Conference on Intelligent Robots and Systems (IROS), pp. 545–551. IEEE (2017)
34. Mitash, C., Boularias, A., Bekris, K.E.: Improving 6D pose estimation of objects in clutter via physics-aware Monte Carlo tree search. In: IEEE International Conference on Robotics and Automation (ICRA) (2018)
35. Qi, C.R., Su, H., Mo, K., Guibas, L.J.: PointNet: deep learning on point sets for 3D classification and segmentation. In: CVPR (2017)
36. Rad, M., Lepetit, V.: BB8: a scalable, accurate, robust to partial occlusion method for predicting the 3D poses of challenging objects without using depth. In: ICCV (2017)
37. Redmon, J., Divvala, S., Girshick, R., Farhadi, A.: You only look once: unified, real-time object detection. In: Proceedings of the IEEE Conference on Computer Vision and Pattern Recognition, pp. 779–788 (2016)
38. Ren, S., He, K., Girshick, R., Sun, J.: Faster R-CNN: towards real-time object detection with region proposal networks. In: Advances in Neural Information Processing Systems, pp. 91–99 (2015)
39. Rennie, C., Shome, R., Bekris, K.E., De Souza, A.F.: A dataset for improved RGBD-based object detection and pose estimation for warehouse pick-and-place. Robot. Autom. Lett. 1, 1179–1185 (2016)
40. Rethage, D., Wald, J., Sturm, J., Navab, N., Tombari, F.: Fully-convolutional point networks for large-scale point clouds. In: Ferrari, V., Hebert, M., Sminchisescu, C., Weiss, Y. (eds.) ECCV 2018. LNCS, vol. 11208, pp. 625–640. Springer, Cham (2018). https://doi.org/10.1007/978-3-030-01225-0_37
41. Rusu, R.B., Blodow, N., Beetz, M.: Fast point feature histograms (FPFH) for 3D registration. In: ICRA (2009)
42. Tan, D.J., Navab, N., Tombari, F.: Looking beyond the simple scenarios: combining learners and optimizers in 3D temporal tracking. IEEE Trans. Vis. Comput. Graph. 1, 1 (2017)
43. Tateno, K., Tombari, F., Laina, I., Navab, N.: CNN-SLAM: real-time dense monocular slam with learned depth prediction. In: CVPR (2017)
44. Tejani, A., Tang, D., Kouskouridas, R., Kim, T.-K.: Latent-class hough forests for 3D object detection and pose estimation. In: Fleet, D., Pajdla, T., Schiele, B., Tuytelaars, T. (eds.) ECCV 2014. LNCS, vol. 8694, pp. 462–477. Springer, Cham (2014). https://doi.org/10.1007/978-3-319-10599-4_30
45. Tekin, B., Sinha, S.N., Fua, P.: Real-time seamless single shot 6D object pose prediction. In: CVPR (2018)
46. Tombari, F., Salti, S., Di Stefano, L.: Unique signatures of histograms for local surface description. In: Daniilidis, K., Maragos, P., Paragios, N. (eds.) ECCV 2010. LNCS, vol. 6313, pp. 356–369. Springer, Heidelberg (2010). https://doi.org/10.1007/978-3-642-15558-1_26
47. Vidal, J., Lin, C.Y., Martí, R.: 6D pose estimation using an improved method based on point pair features. In: ICCAR (2018)

48. Xiang, Y., Schmidt, T., Narayanan, V., Fox, D.: PoseCNN: a convolutional neural network for 6D object pose estimation in cluttered scenes. arXiv preprint arXiv:1711.00199 (2017)
49. Xiang, Y., Schmidt, T., Narayanan, V., Fox, D.: PoseCNN: a convolutional neural network for 6D object pose estimation in cluttered scenes. In: RSS (2018)
50. Wang, Y., Sun, Y., Liu, Z., Sarma, S.E., Bronstein, M.M., Solomon, J.M.: Dynamic graph CNN for learning on point clouds. arXiv preprint arXiv:1801.07829 (2018)
51. Zeng, A., et al.: Multi-view self-supervised deep learning for 6D pose estimation in the Amazon picking challenge. In: IEEE International Conference on Robotics and Automation (ICRA) (2017)
52. Zeng, A., Song, S., Nießner, M., Fisher, M., Xiao, J., Funkhouser, T.: 3DMatch: learning local geometric descriptors from RGB-D reconstructions. In: CVPR (2017)

Image-to-Voxel Model Translation
with Conditional Adversarial Networks

Vladimir A. Knyaz[1,2](✉) ⓘ, Vladimir V. Kniaz[1,2] ⓘ, and Fabio Remondino[3] ⓘ

[1] State Research Institute of Aviation Systems (GosNIIAS), Moscow, Russia
{knyaz,vl.kniaz}@gosniias.ru
[2] Moscow Institute of Physics and Technology (MIPT), Dolgoprudny, Russia
[3] 3D Optical Metrology (3DOM) unit, Bruno Kessler Foundation (FBK),
Trento, Italy
remondino@fbk.eu

Abstract. We present a single-view voxel model prediction method that uses generative adversarial networks. Our method utilizes correspondences between 2D silhouettes and slices of a camera frustum to predict a voxel model of a scene with multiple object instances. We exploit pyramid shaped voxel and a generator network with skip connections between 2D and 3D feature maps. We collected two datasets VoxelCity and VoxelHome to train our framework with 36,416 images of 28 scenes with ground-truth 3D models, depth maps, and 6D object poses. We made the datasets publicly available (http://www.zefirus.org/Z_GAN). We evaluate our framework on 3D shape datasets to show that it delivers robust 3D scene reconstruction results that compete with and surpass state-of-the-art in a scene reconstruction with multiple non-rigid objects.

Keywords: Conditional GAN · Voxel model · 6D pose estimation

1 Introduction

Does a voxel model with a shape $128 \times 128 \times 1$ provide any information about a 3D object? If the XY plane of the voxel model is normal to a camera optical axis, the voxel model is similar to the object's semantic segmentation.

Modern methods [27,34] demonstrate the state-of-art results on the task of semantic segmentation. Although deep networks trained for segmentation provide the resolution of an input color image, the resolution of a voxel model output produced by modern networks is lower than the resolution of an input image [26,53,58,59,61].

We hypothesize that a pixel correspondence between an input color image and slices of a voxel model can improve the quality of fine details in a voxel output. The necessary correspondences are found using three interconnected steps: (1) we provide an aligned voxel model for each color image, (2) we use

ⓒ Springer Nature Switzerland AG 2019
L. Leal-Taixé and S. Roth (Eds.): ECCV 2018 Workshops, LNCS 11129, pp. 601–618, 2019.
https://doi.org/10.1007/978-3-030-11009-3_37

 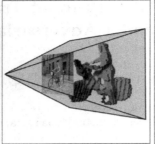 

Fig. 1. Results of our image-to-voxel translation based on generative adversarial network (GAN) and frustum voxel model. Input color image (left). Ground truth frustum voxel model slices colored as a depth map (middle). The voxel model output (right). (Color figure online)

slices of a camera's frustum to built the voxel space, (3) we use a generator network with skip connections [27,46] to feed high-resolution image features to 3D deconvolutional layers of a generator network (Fig. 1).

It is challenging to predict a voxel model from a single color image. The color-to-voxel model translation problem has received a lot of scholar attention in recent time [9,17,26,44,48,53,58,59,61]. The trained models have demonstrated state-of-the-art results on large datasets with 3D object annotations [33,60]. Main limitations of the existing models are a single object focused prediction and limited generalization ability.

A research project has recently been started by the authors. The project is focused on the development of a low-cost driver assistance system. We developed two new 3D shape datasets VoxelCity and VoxelHome to train our framework. The datasets include 36,416 images of 28 scenes with ground-truth 3D models, depth maps, and 6D object poses.

The results of the trained Z-GAN model are encouraging. We experimented with high-resolution voxel outputs of $128 \times 128 \times 128$ and were able to predict the shape of multiple objects accurately. We evaluated our Z-GAN model using the Pascal 3D+ [60] and the IKEA [33] datasets. The comparison with the state-of-the-art has demonstrated that the Z-GAN effectively outperforms modern models in the number of reconstructed objects, the generalization ability, and the resolution of the output voxel model. The Z-GAN model can be used in the 3D vision applications such as robot vision, 6D pose estimation, and 3D model reconstruction.

The rest of the paper is organized as follows. Section 2 outlines modern approaches to voxel model reconstruction. In Sect. 3 we describe the structure of our VoxelCity and VoxelHome datasets. In Sect. 4 the developed conditional Z-GAN model is presented. Section 5 presents the evaluation of baselines and the developed model.

1.1 Contributions

The key contributions of this paper are: (1) the conditional adversarial volumetric Z-GAN framework for the generation of a voxel model from a single-view color image, (2) VoxelCity and VoxelHome datasets with 36,416 color images, ground-truth voxel models, depth maps and camera orientations of 21 outdoor and 7 indoor scenes, (3) an evaluation of baselines and our framework on 3D shape datasets.

2 Related Work

Generative Adversarial Networks. Recently proposed Generative Adversarial Networks (GANs) [18] provide a mapping from a random noise vector to a domain of the desired outputs (e.g., images, voxel models). GANs are gaining increasing attention in recent years. They provide encouraging results in tasks like image-to-image translation [27] and voxel model generation [59].

Single-Photo 3D Model Reconstruction. Accurate 3D reconstruction is challenging if only a single color image is provided. This problem was always of great interest for the research community [12,42,43] and in the last years many new approaches were proposed based on the use of deep learning [9,17,26,44,48,53,58,59,61]. While a number of methods were proposed for prediction of unobserved voxels from a single depth map [15,51,62–64], prediction of the voxel model of a complex scene from a single color (RGB) image is more ambiguous. Prior knowledge of 3D shape is required for the robust performance of a single-image method. Hence, most of the methods split the problem into two steps: object recognition and a 3D shape reconstruction. In [17] a deep learning method for a single image voxel model reconstruction was proposed. The method leverages an auto-encoder architecture for a voxel model prediction. While the model has demonstrated promising results, the resolution of the voxel model was limited to $20 \times 20 \times 20$ elements. An approach that combines single-view and multi-view reconstruction modes was proposed in [9]. In [44] a new voxel decoder architecture was proposed that leverages voxel tube and shape layers to increase the resulting voxel model resolution. A comparison of surface-based and volumetric 3D model prediction is performed in [48].

3D shape synthesis from a latent space has received a lot of scholar attention recently [7,17,59]. Wu et al. have proposed a GAN model [59] for a voxel model generation (3D-GAN). The model was capable to predict voxel models with resolution $64 \times 64 \times 64$ from a randomly sampled noise vector. 3D-GAN was used for a single-image 3D reconstruction using an approach proposed in [17]. While 3D models produced by the 3D-GAN model provided more details compared to [17], the generalization ability of the approach was insufficient to predict voxel models of previously unseen 3D shapes.

3D Shape Datasets. Multiple 3D shape datasets were designed [8,33,52,60] for training deep models. Manual annotation was performed for the Pascal VOC dataset [14] to align a set of CAD models with color photos. The extended dataset was termed Pascal 3D+ [60]. While many models were trained using the Pascal 3D+ dataset, it provides a coarse correspondence between a 3D model and a photo. A large ShapeNet dataset [8] was collected to address the problems of shape recognition and generative modeling. However, training for single photo 3D model reconstruction is possible only with synthetic data. Hinterstoisser et al. have designed a large Linemod dataset [20] with aligned RGB-D data. The dataset is focused on object recognition in the indoor setting. The Linemod dataset was intensively used for training 6D pose estimation algorithms [2,3,5,6,10,22,23,32,35,40,50,55]. In [21] a large dataset for 6D pose estimation of texture-less objects was developed. An MVTec ITODD dataset [11] addresses the challenging problem of 6D pose prediction in industrial application.

The 6D pose estimation has received a lot of scholar attention recently [2,3,5, 6,10,22,23,29,31,32,35,40,50,55]. Accurate estimation of camera pose relative to an object is of primary importance in such fields as an autonomous driving [1,4,36,39] and Simultaneous Localization and Mapping (SLAM) [13,57]. However, most of the datasets contain 3D data as LIDAR range scans. As no complete 3D shapes are provided in the existing datasets, they require an additional annotation for single-photo 3D reconstruction.

3   Dataset

We collected two new datasets VoxelCity and VoxelHome to train our Z-GAN model. The primary motivation for the creation of new datasets was an absence of large 3D shape datasets with pixel-level 3D object annotations. Annotations provided in Pascal 3D+ dataset [60] present CAD models of abstract classes that do not provide real silhouettes of 3D objects.

We capture multi-view images of scenes to generate our datasets (Sects. 3.2 and 3.3), composed of images, depth maps, reconstructed 3D models and ground-truth 3D CAD models. We recover 6D camera poses for each image and textured 3D models using state-of-the-art SfM algorithms [30,38,41,54]. Then we manually annotated all objects in a scene to provide multi-object 6D poses. The SfM-based approach provides two benefits. Firstly, SfM models present real configuration of objects in a scene that provides a pixel-level correspondence between images and a 3D model (Fig. 2). Secondly, SfM provides a 6D camera pose for each image. We made the datasets compliant with the SIXD Challenge dataset format [24].

3.1   3D Model Generation Using SfM

The multi-view image-based 3D reconstruction pipeline, generally called Structure from Motion (SfM), based on the integration of photogrammetric and computer vision algorithms, has become in the last years a powerful and valuable

    (a)   (b)   (c)   (d)

Fig. 2. Comparison of an alignment of 3D models in the Pix3D (a) and our VoxelHome (b) datasets and in the Pascal 3D+ (c) and our VoxelCity (d) datasets. Please note that (a) and (c) do not provide perfect alignment of the contours.

approach for 3D modeling purposes. It generally ensures sufficient automation, low cost, efficient results and ease of use, even for non-expert users. SfM now successfully reconstructs scenes containing hundred thousands or even millions of images [19,47]. Available online reconstruction services decoupled the user from a powerful hardware that carried out the reconstructions, only requiring to upload the images on a Cloud server [54]. Recently, online SfM methods demonstrated that it is possible to add new images to existing 3D reconstructions and build an incremental surface model [25,38]. We manually created 3D CAD models using the coarse 3D models reconstructed using SfM as a baseline. We use the CAD models to generate the voxel models for network training.

3.2   VoxelCity

Our VoxelCity dataset includes 3D models of 21 scenes, composed of 18,836 color images with reconstructed 3D models, ground-truth 3D CAD models, depth maps and 6D poses of seven object classes: human, car, bicycle, truck, van. Examples of 3D scenes and object pose annotations for various object classes are presented in Fig. 3. Comparison to previous 3D shape datasets regarding outdoor scenes is presented in Table 1.

Table 1. Comparison to previous outdoor 3D shape dataset. The type of data provided is listed: dense (D), coarse (C).

Dataset	#scene	#image	#class	#3D model	6D pose	P. cloud	Depth
KITTI [16]	×	15,001	3	×	✓	×	×
Pascal 3D+ [60]	×	30,364	12	77	✓	C	C
CL [28]	6	12,000	×	×	✓	D	×
VoxelCity	21	18,836	7	38	✓	D	D

Fig. 3. Examples of color images with 6D pose annotations and ground truth dense point clouds from our VoxelCity dataset. (Color figure online)

3.3   VoxelHome

Our VoxelHome dataset presents 3D models of 7 indoor scenes, composed of 17,580 color images with reconstructed 3D models, ground-truth 3D CAD models, depth maps and 6D poses of nine object classes: chair, table, armchair, sofa, stool, cupboard, vase, washing machine, oven. Examples of 3D models and object pose annotations for various object classes are presented in Fig. 4. We present comparison to previous datasets regarding indoor scenes in Table 2.

Table 2. Comparison to previous outdoor 3D shape dataset. The type of data provided is listed: dense (D), coarse (C).

Dataset	#scene	#image	#class	#3D model	6D pose	P. cloud	Depth
IKEA [33]	×	759	7	219	✓	×	×
Linemod [20]	1	18,241	15	15	✓	×	×
T-LESS [21]	20	$3 \times 49,000$	26	30	✓	D	D
7 scenes [49]	7	43,000	×	×	✓	D	D
12 scenes [56]	12	246,673	×	×	✓	C	C
VoxelHome	7	17,580	9	64	✓	D	D

4   Method

The aim of the present research is to apply conditional generative adversarial network to the color image-to-voxel model translation task. The straightforward

Fig. 4. Examples of color images with 6D pose annotations and ground truth dense point clouds from our VoxelHome dataset.

approach is to change the network output from an image to a voxel model. However, the convergence of the training process is poor for such setting. We hypothesize that the performance can be improved if the voxel model will be aligned with the input image.

A depth map is an example of an aligned 3D representation of the color image. While the depth map provides the 3D shape only for the visible surface of objects, the voxel model encodes the complete 3D model of the scene. We use assumptions made by [58] as the starting point for our 3D model representation. To provide the aligned voxel model, we combine depth map representation with a voxel grid. We term the resulting 3D model as a Frustum Voxel model (Fruxel model).

4.1 Frustum Voxel Model

The main idea of the fruxel model is to provide precise alignment of voxel slices with contours of a color image. Such alignment can be achieved with a common voxel model if the camera has an orthographic projection and its optical axis coincides with the Z-axis of the voxel model (see Fig. 5, left). We generalize such alignment to the perspective projection. As the camera frustum is no longer corresponding to the cube voxel elements, we use sections of a pyramid.

Fruxel model representation provides multiple advantages. Firstly, each XY slice of the model is aligned with some contours on a corresponding color photo (some parts of them can be invisible). Secondly, a fruxel model encodes a shape of both visible and invisible surfaces. Hence, unlike the depth map, it contains complete information about the 3D shapes. In other words, the fruxel model is similar to theatre scenery composed of flat screens with drawings of objects that imitate perspective space. Please note, that while fruxel elements have different dimensions in object space, all slices of the fruxel model have the same number of fruxel elements (e.g., $128 \times 128 \times 1$).

A fruxel model is characterized by a following set of parameters: $\{z_n, z_f, d, \alpha\}$, where z_n is a distance to a near clipping plane, z_f is a distance to a far clipping plane, d is the number of frustum slices, α is a field of view of a camera.

While fruxel model provides contour correspondence with a color image, its interpretation by a human may be complicated. We consider fruxel models as a

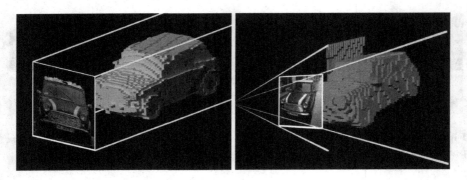

Fig. 5. Comparison between voxel model (left) and the proposed frustum voxel model (right) with shape $64 \times 64 \times 64$ fruxel elements.

special representation of a voxel model optimized for the training of conditional adversarial networks. Nevertheless, a fruxel model can be converted into three common data types: (1) voxel model, (2) depth map, (3) object annotation.

A voxel model can be produced from the fruxel model by scaling each consequent layer slice by the coefficient k defined as follows:

$$k = \frac{z_n}{z_n + s_z}, \tag{1}$$

where $s_z = \frac{z_f - z_n}{d}$ is the size of the fruxel element along the Z-axis.

To generate a depth map P from the fruxel model, we multiply indices of the frontmost non-empty elements by the step s_z.

$$P(x, y) = \text{argmax}_i[F_i(x, y) = 1] \cdot s_z \tag{2}$$

where $P(x, y)$ is an element of a depth map, $F_i(x, y)$ vector of elements in a fruxel model at slice i.

An object annotation is equal to a product of all elements with given x, y coordinates

$$A(x, y) = \prod_{i=0}^{d} F(x, y, i) \tag{3}$$

We use boolean operations to generate the fruxel model from a 3D scene. Firstly, we set the desired position of a virtual camera. After that, we find a boolean intersection between the 3D scene and XY slices of the frustum space. We render each intersection using white emission shader. We combine all slices in a single 3D array with dimensions $w \times h \times d$, where w is the width, h is the height of the color image, d is the number of slices. We term the resulting 3D array as a fruxel model. We generate fruxel models for real photos using 3D models generated with the structure-from-motion (SfM) algorithm. The SfM approach provides an estimation of camera poses with respect to the reconstructed 3D model. We place the virtual camera in the estimated pose and render the slices of the reconstructed model.

4.2 Conditional Adversarial Networks

Generative Adversarial Networks (GAN) generate a signal $\hat{B}$ for a given random noise vector z, $G : z \rightarrow \hat{B}$ [18,27]. Conditional GAN transforms an input image A and the vector z to an output $\hat{B}$, $G : \{A, z\} \rightarrow \hat{B}$. The input A can be an image that is transformed by the generator network G. The discriminator network D is trained to distinguish "real" signals from target domain B from the "fakes" $\hat{B}$ produced by the generator. Both networks are trained simultaneously. Discriminator provides the adversarial loss that enforces the generator to produce "fakes" $\hat{B}$ that cannot be distinguished from "real" signal B.

We train a generator $G : \{A\} \rightarrow \hat{B}$ to synthesize a fruxel model $\hat{B} \in \mathbb{R}^{w \times h \times d}$ conditioned by a color image $A \in \mathbb{R}^{w \times h \times 3}$.

4.3 Z-GAN Framework

We use pix2pix [27] framework as a starting point to develop our Z-GAN model. We keep the encoder part of the generator unchanged. We change 2D convolution kernels with 3D deconvolution kernels to encode a correlation between neighbor slices along the Z-axis.

We keep the skip connections between the layers of the same depth that was proposed in the U-net model [46]. We believe that skip connections help to transfer high-frequency components of the input image to the high-frequency components of the 3D shape. The resulting architecture of our Z-GAN model is presented in Fig. 6.

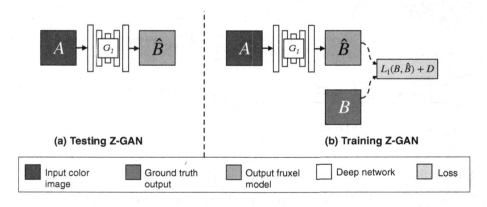

(a) Testing Z-GAN   (b) Training Z-GAN

| | Input color image | | Ground truth output | | Output fruxel model | | Deep network | | Loss |

Fig. 6. Z-GAN framework.

4.4 Volumetric Generator

The main idea of our volumetric generator G is to use the correspondence between silhouettes in a color image and slices of a fruxel model. We used the U-Net generator [46] as a starting point to develop our model. The original U-Net generator leverages skip connections between convolutional and deconvolutional layers of the same depth to transfer fine details from the source to the target domain effectively.

We added two contributions to the original U-Net model. Firstly, we replaced the 2D deconvolutional filters with 3D deconvolutional filters. Secondly, we modified the skip connections to provide the correspondence between shapes of 2D and 3D features. The outputs of 2D convolutional filters in the left (encoder) side of Z-Net generator are $F_{2D} \in \mathbb{R}^{w \times h \times c}$ tensors, where w, h is the width and the height of a feature map and c is the number of channels. The output of 3D deconvolutional filters in the right (decoder) side are $F_{3D} \in \mathbb{R}^{w \times h \times d \times c}$ tensors. We use d copies of each channel of F_{2D} to fill the third dimension of F_{3D}. We term this operation as "copy inflate". The architecture of the generator is presented in Fig. 7.

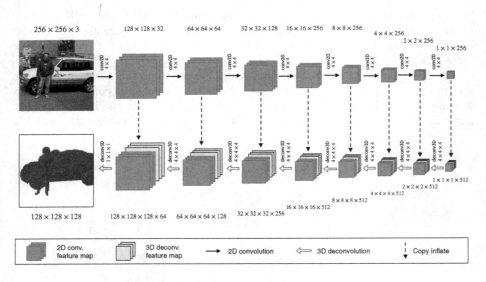

Fig. 7. The architecture of the generator.

4.5 Volumetric Discriminator

We modify the PatchGAN discriminator [27] to process the 3D slices efficiently. The original PatchGAN discriminator is based on the assumption of the markovian independence of the local image patches. Therefore the discriminator penalizes the image structure only at the scale of local patches.

The PatchGAN discriminator consists of a stack of convolutional layers with a constant kernel size. The stride of each layer is balanced with a kernel size in such way that the layer output size remains corresponding to the size of the input image. In other words, each convolutional layer takes the input with the size equal to the size of the input color image and produces a feature map. The sequential application of the convolutions with constant kernel size increases the "aperture" of the discriminator. For example, sequential application of seven convolutional layers results in the feature "aperture" of 140 pixels.

Our Z-Patch discriminator has a similar structure to the PatchGAN discriminator [27]. We replaced all 2D convolutional layers with 3D convolutional layers to process 3D shapes.

5   Evaluation

We evaluate baseline models and our Z-GAN framework on a task of generation of a voxel model from a single-view color image. We use two 3D shape datasets for the evaluation: Pascal 3D+ [60] and Pix3D [52]. All datasets include real images with 6D object poses.

We use two metrics to provide a quantitative evaluation of 3D object reconstruction quality: (*i*) an Intersection over Union (IoU) metric to measure a difference between a ground-truth 3D model and an output of a method and (*ii*) a surface distance metric similar to [45] to evaluate an accuracy of camera pose estimation for the 3D-R2N2 and our Z-GAN models. We also provide images of resulting voxel models for qualitative evaluation.

5.1   Baselines

We compare our model with three baselines: 3D-R2N2 [9,48], TL-network [17], and MarrNet [58]. To the best of our knowledge, there are no baselines to date capable of predicting voxel models of multiple objects from a single image. TL-network and MarrNet perform object-centered [48] prediction of voxel models with resolutions of $20 \times 20 \times 20$ and $128 \times 128 \times 128$. 3D-R2N2 provides a view-centered prediction with resolution $32 \times 32 \times 32$. Our Z-GAN model predicts a view-centered fruxel model with resolution $128 \times 128 \times 128$.

5.2   Training Details

Our Z-GAN framework was trained on the VoxelCity and VoxelHome datasets using PyTorch library [37]. We use VoxelCity dataset for the evaluation on Pascal 3D+ with fruxel model parameters $\{z_n = 2, z_f = 12, d = 128, \alpha = 40°\}$. For the evaluation on Pix3D dataset, we train our model on the VoxelHome dataset with fruxel model parameters $\{z_n = 0.5, z_f = 5.5, d = 128, \alpha = 40°\}$. The training was performed using the NVIDIA 1080 Ti GPU and took 11 h for G, D. For network optimization, we use minibatch SGD with an Adam solver. We set the learning rate to 0.0002 with momentum parameters $\beta_1 = 0.5$, $\beta_2 = 0.999$ similar to [27].

5.3 3D Reconstruction on Pascal 3D+

Qualitative Evaluation. We show results of single-view voxel model generation in Fig. 8. We use three object classes: car, bicycle, human. We selected 2,762 images from Pascal 3D+ image sets with a field of view similar to our trained model. We manually annotated the images with human 3D models from the ShapeNet dataset [8]. The qualitative evaluation demonstrates that models predicted by TL-network and MarrNet models have limited resolution and do not demonstrate new details compared to ground-truth models from the training set. While 3D-R2N2 shows more diversity in the output, it is capable of predicting only a single object in a scene. Our Z-GAN model produces voxel models of the whole scene with multiple object instances.

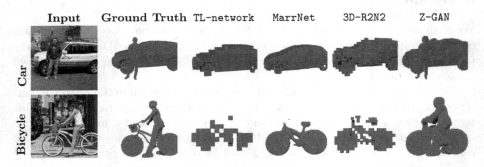

Fig. 8. An example of 3D reconstruction using TL-network,MarrNet,3D-R2N2 and Z-GAN on Pascal 3D+ [60] dataset and considering three object classes: car, bicycle, human.

Quantitative Evaluation. We evaluate the results of the proposed Z-GAN method in terms of IoU and surface distance in Tables 3 and 4.

Table 3. Intersection over union metric for different object classes for Pascal 3D+ images.

Method	Object class		
	Car	Bicycle	Mean
TL-network [17]	0.301	0.117	0.209
MarrNet [58]	0.321	0.156	0.239
3D-R2N2 [48]	0.582	0.212	0.397
Z-GAN	**0.612**	**0.398**	**0.505**

Table 4. Surface distance metric [45] for different object classes for Pascal 3D+ images.

Method	Object class		
	Car	Bicycle	Mean
3D-R2N2 [48]	0.151	0.701	0.426
Z-GAN	**0.091**	**0.356**	**0.224**

5.4 3D Reconstruction on Pix3D

Qualitative Evaluation. Evaluation results of single-view voxel model generation are presented in Fig. 9. We use two object classes: chair and table. We selected 1,512 images from Pix3D image sets with a field of view similar to our model trained on VoxelHome dataset. We made the following conclusions from the qualitative evaluation. Firstly, TL-network predicts the object as the voxel model from the training set. While MarrNet tries to imitate the shape of the object in the input, it is confused on images with multiple objects. 3D-R2N2 reconstructs view-centered object voxel model but the resolution of the model is not enough to show details of multiple objects. Results of our Z-GAN model demonstrate fine object details and correct poses of multiple objects.

Input   Ground Truth TL-network   MarrNet   3D-R2N2   Z-GAN

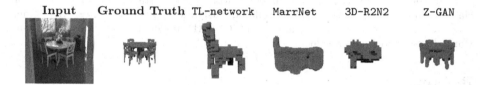

Fig. 9. Example of 3D reconstructions using the Pix3D dataset.

Quantitative Evaluation. We evaluate the results of the proposed Z-GAN method in terms of IoU and surface distance in Tables 5 and 6.

Table 5. Intersection over union metric for different object classes for Pix3D images.

Method	Object class		
	Chair	Table	Mean
TL-network [17]	0.190	0.211	0.201
MarrNet [58]	0.241	0.376	0.309
3D-R2N2 [48]	0.289	0.251	0.270
Z-GAN	**0.461**	**0.612**	**0.536**

Table 6. Surface distance metric [45] for different object classes for Pix3D images.

Method	Object class		
	Chair	Table	Mean
3D-R2N2 [48]	0.201	0.691	0.446
Z-GAN	**0.121**	**0.467**	**0.294**

6 Conclusions

The paper presented a new approach based on conditional generative adversarial networks capable of prediction of a voxel model from a single image. We showed that conditional adversarial volumetric networks can generate voxel models of complex scenes with multiple objects. We demonstrated that skip connections between 2D convolutional and 3D deconvolutional layers facilitate reconstruction of fine details. Furthermore, models utilizing skip connections require less training parameters for high-quality reconstruction of cluttered scenes with multiple 3D shapes of different classes.

We developed a new Z-GAN framework for translation of a single color image to a voxel model of a scene. We collected two datasets VoxelCity and VoxelHome to train our model. Datasets include fine-grade scene models, color images, depth maps and 6D object poses. We evaluated baselines and our model on multiple 3D shape datasets to show that it achieves and surpasses the state-of-the-art in terms of the number of reconstructed objects and their details.

Acknowledgments. The reported study was funded by Russian Foundation for Basic Research (RFBR) according to the research project N° 17-29-04509 and the Russian Science Foundation (RSF) according to the research project N° 16-11-00082.

We would like to thank the volunteers, who acted as statues for 3D models for class "human": Zoya Kniaz, Lena Metelkina, Nastya Metelkina, and Anya Metelkina. Also we would like to thank the authors of 3D CAD models for the dataset: Artyom Bordodymov and Pyotr Moshkantsev.

References

1. Alhaija, H.A., Mustikovela, S.K., Mescheder, L., Geiger, A., Rother, C.: Augmented reality meets computer vision: efficient data generation for urban driving scenes. Int. J. Comput. Vis. (2018). https://doi.org/10.1007/s11263-018-1070-x
2. Balntas, V., Doumanoglou, A., Sahin, C., Sock, J., Kouskouridas, R., Kim, T.: Pose guided RGBD feature learning for 3D object pose estimation. In: 2017 IEEE International Conference on Computer Vision, ICCV 2017, Venice, Italy, 22–29 October, pp. 3876–3884 (2017). https://doi.org/10.1109/ICCV.2017.416
3. Balntas, V., Doumanoglou, A., Sahin, C., Sock, J., Kouskouridas, R., Kim, T.K.: Pose guided RGBD feature learning for 3D object pose estimation. In: The IEEE International Conference on Computer Vision (ICCV), October 2017
4. Behl, A., Hosseini Jafari, O., Karthik Mustikovela, S., Abu Alhaija, H., Rother, C., Geiger, A.: Bounding boxes, segmentations and object coordinates: how important is recognition for 3D scene flow estimation in autonomous driving scenarios? In: The IEEE International Conference on Computer Vision (ICCV), October 2017
5. Brachmann, E., et al.: DSAC - differentiable RANSAC for camera localization. In: The IEEE Conference on Computer Vision and Pattern Recognition (CVPR), July 2017
6. Brachmann, E., Rother, C.: Learning less is more - 6D camera localization via 3D surface regression. In: The IEEE Conference on Computer Vision and Pattern Recognition (CVPR), June 2018
7. Brock, A., Lim, T., Ritchie, J., Weston, N.: Generative and discriminative voxel modeling with convolutional neural networks. pp. 1–9 December 2016. https://nips.cc/Conferences/2016. workshop contribution; Neural Inofrmation Processing Conference : 3D Deep Learning, NIPS; Conference date: 05–12-2016 Through 10–12-2016
8. Chang, A.X., et al.: ShapeNet: an information-rich 3D model repository. CoRR abs/1512.03012 (2015)

9. Choy, C.B., Xu, D., Gwak, J., Chen, K., Savarese, S.: 3D-R2N2: a unified approach for single and multi-view 3D object reconstruction. In: Proceedings of the European Conference on Computer Vision (ECCV) (2016)

10. Doumanoglou, A., Kouskouridas, R., Malassiotis, S., Kim, T.: Recovering 6D object pose and predicting next-best-view in the crowd. In: 2016 IEEE Conference on Computer Vision and Pattern Recognition, CVPR 2016, Las Vegas, NV, USA, 27–30 June 2016, pp. 3583–3592 (2016). https://doi.org/10.1109/CVPR.2016.390

11. Drost, B., Ulrich, M., Bergmann, P., Hartinger, P., Steger, C.: Introducing MVTec ITODD - a dataset for 3D object recognition in industry. In: The IEEE International Conference on Computer Vision (ICCV) Workshops, October 2017

12. El-Hakim, S.: A flexible approach to 3D reconstruction from single images. In: ACM SIGGRAPH, vol. 1, pp. 12–17 (2001)

13. Engel, J., Stueckler, J., Cremers, D.: Large-scale direct slam with stereo cameras (2015)

14. Everingham, M., Van Gool, L., Williams, C.K.I., Winn, J., Zisserman, A.: The pascal visual object classes (VOC) challenge. Int. J. Comput. Vis. **88**(2), 303–338 (2009)

15. Firman, M., Mac Aodha, O., Julier, S., Brostow, G.J.: Structured prediction of unobserved voxels from a single depth image. In: The IEEE Conference on Computer Vision and Pattern Recognition (CVPR), June 2016

16. Geiger, A., Lenz, P., Stiller, C., Urtasun, R.: Vision meets robotics: the KITTI dataset. Int. J. Robot. Res. (IJRR) **32**(11), 1231–1237 (2013)

17. Girdhar, R., Fouhey, D.F., Rodriguez, M., Gupta, A.: Learning a predictable and generative vector representation for objects. In: Leibe, B., Matas, J., Sebe, N., Welling, M. (eds.) ECCV 2016. LNCS, vol. 9910, pp. 484–499. Springer, Cham (2016). https://doi.org/10.1007/978-3-319-46466-4_29

18. Goodfellow, I., et al.: Generative adversarial nets. In: Advances in Neural Information Processing Systems, pp. 2672–2680 (2014)

19. Heinly, J., Schonberger, J.L., Dunn, E., Frahm, J.M.: Reconstructing the world* in six days *(as captured by the Yahoo 100 million image dataset). In: The IEEE Conference on Computer Vision and Pattern Recognition (CVPR), June 2015

20. Hinterstoisser, S., et al.: Model based training, detection and pose estimation of texture-less 3D objects in heavily cluttered scenes. In: Lee, K.M., Matsushita, Y., Rehg, J.M., Hu, Z. (eds.) ACCV 2012. LNCS, vol. 7724, pp. 548–562. Springer, Heidelberg (2013). https://doi.org/10.1007/978-3-642-37331-2_42

21. Hodaň, T., Haluza, P., Obdržálek, Š., Matas, J., Lourakis, M., Zabulis, X.: T-LESS: an RGB-D dataset for 6D pose estimation of texture-less objects. In: IEEE Winter Conference on Applications of Computer Vision (WACV) (2017)

22. Hodan, T., Haluza, P., Obdrzálek, S., Matas, J., Lourakis, M.I.A., Zabulis, X.: T-LESS: an RGB-D dataset for 6D pose estimation of texture-less objects. In: 2017 IEEE Winter Conference on Applications of Computer Vision WACV 2017, Santa Rosa, CA, USA, 24–31 March 2017, pp. 880–888 (2017). https://doi.org/10.1109/WACV.2017.103

23. Hodaň, T., Matas, J., Obdržálek, Š.: On evaluation of 6D object pose estimation. In: Hua, G., Jégou, H. (eds.) ECCV 2016. LNCS, vol. 9915, pp. 606–619. Springer, Cham (2016). https://doi.org/10.1007/978-3-319-49409-8_52

24. Hodaň, T., Michel, F., Sahin, C., Kim, T.K., Matas, J., Rother, C.: SIXD Challenge 2017. http://cmp.felk.cvut.cz/sixd/challenge_2017/. Accessed 01 July 2018

25. Hoppe, C., Klopschitz, M., Donoser, M., Bischof, H.: Incremental surface extraction from sparse structure-from-motion point clouds. In: Proceedings of the British Machine Vision Conference 2013, pp. 94:1–94:11, British Machine Vision Association (2013)
26. Huang, Q., Wang, H., Koltun, V.: Single-view reconstruction via joint analysis of image and shape collections. ACM Trans. Graph. **34**(4), 87:1–87:10 (2015)
27. Isola, P., Zhu, J.Y., Zhou, T., Efros, A.A.: Image-to-image translation with conditional adversarial networks. In: 2017 IEEE Conference on Computer Vision and Pattern Recognition (CVPR), pp. 5967–5976. IEEE (2017)
28. Kendall, A., Grimes, M., Cipolla, R.: PoseNet: a convolutional network for real-time 6-DOF camera relocalization. In: Proceedings of the IEEE International Conference on Computer Vision, University of Cambridge, Cambridge, United Kingdom, pp. 2938–2946. IEEE, February 2015
29. Kniaz, V.V.: Robust vision-based pose estimation algorithm for an UAV with known gravity vector. ISPRS-Int. Arch. Photogram. Remote Sens. Spat. Inf. Sci. **XLI-B5**, 63–68 (2016). https://doi.org/10.5194/isprs-archives-XLI-B5-63-2016
30. Knyaz, V., Zheltov, S.: Accuracy evaluation of structure from motion surface 3D reconstruction. In: Proceedings of SPIE, vol. 10332, pp. 10332-1–10332-10 (2017). https://doi.org/10.1117/12.2272021
31. Knyaz, V.A., et al.: Deep learning of convolutional auto-encoder for image matching and 3d object reconstruction in the infrared range. In: The IEEE International Conference on Computer Vision (ICCV) Workshops, pp. 2155–2164 (2017). https://doi.org/10.1109/ICCVW.2017.252
32. Krull, A., Brachmann, E., Nowozin, S., Michel, F., Shotton, J., Rother, C.: PoseAgent: budget-constrained 6d object pose estimation via reinforcement learning. In: The IEEE Conference on Computer Vision and Pattern Recognition (CVPR), July 2017
33. Lim, J.J., Pirsiavash, H., Torralba, A.: Parsing IKEA objects: fine pose estimation. In: ICCV (2013)
34. Long, J., Shelhamer, E., Darrell, T.: Fully convolutional networks for semantic segmentation. In: 2015 IEEE Conference on Computer Vision and Pattern Recognition (CVPR), pp. 3431–3440. IEEE (2015)
35. Ma, M., Marturi, N., Li, Y., Leonardis, A., Stolkin, R.: Region-sequence based six-stream CNN features for general and fine-grained human action recognition in videos. Pattern Recogn. **76**(11), 506–521 (2017)
36. Menze, M., Geiger, A.: Object scene flow for autonomous vehicles. In: CVPR, pp. 3061–3070 (2015)
37. Paszke, A., et al.: Automatic differentiation in pyTorch (2017)
38. Poiesi, F., Locher, A., Chippendale, P., Nocerino, E., Remondino, F., Van Gool, L.: Cloud-based collaborative 3D reconstruction using smartphones. In: the 14th ACM European Conference on Visual Media Production (CVMP), pp. 1–9. ACM Press, New York (2017)
39. Qi, C.R., Liu, W., Wu, C., Su, H., Guibas, L.J.: Frustum pointNets for 3D object detection from RGB-D data. arXiv preprint arXiv:1711.08488 (2017)
40. Rad, M., Lepetit, V.: BB8: a scalable, accurate, robust to partial occlusion method for predicting the 3D poses of challenging objects without using depth. In: IEEE International Conference on Computer Vision, ICCV 2017, Venice, Italy, 22–29 October 2017, pp. 3848–3856 (2017). https://doi.org/10.1109/ICCV.2017.413

41. Remondino, F., Nocerino, E., Toschi, I., Menna, F.: A critical review of automated photogrammetric processing of large datasets. ISPRS - Int. Arch. Photogram. Remote Sens. Spat. Inf. Sci. **42**, 591–599 (2017). XLII-2/W5. https://doi.org/10.5194/isprs-archives-XLII-2-W5-591-2017

42. Remondino, F., Roditakis, A.: Human figure reconstruction and modeling from single image or monocular video sequence. In: 2003 Fourth International Conference on 3-D Digital Imaging and Modeling, 3DIM 2003, pp. 116–123. IEEE October 2003

43. Remondino, F., El-Hakim, S.: Image-based 3D modelling: a review. Photogram. Rec. **21**(115), 269–291 (2006)

44. Richter, S.R., Roth, S.: Matryoshka networks: predicting 3D geometry via nested shape layers. arXiv.org, April 2018

45. Rock, J., Gupta, T., Thorsen, J., Gwak, J., Shin, D., Hoiem, D.: Completing 3D object shape from one depth image. In: 2013 IEEE Conference on Computer Vision and Pattern Recognition, pp. 2484–2493. University of Illinois at Urbana-Champaign, Urbana, IEEE, October 2015

46. Ronneberger, O., Fischer, P., Brox, T.: U-Net: convolutional networks for biomedical image segmentation. In: Navab, N., Hornegger, J., Wells, W.M., Frangi, A.F. (eds.) MICCAI 2015. LNCS, vol. 9351, pp. 234–241. Springer, Cham (2015). https://doi.org/10.1007/978-3-319-24574-4_28

47. Schonberger, J.L., Frahm, J.M.: Structure-from-motion revisited. In: The IEEE Conference on Computer Vision and Pattern Recognition (CVPR), June 2016

48. Shin, D., Fowlkes, C., Hoiem, D.: Pixels, voxels, and views: a study of shape representations for single view 3D object shape prediction. In: IEEE Conference on Computer Vision and Pattern Recognition (CVPR) (2018)

49. Shotton, J., Glocker, B., Zach, C., Izadi, S., Criminisi, A., Fitzgibbon, A.: Scene coordinate regression forests for camera relocalization in RGB-D images. In: Proceedings of the 2013 IEEE Conference on Computer Vision and Pattern Recognition, CVPR 2013, pp. 2930–2937. IEEE Computer Society, Washington (2013). https://doi.org/10.1109/CVPR.2013.377

50. Sock, J., Kim, K.I., Sahin, C., Kim, T.K.: Multi-task deep networks for depth-based 6D object pose and joint registration in crowd scenarios. arXiv.org, June 2018

51. Song, S., Yu, F., Zeng, A., Chang, A.X., Savva, M., Funkhouser, T.: Semantic scene completion from a single depth image. In: The IEEE Conference on Computer Vision and Pattern Recognition (CVPR), July 2017

52. Sun, X., et al.: Pix3D: dataset and methods for single-image 3D shape modeling. In: IEEE Conference on Computer Vision and Pattern Recognition (CVPR) (2018)

53. Tatarchenko, M., Dosovitskiy, A., Brox, T.: Multi-view 3D models from single images with a convolutional network. arXiv.org, November 2015

54. Tefera, Y., Poiesi, F., Morabito, D., Remondino, F., Nocerino, E., Chippendale, P.: 3DNOW: image-based 3D reconstruction and modeling via web. ISPRS - Int. Arch. Photogram. Remote Sens. Spat. Inf. Sci. 1097–1103 (2018). XLII-2. https://doi.org/10.5194/isprs-archives-XLII-2-1097-2018

55. Tejani, A., Kouskouridas, R., Doumanoglou, A., Tang, D., Kim, T.: Latent-class hough forests for 6 DoF object pose estimation. IEEE Trans. Pattern Anal. Mach. Intell. **40**(1), 119–132 (2018). https://doi.org/10.1109/TPAMI.2017.2665623

56. Valentin, J., et al.: Learning to navigate the energy landscape. In: Proceedings - 2016 4th International Conference on 3D Vision, 3DV 2016, University of Oxford, Oxford, United Kingdom, pp. 323–332. IEEE, December 2016

57. Walas, K., Nowicki, M., Ferstl, D., Skrzypczynski, P.: Depth data fusion for simultaneous localization and mapping - RGB-DD SLAM. In: 2016 IEEE International Conference on Multisensor Fusion and Integration for Intelligent Systems, MFI 2016, Baden-Baden, Germany, 19–21 September 2016, pp. 9–14 (2016). https:// doi.org/10.1109/MFI.2016.7849459
58. Wu, J., Wang, Y., Xue, T., Sun, X., Freeman, W.T., Tenenbaum, J.B.: MarrNet: 3D shape reconstruction via 2.5D sketches. arXiv.org November 2017
59. Wu, J., Zhang, C., Xue, T., Freeman, B., Tenenbaum, J.: Learning a probabilistic latent space of object shapes via 3D generative-adversarial modeling, pp. 82–90 (2016)
60. Xiang, Y., Mottaghi, R., Savarese, S.: Beyond PASCAL: a benchmark for 3D object detection in the wild. In: IEEE Winter Conference on Applications of Computer Vision (WACV) (2014)
61. Yan, X., Yang, J., Yumer, E., Guo, Y., Lee, H.: Perspective transformer nets: Learning single-view 3D object reconstruction without 3D supervision (2016). papers.nips.cc
62. Yang, B., Rosa, S., Markham, A., Trigoni, N., Wen, H.: 3D object dense reconstruction from a single depth view. arXiv preprint arXiv:1802.00411 (2018)
63. Yang, B., Wen, H., Wang, S., Clark, R., Markham, A., Trigoni, N.: 3D object reconstruction from a single depth view with adversarial learning. In: The IEEE International Conference on Computer Vision (ICCV) Workshops, October 2017
64. Zheng, B., Zhao, Y., Yu, J.C., Ikeuchi, K., Zhu, S.C.: Beyond point clouds: scene understanding by reasoning geometry and physics. In: The IEEE Conference on Computer Vision and Pattern Recognition (CVPR), June 2013

3D Pose Estimation for Fine-Grained Object Categories

Yaming Wang[1]([✉]), Xiao Tan[2], Yi Yang[2], Xiao Liu[2], Errui Ding[2], Feng Zhou[2], and Larry S. Davis[1]

[1] University of Maryland, College Park, MD 20742, USA
{wym,lsd}@umiacs.umd.edu
[2] Baidu, Inc., Beijing, China
{tanxiao01,yangyi05,liuxiao12,dingerrui,zhoufeng09}@baidu.com

Abstract. Existing object pose estimation datasets are related to generic object types and there is so far no dataset for fine-grained object categories. In this work, we introduce a new large dataset to benchmark pose estimation for fine-grained objects, thanks to the availability of both 2D and 3D fine-grained data recently. Specifically, we augment two popular fine-grained recognition datasets (StanfordCars and CompCars) by finding a fine-grained 3D CAD model for each sub-category and manually annotating each object in images with 3D pose. We show that, with enough training data, a full perspective model with continuous parameters can be estimated using 2D appearance information alone. We achieve this via a framework based on Faster/Mask R-CNN. This goes beyond previous works on category-level pose estimation, which only estimate discrete/continuous viewpoint angles or recover rotation matrices often with the help of key points. Furthermore, with fine-grained 3D models available, we incorporate a dense 3D representation named as *location field* into the CNN-based pose estimation framework to further improve the performance. The new dataset is available at www.umiacs.umd.edu/~wym/3dpose.html.

1 Introduction

In the past few years, the fast-pacing progress of generic image recognition on ImageNet [11] has drawn increasing attention of research in classifying fine-grained object categories [9,26], *e.g.* bird species [27], car makes and models [10]. However, simply recognizing object labels is still far from solving many industrial problems where we need to have a deeper understanding of other attributes of the object [12]. In this work, we study the problem of estimating 3D pose for fine-grained objects from monocular images. We believe this will become an indispensable component in some broader tasks. For example, to build a vision-based car damage assessment system, an important step is to estimate the exact pose of the car so that the damaged part can be well aligned for further detailed analysis.

© Springer Nature Switzerland AG 2019
L. Leal-Taixé and S. Roth (Eds.): ECCV 2018 Workshops, LNCS 11129, pp. 619–632, 2019.
https://doi.org/10.1007/978-3-030-11009-3_38

Fine-Grained 2D Image   Fine-Grained 3D Model   Pose

Fig. 1. For an image from a fine-grained category (Left), we find its corresponding fine-grained 3D model (Middle) and annotate its pose (Right). The problem is to estimate the pose such that the projection of the 3D model align with the image as well as possible.

To address this task, collecting suitable data is of vital importance. However, large-scale as they are, recent category-level pose estimation datasets are typically designed for generic object types [29,30] and there is so far no large-scale pose dataset for fine-grained object categories. Although datasets on generic object types could contain decent information for pose, they lack of fine-detailed matching of object shapes during annotation, since they usually use only a few universal 3D object models to match a group of objects with different shapes in one hyper class [30]. In this work, we introduce a new dataset that is able to benchmark pose estimation for fine-grained objects. Specifically, we augment two existing fine-grained recognition datasets, StanfordCars [10] and CompCars [32], with two types of useful 3D information: (i) for each car in the image, we manually annotate the pose parameters for a full perspective projection; (ii) we provide an accurate match of the computer aided design (CAD) model for each category. The resulting augmented dataset consists of more than 20,000 images for over 300 fine-grained categories.

To our best knowledge, this is the first work for fine-grained object pose estimation. Given the built dataset with high-quality pose annotations, we show that the pose parameters can be predicted from a single 2D image with only appearance information. Compared to most previous works [17,25,33], our method does not require the intermediate prediction of 2D/3D key points. In addition, we assume a full perspective model, which is a more challenging setting than previous works of estimating discrete/continuous viewpoint angles (azimuth) [4] or recovering the rotation matrices only [14]. Our expected goal is that by projecting the fine-grained 3D model according to the regressed pose estimation, the projection can align well with the object in the 2D image. To tackle this problem, we integrate pose estimation into the Faster/Mask R-CNN framework [7,19] by sharing information between the detection and pose estimation branches. However, a simple extension leads to inaccurate prediction result. Therefore, we introduce dense 3D representation into the end-to-end deep framework named *3D location field* that maps each pixel to the 3D location on the model surface. The idea of using pixel-3D coordinates correspondences was explored on multi-stage frameworks using RGB-D input [1,21,24]. Under end-to-end deep framework with RGB input at category-level, we show that this representation can provide powerful supervision for the CNNs to efficiently capture the 3D shape of objects. Additionally, it requires no rendering such that there is no domain gap between real-world annotated data and synthetic data. Using large amount of synthetic location fields for pre-training, we overcome the problem of data shortage as well as the domain gap caused by rendering.

Our contribution is three-fold. First, we collect a new large 3D pose dataset for fine-grained objects with a better match to the fine-detailed shapes of objects. Second, we propose a system based on Faster/Mask R-CNN that estimates a full perspective model parameters on our dataset. Third, we integrate *location field*, a dense 3D representation that efficiently encodes the object 3D shapes, into deep framework in an end-to-end fashion. This goes beyond previous works on category-level pose estimation, which only estimate discrete/continuous viewpoint angles or recover rotation matrices often with the help of key points.

Table 1. We provide a larger-scale pose annotation than most existing datasets. Although ObjectNet3D also annotates 100 classes with more than 90,000 images, their CAD models are for generic objects, not in fine-grained details.

Dataset	# class	# image	Annotation	Fine-grained
3D Object [20]	10	6,675	Discretized view	✗
EPFL Cars [16]	1	2,299	Continuous view	✗
Pascal 3D+ [30]	12	30,899	2d-3d alignment	✗
ObjectNet3D [29]	100	90,127	2d-3d alignment	✗
StanfordCars 3D (Ours)	196	16,185	2d-3d alignment	✓
CompCars 3D (Ours)	113	5,696	2d-3d alignment	✓
Total (Ours)	309	21881	2d-3d alignment	✓

2   Related Work

Dataset. Earlier object pose datasets are limited not only in their dataset scales but also in the types of annotation they covered. Table 1 provides a quantitative comparison between our dataset and previous ones. For example, 3D Object [20] dataset only provides viewpoint annotation for 10 object classes with 10 instances for each class. EPFL Car dataset [16] consists of 2,299 images of 20 car instances captured at multiple azimuth angles; moreover, the other parameters including elevation and distance are kept almost the same for all the instances in order to simplify the problem [16]. Pascal 3D+ [30] is perhaps the first large-scale 3D pose dataset for generic object categories, with 30,899 images from 12 different classes of the Pascal VOC dataset [3]. Recently, ObjectNet3D dataset [29] further extends the scale to 90,127 images of 100 categories. Both Pascal 3D+ and ObjectNe3D datasets assume a camera model with 6 parameters to annotate.

However, different images in one hyper class (*i.e.*, cars) are usually matched with a few coarse 3D CAD models, thereby the projection error might be large due to the lack of accurate CAD models in some cases. Being aware of these problems, we therefore project fine-grained CAD models to match with images. In addition, our datasets surpass most of previous ones in both scales of images and classes.

Pose Estimation. Despite the fact that continuous pose parameters are available for dataset such as Pascal 3D+, a majority of previous works [4,18,23,25,30] still casts the pose estimation problem as a multi-class classification of discrete viewpoint angles, which can be further refined as shown in [6,31]. There are very few works except [14,17] that directly regresses the continuous pose parameters. Although [17] estimates a weak-perspective model for object categories and is able to lay the 3D models onto 2D images for visualization, its quantitative evaluation is still limited to 3D rotations. In contrast, we tackle a more challenging problem that estimates the full perspective matrices from a single image. Our new dataset allows us to quantitatively evaluate the estimated perspective projection. Based on this, we design a new efficient CNN framework as well as a new 3D representation that further improves the pose estimation accuracy.

Fine-Grained Recognition. Fine-grained recognition refers to the task of distinguishing sub-ordinate categories [10,26,27]. In earlier works, 3D information is a common source to gain recognition performance improvement [15,22,28,34]. As deep learning prevails and fine-grained datasets become larger [9,13], the effect of 3D information on recognition diminishes. Recently, [22] incorporate 3D bounding box into deep framework when images of cars are taken from a fixed camera. On the other hand, almost all existing fine-grained datasets are lack of 3D pose labels or 3D shape information [10], and pose estimation for fine-grained object categories are not well-studied. Our work fills this gap by annotating poses and matching CAD models on two existing popular fine-grained recognition datasets and performing the new task of pose estimation based on the augmented annotations.

3   Dataset

Our dataset annotation process is similar to ObjectNet3D [29]. We first select the most appropriate 3D car model from ShapeNet [2] for each category in the fine-grained image dataset. For each image, we then obtain its pose parameters by asking the annotators to align the projection of the 3D model with the image using our designed interface.

3.1   3D Models

We build two fine-grained 3D pose datasets for vehicles. Each dataset consists of two parts, *i.e.*, 2D images and 3D models. The 2D images of vehicles are collected from StanfordCars [10] and CompCars [32] respectively. Target objects in most images are non-occluded and easy to identify. In order to distinguish between fine-grained categories, we adopt a distinct model for each category. Thanks to ShapeNet [2], a large number of 3D models for fine-grained vehicles are available with make/model names in their meta data, which are used to find the corresponding 3D model given an image category name. If there is no exact match between a category name and meta data, we manually select a visually similar 3D model for that category. For StanfordCars, we annotate images for all 196 categories, where 148 categories have exact matched models. For CompCars, we only include 113 categories with matched 3D models in ShapeNet. To our best knowledge, our dataset is the very first one which employs fine-grained category aware 3D model in 3D pose estimation.

3.2 Camera Model

The world coordinate system is defined in accordance with the 3D model coordinate system. In this case, a point $\mathbf{X}$ on a 3D model is projected onto a point $\mathbf{x}$ on a 2D image:

$$\mathbf{x} = \mathcal{P}\mathbf{X}, \tag{1}$$

via a perspective projection matrix:

$$\mathcal{P} = K\left[R|T\right], \tag{2}$$

where K denotes the intrinsic parameter:

$$K = \begin{bmatrix} f & 0 & u \\ 0 & f & v \\ 0 & 0 & 1 \end{bmatrix}, \tag{3}$$

and R encodes a 3×3 rotation matrix between the world and camera coordinate systems, parameterized by three angles, i.e., elevation e, azimuth a and in-plane rotation θ. We assume that the camera is always facing towards the origin of the 3D model. Hence the translation $T = [0, 0, d]^{\mathrm{T}}$ is only defined up to the model depth d, the distance between the origins of two coordinate systems, and the principal point (u, v) is the projection of the origin of world coordinate system on the image. As a result, our model has 7 parameters in total: camera focal length f, principal point location u, v, azimuth a, elevation e, in-plane rotation θ and model depth d. Note that, since the images are collected online, even the annotated intrinsic parameters (u, v and f) are approximation. Compared with previous annotations [29,30] with 6 parameters (f fixed), our camera model considers both the camera focal length f and object depth d in a full perspective projection for finer 2D-3D alignment.

3.3 2D-3D Alignment

We annotate 3D pose information for all 2D images in our datasets through crowd-sourcing. To facilitate the annotation process, we develop an annotation tool illustrated in Fig. 2. For each image during annotation, we choose the 3D model according to the fine-grained car type given beforehand. Then, we ask the annotators to adjust the 7 parameters so that the projected 3D model is aligned with the target object in 2D image. This process can be roughly summarized as follows: (1) shift the 3D model such that the center of the model (the origin of the world coordinate system) is roughly aligned with the center of the target object in the 2D image; (2) rotate the model to the same orientation as the target object in the 2D image; (3) adjust the model depth d and camera focal length f to match the size of the target object in the 2D image. Some finer adjustment might be applied after the three main steps. In this way we annotate all 7 parameters across the whole dataset. On average, each image takes approximately 60 s to annotate by an experienced annotator. To ensure the quality, after one round of annotation across the whole dataset, we perform quality check and let the annotators do a second round revision for unqualified examples.

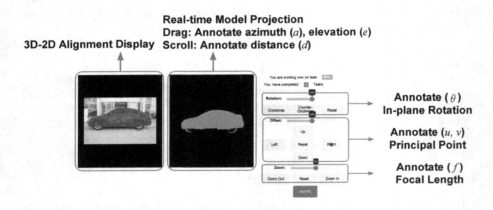

Fig. 2. An overview of our annotation interface.

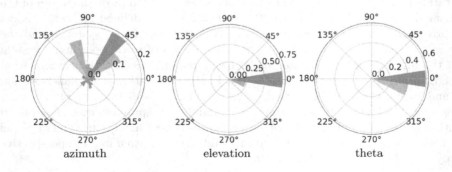

Fig. 3. The polar histogram of the three key pose parameters in our annotated StanfordCars 3D dataset.

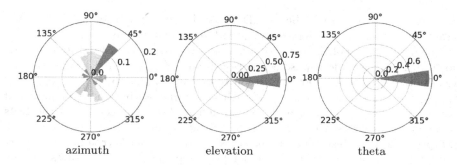

Fig. 4. The polar histogram of the three key pose parameters in our annotated CompCars 3D dataset.

3.4   Dataset Statistics

We plot the distributions of azimuth (a), elevation (e) and in-plane rotation (θ) in Figs. 3 and 4 for StanfordCars 3D and CompCars 3D, respectively. For azimuth, due to the nature of the original fine-grained recognition dataset, we found it is not uniformly distributed, while the distributions of the two dataset are complementary to some degree. Elevations and in-plane rotations are not severe as expected, since the images of cars are usually taken from the ground view.

4   3D Pose Estimation for Fine-Grained Object Categories

Given an input image of a fine-grained object, our task is to predict *all* the 7 parameters related to Eq. (2), *i.e.*, 3D rotation $R(a, e, \theta)$, distance d, principal point (u, v) and f, such that the projected 3D model can align well with the object in the 2D image.

4.1   Baseline Framework

Our baseline method only uses 2D appearance to regress the pose parameters. It is a modified version of Faster R-CNN [19] which was originally designed for object detection. Casting our pose estimation problem into a detection framework is motivated by the relation between the two tasks. Since we are not using key points as an attention mechanism, performing pose estimation within the region of interest (RoI) helps us get rid of unrelated image regions hence make use of 2D information more effectively. In addition, 3D pose estimation is highly related to the detection task, especially the intrinsic parameters in Eq. (3).

We parametrize the 3D rotation using the *quaternion* representation, converted from the angles (a, e, θ). The principal point (u, v) is highly related to RoI center. Therefore, we regress $(\Delta u, \Delta v)$, the offset of the principal point from the RoI center. Such offset exists since the projection of the 3D object center might not necessarily be the 2D center depending on the poses. For other parameters (d and f), we regress the standard format as they are.

The modification of the network architecture is relatively straightforward. As shown in Fig. 5, we add a pose estimation branch along with the existing class prediction and bounding box regression branches. Similar to the bounding box regression branch, the estimation of each group of pose parameters consists of a fully-connected (FC) layer and a smoothed L_1 loss. The centers of the RoIs are also used to adjust the regression targets at training time and generate the final predictions at test time, as discussed above. For each training image, its bounding box is figured out from the perspective projection of the corresponding 3D model. Since we have fine-grained 3D models and high-quality annotations, these bounding boxes are tight to their corresponding objects.

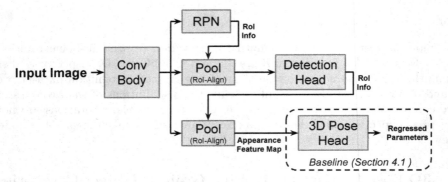

Fig. 5. Our base pose estimation framework. Given an input 2D image, we adapt the Mask R-CNN framework to regress the pose parameters from the pooled appearance feature map with its area determined by the detection module. The whole network is trained end-to-end.

4.2   Improve Pose Estimation via 3D Location Field

The key difference of our dataset to previous ones is that we have fine-grained 3D models such that the projection aligns better with the image. This advantage allows us to explore the usage of dense 3D representations in addition to 2D appearance to regress the pose parameters.

Given an object in an image and its 3D model, our representation, named as *3D location field*, maps every foreground pixel to its corresponding location on the surface of the 3D model, *i.e.*, $f(x, y) = (X, Y, Z)$. The resulting field has the same size as the image and has three channels containing the X, Y and Z coordinates respectively. A sample image with corresponding 3D location field can be seen in Fig. 6. The 3D location field is a dense representation of 3D information which can be directly used as network input.

Fig. 6. A sample image and its corresponding 3D location field. The location field is a 3-dimensional tensor with the same size as an image. The last channel encodes the 3d locations of a pixel on the visible surface of the 3D model. (Color figure online)

We explore the usage of 3D location field to improve pose estimation based on Mask R-CNN. We would still expect only 2D image input at test time, therefore we regress 3D location field and use the regressed field for pose estimation. Based on the framework in Fig. 5, we add a branch to regress 3D location field (instead of regressing binary masks in Mask R-CNN). The regressed location fields are fed into a CNN consisting of additional convolutional layers followed by layers to regress the pose parameters. The regressions from 2D appearance (as part of Fig. 5) and 3D location field are later combined to produce the final pose parameters. Figure 7 shows the detailed network structure.

We train the pose regression from location fields using a large amount of synthetic data. The synthetic location fields are generated from the 3D models with various pre-defined poses. The location field is a very suitable representation for synthetic data augmentation due to the following reasons: (i) the field only encodes 3D location information without any rendering of 3D models and naturally avoids the domain gap between synthetic data and photo-realistic data; (ii) the field is invariant to color, texture and scale of the images.

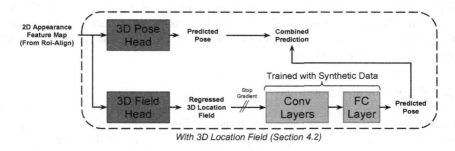

Fig. 7. Our improved network architecture of using 3D location field to help pose estimation. The block in the dash-line box is to replace the corresponding base network in Fig. 5. The key difference is that we add a 3D field branch that also estimates the pose parameters.

5 Experiments

5.1 Evaluation Metrics

For each test sample, we introduce two metrics to comprehensively evaluate object poses.

Following [17,25], the first metric, **Rotation Error**, focuses on the quality of viewpoint estimation only. Given the predicted and ground truth rotation matrices $\{R, R_{gt}\}$, the difference between the two measured by geodesic distance is $e_R = \frac{1}{\sqrt{2}} \| \log(R^T R_{gt}) \|_F$.

The second metric evaluates the overall quality of perspective projection. Our evaluation metric is based on **Average Distance of Model Points** in [8], which measures the averaged distance between predicted projected points and their corresponding ground truth projections. Concretely, given one test result $\{\mathcal{P}, \mathcal{P}_{gt}, \mathcal{M}\}$, where its predicted pose is $\mathcal{P}$, its ground truth pose $\mathcal{P}_{gt}$ and corresponding 3D model $\mathcal{M}$, the metric is defined as

$$e_{\text{ADD}}(\mathcal{P}, \mathcal{P}_{gt}; \mathcal{M}) = \underset{\mathbf{X} \in \mathcal{M}}{\text{avg}} \| \mathcal{P}\mathbf{X} - \mathcal{P}_{gt}\mathbf{X} \|_2 \tag{4}$$

According to [8], this is the most widely-used error function to evaluate a projection matrix. The unit of the above distance is the number of pixels. To make the metric scale-invariant, we normalize it using the diameter of the 2D bounding box. We denote the normalized distance as $\tilde{e}_{\text{ADD}}$. It is worth mentioning again that the 3D models are only used when computing the evaluation metrics. During test time, only a single 2D image is fed into the network to predict the pose $\mathcal{P}$.

To measure the performance over the whole test set, we compute the mean and median of e_R and $\tilde{e}_{\text{ADD}}$ over all test samples. Also, by setting thresholds on the two metrics, we can get an accuracy number. For e_R, following [17,25], we set the threshold to be $\frac{\pi}{6}$. For $\tilde{e}_{\text{ADD}}$, the common threshold is 0.1, which means that the prediction with average projection error less than 10% of the 2D diameter is considered correct.

5.2 Experimental Settings

Data Split. For StanfordCars 3D, since we have annotated all the images, we follow the standard train/test split provided by the original dataset [10] with 8144 training examples and 8041 testing examples. For CompCars 3D, we randomly sample 2/3 of our annotated data as training set and the rest 1/3 as testing set, resulting in 3798 training and 1898 test examples.

Baseline Implementation. Our implementation is based on the Detectron package [5], which includes Faster/Mask R-CNN implementations. The convolutional body (*i.e.*, the "backbone" in [7]) used for the baseline is ResNet-50. For fair comparison, the convolutional body is initialized from ImageNet pre-trained model, and other layers are randomly initialized (*i.e.*, we are not using COCO pre-trained detectors). Following the setting of Mask R-CNN, the whole network is trained end-to-end. At test time, we adopt a cascaded strategy, where the 3D pose branch is applied only to the highest scoring box prediction.

Comparison to Previous Baselines. It is worth mentioning that, when only evaluating the rotation error in Sect. 5.1, our baseline in Fig. 5 is almost identical to the baselines in Pascal3D+ [30] and ObjectNet3D [29] except that their detection and pose estimation heads are parallel while ours is cascaded.

3D Location Field. In Sect. 4.2, incorporating 3D location fields involves two steps – field regression and pose regression from fields. Field regression is trained together with detection and baseline pose estimation in an end-to-end fashion, similar to Mask R-CNN. The ground truth training fields are generated from the annotations (3D models and poses). The second step, pose regression from fields is trained using the synthetic data generated from the pool of matched 3D models in a dataset (38102/14017 synthetic samples for StanfordCars&CompCars 3D). We only regress the quaternion using the location fields.

Table 2. Experimental results on StanfordCars 3D dataset. The two rows show the baseline results (Sect. 4.1) and the results with 3D location field (Sect. 4.2), respectively. The rotation error e_R is measured in degree ($°$). The accuracy ($Acc_{\frac{\pi}{6}}$ and $Acc_{th=0.1}$) is measured in percentage (%). Please see Sect. 5.1 for details about evaluation metrics.

Method	Median e_R	Mean e_R	$Acc_{\frac{\pi}{6}}$	Median $\tilde{e}_{ADD}$	Mean $\tilde{e}_{ADD}$	$Acc_{th=0.1}$
Baseline	6.68	9.89	96.59	0.0888	0.1087	60.04
w./Field	**5.68**	**7.67**	**98.73**	**0.0834**	**0.0977**	**66.07**

Table 3. Experimental results on CompCars 3D dataset. The last two rows show results fine-tuned (FT) from a StanfordCars 3D pre-trained model.

Method	Median e_R	Mean e_R	$Acc_{\frac{\pi}{6}}$	Median $\tilde{e}_{ADD}$	Mean $\tilde{e}_{ADD}$	$Acc_{th=0.1}$
Baseline	8.09	13.02	93.62	0.1275	0.1580	32.52
w./Field	6.14	8.98	98.00	0.1141	0.1408	40.15
FT Baseline	5.51	8.69	96.84	0.0878	0.1123	58.58
FT w./Field	**4.74**	**7.45**	**98.31**	**0.0836**	**0.1047**	**64.01**

5.3 Results and Analysis

The quantitative results for StanfordCars 3D and CompCars 3D are shown in Tables 2 and 3 respectively. The changes of Acc_{th} *w.r.t* the threshold for the datasets are shown in Fig. 8. For CompCars 3D dataset, besides ImageNet initialization we also report the result finetuned from a StanfordCars 3D pretrained model, since the number of training samples in StanfordCars is relatively larger.

As can be seen in Tables 2 and 3, our baseline performs very well on estimating the rotation matrix for both datasets, with Median e_R less than 10 degrees and $Acc_{\frac{\pi}{6}}$ around 95%. While recovering the full perspective model is a much more challenging task, Table 2 shows that promising performance can be achieved with enough properly annotated training samples. For StanfordCars 3D, Median $\tilde{e}_{ADD}$ (the median of the average projection error) is less than 10% of the diameter of the 2D bounding box. When the training set is limited, from the first and the third row of Table 3, we can see the effectiveness of transfer learning from a larger dataset. Regarding the effectiveness of the 3D location field, we can observe consistent performance gain across all datasets. The main reasons are two-fold: (i) this 3D representation enables the usage of large amounts of synthetic training data with no domain gap; (ii) our field regression adapted from Mask R-CNN works well such that even the pose prediction based on the regressed field can help a lot at test time.

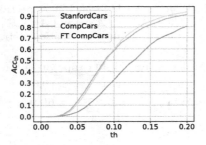 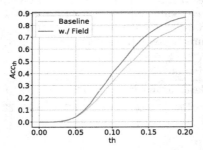

Fig. 8. Left: Plot of Acc_{th} w.r.t. threshold for the three baselines. Right: for CompCars 3D, compare the result using location field to the baseline curve. (Color figure online)

Fig. 9. Visualizations of predicted poses for test examples. For each dataset, we show five examples of successful predictions and two of the failure cases, separated by the solid black line in the figure.

We visualize the predicted poses in Fig. 9. As shown on the left part of Fig. 9, our method is able to handle poses of various orientations, scales and locations of the projection. On the right part of Fig. 9, failure cases exist in our predictions, indicating there are still potential rooms for improvement, especially for the estimation of scale, cases with large perspective distortion and some uncommon poses with few training samples.

6   Conclusion

We study the problem of pose estimation for fine-grained object categories. We annotate two popular fine-grained recognition datasets with fine-grained 3D shapes and poses. We propose an approach to estimate the full perspective parameters from a single image. We further propose 3D location field as a dense 3D representation to facilitate pose estimation. Experiments on our datasets suggest that this is an interesting problem in future.

References

1. Brachmann, E., Krull, A., Michel, F., Gumhold, S., Shotton, J., Rother, C.: Learning 6D Object pose estimation using 3D object coordinates. In: Fleet, D., Pajdla, T., Schiele, B., Tuytelaars, T. (eds.) ECCV 2014. LNCS, vol. 8690, pp. 536–551. Springer, Cham (2014). https://doi.org/10.1007/978-3-319-10605-2_35
2. Chang, A.X., et al.: ShapeNet: an information-rich 3D model repository. arXiv preprint arXiv:1512.03012 (2015)
3. Everingham, M., Van Gool, L., Williams, C.K., Winn, J., Zisserman, A.: The pascal visual object classes (voc) challenge. Int. J. Comput. Vis. **88**(2), 303–338 (2010)
4. Ghodrati, A., Pedersoli, M., Tuytelaars, T.: Is 2D information enough for viewpoint estimation? In: BMVC (2014)
5. Girshick, R., Radosavovic, I., Gkioxari, G., Dollár, P., He, K.: Detectron. https://github.com/facebookresearch/detectron (2018)
6. Hara, K., Vemulapalli, R., Chellappa, R.: Designing deep convolutional neural networks for continuous object orientation estimation. arXiv preprint arXiv:1702.01499 (2017)
7. He, K., Gkioxari, G., Dollár, P., Girshick, R.: Mask R-CNN. In: ICCV (2017)
8. Hodaň, T., Matas, J., Obdržálek, Š.: On evaluation of 6D object pose estimation. In: Hua, G., Jégou, H. (eds.) ECCV 2016. LNCS, vol. 9915, pp. 606–619. Springer, Cham (2016). https://doi.org/10.1007/978-3-319-49409-8_52
9. Krause, J., et al.: The unreasonable effectiveness of noisy data for fine-grained recognition. In: Leibe, B., Matas, J., Sebe, N., Welling, M. (eds.) ECCV 2016. LNCS, vol. 9907, pp. 301–320. Springer, Cham (2016). https://doi.org/10.1007/978-3-319-46487-9_19
10. Krause, J., Stark, M., Deng, J., Fei-Fei, L.: 3D object representations for fine-grained categorization. In: ICCV Workshops on 3D Representation and Recognition (2013)
11. Krizhevsky, A., Sutskever, I., Hinton, G.E.: ImageNet classification with deep convolutional neural networks. In: NIPS (2012)
12. Lim, J.J., Pirsiavash, H., Torralba, A.: Parsing IKEA objects: fine pose estimation. In: ICCV (2013)

13. Lin, T.Y., RoyChowdhury, A., Maji, S.: Bilinear CNN models for fine-grained visual recognition. In: ICCV (2015)
14. Mahendran, S., Ali, H., Vidal, R.: 3D pose regression using convolutional neural networks. In: ICCV, vol. 1, p. 4 (2017)
15. Mottaghi, R., Xiang, Y., Savarese, S.: A coarse-to-fine model for 3D pose estimation and sub-category recognition. In: CVPR (2015)
16. Ozuysal, M., Lepetit, V., Fua, P.: Pose estimation for category specific multiview object localization. In: CVPR (2009)
17. Pavlakos, G., Zhou, X., Chan, A., Derpanis, K.G., Daniilidis, K.: 6-DoF object pose from semantic keypoints. In: ICRA, pp. 2011–2018 (2017)
18. Pepik, B., Stark, M., Gehler, P., Schiele, B.: Teaching 3D geometry to deformable part models. In: CVPR (2012)
19. Ren, S., He, K., Girshick, R.B., Sun, J.: Faster R-CNN: towards real-time object detection with region proposal networks. In: NIPS (2015)
20. Savarese, S., Fei-Fei, L.: 3D generic object categorization, localization and pose estimation. In: ICCV (2007)
21. Shotton, J., Glocker, B., Zach, C., Izadi, S., Criminisi, A., Fitzgibbon, A.W.: Scene coordinate regression forests for camera relocalization in RGB-D images. In: CVPR (2013)
22. Sochor, J., Herout, A., Havel, J.: BoxCars: 3D boxes as CNN input for improved fine-grained vehicle recognition. In: CVPR (2016)
23. Su, H., Qi, C.R., Li, Y., Guibas, L.J.: Render for CNN: viewpoint estimation in images using CNNs trained with rendered 3D model views. In: ICCV (2015)
24. Taylor, J., Shotton, J., Sharp, T., Fitzgibbon, A.W.: The vitruvian manifold: inferring dense correspondences for one-shot human pose estimation. In: CVPR (2012)
25. Tulsiani, S., Malik, J.: Viewpoints and keypoints. In: Proceedings of the IEEE Conference on Computer Vision and Pattern Recognition, pp. 1510–1519 (2015)
26. Van Horn, G., et al.: The iNaturalist challenge 2017 dataset. arXiv preprint arXiv:1707.06642 (2017)
27. Wah, C., Branson, S., Welinder, P., Perona, P., Belongie, S.: The Caltech-UCSD Birds-200-2011 Dataset. Technical report (2011)
28. Xiang, Y., Choi, W., Lin, Y., Savarese, S.: Data-driven 3D voxel patterns for object category recognition. In: Proceedings of the IEEE Conference on Computer Vision and Pattern Recognition, pp. 1903–1911 (2015)
29. Xiang, Y., et al.: ObjectNet3D: a large scale database for 3D object recognition. In: ECCV (2016)
30. Xiang, Y., Mottaghi, R., Savarese, S.: Beyond PASCAL: a benchmark for 3D object detection in the wild. In: WACV (2014)
31. Yang, L., Liu, J., Tang, X.: Object detection and viewpoint estimation with auto-masking neural network. In: Fleet, D., Pajdla, T., Schiele, B., Tuytelaars, T. (eds.) ECCV 2014. LNCS, vol. 8691, pp. 441–455. Springer, Cham (2014). https://doi.org/10.1007/978-3-319-10578-9_29
32. Yang, L., Luo, P., Change Loy, C., Tang, X.: A large-scale car dataset for fine-grained categorization and verification. In: CVPR (2015)
33. Zhou, X., Leonardos, S., Hu, X., Daniilidis, K., et al.: 3D shape estimation from 2D landmarks: a convex relaxation approach. In: CVPR (2015)
34. Zia, M.Z., Stark, M., Schiele, B., Schindler, K.: Detailed 3D representations for object recognition and modeling. PAMI 35(11), 2608–2623 (2013)

Seamless Color Mapping for 3D Reconstruction with Consumer-Grade Scanning Devices

Bin Wang[1(✉)], Pan Pan[1], Qinjie Xiao[2], Likang Luo[2], Xiaofeng Ren[1], Rong Jin[1], and Xiaogang Jin[2]

[1] Machine Intelligence Technology Lab, Alibaba Group, Hangzhou, China
{ganfu.wb,panpan.pp,x.ren,jinrong.jr}@alibaba-inc.com
[2] State Key Lab of CAD&CG, Zhejiang University, Hangzhou, China
826464268@qq.com, style_luo@163.com, jin@cad.zju.edu.cn

Abstract. Virtual Reality provides an immersive and intuitive shopping experience for customers. This raises challenging problems of reconstructing real-life products realistically in a cheap way. We present a seamless texturing method for 3D reconstructed objects with inexpensive consumer-grade scanning devices. To this end, we develop a two-step global optimization method to seamlessly texture reconstructed models with color images. We first perform a seam generation optimization based on Markov random field to generate more reasonable seams located at low-frequency color areas. Then, we employ a seam correction optimization that uses local color information around seams to correct the misalignments of images used for texturing. In contrast to previous approaches, the proposed method is more computationally efficient in generating seamless texture maps. Experimental results show that our method can efficiently deliver a seamless and high-quality texture maps even for noisy data.

Keywords: Texture mapping · Markov random field ·
Seamless color optimization

1 Introduction

Texture mapping plays an important role in reconstructing virtual versions of real-life products for E-Commerce applications with inexpensive consumer-grade scanning devices. This raises challenging problems to reconstruct seamless, high-quality texture maps from noisy data, such as inaccurate geometry, imprecise camera poses, and optical distortions of consumer-grade cameras. Existing methods such as Waechter *et al.* [24] efficiently select suitable images to texture faces

Electronic supplementary material The online version of this chapter (https://doi.org/10.1007/978-3-030-11009-3_39) contains supplementary material, which is available to authorized users.

L. Leal-Taixé and S. Roth (Eds.): ECCV 2018 Workshops, LNCS 11129, pp. 633–648, 2019.
https://doi.org/10.1007/978-3-030-11009-3_39

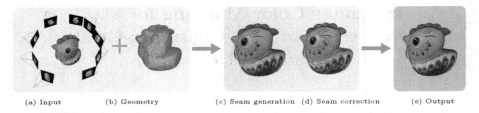

(a) Input   (b) Geometry   (c) Seam generation   (d) Seam correction   (e) Output

Fig. 1. The pipeline of our texture mapping process: (a) a set of images registered to a corresponding geometry (b) are taken as input, then the seam generation process (c) selects suitable images to texture faces on geometry, which creates most of the seams across low-frequency color areas. Finally, a seam correction optimization (d) corrects misalignments around seams (shown in translucent orange blocks) and generates a high-quality texture mapping output (e) (Color figure online)

on geometric models, but their method may generate visible seams, blurring and ghosting artifacts on the generated texture maps. Recently, Zhou and Koltun [26] use dense, global color information to correct the misalignments of images used for texturing, which produces impressive color maps. However, their approach suffers from large computational consumption. In this paper, we improve seamless texture maps by generating optimal seams with a bypass optimization and correcting the misaligned seams efficiently using local color information.

Our approach achieves both efficiency and seamless texture maps by a two-step global optimization. For the first step, we present a novel optimization based on Markov random field (MRF) that selects suitable images to texture geometric meshes and generates optimal seams located at low-frequency texture regions on texture maps. Our optimization incorporates color discrepancies between the textures of adjacent faces on meshes. As a result, low-frequency texture regions will be more appropriate to create seams, which results in lower energy for MRF-based optimization, and visible seams are thus diminished. As the seams cannot be completely eliminated by the first step, we perform a joint optimization in the second step in order to maximize the color consistency around the seams, which further eliminates the misaligned seams. We estimate camera poses and local warping of images used for texturing geometry. Specially, we only estimate the color consistency of vertices around seams and warp local image patches where seams exist for efficiency.

The contributions of our approach can be summarized as follows. Firstly, we present a seam generation optimization based on MRF to create optimal seams on low-frequency color areas. Then, we propose a seam correction optimization which can efficiently correct misaligned errors. Finally, we present a two-step optimization framework that can efficiently generate seamless texture maps, a main problem of texture mapping. Experimental results demonstrate that our approach can provide a better color representation with much lower computational cost compared to existing methods.

2   Related Works

3D Acquisition. As consumer-grade depth cameras make 3D acquisition more and more affordable and convenient, geometric acquisition using RGB-D is highly anticipated [19,23,25]. The pioneer work of KinectFusion proposed by Izadi *et al.* [11] reconstructs the scene's geometry with a volumetric representation. Nießner *et al.* [20] propose a real-time online 3D reconstruction system using an efficient geometric representation based on hashing. Zhou and Koltun [25] reconstruct dense scenes with points of interest using RGB-D cameras. Another popular method of geometric reconstruction is structure from motion. Ackermann *et al.* [1] propose a photometric stereo technique to reconstruct outdoor scenes. These methods based on structure from motion and RGB-D images are flexible enough to reconstruct geometry ranging from fine-scale objects to large-scale scenes. However, they generate 3D models with much noises [4,10,14]. Accurate geometric reconstruction can be obtained by structured light scanning systems [9,18]. Gupta *et al.* [8] present a structured light system to reconstruct high-quality geometry with global illumination. In this paper, we use data scanned from a low-cost structured light system, which consists of an ordinary projector and a RGB industry camera.

Vertex Texturing Methods. Vertex texturing methods encode color information as per-vertex color. Nießner *et al.* [20] and Shan *et al.* [22] integrate multi-view color samples, which lead to blurring and ghosting artifacts due to the misaligned errors. Zhou and Koltun [26] use dense, global color information to estimate the photometric consistency of all vertices on the object's mesh. Their method corrects misaligned errors and improves texture mapping fidelity. However, in order to describe the high-quality details of objects, their approach estimates the color for lots of vertices on the objects' meshes, which is time-consuming and may lose the advantage of texture mapping that represents high-quality details with low geometric representations.

Face Texturing Methods. Face texturing methods such as [7,15,24] are based on Markov random field, and they select one single image to texture each face on the objects' meshes. These methods can generate texture maps with lots of details. However, these methods cannot perfectly address the misalignments of images resulting in blurring and ghosting artifacts. Lempitsky and Ivanov [15] diminish visible seams by performing a global color adjustment following with Poisson editing [21]. However, blurring and ghosting artifacts around seams may still occur due to noisy input data. Other approaches are proposed to generate seamless texture maps using geometry information. For example, Barnes *et al.* [3] provide an interactive method to manually correct misaligned errors between the geometry model and images, which is not suitable for E-Commerce applications. Bi *et al.* [5] propose a patch-based optimization that incorporates geometry information. Their method estimates the bidirectional similarity of different images, which suffers from high computational cost. Recently, some deep learning-based approaches are developed for real-world texture reconstruction using texture synthesis [16, 17].

3   Overview

As shown in Fig. 1, our pipeline takes an object's mesh and a set of images registered to the mesh as input, and generates a high-quality and seamless texture map for the object. Our approach starts with the seam generation process that takes advantage of a novel MRF formulation to select the "best view" texturing per face on the mesh. Existing methods consider "best view" selection as a Graph Cuts optimization [6]. The main idea of our seam generation optimization formulation consists of two energy terms. The first term (data term) selects high-resolution images to texture each face, and the second term (smooth term) provides a smooth representation. The energy function can be solved by a MRF solution [13]. However, traditional methods are not robust for noisy data, resulting in blurring and ghosting artifacts [24]. We redefine the energy function of MRF by employing an easy-to-compute data term and a smooth term by taking advantage of the color differences between adjacent faces, which generates more reliable invisible seams. Details of our seam generation are presented in Sect. 4.1.

To reduce the remaining visible seams that cannot be fully diminished by the seam generation step, we develop a seam correction optimization to deal with misalignments in Sect. 4.2. Inspired by Zhou and Koltun [26] and Bi et al. [5], we correct the texture regions around the seams to generate a consistent color 3D representation. Compared to the existing method [24], we design a close-form solution (Fig. 1(d)) to obtain plausible results with a low computational cost. Finally, we use the color adjustment method of Waechter et al. [24] to deal with luminance inconsistency caused by variance of lighting on the textured results.

4   Approach

Our approach can texture a 3D object with less perceptible texture seams and higher fidelity. This section details the two key steps. Section 4.1 describes the seam generation optimization step, and Sect. 4.2 describes the seam correction step.

4.1   Seam Generation Optimization

Our seam generation optimization divides the mesh into blocks of faces (as shown in Fig. 2), and the faces in a block corresponds to the same image. The boundaries between blocks are perceived as texture seams in the textured mesh. The input of our method includes an object's triangle mesh and a set of object's images registered to the object mesh. We represent the triangle faces on the mesh as $F = \{F_1, F_2, \cdots, F_m\}$, and the corresponding texture images as $I = \{I_1, I_2, \cdots, I_n\}$, where I_i is the texture image for view i. The projection between images and faces are calculated according to camera intrinsic and extrinsic parameters.

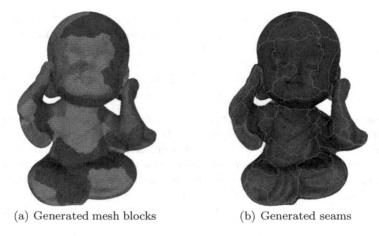

(a) Generated mesh blocks   (b) Generated seams

Fig. 2. A mesh labeling example. Each color block in (a) represents a rendering texture to a face, and (b) shows the texturing result where pink contours indicate seams (Color figure online)

The generation of optimized blocks of faces or texture seams is formulated as a labeling problem, and we label each face F_j with a suitable image I_{l_i}. We assume a vector to represent the label relationship $L = \{L_1, L_2, \cdots, L_j, \cdots, L_m\} \in \{1, 2, \cdots, i, \cdots, n\}^m$, and $L_j = i$ indicates that image I_i is used for texturing face F_j. As multiple images may correspond to one face, we should select the best candidate image view for each face. Here, we adopt MRF to solve this problem, and a common MRF energy function can be defined as:

$$E(L) = E_d(L) + \alpha \cdot E_s(L). \tag{1}$$

The first energy term, namely the data term $E_d(L)$ represents the cost of texturing faces with texture images from a certain selection of views. The second term $E_s(L)$ represents the energy measuring the smooth level of the generated texture. α is a parameter to adjust the weight. In this paper, we propose a novel data term and a smooth term to effectively generate more accurate seams at low-frequency color areas, which cannot be solved by existing MRF techniques.

We aim to reconstruct textures of objects with an ordinary size, and there are no scaling issues in our image data. Thus, it's not necessary to consider scaling in the data term as in Waechter $et\ al.$ [24] which is time-consuming. Besides, Allene $et\ al.$ [2] utilize a projected size as the data term, which is easy to calculate, but they cannot deal with blurring artifacts. Inspired by the method in [15], the metric employed by our data term is to measure the angle between the normal of a face and the camera view direction of an image. This metric accelerates our algorithm since it is computationally efficient. For face $F_j \in F$, we use $f(L_j)$ to evaluate the texturing quality of F_j with view image $I_{L_j} \in I$ ($L_j = i$). If we can observe F_j from image I_{L_j}, we have $f(L_j) = 1 - (n_j \cdot n_{L_j})^2$; otherwise,

$f(L_j) = \infty$, where n_j is the normal vector of face F_j and n_{L_j} is the unit camera view vector of image I_{L_j}. We then have our data term $E_d(\boldsymbol{L})$ as follows:

$$E_d(\boldsymbol{L}) = \sum_{j=1}^{j=m} f(L_j). \tag{2}$$

For the smooth term, we minimize the average color difference between co-edged faces along the texture seams. We suppose that $e_{jk} \in \boldsymbol{E}_{dge}$ is the edge shared by face F_j and face F_k, $\boldsymbol{E}_{dge}$ is the set of edges shared by adjacent faces of the mesh. Since faces have greater color differences than edges, the average color of faces can better express discrepancies than method [15], which utilizes color discrepancies on the edges. Let $\boldsymbol{C}_{L_j}$ be the average color of pixels on the area where F_j is projected onto an image I_{L_j}, we use the following function to measure the cost of edge e_{jk}:

$$D(L_j, L_k) = \begin{cases} 0, & \text{if } L_j = L_k \\ d(\boldsymbol{C}_{L_j}, \boldsymbol{C}_{L_k})^2, & \text{otherwise,} \end{cases} \tag{3}$$

where $d(\cdot, \cdot)$ is the Euclidean distance on RGB color space. Thus, we have the smooth term $E_s(\boldsymbol{L})$:

$$E_s(\boldsymbol{L}) = \alpha \cdot \sum_{e_{jk} \in \boldsymbol{E}_{dge}} D(L_j, L_k). \tag{4}$$

The overall seam generation energy in Eq. (1) can be re-written as:

$$E(\boldsymbol{L}) = \sum_{j=1}^{j=m} f(L_j) + \alpha \cdot \sum_{e_{jk} \in \boldsymbol{E}_{dges}} D(L_j, L_k). \tag{5}$$

The energy function in Eq. (5) can be formulated as a probability distribution problem with Markov random field, which can be efficiently solved by the α-expansion Graph Cuts [6].

4.2   Seam Correction Optimization

Seam generation optimization produces reasonable seams that are less perceptible. There are still some noticeable seams as shown in Fig. 4 in the reconstructed model due to large misalignments of images. Seam correction optimization is designed to correct such seams by adjusting the content of selected images used for textures. Different from other global optimization methods such as Zhou and Koltun [26] that estimate colors for all vertices, our approach is more efficient since our optimization is only performed for a small set of vertices around seams.

When performing seam correction optimization, we take the following two factors into consideration. First, the color along seams should be consistent. Second, the textured appearance of the area around seams should be similar to the corresponding area in the selected images. To this end, we estimate the colors

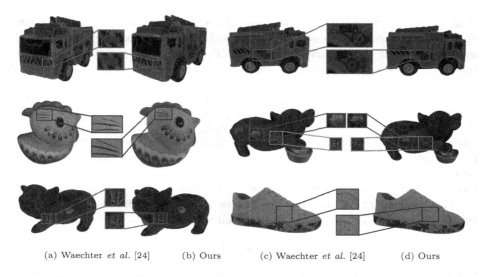

(a) Waechter *et al.* [24]   (b) Ours   (c) Waechter *et al.* [24]   (d) Ours

Fig. 3. The seam generation results of our method are tested on several datasets. We compare our results with Waechter *et al.* [24]. Our method outperforms the state-of-the-art view selection methods

for all vertices within the ranges on geometry where seams exist, as well as the camera poses for all images used for texturing geometry and the local warping of images patches that contain the seams to maximize the color similarity of the mapping around seams.

After seam generation, we divide the mesh into different blocks textured with some selected images. We represent the image patch corresponding to each mesh block respectively as $P = \{P_1, P_2, \cdots, P_k\}$. One image can be used to texture multiple blocks (e.g. $\{P_1, P_2, P_3\} \in I_i$). We define the mesh blocks as $B = \{B_1, B_2, \cdots, B_k\}$. The relationship between an image patch and its corresponding mesh block is a perspective transformation calculated as $P_k = \mathcal{K}T_k B_k$ ($T = \{T_1, T_2, \cdots, T_k\}$ denotes the external camera parameters, and $\mathcal{K}$ denotes the internal camera parameters). $E = \{E_1, E_2, \cdots, E_k\}$ denotes the edges set for each mesh block B_k. $F = \{F_1, F_2, \cdots, F_k\}$ denotes the control lattices for each image patch P_k, which is used to warp image patch P_k. We choose a vertex $v \in B_k$ as a candidate vertex for optimization, and the shortest geodetic distance from vertex v to edge set E_k is defined as $g(v, E_k)$. We define a proper control range in each image patch for correction, in which only the vertex v with $g(v, E_k)$ less than γ is used. The objective function can then be described as:

$$E_{correction}(C, F, T) = \sum_k (\sum_{\substack{v \in B_k, \\ g(v, E_k) < \gamma}} w(v) \cdot e^2 + \beta \cdot F_k^\top F_k), \qquad (6)$$

where $C = \{C_v | g(v, E_k) < \gamma\}$ denotes the set of gray-scale color estimated for vertices around seams on the mesh, F denotes the pixel color corrections and T

denotes the camera pose transformations. During optimization, the variables are optimized to correct visible seams. The second term is a regular term penalizing image patches from excessive deformation F. $w(v)$ is the weight of vertex v representing the color discrepancies of the faces around vertex v:

$$w(v) = \frac{1}{|\mathcal{E}(v)|} \sum_{e_{jk} \in \mathcal{E}(v)} d(C_{L_j}, C_{L_k})^2, \tag{7}$$

where $\mathcal{E}(v)$ is the set of edges that connect with vertex v. Since we texture each face on geometry in the seam generation step, $w(v)$ can be precomputed and is constant in the seam correction step, which gives more weight to the vertex located at high-frequency color areas around seams.

The first term of the objective function estimates the color similarity for each vertex in $\{v|g(v, E_k) < \gamma\}$, e^2 is the residual value, and is described as:

$$e = C_v - \mathcal{L} \circ \mathcal{F}_k(\mathcal{K} \cdot T_k \cdot v). \tag{8}$$

For each vertex v, we project v into the image plane of P_k according to camera intrinsic parameter $\mathcal{K}$ and camera poses T_k (we assume that $u = \mathcal{K} \cdot T_k \cdot v$), and then warp image patch P_k according to the following color correction function:

$$\mathcal{F}_k(u) = u + B(u) \cdot F_k, \tag{9}$$

where $B(u)$ is a vector of B-spline base function which controls the vector of control lattices. To this end, we use $\mathcal{L}(u)$ to evaluate the gray-scale intensity of the projective point of vertex v.

We solve Eq. (6) using an alternating optimization approach to optimize the image correction inspired by Zhou $et\ al.$ [27]. We first fix F and T to optimize C, then fix C to optimize F and T, and vice versa. When F and T are fixed, Eq. (6) degenerates to a least-square optimization problem, and we use the following equation to calculate the average gray-scale value of vertex v:

$$C_v = \frac{1}{|\mathcal{I}_v|} \sum_{\substack{k, \\ P_k \in \mathcal{I}_v}} \mathcal{L} \circ \mathcal{F}_k(\mathcal{K} \cdot T_k \cdot v), \tag{10}$$

where $\mathcal{I}_v$ is the set of image patches that can observe v.

When C is fixed, we perform an inner iterative strategy to solve F and T. We fix F and assume that we perform little rotation for each image. With this assumption, we can solve the camera pose as a linear system. By approximating the external camera matrix as a 6-vector $T_k = \{\alpha_k, \beta_k, \lambda_k, a_k, b_k, c_k\}$, we can independently solve a linear system with 6 parameters for each image patch P_k.

After that, we fix C and T to optimize F. Then $u = \mathcal{K} \cdot T_k \cdot v$ is a constant, and $\mathcal{F}_k(u)$ is a linear combination of F_k, and we have:

$$E_{correction}(F) = \sum_k (\sum_{\substack{v \in B_k, \\ g(v, E_k) < \gamma}} w(v) \cdot (C_v - \mathcal{L} \circ \mathcal{F}_k(F_k))^2 + \beta \cdot F_k^\top F_k). \tag{11}$$

Equation (11) is a least-square system and can be efficiently solved. We continue the alternating optimization iteratively until it converges.

5   Results

We evaluated the performance of our proposed method using our test datasets. All experiments were performed on a commodity workstation with an Intel i5 3.2 GHz CPU and 8 GB of RAM. We first presented details about the test data, and then evaluated the seam generation process and seam correction process. Finally, we compare our method to the state-of-the-art approaches.

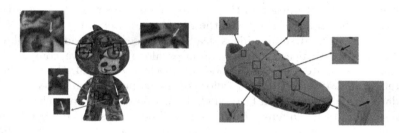

Fig. 4. Some noticeable seams still remain in the textured object due to the misalignment of texture images that cannot be completely avoided by seam generation optimizations

Test Datasets. Our datasets were captured from real-life products (shoes, arts, crafts, etc.) and were reconstructed by the following steps. For each object, we first used a consumer-level structured light 3D scanner to generate a registered point cloud. The scanner contained an RGB industry camera and a normal projector, which was inexpensive. Calibration was performed before the scanning procedure. Then we meshed the point cloud by surface reconstruction [12]. Since the calibrated parameters changed slightly due to the heat transfer in the environment (especially for the parameters of projector), the reconstructed 3D geometry, camera poses and images suffered from noises. Besides, geometric errors would also be introduced by the point cloud registration step. In general, the error of the geometry model was about 3 mm to 5 mm, and the texture reprojection error was about 5 pixels to 15 pixels (the resolution of the captured images was 3456 × 2304).

Seam Generation Evaluation. We first evaluated the contribution of the weight α in Eq. (1). As discussed in Sect. 4.1, the weight α kept a balance between the data term and the smooth term. As shown in Fig. 6, we found that seams will bypass most of the high-frequency color areas on texture images if we set a larger α. Since a larger weight of $E_s(L)$ might result in a larger value of $E_d(L)$, the resolution of texture might be reduced. Hence, we need to find an appropriate α value which will not increase $E_d(L)$ significantly. We estimated the incremental percentage of $E_d(L)$ for different values of α:

$$\Delta E_{d,\alpha_i}(L) = \frac{E_{d,\alpha_i}(L) - E_{d,\alpha_{i-1}}(L)}{E_{d,\alpha_{i-1}}(L)}(i \geqslant 2). \tag{12}$$

We set different α values (from 50 to 300) marked as α_i, and tested its influence on $E_d(L)$. Estimated data were shown in Table 1 and Fig. 5, when $\alpha \leqslant 200$, the average incremental percentage of $E_d(L)$ was about 5% and increased to about 15% when $\alpha > 200$. It meant that if we set α too large for the seam generation optimization, the optimization will select images with larger intersection angles between the view direction and the face normal to texture geometric meshes, which decreased the resolution of the texture. Thus, we set $\alpha = 200$ as a trade-off to balance the seam visibility and the resolution of texture.

Since [7,15,24] used similar ideas dealing with seams considering color differences, labels of vertices or edges for faces along seams, we compared our seam generation strategy to the method of Waechter et al. [24]. The method of Waechter et al. [24] integrated the colors of image patches projected to a face as the data term energy, which favored close-up views. This approach is suitable for large-scale models. Different from their method, we used the angle between the face normal and the camera view direction for the data term. In addition, the smooth term in [24] is based on the Potts model, while our smooth term was based on the color difference between faces adjacent to seams. As shown in Figs. 3 and 8, our method can generate more reasonable seams.

We also compared the computational cost of the MRF-based optimization between Waechter et al.' method and our approach. As the authors described in [24], their main computational bottleneck relied on the data term, while the main computational cost of our MRF-based optimization relied on the smooth term, which calculates the average color of each face. Theoretically, the computation of average color was cheaper to calculate than the computation of Waechter et al.'

Table 1. Some experimental examples of α in Eq. (1). For our datasets, we set $\alpha = 200$ as a trade-off to balance the seam effect and the resolution of texture

α_i value	$E_d(L)$ for different test data					
	car	chicken	pig	doll1	shoes1	doll2
50	47,612	29,041	55,178	29,194	100,692	68,859
100	47,633	30,582	56,603	29,512	101,789	69,503
150	48,310	32,477	57,420	30,368	105,036	71,893
200	**48,826**	**34,698**	**59,387**	**32,152**	**108,605**	**74,337**
250	55,781	38,424	69,164	34,896	157,398	80,641
300	65,812	52,109	82,636	48,177	212,607	89,603

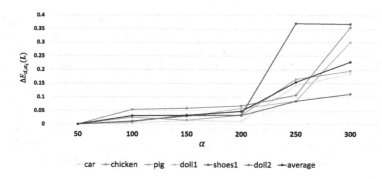

Fig. 5. The incremental percentages of $E_d(L)$

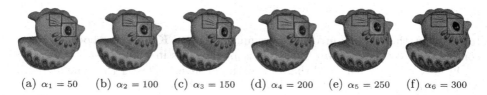

(a) $\alpha_1 = 50$ (b) $\alpha_2 = 100$ (c) $\alpha_3 = 150$ (d) $\alpha_4 = 200$ (e) $\alpha_5 = 250$ (f) $\alpha_6 = 300$

Fig. 6. The seam generation results. The seam generation scheme can bypass more high-frequency color areas as α increases

data term, which needs to compute the projected size and integrate pixel colors. In Table 2, we compared the MRF computational cost between our method and Waechter *et al.*' method quantitatively. The listed statistics conform to our theoretical analysis. Our computational advantage is more obvious when the data size grows large.

Table 2. The comparison of computational cost between our seam generation and Waechter *et al.* [24] for datasets with different sizes (Ours/Waechter *et al.*' method). Our approach is more computationally efficient than Waechter *et al.* [24] ("k", "m" represent thousand and million, respectively)

View number	Computational cost for different numbers of views and faces					
	50k	0.1m	0.2m	0.5m	1m	2m
8	6.2s/6.8s	7.2s/9.6s	8.7s/12.2s	12.5s/15.4s	14.5s/19.2s	23.9s/35.2s
12	8.9s/10.7s	10.5s/13.9s	13.8s/16.1s	18.5s/23.9s	21.7s/28.4s	37.8s/53.1s
24	19.6s/21.3s	22.4s/29.7s	27.2s/37.4s	38.1s/49.5s	44.6s/58.5s	75.2s/108.2s
32	25.1s/27.6s	29.1s/38.7s	35.2s/50.3s	51.4s/63.6s	58.3s/78.3s	96.7s/143.8s
48	41.4s/46.8s	48.2s/61.1s	51.6s/70.4s	73.6s/98.5s	87.3s/114.4s	152.8s/225.1s

Seam Correction Evaluation. We first compared our results to the approach of Zhou and Koltun [26]. Their approach used images of all views to optimize color for each vertex. However, if some images were blurred, it generated blurring artifacts. Different from them, our approach selected the best images to texture faces on meshes. As a result, our method can avoid blurring effects effectively. Moreover, since we used high-resolution images to texture faces, we can generate high-quality texture maps even for low-resolution meshes. Results shown in Fig. 7 indicate that our approach can generate better results for blurring cases.

To evaluate the optimization performance quantitatively, we defined a normalized residual error by dividing it with the number of vertices used for optimization, and was described as:

$$RE_{normalized} = \frac{\sum_{i=1}^{k} \sum e^2}{|v|}. \tag{13}$$

In this way, the residual errors of ours and Zhou and Koltun' method [26] were comparable. We have shown the $RE_{normalized}$ results in Table 3.

From Table 3, we can find that our method converges faster than the method by Zhou and Koltun [26] (see the column named "Time per iter." and "# of iter."). Moreover, the computational cost of our approach outperforms Zhou and Koltun' method [26], especially for high-resolution meshes (see the column named "Total time" in Table 3). This can be explained as follows. Zhou and Koltun [26] utilized all vertices for optimization. Different from them, we only utilized related pixels around the seams for color optimization, and our computational cost was related to the number of edges of seams instead of the number of vertices.

Texture Maps Evaluation. Finally, we compared our final results to the approaches of Shan et al. [22], Waechter et al. [24] and Zhou and Koltun [26] qualitatively. For a fair comparison, all methods shared the same inputs. The results were shown in Fig. 8. Both [22] and [26] produced color for all vertices only. Shan et al. [22] blended color for vertices from views, resulting in blurry and ghosting artifacts shown in Fig. 8(a) and (e). Zhou and Koltun [26] generated

Table 3. Normalized residual error and average time cost per iteration. Our optimization converges faster and has a lower computational cost in each iteration

Model	Method/# of vertices	Normalized residual error					Time per iter.	# of iter.	Total time
		Initial	50 iter.	100 iter.	200 iter.	final			
Fig. 7(a)	Zhou et al./50k	0.061	0.043	0.031	0.022	0.018	0.062s	302	18.8s
	Ours/50k	0.061	0.033	0.021	0.020	0.018	0.042s	276	11.6s
Fig. 7(b)	Zhou et al./0.2m	0.065	0.047	0.038	0.028	0.019	0.180s	353	63.5s
	Ours/0.2m	0.065	0.039	0.029	0.020	0.019	0.046s	298	13.7s
Fig. 7(d)	Zhou et al./1m	0.063	0.051	0.045	0.037	0.018	0.420s	868	364.5s
	Ours/1m	0.063	0.038	0.027	0.021	0.018	0.058s	325	18.85s

better results in Fig. 8(b) and (f), but their performance was limited by the number of vertices. Waechter *et al.* [24] performed texturing per face on mesh with a single image, their approach generated obvious seams because of noises (shown in Fig. 8(c) and (g)). With our two-step optimization, our approach was able to produce visually seamless texture maps (see Fig. 8(d) and (h)). The comparison results show that our approach can substantially improve texture mapping.

6   Conclusions

It is a challenging problem to reconstruct virtual versions of real-life products realistically with inexpensive consumer-grade scanning devices. We have presented a two-step optimization solution for seamless texture mapping with noisy data. The seams are generated from imperceptible texture regions, and the seam misalignments are corrected by the color consistency strategy. We evaluate our approach on a number of objects. Experimental results have shown that our method can efficiently generate visually seamless high-fidelity texture maps with realistic appearance at a low cost. More experimental results are shown in the supplementary video.

It is worth noting that our approach uses a small set of data around seams to correct misalignments, and thus may not be able to correct large noisy data. We mainly focus on indoor objects, and the occlusion problem is not yet addressed. We plan to extend our approach to data with even larger noises in our future work.

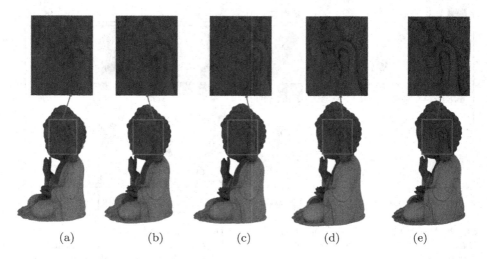

| (a) | (b) | (c) | (d) | (e) |

Fig. 7. (a)–(d) are the results of Zhou and Koltun' method by rendering meshes with vertex color. From left to right, the number of vertices of the models are 0.05 million, 0.2 million, 0.5 million, and 1 million, respectively. (e) is our result with 0.05 million vertices. We reconstruct high-quality texture maps with low geometric complexity

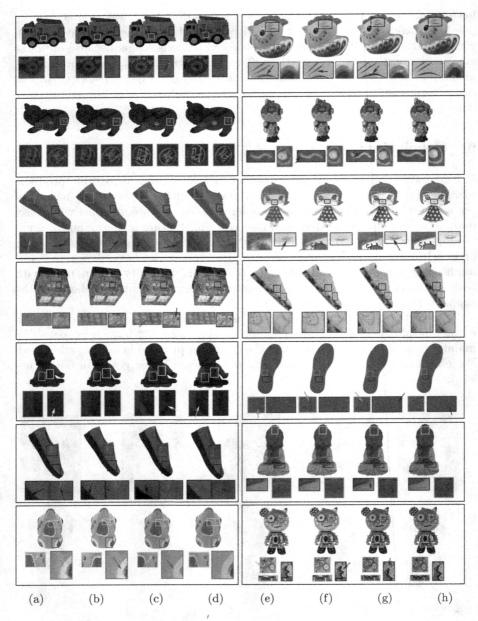

(a)   (b)   (c)   (d)   (e)   (f)   (g)   (h)

Fig. 8. We compare our method to the state-of-the-art methods with the same inputs. Shan *et al.* [22] (a, e) generate blurring and ghosting artifacts for noise data. Zhou and Koltun [26] perform better, but their results suffer from low-resolution geometry (b, f). Waechter *et al.* [24] select an image texturing per face by penalizing a global optimization, resulting in visible seams for noisy data (c, g). Our method can produce realistic and high-fidelity texture maps (d, h)

Acknowledgments. Xiaogang Jin is supported by the National Key R&D Program of China (No. 2017YFB1002600).

References

1. Ackermann, J., Langguth, F., Fuhrmann, S., Goesele, M.: Photometric stereo for outdoor webcams. In: IEEE Conference on Computer Vision and Pattern Recognition (CVPR) (2012)
2. Allene, C., Pons, J.P., Keriven, R.: Seamless image-based texture atlases using multi-band blending. In: 19th International Conference on Pattern Recognition (ICPR) (2008)
3. Barnes, C., Goldman, D.B., Shechtman, E., Finkelstein, A.: The patchmatch randomized matching algorithm for image manipulation. Commun. ACM **54**(11), 103–110 (2001)
4. Bernardini, F., Martin, I.M., Rushmeier, H.: High-quality texture reconstruction from multiple scans. IEEE Trans. Vis. Comput. Graph. **7**(4), 318–332 (2001)
5. Bi, S., Kalantari, N.K., Ramamoorthi, R.: Patch-based optimization for image-based texture mapping. ACM Trans. Graph. **36**(4), 106:1–106:11 (2017)
6. Boykov, Y., Veksler, O., Zabih, R.: Fast approximate energy minimization via graph cuts. IEEE Trans. Pattern Anal. Mach. Intell. **23**(11), 1222–1239 (2001)
7. Gal, R., Wexler, Y., Ofek, E., Hoppe, H., Cohen-Or, D.: Seamless montage for texturing models. In: Computer Graphics Forum, pp. 479–486 (2010)
8. Gupta, M., Agrawal, A., Veeraraghavan, A., Narasimhan, S.G.: Structured light 3D scanning in the presence of global illumination. In: IEEE Conference on Computer Vision and Pattern Recognition (CVPR) (2011)
9. Gupta, M., Nayar, S.K.: Micro phase shifting. In: IEEE Conference on Computer Vision and Pattern Recognition (CVPR) (2012)
10. Henry, P., Krainin, M., Herbst, E., Ren, X., Fox, D.: RGB-D mapping: using depth cameras for dense 3D modeling of indoor environments. In: Khatib, O., Kumar, V., Sukhatme, G. (eds.) Experimental Robotics, pp. 477–491. Springer, Heidelberg (2014). https://doi.org/10.1007/978-3-642-28572-1_33
11. Izadi, S., et al.: KinectFusion: real-time 3D reconstruction and interaction using a moving depth camera. In: Proceedings of the 24th Annual ACM Symposium on User Interface Software and Technology (UIST) (2011)
12. Kazhdan, M., Hoppe, H.: Screened poisson surface reconstruction. ACM Trans. Graph. **32**(3), 29:1–29:13 (2013)
13. Kindermann, R., Snell, J.L.: Markov Random Fields and Their Applications, vol. 1. American Mathematical Society, Providence (1980)
14. Lai, K., Bo, L., Ren, X., Fox, D.: A large-scale hierarchical multi-view RGB-D object dataset. In: IEEE International Conference on Robotics and Automation (ICRA) (2011)
15. Lempitsky, V., Ivanov, D.: Seamless mosaicing of image-based texture maps. In: IEEE Conference on Computer Vision and Pattern Recognition (CVPR) (2007)
16. Li, C., Wand, M.: Combining Markov random fields and convolutional neural networks for image synthesis. In: IEEE Conference on Computer Vision and Pattern Recognition (CVPR) (2016)
17. Li, C., Wand, M.: Precomputed real-time texture synthesis with markovian generative adversarial networks. In: Leibe, B., Matas, J., Sebe, N., Welling, M. (eds.) ECCV 2016. LNCS, vol. 9907, pp. 702–716. Springer, Cham (2016). https://doi.org/10.1007/978-3-319-46487-9_43

18. Moreno, D., Son, K., Taubin, G.: Embedded phase shifting: robust phase shifting with embedded signals. In: The IEEE Conference on Computer Vision and Pattern Recognition (CVPR), June 2015

19. Mur-Artal, R., Tardós, J.D.: ORB-SLAM2: an open-source SLAM system for monocular, stereo, and RGB-D cameras. IEEE Trans. Robot. **33**(5), 1255–1262 (2017)

20. Nießner, M., Zollhöfer, M., Izadi, S., Stamminger, M.: Real-time 3D reconstruction at scale using voxel hashing. ACM Trans. Graph. **32**(6), 169:1–169:11 (2013)

21. Pérez, P., Gangnet, M., Blake, A.: Poisson image editing. In: ACM SIGGRAPH 2003 Papers (2003)

22. Shan, Q., Adams, R., Curless, B., Furukawa, Y., Seitz, S.M.: The visual turing test for scene reconstruction. In: International Conference on 3D Vision (3DV) (2013)

23. Song, S., Xiao, J.: Tracking revisited using RGBD camera: unified benchmark and baselines. In: Proceedings of the 2013 IEEE International Conference on Computer Vision (ICCV) (2013)

24. Waechter, M., Moehrle, N., Goesele, M.: Let there be color! Large-scale texturing of 3D reconstructions. In: Fleet, D., Pajdla, T., Schiele, B., Tuytelaars, T. (eds.) ECCV 2014. LNCS, vol. 8693, pp. 836–850. Springer, Cham (2014). https://doi.org/10.1007/978-3-319-10602-1_54

25. Zhou, Q., Koltun, V.: Dense scene reconstruction with points of interest. ACM Trans. Graph. **32**(4), 112:1–112:8 (2013)

26. Zhou, Q., Koltun, V.: Color map optimization for 3D reconstruction with consumer depth cameras. ACM Trans. Graph. **33**(4), 155:1–155:10 (2014)

27. Zhou, Q.-Y., Park, J., Koltun, V.: Fast global registration. In: Leibe, B., Matas, J., Sebe, N., Welling, M. (eds.) ECCV 2016. LNCS, vol. 9906, pp. 766–782. Springer, Cham (2016). https://doi.org/10.1007/978-3-319-46475-6_47

Plane-Based Humanoid Robot Navigation and Object Model Construction for Grasping

Pavel Gritsenko[2], Igor Gritsenko[2], Askar Seidakhmet[2], and Bogdan Kwolek[1(✉)]

[1] AGH University of Science and Technology, 30 Mickiewicza, 30-059 Krakow, Poland
bkw@agh.edu.pl
http://home.agh.edu.pl/~bkw/contact.html
[2] Al-Farabi Kazakh National University, Prospect al-Farabi 71, Almaty, Kazakhstan

Abstract. In this work we present an approach to humanoid robot navigation and object model construction for grasping using only RGB-D data from an onboard depth sensor. A plane-based representation is used to provide a high-level model of the workspace, to estimate both the global robot pose and pose with respect to the object, and to determine the object pose as well as its dimensions. A visual feedback is used to achieve the desired robot pose for grasping. In the pre–grasping pose the robot determines the object pose as well as its dimensions. In such a local grasping approach, a simulator with our high-level scene representation and a virtual camera is used to fine-tune the motion controllers as well as to simulate and validate the process of grasping. We present experimental results that were obtained in simulations with virtual camera and robot as well as with real humanoid robot equipped with RGB-D camera, which performed object grasping in low-texture layouts.

Keywords: Object grasping · Humanoid robot · Pose recovery

1 Introduction

Humanoid robotics technology has recently made rapid progress. However, object grasping by humanoid robots is still a challenging problem due to complex mechanical structures, long kinematic chains, occlusions and noisy camera observations. Conventional approaches to object grasping can fail when the shape, dimension or pose of the objects are missing or are not precise enough. Grasping of unknown objects with neither 3D models nor appearance data is very important for humanoid robots that by definition should work in unknown and unstructured environments. Moreover, any humanoid robot should automatically determine best grasping pose, i.e. be able to approach the object as well avoid obstacles while moving towards the object of interest, and finally take the best pose with respect to the object. As noticed in a recent survey [1], very few works employ visual feedback during the reaching and grasping. Most approaches rely

© Springer Nature Switzerland AG 2019
L. Leal-Taixé and S. Roth (Eds.): ECCV 2018 Workshops, LNCS 11129, pp. 649–664, 2019.
https://doi.org/10.1007/978-3-030-11009-3_40

on open-loop algorithms, where the robot takes a single shot of the scene, determines the relative poses between the hands and the object of interest, and finally without a visual feedback drives the arms towards the object.

In real grasping scenarios with humanoid robots, particularly with robots that act as human assistants, the robot should be able to detect the object on the basis of a description provided by the user, or alternatively, it should recognize the object of interest or acquire information about the object on the basis of pointing gestures. Given the object of interest determined with such a user-friendly interface, the humanoid robot should approach the object and take the pre-grasping pose. Finally, it should determine object dimensions, best grasping points, calculate arm motions and execute grasping task. While approaching the object the robot should, among others, simultaneously build or update the map of the environment, construct high level-representation of the environment, determine its own pose in the map and with respect to the object, detect and avoid obstacles, etc.

Navigating in unknown environment towards the object to be grasped requires a SLAM (Simultaneous Localization and Mapping) system. Several approaches to solve SLAM problem have been proposed in the last two decades [2]. Most existing SLAM systems use RGB cameras or RGB-D cameras to perceive the scene. Traditional RGB image-based SLAM might fail in challenging low-texture cases. The reason for this is that in low-texture scenes it is often difficult to find a sufficient number of reliable point features and, as a consequence, the performance of such SLAM algorithms degrades. In such low-texture scenarios, in addition to points, lines, planes and objects should be utilized. Moreover, reasoning about 3D objects and layouts should be carried out for better scene understanding. The RGB-D SLAM systems built on point clouds require substantial amount of memory. Even when mapping a simple scene, for instance an empty room, in mentioned above representation the memory demands grow quickly with scene complexity and time.

In general, the existing approaches for unknown object grasping can be divided into two groups: global and local grasping approaches. Global grasping approaches employ the full 3D model of the unknown object to find appropriate grasps. The model can be constructed by the use of multiple views of the object, for instance, by using structure from motion to refine existing model, by using point clouds to infer 3D structure and/or model, or by decomposition the object into 3D shapes, etc. In contrast, local grasping approaches only utilize available data to accomplish suitable grasps using information like edges, silhouettes, boundaries, etc.

In this work we present an approach to humanoid robot navigation and object model construction for grasping using only RGB-D data from an onboard depth sensor. A plane-based representation is used to provide a high-level model of the workspace, i.e. the world in which the robot performs the task and occupies space, to estimate both the global robot pose and pose with respect to the object, and to determine the object pose as well as its dimensions. A visual feedback is used to achieve the desired robot pose for grasping. In the first stage, error between robot position and desired path is calculated, whereas in the last stage, error between robot pose and object pose is calculated for visual controller, which allows the robot reaching a pre-grasping pose. In the pre–grasping pose the robot determines the object pose as well as its dimensions. In such a local grasping approach, a simulator with our high-level scene representation and a virtual camera is used to fine-tune the motion controllers as well as to simulate and validate the process of grasping. We present experimental results that were obtained in simulations with virtual camera and robot as well as with real humanoid robot equipped with RGB-D camera, which performed object grasping in low-texture layouts.

2   Relevant Work and Our Contribution

2.1   Relevant Work

Contrary to analytic approaches to object grasping, approaches following the data-driven paradigm focus on object representation and extraction of perceptual information [1]. Data-driven grasp synthesis started to be used more broadly with the availability of GraspIt! [3], which is an interactive simulation, planning, analysis, and visualization tool to determine stable grasp for a mechanical hand. In [4], Kragic et al. presented a visual tracking system that was capable of recognizing objects. Once an object was recognized the model and object pose have been sent to GraspIt!. Then, a human operator utilized the discussed tool to design motion strategies for grasping of the considered object. The latest version of the discussed simulator can accommodate arbitrary hand as well as load objects and obstacles of arbitrary geometry.

In grasping system of a humanoid robot we can distinguish units responsible for navigation of the robot, acquisition of the object model and determining grasping points from the acquired data. Usually, the navigation unit is considered separately or it is assumed that the robot is placed in vicinity of the object, i.e. it is already located in a pre-grasping position. In [5] a SLAM-based grasping framework for robotic arm navigation and object model construction is presented. Authors of discussed work argue that although improving the object model is beneficial, it is not enough to achieve stable grasping. Thus, a correction of robot pose has been one of the key aspect of the proposed framework. They demonstrated the influence of the accuracy of the robot pose on the process of grasping. A simple object constructed from three planes attached together has been used in all experiments. The features of the object were defined as the intersection between these planes.

In approaches belonging to local grasping category, RGB-D cameras are usually used to provide information required for completing the task. An approach [6] uses object edges to determine grasping locations by fitting a so-called ?grasping rectangle? on image plane. Such a rectangle is used to describe gripper configuration. A learning algorithm has been investigated to select the best grasping location depending on the object shape. In a later work [7], the presented above idea has been extended by looking at the contact area of the grasping rectangle.

For instance, if the contact area appears to be too small, the grasp task is likely to fail and a better grasp is searched. An approach proposed by Ala et al. [8] retrieves graspable boundaries and convex segments of unknown object. In point clouds acquired by a 3D camera a scene segmentation is conducted to determine point cloud belonging to the object. With the help of blob detection, the object boundaries are determined to extract the boundary edges. The grasp planner determines one contact point in order to execute a boundary grasp. In [9], the algorithm fits the gripper shape to point cloud that belongs to the object. It utilizes a segmentation to delineate object from the scene as well as incorporates learning to improve the grasp success rate. In approach of Navarro [10], object center is estimated on the basis of point cloud. A tracking algorithm has been used to extract objects on a conveyer belt and then grasp them by a gripper. In [11] the principal axis and centroid of unknown object are estimated on the basis of point cloud to determine a stable grasp. A high success rate has been demonstrated for a set of household objects.

On the basis of a bottom-up hierarchical clustering approach, which is able to segment objects and parts in a scene, a transform from such a segmentation into a corresponding, hierarchical saliency function has been proposed in [12]. This hierarchical saliency characterizes most salient corresponding region (scale) for each point in the image. The discussed algorithm has been evaluated on an easy-to-use pick and place manipulation system.

2.2 Differences with Relevant Approaches

Our approach to scene and object representation differs in several aspects from approaches discussed in relevant work. The first difference is that our algorithm does not decompose point clouds onto sets of separate primitives, but instead it aggregates detected in advance planes onto objects and builds complex representations comprising plane-based objects and point clouds. The second difference is that our algorithm reconstructs any type plane-based objects consisting of any number of faces. Thus, it differs from widely used RANSAC algorithm, which can extract objects described mathematically. It can employ any of the state-of-the-art closed-form solutions [13–18] to estimate the robot pose. The use of trihedral angles (corners) to represent plane-based objects permits the discussed capability. Trihedral angles permit the use of all three types of primitives: point, line, plane, as well as point-to-point [15], line-to-line [14], plane-to-plane [13], point-to-line [17], point-to-plane [18], and line-to-plane [16] correspondences and their closed-form solutions. Owing to use of graph patterns it can be used to perform classification of objects.

Another important point is that there exist no state-of-the-art representation providing high-level information about the environment to allow a robot to distinguish between objects, their sizes and types [19]. With the ability to extract objects and their physical sizes, our high-level map representation provides additional information and opportunities for higher level understanding of the scene and object geometries.

3   Algorithm Overview

The plane object-based map representation is built on point cloud, which is calculated on the basis of RGB-D streams delivered by the Xtion sensor. Upon the segmented planes in the point cloud we build a graph, where a node and edge represent a plane and its real intersection with other plane, respectively. Afterwards, we extract all trihedral angles, i.e. corners represented by 3rd order cycles in the graph. Next, we carry out systematic aggregation of trihedral angles onto object such as trihedral angles belonging to the same plane-based object have common edges. At the end, we perform object classification using simple subgraph patterns and calculate their physical sizes. During approaching the object by a humanoid robot with the onboard RGB-D sensor, the point could is segmented, planes are extracted, correspondences between planes are determined, and relative poses (rotations and translations) between current and previous point clouds are determined using RANSAC algorithm, which is initialized in each frame with a direct pose estimate [20]. On the basis of the initial pose of the robot in real world coordinates, which is determined automatically on the basis of visual data, as well as object position that can be determined automatically or specified by the user, the robot calculates a collision free path, and then follows it using a visual feedback. A controller responsible for path following and reaching the desired pose uses the robot pose as well as object location. In the vicinity of the object the controller employs the object pose to achieve best grasping pose. It is determined by a simulator, which on the basis of our high-level object representation, the kinematic model of the humanoid robot, as well as virtual camera, performs a simulation of reaching and grasping the object. This means that the 3D scene fragments that are located in the field of view of the virtual camera can be extracted and then projected into the image plane of the camera. The simulations were done using Webots robot simulator [21,22], which provides a complete development environment to model, program and simulate robots and our scripts in Python language. In the simulation experiments an ArUco marker [23], which was attached to the object of interest has been detected and then used to determine the pose of Nao robot acting in virtual world. The parameters obtained in the simulation were then used in real experiments. Given a motion controller tuned by the discussed tool, the robot can follow any feasible path towards the pre-grasping position. The main role of our tool is simulation and visualization of the grasping process given the real pose of the robot as well as pose of the object together with its dimensions. We assume that the objects undergoing grasping are located on the floor and are composed of planes.

Figure 1 depicts step–by–step transition from simple point cloud to classified plane–based object representation with sizes (edge lengths). In the algorithm we can distinguish seven major steps. In the first step, RGB-D data stream consisting of a pair of a color image and a depth map is acquired. After that, colored point cloud is reconstructed on the basis of the RGB-D stream and intrinsic calibration parameters. The colored point cloud is an initial representation of the observed scene. In the next step, M-estimator SAmple Consensus (MSAC) is executed to perform plane segmentation. Afterwards, real planes intersections with their lengths are calculated. At the end, on the basis of segmented planes and their intersections a graph is being built. This leads to second map representation that comprises plane equations and point clouds representing objects of complex shape (not plane-based objects). Due to substitution of point clouds representing plane equations the map representation gets compact. In the following step, extraction of trihedral angles that are represented by 3rd order cycles from the constructed graph takes place (Fig. 2). After determining the trihedral angles, their aggregation can be performed as the trihedral angles of the same plane-based object have common edges. Finding common edges for trihedral angles is performed using the constructed graph. Through aggregating all trihedral angles with common edges we get abstract plane-based objects. This means that at this stage we have a structure that describes which planes belong to which object, the number of such objects, their dimensions, but no types. Therefore, this representation is called as abstract plane-based objects, see also Fig. 1. The last step is devoted to classification. The classification relies on matching graph patterns with a subgraph from the extracted graph. The resulting algorithm is simple and effective.

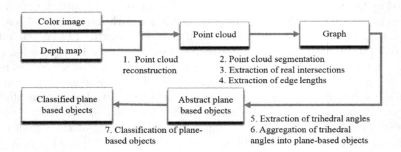

Fig. 1. Diagram illustrating transition from colored point cloud to classified plane object-based high-level map representation.

4   The Algorithm

4.1   Object Model and Its Dimensions

Determining Physical Object Size. Let us consider how the real intersection of two planes and their length can be extracted. Let's assume that we have two planes: $P_1 = A_1x + B_1y + C_1z + D_1$ and $P_2 = A_2x + B_2y + C_2z + D_2$. According to algorithm in Fig. 1, after point cloud segmentation we determine the plane intersections. Thus, after this step we have in disposal planes and their inliers, i.e. array of points representing them. Let's denote P_1 inliers as $\{p_{plane1,1} \cdots p_{plane1,i}\}$ and P_2 inliers as $\{p_{plane2,1} \cdots p_{plane2,i}\}$. According to definition of the intersection, which states that if planes P_1 and P_2 have real intersection then they should have common inliers $\{p_{edge,1} \ldots p_{edge,i}\}$, i.e. array of points belonging to P_1 and P_2 simultaneously, see (1):

$$\{p_{edge,1} \ldots p_{edge,i}\} = \{p_{plane1,1} \ldots p_{plane1,i}\} \cap \{p_{plane2,1} \ldots p_{plane2,i}\} \quad (1)$$

However, $p_{edge,1} \ldots p_{edge,i} = \emptyset$, because a point can be among inliers of only single plane. Thus, we reformulate this definition and state that the points representing real intersection $p_{edge,1} \ldots p_{edge,i}$ will be simultaneously close to planes P_1 and P_2. Therefore, on the basis of Eqs. (2)–(5) we determine the point-to-plane distance for both sets of inliers to both planes.

$$\{d_{plane1-plane1,1} \ldots d_{plane1-plane1,i}\} = |A_1 p_{plane1,i,x} + B_1 p_{plane1,i,y}$$
$$+ C_1 p_{plane1,i,z} + D_1| * (A_1^2 + B_1^2 + C_1^2)^{1/2} \quad (2)$$

$$\{d_{plane1-plane2,1} \ldots d_{plane1-plane2,i}\} = |A_2 p_{plane1,i,x} + B_2 p_{plane1,i,y}$$
$$+ C_2 p_{plane1,i,z} + D_2| * (A_2^2 + B_2^2 + C_2^2)^{1/2} \quad (3)$$

$$\{d_{plane2-plane2,1} \ldots d_{plane2-plane2,i}\} = |A_2 p_{plane2,i,x} + B_2 p_{plane2,i,y}$$
$$+ C_2 p_{plane2,i,z} + D_2| * (A_2^2 + B_2^2 + C_2^2)^{1/2} \quad (4)$$

$$\{d_{plane2-plane1,1} \ldots d_{plane2-plane1,i}\} = |A_1 p_{plane2,i,x} + B_1 p_{plane2,i,y}$$
$$+ C_1 p_{plane2,i,z} + D_1| * (A_1^2 + B_1^2 + C_1^2)^{1/2} \quad (5)$$

After that we determine all points that have the distance to both planes smaller than d_{thresh} and grater than d_{min}. d_{min} is utilized to cope with noise.

In order to define edge length d_{edge} we take two points from $p_{edge,1} \ldots p_{edge,i}$ with maximum distance to each other. The distance between the points represents diagonal length $d_{diagonal}$ of the cylinder of radius d_{thresh}. Thus, the edge length is determined on the basis of (6):

$$4 * d_{tresh}^2 + d_{edge}^2 = d_{diagonal}^2 \quad (6)$$

Aggregation of Planes into Object. After determining plane intersections we can build a graph whose node and edge represent a plane and its real intersection with other plane, respectively. The graph permits us to determine in a fast manner all trihedral angles as 3rd order cycles in the graph, see also Fig. 2. Subsequently, we assume that all trihedral angles of the same plane-based object have common edges.

If the object is presented by several trihedral angles the assumption mentioned above allows us to merge them angle-by-angle and extract plane-based object. If the trihedral angle has no common edges then the object is represented by single trihedral angle. All trihedral angles are represented by three planes, see also Fig. 2. Let's denote them by indexes of planes. Thus, the trihedral angle

1-4-7 has no common edges. Therefore, Box object from Fig. 2 is plane-based object and is represented by single trihedral angle, whereas Locker 2 object is represented by single trihedral angle 1-3-6. Locker 1 object from Fig. 2 consist of two trihedral angles 1-8-9 and 1-5-8. These trihedral angles have common edge 1-8, so that Locker 1 is plane-based object represented by two trihedral angles. In this way the aggregation is capable of adding trihedral angles, angle-by-angle.

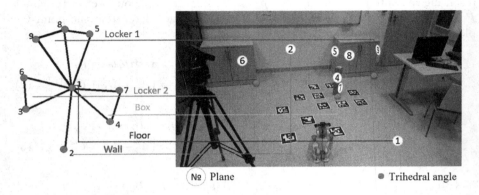

Fig. 2. Graph representing scene that is observed by Nao robot with onboard Xtion sensor. Orange stands for centers of trihedral angles. Circles with numbers stand for segmented planes, whereas blue color points on the graph vertices. Black edges between blue nodes on the graph represent real intersections between segmented planes. For visualization purposes only selected trihedral angles were used for graph construction. (Color figure online)

Classification of Objects. After extracting all plane-based objects, a classification step is executed. This step boils down to splitting the graph into subgraphs (for instance plane one in Fig. 2), and then matching the predefined patterns, see Fig. 3.

Fig. 3. Predefined patterns to match objects in the graph representation.

Merging Plane Object-Based High-Level Map Representation. Merging a pair of plane object-based high-level map representation is performed using a graph representation. At the beginning, data association is performed, and plane-to-plane correspondence is determined on the basis of matching normals and distances between the considered planes. Afterwards, a transformation matrix between frames is determined on the basis of closed-form solution for plane-to-plane correspondence [20]. The transformation matrix is then refined by the ICP algorithm. Next, frames are aligned. Subsequently, on the basis of plane-to-plane correspondences we merge graph representations. This is done under assumption that each edge length is the longest one from corresponding edges in pair of frames. In this way the graph is reconstructed. In the last stage, we reinitialize the plane-based object structure and execute classification, see Fig. 4.

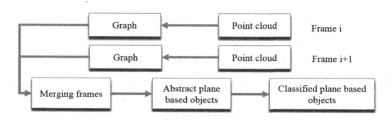

Fig. 4. Algorithm of merging plane object-based high-level map representations.

Determining the Main Axis of the Object. Let's denote center of trihedral angle as $T_c(x_{T_c}, y_{T_c}, z_{T_c})$, and the three edge vectors containing edge length and its direction as (e_1, e_2, e_3). Then central point of the object $C(x_c, y_c, z_c)$ can be calculated as follows:

$$C = T_c + (e_1 + e_2 + e_3)/2 \tag{7}$$

If object includes several trihedral angles then central point of the object is identified as mean of central points of all trihedral angles in this object. The axis is defined as normal $N(A, B, C)$ of the plane described by the equation $P = Ax + By + Cz + D$ and representing object side chosen for grasping. From one hand, the proposed algorithm can identify central point and appropriate sides for grasping, as well as their axes for any plane-based object. From the other hand, complex plane-based objects require complex control strategy for grasping and it is an open problem. Figure 5 illustrates identification of sides and axes of the object, which are appropriate for grasping, as well as calculating object's central point.

4.2   Navigation and Grasping

Given the point cloud, the robot extracts planes from it and identifies correspondences between planes. Then, on the basis of such plane correspondences, not less than three, not parallel planes are used for direct 6-DoF pose estimation [20]. This pose is used as an initial point for further refinement by the ICP algorithm. It is worth noting that the ICP algorithm uses no initial point cloud, but it uses reconstructed point cloud on the basis of inliers of all extracted

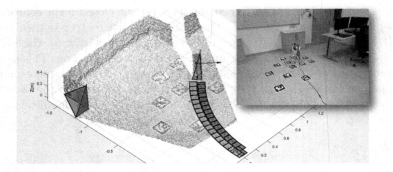

Fig. 5. Identification of sides and axes of the object, which are appropriate for grasping, as well as calculating object central point. Motion planning was done on the basis of extracted central point and axis of proper side. Red patches represent footsteps of right leg, while green patches represent footsteps of left leg. Different objects on the scene are represented by different colors, e.g. Box from Fig. 2 is represented by green color, while Locker 2 is represented by red color. No axis is presented for Locker 2 because no side is appropriate for the grasping. (Color figure online)

planes. Such point cloud is constructed for the current frame and for the target frame to align. After alignment, not associated plane equations are added to the first frame together with their inliers. The transformation for the next frame is calculated with regard to the updated first frame. Therefore, transformation is calculated not in frame-by-frame manner, but all frames are aligned to the updated first frame. As a result of the alignment, final transformation matrix and robot pose are determined. To cope with data association we keep transformation matrix for the last used frame, so that each new frame is firstly transformed by this matrix.

5   Experimental Results

Our system is conceived to work with any RGB-D sensor. In the experiments we utilized ASUS Xtion sensor, which has been mounted on the Nao humanoid robot. It works at a frame rate of 30 Hz and delivers stream of color images of size 320×240 and depth map stream, whose images have resolution of 640×480 pixels. The system has been tested in scenarios similar to scenario shown on Fig. 2. Figure 6 illustrates constructing plane object-based high-level map representation and merging it frame-by-frame. Figure 6a shows results of reconstruction of point cloud using color image, depth map and intrinsic calibration parameters. Figure 6b depicts extraction of planes from the reconstructed point cloud using MSAC. Figure 6c shows results of systematic aggregation of trihedral angles into objects. The top row presents results that were obtained for the first frame, whereas bottom row presents results that were obtained in frame tenth. In the discussed experiment we merged point clouds that were reconstructed step-by-step from color images and depth maps, using estimated robot poses.

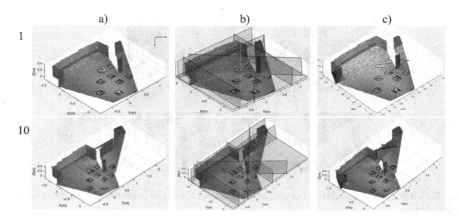

Fig. 6. An example of constructing plane object-based high-level map representation and merging it frame-by-frame. (a) Reconstructed point cloud using color image, depth map and intrinsic calibration data of the sensor. (b) Extracted planes from point cloud using MSAC. (c) Systematic aggregation of trihedral angles into objects. Green points of the graph denote centers of trihedral angles, while blue points denote estimated centers of objects. Edges of trihedral angles are represented by black line segments, while axis of objects appropriate for grasping are represented by black arrows. (Color figure online)

As we can observe on Fig. 6b–c, the proposed algorithm for extraction of real intersections of planes from point cloud gave satisfactory results. It is worth noting that the trihedral angle permits the use of all three types of basic geometric primitives: point, line and plane. However, how to combine transformation matrices, which are calculated using different closed form solutions for our high-level map representation is an open problem. In the discussed experiment we have utilized plane-to-plane [13] correspondence in order to find the transformation matrix between frames.

In the next stage we conducted experiments consisting in grasping the objects by Nao robot. At the beginning we performed simulations to tune controllers for path following. Afterwards, simulations aiming at tuning arm controllers were conducted. Finally, Nao humanoid robot has been utilized in experiments with object grasping. Figure 7a shows view of the simulated scene using Webots API (see also images acquired by virtual cameras), Fig. 7b depicts view of the real scene, whereas Fig. 7c contains example images that were obtained in simulation of object grasping. In Fig. 7a there are three sub-images that were acquired by virtual cameras that the Nao robot was equipped with. The left sub-image was acquired by camera (bottom) that is located in the Nao's head, the middle sub-image contains depth map that was grabbed by simulated RGB-D sensor, whereas right sub-image depicts RGB image acquired by RGB-D sensor. As we can notice, the RGB-D sensor has been mounted on the Nao's head.

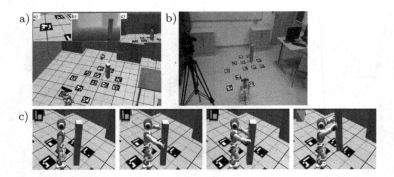

Fig. 7. View of the simulated scene (a), real scene view (b), simulated grasping of the object (c).

In order to show potential of the presented approach we calculated errors in three scenarios. In the first one the Nao robot approached the object without visual feedback using only footsteps determined in advance. In the second scenario the robot followed path that was determined in advance. In the discussed scenario the robot pose has been corrected using visual feedback in a predefined number of control points. In the last scenario the robot followed first part of the path using visual feedback in the predefined number of control points, whereas in the last part of the path the information about the relative robot-object poses was used to correct the robot motion. The actual robot pose in the world coordinates has been determined on the basis of images acquired from on-board camera, using algorithm discussed in Subsect. 4.2. The pose and main axis of the object were determined using algorithm described in Subsect. 4.1. Figure 8 depicts representative results that were obtained in one of the simulations.

Figure 8a depicts distance between estimated position and the reference path vs. control point number in three scenarios. In the first scenario the robot walked towards the object using motions that were determined in advance by

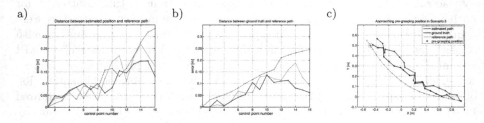

Fig. 8. Left plot: distance between estimated position and the reference path vs. control point number. Middle plot: distance between ground-truth and the reference path. Red - no correction of Nao pose, green - path following using visual feedback, blue – path following in the first eight control points and object approaching in remaining points. Right plot: approaching pre-grasping position in Scenario 3. (Color figure online)

the footstep planner. As we can notice, without a visual feedback the error grows over time. Owing to using P controllers that were responsible by steering the robot towards the reference path, the error between the reference path and the estimated pose has been reduced. The control corrections have been calculated using the estimated robot position and orientation with respect to reference position and orientation and then used in moveTo function to correct robot motion. In the discussed scenario, in each control point the robot corrects its motion to follow the reference path using visual feedback. In the third scenario, the robot followed first part of the path using the same control strategy as in scenario two, whereas in the last part of the path the robot used information about the object location. This means that in the control point the robot estimated relative position and orientation with respect to the object of interest. On the basis of estimated object position and orientation the robot exploited P controllers to reduce distance to the object and angle between camera main axis and object main axis. As we can notice on the plot shown on Fig. 8a, in the discussed scenario the error at the pre-grasping position has been further reduced.

Figure 8b depicts distance between the reference path and the ground-truth, i.e. distance between the reference path and the real position of the robot in three scenarios. As we can notice, in the third scenario, in the pre-grasping position the error between the robot and the desired position is equal to 6.6 cm. Table 1 contains errors that were obtained in discussed experiment. As we can see on Fig. 8c the robot was able to achieve a pre-grasping position that was quite close to desired one.

Table 1. Errors that were obtained in the simulated environment, c.f. plot on Fig. 8b.

Error [cm]	Scenario 1	Scenario 2	Scenario 3
Average error	13.0	8.3	6.6
Error in pre-grasping position	24.5	9.1	6.1

Figure 9 depicts some color images with corresponding depth maps that were acquired by virtual RGB-D camera mounted on Nao's head in an experiment in 3rd scenario. The advantage of our simulator is that it not only provides precise ground-truth for both the robot and the camera but it allows also contamination of images and depth maps by noise that can arise during real experiments. This means that it allows to investigate the influence of blur motion, rapid movements and rotations as well as depth error on the performance of the object grasping.

Next, we conducted experiments using real humanoid robot. The ground-truth of the robot pose has been determined using ArUco markers [23], which were placed on the floor, see also Fig. 2. In 3rd scenario the error at the pre-grasping position was between five and eight centimeters. The average error in determining the physical dimensions of the rectangular object from Fig. 2 is about two centimeters, whereas the average error of the main axis is below three

Fig. 9. Images acquired by virtual RGB-D camera mounted on Nao's head in control point #1, #6, #11 and #16, respectively.

degrees. Figure 10 depicts sample images that were acquired in one of the experiments. As we can notice, due to rapid rotations the images are contaminated by motion blur, and thus the ground-truth that has been calculated on the basis of ArUco markers was not accurate enough to calculate supplementary quantitative results. The system operates at frame rate of about 5 Hz at Intel I7 CPU. Supplemental material from experiments with real robot is available at: http:// bit.ly/ECCV2018_Wksp_6DObjectPose.

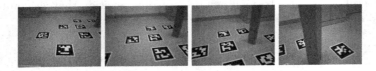

Fig. 10. Images acquired by Xtion sensor mounted on Nao's head in control point #1, #6, #11 and #16, respectively.

6   Conclusions

We presented an approach for plane-based humanoid robot navigation towards the object as well as object model construction for grasping. We presented a novel algorithm for constructing plane object-based high-level scene representation. We discussed determining the object model and its dimensions, aggregation of planes into object, and determining the main axis of the object. We presented experimental results that were achieved in simulations with virtual camera and robot as well as with real humanoid robot equipped with RGB-D camera, which performed object grasping in low-texture layouts. The visual feedback acknowledged its usefulness in achieving the pre-grasping pose by the robot.

Acknowledgment. This work was supported by Polish National Science Center (NCN) under research grants 2014/15/B/ST6/02808 and 2017/27/B/ST6/01743.

References

1. Bohg, J., Morales, A., Asfour, T., Kragic, D.: Data-driven grasp synthesis - a survey. IEEE Trans. Robot. **30**(2), 289–309 (2014)
2. Bresson, G., Alsayed, Z., Yu, L., Glaser, S.: Simultaneous localization and mapping: a survey of current trends in autonomous driving. IEEE Trans. Intell. Veh. **2**(3), 194–220 (2017)
3. Miller, A.T., Allen, P.K.: Graspit! A versatile simulator for robotic grasping. IEEE Robot. Autom. Mag. **11**(4), 110–122 (2004)
4. Kragic, D., Miller, A.T., Allen, P.K.: Real-time tracking meets online grasp planning. In: Proceedings of IEEE International Conference on Robotics and Automation, vol. 3, pp. 2460–2465 (2001)
5. Wongwilai, N., Niparnan, N., Sudsang, A.: SLAM-based grasping framework for robotic arm navigation and object model construction. In: IEEE International Conference on Cyber Technology in Automation, Control and Intelligent, pp. 156–161 (2014)
6. Jiang, Y., Moseson, S., Saxena, A.: Efficient grasping from RGBD images: learning using a new rectangle representation. In: IEEE International Conference on Robotics and Automation, pp. 3304–3311 (2011)
7. Lin, Y.C., Wei, S.T., Fu, L.C.: Grasping unknown objects using depth gradient feature with eye-in-hand RGB-D sensor. In: IEEE International Conference on Automation Science and Engineering (CASE), pp. 1258–1263 (2014)
8. Ala, R., Kim, D.H., Shin, S.Y., Kim, C., Park, S.K.: A 3D-grasp synthesis algorithm to grasp unknown objects based on graspable boundary and convex segments. Inf. Sci. **295**(C), 91–106 (2015)
9. ten Pas, A., Platt, R.: Using geometry to detect grasp poses in 3D point clouds. In: Bicchi, A., Burgard, W. (eds.) Robotics Research. SPAR, vol. 2, pp. 307–324. Springer, Cham (2018). https://doi.org/10.1007/978-3-319-51532-8_19
10. Navarro, S.E., Weiss, D., Stogl, D., Milev, D., Hein, B.: Tracking and grasping of known and unknown objects from a conveyor belt. In: 41st International Symposium on Robotics ISR/Robotik 2014, pp. 1–8 (2014)
11. Suzuki, T., Oka, T.: Grasping of unknown objects on a planar surface using a single depth image. In: IEEE International Conference on Advanced Intelligent Mechatronics (AIM), pp. 572–577 (2016)
12. Klein, D.A., Illing, B., Gaspers, B., Schulz, D., Cremers, A.B.: Hierarchical salient object detection for assisted grasping. In: IEEE International Conference on Robotics and Automation (ICRA), pp. 2230–2237 (2017)
13. Grimson, W., Lozano-Perez, T.: Model-based recognition and localization from sparse range or tactile data. Int. J. Robot. Res. **3**(3), 3–35 (1984)
14. Zhang, Z., Faugeras, O.: Determining motion from 3D line segment matches: a comparative study. Image Vis. Comput. **9**(1), 10–19 (1991)
15. Umeyama, S.: Least-squares estimation of transformation parameters between two point patterns. IEEE Trans. Pattern Anal. Mach. Intell. **13**(4), 376–380 (1991)
16. Chen, H.: Pose determination from line-to-plane correspondences: existence condition and closed-form solutions. IEEE Trans. Pattern Anal. Mach. Intell. **13**(6), 530–541 (1991)
17. Nister, D.: A minimal solution to the generalised 3-point pose problem. In: IEEE Conference on Computer Vision and Pattern Recognition (CVPR), pp. 560–567, June 2004

18. Ramalingam, S., Taguchi, Y.: A theory of minimal 3D point to 3D plane registration and its generalization. Int. J. Comput. Vis. **102**, 73–90 (2012)
19. Cadena, C., et al.: Past, present, and future of simultaneous localization and mapping: toward the robust-perception age. IEEE Trans. Robot. **32**(6), 1309–1332 (2016)
20. Khoshelham, K.: Direct 6-DoF pose estimation from point-plane correspondences. In: International Conference on Digital Image Computing: Techniques and Applications (DICTA), pp. 1–6 (2015)
21. Michel, O.: Webots: professional mobile robot simulation. J. Adv. Robot. Syst. **1**(1), 39–42 (2004)
22. Webots. Commercial Mobile Robot Simulation Software. http://www.cyberbotics.com
23. Romero-Ramirez, F.J., Muñoz-Salinas, R., Medina-Carnicer, R.: Speeded up detection of squared fiducial markers. Image Vis. Comput. **76**, 38–47 (2018)

Category-Level 6D Object Pose Recovery
in Depth Images

Caner Sahin[(✉)] and Tae-Kyun Kim

ICVL, Imperial College London, London, UK
c.sahin14@imperial.ac.uk

Abstract. Intra-class variations, distribution shifts among source and target domains are the major challenges of category-level tasks. In this study, we address category-level full 6D object pose estimation in the context of depth modality, introducing a novel part-based architecture that can tackle the above-mentioned challenges. Our architecture particularly adapts the distribution shifts arising from shape discrepancies, and naturally removes the variations of texture, illumination, pose, etc., so we call it as "Intrinsic Structure Adaptor (ISA)". We engineer ISA based on the followings: (i) "Semantically Selected Centers (SSC)" are proposed in order to define the "6D pose" at the level of categories. (ii) 3D skeleton structures, which we derive as shape-invariant features, are used to represent the parts extracted from the instances of given categories, and privileged one-class learning is employed based on these parts. (iii) Graph matching is performed during training in such a way that the adaptation/generalization capability of the proposed architecture is improved across unseen instances. Experiments validate the promising performance of the proposed architecture using both synthetic and real datasets.

Keywords: Category-level · 6D object pose · 3D skeleton ·
Graph matching · Privileged one-class learning

1 Introduction

Accurate 3D object detection and pose estimation, also known as 6D object pose recovery, is an essential ingredient for many practical applications related to scene understanding, augmented reality, control and navigation of robotics, *etc*. While substantial progress has been made in the last decade, either using depth information from RGB-D sensors [1–8] or even estimating pose from a single RGB image [9–12], improved results have been reported for instance-level recognition where source data from which a classifier is learnt share the same statistical distributions with the target data on which the classifiers will be tested. Instance-based methods cannot easily be generalized for category-level tasks, which inherently involve the challenges such as distribution shift among source and target domains, high intra-class variations, and shape discrepancies between objects, *etc*.

© Springer Nature Switzerland AG 2019
L. Leal-Taixé and S. Roth (Eds.): ECCV 2018 Workshops, LNCS 11129, pp. 665–681, 2019.
https://doi.org/10.1007/978-3-030-11009-3_41

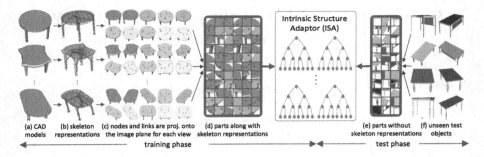

Fig. 1. Intrinsic Structure Adaptor (ISA) is trained based on parts extracted from instances of a given category. CAD models in (a) are represented with skeletons in (b). Nodes and links are projected onto the image plane in (c) for each view. Parts along with skeletal representations in (d) are fed into the forest. In the test, appearances of the parts (e) that are extracted from depth images of unseen instances (f) are used in order to hypothesise 6D pose.

At the level of categories, Sliding Shapes (SS) [13], an SVM-based method enlarging search space to 3D, detects objects in the context of depth modality naturally tackling the variations of texture, illumination, and viewpoint. The detection performance of this method is further improved in Deep Sliding Shapes (Deep SS) [14], where more powerful representations encoding geometric shapes are learned in ConvNets. These two methods run sliding windows in the 3D space mainly concerning 3D object detection rather than full 6D pose estimation. The system in [15], inspired by [13], further estimates detected and segmented objects' rotation around the gravity axis using a CNN. The system is the combination of individual detection/segmentation and pose estimation frameworks. Unlike these methods, we aim to directly hypothesise full 6D poses in a single-shot operation. The ways the methods above [13–15] address the challenges of categories are relatively naive. Both SS and the method in [15] rely on the availability of large scale 3D models in order to cover the shape variance of objects in the real world. Deep SS performs slightly better against the categories' challenges, however, its effort is limited to the capability of ConvNets.

In this study, we engineer a dedicated architecture that directly tackles the challenges of categories while estimating objects' 6D. To this end, we utilize *3D skeleton structures*, derive those as shape-invariant features, and use those as privileged information during the training phase of our architecture. *3D skeleton structures* are frequently used in the literature in order to handle shape discrepancies [16–19]. We introduce "Intrinsic Structure Adaptor (ISA)", a part-based random forest architecture, for full 6D object pose estimation at the level of categories in depth images. ISA works in the 6D space. It neither requires a segmented/cropped image as in [15], nor asks for 3D bounding box proposals as in [14]. Unlike [13,14], instead of running sliding windows, ISA extracts parts from the input depth image, and feeding all those down the forest, directly votes for the 6D pose of objects. Its training phase is processed so that the challenges of the categories can successfully be tackled. 3D skeleton structures are used to represent the parts extracted from the instances of given categories, and privileged learning is employed based on these parts. Graph matching is performed during the splitting processes of random forest in such a way that the adaptation/generalization capability of the proposed architecture is improved across unseen instances. Note that, unlike [13–15], this is one-class learning, and a single classifier is learnt for all instances of the given category. Figure 1 depicts the whole system of our architecture. To summarize, our main contributions are as follows:

Contributions. "Semantically Selected Centers (SSC)" are proposed in order to define the "6D pose" at the level of categories. 3D skeleton structures, which we derive as shape-invariant features, are used to represent the parts extracted from the instances of given categories, and privileged one-class learning is employed based on these parts. Graph matching is performed during training in such a way that the adaptation/generalization capability of the proposed architecture is improved across unseen instances.

2   Related Work

A number of methods have been proposed for 3D object detection and pose estimation, and for skeleton representations. For the reader's convenience, we only review 6D case for instance-level object detection and pose estimation, and keep category-level detection broader.

2.1   Object Detection and Pose Estimation

Instance-Level (6D): State-of-the-art methods for instance-level 6D object pose estimation report improved results tackling the problem's main challenges, such as occlusion and clutter, and texture-less objects, *etc.* The holistic template matching approach, Linemod [20], estimates cluttered object's 6D pose using color gradients and surface normals. It is improved by discriminative learning in [21], and later been utilized in a part-based random forest method [22] in order to provide robustness across occlusion. Occlusion aware features [23] are further formulated, and more recently feature representations are learnt in an unsupervised fashion using deep convolutional networks [1,24]. The studies in [2,3] cope with texture-less objects. Whilst these methods fuse data coming from RGB and depth channels, a local belief propagation based approach [25] and an iterative refinement architecture [26,27] are proposed in depth modality [28]. 6D pose estimation is recently achieved from RGB only [9–12]. Despite being successful, instance-based methods cannot easily be generalized for category-level tasks, which inherently involve the challenges such as distribution shift among source and target domains, high intra-class variations, and shape discrepancies between objects, *etc.*

Category-Level: At the level of categories, several studies combine depth data with RGB. Depth images are encoded into a series of channels in [29] in such a way that R-CNN, the network pre-designed for RGB images, can represent that encoding properly. The learnt representation along with the features extracted from RGB images are then fed into an SVM classifier. In another study [30], annotated depth data, available for a subset of categories in Imagenet, are used to learn mid-level representations that can be fused with mid-level RGB representations. Although promising, they are not capable enough for the applications beyond 2D.

Sliding Shapes (SS) [13], an SVM-based method, hypothesises 3D bounding boxes of the objects, and naturally tackles the variations of texture, illumination, and viewpoint, since it works in depth images. However, hand-crafted features used by the method, being unable to reasonably handle the challenges of categories, limit the method's detection performance across unseen instances. Deep Sliding Shapes (Deep SS) [14], the method based on 3D convolutional neural networks (CNN), learns more powerful representations for encoding geometric shapes further improving SS. However, the improvement is architecture-wise, and Deep SS encodes a 3D space using Truncated Signed Distance Functions (TSDF), similar to SS. Although promising, both methods concentrate on hypothesising 3D bounding boxes, running sliding windows in the 3D space. Our architecture, ISA, works in the 6D space. Instead of running sliding windows, it directly votes for the 6D pose of the objects by passing the parts extracted from the input depth image down all the trees in the forest. The system in [15], inspired by [13], further estimates detected and segmented objects rotation around gravity direction using a CNN, which is trained using pixel surface normals. A relative improvement is observed in terms of accuracy, however, the system is built integrating individual detection/segmentation and pose estimation frameworks. ISA neither requires a segmented/cropped image as in [15], nor asks for 3D bounding box proposals as in [14].

Despite being proposed to work in large-scale scenarios, the methods [13–15] do not have specific designs that can explicitly tackle the challenges of categories. SS relies on the availability of large scale 3D models in order to handle distribution shifts arising from shape discrepancies. Deep SS learns powerful 3D features from the data via a CNN architecture, however, the representation used to encode a 3D space is similar to the one used in SS, that is, the improvement on the feature representation arises from the CNN architecture. Gupta et al. [15] use objects' CAD models at different scales in order to cover the shape variance of the objects in the real world while estimating objects' rotation and translation. Unlike these methods, ISA is a dedicated architecture that directly tackles the challenges of the categories while estimating objects 6D. It employs graph matching during forest training based on the parts represented with skeleton structures in such a way that the adaptation/generalization capability is improved across unseen instances.

2.2   Skeleton Representation

Skeletal structures have frequently been used in the literature, particularly to improve the performance of action/activity recognition algorithms. Baek et al. [31] consider the geometry between scene layouts and human skeletons and propose kinematic-layout random forests. Another study [17] utilizes skeleton joints as privileged information along with raw depth maps in an RNN framework in order to recognise actions. The study in [18] shows that, one can effectively utilize 3D skeleton structures for overcoming intra-class variations, and for building a more accurate classifier, advocating the idea, domain invariant features increase generalization, stated in [19].

3   Proposed Architecture

This section presents the technologies top of which the proposed architecture, ISA, is based on. We firstly define the "pose" for the category-level 6D object pose estimation problem, and demonstrate the dataset and annotations discussing shape-invariant feature representations. We next present privileged one-class learning where we employ graph matching, and lastly we describe the test step, category-level 6D object pose estimation.

3.1   Pose Definition: Semantically Selected Centers (SSC)

A method designed for 6D pose estimation outputs the 3D position and 3D rotation of an object of interest in camera-centered coordinates. According to this output, it is important to precisely assign the reference coordinate frame to the interested object. When the method is proposed for instance-level 6D object pose estimation tasks, the most common approach is to assign the reference coordinate frame to the center of mass (COM) of the object's model. At the level of instances, source data from which a classifier is learnt share the same statistical distributions with the target data on which the classifiers will be tested, that is, training and test samples are of the same object. Hence, instance-level 6D pose estimators output the relative orientation between the COM of the object and the camera center. At the level of categories, in turn, this 6D pose definition cannot be directly utilised, since significant distribution shifts arise between training and test data.

An architecture engineered for the category-level 6D object pose estimation problem should hypothesise 6D pose parameters of unseen objects. Objects from the same category typically have similar physical sizes [14]. However, investigations over 3D models of the instances demonstrate that each instance has different COM, thus making the utilization of conventional 6D pose definition to malfunction for category-level tasks. In such a case, we reveal Semantically Selected Centers (SSC), which allow us to redefine the "6D pose" for the category-level 6D object pose estimation problem. For every category we define only one SSC performing the following procedure:

Fig. 2. Semantically Selected Centers (SSC): top row shows centers of mass of the instances, while the bottom row depicts SSCs of the corresponding instances (views best describing the difference selected).

- For each instance, skeletal graph representation is extracted, and the COM is found over 3D model. 3D distances between the nodes of the representation and the COM is computed.
- Between all instances, the skeleton nodes are topologically matched, and the most repetitive node is determined.
- In case there are more than 1 repetitive node computed, the SSCs are determined by interpolating between the repetitive nodes.

Note that, this repetitive node is also the one closest to the COMs of the instances. As the last step, we assign reference coordinate frames to the related parts of the objects given in the category. Figure 2 shows SSCs for the chair category. Despite the fact that COMs of the models are individually different, the 6D pose of each chair is defined with respect to Semantically Selected Centers (bottom row of the figure).

The metric proposed in [20], Average Distance (AD), is designed to measure the performance of instance-level object detectors. In order to evaluate our architecture, we modify AD making this metric work at the level of categories via the Semantically Selected Centers (SSC) of the instances of the given category. $M_c^{SSC_i}$ is the 3D model of the instance i that belongs to the category c, and the set of $M_c^{SSC_i}$ of the test instances form $\mathcal{M}_c$: $\mathcal{M}_c = \{M_c^{SSC_i} | i = 1, 2, ...\}$. $X_c^{SSC_i}$ is the point cloud of the model $M_c^{SSC_i}$. Having the ground truth rotation R and translation T, and the estimated rotation $\tilde{R}$ and translation $\tilde{T}$, we compute the average distance over $X_c^{SSC_i}$:

$$\omega_i = avg||(RX_c^{SSC_i} + T) - (\tilde{R}X_c^{SSC_i} + \tilde{T})||. \tag{1}$$

Fig. 3. Skeletal graph representation: skeleton nodes are determined with respect to model coordinate frame. Skeletal nodes and links are projected onto the image plane for each viewpoint at which a synthetic depth image is rendered.

ω_i calculates the distance between the ground truth and estimated poses of the test instance i. The detection hypothesis that ensures the following inequality is considered as correct:

$$\omega_i \leq z_{\omega_i} \Phi_i \tag{2}$$

where Φ_i is the diameter of $M_c^{SSC_i}$, and z_{ω_i} is a constant that determines the coarseness of an hypothesis that is assigned as correct.

3.2 Dataset and Part Representations

The training dataset $\mathcal{S}$ involves synthetic data that are of c_s instances of a given category. Using the 3D CAD models of these c_s instances, we render foreground synthetic depth maps from different viewpoints and generate annotated parts in order to form $\mathcal{S}$:

$$\mathcal{S} = \{\mathcal{P}_i | i = 1, 2, ..., c_s\}$$
$$\mathcal{P}_i = \{\cup_{j=1}^n P_j\} = \{\cup_{j=1}^n (\mathbf{c}_j, \Delta\mathbf{x}_j, \theta_j, \mathbf{a}_j, \mathbf{s}_j, D_{P_j})\} \tag{3}$$

where $\mathcal{P}_i$ involves the set of parts $\{P_j | j = 1, 2, ..., n\}$ that are extracted from the synthetic images of the object instance i. $\mathbf{c}_j = (c_{x_j}, c_{y_j}, c_{z_j})$ is the part centre in $[px, px, m]$. $\Delta\mathbf{x}_j = (\Delta x, \Delta y, \Delta z)$ presents the 3D offset between the centre of the part and the SSC of the object, and $\theta_j = (\theta_r, \theta_p, \theta_y)$ depicts the 3D rotation parameters of the point cloud from which the part P_j is extracted. $\mathbf{a}_j$ describes the vector of the skeletal link angles. $\mathbf{s}_j$ is the skeletal node offset matrix representation, and D_{P_j} is the depth map of the part P_j.

We next briefly mention how we derive $\mathbf{a}_j$ and $\mathbf{s}_j$ based on skeletal graph representation extracted from 3D model of an instance.

Derivation of $\mathbf{a}_j$ and $\mathbf{s}_j$. The algorithm in [32] is utilized in order to extract the skeletal graph of an instance from its 3D model. Once the skeletal graph is extracted, we next project both the nodes and the links onto the image plane for every viewpoint at which synthetic depth maps are rendered. At each viewpoint, we measure the angles that the links of the graph representation make with the x direction, and stack them into the vector of skeletal link angles $\mathbf{a}_j$ (see Fig. 3). All of the parts extracted at a specific viewpoint have the same representation $\mathbf{a}$. The distances between the centre $\mathbf{c}_j$ of each part P_j and skeleton nodes are

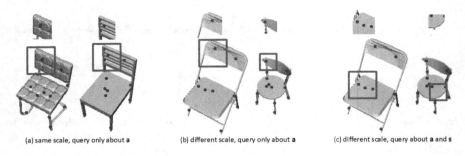

(a) same scale, query only about **a**   (b) different scale, query only about **a**   (c) different scale, query about **a** and **s**

Fig. 4. Parts in (a) and (b) are topologically at the same location, having the same **a**. Parts in (c) are topologically at different location, having the same **a**, the case which is undesired. Hence the parts are further questioned with **s**, the representation that removes mismatches.

measured in image pixels along x and y, and in metric coordinates along z direction in order to derive the skeletal node offset matrix $\mathbf{s}_j$:

$$\mathbf{s}_j = [\Delta x_{j_i}, \Delta y_{j_i}, \Delta z_{j_i}]_{s_n \times 3}, \quad i = 1, 2, ..., s_n. \tag{4}$$

Figure 3 shows an example skeletal graph and its projection onto 2D image plane for several viewpoints. In this representation, we compute 19 nodes in total and project onto the image plane 11 of those.

We next discuss how to handle shape discrepancies between the parts extracted from the instances of a given category using the representations **a** and **s**.

Privileged Data: Shape-Invariant Skeleton Representations. We start our discussion by firstly representing the parts with **a**. The study in [14] states that objects from the same category typically have similar physical size, however, the appearances of the objects are relatively different. Figure 4(a) depicts the parts extracted from 2 different objects, belonging to the same category. Despite the fact that both parts have different shapes in depth channel, their representations **a** are the same, tackling the discrepancy in shape.

There are also cases where some instances are relatively larger in the given category. The vector of skeletal link angles, **a**, readily handles the scale variation between the instances. In Fig. 4(b), the objects from which the parts extracted are different in both shape and in scale, however, the parts have the same representations **a**. One drawback of this representation is that it is not sufficient enough to match topologically correct parts. In Fig. 4(c), the parts are semantically at different locations of the objects, however, they have the same **a**. Hence, we additionally represent the parts with the skeletal node offset matrix **s**. **s** along with **a** are used to adapt the intrinsic structures of the instances while topologically constraining the structures. In Fig. 4(c), when we query about **s**, in addition to **a**, the mismatch between the parts disappears, since both parts have different skeletal node offset matrix representation **s**.

3.3   Privileged One-Class Learning

ISA, being a part-based random forest architecture, is the combination of randomized binary decision trees. Employing one-class learning, it is trained only on positive samples, rather than explicitly collecting representative negative samples. The learning scheme is additionally privileged. The part representations $\mathbf{a}$ and $\mathbf{s}$ are only available during training, and not required during testing. This is achieved by using them in the split criteria (Eq. 7), but not in the split function (Eq. 5). We use the dataset S in order to train ISA employing simple depth comparison features (2-pixel test) in the split nodes. At a given pixel $\mathbf{w}$, the features compute:

$$f_\psi(D_P, \mathbf{w}) = D_P(\mathbf{w} + \frac{\mathbf{u}}{D_P(\mathbf{w})}) - D_P(\mathbf{w} + \frac{\mathbf{v}}{D_P(\mathbf{w})}) \tag{5}$$

where $D_P(\mathbf{w})$ is the depth value of the pixel $\mathbf{w}$ in part P, and the parameters $\psi = (\mathbf{u}, \mathbf{v})$ depict offsets $\mathbf{u}$ and $\mathbf{v}$. Each tree is constructed by using a randomly selected subset $\mathcal{W} = \{P_j\}$ of the annotated training parts $\mathcal{W} \subset S$. Starting from the root node, a group of splitting candidates $\{\phi = (\psi, \tau)\}$, where ψ is the feature parameter and τ is the threshold, are randomly produced. The subset $\mathcal{W}$ is partitioned into left $\mathcal{W}_l$ and right $\mathcal{W}_r$ by each ϕ:

$$\mathcal{W}_l(\phi) = \{\mathcal{W} | f_\theta(D_P, \mathbf{w}) < \tau\}$$
$$\mathcal{W}_r(\phi) = \mathcal{W} \setminus \mathcal{W}_l. \tag{6}$$

The ϕ that best optimizes the following entropy is determined:

$$\phi^* = \arg\max_\phi(Q(\phi))$$
$$Q = Q_1 + Q_2 + Q_3 \tag{7}$$

where Q_1, Q_2, and Q_3 are the 6D pose entropy, the skeletal link angle entropy, and the skeletal node offset entropy, respectively. Each tree is grown by repeating this process recursively until the forest termination criteria are satisfied. When the termination conditions are met, the leaf nodes are formed and they store votes for both the object center $\Delta\mathbf{x} = (\Delta x, \Delta y, \Delta z)$ and the object rotation $\theta = (\theta_r, \theta_p, \theta_y)$.

Matching Skeletal Graphs. When we build ISA, our main target is to provide adaptation between the instances, and to improve the generalization across unseen objects. Apart from the data used to train the forest, the quality functions we introduce play an important role for these purposes. The quality function Q_1, optimizing data with respect to only 6D pose parameters, is given below:

$$Q_1 = log(|\Sigma^{\Delta\mathbf{x}}| + |\Sigma^\theta|) - \sum_{i \in (L,R)} \frac{S_i}{S} log(|\Sigma_i^{\Delta\mathbf{x}}| + |\Sigma_i^\theta|) \tag{8}$$

where $|\Sigma^{\Delta\mathbf{x}}|$, $|\Sigma^\theta|$ show the determinants of offset and pose covariance matrices, respectively. S_i depicts the synthetic data sent either to the left L or to the right

R child node. In case the architecture is trained only using parts extracted from 1 instance, Q_1 successfully works. We train ISA using multiple instances, targeting to improve the adaptation/generalization capability across unseen instances. In order to achieve that, we propose the following quality function in addition to Q_1:

$$Q_2 = log(|\Sigma^{\mathbf{a}}|) - \sum_{i \in (L,R)} \frac{S_i}{S} log(|\Sigma_i^{\mathbf{a}}|) \tag{9}$$

where $|\Sigma^{\mathbf{a}}|$ shows the determinant of the skeletal link angle covariance matrix. This function measures the similarity of the parts regarding the angles that the links of the skeleton representations make with the x direction. The main reason why we use this function is to handle shape discrepancies in depth channel between parts, even if the parts are extracted from relatively large scale objects. Let's suppose that if all parts under query are extracted from topologically same locations of the instances, the combination of Q_1 and Q_2 would be sufficient. On the other hand, the combination of these two functions is not sufficient, since the parts are extracted from the complete structures of the instances. In such a scenario, the parts coming from topologically different locations, but with similar **a** are tend to travel to the same child node, if the features used in the split function fails to correctly separate the data. Hence, we require the following function that prevents this drawback:

$$Q_3 = log(|\Sigma^{\mathbf{s}}|) - \sum_{i \in (L,R)} \frac{S_i}{S} log(|\Sigma_i^{\mathbf{s}}|) \tag{10}$$

where $|\Sigma^{\mathbf{s}}|$ shows the determinant of the skeletal node offset covariance matrix. The main reason why we use Q_3 is to prevent topologic mismatches in between the parts extracted from different instances of the given category.

3.4   Category-Level 6D Object Pose Estimation

Given a category of interest c, and a depth image I^t in which an unseen instance of the interested category exists, the proposed architecture, ISA, targets to maximize the joint posterior density of the object position $\Delta\mathbf{x}$ and the rotation θ:

$$(\Delta\mathbf{x}, \theta) = \arg\max_{\Delta\mathbf{x}, \theta} p(\Delta\mathbf{x}, \theta | I^t, c). \tag{11}$$

Since ISA is based on parts, and the parts extracted from I^t are passed down all the trees by the split function in Eq. 5, we can calculate the probability $p(\Delta\mathbf{x}, \theta | I^t, c)$ for a single tree T aggregating the conditional probabilities $p(\Delta\mathbf{x}, \theta | P, c)$ for each part P:

$$p(\Delta\mathbf{x}, \theta | I^t, c; T) = \sum_i p(\Delta\mathbf{x}, \theta | P_i, c, D_{P_i}; T). \tag{12}$$

In order to hypothesise the final pose parameters, we average the probabilities over all trees using the information stored in the leaf nodes for a given forest F:

$$p(\Delta\mathbf{x}, \theta|I^t, c; F) = \frac{1}{|F|} \sum_t^{|F|} \sum_i p(\Delta\mathbf{x}, \theta|P_i, c, D_{P_i}; T_t). \tag{13}$$

Please note that the above pose inference is done using a single depth image, not skeletons and their representations.

4 Experiments

In order to validate the performance of the proposed architecture, we conduct experiments on both synthetic and real data.

Synthetic Dataset. Princeton ModelNet10 dataset [33] contains CAD models of 10 categories, and in each category, the models are divided into train and test. We use the CAD models of the test instances of four categories, *bed, chair, table,* and *toilet,* and render depth images from different viewpoints, each of which is 6D annotated and occlusion/clutter-free. Each category involves 264 images of unseen objects, and there are 1320 test images in total. We compare ISA and instance-based Linemod on the synthetic dataset.

Real Dataset. RMRC [34], involving cluttered real depth images of several object categories, is the dataset on which we test and compare our architecture with the state-of-the-art methods [13–15]. The images in this dataset are annotated only with 3D bounding boxes.

Evaluation Protocols. The evaluation protocol used for the experiments conducted on the synthetic dataset is the one proposed in Subsect. 3.1. We make use of the evaluation metric in [13] when we compare ISA with the state-of-the-art methods on real data.

4.1 Experiments on Synthetic Data

The main reason why we conduct experiments first on synthetic data is to demonstrate the intrinsic structure adaptation performance of the proposed algorithm in order to have a better understanding on its behaviour across unseen instances.

Training ISA. We employ one-class privileged training using only positive synthetic samples and train the classifiers based on parts extracted from the depth images of the instances in the given categories. Note that, the data related to skeletal representation is only available during training, and in the test phase, the parts reach the leaf nodes using depth appearances in order to vote for a

6D pose. The models from which the depth images are synthesised are sorted through the training part of ModelNet10. The number of the instances, the number of the viewpoints from which synthetic depth images are rendered, and the number of the parts used during training are shown in Table 1.

We train 16 different forests each 4 of which are individually trained using the quality functions Q_1, $Q_1\&Q_2$, $Q_1\&Q_3$, and $Q_1\&Q_2\&Q_3$ per category. The instances used to train the forests are shown in Fig. 5.

Linemod Templates. Since Linemod is an instance-based detector, the templates method uses are of the object instance on which the the method is tested. Hence, in order to fairly compare Linemod detector with ISA, we employ the following strategy: on the test images of a given category (*e.g.* chair), we run the Linemod detector using the templates of each training instance (for chair, we run Linemod detector 28 times using 89 templates of each of 28 training instances, see Table 1). We sort the recall values, and report 3 different numbers: Linemod (min) represents the lowest recall obtained by any of the training instances, Linemod (max) depicts the highest recall obtained by any of the training instances, and Linemod (all) shows the mean of recall values obtained by all of the training instances.

Test. Unseen test instances are shown in Fig. 6. The resultant recall values are depicted in Table 2 (left). A short analysis on the table reveals that the ISAs based on the 6D pose entropy Q_1 demonstrate the poorest performance. Thanks to the utilization of the skeletal link angle entropy Q_2, in addition to the 6D quality function, the classifiers reach higher recall values. In case the skeletal node offset entropy Q_3 is used along with the 6D pose entropy, there is a relative improvement if we compare with the classifiers trained only on 6D pose entropy. The combined utilization of 6D pose, skeletal link angle, and skeletal node offset entropies performs best on average.

For the *bed* category, separately using Q_2 and Q_3 along with Q_1 demonstrates approximately the same performance when the classifiers are trained only on the quality function Q_1. However, the combined utilization of Q_1, Q_2, and Q_3 shows the best performance. For the *chair* category, the forest trained on Q_1 and Q_3 generates the highest recall value, describing the positive impact of using the skeleton node offset entropy. Unlike the bed category, exploiting the skeletal link angle entropy Q_2 along with $Q_1\&Q_3$ relatively degrades the performance of ISA. For the *table* category, one can observe that the skeletal link angle entropy and the skeletal node offset entropy contribute the same to the classifiers in order to generalize across unseen instances. Training the forests using both $Q_1\&Q_2$ and $Q_1\&Q_3$ gives rise 3% improvement with respect to the quality function Q_1 only. For the *toilet* category, using Q_1 along with Q_2 outperforms other forests. Despite the fact that adding the last term Q_3 into the combined quality function relatively decreases the recall value, the resultant performance is still better that the classifier trained Q_1 only. Figure 7 depicts sample hypotheses of unseen instances with ground truth poses in red. The forests based on $Q_1\&Q_2\&Q_3$

Table 1. Numbers on training samples

	Bed	Chair	Table	Toilet
#instances	2	28	8	7
#view (per inst.)	89	89	89	89
#parts (total)	∼600k	∼1m	∼900k	∼800k

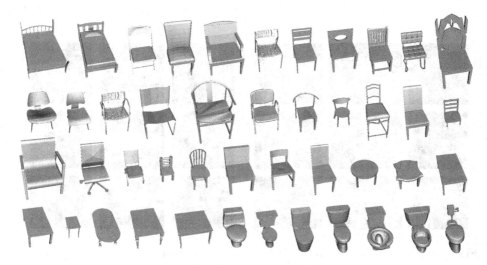

Fig. 5. Instances used to train a separate ISA for each category. These training instances are used to generate templates for testing Linemod.

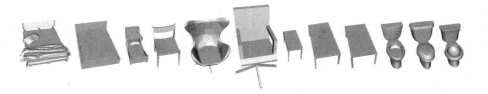

Fig. 6. Unseen object instances on which ISA and Linemod are tested

hypothesise the green estimations which are considered as true positive, and the forests based on Q_1 hypothesise the blue estimations which are considered as false positive. Note that, both 3D position and 3D orientation of an estimation are used when deciding whether the object is correctly estimated.

In Table 2 (left), we report recall values for the Linemod detector. Using the templates of each training instance of the given category, we run Linemod, and sort the recall values. According to the Linemod (min) recall values, Linemod worst performs on the *chair* category, whilst it shows best performance on the

Table 2. (left) Comparison on 6D object pose using the evaluation metric in Subsect. 3.1. (right) Comparison on 3D object detection using the evaluation metric in [13].

Method	bed	chair	table	toilet	average	Method	input channel	bed	chair	table	toilet	mean
ISA (Q_1)	39	40	50	80	52.25							
ISA (Q_1 & Q_2)	41	37	53	89	55.0	Sliding Shapes [13]	depth	33.5	29	34.5	67.3	41.075
ISA (Q_1 & Q_3)	39	46	53	82	55.0	[15] on instance seg.	depth	71	18.2	30.4	63.4	45.75
ISA (Q_1 & Q_2 & Q_3)	46	42	52	87	56.75	[15] on estimated model	depth	72.7	47.5	40.6	72.7	58.375
Linemod (min)	58	5	9	27	25	Deep Sliding Shapes [14]	depth	83.0	58.8	68.6	79.2	72.40
Linemod (max)	62	51	69	83	66	ISA based on Q_1&Q_2&Q_3	depth	52.0	36.0	46.5	67.7	50.55
Linemod (all)	60	32	37	58	47							

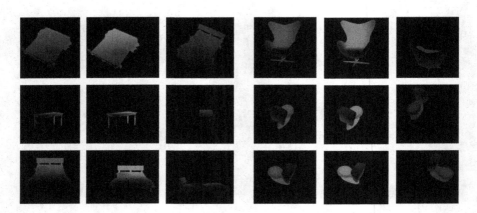

Fig. 7. Sample results generated by ISA on synthetic data: (for each triplet) each row is of per viewpoint, red is ground truth, green is estimation based on the quality function Q_1&Q_2&Q_3, blue is estimation based on the quality function Q_1 only. (Color figure online)

toilet category. The maximum recall value that Linemod achieve is of the *toilet* category. When we compute the mean for all recall values, Linemod best performs on the *bed* category.

4.2 Experiments on Real Data

Table 2 (right) depicts the comparison on 3D object detection. A short analysis on the table reveals that our architecture demonstrate 50% average precision. The highest value ISA reaches is on the *toilet* category, mainly because of the limited deviation in shape in between the instances. ISA next best performs on *bed*, with 52% mean precision. The accuracy on both the categories *bed* and *table* are approximately the same. Despite the fact that all forests used in the experiments undergo relatively a naive training process, the highest number of the instances during training are used for the chair category. However, ISA worst performs on this category, since the images in the test dataset have strong challenges of the instances, such as occlusion, clutter, and high diversity from the shape point of view. We lastly present sample results in Fig. 8. In these figures, the leftmost images are the inputs of our architecture, and the 2nd and the 3rd columns demonstrate the estimations of the forests based on $Q_1 \& Q_2 \& Q_3$ and Q_1 only, respectively.

Fig. 8. Sample results generated by ISA on real data: (for each triplet) each row is for per scene. First column depicts depth images of scenes. Estimations in the middle belong to ISAs trained using $Q_1 \& Q_2 \& Q_3$, and hypotheses on the right are of ISAs trained on Q_1 only.

5 Conclusion

In this paper we have introduced a novel architecture, ISA, for category-level 6D object pose estimation from depth images. We have designed the proposed architecture in such a way that the challenges of the categories, intra-class variations, distribution shifts among source and target domains, can successfully be tackled while the 6D pose of unseen objects are estimated. To this end, we have engineered ISA based on the following technologies: We have firstly presented Semantically Selected Centers (SSC) for the category-level 6D object pose estimation problem. We next have utilized 3D skeleton structures and derived those as shape-invariant features. Using these features, we have represented the parts extracted from the instances of given categories, and employed privileged one-class learning based on these parts. We have performed graph matching during training so that the adaptation capability of the proposed architecture is improved across unseen instances. Experiments conducted on test images validate the promising performance of ISA. In the future, we are planning to improve the performance of ISA approaching the problem from transfer learning point of view.

References

1. Doumanoglou, A., Kouskouridas, R., Malassiotis, S., Kim, T.K.: Recovering 6D object pose and predicting next-best-view in the crowd. In: CVPR (2016)
2. Brachmann, E., Krull, A., Michel, F., Gumhold, S., Shotton, J., Rother, C.: Learning 6D object pose estimation using 3D object coordinates. In: Fleet, D., Pajdla, T., Schiele, B., Tuytelaars, T. (eds.) ECCV 2014. LNCS, vol. 8690, pp. 536–551. Springer, Cham (2014). https://doi.org/10.1007/978-3-319-10605-2_35
3. Krull, A., Brachmann, E., Michel, F., Yang, M.Y., Gumhold, S., Rother, C.: Learning analysis-by-synthesis for 6D pose estimation in RGB-D images. In: ICCV (2015)
4. Wohlhart, P., Lepetit, V.: Learning descriptors for object recognition and 3D pose estimation. In: CVPR (2015)
5. Hodaň, T., et al.: BOP: benchmark for 6D object pose estimation. In: Ferrari, V., Hebert, M., Sminchisescu, C., Weiss, Y. (eds.) ECCV 2018. LNCS, vol. 11214, pp. 19–35. Springer, Cham (2018). https://doi.org/10.1007/978-3-030-01249-6_2
6. Michel, F., et al.: Global hypothesis generation for 6D object pose estimation. In: CVPR (2017)
7. Balntas, V., Doumanoglou, A., Sahin, C., Sock, J., Kouskouridas, R., Kim, T.K.: Pose guided RGBD feature learning for 3D object pose estimation. In: ICCV (2017)
8. Sock, J., Kasaei, S.H., Lopes, L.S., Kim, T.K.: Multi-view 6D object pose estimation and camera motion planning using RGBD images. In: 3rd International Workshop on Recovering 6D Object Pose (2017)
9. Brachmann, E., Michel, F., Krull, A., Yang, M., Gumhold, S., Rother, C.: Uncertainty-driven 6D pose estimation of objects and scenes from a single RGB image. In: CVPR (2016)
10. Kehl, W., Manhardt, F., Tombari, F., Ilic, S., Navab, N.: SSD-6D: making RGB-based 3D detection and 6D pose estimation great again. In: CVPR (2017)
11. Rad, M., Lepetit, V.: BB8: a scalable, accurate, robust to partial occlusion method for predicting the 3D poses of challenging objects without using depth. In: ICCV (2017)
12. Tekin, B., Sinha, S.N., Fua, P.: Real-time seamless single shot 6D object pose prediction. arxiv (2017)
13. Song, S., Xiao, J.: Sliding shapes for 3D object detection in depth images. In: Fleet, D., Pajdla, T., Schiele, B., Tuytelaars, T. (eds.) ECCV 2014. LNCS, vol. 8694, pp. 634–651. Springer, Cham (2014). https://doi.org/10.1007/978-3-319-10599-4_41
14. Song, S., Xiao, J.: Deep sliding shapes for amodal 3D object detection in RGB-D images. In: CVPR (2016)
15. Gupta, S., Arbelez, P., Girshick, R., Malik, J.: Aligning 3D models to RGB-D images of cluttered scenes. In: CVPR (2015)
16. Garcia-Hernando, G., Kim, T.K.: Transition forests: learning discriminative temporal transitions for action recognition. In: CVPR (2017)
17. Shi, Z., Kim, T.K.: Learning and refining of privileged information-based RNNs for action recognition from depth sequences. In: CVPR (2017)
18. Lin, Y.Y., Hua, J.H., Tang, N.C., Chen, M.H., Liao, H.Y.M.: Depth and skeleton associated action recognition without online accessible RGB-D cameras. In: CVPR (2014)
19. Ben-David, S., Blitzer, J., Crammer, K., Pereira, F.: Analysis of representations for domain adaptation. In: NIPS (2007)

20. Hinterstoisser, S., et al.: Model based training, detection and pose estimation of texture-less 3D objects in heavily cluttered scenes. In: Lee, K.M., Matsushita, Y., Rehg, J.M., Hu, Z. (eds.) ACCV 2012. LNCS, vol. 7724, pp. 548–562. Springer, Heidelberg (2013). https://doi.org/10.1007/978-3-642-37331-2_42
21. Rios-Cabrera, R., Tuytelaars, T.: Discriminatively trained templates for 3D object detection: a real time scalable approach. In: ICCV (2013)
22. Tejani, A., Tang, D., Kouskouridas, R., Kim, T.-K.: Latent-class hough forests for 3D object detection and pose estimation. In: Fleet, D., Pajdla, T., Schiele, B., Tuytelaars, T. (eds.) ECCV 2014. LNCS, vol. 8694, pp. 462–477. Springer, Cham (2014). https://doi.org/10.1007/978-3-319-10599-4_30
23. Bonde, U., Badrinarayanan, V., Cipolla, R.: Robust instance recognition in presence of occlusion and clutter. In: Fleet, D., Pajdla, T., Schiele, B., Tuytelaars, T. (eds.) ECCV 2014. LNCS, vol. 8690, pp. 520–535. Springer, Cham (2014). https://doi.org/10.1007/978-3-319-10605-2_34
24. Kehl, W., Milletari, F., Tombari, F., Ilic, S., Navab, N.: Deep learning of local RGB-D patches for 3D object detection and 6D pose estimation. In: Leibe, B., Matas, J., Sebe, N., Welling, M. (eds.) ECCV 2016. LNCS, vol. 9907, pp. 205–220. Springer, Cham (2016). https://doi.org/10.1007/978-3-319-46487-9_13
25. Zach, C., Penate-Sanchez, A., Pham, M.: A dynamic programming approach for fast and robust object pose recognition from range images. In: CVPR (2015)
26. Sahin, C., Kouskouridas, R., Kim, T.K.: A learning-based variable size part extraction architecture for 6D object pose recovery in depth images. J. Image Vis. Comput. 63, 38–50 (2017)
27. Sahin, C., Kouskouridas, R., Kim, T.K.: Iterative hough forest with histogram of control points for 6 DoF object registration from depth images. In: IROS (2016)
28. Sock, J., Kim, K., Sahin, C., Kim, T.K.: Multi-task deep networks for depth-based 6D object pose and joint registration in crowd scenarios. In: BMVC (2018)
29. Gupta, S., Girshick, R., Arbeláez, P., Malik, J.: Learning rich features from RGB-D images for object detection and segmentation. In: Fleet, D., Pajdla, T., Schiele, B., Tuytelaars, T. (eds.) ECCV 2014. LNCS, vol. 8695, pp. 345–360. Springer, Cham (2014). https://doi.org/10.1007/978-3-319-10584-0_23
30. Hoffman, J., Gupta, S., Leong, J., Guadarrama, S., Darrell, T.: Cross-modal adaptation for RGB-D detection. In: ICRA (2016)
31. Baek, S., Shi, Z., Kawade, M., Kim, T.K.: Kinematic-layout-aware random forests for depth-based action recognition. In: BMVC (2017)
32. Cao, J., Tagliasacchi, A., Olson, M., Zhang, H., Su, Z.: Point cloud skeletons via Laplacian based contraction. In: Shape Modeling International Conference (SMI) (2010)
33. Wu, Z., et al.: 3D ShapeNets: a deep representation for volumetric shape modeling. In: CVPR (2015)
34. Silberman, N., Hoiem, D., Kohli, P., Fergus, R.: Indoor segmentation and support inference from RGBD images. In: Fitzgibbon, A., Lazebnik, S., Perona, P., Sato, Y., Schmid, C. (eds.) ECCV 2012. LNCS, vol. 7576, pp. 746–760. Springer, Heidelberg (2012). https://doi.org/10.1007/978-3-642-33715-4_54

On Pre-trained Image Features and Synthetic Images for Deep Learning

Stefan Hinterstoisser[1](✉), Vincent Lepetit[2](✉), Paul Wohlhart[1](✉),
and Kurt Konolige[1](✉)

[1] X, Mountain View 94043, USA
{hinterst,wohlhart,konolige}@google.com
[2] University of Bordeaux, 33405 Bordeaux, France
vincent.lepetit@u-bordeaux.fr

Abstract. Deep Learning methods usually require huge amounts of training data to perform at their full potential, and often require expensive manual labeling. Using synthetic images is therefore very attractive to train object detectors, as the labeling comes for free, and several approaches have been proposed to combine synthetic and real images for training. In this paper, we evaluate if 'freezing' the layers responsible for feature extraction to generic layers pre-trained on real images, and training only the remaining layers with plain OpenGL rendering may allow for training with synthetic images only. Our experiments with very recent deep architectures for object recognition (Faster-RCNN, R-FCN, Mask-RCNN) and image feature extractors (InceptionResnet and Resnet) show this simple approach performs surprisingly well.

1 Introduction

The capability of detecting objects in challenging environments is a key component for many computer vision and robotics task. Current leading object detectors—Faster-RCNNs [2], SSD [3], RFCN [4], Yolo9000 [5]—all rely on convolutional neural networks. However, to perform at their best, they require huge amounts of labeled training data, which is usually time consuming and expensive to create (Fig. 1).

Using synthetic images is therefore very attractive to train object detectors, as the labeling comes for free. Unfortunately, synthetic rendering pipelines are usually unable to reproduce the statistics produced by their real-world counterparts. This is often referred to as the 'domain gap' between synthetic and real data and the transfer from one to another usually results in deteriorated performance, as observed in [6] for example.

Several approaches have tried to overcome this domain gap. For instance, [7–9] use synthetic images in addition to real ones to boost performance. While

Electronic supplementary material The online version of this chapter (https://doi.org/10.1007/978-3-030-11009-3_42) contains supplementary material, which is available to authorized users.

L. Leal-Taixé and S. Roth (Eds.): ECCV 2018 Workshops, LNCS 11129, pp. 682–697, 2019.
https://doi.org/10.1007/978-3-030-11009-3_42

Fig. 1. We show that feature extractor layers from modern object detectors pre-trained on real images can be used on synthetic images to learn to detect objects in real images. The top-left image shows the CAD model we used to learn to detect the object in the three other images.

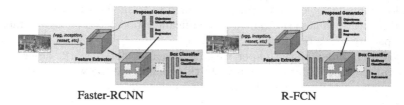

Faster-RCNN   R-FCN

Fig. 2. The architectures of two recent object detectors with their feature extractors isolated as described in [1] (Figure taken from [1]).

this usually results in good performance, it is still dependent on real world labeled data. Transfer learning approaches are also possible [10–12], however they also require real images of the objects to detect. [13,14] create photo-realistic graphics renderings and [8,13–15] compose realistic scenes for improved performance. Unfortunately, these strategies are usually difficult to engineer, need domain specific expertise and require some additional data such as illumination information and scene labeling to create realistic scenes. [6] uses 'domain randomization' to narrow the gap. While this has shown very promising results, it has mainly been demonstrated to work with simple objects and scenarios. Other works [16,17] use Generative Adversarial Networks (GANs) to remove the domain gap, however, GANs are still very brittle and hard to train, and to the best of our knowledge they have not been used for detection tasks yet.

In this paper we consider a simple alternative solution. As shown by [1] and illustrated in Fig. 2, many of today's modern feature extractors can be split into a feature extractor and some remaining layers that depend on the meta-architecture of the detector. Our claim is twofold: (a) the pre-trained feature extractors are already rich enough and do not need to be retrained when considering new objects to detect; (b) when applied to an image synthetically generated using simple rendering techniques, the feature extractors work as a "projector" and output image features that are close to real image features.

Therefore, by freezing the weights of feature extractor pre-trained on real data and by only adapting the weights of the remaining layers during training, we are able to train state-of-the-art object detectors purely on synthetic data.

While using pre-trained layers for feature extraction and finetuning them on a different task is not new (for example, VGG [18] has been used extensively for this purpose, our contribution is to show that this approach also enables us to train on synthetic data only if the pre-trained weights of the feature extractor are frozen. Since we have not found any reference on this particular approach, we evaluated it and report the results here as we thought it could be very useful for the community. We also show that this observation is fairly general and we give both qualitative and quantitative experiments for different detectors—Faster-RCNN [2], RFCN [4] and Mask-RCNN [19]—and different feature extraction networks—InceptionResnet [20] and Resnet101 [21].

Furthermore, we show that different cameras have different image statistics that allow different levels of performance when re-trained on synthetic data. We will demonstrate that performance is significantly boosted for these cameras if this simple approach is applied.

In the remainder of the paper we first discuss related work, describe how we generate synthetic data, demonstrate the domain gap between synthetic and real data, and detail our experiments and conclusions.

2   Related Work

Mixing real and synthetic data to improve detection performance is a well established process. Many approaches such as [7,8,22], to mention only very recent ones, have shown the usefulness of adding synthetic data when real data is limited. In contrast to [7,8] which use real masked image patches, [22] uses 3D CAD models and a structure-preserving deformation pipeline to generate new synthetic models to prevent overfitting. However, while these approaches obtain better results compared to detectors trained on real data only, they still require real data.

In order to avoid expensive labeling in terms of time and money, some approaches learn object detectors purely from synthetic data. For instance, a whole line of work uses photo-realistic rendering [13,14] and complex scene composition [8,13–15] to achieve good results, and [23] stresses the need for photo-realistic rendering. Some approaches even use physics engines to enable realistic placing of objects [24]. This requires significant resources and highly elaborate pipelines that are difficult to engineer and need domain specific expertise [25]. Furthermore, additional effort is needed to collect environment information like illumination information [14] to produce photo-realistic scenes. For real scene composition, one also needs to parse real background images semantically in order to place the objects meaningful into the scene.

This usually needs manual post-processing or labeling which is both expensive and time consuming. While these graphics based rendering approaches already show some of the advantages of learning from synthetic data, they usually suffer from the domain gap between real and synthetic data.

To address this, a new line of work [7–9] moves away from graphics based renderings to composing real images. The underlying theme is to paste masked patches of objects into real images, and thus reducing the dependence on graphics renderings. This approach has the advantage that the images of the objects are already in the right domain—the domain of real images—and thus, the domain gap between image compositions and real images is smaller than the one of graphics based rendering and real images. While this has shown quite some success, the amount of data is still restricted to the number of images taken from the object in the data gathering step and therefore does not allow to come up with new views of the object. Furthermore, it is not possible to generate new illumination settings or proper occlusions since shape and depth are usually not available. In addition, this approach is dependent on segmenting out the object from the background which is prone to segmentation errors when generating the object masks.

Recently, several approaches [16,17] tried to overcome the domain gap between real and synthetic data by using generative adversarial networks (GANs). This way they produced better results than training with real data. However, GANs are hard to train and up to now, they have mainly shown their usefulness on regression tasks and not on detection applications.

Yet another approach is to rely on transfer learning [10–12], to exploit a large amount of available data in a source domain, here the domain of synthetic images, to correctly classify data from the target domain, here the domain of real images, for which the amount of training data is limited. This is typically done by tighting two predictors together, one trained on the source domain, the other on the target domain or by training a single predictor on the two domains. This is a general approach as the source and target domains can be very different, compared to synthetic and real images, which are more related to each other. In this paper, we exploit this relation by applying the same feature extractor to the two domains. However, in contrast to [10–12] we do not need any real images of the objects of interest in our approach.

As mentioned in the introduction, finetuning pre-trained object detection networks [26] and freezing intermediate level layers during fine-tuning [27] is not new. However, to the best to our knowledge, no paper has shown that these two techniques when combined can help to bridge the domain gap between real and synthetic data and enable state-of-the-art object detectors to be trained only from synthetically rendered data with only little degradation compared to models trained on real data only. For instance, [28] discusses finetuning the hidden layers and is not about freezing layers. Also, it only tackles the classification part of RCNN, as the object proposal component of RCNN is not deep. In addition, its training dataset is not purely synthetic and contains real images, too. [7,9,22] also use fine-tuning but no freezing of layers. In addition, while [22] renders CAD models, [7,9] are only about composing images only.

3   Method

In this section, we will present our simple synthetic data generation pipeline and describe how we change existing state-of-the-art object detectors to enable them to learn from synthetic data. In this context, we will focus on object instance detection. Throughout this paper, we will mainly consider Faster-RCNN [2] since it demonstrated the best detection performance among a whole family of object detectors as shown in [1]. However, in order to show the generability of our approach, we will also present additional quantitative and qualitative results of other detectors (RFCN [4] and Mask-RCNN [19]) in Sect. 4.7.

3.1 Synthetic Data Generation Pipeline

Similar to [7], we believe that while global consistency can be important, local appearance—so called patch-level realism—is also important. The term patch-level realism refers to the observation that the content of the bounding box framing the rendered object looks realistic.

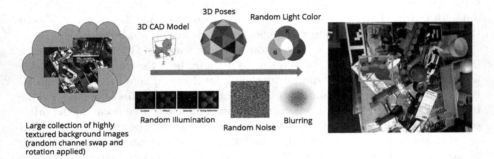

Fig. 3. Our synthetic data generation pipeline. For each generated 3D pose and object, we render the object over a randomly selected cluttered background image using OpenGL and the Phong illumination model [29]. We use randomly perturbed light color for rendering and add image noise to the rendering. Finally, we blur the object with a Gaussian filter. We also compute a tightly fitting bounding box using the object's CAD model and the corresponding pose. (Color figure online)

This principle is an important assumption for our synthetic data generation pipeline, shown in Fig. 3. For each object, we start by generating a large set of poses uniformly covering the pose space in which we want to be able to detect the corresponding object. As in [30], we generate rotations by recursively dividing an icosahedron, the largest convex regular polyhedron. We substitute each triangle into four almost equilateral triangles, and iterate several times. The vertices of the resulting polyhedron give us then the two out-of-plane rotation angles for the sampled pose with respect to the coordinate center. In addition to these two out-of-plane rotations, we also use equally sampled in-plane rotations. Furthermore, we sample the scale logarithmically to guarantee an approximate linear change in pixel coverage of the reprojected object between consecutive scale levels.

The object is rendered at a random location in a randomly selected background image using a uniform distribution. The selected background image is part of a large collection of highly cluttered real background images taken with the camera of choice where the objects of interest are not included. To increase the variability of the background image set, we randomly swap the three background image channels and randomly flip and rotate the images ($0°$, $90°$, $180°$ and $270°$). We also tried to work without using real background images and experimented with backgrounds only exhibiting one randomly chosen color, however, that did not lead to good results.

We use plain OpenGL with simple Phong shading [29] for rendering where we allow small random perturbations of the ambient, the diffuse and the specular parameters. We also allow small random perturbations of the light color. We add random Gaussian noise to the rendered object and blur it with a Gaussian kernel, including its boundaries with the adjacent background image pixels to better integrate the rendering with the background. We also experimented with different strategies for integrating the rendered object in images as [7], however this did not result in significant performance improvements.

3.2   Freezing a Pre-trained Feature Extractor

As shown in [1] and illustrated in Fig. 2, many state-of-the-art object detectors including Faster-RCNN [2], Mask-RCNN [19], and R-FCN [4] can be decoupled as a 'meta-architecture' and a feature extractor such as VGG [18], Resnet [21], or InceptionResnet [20].

While the meta-architecture defines the different modules and how they work together, the feature extractor is a deep network cut at some selected intermediate convolutional level. The remaining part can be used as part of the multi-way classification+localization of the object detector. As discussed in the introduction, for the feature extractor, we use frozen weights pre-learned on real images, to enable training the remaining part of the architecture on synthetic images only.

In practice, we use the Google's public available OpenSource version [1] of Faster-RCNN and RFCN, and our own implementation of Mask-RCNN. The 'frozen' parts are taken according to [1], by training InceptionResnet and Resnet101 on a classification task on the ImageNet-CLs dataset. We freeze InceptionResnet (v2) after the repeated use of block17 and right before layer Mixed_7a and Resnet101 after block3. All other remaining parts of the networks are not 'frozen', meaning their weights are free to adapt when we train the detector on synthetic images.

We evaluate this approach in the next section.

4   Experiments

In this section, we first describe the dataset we created for these evaluations, made of synthetic and real images of 10 different objects. We also considered two different cameras, as the quality of the camera influences the recognition results as we will show. The rest of the section reports our experiments and the conclusions we draw from them.

(a) Real Objects   (b) 3D CAD Models

Fig. 4. (a) The real objects used in our experiments and (b) their CAD models. We chose our objects carefully to represent different colors and 3D shapes and to cover different fields of applications (industrial objects, household objects, toys). (Color figure online)

4.1   Objects and 3D CAD Models

As shown in Fig. 4, we carefully selected the objects we used in our experiments: We tried to represent different colors, textures (homogeneous color versus highly textured), 3D shapes and material properties (reflective versus non-reflective). Except for the mug and the bottle, the 3D shapes of the objects we selected can look very different from different views. We also tried to consider objects from different application fields (industrial objects, household objects, toys). For each real object we have a textured 3D CAD model at hand which we generated using our in-house 3D scanner.

4.2   Cameras

We consider two cameras, an AsusXtionPROLive and a PtGreyBlackfly. For each camera, we generated a training dataset and an evaluation dataset. The training datasets consist of approximatively 20 K and the evaluation datasets of approximatively 1 K manually labeled real world images. Each sample image contains one of the 10 objects shown in Fig. 4 in challenging environments: heavy background clutter, illumination changes, etc. In addition, we made sure that each object is shown from various poses as this is very important for object instance detection. Furthermore, for each dataset all objects have the same amount of images.

4.3   Freezing the Feature Extractor

Figure 5 shows that when Faster-RCNN is trained on synthetic images and tested on real images, it performs significantly worse than when trained on real data. By

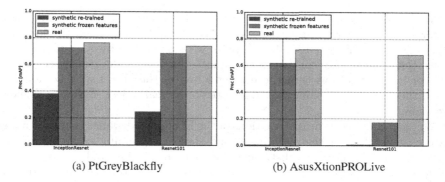

(a) PtGreyBlackfly   (b) AsusXtionPROLive

Fig. 5. The effect of freezing the pre-trained feature extractor, for two different cameras. Training the feature extractors on synthetic images performs poorly, and totally fails in the case of the AsusXtionPROLive camera. When using feature extractors pre-trained on real images without retraining them, the performances of detectors trained on synthetic data are almost as good as when training them on real data, except when ResNet101 is used with images from the AsusXtionPROLive camera.

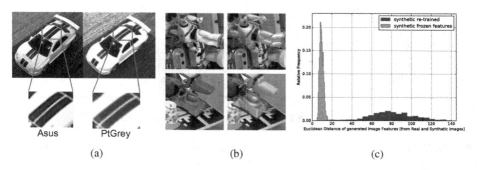

(a)   (b)   (c)

Fig. 6. (a) Debayering Artefacts of the AsusXtionPROLive camera (zoom for better view). (b) Two examples of pairs of a real image and a synthetic one for the same object under the same pose. (c) Distributions of the Euclidean distances between image features generated for the real images and the corresponding synthetic images. See text in Sect. 4.3 for details. (Color figure online)

contrast, when we freeze the feature extractor's weights during training to values pre-trained on real images, and only train the remaining parts of the detector, we get a significant performance boost. We even come close to detectors trained purely on real world data, as we typically obtained up to 95% of the performance when trained on synthetic data.

In general, we observe that our method exhibits better results for the PtGrey-Blackfly camera than for the AsusXtionPROLive camera. In contrast to the PtGrey camera, the Asus camera exhibits 'debayering artefacts' along edges that we do not simulate. We believe that this debayering artefact is the main reason for the differences between the two cameras (see Fig. 6(a)).

To get a better intuition why freezing the feature extractor gives significant better results than retraining it on synthetic data, we performed the following experiment: We created 1000 image pairs with different objects under various poses. Each image pair consists of one image that shows the real object and of another image where we superpose a rendering of the object's CAD model on top of the real image, under the same pose as the real object. Figure 6(b) shows two examples.

We then compared the distributions of the Euclidean distances between image features generated for the real images and the corresponding synthetic images. As we can see Fig. 6(c), the distribution is much more clustered around 0 when the features are computed using a frozen feature extractor pre-trained on real images (red) compared to the distribution obtained when the pre-trained feature extractor is finetuned on synthetic images (blue).

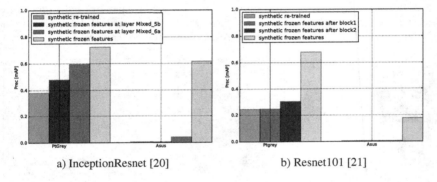

a) InceptionResnet [20]   b) Resnet101 [21]

Fig. 7. We freeze features at different layers of InceptionResnet [20] and Resnet101 [21]. We can see that freezing the full feature extractor performs best (yellow). (Color figure online)

4.4   Freezing the Feature Extractor at Different Layers

We also performed experiments where we freeze the feature extractor at different intermediate layers i.e. layers lying between the input and the output layers of the feature extractor as specified in Sect. 3.2. As can be seen in Fig. 7, freezing the full feature extractor always performs best. For the AsusXtionPROLive camera, freezing the feature extractor on intermediate levels even results in a dramatic loss of performance.

4.5   On Finetuning the Feature Extractor

One may wonder if the domain shift between synthetic and real images still leads to decreased performance after the detector was trained for some time with the pre-trained feature extractor frozen. One could argue that all remaining detector

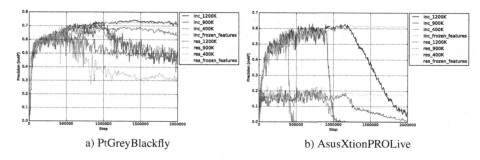

a) PtGreyBlackfly   b) AsusXtionPROLive

Fig. 8. Finetuning the feature extractor after 400K, 900K and 1200K steps where the pre-trained feature extractor was frozen for the PtGreyBlackfly and the AsusXtion-PROLive cameras. We show results for the InceptionResnet [20] and Resnet101 [21] architectures.

weights have already started to converge and therefore, the domain shift is far less influential. As a result, the frozen feature extractor could be unfrozen to finetune its weights to adapt to the learning task.

However, as we show in Fig. 8, this is not true. Even after 1200K training steps where the feature extractor was frozen and the detection performance starts to plateau the detector's performance degrades significantly if the frozen feature extractor is unfrozen and its weights are finetuned. Table 1 gives the corresponding numbers.

Table 1. Outcomes of all our experiments. We give numbers for InceptionResnet [20]/Resnet101 [21]. Except for the experiments with real data (last column), all experiments were performed on synthetic data only. We emphasized the best results trained on synthetic data.

		Synthetic	Frozen	400K	900K	1200K	Real
Asus	Prec [mAP]	.000/.000	**.617**/.171	.000/.000	.000/.000	.061/.006	.719/.681
	Prec [mAP@0.5]	.000/.000	**.948**/.385	.000/.000	.000/.000	.114/.016	.983/.988
	Prec [mAP@0.75]	.000/.000	**.733**/.130	.000/.000	.000/.000	.064/.004	.872/.844
	Acc [@100]	.000/.010	**.686**/.256	.000/.000	.000/.000	.079/.007	.772/.742
PtGrey	Prec [mAP]	.374/.243	**.725**/.687	.426/.317	.514/.485	.709/.626	.764/.742
	Prec [mAP@0.5]	.537/.410	**.971**/.966	.606/.491	.717/.685	.936/.912	.987/.987
	Prec [mAP@0.75]	.431/.239	**.886**/.844	.495/.355	.593/.564	.835/.756	.908/.916
	Acc [@100]	.461/.324	**.771**/.736	.483/.384	.577/.551	.768/.695	.808/.804

4.6 Ablation Experiments

In the following experiments, we investigated the influence of the single steps in the image generation pipeline. For all these experiments we used InceptionResnet [20] as feature extractor. The feature extractor itself was frozen. We found out that blurring the rendered object and its adjacent image pixels gives a huge performance boost. Adding noise to the rendered object or enabling random light color did not give much improvement in performance and its influence depends on the camera used. As already mentioned, we also experimented with different blending strategies as in [7], that is using different blending options in the same dataset: no blending, Gaussian blurring and Poisson blending, however we could not find significant performance improvements.

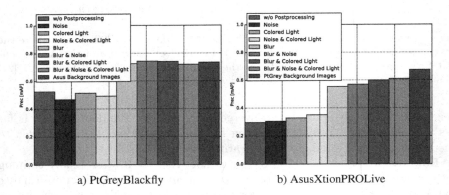

a) PtGreyBlackfly   b) AsusXtionPROLive

Fig. 9. Influences of the different building blocks for synthetic rendering for the PtGrey-Blackfly and the AsusXtionPROLive cameras. Results were obtained with Inception-Resnet [20] as the feature extractor. Blurring is clearly a useful yet simple operation to apply to the synthetic images to improve the results.

We also investigated what happens if we use the internal camera parameter of our target camera but a background dataset taken with another camera. As we can see in Fig. 9, results seem to stay approximately the same for the PtGreyBlackfly camera and seem to improve for the AsusXtionPROLive camera. The later seems reasonable since the background images taken with the PtGreyBlackfly camera are more cluttered and are showing more background variety than the background images taken with the AsusXtionPROLive camera. These results suggest that the camera images can be taken from an arbitrary source and we only have to make sure that a high amount of background variety is provided.

4.7   RFCN, MASK-RCNN and the Dishware Dataset

To show the generality of our approach, we also performed several addition experiments. Figure 10(a) shows the results for RFCN [4] trained only on synthetic data with the feature extractor frozen and compares them with those using RFCN trained on real data and and those using RFCN re-trained on synthetic data. Freezing the feature extractor helps to unlock significant performance improvements also here.

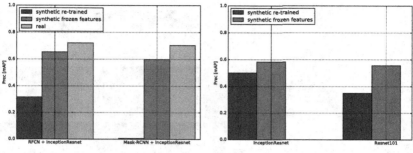

a) Results of RFCN and Mask-RCNN   b) Results on the Dishware dataset

Fig. 10. Left: Results using RFCN [4] on the PtGreyBlackfly dataset. Freezing the feature extractor boosts performance significantly on this method as well. We observe the same results if we train Mask-RCNN on the AsusXtionPROLive dataset. Right: We also performed experiments on the Dishware dataset using the PtGreyBlackfly camera. Since we have only real evaluation data and no real labeled training data we show the difference between training purley on synthetic data with non-frozen and frozen features. While one can observe a significant gap between the two approaches, the gap is not as large as in previous experiments. We believe that this is because the dataset contains mostly uniform and little textured objects and thus, is less prone to synthetic image statistics generated by rendering.

Figure 10(a) also shows quantitative results of Mask-RCNN [19] trained only on synthetic data with the feature extractor frozen. Similar to what we observed with Faster-RCNN and RFCN, freezing the feature extractor significantly boosts the performance when trained on synthetic data. Figure 13 shows that we are able to detect objects in highly cluttered environments under various poses and get reasonable masks. This result is especially important since it shows that exhaustive (manual) pixel labeling is made redundant by training from synthetic data.

We also show results of Faster-RCNN on another dataset depicted in Fig. 11 that we created with the PtGreyBlackfly camera. We call this dataset the Dishware dataset as it contains 9 dishware objects (*i.e.* plates, cups, bowls) and their corresponding 3D CAD models. For this dataset, in addition to the 3D CAD models of the nine objects, we also have real evaluation data, but no real training data at hand. Therefore, we only show the gap between training with re-trained and frozen features on synthetic training data. The evaluation dataset consists of approximatively 1K manually labeled real world images where objects are seen in different cluttered environments under various poses and severe illumination changes. Each object has the same number of evaluation images. As one can see in Fig. 10(b), freezing the features helps to significantly increase performance. While the gap between these two approaches is significant, it is less than what we observed on our first dataset (see Fig. 5). We believe that this is because the dataset contains mostly uniform or little textured objects and thus, is less prone to synthetic image statistics generated by rendering.

(a) Real Dishware Objects   (b) 3D CAD Dishware Models

Fig. 11. (a) The real objects of our second dataset (dishware dataset) used in Fig. 10 and (b) their CAD models.

Fig. 12. Results of Faster-RCNN trained on synthetic images only with the feature extractor frozen. The objects are detected in highly cluttered scenes and many different instances are available in one image. Note that the different objects are seen in different arbitrary poses.

Fig. 13. Results of Mask-RCNN [19] trained on synthetic images only with the feature extractor frozen. The images were taken with the AsusXtionPROLive camera in a highly cluttered environment under various poses.

Fig. 14. Objects with similar shapes and colors detected in challenging environments. The detector was trained on synthetic images only. (Color figure online)

4.8   Qualitative Results

Figure 12 shows some qualitative results on images exhibiting several of the 10 objects we considered in various poses with heavy background clutter and illumination changes. We use Faster-RCNN [2] with the InceptionResnet [20] as feature extractor and trained the rest of the network on synthetic images only. Figure 13 shows results of Mask-RCNN [19] trained on synthetic images only. Figure 14 shows some other objects trained with the method presented in this paper.

5   Conclusion

We have shown that by freezing a pre-trained feature extractor we are able to train state-of-the-art object detectors on synthetic data only. The results are close to approaches trained on real data only. While we have demonstrated that object detectors re-trained on synthetic data lead to poor performances and that images from different cameras lead to different results, freezing the feature extractor always gives a huge performance boost.

Our experiments suggest that simple rendering is sufficient to achieve good performances and that complicated scene composition does not seem necessary. Training from rendered 3D CAD models allows us to detect objects from all possible viewpoints which makes the need for a real data generation and expensive manual labeling pipeline redundant.

Acknowledgments. The authors thank Google's VALE team for tremendous support using the Google Object Detection API, especially Jonathan Huang, Alireza Fathi, Vivek Rathod, and Chen Sun. In addition, we thank Kevin Murphy, Vincent Vanhoucke, and Alexander Toshev for valuable discussions and feedback.

References

1. Huang, J., et al.: Speed and accuracy trade-offs for modern convolutional object detectors. In: Conference on Computer Vision and Pattern Recognition (2017)
2. Ren, S., He, K., Girshick, R., Sun, J.: Faster R-CNN: towards real-time object detection with region proposal networks. In: Advances in Neural Information Processing Systems (2015)
3. Liu, W., et al.: SSD: single shot multibox detector. In: Leibe, B., Matas, J., Sebe, N., Welling, M. (eds.) ECCV 2016. LNCS, vol. 9905, pp. 21–37. Springer, Cham (2016). https://doi.org/10.1007/978-3-319-46448-0_2
4. Dai, J., Li, Y., He, K., Sun, J.: R-FCN: object detection via region-based fully convolutional networks. In: Advances in Neural Information Processing Systems (2016)
5. Redmon, J., Farhadi, A.: YOLO9000: better, faster, stronger. In: Conference on Computer Vision and Pattern Recognition (2017)
6. Tobin, J., Fong, R., Ray, A., Schneider, J., Zaremba, W., Abbeel, P.: Domain randomization for transferring deep neural networks from simulation to the real world. In: International Conference on Intelligent Robots and Systems (2017)

7. Dwibedi, D., Misra, I., Hebert, M.: Cut, paste and learn: surprisingly easy synthesis for instance detection. arXiv Preprint (2017)
8. Georgakis, G., Mousavian, A., Berg, A.C., Kosecka, J.: Synthesizing training data for object detection in indoor scenes. In: Robotics: Science and Systems Conference (2017)
9. Rad, M., Lepetit, V.: BB8: a scalable, accurate, robust to partial occlusion method for predicting the 3D poses of challenging objects without using depth. In: International Conference on Computer Vision (2017)
10. Rozantsev, A., Salzmann, M., Fua, P.: Beyond sharing weights for deep domain adaptation. In: Conference on Computer Vision and Pattern Recognition (2017)
11. Bousmalis, K., Trigeorgis, G., Silberman, N., Krishnan, D., Erhan, D.: Domain separation networks. In: Advances in Neural Information Processing Systems (2016)
12. Ganin, Y., et al.: Domain-adversarial training of neural networks. J. Mach. Learn. Res. (2016)
13. Gupta, A., Vedaldi, A., Zisserman, A.: Synthetic data for text localisation in natural images. In: Conference on Computer Vision and Pattern Recognition (2016)
14. Alhaija, H.A., Mustikovela, S.K., Mescheder, L., Geiger, A., Rother, C.: Augmented reality meets deep learning for car instance segmentation in urban scenes. In: British Machine Vision Conference (2017)
15. Varol, G., et al.: Learning from synthetic humans. In: Conference on Computer Vision and Pattern Recognition (2017)
16. Shrivastava, A., Pfister, T., Tuzel, O., Susskind, J., Wang, W., Webb, R.: Learning from simulated and unsupervised images through adversarial training. In: Conference on Computer Vision and Pattern Recognition (2017)
17. Bousmalis, K., Silberman, N., Dohan, D., Erhan, D., Krishnan, D.: Unsupervised pixel-level domain adaptation with generative adversarial networks. In: Conference on Computer Vision and Pattern Recognition (2017)
18. Simonyan, K., Zisserman, A.: Very deep convolutional networks for large-scale image recognition. In: International Conference for Learning Representations (2015)
19. He, K., Gkioxari, G., Dollár, P., Girshick, R.: Mask R-CNN. arXiv Preprint (2017)
20. Szegedy, C., Ioffe, S., Vanhoucke, V., Alemi, A.A.: Inception-V4, inception-resnet and the impact of residual connections on learning. In: American Association for Artificial Intelligence Conference (2017)
21. He, K., Zhang, X., Ren, S., Sun, J.: Deep residual learning for image recognition. In: Conference on Computer Vision and Pattern Recognition (2016)
22. Su, H., Qi, C.R., Li, Y., Guibas, L.J.: Render for CNN: viewpoint estimation in images using CNNs trained with rendered 3D model views. In: ICCV (2015)
23. Movshovitz-attias, Y., Kanade, T., Sheikh, Y.: How useful is photo-realistic rendering for visual learning? In: European Conference on Computer Vision (2016)
24. Mitash, C., Bekris, K.E., Boularias, A.: A self-supervised learning system for object detection using physics simulation and multi-view pose estimation. In: International Conference on Intelligent Robots and Systems (2017)
25. Richter, S.R., Vineet, V., Roth, S., Koltun, V.: Playing for data: ground truth from computer games. In: Leibe, B., Matas, J., Sebe, N., Welling, M. (eds.) ECCV 2016. LNCS, vol. 9906, pp. 102–118. Springer, Cham (2016). https://doi.org/10.1007/978-3-319-46475-6_7
26. Girshick, R.B., Donahue, J., Darrell, T., Malik, J.: Rich feature hierarchies for accurate object detection and semantic segmentation. In: Conference on Computer Vision and Pattern Recognition (2014)

27. Ouyang, W., Wang, X., Zhang, C., Yang, X.: Factors in finetuning deep model for object detection with long-tail distribution. In: Conference on Computer Vision and Pattern Recognition (2016)

28. Peng, X., Sun, B., Ali, K., Saenko, K.: Learning deep object detectors from 3D models. In: International Conference on Computer Vision (2015)

29. Phong, B.T.: Illumination for computer generated pictures. Commun. ACM **18**, 311–317 (1975)

30. Hinterstoisser, S., et al.: Model based training, detection and pose estimation of texture-less 3D objects in heavily cluttered scenes. In: Lee, K.M., Matsushita, Y., Rehg, J.M., Hu, Z. (eds.) ACCV 2012. LNCS, vol. 7724, pp. 548–562. Springer, Heidelberg (2013). https://doi.org/10.1007/978-3-642-37331-2_42

Convolutional Networks for Object Category and 3D Pose Estimation from 2D Images

Siddharth Mahendran$^{(\boxtimes)}$, Haider Ali, and René Vidal

Center for Imaging Science, Johns Hopkins University, Baltimore, USA
{siddharthm,hali,rvidal}@jhu.edu

Abstract. Current CNN-based algorithms for recovering the 3D pose of an object in an image assume knowledge about both the object category and its 2D localization in the image. In this paper, we relax one of these constraints and propose to solve the task of joint object category and 3D pose estimation from an image assuming known 2D localization. We design a new architecture for this task composed of a feature network that is shared between subtasks, an object categorization network built on top of the feature network, and a collection of category dependent pose regression networks. We also introduce suitable loss functions and a training method for the new architecture. Experiments on the challenging PASCAL3D+ dataset show state-of-the-art performance in the joint categorization and pose estimation task. Moreover, our performance on the joint task is comparable to the performance of state-of-the-art methods on the simpler 3D pose estimation with known object category task.

Keywords: 3D pose estimation · Category-dependent pose networks · Multi-task networks · ResNet architecture

1 Introduction

Object pose estimation is the task of estimating the relative rigid transformation between the camera and the object in an image. This is an old and fundamental problem in computer vision and a stepping stone for many other problems such as 3D scene understanding and reconstruction. Recently, this problem has enjoyed renewed interest due to the emergence of applications in autonomous driving and augmented reality, where the ability to reason about objects in 3D is key.

As with many computer vision tasks, methods based on convolutional neural networks (CNNs) have been shown to work really well for object pose estimation [1–6]. However, these methods often assume knowledge

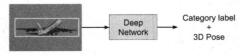

Fig. 1. Overview of our problem

about the object category and its 2D localization in the image. In this paper, we relax one of these constraints and propose to solve the problem of joint object

© Springer Nature Switzerland AG 2019
L. Leal-Taixé and S. Roth (Eds.): ECCV 2018 Workshops, LNCS 11129, pp. 698–715, 2019.
https://doi.org/10.1007/978-3-030-11009-3_43

category and 3D pose estimation from 2D images assuming known localization of the object in the image. More specifically, we assume that the bounding box around an object in the image is provided to us by an oracle and we learn a deep network that predicts the category label and 3D pose of the object, as illustrated in Fig. 1.

One approach to object category and 3D pose estimation is to learn independent networks for each task, as illustrated in Fig. 2a. However, this approach does not exploit the fact that some parts of the representation could be shared across multiple tasks [7]. To address this

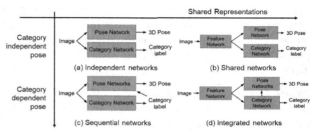

Fig. 2. Different network architectures for joint object category and 3D pose estimation

issue, [8] designs independent pose and category networks, but each one is built on top of a feature network that is shared by both tasks, as shown in Fig. 2b. However, one issue with both independent and shared networks is that they predict pose in a category agnostic manner, which may not always be possible because in some cases it may be difficult to define a universal reference frame (or characteristic pose) for all object categories.[1] To address this issue, we could train a category dependent pose network, i.e., a collection of pose networks (one per object category), each of which takes as input the 2D image and predicts a 3D pose, as shown in Fig. 2c. The final 3D pose predicted by this sequential network is the pose predicted by the network corresponding to the predicted category label. However, as is the case for independent networks, sequential networks do not take advantage of shared representations.

Paper Contributions. We propose an integrated architecture that provides the best of both worlds by integrating (1) a shared feature representation for both tasks and (2) a category dependent pose network. The proposed architecture consists of a shared feature network, whose output is used as an input to both a category network and a category dependent pose network, as shown in Fig. 2d. The feature network is a residual network learned so that it captures properties of the image that are relevant to both categorization and pose estimation. The category network is also a residual network applied to the output of the feature network. Finally, the category dependent pose network is a collection of fully connected networks (one per object category) that receives the outputs of both the feature and categorization networks as inputs. Since the latter is a class probability vector, it can be used to predict the final pose by fusing pose from individual categories, thereby being potentially more robust to errors in the estimation of the object category. We also devise a new training algorithm for

---

[1] A natural choice is the center of gravity of the object and the three principal directions (PDs), but even PDs cannot be consistently defined across object categories.

our proposed architecture. Our experiments show that the proposed approach achieves state-of-the-art performance on the challenging Pascal3D+ [9] dataset for the joint categorization and pose estimation task; which is comparable to the performance of state-of-the-art methods on the simpler 3D pose estimation with known object category task. We also present an ablative analysis that provides empirical justification for our design choices such as (i) network architecture, (ii) feature representations, (iii) training method, etc. To the best of our knowledge, our work is the first to use residual networks [10] –that have worked very well for the task of image classification– for 3D pose estimation. We do note that [11] also use residual networks but for azimuth or orientation estimation.

Paper Outline. We first review related work in Sect. 2. We then describe our model for joint object category and 3D pose estimation in Sect. 3, including the proposed architecture in Sect. 3.1, loss functions in Sect. 3.2, and training procedure in Sect. 3.3. Finally, we describe our experimental evaluation and analysis in Sect. 4.

2   Related Work

There are two main lines of research that are relevant to our work: (i) 3D pose estimation given object category label and (ii) joint object category and pose estimation. There are many non-deep learning based approaches such as [12–19], which have designed systems to solve these two tasks. However, due to space constraints, we restrict our discussion to deep learning based approaches.

3D Pose Estimation Given Object Category Label. Current literature for this task can be grouped into two categories: (1) predict 2D keypoints from images and then align 3D models with these keypoints to recover 3D pose and (2) predict 3D pose directly from 2D images. The first category includes methods like Pavlakos *et al.* [4] and Wu *et al.* [5], which recover a full 6-dimensional pose (azimuth, elevation, camera-tilt, depth, image-translation). Both methods train on images that have been annotated with 2D keypoints that correspond to semantic keypoints on 3D object models. Given a 2D image, they first generate a probabilistic heatmap of 2D keypoints and then recover 3D pose by aligning these 2D keypoints with the 3D keypoints. The second category includes methods like Tulsiani and Malik [1], Su *et al.* [2], Mahendran *et al.* [6], Mousavian *et al.* [3] and Wang *et al.* [20], where they recover the 3D rotation between the object and the camera which corresponds to a 3-dimensional pose (azimuth, elevation, camera-tilt). We also aim to predict a 3-dof pose output in this work. [1, 2] setup a pose-classification problem by discretizing the euler angles into pose-labels and minimize the cross-entropy loss during training. [3] solves a mixed classification-regression problem by returning both pose-label and a residual angle associated with every pose-label, such that the predicted angle is the sum of the center of pose-bin and the corresponding residual angle with the highest confidence. [6, 20] on the other hand, solve a pose regression problem. While [20] directly regresses the three angles with mean squared loss, [6] uses axis-angle or quaternion representations of 3D rotations and minimizes a geodesic loss during training. Our work is closest to [6] in that we also use an axis-angle representation and geodesic loss function while solving a 3D pose regression problem. However, there are three key differences between our work and [6]: (i) we solve the harder task of joint category and pose estimation, (ii) we design a new integrated architecture for the joint task, and (iii) our feature network architecture is based on residual networks [10,21] whereas the feature network of [6] uses VGG-M [22]. We refer the reader to [23] for a more detailed review of the current literature on 3D pose estimation using deep networks.

Joint Object Category and Pose Estimation. Braun *et al.* [24], Massa *et al.* [25,26] and Oñoro-Rubio *et al.* [27] work on the problem of joint object detection and pose estimation, while Elhoseiny *et al.* [8] and Afifi *et al.* [28] work on the problem of joint object category and pose estimation. However in all these works, the pose is restricted to just the azimuth or yaw angle. We, on the other hand, recover the full 3D rotation matrix which is a much harder problem. Also, these works all consider pose to be independent of category, *i.e.* they set up a multi-task network that has separate branches for pose and category label, which are then treated independently. While [27] proposes various network architectures, all of them are variations of shared networks (Fig. 2b) or independent networks (Fig. 2a). We, on the other hand, design an integrated network architecture (Fig. 2d) with a category-dependent pose network.

3   Joint Object Category and Pose Estimation

In this section, we describe the proposed integrated architecture for joint object category and 3D pose estimation, which consists of a feature network, a category network and a category dependent pose network, as shown in Fig. 2d. In addition, we describe our loss functions and proposed training algorithm.

3.1   Integrated Network Architecture

Feature and Category Networks. Observe that the combination of our feature network and our categorization network resembles a standard categorization network in the image classification literature. Therefore, when designing our feature and categorization networks, we consider existing categorization architectures as our starting point. The recently introduced residual networks [10,21] have been shown to work remarkably well for image classification as well as object detection. Taking inspiration from their success and good optimization properties [29], we use residual networks (specifically the ResNet-50 network) in our work.

In image classification works, the last linear layer is considered a 'categorization' network and everything before that is considered the 'feature' network. In our case though, we are also interested in the 3D pose and such a splitting is not feasible because the image representations learned by such a feature network is highly specialized for categorization. We need to look at intermediate layers to find a suitable splitting point for our feature network and categorization network such that the image representations contain some pose information. Our experiments (in Sect. 4.2) show that stage-4 is an appropriate splitting point and hence, we choose the ResNet-50 network upto stage-4 as our feature network and the stage-5 block of the ResNet-50 network as our categorization network.

Category Dependent Pose Network. The proposed category dependent pose network is a collection of 3-layer fully connected (FC) pose networks (one per object category) that take in as input the output of the feature network and the probability vector output by the category network. An example is shown in Fig. 3a, where the output of the feature network $\phi(I)$ for image I is input to K FC pose networks. Each individual pose network (shown in Fig. 3b) consists of 3 FC layers (FC1, FC2 and FC3) with batch normalization (BN) and rectified linear units (ReLU) interspersed between them and a nonlinearity at the output. The outputs of these pose networks $\{\mathbf{y}_i\}_{i=1}^K$ correspond to some representation of the object pose (see below for details). The category probability vector is denoted by $\mathbf{p}$ where $\mathbf{p}_i = P(c = i \mid I)$ is the probability of assigning the i-th category label to the image I. The K category-dependent pose representations are fused together with the category probability vector $\mathbf{p}$ to predict the final 3D pose using either a weighted or top-1 fusion strategy (see below for details).

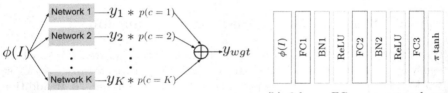

(a) Overview with weighted fusion

(b) 3-layer FC pose network per object category (adapted from [6])

Fig. 3. Category dependent pose network

Representation of 3D Pose. Each pose network predicts a 3D pose (a rotation matrix R) for a given object category label c. We use the axis-angle representation, $R = \text{expm}(\theta[\mathbf{v}]_\times)$, where $\mathbf{v}$ corresponds to the axis of rotation and θ is the angle of rotation. $[\mathbf{v}]_\times$ is the skew-symmetric matrix generated from vector $\mathbf{v} = [v_1, v_2, v_3]^T$, i.e. $[\mathbf{v}]_\times = \begin{pmatrix} 0 & -v_3 & v_2 \\ v_3 & 0 & -v_1 \\ -v_2 & v_1 & 0 \end{pmatrix}$. By restricting $\theta \in [0, \pi)$, we create a one-to-one correspondence between a rotation R and its axis-angle vector $\mathbf{y} = \theta\mathbf{v}$. Let $\mathbf{y}_i$ be the output of the i-th pose network. When the object category is known, we can choose the output $\mathbf{y}_{c^*}$ corresponding to the true category c^* and apply the exponential map $R_{c^*} = \text{expm}([\mathbf{y}_{c^*}]_\times)$ to obtain a rotation. Since in our case we do not know the category, the outputs of the K pose networks need to be fused. Because the space of rotations is non-Euclidean, fusion is more easily done in the axis-angle space. Therefore, to obtain the final rotation, we first fuse the outputs of the K pose networks and then apply the exponential map.

Pose Fusion. Given K category-dependent pose predictions $\{y_i\}_{i=1}^{K}$ obtained by the K pose networks and a category probability vector $\mathbf{p}$ obtained from the category network, we propose two simple fusion strategies.

- *Weighted fusion:* The fused pose output is a weighted sum of the individual pose predictions, with the weights determined by the category probability vector:

$$y_{wgt} = \sum_i y_i \mathbf{p}_i. \tag{1}$$

This kind of fusion of pose outputs has some interesting properties:

1. In the special case of know object category label, the category probability vector $\mathbf{p} = \delta(c^*)$ and Eq. 1 naturally simplifies to $y_{wgt} = y_{c^*}$
2. It is valid to define $y_{wgt} = \sum_i y_i \mathbf{p}_i$ because a weighted sum of axis-angle vectors is still an axis-angle vector (axis-angle vectors are elements of the convex set $\{x \in \mathbb{R}^3 | \|x\|_2 < \pi\}$ and the weighted sum is a convex combination of elements of this convex set). On the other hand, a weighted sum of rotation matrices is not guaranteed to be a rotation matrix.

- *Top1 fusion:* Instead of marginalizing out the category label, we can choose the final pose as the output corresponding to the mode of the category probability distribution. Effectively in this fusion, we are first estimating the object category label $\hat{c} = \text{argmax}_i\, \mathbf{p}_i$ and predicting pose accordingly

$$y_{top1} = y_{\hat{c}}. \tag{2}$$

3.2   Loss Functions

In general, a loss function between ground-truth pose R^*, ground-truth category label c^* and our network output (R, c), can be expressed as $\mathcal{L}(R, c, R^*, c^*)$. A simple choice of the overall loss is to define it as a sum of a pose loss and a category loss, *i.e.* $\mathcal{L}(R, c, R^*, c^*) = \mathcal{L}_{pose}(R(c), R^*) + \lambda \mathcal{L}_{category}(c, c^*)$, where the notation $R(c)$ explicitly encodes the fact that our pose output depends on the estimated category. We use the categorical cross-entropy loss as our category loss, and the geodesic distance between two rotation matrices R_1 and R_2,

$$\mathcal{L}_{pose}(R_1, R_2) = \frac{\| \log(R_1 R_2^T) \|_F}{\sqrt{2}}, \tag{3}$$

as our pose loss. The pose loss between two axis-angle vectors y_1 and y_2 is now defined as $\mathcal{L}_p(y_1, y_2) \equiv \mathcal{L}(R_1, R_2)$ where R_1 and R_2 are the corresponding rotation matrices. Pose loss for the weighted fusion and top1 fusion pose outputs is now given by $\mathcal{L}_p(y^*, y_{wgt})$ and $\mathcal{L}_p(y^*, y_{top1})$ respectively.

In this paper, for our choice of representation and loss function, we do not observe a significant difference between the weighted and top1 fusion of pose outputs and report performance on both for all our experiments. However, for a different choice of representation, one might be better than the other.

3.3   Network Training

The overall network architecture has three sub-networks: the feature network (FN), the category network (CN) and the category dependent pose network (PN) consisting of one FC pose network per object category. A natural way to train this integrated network is to fix the feature network using weights from a pre-trained ResNet-50, train the category network & each pose network independently and then finetune the overall network using our joint loss. This is called the "balanced" training approach where category and pose are treated in a balanced way. The fundamental problem with the balanced approach is that the feature network initialized with pre-trained weights is biased to categorization. And since we are solving a joint task with competing objectives where initialization is important, we end up with good categorization performance at the cost of pose estimation performance. Therefore, we propose a different approach to training the overall network called "pose-first" training.

In this approach, we try to bias the feature network towards 3D pose estimation. We do this by first training our proposed network with an oracle category network *i.e.* train the feature network and category dependent pose network, by minimizing the pose loss, with ground-truth object

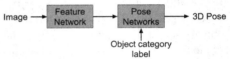

Fig. 4. Training feature network + pose networks with oracle category network

category labels (as shown in Fig. 4). For every training image, the oracle category network returns a probability vector $\mathbf{p} = \delta(c^*)$ that selects the pose network corresponding to its category label and updates only that pose network. In the process, we are also updating the feature network for the task of 3D pose estimation. With this updated feature network and category dependent pose network fixed, we now train the category network by minimizing the category loss. Then the overall network is finetuned end-to-end with both category and pose losses jointly. We also manually balance our training batch so that every batch has roughly the same number of training images per object category, which is an alternative implementation of the recommendation in [7] where they recommend asynchronous gradient updates to balance the variability of data across various tasks and datasets. We show in our experiments in Sect. 4.4 that "pose-first" training achieves significantly better results for pose estimation compared to "balanced" training while achieving the marginally better results for category estimation. The "pose-first" training encodes what we set out to do, learn a 3D pose estimation system with known object category labels and then relax that constraint by replacing the oracle with a category estimation network.

As mentioned earlier, we use the categorical cross-entropy loss for our category loss and the geodesic distance between rotation matrices for our pose loss. For evaluation, we use two metrics, (i) *cat-acc*: the average accuracy in estimating the object category label (higher is better) and (ii) *pose-err*: the median viewpoint error in degrees between the ground-truth and estimated rotations (lower is better). The viewpoint error between rotation matrices, Eq. 3, can be

Table 1. Table outlining the steps to train the overall network in two ways

Step	Balanced	Pose-first
1	Fix FN using weights from the pre-trained ResNet-50	
2	Learn PN per object category independent of each other	
3	Learn CN	Finetune FN+PN jointly with oracle CN
4	Finetune FN+CN+PN jointly	Learn CN with updated FN fixed
5	-	Finetune FN+CN+PN jointly

simplified using the Rodrigues' rotation formula to get viewpoint angle error (in degrees) between ground-truth rotation R^* and predicted rotation R,

$$\Delta(R, R^*) = |\cos^{-1}\left[\frac{\text{trace}(R^T R^*) - 1}{2}\right]|. \qquad (4)$$

We use Adam optimizer [30] in all our experiments and our code was written in Keras [31] with TensorFlow backend [32].

4   Results and Discussion

We first present the dataset we use for our experimental evaluation in Sect. 4.1. Then, in Sect. 4.2, we produce an investigation of features learned by a pre-trained ResNet-50 network for the task of 3D pose estimation. In Sect. 4.3 we empirically verify a key assumption we make, that category dependent networks work better than category independent networks. Then, in Sect. 4.4 we report our experiments on the joint object category and pose estimation task. We demonstrate significant improvement upon state-of-the-art on the joint task and achieve performance comparable to methods that solve for 3D pose with known object category. Finally, we also present an extensive ablative analysis of many decisions choices like network architecture, feature representations, training protocol and relative weighting parameter.

4.1   Datasets

For our experiments, we use the challenging Pascal3D+ dataset (release version 1.1) [9] which consists of images of 12 common rigid object categories of interest: aeroplane (aero), bicycle (bike), boat, bottle, bus, car, chair, diningtable (dtable), motorbike (mbike), sofa, train and tvmonitor (tv). The dataset includes Pascal VOC 2012 images [33] and ImageNet images [34] annotated with 3D pose annotations that describe the position of the camera with respect to the object in terms of azimuth, elevation, camera-tilt, distance, image-translation and focal-length. We use the ImageNet-training+validation images as our training data, Pascal-training images as our validation data and Pascal-validation images as our testing data. Like we mentioned earlier, we concentrate on the problem of joint object category and 3D pose estimation assuming we have bounding boxes around objects returned by an oracle. We use images that contain un-occluded and un-truncated objects that have been annotated with ground-truth bounding boxes. There are a total of 20,843 images that satisfy this criteria across these 12 categories of interest, with the number of images across the train-val-test splits detailed in Table 2. We use the 3D pose jittering data augmentation proposed in [6] and the rendered images[2] provided in [2] to augment our training data.

Table 2. Number of images in Pascal3D+ v1.1 [9] across various splits as well as rendered images provided by Su *et al.* [2].

Category	aero	bike	boat	bottle	bus	car	chair	dtable	mbike	sofa	train	tv	Total
Train	1765	794	1979	1303	1024	5287	967	737	634	601	1016	1195	17302
Val	242	108	177	201	149	294	161	26	119	38	100	167	1782
Test	244	112	163	177	144	262	180	17	127	37	105	191	1759
Rendered	198k	200k	199k	200k	199k	195k	197k	196k	200k	200k	200k	199k	2.381m

4.2 Residual Networks for 3D Pose Estimation

One of our contributions in this work is the use of the very popular residual networks designed by He *et al.* [10,21] for the task of 3D pose estimation. As described in Sect. 3.3, we initialize our overall network with pre-trained ResNet-50 networks. Before we present our experimental results though, we would like to answer the question: Can we adapt residual networks trained for the task of image classification to the task of pose estimation? Networks learned for the task of image classification are trained to be invariant to pose. However, previous works like [8] (for AlexNet [35]) and [6] (for VGG-M [22]) have shown that features extracted from intermediate layers retain information relevant to pose estimation. For our specific case, we are also interested in knowing at what intermediate stage does a pre-trained ResNet-50 have relevant pose information.

We extract features at different stages of the ResNet-50 architecture with pre-trained weights. We then learn 3-layer FC networks per object category of size d-1000-500-3 using these features. As can be seen in Fig. 5 and Table 3, we find that features extracted at the end of stage-4 are better than the features extracted at the end of stages-3 and 5. This is consistent with previous findings that show that (i) features become more specialized for the task they were trained for

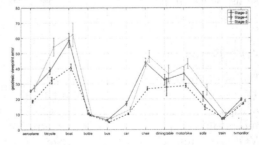

Fig. 5. Median viewpoint error (in degrees) with features extracted from different stage of the pre-trained ResNet-50. Lower is better. Best seen in color.

---

[2] https://shapenet.cs.stanford.edu/media/syn_images_cropped_bkg_overlaid.tar.

(image classification in this case) the deeper they are in the network, which explains why stage-4 features are better than stage-5, and (ii) deeper layers capture more complex information compared to simple edge detectors at the first few layers, which explains why stage-4 features are better than stage-3.

Table 3. Median viewpoint error (in degrees) after learning pose networks using features extracted from pre-trained networks. Pose networks are of size 512/1024/2048-1000-500-3 for ResNet-50 Stages-3/4/5 respectively. Lower is better and best results in bold.

Network	Feats.	aero	bike	boat	bottle	bus	car	chair	dtable	mbike	sofa	train	tv	mean
ResNet-50	Stage-3	25.3	38.6	58.6	10.5	6.4	17.0	44.1	32.6	36.7	21.6	**7.1**	19.7	26.51
	Stage-4	**18.4**	**32.3**	**40.9**	9.6	**5.0**	**10.4**	**26.8**	**27.8**	**28.7**	**14.6**	7.3	**16.9**	**19.91**
	Stage-5	27.1	54.3	62.4	**9.2**	7.6	13.3	47.8	36.7	43.1	26.0	9.8	18.8	29.67

4.3   Category-Dependent Pose Networks

An implicit assumption we have made in our work is that our choice of category-dependent pose network architecture (with per-category pose networks) is better than the choice of a category-independent pose network (the choice of [8,24]). In our architecture, the feature network is shared between all object categories and the pose networks are specific to each category. [8] discusses where the branching between category and pose estimation tasks should occur in their early branching (EBM) and late branching (LBM) models, but they do not discuss why they choose a category-independent pose network. We now validate our decision choice of category-dependent pose networks empirically. For this experiment, we use the features extracted from ResNet-50 stage-4. We then learn twelve 3-layer pose networks, one for each object category, of size 1024-1000-500-3 (Row 1 of Table 4). To compare with a category independent pose network, we use these same features to learn a single pose network of size 1024-12000-500-3 (Row 2 of Table 4). Note that the intermediate layer is of size 12000 to have roughly the same number of total parameters as the 12 independent pose networks. We also show performance on two smaller intermediate sizes and as can be seen in Table 4, solving for the pose in a per-category manner is better.

Table 4. Median viewpoint error (in degrees) for category-dependent and category-independent pose networks. For the category-dependent network, there are 12 networks of size 1024-1000-500-3. We evaluate three sizes of category-independent networks: 1024-12000-500-3 (12k), 1024-5000-500-3 (5k) and 1024-1000-500-3 (1k). Lower is better and best results in bold.

Type	aero	bike	boat	bottle	bus	car	chair	dtable	mbike	sofa	train	tv	Mean
Cat-dep.	**18.4**	**32.3**	**40.9**	9.6	**5.0**	**10.4**	**26.8**	27.8	**28.7**	14.6	**7.3**	**16.9**	**19.91**
Cat-ind. (12k)	23.9	40.9	54.7	12.1	5.8	11.6	41.8	26.9	31.0	20.3	10.0	18.9	24.83
Cat-ind. (5k)	22.3	39.6	52.6	12.4	5.5	12.2	44.1	27.4	32.4	**14.6**	10.2	18.7	24.3
Cat-ind. (1k)	22.9	36.6	55.4	10.8	5.5	10.6	36.9	**26.3**	32.4	18.5	9.4	18.8	23.69

4.4   Joint Object Category and Pose Estimation

We now present the results of our experiments on the task of joint object category and pose estimation. As mentioned earlier in Sect. 3.3 we train the overall network using the "pose-first" approach with both weighted and top1 fusion strategies of Sect. 3.1. To evaluate our performance we report the object category estimation accuracy (cat-acc) and the median viewpoint error (pose-err), across all object categories. As can be seen in Table 5, we achieve close to 90% category estimation accuracy and slightly more than 16° median viewpoint error averaged across object categories in both models when training on only real images. Using rendered images to augment training data leads to significant improvement in pose estimation performance, with pose viewpoint error decreasing by ~2.4° in the Weighted model and ~2.7° in the Top1 model, and an improvement of ~2% in the category estimation accuracy for both models. Note that rendered images are valid only for the pose estimation part of our problem and not the category estimation part. In the "pose-first" training method, we use these rendered images in steps 2&3 of Table 1. This is used to initialize the joint network which is subsequently trained using only real (original + flipped) images from PAS-CAL3D+. Our results are consistent with those of [2] and [6] who also observed improved performance by using rendered images for data augmentation.

Table 5. Object category estimation accuracy (percentage, higher is better) and pose viewpoint error (degress, lower is better) for experiments with joint networks using real and rendered images. Best results are in bold.

Metric	Data	Model	aero	bike	boat	bottle	bus	car	chair	dtable	mbike	sofa	train	tv	mean
pose-err	Only real images	Weighted	13.6	21.3	34.8	9.0	3.4	7.8	26.6	**20.8**	17.6	15.8	6.9	15.2	16.07
		Top1	13.4	22.2	33.5	9.2	3.3	7.7	26.2	24.0	17.8	16.5	**6.6**	15.2	16.29
	Real and rendered	Weighted	11.5	**15.7**	30.5	9.0	2.9	6.8	16.2	22.5	14.4	**13.8**	7.3	13.4	13.67
		Top1	**10.2**	17.1	**29.2**	**8.1**	**2.6**	**6.0**	**13.8**	26.7	**14.1**	14.3	7.1	13.5	**13.56**
cat-acc	Only real images	Weighted	0.94	0.89	0.95	0.98	0.96	0.94	0.83	0.67	0.93	0.78	0.94	0.93	0.8944
		Top1	**0.97**	0.87	0.94	0.96	0.96	0.95	0.84	0.62	**0.96**	0.78	0.94	0.93	0.8930
	Real and rendered	Weighted	0.96	**0.94**	0.97	**1.00**	0.95	**0.96**	0.87	0.71	**0.96**	0.77	**0.95**	**0.95**	0.9150
		Top1	0.96	0.92	**0.98**	0.98	**0.97**	**0.96**	**0.89**	**0.76**	0.93	**0.82**	0.88	**0.95**	**0.9181**

Comparison with State-of-the-Art. To the best of our knowledge, Elhoseiny *et al.* [8] are the current state-of-the-art on the PASCAL3D+ dataset for the task of joint object category and azimuth estimation given ground-truth bounding boxes. We do not use any rendered images in these experiments to ensure a fair comparison. They report the performance of their models using the following metrics: (i) P%($<22.5°/45°$): percentage of images that have pose error less than $22.5°/45°$ and (ii) AAAI: $1 - [\min(|err|, 2\pi - |err|)/\pi]$. We evaluate our models using these metrics for both azimuth error $|az - az^*|$ and 3D pose error $\Delta(P, R^*)$. For azimuth estimation, we predict 3D rotation matrix and then retrieve the azimuth angle. For a fair comparison between their method and ours, we re-implemented their algorithm with our network architecture *i.e.* feature network is ResNet-50 upto Stage-4, category network is ResNet-50 Stage-5 and pose network is a 3-layer FC network of size 1024-1000-500-3. This size of the pose network was chosen based on Table 4. As can be seen in Tables 6 and 7, we perform significantly better than [8] in pose estimation accuracy under different metrics while performing marginally worse (0.3−0.6%) in category accuracy.

Table 6. Comparing our joint networks with weighted (wgt) and top1 pose output with [8]* (our re-implementation of [8], see text for details). Higher is better for the cat-acc, lower is better for pose-err metric. Best results in bold.

Metric	Model	aero	bike	boat	bottle	bus	car	chair	dtable	mbike	sofa	train	tv	Mean
pose-err	[8]*	17.7	24.7	41.6	9.9	3.6	12.2	31.9	20.8	20.2	26.7	6.9	16.0	19.35
	Ours-Wgt	11.5	**15.7**	30.5	9.0	2.9	6.8	16.2	**22.5**	14.4	**13.8**	7.3	**13.4**	13.67
	Ours-Top1	**10.2**	17.1	**29.2**	**8.1**	**2.6**	**6.0**	13.8	26.7	14.1	14.3	**7.1**	13.5	**13.56**
cat-acc	[8]*	0.95	**0.94**	**0.98**	0.98	**0.99**	**0.96**	**0.89**	0.57	**0.96**	**0.90**	**0.97**	**0.96**	**0.9215**
	Ours-Wgt	**0.96**	**0.94**	0.97	**1.00**	0.95	**0.96**	0.87	0.71	**0.96**	0.77	0.95	0.95	0.9150
	Ours-Top1	**0.96**	0.92	**0.98**	0.98	0.97	**0.96**	**0.89**	**0.76**	0.93	0.82	0.88	0.95	0.9181

Table 7. Comparing our joint networks with weighted (wgt) and top1 pose output with [8]* under their metrics. Higher is better, Best results in bold.

Error	Model	cat-acc	P%(<22.5°)	P%(<45°)	AAAI
$\Delta(R, R^*)$	[8]*	**0.9215**	0.5759	0.7647	0.8128
	Ours-Weighted	0.9150	0.6853	0.8370	0.8495
	Ours-Top1	0.9181	**0.7054**	**0.8436**	**0.8526**
$\Delta(az, az^*)$	[8]*	**0.9215**	0.5009	0.6939	0.7692
	Ours-Weighted	0.9150	0.6627	0.7797	0.8130
	Ours-Top1	0.9181	**0.7287**	**0.8170**	**0.8333**
	[8]	0.8379	0.5189	0.6074	0.7539

In Table 8, we compare with state-of-the-art methods on pose estimation with known object category and observe that we achieve competitive performance even though we are solving a harder problem of joint object category and pose estimation. We would like to explicitly mention that, by solving the joint task, we are not trying to achieve improved performance relative to pose estimation with known object category. As we shall show later, the fine-tuning step where we jointly minimize pose and category losses shows a trade-off between pose estimation and category estimation performance, further proving our intuition that pose estimation and categorization are competing (not synergistic) tasks. Our motivation is to relax the known object category label constraint and still achieve comparable results.

Table 8. Median viewpoint error (in degrees, lower is better) across 12 object categories on Pascal3D+ dataset. First four rows are 3D pose estimation methods with known object category and the last two rows (ours) are joint object category and 3D pose estimation methods. Best results are highlighted in bold and second best are in red. Best seen in color.

Methods	aero	bike	boat	bottle	bus	car	chair	dtable	mbike	sofa	train	tv	Mean
Viepoints & Keypoints [1]	13.8	17.7	**21.3**	12.9	5.8	9.1	14.8	15.2	14.7	13.7	8.7	15.4	13.59
Render-for-CNN [2]	15.4	14.8	25.6	9.3	3.6	6.0	**9.7**	**10.8**	16.7	**9.5**	**6.1**	12.6	11.67
3D-pose-regression [6]	13.97	21.07	35.52	8.99	4.08	7.56	21.18	17.74	17.87	12.70	8.22	15.68	15.38
Multibin [3]	13.6	**12.5**	22.8	8.3	3.1	**5.8**	11.9	12.5	**12.3**	12.8	6.3	**11.9**	**11.1**
Ours-Weighted	11.5	15.7	30.5	9.0	2.9	6.8	16.2	22.5	14.4	13.8	7.3	13.4	13.67
Ours-Top1	**10.2**	17.1	29.2	**8.1**	**2.6**	6.0	13.8	26.7	14.1	14.3	7.1	13.5	13.56

Choice of Network Architecture. In Sect. 1, we introduced four possible network architectures to solve a joint task and advocated for Integrated network over other choices. We experimentally validate that choice by comparing it with a Sequential network and Shared network. Like we mention earlier, [8] is a Shared network. For a Sequential network, we use a second ResNet-50 network and finetune different parts of the network for categorization on the Pascal3D+ dataset.

Table 9. Comparison between Sequential, Shared and Integrated networks.

Metric	Network	Model	aero	bike	boat	bottle	bus	car	chair	dtable	mbike	sofa	train	tv	Mean
pose-err	Sequential	Everything	11.7	17.5	27.4	8.4	3.3	**5.9**	14.5	24.8	15.0	**11.1**	6.3	**13.2**	**13.25**
		FC	11.7	17.7	**27.1**	8.5	3.2	6.4	16.7	24.8	15.0	**11.1**	6.9	**13.2**	13.54
		FC+Stage5	11.7	17.6	27.3	8.2	3.2	**5.9**	14.5	24.8	14.3	12.7	**6.3**	**13.2**	13.30
	Integrated	Ours-Wgt	11.5	**15.7**	30.5	9.0	2.9	6.8	16.2	22.5	14.4	13.8	7.3	13.4	13.67
		Ours-Top1	**10.2**	17.1	29.2	**8.1**	**2.6**	6.0	**13.8**	26.7	**14.1**	14.3	7.1	13.5	13.56
	Shared	[8]*	17.7	24.7	41.6	9.9	3.6	12.2	31.9	**20.8**	20.2	26.7	6.9	16.0	19.35
cat-acc	Sequential	Everything	0.96	0.92	**0.98**	0.98	0.95	**0.97**	0.88	**0.76**	0.93	0.85	**0.97**	0.97	0.9275
		FC	0.94	0.92	0.96	0.97	0.97	0.88	0.81	0.62	0.93	**0.95**	0.95	0.95	0.9033
		FC+Stage5	**0.98**	0.92	**0.98**	0.99	0.97	**0.97**	**0.90**	0.67	**0.96**	0.92	**0.99**	0.96	**0.9348**
	Integrated	Ours-Wgt	0.96	**0.94**	0.97	**1.00**	0.95	0.96	0.87	0.71	**0.96**	0.77	0.95	0.95	0.9150
		Ours-Top1	0.96	0.92	**0.98**	0.98	0.97	0.96	0.89	**0.76**	0.93	0.82	0.88	0.95	0.9181
	Shared	[8]*	0.95	**0.94**	**0.98**	0.98	**0.99**	0.96	0.89	0.57	**0.96**	0.90	0.97	0.96	0.9215

As can be seen in Table 9, our Integrate networks are clearly better than the Shared network. They are comparable to Sequential networks in pose estimation performance and slightly worse in categorization accuracy while being significantly cheaper computationally. The Sequential network has to maintain two ResNet-50 networks compared to a single one for our Integrated networks.

Choice of Training Protocol. In Sect. 3.3, we proposed two approaches to train the overall network. As can be seen in Table 10, averaged across all object categories, the joint models trained using the "pose-first" approach are better than those trained using the "balanced" one. This means that learning the best possible feature + pose models for the task of 3D pose estimation first and then relaxing them to solve the joint category and pose estimation task is better than solving category and pose estimation tasks independently with fixed feature network and then training everything jointly.

Table 10. Object category estimation accuracy (percentage, higher is better) and pose viewpoint error (degrees, lower is better) using the two training approaches described in Sect. 3.3 for Real Images. Best results in bold.

Metric	Expt.	Type	aero	bike	boat	bottle	bus	car	chair	dtable	mbike	sofa	train	tv	mean
pose-err	Balance	Weighted	13.9	24.1	35.4	9.6	4.1	8.8	33.5	24.1	19.5	17.7	7.6	15.9	17.86
		Top1	13.7	23.9	**32.4**	10.6	3.8	8.0	32.5	26.3	17.8	18.0	7.6	15.4	17.51
	Pose-first	Weighted	13.6	**21.3**	34.8	**9.0**	3.4	7.8	26.6	**20.8**	17.6	**15.8**	6.9	**15.2**	**16.07**
		Top1	**13.4**	22.2	33.5	9.2	**3.3**	**7.7**	**26.2**	24.0	17.8	16.5	**6.6**	15.2	16.29
cat-acc	Balance	Weighted	0.92	**0.89**	0.96	0.96	0.95	0.81	0.73	0.71	0.94	**0.87**	**0.96**	**0.96**	0.8889
		Top1	0.90	**0.89**	**0.97**	0.88	0.94	0.79	0.70	**0.73**	0.95	**0.87**	0.95	0.95	0.8760
	Pose-first	Weighted	0.94	**0.89**	0.95	**0.98**	**0.96**	0.94	0.83	0.67	0.93	0.78	0.94	0.93	**0.8944**
		Top1	**0.97**	0.87	0.94	0.96	**0.96**	**0.95**	0.84	0.62	**0.96**	0.78	0.94	0.93	0.8930

Effect of Finetuning the Overall Network with the Joint Losses. The tasks of object category estimation (which requires the network to be invariant to pose) and 3D pose estimation (which is invariant to object sub-category) are competing with each other and during joint training, the feature network tries to learn a representation that is suitable for both tasks. In doing so, we expect a the trade-off between cat-acc and pose-err performance. This trade-off is observed explicitly when trying to learn the overall model using the "balanced" approach. We first do steps 1–3, where we fix the feature network to the pre-trained weights and train the pose and category networks independently. Rows 1–3 of Table 11 show that the original feature network with pre-trained weights has features that are very good for category estimation but not for pose estimation. We then do step 4, where we finetune the overall network with our joint loss. As can be seen in Table 11, there is a trade-off between the two tasks of object category estimation & 3D pose estimation and we lose some category estimation accuracy while improving the pose estimation performance.

Table 11. Object category estimation accuracy (percentage, higher is better) and pose viewpoint error (degrees, lower is better) before (Steps 1–3) and after (Step 4) finetuning the overall network in "balanced" training. Best results in bold.

Metric	Expt.	Type	aero	bike	boat	bottle	bus	car	chair	dtable	mbike	sofa	train	tv	mean
pose-err	Before	Weighted	25.5	39.0	47.6	13.4	9.7	15.2	34.6	38.2	37.5	21.5	9.6	16.6	25.70
		Top1	25.5	38.9	49.5	13.4	9.4	14.5	35.8	38.2	37.2	21.5	8.9	16.7	25.79
	After	Weighted	13.9	24.1	35.4	9.6	4.1	8.8	33.5	24.1	19.5	17.7	7.6	15.9	17.86
		Top1	**13.7**	**23.9**	**32.4**	10.6	**3.8**	8.0	**32.5**	26.3	**17.8**	18.0	**7.6**	**15.4**	**17.51**
cat-acc	Before	Both	0.97	0.91	0.97	0.98	0.95	0.92	0.90	0.71	0.97	0.85	0.95	0.99	0.9226
	After	Weighted	0.92	0.89	0.96	0.96	0.95	0.81	0.73	0.71	0.94	**0.87**	**0.96**	0.96	0.8889
		Top1	0.90	0.89	**0.97**	0.88	0.94	0.79	0.70	**0.73**	0.95	**0.87**	0.95	0.95	0.8760

Choice of λ. In Table 12, we compare the performance of models learned with different choices of λ. The λ parameter controls the relative importance of the category loss (categorical cross-entropy) w.r.t. the pose loss (geodesic loss). Recall that $\mathcal{L}(R, c, R^*, c^*) = \mathcal{L}_{pose}(R(c), R^*) + \lambda\mathcal{L}_{category}(c, c^*)$. The smaller value of $\lambda = 0.1$ lead to better joint models and unless mentioned otherwise all the models were trained with that choice of λ.

Table 12. Object category estimation accuracy (percentage, higher is better) and pose viewpoint error (degrees, lower is better) under the two joint losses for different λ trained using the pose-first approach. Best results in bold.

Metric	Expt.	Type	aero	bike	boat	bottle	bus	car	chair	dtable	mbike	sofa	train	tv	mean
pose-err	$\lambda = 0.1$	Weighted	13.6	**21.3**	34.8	**9.0**	3.4	7.8	26.6	20.8	**17.6**	**15.8**	6.9	**15.2**	**16.07**
		Top1	13.4	22.2	**33.5**	9.2	**3.3**	**7.7**	**26.2**	24.0	17.8	16.5	**6.6**	**15.2**	16.29
	$\lambda = 1$	Weighted	14.5	23.8	38.4	9.5	3.4	8.4	28.4	**18.6**	**17.6**	17.4	7.3	15.4	16.89
		Top1	**13.4**	22.8	36.8	10.2	3.4	8.5	30.2	19.2	18.7	15.8	6.7	15.4	16.74
cat-acc	$\lambda = 0.1$	Weighted	0.94	0.89	0.95	**0.98**	**0.96**	0.94	0.83	0.67	0.93	0.78	0.94	0.93	**0.8944**
		Top1	**0.97**	0.87	0.94	0.96	**0.96**	**0.95**	**0.84**	0.62	**0.96**	0.78	0.94	0.93	0.8930
	$\lambda = 1$	Weighted	0.92	**0.91**	**0.96**	0.91	0.94	0.82	0.80	0.70	0.85	0.75	0.91	0.93	0.8678
		Top1	0.92	0.90	0.93	0.88	0.95	0.85	0.73	**0.71**	0.91	**0.87**	**0.95**	**0.94**	0.8775

Top-k Category Labels: We also analyze performance when instead of the most-likely (top1) category label, the category network returns multiple labels (top2/3). To compute the pose error with multiple predicted category labels, we compute the viewpoint error with the pose output of every predicted category and take the minimum value. For example, the pose error for the top3 category labels (c_1, c_2, c_3) using the notation of Sect. 3.2 is given by $\mathcal{L}_p(y^*, y(c_1, c_2, c_3)) = \min_{i=1..3} \mathcal{L}_p(y^*, y_{c_i})$.

As can be seen in Table 13, increasing the number of possible category labels leads to an increase in both category estimation accuracy and reduction in pose estimation error. However, it must also be noted that this reduction of pose error is very likely an artifact of the above metric ($\min_{i=1..3} \mathcal{L}_p(y^*, y_{c_i}) \leq \min_{i=1,2} \mathcal{L}_p(y^*, y_{c_i}) \leq \mathcal{L}_p(y^*, y_{c_1})$) because when we use an oracle for category estimation (GT), the viewpoint error is higher than top-2/3 error. At the same time, improving category estimation accuracy (comparing top1 and GT, $89.30 \rightarrow 100$) leads to better performance in pose estimation ($16.29 \rightarrow 15.28$).

Table 13. Object category estimation accuracy and median viewpoint error when Top1/2/3 predicted labels are returned by the category network.

Top1		Top-2		Top-3		GT	
cat-acc	pose-err	cat-acc	pose-err	cat-acc	pose-err	cat-acc	pose-err
0.8930	16.29	0.9455	14.08	0.9595	13.15	100	15.28

5   Conclusion and Future Work

We have designed a new integrated network architecture consisting of a shared feature network, a categorization network and a new category dependent pose network (per-category collection of fully connected pose networks) for the task of joint object category and 3D pose estimation. We have developed two ways of fusing the outputs of individual pose networks and the output of the category network to predict 3D pose of an object in the image when its category label is not known. We have proposed a training algorithm to solve our joint network with suitable pose and category loss functions. Finally, we have shown state-of-the-art results on the PASCAL3D+ dataset for the joint task and have shown pose estimation performance comparable to state-of-the-art methods that solve the simpler task of 3D pose with known object category.

Future Work. We are exploring two avenues of future research. (1) We have used a pose regression formulation for our fusion techniques but they can be extended to pose classification problems and a natural question is to ask how well our proposed network architecture performs for the joint task of pose label and category label estimation. (2) An extension of this work to the joint object detection and pose estimation task by incorporating the category dependent pose network into existing architectures.

Acknowledgement. This research was supported by NSF grant 1527340.

References

1. Tulsiani, S., Malik, J.: Viewpoints and keypoints. In: 2015 IEEE Conference on Computer Vision and Pattern Recognition (CVPR), pp. 1510–1519, June 2015
2. Su, H., Qi, C.R., Li, Y., Guibas, L.J.: Render for CNN: viewpoint estimation in images using CNNs trained with rendered 3D model views. In: 2015 IEEE International Conference on Computer Vision (ICCV), pp. 2686–2694, December 2015
3. Mousavian, A., Anguelov, D., Flynn, J., Košecká, J.: 3D bounding box estimation using deep learning and geometry. In: 2017 IEEE Conference on Computer Vision and Pattern Recognition (CVPR), pp. 5632–5640, July 2017
4. Pavlakos, G., Zhou, X., Chan, A., Derpanis, K.G., Daniilidis, K.: 6-DoF object pose from semantic keypoints. In: 2017 IEEE International Conference on Robotics and Automation (ICRA), pp. 2011–2018, May 2017
5. Wu, J., et al.: Single image 3D interpreter network. In: Leibe, B., Matas, J., Sebe, N., Welling, M. (eds.) ECCV 2016. LNCS, vol. 9910, pp. 365–382. Springer, Cham (2016). https://doi.org/10.1007/978-3-319-46466-4_22
6. Mahendran, S., Ali, H., Vidal, R.: 3D pose regression using convolutional neural networks. In: IEEE International Conference on Computer Vision Workshop on Recovering 6D Object Pose (2017)
7. Kokkinos, I.: UberNet: training a 'universal' convolutional neural network for low-, mid-, and high-level vision using diverse datasets and limited memory. In: IEEE Conference on Computer Vision and Pattern Recognition (2017)

8. Elhoseiny, M., El-Gaaly, T., Bakry, A., Elgammal, A.: A comparative analysis and study of multiview CNN models for joint object categorization and pose estimation. In: Proceedings of the 33rd International Conference on International Conference on Machine Learning. ICML 2016, vol. 18, pp. 888–897. JMLR.org (2016)
9. Xiang, Y., Mottaghi, R., Savarese, S.: Beyond PASCAL: a benchmark for 3D object detection in the wild. In: IEEE Winter Conference on Applications of Computer Vision, pp. 75–82, March 2014
10. He, K., Zhang, X., Ren, S., Sun, J.: Deep residual learning for image recognition. In: 2016 IEEE Conference on Computer Vision and Pattern Recognition (CVPR), pp. 770–778, June 2016
11. Hara, K., Vemulapalli, R., Chellappa, R.: Designing deep convolutional neural networks for continuous object orientation estimation. CoRR abs/1702.01499 (2017)
12. López-Sastre, R.J., Tuytelaars, T., Savarese, S.: Deformable part models revisited: a performance evaluation for object category pose estimation. In: 2011 IEEE International Conference on Computer Vision Workshops (ICCV Workshops), pp. 1052–1059, November 2011
13. Hejrati, M., Ramanan, D.: Analysis by synthesis: 3D object recognition by object reconstruction. In: 2014 IEEE Conference on Computer Vision and Pattern Recognition, pp. 2449–2456, June 2014
14. Aubry, M., Maturana, D., Efros, A.A., Russell, B.C., Sivic, J.: Seeing 3D chairs: exemplar part-based 2D–3D alignment using a large dataset of CAD models. In: 2014 IEEE Conference on Computer Vision and Pattern Recognition, pp. 3762–3769, June 2014
15. Pepik, B., Stark, M., Gehler, P., Schiele, B.: Teaching 3D geometry to deformable part models. In: 2012 IEEE Conference on Computer Vision and Pattern Recognition, pp. 3362–3369, June 2012
16. Savarese, S., Fei-Fei, L.: 3D generic object categorization, localization and pose estimation. In: 2007 IEEE 11th International Conference on Computer Vision, pp. 1–8, October 2007
17. Bakry, A., El-Gaaly, T., Elhoseiny, M., Elgammal, A.: Joint object recognition and pose estimation using a nonlinear view-invariant latent generative model. In: IEEE Winter Applications of Computer Vision Conference (2016)
18. Mottaghi, R., Xiang, Y., Savarese, S.: A coarse-to-fine model for 3D pose estimation and sub-category recognition. In: IEEE Conference on Computer Vision and Pattern Recognition (2015)
19. Juranek, R., Herout, A., Dubska, M., Zemcik, P.: Real-time pose estimation piggybacked on object detection. In: IEEE International Conference on Computer Vision (2015)
20. Wang, Y., Li, S., Jia, M., Liang, W.: Viewpoint estimation for objects with convolutional neural network trained on synthetic images. In: Chen, E., Gong, Y., Tie, Y. (eds.) PCM 2016. LNCS, vol. 9917, pp. 169–179. Springer, Cham (2016). https://doi.org/10.1007/978-3-319-48896-7_17
21. He, K., Zhang, X., Ren, S., Sun, J.: Identity mappings in deep residual networks. In: Leibe, B., Matas, J., Sebe, N., Welling, M. (eds.) ECCV 2016. LNCS, vol. 9908, pp. 630–645. Springer, Cham (2016). https://doi.org/10.1007/978-3-319-46493-0_38
22. Chatfield, K., Simonyan, K., Vedaldi, A., Zisserman, A.: Return of the devil in the details: delving deep into convolutional nets. In: British Machine Vision Conference (2014)
23. Li, W., Luo, Y., Wang, P., Qin, Z., Zhou, H., Qiao, H.: Recent advances on application of deep learning for recovering object pose. In: International Conference on Robotics and Biomimetics (2016)

24. Braun, M., Rao, Q., Wang, Y., Flohr, F.: Pose-RCNN: joint object detection and pose estimation using 3D object proposals. In: International Conference on Intelligent Transportation Systems (2016)
25. Massa, F., Aubry, M., Marlet, R.: Convolutional neural networks for joint object detection and pose estimation: a comparative study. CoRR abs/1412.7190 (2014)
26. Massa, F., Marlet, R., Aubry, M.: Crafting a multi-task CNN for viewpoint estimation. In: British Machine Vision Conference (2016)
27. Oñoro-Rubio, D., López-Sastre, R.J., Redondo-Cabrera, C., Gil-Jiménez, P.: The challenge of simultaneous object detection and pose estimation: a comparative study. cORR abs/1801.08110 (2018)
28. Afifi, A.J., Hellwich, O., Soomro, T.A.: Simultaneous object classification and viewpoint estimation using deep multi-task convolutional neural network. In: The 13th International Joint Conference on Computer Vision, Imaging and Computer Graphics Theory and Applications (2018)
29. Li, C., Bai, J., Hager, G.D.: A unified framework for multi-view multi-class object pose estimation. cORR abs/1801.08103 (2018)
30. Kingma, D., Ba, J.: Adam: a method for stochastic optimization. In: International Conference on Learning Representations (2014)
31. Chollet, F.: Keras (2015). https://github.com/fchollet/keras
32. TensorFlow: large-scale machine learning on heterogeneous systems (2015). tensorflow.org
33. Everingham, M., Eslami, S.M.A., Van Gool, L., Williams, C.K.I., Winn, J., Zisserman, A.: The pascal visual object classes challenge: a retrospective. Int. J. Comput. Vis. 111(1), 98–136 (2015)
34. Deng, J., Dong, W., Socher, R., Li, L.J., Li, K., Fei-Fei, L.: ImageNet: a large-scale hierarchical image database. In: 2009 IEEE Conference on Computer Vision and Pattern Recognition, pp. 248–255, June 2009
35. Krizhevsky, A., Sutskever, I., Hinton, G.E.: ImageNet classification with deep convolutional neural networks. In: Neural Information Processing Systems (2012)

Occlusion Resistant Object Rotation Regression from Point Cloud Segments

Ge Gao[⊠][iD], Mikko Lauri, Jianwei Zhang, and Simone Frintrop

Department of Informatics, University of Hamburg, Hamburg, Germany
{gao,lauri,zhang,frintrop}@informatik.uni-hamburg.de

Abstract. Rotation estimation of known rigid objects is important for robotic applications such as dexterous manipulation. Most existing methods for rotation estimation use intermediate representations such as templates, global or local feature descriptors, or object coordinates, which require multiple steps in order to infer the object pose. We propose to directly regress a pose vector from point cloud segments using a convolutional neural network. Experimental results show that our method achieves competitive performance compared to a state-of-the-art method, while also showing more robustness against occlusion. Our method does not require any post processing such as refinement with the iterative closest point algorithm.

Keywords: 6D pose estimation · Convolutional neural network · Point cloud · Lie algebra

1 Introduction

The 6D pose of an object is composed of 3D location and 3D orientation. The pose describes the transformation from a local coordinate system of the object to a reference coordinate system (e.g. camera or robot coordinate) [20], as shown in Fig. 1. Knowing the accurate 6D pose of an object is necessary for robotic applications such as dexterous grasping and manipulation. This problem is challenging due to occlusion, clutter and varying lighting conditions.

Many methods for pose estimation using only color information have been proposed [17,21,25,32]. Since depth cameras are commonly used, there have been many methods using both color and depth information [1,15,18]. Recently, there are also many CNN based methods [15,18]. In general, methods that use depth information can handle both textured and texture-less objects, and they are more robust to occlusion compared to methods using only color information [15,18].

The 6D pose of an object is an inherently continuous quantity. Some works discretize the continuous pose space [8,9], and formulate the problem as classification. Others avoid discretization by representing the pose using, e.g., quaternions [34], or the axis-angle representation [4,22]. Work outside the domain of pose estimation has also considered rotation matrices [24], or in a more general case parametric representations of affine transformations [14]. In these cases the

© Springer Nature Switzerland AG 2019
L. Leal-Taixé and S. Roth (Eds.): ECCV 2018 Workshops, LNCS 11129, pp. 716–729, 2019.
https://doi.org/10.1007/978-3-030-11009-3_44

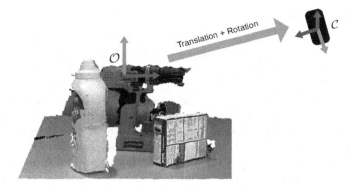

Fig. 1. The goal of 6D pose estimation is to find the translation and rotation from the object coordinate frame $\mathcal{O}$ to the camera coordinate frame $\mathcal{C}$.

problem is often formulated as regression. The choice of rotation representation has a major impact on the performance of the estimation method.

In this work, we propose a deep learning based pose estimation method that uses point clouds as an input. To the best of our knowledge, this is the first attempt at applying deep learning for directly estimating 3D rotation using point cloud segments. We formulate the problem of estimating the rotation of a rigid object as regression from a point cloud segment to the axis-angle representation of the rotation. This representation is constraint-free and thus well-suited for application in supervised learning.

Our experimental results show that our method reaches state-of-the-art performance. We also show that our method exceeds the state-of-the-art in pose estimation tasks with moderate amounts of occlusion. Our approach does not require any post-processing, such as pose refinement by the iterative closest point (ICP) algorithm [3]. In practice, we adapt PointNet [24] for the rotation regression task. Our input is a point cloud with spatial and color information. We use the geodesic distance between rotations as the loss function.

The remainder of the paper is organized as follows. Section 2 reviews related work in pose estimation. In Sect. 3, we argue why the axis-angle representation is suitable for supervised learning. We present our system architecture and network details in Sect. 4. Section 5 presents our experimental results. In Sect. 6 we provide concluding remarks and discuss future work.

2   Related Work

6D pose estimation using only RGB information has been widely studied [17, 21, 25, 32]. Since this work concentrates on using point cloud inputs, which contain depth information, we mainly review works that also consider depth information. We also review how depth information can be represented.

2.1   Pose Estimation

RGB-D Methods. A template matching method which integrates color and depth information is proposed by Hinterstoisser et al. [8,9]. Templates are built with quantized image gradients on object contour from RGB information and surface normals on object interior from depth information, and annotated with viewpoint information. The effectiveness of template matching is also shown in [12,19]. However, template matching methods are sensitive to occlusions [18].

Voting-based methods attempt to infer the pose of an object by accumulating evidence from local or global features of image patches. One example is the Latent-Class Hough Forest [30,31] which adapts the template feature from [8] for generating training data. During inference stage, a random set of patches is sampled from the input image. The patches are used in Hough voting to obtain pose hypotheses for verification.

3D object coordinates and object instance probabilities are learned using a Decision Forest in [1]. The 6D pose estimation is then formulated as an energy optimization problem which compares synthetic images rendered with the estimated pose with observed depth values. 3D object coordinates are also used in [18,23]. However, those approaches tend to be very computationally intensive due to generation and verification of hypotheses [18].

Most recent approaches rely on convolutional neural networks (CNNs). In [20], the work in [1] is extended by adding a CNN to describe the posterior density of an object pose. A combination of using a CNN for object segmentation and geometry-based pose estimation is proposed in [16]. PoseCNN [34] uses a similar two-stage network, in which the first stage extracts feature maps from RGB input and the second stage uses the generated maps for object segmentation, 3D translation estimation and 3D rotation regression in quaternion format. Depth data and ICP are used for pose refinement. Jafari et al. [15] propose a three-stage, instance-aware approach for 6D object pose estimation. An instance segmentation network is first applied, followed by an encoder-decoder network which estimates the 3D object coordinates for each segment. The 6D pose is recovered with a geometric pose optimization step similar to [1]. The approaches [15,20,34] do not directly use CNN to predict the pose. Instead, they provide segmentation and other intermediate information, which are used to infer the object pose.

Point Cloud-Based. Drost et al. [5] propose to extract a global model description from oriented point pair features. With the global description, scene data are matched with models using a voting scheme. This approach is further improved by [10] to be more robust against sensor noise and background clutter. Compared to [5,10], our approach uses a CNN to learn the global description.

2.2   Depth Representation

Depth information in deep learning systems can be represented with, e.g., voxel grids [26,28], truncated signed distance functions (TSDF) [29], or point clouds [24]. Voxel grids are simple to generate and use. Because of their regular grid structure, voxel grids can be directly used as inputs to 3D CNNs. However, voxel grids are inefficient since they also have to explicitly represent empty space. They also suffer from discretization artifacts. TSDF tries to alleviate these problems by storing the shortest distance to the surface represented in each voxel. This allows a more faithful representation of the 3D information. In comparison to other depth data representations, a point cloud has a simple representation without redundancy, yet contains rich geometric information. Recently, Point-Net [24] has allowed to use raw point clouds directly as an input of a CNN.

3 Supervised Learning for Rotation Regression

The aim of object pose estimation is to find the translation and rotation that describe the transformation from the object coordinate system $\mathcal{O}$ to the camera coordinate system $\mathcal{C}$ (Fig. 1). The translation consists of the displacements along the three coordinate axes, and the rotation specifies the rotation around the three coordinate axes. Here we concentrate on the problem of estimating rotation.

For supervised learning, we require a loss function that measures the difference between the predicted rotation and the ground truth rotation. To find a suitable loss function, we begin by considering a suitable representation for a rotation. We argue that the axis-angle representation is the best suited for a learning task. We then review the connection of the axis-angle representation to the Lie algebra of rotation matrices. The Lie algebra provides us with tools needed to define our loss function as the geodesic distance of rotation matrices. These steps allow our network to directly make predictions in the axis-angle format.

Notation. In the following, we denote by $(\cdot)^T$ vector or matrix transpose. By $\|\cdot\|_2$, we denote the Euclidean or 2-norm. We write $I_{3\times3}$ for the 3-by-3 identity matrix.

3.1 Axis-Angle Representation of Rotations

A rotation can be represented, e.g., as Euler angles, a rotation matrix, a quaternion, or with the axis-angle representation. Euler angles are known to suffer from gimbal lock discontinuity [11]. Rotation matrices and quaternions have orthogonality and unit norm constraints, respectively. Such constraints may be problematic in an optimization-based approach such as supervised learning, since they restrict the range of valid predictions. To avoid these issues, we adopt the axis-angle representation. In the axis-angle representation, a vector $\mathbf{r} \in \mathbb{R}^3$ represents a rotation of $\theta = \|\mathbf{r}\|_2$ radians around the unit vector $\frac{\mathbf{r}}{\|\mathbf{r}\|_2}$ [7].

3.2 The Lie Group $SO(3)$

The special orthogonal group $SO(3) = \{R \in \mathbb{R}^{3\times3} \mid RR^T = I_{3\times3}, \det R = 1\}$ is a compact Lie group that contains the 3-by-3 orthogonal matrices with determinant one, i.e., all rotation matrices [6]. Associated with $SO(3)$ is the Lie algebra $so(3)$, consisting of the set of skew-symmetric 3-by-3 matrices.

Let $\mathbf{r} = \begin{bmatrix} r_1 & r_2 & r_3 \end{bmatrix}^T \in \mathbb{R}^3$ be an axis-angle representation of a rotation. The corresponding element of $so(3)$ is the skew-symmetric matrix

$$\mathbf{r}_\times = \begin{bmatrix} 0 & -r_3 & r_2 \\ r_3 & 0 & -r_1 \\ -r_2 & r_1 & 0 \end{bmatrix}. \tag{1}$$

The *exponential map* $\exp : so(3) \to SO(3)$ connects the Lie algebra with the Lie group by

$$\exp(\mathbf{r}_\times) = I_{3\times 3} + \frac{\sin\theta}{\theta}\mathbf{r}_\times + \frac{1-\cos\theta}{\theta^2}\mathbf{r}_\times^2, \tag{2}$$

where $\theta = \mathbf{r}^T\mathbf{r} = \|\mathbf{r}\|_2$ as above[1].

Now let R be a rotation matrix in the Lie group $SO(3)$. The *logarithmic map* $\log : SO(3) \to so(3)$ connects R with an element in the Lie algebra by

$$\log(R) = \frac{\phi(R)}{2\sin(\phi(R))}(R - R^T), \tag{3}$$

where

$$\phi(R) = \arccos\left(\frac{\operatorname{trace}(R) - 1}{2}\right) \tag{4}$$

can be interpreted as the magnitude of rotation related to R in radians. If desired, we can now obtain an axis-angle representation of R by first extracting from $\log(R)$ the corresponding elements indicated in Eq. (1), and then setting the norm of the resulting vector to $\phi(R)$.

3.3   Loss Function for Rotation Regression

We regress to a predicted rotation $\hat{\mathbf{r}}$ represented in the axis-angle form. The prediction is compared against the ground truth rotation $\mathbf{r}$ via a loss function $l : \mathbb{R}^3 \times \mathbb{R}^3 \to \mathbb{R}_{\geq 0}$. Let $\hat{R}$ and R denote the two rotation matrices corresponding to $\hat{\mathbf{r}}$ and $\mathbf{r}$, respectively. We use as loss function the geodesic distance $d(\hat{R}, R)$ of $\hat{R}$ and R [7,13], i.e.,

$$l(\hat{\mathbf{r}}, \mathbf{r}) = d(\hat{R}, R) = \phi(\hat{R}R^T), \tag{5}$$

where we first obtain $\hat{R}$ and R via the exponential map, and then calculate $\phi(\hat{R}R^T)$ to obtain the loss value. This loss function directly measures the magnitude of rotation between $\hat{R}$ and R, making it convenient to interpret. Furthermore, using the axis-angle representation allows to make predictions free of constraints such as the unit norm requirement of quaternions. This makes the loss function also convenient to implement in a supervised learning approach.

---

[1] In a practical implementation, the Taylor expansions of $\frac{\sin\theta}{\theta}$ and $\frac{1-\cos\theta}{\theta^2}$ should be used for small θ for numerical stability.

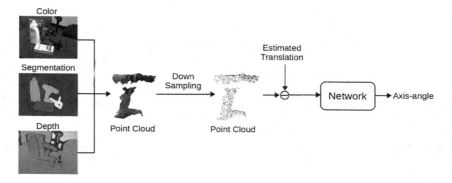

Fig. 2. System overview. The color and depth images together with a segmentation of the target object are used to create a point cloud. The segment is randomly downsampled, and the estimated translation of the down-sampled segment is removed. The normalized segment is fed into a network for rotation prediction.

4   System Architecture

Figure 2 shows the system overview. We train our system for a specific target object, in Fig. 2 the drill. The inputs to our system are the RGB color image, the depth image, and a segmentation mask indicating which pixels belong to the target object. We first create a point cloud segment of the target object based on the inputs. Each point has 6 dimensions: 3 dimensions for spatial coordinates and 3 dimensions for color information. We randomly sample n points from this point cloud segment to create a fixed-size downsampled point cloud. In all of our experiments, we use $n = 256$. We then remove the estimated translation from the point coordinates to normalize the data. The normalized point cloud segment is then fed into a network which outputs a rotation prediction in the axis-angle format. During training, we use the ground truth segmentation and translation. As we focus on the rotation estimation, during testing, we apply the segmentation and translation outputs of PoseCNN [34].

We consider two variants for our network presented in the following subsections. The first variant processes the point cloud as a set of independent points without regard to the local neighbourhoods of points. The second variant explicitly takes into account the local neighbourhoods of a point by considering its nearest neighbours.

4.1   PointNet (PN)

Our PN network is based on PointNet [24], as illustrated in Fig. 3. The PointNet architecture is invariant to all $n!$ possible permutations of the input point cloud, and hence an ideal structure for processing raw point clouds. The invariance is achieved by processing all points independently using multi-layer perceptrons (MLPs) with shared weights. The obtained feature vectors are finally max-pooled to create a global feature representation of the input point cloud. Finally, we attach a three-layer regression MLP on top of this global feature to predict the rotation.

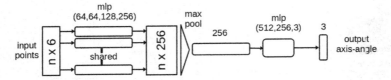

Fig. 3. Network architecture. The numbers in parentheses indicate number of MLP layers, and numbers not in parentheses indicate intermediate vector dimensionality. A feature vector for each point is learned using shared weights. A max pooling layer then aggregates the individual features into a global feature vector. Finally, a regression network with 3 fully-connected layers outputs the rotation prediction.

4.2   Dynamic Nearest Neighbour Graph (DG)

In the PN architecture, all features are extracted based only on a single point. Hence it does not explicitly consider the local neighbourhoods of individual points. However, local neighbourhoods can contain useful geometric information for pose estimation [27]. The local neighbourhoods are considered by an alternative network structure based on the dynamic nearest-neighbour graph network proposed in [33]. For each point P_i in the point set, a k-nearest neighbor graph is calculated. In all our experiments, we use $k = 10$. The graph contains directed edges $(i, j_{i1}), \ldots, (i, j_{ik})$, such that $P_{j_{i1}}, \ldots, P_{j_{ik}}$ are the k closest points to P_i. For an edge e_{ij}, an edge feature $[P_i, (P_j - P_i)]^T$ is calculated. The edge features are then processed in a similar manner as in PointNet to preserve permutation invariance. This dynamic graph convolution can then be repeated, now calculating the nearest neighbour graph for the feature vectors of the first shared MLP layer, and so on for the subsequent layers. We use the implementation[2] provided by authors from [33], and call the resulting network DG for dynamic graph.

5   Experimental Results

This section shows experimental results of the proposed approach on the YCB video dataset [34], and compares the performance with state-of-the-art PoseCNN method [34]. Besides prediction accuracy, we investigate the effect of occlusions and the quality of the segmentation and translation estimates.

5.1   Experiment Setup

The YCB video dataset [34] is used for training and testing with the original train/test split. The dataset contains 133,827 frames of 21 objects selected from the YCB object set [2] with 6D pose annotation. 80,000 frames of synthetic data are also provided as an extension to the training set.

We select a set of four objects to test on, shown in Fig. 4. As our approach does not consider object symmetry, we use objects that have 1-fold rotational

---

[2] https://github.com/WangYueFt/dgcnn.

Fig. 4. Testing objects. From left to right: power drill, extra large clamp, banana, pitcher base.

symmetry (power drill, banana and pitcher base) or 2-fold rotational symmetry (extra large clamp).

We run all experiments using both the PointNet based (PN) and dynamic graph (DG) networks. During training, Adam optimizer is used with learning rate 0.008, and batch size of 128. Batch normalization is applied to all layers. No dropout is used.

For training, ground truth segmentations and translations are used as the corresponding inputs shown in Fig. 2. While evaluating 3D rotation estimation in Subsect. 5.3, the translation and segmentation predicted by PoseCNN are used.

5.2 Evaluation Metrics

For evaluating rotation estimation, we directly use geodesic distance described in Sect. 3 to quantify the rotation error. We evaluate 6D pose estimation using average distance of model points (ADD) proposed in [9]. For a 3D model $\mathcal{M}$ represented as a set of points, with ground truth rotation R and translation $\mathbf{t}$, and estimated rotation $\hat{R}$ and translation $\hat{\mathbf{t}}$, the ADD is defined as:

$$\text{ADD} = \frac{1}{m} \sum_{\mathbf{x} \in \mathcal{M}} \left\| (R\mathbf{x} + \mathbf{t}) - (\hat{R}\mathbf{x} + \hat{\mathbf{t}}) \right\|_2 , \qquad (6)$$

where m is the number of points. The 6D pose estimate is considered to be correct if ADD is smaller than a given threshold.

5.3 Rotation Estimation

Figure 5 shows the estimation accuracy as function of the rotation angle error threshold, i.e., the fraction of predictions that have an angle error smaller than the horizontal axis value. Results are shown for PoseCNN, PoseCNN with ICP refinement (PoseCNN + ICP), and our method with PointNet structure (PN), and with dynamic graph structure (DG). To determine the effect of the translation and segmentation input, we additionally test our methods while giving the ground truth translation and segmentation as input. The cases with ground truths provided are indicated by +gt, and shown with a dashed line.

With translation and segmentation results from PoseCNN, our methods show competitive or superior results compared to PoseCNN with ICP refinement. This

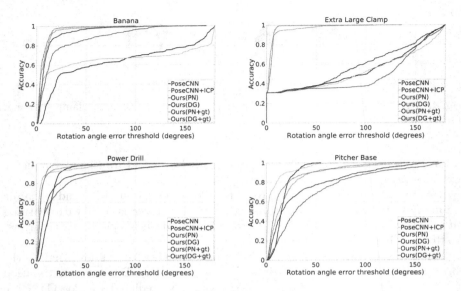

Fig. 5. Accuracy of rotation angle prediction shows the fraction of predictions with error smaller than the threshold. Results are shown for our method and PoseCNN [34]. The additional +gt denotes the variants where ground truth segmentation is provided.

demonstrates that our network is able to accurately predict rotation, and is able to do so without any post-processing or ICP-based pose refinement. We also note that in cases where our method does not work very well (e.g., extra large clamp), by providing the ground truth translation and segmentation (+gt), the results are greatly improved. This shows that good translation and segmentation are crucial for accurate rotation estimation. For pitcher base, our method does not perform well. One possible explanation is that information about the handle and water outlet parts of the pitcher, which are very discriminative for determining the pitcher's rotation, may be lost in our downsampling step. In future work, we are planning to investigate other sampling methods such as farthest point sampling to ensure a full view of the object is preserved even with downsampling.

The results also confirm the fact that ICP based refinement usually only improves the estimation quality if the initial guess is already good enough. When the initial estimation is not accurate enough, the use of ICP can even decrease the accuracy, as shown by the PoseCNN + ICP curve falling below the PoseCNN curve for large angle thresholds.

Effect of Occlusion. We quantify the effect of occlusion on the rotation prediction accuracy. For a given frame and target object, we estimate the occlusion factor O of the object by

$$O = 1 - \frac{\lambda}{\mu}, \tag{7}$$

Table 1. Average rotation angle error in degrees with 95% confidence interval in frames with low ($O < 0.2$) and moderate (mod, $O \geq 0.2$) occlusion

Object	Banana		Power drill		Extra large clamp	
Occlusion	low	mod	low	mod	low	mod
PoseCNN [34]	$62.0° \pm 3.1°$	$8.2° \pm 0.25°$	$14.7° \pm 0.3°$	$37.4° \pm 2.4°$	$109.8° \pm 2.0°$	$151.0° \pm 3.6°$
PoseCNN+ICP	$56.5° \pm 3.4°$	$7.1° \pm 0.9°$	$6.9° \pm 0.4°$	$44.1° \pm 3.5°$	$115.5° \pm 2.0°$	$140.5° \pm 6.0°$
Ours (PN)	$25.1° \pm 1.4°$	$53.5° \pm 3.8°$	$23.2° \pm 0.8°$	$34.8° \pm 6.2°$	$125.7° \pm 1.8°$	$158.1° \pm 2.3°$
Ours (DG)	$\mathbf{12.6° \pm 0.8°}$	$\mathbf{6.7° \pm 0.4°}$	$18.6° \pm 0.8°$	$49.1° \pm 6.7°$	$\mathbf{96.9° \pm 1.9°}$	$\mathbf{100.8° \pm 6.1°}$
Ours (PN+gt)	$8.6° \pm 0.5°$	$10.6° \pm 1.8°$	$7.0° \pm 0.3°$	$\mathbf{3.8° \pm 0.3°}$	$6.2° \pm 0.4°$	$36.4° \pm 3.7°$
Ours (DG+gt)	$\mathbf{7.4° \pm 0.4°}$	$\mathbf{4.3° \pm 0.2°}$	$\mathbf{5.8° \pm 0.3°}$	$5.3° \pm 0.6°$	$\mathbf{4.7° \pm 0.1°}$	$\mathbf{3.5° \pm 0.1°}$

where λ is the number of pixels in the 2D ground truth segmentation, and μ is the number of pixels in the projection of the 3D model of the object onto the image plane using the camera intrinsic parameters and the ground truth 6D pose, when we assume that the object would be fully visible. We noted that for the test frames of the YCB-video dataset O is mostly below 0.5. We categorize $O < 0.2$ as low occlusion and $O \geq 0.2$ as moderate occlusion.

Table 1 shows the average rotation angle error (in degrees) and its 95% confidence interval[3] for PoseCNN and our method in the low and moderate occlusion categories. We also investigated the effect of the translation and segmentation by considering variants of our methods that were provided with the ground truth translation and segmentation. These variants are shown in the table indicated by +gt. We observe that in the moderate occlusion category, our methods have significantly better performance than PoseCNN. We note that for the extra large clamp, the results are greatly improved if the ground truths are provided. This indicates that the failure of both PoseCNN and our method for extra large clamp is due to the poor quality translation and segmentation. Furthermore, with the dynamic graph architecture (DG), the average error tends to be lower. This shows the local neighbourhood information extracted by DG is useful for rotation estimation. One observation is that for banana, the rotation error in low occlusion is significantly higher than it is in the moderate case for PoseCNN. This is because near 25% of the test frames in low occlusion case present an rotation error in range of 160° to 180°.

Qualitative results for rotation estimation are shown in Fig. 6. In the leftmost column, the occlusion factor O of the target object is denoted. Then, from left to right, we show the ground truth, PoseCNN+ICP, and our method using DG and our method using DG with ground truth translation and segmentation (DG+gt) results. In all cases, the ground truth pose, or respectively, the pose estimate, are indicated by the green overlay on the figures. To focus on the difference in the rotation estimate, we use the ground truth translation for all methods for the visualization. The rotation predictions for Ours (DG) are still based on translation and segmentation from PoseCNN.

---

[3] The results for pitcher base are not reported here since all samples in testing set for pitcher base have low occlusion.

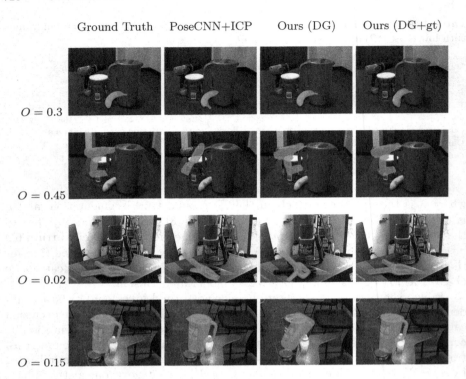

Fig. 6. Qualitative results for rotation estimation. The number on the left indicates the occlusion factor O for the target object. Then, from left to right: ground truth, PoseCNN [34] with ICP refinement, our method using dynamic graph (DG) with PoseCNN segmentation, and dynamic graph with ground truth segmentation (DG+gt). The green overlay indicates the ground truth pose, or respectively, the predicted pose of the target object. Ground truth translation is used in all cases.

The first two rows of Fig. 6 show cases with moderate occlusion. When the discriminative part of the banana is occluded (top row), PoseCNN can not recover the rotation, while our method still produces a good estimate. The situation is similar in the second row for the drill. The third row illustrates that the quality of segmentation has a strong impact on the accuracy of rotation estimation. In this case the segmentation fails to detect the black clamp on the black background, which leads to a poor rotation estimate for both PoseCNN and our method. When we provide the ground truth segmentation (third row, last column), our method is able to recover the correct rotation. The final fourth row shows a failure case for the pitcher base. Our method fails while it loses information about the discriminative handle and water outlet parts of the pitcher in the subsampling phase.

6   Conclusion

We propose to directly predict the 3D rotation of a known rigid object from a point cloud segment. We use axis-angle representation of rotations as the regression target. Our network learns a global representation either from individual input points, or from point sets of nearest neighbors. Geodesic distance is used as the loss function to supervise the learning process. Without using ICP refinement, experiments shows that the proposed method can reach competitive and sometimes superior performance compared to PoseCNN.

Our results show that point cloud segments contain enough information for inferring object pose. The axis-angle representation does not have any constraints, making it a suitable regression target. Using Lie algebra as a tool provides a valid distance measure for rotations. This distance measure can be used as a loss function during training.

We discovered that the performance of our method is strongly affected by the quality of the target object translation and segmentation, which will be further investigated in future work. We will extend the proposed method to full 6D pose estimation by additionally predicting the object translations. We also plan to integrate object classification into our system, and study a wider range of target objects.

Acknowledgments. This work was partially funded by the German Science Foundation (DFG) in project Crossmodal Learning, TRR 169.

References

1. Brachmann, E., Krull, A., Michel, F., Gumhold, S., Shotton, J., Rother, C.: Learning 6D object pose estimation using 3D object coordinates. In: Fleet, D., Pajdla, T., Schiele, B., Tuytelaars, T. (eds.) ECCV 2014. LNCS, vol. 8690, pp. 536–551. Springer, Cham (2014). https://doi.org/10.1007/978-3-319-10605-2_35
2. Calli, B., Walsman, A., Singh, A., Srinivasa, S., Abbeel, P.: Benchmarking in manipulation research using the Yale-CMU-Berkeley object and model set. Robot. Autom. Mag. IEEE **22**(3), 36–52 (2015)
3. Chen, Y., Medioni, G.: Object modelling by registration of multiple range images. Image Vis. Comput. **10**(3), 145–155 (1992)
4. Do, T., Cai, M., Pham, T., Reid, I.: Deep-6DPose: recovering 6D object pose from a single RGB image. arXiv preprint arXiv:1802.10367 (2018)
5. Drost, B., Ulrich, M., Navab, N., Ilic, S.: Model globally, match locally: efficient and robust 3D object recognition. In: CVPR (2010)
6. Hall, B.C.: Lie Groups, Lie Algebras, and Representations. GTM, vol. 222. Springer, Cham (2015). https://doi.org/10.1007/978-3-319-13467-3
7. Hartley, R., Trumpf, J., Dai, Y., Li, H.: Rotation averaging. Int. J. Comput. Vis. **103**(3), 267–305 (2013)
8. Hinterstoisser, S., et al.: Multimodal templates for real-time detection of textureless objects in heavily cluttered scenes. In: ICCV (2011)

9. Hinterstoisser, S., et al.: Model based training, detection and pose estimation of texture-less 3D objects in heavily cluttered scenes. In: Lee, K.M., Matsushita, Y., Rehg, J.M., Hu, Z. (eds.) ACCV 2012. LNCS, vol. 7724, pp. 548–562. Springer, Heidelberg (2013). https://doi.org/10.1007/978-3-642-37331-2_42

10. Hinterstoisser, S., Lepetit, V., Rajkumar, N., Konolige, K.: Going further with point pair features. In: Leibe, B., Matas, J., Sebe, N., Welling, M. (eds.) ECCV 2016. LNCS, vol. 9907, pp. 834–848. Springer, Cham (2016). https://doi.org/10. 1007/978-3-319-46487-9_51

11. Hoag, D.: Apollo guidance and navigation: considerations of Apollo IMU gimbal lock, pp. 1–64. MIT Instrumentation Laboratory, Cambridge (1963)

12. Hodaň, T., Zabulis, X., Lourakis, M., Obdržálek, S., Matas, J.: Detection and fine 3D pose estimation of texture-less objects in RGB-D images. In: IROS (2015)

13. Huynh, D.Q.: Metrics for 3D rotations: comparison and analysis. J. Math. Imag. Vis. **35**(2), 155–164 (2009)

14. Jaderberg, M., Simonyan, K., Zisserman, A., Kavukcuoglu, K.: Spatial transformer networks. In: NIPS (2015)

15. Jafari, H., Mustikovela, S.K., Pertsch, K., Brachmann, E., Rother, C.: iPose: instance-aware 6D pose estimation of partly occluded objects. arXiv preprint arXiv:1712.01924 (2018)

16. Jafari, O.H., Mustikovela, S.K., Pertsch, K., Brachmann, E., Rother, C.: The best of both worlds: learning geometry-based 6D object pose estimation. arXiv preprint arXiv:1712.01924 (2017)

17. Kehl, W., Manhardt, F., Tombari, F., Ilic, S., Navab, N.: SSD-6D: making RGB-based 3D detection and 6D pose estimation great again. In: ICCV (2017)

18. Kehl, W., Milletari, F., Tombari, F., Ilic, S., Navab, N.: Deep learning of local RGB-D patches for 3D object detection and 6D pose estimation. In: Leibe, B., Matas, J., Sebe, N., Welling, M. (eds.) ECCV 2016. LNCS, vol. 9907, pp. 205–220. Springer, Cham (2016). https://doi.org/10.1007/978-3-319-46487-9_13

19. Kehl, W., Tombari, F., Navab, N., Ilic, S., Lepetit, V.: Hashmod: a hashing method for scalable 3D object detection. In: BMVC (2015)

20. Krull, A., Brachmann, E., Michel, F., Yang, M.Y., Gumhold, S., Rother, C.: Learning analysis-by-synthesis for 6D pose estimation in RGB-D images. In: ICCV (2015)

21. Li, Y., Wang, G., Ji, X., Xiang, Y., Fox, D.: DeepIM: deep iterative matching for 6D pose estimation. arXiv preprint arXiv:1804.00175 (2018)

22. Mahendran, S., Ali, H., Vidal, R.: 3D pose regression using convolutional neural networks. In: ICCV (2017)

23. Michel, F., et al.: Global hypothesis generation for 6D object pose estimation. In: CVPR (2017)

24. Qi, C.R., Su, H., Mo, K., Guibas, L.J.: PointNet: deep learning on point sets for 3D classification and segmentation. In: CVPR (2017)

25. Rad, M., Lepetit, V.: BB8: a scalable, accurate, robust to partial occlusion method for predicting the 3D poses of challenging objects without using depth. In: ICCV (2017)

26. Riegler, G., Ulusoy, A.O., Geiger, A.: OctNet: learning deep 3D representations at high resolutions. In: CVPR (2017)

27. Rusu, R., Bradski, G., Thibaux, R., Hsu, J.: Fast 3D recognition and pose using the viewpoint feature histogram. In: IROS (2010)

28. Sedaghat, N., Zolfaghari, M., Amiri, E., Brox, T.: Orientation-boosted voxel nets for 3D object recognition. In: BMVC (2017)

29. Song, S., Xiao, J.: Deep sliding shapes for Amodal 3D object detection in RGB-D images. In: CVPR (2016)

30. Tejani, A., Kouskouridas, R., Doumanoglou, A., Tang, D., Kim, T.: Latent-class Hough forests for 6 DoF object pose estimation. PAMI **40**(1), 119–132 (2018)
31. Tejani, A., Tang, D., Kouskouridas, R., Kim, T.-K.: Latent-class Hough forests for 3D object detection and pose estimation. In: Fleet, D., Pajdla, T., Schiele, B., Tuytelaars, T. (eds.) ECCV 2014. LNCS, vol. 8694, pp. 462–477. Springer, Cham (2014). https://doi.org/10.1007/978-3-319-10599-4_30
32. Tekin, B., Sinha, S.N., Fua, P.: Real-time seamless single shot 6D object pose prediction. In: CVPR (2018)
33. Wang, Y., Sun, Y., Liu, Z., Sarma, S.E., Bronstein, M.M., Solomon, J.M.: Dynamic graph CNN for learning on point clouds. arXiv preprint arXiv:1801.07829 (2018)
34. Xiang, Y., Schmidt, T., Narayanan, V., Fox, D.: PoseCNN: a convolutional neural network for 6D object pose estimation in cluttered scenes. In: RSS (2018)

Camera Tracking for SLAM
in Deformable Maps

Jose Lamarca$^{(\boxtimes)}$ ⓘ and J. M. M. Montiel$^{(\boxtimes)}$ ⓘ

Instituto de Investigación en Ingeniería de Aragón (I3A), Universidad de Zaragoza,
50018 Zaragoza, Spain
{jlamarca,josemari}@unizar.es

Abstract. The current SLAM algorithms cannot work without assuming rigidity. We propose the first real-time tracking thread for monocular VSLAM systems that manages deformable scenes. It is based on top of the Shape-from-Template (SfT) methods to code the scene deformation model. Our proposal is a sequential method that manages efficiently large templates, i.e. deformable maps estimating at the same time the camera pose and deformation. It also can be relocated in case of tracking loss. We have created a new dataset to evaluate our system. Our results show the robustness of the method in deformable environments while running in real time with errors under 3% in depth estimation.

Keywords: Non Rigid Structure-from-Motion ·
Shape-from-Template · Deformation models · Deformable SLAM ·
Non-rigid SLAM

1 Introduction

Recovering 3D scenes from monocular RGB-only images is a significantly challenging problem in Computer Vision. Under the rigidity assumption, Structure-from-Motion (SfM) methods provide the theoretical basis for the solution in static environments. Nonetheless, this assumption renders invalid for deforming scenes as most medical imaging scenarios. In the case of the non-rigid scenes the theoretical foundations are not yet well defined.

We can distinguish two types of algorithms that manage non rigid 3D reconstruction: Non-Rigid Structure-from-Motion (NRSfM), which are mostly batch processes, and Shape-from-Template (SfT), which work frame-to-frame. The main difference between these methods is that NRSfM learns the deformation model from the observations while SfT assumes a previously defined deformation model to estimate the deformation for each image.

Rigid methods like Visual SLAM (Simultaneous Localisation and Mapping) have made headway to work sequentially with scenes bigger than the camera field of view [7,8,13,16]. Meanwhile, non-rigid methods are mostly focused on reconstructing structures which are entirely imaged and tracked, for example, surfaces, [6,17,24], faces [2,4,20,25], or articulated objects [15,23].

© Springer Nature Switzerland AG 2019
L. Leal-Taixé and S. Roth (Eds.): ECCV 2018 Workshops, LNCS 11129, pp. 730–737, 2019.
https://doi.org/10.1007/978-3-030-11009-3_45

We conceive the first real-time tracking thread integrated in a SLAM system that can locate the camera and estimate the deformation of the surface based on top of a SfT algorithm following [3,17,21,24]. Our method includes automatic data association and PnP + RANSAC relocalisation algorithm. We code the deformable map as a template which consists of a mesh with a deformation model. Our template is represented as a 3D surface triangular mesh with spatial and temporal regularisers that are rotation and translation invariant. We have selected it because it is suitable for implementing physical models and with barycentric coordinates we can relate the observations with the template.

We evaluate our algorithm with experimental validation over real data both for camera location and scene deformation. This is the first work that focuses on recovering the deformable 3D just from partial images. Thus, we have created a new dataset to experiment with partially-imaged template for sake of future comparison.

2   Problem Formulation

2.1   Template Definition

We code the deformable structure of the scene as a known template $T \subset \mathbb{R}^3$. The template is modelled as a surface mesh composed of planar triangular facets $\mathcal{F}$ that connect a set of nodes $\mathcal{V}$. The facet f is defined in the frame i by its three nodes $V_{f_j}^i = \{V_{f,h}^i\}$ $h = 1 \ldots 3$. The mesh is measured through observable points $\mathcal{X}$ which lie inside the facets. To code a point $X_j \in \mathcal{X}$ in frame i wrt. its facet f_j nodes, we use a piecewise linear interpolation through the barycentric coordinates $\mathbf{b}_j = [b_{j,1}, b_{j,2}, b_{j,3}]^\top$ by means of the function $\varphi : [\mathbb{R}^3, \mathbb{R}^{3x3}] \to \mathbb{R}^3$:

$$\mathbf{X}_j^i = \varphi(\mathbf{b}_j, \mathbf{V}_{f_j}^i) = \sum_{h=1}^{3} b_{j,h} \mathbf{V}_{f_j,h}^i \tag{1}$$

The camera is assumed projective, the observable point $\mathbf{X}_j^i \in T$ defined in $\mathbb{R}^3$ is viewed in the frame i with the camera located in the pose $\mathbf{T}_i$ through the projective function $\pi : [\mathrm{Sim}\,(3), \mathbb{R}^3] \to \mathbb{R}^2$.

$$\pi\left(\mathbf{T}_i, \mathbf{X}_j^i\right) = \begin{bmatrix} f_u \frac{x_j^i}{z_j^i} + c_u \\ f_v \frac{y_j^i}{z_j^i} + c_v \end{bmatrix} \tag{2}$$

$$\begin{bmatrix} x_j^i & y_j^i & z_j^i \end{bmatrix}^T = \mathbf{R}^i \mathbf{X}_j^i + \mathbf{t}^i \tag{3}$$

Where $\mathbf{R}^i \in SO(3)$ and $\mathbf{t}^i \in \mathbb{R}^3$ are respectively the rotation and the translation of the transformation $\mathbf{T}_i$ and $\{f_u, f_v, c_u, c_v\}$ are the focal lengths and the principal point that define the projective calibration for the camera. The algorithm works under the assumption of previously knowing the template. This is a common assumption of template methods. We effectively compute it by means

of a rigid VSLAM algorithm [16]. We initialise the template from a 3D reconstruction of the shape surface at rest. We use Poisson surface reconstruction
as it is proposed in [12] to construct the template triangular mesh from the
sparse point cloud. Once the template is generated, only cloud points which lie
close to a facet are retained and then projected into the mesh facets where their
barycentric coordinates are computed.

3   Optimisation

We recover the camera pose and the deformation only in the template region
detected by the camera. We define the *observation region*, $\mathcal{O}_i$, as the template
nodes belonging to a facet with one or more matched observations in the current
image i. We dilate the $\mathcal{O}_i$ region with a layer that we call *thickening layer*, $\mathcal{K}_i$
whose thickness is $d_\mathcal{K}$. We call the template region estimated in the local step
local map, $\mathcal{L}_i$. It is defined as $\mathcal{L}_i = \mathcal{O}_i \cup \mathcal{K}_i$ (Fig. 1).

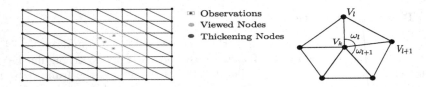

Fig. 1. Left: Two step region definition for the case of three observations inside two
unconnected facets. $d_\mathcal{K} = 1$ for the thickening $\mathcal{K}_i$. Right: Ring of neighbours $\mathcal{N}_k$ of the
node K.

We propose the next optimisation to recover both the camera pose T_i and
the position of the local map nodes $V_k^i \in \mathcal{L}_i$, in frame i:

$$
\arg\min_{T_i, V_k^i \in \mathcal{L}_i} \frac{1}{N_\bullet} \sum_j \rho \left(\left\| \pi_i \left(T_i, \varphi(\mathbf{b}_j, V_{f_j}^i) \right) - x_j^i \right\|^2 \right)
$$

$$
+ \frac{\lambda_d}{N_\bullet} \sum_k \sum_{l \in \mathcal{N}_k} \left(\frac{\left\| V_k^i - V_l^i \right\| - \left\| V_k^0 - V_l^0 \right\|}{\left\| V_k^0 - V_l^0 \right\|} \right)^2
$$

$$
+ \frac{\lambda_L}{N_\bullet} \sum_k \left(\|\delta_k^i\| - \|\delta_k^0\| \right)^2 \sum_{l \in \mathcal{N}_k} \frac{1}{\left\| V_k - V_l \right\|^2} \tag{4}
$$

$$
+ \frac{\lambda_T}{S N_\bullet} \sum_k \left\| V_k^i - V_k^{i-1} \right\|
$$

The weights of the regularisers $\lambda_L, \lambda_d, \lambda_t$ are defined with respect to a unit
weight for the data term. Additionally, we consider different normalisation factors to correct the final weight assigned to each term. We consider a correction

depending on the number of addends, denoted as $N_\bullet$, in the summation of the corresponding regularising term and a scale correction for the temporal term.

The nodes not included in the optimisation, whose position is fixed, $V_k^i \in \{\mathcal{T} \setminus \mathcal{L}_i\}$, are linked with those optimised, hence they are acting as boundary conditions. As a consequence most of the rigid motion between the camera and the template is included in the camera motion estimate $\mathbf{T}_i$.

The regularisers code our deformation model, they are inspired in continuum mechanics where bodies deform generating internal energies due to normal strain and shear strain. The first term is the Cauchy or engineering strain:

$$\sum_k \sum_{l \in \mathcal{N}_k} \left(\frac{\|V_k^i - V_l^i\| - \|V_k^0 - V_l^0\|}{\|V_k^0 - V_l^0\|} \right)^2 \tag{5}$$

It penalises the normal strain energy. Per each node V_k^i we consider a summation over the ring of its neighbours N_k. Per each neighbour the deformation energy is computed as proportional to the squared ratio between the distance increment and the distance at rest. Unlike other isometry or inextensibility regularisers, [10, 17], it is a dimensionless magnitude, invariant with respect to the facet size. Per each node V_k^i we consider its ring of neighbours $\mathcal{N}_k$ in the computation.

The second regulariser is the bending energy:

$$\sum_k \left(\|\delta_k^i\| - \|\delta_k^0\| \right)^2 \sum_{l \in \mathcal{N}_k} \frac{1}{\|V_k - V_l\|^2} \tag{6}$$

It penalises the shear strain energy. It is coded as the squared ratio between the deflection change and the mean edge length in its ring of neighbours $\mathcal{N}_k$. We use the ratio in order to get dimensionless magnitude invariant to the facet size. The deflection δ_k^i also represents the mean curvature, it is computed by means of the discrete Laplace-Beltrami operator:

$$\delta_k^i = V_k^i - \frac{1}{\sum_{l \in \mathcal{N}_j} \omega_l} \sum_{l \in \mathcal{N}_j} \omega_l V_l^i \tag{7}$$

in order to cope with irregular and obtuse meshes, ω_l is defined by the so-called mean-value coordinates [9]:

$$\omega_l = \frac{\tan(\Omega_{k,l}^1/2) + \tan(\Omega_{k,l}^2/2)}{\|V_k^0 - V_l^0\|} \tag{8}$$

The $\Omega_{k,l}^1$ and $\Omega_{k,l}^2$ angles are defined in Fig. 1.

The last term codes a temporal smoothing between the nodes in $\mathcal{L}_i$. This term is dimensionless with the term S. This term is the average length of the arcs in the mesh. We optimise with the Levenberg–Marquardt algorithm implemented in the library g2o [14].

4   SLAM Pipeline

To compose the entire tracking thread, we integrate the optimisation in a pipeline with automatic data association working with ORB points, and a DBoW keyframe database [11] that allows relocalisation in case of losing the tracking.

Our optimisation method uses as input the observations of the template points in the current frame. Specifically, multiscale FAST corner to detect the observations, and the ORB descriptor [22] to identify the matches. We apply the classical in VSLAM *active matching*, that sequentially process the image stream. First, the ORB points are detected in the current image. Next, with a camera motion model, it is predicted the camera pose as a function of the past camera poses. Then the last template estimate and the barycentric coordinates, are used to predict where the template points would be imaged. Around the template point prediction it is defined a search region. Among the ORB points inside the search region, the one with the closest ORB descriptor is selected as the observation. We apply a threshold on the ORB similarity to definitively accept a match. The ORB descriptor of the template point is taken from the template initialisation. The similarity is estimated as the Hamming distance between the ORB descriptors. To reduce the number of false negatives, we cluster the matches according to their geometrical innovation, difference between the predicted template point in the image and the detected one. Only the three main clusters of matches are retained.

As an approach of relocalisation algorithm, we use a relaxed rigid PnP + RANSAC algorithm. We test the original rigid PnP in five thousand images that contain deformation and we got a recall of 26% successful relocalisation, with the relaxed method up to a 49%. The precision in the relocalisation is close to the 100%.

5   Experiments

Comparison with State of the Art SfT. We benchmark our proposal with the standard *Kinect paper dataset*, to compare the performance of our deformation model with respect to state-of-the-art template-based algorithms. Kinect paper dataset is composed of 193 frames, each frame contains around 1300 observations coming form SIFT points. The matches for the observations are also provided. The ground truth for the matched points are computed from a Kinect RGB-D sensor. The benchmark considers a template that can be fit within the camera field of view. To make an homogeneous comparison we fixed the camera and leave the boundaries of the mesh free. In Table 1 we show the mean RMS error along the sequence compared with respect to some popular methods [3, 6, 18, 19, 24], results are taken from [19]. Ours gets 4.86 mm at 13 ms per frame, what is comparable with the similar state-of-the-art algorithms [18, 24].

Experimental Validation. To analyse the performance of our system, we have created the *mandala dataset*. In this dataset, a mandala blanket is hanged and

Table 1. RMSE averaged over all the frames in the sequence.

	[6]	[3]	[19]	[24]	[18]	[5]	Ours
Mean RMSE (mm)	3.97	4.56	3.78	7.47	4.82	3.86	4.86
Runtime per frame (ms)	2	0.7	7	5	30	116	13

deformed manually from its back surface, meanwhile a hand-held RGB-D camera closely observes the mandala surface mimicking a scanning movement in circles. Due to the limited field of view of the camera and its proximity to the cloth, the whole mandala is never completely imaged. We run the experiments in a Intel Core i7-7700K CPU @ 4.20 GHz 8 with a 32 GB of RAM memory.

The sequence is composed of ten thousand frames, there is a first part for initialisation where the cloth remains rigid. After that, the level of hardness of the deformation is progressively increased. The video captures from big displacements in different points of the mandala to wrinkled moments and occlusions.

We evaluate the influence of the thickening layer size, $d_{\mathcal{K}}$. As result of the experiment, we get a system that can run in real-time and have an RMS error of 2.30%, 2.22%, and 2.32% for $d_{\mathcal{K}} = 0, 1$ and 2 respectively. When it comes to runtime, the optimisation algorithm is taking 17, 19 and 20 ms, and the total times per frame are 39, 40 and 41 ms. With $d_{\mathcal{K}} = 1$ we get to reduce the error without increasing excessively the time (Fig. 2).

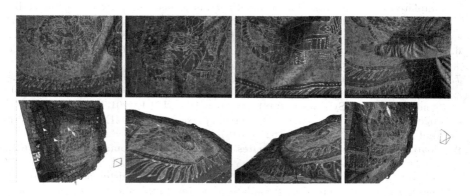

Fig. 2. From left to right: frames #1347, #2089, #9454, #10739, corresponding to the shape at rest and different deformations. Top: 2D image Bottom: 3D reconstruction

6   Discussion

We present a new tracking method able to work in deformable environment incorporating SfT techniques to a SLAM pipeline. We have developed a full-fledged SLAM tracking thread that can robustly operate with an average time budged of 39 ms per frame in very general scenarios with an error under 3% in a real scene and with a relocalisation algorithm with a recall of a 46% in deformable environments with a precision close to the 100%.

Acknowledgements. The authors are with the I3A, Universidad de Zaragoza, Spain. This research was funded by the Spanish government with the projects DPI2015-67275-P and the FPI grant BES-2016-078678.

References

1. Bartoli, A., Grard, Y., Chadebecq, F., Collins, T.: On template-based reconstruction from a single view: analytical solutions and proofs of well-posedness for developable, isometric and conformal surfaces. In: 2012 IEEE Conference on Computer Vision and Pattern Recognition, pp. 2026–2033, June 2012. https://doi.org/10.1109/CVPR.2012.6247906
2. Bartoli, A., Gay-Bellile, V., Castellani, U., Peyras, J., Olsen, S., Sayd, P.: Coarse-to-fine low-rank structure-from-motion. In: 2008 IEEE Conference on Computer Vision and Pattern Recognition. CVPR 2008, pp. 1–8. IEEE (2008)
3. Bartoli, A., Gérard, Y., Chadebecq, F., Collins, T., Pizarro, D.: Shape-from-template. IEEE Trans. Pattern Anal. Mach. Intell. **37**(10), 2099–2118 (2015)
4. Bregler, C., Hertzmann, A., Biermann, H.: Recovering non-rigid 3D shape from image streams. In: 2000 Proceedings of IEEE Conference on Computer Vision and Pattern Recognition, vol. 2, pp. 690–696. IEEE (2000)
5. Brunet, F., Hartley, R., Bartoli, A., Navab, N., Malgouyres, R.: Monocular template-based reconstruction of smooth and inextensible surfaces. In: Kimmel, R., Klette, R., Sugimoto, A. (eds.) ACCV 2010. LNCS, vol. 6494, pp. 52–66. Springer, Heidelberg (2011). https://doi.org/10.1007/978-3-642-19318-7_5
6. Chhatkuli, A., Pizarro, D., Bartoli, A.: Non-rigid shape-from-motion for isometric surfaces using infinitesimal planarity. In: BMVC (2014)
7. Concha, A., Civera, J.: DPPTAM: dense piecewise planar tracking and mapping from a monocular sequence. In: 2015 IEEE/RSJ International Conference on Intelligent Robots and Systems (IROS), pp. 5686–5693. IEEE (2015)
8. Engel, J., Koltun, V., Cremers, D.: Direct sparse odometry. IEEE Trans. Pattern Anal. Mach. Intell. **40**(3), 611–625 (2018)
9. Floater, M.S.: Mean value coordinates. Comput. Aided Geom. Des. **20**(1), 19–27 (2003)
10. Gallardo, M., Collins, T., Bartoli, A.: Can we jointly register and reconstruct creased surfaces by shape-from-template accurately? In: Leibe, B., Matas, J., Sebe, N., Welling, M. (eds.) ECCV 2016. LNCS, vol. 9908, pp. 105–120. Springer, Cham (2016). https://doi.org/10.1007/978-3-319-46493-0_7
11. Gálvez-López, D., Tardós, J.D.: Bags of binary words for fast place recognition in image sequences. IEEE Trans. Rob. **28**(5), 1188–1197 (2012). https://doi.org/10.1109/TRO.2012.2197158
12. Kazhdan, M., Bolitho, M., Hoppe, H.: Poisson surface reconstruction. In: Proceedings of the fourth Eurographics Symposium on Geometry Processing, pp. 61–70. Eurographics Association (2006)
13. Klein, G., Murray, D.: Parallel tracking and mapping for small AR workspaces. In: 2007 6th IEEE and ACM International Symposium on Mixed and Augmented Reality. ISMAR 2007, pp. 225–234. IEEE (2007)

14. Kümmerle, R., Grisetti, G., Strasdat, H., Konolige, K., Burgard, W.: g2o: a general framework for graph optimization. In: 2011 IEEE International Conference on Robotics and Automation (ICRA), pp. 3607–3613. IEEE (2011)
15. Lee, M., Choi, C.H., Oh, S.: A procrustean Markov process for non-rigid structure recovery. In: Proceedings of the IEEE Conference on Computer Vision and Pattern Recognition, pp. 1550–1557 (2014)
16. Mur-Artal, R., Montiel, J.M.M., Tardos, J.D.: ORB-SLAM: a versatile and accurate monocular SLAM system. IEEE Trans. Rob. 31(5), 1147–1163 (2015)
17. Ngo, D.T., Östlund, J., Fua, P.: Template-based monocular 3D shape recovery using laplacian meshes. IEEE Trans. Pattern Anal. Mach. Intell. 38(1), 172–187 (2016)
18. Östlund, J., Varol, A., Ngo, D.T., Fua, P.: Laplacian meshes for monocular 3D shape recovery. In: Fitzgibbon, A., Lazebnik, S., Perona, P., Sato, Y., Schmid, C. (eds.) ECCV 2012. LNCS, vol. 7574, pp. 412–425. Springer, Heidelberg (2012). https://doi.org/10.1007/978-3-642-33712-3_30
19. Özgür, E., Bartoli, A.: Particle-SfT: a provably-convergent, fast shape-from-template algorithm. Int. J. Comput. Vision 123(2), 184–205 (2017)
20. Paladini, M., Bartoli, A., Agapito, L.: Sequential non-rigid structure-from-motion with the 3D-implicit low-rank shape model. In: Daniilidis, K., Maragos, P., Paragios, N. (eds.) ECCV 2010. LNCS, vol. 6312, pp. 15–28. Springer, Heidelberg (2010). https://doi.org/10.1007/978-3-642-15552-9_2
21. Perriollat, M., Hartley, R., Bartoli, A.: Monocular template-based reconstruction of inextensible surfaces. Int. J. Comput. Vision 95(2), 124–137 (2011)
22. Rublee, E., Rabaud, V., Konolige, K., Bradski, G.: ORB: an efficient alternative to SIFT or SURF. In: 2011 IEEE International Conference on Computer Vision (ICCV), pp. 2564–2571. IEEE (2011)
23. Russell, C., Fayad, J., Agapito, L.: Energy based multiple model fitting for non-rigid structure from motion. In: 2011 IEEE Conference on Computer Vision and Pattern Recognition (CVPR), pp. 3009–3016. IEEE (2011)
24. Salzmann, M., Fua, P.: Linear local models for monocular reconstruction of deformable surfaces. IEEE Trans. Pattern Anal. Mach. Intell. 33(5), 931–944 (2011)
25. Torresani, L., Hertzmann, A., Bregler, C.: Nonrigid structure-from-motion: estimating shape and motion with hierarchical priors. IEEE Trans. Pattern Anal. Mach. Intell. 30(5), 878–892 (2008)

RPNet: An End-to-End Network for Relative Camera Pose Estimation

Sovann En$^{(\boxtimes)}$, Alexis Lechervy, and Frédéric Jurie

Normandie Univ, UNICAEN, ENSICAEN, CNRS—UMR GREYC, Caen, France
{sovann.en,alexis.lechervy,frederic.jurie}@unicaen.fr

Abstract. This paper addresses the task of relative camera pose estimation from raw image pixels, by means of deep neural networks. The proposed RPNet network takes pairs of images as input and directly infers the relative poses, without the need of camera intrinsic/extrinsic. While state-of-the-art systems based on SIFT + RANSAC, are able to recover the translation vector only up to scale, RPNet is trained to produce the full translation vector, in an end-to-end way. Experimental results on the Cambridge Landmark data set show very promising results regarding the recovery of the full translation vector. They also show that RPNet produces more accurate and more stable results than traditional approaches, especially for hard images (repetitive textures, textureless images, *etc.*). To the best of our knowledge, RPNet is the first attempt to recover full translation vectors in relative pose estimation.

Keywords: Relative pose estimation · Pose estimation · PoseNet

1 Introduction

In this paper, we are interested in *relative camera pose estimation*—a task consisting in accurately estimating the location and orientation of the camera with respect to another camera's reference system. Relative pose estimation is an essential task for many computer vision problems, such as Structure from Motion (SfM), Simultaneous Localisation And Mapping (SLAM), *etc.* Traditionally, this task can be accomplished by (i) extracting sparse keypoints (e.x. SIFT, SURF), (ii) establishing 2D correspondences between keypoints and (iii) estimating the essential matrix using 5-points or 8-point algorithms [13]. RANSAC is very often used to reject outliers in a robust manner.

This technique, although it has been considered as the de facto standard for many years, presents two main drawbacks. First, the quality of the estimation depends heavily on the correspondence assignment. This is to say, too few correspondences (textureless objects) or too many noisy correspondences (repetitive texture or too much viewpoint change) can lead to surprisingly bad results. Second, the traditional method is able to estimate the translation vector only up to scale (directional vector).

L. Leal-Taixé and S. Roth (Eds.): ECCV 2018 Workshops, LNCS 11129, pp. 738–745, 2019.
https://doi.org/10.1007/978-3-030-11009-3_46

In this paper, our objective is three folds: (i) we propose a system producing more stable results (ii) recovering the full translation vector (iii) and we provide insights regarding relative pose inference (*i.e.* from absolute pose, regressor *etc.*).

As pointed out in [20], CNN based methods are able to produce pretty good results in some cases where SIFT-based methods fail (*i.e.* texture less images). This is the reason why we opted for a global method based on CNN. Inspired by the success of PoseNet [9], we propose a modified Siamese PoseNet for relative camera pose estimation, dubbed as RPNet, with different ways to infer the relative pose. To the best of our knowledge, [12] is the only end-to-end system aiming at solving relative camera pose using deep learning approach. However, their system estimate the translation vector up to scale, while ours produces full translation vectors.

The rest of the paper is organized as follows: Sect. 2 presents the related work. Section 3 introduces the network architecture and the training methodology. Section 4 discusses the datasets and presents the experimental validation of the approach. Finally, Sect. 5 concludes the paper.

2 State of the Art

Local Keypoint-Based Approaches. They address relative camera pose estimation using the epipolar geometry between 2D-2D correspondences of keypoints. Early attempts aimed at better engineering interest point detectors to focus on interesting image properties such as corners [6], blobs in scale-space [10], regions [11], or speed [2,16,18] *etc.* More recently, there is a growing interest to train interest point detectors together with the matching function [4,5,17,19,23]. LIFT [21] adopted the traditional pipeline combining a detector, an orientation estimator, and a descriptor, tied together with differentiable operations and learned end-to-end. [1] proposed a multitask network with different sub-branches to operate on varying input sizes. [4] proposed a bootstrapping strategy by first learning on simple synthetic data and increasing the training set with real images in a second time.

End-to-End Pose Estimation. The first end-to-end neural network for camera pose estimation from single RGB images is PoseNet [9]. It is based on GoogLeNet with two output branches to regress translations and rotations. PoseNet follow-up includes: Baysian PoseNet [7], Posenet-LSTM [20] where LSTM is used to model the context of the images, Geometric-PoseNet where the loss is calculated using the re-projection error of the coordinates using the predicted pose and the ground truth [8]. Since all the 3D models used for comparisons are created using SIFT-based techniques, traditional approach seems more accurate. [20] showed that the classical approaches completely fail with less textured datasets such as the proposed TMU-LSI dataset. [14] is an end-to-end system for pose regression taking sparse keypoint as inputs. Regarding relative pose estimation, [12] is the only system we are aware of. Their network is based on ResNet35 with FCs layers acting as pose regressor. Similar to the previous networks, the authors formulate the loss function as minimising the L2-distances between the ground truth

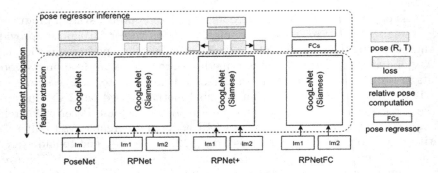

Fig. 1. Illustration of the proposed system

and the estimated pose. Unfortunately, several aspects of their results (including their label generation, experimental methodology and the baseline system) make comparisons difficult. Along side with pose regression problems, another promising works from [15] showed that an end-to-end neural network can effectively be trained to regress to infer the homography between two images. Finally, two recent papers [3,22] made useful contributions to the training of end-to-end systems for pose estimation. [22] proposed a regressor network to produce essential matrix which can be then used to find the relative pose. However, their system is able to find the translation up to scale which is completely different from our objective. In [3], a differentiable RANSAC is proposed for outlier rejection and can be a plug-and-play component into an end-to-end system.

3   Relative Pose Inference with RPNet

Architecture. The architecture of the proposed RPNet, illustrated Fig. 1, is made of two building blocks: (i) a Siamese Network with two branches regressing one pose per image, (ii) a pose inference module for computing the relative pose between the cameras. We provide three variants of the pose inference module: (1) a parameter-free module, (2) a parameter-free module with additional losses (same as PoseNet loss [9]) aiming at regressing the two camera poses as well as the relative pose, and (3) a relative pose regressor based on FC layers. The whole network is trained end-to-end for relative pose estimation. Inspired by PoseNet [9], the feature extraction network is based on the GoogLeNet architecture with 22 CNN layers and 6 inception modules. We only normalize the quaternion during test time. It outputs one pose per image.

For RPNet and RPNet$^+$, the module for computing the relative pose between the cameras is straightforward and relies on simple geometry. Following the convention of OpenCV, the relative pose is calculated in the reference system of the 2nd camera. Let (R_1, t_1, R_2, t_2) be the rotation matrices and translation vectors used to project a point X from world coordinate system to a fixed camera system (camera 1 & 2). Let (q_1, q_2) be the corresponding quaternions of (R_1, R_2).

Table 1. Number of training and testing pairs for Cambridge Landmark dataset. SE stands for spatial extent, measured in meter.

Scene	Train	Test	SE	Scence	Train	Test	SE
Kings College	9.1k	2.4k	140×40	Shop Facade	1.6k	0.6k	35×25
Old Hospital	6.5k	1.2k	50×40	St Marys Church	11k	4.1k	80×60

The relative pose is calculated as followed:

$$R_{1,2} = q_2 \times q_1^* \quad \text{and} \quad T_{1,2} = R_2(-R_1^T t_1) + t_2 \tag{1}$$

where q_1^* is the conjugate of q_1, and $\times$ denotes the multiplication in the quaternion domain. Both equations are differentiable. For RPNetFC, the pose inference module is a simple stacked fully connected layers with *relu* activation. To limit over-fitting, we modified the output of the Siamese network by reducing its output dimension from 2048 to 256. This results in almost 50% reduction of the number of parameters compared to PoseNet, RPNet and RPNet$^+$ network. The pose regressor network contains two FC layers (both with 128 dimensions) (Table 1).

Losses. The loss function uses the Euclidean distance to compare predicted relative rotation $\hat{q}_{1,2}$ and translation $\hat{T}_{1,2}$ with ground truth $\hat{q}_{1,2}$ and $q_{1,2}$: $loss = \sum_i (||\hat{T}_{1,2}^i - T_{1,2}^i||_2 + \beta * ||\hat{q}_{1,2}^i - q_{1,2}^i||_2)$. Quaternions are unit quaternions. The original PoseNet has a β term in front of quaternions to balance the loss values between the translation and rotation. To find the most suitable value of β, we cross-validated on our validation set. Please refer to our codes for different hyper-parameter values on different subsets.

4 Experimentations

4.1 Experimental Setup

Dataset. Experimental validation is done on the Cambridge Landmark dataset[1]. Each image is associated with a ground-truth pose. We provide results on 4 of the 5 subsets (scenes). As discussed by several people, the 'street' scene raises several issues[2].

Pair Generation. For each sequence of each scene, we randomly pair each image with eight different images of the same sequence. For a fair comparison with SURF, the pair generation is done by making sure that they overlap enough. We followed the train-test splits defined with the data set. Images are scaled so that the smallest dimension is 256 pixels, keeping its original aspect ratio. During training, we use 224 * 224 random crops and feed them into the network. During test time, we center crop the image.

---

[1] http://mi.eng.cam.ac.uk/projects/relocalisation.
[2] https://github.com/alexgkendall/caffe-posenet/issues/2.

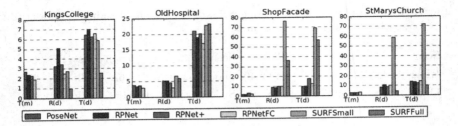

Fig. 2. Translation and rotation errors (median) of the different approaches

Baseline. The baseline is a traditional keypoint-based method (SURF). The focal length and the principle point are provided by the dataset. Other parameters are cross-validated on the validation set. For a fair comparison, we provide two scenarios for baselines: (1) the image are scaled to be 256 * 455 pixels, followed by a center-crop (224 * 224 pixels) to produce the same image pairs as tested with our networks and (2) the original images without down-sampling. We named these two scenarios as 'SURFSmall' and 'SURFFull'. All the camera parameters are adapted to the scaling and cropping we applied.

Evaluation Metric. We measured 3 different errors: (i) translation errors, in meters (ii) rotation errors, in degrees and (iii) translation errors in degrees. We report the median for all the measurements.

4.2 Experimental Results

Relative Pose Inference Module. Figure 2 compares the performance of the different systems and test scenarios. Based on these experimental results, RPNetFC and RPNet$^+$ are the most efficient ways to recover the relative pose. On easy dataset (*i.e.* KingsCollege and OldHospital), where there is no ambiguity textures, using pose regressor (RPNetFC) produces slightly better results than inferring the relative pose from the two images (PoseNet/RPNet/RPNet$^+$). On the contrary, on hard datasets (*i.e.* ShopFacade and StMarysChurch), RPNet-family outperforms RPNetFC. This behavior is also true for relative rotation and relative translation measured in degree. Globally, RPNetFC produces the best results followed by RPNet$^+$, PoseNet and finally, RPNet. The differences of their results are between 0 and 8°. Regarding technical aspect, RPNetFC is a lot easier to train than RPNet$^+$/RPNet since it does not involve multiple hyper-parameters to balance the different losses. It also converges faster.

Comparison with Traditional Approaches. We will start by discussing the SURFSmall scenario first. In general, the error on both translation and rotation can be reduced between 5 to 70% using RPNet family, except on KingsCollege where the traditional approach slightly outperforms RPNet-based methods. We observed that the performance of the traditional approaches varies largely from one subset to another, while RPNet$^+$/RPNetFC are more stable. In addition, the

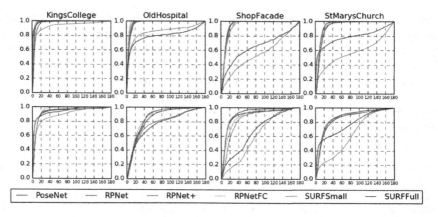

Fig. 3. Accumulative hist. of errors in rotation (1st row, d), translation (2nd row, m).

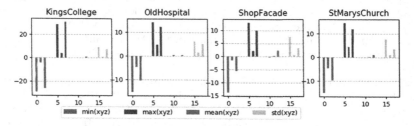

Fig. 4. Min/Max/Mean/STD relative translations (ground truth), w.r.t. XYZ axis (m).

traditional approach requires camera information for each image in order to correctly estimate the pose. In contrast, RPNet-based does not require any specific information at all. Using the original image size (SURFFull) significantly boost the performance of the traditional approach. However, RPNetFC still enjoy a significant gain in performance on OldHospital and ShopFacade, while performing slightly worse than SURFFull on KingsCollege and StMarysChurch. The difference in performance between SURFFull and RPNetFC is even more significant when the images contain large view point changes (see Fig. 3).

Full Translation Vector. One of our objectives is to provide a system able to estimate the full translation vector. On average, we observed that the median error ranges between 2 to 4 m, using RPNetFC. Figure 4 gives an idea of ground truth translations w.r.t. reference axes (xyz). For instance, on KingsCollege, the values of X-axis can range from -29 m to 30 m with an STD of 7 m. Interestingly, our network has a translation error of only 2.88 m.

5 Conclusions

This paper proposed a novel architecture for estimating full relative poses using an end-to-end neural network. The network is based on a Siamese architecture, which was experimented with different ways to infer the relative poses. In addition, to produce competitive or better results over the traditional SURF-based approaches, our system is able to produce an accurate full translation vector. We hope this paper will provide more insight and motivate other researchers to focus on global end-to-end system for relative pose regression problems.

Acknowledgements. This work was partly funded by the FrenchUK MCM ITP program and by the ANR-16-CE23-0006 program.

References

1. Altwaijry, H., Veit, A., Belongie, S.J.: Learning to detect and match keypoints with deep architectures. In: Proceedings of the British Machine Vision Conference 2016, BMVC 2016, 19–22 September 2016, York, UK (2016)
2. Bay, H., Tuytelaars, T., Van Gool, L.: SURF: speeded up robust features. In: Leonardis, A., Bischof, H., Pinz, A. (eds.) ECCV 2006. LNCS, vol. 3951, pp. 404–417. Springer, Heidelberg (2006). https://doi.org/10.1007/11744023_32
3. Brachmann, E., et al.: DSAC-differentiable RANSAC for camera localization. In: IEEE Conference on Computer Vision and Pattern Recognition (CVPR), vol. 3 (2017)
4. DeTone, D., Malisiewicz, T., Rabinovich, A.: Superpoint: self-supervised interest point detection and description. arXiv preprint arXiv:1712.07629 (2017)
5. Han, X., Leung, T., Jia, Y., Sukthankar, R., Berg, A.C.: MatchNet: unifying feature and metric learning for patch-based matching. In: 2015 IEEE Conference on Computer Vision and Pattern Recognition (CVPR), pp. 3279–3286 (2015)
6. Harris, C.G., Stephens, M.: A combined corner and edge detector. In: Proceedings of the Alvey Vision Conference, AVC 1988, September 1988, Manchester, UK, pp. 1–6 (1988)
7. Kendall, A., Cipolla, R.: Modelling uncertainty in deep learning for camera relocalization. In: 2016 IEEE International Conference on Robotics and Automation (ICRA), pp. 4762–4769 (2016)
8. Kendall, A., Cipolla, R.: Geometric loss functions for camera pose regression with deep learning. In: 2017 IEEE Conference on Computer Vision and Pattern Recognition, CVPR 2017, 21–26 July 2017, Honolulu, HI, USA, pp. 6555–6564. IEEE Computer Society (2017). https://doi.org/10.1109/CVPR.2017.694
9. Kendall, A., Grimes, M., Cipolla, R.: PoseNet: a convolutional network for real-time 6-DOF camera relocalization. In: 2015 IEEE International Conference on Computer Vision (ICCV), pp. 2938–2946 (2015)
10. Lowe, D.G.: Distinctive image features from scale-invariant keypoints. Int. J. Comput. Vis. **60**(2), 91–110 (2004)
11. Matas, J., Chum, O., Urban, M., Pajdla, T.: Robust wide-baseline stereo from maximally stable extremal regions. Image Vis. Comput. **22**(10), 761–767 (2004)
12. Melekhov, I., Ylioinas, J., Kannala, J., Rahtu, E.: Relative camera pose estimation using convolutional neural networks. In: Blanc-Talon, J., Penne, R., Philips, W., Popescu, D., Scheunders, P. (eds.) ACIVS 2017. LNCS, vol. 10617, pp. 675–687. Springer, Cham (2017). https://doi.org/10.1007/978-3-319-70353-4_57
13. Nistér, D.: An efficient solution to the five-point relative pose problem. IEEE Trans. Pattern Anal. Mach. Intell. **26**(6), 756–770 (2004)

14. Purkait, P., Zhao, C., Zach, C.: SPP-Net: deep absolute pose regression with synthetic views. arXiv preprint arXiv:1712.03452 (2017)
15. Rocco, I., Arandjelovic, R., Sivic, J.: Convolutional neural network architecture for geometric matching. In: 2017 IEEE Conference on Computer Vision and Pattern Recognition, CVPR 2017, 21–26 July 2017, Honolulu, HI, USA, pp. 39–48. IEEE Computer Society (2017). https://doi.org/10.1109/CVPR.2017.12
16. Rublee, E., Rabaud, V., Konolige, K., Bradski, G.: ORB: an efficient alternative to SIFT or SURF. In: 2011 IEEE International Conference on Computer Vision (ICCV), pp. 2564–2571 (2011)
17. Tian, Y., Fan, B., Wu, F., et al.: L2-Net: deep learning of discriminative patch descriptor in euclidean space. In: Conference on Computer Vision and Pattern Recognition (CVPR), vol. 2 (2017)
18. Tola, E., Lepetit, V., Fua, P.: Daisy: an efficient dense descriptor applied to wide-baseline stereo. IEEE Trans. Pattern Anal. Mach. Intell. **32**(5), 815–830 (2010)
19. Trujillo, L., Olague, G.: Using evolution to learn how to perform interest point detection. In: 2006 18th International Conference on Pattern Recognition, ICPR 2006, vol. 1, pp. 211–214 (2006)
20. Walch, F., Hazirbas, C., Leal-Taixé, L., Sattler, T., Hilsenbeck, S., Cremers, D.: Image-based localization using LSTMs for structured feature correlation. In: IEEE International Conference on Computer Vision, ICCV 2017, 22–29 October 2017, Venice, Italy, pp. 627–637. IEEE Computer Society (2017). https://doi.org/10.1109/ICCV.2017.75
21. Yi, K.M., Trulls, E., Lepetit, V., Fua, P.: LIFT: learned invariant feature transform. In: Leibe, B., Matas, J., Sebe, N., Welling, M. (eds.) ECCV 2016. LNCS, vol. 9910, pp. 467–483. Springer, Cham (2016). https://doi.org/10.1007/978-3-319-46466-4_28
22. Yi, K.M., Trulls, E., Ono, Y., Lepetit, V., Salzmann, M., Fua, P.: Learning to find good correspondences. In: Proceedings of the 2018 IEEE/CVF Conference on Computer Vision and Pattern Recognition (CVPR), vol. 3 (2018)
23. Zagoruyko, S., Komodakis, N.: Learning to compare image patches via convolutional neural networks. In: 2015 IEEE Conference on Computer Vision and Pattern Recognition (CVPR), pp. 4353–4361 (2015)

Author Index

Printed in the United States
By Bookmasters